WHO'S WHO
ON TELEVISION

WHO'S WHO
ON TELEVISION

The comprehensive guide to the stars of the small screen

BOXTREE

First published 2000 by Boxtree
an imprint of Macmillan Publishers Ltd
25 Eccleston Place, London SW1W 9NF
Basingstoke and Oxford

www.macmillan.co.uk

Associated companies throughout the world

ISBN 0 7522 1821 2

9 8 7 6 5 4 3 2 1

A CIP catalogue record for this book is available from
the British Library.

Designed and typeset by Blackjacks
Printed in Great Britain by The Bath Press

CONTENTS

FOREWORD

We all know the feeling – you're relaxing watching TV, you notice an actor on screen and ask yourself, 'Where have I seen *him* before? Wasn't he in that series last year on BBC2?'

Whether you're an armchair fan or you're in the entertainment business, there's never been a more appropriate time for this much-expanded, all-new edition of *TVTimes Who's Who on Television*.

As our choice of TV channels expands rapidly in the digital age, we now have endless opportunities to see classic comedy and drama repeats as well as a wonderfully rich diet of fresh television. This book offers the TV addict and the professional alike an invaluable aid in providing a fascinating record of the careers and backgrounds of those who appear regularly on our screens.

TV Times Who's Who on Television, produced by a team of journalists who live and breathe TV every day of the year, is a unique reference guide to the work of more than 2,000 actors and actresses who make British TV, with its superb variety and quality of choice, the envy of the world.

PETER GENOWER
Editor-in-Chief

ACKNOWLEDGEMENTS
The Editor would like to thank the following for their fortitude, perseverance, and skill in compiling this book: Philippa Clarke, Luke Genower, Polly Horne, Nicola Jenkins, Eloise Maynard, Kim Palfrey, William Preston, Michael Ripley and David Byers.

A

ABBOT, Russ

Russ Abbot. Actor/Comedian (M).
b. Chester, 18 September 1948.
TV: *London Night Out; What's On Next?; Who Do You Do?; The Comedians; Bruce Forsyth's Big Night; Russ Abbot's Madhous; Des O'Connor Now; Live From her Majesty's; Tarby and Friends; Wogan; The Bob Monkhouse Show; Live from the Palladium; Stars in Their Eyes – Elvis Special; The Russ Abbot Show;* Ted Fenwick in *September Song;* Ted Butler in *Married for Life.*
Address: c/o Mike Hughes Entertainments, c/o Gerald Goss Ltd, Dudley House, 169 Piccadilly, London W1V 9DD. m. Trisha; 3 s. Gary, Richard and Christopher; 1 d. Erika

ACTON, Dawn

Dawn Acton. Actor (F)
b. Ashton-under Lyne, Lancashire, 15 March 1977.
TV: Tracy Preston nee Barlow in *Coronation Street.*
Address: c/o Granada Television, Quay Street, Manchester, M60 9EA.

ADAMS, Rick

Rick Adams. Presenter/Actor (M).
b. 16 October 1971.
TV: *Breakfast Show; Highly Sprung; Live; Reactive.*
Address: c/o James Grant Management Ltd, Syon Lodge, England Road, Isleworth, Middlesex TW7 5BH.

ADAMS, Tom

Tom Adams. Actor (M).
b. London, 3 September 1938.
TV: Villain in *Dixon of Dock Green; Emergency Ward 10;* Mal Bates in *Emmerdale; Focus North;* Dr Wallman in *General Hospital; Journey into Midnight; Madigan;* Calico Jack in *Pyrates;* John Ross in *Remington Steele;* Major Sullivan in *Spy Trap;* Ken Stevenson in *Strike it Rich; Ted Viles TV;* Nick Lewis in *The Enigma Files; The Lisbon Beat;* Daniel Fogarty in *The Onedin Line;* Bernard in *Villains; Westcountry Tales: The Hard Man; Would I Lie to You?*
Films: *Das Ist dein Ende; Duel of Love; Fathom; Licence To Kill; Somebody's Stolen Our Russian Spy; Subterfuge; The Fast Kill; The Fighting Prince of Donegal; The Great Escape; The House that Dripped Blood; The Peaches; The Red Baron; This is My Street;* Charles Vince in *Where The Bullets Fly.*
Address: c/o Langford Associates, 17 Westfields Avenue, London SW13 0AT. Hobbies: Cricket, golf, most sports.

ADIE, Kate

Kate Adie. Reporter. b. Sunderland, 19 October 1945.
TV: Director BBC Outside Broadcast Sports and Religion, BBC TV News Reporter, Court Correspondent, Chief News Correspondent.
Address: Contact via BBC, Union House, 65–69, Shepherds Bush Green, London W12 8TX.

ADUDU, Trish

Trish Adudu. Sports Presenter. b. 1959.
TV: Assistant Producer *Grandstand, Reportage; All Black,* Reporter on *Good Morning;* Presenter *Channel One;* Sports Presenter *5 News.*

AHERNE, Caroline

Caroline Aherne. Actor (F)/Writer.
b. Manchester, 24 December 1963.
TV: *Dead Good Show; The Fast Show Christmas Special; It's a Mad World, World, World World; Mrs Merton; Mrs Merton Christmas Special; Mrs Merton in Las Vegas; Mrs Merton and Malcom; Paramount City; The Comedy Club; The Fast Show; The Royle Family; Up Front.*
Address: c/o McIntyre Management Ltd, 2nd Floor, 35 Soho Square, London W1V 5DG.

AINSWORTH, Kacey

Kacey Ainsworth. Actor (F).
b. London, 19 October 1970.
TV: Carol Nash in *A Touch of Frost;* Tina in *Beggar Bride;* Loretta in *Cone Zone;* Julia in *Peak Practice;* Kitty in *Sin of Gluttony;* Mrs Hughes in *Soldier, Soldier;* Rosie Murray in *The Accused;* Gail Painter in *The Bill;* Paula Sheraton in *The Bill;* Drucilla Clark in *The Moonstone;* Val in *Touch and Go;* Sarah in *Under the Moon.*
Films: Dorothea Fitzherbert in *Topsy Turvy.*
Address: c/o Cassie Mayer Ltd, 34 Kingly Court, London W1R 5LE. Hobbies: Running, yoga, organic gardening.

AIR, Donna

Donna Air. Actor/Presenter (F).
b. Newcastle, 1979.
TV: Charlie in *Byker Grove*; *MTV Select*; Lucy in *Supply & Demand*; *The Big Breakfast*.
Films: Dutch hitchhiker in *Still Crazy*; Louise in *Truth Or Dare*.
Address: c/o William Morris Agency (UK) Ltd, 1 Stratton Street, London W1X 6HB.

AIRD, Holly

Holly Aird. Actor (F). b. Hampshire, 18 May 1969.
TV: *The Flame Trees of Thika*; *The Life and Tales of Beatrix Potter*; *Seal Morning*; *Happy Valley*; *Inspector Morse*; *Mother Love*; Nancy in *Soldier, Soldier*; *The Life and Death of Philip Knight*; *Kavanagh QC*; *Have Your Cake*; *Dressing for Breakfast*; *Rules of Engagement*.
Films: *Carry on Columbus*; *Intimate Relations*; *Fever Pitch*; *Theory of Flight*; *Dreaming of Joseph Lees*; *The Criminal*.
Address: c/o Ken McReddie, 91 Regent Street, London W1R 7TB.

AITKEN, Maria

Maria Aitken. Actor/Chat Show Host (F).
b. Dublin, 11 September 1945.
TV: *A Bit of Fry and Laurie*; *Armchair Thriller*; *Bedroom Farce*; *Company & Co.*; *Crown Court*; *Fall in the Stars*; *Love on a Branch Line*; *Play for Today*; *Poor Little Rich Girls*; *Private Lives*; *Ripping Yarns*; *Romance Moths*; *Shelley*; *Sidney You're A Genius*; *South Bank Show*; *The Good Guys*.
Films: *A Fish Called Wanda*; *Dr Faustus*; *Fierce Creatures*; *Half Moon Street*; *Jinnah*; *Mary Queen of Scots*; *Melba*; *The Fool*; *The Grotesque*.
Address: c/o Whitehall Artists, 125 Gloucester Road, London SW7 4TE.

AKHURST, Lucy

Lucy Akhurst. Actor (F). b. Newcastle, 1970.
TV: Laura Delooze in *All Quiet on the Preston Front*; Polly Benton in *The Cinder Path*; Alic Grant in *The Vanishing Man*; Lead character in *Wonderful You*; *Longitude*.
Films: Spider Woman in *Big City Blue*; *Circus*; Janet in *Landgirls*.
Address: c/o Roxane Vacca Management, 73 Beak Street, London W1R 3LF. m., 1 child. Hobbies: Swimming, horse riding.

ALAN, Ray

Ray Alan. Writer/Ventriloquist.
b. Greenwich, London, 18 September 1930.

TV: *A Gottle of Geer*; *Bob Hope's Birthday Show*; *Ice Show*; *It's Your World*; *Magic Circle*; *The Good Old Days*; *The Magic Show*; *Three Little Words*; *Titch and Quackers*; *Where in the World*.
Address: International Artistes Ltd, Regent House, 235 Regent Street, London W1R 8AX. Family: m. Jane.

ALCOCK, Victoria

Victoria Alcock. Actor (F).
TV: *Castles*; *Chillers*; *Coronation Street*; *EastEnders*; *Far From the Madding Crowd*; *Grange Hill*; *The House of Elliott*; *Jailbirds*; *Lovejoy*; *Poirot*; *The Bill*.
Address: c/o The Narrow Road Company, 21–22 Poland Street, London W1V 3DD. Hobbies: Horse riding, tap dancing.

ALDERTON, John

John Alderton. Actor (M).
b. Gainsborough, Lincolnshire, 27 November 1940.
TV: *Father's Day*; *Forever Green*; *The Mrs Bradley Mysteries*; *My Wife Next Door*; *No, Honestly*; *Please Sir*; *The Upchat Line*; *Thomas and Sarah*; *Upstairs Downstairs*; *Wodehouse Playhouse*.
Films: *It Shouldn't Happen to a Vet*; *Zardoz*.
Address: c/o Whitehall Artists, 125 Gloucester Road, London SW7 4TE.

ALDERTON, Terry

Terry Alderton. Comedian/Presenter.
b. Southend.
TV: *First Impressions*; *Glamorama with Jack Dee*; *National Lottery*; *Saturday Live*; *The Comedy Store*; *Viva Cabaret*; *Red Alert*.
Address: c/o Off the Kerb Productions, 3rd Floor, Hammer House, 113–117 Wardour Street, London W1V 3TD.

ALDRED, Sophie

Sophie Aldred. Actor/Presenter (F).
b. Greenwich, London, 20 August 1962.
TV: *Bitesize*; *Carlton Country*; *Corners*; Dorothy 'Ace' McShane in *Doctor Who*; Suzie in *EastEnders*; *Heart of the Country*; *It's a Mystery*; *Live Wire*; *Love Call Live*; *Numbertime*; *Tiny and Crew*; *Under the Influence*; *Words and Pictures*; *Wow!*.
Address: c/o Michael Ladkin Personal Management, Suite One, Ground Floor, 1 Duchess Street, London W1N 3DE. Hobbies: Trumpet, piano, most sports.

ALEXANDER, Jean

Jean Alexander. Actor (F).
b. 56 Parkdale Road, Liverpool, 24 February 1926.
TV: Mrs Whisper in *Adam's Family Tree*; *Boon*; Marjory

Hunt in *Cluedo* (1993); Hilda Ogden in *Coronation Street*; *Deadline Midnight* (1961); Irene Patterson in *Harry*; *Jacks and Knaves*; Auntie Wainwright in *Last of the Summer Wine*; Lily in *The Phoenix and the Carpet*; *Top Secret*; *Woof*; *Z Cars*.
Films: Mrs Keeler in *Scandal*; *Willie's War*; *The Phoenix and the Carpet*.
Address: c/o Joan Reddin; Hazel Cottage, Wheeler End Common, Wheeler End, High Wycombe, Buckinghamshire HP14 3NL.

ALEXANDER, Maev

Maev Alexander. Actor/Presenter (F).
b. Glasgow, 2 March 1948.
TV: *A Christmas Carol*; *A Leap in the Dark*; *Angels*; *By the Sword Divided*; *EastEnders*; *Hazell*; Jen-Jen in *Holding the Fort*; *Inspector Ghote Moves In*; *Kids*; *Pictures*; *Scoop*; *Smeddum*; *Sutherland's Law*; *Take the Stage*; *That's Life* (1985); *The Befrienders*; *The Borders*; *The Fools on the Hill*; *The Gentle Touch*; *The Kit Curran Radio Show*; *The Main Chance*; *The New Avengers*; *The New Road*; *The Revenue Man*; *The Standard*; *This Man Craig*; *Visitors*.
Address: c/o Brian Taylor – Nina Quick Associates, 50 Pembroke Road, Kensington, London W8 6NX. Family: 1 d. Alix. Hobbies: Running a small textiles design company called 'Pure Fabrication'.

ALEXANDER, Peter

Peter Alexander. Actor (M).
b. Midsomer Norton, Somerset, 15 October 1952.
TV: *Affairs of the Heart*; *All Creatures Great and Small*; *Brookside*; *Chess Game*; *Coronation Street*; *EastEnders*; Phil Pearce in *Emmerdale Farm*; *Disasters*; *Family Man*; *Heartbeat*; *Medics*; *Minder*; *Mission Top Secret*; *Singles*; *The Bill*; *The Practice*; *Travelling Man*; *Tuesdays and Thursdays*; *Winning Streak*.
Address: c/o Burnett Granger Associates Ltd, Prince Of Wales Theatre, 31 Coventry Street, London W1V 8AS. m. Penny Stevenson; 1 d. Emily; 1 s. Nicholas. Hobbies: Golf, music, wine, food.

ALEXANDROU, James

James Alexandrou. Actor(M). b. 12 April 1985.
TV: *Diggit*; *Disney Club Christmas Special*; Martin Fowler in *EastEnders*.
Address: c/o Anna Scher Theatre Managment Ltd, 70–72 Barnsbury Road, London N1 OES. Hobbies: Swimming, football, basketball.

ALLDRIDGE, Arin

Arin Alldridge. Actor (M).
TV: Joe in *Deadman's Tales*; Daniel in *Heterosexual*;

Scientist in *Oktober*; Gerry in *Press Gang*; P.C. Phil Young in *The Bill*.
Address: Argyle Associates, 86 Goswell Road, London EC1V 7DR. Hobbies: Guitar, various sports.

ALLEN, Dave

David Tynan O'Mahony. Comedian/Presenter.
b. Tallaght, Co. Dublin, 6 July 1936.
TV: *Clive Anderson* (1998); *Clive James* (1995); *Dave Allen* (1992); *Dave Allen at Large* (1979); *Des O'Connor* (1996); *Eccentrics at Play* (1974); *In Search of the Great British Eccentric* (1974); *New Faces* (1959); *One Fine Day* (1978); *Salute to Sir Lew Grade* (1975); *Sunday Night at the London Palladium*; *This Morning* (1996); *Tonight with Dave Allen*.
Address: c/o The Richard Stone Partnership, 2 Henrietta Street, London WC2E 8PS.

ALLEN, Keith

Keith Allen. Actor (M). b. 1952.
TV: *A Very British Coup*; *The Beat Generation*; *Between the Lines*; *Born to Run*; *Breaking Rank*; *Class Act*; *Dangerfield*; *Detectives on the Verge of a Nervous Breakdown*; *Faith*; *Fistful of Traveller's Cheques*; *Gino*; *Gregory – Video Diary of a Nutcase*; *I Love Keith Allen*; *Inspector Morse*; *It's Keith Allen*; *Jack of Hearts*; *Making Out*; *Martin Chuzzlewit*; *One More Thing*; *Preston Front*; *Red Nose of Courage*; *Roger Roger*; *Samson & Delilah*; *Secret Ingredient*; *Sharman*; *Shooting Stars*; *Space Virgins from the Planet Sex*; *The Bite*; *The Bullshitters*; *The Crying Game*; *The Life of William Palmer*; *The Strike*; *The Yob*; *Ticket to Ride*; *Walter*; *Whatever You Want*; *You Are Here*; *Young Person's Guide to Becoming a Rock Star*.
Films: *Beyond Bedlam*; *Blue Juice*; *Captives*; *Carry On Colombus*; *Chicago Joe and the Showgirl*; *Comrades*; *Kafka*; *Loch Ness*; *Preaching to the Perverted*; *Rancid Aluminium*; *Rebecca's Daughters*; *Robinson Crusoe*; *Scandal*; *Second Best*; *Shallow Grave*; *Supergrass*; *Trainspotting*; *Twin Town*; *The Wrong Blonde*; *Young Americans*.
Address: c/o ICM, Oxford House, 76 Oxford Street, London W1N 0AX.

ALLEN, Patrick

Patrick Allen. Actor (M). b. 17 March 1927.
TV: *Bergerac*; *Body and Soul*; *Brett*; *Churchill and the Generals*; *Crane*; *East Lynne*; Major Ferguson in *Fergie and Andrew: Behind the Palace Doors*; *Hamlet*; *Hard Times*; *Kidnapped*; Major Horton in *Murder is Easy*; *Pericles*; *Roman Holiday*; *Sea Wolves*; *Blackadder*; *The Return of Sherlock Holmes*.
Films: *Caligula*; *Captain Clegg*; *Carry On Doctor*; *Confession*; *Cross Channel*; *Dial M for Murder*; *Diamonds*

on Wheels; Dunkirk; Flight from Singapore; High Tide at Noon; I Was Monty's Double; Jet Storm; Never Take Sweets From a Stranger; Night of the Big Heat; Persecution; Puppet on a Chain; Sinister Man; The Long Haul; The Man Who Wouldn't Talk; The Night of the Generals; The Traitors; The Wilby Conspiracy; The Wild Geese; The World At their Feet; Thin Air; Tread Softly Stranger; When Dinosaurs Ruled the Earth.
Address: c/o ICM, Oxford House, 76 Oxford Street, London W1N 0AX.

ALLEN, Sheila

Sheila Allen. Actor (F).
b. Chard, Somerset, 22 October 1932.
TV: A Bouquet of Barbed Wire; A Portrait of Marion Evans; Act of Will; Antonia and Jane; Casualty; Danger Man; Dangerfield; Mothertime; Old Devils; Poirot; Shoulder to Shoulder; Stolen; Shroud for a Nightingale; The Four Just Men; The Hedgehog Wedding; The Prisoner; The Regiment; The Ring; The Trial of Lady Chatterley.
Films: Mrs Freidan in Fire of the Dark; Liz West in Northern Crescent; Mrs Marchant in Pascali's Island; Olga in Shining Through; The A.B.C. Murders; Mary Tudor in The Prince and the Pauper.
Address: c/o Cassie Mayer Ltd, 34 Kingly Court, London W1R 5LE.

ALLEN, Tim

Timothy Allen Dick. Actor (M).
b. Denver, Colorado, USA, 13 June 1953.
TV: Tim 'The Tool Man' Taylor in Home Improvement; Just For Laughs Festival (1991); Men Are Pigs (1990); Showtime Comedy Club All-Stars II (1988); Tim Taylor in Soul Man (1997); Rags in Spin City (1998); Himself in The Drew Carey Show (1996); Pilot in The Flying Doctors (1985).
Films: Brad Sexton in For Richer or Poorer; Jason Nesmith/Commander Peter Quincy Taggart in Galaxy Quest; Michael Cromwell in Jungle2Jungle; himself in Meet Wally Sparks; Fringe Theatre Director in The Girl Who Came Late; Scott Calvin in The Santa Clause; Buzz Lightyear in Toy Story; Buzz Lightyear in Toy Story 2; Baggage Handler in Tropical Snow; Interviewer in What Do You Say To A Naked Lady?.
Address: c/o Messina Baker Agency, 955 South Carillo Drive, Suite 100, Los Angeles, CA 90048, USA. m. Laura Deibel; 1 d. Kady. Hobbies: Writing, cars, DIY.

ALLEY, Kirstie

Kirstie Alley. Actor (F).
b. Wichita, Kansas, USA, 12 January 1955.
TV: Gloria Steinem in A Bunny's Tale (1985); Rebecca

Howe in Cheers (1987); Sally Goodson in David's Mother (1994); Ellie Denato in Infidelity (1987); Le Voyageur (1990); Casey Collins in Masquerade (1983); Masquerade (1990); Match Game 73 (1973); Virgilia Hazard in North and South II; Annie in Peter and the Wolf (1996); Gloria Goodman in Radiant City (1996); Patrice Cantwell in Sins of the Past (1984); The Hitch Hiker (1983); Rose Marie Clericuzio in The Last Don (1997); Rose Marie Clericuzio in The Last Don II (1998); Catherine Lewis in Toothless (1997); Veronica Chase in Veronica's Closet.
Films: Barbara in Champions; Joan in Deconstructing Harry; Gladys Leeman in Drop Dead Gorgeous; Caroline Sexton in For Richer or Poorer; Diane Barrows in It Takes Two; Mollie in Look Who's Talking; Mollie in Look Who's Talking Now; Mollie in Look Who's Talking Too; Joyce Palmer in Loverboy; Jessie Bannister in Madhouse; McGill in Nevada; One More Chance; Jackie Rogers in Runaway; She's Having A Baby; Sarah in Shoot to Kill; Marjorie Turner in Sibling Rivalry; Lt. Saavik in Star Trek: The Wrath of Khan; Joey's Mum in Sticks and Stones; Robin Bishop in Summer School; Vanessa Bartholemew in The Mao Game; Three Chains O'Gold; Dr Susan Verner in Village of the Damned.
Address: Metropolitan Agency, 4526 Wilshire Blvd, Los Angeles, CA 90010, USA. Partner James Wilder; 1 s. William True Stevenson, 1 d. Lillie Price Stevenson.

ALLISS, Peter

Peter Alliss. Presenter. b. Berlin 1931.
TV: A Round with Alliss; Pro-Celebrity.
Address: c/o BBC, Union House, 65–69 Shepherds Bush Green, London W12 8TX. Hobbies: Yoga, meditation, keep fit.

AMORY, Peter

Peter Amory. Actor (M). b. 2 November 1962.
TV: Parrott in Boon; Guy in Casualty; Christopher Tate in Emmerdale; Andrew Craig-Allen in Gentlemen and Players; DC Hilaire in Inspector Morse; Rob in Running Wild; Robbie in The Chelworth Inheritance; The Chief.
Address: c/o David Daly Associates, 586a Kings Road, Fulham, London SW6 2DX. m. Claire King.

AMOS, Emma

Emma Amos. Actor (F). b. Newcastle-under Lyme, Staffordshire, 18 August 1967.
TV: Alas Smith and Jones; Yvonne Sparrow in Goodnight Sweetheart; Sonia in The Alleyn Mysteries; Samantha Connors in Madson; Mandy in Men Behaving Badly; Kathy in Moving Story; Murder Most Horrid II; Dawn in Passion Killers; The Perfect State.

Films: *A Ghost in Monte Carlo;* Dawn in *Buddy's Song;* Ellen in *Firelight; Rowing with the Wind; Secrets and Lies;* Diana in *The Tribe.*
Address: c/o Peters, Fraser and Dunlop, Drury House, 34–43 Russell Street, London WC2B 5HA. m. Jonathan Coy; 1 d. Esme.

ANDERSON, Clive

Clive Anderson. Presenter. b. 10 December 1952.
TV: *Clive Anderson All Talk; Have I Got News For You; Not the Nine O'Clock News; Notes and Queries; Whose Line is it Anyway?; Wogan; The Not the Nine O'Clock News Story.*
Address: c/o London Management, Noel House, 2–4 Noel Street, London W1V 3RB.

ANDERSON, Georgine

Georgine Anderson. Actor (F).
TV: *A Pin To See The Peep Show; An Unsuitable Job for a Woman; Angels; Auf Wiedersehn, Pet; Blott on the Landscape; Casualty; Century Falls; Coronation Street; Cousin Phyllis; Cruelty To Prawns; Do Not Disturb; Douglas; Enemy at the Door; Esther Waters; Family; Family at War; Glittering Prizes; Growing Pains; Hinckley House; Jonathan Creek; Love for Lydia; Marked Personnel; Matilda's England; Midnight Movie; Miss Marple:; Never the Twain; Sharing Time; Sister Dora; Taggart; The Hanged Man; The Jewel in the Crown; The Prime of Miss Jean Brodie; The Woman in White; Time For Murder; Upstairs Downstairs; Very Big, Very Soon; Wycliffe.*
Films: *Dardanelles; Secrets; The Innocent Sleep.*
Address: c/o Conway Van Gelder, 18–21 Jermyn Street, London SW1Y 6HP.

ANDERSON, Gillian

Gillian Anderson. Actor (F).
b. Chicago, Illinois, USA, 9 August 1968.
TV: *Class of '96* (1993); Agent Scully (voice) in *Eek! The Cat* (1995); Jenny (voice) in *Frasier* (1999); *Future Fantastic* (1996); Video narrator in *Harsh Realm* (1999); Data Nully in *Reboot* (1996); *Spies Above* (1996); Dana Scully in *The Simpsons* (1997); Special Agent Dana Katherine Scully in *The X-Files* (1993); *Why Planes Go Down* (1996).
Films: Southside girl in *Chicago Cab;* Meredith in *Playing By Heart;* Lily Bart in *The House of Mirth;* Loretta Lee in *The Mighty;* April Cavanaugh in *The Turning;* Agent Dana Scully in *The X-Files Movie.*
Address: c/o Steve Glick at William Morris Agency, 151 El Camino Drive, Beverly Hills, CA 90210, USA 90210. m. 1st Errol Clyde Kotz (sep); 1 d. Piper Maru. Hobbies: Scuba diving, collecting art.

ANDERSON, Miles

Miles Anderson. Actor (M). b. 1953.
TV: *A Certain Justice; A Touch of Frost; All in the Game; Bliss; Chiller;* Bailey in *Dangerfield;* Toby Ross in *Doomwatch;* Ian in *Every Woman Knows a Secret; Fall of Eagles;* Sam Dawson in *Have Your Cake and Eat It;* Roger O'Neill in *House of Cards; In Your Dreams;* Dr Peter Kingdom in *Into the Blue;* Tom Faggus in *Lorna Doone;* Guy Gamelin in *Midsomer Murders;* Poseidon in *Odyssey;* Baron Kite *Oliver's Travels; People Like Us;* Robin Hood; *Soldier, Soldier;* Patrick O'Sullivan in *The Rector's Wife;* Inspector Gary Harmer in *The Scold's Bridle; The Sweeney; What If It's Raining;* Charles Hudson in *A Wing and a Prayer.*
Films: Jardin in *A Far Off Place;* Lemick in *Cry Freedom;* Bannock in *Fast Food; Gunbus; Joseph Andrews;* The Sheriff in *Riddler's Moon;* David Hamilton in *The Thirty-Nine Steps;* Jack in *The King is Alive.*
Address: c/o CDA 19 Sydney Mews, London SW3 6HL.

ANDERSON, Pamela

Pamela Anderson. Actor (F).
b. Ladysmith, British Colombia, Canada, 1 July 1967.
TV: C.J. Parker in *Baywatch;* C.J. Parker in *Baywatch: River of No Return* (1995); Chris in *Charles in Charge* (1990); Velda in *Come Die with Me: A Mickey Spillane's Mike Hammer Mystery* (1994); Cindy in *Days of Our Lives* (1992); Herself *in Futurama* (1999); Lisa, the 'Tool Time Girl' in *Home Improvement* (1991); *Married with Children* (1990); Heather Biblow-Imperiali in *The Nanny* (1993); Romana in *Top of the Heap* (1992); Vallery Irons in *VIP.*
Films: Barbara Kopetski in *Barb Wire;* Britt in *Naked Souls;* Sarah in *Raw Justice;* Felicity in *Snapdragon; The Taking of Beverly Hills.*
Address: c/o Publicist Suzanne Austin, Columbia Pictures Television, 10202, W. Washington Bldg, SPP RM 4188, Culver City, CA 90232, USA. m. Tommy Lee (dis.); 2 s. Thomas, Dylan Jagger. Hobbies: Volleyball.

ANDREWS, Anthony

Anthony Andrews. Actor (M). b. 12 January 1948.
TV: *A War of Children; Bluegrass; Brideshead Revisited; Columbo: Columbo Goes to the Guillotine; Danger UXB; David Copperfield; Hands of a Murderer; Heartstones; Ivanhoe; Jewels; Mistress of Paradise; Mothertime; Much Ado About Nothing; Romeo and Juliet; Sparkling Cyanide; Suspicion; The Country Wife; The Scarlet Pimpernel; The Strange Case of Dr Jekyll and Mr Hyde; The Woman He Loved; Upstairs Downstairs; Z for Zachariah.*

Films: *AD; French Without Tears; Hannah's War; Innocent Heroes; Las Adolescentes; Operation Daybreak; Percy's Progress; QB VII; Take Me High; The Holcroft Covenant; The Lighthorsemen; The War Lord; Under the Volcano.*
Address: c/o PFD, Drury House, 34–43 Russell Street, London WC2B 5HA.

ANGELIS, Michael
Michael Angelis. Actor (M).
TV: *A Nightingale Sang in Berkeley Square; Bergerac; Boon; Boys from the Blackstuff; Casualty; GBH; George and Mildred; Luv; Melissa; No Surrender; Reilly, Ace of Spies; The Liver Birds;* Voice in *Thomas the Tank Engine.*
Address: c/o London Management, Noel House, 2–4 Noel Street, London W1V 3RB.

ANGELIS, Paul
Paul Angelis. Actor (M).
TV: *Black Beauty;* Robbie in *Brookside; The Brothers McGregor; Bullman; Callan;* Robert Layton in *Casualty; Conan Doyle;* Brian Bowes in *Coronation Street; Dick Turpin;* D.S. Barnes in *EastEnders; George and Mildred; Juliet Bravo; Kidnapped; Man about the House; Moon and Son; Porridge; Public Eye; Robin's Nest; Softly, Softly;* Fielding in *The Bill;* Mentorn in *The Bullion Boys; The Gentle Touch;* Big Reg Titley in *The Grimleys;* John Tideway in *The Hunt for the Yorkshire Ripper;* Connie Devooght in *The Knock; The Liver Birds; The Saint* (1989); *The Vice; Truckers; Tucker's Luck; Z Cars.*
Films: *For Your Eyes Only; Force 10 to Navarone; Hussey; Inadmissable Evidence; Otley; Runners; The Battle of Britain; The Garnet Saga; Yellow Submarine.*
Address: c/o Burdett-Coutts Associates, Riverside Studios, Crisp Road, London W6 9RL. Hobbies: Fencing, ballroom dancing.

ANHOLT, Christien
Christien Anholt. Actor (M).
TV: *Appetite; Cadfael; Felicity; Hard Times; Money for Nothing; Nightworld; The Relic Hunter; The Waiting Time.*
Films: *Blackheath Poisonings; Hamlet; Meter Running; One Against the Wind; Passmore; Power of One; Preaching to the Perverted; Reunion; Seventeen; Speilberg; The Harpist; The Ruby Ring; Thurn; Zefferelli.*
Address: c/o Roger Carey Associates, 7 St George's Square, London SW1V 2HX.

ANISTON, Jennifer
Jennifer Aniston. Actor/Voice artist (F).
b. Sherman Oaks, California, 11 February 1969.
TV: Suzie Brooks in *Herman's Head* (1992, 1993); Courtney in *Molloy* (1990); Madeline Drego Cooper in *Muddling Through* (1994); CPA Suzanne in *Partners* (1996); Kiki Wilson in *Quantum Leap* (1992); Miss Stevens, The Choir Teacher in *South Park* (1999); various, *The Edge* (1992); *The Larry Sanders Show* (1995); Linda Campbell in *Burke's Law* (1994); Ava in *Camp Cucamonga* (1990); Gallitea in *Disney's Hercules* (1998); Jeanie Bueller in *Ferris Bueller* (1990); Rachel Karen Green in *Friends* (1994); Suzie Brooks in *Herman's Head* (1992).
Films: Debbie in *'Til There Was You;* Allison in *Dream For An Insomniac;* Tory in *Leprechaun;* Joanna in *Office Space;* Kate Mosley in *Picture Perfect;* Renee Fitzpatrick in *She's The One;* Laura in *Steven Spielberg's Director's Chair;* Annie Hughes (voice) in *The Iron Giant;* Nina Borowski in *The Object of My Affection;* herself in *Waiting For Woody.*
Address: c/o Creative Artists Agency, 9830 Wilshire Boulevard, Beverly Hills, CA 90212, USA. Partner Brad Pitt; father John Aniston; mother Nancy Aniston; godfather Telly Savalas. Hobbies: Growing roses, collecting antiques.

ANNETT, Chloe
Chloe Annett. Actor (F). b. 25 July 1970.
TV: *All Creatures Great and Small; Byker Grove; Cadfael; Crime Traveller; Doctors at the Top; Families; Jewels; Red Dwarf; Ruth Rendell Mysteries; Spatz.*
Films: *Airs and Graces; Covington Cross;* Sarah in *Double X;* Mary in *How To Speak Japanese;* Emma in *Teacher's Pet;* Rose in *The Asylum.*
Address: Noel Gay Artists, Albion Court, Albion Place, Galena Road, London W6 0QZ. Partner Alec McKinlay; father Paul Annett; mother Margo Annett; brother Jamie.

ANNIS, Francesca
Francesca Annis. Actor (F). b. London, 19 May 1944.
TV: *A Pin to See the Peep Show; Absolute Hell; ARI; Between the Lines; Caversbridge; Comedy of Errors; Dalziel and Pascoe; Deadly Summer; Death of an Old-fashioned Girl; Debt Collector; Deceit; Edward VII; Gravy Train II; Haunting Harmony; Headhunters; Inside Story; Lillie; Madame Bovary; Magnum PI – Déjà Vu; Once Upon a Time; Parnell; Partners in Crime; Peer Gynt; Reckless; Schumann; Shades of Darkness – The Maze; Tales from the Crypt; The Chinese Prime Minister; The Couch; The Family is a Vicious Circle; The Ragazza; The Secret Adversary; The Way of the World; The Wood Demon; Weep No More, My Lady; Why Didn't They Ask Evans?; Wives and Daughters.*
Films: Clare in *Big Mack and Poor Clare; Coming out of the Ice;* Lady Jessica in *Dune; El Rio De Oro;* Tina

in *Gemini; Krull;* Lady Macbeth in *Macbeth;* Harriet in *Milk;* Katiusha in *Onegin; Penny Gold;* Arabella in *The Walking Stick;* Mrs Wellington in *Under the Cherry Moon.*
Address: c/o ICM, Oxford House, 76 Oxford Street, London W1N 0AX.

ANNOBIL-DODOO, Freddie
Freddie Annobil-Dodoo. Actor (M).
TV: Saul in *Grange Hill;* Karinde in *Heat of the Sun;* Marcus in *Holding On;* Romeo in *Shakespeare Shorts;* Richie Hutchin in *The Bill.*
Films: Elray in *Greenwich Mean Time;* Jason in *Jump Boys;* Fancy Man in *The Final Passage;* Paul in *Three Steps to Heaven.*
Address: c/o Sandra Boyce Management, 1 Kingsway Parade, Albion Road, London N16 0TA.

APSION, Annabelle
Annabelle Apsion. Actor (F).
TV: *Alive and Kicking; Big Women; Casualty; Framed; Goodnight Mister Tom;* Jenny in *Hillsborough; Killing Me Softly;* Jane Cavindish in *Midsomer Murders;* Mona Bunting in *Mrs Bradley;* Betty in *My Good Friend;* Joy in *Soldier, Soldier; Sunburn; The Lakes II; The Widow Maker.*
Films: *Lolita; The Wrong Blonde; This Year's Love; War Zone.*
Address: c/o PFD, Drury House, 34–43 Russell Street, London WC2B 5HA. Hobbies: Swimming, running, playing violin and piano, boxing.

ARIS, Ben
Ben Aris. Actor (M).
b. Chelsea, London, 16 March 1937.
TV: *Boon; Call Me Mister; Charlie the Kid; Clouds of Glory; Eldorado; First of the Summer Wine; Further Up Pompeii; A Hazard of Hearts;* Hercule Poirot; Julian Dalrymple-Sykes in *Hi De Hi; Hope it Rains; In Sickness and in Health; In Suspicious Circumstances; King of Chaos; King of the Wind; Lady Chatterley; No Job for a Lady;* Simon Anderson in *September Song; The Bill; The Falklands Factor; The Good Guys; The Last Englishman;* Spalding in *To the Manor Born.*
Films: *Charge of the Light Brigade; Didn't You Kill My Brother?; Get Carter; Hold the Dream; If...; O Lucky Man!; Relative Values; Royal Flash; The Fool; The Ritz; The Savage Messiah; The Three Musketeers; Tom Brown's Schooldays; Up the Villa.*
Address: c/o Barry Brown & Partner, 47 West Square, London SE11.

ARIS, Gina
Gina Aris. Actor (F).
TV: Frankie in *Emmerdale;* Maxine in *In the Pink;* Katy in *Peak Practice;* Elaine Beckett in *The Bill;* Samantha in *Them And Us;* Nurse Cox in *Woof; Your Mother Wouldn't Like It.*
Films: Ruby in *Small Time;* Sharon in *TwentyFour Seven.*
Address: c/o William Morris Agency, 1 Stratton Street, London W1X 6UB.

ARMSTRONG, Alun
Alun Armstrong. Actor (M).
b. Anfield Plain, 17 July 1946.
TV: The Father in *All Day at the Sands;* Henry Fox in *Aristocrats;* Jimmy Hardcastle in *Brazen Hussies;* Singer in *Caucasian Chalk Circle;* Shep in *Days of Hope;* Gerald in *Goggle Eyes;* Jefferson in *In the Red;* Thenardier in *Les Miserables;* Barnardio in *Measure for Measure;* Squeers in *Nicholas Nickelby;* Mr Flemming in *Oliver Twist;* Lead in *Only Make Believe;* Mr Briggs in *Our Day Out;* Austin Donoghue in *Our Friends in the North;* Mickey in *Sorry About Last Night;* Herbert in *Tales from the Crypt;* Uncle Teddy in *The Life and Times of Henry Pratt;* Badger *in This is Personal;* Middlemas in *Underworld;* Fr Harold Poulchau in *Witness Against Hitler.*
Films: Weeks in *American Friends;* Uncle Vernon in *An Awfully Big Adventure;* Reuben in *Black Beauty;* Osgood in *Blue Ice;* Mornay in *Braveheart;* Keith in *Get Carter;* Samuel Brubeck in *Harrison Flowers;* Stone in *London Kills Me;* Sammy in *Old New Borrowed Blue;* Zaretsky in *Onegin;* Owen in *Patriot Games;* Louis Mayer in *RKO 281;* Thrasher in *Split Second;* Stefano in *The Child Eater;* Inspector Teale in *The Saint;* The Father in *The Widow Maker;* Lockheart in *White Hunter, Black Heart;* Zemba in *White Roses.*
Address: c/o Markham & Froggatt Ltd, 4 Windmill Street, London W1P 1HF.

ARMSTRONG, Fiona
Fiona Armstrong. Journalist/Presenter.
b. Preston, Lancashire, 28 November 1956.
TV: *Border Television News; Lookaround* (1985); *Northwest Tonight* (1982); *The Prince and Princess of Wales In Western Africa* (1990); *Under the Hammer; ITN News.*
Address: c/o Knight Ayton Management, 10 Argyll Street, London W1V 1AB.

ARMSTRONG, Linda
Linda Armstrong. Actor (F).
TV: F.S.O. Nichols in *Brookside;* Prison Guard in

BUGS; D.S. Kate Morgan in *The Bill*; Dr Beth Hardwick in *The Millennium Bug*; Lisa Jenson in *Casualty*; Jill in *Dangerfield*; Christine in *Emma's Story*; D.I. Alice Beale in *Frost*; Car Darch in *Tess of the D'Urbervilles*.
Address: c/o Barry Brown & Partner, 47 West Square, London SE11.

ARNOLD, Debbie
Debbie Arnold. Actor (F).
b. Sunderland, 14 June 1957.
TV: *A Turn for the Worse; All Creatures Great and Small; Birds of a Feather; Bottle Saddles; C.A.T.S. Eyes; Coronation Street; Don't Wait Up; EastEnders; Emmerdale; Four in a Million; Hollyoaks; Jonathan Creek; Minder; Miss Marple; Now Who Do You Do; Once in a Lifetime; Real Women; Rockliffe's Babies; The Bill; The Dick Emery Show; The Funny Side; The Good Sex Guide; The Jim Davidson Show; The Liver Birds; The Russ Abbot Show; The Two Ronnies; Ticket to Ride; Virtual Murder.*
Address: c/o Whitehall Artists, 125 Gloucester Road, London SW7 4TE.

ARNOLD, Steven
Steven Arnold. Actor (M).
b. Warrington, 12 December 1974.
TV: Joe Lloyd in *Children's Ward*; Stanty in *Common As Muck*; Ashley Peacock in *Coronation Street*; Courier in *Hetty Wainthropp Investigates*; Darren in *Medics*; Rob in *The Bill*; *You, Me and Marley*.
Films: *Growing Pains*; Lloyd in *This Boy's Story*.
Address: c/o Pemberton Associates, 193 Wardour Street, London W1V 3FA.

ASH, Leslie
Leslie Ash. Actor (F). b. 1960.
TV: *The Happy Apple; The Marksman; The Tube; BUGS; C.A.T.S. Eyes; Going for a Song; Haggard; Harry Enfield's Television Programme; Home to Roost; La Ronde; Love Hurts; Men Behaving Badly; Murder – Ultimate Grounds for Divorce; Natural Causes; Outside Edge; Perfect Scoundrels; Seconds Out; Shelley; Sporting Chance II; Stay Lucky; The Balance of Nature; The Bill.*
Films: *Quadrophenia; Shadey; The Curse of the Pink Panther; The Nutcracker.*
Address: c/o International Artistes Ltd, Mezzanine Floor, 235 Regent Street, London W1R 8AX. m. Lee Chapman.

ASHBOURNE, Jayne
Jayne Ashbourne. Actor (F). b. 10 February 1969.
TV: *Band of Gold; Big Women; Blood and Peaches; Coronation Street; The Alleyn Mysteries; Lost in France;*

Madson; Money for Nothing; Pale Horse; Respect; Sharpe's Gold; Little Orphan Annie in *Sir Daddy; The Grand; The Life of William Palmer; The Riff-Raff Element; The Young Indiana Jones Chronicles.*
Films: *Honest; Loop.*
Address: c/o ICM, Oxford House, 76 Oxford Street, London W1N 0AX.

ASHBOURNE, Lorraine
Lorraine Ashbourne. Actor (F).
TV: *3-7-11; Chiller; City Central; Fighting For Gemma; In Suspicious Circumstances; Life's a Bitch; Mr Wroe's Virgins; Pie in the Sky; Playing the Field; Rich Tea and Sympathy.*
Films: *Distant Voices, Still Lives; Fever Pitch; Jack And Sarah; Resurrected; The Dressmaker.*
Address: c/o ICM, Oxford House, 76 Oxford Street, London W1N 0AX.

ASHCROFT, Ray
Ray Ashcroft. Actor (M). b. Yorkshire, 28 June 1952.
TV: DS Geoff Daly in *The Bill; Emmerdale; Chandler & Co; Hetty Wainthropp; Heartbeat; The Chief; Prime Suspect; September Song*
Films: Ringo in *Birth of the Beatles; Diamonds in Brown Paper.*
Address: c/o Tim Scott Personal Management, 5 Cloisters Business Centre, 8 Battersea Park Road, London, SW8 4BG.

ASHE, Anna Maria
Anna Maria Ashe. Presenter (F)/Newsreader.
TV: *Can't Stand the Heat; Health Matters; London Today; London Tonight; Summer Dream Ticket; The Telethon.*
Address: c/o The Roseman Organisation, Suite 9, The Power House, 70 Chiswick Road, London W4 1SY. Hobbies: Interior design, theatre, cinema, singing.

ASHE, Daniela
Daniela Ashe. Actor (F).
TV: *Absolutely Fabulous; Crime Limited; Crimewatch; Desmonds;* Sarah Hills in *EastEnders; Kevin and Co.; The New Adventures of Molly.*
Address: c/o Ravenscourt Management, Tandy House, 30–40 Dalling Road, London W6 0JB.

ASHER, Jane
Jane Asher. Actor (F)/Presenter.
b. London, 5 April 1946.
TV: *A Voyage Around My Father;* Celia Ryder in *Brideshead Revisited;* Emma Vane in *East Lynne; French & Saunders; Good Living;* Lydia Howling in

Murder Most Horrid; Rumpole of the Bailey; Felicity Troy in *The Choir;* Helen in *The Mistress;* Faith Ashley in *Wish Me Luck.*

Films: *Adventure in the Hopfields;* Annie in *Alfie;* Anna in *Closing Numbers; Dance Little Lady;* Susan in *Deep End;* Mrs Liddell in *Dreamchild;* Lindy Birkett in *Girl In The Headlines;* Jane Seymour in *Henry VIII and His Six Wives;* Nina in *Mandy;* Pauline in *Paris By Night; Runners;* Bank Manager in *Success is the Best Revenge;* Margaret in *The Buttercup Chain;* Hester in *The Greengage Summer;* Francesca in *The Masque of the Red Death;* Lady Jane Grey in *The Prince and The Pauper;* Little Girl in *The Quatermass Experiment;* Perdita in *The Winter's Tale.*

Address: c/o Chatto & Linnit Ltd, 123a Kings Road London SW3 4PL. m. Gerald Scarfe; 1 d. Katie; 2 s. Alexander, Rory.

ASHFORDE, Matthew

Matthew Ashforde. Actor (M).

TV: Biker in *Drop the Dead Donkey;* Millwall supporter in *Gone to Seed; Harry Enfield and Chums;* The Engineer in *Heroes and Villains;* Darren in *Is it Legal?; London's Burning;* The Porter in *Mr Bean;* Gordon in *Paul Merton (Don't Dilly Dally);* Roger in *Press Gang;* Tel in *Shelley; Sitcom Festival;* Doggy Bag in *Stonecold;* William in *Wonderful You;* Phil in *You, Me and Him.*

Films: Marine Farnworth in *An Ungentlemanly Act;* Bell Boy in *London Suite; Luxury Tug;* Martin in *On the Roof;* Billy in *The Key to Life Itself.*

Address: c/o Annette Stone Associates, 2nd Floor, 22 Great Marlborough Street, London W1V 1AF.

ASHPITEL, Ian

Ian Ashpitel. Actor (M).

b. Leigh, Lancashire, 15 February 1957.

TV: Mr Blunlett in *EastEnders;* Chris Hart in *Family Affairs; Fist of Fun; Saturday Night Armistice; The Bill;* Lennox in *The Knock.*

Films: *The Pill.*

Address: c/o Sandra Griffin Management, 6 Ryde Place, Richmond Road, Twickenham, Middlesex TW1 2EH. Hobbies: Golf, cooking, reading (particulary books on Napoleon).

ASHTON, Al Hunter

Al Hunter Ashton. Actor (M). b. Liverpool.

TV: *Back Up; Bergerac; Birds of a Feather; Bread; Broker's Man; Bullion Boys; Casualty; Devices and Desires; Duck Patrol; Emmerdale; Holby City; Inspector Morse; Kinsey; London's Burning; Lost Empires; Lytton's Diary; Mr Bean; Oh, Doctor Beeching!; Out of Sight; Raw Talent; Rumble; See How They Run; Surgical Spirit;*

Teaching Matthew; Tenth Kingdom; The Brittas Empire; The Chief; Time After Time; Walk to Fly; Watching; White Goods.

Films: *A Fish Called Wanda; Arthur's Hollowed Ground; Endless Game; Femme Fatale; Remembrance;* George Merry in *Treasure Island; Widow Maker.*

Address: The Narrow Road Company, 21–22 Poland Street, London W1V 3DD. Hobbies: Karate (green belt), squash, tennis, football.

ASHTON, John

John Ashton. Actor (M). b. 29 November 1950.

TV: Detective Sgt. Anderson in *Brookside;* Corby in *EastEnders;* Cushing in *Family Affairs;* Tim in *Gold; Grange Hill;* Beardsall in *Hippies;* Robinson in *London's Burning;* Graham Ridley in *Love Hurts; Michael Winner's True Crimes; Out of Court; Possessions;* Hodge in *Shine on Harvey Moon;* Brooks/ Coughlin/Durrant/Micky in *The Bill; The Discovery of Animal Behaviour;* Det. Supt. Ferman in *UltraViolet;* Roy Bennet in *Up Rising;* Chief Supt. Don Henderson in *Waterfront Beat.*

Films: *Demolition Man.*

Address: c/o Sandra Griffin Management, 6 Ryde Place, Richmond Road, Twickenham, Middlesex TW1 2EH. Hobbies: Guitar, various sports.

ASHTON, Marcia

Marcia Ashton. Actor (F). b. Sheffield, 1 July 1932.

TV: Miss Temple in *Bernard and the Genie;* Jean Crosbie in *Brookside;* Mrs Chalmers in *Collision Course; Father, Dear Father;* Grace Lyndon in *Holby City;* Matilda in *Mattspy;* Karaoke Woman in *Men Behaving Badly; On the Buses; Play for Today; Pulaski;* Mrs Dankwerts in *Rumpole of the Bailey;* Maggie Shallworth in *The Bill; The Brothers; Upstairs Downstairs; Z Cars.*

Address: c/o Glenn Bexfield Personal Management, 55 Kenilworth Road, London E3 5RH.

ASHWORTH, Dicken

Dicken Ashworth. Actor (M).

b. Todmorden, Yorkshire.

TV: *Bat Out Of Hell; Better Days; Boon; Casualty; Common as Muck; Coronation Street; Grange Hill; I Lovett; Inspector Morse; Madson; Making Out; Minder; Return to Treasure Island; Revenger's Comedy; Riff Raff Element; Scab; The Bill; The Detectives; The Lakes; The Luddites; Thin Blue Line; Vroom; We are Seven.*

Films: *Blood and the Dole; Chariots of Fire; Force 10 From Navarone; Krull; Remembrance; Tess; The Biggest Bank Robbery.*

Address: c/o The Narrow Road Company, 21–22 Poland Street, London W1V 3DD.

ASPEL, Michael
Michael Aspel. Announcer/Presenter.
b. London, 12 January 1933.
TV: *Ask Aspel* (1968); *Aspel and Co.* (1984); *BBC News*; *Child's Play* (1982); *Strange But True* (1996); *Telethon* (1988, 1990, 1992); *This is Your Life.*
Address: c/o Shepherd & Ford, 13 Radnor Walk, London SW3 4BP. m. 3 Elizabeth; 4 s. Richard (from 1st m.), Edward (from 2nd m.), Daniel (from 3rd m.), Patrick (from 3rd m.); 1 d. Jane (from 2nd m.). Hobbies: cars, films, drawing cartoons.

ASPINALL, Ian
Ian Aspinall. Actor (M). b. 1971.
TV: Dr Memarzia in *Band of Gold II*; Hassan in *Body and Soul*; Kumar Kaul in *Casualty*; Barney in *Gigglish Allsorts*; *How to be Cool*; Fighter Controller in *Invasion Earth*; Simon Rollanson in *Peak Practice*; Anthony in *Supply and Demand*; Anil in *The Bill*; Dilip in *The Fragile Heart*; Pony in *The King of Farawania.*
Films: Nazir Khan in *East is East.*
Address: c/o CDA, 19 Sydney Mews, London SW3 6HL. Hobbies: Guitar, fencing.

ASPREY, George
George Asprey. Actor (M). b. London 1966.
TV: Lieutenant in *A Breed of Heroes*; *An Independent Man*; Jeremy in *Coming Home*; *Nancherrow*; *Supply & Demand*; *The Bill*; Sean Devereux in *The Dying of the Light*; Frank in *The Peter Principle*; *Trial and Retribution.*
Address: c/o Jonathan Altaras Associates, 13 Short Gardens, London WC2H 9AT.

ATKINS, Eileen
Eileen Atkins. Actor/Creator (F).
b. London, 16 June 1934.
TV: *A Dance to the Music of Time*; *A Hazard of Hearts*; *A Midsummer Night's Dream*; *Cold Comfort Farm*; *Oliver Twist*; *Roman Holiday*; *She Fell Among Thieves*; *Smiley's People*; *Talking Heads*; *The Burston Rebellion*; *The Duchess of Malfi*; *The Ghost Hunter*; *The House of Elliott*; *The Lady from the Sea*; *The Lost Languages of Cranes*; *The Three Sisters*; *Titus Andronicus*; *Upstairs Downstairs* (co-creator).
Films: *Let Him Have It*; Nelly in *Nelly's Version*; *The Devil Within Her*; *The Dresser*; *The Vision.*
Address: c/o ICM, Oxford House, 76 Oxford Street, London W1N 0AX. m. Bill Shephard.

ATKINS, Holly
Holly Atkins. Actor (F).
TV: Carrie in *EastEnders*; Alex in *Kiss Me Kate.*
Films: Elizabeth in *Belles of the Black Diamond Field.*
Address: c/o Garricks, 7 Garrick Street, London WC2E 9AR.

ATKINSON, Rowan
Rowan Atkinson. Actor (M).
b. Co. Durham, 6 January 1955.
TV: Blackadder in *Blackadder*; Mr Bean in *Mr Bean*; *Not the Nine O'Clock News* (1978); *Rowan Atkinson on location in Boston* (1993); Inspector Raymond Fowler in *The Thin Blue Line* (1995).
Films: *Blackadder, Back and Forth* (1999); Mr Bean in *Bean – The Ultimate Disaster Movie* (1997); *Hot Shots – Part Deux*; *Never Say Never Again*; *The Appointments of Dennis Jennings* (1989); Zazu in *The Lion King* (1996); *The Tall Guy*; *The Witches.*
Address: c/o PBJ Management, 5 Soho Square, London W1V 5DE. m. Sunetra Sastry; 1 child.

ATKINSON WOOD, Helen
Helen Atkinson Wood. Actor/Presenter (F).
b. Cheadle Hulme, 14 March 1955.
TV: *Alfresco*; Mrs Miggins in *Blackadder III*; *Collector's Lot*; Anna Daptor in *KYTV*; *OTT*; *Style Trial*; Blackheart in *Tales from the Poopdeck*; *The Good Life Gourmet Guide*; *The Story of Bean*; Tamara Magaskill in *Your Cheatin' Heart.*
Films: *Chasing the Bandwagon*; *Consuela.*
Address: c/o Shepherd & Ford, 13 Radnor Walk, Chelsea, London SW3 4BP. m. John Morton.

ATTENBOROUGH, David
David Attenborough. Presenter-Writer/Producer.
b. London, 8 May 1926.
TV: *Life in the Freezer* (1993); *Life on Earth* (1979); *Lost World* (1989); *The First Eden* (1987); *The Life of Birds* (1998); *The Living Planet* (1984); *The Private Life of Plants* (1995); *The Trials of Life* (1990); *Tribal Eye* (1976); *Vanished Lives* (1989); *Wildlife on One.*
Address: Contact via BBC, Union House, 65–69 Shepherds Bush Green, London W12 8TX. Brother Richard Attenborough. Hobbies: Music, tribal art, natural history.

AUBREY, James
James Aubrey. Actor (M). b. Klangenfurt 1947.
TV: *A Fatal Inversion*; Gavin in *Another Bouquet*; *Apocalypse Watch*; Gavin in *Bouquet of Barbed Wire*; *Brookside*; *Casualty*; *Danton's Death*; *Figure in a Landscape*; *Full Stretch*; *Great Writers*; *Harry*; *Infidelities*; *Inspector Morse*; *Lovejoy*; *Lytton's Diary*; *Minder*; *Mission Eureka*; *Return of the Saint*; *Rockliffe's Babies*; *Selling Hitler*; *Shackleton*; *Silent Witness*; *St. Joan*; *Tecx*; *The Bill*; *The*

Choir; *The Cleopatras*; Tom in *The Glass Menagerie*; *The Men's Room*; *The Mountain and the Molehill*; *The Sweeney*; *Thin Air*; *Van Der Valk*; *Variety of Passion*; *Voice from the Gallows*.

Films: *Buddy's Song*; *Cry Freedom*; *Forever Young*; *Galileo*; *Home Before Midnight*; *Terror*; *The American Way*; *The Final Frame*; *The Great Rock 'n' Roll Swindle*; *The Hunger*.

Address: c/o Conway Van Gelder, 18–21 Jermyn Street, London SW1Y 6HP.

AUSTIN, Mark

Mark Austin. News Correspondent. b. 1959.

TV: News Correspondent for ITN; Asia Correspondent; Africa Correspondent; BBC Sports Correspondent; Sports reporting for ITN.

Address c/o ITN, 200 Gray's Inn Road, London, WC1X 8XZ.

AYOLA, Rakie

Rakie Ayola. Actor (F). b. 1968.

TV: Lauren in *A Better Life Than Mine*; Karen Goddard in *Casualty*; Helen Tomlin in *Maisie Raine*; *Night Shift*; Pansy in *Scarlett*; Bernie Roberts in *Soldier, Soldier*; Helen Jarrett in *Tiger Bay*.

Films: Gabriel in *Great Moments in Aviation*; Housing Officer in *Horse*; *The Secret Laughter of Women*.

Address: c/o Marina Martin Associates, 12–13 Poland Street, London W1V 3DE. Hobbies: Singing, jazz dancing.

AYRES, Rosalind

Rosalind Ayres. Actor (F). b. 7 December 1944.

TV: *Afternoon at the Festival*; *Agony*; *Better Than the Movies*; *Casualty*; *Charades*; *Chicago Hope*; *Coronation Street*; *Country Matters*; *Family at War*; *Father Brown*; *Father's Day*; *General Hospital*; Anne Foxton in *Heartbeat*; *Hindle Wakes*; *Holding On*; *Home and Away*; *Juliet Bravo*; Doreen Anderson in *Midsomer Murders*; *Milly*; *Mistress of Suspense*; *Nearest and Dearest*; *New World*; *Nurses Do*; *Old Man's Hat*; *Only When I Laugh*; *Penmarric*; *PSY Warriors*; *Public Eye*; *Rings on their Fingers*; *Shoulder to Shoulder*; *The Bounder*; Mrs McFell in *The Cinder Path*; *The Dick Emery Show*; *The Gay Lord Quex*; *The Gentle Touch*; *The Good Guys*; *The House of Bernarda Alba*; *The Late Wife*; *The Limbo Connection*; *The Lovers*; *The Saliva Milkshake*; *The Stretch*; *The Weather in the Streets*; *The Widowing of Mrs Holroyd*; Doctor in *The Upper Hand*; *Thrills Galore*; *Two's Company*; *Warship*; *Who Dares Wins*; *Within These Walls*; *Women of Durham Jail*.

Films: Mrs Travers in *A Face to Die For*; Jasmine Dizdar in *Beautiful People*; *Black Beauty*; *Cry Wolf*; *Emily's Cost*; Elsa Lanchester in *Gods and Monsters*; *Little Malcolm*; *Mr Smith*; *Stardust*; *Tales From Beyond the Grave*; *That'll be the Day*; *The Lovers*; *The Slipper and the Rose*; Lady Lucille Duff Gordon in *Titanic*.

Address: c/o Lou Coulson, 37 Berwick Street, London W1V 3RF.

B

BACON, Richard

Richard Bacon. Presenter/Reporter.
b. Mansfield, 30 November 1975.
TV: *The Big Breakfast; Blue Peter.*
Address: c/o Marquee Group (UK) Ltd, 21 The Green, Richmond, Surrey TW9 1PX.

BADDIEL, David

David Baddiel. Presenter/Writer/Comedian.
b. 28 May 1964.
TV: *Fantasy Football League* (1994); *Fantasy World Cup* (1998); *Newman and Baddiel in Pieces* (1993); *The Mary Whitehouse Experience* (1991); *World Cup Grandstand* (1994).
Music: *It's Coming Home.*
Address: c/o Avalon Promotions, 2nd Floor, Queen's House, Leicester Place, Leicester Square, London WC2H 7BP.

BADEL, Sarah

Sarah Badel. Actor (F). b. London, 30 March 1943.
TV: Lady Molly in *A Dance to the Music of Time*; Baroness Weber in *A Perfect Spy*; Sister Madelaine in *Cadfael*; Flora Post in *Cold Comfort Farm*; Rosa in *Midsomer Murders*; Joy/Hilary in *Small World*; Angela in *The Cloning of Joanna May*; Babs in *The Irish RM*; Lizzie Eustace in *The Pallisers*; Katherine in *The Taming of the Shrew*; Rachel in *The Tenant of Wildfell Hall.*
Films: Gladys Evans in *Cotton Mary*; Sally Seton in *Mrs Dalloway*; Swiss Consul in *Not Without My Daughter*; Ida in *The Shooting Party.*
Address: c/o PFD, Drury House, 34–43 Russell Street, London WC2B 5HA. Father Alan Badel; mother Yvonne Owen. Hobbies: Cooking, travel, writing.

BADEN-SEMPER, Nina

Nina Baden-Semper. Actor (F). b. 1953.
TV: *Armchair Theatre; Brothers and Sisters; Callan; Children's Ward; Comedy Hour; Five to Eleven; George and Mildred; It's a Girl; Little Napoleons; Love Story; Love Thy Neighbour; Machinegunner; Private Eye; Take Three Girls; The Bill; The Corridor People; The Doctors; The Story of Caedman; Thick as Thieves; This is Your Life.*

Films: *Kongi's Harvest; Love Thy Neighbour;* Godwin's Mother in *Rage; The Hand of Night; The Love Bug.*
Address: c/o Collis Management, 182 Trevelyan Road, London SW17 9LW.

BAEZA, Paloma

Paloma Baeza. Actor (F). b. 1974.
TV: *Anna Karenina;* Bathsheba in *Far From the Madding Crowd;* Rose Grant in *No Bananas;* Rose Markham in *The Tenant of Wildfell Hall;* Rachel in *A Touch of Frost.*
Films: Voice of Sandy in *A Connecticut Yankee in the Court of King Arthur* (Animation*)*; Katie in *A Kid in King Arthur's Court*; Mashenka in *All Forgotten*; Dinah in *Joseph*; Paula in *Look Me in the Eye*; Aideen in *Sunburn; The Longest Memory*; Melanthe in *The Odyssey.*
Address: c/o PFD, Drury House, 34–43 Russell Street, London WC2B 5HA. Hobbies: Languages (Spanish and French); horse riding, guitar, fencing.

BAILEY, Bill

Bill Bailey. Comedian. b. Bath, Somerset 1964.
TV: *April Fool's Day* (1995); *Blue Heaven; Bring Me the Head of Light Entertainment* (1997); *Des O'Connor Tonight* (1996); *Edinburgh Nights* (1997); *Hogmanay Show* (1997); *Is it Bill Bailey?* (1998); *Jo Brand Christmas Special* (1996); *Monster Night* (1998); *Packing them In; Phil Kay Feels* (1997); *Raw Soup; Spaced Out* (1997); *That's Showbusiness* (1995); *The Happening; The Stand Up Show* (1995, 1996); *What's New?; Wow-FabGroovy* (1997).
Address: c/o International Artistes Ltd, Mezzanine Floor, 235 Regent Street, London W1R 8AX.

BAIRSTOW, Amanda

Amanda Bairstow. Actor (F).
b. Bingley, West Yorkshire, 12 November 1960.
TV: Sheila Simmonds in *3-7-11* (1995); Jane in *Bramwell* (1997); Jacqueline Phelps in *Cockles*; Susan Denton in *Coronation Street*; Maggie Norman in *Juliet Bravo*; Sophie in *Lytton's Diary*; Jane in *Mulberry* (1994); Debbie in *Only Children*; Fiona in *Salad Days*; Victoria in *Tears Before Bedtime*; Alison in *The Bill* (1993).

Films: Karen in *Coming Home* (1997).
Address: c/o McIntosh Rae Management, Thornton House, Thornton Road, London SW19 4NG.

BAKER, Colin

Colin Baker. Actor (M). b. London, 8 June 1943.
TV: Canon Fenneau in *A Dance to the Music of Time* (1997); David Robinson in *A Seat on the Board* (1995); Colin Miles in *Casualty* (1989); David Vincent in *Casualty* (1997); Count Wenceslas Steinbock in *Cousin Bette* (1971); Mr Biffen in *Cuckoo* (1988); Vicar in *Dangerfield* (1999); The Doctor in *Doctor Who* (1983); W.P. Frith in *Eureka* (1995); The Fake Mr Brent in *Five go to Billycock Hill* (1996); Mr Perkins in *Harry's Mad* (1995); The Judge in *Hollyoaks* (1997); Hedley Shale in *Jonathan Creek* (1996); Frankie Miller in *Juliet Bravo* (1982); Claude in *Roads to Freedom* (1970); Galico in *Souls Ark* (1999); *Sunburn* (1998); Dr Dudgeon in *Swallows and Amazons For Ever* (1983); Arbuthnot in *The Asylum* (1999); William in *The Bill* (1997); Paul Merroney in *The Brothers* (1973); Joseph Laycock in *The Edwardians* (1972); Herr Rupitsch in *The Harpist* (1997); Desmond Dewhurst in *The Knock* (1997); Fleming in *The Waiting Time* (1999); V.E. Day Celebrations – Hyde Park (1995); Anatol Kuragin in *War and Peace* (1972); General Chauvel in *The Young Indiana Jones Chronicles* (1995).
Address: c/o Evans & Reiss, 100 Fawe Park Road, London SW15 2EA. m. Marion; 4 d. Lucy, Bindy, Lally, Rosie. Hobbies: columnist for his local paper, chairman of the Foundation for the Study of Infant Deaths.

BAKER, George

George Baker. Actor (M).
b. Varna, 1 April 1931.
TV: *A Question of Disposal; Alice; Any Other Business; Boule de Suif; Candida; Click; Common Ground; Curtain of Fear; Days in the Trees; Death of a Salesman; Dial M for Murder; Doomsday for Dyson; Faraway Music; Four Triumphant; Fraud Squad; Games People Play; Gideon's Way; Girls About Town; Glide Path; Happiness is £ Shaped; I, Claudius; Little Lord Fauntleroy; Love Life; Maigret; Mary Stuart; Medea; Mrs Capper's Birthday; Myself, I've Got Nothing; Nick of the River; On with the Show; One Good Turn; Paul Temple; Pillars of Midnight; Probation Officer; Rupert of Hentzau;* Insp. Wexford in *Ruth Rendell Mysteries; So Dark the Night; Some Mothers Do 'Ave 'Em; Spy Trap; Square Ring; Stiff Upper Lip; Sullivan Brothers; Surface of Innocence; Survivors; The Big Man Coughed and Died; The Bonegrinder; The Dickie Henderson Show; The Goodies; The Guinea Pig; The Harry Worth Show; The Hidden Witness; The Master; The Navigators; The Paraffin Season; The Persuaders; The Prisoner; The Queen & Jackson; The Sex Game; The Truth About Melandrinos; Undermind Myself; Up and Down; Up Pompeii; Voyage in the Dark; Z Cars; Zodiak.*
Films: *A Hill in Korea; A Warm December; A Woman for Joe; For Queen and Country; Goodbye, Mr Chips; Hopscotch; Justine; Lancelot and Guinevere; Mister Ten Percent; Moonraker; No Time for Tears; North Sea Hijack; On Her Majesty's Secret Service; The Thirty-Nine Steps; The Canterville Ghost; The Curse of the Fly; The Dambusters; The Executioner; The Extra Day; The Feminine Touch; The Intruder; The Ship that Died of Shame; The Spy Who Loved Me; These Dangerous Years; Tread Softly Stranger.*
Address: c/o Shepherd & Ford, 13 Radnor Walk, London SW3 4BP. m. 3 Louie Ramsay; 5 d. Candy (1st m.), Tessa (1st m.), Ellie (1st m.), Charlie (1st m.), Sarah (2nd m.).

BAKER, Nick

Nick Baker. Presenter. b. 1973.
TV: *Blue Peter; Holiday; Live & Kicking; Nature Detectives; Nick Quest; Playdays; The Big Breakfast; The Really Wild Guide to Britain; The Really Wild Show; Tomorrow's World; Twister; Watch Out; West Watch.*
Address: c/o Arlington Enterprises Ltd, 1–3 Charlotte Street, London W1P 1HD. Hobbies: Natural history, blues and jazz, harmonica, cycling, jeeps, performing in his band.

BAKER, Tina

Tina Baker. Presenter/Guest expert.
b. Kirby Muxloe, Leicester, 4 May 1958.
TV: *Blankety Blank; Breakfast News; Daytime Live; Exclusive; The Club; This Morning; The Truth About Soap Stars; TV-am; TV Unzipped; TV Weekly; Vanessa;* various.
Address: c/o Take 3 Management, Osbourne House, 111 Bartholemew Road, London NW5 2BJ. Hobbies: Cats, meditation, chasing men.

BAKER, Tom

Tom Baker. Actor(M). b. 20 January 1934.
TV: Professor Plum in *Cluedo;* Doctor Who in *Doctor Who; The Tom Baker Years; Doctor... Who on Earth is Tom Baker; Dungeons and Dragons;* Sea Captain in *Frankenstein: The True Story; Have I Got News For You;* Sherlock Holmes in *The Hound of the Baskervilles; Medics; Randall & Hopkirk (Deceased); Selling Hitler; The Golden Voyage of Sinbad; The Lives and Loves of a She Devil;* Lynch in *The Mutations;* Moore in *The Vault of Horror.*
Films: Rasputin in *Nicholas and Alexandra.*
Address: c/o JM Associates, 77 Beak Street, London W1R 3LF.

BALDWIN, Peter

Peter Baldwin. Actor (M).
b. Chichester, Sussex, 29 July 1933.
TV: Prior Mortimer in *Cadfael* (1997); Derek Wilton in *Coronation Street* (1976); *Harry Hill Show* (1998); Uncle Gus in *Out of Sight* (1997).
Address: c/o Shepherd & Ford, 13 Radnor Walk London SW3 4BP. Hobbies: Tennis, collecting old toy theatres.

BALL, Johnny

Johnny Ball. Presenter. b. Bristol, 23 May 1938.
TV: *Away with Numbers; Bouncing Back; Christmas Night Spectacular; Johnny Ball Reveals All; Knowhow; Late Date with Johnny Ball; Odds and Probability; Playaway; The Harry Secombe Show; The Val Doonican Show; Think Again; Think of a Number.*
Address: c/o Downes Presenters Agency, 96 Broadway, Bexley Heath, Kent DA6 7DE. m. Di; 1 d. Zoe; 2 s. Nick, Dan.

BALL, Martin

Martin Ball. Actor (M). b. 1965.
TV: Simon Lester in *Anna Lee*; Dennis Cooke in *Badger*; Dave Masters in *Casualty*; Dan McGill in *Chalk*; Herr Koch in *Genghis Cohen*; Dad in *Home Farm Twins*; Waiter in *Indiscreet*; Andrew in *Keeping Mum*; Mordaunt in *Little Lord Fauntleroy*; Daniel in *Play it Again, Dan*; Presenter in *Say it in English*; Jeff Hawkes in *The Bill*; Simon Maughan in *The Missing Postman*; Harper in *Wycliffe*.
Address: c/o Barry Brown & Partner, 47 West Square, London SE11.

BALL, Zoë

Zoë Ball. Presenter.
TV: *Broom Cupboard; Cool Cube; Fully Booked* (1995); *Live and Kicking* (1996); *Playdays; Short Change; Smart* (1995); *The Big Breakfast* (1996); *The Ozone; The Priory.*
Address: c/o James Grant Management Ltd, Syon Lodge, England Road, Syon Park; Middlesex TW7 5BH. m. Norman 'Fat Boy Slim' Cook; father Johnny Ball.

BAMBER, David

David Bamber. Actor (M). b. 1954.
TV: Fred Hurley in *Call Me Mister*; Eric Slatt in *Chalk*; Shaw in *Heartbeat*; Pilbeam in *Heavy Weather*; Ray in *Murder Most Horrid*; Dad in *My Dad's a Boring Nerd*; Guy in *My Night With Reg*; Angus in *Neville's Island*; *Out of the Past*; Reverend Collins in *Pride and Prejudice*; Prof in *Stalag Luft*; Shadwell in *The Buddha of Suburbia*; Chris in *The Complete Guide to Relationships*; Tony in *The Good Guys*; Dr Forrest in *The Railway*

Children (1999); Guy Bottrell in *Wycliffe*.
Films: Simon in *Dakota Road*; Rupert in *High Hopes*; Charles Bishop in *Privates on Parade*; Potter in *The Year of the Comet; Wet & Dry.*
Address: c/o Jonathan Altaras Associates, 13 Shorts Gardens, London WC2H 9AT. m. Julia Swift.

BANKS, Morwenna

Morwenna Banks. Actor (F)/Presenter.
b. Flushing, Cornwall.
TV: *Absolutely; Bang Bang, It's Reeves and Mortimer; Big Nights; Dream On;* Goldilocks in *Jack and the Beanstalk;* Sabrina, *The Teenage Witch; Saturday Night Live; Stressed Eric; The Jack Docherty Show; The Man from Auntie; The Morwenna Banks Show; The Outlaw.*
Address: c/o PBJ Management, 5 Soho Square, London W1V 5DE.

BANNERMAN, Marc

Marc Bannerman. Actor (M). b. 1972.
TV: Malcolm in *Chalk*; Gianni in *EastEnders*; Policeman in *Legal Affairs*; Phil in *The Bill*; Paul in *The Stalker's Apprentice.*
Films: Gangster in *On The Eight Ball.*
Address: c/o Associated International Management, 5 Denmark Street, London WC2H 8LP.

BARBER, Frances

Frances Barber. Actor (F).
b. Wolverhampton, 13 May 1958.
TV: *Men Behaving Badly; Clem; Dalziel and Pascoe; Do Not Disturb; Hancock; Home Sweet Home;* Gloria Twigge in *Murder Most Horrid; Orchid House; Plastic Man;* Anna in *Real Women; Rhodes; The Ice House; The Leaving of Liverpool; The Nightmare Years; This is David Lander; Three Steps to Heaven.*
Films: *A Zed and Two Noughts; Acceptable Levels; Chambre a Part; Prick Up Your Ears; Sammy and Rosie Get Laid; Soft Top, Hard Shoulder; The Grasscutter; The Missionary; Three Steps to Heaven; We Think the World of You; White City; Young Rebels.*
Address: c/o London Management, Noel House, 2–4 Noel Street, London W1V 3RB.

BARBER, Glynis

Glynis Van Der Reit. Actor (F). b. 25 October 1955.
TV: *The Mirror Crack'd; Visitors; Highlander; Babes in the Wood;* D.S. Makepeace in *Dempsey & Makepeace; The Bill; Hound of the Baskervilles; Jane; Blake's 7; The Sandbaggers; Tales of the Unexpected.*
Films: *Beings; Deja Vu; Edge of Sanity; The Wicked Lady; Horror Safari; Terror; Duel.*
Address: c/o Susan Shaper, Queen's House, 1 Leices-

ter Place, London WC2H 7BP. m. Michael Brandon (dis.); 1 s. Alexander.

BARDON, John

John Bardon. Actor (M). b. 25 August 1939.
TV: William Cole in *A Royal Scandal*; *After Henry*; Les in *Birds of a Feather*; *Bramwell*; Ted Clark in *Broker's Man*; *Campion*; *Casualty*; Jim Branning in *EastEnders*; John Campbell in *Frontiers*; Bernie Sweet in *Get Back*; Stan Gale in *Giving Tongue*; *Gobble*; *Goodnight Sweetheart*; Grandad Rowan in *Heartbeat*; Mr Jarvis in *Johnny Jarvis*; Sam Carver in *Love Hurts*; Walter in *Lovejoy*; Mr Belgrove in *Midsomer Murders*; Sir Stanley Swan in *Mike and Angelo*; *Minder*; *Mrs Shaw's Missing Millions*; Jim in *Polterguests*; *Return of the Antelope*; Fred Timson in *Rumpole of the Bailey*; *Seconds Out*; *Spatz*; *The Bill*; Mr Blanchfield in *Darling Buds of May*; Billy in *The Detectives*.
Films: *84 Charing Cross Road*; *Clockwise*; *East is East*; *Fierce Creatures*; *Fords on Water*; *Gulliver's Travels*; *Ordeal by Innocence*; *S.P.Y.S.*; *Seasick*; *The Keeper*;
Address: c/o Barry Brown & Partner, 47 West Square, London SE11.

BARKER, Ronnie

Ronnie Barker. Actor (M)/Comedian.
b. Bedford, Bedfordshire, 25 September 1929.
TV: Clarence Sale in *Clarence* (1988); Norman Stanley Fletcher in *Going Straight* (1978); Lord Rustless in *Hark At Barker* (1969); Lord Rustless in *His Lordship Entertains* (1972); Arkwright in *Open All Hours* (1976); Norman Stanley Fletcher in *Porridge* (1974); *Six Dates With Barker* (1971); *The Frost Report* (1966); *Plantagenet*; *The Magnificent Evans* (1984); *The Two Ronnies* (1971).
Films: The General in *By The Sea* (1982); Norman Stanley Fletcher in *Porridge* (1979); Friar Tuck in *Robin and Marian* (1976); Ronnie in *The Bargee* (1964).
Address: Currently retired. m. Joy Barker; 1 d. Charlotte; 2 s. Adam, Larry. Hobbies: Collecting antiques and postcards.

BARKER, Sue

Sue Barker. Commentator/Presenter.
b. Paignton, Devon, 19 April 1956.
TV: *A Question of Sport*; *Olympics Coverage* (1988); various BBC sports programmes; *Wimbledon*.
Address: c/o Professional Sports Partnership Ltd, 8 Chertsey Road, Chobham, Surrey GU24 8NB.

BARKWORTH, Peter

Peter Barkworth. Actor (M).
b. Margate, Kent, 14 January 1929.

TV: *Heartbeat*; Professor Edward Brett in *Late Starter*; *Maigret*; *Manhunt*; *Meditations*; Telford in *Telford's Change*; *The Gospel According to St Matthew*; *The Power Game*; Geoffrey Carr in *The Price*; Stanley Baldwin in *Winston Churchill – The Wilderness Years*.
Films: *Escape from the Dark*; *Mr Smith*; *Where Eagles Dare*; *Wilde*.
Address: c/o Jonathan Altaras Associates, 13 Shorts Gardens, London WC2H 9AT.

BARLOW, Jonathan

Jonathan Barlow. Actor (M).
b. Ironbridge, Shropshire, 3 January 1956.
TV: Roy Harrison in *Albion Market*; Gil Baker in *Birds of a Feather*; *Brideshead Revisited*; D.J.N. Summerhill in *Brookside*; *Casualty*; Jeff Singleton in *Coronation Street*; Ken Hopkins in *Fallen Hero*; Terru Prince in *Feet First*; Gordon Harris in *Making Out*; *Minder*; *Poirot*; Jack Pertwee in *Ruth Rendell Mysteries*; Insp. Summerbee in *Sherlock Holmes*; Jack Freeman in *Springhill*; *The Practice*; Uncle George in *The Wild House*
Films: Young Medic in *Rosie Dixon: Night Nurse*; Captain Hardy in *Scandalous*.
Address: c/o Shane Collins Associates, 39–41 New Oxford Street, London WC1A 1BH. m. Sally; 1 s. Jake. Hobbies: Musician (drummer, guitarist and vocalist), writing, football, squash, tennis.

BARLOW, Thelma

Thelma Barlow. Actor (F)/Presenter.
b. Middlesborough, 19 June 1929.
TV: *Call My Bluff*; Mavis Wilton in *Coronation Street*; *David Copperfield*; Dolly in *dinnerladies*; *Murder Most Horrid*; *The Garden Party*; *The Holiday Programme*.
Address: c/o April Young, 11 Woodlands Road, London SW13 0JZ.

BARNES, Carol

Carol Barnes. Presenter/Reporter.
b. 13 September 1944.
TV: *5.40 News*; *7 Days*; Budget Specials; Election Specials; *ITN Lunchtime News*; *News At Ten*; *The Sharp End*.
Address: c/o Knight Ayton Management, 10 Argyll Street, London W1V 1AB.

BARNES, Michael

Michael Barnes. Actor (M).
b. London, 25 August 1945.
TV: Willy Roper in *EastEnders*; *Head over Heels*; *Hope it Rains*; *Poirot*; *Second Verdict*; *The Bill*; *The Gentle Touch*; Ponting in *The Last Place on Earth*; *The Merchant of Venice*; *The Trials of Oz*.

Films: *Melody is Her Second Name; Night Swimming.*
Address: c/o Langford Associates, 17 Westfields
Avenue, London SW13 0AT.

BARON, Lynda

Lynda Baron. Actor (F).
b. Manchester, 24 March 1939.
TV: *Alas Smith and Jones;* Auntie Mabel in *Come Out-
side;* Renee Turnbull in *Coronation Street;* Carmel in
dinnerladies; Mrs Green in *Goodnight Sweetheart;*
Grundy; Stella Mitchell in *Insiders; KYTV;* Lily Bless'er
in *Last of the Summer Wine; Mesmerist; Minder; Mr
Gurney and the Brighton;* Dashaa in *Nancherrow; Oh
No, It's Selwyn Froggitt;* Nurse Gladys in *Open All
Hours;* Paul's Mother in *Paul Merton in 'Visiting Day';
Roof Over My Head;* Sandra in *Sunburn;* Auntie Pat in
The Upper Hand; Barmaid in *Two Minutes.*
Films: Meg in *Carry On Columbus; Hands of the
Ripper; Hot Millions;* English Woman in *Masquerade;
Mrs Brown, You've Got a Lovely Daughter; Tiffany Jones;
Universal Soldier;* Baker's Widow in *Yentl.*
Address: c/o Marina Martin Associates, 12–13
Poland Street, London W1V 3DE.

BARR, Roseanne

Roseanne Barr. Actor (F)/Executive producer/Voice
artist. b. Salt Lake City, Utah, USA, 3 November 1952.
TV: Janet in *3rd Rock from the Sun* (1997); Herself
in *A Century of Women* (1994); Nancy Seavers in
Backfield In Motion (1991); Jennifer Smith in *Gen-
eral Hospital* (1994); Herself in *Happy Birthday Eliz-
abeth: A Celebration of Life* (1997); *I am Your Child*
(1997); Little Rosie in *Little Rosie* (1990);
Roseanne Conner in *Roseanne* (1988); Rosey in
Rosey and Buddy Show (1992); Herself in *Ruby Wax
Meets; Saturday Night Special* (1996); Herself in
Seriously Funny: An Argument For Comedy (1996);
Herself in *Sinatra: 80 Years My Way* (1995); Herself
in *The Ben Stiller Show;* herself in *The Dennis Miller
Show;* Herself in *The Jackie Thomas Show;* Herself in
The Larry Saunders Show; Fran's Cousin Sheila in
The Nanny (1997); *The Roseanne Show* (1998);
Joyce in *The Woman Who Loved Elvis* (1993); her-
self in *Woman of The House.*
Films: Vinnie's Wife in *Blue in the Face* (1995);
Madame Zoe in *Even Cowgirls Get the Blues* (1993);
Childless Woman in *Freddy's Dead: The Final Night-
mare* (1991); *Get Bruce* (1999); Voice of Julie in *Look
Who's Talking Too* (1990); herself in *Meet Wally Sparks*
(1997); The Wicked Witch of the West in *Oz: The
American Fairyland* (1997); Ruth in *She-Devil* (1989).
Address: William Morris Agency, 151 El Camino
Drive, Beverly Hill, CA 90210, USA. m. 1 Bill Pentland

(div.); m. 2 Tom Arnold; m. 3 Ben Thomas. 2 d. Jessica, Jennifer; 3 s. Brandi, Jake, Thomas.

BARRACLOUGH, Roy

Roy Barraclough. Actor (M).
b. Preston, Lancashire, 12 July 1935.
TV: *A Different Way Home; Bingo;* Arthur Swarbrick in
Bostock's Cup (1999); *Cadfael; Castlehaven;* Arthur
Lyle in *Casualty* (1998); *Celebration;* Alec Gilroy in
Coronation Street; SS Titanic-Award Show Host in *Dr
Willoughby* (1999); *Galton & Simpson Playhouse; Gold
Medal Travel; Granada Television's 40th Anniversary
Celebration; The Krypton Factor; Les Dawson Tribute;
Lost Empires; Mother's Ruin;* Dr Simms in *The Mrs
Bradley Mysteries* (1999); *Pardon My Genie; Peak Prac-
tice; Woof.*
Films: *Car Trouble; The Slipper and the Rose.*
Address: c/o PBR Management, 26 Foubert's Place,
Regent Street, London W1V 1HG.

BARRIE, Amanda

Shirley Ann Broadbent. Actor (F). b. Ashton-under-
Lyne, Staffordshire, 14 September 1939.
TV: Hermia in *A Midsummer Night's Dream; Are You
Being Served?;* Alma in *Coronation Street;* Sally in *L for
Lester; Sanctuary; Spooner's Patch; Struggles.*
Films: *Carry On Cabby;* Cleopatra in *Carry On Cleo; I
Gotta Horse; One of Our Dinosaurs is Missing.*
Address: c/o Peter Charlesworth & Associates, 68
Old Brompton Road, London SW7 3LQ. Hobbies:
Horse racing, riding and betting! Collecting Victo-
rian toys, especially wooden horses and teddy bears.

BARRIE, Chris

Chris Barrie. Actor (M)/Voice artist.
b. 28 March 1960.
TV: Gary Prince in *A Prince Among Men;* Abassador/
Revolutionary in *Blackadder the Third;* Chris Barrie's
Motoring Wheel Nuts; Gordon Brittas in *Get Fit with
Brittas;* Arnold J. Rimmer in *Red Dwarf;* A.J.
Rimmer/himself in *Red Dwarf Smeg Outs; Spitting
Image;* Gordon Brittas in *The Brittas Empire.*
Address: c/o Jeremy Lee Associates, 13 Shorts Gar-
dens, London WC2H 9AT. Hobbies: Dogs.

BARRON, John

John Barron. Actor (M).
b. St Marylebone, 24 December 1920.
TV: *All Gas and Gaiters; Crown Court; Doomwatch;
Emergency Ward 10; The Kelly Monteith Show; Othello;
Potter; Softly, Softly; The Fall and Rise of Reginald
Perrin; The Taming of the Shrew; To the Manor Born;
Whoops, Apocalypse!; Yes, Minister.*

Address: c/o Green & Underwood, 2 Conduit Street, London W1R 9TG.

BARRON, Keith

Keith Barron. Actor (M).
b. Mexborough, Yorkshire, 8 August 1934.
TV: Jack Bentham in *1996*; Eddie in *20:20*; Inspector Masters in *A Case of Coincidence*; *About Face*; *All Night Long*; Gordon in *Close Relations*; Dick Elgood in *Dalziel and Pascoe*; Sir Thomas in *Drovers Gold*; *Duty Free*; Arthur Hedley in *Gobble*; Squire, Amos Haggard in *Haggard*; Gordon Gregson in *Hetty Wainthropp Investigates*; *Holding the Fort*; *I've Been Eddie Mostyn*; Jim Wilkes in *In the Red*; *Island Gardens*; *Late Expectations*; *Lifeboat*; L'Heureux in *Madame Bovary*; *Only Make Believe*; Eric Dunfries in *Pie in the Sky*; *Room at the Bottom*; Frank in *Scene – A Man of Letters*; Bob Ferguson in *Sherlock Holmes*; Nigel Barton in *Stand Up for Nigel Barton*; *Stay With Me 'Til Morning*; Tom in *Take Me Home*; *Telford's Change*; *The Further Adventures of Lucky Jim*; Guy Lofthouse in *The Good Guys*; *The Prince Regent*; Jonathan Ratcliffe in *The Round Tower*; Glyn in *This Could Be the Last Time*; *Under the Hammer*; Mr Davies in *Verdict*; Nigel Barton in *Vote, Vote, Vote for Nigel Barton*.
Films: Dowsett in *At the Earth's Core*; *Con Man*; Roy in *La Passione*; Dr Haynes in *Nothing But the Night*; *She'll Follow You Anywhere*; Jim Maxwell in *The Firechasers*; Bradley in *The Land That Time Forgot*; Jack Braid in *The Man Who Had Power Over Women*; Purser Mueller in *The Voyage of the Damned*.
Address: c/o CDA, 19 Sydney Mews, London SW3 6HL.

BARROW, Andrew

Andrew Barrow. Actor (M).
b. Doncaster, South Yorkshire, 18 January 1964.
TV: *Drop the Dead Donkey*; Jakin in *Five Children and It*; Dean Scholes in *Hetty Wainthropp Investigates*; Lovegrove in *The Bill*.
Films: *Love and Death on Long Island*.
Address: c/o Hobsons, 62–64 Chiswick High Road, London W4. Partner Elli MacKenzie; 1 s. Felix. Hobbies: Cycling, walking, DIY, rugby.

BARROWMAN, John

John Barrowman. Actor (M)/Presenter.
TV: Peter Fairchild in *Central Park West*; *Electric Circus*; *Five's Company*; *Live & Kicking*; *The Movie Game*.
Music: *Godspell*; *Grease*; *Hair: Album of the Production*; *John Barrowman: Aspects of Lloyd-Webber* (solo recording); *Matador*; *Phantom of the Opera*; *Red Red Rose*; *Reflections from Broadway* (solo recording); *The*

Fix: Album of the production; *The Music of Andrew Lloyd-Webber*.
Address: c/o Eric Glass Ltd, 28 Berkeley Square, London W1X 6HD.

BARRY, David

David Barry. Actor (M). b. 30 April 1943.
TV: Tony Hillyer in *A Mind to Kill*; John Laird in *Brookside*; Joe in *It's a Mystery*; Norman in *Never the Twain*; 2nd Soldier in *Owain Glyndwr*; Usher in *The Bill*; Mr Edwards in *The Bill*; Patient in *The Lost Secret*; Pearson in *The Woman in White*; Len in *We'll Think of Something*.
Films: Carlos in *Captain Stirrock*; Elvis in *George and Mildred*; Abbott in *Please, Sir!*; Jones the Milk in *The Gingerbread House*; Reg Pepper in *The Impersonation*.
Address: c/o Pelham Associates, 9–12 Middle Street, Brighton BN1 1AL.

BARRY, Jason

Jason Barry. Actor (M).
TV: *A Very Open Prison*; *An Unsuitable Job for a Woman*; *EastEnders*; *McCallum*; *Metropolis*; Mickey in *O Mary This London*; *Roughnecks*; *Scratch Saturday*; *The Bill*.
Films: *Circle of Friends*; *Last of the High Kings*; *Monument Avenue*; *Muggers*; *Though the Sky Falls*; *Titanic*.
Address: William Morris Agency (UK) Ltd, 1 Stratton Street, London W1X 6HB.

BARRYMORE, Michael

Michael Barrymore. Actor (M)/Host/Presenter.
b. Bermondsey, London, 4 May 1952.
TV: *Barrymore*; *Barrymore Show*; *Bob Martin*; *Kids Say the Funniest Things*; *My Kind of Music*; *My Kind of People*; *Russ Abbot's Madhouse*; *Strike it Lucky* (1987); *Strike it Rich*; *The Michael Barrymore Show*.
Films: *Spice World*.
Address: c/o Hazemead Ltd, 3rd floor, 18 Hanover Street, London W1R 9HG. Hobbies: Fishing, cooking, cars.

BARTON, Tony

Tony Barton. Actor (M). b. Yorkshire.
TV: Arnold in *Always and Everyone*; Compere in *City Central*; Pub Landlord in *Common as Muck*; Pat Hegarty in *Coronation Street*; Railway Man in *Crewe Stories*; Bazza in *Emmerdale*; Tilley in *Harbour Lights*; Loan Shark in *Hetty Wainthropp Investigates*; Bazza in *New Voices*; Herbert Sidebottom in *Our Friends in the North*; Jockey Megson in *Out of the Blue*; Alan Thompson in *Peak Practice*; Decorator in *Reckless*; Rustler in *Rhinoceros*; Dobbo in *The Things You Do for Love*; Bill in *Where the Heart Is*.

Films: *Between Two Women; Funny Bones; Never Better.*
Music: *Stoned.*
Address: c/o Sharron Ashcroft Management, Dean Clough, Halifax, Yorkshire HX3 5AX. Hobbies: Gliding, pool, darts, golf, dancing, flying aeroplanes, rugby.

BASHIR, Martin

Martin Bashir. Presenter/Reporter. b. 19 January 1963.
TV: *East; Just One Chance; News At 12.30* (1986); *Panorama; Public Eye* (1989); *Regional News* (1987); *Songs of Praise* (1989); *The Midnight Hour.*
Address: c/o John Miles Organisation, Cadbury, Camp Lane, Clapton in Gordano, Bristol BS20 7SB. 3 children.

BASTEDO, Alexandra

Alexandra Bastedo. Actor (F)/Writer.
b. Hove, East Sussex, 9 March 1946.
TV: *Absolutely Fabulous; Boon; Europe on the Brink; Scobie Man; The Aphrodite Inheritance; The Champions; The Code Name; The Horseman; The House of Pride.*
Films: *Casino Royale; Draw; Find the Lady; Hushabye; The Ghoul.*
Address: c/o Peter Charlesworth & Associates, 68 Old Brompton Road, London SW7 3LQ. Hobbies: Animal welfare.

BATE, Anthony

Anthony Bate. Actor (M).
b. Stourbridge, Worcestershire, 1934.
TV: Soranzo in *'Tis Pity She's a Whore* (1979); *A Case of No Resolution* (1972); *A Nice Little Business* (1965); Col. Charlie Lawson in *A Touch of Frost* (1996); Harold Nicholson in *All Passion Spent* (1981); *All the World's a Stage* (1981); Harmer in *An Englishman's Castle* (1978); Golspie in *Angel Pavement* (1967); Ingres in *Artists and Models – Ingres* (1983); *Attorney General* (1961); *Beasts* (1975); *Beyond Our Means* (1973); Glennie in *Bodyguards* (1996); *Botany Bay* (1962); *Boyd Q.C.* (1961); Shevardnadse in *Breakthrough at Reykjavik* (1987); *Call Me Mister* (1986); Graham Greene in *Chagrin in Three Parts* (1975); Sir John Simon in *Countdown to War* (1989); *Couples* (1975); Svidrigailov in *Crime and Punishment* (1979); *Crimes of Persuasion* (1977); David Rockwell Q.C. in *Crown Court* (1976); *Dackson's Wharf* (1962); Captain Done in *Dalhouse's Luck* (1979); T. H. Huxley in *Darwin's Bulldog* (1971); *Double Echo* (1976); Charlie Appleby in *Eden End* (1963); Myers in *Edmund Guerney and the Brighton Mesmerist* (1967); Victor Hugo in *Ego Hugo* (1973); Clive Seymour in *Fanny by Gaslight* (1981); Nikolia in *Fathers and Sons* (1971); Bret Rensselaer in *Game, Set and Match* (1987); Grady in *Grady* (1970); *Guilty* (1963); Brutus in *Hail Caesar* (1973); *Helen, A Woman of Today* (1973); *Henry the Incredible Bore* (1968); *Highway* (1992); Neils Bohr in *Horizon* (1991); *I Can't Bear Violence* (1963); *I'll Go Along with That* (1971); *Inside Man* (1969); Bernard Crowther in *Inspector Morse* (1987); Harry Paynter in *Intimate Strangers* (1974); Templar in *Ivanhoe* (1969); *Julius Caesar* (1968); Creon in *King Oedipus* (1972); Javert in *Les Miserables* (1966); The General in *Level Seven* (1966); Macduff in *Macbeth* (1966); *Maybury* (1983); Reginald Girling in *Medics* (1991); *Mr Irtin* (1966); *Nanny's Boy* (1976); *No Hiding Places* (1962); *Nobody's Conscience* (1976); Kim Philby in *Philby, Burgess and Maclean* (1977); *Poirot* (1989); James Greenlees in *Prime Suspect* (1994); Colonel Julian in *Rebecca* (1996); James in *Rediffusion; Second Time Around* (1971); Lord Curzon in *Shackleton* (1982); Professor Leon Forman in *Silent Witness* (1997); Lacon in *Smiley's People* (1981); Eddie Edwards in *Spindhoe* (1968); *Sutherland's Law* (1973); *The Avengers; The Big Boys* (1961); Surgeon in *The Calling of C. H. Surgeon* (1975); Pinter in *The Collection* (1961); *The Human Crocodile* (1980); Rogojin in *The Idiot* (1966); *The Intrigue* (1962); *The Last Witness* (1971); *The Nature of the Beast* (1971); *The Saint;* Galileo/Huxley in *The Scientists* (1978); Dr Dorn in *The Seagull* (1977); Paul Sullavan in *The Sullavan Brothers* (1964); Gerard Vaders in *The Train that Never Arrived* (1977); Dr Halliday Sutherland in *The Trial of Marie Stopes* (1970); Uri Orlov in *The Trial of Uri Orlov* (1978); *The Truth about Alan* (1963); Van Daker in *The World of Tim Frazer* (1961); *The Youngest Profession* (1963); Lacon in *Tinker, Tailor, Soldier, Spy 1978*); Harry in *To Kill a King* (1980); *Top Secret* (1962); Dr Livesey in *Treasure Island* (1968); *Visitor from Outer Space* (1983); *Whose Child* (1970).
Films: General Ross in *A Woman Called Golda* (1981); *Act of Murder* (1964); Bismarck in *Bismarck* (1975); *Davey Jones' Locker* (1964); Dr John Irvin in *Eminent Domain* (1990); *Exploits at West Poley* (1985); *Ghost Story* (1973); *Give My Regards to Broad Street* (1982); *Stopover Forever* (1963); *The Set Up* (1962); *Two Guys Abroad* (1962); Von Runstedt in *War and Remembrance* (1986).
Address: c/o Ken McReddie Ltd, 91 Regent Street, London W1R 7TB. m. Diana Fay; 1 s. Gavin Watson. Hobbies: Music, painting.

BATESON, Timothy

Timothy Bateson. Actor (M). b. 3 April 1926.
TV: Mr Beckwith in *All Creatures Great and Small; As Time Goes By;* Sir Oliver in *As You Like It;* Stieglitz in *Bach;* Mr Jorry in *Bird of Pray;* Wigley in *Bonjour La Classe;* Arthur Gordon-Davis in *Brookside;* Ronald in *Casualty;* Foster in *Chintz;* Medick in *David Copper-*

field; Cummings in *Diary of a Nobody*; Mr Burton in *Don't Wait Up*; Sainsbury in *Donkey's Years*; Binro in *Doctor Who*; Keeper in *Dramarama – The Frog*; Mr Bream in *The Duchess of Duke Street*; Mr Macklin in *East of Ipswich*; Laurence Tredwell in *Ever Decreasing Circles*; Moxey in *Flayed*; Arthur in *Gate of Eden*; Oaksie in *Going Straight*; Mr Thompson in *Grange Hill*; Mr Pocket in *Great Expectations*; Eric Childers in *Hard Times*; Walter Lowe in *Health and Efficiency*; Charlie Rose in *Hi De Hi*; Mr Bottomley in *In Loving Memory*; Amos in *Last of the Summer Wine*; Derwood in *Little Orphan Annie*; Father Abbott in *Merlin*; *Minder*; *Morris Minor and the Majors*; *Mother & Son*; Mr Poole in *Never Come Back*; Halvard in *Neverwhere*; Herbert Morrison in *Nye*; Grandfather in *Paul Merton's Life of Comedy*; *Paying Guests*; Schoolmaster in *Pinocchio*; Pond in *Strong Poison*; Mervin in *Terry and June*; Colin Hammond in *That's Love*; Frank Winston in *The Bill*; Davey in *The Bell Run*; Eddie in *The Bill*; Under Prompter in *The Critic*; Professor Hayling in *The Famous Five*; Mr Bailey in *The Good Life*; *Midsomer Murders*; Albert Hayes in *The Sculptress*; Harold Searle in *The Square Leopard*; Printer in *The Tale of Beatrix Potter*; Grivet in *Thérèse Raquin*; Arnold Broadhurst in *Thicker Than Water*; Jack Cumberpatch in *Within These Walls*; Mr James in *Wurzel Gummidge*; Melas in *Yours Sincerely*; Monk in *Zorro*.

Films: *101 Dalmatians*; Mr Fezziwig in *A Christmas Carol*; MacDoug in *A Handful of Dust*; Max Liebman in *For My Baby*; Bettleman in *Foreign Body*; *Heart of Darkness*; Wentworth in *High Road to China*; Commerce in *The Hunchback of Notre Dame*; Priest in *Joseph*; *Les Miserables*; *Loophole*; *The Anniversary*; *The Horse's Mouth*; *True Blue*; *Twisted Nerve*.

Address: c/o Ken McReddie Ltd, 91 Regent Street, London W1R 7TB.

BATHURST, Robert

Robert Bathurst. Actor (M).
TV: Major Edward Lumley in *A Breed of Heroes*; *About Face*; *All in Good Faith*; *Anything More*; *Blind Justice*; *Chelmsford 123*; David Marsden in *Cold Feet*; *Comic Relief*; *District Nurse*; Gribble in *Get Well Soon*; Lt. Ecclestone in *Hornblower*; *Joking Apart*; *Lazarus and Dingwall*; *New World*; *No Job for a Lady*; *Red Dwarf*; *Starting Out*; *The Detectives*; James in *The Good Sex Guide*; *The House of Eliott*; *The Lenny Henry Show*; *Timeline*; *Who Dares Wins*; *Would Be Greedy*.
Films: *Just Ask for Diamond*; *Twenty-One*; *Whoops Apocalypse*; *Wind in the Willows*.
Address: c/o William Morris Agency (UK) Ltd, 1 Stratton Street, London W1X 6HB.

BATTIE, David

David Battie. Antiques expert.
TV: *The Antiques Roadshow*.
Address: Contact via BBC, Union House, 65–69 Shepherds Bush Green, London W12 8TX.

BAXENDALE, Helen

Helen Baxendale. Actor (F). b. 1971.
TV: *An Unsuitable Job for a Woman*; *Cardiac Arrest*; *Cold Feet*; *Crossing the Floor*; Emily in *Friends*; *Marshal and the Madwoman*; *The Investigator*; *Truth or Dare*.
Films: *Bolshe Vita*; *Love's Lost Hour*; *Macbeth*; *Ordinary Decent Criminal*.
Address: c/o William Morris Agency (UK) Ltd, 1 Stratton Street, London W1X 6HB.

BAXTER, Lynsey

Lynsey Baxter. Actor (F). b. 1961.
TV: Angela in *Accidental Death*; Jane in *Act of Will*; Catherine in *An Evil Streak*; Laura in *Bramwell*; Duchess of Beaufort in *Broken Lives*; Victoria in *Chancer*; Bella in *Clarissa*; Beth in *Dangerfield*; Cora in *Gormenghast*; Miss Baxter in *The Harry Enfield Show*; Mariella in *Hedgehog Wedding*; Lucy in *Natural Lives*; Karen in *Psychos*; Juliet in *Saracen*; Serena in *Snakes and Ladders*; Elizabeth in *Starlings*; Lucy in *Succubus*; Polina Andrevna in *The Gambler*; Marianna in *The Grass Arena*; Clea in *The Mushroom Picker*; Lucretia Borgia in *The Night Show*; Lady Lucan in *The Trial of Lord Lucan*; Zoe in *The Ultimate Object of Desire*; Nancy Ramsey in *To The Lighthouse*; Margaret in *The Young Indiana Jones Chronicles*.
Films: Emma in *Real Life*; Milena in *The Cold Light of Day*; Ernestina in *The French Lieutenant's Woman*; Jane in *The Girl in a Swing*; Sammy in *The Pleasure Principle*; Natasha in *The Return of I Spy*.
Address: c/o Amanda Howard Associates Ltd, 21 Berwick Street, London W1V 3RG.

BAXTER, Sally

Sally Baxter. Actor (F).
TV: *Albion Market*; *Anna Lee*; *Cadfael*; *French Fields*; *Home is the Sailor*; *On the Line*; *Out of Line*; *Out on the Floor*; *Peak Practice*; *Que Sera*; *Rainy Day Woman*.
Address: c/o Crouch Associates, 9–15 Covent Garden, London WC2H 9PF.

BAYLDON, Geoffrey

Geoffrey Bayldon. Actor (M).
b. Leeds, Yorkshire, 7 January 1924.
TV: *Abide with Me*; *All Creatures Great and Small*; *All Passion Spent*; *Blott on the Landscape*; *Campion*; *Casualty*; *Catweazle*; *Cause Célèbre*; *Chronicles of Narnia*;

Cut; Devenish; Doctor Who; The Duchess of Duke Street; Faith in the Future; The Famous Five; Frontiers of War; Hallelujah; Heat of the Sun; Hold the Back Page; In Loving Memory; Just Dessert; Just William; Knight School; Little Pig Robinson; Look and Learn; Peak Practice; Pie in the Sky; Pisces Connection; The Return of Sherlock Holmes; Rumpole of the Bailey; Sergeant Cribb; Soldier, Soldier; Space 1999; Starcops; Tales of the Unexpected; Tecx; The Biz; The Last of the Summer Wine; The New Adventures of Robin Hood; The Prince and the Hedgehog; The Prince and the Pauper; The Secret of Adlington Hall; The Trial of Lady Chatterley; There Comes a Time; This Office Life; Tomorrow People; Watching; Where the Heart Is; The Crowman in *Worzel Gummidge.*
Films: *Bullshot; Casino Royale; Dandy in Aspic; Ebenezer Scrooge; Inspector Clouseau; King Rat; Madame Sousatzka; Necessary Love; Say Hello to Yesterday; Skywest and Crooked; The Beggar's Opera; The Tenth Man; To Sir With Love; Tom and Viv.*
Address: c/o Joy Jameson Ltd, 2.19 The Plaza, 535 Kings Road, London SW10 0SZ.

BEACH, Ann
Ann Beach. Actor (F). b. Wolverhampton, 7 June 1938.
TV: Mrs Chubb in *A Question of Attribution;* Blodwen in *Blodwen, Home from Rachel's Marriage; Brecht on Brecht;* Jane Harper in *Brookside;* Sonia in *Fresh Fields;* Mrs ET in *Gwyn Thomas;* Phyllis Shore in *Lifeboat;* Freda in *Service Not Included;* Lorinda in *Stick With Me Kid;* Nurse Peters in *Tandoori Nights;* Mrs Davies in *That Uncertain Feeling;* Mrs Parker in *The Bill;* Anna in *The Government Inspector;* Mrs Leveller in *Two Golden Balls;* Mrs Wimble in *Wycliffe.*
Films: Victoire in *Hotel Paradiso;* Miranda's Mother in *King Rufus; Never Mind the Quality, Feel the Width;* Mrs Sowerby in *Oliver Twist;* William's Mother in *The Notting Hill Film;* Polly Garter in *Under Milk Wood.*
Address: c/o Barry Brown & Partner, 47 West Square, London SE11.

BEACHAM, Stephanie
Stephanie Beacham. Actor (F). b. 28 February 1947.
TV: *Beverly Hills 90210; Callan; Cluedo; Connie; Dynasty; French & Saunders; No Bananas; Noel's House Party; Riders; SeaQuest DSV; Secrets; Tenko; The Colbys; The Protectors; The Saint; To Be the Best; UFO.*
Films: *And Now the Screaming Starts!; Dracula A.D.* (1972); *Nightcomers; Schizo; Tam Lin; The Confessional; The Games; The Wolves of Willoughby Chase.*
Address: c/o PFD, Drury House, 34–43 Russell Street, London WC2B 5HA.

BEADLE, Jeremy
Jeremy Beadle. Presenter. b. London, 12 April 1948.
TV: *Beadle's About; Beadle's Box of Tricks; Beadle's Hot Shots; Game for a Laugh; It's Beadle; People Do the Funniest Things; Win Beadle's Money; You've Been Framed.*
Address: c/o MPC Entertainment, MPC House, 15–16 Maple Mews, London NW6 5UZ.

BEAMISH, Oliver
Oliver Beamish. Actor (M).
TV: *Brookside;* Richard Willmore in *Coronation Street; The Darling Buds of May; La Reincarnation; Poirot; Stay Lucky.*
Address: c/o John Markham Associates, 1a Oakwood Avenue, Purley, Surrey CR8 1AR.

BEAN, Sean
Sean Bean. Actor (M). b. Sheffield, 17 April 1958.
TV: *A Woman's Guide to Adultery; Bravo Two Zero; Clarissa; Extremely Dangerous; Fools Gold; Inspector Morse; Jacob; Lady Chatterley; My Kingdom for a Horse; Prince; Samson & Delilah; Sharpe's Rifles; Small Zones; Tell Me That You Love Me; The Loser; The True Bride; Troubles; War Requiem; Wedded; Winter Flight.*
Films: *Airbourne; Anna Karenina; Black Beauty;* Renuncio in *Caravaggio; Essex Boys;* Alex Trevelyan in *Goldeneye;* Carver Doone in *Lorna Doone;* Miller in *Patriot Games; Ronin; Scarlett; Shopping;* Brendan in *Stormy Monday;* Tadgh in *The Field; When Saturday Comes; Windprints.*
Address: c/o ICM, Oxford House, 76 Oxford Street, London W1N 0AX.

BEARD, Tom
Tom Beard. Actor (M).
TV: Roger Horace Brown in *Ain't Misbehavin';* Charles, 3rd Duke in *Aristocrats;* Dave Gregg in *Bad Girl; Boon;* Robert in *Harnessing Peacocks; Heartbeat;* Captain Rodgers in *Holby City; Jewels;* George Forbes in *McCallum;* Dr Acres in *Peak Practice;* Duke of Merton in *Poirot;* Major Smith in *Soldier, Soldier;* Miles Vincent in *Staying Alive;* Major Clements in *The Investigator;* Gerry in *Unnatural Pursuits;* Major Mike Brewster in *A Wing and a Prayer.*
Address: c/o Rebecca Blond Associates, 69a Kings Road, London SW3 4NX. Hobbies: Languages (French).

BEATTIE, Louise
Louise Beattie. Actor (F).
TV: *Emmerdale Farm; The Broker's Man; The Bill; Tears Before Bedtime; The Long Roads; Inspector Morse;*

Taggart; The Woman He Loved; Extras; A Very Peculiar Practice; Tutti Frutti; City Lights; Naked Video; Rab C. Nesbitt; The Ferguson Theory; The Baldy Man; N7.
Films: Bessie Gordon in *Blood Red Roses*; Margaret in *Brond*; Julie in *Jones Alabama*.
Address: c/o The Narrow Road Company, 21/22 Poland Street, London W1V 3DD.

BEATTIE, Maureen
Maureen Beattie. Actor (F).
TV: Anna in *A Wing and a Prayer*; Vanda in *All Night Long; Boon; Bramwell*; Nurse Sandra Nicholl in *Casualty; City Central; City Lights; Hard to Get*; Beattie in *Ruffian Hearts*; Jess in *Taggart; The Bill; The Campbells*; Gemma Marshall in *The Chief; The Daftie; The Donegals*; Marie in *The Long Roads; The Lost Tribe; The People Versus Scott.*
Address: c/o Jonathan Altaras Associates, 13 Shorts Gardens, London WC2H 9AT. 1 sister Louise.

BEAUMONT, Debra
Debra Beaumont. Actor (F).
b. Cuckfield, West Sussex, 2 May 1967.
TV: Sheila in *Birds of a Feather*; Melanie in *Boon*; Debra in *Brookside*; Hayley in *EastEnders*; Paula in *Gentlemen and Players*; Emma Casson in *The House of Eliott*; Nicola Maitland in *The Alleyn Mysteries*; Yvette in *It's Tuesday, It Still Must Be Belgium*; Nina in *Lipstick On My Collar*; Pat in *Men Behaving Badly*; Sally Hawkins in *Soldier, Soldier.*
Films: Queen Victoria in *The Opium Wars.*
Address: c/o Jane Lehrer Associates, 100a Chalk Farm Road, London NW1 8EH.

BECK, Robert
Robert Beck. Actor (M). b. London, 1 August 1970.
TV: Peter Harrison in *Brookside; Cone Zone; Dangerfield*; Gavin Ferris in *Emmerdale*; Dominic in *London Bridge; Princess in Love; Surprise, Surprise; The Bill*; Dan in *The Upper Hand; The X-Files; Thief Takers*; Harris in *Three Men and Another Boat; Wilde.*
Films: Nathan in *Pressing Engagement; Random Acts of Intimacy; The Harpist.*
Address: c/o Langford Associates, 17 Westfields Avenue, London SW13 0AT. Hobbies: Watching films, football, hockey (plays for his county team); tennis.

BECKETT, Tanya
Tanya Beckett. Presenter.
TV: *Business Breakfast; FT Business Daily; FT Business Today; FT Reports; Squawkbox; The Moneywheel; VIP.*
Address: c/o Jane Hughes Management, The Coach House, PO Box 123, Knutsford, Cheshire WA16

9HX. Hobbies: Theatre acting and directing, fencing (former member of the national squad), tennis, running, languages (French and German).

BECKINSALE, Kate
Kate Beckinsale. Actor (M). b. 1974.
TV: *Alice Through the Looking Glass; Anna Lee*; Flora Poste in *Cold Comfort Farm; Devices and Desires; Emma; One Against the Wind; Rachel's Dream.*
Films: *Brokedown Palace; Marie Louise; Much Ado About Nothing; Shooting Fish; The Golden Bowl; The Last Days of Disco; The Prince Of Jutland.*
Address: c/o ICM, Oxford House, 76 Oxford Street, London W1N 0AX. Father Richard Beckinsale; 1 sister Samantha.

BECKINSALE, Samantha
Samantha Beckinsale. Actor (F). b. 1968.
TV: *Dangerfield; London's Burning; Time After Time; Get Well Soon; Duck Patrol; Jake's Progress.*
Address: c/o London Management, Noel House, 2–4 Noel Street, London W1V 3RB. Hobbies: Decorating and designing houses, reading, various sports. Father Richard Beckinsdale; 1 sister Kate.

BEDDARD, Jamie
Jamie Beddard. Actor (M).
TV: Roland Adams in *All the King's Men*; Gavin in *Common As Muck*; Arthur in *Scallagrigg*; John Hunter in *Sky High.*
Films: Mike Bradley in *No One Likes Us; Quills*; Terry in *The Trouble With Terry*; Nobby in *Wonderful You.*
Address: c/o Amanda Howard Associates Ltd, 21 Berwick Street, London W1V 3RG.

BEENEY, Christopher
Christopher Beeney. Actor (M). b. 7 July 1941.
TV: *Armchair; Dixon of Dock Green; Emergency Ward 10; Grandad*; Billy in *In Loving Memory*; Geoffrey in *Miss Jones and Son; Rivals of Sherlock Holmes; Softly Softly*; Lennie Grove in *The Grove Family; The Plane Makers*; Tony in *The Rag Trade*; Edward in *Upstairs Downstairs; Whodunnit?; Z Cars.*
Address: c/o Roger Carey Associates, 7 St George's Square, London SW1V 2HX.

BEER, Alice
Alice Beer. Presenter/Reporter. b. 1965.
TV: *Face Value; Families at War; Gloria Live; Healthcheck; The Holiday Programme; Kilroy; Real Rakeovers; That's Life; Watchdog.*
Address: c/o Unique Artistes, Avon House, Kensington Village, London W14 8TS.

BEESLEY, Max

Max Beesley. Actor (M).

TV: *The Broker's Man; Thief Takers;* Tom Jones in *Tom Jones.*

Films: *Five Seconds to Spare; The Beautiful Game.*

Address: c/o ICM, Oxford House, 76 Oxford Street, London W1N 0AX. Hobbies: Meditation.

BEGLEY, Michael

Michael Begley. Actor (M). b. London.

TV: George in *Amongst Barbarians;* Richard Law in *City Central;* P.C. Bentley in *Coronation Street;* Terry in *Grafters; Hillsborough;* Casca in *Julius Caesar;* Teflon in *London's Burning;* John Bruton in *McLibel!; See You Friday;* Lee Gallagher in *The Bill;* Jim in *The Grand;* Terry Cole in *This Life.*

Address: c/o John Markham Associates, 1a Oakwood Avenue, Purley, Surrey CR8 1AR.

BEHR, Dani

Dani Behr. Actor (F)/Presenter.

b. London, 9 Juy 1974.

TV: *Absolutely Animals; Access All Areas;* Jackie in *Babes in the Wood; Big Breakfast;* Dani in *Bob Martin; Capital Café; Comedy Lab; Dani Dares;* Shelley in *Frank Dance Is Dead; Hotel Babylon; Ice Warriors; Live in Your Living Room; Metro Café; Surf Potatoes; The Brit Awards; The Mix; The Word; Wish You Were Here...?; World Premiere of Paris.*

Films: Dani in *Bolt;* Charlie in *Like It Is;* Candy in *Party On;* Charlie in *Rancid Aluminium;* Jessica in *Strong Boys.*

Address: c/o William Morris Agency (UK) Ltd, 1 Stratton Street, London W1X 6HB. Hobbies: Interior design, yoga, cinema.

BELL, Ann

Ann Bell. Actor (F).

b. Wallasey, Cheshire, 29 April 1940.

TV: Eve Lambert in *Anna Lee* (1993); Casting Director in *Blackeyes* (1989); Caroline in *Callan* (1967); Mrs Burton in *Christabel* (1988); May in *Department S* (1969); Mary in *Double First* (1988); Jean Bailey in *Out of this World* (1962); Lady Astwell in *Poirot* (1993); Receptionist in *Shaggy Dog* (1968); Anitra Cyon in *Spectre* (1977); Marion Jefferson in *Tenko Reunion* (1984); Nikki Holz in *The Baron* (1966); Joyce in *The Black Knight* (1977); Molly Phillips in *The Ice House* (1997); Sylvia Llewelyn in *The Lost Boys* (1978); Natasja in *The Saint* (1962); Katrina in *The Sentimental Agent* (1963); Mrs Rideout in *The Woman in White* (1997); Helen Stubbs in *Tumbledown* (1989).

Films: *Cartel;* Valda Embiricos in *Champions;* Ann Rogers in *Dr Terror's House of Horrors;* Susan in *Flat Two; Savage Harvest; The Land Girls;* Sally in *The Witches;* Mrs Dare in *To Sir With Love;* Sarah Muir in *When Saturday Comes.*

Address: c/o Julian Belfrage Associates, 46 Albemarle Street, London W1X 4PP.

BELL, Duncan

Duncan Bell. Actor (M).

TV: Peter Winrow in *A Touch of Frost;* Insp. Pollock in *Between the Lines; Blind Justice; Boon;* Bertie Armstrong in *Bramwell;* Dr Rankin in *Brave New World; Doctor Finlay's Casebook; Head Hunters;* Lt. Clayton in *Hornblower; Medics; Rik Mayall Presents;* Lt. Col Phillips in *Soldier, Soldier;* Dr Sutherland in *Taggart;* Alan Forrester in *Taggart;* Tom McAllister in *Taggart;* Stuart Gaunt in *The Bill; The Bill;* Nick Black in *The Countess Alice; The Lawlord; The Strauss Dynasty;* The Zebra Man in *The Zebra Man; Troubles;* Sir Miles Chandon in *True Tilda;* Roy Price in *Where the Heart Is.*

Address: c/o The Richard Stone Partnership, 2 Henrietta Street, London WC2E 8PS.

BELL, Tom

Tom Bell. Actor (M). b. Liverpool 1932.

TV: *Angels Are So Few; Chancer; Hedda Gabler; Holocaust; Hope it Rains; No Bananas; Out; Prime Suspect; Prime Suspect III; Red King, White Knight; Reilly Ace of Spies; Stronger Than the Sun; The Cinder Path; The Detective; The Great Kandinsky; The Rainbow; The Virginian; The Young Indiana Jones Chronicles.*

Films: *Lock Up Your Daughters!; Payroll; Prospero's Books; Sands of Beersheba; Seconds Out; Straight on Till Morning; The Criminal; The Kitchen; The Krays; The L-Shaped Room; The Long Day's Dying; The Sailor's Return; The Violent Enemy; A Prize of Arms; All The Right Noises; Ballad in Blue; Echo of Barbara; He Who Rides a Tiger; HMS Defiant; In Enemy Country.*

Address: c/o Shepherd & Ford, 13 Radnor Walk, London SW3 4BP.

BELLAMY, David

David Bellamy. Presenter. b. London, 18 January 1933.

TV: *An Island Called Danger; Backyard Safari; Bellamy on Botany; Bellamy on Top of the World; Bellamy Rides Again; Bellamy's Birds Eye View; Bellamy's Border Raids; Bellamy's Britain; Bellamy's Bugle; Bellamy's Europe; Bellamy's New World; Bellamy's Singapore; Blooming Bellamy; Botanic Man; Don't Ask Me; England's Last Wilderness; England's Lost Wilderness; It's Life; It's More Life; Journey to the Centre of the World;*

Life in Our Sea; Moa's Ark; Paradise Ploughed; Routes of Wisdom; Seaside Safari; Swallow; The End of the Rainbow Show; The Gene Machine; The Great Seasons; The Owl and the Woodsman; Turning the Tide; Up a Gum Tree; Wheat Today What Tomorrow?; You Can't See The Wood.

Address: c/o Jonathan Clowes, 10 Iron Bridge House, Bridge Approach, London NW1 8BB. m. Rosemary; 3 d. Henrietta, Brighid, Hannah; 2 s. Rufus, Eoghain. Hobbies: Ballet, conservation.

BELLINGHAM, Lynda

Lynda Bellingham. Actor (F).
b. Montreal, Quebec, 31 May 1948.
TV: Helen Herriott in *All Creatures Great and Small; At Home with the Braithwaites;* Faith in *Faith in the Future; Reach for the Moon;* Faith in *Second Thoughts; Bob Martin; Sisters Rosensweig; Martin Chuzzlewit; Filthy; Rich and Catflap; Doctor Who; The Gentle Touch; Angels; Murphy's Mob; McKenzie.*
Films: *Bodyworks; Confessions of a Driving Instructor; Don't Go Breaking My Heart; Stand Up Virgin Soldiers;* Czarina Alexandra in *The Romanovs; The Scarlet Tunic; The Sweeney; Waterloo Bridge Handicap.*
Address: c/o William Morris Agency (UK) Ltd, 1 Stratton Street, London W1X 6HB.

BELZER, Richard

Richard Belzer. Actor (M).
b. Bridgeport, Connecticut, USA, 4 August 1944.
TV: Big Bob in *Bandit: Bandit Bandit* (1994); *Crime Stories;* Mariano in *Deadly Pursuits* (1996); Detective Giordano in *Hart to Hart: Crimes of the Hart* (1994); *The David Letterman Show; HBO Comedy Special: Another Lone Nut; Homicide;* Det. John Munch in *Lie on the Street; Hot Properties;* himself in *It's Just a Ride* (1994); Det. John Munch in *Law and Order: Special Victims Unit* (1999); Inspector Henderson in *Lois & Clark: The New Adventures of Superman;* Bernie in *Prince for a Day* (1995); Joe Kline in *The Flash* (1990); Randy Stein in *The Invaders* (1995); himself in *The Playboy Comedy Roast/Tommy Chong* (1986); *The Richard Belzer Show;* himself in *Thick of the Night* (1983); *When Cars Attack* (1997).
Films: Detective in *A Very Brady Sequel;* Gypsy Beam in *America;* Seth Shapiro in *Author! Author!;* Cameo in *Dangerous Games;* Conferencier in *Fame;* Phil in *Fletch Lives;* Stone in *Flicks;* Doctor David Lazarus in *Freeway;* Rick in *Get on the Bus;* Caller 1, Beach in *Girl 6;* M.C./Comic in *Mad Dog and Glory;* Baldesan in *Missing Pieces;* Pig in *Night Shift;* Barker in *North;* Jeremy in *Not of This Earth;* Milt Zoloth in *Off and*

Running; M.C. at Babylon Club in *Scarface;* President in *Species II;* Video Show Host in *The Big Picture;* Television Producer in *The Bonfire of the Vanities;* Rodriguez/Leo Batfish/The President/The Hooker in *The Groove Tube;* Jarvis in *The Puppet Masters;* Belz in *The Wrong Guys.*
Address: c/o Don Buchwald and Associates, 10 East 44th Street, New York, New York 10017, USA. m. 1 Gail Susan Ross (dis); m. 2 Dalia Danoch (dis); m. 3 Harlee McBride; 2 Step-d. Jessica, Bree.

BENJAMIN, Christopher

Christopher Benjamin. Actor (M).
b. 27 December 1934.
TV: *Double Dealer; London's Burning; Pride and Prejudice; See Saw; The Last Salute; The Tomorrow People.*
Address: c/o Scott Marshall, 44 Perryn Road, London W3 7NA.

BENJAMIN, Lucy

Lucy Benjamin. Actor (F).
b. Sutton Coldfield, West Midlands, 25 June 1970.
TV: Young Claudia in *Beau Geste;* Nurse in *Bottom;* Beryl in *Class Act;* Kate Shephard in *Close to Home;* Audrey in *Dangerfield;* Young Nyssa in *Doctor Who;* Lisa in *EastEnders;* Fiona McBride in *Jupiter Moon;* Gemma Tindle in *Me and My Girl;* Katherine in *Murder Most Horrid;* Julie in *Press Gang;* Nancy in *Star Trap;* Zoe in *Staying Alive;* Miss Faulkner Green in *Stig of the Dump;* Cynthia Sunday in *Teleganticmegavision;* Joey in *The Bill;* Ingrid in *The Bill;* Amy/Amelia in *The Exorcism of Amy;* Pam in *Time on Your Hands;* Kate in *Up the Elephant and Round the Castle.*
Address: c/o CAM London, 19 Denmark Street, London WC2H 8NA.

BENNETT, Alan

Alan Bennett. Writer/Actor (M).
b. Leeds, Yorkshire, 9 May 1934.
TV: *A Dance to the Music of Time; A Day Out; A Question of Attribution; A Visit from Mrs Prothero; A Woman of No Importance; Afternoon Off; All Day at the Sands; An Englishman Abroad; Doris and Doreen; Intensive Care; Marks; Me! I'm Afraid of Virginia Woolf; One Fine Day; Our Winnie; Poetry in Motion; Rolling Home; Say Something Happened; Sunset Across the Bay; Talking Heads; Talking Heads II; The Insurance Man; The Old Crowd.*
Films: *A Private Function; Prick Up Your Ears; The Madness Of King George.*
Address: c/o Chatto & Linnit Ltd, 123a Kings Road, London SW3 4PL.

BENNETT, Hywel

Hywel Bennett. Actor (M).

b. Garnant, Amman Valley, Wales, 8 April 1944.

TV: *A Mind to Kill; A Month in the Country; Absent Friends; Artemis 81; Boon; Checkpoint Chiswick; Coming Out; Death of a Teddy Bear; Frank Stubbs Promotes; Frankie & Johnny; Frontiers;* Iles in *Harpur and Iles;* Arthur 'Pig' Malion in *Karaoke;* Dr Brickleigh in *Malice Aforethought; Murder Most Horrid;* Croup in *Neverwhere;* Tom the Pimp in *Pennies from Heaven;* Romeo in *Romeo and Juliet;* Shelley in *Shelley; The Consultant;* Mr Puff in *The Critic; The Idiot; The Secret Agent; Tinker, Tailor, Soldier, Spy; Trust Me; Unman, Wittering and Zigo; Virtual Murder; Where the Buffalo Roam.*

Films: *Age Unknown; Alice in Wonderland; Deadly Advice; Endless Night; Loot;* Reg in *Married to Malcolm;* Herod in *Mary, Mother of Jesus;* The Sea Captain in *Misery Harbour; Murder Elite;* David Withers in *Nasty Neighbours; Percy; The Buttercup Chain;* Arthur in *The Family Way;* Purvis in *The Other Side of Paradise; The Twilight Zone; The Twisted Nerve; The Virgin Soldiers; Vetel; War Zone.*

Address: c/o Gavin Barker Associates Ltd, 45 South Molton Street, London W1Y 1HD.

BENNETT, Rosalind

Rosalind Bennett. Actor (F). b. 13 May 1966.

TV: *An Evil Streak;* Rose in *Campaign;* Tina Wagstaff in *Coronation Street;* Genevieve in *Covington Cross;* Carmen in *Growing Rich;* Carol Reed in *Guardians;* Flora in *Heart of the Country;* Niza in *Incident in Judea; Mothertime;* Marie in *Poirot;* Penny in *Shrinks;* Sue in *Statement of Affairs;* Zoe in *The Facts of Life;* Colette in *The Fear;* Pauline Wilson in *The Manageress; Time and Motion.*

Films: Miss Pickwick in *American Roulette;* Bonnie in *Dealers; Halcyon Days; In the Time of Angels;* Eleanor in *Restoration;* Elisabeth in *Smack and Thistle;* Kate in *The Grass Arena;* Lyn in *VROOM!.*

Address: c/o ICM, Oxford House, 76 Oxford Street, London W1N 0AX.

BENNETT, Tracie

Tracie Bennett. Actor (F). b. 17 June 1961.

TV: *Alas Smith and Jones; Black Silk; Boon;* Miss Wilson in *Brush Strokes;* Sally in *Casualty;* Sharon Gaskell in *Coronation Street; Going Out;* Lieutenant in *Heartbeat;* Rita in *Heartburn Hotel;* Tracy in *Joking Apart; Knock Knock;* Monica in *Made in Heaven;* Norma in *Making Out;* Liz in *Next of Kin; Relative Strangers;* Nicky in *Rich Tea and Sympathy;* Monica in *Ruth Rendell Mysteries; Shame;* Annette in *The Ambas-sador;* Lisa Brooks in *The Bill;* Connie Fazakerly in *The Bretts;* Stella in *The Gingerbread Girl; The Rector of Stifkey;* June in *The Refuge;* Angie in *The Ritz;* Michelle in *The Upper Hand;* Cheryl in *Unnatural Causes;* Sally in *Verdict.*

Films: Ana in *Deep Red Instant;* Tina in *Knights and Emeralds;* Milandra in *Shirley Valentine.*

Address: c/o Conway Van Gelder, 18–21 Jermyn Street, London SW1Y 6HP.

BENSON, Kim

Kim Benson. Actor (F).

TV: Christine in *2point4 children;* Tracey in *A Taste for Death;* Sue in *Big Deal;* Kay in *I Like Here;* Angela in *Made in Britain;* Young Mum in *Mr Wakefield's Crusade;* Agnes Tebbitt in *The New Statesman.*

Films: *Paradise Postponed; Wings of Death.*

Address: c/o Hillman Threlfall, 33 Brookfield, Highgate West Hill, London N6 6AT.

BENSON-PHILLIPS, Dave

Dave Benson-Phillips. Presenter.

TV: *1,2,3,4,5; Bitesize; Cat's Eyes; Dave's Summer Party; Disney's Wake Up in the Wild Room;* Jack Hammer in *Dream Street; Get Your Own Back,* (1999); *Go for It; Hunny Pot* (1997); *Jack in the Box; Nick Jnr; Playdays; Playtime; Q&A; Ratkan II; Saturday Action; Stories and Rhymes; The Fun Song Factory.*

Address: c/o AMG Ltd, 8 King Street, London WC2E 8HN. Hobbies: Guitar, drums, ukulele, harmonica, juggling, magic, balloon modelling, stilt walking, roller-skating, dancing, photography, horse riding.

BENTINCK, Timothy

Timothy Bentinck. Actor (M).

b. Tasmania, Australia, 1 June 1953.

TV: Mark in *A Prince Among Men;* Keen in *Boon;* Tom Lacey in *By the Sword Divided;* McDermot in *Casualty;* Announcer in *Four Minute Mile;* Mr Mitchell in *Grange Hill;* Garth Stanford in *Griffiths;* Gosling in *Kavanagh QC;* Steve in *Made in Heaven;* Montague in *Melba;* Captain Murray in *Sharpe's Rifles;* Nigel in *Square Deal;* Raikes in *Strike Force;* Count Frederick in *The New Adventures of Robin Hood;* Meech in *The Stinker;* George in *Three Up, Two Down;* Baines in *Tiger of Kumaon;* David Boutflour in *White House Farm Murders.*

Films: Harris in *North Sea Hijack;* Pirate in *Pirates of Penzance;* Pieter in *Success is the Best Revenge;* Richard in *The Year of the Comet;* Captain in *Twelfth Night;* Lt. Flynn in *Winter Flight.*

Address: c/o JM Associates, 77 Beak Street, London W1R 3LF.

BENTON, Mark

Mark Benton. Actor (M).

b. Guisborough, Cleveland, 16 November 1965.

TV: Mickeyo in *Ballykissangel*; Martin Pond in *Barbara*; Chukie in *Eureka Street*; Bernie in *Finney*; Fred in *Nature Boy*; Harry Wallis in *Randall & Hopkirk (Deceased)*; Bernie in *See You Friday*; Fred in *The Girl*; Jimmy in *The Jump*; Hawkshaw in *This is Personal*.

Films: Ricky in *Career Girls*; Topsy Turvy in *Sydney Price*; Giant in *The Lost Son*.

Address: c/o London Management, Noel House, 2–4 Noel Street, London W1V 3RB. Partner Sarah Gardner; 1 s. Archie; uncle Michael Gunn. Hobbies: Guitar, writing.

BERGLAS, Ron

Ron Berglas. Actor (M).

TV: Pyrus Bonnington in *Another Flip for Dominic*; Wadkins in *Boon*; Kenneth Adelman in *Breakthrough at Reykjavik*; Gino in *C.A.T.S. Eyes*; TV Host in *Exit*; Jeb Faulkner in *Heartbeat*; Dr Curchin in *Jonathan Creek*; Buford in *Kavanagh QC*; Uncle Bob in *Mike and Angelo*; Louis Finkel in *Murder Most Horrid*; Richard Arens in *Naming Names*; John Manley in *Oppenheimer*; Rev. De Angelis in *Perfect Scoundrels*; Solly Granger in *Pulaski*; Maurice Fishbourne in *Rumpole of the Bailey*; Sam in *Saigon – The Last Day*; Mel Burger/Capt. Ahab in *She-Wolf of London*; Elkin in *The Glory Boys*; Patton in *The Last Days of Patton*; Edmonds in *The Missing Reel*; Forrester in *The Professionals*; Frank in *Tomorrow People*; Kahnweiler in *The Young Indiana Jones Chronicles*.

Films: Max in *Crime Time*; Roger Flint in *Death Train*; Sam in *Dreamchild*; Harry Flood in *Eye of the Storm*; Richards in *Helen and the Teacher*; Erik in *Highlander*; Mike Bohn in *Hostile Waters*; Jeff in *Ishtar*; *Jilting Joe*; Williams in *Red Eagle*; Selznick in *RKO 281*; Bennett in *Vengeance*; Stampler in *Woman Called Golda*.

Address: c/o Kerry Gardner Management, 7 St George's Square, London SW1V 2HX.

BERRINGTON, Elizabeth

Elizabeth Berrington. Actor (F).

TV: *Between the Lines*; *Casualty*; Marie Antoinette in *Let Them Eat Cake*; Marina in *My Wonderful Life*; *Nature Boy*; *Nurses*; *Silent Witness*; *The Bill*; Ruth in *The Lakes*; Limping Lucy in *The Moonstone*.

Films: Mrs Ash in *An Urban Ghost Story*; Celeste in *Eight and a Half Women*; Mlle Volonsky in *Onegin*; Pru in *Mad Cows*; Giselle in *Naked*; Jane in *Secrets and Lies*.

Address: c/o Roxane Vacca Management, 73 Beak Street, London W1R 3LF. Hobbies: Horse riding, dancing, singing.

BERRY, Nick

Nick Berry. Actor (M).

b. Woodford, Essex, 16 April 1963.

TV: *Black Velvet Band*; *Box of Delights*; *Cluedo*; *Cover Her Face*; *Dramarama*; Simon Wicks in *EastEnders*; Mike Nicholls in *Harbour Lights*; P.C. Nick Rowan in *Heartbeat*; *Paparazzo*; *Respect*; *The Grove Family*; Colin in *The Mystery of Men*.

Films: *Party Party*; *Tank Malling*.

Address: c/o ICM, Oxford House, 76 Oxford Street, London W1N 0AX.

BERTISH, Jane

Jane Bertish. Actor (F).

TV: *Broker's Man*; *French & Saunders*; *Girls on Top*; *Inspector Morse*; *Life After Life*; *Parker*; *Quatermass*; *Sam Saturday*; *Seeing in the Dark*; *The Lenny Henry Show*; *The Passion*; *Vanity Fair*.

Films: *Bodywork*; *Dance with Strangers*; *Paperhouse*; *Smart Money*; *The Reef*.

Address: c/o Barry Brown & Partner, 47 West Square, London SE11.

BERTISH, Suzanne

Suzanne Bertish. Actor (F). b. 7 August 1953.

TV: *A Day in Summer*; *Absolutely Fabulous*; *Girls on Top*; *Mr Bean*; *Shine on Harvey Moon*; *The Comedy of Errors*; *The Life and Adventures of Nicholas Nickleby*; *The Scarlet Pimpernel*; *To The Lighthouse*.

Films: *Bent*; *Crimetime*; *Hanover Street*; *The Hunger*.

Address: c/o London Management, Noel House, 2–4 Noel Street, London W1V 3RB.

BEVAN, Gillian

Gillian Bevan. Actor (F). b. Stockport, Cheshire.

TV: *A Dance to the Music of Time*; *A Touch of Frost*; *Act of Will*; *Chillers*; Sharon in *Coppers*; Professor Lin Pascoe in *Ghostwatch*; *Kiss and Tell*; Cissie Mapes in *Lost Empires*; *Loved By You*; *No Job for a Lady*; *Peak Practice*; *Pie in the Sky*; *Screaming*; Beryl Wainwright in *Sharon and Elsie*; *Sunburn*; DS Rose Penfold in *The Chief*.

Address: c/o ICM, Oxford House, 76 Oxford Street, London W1N 0AX.

BEWES, Rodney

Rodney Bewes. Actor (M)/Co-producer.

b. Bingley, Yorkshire, 27 November 1938.

TV: *'Tis Pity She's a Whore*; *The Basil Brush Show*; *Camera Club*; *Dear Mother... Love Albert*; *Doctor Who*; *Emergency Ward 10*; *Love Story*; *Spender*; *The Likely Lads*; *Whatever Happened to the Likely Lads*; *The Plane Makers*.

Films: *Alice in Wonderland*; *Billy Liar*; *Saint Jack*;

Spring and Port Wine; St Trinian's; The Gothic Chimney; The Spaceman and King Arthur; The Wild Cats of St Trinian's; We Joined the Navy.
Address: c/o Michelle Braidman Associates, 10–11 Lower John Street, London W1R 3PE. Hobbies: Oarsman for 'The London Rowing Club' and for 'Cadgwith Cove' in Cornwall.

BHASKAR, Sanjeev

Sanjeev Bhaskar. Actor (M). b. 1964.
TV: Adel in *Captain Butler; Diwali Lights; In the Mix; Jo Brand – Through the Cakehole;* Steve McCrum in *Keeping Mum;* Sanjay in *Pork Pie; Small Potatoes;* Dr Patel in *The Grimleys.*
Films: *Notting Hill;* Rai in *The Dance of Shiva.*
Address: c/o Lou Coulson, 37 Berwick Street, London W1V 3RF.

BHATTACHARJEE, Paul

Paul Bhattacharjee. Actor (M).
TV: *A Summer Day's Dream;* Jaz in *Albion Market;* Old Man in *Ancestral Voices;* Reg Ferney in *Bergerac; Black and Blue;* Jag in *Chilli in Your Eyes; Clubland;* Steve in *Here is the News;* General Dyer in *Inkalaab;* Ranjit in *Johnny Jarvis;* Querishi in *Love Birds;* Valet in *Maigret; Navy in Action; Northern Crescent;* Maganlal in *Pravina's Wedding;* Prince Javad in *Saracen;* Said Farrukh in *Shalom Shalaam; Sister Wife;* Ramiz in *The Bill; Thief Takers; Two Oranges and a Mango; A Wing and a Prayer.*
Films: *Jinnah; Wild West.*
Address: c/o ICM, Oxford House, 76 Oxford Street, London W1N 0AX.

BIAGI, Simon

Simon Biagi. Presenter.
b. Southampton, Hampshire, 18 September 1961.
TV: *Backstage; Café Biagi; Close Shave; Decision Time; Eikon; Friday Live Show; GMTV; Great Escapes; Gridlock; Heaven and Earth Show; Live Wire; Real Rooms; The Mysterious North; The Terrace.*
Address: c/o David Anthony Promotions, PO Box 286, Warrington, Cheshire WA2 6GA. Partner Tove; 1 sister Leigh. Hobbies: Dogs (field trials and shows), most sports, diving, mountain biking.

BIBBY, Andrew

Andrew Bibby. Actor (M).
TV: *A Country Practice; Blue Heelers;* Lance Wilkinson in *Neighbours; Ocean Girl 2.*
Films: *Computer Kids; Hotel de Love.*
Address: c/o Pearson Television, 1 Stephen Street, London W1P 1PJ.

BIGGINS, Christopher

Christopher Biggins. Actor (M).
b. Oldham, Lancashire, 16 December 1948.
TV: *Absolutely Fabulous;* The Sorceror in *Adam's Family Tree; Alfresco; Brontë Connection;* Reverend Green in *Cluedo; Five's Company; French & Saunders; Gay TV;* Emperor Nero in *I, Claudius; Infidelities; Man of Straw; Masada; Monster TV;* Reverend Ossie Whitworth in *Poldark;* Lukewarm in *Porridge; Some Mothers Do 'Ave 'Em; Surprise, Surprise; The Likely Lads; The Sooty Show; Weekend Plus.*
Films: *Applause; Caught in the Act; Cold Fish; Decadence; Eskimo Nell; The Rocky Horror Picture Show; The Tempest.*
Address: c/o Jonathan Altaras Associates, 13 Shorts Gardens, London WC2H 9AT.

BILLINGTON, Michael

Michael Billington. Actor (M).
TV: Ventidius in *Antony and Cleopatra;* Czar Nicholas II in *Edward the King; Fantasy Island; Gavilan; Greatest American Hero;* Freddie Hepton in *Hadleigh; Hart to Hart; Magnum PI;* Oscar in *Maigret and the Nightclub Dancer; Philip Marlowe PI;* Kenyon Jones in *Sister Dora;* Col-Sgt. Jackson in *Spearhead;* Catoline (Arthur Becker) in *Stick With Me Kid;* Tom Gibbons in *The Collectors;* Daniel Fogarty in *The Onedin Line;* John Coogan in *The Professionals; The Quest* (lead); Ben Adams in *Thundercloud; Today's FBI;* Paul Foster in *U.F.O.;* Alphons Berg in *War and Peace;* Mr Fainall in *Way of the World.*
Films: *KGB – The Secret War* (lead); Sergei in *The Spy Who Loved Me.*
Address: c/o Brunskill Management, Suite 8a, 169 Queen's Gate, London SW7 5HE.

BILLINGTON, Stephen

Stephen Billington. Actor (M). b. 1972.
TV: Greg Kelly in *Coronation Street;* Derrick in *Highlander;* Neville in *Jonathan Creek;* Gary in *Rules of Engagement;* Ross in *Space Precinct;* L.T. James in *The Buccaneers;* Lysander in *The Man Who Made Husbands Jealous.*
Films: Philip in *Braveheart.*
Address: c/o Markham & Froggatt Ltd, 4 Windmill Street, London W1P 1HF.

BIRCH, Leila

Leila Birch. Actor (F). b. London.
TV: Teresa di Marco in *EastEnders;* Gina in *Renford Rejects;* Sheena in *Thief Takers.*
Films: Ellen/Sonia in *Broken Thread;* Sonia in *Gas Menagerie;* Claudia in *More Than Dreams.*

Address: c/o Burdett-Coutts Associates, Riverside Studios, Crisp Road, London W6 9RL.

BIRD, John

John Bird. Actor (M)/Comedian/Presenter.
b. Nottingham, 22 November 1936.
TV: *A Travelling Man; A Very Peculiar Practice; Blue Money; Carrington of the Foreign Office; C.A.T.S. Eyes; Crown Court* (1977); Dougherty in *Dead Entry; Educating Marmalade* (1977); *El C.I.D.;* Dingo Wucker in *Filthy Rich and Catflap; Fry and Laurie; Giving Tongue;* Frank in *God's Chosen Car Park; Healthwatch; Home to Roost; In the Looking Glass* (1976); *In the Red; Inspector Morse; Jane* (1977); *John Bird/John Fortune Show* (1975); *Joint Account; King Lear* (1977); *London Scene* (1976); *Lytton's Diary; Marmalade Atkins in Space* (1977); *Mrs Capper's Birthday; One Foot in the Grave; Oxbridge Blues* (1977); *Rory Bremner... Who Else?; Round and Round* (1977); *Saturday Night Live; Ten Glorious Years; The Ballad of Johnny Vanguard; The Chamber; The Children of Dynmouth; The Combination* (1977); *The Galton and Simpson Playhouse* (1975); *The Growing Pains of Adrian Mole; The Little Princess; The Long Johns; The Melting Pot* (1975); *The Mistress; The Punch Review* (1975); *The Rory Bremner Show; The Two Johns; The Wild West Show* (1977); *The Year of the Blair; Timon of Athens* (1977); *Variations on a Theme* (1976).
Films: *Dick Turpin; Help!; Jabberwocky; The Seven Per Cent Solution; Yellow Pages.*
Address: c/o Chatto & Linnit Ltd, 123a Kings Road, London SW3 4PL.

BIRDSALL, Jesse

Jesse Birdsall. Actor (M).
b. London, 13 February 1963.
TV: *A Sudden Wrench; Anna Lee;* Pete in *Annika;* Phil in *Blind Men;* Jordan in *Boon;* Beckett in *BUGS; Casualty; Eldorado;* Elvis in *Elvis;* Des Lewis in *Kavanagh QC;* Julian in *Rides; Sean's Show;* Neil in *September; Shrinks; Silent Witness; Tales out of School;* Marty in *The Fear;* Sgt. Baker in *The Lord Lucan Case; Thief Takers.*
Films: Kid Divine in *The Ballad of Kid Divine; Bedlam; Bloody Kids;* Gavin in *Getting it Right; Revolution;* Carl in *Shadey;* Dave in *Wish You Were Here.*
Address: c/o Conway Van Gelder, 18–21 Jermyn Street, London SW1Y 6HP.

BISSON, Chris

Chris Bisson. Actor (M). b. 21 July 1975.
TV: JJ in *Children's Ward;* Omar Assi in *Cops;* Vikram Desai in *Coronation Street;* Nazir Ahmed in *Prime Suspect V.*
Films: Saleem Khan in *East is East.*
Address: c/o Stephen Hatton Management Suite, 24 London Fruit and Wool Exchange, Brushfield Street, London E1 6HB.

BLACK, Cilla

Priscilla White. Host/Singer/Actor (F).
b. Liverpool, Merseyside, 27 May 1943.
TV: *Blind Date; Juke Box Jury; Surprise, Surprise; The Moment of Truth.*
Music: *Alfie; Anyone Who Had A Heart; Something Tells Me; Step Inside Love; You're My World.*
Address: c/o Bobsons Productions, The Penthouse, 10 Abbey Orchard Street, London SW1P 2JP.

BLACK, Denise

Denise Black. Actor (F).
b. Emsworth, Hampshire 1958.
TV: *A Touch of Frost;* Jessie in *Bad Girls; Between the Lines; Call My Bluff; Casualty; Coronation Street; Dangerfield; Dead Romantic;* Aunt Jill in *Dear Nobody; How to do Love in the 21st Century; Josie;* Witch in *Macbeth; Nazi Germany; Play Dead;* Hazel in *Queer as Folk; Saturday Live; Sherlock Holmes; The Bill;* Madame Guillotine in *The Scarlet Pimpernel;* Pat Phoenix in *The Things You Do For Love;* Maggie in *Vanishing Man; What's My Line?.*
Address: c/o Emptage Hallett, 24 Poland Street, London W1V 3DD.

BLACK, Leon

Leon Black. Actor (M).
TV: *Demon in My View; The Real McCoy; Desmonds; Go Wild; The Pirate Prince; Oasis; Lenny Henry Show; Gimme 5; Casualty; Ronson's Mission; The Honeymoon is Over; Live in Babylon; Children's Society; Game On; LRTV; Marvin; The Bill;* Graffiti Punk in *Toon Box – I Dent; Unsuitable Job for Woman;* Stephen Lawrence in *The Stephen Lawrence Story;* Brian in *Maisie Raine.*
Films: *Face; Clockwork Mice; Shopping.*
Address: c/o Anna Scher Theatre Management Ltd, 70–72 Barnsbury Road, London N1 0ES.

BLACKMAN, Honor

Honor Blackman. Actor (F). b. 22 August 1926.
TV: *Doctor Who; First Olympics: Athens 1896; Ghost Squad; Lace; Minder on the Orient Express; Probation Officer;* Cathy Gale in *The Avengers; The Four Just Men; The Secret Adversary;* Laura West in *The Upper Hand; Voice of the Heart.*

Films: *A Boy, a Girl and a Bike; A Matter of Who; A Night to Remember; A Twist of Sand; Account Rendered; Age of Innocence; Breakaway; Conspirator; Daughter of Darkness; Delavine Affair; Diamond City; Diplomatic Passport; Fame is the Spur; Fright;* Pussy Galore in *Goldfinger; Green Grow the Rushes; Jason and the Argonauts; Moment to Moment; Quartet; Serena; Shalako; So Long at the Fair; Something Big; Suspended Alibi; The Cat and The Canary; The Glass Cage; The Last Grenade; The Rainbow Jacket; The Secret of My Success; The Square Peg; The Virgin and the Gypsy; To The Devil a Daughter; Walking With Lions.*
Address: c/o London Management, Noel House, 2–4 Noel Street, London W1V 3RB.

BLACKWOOD, Richard
Richard Blackwood. Comedian/Presenter.
b. Streatham, South London.
TV: *Club Class; Five Night Stand; Full On For Less; MTV Base; MTV Hot; Richard Blackwood Show; Singled Out; The Real McCoy.*
Address: Contact via Channel 5, 22 Long Acre, London WC2E 9LY.

BLAIR, David
David Blair. Actor (M). b. Surrey 19 April 1973.
TV: PC Martins in *A Touch of Frost;* Herbert Batty in *Dalziel and Pascoe;* Stuart in *Island;* Gavin in *The Wild House III.*
Address: c/o Dennis Lyne Agency, 108 Leonard Street, London EC2A 4RH.

BLAIR, Isla
Isla Blair. Actor (F).
b. Bangalore, 29 September 1946.
TV: *A Touch of Frost; An Englishman's Castle; Bookie; Boon; C.A.T.S. Eyes; The Darling Buds of May; Doctor Finlay's Casebook; Final Cut; Haggard;* Elaine Aubrey in *Heartbeat;* Mary Weston in *Heaven on Earth; Inspector Morse; The Prime of Miss Jean Brodie; Love Story; Medics; Mother Love;* Myrtle Quincy in *The Mrs Bradley Mysteries; Off Peak; Present Laughter; Story Book; Taggart; The Advocates; The Beggar's Opera; The Bounder; The Good Guys; The History Man; The Liars; When the Boat Comes In; Wilde Alliance.*
Films: *Battle of Britain; Indiana Jones and The Last Crusade; Taste the Blood of Dracula;* Sheila in *The Match; The Monk; The Tennis Court; Treasure Island; True Tilda; Valmont.*
Address: c/o Shepherd & Ford, 13 Radnor Walk, London SW3 4BP. m. Julian Glover; 1 s. Jamie.

BLAIR, Lionel
Lionel Ogus. Dancer/Panellist.
b. Montreal, 12 December 1931.
TV: *Give Us a Clue.*
Films: *Absolute Beginners.*
Address: c/o Peter Charlesworth & Associates, 68 Old Brompton Road, London SW7 3LQ.

BLAKE, Christopher
Christopher Blake. Actor (M).
b. London, 23 August 1949.
TV: *Anne of Avonlea; Brookside; Death or Glory Boys;* Richardson in *Love for Lydia;* Tom Tulliver in *The Mill on the Floss;* Tom in *Mixed Blessings;* Robert in *That's My Boy;* Robert in *The Lost Boys.*
Films: *Aces High; Faith; Hennessy.*
Address: c/o Ken McReddie Ltd, 91 Regent Street, London W1R 7TB. 2 d. Charlotte, Louise; s. Sean. Hobbies: Supporter of Arsenal FC, cricket, rock music.

BLAKE, Katie
Katie Blake. Actor (F).
TV: Julie Bird in *City Central;* Aida in *Dalziel and Pascoe;* Helen in *Dear Nobody;* Nicola in *Microsoap;* Emma in *See How They Run;* Eden in *Verdict.*
Address: c/o William Morris Agency (UK) Ltd, 1 Stratton Street, London W1X 6HB.

BLAKE, Susie
Susie Blake. Actor (F). b. Highgate, London.
TV: *A Dog's Ransom;* Beverley in *A Prince Among Men;* Susan Hopkins in *A Year in Provence;* Louise in *April Fools Day; Blore; Born and Bred; Comet Amongst the Stars; Drop the Dead Donkey; Eleven Men Against Eleven; Ghost Sonata; Love School; Mud; Paradise Postponed; Return to Blood River;* Eve Beckett in *Roger, Roger; Russ Abbot's Madhouse; Singles;* Mrs Buchanan in *Sunburn; Thank You Miss Jones;* Mrs Jerebohm in *The Darling Buds of May; The Gang Show; The Jim Davidson Show; The Stanley Baxter Show; The Victoria Wood Show;* Fay Morgan in *The Wail of the Banshee; Wake Up With...; Zodiac.*
Films: The Woman in Red in *Fierce Creatures.*
Address: c/o Gavin Barker Associates Ltd, 45 South Molton Street, London W1Y 1HD. m. Martin Potter.

BLAKELY, Lucy
Lucy Blakely. Actor (F).
TV: Tania in *Babes in the Wood;* Kate in *Days Like These;* Stephanie Cockerill in *Family Affairs; Kids Court;* Nicki in *Married for Life; The Pyjama Party.*
Address: c/o Sandra Boyce Management, 1 Kingsway Parade, Albion Road, London N16 0TA.

BLAKISTON, Caroline

Caroline Blakiston. Actor (F).

b. London, 13 February 1933.

TV: Lady Patience Hardacre in *As Time Goes By*; *Brass*; *Charters & Caldicott*; Judith Villiers in *Children of the New Forest*; *Crown Court*; *Life After Death*; Lady Bess Sedgwick in *Miss Marple*; *Mr Palfrey of Westminster*; *Nanny*; *Not So Much a Programme*; *Private Schultz*; Scarlet O'Hara in *Rides*; *Shoestring*; *Shrinks*; Mrs Armitage in *Sunburn*; *The Avengers*; *The Caesars*; *The Forsyte Saga*; Isobel Crawford in *The Grand*; *The Last Song*; *The Mallens*; *The Racing Game*; Helen Crichton-Crick in *The Refuge*; *The Saint*; *Wives and Daughters*.

Films: *Knots*; *Sunday, Bloody Sunday*; *The Fourth Protocol*; *The Magic Christian*; *The Return of the Jedi*; *The Trygon Factor*; *Yanks*.

Address: c/o CDA, 19 Sydney Mews, London SW3 6HL.

BLANCH, Dennis

Dennis Blanch. Actor (M).

b. Barnet, Herefordshire, 4 February 1947.

TV: Vic Deardon in *Blood and Peaches*; Dennis Evans in *Casualty*; Bill Starkey in *Chandler and Co*; George in *Dream Team*; Des Warner in *Emmerdale*; Tom Gordon in *Heartbeat*; Peter Logg in *Hillsborough*; Morris Hartley in *Lost for Words*; Kev Bailey in *Love and Reason*; Sgt. Trunch in *Making Out*; Billy Roache in *Meat*; DS Willis in *Strangers*; D.I. Winley in *The Broker's Man*; Alan in *The Smiths*.

Films: Tom Hudson in *International Velvet*; Brewer in *Permission to Kill*; Sgt. Bell in *The Eagle Has Landed*; Alan Wheeler in *The Full Monty*; Private David in *The Spy Who Loved Me*.

Address: c/o John Markham Associates, 1a Oakwood Avenue, Purley, Surrey CR8 1AR.

BLEASDALE, Ian

Ian Bleasdale. Actor (M). b. 1954.

TV: Police Officer in *A Sense of Guilt*; David Braithwaite in *All Creatures Great and Small*; The Milkman in *Andy Capp*; Simon Danneflower in *Boon*; Stan McHugh in *Brookside*; Josh in *Casualty*; Chief Inspector Frost in *Drop the Dead Donkey*; *Emmerdale*; *First of the Summer Wine*; Gordon Briggs in *Heartbeat*; Ron in *Making News*; Jimmy in *Mission Top Secret*; *No Job for a Lady*; *Ruth Rendell Mysteries*; *Sherlock Holmes*; Daz in *Soldier, Soldier*; Joe Reilly in *Take the High Road*; Roy Beamish in *The Bill*; *The Brittas Empire*; *The World of Eddie Weary*.

Films: *Last Bus to Woodstock*; *To be the Best*.

Address: c/o Barry Brown & Partner, 47 West Square, London SE11.

BLESSED, Brian

Brian Blessed. Actor (M).

b. Mexborough, Yorkshire, 9 October 1937.

TV: Laughing Cavalier in *Adam's Family Tree*; *Arthur of the Britons*; The King in *Blackadder*; *Blake's 7*; Lambert Sampson in *Boon*; Brahms in *Brahms*; King Guthrum in *Churchill's People*; Reuben in *Cold Comfort Farm*; Captain in *Dennis the Menace and Gnasher*; *Doctor Who*; Prince Albert in *George Sand*; Augustus Caesar in *I, Claudius*; William Stickers in *Johnny and the Dead*; Fawcett (the explorer) in *Love Story*; Detective Freddie Dyer in *Minder*; Spiro in *My Family and Other Animals*; Courbet in *Omnibus – Courbet*; John Bunyan in *Omnibus – John Bunyan*; Father Xmas in *Sooty Swiss Alps*; *Space 1999*; *St Vitus Dance*; Inspector Smith in *Tales of the Unexpected*; *The Avengers*; Morris in *The Big Knights*; William Woodcock in *The Boy Dominic*; Mr Scottley in *The Greatest Store in the World*; Naputo in *The Half Gods*; Villain in *The Hound of the Baskervilles*; Pepone in *The Little World of Don Comillo*; Sergeant Kita in *The Recruiting Officer*; Sugden in *The Secret Agent*; Kembel in *The Sweeney*; Porthos in *The Three Musketeers*; Porthos in *The Three Musketeers: Twenty Years After*; Andrew in *The Wine of India*; Squire Western in *Tom Jones*; P.C. Fancy Smith in *Z Cars*.

Films: Bestuzhev in *Catherine the Great*; Captain Elliot in *Chasing the Deer*; Jock the Cock in *Country Dance*; Vultan, King of the Hawkmen in *Flash Gordon*; The Ghost/The King in *Hamlet*; The Duke of Exeter in *Henry V*; Suliman Khan in *High Road to China*; Black Beard in *Into Infinity*; Cluny in *Kidnapped*; King Lear in *King Lear*; Professor Atticus in *MacGyver*; Pedro in *Man of La Mancha*; Antonio in *Much Ado About Nothing*; Long John Silver in *Return to Treasure Island*; Lord Locksley in *Robin Hood: Prince of Thieves*; Boss Nass in *Star Wars: The Phantom Menace*; Clayton in *Tarzan*; Edward I in *The Bruce*; Bach in *The Joy of Bach*; Olinthus in *The Last Days of Pompeii*; Corski in *The Last Valley*; Talthybius in *The Trojan Women*; *The Young Persons Guide to the Orchestra*; General Yevlenko in *War and Remembrance*.

Address: c/o Associated International Management, 5 Denmark Street, London WC2H 8LP.

BLETHYN, Brenda

Brenda Blethyn. Actor (F).

b. Ramsgate, 20 February 1946.

TV: *Alas Smith and Jones*; *All Good Things*; *Bedroom Farce*; *The Buddha of Suburbia*; *Chance in a Million*; *Claws*; *Death of an Expert Witness*; *Floating Off*; *Grown Ups*; *Henry VI*; *In the World*; *Mona*; *Outside Edge*; *Sheppy*; *Singles Weekend*; *Tales of the Unexpected*; *That Uncertain Feeling*; *The Bullion Boys*; *The Imitation*

Game; The Richest Woman; The Storyteller; Yes, Minister.
Films: *A River Runs Through It; Daddy and Them; Girls' Night; Little Voice; Night Train; Remember Me; Secrets and Lies; Witches.*
Address: c/o ICM, Oxford House, 76 Oxford Street, London W1N 0AX.

BLOOM, Claire

Claire Bloom. Actor (F).
b. London, 15 February 1931.
TV: *A Village Affair; Anastasia; Anne and Debbie; Brideshead Revisited; Cymbeline; Family Money; Hamlet; Henry VIII; Imogen's Face; Intimate Contact; King John; Liberty; Miss Marple:; Oedipus the King; Queenie; Remember; Shadowlands; The Belle of Amhurst; The Camomile Lawn; The Ghost Writer; Time and the Conways.*
Films: *A Doll's House; Alexander the Great; Charly; Clash of the Titans; Crimes and Misdemeanours; Daylight; Islands in the Stream; Limelight; Look Back in Anger; Love And Murder; Mad Dogs and Englishmen; Mighty Aphrodite; Richard III; Sammy and Rosie Get Laid; The Brothers Karamazov; The Brothers Grimm; The Buccaneer; The Man Between; The Outrage; The Spy Who Came in from the Cold.*
Address: c/o Conway Van Gelder, 18–21 Jermyn Street, London SW1Y 6HP.

BLOOM, Marston

Marston Bloom. Actor (M).
TV: Pringle in *The Writing on the Wall;* Parson Maybell in *The Wyvern Mystery;* Blair in *A Touch of Frost;* Simon Hawkes in *Fair Game;* Lampo Davey in *Henry Pratt;* Ben Hamilton in *Preston Front;* Cpt. Russell in *Soldier, Soldier;* Einstein in *Stalag Luft;* Michael Seals in *The Alchemist;* Alan Holmes in *The Hummingbird Tree;* Arnie Rheinhardt in *The Knock III.*
Address: c/o Storm Artists Management, 47 Brewer Street, London W1R 3FD.

BLOWERS, Sean

Sean Blowers. Actor (M). b. 1961.
TV: Bill Parkes in *Bluebirds;* Ivor in *C.A.T.S. Eyes;* Slug in *Deptford Graffiti;* Rebel Leader in *Doctor Who;* Ivor in *Emergency 999;* Joe Garey in *Great Expectations;* Rodney in *Heartbeat;* Photographer in *Hot Metal;* Sub officer John Hallam in *London's Burning;* Cornflakes in *Me and My Girl;* Nick Bale in *Rockliffe's Babies;* Gordon in *Staying Alive;* Brian Case in *The Bill;* DCI Cudlip in *The Chief;* Carfard in *The Pirate Prince;* Celebrity in *The Time of Your Life;* John in *To Have and To Hold.*
Films: Bookie in *Best;* Black Beauty; Caradoss in *First*

Knight; *Foreign* Talbot in *Bodies;* Agent Dooley in *Tank Malling;* Chris Ripley in *The Krays;* Sgt. Price in *Tree of Hands.*
Address: c/o Lou Coulson, 37 Berwick Street, London W1V 3RF.

BLUMENAU, Jack

Jack Blumenau. Actor (M).
b. London, 22 November 1986.
TV: Danny in *Microsoap;* Kyle in *Reach for the Moon;* Peter in *The Railway Children.*
Address: c/o Italia Conti Agency Ltd, 23 Goswell Road, London EC1M 7AJ.

BLUTHAL, John

John Bluthal. Actor (M). b. 12 August 1939.
TV: *A View from the Bridge; Birds of a Feather; Design for Living; Home Sweet Home; Inspector Morse; Jonathan Creek; Man in a Suitcase; Minder; Never Mind the Quality, Feel the Width; Pathfinder; Q; Reilly Ace of Spies; Taggart; The Avengers; The Lives and Loves of a She Devil; The Saint;* Frank Pickle in *The Vicar of Dibley.*
Films: *A Funny Thing Happened on the Way to the Forum; A Hard Day's Night; Carry On Henry; Carry On Spying; Casino Royale; Dark City; Follow that Camel; Help!; Leapin' Leprechauns; RPM;* Stan in *Stan and George's New Life; Superman III; The Fifth Element; The Great McGonagall; The Knack; The Return of the Pink Panther;* Harry in *Time and Tide.*
Address: c/o Ken McReddie Ltd, 91 Regent Street, London W1R 7TB.

BLY, John

John Bly. Antiques expert.
TV: *The Antiques Roadshow.*
Address: Contact via BBC, Union House, 65–69 Shepherds Bush Green, London W12 8TX.

BOATMAN, Ross

Ross Boatman. Actor (M). b. 1964.
TV: Leo Arnfield in *A Touch of Frost; All in Good Faith;* Alan in *Daylight Robbery;* Gary Austin in *Death of a Son;* Kevin Medhurst in *London's Burning; The Finding.*
Films: Bear in *Hard Men;* Newsboy in *Maurice;* Rock star in *Mavis Davis; The Page* in *The Storyteller.*
Address: c/o Marina Martin Associates, 12–13 Poland Street, London W1V 3DE.

BOHT, Jean

Jean Boht. Actor (F). b. 6 March 1936.
TV: Madame Joliet in *4.50 From Paddington* (1987); Mrs Farrell in *Bergerac* (1981); Miss Sutcliffe in *Boys from the Blackstuff* (1980); Nellie Boswell in *Bread*

(1986); Josephine in *Brighton Belles* (1993); Mrs Fairchild in *Juliet Bravo (1980)*; Neighbour in *The Sweeney* (1975); Mary Teague in *Where Adam Stood* (1976).
Films: Betty in *Arthur's Hallowed Ground*; Aunty Nell in *Distant Voices, Still Lives*; Mrs Taswell in *The Girl in a Swing*.
Address: c/o Kremer Associates, Cameo House, 11 Bear Street, London WC2H 7AS. m. Carl Davies.

BOLAM, James
James Bolam. Actor (M). b. Sunderland, 16 June 1938.
TV: *Andy Capp; As You Like It; Eleven Men Against Eleven; Have Your Cake and Eat it Too; Macbeth; Only When I Laugh; Out of Sight; Room at the Bottom; Second Thoughts; Sticky Wickets; The Beiderbecke Connection/Tapes/Affair;* Terry in *The Likely Lads; The Limbo Connection; The Maze; The Missing Postman; The Stalker's Apprentice; When the Boat Comes In.*
Films: *A Kind of Loving; Clockwork Mice; End of the Affair; Half a Sixpence; In Celebration; Island on Bird Street; Murder Most Foul; O Lucky Man!; Otley; Stella Does Tricks; Straight on Till Morning; The Great Question; The Loneliness of the Long Distance Runner.*
Address: c/o ICM, Oxford House, 76 Oxford Street, London W1N 0AX.

BOLAND, Eamon
Eamon Boland. Actor (M).
b. Manchester, 15 July 1947.
TV: *A Raging Calm;* Graham Keegan in *Annie's Bar; Bare Necessities; Between the Lines; Blonde Bombshell; Bramwell;* Tony Walker in *Casualty;* Ross in *Crossfire; Crossing the Line; Fair Game;* Dave Ashton in *Fell Tiger;* Phil in *Fox; Frontiers; Harry II; Heartbeat; Hot Dog Wars;* Gerry Hollis in *Kinsey;* Hill in *Liverpool One; Missing Persons; Peak Practice; Pie in the Sky;* Clive in *Singles; Soldier, Soldier; Spearhead; Stay Lucky; The Beiderbecke Connection;* DCI Jim Gray in *The Chief; The Fragile Heart; The Grand; The Uninvited; The Vanishing Man; The Vet; This is David Lander;* Ken in *To Have and To Hold; A Wing and a Prayer;* Laurie in *Winter Sunlight; Woof.*
Films: *Business as Usual; Red Tuesday.*
Address: c/o Barry Brown & Partner, 47 West Square, London SE11.

BOND, Denis
Denis Bond. Actor (M)/Writer.
b. London, 22 November 1952.
TV: *A Day on the Sands;* Ron in *Beryl's Lot; Don't Forget to Write;* Corporal Higgins in *It Ain't Half Hot Mum; Jubilee; Juliet Bravo;* Mike in *Keeping up Appearances;*

The Kelly Monteith Show; Mervyn in *No Appointment Necessary; Oh Happy Band; Pipkin's; Rainbow; Rings on Their Fingers; The Bill; The Chinese Detective; The Cuckoo Calls; The Kenny Everett Show; The Knowledge; The Legend of Robin Hood; The New Adventures of Robin Hood; The Professionals.*
Films: Potts in *A Bridge Too Far;* Ted in *Follow Me.*
Address: c/o Langford Associates, 17 Westfields Avenue, London SW13 0AT. Hobbies: Teaching Spanish.

BOND, Philip
Philip Bond. Actor (M).
b. Burton-on-Trent, Staffordshire.
TV: *An Englishman's Castle; Bergerac; Brookside; Crown Court; Dial M for Murder; Doctor Who; Forever Green; General Hospital; Hedda Gabler; Home is the Sailor; The Hound of the Baskervilles; Howards Zero; Lillie; Lovejoy; Only Fools and Horses; St. Joan; The Champions; The Main Chance; The Oldest Goose in the Business; The Onedin Line; The Saint; The Sandbaggers; The Scott Enquiry; The Vortex; Travellers by Night; Warship; Z-Cars.*
Films: *Count 5 or Die; Fever Pitch; Foxhole in Cairo; Hell is a City; I Know What I Want; John Paul Jones; Our Boy; Sleep Well My Love.*
Address: c/o Hillman Threlfall, 33 Brookfield, Highgate West Hill, London N6 6AT. m. Pat Sandys; 1 d, Samantha Bond.

BONHAM-CARTER, Crispin
Crispin Bonham-Carter. Actor (M).
TV: Ralph in *Accused;* Robert in *Brighton Bubble;* Miles Coliar in *Cadfael;* Burn in *Full Throttle;* Archie Glenister in *Game On;* Danny in *Highlander;* Charlie in *Honey for Tea;* Bingley in *Pride and Prejudice;* Conte de Croisenois in *Scarlet and Black;* Dr Hill in *The Gift;* Bernard in *The Rag Nymph;* Edgar in *Wuthering Heights.*
Films: Ralph in *Basil;* Albert in *Howard's End;* Rupert in *Little Orphan Annie.*
Address: c/o William Morris Agency (UK) Ltd, 1 Stratton Street, London W1X 6HB.

BONHAM-CARTER, Helena
Helena Bonham-Carter. Actor (F). b. 26 May 1966.
TV: *A Dark Adapted Eye; Absolutely Fabulous; Arms and the Man; Dancing Queen; Jo Brand – Through the Cakehole; Merlin; Miami Vice; The Vision.*
Films: *A Room with a View; Butter; Chinese Portraits; Fatal Deception; Frankenstein; Getting it Right; Hamlet; Howard's End; Keep the Aspidistra Flying; Lady Jane; Margaret's Museum; Mighty Aphrodite; St Francis of*

Assisi; The Fight Club; The Gallery; The Revenger's Comedies; Theory of Flight; Twelfth Night; Where Angels Fear to Tread; The Wings of the Dove.
Address: c/o Conway Van Gelder, 18–21 Jermyn Street, London SW1Y 6HP.

BONNEVILLE, Hugh

Hugh Bonneville. Actor (M).
TV: Henry Oakes in *Between the Lines;* Peter Schneider in *Breakout;* Pym in *BUGS;* Daniel Aurifaber in *Cadfael;* Jazz in *Chancer;* Rick in *Dodgem;* Headmaster in *EastEnders;* Jeremy in *Fair Game;* Tucker in *Get Well Soon;* Edward Hibbard in *Heat of the Sun;* Gordon in *Holding the Baby;* Charles Bovary in *Madame Bovary;* Steve in *Married for Life;* Bob Boosley in *Mosley;* Dawson in *Murder Most Horrid;* Robert Ford in *My Night With Reg;* Dominic Kent in *Peak Practice;* Commander Striker in *Punt and Dennis;* Daniel in *See You Friday;* Victor Savage in *Sherlock Holmes;* Squadron Leader Barton in *Stalag Luft;* Robin Fuckle in *Stick With Me Kid; The Man Who Made Husbands Jealous; The Paul Merton Show;* Guy Duggen in *The Scold's Bridle;* Alan in *The Vet.*
Films: Rushworth in *Mansfield Park;* Schiller in *Mary Shelley's Frankenstein;* Louis in *Never Better;* Bernie in *Notting Hill;* CAWO in *Tomorrow Never Dies.*
Address: c/o Marina Martin Associates, 12–13 Poland Street, London W1V 3DE.

BOOTH, Connie

Connie Booth. Actor (F).
TV: Linda in *Caring; Crown Court; Every Breath You Take;* Pat in *Faith;* Polly in *Fawlty Towers; Floodtide; Glittering Prizes; Hello Comrades; Monty Python's Flying Circus; Readings from Dorothy Parker; Redundant; Rocket to the Moon; Spaghetti Two Step;* Mrs March in *The Buccaneers; The Deadly Game;* Naomi Balliol in *The Greater Good; The Hound of the Baskervilles; The Return of Sherlock Holmes; The Ronnie Corbett Show; The Story of Ruth;* Dr Connor in *The Tomorrow People; The Unmade Bed;* Madge in *The World of Eddie Weary; Voice From The Gallows; Why Didn't They Ask Evans?; Worzel Gummidge.*
Films: *84 Charing Cross Road;* Caroline Hartley in *American Friends; And Now For Something Completely Different;* Nurse Jarvis in *Hawks;* Margie Clay in *High Spirits;* Yvonne in *Leon the Pig Farmer; Little Lord Fauntleroy; Romance with a Double Bass; The Revolutionaries.*
Address: c/o Kate Feast Management, 10 Primrose Hill Studios, Fitzroy Road, London NW1 8TR.

BOOTH, Lauren

Sarah Jane Booth. Presenter/Reporter/ Reviewer.
b. 22 July 1967.
TV: *Breakfast News; Lorraine Live; News 24.*
Address: c/o Noel Gay Artists, 19 Denmark Street, London WC2H 8NA. Half-sister Cherie Blair; father Tony Booth. Hobbies: Languages (French and German), horse riding, skiing, rally driving.

BOUGH, Frank

Frank Bough. Commentator/Presenter.
b. Stoke, 15 November 1933.
TV: *Breakfast Time; FBI – The Frank Bough Interview; Grandstand; Holiday Programme; Hospital Watch; Moneywise; Nationwide; Rugby Union World Cup; Six O'Clock Live; The Cenotaph Memorial Service; The Travel Channel.*
Address: c/o The Roseman Organisation, Suite 9, The Power House, 70 Chiswick Road, London W4 1SY.

BOVELL, Brian

Brian Bovell. Actor (M).
b. London, 26 October 1959.
TV: *A Touch of Frost; Armed & Dangerous; Between the Lines; Drop the Dead Donkey; Felix Dexter on TV; Gimme, Gimme, Gimme; Inspector Morse; Maisie Raine; Mash & Peas; Running Late; The Bill; The Chief; The Smiths; True Crimes; Wall of Silence; Whizziwig.*
Films: *A Demon in My View; Babylon; Burning an Illusion; Final Passage; Lord of Misrule; Playing Away; Public Enemy, Private Friends; Real Life; Secrets and Lies; The Stephen Lawrence Story; Welcome II the Terrordrome; When Love Dies; Wrangle.*
Address: c/o International Artistes Ltd, Mezzanine Floor, 235 Regent Street, London W1R 8AX.

BOWE, John

John Bowe. Actor (M). b. 1 February 1950.
TV: *Body and Soul; Boon; Bright Hair; Capital City; Class Act; Clem;* Duggie Ferguson in *Coronation Street* (1999); *Cyrano de Bergerac; Families; Imogen's Face; Lovejoy; Poldark; Precious Bane; Prime Suspect; Soldier, Soldier; Stalin; Trainer; Verdict; Wall of Silence.*
Films: *Resurrected; The Living Daylights.*
Address: c/o Shepherd & Ford, 13 Radnor Walk, London SW3 4BP. m. Emma Harbour; 2 d. Aimee May, Maddie; 1 s. (1st m.) Joseph.

BOWEN, Jeremy

Jeremy Bowen. Presenter/Reporter.
b. Cardiff, 6 February 1960.
TV: BBC News Middle East Correspondent, Presenter on BBC Breakfast News.
Address: Contact via BBC News Union House,

65–69 Shepherds Bush Green, London W12 8TX.

BOWLER, Norman
Norman Bowler. Actor (M).
b. London, 1 August 1932.
TV: *A Little Silver Trumpet; Casualty; Cousin Kit; Cross-roads;* Frank Tate in *Emmerdale; Escape to the West; Exeter Fire; Gideon's Way; Into the Labyrinth; Jamaica Inn; Letters from the Dead; Love Story; Maggie's Moor; Masterspy; Mogul; Mountain Men; Park Ranger; Robin of Sherwood; Sherlock Holmes; Softly, Softly; Soldiers from the Wars Returning; The Amazing Avon; The Avengers; The Forgotten Story; The Good Doctor Bodkin Adams; The Joel Brandt Story; The Magic Carpet; The Square Leopard; The Unusual Miss Mulberry; The Winds of War; Whodunnit?*
Films: *Naval Patrol; Passion of Christ; Renegade; Shameless; Submarine X-1; The Grass is Greener; The Island of Treasure; Tom Thumb; Von Ryan's Express.*
Address: c/o Rebecca Blond Associates, 69a Kings Road, London SW3 4NX.

BOWLES, Peter
Peter Bowles. Actor (M). b. 16 October 1936.
TV: *Randall & Hopkirk (Deceased); Rumpole of the Bailey; To The Manor Born; Only When I Laugh; Pennies from Heaven; Tales of the Unexpected; Rising Damp; Vice Versa; The Bounder; The Irish PM; Lytton's Diary; Executive Stress; Perfect Scoundrels; Running Late; Little White Lies.*
Films: *Blow Up; A Day in the Death of Joe Egg; Isadora; Laughter in the Dark; Masquerade; Shadow of the Sun; The Charge of the Light Brigade; The Disappearance; The Informers; The Offence; The Quarry; The Steal; Try This One For Size.*
Address: c/o Conway Van Gelder, 18–21 Jermyn Street, London SW1Y 6HP.

BOWN, Paul
Paul Bown. Actor (M).
b. Staffordshire, 11 October 1957.
TV: Detective in *All Proceeds to the Beast;* D.S. Parker in *And the Beat Goes On;* P.C. Williams in *Coast to Coast;* Ivanov in *Heartbeat;* Stranger (guest star) in *Last of the Summer Wine;* Mr Bean (examination sketch); James Macarty in *Peak Practice;* Roger Bones in *Pirates;* Investigative Journalist in *Reasonable Force;* Tony Dean in *Staying Put; The Bill;* Harry in *The Last Salute;* Captain in *Time Riders;* Victor Technology in *Upline;* Malcolm in *Watching.*
Films: Gary in *Butterfly Kiss;* Uncle Jim in *Jude;* Julian in *Morons from Outer Space; The Assam Garden;* Nygard in *Underworld;* Bassous in *Young Blades.*

Address: c/o Brunskill Management, Suite 8a, 169 Queen's Gate, London SW7 5HE.

BOXLEITNER, Bruce
Bruce Boxleitner. Actor (M).
b. Elgin, Ilinois, USA, 12 May 1950.
TV: Richie Danko in *A Cry for Help;* Captain William Wicker in *Angel in Green;* John Sheridan in *Babylon 5;* Chase Marshall in *Bare Essences;* Frank Buck in *Bring 'Em Back Alive;* Jack Hart in *Double Jeopardy;* Charles Trask in *East of Eden; Fly Away Home;* Mark Ettinger in *Freefall;* Peter Langford in *From the Dead of Night;* Billy Montana in *Gambler 5;* David Healey in *Gunsmoke;* Dr Frank Ravinel in *House of Secrets;* Luke Macahan in *How the West Was Won;* Wyatt Earp in *I Married Wyatt Earp;* Bill Montana in *Kenny Rogers as the Gambler;* Douglas Lane in *Kiss Me, Kill Me;* Scott Collins in *Louis L'Amour's Down the Hills;* Det. Kyle Robeshaw in *Murderous Vision;* Cadet in *North and South;* Larry Janson in *Passion Flower;* Allan Bodine in *Perfect Family;* Matthew Garth in *Red River;* himself in *The Return of Mickey Spillane's Mike Hammer;* Lee Stetson in *Scarecrow and Mrs King;* Danny in *The Chadwick Family;* Billy Montana in *The Gambler Part III: The Legend Continues;* George Virdon in *The Last Convertible;* Seth Macahan in *The Macahans;* Patrick O'Riley in *The Maharaja's Daughter;* Rick in *The Mary Tyler Moore Show;* Charlie in *The Road Raiders;* Patrick Dunmore in *The Secret;* Robert Doniger in *The Town Bully; Till We Meet Again;* Vern Tyree in *Wild Times;* Clayton Andrews in *Zoya.*
Films: Joey in *Breakaway;* Cole Hickel in *Diplomatic Immunity;* Michael Shafer in *Flight from Justice;* Brad Kuffs in *Kuffs;* Bobby Joe in *Six Pack Annie;* Jumpin' Joe Dugan in *The Babe;* Billie Joe Robbins in *The Baltimore Bullet;* Alan Bradley/Tron in *Tron; Wyatt Earp: Return To Tombstone.*
Address: c/o David Shipera, Suite 235, 15821 Ventura Blvd., Encino, CA 91436, USA. 1st m. Kathryn Holcomb, m. Melissa Gilbert; 3 s. Sam, Lee (1st m.); Michael (2nd m.).

BOYD, Darren
Darren Boyd. Actor (M). b. 1970.
TV: *Hippies; Kiss Me Kate; Los Dos Bros; Riverside Sitcom Festival* (1998), *Smack the Pony.*
Address: c/o Amanda Howard Associates Ltd, 21 Berwick Street, London W1V 3RG.

BOYD, Roy
Roy Boyd. Actor (M). b. 18 August 1938.
TV: *A Bridge Too Far; A Hazard of Hearts; A Nightingale Sang in Berkeley Square;* Gregorio in *Adventures*

of *William Tell*; *Biggles*; *The Black Arrow*; *Blake's 7*; Tam in *Casualty*; Proffesor Draycott in *Chocky's Challenge*; *Colditz*; Casey in *Coronation Street*; Tilden in *Covington Cross*; Eddie Lee in *Crossroads*; *Dangerous Love*; *Dempsey and Makepeace*; Footman in *Duel for Love*; *EastEnders*; Dryden Hogbin in *Emmerdale*; Captain McCallum in *Enemy of the People*; *Goodbye Darling*; Joseph Laslo in *Heartbeat*; Patterson in *House of Men*; Fen in *Knights of God*; *Minder*; Marner in *Natural Lies*; Horace in *Pennies from Heaven*; Stoddard in *Poirot*; *Secret Army*; *Sitting Target*; Inspector Nichols in *Stick By Me Kid*; Tilley in *Survivors*; *The Bill*; Ranulf in *The Devil's Crown*; Paul Lamboit in *The Fourth Arm*; *The Mystery of Hunters*; *The Professionals*; Lord Drinian in *The Silver Chair*; George Merry in *Treasure Island*; *Tuxedo Warrior*.
Films: Harry Hyde in *The Promise*.
Address: c/o Peter Browne Management, Pebro House, 13 St Martin's Road, London SW9 0SP. Hobbies: Horse riding.

BOYLE, Tommy

Tommy Boyle. Actor (M). b. Manchester, 3 May 1948.
TV: *A Woman Sobbing*; *All at Number 20*; *Beneath the News*; *Benny Lynch*; *Brick is Beautiful*; *Brookside*; *Bulman*; *Came the Rapper*; *Coasting*; *Coronation Street*; *Crown Court*; *From the Roots*; *Hard Cases*; *Hollyoaks*; *Home and Away*; *The Racing Game*; *House of Cards*; *Juliet Bravo*; *Mrs Podmore's Cat*; *The New Avengers*; *Over There*; *Poor Girl*; *Raging Calm*; *Slattery's Mounted Foot*; *Starlings*; *Strangers*; *Summer Season*; *Taggart*; *The Bill*; *The Professionals*; *The Wackers*; *Travelling Man*; *Watching and Witching*; *Waterfront Beat*; *William Tell*; *Z Cars*; *Zatchi and Zatchi*.
Address: c/o Roger Carey Associates, 7 St George's Square, London SW1V 2HX.

BRABIN, Tracy

Tracy Brabin. Actor (F). b. Batley, Yorkshire 1961.
TV: *Sandra in A Bit of a Do*; Tricia Armstrong in *Coronation Street*; Fran in *El C.I.D.*; Doreen in *Hale and Pace*; Terry in *In the Dark*; Ginne in *Outside Edge*; Lou in *Peak Practice*; Sheila in *Sunburn*; Mrs Oliver in *The Ghostbuster*; Barbara in *The Gift*.
Films: Fergie in *A Palace Divided*; Florence in *Diamonds in Brown Paper*; Sylvia in *Mayday Mayday*; Josie in *Riff Raff*.
Address: c/o Barry Brown & Partner, 47 West Square, London SE11.

BRACKNELL, Leah

Leah Bracknell. Actor (F). b. London, 12 July 1964.
TV: Zoe in *Emmerdale*; *The Bill*; *The Cannon and Ball*

Show; *The Chiffy Kids*.
Address: c/o Elspeth Cochrane, 11–13 Orlando Road, London SW4 0LE.

BRADBURY, Julia

Julia Bradbury. Co-presenter/L.A Correspondent/Presenter. b. Dublin.
TV: *Backstage* (1999); *Carlton Country* (1999); *Exclusive* (1998); *GMTV*; *Moral Dilemmas* (1999); *Movie Café* (1998); *The National Lottery* (1999); *Top Gear* (1999).
Address: c/o William Morris Agency (UK) Ltd, 1 Stratton Street, London W1X 6HB. Hobbies: Films, tennis, skiing, avoiding sharks.

BRADLEY, David

David Bradley. Actor (M)/Voice-over.
b. Sheffield 1955.
TV: Les James in *A Touch of Frost*; Pilate in *Animated World Faiths*; Mike Preach in *Bad Girl*; Alf Leavey in *Band of Gold*; Sgt. Harry Ross in *Between the Lines*; *Bill Brand*; Charles Matthews in *Bramwell*; Mr Stanmore in *Casualty*; *Clapperclaw*; Carter in *Cracker*; Headmaster in *Criminal*; Roper in *Eurocops*; Fred in *Fair Game*; Don Naylor in *Full Stretch*; John Quesked in *In Your Dreams*; *King of the Ghetto*; Sup. Int. Cooper Hines in *Kiss and Tell*; Mike Preach in *Maggie's Baby*; David Crimple in *Martin Chuzzlewit*; Harry in *Master of Marionettes*; Barnadine in *Measure for Measure*; *Molière*; *One by One*; Eddie Wells in *Our Friends in the North*; Rogue Riderhood in *Our Mutual Friend*; Arnold Springer in *Reckless*; Edward in *Shadow of the Noose*; Hairy Back in *The Buddha of Suburbia*; Dave Waters in *The Moth*; *The Pickersgill Primitive*; Grandad Burns in *The Star*; Farmer in *The Vet*; Dad in *The Wilsons*; Sir Pitt Crawley in *Vanity Fair*; Derek Woodford in *Where the Heart Is*; Joe in *Wycliffe*.
Films: Mr MacAleese in *Kangaroo Palace*; Concierge in *Left Luggage*; Noah in *Never Better*; Undertaker in *Prick Up Your Ears*; Henry in *The Promised End*; Abel in *Tom's Midnight Garden*.
Address: c/o Kate Feast Management, 10 Primrose Hill Studios, Fitzroy Road, London NW1 8TR.

BRADLEY, Elizabeth

Elizabeth Bradley. Actor (F). b. London 1922.
TV: Great Aunt Annie in *A Little Bit of Lippy*; *A Small Mourning*; *A Traveller in Time*; *An English Christmas*; Nanny in *An Ungentlemanly Act*; *Bergerac*; Gladys in *Boon*; *Casualty*; Maud in *Coronation Street*; *Doctor Finlay's Casebook*; *God Speed Co-operation*; *Going Home*; *Juliet Bravo*; *Late Expectations*; *Leaving*; *Living Lies Lately*; *London's Burning*; *London's Drowning*;

Louise; Mrs Anthony in *Memento Mori*; Vera Barnet in *Pass More*; Resnick; *Shine on Harvey Moon*; *Softly, Softly*; *Spring Birthday*; *Take Three Girls*; *Tales of the Unexpected*; *The Bill*; *The Cartland Murder*; *The Citadel*; *The Devil's Crown*; Mrs Swinhoe in *The Men's Room*; *The Mistress*; *The Piglet Files*; *The Sweeney*; *Waterloo Sunset*.
Films: *An American Werewolf in London*; *Brimstone and Treacle*.
Address: c/o Kate Feast Management, 10 Primrose Hill Studios, Fitzroy Road, London NW1 8TR.

BRADSHAW-WHITE, Luisa
Luisa Bradshaw-White. Actor (F).
TV: Lorna Rose in *Bad Girls* (1999); Samantha in *Big Bad World* (1999); Dawn in *Birds of a Feather* (1998); Groupie in *Faith in the Future* (1995); Rachel in *Grange Hill* (1987–1992); Shelley in *The Bill* (1998); Judy Killick in *The Bill* (1996); Paula Davies in *The Bill* (1997); Angie in *The Brittas Empire* (1996); Kira in *This Life* (1997); Joanna in *A Touch of Frost* (1996).
Films: Herte in *A Friendship In Vienna*; Evits in *The Wrong Blonde*.
Address: c/o London Management, Noel House, 2–4 Noel Street, London W1V 3RB.

BRADY, Joseph
Joseph Brady. Actor (M). b. Glasgow.
TV: *Airport Chaplain*; *All in Good Faith*; *Angels*; *Attachments*; *Boon*; *Brideshead Revisited*; *Casualty*; *Class of His Own*; *Dead on Arrival*; *Dramarama*; *The Famous Five*; *Highway*; *Holy City*; *The House with Green Shutters*; *If You Go Down in the Woods*; *Ill Fares the Land*; *It Could Happen to Anyone*; *Justice*; *Kidnapped*; *King of the River*; *Ladykillers*; *Main Chance*; *Majorie and Men*; *Nervous Energy*; *Old Master*; *The Prime of Miss Jean Brodie*; *Print Out*; *Reginald Perrin*; *Scene*; *Secret Advisary*; *Send in the Girls*; *Song and Dance Man*; *Stories of Orkney*; *Sutherland's Law*; *Taggart*; *Take the High Road*; *Tell-Tale Heart*; *The Assailants*; *The Bill*; *The Borderers*; *The Boy Who Wanted Peace*; *The Ship*; *Time to Think*; *View from Daniel Pike*; *Vote for Them*; *Who'll Take the Low Road?*; *Willie Rough*; P.C. Jock Weir in *Z Cars*.
Films: *Cause for Alarm*; *Cry Wolf*; *The Fourth Protocol*.
Address: c/o Bryan Drew Ltd, Quadrant House, 80–82 Regent Street, London W1X 3TB.

BRADY, Orla
Orla Brady. Actor (F). b. Dublin 1963.
TV: *Absolutely Fabulous*; *Dangerfield*; *Leprechauns*; *Noah's Ark*; *Out of the Blue*; *Pure Wickedness*; *So You Think You've Got Troubles*; *The Heart Surgeon*; *The Rector's Wife*; *The Vicar of Dibley*; *Wuthering Heights*.
Films: *A Love Divided*; *Luzhin Defense*; *Words Upon the Window Pane*.
Address: c/o ICM, Oxford House, 76 Oxford Street, London W1N 0AX.

BRAGG, Melvyn
Lord Bragg of Wigton. Writer/Broadcaster/Presenter. b. Wigton, Cumbria, 6 October 1939.
TV: *In the Picture* (1971); *Monitor* (1963); *New Release* (1964); *Read All About It* (1974); *Second House* (1974); *Take it Or Leave it* (1964); *The South Bank Show*; *Tonight with Dave Allen* (1974); *Writer's World*.
Films (as screenwriter): *A Time to Dance*; *Debussy*; *Isadora*; *Jesus Christ Superstar*; *The Music Lovers*.
Address: Contact via LWT, London Television Centre, Upper Ground, London SE1 9LT. m. Catherine Mary; 2 d. Marie-Elsa (1st m.), Alice (2nd m.); 1 s. Tom (2nd m.). Hobbies: Walking. Became Lord Bragg of Wigton, 1998.

BRAID, Hilda
Hilda Braid. Actor (F).
b. Gravesend, Kent, 3 March 1934.
TV: Mrs Larwood in *Anglo-Saxon Attitudes*; Florence in *Citizen Smith*; Louisa Chick in *Dombey and Son*; Gran in *Gogglewatch*; Doreen Beavis in *Midsomer Murders*; Nurse Page in *On Giant's Shoulders*; Mrs Dawson in *One Foot in the Grave*; Edith in *The Ten Percenters*; Tabitha in *The Two Ronnies*.
Films: Mrs B in *101 Dalmatians*; Levilla's Handmaiden in *AD*; Polly in *Dick Turpin*; Guest in *Mrs Dalloway*; Fiaaiwig Guest in *Scrooge*; School Secretary in *The Wildcats of St Trinian's*.
Address: c/o Ken McReddie Ltd, 91 Regent Street, London W1R 7TB. m. Brian Badcoe; 1 d. Penny; 1 s. Robin; Father-in-Law Louis Raymond. Hobbies: Gardening, tapestry, 'scribbling'.

BRAILEY, Gil
Gil Brailey. Actor (F). b. Liverpool.
TV: *Adventures of Billy Webb*; Mrs Godfrey in *Broker's Man*; Dr Clucas in *Brookside*; Mary Reardon in *Casualty*; *Checkpoint Chiswick*; *Hard Cases*; Mrs Holt in *Madson*; *Men of the World*; *Stay Lucky*; Susan Clyde in *Taggart*; Mrs O'Rourke in *The Anorak*; *The Bill*; Connie Davies in *The Bill*; Kerry's Mum in *The Biz*; Jan James in *The Ward*; *Think About Science*.
Films: *The Samaritans*; *Yanks*.
Address: c/o Tim Scott Personal Management, 5 Cloisters Business Centre, 8 Battersea Park Road, London SW8 4BG. Hobbies: Swimming, cycling.

BRAKE, Patricia

Patricia Brake. Actor (F). b. 25 June 1942.

TV: *2point4 children; A Seat on the Board; Brigadista; Campion; Casualty; Eldorado; Escape to the West; Fat; Forget Me Not; Going Straight; Madge; Mann's Best Friend; Me and My Girl; Midsomer Murders; Morecambe and Wise; Nicholas Nickelby; Porridge; Second Time Around; Speak for Yourself; Taylors; The Bill; The Bouncing Boy; The Glums; The Good Companions; The Kept Man; The Refuge; The Two Ronnies; Trelawny of the Wells; Troubles and Strife.*

Address: c/o Scott Marshall, 44 Perryn Road, London W3 7NA.

BRANAGH, Kenneth

Kenneth Branagh. Actor (M)/Director/Narrator.
b. Belfast, County Antrim, 10 December 1960.

TV: *Anne Frank Remembered* (1995); *Cinema Europe – the Other Hollywood* (1995); *Coming Through* (1985); *Derek* (1983); *Fortunes of War* (1986); *Ghost* (1985); *Maybury* (1982); *Shadow of a Gunman* (1995); *Strange Interlude* (1987); *The Billy Plays* (1981); *The Boy in the Bush* (1983); *The Cold War* (1998); *The Great Composers* (1998); *The Lady's Not for Burning* (1987); *To the Lighthouse* (1982); *Universal Horror* (1998); *Walking with Dinosaurs.*

Films: *A Month in the Country; Alien Love Triangle; Celebrity; Dead Again; Hamlet; Henry V; High Season; In the Bleak Midwinter; Mary Shelley's Frankenstein; Much Ado About Nothing; Othello; Peter's Friends; Swan Song; Swing Kids; The Gingerbread Man; The Proposition; Theory of Flight; Wild Wild West.*

Address: c/o Kenneth Branagh Ltd, Shepperton Studios, Studio Road, Shepperton, Middlesex TW17 0QD. m. Emma Thompson (div).

BRAND, Jo

Jo Brand. Actor (F)/Comedian.
b. Hastings, East Sussex, 1957.

TV: *Absolutely Fabulous; All the Way to Worcester* (1996); *Alternative Comedy; Ant and Dec Unzipped* (1997); *Auntie's TV Favourites* (1997); *Bad Sports; Books of the Century* (1996); *Call My Bluff; Celebrity Countdown* (1998); *Challenge Anneka; Clive James on Television; Countdown; Country Tracks* (1999); *Danny Baker Show; Edinburgh Nights* (1995); *Election Night Armistice* (1997); *Fantasy Football* (1995); *Glam-O-Rama* (1995); *History of Alternative Comedy* (1998); *I'm Glad You Asked Me That* (1999); *It's a Girl; It's Been a Bad Week* (1999); *Jo Brand – Through the Cakehole* (1993); *Jo Brand Through the Christmas Cakehole* (1994); *Jo Brand's Christmas Log* (1998); *Just a Minute* (1999); *Late Lunch* (1998); *Leviathan: International*

Debt (1999); *Light Lunch* (1997); *Like It or Lump It* (1997); *McCoist and MacAuley* (1998); *Monday Night Clive* (1999); *The Mrs Merton Show* (1995); *Never Mind the Buzzcocks; Newsnight* (1997); *Question Time; Relatively Speaking* (1997); *Rock and Goal Years* (1996); *Room 101; Shooting Stars* (1996); *Six of One; Soul II Soul* (1999); *The South Bank Show; Standing Room Only; Sunday Night Clive; Taking the Mike* (1999); *T.F.I. Friday* (1996); *The Art of Gagging; The Big Question* (1998); *The Brain Drain; The Comedy Store* (1996); *The Full Mountie* (1999); *The Jack Docherty Show* (1997); *The Nation's Favourite Love Poem* (1997); *They Think tt's All Over; This Morning; Top of the Pops* (1995); *Under the Moon* (1997); *Win, Lose or Draw; You Can't be Serious* (1999).

Address: c/o The Richard Stone Partnership, 2 Henrietta Street, London WC2E 8PS.

BRANDON, Michael

Michael Brandon. Actor (M)/Director.
b. Brooklyn, New York, USA, 20 April 1945.

TV: *Comedy Company; Dempsey and Makepeace; Emerald Point; Hitch Kike; Home Fries; Perfect Match; Queen of the Stardust Ballroom; Red Alert; Red Badge of Courage; Tales of the Unexpected; The Care of Time; The Visitors; Third Girl from the Left.*

Films: *A Change of Seasons; Four Flies on Grey Velvet; Lovers and Other Strangers; Promises in the Dark; Rich and Famous; The Touch.*

Address: c/o Storm Artists Management, 47 Brewer Street, London W1R 3FD. m. Glynis Barber; 1 s. Hobbies: Skiing.

BRAUGHER, Andre

Andre Braugher. Actor (M)/Director/Narrator.
b. Chicago, Illinois, USA, 1 July 1962.

TV: *Arson: Clues in the Ashes* (1996); Lucius in *Class of '61* (1993); Det. Frank Xavier (Frank Pembleton) in *Homicide: Life on the Street;* Detective Winston Blake in *Kojak;* Frank Pembleton in *Law & Order* (1996); Ellis in *Love Songs* (1999); Dennis in *Murder in Mississippi* (1990); Father Joseph Verrett in *Passing Glory* (1999); Robert Carter in *Simple Justice* (1993); Dan Weston in *Somebody Has to Shoot the Picture* (1990); Jackie Robinson in *The Court Martial of Jackie Robinson* (1990); Lt. Col. Benjamin O. Davies in *The Tuskegee Airmen* (1995); *Without Warning: Terror in The Towers* (1993).

Films: *A Better Way to Die;* Tim Sullivan in *All the Rage;* Cassiel in *City of Angels;* Reggie in *Duets;* Satch in *Frequency;* Flip in *Get on the Bus;* Thomas Searles in *Glory; Louisville;* Tommy Goodman in *Primal Fear;* District Attorney Frank Morris in *Striking Distance;*

The Black Picture Show; Dink in *Thick as Thieves*; *Wildlife: Feel the Heat* (narrator).
Address: c/o Creative Artists Agency, 9830 Wilshire Boulevard, Beverly Hills, CA 90212, USA. m. Ami Brabson; 2 s. Michael, Isaiah.

BREMNER, Rory
Rory Bremner. Impressionist.
b. Edinburgh, 6 April 1961.
TV: *And There's More; Beware of Imitations; From Blair To Here; Rory Bremner... Who Else?; Survival Special; The Great Fog; The Tube; Year of Blair II.*
Address: c/o The Richard Stone Partnership, 2 Henrietta Street, London WC2E 8PS. Hobbies: Cricket – plays for 'Lord's Taveners', golf, tennis, horse riding, horse racing (co-owns two horses), food and drink.

BRENT, Dannielle
Dannielle Brent. Actor (F). b. 19 September 1979.
TV: Gina Patrick in *Hollyoaks*; Kelly Sumner in *The Bill*.
Films: Big Feet in *Big Feet*; Lucy in *WOW!*.
Address: c/o Italia Conti Agency Ltd, 23 Goswell Road, London EC1M 7AJ.

BREWSTER, Yvonne
Yvonne Brewster. Actor (F).
TV: Linda in *Holby City*; Patience Divine in *A Wing and a Prayer*; Mrs Ambrose in *The Bill: 'Tainted Love'; The Chinese Detective; The English Programme*; Mrs Jordan in *Perfect Blue*; The Groit (storyteller) in *History File*; Betty Coogan in *Between the Lines; The Late Show*.
Address: c/o Sandra Boyce Management, 1 Kingsway Parade, Albion Road, London N16 0TA.

BRIERLEY, Roger
Roger Brierley. Actor (M).
TV: Disraeli in *A Business Affair*; Gough in *A Kind of Living*; Sir Roger in *Bottom*; Ferneyhough in *Casualty*; Mr Stringer in *Children of Dynmouth*; Drathro in *Doctor Who*; Rev. Phelps in *East of Ipswich*; Steve Nicklin in *Expert Witness*; Simpkins in *Foreign Affairs*; Middleton in *Have Your Cake and Eat It*; Montague in *The House of Elliott*; Sir Roderick Glossop in *Jeeves and Wooster*; Harvey Swainton in *Lovejoy*; Neville Chamberlain in *Mosley*; Hotel Manager in *Pat and Margaret*; Cursitor in *Rumpole of the Bailey*; Dr Fenton in *Seaforth*; Mr Evans in *Sex and Chocolate*; Prof Watney in *Surgical Spirit*; Mr Curd in *Tales from the Crypt*; Allnut in *The Bill*; Ramsden in *The Franchise Affair*; Alan Maseby in *The Legacy of Reggie Perrin*; *The Lenny Henry Series*; Richard Pearson in *The Politician's Wife*; The Head in *The Vanishing Man*; *The Victoria Wood Show*; Rev. Mercer in *When We Are Married*.

Films: Davidson in *A Fish Called Wanda*; Andrews in *A Very British Coup*; L'Impremeur in *Beaumarchais*; District Judge in *Bodywork*; The Judge in *Jinnah*; Hotel Manager in *Killing Dad*; *Superman II*; *The Adventures of Barry MacKenzie*; Ganza in *The She Wolf of London*; *The Wicked Lady*; *Young Sherlock Holmes*.
Address: c/o Barry Brown & Partner, 47 West Square, Southwark, London SE11.

BRIERS, Lucy
Lucy Briers. Actor (F). b. 19 August 1967.
TV: Student in *A Masculine Ending*; 'Maid' in *The Blackheath Poisonings*; Wendy in *The Brittas Empire*; Joanna in *Casualty*; Adele Griffiths in *Dangerfield*; Lulu Glenister in *Game On*; Janet in *Imogen's Face*; Marnie in *Only You*; Mary Bennett in *Pride and Prejudice*; Harrison in *Red Dwarf*; Jennifer in *Screaming*; Sarah Beecham in *The Bill*; Psychiatrist in *The Ten Percenters*; *Unfinished Business*; Eliza Marley in *Unnatural Causes*.
Address: c/o Hamilton Asper, 24 Hanway Street, London W1P 9DD. Father Richard Briers. Hobbies: Music (plays piano and flute).

BRIERS, Richard
Richard Briers. Actor (M).
b. Merton, Surrey, 14 January 1934.
TV: *A Respectable Trade; All in Good Faith; Arms and the Man; Down to Earth; Doctor Who; Ever Decreasing Circles; Goodbye Mr Kent; Heavy Weather*; Godfrey in *If You See God, Tell Him; Inspector Morse; Just Between Ourselves; Lovejoy; Middle Age Spread*; Hector in *Monarch of the Glen; One Flesh and Blood; One-Upmanship; Play for Today; PQ 17; Run for Your Wife*; Arthur/George in *Scallagrigg; Spring into Summer; Swop You One of These for One of Those; The Family Dance*; Tom in *The Good Life; The Other One; The Verger; Twelfth Night; Village Wooing; Why Me?*.
Films: *A Chorus of Disapproval*; Polonius in *Hamlet*; Bardolph in *Henry V*; *In the Bleak Midwinter*; Nathaniel in *Love's Labours Lost*; *Mary Shelley's Frankenstein*; Leonato in *Much Ado About Nothing*; *Watership Down*.
Address: c/o Hamilton Asper, 24 Hanway Street, London W1P 9DD. m. Anne; 1 d. Lucy

BRIGGS, Johnny
Johnny Briggs. Actor (M).
b. Battersea, London, 5 September 1935.
TV: Mike Baldwin in *Coronation Street*; Clifford Leyton in *Crossroads; Department S; Devil's Disciple; Love Thy Neighbour; My Wife Next Door; No Hiding Place; No Honestly; Softly, Softly; The Avengers; The Man With the Power; The Persuaders; The Plane*

Makers; The Saint; The Younger Generation; Thick as Thieves; Yus My Dear; Z Cars.
Films: 633 Squadron; Au Pair Girls; Carry On Behind; Carry On Regardless; Carry On Up the Khyber; Cosh Boy; Devil Ship Pirates; Doctor on the Go; Doctor in Charge; Doctor in Love; Doctor in the House; HMS Defiant; Light Up the Sky of the Day; Office Party; Perfect Friday; Quartet; Rosie; Sink the Bismark!; C'est Pour la Bonne Cause; The Best Pair of Legs; The Last Escape.
Address: c/o Marina Martin Associates, 12–13 Poland Street, London W1V 3DE. Contact via Granada Television, Quay Street, Manchester M60 9EA. m. 1 Carole (div); 1 d. Karen; 1 s. Mark; m. 2 Christine; 2 d. Jennifer, Stephanie; 2 s. Michael, Anthony.

BRIGHT, Kellie

Kellie Bright. Actor (F). b. 1 July 1976.
TV: Claire in Alison; Alexandra in It Must Be Love; Nettles in Maid Marion and her Merry Men; Katy in Nature Boy; Sally Simpkins in T-Bag; Sally Simpkins in T-Bag's Christmas Carol; Daphne Grove in The Lime Grove Story; Joanna Burrows in The Upper Hand.
Address: c/o Marina Martin Associates, 12–13 Poland Street, London W1V 3DE.

BRITTON, Fern

Fern Britton. Presenter. b. Ealing, London.
TV: After Five; Celebrity Ready, Steady, Cook; Coast to Coast; Coast to Coast People; Holiday; London Tonight; Magic Moments; News Afternoon; Ready, Steady, Cook; Spotlight South West; This Morning; Top of the Morning.
Address: c/o The Roseman Organisation, Suite 9, The Power House, 70 Chiswick Road, London W4 1SY. Father Tony Britton.

BRITTON, Tony

Tony Britton. Actor (M). b. Birmingham, 9 June 1924.
TV: Vivian Bancroft in Don't Tell Father; Dr Toby Latimer in Don't Wait Up; James Nicholls in Robin's Nest; Romeo in Romeo and Juliet; The Nearly Man; The Saint.
Films: Dr Syn, Alias the Scarecrow; Mr Forbrush and the Penguins; Night Watch; Sunday Bloody Sunday; The Day of the Jackal; There's a Girl in My Soup.
Address: c/o Chatto & Linnit Ltd, 123a Kings Road, London SW3 4PL. m. Eve; 2 d. Cherry and Fern (both 1st m.); 1 s. Jasper.

BROADBENT, Jim

Jim Broadbent. Actor (M). b. 1949.
TV: Alter; Bird of Pray; Birth of a Nation; Blackadder; Conrad; Detectives on the Verge of a Nervous Breakdown; Games Without Frontiers; Gone to Seed; Gone to

the Dogs; Great Masters; Happy Families; Happy Feet; Heroes and Villains – The Last Englishman; Inspector Morse; Intensive Care; La Nona; Murder Most Horrid; Only Fools and Horses; Picture Friend; Revolution – National Theatre of Brent; Sheppey; Silas Marner; The Adventures of Frank; The Country Churchyard; The Last Company Car; The Long Distance Information; The Messiah; The Miser; The Peter Principle; Winnie; Work;
Films: A Day in the Life of Bernard Frip; Brazil; Breaking Glass; Bullets Over Broadway; Dogs of War; Enchanted April; Life is Sweet; Princess Caraboo; Richard III; Rough Magic; Secret Agent; Smilla's Sense of Snow; Superman IV; The Avengers; The Borrowers; The Crying Game; The Good Father; The Man Who Shot Christmas; The Passage; Little Voice; The Shout; Time Bandits; Topsy Turvy; Wide Eyed and Legless; Widow's Peak.
Address: c/o ICM, Oxford House, 76 Oxford Street, London W1N 0AX.

BROOK, Kelly

Kelly Brook. Actor (F)/Presenter.
b. Chatham, Kent, 23 November 1979.
TV: Babewatch; The Big Breakfast; Fist of Fun; No Worries; Select; Shift; Short Change; The T-Spot; VPL.
Films: Mojo; Sarah in Sorted.
Address: c/o William Morris Agency (UK) Ltd, 1 Stratton Street, London W1X 6HB. Hobbies: Dogs.

BROOKE-TAYLOR, Tim

Tim Brooke-Taylor. Actor (M)/Writer.
b. Buxton, Derbyshire, 17 July 1940.
TV: Assaulted Nuts; At Last the 1948 Show; Broaden Your Mind (1968); Does the Team Think; The Frost Programme; Loose Ends; Marty; Me and My Girl; On The Braden Beat (1965); One Foot in the Grave – Christmas Special (1997); Possibilities; QD The Master Game; The Fame Game; The Goodies; The Overnight Bag; various (1964); You Must Be the Husband.
Music: The Funky Gibbon; The In Betweenies.
Address: c/o Jill Foster Ltd, 9 Barb Mews, Brook Green, London W6 7PA.

BROOKING, Trevor

Trevor Brooking. Commentator.
b. Barking, Essex, 2 April 1948.
TV: Match of the Day.
Address: c/o Jane Morgan Management, Café Royal, 68 Royal Street, London W1R 6FI.

BROOKS, Charlene

Charlene Brooks. Actor (F).
b. Barmouth, N. Wales, 3 May 1981.
TV: Karen in Dispatches; Janine Butcher in EastEnders;

Emma in *Emma's Story*; *Jonathan Creek*; Mandy in *London's Burning*; Carol in *Out of Tune*; Claire in *The Bill*; Miriam in *The Bill*; The Brains in *The Demon Headmaster*.
Address: c/o Ravenscourt Management, Tandy House, 30–40 Dalling Road, London W6 0JB. Brother Ben Brooks.

BROOKS, Nikki

Nikki Brooks. Actor (F). b. 29 June 1968.
TV: Rosie Harding in *Crossroads*; Karen in *Inspector Morse*; Herline Gothard in *Jupiter Moon*; *Make Believe*; Beverley Dexter in *The Bill*; Carmen in *The Fear*; The Girl in *The Kid*; Lisa Marlow in *The Marlows*; Clare Neilson in *The Secret Diary of Adrian Mole*.
Films: Janet in *Bloody New Year*; Georgina in *Cresta Run*; Patricia Lewis in *Morning, Night and Noon*; Mary in *Transference*.
Address: c/o Andrew Manson Personal Management, 288 Munster Road, London SW6 6BQ. Hobbies: Singing, dancing.

BROOKS, Ray

Ray Brooks. Actor (M)/Narrator/Voice artist.
b. Brighton, East Sussex, 20 April 1939.
TV: *A Touch of the Tiny Hacketts*; *All Aboard the Cat Bus*; *Aspects of Love*; Robby Box in *Big Deal*; *Black & Blue*; *Brotherly Love*; *Cathy Come Home*; *Couples*; *Death of an Expert Witness*; *Doomwatch*; Tom in *Growing Pains*; *Jackanory*; *Play of the Month*; *Rumpole of the Bailey*; Max Wild in *Running Wild*; *Skimp*; *Softly, Softly*; *The Expert*; *The Office Party*; *The Raging Moon*; Eddie Weary in *The World of Eddie Weary*; *Two People*; *Woof*.
Music: *Album – 'Lend Me Some Of Your Time'.*
Address: c/o Marmont Management Ltd, Langham House, 308 Regent Street, London W1R 5AL.

BROUGHTON, Paul

Paul Broughton. Actor (M).
b. Liverpool, 21 January 1957.
TV: *Between the Lines*; Eddie Banks in *Brookside*; *Cadfael*; *Casualty*; *Heartbeat*; Frank in *Liverpool One*; *Minder*; Pete in *Needle*; *Peak Practice*; *Terraces*; *The Bill*; *Trial by Fire*.
Address: c/o Scott Marshall, 44 Perryn Road, London W3 7NA. Hobbies: golf, cricket, horse riding, singer, amateur boxer.

BROWN, Collette

Collette Brown. Actor (F).
TV: *A Touch of Frost*; *Casualty*; Kirsty Maine in *City Central*; *Dangerfield*; *Holding the Baby*; *Our Friends in the North*; *Sunburn*.

Films: *Blue Juice*.
Address: c/o Scott Marshall, 44 Perryn Road, London W3 7NA.

BROWN, David

David Brown. Actor (M).
TV: Adam Morgan in *Hollyoaks*.
Address: c/o PHA Casting Management, Tanzaro House, Ardwick Green North, Manchester M12 6FZ.

BROWN, Duggie

Duggie Brown. Actor (M). b. 7 August 1940.
TV: Brian Appleby in *All Creatures Great and Small*; *Another Sunday and Sweet FA*; Hugh in *Combination*; Windows Man in *Common As Muck*; George Freeman in *Coronation Street*; *Crown Court*; *Cuckoo Waltz*; *Days of Hope*; Sam Weir in *Ellington*; Phil Strong in *The Enigma Files*; Wilfred in *Heartbeat*; Joe Badger in *House of Cards – The Final Cut*; Verny in *Last of the Summer Wine*; *Leeds United*; *Minder*; *My Brother's Keeper*; Brian Neale in *Peak Practice*; *Price of Coal*; *Say Goodnight to Grandma*; *Send in the Girls*; *Slattery's Mounted Foot*; *Stay Lucky*; Harvey Hall in *Take My Wife*; *The Bill*; Ernest Garstang in *The Glamour Girls*; Billy Cough in *The Hard Word*; Jack in *The House That Jack Built*.
Films: Mr Britchenor in *Between Two Women*; Duggie the Hairdresser in *For the Love of Ada*; Tom the Milkman in *Kes*.
Address: c/o Sharron Ashcroft Management, Dean Clough, Halifax, Yorkshire HX3 5AX. Hobbies: golf, snooker, darts, guitar.

BROWN, June

June Brown. Actor (F)/Performer.
b. Needham Market, Suffolk, 16 February 1927.
TV: *A Christmas Carol*; *Angels*; Sheila Heron in *Broken Glass*; Eileen Allcock in *Churchill's People*; *Clayton Close*; *Couples*; Dot Cotton in *EastEnders*; Elsie Grant in *God's Wonderful Railway*; *Home and Away*; Cleaner in *Hospital*; Joany in *Hypnotising Rita*; Mrs Trelawny in *Lace*; Emma Saxon in *Lady's Maid Bell*; Fan Dancer in *The Lily Savage Show*; Aunt Sadie in *Now and Then*; June in *Oranges and Lemons*; *Play for Today*; Agnes in *Relative Strangers*; Nell Latimore in *Rules of Justice*; Mrs Donn in *Shadows and Substance*; *Shining Pyramid*; *South Riding*; Mrs Doleman in *The Bill*; *The Duchess of Duke Street*; Mother in *The Prince and the Pauper*; *The Sweeney*; Amelia Sayers in *Verdict*; Lizzie in *Young at Heart*; *Gormenghast*.
Films: Mrs Paley in *Misunderstood*; Stephanova in *Nijinski*; *Sherlock Holmes*; Mother in *The Fourteen*; 2nd Woman in *The Hunchback of Notre Dame*.

Address: c/o Associated International Management, 5 Denmark Street, London WC2H 8LP.

BROWN, Phillip

Phillip Brown. Actor (M). b. Manchester, 9 July 1956.
TV: John Daley in *A Wing and a Prayer*; *All Creatures Great and Small*; *Band of Gold*; *Between the Lines*; Sgt. Dobson in *City Central*; *Coming Through*; *Coogan's Run*; *Hetty Wainthropp Investigates*; *Minder*; *Murder Most Horrid*; *Playing the Field*; *The Monocled Mutineer*; *The Paradise Club*.
Films: *Bring Me the Head of Mavis Davis*; *Hostile Waters*; *Party Party*; *The Bounty*; *The Eye of the Needle*.
Address: c/o William Morris Agency (UK) Ltd, 1 Stratton Street, London W1X 6HB. m. Elizabeth; 1 s. Rupert William; 1 d. Jodie Rebecca. Hobbies: Gardening, cooking, piano.

BROWN, Ralph

Ralph Brown. Actor (M).
TV: *A Curious Suicide*; *Christabel*; *Cleopatra*; Keating in *Coppers*; *Dalziel and Pascoe*; *Devil's Advocate*; *Extremely Dangerous*; *Ivanhoe*; *Last Train*; *Peak Practice*; Derek Brasher in *Piggybank*; *Place of the Dead*; *Respectable Trade*; *Rules of Engagement*; *Say Hello to the Real Dr Snide*; Inspector Drury in *The Black and Blue Lamp*; *The Merry Wives of Windsor*; *Van Der Valk*; Ted in *West*.
Films: Aaron in *Alien III*; *Amistad*; Ronnie Biggs in *Buster*; Jack in *Diamond Skulls*; Eugene in *Impromptu*; *New Year's Day*; *Psychotherapy*; Paul Mann in *Scandal*; *Star Wars – The Phantom Menace*; Dave in *The Crying Game*; *Under Cover Blues*; *Up 'n' Under*; *Wayne's World II*; Danny in *Withnail & I*.
Address: c/o ICM Oxford House, 76 Oxford Street, London W1N 0AX.

BROWN, Susan

Susan Brown. Actor (F). b. Bristol, Avon, 6 May 1946.
TV: *A Touch of Frost*; Bill in *Absolute Hell*; Ruby in *Andy Capp*; Mrs Gascoine in *Anorak of Fire*; *Casualty*; Connie Clayton in *Coronation Street*; Mrs Bassett in *Dangerfield*; *EastEnders*; *Kissing the Gunner's Daughter*; Marjorie Scrope in *Knight School*; Avril in *Making Out*; Maria in *Nona*; *Pinch of Snuff*; *Prime Suspect*; Mrs Hope in *Randall & Hopkirk (Deceased)*; Helen in *Road*; Cilla in *September Song*; *Stay Lucky*; Jan Dickson in *Taggart*; *The Bill*; Maggie Belcher in *The Riff Raff Element*; June Wrekin in *Where the Heart Is*; Jacqui in *Wokenwell*.
Films: Mrs Evans in *Hope and Glory*; *The Year of the Bodyguard*.
Address: c/o Barry Brown & Partner, 47 West Square, London SE11.

BROWNING, Michael

Michael Browning. Actor (M). b. 15 May 1930.
TV: Tom Fisher in *Trainer*; George Newton in *Coronation Street*; Prison Govenor in *Crime Traveller*; Henry Carter in *Crossroads*; Mr Fawcett in *Emmerdale*; Dr Haydock in *Murder at the Vicarage*; Sir John Ross-Pifford in *Take the High Road*; Philip Stone in *The Bill*; Dr Hughes in *The Famous Five*.
Films: Philip in *Night Without Pity*; Jenkins in *The Four Feathers*.
Address: c/o ALW Associates, 70 Mildmay Road, London N1 4NG.

BRUCE, Fiona

Fiona Bruce. Presenter. b. 25 April 1964.
TV: *6 O'Clock News*; *Newsnight*; *Panorama*; *The Antiques Show*.
Address: c/o Knight Ayton Management, 10 Argyll Street, London W1V 1AB. Partner Nigel; 1 s. Sam.

BRUNO, Frank

Frank Bruno. Actor (M)/Presenter.
b. Hammersmith, London, 16 November 1961.
TV: *Cannon and Ball*; *Fort Boyard*; *Freddie Starr*; *It's a Knockout*; *Lenny Henry*; *People*; *This is Your Life*; *Wogan*.
Address: c/o International Artistes Ltd, Mezzanine Floor, 235 Regent Street, London W1R 8AX. m. Laura Bruno; 2 d. Nicola, Rachel; 1 s. Franklin. Hobbies: Swimming, training.

BRUNSON, Michael

Michael Brunson. Political editor/Reporter.
b. Norwich, Norfolk, 12 August 1940.
TV: Independent Television News; Independent Television News (Washington Correspondent) (1972); Independent Television News reader.
Address: c/o Knight Ayton Management, 10 Argyll Street, London W1V 1AB.

BRUNT, Dominic

Dominic Brunt. Actor (M).
TV: Petrol Pump Attendant in *2point4 children*; Gary Bryant in *Crimewatch File*; Witness in *Crimewatch UK*; Vince in *EastEnders*; Paddy in *Emmerdale*; Policeman in *Holding On*; Detective Jim in *Inspector Morse*; Juror in *Paul Merton*; Ron Jarvis in *Soldier, Soldier*; Shop Assistant in *The Bill*.
Films: Martin in *Skin*; Fred in *You Can Keep the Animals*.
Address: c/o Michelle Braidman Associates, 10–11 Lower John Street, London W1R 3PE.

BRYAN, Dora

Dora Bryan. Actor (F). b. Southport, Lancashire, 7 February 1923.

TV: *Absolutely Fabulous; Boon; Casualty; dinnerladies; Frank Stubbs Promotes; Heartbeat; Mother's Ruin; The Last of the Summer Wine; Virtual Murder.*

Films: *A Taste of Honey; Apartment Zero; Cure for Love; Fallen Idol; Odd Man Out; The Blue Lamp; The Squealer.*

Address: c/o Burnett Granger Associates, Prince Of Wales Theatre, 31 Coventry Street, London W1V 8AS.

BRYER, Tania

Tania Bryer. Presenter. b. London, 5 July 1962.

TV: *Tania Bryer's Showbiz Weekly.*

Address: c/o William Morris Agency (UK) Ltd, 1 Stratton Street, London W1X 6HB. m. Tim Moufarrige; 1 d. Natasha Joy. Hobbies: Most sports, theatre, music, opera.

BRYON, Antoinette

Antoinette Bryon. Actor (F).

TV: *All My Children; Baywatch; E-Street;* Natalie Nash in *Home and Away; Jake and the Fat Man; Melrose Place; Neighbours; Pacific Paradise; Savannah; Scales of Justice; Skin Deep; The Bold and The Beautiful; The Henderson Kids.*

Films: *Death of a Soldier; Fast Talking; Rebel; Winter in Our Dreams.*

Address: Contact via Seven Network Ltd, Mabbs Lane, Epping, New South Wales 2121, Australia.

BRYSON, Ann

Ann Bryson. Actor (F).

TV: *City Lights;* Kitty in *Days Like These; Glam Metal Detectives; Inspector Morse; KYTV; Murder Most Horrid; Now, Something Else; Only Fools and Horses; Sometime, Never; Space Vets.*

Films: Andrea in *My Hero;* Avril in *Road Trip; Six Thirty Something;* Sally in *The Steal.*

Address: c/o Amanda Howard Associates Ltd, 21 Berwick Street, London W1V 3RG.

BUCHANAN, Katrina

Katrina Buchanan. Actor (F)/Presenter/Singer. b. Ealing, London, 1 November 1963.

TV: *Cheap Chic; Gaytime TV; Late and Live; Living It Up; Lovejoy; Recipe for Disaster; Sex Files; Sex Zone; Sextasy; She's Out.*

Address: c/o Unique Artistes, Avon House, Kensington Village, London W14 8TS. Hobbies: Reading, theatre, cinema, concerts, eating (preferably chocolate and ice cream).

BUCHANAN, Neil

Neil Buchanan. Creator/Presenter. b. Liverpool, 11 October 1962.

TV: *Animal Crazy; Art Attack; Craft, Design and Technology; Finders Keepers; It's a Mystery; Motormouth; No. 73; Quids In; Terror Towers; The Body Works* (1990); *Wow!; You'll Never Believe It; Your Number Please;* Smarty Arty in *ZZZZAP!.*

Address: Contact via ITV Sport, 200 Grays Inn Road, London WC1X 8XZ. Hobbies: Bird watching, flying.

BUCKFIELD, Clare

Clare Buckfield. Actor (F). b. 1976.

TV: Jenny Porter in *2point4 Children;* Jackie in *Dangerfield;* Natasha Stevens in *Grange Hill;* Wendy in *Labours of Erica.*

Address: c/o Emptage Hallett, 24 Poland Street, London W1V 3DD. 1 sister Julie Buckfield.

BUCKFIELD, Julie

Julie Buckfield. Actor (F)/Presenter. b. 1976.

TV: *Disney Club;* Amanda in *Expert Witness;* Natalie Stevens in *Grange Hill;* Julie Mathews in *Hollyoaks;* Nicola in *London's Burning;* Maddy in *Pie in the Sky;* Nurse Price in *The Bill.*

Address: c/o The Narrow Road Company, 21–22 Poland Street, London W1V 3DD. 1 sister Clare. Hobbies: Roller skating, ice skating, football, flute, dancing.

BUERK, Michael

Michael Buerk. Correspondent/Presenter/Reporter. b. 18 February 1946.

TV: *999; Nature; News* (1983) (Southern Africa Correspondent); *News* (1980) (Special Correspondent); *News* (1977) (Energy Correspondent); *News* (1979) (Scotland Correspondent); *News* (1976) (Industrial Correspondent); *News* (1973) (Network Reporter); *The Nine O'Clock News.*

Address: c/o Knight Ayton Management, 10 Argyll Street, London W1V 1AB.

BUFFERY, Kate

Kate Buffery. Actor (F). b. 23 July 1957.

TV: *A Taste of Death; Boon;* Charlotte in *Call Me Mister; Close Relations; Come Back; Frankenstein's Baby; Love After Lunch; Medics; Perseus and the Gorgon; Poirot; Sam Saturday; Strife; The Orchid House; The Man Who Cried; The Miser;* Winifred in *The Rainbow; Trial and Retribution; A Wing and a Prayer; Wish Me Luck.*

Films: *Dark River; Halcyon Days; Swing Kids; The Long Way Home.*

Address: c/o ICM, Oxford House, 76 Oxford Street, London W1N 0AX.

BULLER, James

James Buller. Actor (M).
b. Burnley, Lancashire, 4 April 1970.
TV: Mike in *Grafters;* Greg in *Sunburn.*
Address: c/o London Management Noel House, 2–4 Noel Street, London W1V 3RB. Hobbies: Football, music, festivals, films.

BULLMORE, Amelia

Amelia Bullmore. Actor (F). b. 31 January 1964.
TV: *Big Train;* Stephanie Barnes in *Coronation Street;* Catriona Billborough in *Cracker;* Ros in *Faith;* Caroline Poole in *Frontiers;* Karen Parmenter in *Hetty Wainthropp Investigates;* Paula Green in *Insiders;* Beth in *Stuck on You; The Bill;* Eileen Sopwith in *Tilly Trotter;* Social Worker in *Trip TV;* Turning Worlds.
Films: Rezia Warren-Smith in *Mrs Dalloway;* Madame Plaisir in *Woman of the Wolf.*
Address: c/o Lou Coulson, 37 Berwick Street, London W1V 3RF.

BULLOCH, Jeremy

Jeremy Bulloch. Actor (M).
b. Market Harborough, 16 February 1945.
TV: George in *After Henry;* Rob in *Agony; All in Good Faith;* George Napier in *Aristocrats;* DS Gower in *Boon;* Rodney Mulligan in *Casualty; Chocky;* Jacklin in *Dangerfield;* Ried in *Disaster;* Pearson in *Do the Right Thing;* David Reckitt in *Faith in the Future; The Harry Enfield Show;* Paul Schroeder in *Jenny's War; Kiss Me Goodnight;* Princess of Wales' Lawyer in *Princess in Love;* Edward in *Robin of Sherwood;* Paul in *Singles;* Barry Higgs in *Sloggers;* Mr Matthews in *The Bill; The Captain's Tale;* Jack Bertrand in *The Chief;* Scott in *The Scott Inquiry.*
Films: M's Assistant in *For Your Eyes Only;* M's Assistant in *Octopussy; Summer Holiday; Swing Kids;* Boba Fett in the *Star Wars* trilogy.
Address: c/o Barry Brown & Partner, 47 West Square, Southwark, London SE11.

BUNTON, Emma

Emma Bunton. Presenter/Singer.
b. Hastings, Sussex, 21 January 1979.
TV: *Babes Behaving Badly; Emma; Flying Start; The Mix.*
Music: Various; *What I Am* (UK number 2).
Address: c/o Panic, 2 Mortimer House, Furmage Street, London SW18 4DF.

BURDEN, Paul

Paul Burden. Co-presenter/Reporter.
TV: *Money Programme* (1986); *Newsnight; What Do You Watch?.*
Address: c/o Knight Ayton Management, 10 Argyll Street, London W1V 1AB.

BURDEN, Ross

Ross Burden. Presenter-Chef. b. 1968.
TV: *All Over the Shop; Celebrity Ready, Steady, Cook; Explorer's Journal; GMTV; Good Food Show; Light Lunch; Ready, Steady, Cook; Ross' Foreign Assignment; Ross in Thailand; Ross on the Range; The Big Breakfast.*
Address: c/o Carolynne Wyper Management, 25 Ives Street, London SW3 2ND. Hobbies: Penguins, travel, natural history.

BURDEN, Suzanne

Suzanne Burden. Actor (F). b. 1958.
TV: *A Mind to Murder; An Office Romance; Between the Lines; Bleak House; Campion; Hard Travelling; Love in a Cold Climate; Microsoap; Poirot; Secret Orchards; Sharma And Beyond; Soldier, Soldier; The Cherry Orchard; The Rivals; The Vet; 'Tis Pity She's a Whore; Troilus And Cressida; You, Me and It.*
Films: *Gertler; Strapless; The Devotee; Very Like a Whale.*
Address: c/o ICM, Oxford House, 76 Oxford Street, London W1N 0AX.

BURFIELD, Ian

Ian Burfield. Actor (M)/Guest lead. b. London.
TV: Gerry in *Casualty;* DS Ray Pickering in *City Central; EastEnders;* Kendall in *Heartbeat;* Jimmy in *Hero to Zero;* Martin Kenyon in *Hetty Wainthropp Investigates;* Nobby in *Johnny Loves Suzy;* Jos in *Longitude;* Mike Ryder in *Out of Line;* Steve Mellor in *Peak Practice;* Andrew Fern in *The Bill;* David Rigg in *The Bill;* Alex Clements in *The Broker's Man;* Tommy Madden in *The Knock;* Frankie Stevens in *A Wing and a Prayer;* Roy Crowe in *Wokenwell.*
Films: Caspar in *Circus;* Crick in *Confession;* Whip in *The Krays.*
Address: c/o CDA, 19 Sydney Mews, London SW3 6HL.

BURGESS, John

John Burgess. Actor (M).
TV: Dr Fettes in *Albert Campion; Big Deal;* David Crosby in *Brookside;* Gordon Diamond in *Casualty;* Driving Examiner in *Chancer;* Neisse in *Christabel;* Sicinus in *Coriolanus;* Mr Ludlow in *EastEnders;* Shadow Chancellor in *First Among Equals;* Solly in *From the Top;* Stuart in *Grange Hill;* Father in *Hale and*

Pace; Mr Bradshaw in *Josie Lawrence*; Bert in *Laura Disorder*; Popov in *Lovejoy*; Sir Nathaniel in *Love's Labours Lost*; Minister of Defence in *Master of Innocents*; Mr Harrison in *Murphy's Mob*; *Poirot*; Dr Crocker in *Ruth Rendell Mysteries*; Rabbi Levine *in Sam Saturday*; Chalky White in *The Bill*; *The Greeks*; Williams in *The Green Man*; Benjamin Kendrick in *The House of Elliott*; Dougie Webber in *Together*; Judge in *Trust*; Sydney Bankhead in *Up Line*; Defence Counsel in *Wiesenthal*.

Films: Chauffeur in *Give My Regards to Broad Street*; Ambassador in *Rosencrantz and Guildenstern Are Dead*; Station Master in *Sakharov*.

Address: c/o L'Epine Smith & Carney Associates, Suite 61–63, Kent House, 87b Regent Street, London W1R 7HF.

BURKE, Diane

Diane Burke. Actor (F). b. 17 July 1976.
TV: Katie Rogers in *Brookside*.
Address: Contact via Mersey Television Campus Manor, Chidwall Abbey Road, Chidwall, Liverpool L16 OJP.

BURKE, Kathy

Kathy Burke. Actor (F). b. 13 June 1964.
TV: Alice in *A Very Peculiar Practice*; Magda in *Absolutely Fabulous*; *Common As Muck*; *Fantasy World Cup*; *French and Saunders*; Linda La Hughes in *Gimme, Gimme, Gimme*; *Harry Enfield and Chums* (various); Waynetta Slob in *Harry Enfield's Television Programme*; Girl in *Life's a Bitch*; Martha in *Mr Wroe's Virgins*; Helen in *Murder Most Horrid*; *Never Mind the Buzzcocks*; Mrs Ted in *Ted and Ralph*; Waitress in *The Comic Strip Presents...*; Honour in *Tom Jones*.
Films: Christine in *After Miss Julie*; Kathy in *Eat the Rich*; Queen Mary Tudor in *Elizabeth*; Perry in *Kevin and Perry*; Valery in *Nil By Mouth*; Glennis in *Scrubbers*; Brenda Winczor in *Sid and Nancy*; Mary in *This Year's Love*; *Work Experience*.
Address: c/o Stephen Hatton Management, Suite 24, London Fruit and Wool Exchange, Brushfield Street, London E1 6HB.

BURNS, Gordon

Gordon Burns. Presenter. b. Belfast, 10 June 1942.
TV: *A Way of Life*; *A Word in Your Ear*; *Future Perfect*; *Granada Reports*; *Irish Angle*; *The Krypton Factor*; *North West Tonight*; *Password*; *Relatively Speaking*; *Reports Politics*; *Situations Vacant*; *Surprise, Surprise*; *The Gordon Burns Hour*; *The Kick Off Match*; *Time Out of Mind*; *UTV Reports*; various; *World in Action*.
Address: c/o David Anthony Promotions, PO Box

286, Warrington, Cheshire WA2 6GA. Hobbies: Watching football, cricket, golf.

BURNS, Terry

Terry Burns. Actor (M).
TV: Josh Matthews in *Family Affairs*.
Address: c/o L'Epine Smith & Carney Associates, Suite 61–63, Kent House, 87b Regent Street, London W1R 7HF.

BURRELL, Sheila

Sheila Burrell. Actor (F).
b. Blackheath, London, 9 May 1922.
TV: Mrs Lomax in *Bramwell*; Agnes Spencer in *Casualty*; Aunt Ada Doom in *Cold Comfort Farm*; *The Darling Buds of May*; *Devices and Desires*; *Frost in May*; *Gaudy Night*; Mrs Hutton in *Heartbeat*; Agnes Stubbs in *Hetty Wainthropp Investigates*; Rosie Brennan in *The Bill*; *The Six Wives of Henry VIII*; *The Tribute*; Mrs Greenway in *Trial & Retribution*; *Trial of Klaus Barbie*.
Films: *Afraid of the Dark*; Mrs Eshton in *Jane Eyre*; Grandma Oliver in *The Woodlanders*.
Address: c/o Burnett Granger Associates, Prince Of Wales Theatre, 31 Coventry Street, London W1V 8AS.

BURROWS, Malandra

Malandra Burrows. Actor (F). b. Woolton, Liverpool, 4 November 1966.
TV: *Brookside*; Kathy Bates in *Emmerdale*.
Music: *Carnival in Heaven*; *Just this Side of Love*.
Address: c/o International Artistes Ltd, Mezzanine Floor, 235 Regent Street, London W1R 8AX.

BURTON, Amanda

Amanda Burton. Actor (F).
b. Londonderry, 10 October 1956.
TV: *A Casualty of War*; Margaret in *Boon*; Heather in *Brookside*; *Forgotten*; *Inspector Morse*; *Lovejoy*; *Minder*; Beth Glover in *Peak Practice*; Dr Sam Ryan in *Silent Witness*; *Stay Lucky*; *Summer School*; Roisin Browne in *The Blood of the Lamb*; *The Gift*; *The Greek Myths – Theseus and the Minotaur*; *Van Der Valk*; *Where There's a Will*.
Address: c/o ICM, Oxford House, 76 Oxford Street, London W1N 0AX.

BUTCHER, Tom

Tom Butcher. Actor (M).
TV: Terry Williams in *BUGS*; Alan in *Heartbeat*; Bertie in *The Mrs Bradley Mysteries*; Mike Parker in *Peak Practice*; P.C. Loxton in *The Bill*; *The Tim Vine Show*; *A Wing and a Prayer*.
Films: Miles in *Dope Opera*; *Melt*.

Address: c/o Evans & Reiss, 100 Fawe Park Road, London SW15 2EA. Hobbies: Singing, guitar, drums, French horn, cello, golf, waterskiing, cricket, snooker, darts, swimming.

BUTLER, Brett

Brett Anderson. Actor (F).
b. Montgomery, Alabama, USA, 30 January 1958.
TV: Grace Kelly in *The Drew Carey Show* (1997); Grace Kelly in *Ellen* (1997); Grace Kelly in *Grace under Fire*; herself in *The Larry Saunders Show* (1995); herself in *Women of The House* (1995).
Address: c/o ICM Agency, 8942 Wilshire Blvd, Beverly Hills, CA 90211, USA. m. 1 Charles Michael Wilson (dis); m. 2 Ken Ziegler. Hobbies: Reading, politics.

BUTLER, Rob

Rob Butler. Presenter/Reporter.
TV: *BBC Business Breakfast*; *BBC World Business News*; *BBC World Television News*; Presenter *5 News at Noon*.
Address: c/o ITN Press Office, 200 Gray's Inn Road, London, WC1X 8XZ.

BUTTERWORTH, Tyler

Tyler Butterworth. Actor (M). b. 6 December 1969.
TV: Miller in *Artrageous*; *Bergerac*; *Birds of a Feather*; *Boon*; *Casualty*; *Chance in a Million*; Osbourne in *Fiddlers Three*; *Hetty Wainthropp Investigates*; Angelo in *Mike and Angelo*; *Minder*; *Murder of a Moderate Man*; *Nature's Morphine*; *Rumpole of the Bailey*; *Singles*; *The Bill*; Reverend Candy in *The Two Gentlemen of Verona*; Nick in *What the Butler Saw*; Mr Archer in *Whizziwig*.
Films: Phipps in *An Ideal Husband*; *Consuming Passions*.
Address: c/o Kerry Gardner Management, 7 St. George's Square, London SW1V 2HX. Father Peter Butterworth.

BYATT, Paul

Paul Byatt. Actor (M). b. 22 December 1971.
TV: Mike Dixon in *Brookside*.
Address: Contact via Mersey Television Campus Manor, Chidwall Abbey Road, Childwall, Liverpool L16 OJP. 1 sister Michelle Byatt.

BYFIELD, Trevor

Trevor Byfield. Actor (M).
TV: *A People's War*; George English in *A Touch of Frost*; *A Wanted Man*; *Animal Ark*; Gifford in *Backup*; Sgt. Rodney Miller in *Bermuda Grace*; *Between the Lines*; *Birds of a Feather*; *Boon*; *Bust*; *Casualty*; *C.A.T.S. Eyes*; *Chancer*; Benny Robinson in *City Central*; Connors in *Crocodile Shoes*; Jim Massey in *Dangerfield*; *Dempsey and Makepeace*; *El C.I.D.*; Kimpton in *Fool's Gold*; *Ghosthunter*; *Holding the Baby*; *Inspector Morse*; Skolly in *Junk*; *Lovejoy*; *Metal Mickey*; *Minder*; *New Scotland Yard*; Troy in *No Sweat*; *One Foot in the Grave*; *Only Fools and Horses*; *Pleasure*; *Pursuit*; Hal Goldie in *Rides*; Perkins in *Rough Justice*; Howson in *Seaforth*; Leyton in *Simisola*; *So Haunt Me*; *Sunday Night Thriller*; Bob Rosen in *Taggart*; *The Bill*; Frank Mortimer in *The Broker's Man*; DCI George Hayes in *The Chief*; *The Gentle Touch*; Jim Scudamore in *The Knock*; *The Lotus Eaters*; Fred Taylor in *The Manageress*; *The Money Men*; Inspector Le Jeune in *The Pale Horse*; *The Professionals*; Jack Villiers in *Thief Takers*; George Rice in *A Wing and a Prayer*; *Yesterday's Dreams*; Ralph Martin in *Young Man in a Hurry*.
Films: *Crime in the City*; John Clay in *Distant Shadow*; *Goldeneye*; Brian in *Greenwich Mean Time*; *Nasty Neighbours*; *Riding High*; *Sexy Beast*; *Shock Treatment*; *Slayground*; *Who Dares Wins*; *The Wolves of Willoughby Chase*.
Address: c/o CDA, 19 Sydney Mews, London SW3 6HL.

BYRNE, Patsy

Patsy Byrne. Actor (F). b. Ashford, Kent, 13 July 1933.
TV: *2point4 children*; *A Taste of Death*; *Adam Bede*; *Blackadder*; *Blackadder Millennium Special*; *Bleak House*; *Bramwell*; *Casualty*; *David Copperfield*; *Early Travellers in North America*; *Hard Times*; *Heartbeat*; *Hotel Du Lac*; *In Sickness and in Health*; *The Alleyn Mysteries*; *Inspector Morse*; *Just William*; *Les Misérables*; *Maid Marian and her Merry Men*; *Marmalade at Work*; *Miracles Take Longer*; *Peak Practice*; *Road Rage*; *The Chronicles of Narnia*; *The Higher Mortals*; *The Treasure Seekers*; *Think About Science*; *Watching*; *Why Bird*.
Films: *Britannia Hospital*; *Hannah's War*; *Kevin and Perry*; *Mr Love*; *Stealing Heaven*; *The Class of Miss MacMichael*; *The Ghost in the Machine*; *Undying Love*.
Address: c/o Crouch Associates, 9–15 Neal Street, London WC2H 9PF.

BYRNE, Peter

Peter Byrne. Actor (M). b. 29 January 1928.
TV: Justin in *Blake's 7*; *Bluebirds*; Derek in *Bread*; P.C./D.S. Andy Crawford in *Dixon of Dock Green*; *Mutiny at Spithead*; *The Cinderella Gang*; *The New Canadians*; *The Pattern of Marriage*; *Three Live Wires*.
Films: Bridegroom in *Carry On Cabby*; *Raising the Wing*; *Reaching for the Sky*; *The Case of the Second Shot*; *The Large Rope*.
Address: c/o Bill McLean Personal Management, 23b Deodar Road, London SW15 2NP.

BYRON, Kathleen

Kathleen Byron. Actor (F). b. London, 11 January 1923.
TV: *An Englishman's Castle; Breaking Point; Callan; Casualty; Crown Court; Dearly Beloved; Edward the Seventh; Emergency Ward 10; Emmerdale; General Hospital; God Speed Co-operation; Hedda Gabler; Howard's Way; In a Land of Plenty; Midsomer Murders; Minder; Moon & Son; Moonstone; Nancy Astor; Not Proven; On Call; Paul Temple; Play to Win; Portrait of a Lady; Portrait of a Marriage; Probation Officer; Secret Army; Sherlock Holmes; Take Three Girls; The Bill; The Brontës of Haworth; The Challengers; The Golden Bowl; The Main Chance; The Professionals; The Rivals of Sherlock Holmes; The Visitors; Thunder Rock; Together; Trainer; Who is Sylvia?; Within These Walls; Wolfshead; The Haunting.*

Films: *A Matter of Life and Death; Emma; Four Days; From a Far Country; Hammerhead; Hand in Hand; Hell is Sold Out; Les Misérables; Life in Her Hands; Madness of the Heart; My Death is a Mockery; Night of the Eagle; Night of the Silvery Moon; Nothing But the Night; One of Our Dinosaurs is Missing; Prelude to Fame; Private Road; Profile; Saving Private Ryan; Secret Venture; The Abdication; The Elephant Man; The Gambler and the Lady; The House on the Square; The Reluctant Widow; The Scarlet Thread; The Small Black Room; Tom Brown's School Days; Twins of Evil; Young Bess.*

Address: c/o L'Epine Smith & Carney Associates, Suite 61–63, Kent House, 87b Regent Street, London W1R 7HF.

C

CAESAR, Johnny

Johnny Caesar. Actor (M)/Voice artist.
b. Southfields, London, 30 October 1936.
TV: Shoplifter's Husband in *Coronation Street*; Bill Middleton in *Emmerdale*; Micky Madden in *Group Practice*; Eric Burdon in *Our Friends in the North*; Slogger in *Stars Look Down*; *Stay Lucky*; Mr Grable in *The Gambling Man*; Freezer Store Manager in *Truckers*.
Address: c/o Anna Scher Theatre Management Ltd, 70–72 Barnsbury Road, London N1 0ES. Hobbies: Guitar, football, swimming, diving.

CAINE, Michael

Maurice Joseph Micklewhite. Actor (M).
b. Bermondsey, London, 14 March 1933.
TV: Capt. Nemo in *20,000 Leagues Under the Sea* (1997); Horatio in *Hamlet* (1964); Insp. Frederick Abberline in *Jack the Ripper* (1988); Dr Henry Jekyll/Mr Edward Hyde in *Jekyll & Hyde* (1990); F. W. de Klerk in *Mandela and de Klerk* (1997); Folsham in *Saber of London* (1958); Josef Stalin in *Then There Were Giants* (1994); Josef Stalin in *World War II: When Lions Roared* (1994).
Films: *A Bridge Too Far*; *A Hill in Korea*; *A Shock to the System*; Alfie in *Alfie*; *Ashanti*; *Battle of Britain*; *Beyond the Poseidon Adventure*; Harry Palmer in *Billion Dollar Brain*; *Blame it on Rio*; *Blindspot*; *Blood and Wine*; Harry Anders in *Blue Ice*; *Bullet to Beijing*; *Bullseye!*; *California Suite*; *Ciderhouse Rules*; *Deadfall*; *Deathtrap*; *Dirty Rotten Scoundrels*; *Dressed to Kill*; *Educating Rita*; *Escape to Victory*; *Foxhole in Cairo*; Harry Palmer in *Funeral in Berlin*; *Gambit*; Jack Carter in *Get Carter*; *Half Moon Street*; *Hannah and Her Sisters*; *Harry and Walter Go to New York*; *Harry Sundown*; *How To Murder a Rich Uncle*; *Jaws: The Revenge*; *Kidnapped*; *Little Voice*; *Midnight in Moscow*; Mortwell in *Mona Lisa*; *Mr Destiny*; *Peeper*; *Play Dirty*; *Pulp*; *Quills*; *Shadow Run*; *Simon, Simon*; *Sleuth*; *Solo for Sparrow*; *Surrender*; *Sweet Liberty*; *The Black Windmill*; *The Bulldog Breed*; *The Day the Earth Caught Fire*; *The Debtor*; *The Eagle Has Landed*; John Preston in *The Fourth Protocol*; *The Hand*; *The Holcroft Covenant*; *The Honorary Consul*; Harry Palmer in *The Ipcress File*; *The Island*; *The Italian Job*; *The Jigsaw Man*; *The Key*; *The Last Valley*; *The Magus*; *The Man Who Would Be King*; *The Marseilles Contract*; *The Romantic Englishwoman*; *The Swarm*; *The Two-Headed Spy*; *The Whistle Blower*; *The Wilby Conspiracy*; *The Wrong Arm of the Law*; *The Wrong Box*; *Too Late The Hero*; *Water*; *Without a Clue*; *Women Times Seven*; *Zee & Co.*; *Zulu*.
Address: c/o ICM, Oxford House, 76 Oxford Street, London W1N 0AX. m. 1 Patricia Haines; m. 2 Shalara; 1 d. Natascha.

CAKE, Jonathan

Jonathan Cake. Actor (M).
b. Worthing, Sussex, 1968.
TV: Peter Templar in *A Dance to the Music of Time*; Ned Ridley in *Catherine Cookson's The Girl*; Nat in *Cold Lazarus*; Rex Johnson in *Cows*; Gareth in *Degrees of Error*; Regan Montana in *Diamond Girl*; Jerome in *Frank Stubbs Promotes*; Ludo in *Goodnight Sweetheart*; Oswald Mosley in *Mosley*; Advocate in *Nightlife*; Japhet in *Noah's Ark*; Ed in *Press Gang*; Jack Favell in *Rebecca*; George Brunos in *The Jump*; Hattersley in *The Tenant of Wildfell Hall*; Stallion in *The Thin Blue Line*.
Films: Sir Gareth in *First Knight*; *Honest*; Patrick Connor in *True Blue*.
Address: c/o Scott Marshall, 44 Perryn Road, London W3 7NA.

CALLARD, Beverley

Beverley Callard. Actor (F).
TV: Liz McDonald in *Coronation Street*; *Emmerdale*; *Hell's Bells*; *The Peter Principle*; *The Practice*; *Will You Love Me Tomorrow?*.
Address: c/o Arena Entertainment, Regents Court, 39 Harrogate Road, Leeds, West Yorkshire. 1 d. Rebecca Callard.

CALLARD, Rebecca

Rebecca Callard. Actor (F). b. 1975
TV: *Band of Gold*; *Bonjour La Classe*; Connie in *Casualty*; *Chillers*; Lisa in *Life Support*; *Missing Persons*; *Peak Practice*; Harriet in *Plotlands*; *September Song*; Laura in *Sunburn*; *The Borrowers*; Kate Morris in *The Grand*; Cecil Moody in *The Mrs Bradley Mysteries*; *Will You Still Love Me Tomorrow?*
Films: *The Wolves of Willoughby Chase*.
Address: c/o Gavin Barker Associates Ltd, 45 South Molton Street, London W1Y 1HD.

CALLOW, Simon

Simon Callow. Actor (M). b. London, 13 June 1949.
Films: Reverend Beebe in *A Room with a View*; Vincent Cadby in *Ace Ventura: When Nature Calls*; Emanuel Schikaneder in *Amadeus*; *Bedrooms and Hallways*; *Crucifer of Blood*; Richard Spenser in *Deadly Appearances*; Gareth in *Four Weddings and a Funeral*; Richard Cosway in *Jefferson in Paris*; *Manifesto*; Mr Ducie in *Maurice*; *Mr and Mrs Bridge*; Simon Markham in *Postcards from the Edge*; Charles II in *Purcell*; Tilney in *Shakespeare in Love*; Eddie Cheese in *Soft Top, Hard Shoulder*; Major Owen in *Stowaway*; *Streetfighter*; *The Good Father*; Capt. Fairfax in *The Scarlet Tunic*; Ziagiacomo in *Victory*; Fosco in *The Woman in White*.
Address: c/o Marina Martin Associates, 12–13 Poland Street, London W1V 3DE.

CALVERT, Jennifer

Jennifer Calvert. Actor (F)/Presenter.
b. London, Ontario, 7 December 1963.
TV: Cheryl Boyanowsky in *Brookside*; Delphine in *Come Home Charlie and Face Them*; *Deadly Earnest Horror Show*; *Emily Climbs*; *Go Getters*; *Mike and Angelo*; *Randall & Hopkirk (Deceased)*; *Red Dwarf*; Karen Hansson in *Spatz*; *T-Bag*; *The Bill*; *The Fast Show*; Susannah Barton in *The Knock*; *Trouble in Mind*; *West Beach*.
Films: *Jim's Gift*; *Proteus*; *Sex Drive*; *The Magician*; *Trying to Kiss the Moon*.
Address: c/o Shepherd & Ford, 13 Radnor Walk, London SW3 4BP. m. Matthew Rose (sep.); 1 d. Georgia Rose. Hobbies: Fly fishing, swing and salsa dancing, dog walking.

CAMERON, Rhona

Rhona Cameron. Comedian/Presenter.
b. Musselburgh, 1965.
TV: *BBC Comedy Awards*; *Blankety Blank*; *Comedy Rules*; *Edinburgh Nights*; *Gaytime TV*; *Have I Got News For You*; *Jackie Mason Show*; *Ruby Wax – Stripped*; *Saturday Live*; *The Stand Up Show*; *The Funny Farm*; *Top of the Pops*; *TXT*.
Films: Velma in *The Funny Man*.
Address: c/o Jeremy Hicks Associates, 12 Ogle Street, London W1P 7LG. Hobbies: Cinema and psychology.

CAMPBELL, Cheryl

Cheryl Campbell. Actor (F). b. 22 May 1949.
TV: *A Sort of Innocence*; *A Touch of Frost*; *A Wing and a Prayer*; *A Winter's Harvest*; *Absurd Person Singular*; *Affairs of the Heart*; *Boon*; *Bramwell*; *Centrepoint*; *Inspector Morse*; *Jackanory*; *Malice Aforethought*; *Miss Marple*:; *Monsignor Renard*; *Pennies from Heaven*; *Rain On The Roof*; *Ruth Rendell Mysteries*; *Shadowy Third*; *Testament of Youth*; *The Casebook of Sherlock Holmes*; *Midsomer Murders*; *The Secret Agent*.
Films: *Chariots of Fire*; *Greystoke*; *The Mill on the Floss*; *The Shooting Party*.
Address: c/o Rebecca Blond Associates, 69a Kings Road, London SW3 4NX.

CAMPBELL, Colin

Colin Campbell. Actor (M).
b. Twickenham, Middlesex, 17 January 1937.
TV: David Ashton in *A Family At War* (lead); *Minder*; Straker in *Playthings*; Simon the Barrister in *Rough Justice*; Sgt. Willoughby in *Ruth Rendell Mysteries*; Batman Jones in *Sherlock Holmes*; *The Bill*.
Address: c/o MGA, Concorde House, 18 Margaret Street, Brighton, Sussex BN2 1TS.

CAMPBELL, Joanne

Joanne Campbell. Actor (F)/Presenter.
b. Northampton, 8 February 1964.
TV: *All Electric Amusement*; *Alphabet Castle*; Deshaun in *Arcade*; Janis in *Birds of a Feather*; Tessa Parks in *Blind Justice*; Mavis in *Bodger & Badger*; Betty Lee in *Chalkface*; Guest in *David Copperfield*; Jevan in *Frighteners*; Rose in *Home James*; Phoebe in *Love Hurts*; Liz in *Me and My Girl*; *MegaMaths*; *Musix Box*; Mandy in *Night Kids* (lead); Jackie in *Parents and Teenagers* (lead); Bella in *Que Sera*; Boatwoman in *Ragtime*; *Saturday AM Show*; Echo in *The South Bank Show*; Bermuda Schultz in *T-Bag Takes off*; *The Bill*; Rita in *The Record*; *Watch: Faith Stories*.
Films: Staff Nurse Simpson in *Nuns on the Run*.
Address: c/o London Management, Noel House, 2–4 Noel Street, London W1V 3RB. Hobbies: Going to the gym, collecting African stone statues.

CAMPBELL, Nicky

Nicky Campbell. Presenter.
b. Edinburgh, 10 April 1961.
TV: *Central Weekend Live*; *European Election Programme*; *Late Night Live*; *Leviathan*; *Newsnight*; *Ride On*; *Talk About*; *The Big Race*; *The Nicky Campbell Show*; *The Travelling Talk Show*; *Thursday Night Live*; *Wheel of Fortune*.
Address: c/o Avalon Promotions, 2nd Floor, Queens House, Leicester Place, Leicester Square, London WC2H 7BP. m. Tina Richie.

CAMPI, Marji

Marji Campi. Actor (F).
TV: *All the World's a Stage*; Betty Hunt in *Brookside*;

Jessie Shadwick in *Brookside*; Dulcie Froggatt in *Coronation Street*; Avis in *Heartbeat*; Beryl in *Picking Up The Pieces*; *Play for Today*; Joyce Watson in *Surgical Spirit*; Gina Lloyd in *The Bill*; *The Man from the Pru*; *The Setbacks*; Beryl Joy in *The Things You Do for Love*; *Wednesday Play*; Mrs Mac in *What Now?*; Elaine Trafford in *Where the Heart Is*.
Address: c/o The Narrow Road Company, 21–22 Poland Street, London W1V 3DD.

CANT, Brian
Brian Cant. Actor (M)/Presenter.
b. Ipswich, Suffolk, 12 July 1933.
TV: *Animal Families*; *Bric à Brac*; *Camberwick Green*; *Chigley*; *Dappledown Farm*; *Dixon of Dock Green*; *Doctor Who*; *Mousetown*; *Teletubbies*; *Trumpton*; *Z-Cars*.
Address: c/o Amanda Howard Associates Ltd, 21 Berwick Street, London W1V 3RG.

CAPRON, Brian
Brian Capron. Actor (M).
b. Woodbridge, Suffolk, 11 February 1949.
TV: Damien/Quentin Bine in *Action Stations*; Martin Smith in *After Martin*; Jim in *Angels*; Fred in *Around the Corner*; Lee Houghton in *Bergerac*; Jack in *Beryl's Lot*; Bill in *Birds of a Feather*; Herald in *Carry on Laughing*; Registrar in *Casualty*; Jimmy in *Class Act*; *Clubs*; Donald Worthington in *Coronation Street*; Rex in *Crocodile Shoes*; Jerry McKenzie in *EastEnders*; Jirka in *Enemies of the State*; Murray in *Full House*; Mr Hopwood in *Grange Hill*; Roland in *Growing Pains*; Ernest Vincze in *Henry Intervening*; Sgt. Godley in *Jack the Ripper*; Ron in *Just Liz*; Victor in *Love letters on Blue Paper*; Bucknall in *Moon & Son*; Chris in *Murder Most Horrid*; Napoleon in *Nelson*; Plain Clothes DC in *Never Come Back*; Dennis in *Never Say Die*; Henry in *Peak Practice*; Phil in *Return to Blood River*; Seb Christie in *Side by Side*; Stephen Smith in *Smiffs*; *Stanley Baxter's Christmas Hamper*; Lester Purdy in *Steven Waldorf*; Andrew Donaldson in *Taggart*; Antonio Mancini in *The Bill*; Toby in *The Gentle Touch*; Dealer in *The Squad*; Colin in *The Sweeney*; Dad in *Uncle Jack*; Tosh in *Up the Elephant and Round the Castle*; Ted in *Way Up To Heaven*.
Films: News Reporter in *101 Dalmatians*; John Knightley in *Emma*; Morris in *Soup*; Sales Exec in *Still Crazy*; Sid in *The Chiffy Kids*; Clay in *The Hope Machine*.
Address: c/o Markham & Froggatt Ltd, 4 Windmill Street, London W1P 1HF. m. Jeanette Legge.

CAPSTICK, Tony
Tony Capstick. Actor (M).
TV: Harvey Nuttall in *Coronation Street*; Alfie Alker in

Heartbeat; Bookie in *Soul Survivors*; Des in *Out of the Blue*; Councillor Baker in *Band of Gold*; Mr Adlard in *Common as Muck*; *Earthfasts*; *Love and Reason*; *Last of the Summer Wine*.
Films: *Resurrection*.
Address: c/o ATS Casting Ltd, 26 St Michael's Road, Headingley, Leeds, LS6 3AW.

CARBY, Fanny
Fanny Carby. Actor (F). b. Sutton, Surrey, 2 February.
TV: *Birds of a Feather*; Amy Burton in *Coronation Street*; Mrs Crupp *in David Copperfield*; Alice in *Drummonds*; *Forgive Our Foolish Ways*; *Goodnight Sweetheart*; *Heartbeat*; *I'm Alan Partridge (Knowing Me, Knowing You)*; *Juliet Bravo*; *Love Story*; Mrs Kell in *Middlemarch*; *Mitch*; *Only Fools and Horses*; *Private Schultz*; *The Bill*; Nurse Randau in *The Good Doctor Bodkin Adams*; *The History of Mr Polly*; Mrs Grant in *The House Plant*; *The Legacy of Reggie Perrin*.
Films: *Bert Rigby*; *Carry On* films; *Crossbow*; *The Elephant Man*; *Indiscreet*; *Loophole*; *Mrs Dalloway*; *Queenie*; *William Tell*; *The Doctor and the Devils*; *You're a Fool*.
Address: c/o Burnett Granger Associates, Prince of Wales Theatre, 31 Coventry Street, London W1V 8AS.

CARLING, Elizabeth
Elizabeth Carling. Actor (F).
b. Middlesbrough, June 1968
TV: Linda Pond in *Barbara*; Laura Marsh in *Boon*; Wendy Cunningham in *Crocodile Shoes*; Esta Frasier in *Frankenstein's Baby*; Phoebe in *Goodnight Sweetheart*; Anna Mordant in *Medics*; Carol in *Men Behaving Badly*.
Address: c/o London Management, Noel House, 2–4 Noel Street, London W1V 3RB.

CARLING, Julia
Julia Carling. Presenter. b. 1963.
TV: *1998 Cable TV Awards*; *The Big Breakfast*; *Bon Voyage*; *Capital Woman*; *Dream Ticket*; *Julia Carling's Style Guide*; *Livetime*; *Shop*; *Something for the Weekend*; *This Morning*; *VH1*.
Address: c/o Take 3 Management, Osborne House, 111 Bartholomew Road, London NW5 2BJ. m. Will Carling (dis).

CARLTON, James
James Carlton. Actor (M)/Presenter.
b. Bolton, Lancashire, 16 November 1977.
TV: *Agony*; Rick in *At Home with the Braithwaites*; Drew in *Casualty*; Waiter in *Cold Feet*; Craig in *Cops*; Maguire in *Days Like These*; *Emmerdale* (1999);

Bobby Chuckles in *Horror of the House of Goggle; Moviewatch.*

Address: c/o The Actors List, Half Moon Chambers, Chapel Walks, Manchester M2 1HN. Hobbies: Basketball, disc jockey, drums, outdoor pursuits and extreme sports, dance music, motorcross.

CARLYLE, Robert

Robert Carlyle. Actor (M). b. Glasgow, 14 April 1961.
TV: Preston in *99-1;* Spankie in *Arena – Byrne on Byrne;* Albie in *Cracker* (1993); Nick Cameron in *Go Now* (1995); Hamish Macbeth in *Hamish Macbeth;* John Joe 'Jo Jo' McCann in *Looking After Jo Jo; Safe;* Gordon in *Taggart;* PC Murray in *The Advocates;* Tom Ward in *The Bill* (1991).
Films: Dad in *Angela's Ashes; Apprentices;* Prehistoric Shamen in *Being Human;* George in *Carla's Song;* Ray in *Face; Marooned;* Graham in *Priest;* Colquhoun in *Ravenous;* Steve in *Riff Raff;* Big Woodsy in *Silent Scream;* Daffy in *The Beach;* Gary Schofield in *The Full Monty;* Renard in *The World is Not Enough;* Francis 'Franco' Begbie in *Trainspotting.*
Address: c/o ICM, Oxford House, 76 Oxford Street, London W1N 0AX.

CARMICHAEL, Katy

Katy Carmichael. Actor (F).
TV: *A Wing and a Prayer; An Independent Man; And the Beat Goes On; Bread; Casualty; Death of Salesman; Holding the Baby; Joking Apart; Karaoke; Liverpool 1; Men of the World; Paul Merton; Scarlett; Six Pairs of Pants; Spaced; Starstruck; Success; Sunnyside Farm.*
Films: *In the Bleak Midwinter.*
Address: c/o ICM, Oxford House, 76 Oxford Street, London W1N 0AX.

CARR, Jack

Jack Carr. Actor (M). b. Norfolk, 21 November 1944.
TV: *Bleak House;* James Taylor in *Casualty; Chancer; Coronation Street; Covington Cross; Death of an Expert Witness; EastEnders;* DS Brown in *Guardians;* Dave Brewis in *Heartbeat;* Jack Doolan in *Hetty Wainthropp Investigates;* Moran in *Love and Reason; Making Out;* Atherton in *Medics; Never the Twain;* Norman Spears in *Out of the Blue; Private Practice;* Terry in *Sharman; Snakes & Ladders; Stay Lucky; Tales of Sherwood;* Frank Reynolds in *The Bill;* Riper in *The Dwelling Place; The Thief; Truckers; True Tilda;* William Petherick in *Wycliffe.*
Films: *Business as Usual;* Lennie in *Suspect;* Franknum in *The Crying Game.*
Address: c/o Barry Brown & Partner, 47 West Square, Southwark, London SE11 4SP.

CARROTT, Jasper

Robert Davis. Actor (M)/Comedian/Presenter.
b. Birmingham, 14 March 1945.
TV: *An Audience with Jasper Carrott* (1978); *Back to the Front* (1999); *Beat the Carrott* (1981); *Canned Carrott; Carrott Confidential; Carrott gets Rowdy* (1979); *Carrott's Commercial Breakdown* (1990–3); *Carrott's Commercial Breakdown* (1995); *Carrott's Lib* (1982); *Cool It* (1985); *One Jasper Carrott* (1992); *Stand Up America* (1986); DC Bob Louis in *The Detectives; The Unrecorded Jasper Carrott* (1979).
Films: Heinrich in *Jane and the Lost City; The Secret Policeman's Other Ball.*
Music: *Funky Moped/Magic Roundabout.*
Address: c/o Highfield Productions, PO Box 46, Cirencester, Gloucestershire GL7 5YD.

CARTER, Jim

Jim Carter. Actor (M).
TV: *Harry's Kingdom; Fox; Not the Nine O'clock News; Marmalade Atkins; What the Dickens; The Big II; December Flower;* Detective Inspector Frinton in *Widows; Hiawatha; The Monocled Mutineer; The Singing Detective; The First Kangaroos; A Very British Coup; Christabel; The Tenth Man; Precious Bane; Startrap; A Sense of Guilt; Here is the News; Crimestrike – The Detective; The Gravy Train; Pontius Pilate; Hancock; Casualty; A Dangerous Man; Murder Most Horrid; Soldier, Soldier; Stalin; Resnick; Rough Treatment; A Year in Provence; Between the Lines; Lipstick On Your Collar; Minder; Detectives on the Edge of a Nervous Breakdown; Medics; Pie in the Sky; Young Man in a Hurry; Screen 2 – In the Cold Light of Day; Dangerfield; Cracker II – The Big Crunch; The Egg man, Sophie's World, Mrs Hartley and the Growth Centre, Coogan's Run It Might be You, The Chest; Ain't Misbehavin';* Harpur & Iles; The Missing Postman; Bill's New Frock;* Norman Devenish in *Bright Hair; Murder Most Horrid; Arabian Nights;* Geoffrey Bailey in *Trial by Fire.*
Films: *Top Secret; A Private Function; Ruthless Rhapsody; Haunted Honeymoon; A Month in the Country; Raggedy Tawney; Sweet & Sour; Duck; Witches; The Rainbow; Erik the Viking; The Fool; Blame it on the Bellboy; Hour of the Pig; Midnight Movie; Black Beauty; The Madness of King George; The Grotesque; Richard III; Brassed Off; Vigo Keep the Aspidistra Flying; Legionnaire; Shakespeare in Love; The Bass Player; The Little Vampire.*
Address: c/o CDA, 19 Sydney Mews, London SW3 6HL.

CARTERET, Anna

Anna Carteret. Actor (F).
b. Bangalore, 11 December 1942.
TV: Harriet Lloyd in *Cold Enough for Snow* 1997;

EastEnders; Kate Longton in *Juliet Bravo* 1983; *Send in the Girls* 1978; Anna in *The Memoirs Of Sherlock Holmes* 1994; Nerissa in *The Merchant of Venice* 1973; *Peak Practice*.
Films: Gay in *Dateline Diamonds* 1965.
Address: Peters, Fraser and Dunlop, Drury House, 34–43 Russell Street, London WC2B 5HA. m. Christopher Morahan; 2 d. Rebecca, Hattie.

CARTWRIGHT, Rebecca
Rebecca Cartwright. Actor (F). b. 23 July 1981.
TV: Hayey Smith in *Home and Away*; *Water Rats*; *Police Rescue*.
Address: Seven Network Ltd, Mabbs Lane, Epping, New South Wales 2121, Australia. Hobbies: Dancing; jazz, tap, ballet, and street dancing, swimming, roller skating, ice skating, horse riding, aerobics, acrobatics, Winnie the Pooh!

CARTY, Todd
Todd Carty. Actor (M). b. 31 August 1962.
TV: *Driving Mum Crazy*; *Drummer*; Mark Fowler in *EastEnders*; *Focus on Britain*; Tucker in *Grange Hill* and *Tucker's Luck*; *Headmaster*; *Jim'll Fix It*; *The Multi-Coloured Swap Shop*; *Our Mutual Friend*; *Scene in New York*; *Snapshot – Eddie Kidd*; *Streets Apart*; *The Black Velvet Band*, (1997); *The Fame Game*; *The Idle Bunch*; *The Jungle Creatures*; *We're Happy*; *Z-Cars*.
Films: *A Question of Balance*; Oswin in *Krull*; *Please Sir!*; *Professor Popper's Problems*; *Serve them Right*; *The Gang's OK*; *The Magic Trip*; *What's In It for You?*.
Address: c/o John Redway Associates, 5 Denmark Street, London WC2H 8LP.

CASEY, Daniel
Daniel Casey. Actor (M).
TV: Ian Graft in *A Touch of Frost*; Robbie Felton in *Catherine Cookson's Wingless Bird*; *Harry*; Sgt. Troy in *Midsomer Murders*; Anthony in *Our Friends in the North*; Colin Bentley in *Peak Practice*; *The Phoenix and the Carpet*; *Polterguests*; Pete in *The Bill*; James Cornell in *The Grand*.
Address: c/o Susan Angel Associates, 1st Floor, 12 D'Arblay Street, London W1V 3FP. Hobbies: Violin, sports, horse riding, singing.

CASEY, Natalie
Natalie Casey. Actor (F)/Dancer. b. 15 April 1980.
TV: *8:15 From Manchester*; *Death in Venice*; *Going Live*; *Russell Harty*; *Saturday Superstore*.
Films: Shirley Temple in *Chicago Joe and the Showgirl*.
Music: *Chick Chick Chicken* (reached number 72 in UK charts).

Address: Mersey Television, Campus Manor, Childwall Abbey Road, Childwall, Liverpool L16 OJP.

CASSIDY, Natalie
Natalie Cassidy. Actor (F)/Presenter. b. 13 May 1983.
TV: *Blankety Blank*; *Boiled Eggs and Soldiers*; *Blue Peter*; *Diggit*; *The Disney Club*; Sonia in *EastEnders*; *Electric Circus*; *Fully Booked*; *Hype*; *Live and Kicking*; *The Rick Adams Show*.
Address: c/o Anna Scher Theatre Managment Ltd, 70–72 Barnsbury Road, London N1 0ES. Hobbies: Singing, swimming, football, tennis, trumpet.

CASTLE, John
John Castle. Actor (M).
b. Croydon, Surrey, 14 January 1940.
TV: *Ben Hall*; *Bramwell*; *Dark Blue Perfume*; *I, Claudius*; *Inspector Morse*; *Lillie*; *Little Lord Fauntleroy*; *Lost Empires*; *Lovejoy*; *Miss Marple*; *Poirot*; *Reilly, Ace of Spies*; *Sherlock Holmes*; *Tales of the Unexpected*; *Tecs*; *The Cater Street Hangman*; *The Fight Against Slavery*; *The Heart Surgeon*; *The Prime of Miss Jean Brodie*; *The Professionals*; *Thief Takers*; *The Three Hostages*; *The Vanishing Man*; *The Wings of a Dove*; *Travels With a Donkey*; *Wycliffe*.
Films: *Antony and Cleopatra*; *Blow Up*; *Eagle's Wing*; *Eliza Fraser*; *King David*; *Made*; *Man of La Mancha*; *The Lion in Winter*; *The Sparrow*.
Address: c/o Dalzell and Beresford Ltd, 91 Regent Street, London W1R 7TB.

CATHERWOOD, Andrea
Andrea Catherwood. Reporter/Presenter.
b. Belfast, 1968.
TV: Co-presenter *Up Front*; News Reporter Ulster Television; Reporter *News at Ten*; Medical Correspondent ITN; Presenter *ITV Lunchtime News*; Anchorwoman *Channel 5 News*.
Address: c/o ITN Press Office, 200 Gray's Inn Road, London WC1X 8XZ.

CATZ, Caroline
Caroline Catz. Actor (F). b. 1970.
TV: Dawn in *All Quiet on the Preston Front*; Caroline in *Moving Story*; Helen in *Peak Practice*; WPC Fox in *The Bill*; Nikkei in *The Guilty*; Cheryl in *The Vice*.
Films: China in *China*; Kitty in *Déjà Vu*; Ruth/Sian in *Look Me in the Eye*; Rebecca in *The Curious*; Jessica in *The Merchant of Venice*; Lynda in *Under the Sun*.
Address: c/o Peters, Fraser and Dunlop, Drury House, 34–43 Russell Street, London WC2B 5HA. Hobbies: Singing, flying trapeze, dancing.

CAUNTER, Tony

Tony Caunter. Actor (M). b. 22 September 1937.

TV: *A Class of His Own; A Crack in the Ice; A Touch of Spice; Angels; Anna Lee; Bad Boys; Big Deal; Blake's 7; Boon; Bust II; The Chinese Detective; Closing Ranks; Departments 'S'; Dixon of Dock Green; Doggin Around; Don't Wait Up; Doctor Who;* Roy Evans in *EastEnders; Farmer's Arms; Gems; Heroes; Home to Roost; Hot Dog Wars; Howard's Way; Juliet Bravo; Kinsey; London's Burning; Lovejoy; Magic Moments; Marked Personal; May to December; Minder; Miracles Take Longer; On Your Todd; Owen MD; Pennies from Heaven; PQ 17; Rivals of Sherlock Holmes; Rumpole of the Bailey; Running Scared; Scarlet Pimpernel; Silas Marner; Softly, Softly; S.O.S. Titanic; Stay Lucky; Take the High Road; The Avengers; The Baron; The Bill; The Blues; The Brief; The Champions; The Chief; The Cleopatra Files; The Expert; The Main Chance; The Professionals; The Queen's Arms; The Saint; The Sweeney; Thicker Than Water; True Crimes; Tumbledown; United; Virtual Murder; Wallpaper Warrior; War and Peace; West Beach; Z-Cars.*

Films: *Cromwell; The Ipcress File; Killing the Beast; The Mind of Mr Soames; Mr Quip; The Hill; Twist of Sand.*

Address: c/o CCA Management, 7 St George's Square, London SW1V 2HX. 1 s. Nicholas Caunter.

CAVEN, Mark

Mark Caven. Actor (M).

b. London, Ontario, Canada, 24 April 1958.

TV: *Alas Smith and Jones; Data Run; Detectives on the Verge of a Nervous Breakdown; Diary of a Nutcase;* Anthony in *Executive Stress; Follow the Star; Hale and Pace; Jonathan Creek; Lust for Glorious; Red Dwarf; Red Nose of Courage; Space Virgins from the Planet Sex; The Crying Game; The Glam Metal Detectives* (lead); *The Upper Hand; Comic Strip Films* (various); *Unnatural Acts; Who Dealt?* (lead); *Wilderness.*

Films: Sam in *Dead Lucky;* Henry in *Monk Dawson; Night Season; Razor Blade Smile; Superman IV;* Don in *The American Way;* Michael in *The Big Swap; The Pope Must Die.*

Address: c/o Elaine Murphy Associates, 310 Aberdeen House, 22–24 Highbury Grove, London N52 EA.

CAWLEY, Richard

Richard Cawley. Chef/Presenter.

b. Doncaster, Yorkshire.

TV: *A China Scrapbook; Can't Cook, Won't Cook; Carlton Food Daily; Food and Drink; GMTV; Guess Who's Coming To Dinner; Mixing It; Parallel 9; Ready Steady Cook; That's Entertaining; The Big Breakfast; The Travel Show; This Morning.*

Address: c/o Curtis Brown, Haymarket House, 28–29 Haymarket, London SW1Y 4SP.

CAWOOD, Sarah

Sarah Cawood. Presenter.

TV: *It's Not Just Saturday; Nickelodeon Live; Night Fever; Party in the Park* (1999); *Reading Festival* (1999); *Select; Singled Out; Tea in the Park* (1999); *That's Rubbish; The Mix; The Ticket; Top of the Pops; V99* (1999); *Videotech.*

Films: PR rep in *Velvet Goldmine.*

Address: c/o John Noel Management, 10a Belmont Street, London NW1 8HH. Hobbies: Going to gigs, gym training, reading, swimming.

CAZLET, Lara

Lara Cazlet. Actor (F).

TV: Zandra Plackett in *Bad Girls;* Nikki in *Harbour Lights;* Carol Harbottle in *Kavanagh QC;* Rachel in *The Alchemist;* Sammy Adams in *The Bill;* Mandy Sharp in *The Bill.*

Address: c/o Ken McReddie Ltd, 91 Regent Street, London W1R 7TB. Hobbies: Singing, piano, dance: rock and roll, salsa, lambada, tap.

CECIL, Jonathan

Jonathan Cecil. Actor (M)/Presenter.

b. 22 February 1939

TV: *A Picture of Katherine Mansfield;* White Rabbit in *Alice in Wonderland; Alice Through The Looking Glass; Around the World with Sir;* Commentator in *Arthur;* Johnny Howard in *Cynthia;* Cummings in *The Diary of a Nobody;* Edmund Canard; Timothy in *F.L.I.P.;* Mr Brown in *Farmer's Arms; Frank Muir on Children* (revue); *French Cricket;* The Emperor in *Gulliver and Lilliput;* Lanscombe in *Hot Paint;* Vicar in *In Sickness and in Health;* Dave Hutchinson in *Jack Buchman Special;* Lord Hawkespear in *Jackanory Playhouse – The Princess and The Inventor;* Cecil in *Jukes of Piccadilly;* Mr Rawlings in *Just William;* House-owner in *Late Flowering Lust;* Holofernes in *Love's Labours Lost;* Lytton Stachey in *Mad Jack; Maggie* (lead); Holly in *Major Barbara;* Mr Warburton in *Murder Most Horrid;* Watling QC in *No Smoke Without Fire;* Herbert in *Oh Happy Band; Revolutionary Theatre; Romany Jones* (lead); Aristocrat in *Scarfe on Class; Sextet;* Captain Jim in *Spooner's Patch;* Hortensio in *The Taming of the Shrew;* Bertie Wooster in *Thank You, PG Wodehouse; The Entertainers;* Bannard in *The Hospice;* Bishop Wooler in *The House;* Guest Star in *The Kenny Everett Show;* Visitor in *The Lady is a Tramp;* William in *The Puppet Man;* Robert Ramsey in *The*

Rector's Wife; The Venetian Twins; Vile Bodies; White-hall Worrier; Vicar in Wurzel Gummidge; Your Move.
Films: Page in *As You Like It;* Lt. Fakenham in *Barry Lyndon;* Embassy Official in *Catch Me a Spy;* Hastings in *Dead Man's Folly;* Rodney in *The Great St Trinian's Train Robbery;* Chess Player in *History of the World – Part I;* First Fop in *Joseph Andrews;* Pierre in *Kleptophelia;* Bench Magnate in *Little Dorrit;* Schoolmaster in *Lust for a Vampire;* Hastings in *Murder in Three Acts;* Party Guest in *Otley;* Boutique Owner in *Rising Damp;* Lord Baxter in *RMP;* Fatso in *Sink or Swim;* Maitre in *Tchin Tchin;* Reporter in *The Yellow Rolls Royce;* Sir Martin Locket in *The Fool;* Capt Lowell in *The Second Victory;* Powell in *The Sign of Command;* Hastings in *Thirteen at Dinner;* Nigel in *Up the Front.*
Address: c/o Kate Feast Management, 10 Primrose Hill Studios, Fitzroy Road, London NW1 8TR.

CHADBON, Tom
Tom Chadbon. Actor (M). b. Luton, 27 February 1946.
TV: *A Day in Summer; A Touch of Frost; Annie and Fannie; BUGS; Casualty; Country Matters; Crown Prosecutor; Devices and Desires; Doctor Who; Heartbeat; Lovesong; Paradise Postponed; Rebecca; Soldier, Soldier; Space Precinct; Strawberry Tree; Tales of the Unexpected; The Creeper; The Flight of the Heron; The Liver Birds; Triple Exposure.*
Films: *Dance with Strangers; Kiszko; A Room with a View; Sherlock Holmes; Shooting Fish; Tess; Juggernaut; The Tenth Kingdom.*
Address: c/o PFD, Drury House, 34–43 Russell Street, London WC2B 5HA. m. Jane; 2 d. Milly, Felicity; 2 s. Dominic, Nicholas.

CHADWICK, Cy
Cy Chadwick. Actor (M)/Presenter/Producer.
b. Leeds, 2 June 1969.
TV: *A & E,* (1999); *Emmerdale; GMTV; Go Getters; Good Morning; Saturday Disney; Soap Dishes; Telethon; The Big Breakfast; Tonight; Zig & Zag.*
Address: c/o Speak-easy Ltd, 90 St Mary's Road, Market Harborough, Leicestershire LEI6 7DX.

CHAKRABARTI, Lolita
Lolita Chakrabarti. Actor (F).
b. Yorkshire, 1 June 1969.
TV: WPC Jamila Blake in *The Bill.*
Address: c/o Peters, Fraser and Dunlop, Drury House, 34–43 Russell Street, London WC2B 5HA. m. Adrian Lester; sister Reeta Chakrabarti is a BBC political affairs correspondent.

CHALMERS, Judith
Judith Chalmers. Host/Presenter.
b. Manchester, 10 October 1936.
TV: *Afternoon Plus* (1972); *BBC Children's Hour; Hot Property* (1987); *Miss United Kingdom* (1979); *Miss World* (1979); *National News; Panorama; Town and Around; Wish You Were Here...?*
Address: c/o Julie Ivelaw-Chapman, The Chase, Chaseside, Close Cheddington, Bedfordshire LU7 0SA. m. Neil Durden-Smith; 1 d. Emma; 1 s. Mark Durden-Smith.

CHAMBERS, Emma
Emma Chambers. Actor (F).
TV: *Drop the Dead Donkey;* Helen Yardley in *How Do You Want Me?;* Charity Pecksniff in *Martin Chuzzlewit; Skullduggery; The Mixer; The Secret Garden;* Alice Tinker in *The Vicar of Dibley.*
Films: Honey in *Notting Hill; The Clandestine Marriage.*
Address: c/o PFD, Drury House, 34–43 Russell Street, London WC2B 5HA.

CHAMBERS, Janys
Janys Chambers. Actor (F).
b. Nottingham, 14 April 1953.
TV: Eva Krejci in *999;* Mrs Howat in *Brookside;* Christine Bullock in *Coronation Street;* Mrs McGill in *Coronation Street;* Karen Dacre in *Dalziel and Pascoe;* Geraldine's Mum in *Hetty Wainthropp Investigates;* Harriet Huish in *In Suspicious Circumstances;* Katie Purcell in *Out of Hours;* Claris in *The Butterfly Collector.*
Address: c/o Amber Personal Management, 28 St Margaret's Chambers, 5 Newton Street, Manchester M1 1HL. Partner Kevin Dyer; 2 s. Harri, Trystan.
Hobbies: Reading, walking, swimming, history.

CHANCELLOR, Anna
Anna Chancellor. Actor (F). b. 1966.
TV: Celia Morton in *Casualty;* Anna in *Cold Lazarus;* Ally Stone in *Ellington;* Sally Smith in *Inspector Morse;* Mercedes in *Jupiter Moon;* Anna in *Karaoke;* Julia Piper in *Kavanagh QC;* Virginie in *Poirot;* Caroline Bingley in *Pride and Prejudice;* Julia in *The Complete Guide to Relationships;* Christina in *The Vice.*
Films: Peter Pan in *Fairy Tale – One Golden Afternoon;* Henrietta in *Four Weddings and a Funeral;* Nicola in *Heart; Killing Dad;* Mrs Peake in *Princess Caraboo;* Carmen in *Staggered;* Barbra in *The Man Who Knew Too Little.*
Address: c/o ICM, Oxford House, 76 Oxford Street, London W1N 0AX.

CHAPMAN, Tiffany

Tiffany Chapman. Actor (F). b. 3 September 1979.
TV: Rachel Jordache-Wright in *Brookside*.
Address: c/o Laine Management, Matrix House, 301–303 Chapel Street, Manchester M3 5JG. Hobbies: Netball and basketball.

CHARLES, Craig

Craig Charles. Actor (M). b. Liverpool, 11 July 1964.
TV: Eddie in *Business as Usual*; Captain Butler in *Captain Butler*; *Funky Bunker*; *Ghost Watch*; *Night Fever*; Dave Lister in *Red Dwarf*; Dave Lister/Himself in *Red Dwarf Smeg Outs*; Dave Lister/Himself in *Red Dwarf Smeg Ups*; *Robot Wars*; *The Big Breakfast*; *The Governor*.
Address: c/o PFD, Drury House, 34–43 Russell Street, London WC2B 5HA.

CHARLES, Nicola

Nicola Charles. Actor (F)
TV: Sarah Beaumont in *Neighbours*.
Address: Grundy Television, c/o Pearson Television, 1 Stephen Street, London SE1 9PD.

CHARLESTON, Anne

Anne Charleston. Actor (F).
TV: *Antigone*; *Bellbird*; *Class of '75*; *Cop Shop*; *Descant for Gossip*; *Division 4*; *Holiday Island*; *Matlock Police*; Madge Bishop in *Neighbours*; *Possession*; *Prisoner*; *Skyways*; *The Man of Destiny*; *The Shifting Heart*; *The Sullivans*; *The Two-Way Mirror*; *Twenty Good Years*.
Films: *2000 Weeks*; *Country Town*; *I Live With Me Dad*.
Address: Grundy Television, c/o Pearson Television, 1 Stephen Street, London SE1 9PD.

CHARNOCK, Mark

Mark Charnock. Actor (M).
TV: *2point4 Children*; Oswin in *Cadfael*; *Coronation Street*; P.C. Costigan in *EastEnders*; Marlon Dingle in *Emmerdale*; *Ruth Rendell Mysteries*; *Waiting for God*; *Watching*.
Films: *Requiem Apache*.
Address: c/o CDA, 19 Sydney Mews, London SW3 6HL.

CHATER, Geoffrey

Geoffrey Chater. Actor (M). b. 23 March 1921.
TV: *A Married Man*; *A Taste for Death*; *Aerodrome*; *Blunt*; *Bognor*; *Callan*; *Devenish*; *Harry's Game*; *Hotel Du Lac*; *Life Story*; *Mapp and Lucia*; *Northanger Abbey*; *Othello*; *Tales of the Unexpected*; *The Upchat Line*; *Troilus and Cressida*.
Films: *10 Rillington Place*; *Barry Lyndon*; *Crime in the City*; *Ghandi*; *if*; *Sammy Goin' South*.

Address: c/o Bernard Hunter Associates, 13 Spencer Gardens, London SW14 7AH.

CHEGWIN, Keith

Keith Chegwin. Actor (M)/Presenter/Reporter. b. Liverpool, 17 January 1957.
TV: *Anything Goes*; *Black Beauty*; *Cheggers Challenge*; *Cheggers Plays Pop*; *Chegwin Checks Out*; *It's a Knockout*; *The Liver Birds*; *My Old Man*; *Open All Hours*; *Roll With It*; *Sale of the Century*; *Saturday Superstore*; *Star Search*; *The MultiColoured Swap Shop*; *The Big Breakfast*; *The Heat is On*; *The Wackers*; *The Tomorrow People*; *Z Cars*.
Films: *Double Trouble*; *Egg Heads Robot*; *Polanski's Macbeth*; *Robin Hood Jnr*.
Address: c/o Fox Artist Management Ltd, Concorde House, 101 Shepherd's Bush Road, London W6 7LP. m. Maria Fielden; 1 d. Rose; 1 s. Ted. Hobbies: Piano, recording, writing.

CHERITON, Shirley

Shirley Cheriton. Actor (F). b. London, 28 June 1955.
TV: Katy in *Angels*; Debbie in *EastEnders*.
Address: c/o St James's Personal Management Ltd, 19 Lodge Close, Stoke D'Abernon, Cobham, Surrey KT11 2SG. Hobbies: Swimming.

CHILDS, Tracey

Tracey Childs. Actor (F). b. London, 30 May 1963.
TV: Pamela in *A Talent For Murder*; Professor Vana in *Captain Zep*; Sophie Flemyng in *Cold Warrior*; Lucy in *Dempsey and Makepeace*; Jessica in *Gems*; Lynne Howard in *Howard's Way*; Monica in *If You See God, Tell Him*; Camilla in *Lobo's World*; Louise in *Morgan's Boy*; Claire in *Runaway Bay*; Laura Hoskins in *The Bill*; Mrs Hart in *The Bill*; Penelope in *The Shellseekers*; *The Victoria Wood Show*.
Address: c/o Evans & Reiss, 100 Fawe Park Road, London SW15 2EA.

CHITTELL, Christopher

Christopher Chittell. Actor (M). b. 19 May 1948.
TV: Eric Pollard in *Emmerdale*; *Freewheelers*; *The Tomorrow People*; *Tucker's Luck*.
Films: *Games for Vultures*; *Golden Rendezvous*; *The Charge of the Light Brigade*; *To Sir with Love*; *Zulu Dawn*.
Address: c/o David Daly Associates, 586a Kings Road, London SW6 2DX. m. Caroline; 1 d. Rebecca; 1 s. Benjamin.

CHOHAN, Syrah

Syrah Chohan. Presenter.
TV: *By Day By Night*; *Country File*; *East*; *French Fix*;

Q Asia; Stress Busters; The Really Useful Show; The Time... The Place.
Address: c/o John Noel Management, 10a Belmont Street, London NW1 8HH.

CHRISTIAN, Terry

Terry Christian. Presenter. b. Manchester, 8 May 1963.
TV: *Big City* (1995); *Hit Mix; The Best of The Word* (1999); *The Word.*
Address: c/o MPC Entertainment, MPC House, 15–16 Maple Mews, London NW6 5UZ. Hobbies: History, reading.

CHRISTIE, Julie

Julie Christie. Actor (F). b. Assam, 14 April 1941.
TV: *'A' For Andromeda; Fathers and Sons; Separate Tables.*
Films: *A Long Way From Home; Afterglow; Billy Liar; Crooks Anonymous; Darling; Don't Look Now; Dragonheart; Fahrenheit 451; Far From the Madding Crowd; Fools of Fortune; Gold; Hamlet; Heat and Dust; Heaven Can Wait; In Search of Gregory; La Mémoire Tatouée; Lillian Alling; Memories of a Survivor; Miss Mary; Petulia; Power; Return of the Soldier; The Fast Lady; The Railway Station Man; Young Cassidy.*
Address: c/o ICM, Oxford House, 76 Oxford Street, London W1N 0AX.

CHUBB, William

William Chubb. Actor (M).
TV: Lent in *An Independent Man;* Hotel Manager in *As Time Goes By;* D.I. David Matthews in *Break Out;* Richard in *The Buddha of Suburbia;* Cottrell in *BUGS;* Moss in *Capital Lives;* Gareth Peters in *Casualty;* Brian Freed in *Downtown Lagos;* Ericson in *Extremely Dangerous;* John Taylor in *Guardians;* John Krejewski in *House of Cards;* Steve Holdsworth in *Just Us;* Commander Driscoll in *Kavanagh QC – The Burning Deck;* Sebastian Braikes in *Lovejoy;* Dad in *Mike and Angelo;* Man in Taxi in *One Foot in the Grave;* Keith Llewellyn in *Peak Practice;* Crown Prosecuting Solicitor in *Playing the Field;* Blake in *Poirot;* Angus Gill in *Randall & Hopkirk (Deceased);* Beech in *Rocket to the Moon;* Inspector McCarthy in *Ruth Rendell Mysteries;* Piers Dearbourne in *Signs and Wonders;* George Wetherby in *Sleepers;* Stephen Tyler in *The Ambassador;* John Krejewski in *To Play the King;* Gordon Wells in *Vanishing Man.*
Films: Mr Wesley in *Milk;* Auctioneer in *The Woodlanders.*
Address: c/o Brunskill Management, Suite 8a, 169 Queen's Gate, London SW7 5HE. Hobbies: Skiing, sailing, languages (Italian and French).

CHURCH, Suzanne

Suzanne Church. Actor (F). b. 9 October 1951.
TV: Estate Agent in *Big Deal;* Valerie Silverman in *Call Me Mister;* Louise Jordan in *C.A.T.S. Eyes; Chopper Squad;* WPC Hartley in *Crossroads;* Elizabeth in *Dead Man's Tales;* Julia in *Dempsey and Makepeace;* Dr Hunter in *Full House;* PA in *Home James;* Susan in *London's Burning;* Sharon Barrie in *Me and My Girl; Migrant;* Customer in *Never the Twain;* Diane Harrington in *No Place Like Home; Number 96;* Miss Trench in *Press Gang;* Ethne L'Strange in *Rude Health;* Miss Foster in *Slinger's Day;* Annie Lucas in *Surgical Spirit;* Isabel in *The Upper Hand.*
Films: Fiona in *Boston Kickout; Fierce Creatures.*
Address: c/o Rolf Kruger Management Ltd, 205 Chudleigh Road, London SE4 1EG.

CLARK, Ryan

Ryan Clark. Actor (M).
b. Sydney, Australia, 9 April 1983.
TV: Sam in *Home and Away.*
Address: c/o Seven Network Ltd, Mabbs Lane, Epping, New South Wales 2121, Australia.
Hobbies: Rugby, surfing.

CLARKE, Jacqueline

Jacqueline Clarke. Actor (F)/Presenter.
b. Buckinghamshire, 13 February 1942.
TV: Sheila Barnes in *A Sharp Intake of Breath; Battle of the Sexes; Chish and Fips; It's Different For Boys; Last of the Summer Wine; Little and Large; Maxwell's House; Only When I Laugh; Partners; Rings on Their Fingers; Scott On; Slinger's Day; Surgical Spirit; The Adventures of Don Quick; The Basil Brush Show; The Bill; Dave Allen; The Kenny Everett Show; The Mike Yarwood Show; The Young Ones; The Brighton Belles; Thirty Minutes' Worth.*
Address: c/o Burnett Granger Associates, Prince of Wales Theatre, 31 Coventry Street, London W1V 8AS. m. Barrie Gosney.

CLARKE, Margi

Margi Clarke. Actor (F)/Presenter. b. Liverpool, 1954.
TV: Jackie Dobbs in *Coronation Street;* Queenie in *Making Out* (1989); Connie in *Soul Survivors* (1995); *The Good Sex Guide* (1994).
Films: Ronnie in *Blonde Fist;* Teresa in *Letter to Brezhnev.*
Address: c/o Associated International Management, 5 Denmark Street, London WC2H 8LP. 1 d. Rowan Budd; 1 s. Lawrence.

CLARKE, Sharon

Sharon Clarke. Actor (F).
TV: Nurse in *Past Caring*; Receptionist in *Soldier, Soldier*; Night Nurse in *The Singing Detective*; Cook in *Between the Lines*; Mrs Richardson in *Children's Ward*; Lizzie Brown in *EastEnders*; Karen in *Here and Now*.
Films: *Dinner Date; Secret Society*.
Address: c/o Sandra Boyce Management, 1 Kingsway Parade, Albion Road, London N16 0TA.

CLARKE, Warren

Warren Clarke. Actor (M).
b. Oldham, Lancashire 1947.
TV: Josiah Cole in *A Respectable Trade* (1998); *All Creatures Great and Small; All in the Game; Angel Train; Anything Legal Considered; Bergerac; Big Deal; Blackadder; Boon; Cop Out; Crown Court*; Det. Supt. Andrew Dalziel in *Dalziel and Pascoe* (1997–2000); Russell Polin in *Giving Tongue* (1996*); Gone to Seed; Gone to the Dogs; Hallelujah Mary Plum; Hands of a Murderer; Heartland*; Max Kelvin in *House of Windsor* (1994*);* Bob in *I.D.* (1995); *Ice Dance*; George Cragge in *In the Red* (1998); *Jail Diary of Alby Sachs; Jennie*; Ednan in *Joseph* (1995); *Lovejoy*; Bamber in *Moving Story* (1994); Vernon Jones in *The Mystery of Men* (1999); *Never Speak Ill of the Dead; Nice Work; Our Mutual Friend; PSY Warriors; Reilly Ace of Spies; Return to Blood River; The Secret Agent; Shelley; Sleepers; Softly, Softly; Sound of Guns; SS Becker; Stay Lucky; The Battle of Waterloo; The Case of the Frightened Lady; The Comic Strip; The Flying Devils; The Greenhill Pals; The Home Front; The Hunchback of Notre Dame; The Jewel in the Crown*; Ronald Pierce in *The Locksmith* (1997); *The Manageress; The Onedin Line; The Roughest Way; The Russian Soldier; The Sweeney*; Caliban in *The Tempest; The Thirteenth Reunion; The Way of the World; Two Weeks in Winter; Wish Me Luck; Wolcott*.
Films: Dim in *A Clockwork Orange; Antony and Cleopatra; Dirty Money; Enigma; Firefox; From a Far Country; Green Fingers; House Work; Never Better; O Lucky Man!; The Antagonists; The Cold Room; The Virgin Soldiers*.
Address: c/o ICM, Oxford House, 76 Oxford Street, London W1N 0AX.

CLARKSON, Jeremy

Jeremy Clarkson. Presenter.
b. Doncaster, South Yorkshire, 11 April 1960.
TV: *Clarkson* (1999); *Clarkson's Star Cars; Jeremy Clarkson's Motorworld* (1995); *Robot Wars* (1998); *Top Gear*.
Films: *Apocalypse Clarkson; Extreme Machines; Head to Head; Jeremy Clarkson Unleashed; Motorsport Mayhem; The Most Outrageous Jeremy Clarkson Video in the World... Ever.*
Address: BBC, Union House, 65–69 Shepherd's Bush Green, London W12 8TX. m. Francie; 2 d. Emily, Katya; 1 s. Finlo.

CLARY, Julian

Julian Clary. Comedian/Actor (M). b. 25 May 1959.
TV: *Aspel and Co.; BAFTA Awards; Brace Yourself Sidney; Brazen Hussies; First Laughs On Four; Has Anyone Seen My Pussy...; Have I Got News For You; Hospital; Jack Dee's Saturday Night; Plunder; Saturday Night Live; Sticky Moments; Terry and Julian; The Clive James Show; They Think It's All Over; Tonight with Jonathan Ross; Trick or Treat; What's Up Dockers; Whose Line is it Anyway?; Wish You Were Here...; Mr and Mrs*.
Films: *Carry On Columbus*.
Address: c/o International Artistes Ltd, Mezzanine Floor, 235 Regent Street, London W1R 8AX.

CLAY, Nicholas

Nicholas Clay. Actor (M).
b. London, 18 September 1946.
TV: *Berlin Break*; Ethan Rockeridge in *BUGS; Gentlemen and Players; Hotel Shanghai; In a Glass Darkly*; Justice Fulbright in *Kavanagh QC; Love Story; Merlin*; Menclaus in *Odyssey; The Picture of Dorian Gray; Poor Little Rich Girl; Psychos; Russian Night; Saturday, Sunday, Monday; Shakespeare; Sherlock Holmes; Shine on Harvey Moon; Taggart; The New Adventures of Robin Hood; The Unknown Soldier; The Three Musketeers; Virtual Murder*.
Films: Alexander in *Alexander the Great*; Patrick Redfern in *Evil Under the Sun*; Lancelot in *Excalibur*; Sir Hugo in *The Hound of the Baskervilles*; Menclaus in *Lady Chatterley's Lover*; Lionel in *Lionheart*; Cesare Augustus in *Martyrdom of St Sebastian*; Prince in *Sleeping Beauty*; Darwin in *The Darwin Adventure*; Tristan in *Tristan and Isolde*; Lt. Raw in *Zulu Dawn*.
Address: c/o PFD, Drury House, 34–43 Russell Street, London WC2B 5HA. m. Lorna; 2 d. Ella, Madge.

CLAYTON, Edward

Edward Clayton. Actor (M).
b. Sheffield, 9 October 1940.
TV: Mr Hugget in *B & B*; Liaison Officer in *Bad Girl*; D.I. Jenkins in *Calling the Shots*; Tom Casey in *Coronation Street*; James Crowther in *GBH*; Station Guard in *Goodnight Mr Tom*; Jack Siddons in *Heartbeat*; Sgt. Cannon in *Wycliffe*; Roach in *Kinsey*; Caretaker in *London Bridge*; Bradley in *Love Hurts*; Official in *Nature Boy*; Farmer in *Out of Sight*; Ref in *Peak Practice*; Edward Lacey in *Taggart*; Boat

Owner in *The Bill*; Bryant in *Underbelly*; Stubbs in *Wild Oats*; Hollingford in *Wives and Daughters*; Len in *Woof*.
Address: c/o The Narrow Road Company, 21–22 Poland Street, London W1V 3DD.

CLEALL, Peter

Peter Cleall. Actor (M)/Producer.
b. 16 March 1944.
TV: Duffy in *Please Sir!*; Jerry Cruncher in *A Tale of Two Cities*; Arthur in *Big Deal*; Assistant in *A Bit of Fry and Laurie*; Steve Lewis in *Casualty*; Stephen Crane in *Dempsey and Makepeace*; Malcom Morris in *EastEnders*; John Keep in *Grange Hill*; Roy Patrick in *Growing Pains*; Percy Foreman in *London's Burning*; Wally Knowles in *Minder*; Inspector Richards in *Peak Practice*; Head Teacher in *Silent Witness*; *The Bill* (various); Von Trapp in *The Brittas Empire*; Davey in *The Lady is a Tramp*; Michael Vey in *Thief Takers*.
Films: Duffy in *Please, Sir!*; Edgar Wharton in *Seeing God*; Mr Ross in *The Bull*; Jean in *Theatre of Death*.
Address: c/o Pelham Associates, 9–12 Middle Street, Brighton BN1 1AL.

CLEESE, John

John Cleese. Comedian/Actor (M).
b. Weston-Super-Mare, 27 October 1939.
TV: *At Last the 1948 Show* (1967); *Cheers* (1987); Basil Fawlty in *Fawlty Towers*; *Monty Python's Flying Circus*; *The Muppet Show* (1979); *Norway, Land of Giants* (1979); Petruchio in *The Taming of the Shrew* (1980); *The Frost Programme* (1966); *The Frost Report* (1966); *The Great Muppet Caper* (1980); *3rd Rock From the Sun* (1998); *Whoops Apocalypse!*.
Films: *A Fish Called Wanda*; *Clockwise*; *Fierce Creatures*; *Isn't She Great*; *Mary Shelley's Frankenstein*; *Monty Python and the Holy Grail*; *Out of Towners*; *Privates on Parade*; *Romance with a Double Bass*; Sheriff Langston in *Silverado*; *Splitting Heirs*; *The Jungle Book*; *The Life of Brian*; *The Strange Case of the End of Civilization as We Know it*; *Time Bandits*.
Address: c/o David Wilkinson Associates, 115 Hazelbury Road, London SW6 2LX. m. 3 Alyce Faye Eichelberger; 2 d. Cynthia (1st m.), Camilla (2nd m.).

CLIFFORD, Kim

Kim Clifford. Actor (F). b. 27 January 1961.
TV: *Goodnight Sweetheart*; Sandra Hallam in *London's Burning*; *Eye Witness*; Mandy in *Colin's Sandwich*; *In Sickness and in Health*; *Alas Smith and Jones*; *Only Fools and Horses*; *Function Room*; *Tucker's Luck*; *Juliet Bravo*; *Now and Then*; *The Nation's Health*; *Partners in Crime*; *Mitch*; *Going Out*; *The History of Mr Polly*.

Films: *My Dead Buddy*; *Revolution 1776*; *Rebellious Jukebox*; *Runners*; *Chariots of Fire*.
Address: c/o Anna Scher Theatre Management Ltd, 70–72 Barnsbury Road, London N1 0ES.

CLIVE, John

John Clive. Actor (M).
b. London, 6 November 1938.
TV: *A Dream of Alice*; Prudoe in *Bye Bye Baby*; Richard in *Casualty*; Cgfartha in *How Green Was My Valley*; Mr Dumby in *Lady Windermere's Fan*; Rosko in *Perils of Pendragon*; *Rings on Their Fingers*; Dai in *Rising Damp*; Terry in *Ten Percenters*; *The Dick Emery Show*; *The Government Inspector*; Hinks in *The History of Mr Polly*; P.C. Harris in *The Nesbitts are Coming*; *The Sweeney*; Rev Boon in *Tropic*; Clerk in *The Young Indiana Jones Chronicles*; *Z-Cars*.
Films: *A Clockwork Orange*; *Carry On Abroad*; *Great Expectations*; *No Longer Alone*; *The Revenge of the Pink Panther*; *Smashing Time*; *The Chiffy Kids*; *The Italian Job*; John Lennon's Voice in *Yellow Submarine*.
Address: c/o The Narrow Road Company, 21–22 Poland Street, London W1V 3DD.

CLOONEY, George

George Clooney. Actor (M).
b. Lexington, Kentucky, USA, 6 May 1961.
TV: Joe in *Baby Talk*; Det Ryan Walker in *Bodies of Evidence*; Major Biff Woods in *Combat High*; Ace in *ER*; Dr Doug Ross in *ER*; Booker in *Roseanne*; Detective James Falconer in *Sisters*; Chic Chesbro in *Sunset Beach*; George Burnett in *The Facts of Life*; Kevin Shea in *Without Warning: Terror in The Towers*.
Films: Batman/Bruce Wayne in *Batman and Robin*; Seth Gecko in *From Dusk Till Dawn*; himself in *Full Tilt Boogie*; *Metal God*; Ulysses Everett McGill in *O Brother, Where Art Thou*; Jack Taylor in *One Fine Day*; Jack Foley in *Out of Sight*; Remar in *Red Surf*; Matt Stevens in *Return of the Killer Tomatoes!*; Oliver in *Return to Horror High*; Dr Doctor in *South Park: Bigger, Longer and Uncut*; Lip-synching Transvestite in *The Harvest*; Thomas Devoe in *The Peacemaker*; Captain Billy Tyne in *The Perfect Storm*; Capt Charles Bosche in *The Thin Red Line*; Archie Gates in *Three Kings*; *Time Tunnel: The Movie*; Mac in *Unbecoming Age*; himself in *Waiting For Woody*.
Address: c/o William Morris Agency, 151 El Camino Drive, Beverly Hills, CA 90212, USA. His aunt is singer Rosemary Clooney. Hobbies: Baseball, basketball, making furniture, collecting old cars, looking after his potbellied pig.

CLUNES, Martin

Martin Clunes. Actor (M)/Director. b. London 1962.
TV: *About Face; All at No. 20; An Evening with Gary Lineker; Awayday; Bonjour La Classe; Boon; Demob; Doctor Who; Gone to the Dogs; Gormenghast; Hannay; Harry Enfield's Television Programme; Have I Got News For You; Hospital; Hunting Venus; Inspector Morse; Jeeves and Wooster; Jury; Lovejoy;* Gary in *Men Behaving Badly; Moving Story; Never Come Back; Never Mind the Horrocks; Neville's Island; No Place Like Home; Over Here; Rides; Sex 'n' Death; Suspicion; The Upper Hand; The White Guard; Touch and Go.*
Films: *Carry On Columbus; Saving Grace; Shakespeare in Love; Staggered; Swing Kids; The Revenger's Comedies; The Russia House.*
Address: c/o ICM, Oxford House, 76 Oxford Street, London W1N 0AX.

CLYDE, Jeremy

Jeremy Clyde. Actor (M)/One half of the pop duo Chad and Jeremy in the 1960s. b. 22 March 1944.
TV: *A Chink in the Wall; A Rather English Marriage; A Young Person's Guide to Becoming a Rock Star; Affairs of the Heart; Agatha Christie Hour; Aimée; Bergerac; Blott on the Landscape; Blow It; By the Sword Divided; Campaign; Casualty; Class Act; Dial M for Murder; Disraeli; The Duchess of Duke Street; Half the Picture; How Green Was My Valley; In Suspicious Circumstances; Inspector Morse; Is It Legal?; Just William; Ladykillers; Moll Flanders; Noah's Ark; Omnibus; Prometheus; Raffles; Romance; School Play; Sexton Blake and the Demon God; Strife; Taggart; Tales of the Unexpected; The Boy who Won the Pools; The Chief; The Children of the New Forest; The Colour of Justice; The Country Wife; The Hitch-Hiker; The Marrying Kind; Midsomer Murders; The Mixer; The Moth; The Onedin Line; The Racing Game; The Year of the French; William Tell; Wycliffe.*
Films: *An Invitation to the Wedding; Cassini; Gare au Male; Kaspar Hauser; Splitting Heirs; The North Sea Hijack; The Silver Bears; Wilt.*
Address: c/o Joy Jameson Ltd, 2.19 The Plaza, 535 Kings Road, London SW10 0SZ.

COBURN, Norman

Norman Coburn. Actor (M).
b. Sydney, Australia, 6 March 1937.
TV: *1915; A Country Practice; Five Mile Creek;* Donald Fisher in *Home and Away; Land of Hope; Peach's Gold; Possession; Rafferty's Rules; Special Squad; The Young Doctors.*
Address: Seven Network Ltd, Mabbs Lane, Epping, New South Wales 2121, Australia.

COCHRANE, Michael

Michael Cochrane. Actor (M).
TV: *99-1; A Dangerous Man;* Charles Hecht in *A Murder of Quality; Beck;* George in *Big Bad World; Fortunes of War;* Dereck Lightfoot in *Heartbeat; Keeping Up Appearances; King's Royal;* Waddington in *Longitude; Love in a Cold Climate; Master of Innocents;* Sir George Rawlings in *Nancherrow; No Job for a Lady;* Marketing Director in *Perfect World; Pie in the Sky;* Sir Henry Simmerson in *Sharpe's Eagles;* Simmerson in *Sharpe's Regiment;* Major Simmerson in *Sharpe's Sword;* Ruth Rendell's *Simisola; Taggart;* Harston in *The Ambassador;* Nigel Boscombe in *The Bill;* Cecil Addison in *The Broker's Man; The Chelworth Inheritance;* Nigel Crimmond in *The Chief; The Citadel; The Darling Buds of May;* Oliver Brown in *The Uninvited; Uncle Jack and Cleopatra's Mummy; Wings;* Price in *Wycliffe.*
Films: *Escape to Victory;* Det. Insp. Deeks in *Incognito; The Return of the Soldier;* Crimpley in *The Far Pavilions;* Kessler in *The Saint.*
Address: c/o CDA, 19 Sydney Mews, London SW3 6HL.

COCHRANE, Nick

Nick Cochrane. Actor (M)/Presenter.
b. Cheshire, 18 December 1973.
TV: Andy McDonald in *Coronation Street; Heartbeat.*
Address: c/o Hillman Threlfall, 33 Brookfield, Highgate West Hill, London N6 6AT.

COCKERELL, Toby

Toby Cockerell. Actor (M). b. 17 October 1976.
TV: Scott Windsor in *Emmerdale;* Gary in *Within Living Memory; London's Burning; The Bill;* Nick in *Turning Point – Nick's Story;* Ruth Rendell – *Fallen Curtain; The Knock; Boiled Eggs and Soldiers; A Taste for Death; Antonia and Jane;* Can You Hear Me Think; *Sweet Nothing; Ex; Streetwise;* Billy Watkins in *The House of Eliott.*
Films: *Virtual Sexuality; SpiceWorld – the Movie; Shopping; Ailisha's Attic; Smack 'n Thistle.*
Address: c/o Anna Scher Theatre Management Ltd, 70–72 Barnsbury Road, London N1 0ES.

COIA, Paul

Paul Coia. Presenter. b. 18 June 1955.
TV: *A Word in Your Ear; Catchword; Flash in the Pan; Heaven Knows; Tricks of the Trade.*
Address: c/o Arlington Enterprises Ltd, 1–3 Charlotte Street, London W1P 1HD. m. Debbie Greenwood; 2 d. Annalie, Luisa.

COLCLOUGH, Graham

Graham Colclough. Actor (M).
b. Stoke-on-Trent, Staffordshire, 10 June 1938.
TV: *Coronation Street*; Dr Curtis in *Dalziel and Pascoe*; *Emmerdale*; *First Among Equals*; *Floodtide*; *Harry's Mad*; *How We Used to Live*; *Travelling Man*.
Films: Morris in *Morris Loves Birds*.
Address: c/o Circuit Personal Management Ltd, Suite 71, S.E.C. Bedford Street, Stoke-on-Trent, Staffordshire ST1 4PZ. m. Jenny; 2 d. Nikki, Nerys. Hobbies: Birdwatching.

COLE, George

George Cole. Actor (M). b. London, 22 April 1925.
TV: *A Bit of a Holiday*; *A Day to Remember*; *A Man of Our Times*; *A Room in Time*; *An Independent Man*; *Blott on the Landscape*; *Comrade Dad*; *Dad* (lead); *Don't Forget to Write*; *Getting it on Concorde*; *Ginger*; *Heggerty, Haggerty*; *Life After Life*; *Losing Her*; *Menace*; *Minder*; *My Good Friend*; *Natural Causes*; *Of Course We Trust You, Arnold*; *The Return of the Saint*; *Root into Europe*; *Sex Game*; *Shadows of Fear*; *Ten Commandments: Honour Thy Mother and Father*; *The Good Humour Man*; *The Good Life*; *The Right Prospectus*; *Voyage of Charles Darwin*.
Films: *Cleopatra*; *Dr Syn*; *Girl in the Dark*; *Legend of Dick Turpin*; *Mary Reilly*; *Minder on the Orient Express*; *One Way Pendulum*; *The Great St Trinian's Train Robbery*; *The Blue Bird*; *The Vampire Lovers*.
Address: c/o Joy Jameson Ltd, 2.19 The Plaza, 535 Kings Road, London SW10 0SZ. m. Penny Morrell.

COLE, Graham

Graham Cole. Actor (M). b. London, 16 March 1952.
TV: *Casualty*; *Doctor Who*; *The Kenny Everett Show*; *Noel's House Party*; *Only Fools and Horses*; *Secret Army*; PC Tony Stamp in *The Bill*.
Films: *Police Stop*.
Address: c/o Evans & Reiss, 100 Fawe Park Road, London SW15 2EA. m. Cherry Anne. Hobbies: Race driving, tennis, stunts (does his own); family outings.

COLE, Julie Dawn

Julie Dawn Cole. Actor (F).
b. Guildford, Surrey, 26 October 1957.
TV: *3-2-1*; *And Mother Makes Three*; Jo Longhurst in *Angels*; *Animal Ark* (1997); *Bergerac*; *Brian Conley's Christmas Show* (1997); *Brian Conley's Crazy Christmas*; *Casualty*; *Company & Co.*; *Dick Turpin*; *EastEnders*; *Emmerdale*; *The Freddie Starr Show* (1998); *Galloping Galaxies*; *Grandad*; *Grundy*; *How to be a Little Sod* (1995); *Jackanory*; *The Kelly Monteith Show*; Married for Life (1996); Lucy in *The Mill on the Floss*; *Moon & Son*; *Noah's Ark* (1998); *Orson Welles Mystery Plays*; *People Like Us*; Rowella in *Poldark*; *Rings on Their Fingers*; *Tales of Empire* (1995); *Tandoori Nights*; *Terry and June*; *The Bernie Winters' Show*; *The Intruders*; *The Jim Davidson Show*; *The Many Wives of Patrick*; *The Politician's Wife* (1995); *The Upper Hand*; *Up the Elephant and Round the Castle*; *Within these Walls*; *Wysiwyg*.
Films: *Camille*; *That Lucky Touch*; Verucca Salt in *Willy Wonka and the Chocolate Factory*.
Address: c/o Burnett Granger Associates, Prince of Wales Theatre, 31 Coventry Street, London W1V 8AS.

COLE, Stephanie

Stephanie Cole. Actor (F). b. Solihull, 5 October 1941.
TV: Betty Silletoe in *A Bit of a Do*; *Going Gently*; *In the Cold Light of the Day*; Peggy in *Keeping Mum*; *Memento Mori*; Mrs Featherstone in *Open All Hours*; *Poirot*; Muriel in *Soldiering On*; *Tenko*; *The Return of the Antelope*; *Waiting for God* (lead).
Films: *Grey Owl*.
Address: c/o Michael Ladkin Personal Management, Suite One, Ground Floor, 1 Duchess Street, London W1N 3DE.

COLE, Stephen

Stephen Cole. Presenter.
TV: *BBC World Television*; *Central News*; *CNN International*; *Newsline*.
Address: c/o Speak-Easy Ltd, 90 St Mary's Road, Market Harborough, Leicestershire LE16 7DX. Hobbies: tennis, rugby, water polo.

COLEMAN, Charlotte

Charlotte Coleman. Actor (F). b. 3 April 1968.
TV: *A View of Harry Clarke*; *Blackeyes*; *Campaign*; *Danger*; *Marmalade at Work*; *Educating Marmalade*; Freddie in *Freddie and Max*; Liffy Bingley Toffingham in *Gayle Tuesday Special*; Barb in *Giving Tongue*; Lisa in *How Do You Want Me?*; *Inappropiate Behaviour*; Jessica in *Inspector Morse*; Mary in *Low Level Panic*; Louise in *Mrs Hartley and the Growth Centre*; Cathy in *Oliver's Travels*; Sheila in *Olly's Prison*; Jess in *Oranges are Not the Only Fruit*; Gail Fleshly in *Pirates*; *Roadie*; Roz in *Sweet Nothing*; Sharon in *The Bill*; Millie in *The Dark Angel*; *The Insurance Man*; Mary in *The Vacillations of Poppy Carew*; *Two People*; *Wurzel Gummidge*; *Wycliffe*.
Films: *Beautiful People*; Tiffany in *Bodywork*; *Different for Girls*; Scarlet in *Four Weddings and a Funeral*; *If Only*; Julie in *Map of the Human Heart*; Norah in *The Revenger's Comedies*; Lila in *Shark Hunt*; Kate in *The*

Bearskin; Cindy in *The Footing*; *The Saint*; Winnie in *The Young Poisoner's Handbook*.
Address: c/o Peters, Fraser and Dunlop, Drury House, 34–43 Russell Street, London WC2B 5HA. Mother is actress Ann Beach; sister is actress Lisa Coleman. Hobbies: Riding, playing snooker.

COLEMAN, Desune
Desune Coleman. Actor (M). b. 1970.
TV: PC Louis in *Anna Lee*; Lenny Wallace in *EastEnders*.
Films: Don in *Boyfriends*; Danny in *Simple*.
Address: c/o Sandra Boyce Management, 1 Kingsway Parade, Albion Road, Stoke London N16 0TA.

COLEMAN, Jonathan
Jonathan Coleman. Actor (M)/Presenter.
b. London, 29 February 1956.
TV: *Bonkers* (1997); *Exclusive* (1997); *Hit for Six* (1999); *Home and Away*; *Mixing It* (1990); *Power Station* (1990).
Films: *Young Einstein*.
Address: c/o John Noel Management, 10a Belmont Street, London NW1 8HH. m. Margot Fitzpatrick; 1 d. Emily; 1 s. Oscar.

COLEMAN, Lisa
Lisa Coleman. Actor (F). b. London, 10 July 1970.
TV: Jude in *Casualty*; *Crown Court* (1976); *The Scoop* (1997); *The Scoop* (1999); *Sarah* May in *Undercover Heart* (1998).
Films: *Loophole*.
Address: c/o Conway Van Gelder, 18–21 Jermyn Street, London SW1Y 6HP. Mother is actress Ann Beach; sister is actress Charlotte Coleman. Hobbies: Music.

COLL, Christopher
Christopher Coll. Actor (M).
b. Liverpool, 28 January 1938.
TV: Watts in *After the Party*; Mr Parkinson in *Billy's Blues*; *Clayhanger*; Victor Pendlebury in *Coronation Street*; *Follyfoot*; *Grange Hill*; *Jack Be Nimble*; Dad in *Mighty Mum and the Petnappers*; Morley in *Minder*; *Missing Time*; *Orde Wingate*; Adams in *Sink or Swim*; Grp. Capt. Price in *Skylark*; Tom in *Slinger's Day*; *Soft Target*; Det. Chief. Insp. Forrest in *Strangers*; *Suez*; Mr Refers in *The Bill*; *The Cuckoo Waltz*; *The Fatal Spring*; *The Flaxton Boys*; *The Gentle Assassin*; *The Naked Civil Servant*; *To Encourage the Others*; Jacko in *United*; Victorian Scandals; Det. Cons. Kane in *Z-Cars*.
Films: Mr Denby in *Goody Two Shoes*; Lawrence in *Harry*; Watson in *The Jigsaw Man*; Flags in *Whoops Apocalypse*.

Address: c/o Hilda Physick Agency, 78 Temple Sheen Road, London SW14 7RR. m. Elizabeth Weaver; 2 d. Sarah, Harriet; 1 s. Daniel.

COLLINS, Joan
Joan Hennetta. Actor (F)/Writer. b. 23 May 1933.
TV: *Drive Hard, Drive Fast*; Alexis Carrington Colby in *Dynasty*; *Hansel and Gretel*; *Hart to Hart*; *Her Life as a Man*; *Jealousy and Hate*; *Making of a Male Model*; Katrina in *Monte Carlo*; *Pacific Pallisades*; *Paper Dolls* (1982); *Sins* (1986); *So Graham Norton* (1999); Risa's Mother in *Sweet Deception*; *The Cartier Affair*; *The Nanny*; *The Wild Woman of Chastity Gulch*.
Films: Fay in *Alfie Darling*; *Annie: A Royal Adventure*; *Can Hieronymus Merkin Ever Forget Mercy Humppe and Find True Happiness?*; Rene Collins in *Cosh Boy*; Sarah Mondeville in *Dark Places*; *Decadence*; *Decameron Nights*; *Esther and the King*; *Fear in the Night*; Evelyn in *Girl in a Red Velvet Swing*; *Growing Pains*; Norma in *I Believe in You*; Margeretta Davey in *In the Bleak Midwinter*; Jocelyn in *Island in the Sun*; *Joseph and the Amazing Technicolor Dreamcoat*; *La Congiuntura*; Beauty show contestant in *Lady Godiva Rides Again*; Princess Nellifer in *Land of the Pharaohs*; *Nutcracker*; Sadie in *Our Girl Friday*; *Quest for Love*; *Rally Round the Flag Boys*; *Revenge*; *Sea Wife*; Melanie in *Seven Thieves*; Tina in *Stopover Tokyo*; *Subterfuge*; *Sunburn*; Joanne Clayton in *Tales From The Crypt*; *Tales that Witness Madness*; Agnes Locelle in *The Big Sleep*; Fontaine Khaled in *The Bitch*; Josefa Velarde in *The Bravados*; *The Clandestine Marriage*; *The Executioner*; Mary in *The Good Die Young*; Crystal in *The Opposite Sex*; Diana in *The Road to Hong Kong*; Frankie in *The Square Ring*; Fontaine Khaled in *The Stud*; *The Virgin Queen*; Alice in *The Wayward Bus*; Marina in *The Woman's Angle*; *Three in the Cellar*; Stella in *Turn the Key Softly*; Pearl Slaghoope in *The Flintstones in Viva Rock Vegas*; Joanie Valens in *Warning Shot*; *Zero to Sixty*.
Address: c/o Stella Wilson, 130 Calabria Road London N5 1HT. 1 sister Jackie Collins (novelist); m. 1. Maxwell Reed (dis); m. 2 Anthony Newley (dis); 1 d. Tara Cynara; 1 s. Sacha; m. 3 Ron Kass (dis); 1 d. Katyana; m. 4 Peter Holm (dis).

COLLINS, John D.
John D. Collins. Actor (M).
b. London, 2 December 1942.
TV: Medical Officer in *Ain't Misbehavin'* (1996); *'Allo 'Allo*; Mr Stephens in *Birds of a Feather* (1996); *The Brittas Empire* (1991); Douglas McDonnel in *Chucklevision* (1995); Dr Weston in *Family Affairs* (1999); Mr Curtain in *Harry's Mad* (1995); *Jackanory Playhouse*

(1983); *Lovejoy* (1990); Toastmaster in *Mosley* (1997); Jack in *Oh, Doctor Beeching!* (1995); *On the Up* (1992); *Only Fools and Horses* (1979); Dave Cornish in *Peak Practice* (1995); *Secret Army* (1984); *Shine on Harvey Moon* (1980); *Teatime with Tiffin* (1990); Travel Agent in *That's English* (1994); News Reader in *That's English* (1995); Clerk of the Court in *Trial and Retribution* (1998, 1999); Armstrong in *Wycliffe* (1997); *Yes, Minister* (1981); *You Rang, M'Lord*.
Address: c/o McIntosh Rae Management, Thornton House, Thornton Road, London SW19 4NG.

COLLINS, Lewis
Lewis Collins. Actor (M).
b. Bidston Birkenhead, 27 May 1946.
TV: *Cluedo; Confessions; Jack the Ripper; Night on the Town; The Cilla Black Show; Must Wear Tights; The Cuckoo Waltz;* Brian Conley's dad in *The Grimleys; The New Avengers;* Bodie in *The Professionals; The Show*.
Films: *Code Name Wildgeese; Commando – Leopard; The Commander; Who Dares Wins*.
Music: In the 1960s, Lewis was in the rock group, The Mojos.
Address: c/o SJ Management Limited, 15 Maiden Lane, London WC2E 7NA. m. Michelle Larrett; 3 s.

COLLINS, Michelle
Michelle Collins. Actor (F).
b. Hackney, London, 28 May 1963.
TV: Sarah in *Bergerac; Daylight Robbery;* Cindy Beale in *EastEnders;* Jane in *Gems;* Daisy in *Lucky Sunil; The Manageress; Marjorie and Men;* Helen in *Morgan's Boy;* Jackie in *Personal Services;* Susie in *Real Women;* Sophie in *Running Wild; Sunburn; Uprising*.
Films: Emma in *Empire State*.
Address: c/o ICM, Oxford House, 76 Oxford Street, London W1N 0AX. 1 d. Miai.

COLLINS, Pauline
Pauline Collins. Actor (F). b. 3 September 1940.
TV: *Flowers of the Forest; Knockback; The Ambassador; The Black Tower; Thomas and Sarah; Upstairs Downstairs*.
Films: *City of Joy; My Mother's Courage; Paradise Road;* Shirley Valentine in *Shirley Valentine;. Emergency – Ward 10;* Dawn in *The Liver Birds; Country Matters;* Sarah in *Upstairs, Downstairs; No Honestly;* Sarah in *Thomas and Sarah; Tales of the Unexpected; Knockback; Tropical Moon over Dorking; The Black Tower;* Harriet Boult in *Forever Green; Flowers of the Forest; The Ambassador.*.
Address: c/o Whitehall Artists, 125 Gloucester Road,

London SW7 4TE. m. John Alderton; 2 d. Louise (from previous relationship), Catherine; 2 s. Nicholas, Richard.

COLOMBO, Tatyana
Tatyana Colombo. Actor (F). b. 26 November.
TV: Marie-Louise in *After Henry;* Lyn in *Call Me Mister;* Francios in *Capital City;* Maria in *Clubland;* Michelle in *French Fields;* Valentina in *Hale and Pace;* Emma Harkness in *Howard's Way;* Caroline in *I Love Keith Allen;* Piera Conti in *Inspector Morse;* Roz in *Me and My Girl;* Isabella in *Talking in Whispers;* Leni in *Ten Great Writers – Kafka;* Alex in *The Good Guys;* Luciana Fontana in *The Manageress;* Donna Meliflua in *The Pyrates*.
Address: c/o Clive Corner Associates, 73 Gloucester Road, Hampton, Middlesex TW12 2UQ. Hobbies: horse riding, swimming.

COLQUHOUN, Christopher
Christopher Colquhoun. Actor (M).
TV: Sean in *Band of Gold;* Maddy Costello in *Casualty;* Luke Peters in *London Bridge;* McDuff in *Shakespeare Shorts;* Andy in *Silent Witness;* Kevin Mitchell in *The Bill*.
Address: c/o Marina Martin Associates, 12–13 Poland Street, London W1V 3DE.

COLTRANE, Robbie
Anthony McMillan. Actor (M). b. Glasgow, 1950.
TV: *The House with the Green Shutter; Metal Mickey; Tom, Dick and Harriet; Keep it in the Family; Reid the Sheep Stealer; Scotch Myths; Luna; 81 Take 2; Jasper Carrott Live; The Lenny Henry Show; Th Young Ones; Saturday Night Live; Girls on Top; Walking to New Orleans; At Last It's Hogmanay; Hooray, It's Holyrood; The Emma Thompson Show; Alfresco; Laugh, I Nearly Paid My Licence Fee; The Comic Strip Presents; Bullshitters; The Miner's Strike; GLC & South Atlantic Raiders; The Secret Ingredient; Jealousy; The Red Nose of Courage; Blackadder; Midnight Breaks; The Robbie Coltrane Special; Mistero Buffo; Tutti Frutti; alive and Kicking; The Bogie Man; Coltrane in a Cadillac; A Tour of the Western Isles; Coltrane's Plane and Automobiles;* Tweedledum in *Alice in Wonderland; Cracker; Hong Kong Cracker; The Ebb Tide*.
Films: *Young Mental Health; Subway Riders; Balham Gateway to the South; Britannia Hospital; Scrubbers; Krull; ghost Dance; Chinese Boxes; The Supergrass; Defense of the Realm; Revolution; Caravaggio; Absolute Beginners; Mona Lisa; Eat the Rich; The Fruit Machine; Slipstream; Bert Rigby, You're a Fool; Danny, Champiojn of the World; Let it Ride; Henry V; Nuns on the Run;*

Perfectly Normal; the Pope Must Die; Triple Bogey on a Five Par Hole; Oh What a Night; The Adventures of Huckleberry Finn; Goldeneye; Buddy; Montana; Frogs for Snakes; Message in a Bottle; The World is Not Enough.
Address: c/o CDA, 19 Sydney Mews, London SW3 6HL. Partner Rhona Gemmil (sculptor); 1 s. Spencer.

COMAN, Gilly

Gilly Coman. Actor (F).
TV: Julia Ryan in *A Touch of Frost;* Sandra in *And Mum Came Too;* Susannah in *Angels in the Annexe;* Dixie's Clerk in *Boys from the Blackstuff;* Aveline in *Bread;* Denise in *Brookside; Casualty;* Carol in *Children's Ward;* Miss Ketteridge in *Chintz;* Sugar La Marr in *Coronation Street;* Linda in *Emmerdale;* Irene Kilride in *Gathering Seed;* Peggy in *Give Us a Break;* Holly Travers in *Inspector Morse;* Robin in *Long Term Memory;* Esther in *Nature Boy;* Granville's Girlfriend in *Open All Hours;* Marie in *Scully; Stay Lucky; Stepping Up* (lead); Bin Bag in *T-Bag;* Elaine in *The Brick is Beautiful;* Susan in *The Family Rules;* Marigold Lockton in *The Man who Made Husbands Jealous;* Kathy in *The Practice;* Linda in *The Snatch; The Victoria Wood Show;* Linda in *Winter Break.*
Films: Dorothy in *A Private Function;* Miss Pluckley in *Higher Mortals;* Ellie Molly in *Priest;* Joy in *Six of Hearts.*
Address: c/o Joy Jameson Ltd, 2.19 The Plaza, 535 Kings Road, London SW10 0SZ.

COMYN, Alison

Alison Comyn. Presenter.
TV: *Children in Need; Holiday; Live TV; Newsline; Newsline Extra; Saints and Scholars; Summer Holiday.*
Address: c/o David Anthony Promotions, PO Box 286, Warrington, Cheshire WA2 6GA.

CONLEY, Brian

Brian Conley. Actor (M)/Comedian.
b. London, 7 August 1961.
TV: *The Brian Conley Show; Brian Conley – Alive and Dangerous; Brian Conley's Crazy Christmas; The Grimleys;* Kenny Conway in *Time After Time.*
Address: c/o William Morris Agency (UK) Ltd, 1 Stratton Street, London W1X 6HB.

CONLEY, Rosemary

Rosemary Conley. Fitness instructor/Presenter.
b. 19 December 1946.
TV: *This Morning.*
Address: c/o J. Gurnett Personal Management Ltd, 2 New Kings Road, London SW6 4SA. m. Mike Rimmington. 1 d. Dawn. Hobbies: Keep fit, religion.

CONNERY, Jason

Jason Connery. Actor (M).
b. London, 11 January 1963.
TV: James Dunham in *Casualty; Doctor Who; Mountain of Diamonds;* Robin Hood in *Robin of Sherwood; Serenade for Dead Lovers;* Flt. Lt. Jeff Thomas in *The Famous Five;* *The Other Side of Paradise* (lead); *The Train.*
Films: John Fox in *An Urban Ghost Story; Bullet to Beijing* (lead); *Bye Bye Baby; Casablanca Express; La Venexiana; Little Nemo; Lords of Discipline;* Macbeth in *Macbeth;* Merlin in *Merlin; Midnight in St. Petersburg* (lead); *Puss In Boots;* Calvin Andrews in *Shanghai Noon; Sheltering Desert; Spymaker; Tank Malling; The Boy Who Had Everything; The First Olympics; The Successor; Winner Takes All.*
Address: c/o CAM London, 19 Denmark Street, London WC2H 8NA. m. Mia Sara; father Sean Connery. Hobbies: Sports.

CONNOLLY, Billy

Billy Connolly. Actor (M)/Comedian.
b. Anderston, Glasgow, 24 November 1942.
TV: *30 Years of Billy Connolly* (1998); *An Audience with Billy Connolly* (1985); Billy MacGregor in *Billy* (1992); *Billy Connolly's World Tour of Australia* (1996); Des in *Blue Money* (1982); Findlay Crawford in *Columbo: Murder With Too Many Notes* (1999); Deacon Brodie in *Deacon Brodie* (1997); Billy MacGregor in *Head of the Class;* Tick Tack, the Bookmaker in *Minder* (1979); William Pynchon in *Pearl* (1996); Campbell in *Veronica's Closet* (1997).
Films: Blakey in *Absolution; Beautiful Joe;* Mr Brown in *Boondock Saints;* Hawkeye McGillicuddy in *Bullshot;* Auction MC in *Indecent Proposal;* Alibius in *Middleton's Changeling;* John Brown in *Mrs Brown;* Billy Bones in *Muppet Treasure Island;* P.C. in *Paws;* Voice of Ben in *Pocahontas;* Hughie in *Still Crazy;* Frankie in *The Big Man;* Nickie Dryden in *The Debt Collector;* Sparks in *The Impostors;* Caddie in *The Return of the Musketeers; The Secret Policeman's Other Ball; To the North of Katmandu;* Delgado in *Waterloo.*
Address: c/o Julian Belfrage Associates, 46 Albemarle Street, London W1X 4PP. m. Pamela Stephenson. Hobbies: Banjo.

CONTI, Tom

Tom Conti. Actor (M).
b. Paisley, Glasgow, 22 November 1941.
TV: *Adam Smith; Blade on a Feather; Churchill's People; Early Struggles; Fatal Dosage; Friends; Madame Bovary; Mother of Men; Play for Today; The Beate Klarsfeld Story; The Beaux Stratagem; The Glittering Prizes; The Norman*

Conquests; The Rather Reassuring Programme; The Wright Verdicts; Thirty Minute Theatre: Castro; Treats.
Films: *American Dreamer; Beyond Therapy; Crush Depth; Don't Go Breaking My Heart; Eclipse; Flame; Full Circle; Heavenly Pursuits; Merry Christmas, Mr Lawrence; Miracles; Out of Control; Reuben, Reuben; Saving Grace; Shirley Valentine; Someone Else's America; Something To Believe In; That Summer of White Roses; The Duellists; The Dumb Waiter; The Inheritance; The Life of Galileo; The Quick and The Dead; The Siege of Venice; The Wall; Two Brothers Running.*
Address: c/o Chatto & Linnit Ltd, 123a Kings Road, London SW3 4PL. m. Kara Wilson; 1 d. Nina.

CONVILLE, David
David Conville. Actor (M). b. 4 June 1929.
TV: *Bergerac; Call Me Mister; Surgical Spirit; The Good Doctor Bodkin Adams; The Small Problem; Tumbledown; Yes, Prime Minister.*
Films: Headmaster in *Clockwise; Gran Jones; The Fourth Protocol.*
Address: c/o Bernard Hunter Associates, 13 Spencer Gardens, London SW14 7AH. m. Philippa Gail.

CONWELL, Nula
Nula Conwell. Actor (F). b. London, 24 May 1959.
TV: *Bad Blood; Dinner At the Sporting Club; The Eric Sykes Show; Eyes Going Out; Home Cooking; If Only; Magpie; Only a Game; Only Fools and Horses; Out; Playhouse: A Silly Little Habit; Roll Over Beethoven; Shoestring; Stars of the Roller State Disco; Telford's Change;* WDC Viv Martella in *The Bill; The Laughter Show; The Police; The Upper Hand; Vanishing Army; You in Mind.*
Films: *Fords on the Water;* Herself in *Love, Honour and Obey* (2000); *Red Saturday; The Elephant Man.*
Address: Scott Marshall, 44 Perryn Road, London W3 7NA. 1 s. Elliott; 1 d. Hannah. Hobbies: keep fit; walking; cooking.

COOGAN, Steve
Steve Coogan. Comedian/Actor (M).
b. Manchester 1965.
TV: *Coogan's Run; First Exposure;* Policeman in *Harry;* Alan Partridge in *Knowing Me, Knowing You, with Alan Partridge; Live From The London Palladium; London Underground; Paramount City;* Paul Calf in *Saturday Zoo; Spitting Image; Stand Up; Up Front;* Mole in *The Wind in the Willows; Wogan; Word In Your Era.*
Films: WWI soldier in *Indian in the Cupboard; Resurrected; The Fix; The Revenger's Comedies.*
Address: c/o ICM, Oxford House, 76 Oxford Street, London W1N 0AX.

COOK, Roger
Roger Cook. Presenter/Investigative reporter
b. New Zealand, 6 April 1943.
TV: *Nationwide; Newsnight; The Cook Report;* various.
Address: c/o The Roseman Organisation, Suite 9, The Power House, 70 Chiswick Road, London W4 1SY.

COOK, Sue
Sue Cook. Presenter.
b. Ruislip, Middlesex, 30 March 1949.
TV: *Breakfast Time; The Chelsea Flower Show; Children in Need; Collector's Lot; Crimewatch UK; Daytime Live; Great Ormond Street Hospital; Hampton Court Flower Show; Having a Baby; Holiday; Life; Nationwide; Omnibus at The Proms; Out of Court; Out of this World; Sunday Matters; Teacher of the Year Awards; The Children's Royal Variety Performance.*
Address: c/o Curtis Brown, Haymarket House, 28–29 Haymarket, London SW1Y 4SP. Partner Billy Macqueen; 1 d. Megan; 1 s. Charlie.

COOMBS, Pat
Pat Coombs. Actor (F). b. London, 27 August 1926.
TV: *3-2-1; Beggar My Neighbour; Blankety Blank; Davro's Sketchpad; Emu's Wide World; In Sickness and in Health; Jimmy Cricket's Joke Machine; Mr Majeka;* Pru in *Noel's House Party; Playbox; Ragdolly Anna; Roy's Raiders; The Dick Emery Show; The Lady is a Tramp; The World of Pam Ayres; Till Death Us Do Part; What's My Line?; Wogan; You're Only Young Twice.*
Films: *Oh You Are Awful!.*
Address: c/o Burnett Granger Associates, Prince of Wales Theatre, 31 Coventry Street, London W1V 8AS.

COOPER, Kimberley
Kimberley Cooper. Actor (F).
b. Sydney, Australia, 24 April 1980.
TV: Gypsy in *Home and Away.*
Address: Seven Network Ltd, Mabbs Lane, Epping, New South Wales 2121, Australia. Hobbies: Dancing, kickboxing, partying!

COOPER, Trevor
Trevor Cooper. Actor (M). b. London, 21 May 1953.
TV: Bert in *A Perfect State;* Big Bob in *Children's Ward;* Mr Turnball in *Dalziel and Pascoe;* Ron Foreman in *Days Like These;* Olly in *Duck Patrol;* Shrapnel in *Framed; Frank Stubbs Promotes;* Gurth in *Ivanhoe;* Wills in *Longitude;* Bear in *Mother In Love;* Cockburn in *Our Friends in the North;* Vernon in *Redemption;* William in *Sex 'n' Death;* Orvis in *Star Cops;* Gary the Builder in *Underground;* Morrisey in *Uprising.*
Films: *Century; Drowning by Numbers; Firm Warning;*

Moonlight; The Silent Touch; The Whistle Blower; Wuthering Heights.
Address: c/o PFD, Drury House, 34–43 Russell Street, London WC2B 5HA. Hobbies: Baseball, poker.

COPE, Kenneth
Kenneth Cope. Actor (M).
TV: *Goodnight Mrs Clinkscales; Minder; Bootle Saddles; The Levkas Man; Return of the Antelope; The Practice; Miss Marple – Sleeping Murder; Kings and Castles; Bergerac; City Lights; Casualty; Truckers; Hollywood Sports; Making News; Uncle Jack; Blood and Peaches; Lovejoy; Ark Angel; 99–1; Out of the Blue; Medics; Golden Collar; Respect; Goodnight Sweetheart; Last of the Summer Wine; A Touch of Frost; Kavanagh QC;* Jed Stone in *Coronation Street;* Marty Hopkirk in the original *Randall & Hopkirk (Deceased).*
Films: *Captives; The Desperados; Hammerhead; Yanks; Rent-a-Dick; George & Mildred; The Damned; The Criminal; Genghis Khan; Juggernaut; Carry on Matron; Carry on at Your Convenience.*
Address: c/o The Narrow Road Company, 21/22 Poland Street, London W1V 3DD.

COPELAND, Freya
Freya Copeland. Actor (F).
b. Stafford, 3 December 1969.
TV: Sgt. Angie Reynolds in *Emmerdale;* Sgt. Karen Mallett in *The Bill.*
Address: c/o Burnett Granger Associates, Prince Of Wales Theatre, 31 Coventry Street, London W1V 8AS. Hobbies: Reading and music. Partner Toby Walton.

COPLEY, Paul
Paul Copley. Actor (M).
b. Denby Dale, 25 November 1944.
TV: Tom in *A Brush with Mr Porter;* Charlie Hepplewhite in *A Pinch of Snuff; A Room for the Winter;* Daniel Brick in *After Julius;* Jim in *All the Saints;* Jesus in *All the World's a Stage;* Finnegan in *Arnhem – Story of an Escape;* Mal in *Big Deal;* Frederick Chambers in *Casualty;* Judas in *Chester Mystery Plays;* Fred in *A Christmas Carol;* Mr Long in *Clean Slate;* Pathologist in *Cracker;* Andy in *Cries from a Watchtower; Dangerous Journey; Dark Horses;* Ben Matthews in *Days of Hope;* Carpenter in *Death of a Princess;* Paul in *Destiny;* Mr Reed in *Ghost in the Water;* Samuel in *Glad Days; God's Story; Grange Hill;* James in *Growing Pains;* Mr Grucock in *Gruey Twoey;* Vernon in *Happy;* Thomas Thomas in *Harry;* Dick Radcliffe in *Heart of the Country;* Jeff in *Holby City;* Matthews in *Hornblower;* Arthur Steadwell in *Juliet Bravo;* Harold Coop in *Juliet Bravo;*

Cynical Sailor in *Landmarks;* George Palmer in *Minder;* Brian Wilson in *Mucking Out;* Paul in *No Charge;* Local Man in *Oedipus at Colonus;* Tony in *Our Geoff; Paradise Club;* Farmer in *Peak Practice;* Officer Jordan in *PQ 17;* Roy Maloney in *Queer As Folk;* Graham in *Rides II;* Ian Pollard in *Roughnecks;* Father in *Scene – Collision Course;* William Dane in *Silas Marner;* Chris Tillson in *Silent Witness;* Billy in *Sloggers;* Peter in *Some Enchanted Evening; Stay Lucky;* POW in *Tenko;* Gerry in *Testimony of a Child; The Bill;* Roy Pearson in *The Bird Fancier;* Lionel in *The Bright Side;* Father in *The Gathering Seed;* Peter Quinlan in *The Lakes;* Jamie in *The Mistress;* Finch in *The Secret Army; The Seven Deadly Sins;* Bill in *The Turkey Who Lives on a Hill;* Jerry in *This Life;* Briggs in *Thunder Rock;* Stable Lad in *Trainer; Travellers;* Ben Gunn in *Treasure Island;* Dave the Joiner in *Trinity Tales; Young Charlie Chaplin.*
Films: Private Wicks in *A Bridge Too Far;* Bakey in *Alfie Darling;* Jan Worth in *Doll's Eye;* Brian in *Driven;* Boatman in *Ends and Means;* Jack in *How's Business;* Mr Willis in *Jude;* Harry Smith in *The Remains of the Day;* Daggett in *War and Remembrance;* Private Storey in *Zulu Dawn.*
Address: c/o Kate Feast Management, 10 Primrose Hill Studios, Fitzroy Road, London NW1 8TR.

COPLEY, Peter
Peter Copley. Actor (M)/Presenter.
b. Bushey, Hertfordshire, 20 May 1915.
TV: Lord Montgomery in *A Bill Called William* (1997); Mr Garlic in *All, or Nothing at All* (1993); Mr Betts in *An Unwanted Woman* (1992); *Androcles and the Lion;* Abbott Heribert in *Cadfael* (1993); *Casualty* (various); *Churchill and the Generals; Far From The Madding Crowd* (1997); *Géricault; Grange Hill* (1992); Eric in *Jonathan Creek* (1997); Harold Richards in *Lovejoy* (1992); *Miss Marple:;* Colonel Kydd in *Moon and Son* (1991); *One Foot in the Grave;* Burgoyne in *Poirot* (1990); *The Prisoner of Zenda; The Bill* (various); Sam in *Where the Heart Is* (1998); Robinson in *Wives and Daughters* (1999); Venerable Bede in *Zig Zag* (1992).
Films: Sir Louis Maitland in *A Dangerous Man; Empire of the Sun;* Percy in *Second Best;* Mr Ferguson in *South by South East;* Preston Breed in *The Paper Man.*
Address: c/o St James's Personal Management Ltd, 19 Lodge Close, Stoke D'Abernon, Cobham, Surrey KT11 2SG. m. Margaret; 2 d. Frances, Emma; 1 s. Gideon.

CORBETT, Ronnie
Ronnie Corbett. Actor (M)/Comedian.
TV: *An Audience with…; The Ben Elton Show; Corbett's*

Follies; Frost on Sunday; No, That's Me Over Here; Small Talk; Sorry; The Frost Report; The Two Ronnies.
Films: Sea-lion Keeper in *Fierce Creatures.*
Address: c/o International Artistes Ltd, Mezzanine Floor, 235 Regent Street, London W1R 8AX. m. Anne Hart.

CORNES, Lee
Lee Cornes. Actor (M)/Comedian/Writer.
TV: Mr Hankin in *Grange Hill; Highly Sprung; Jack and Jeremy;* Dr Pete in *The Detectives; Jeff Green Live; Loved by You; The Young Ones; The Comic Strip; Doctor Who; The Lenny Henry Show; Saturday Night Live; Red Dwarf;* Graham in *Colin's Sandwich; Blackadder; Rab C Nesbitt; Set of Six; Mornin' Sarge; The Trials of Oz; A Load of Lovett; French and Saunders; Mud; Bottom; Number 73, Addams Family Tree; Up Our Street.*
Address: c/o L'Epine, Smith & Carney Associates, Suite 61/63 Kent House, 87 Regent Street, London W1R 7HF.

CORNWELL, Charlotte
Charlotte Cornwell. Actor (F).
TV: *A Masculine Ending; A Touch of Frost; Bognor; Capital City; Casualty;* Queen Elizabeth I in *Drake; Dressing for Breakfast; Early Struggles; Find Me; Heavy Revie; Love Hurts; Lovejoy;* Shelley Maze in *No Excuses; Only Children;* Anna in *Rock Follies;* Sarah Morris in *Shalom Shalaam; Shoestring; Something's Got To Give; The Governor; The House of Eliott; The Men's Room; The New Professionals;* Svetlana in *Three of a Kind; Where the Heart Is.*
Films: *The Russia House;* Aunt May in *The Krays;* Inspector Rabineau in *The Saint;* Miss Wilding in *White Hunter, Black Heart.*
Address: c/o Ken McReddie Ltd, 91 Regent Street, London W1R 7TB.

CORNWELL, Judy
Judy Cornwell. Actor (F).
b. London, 22 February 1940.
TV: *All the World's a Stage; Bergerac; Boon;* Rosie in *Cakes and Ale;* Miss Smith in *Call Me Daddy;* Miss Matty in *Cranford;* Mrs MacDipper in *December Rose; Doctor Who; Farrington of the F.O.;* Miss Brock in *Good Behaviour;* Miss Trant in *Good Companions; Infidelity took Place; Jane Eyre;* Daisy in *Keeping up Appearances;* Lady Gay Spanker in *London Assurance; Love Story;* Guste Daimchen in *Man of Straw;* May Cuttle in *Midsomer Murders;* Bessie in *The Mill on the Floss;* Miss Pegg in *Moody and Pegg;* Aunt Peggy in *Nice Town; No Decision;* Mrs Bliss in *Paying*

Guests; Poor Cherry; Relatively Speaking; Joyce in *Ruffian on the Stair; Rumpole; The Anniversary;* Brenda in *The Bill; The Chinese Prime Minister; The Cork Moustache;* Lucy in *The Fall of Lucy Hodges; The Feydeau Farces;* Wife in *The Guest;* Mrs Palmer in *The Life of William Palmer; The Rise and Fall of Kelvin Walker; Touch of the Tiny Hackets; Wind in the Tall Paper Chimney.*
Films: Rosie in *Brotherly Love;* Embassy Secretary in *Cry Freedom;* Peggotty in *David Copperfield;* Rosa in *Devil's Lieutenant;* Liz in *Every Home Should Have One;* Mother in *Mad Cows;* Nula in *Paddy;* Mrs Musgrove in *Persuasion;* Lady Electra in *Rocket to the Moon;* Mrs Claus in *Santa Claus: The Movie;* School Girl in *Two for the Road;* Clarissa in *Who Slew Auntie Roo?;* Nellie in *Wuthering Heights.*
Address: c/o Ken McReddie Ltd, 91 Regent Street, London W1R 7TB. m. John K. Parry; 1 s. Edward; grandmother Sarah Bonner (Music Hall singer). Hobbies: Philosophy, travel, history.

COSMO, James
James Cosmo. Actor (M).
TV: *Ain't Misbehavin';* Matt Devlin in *Bad Boys; Between the Lines; Brondo; Casualty; El C.I.D.; Heartbeat; HMS Thundercloud;* James Maxton in *The House of Eliott;* Major Ballantine in *The Inspector Alleyn Mysteries;* Cedric of Rotherwood in *Ivanhoe; Lost Empires; Medics; Midnight is a Place;* Reception Officer in *Pig Boy; Rab C. Nesbitt;* Tom in *Roughnecks; Saracen; Sharp End;* Jerry in *Sin Bin;* Drysdale in *Soldier, Soldier; Stay Lucky; The Sweeney; The Bill; The Castle; The House on the Hill; The Justice Game; The MacKenzie Affair; The Nightmare Man; The Tenth Kingdom;* John Menzies in *The Window Cleaner;* Brig. Mike Calvert in *Wingate; Winners and Losers.*
Films: Minister in *An Urban Ghost Story; Assault; The Battle of Britain;* Zorba in *Billy and Zorba;* Campbell in *Braveheart;* Mr Weston in *Emma; Golden Wedding; Highlander;* Tommy in *Honest;* Frank in *One More Kiss;* Donald Paterson in *Split Second; Stormy Monday;* McDonald in *Sunset Heights; The Fool; The Key;* Bill Bailey in *The Match;* Mr Renton in *Trainspotting; Treasure Island; The Virgin Soldiers; Young Winston.*
Address: c/o Marina Martin Associates, 12–13 Poland Street, London W1V 3DE.

COSTIGAN, George
George Costigan. Actor (M).
TV: *The Barchester Chronicles;* Ben in *The Beiderbecke Connection;* Ollie Sutton in *Bergerac;* Martin Gregory in *Casualty;* Schasser in *Chimera;* Arnie in *Connie;*

Tom Hannaway in *Fame is the Spur*; Steve in *Girls' Night*; Wallace in *Hetty Wainthropp Investigates*; Ron Garrett in *Inspector Morse*; *Kavanagh QC*; Phillip the Bastard in *King John*; Michael in *London's Burning*; Billy in *Minder*; *Safe*; Wilson Kemp in *Sherlock Holmes*; *Sin Bin*; Malcom Grindlay in *Slap*; Sgt. Jones in *Slip Up*; Terry in *Stolen*; Nolan O'Shaughnessy in *Under the Skin*.

Films: Father in *Monster Maker*; Bob in *Rita, Sue and Bob Too*; Dougie in *Shirley Valentine*; *The Sailor's Return*; *Widows*.

Address: c/o Hamilton Asper, 24 Hanway Street, London W1P 9DD.

COTTERILL, Chrissie

Chrissie Cotterill. Actor (F).
b. London, 19 July 1955.

TV: Di Smart in *A Terrible Coldness*; Trish in *Birds of a Feather*; *Boon*; *Bust*; Graham Young in *Crime Story*; Cynthia in *Crossroads*; June Smith in *EastEnders*; Linda Bowman in *Expert Witness*; *Fox*; Lynn in *Hewitt*; *Jo Brand – Through the Cakehole*; *Lindsay*; Annie in *Love Hurts*; Debbie in *May to December*; Wendy in *Minder*; Miss Farly in *Moll Flanders*; *Out of Sight*; Mona in *Prospects*; Babs in *Rides*; Roz Timson in *Rumpole of the Bailey*; Daphne in *Separate Tables*; *Shades of Darkness*; *The Bill*; *The Charmer*; *The Crezz*; *The Jump*; *The Lady*; *The One*; *The Professionals*; Shirley in *Too Late to Talk to Billy*; *Touching Evil*; *Valentine Park*.

Films: Jane in *Adventures of Caleb Williams*; Belle in *Billy the Kid and the Green Baize Vampire*; June Ord in *Honest*; Yvonne in *Look Like the Innocent*; Paula in *Nil By Mouth*; Annette in *Scrubbers*; *Smoke*; Mrs Ralt in *Underground*; Denise in *Weak at Denise*; Judy in *Yanks*.

Address: c/o Langford Associates, 17 Westfields Avenue, London SW13 0AT. m. 1 Edward Heron; 1 d. Jodie; m. 2 Robert Mooney;1 d. Katie. Hobbies: Pets, horse riding, swimming.

COTTLE, Matthew

Matthew Cottle. Actor (M).
b. Henley on Thames, 16 February 1967.

TV: Malcolm in *A Perfect State*; Laurence in *Comin' Atcha*; *Drop the Dead Donkey*; Martin Henson in *Game On*; Roy Osbourne in *Get Well Soon*; *Taking the Floor*.

Films: Dick Wilkins in *A Christmas Carol*; Stan Laurel in *Chaplin*.

Address: c/o PFD, Drury House, 34–43 Russell Street, London WC2B 5HA. m. Sarah; 1 d. Hannah Rebecca. Hobbies: Supporter of Arsenal FC, cinema.

COTTON, Oliver

Oliver Cotton. Actor (M). b. London, 20 June 1944.

TV: Stefan in *C.A.T.S. Eyes*; *David Copperfield*; *Fireworks*; Frank in *Heartbeat*; Frobel in *Lovejoy*; Declan in *All Quiet on the Preston Front*; *Redemption*; Chamberlain in *Rhodes*; *Robin of Sherwood*; *Room at the Bottom*; *Sharpe's Battle*; Cesare Borgia in *The Borgias*; *The Camomile Lawn*; *The Intruder*; *The Party*; *West Beach*; *Wokenwell*.

Films: Hrothgar in *Beowulf*; *Christopher Columbus: The Discovery*; *Eleni*; *Firefox*; *Here We Go Round The Mulberry Bush*; *Hiding Out*; *Let Me Live*; *Oliver Twist*; *Singing For Stalin*; *Son of the Pink Panther*; *The Day Christ Died*; Lusano in *The Innocent Sleep*; George Elliott in *The Opium War*; *The Sicilian*.

Address: c/o William Morris Agency (UK) Ltd, 1 Stratton Street, London W1X 6HB.

COULSON, Lindsey

Lindsey Coulson. Actor (F). b. London 1960.

TV: Lindsey in *A Bear Behind*; Carol Jackson in *EastEnders*; Storyteller in *Harum Scarum*; Cathy Hardy in *Out of Hours*; Mrs Simms in *The Bill*; Judy in *Think About Science*.

Address: c/o CAM London, 19 Denmark Street, London WC2H 8NA.

COUNSELL, Elizabeth

Elizabeth Counsell. Actor (F).
b. Manchester, 7 June 1942.

TV: *Bless This House*; Ivy in *Blue Heaven*; *Boon*; Veronica in *Brush Strokes*; *C.A.T.S. Eyes*; *Dear Lavinia*; Anthea in *Executive Stress*; *Fame is the Spur*; *Geh Kinder Geh*; *Lytton's Diary*; Jackie in *Nelson's Column*; *Partners*; *The Gentle Touch*; *The Many Wives of Patrick*; *The Moving Finger*; *The Return of W.C. Fields*; *The Woman He Loved*.

Films: *Claudia's Story*; *If Tomorrow Comes*.

Address: c/o ICM, Oxford House, 76 Oxford Street, London W1N 0AX.

COURTENAY, Tom

Tom Courtenay. Actor (M).
b. Hull, Yorkshire, 25 February 1937.

TV: *A Rather English Marriage*; *Absent Friends*; *Chekhov in Yalta*; Felix Crawley in *Kavanagh QC*; *Me and the Girls*; Quilp in *The Old Curiosity Shop*; *The Young Indiana Jones Chronicles*.

Films: *A Dandy in Aspic*; *Billy Liar*; *Catch Me a Spy*; *Doctor Zhivago*; *Happy New Year*; *King and Country*; *King Rat*; *Let Him Have It*; *One Day in the Life of Ivan Denisovich*; *Operation Rainbow*; *Otley*; *Private Potter*; *The Boy From Mercury*; *The Day the Fish Came Out*;

The Dresser; The Last Butterfly; The Loneliness of the Long Distance Runner; The Night of the Generals; What Ever Happened to Harold Smith?
Address: c/o Jonathan Altaras Associates, 13 Shorts Gardens, London WC2H 9AT.

COWPER, Nicola
Nicola Cowper. Actor (F).
b. London, 21 December 1967.
TV: *The Burston Rebellion; Casualty; Crimewatch File;* D.S. Helen Diamond in *Dangerfield; Devices and Desires;* Gina (Cindy's sister) in *EastEnders; Home Video; Tears Before Bedtime; The Bill;* Edith West in *The Grand; The Practice; Winter Flight; Inspector Morse; Minder; Pig Boy; Rides; Sea Urchin; Streetwise; Swalk.*
Films: *Dreamchild; Journey to the Centre of the Earth; Lionheart; Underworld.*
Address: c/o Associated International Management, 5 Denmark Street, London WC2H 8LP.

COX, Brian
Brian Cox. Actor (M). b. 1 June 1946.
TV: *Alas Smith and Jones; Bach; Bothwell; Changeling Master of Ballantrae; Churchill's People; Crown Court;* William Wallace in *Dalhouse's Luck; Family Brood;* Aneurin Bevan in *Food for Ravens; Grushko; Home Cooking; Inspector Morse; Jemima Shore;* Lord Morton in *Longitude; The Lost Languages of the Cranes; Minder;* Goering in *Nuremberg; Perfect Scoundrels; Picasso; Pigboy; Rat in the Skull; Red Dwarf; Red Fox; Sean's Show; Secret Weapon; Shadow of the Sun; Sharpe's Rifles; Shoot for the Sun; Six Characters in Search of an Author; The Big Battalions; The Cloning of Joanna May;* Martin Smith in *The Cup; The Devil's Crown; The Fourth Floor; The House on the Hill; The Negotiator; Thérèse Raquin; Van Der Valk;* King Arthur in *Witness Against Hitler.*
Films: *Braveheart; Chain Reaction; Complicity; Desperate Measures; Florence Nightingale; Hidden Agenda; Iron Will; Kiss the Girls; Mad About Mambo; Manhunter; Pope John; Prince of Jutland; Rob Roy; Rushmore; The Boxer; The Corruptor; The Glimmer Man; The Long Kiss Goodnight; The Minus Man.*
Address: c/o Conway Van Gelder, 18–21 Jermyn Street, London SW1Y 6HP. Hobbies: Keep fit.

COX, Claire
Claire Cox. Actor (F).
b. Peterborough 19 December 1975.
TV: *Always and Everyone; Blue Murder; Every Woman Knows a Secret; The Choir; The Last Salute.*
Films: *Shooting Fish; The Leading Man.*
Address: c/o PFD, Drury House, 34–43 Russell Street, London WC2B 5HA. Hobbies: Singing, reading, cinema, dancing.

COX, Courteney
Courteney Cox Arquette. Actor (F).
b. Birmingham, Alabama, USA, 15 June 1964.
TV: Bunny in *As the World Turns* (1984*); Battling for Baby* (1992); Gwen in *Curiosity Kills* (1990); *Dream On* (1992); Lauren Miller in *Family Ties;* Monica in *Friends; I'll Be Home for Christmas* (1988); Hana Wyshocki in *If It's Tuesday, It Still Must be Belgium* (1987); Gloria Dinallo in *Misfits of Science* (1985); Carol Bannister in *Murder, She Wrote (1984);* Jacquie Kimberly in *Roxanne* (1989); Meryl in *Seinfeld* (1994); Emmy O'Connor in *Sketch Artist II: Hands that See* (1995); Gabrielle Easdon in *The Trouble with Larry* (1993); Freddy in *Till We Meet Again* (1989).
Films: Melissa Robinson in *Ace Ventura: Pet Detective;* Lisa Roberts in *Blue Desert;* Sara in *Cocoon: The Return;* Rachel Luce in *Commandments;* Tarah in *Down Twisted;* Julie Winston in *Masters of the Universe;* Jewel Jagger in *Mr Destiny;* Gale Weathers in *Scream;* Gale Weathers in *Scream 2;* Gale Weathers in *Scream 3;* Kathleen in *Shaking the Tree;* Carrie Davenport in *The Opposite Sex (And How to Live With Them);* Karina in *The Runner; The Shrink is In.*
Address: c/o Creative Artists Agency, 9830 Wilshire Boulevard, Beverly Hills, California 90212, USA. m. actor David Arquette; Stuart Copeland of The Police is Courtney's step cousin. Hobbies: Buying and renovating houses, exercising, yoga, reading.

COX, Jane
Jane Cox. Actor (F).
TV: Diana White in *Bulman;* Lisa Dingle in *Emmerdale;* Mrs Berne in *Flip.;* Mrs Roberts in *Radio;* Kitty Harrison in *The Monocled Mutineer.*
Address: c/o Evans & Reiss, 100 Fawe Park Road, London SW15 2EA.

COX, Laura
Laura Cox. Actor (F)/Presenter.
b. London, 12 October 1948.
TV: *Albion Market;* Ruth Simmons in *Back Up; Brookside; Casualty; Coronation Street; Disco;* Brenda Savage in *Heartbeat; London's Burning; Maigret; One Foot in the Grave; Silent Witness; The Asylum Wars; The Bill; The Blind Date; The Cater Street Hangman.*
Films: *Click; I'm Not Like That; Little Dorrit; The Fool;* Ivy Smith in *The Krays; The Visitors; The Turn of the Screw.*
Address: c/o Howard Cooke Associates, 19 Coulson Street, London SW3 3NA. Hobbies: Painting, drawing, singing, cats, cooking, dog walking.

COY, Jonathan

Jonathan Coy. Actor (M)
b. Hammersmith, London, 24 April 1953.
TV: Richard Taylor in *Grafters*; Cloudisley Shovell in *Longitude*; Chatsworth in *The Secret Adventures of Jules Verne*.
Address: c/o PFD, Drury House, 34–43 Russell Street, London WC2B 5HA. m. Emma Amos; 3 d. Charlotte, Jolyon, Esme. Hobbies: cricket, football, reading, wine.

COYLE, Brendan

Brendan Coyle. Actor (M).   .
TV: Liam Flaherty in *Silent Witness*; Gerry in *Soft Sand Blue Sea*; Slattery in *The Full Wax*; Manuel Mendoza in *The Glass Virgin*; Bob Tate in *Thief Takers*.
Films: Miles Butler in *Ailsa*; Francie in *I Could Read the Sky*; Steve Hadden in *Last Bus Home*; Frank in *The Cull*; UVF Leader in *The General*; Leading Seaman in *Tomorrow Never Dies*.
Address: William Morris Agency (UK) Ltd, 1 Stratton Street, London W1X 6HB.

CRAIG, Thomas

Thomas Craig. Actor (M).
b. Sheffield, 4 December 1962.
TV: Gordon Berry in *Madson* (1995); Jacko Barton in *Soldier, Soldier* (1997); Simon Goddard in *Where the Heart Is*.
Address: c/o Shepherd & Ford, 13 Radnor Walk London SW3 4BP.

CRAIG, Wendy

Wendy Craig. Actor (F).
b. County Durham, 20 June 1934.
TV: *The Brighton Belles*; *Butterflies*; *Candida*; *Mother Makes Three, Mother Makes Five*; *Nanny*; *Not in Front of the Children*; *Wings of a Dove*.
Address: c/o Waring & McKenna, Lauderdale House, 11 Gower Street, London WC1E 2HB.

CRANHAM, Kenneth

Kenneth Cranham. Actor (M).
b. Dunfermline, Fife, 12 December 1944.
TV: Giovanni in *'Tis Pity She's a Whore*; Riggie in *A Little Bit of Lippy*; Eric Palmer in *A Sort of Innocence*; Gascoyne in *Bergerac*; Aiden in *Boon*; Mason in *Butterflies Don't Count*; *Canterbury Tales*; James Lawrence in *Casualty*; Henessey in *Chimera*; Salt in *Danger UXB*; *Donkey's Years*; Knee Cap in *Dunrulin'*; Mercer in *El C.I.D.*; Insp. Trussler in *Get Well Soon*; Tony in *Get Away*; Charlie Wallace in *Heartbeat*; Cedric Downes in *Inspector Morse*; Brosch in *Just*

Another Secret; Roy Lawrence in *Kavanagh QC*; Soldier in *La Ronde*; Lord Darlington in *Lady Windermere's Fan*; Litvak in *Lovejoy*; Teddy in *Master of the Marionettes*; Walter in *Minder*; Detective in *Murder Most Horrid*; Peter in *Normal Services*; Pastor Finch in *Oranges are Not the Only Fruit*; Silas Wegg in *Our Mutual Friend*; Lenin in *Reilly, Ace of Spies*; Douglas in *A Royal Celebration*; Mart Goodman in *Rules of Engagement*; Harvey Moon in *Shine On Harvey Moon*; *Sling Your Hook*; Col. Braun in *Tecs – A Question of Chemistry*; Nick in *The Bell*; Stanley in *The Birthday Party*; Superintendent Cherry in *The Black and Blue Lamp*; Aston in *The Caretaker*; George in *The Change*; Chauffeur in *The Chauffeur and The Lady*; Kay in *The Contractor*; Gus in *The Dumb Waiter*; Gratiano in *The Merchant of Venice*; Michael Mansfield in *The Murder of Stephen Lawrence*; Joe in *The Party*; *The Sin Bin*; *The Sound of Guns*; Rev. Millward in *The Tenant of Wildfell Hall*; Dick Naughton in *The Vision Thing*; Camille in *Thérèse Raquin*; Boutsen in *Van Der Valk*; Schmidt in *The Young Indiana Jones Chronicles*.
Films: *Amelia and the King of Plants*; Paulo in *Brother Sun, Sister Moon*; Joe in *Chocolate*; Insp. Brand in *Dead Man's Folly*; Tommy in *Gangster No. 1*; Calvin in *Heart of the High Country*; Channard in *Hellraiser II: Hellbound*; Robert Flaherty in *In The West*; Wicked Squire in *Joseph Andrews*; Noah Claypole in *Oliver*; Brig. Ferguson in *On Dangerous Ground*; Sebastian in *Prospero's Books*; Vice Chancellor Sugar in *Stealing Heaven*; Mat McGuire in *The Boxer*; Joe in *The Clot*; Len in *The Last Yellow*; Frank in *Under Suspicion*; George in *Women Talking Dirty*.
Address: c/o Markham & Froggatt Ltd, 4 Windmill Street, London W1P 1HF. m. 1 Diana Quick (dis); m. 2 Fiona Victory.

CRANITCH, Lorcan

Lorcan Cranitch. Actor (M). b. 30 December 1959.
TV: Sean Dillon in *Ballykissangel*; Prof. Fielder in *Bliss in Memoriam*; Stephen in *Close Relations*; Beck in *Cracker*; Dan in *Dah Dit Dah*; George Smith in *Deacon Brodie*; Leo Doyle in *Life After Life*; Macduff in *Macbeth*; Tim Healy in *Parnell*; *The Bill*; *The Family*; Larry Duigan in *The Heart Surgeon*; Mr Scott in *Venus de Milo Instead*; Father Tom in *You, Me and Marley*.
Films: Danny Bradley in *Dancing at Lughnasa*; Richard in *Empire State*; Chernov in *Final Warning*; Luke in *Food of Love*; Billy in *Night Train*; Francie in *The Magic Toyshop*; Ryan in *The Playboys*; Tony in *Titanic Town*.
Address: c/o Sally Hope Associates, 108 Leonard Street, London EC2A 4XS.

CRAVEN, John

John Craven. Presenter. b. Leeds, 16 August.

TV: *Animal Sanctuary; Country File; Craven's Collectables; John Craven's Newsround; National Lottery Live; Saturday Superstore; Search; The MultiColoured Swap Shop.*

Address: c/o Unique Artistes, Avon House, Kensington Village, London W14 8TS.

CRAWFORD, Michael

Michael Patrick Smith. Actor (M)/Singer.
b. Salisbury, Wiltshire, 19 January 1942.

TV: *Barnum!; Billy Bunter; Chalk and Cheese;* Frank Spencer in *Some Mothers Do 'Ave 'Em.*

Films: *A French Mistress; A Funny Thing Happened on the Way to the Forum; Alice's Adventures in Wonderland; Blow Your Own Trumpet; Condorman; Hello, Dolly!; Hello-Goodbye; How I Won the War; Once Upon a Forest; Soapbox Derby; The Adventures of Sir Francis Drake; The Games; The Jokers; The Knack, and How to Get It; The War Lover; Two Left Feet; Two Living, One Dead.*

Address: c/o Knight Ayton Management, 10 Argyll Street, London W1V 1AB. 2 d. Emma, Lucy.

CREED-MILES, Charlie

Charlie Creed-Miles. Actor (M).   .

TV: Simon Knight in *15: The Life and Death of Philip Knight; A Small Dance; A Touch of Frost; Between the Lines; Casualty;* Carl in *Drop the Dead Donkey;* Jools in *Faith in the Future; Growing Pains; Listen to Me; London's Burning;* Danny in *Loved Up;* Danny McColl in *Press Gang; Sam Saturday; Shrinks; Stanley and the Women; The Bill; The Chief;* Jake in *The Roughest Way;* Al in *The Upper Hand; Trust Me;* Ivor in *Words of Love; Youth Language Programme.*

Films: *Glastonbury: The Movie; Judge Dredd; Let Him Have It; London Kills Me;* Billy in *Nil By Mouth; Skullduggery;* Greg in *Supergrass;* David in *The Fifth Element;* Kenny in *The Last Yellow;* David in *The Punk and the Princess;* Berridge in *The Young Poisoner's Handbook;* Stanley Jardine in *Woundings.*

Address: c/o William Morris Agency (UK) Ltd, 1 Stratton Street, Mayfair, London W1X 6HB.

CRIBBINS, Bernard

Bernard Cribbins. Actor (M).
b. Oldham, Lancashire, 29 December 1928.

TV: Uncle Henry in *Dalziel and Pascoe; Dangerous Davis – The Last Detective; High and Dry; Langley Bottom; The Shillingbury Miracle; The Shillingbury Tinker; Tonight at 8.30; When We Are Married.*

Films: *Carry On Columbus; Carry On Jack; Crooks in*

Cloisters; Mr Perks in *The Railway Children; The Water Babies; The Wrong Arm of the Law; Two Way Stretch.*

Music: *Folksong; Hole in the Ground; Right Said Fred.*

Address: c/o Gavin Barker Associates Ltd, 45 South Molton Street, London W1Y 1HD.

CROFT, Annabel

Annabel Croft. Presenter. b. 12 July 1966.

TV: *Australian Tennis Open; Cudmore's Call; Network 7; Sssports; The Interceptor; Treasure Hunt.*

Address: c/o Lake-Smith Griffin Associates, 15 Maiden Lane, London WC2E 7NA. m. Mel Coleman. Hobbies: Tennis, long-distance running.

CROFT, Emma

Emma Croft. Actor (F).

TV: Morag in *BUGS;* Tessa in *Casualty;* Ann in *Dark Adapted Eye;* Lucy Mann in *Holding On;* Lyn in *Master of the Moor;* Maria in *Snow;* Julie Kelly in *The Bill;* Louise Fuller in *The Bill;* Jackie Steven in *The Bill;* Anna in *The Governor;* Cindy in *Trial & Retribution.*

Films: Rosalind in *As You Like It;* Jackie in *Checkout Girl;* Ruthie in *Kleptophelia;* Benja in *Smilla's Feeling for Snow;* Tess in *The Third Party.*

Address: c/o Kate Feast Management, 10 Primrose Hill Studios, Fitzroy Road, London NW1 8TR.

CROFT, Jaq

Jaq Croft. Actor (F). b. Paris, 4 April 1968.

TV: Felicia in *A Class Act; Bernard's Watch; Coronation Street;* Eve Barton in *Dangerfield;* Betty in *Inspector Shaikh;* Anna in *Making Waves;* Monique in *Stick With Me Kid;* Jean Caulder/Elizabeth Lester in *The Bill;* Sarah Clifton-Jones in *The One;* Rianna in *The Terminal Game.*

Films: Judy Holloway in *Rio;* Juliette in *The Reluctant Stranger.*

Address: c/o Langford Associates, 17 Westfields Avenue, London SW13 0AT. m. Conal Cunningham.

CROPPER, Anna

Anna Cropper. Actor (F). b. 13 May 1938.

TV: Lydia Prosser in *A Day in the Summer;* Eileen Kershaw in *A New Lease of Death;* Sarah Bennett in *A Skirt Through History; Angel Pavement* (lead); *Anna of the Five Towns* (lead); *Birth of a Private Man* (lead); Lilian in *Bloody Tower; Boon;* Margaret Castle in *Castles;* Mrs Chassne in *Casualty;* Mrs McIver in *Chancer; Corbett of Kumaon* (lead); Storyteller in *Early Travellers in North America; Gun Play* (lead); Mrs Lessor in *Heartbeat;* Avis Beechwood in *If You See God, Tell Him; Imperial Palace; In Two Minds; The Inspector Alleyn Mysteries;* Storyteller in *Jane Austen;* Nicky

Panton in *Jewel in the Crown*; Marion Beck in *Kavanagh QC*; Clementina in *Marshal and the Madwoman*; Memento Mori in *Memento Mori*; Mrs Moorey in *Midnight Movie*; *Midsomer Murders*; *Miss Marple*; Arabella in *Mistress of Hardwick*; Mrs Denmark in *Moon and Son*; Francine in *Nativity Blues*; *Père Goriot*; Lady Willard in *Poirot*; Helen Bamber in *Prisoners in Time*; *Robin Redbreast*; Mrs Stanton in *Smokescreen*; Mrs Leyland in *The Affair*; Mrs Jones in *The Child Eater*; *The Insect Play*; Mrs Seid in *The Murderers Among Us*; Gwen in *The Old Devils*; *The Princess and the Inventor*; Lucy in *The Rivals*; *Vacant Possession*; Julie Meijers in *Van Der Valk*; Mother in *Van Gogh*; *Woof*; *Zig Zag*; Rosanna Spearman in *The Moonstone*. Address: c/o Kate Feast Management, 10 Primrose Hill Studios, Fitzroy Road, London NW1 8TR. Her son is actor Linus Roache.

CROSBIE, Annette

Annette Crosbie. Actor (F).
b. Edinburgh, 12 February 1934.
TV: *Auntie's Niece*; *Beyond the Pale*; *Bon Espérance*; *Charles Dilk Trilogy*; *Colin's Sandwich*; *Dr Finlay*; *East Lynne*; *Edward VII*; *Find Me First*; *Flowers of the Forest*; *Game, Set and Match*; *Heartbeat*; *Henrik Ibsen*; *Jessie*; *Jonathan Creek*; *Jute City*; *Langrish Go Down*; *Lilly Langtry*; *Lowry – A Private View*; *Message For Posterity*; *Nervous Energy*; *Nobody's Property*; *Northern Lights*; *Of Mycenae and Men*; *Off Peak*; *Paradise Postponed*; *Paying Guests*; *Pericles*; *Que Sera*; *Richard III*; *Stuart*; *Summer's Lease*; *Sunday Night Thriller*; *Taggart*; *Take Me Home*; *The House on the Hill*; *The Misanthrope*; *The Portrait*; *The Pyramid Game*; *The Seagull*; Catherine of Aragon in *The Six Wives of Henry VIII*; *The Speaker of Mandarin*; *Tolstoy*; *Twelfth Night*; *An Unsuitable Job for a Woman*; *Waste*; *Watch with Mother*.
Films: *Debt Collector*; *Final Warning*; *Hawk the Slayer*; *Leon the Pig Farmer*; *Solitaire for Two*; *The Disappearance of Harry*; *The Pope Must Die*; *The Slipper and the Rose*.
Address: c/o ICM, Oxford House, 76 Oxford Street, London W1N 0AX.

CROSSLEY, Laura

Laura Crossley. Actor (F). b. Oldham, 29 August 1979.
TV: Rachel in *A Touch of Frost* (1996); Natalie in *Anorak of Fire* (1997); Sarah in *Bramwell* (1996); Joanne Lloyd in *Casualty* (1996); Anna Miller in *Heartbeat* (1999); *Hetty Wainthropp Investigates* (1996); Tracy in *This is Personal: The Hunt for the Yorkshire Ripper* (1998); Kim in *London's Burning* (1999); *Susan Jakes in Peak Practice* (1997); Deborah Alliss in *Where the Heart Is* (1998).
Films: Martha in *The Secret Garden*.

Address: c/o Shepherd & Ford, 13 Radnor Walk, London SW3 4BP.

CROWE, Sara

Sara Crowe. Actor (F). b. 1966.
TV: *Alas Smith and Jones*; *Boogie Outlaws*; Luli in *Scarlett*; *Sometime, Never*; *The Harry Enfield Show*; *The Rory Bremner Show*.
Films: *Carry On Columbus*; *Four Weddings and a Funeral*; *The Steal*; *Caught in the Act*.
Address: c/o Jonathan Altaras Associates, 13 Short Gardens, London WC2H 9AT. m. Toby Dale.

CROYDON, Nicky

Nicky Croydon. Actor (F)/Presenter.
TV: *Bobby Davro*; Jean in *Brush Strokes*; Liz Brimlow and Claire Wilson in *Casualty*; *Dear Heart*; Sylvia Thornton in *Heartbeat*; *Hot Machines*; Gwen Farrell in *Maisie Raine II*; *Middle of the Road Show*; *Omnibus*; *Rights and Responsibilities*; *Russ Abbott's Madhouse*; Lorraine in *Say Hello to the Real Dr Snide*; Emily in *The Ballad of Johnny Vanguard*; *The Bill*; Jane in *The Gentle Touch*; Jeannie in *The Missing Postman*; *Victoria Wood – As Seen On TV*; *Wainwright's Law*.
Films: Singing Maid in *Lady Jane Grey*.
Address: c/o Cassie Mayer Ltd, 34 Kingly Court, London W1R 5LE.

CRYER, Barry

Barry Cryer. Comedian/Writer/Actor (M). b. Leeds, Yorkshire, 23 March 1935.
TV: *Blankety Blank*; *Bruce Forsyth's 70th Birthday Concert* (1998); *Countdown*; *Cross Wits*; *Cryer's Crackers*; *Frost on Sunday*; *Frost over England*; *Gibberish*; *Give Us a Clue*; *Hello Cheeky*; *Jokers Wild*; *The Kenny Everett Show*; *Punch Lines*; *Season's Greetings* (1997); *Small Talk*; *Stand Up* (1995); *That's Show Business*; Sergeant Sammy Simpson in *The Detectives*; *The Frost Report*; *The Generation Game*; *The Steam Video Company*; *The Thoughts of Chairman Alf*; *The Two Ronnies*; *This is Your Life* (1995); *What's My Line?*; *What's on Next?*.
Address: c/o Roger Hancock Ltd, 4 Water Lane, London NW1 8NZ.

CUKA, Frances

Frances Cuka. Actor (F). b. 21 August 1936.
TV: *Day of the Tortoise*; Doll Tearsheet in *Henry IV (Part II)*; Angele in *Maigret*; Sister Angelica in *Minder*; *One Day at a Time*; Euridice in *Point of Departure*; Lois Knox in *Ruth Rendell Mysteries*; *The Attic*; *Underground*; Helen Kane in *Wycliffe*; *The Beggar's Opera*; Mrs van Daan in *The Hiding Place*; Frankie in *The Member of the Wedding*; Constance in *The Old Wives' Tale*.

Films: Mrs Dalton in *Afraid of the Dark*; Lady Howton in *Mountain of the Moon*; *Scrooge*; *Six Wives of Henry VIII*; Nannau in *Snow White in the Black Forest*; Lydia in *The Man Who Held His Breath*; *Watcher in the Woods*.
Address: c/o Lou Coulson, 37 Berwick Street, London W1V 3RF.

CULBERTSON, Rod

Rod Culbertson. Actor (M). b. 28 April 1950.
TV: *A Horseman Riding By*; *After Julius*; *Agent Z and the Penguin From Mars*; *Albert and the Lion*; *An Actor's Life For Me*; Howard Winfold in *Bergerac*; *Brookside*; *Bust*; *Casualty*; *Catherine Cookson's 'The Secret'*; *EastEnders*; *Gas and Candles*; *Inspector Mitcham*; *No Further Cause for Concern*; Bede Conner in *Our Friends in the North*; *Spender*; Kevin Redman in *Taggart*; *The Balcony*; *The Bill* (various); *The Dwelling Place*; *The Professionals*; *The Sweeney*; *Village Hall*; *William Tell*; *World Cup – A Captain's Tale*.
Films: Master Ridley in *Elizabeth*; *Porridge*; The Radio Operator in *SOS Titanic*; *Spy Story*; Paul McCartney in *The Birth of the Beatles*; 2nd Officer in *Twelfth Night*.
Address: c/o A.D.A. Enterprises, 78 St Margaret's Road, St Margaret's, Twickenham, Middlesex TW1 2LP.

CULLEN, Ian

Ian Cullen. Actor (M). b. Sunderland.
TV: Flight Sergeant in *Ain't Misbehavin'* (1996); Roberts in *Dalziel and Pascoe* (1996); Corporal in *The Dame of Sark* (1976); Angus Hart in *Family Affairs* (1997); Gyver in *Harry* (1993); Mr Foster in *In Suspicious Circumstances* (1993); Tom Kelly in *Spender* (1991); Frank Collins in *The Bill* (1994); Paddy O'Connor in *The Gambling Man* (1994); Stephen Hopkins in *The New World* (1986); *The Paper Lads* (1978); *The Return of the Saint* (1977); McVicar in *True Crimes* (1992); Ralph Gardiner in *Tyneside Entertainment* (1976); Mr Watson in *When the Boat Comes In* (1977); Skinner in *Z Cars* (1970).
Films: *Burning an Illusion*; *On the Fiddle*; *The Voyage*; *Village of the Damned*.
Address: c/o The Richard Stone Partnership, 2 Henrietta Street, London WC2E 8PS.

CUNLIFFE, Jane

Jane Cunliffe. Actor (F).
b. Oldham, Lancashire, 1 June 1962.
TV: Debbie Sparrow in *Boon*; Laura Gordon Davies in *Brookside*; *Bullman*; School Principal in *Cold Feet*; *Conjugal Rights*; Carol Longhorne in *Emmerdale*; *Hale and Pace*; Francesca in *Hollywood Sports*; *She-Wolf of London*; *Strike It Rich*; *The Bill*; D.S. Scarlett in *The Ireland Project*; Penelope in *Trouble in Mind*.
Address: c/o Green & Underwood, 2 Conduit Street, London W1R 9TG.

CUNNINGHAM, Emma

Emma Cunningham. Actor (F).
b. Lee Green, London, 2 April 1968.
TV: *Casualty*; *Inspector Morse*; Dr Gail Benson in *Medics*; Gloria in *Minder*; *Sharman*; *The Bill*; *Van Der Valk*; Sally in *Wonderful You*.
Address: c/o Scott Marshall, 44 Perryn Road, London W3 7NA. Hobbies: Skiing, water-skiing, travelling, salsa dancing.

CUNNINGHAM, Liam

Liam Cunningham. Actor (M). b. 1960.
TV: *20:20*; Stapler in *A Handful of Stars*; *Cracker*; Mossie Sheehan in *Falling for a Dancer*; Danger Doyle in *Poor Beast in the Rain*; Frank in *Private Lives*; The Soldier in *Rewind*; Gregg Toland in *RKO 281*; Chris in *Roughnecks*; Christopher Anderson in *Shooting the Past*; Alec Cunningham-Reid in *Too Rich: The Secret Life of Doris Duke*.
Films: Sean Cloney in *A Love Divided*; Sean in *Breach of Faith*; Agravaine in *First Knight*; Policeman in *Into the West*; Phillotson in *Jude*; Sneddon in *Life of Stuff*; Billy O'Connell in *Police 2020*; Detective Bone in *Tale of Sweety Barrett*; Capt. Crewe/Prince Rama in *The Little Princess*; Greg Laughton in *Undercurrent*; *Veronica Guerin*; The Master in *War of the Buttons*.
Address: Marina Martin Associates, 12-13 Poland Street, London W1V 3DE.

CURLING, Rob

Rob Curling. Presenter.
TV: *Farnborough*; *International Aerospace*; *International Air Tattoo*; *Into Music*; *The Geography Programme*; *The International Boat Show*; *Turnabout*; *V.E. Day Celebrations – Hyde Park*.
Address: c/o Speak-easy Ltd, 90 St Mary's Road, Market Harborough, Leicestershire LEI6 7DX.

CURRAN, Paul

Paul Curran. Actor (M). b. 1913.
TV: King Arthur in *Merlin*; Simon Travis in *Nancherrow*.
Films: France in *King Lear*.
Address: c/o Marmont Management Ltd, Langham House, 308 Regent St., London W1R 5AL.

CURRY, Mark

Mark Curry. Presenter/Reporter.
b. Stafford, 27 August 1961.

TV: *Blue Peter* (1986); *Careering Ahead; Change That; Get Set For the Summer* (1981); *Get the Grammar; Junior Showtime; Make 'Em Laugh; Record Breakers* (1994); *Screen Test; The Saturday Picture Show; Treasure Houses.*
Address: c/o The Roseman Organisation, Suite 9, The Power House, 70 Chiswick Road, London W4 1SY. Hobbies: Tennis.

CURRY, Tim

Tim Curry. Actor (M). b. Cheshire, 19 April 1946.
TV: Larry Gormley in *Blue Money; City Sugar; Gai-Jin;* Bill Sikes in *Oliver Twist;* Simon Ferguson in *Over The Top; Rock Follies; Roseanne; Saturday Night Live;* Shakespeare in *The Life of Shakespeare; Stephen King's IT; Tales from the Crypt;* Jerome K Jerome in *Three Men in a Boat; Video Star;* Winston Newquay in *Wiseguy.*
Films: Rooster Hannigan in *Annie;* Wadsworth in *Clue;* Herkermer Homolka in *Congo;* Mr Hector, Concierge in *Home Alone II; Legend;* Maj Vladikov in *McHale's Navy;* Long John Silver in *Muppet Treasure Island;* Jigsaw in *National Lampoon's Loaded Weapon I;* Dr Thornoton Poole in *Oscar;* Rev Ray Porter in *Pass the Ammunition;* Dr Petrov (Red October) in *The Hunt for Red October;* Doctor Frank N Furter in *The Rocky Horror Picture Show;* Farley Claymore in *The Shadow;* Robert Graves in *The Shout;* Cardinal Richelieu in *The Three Musketeers;* Johnny LaGuardia in *Times Square.*
Address: c/o William Morris Agency, 151 El Camino Drive, Beverly Hills, California 90212, USA.

CURTIN, Jane

Jane Curtin. Actor (F)/Host/Voice artist.
b. Cambridge, Massachusetts, USA, 6 September 1947.
TV: *Bob and Ray & Jane, Laraine and Gilda* (1979); *Christmas in Washington* (1996); Alice McGoff in *Common Ground* (1990); Vickey Sturgess in *Divorce Wars: A Love Story* (1982); *Don't Try This at Home* (1990); Allie Lowell in *Kate & Allie* (1984); Julia Gilbert in *Maybe Baby* (1988); Mrs Clemperer in *Recess* (1997); *Saturday Night Live* (1975) (Various routines/sketches); Mary Todd Lincoln in *Tad* (1995); Mary Albright in *Third Rock from the Sun* (1996–9); Sarah Marshall in *Working Out* (1990).
Films: Voice of 'Muffy' in *ANTZ; Coneheads;* Elaine in *How to beat the High Co$t of Living;* herself in *Mr Mike's Mondo Video; O.C. & Stiggs;* Lina McLaidlaw in *Suspicion.*
Address: c/o ICM Agency, 8942 Wilshire Blvd., Beverly Hills, California 90211, USA.

CURTIS, Ian

Ian Curtis. Actor (M). b. Manchester, 1972.
TV: John Branigan in *Cracker;* Guy in *Crocodile Shoes;* P.C. Wainwright in *Frontiers;* Ray Sykes in *Holby City;* David in *Medics;* Jack Barnes in *No Bananas;* P.C. Cobbett in *Pie in the Sky;* Corporal Hobbs in *Soldier, Soldier;* Paul Webster in *The Governor;* Gareth King in *A Touch of Frost.*
Films: *A Twist of Fate* (lead); Legs in *Bravo Two Zero* (lead); *Dave in Dot Dot Dot* (lead); Mike in *Visual Pleasure.*
Address: c/o CAM London, 19 Denmark Street, London WC2H 8NA. Hobbies: Karate, fencing, football, swimming.

CUSACK, Catherine

Catherine Cusack. Actor (F).
TV: *Ho, Ho, Ho;* Frankie in *Ballykissangel; The Bill; Cadfael; Dressing for Breakfast;* Hilary Scott in *The Chief;* Carmel Finnan in *Coronation Street; Doctor Who; Sophia and Constance.*
Address: c/o London Management, 2 –4 Noel Street, London, W1V 3RB. Father Cyril Cusack; sisters Niamh, Sorcha, Sinead.

CUSACK, Niamh

Niamh Cusack. Actor (F). b. Dublin 1961.
TV: *A Marriage of Inconvenience;* Mary in *Angel Train; Chalk Face;* Bridget Patterson in *Colour Blind;* Josephine in *Fools of Fortune; Heartbeat;* Bobby in *Jeeves and Wooster; Rhinoceros; Till We Meet Again;* Jane in *Trauma.*
Films: Clara in *Paris By Night; Playboys;* Clara in *Shadow Under the Sun; Untitled Comedy.*
Address: c/o PFD, Drury House, 34–43 Russell Street, London WC2B 5HA. m. Finbar Lynch, her acting sisters are Sinead, Sorcha and Catherine; her father was actor Cyril Cusack.

CUSACK, Sinead

Sinead Cusack. Actor (F).
b. Dalkey, Ireland, 18 February 1948.
TV: Charlotte in *Have Your Cake and Eat It; Miriad, A Boy From Bosnia; Oliver's Travels; Tales from Hollywood; God on the Rocks;* Olivia in *Twelfth Night; Tthe Henhouse; Scoop; Romance: The Black Night;* Trilby in *Trilby;* Rosaline in *Love's Labours Lost; Shadow of a Gunman; Playboy of the Western World; The Kitchen; Supernatural – Ghost in Venice; Quiller; Affairs of the Heart; George Sand: Notorious Woman; Menace: the Solarium; The Eyes Have It.*
Films: *My Mother Frank; Passion in Mind; The Nephew; Stealing Beauty; The Flemish Board; The*

Sparrow; The Cement Garden; Bad Behaviour; Waterland; David Copperfield; Venus Peter; Rocket Gibraltar; The Last Remake of Beau Geste; Horowqitz in Dublin Castle; Hoffman; Tamlyn; Alfred the Great.
Address: c/o Markham & Froggatt, 4 Windmill Street, London, W1P 1HF. Father Cyril Cusack; sisters Niamh, Sorcha, Catherine.

CUSACK, Sorcha
Sorcha Cusack. Actor (F).
TV: *Jane Eyre; Napoleon and Love; Within These Walls; Rooms; Married Love; Murder Machine; The Gates; Private Affairs; Jackanory; Rainbow; Ulysses; Hold the Dream; Confessional; The Real Charlotte; August Saturday; Shoot the Revolution; Boon; Inspector Morse; Brookside; Rides; Poirot – Jewel Robbery at the Grand Metropolitan; Maigret;* Kate Wilson in *Casualty; The Corn Devils; Plastic Man.*
Films: *A Hitch in Time; Angel.*
Address: c/o PFD, Drury House, 34– 43 Russell Street, London, WC2B 5HA. Father Cyril Cusack; sisters Niamh, Sinead, Catherine.

D

D'ARBY, Josephine
Josephine D'Arby. Actor (F)/Presenter.
TV: *Broom Cupboard*; Sarah in *Casualty*; *Children's Comic Relief*; *Friday Zone*; *Live and Kicking*; *Smart*; Lee in *Spywatch*; *Talkabout*; *The Bigger Breakfast*; *The Mag*; *The Music Room*.
Address: c/o William Morris Agency (UK) Ltd, 1 Stratton Street, London W1X 6HB.

DALE, Charles
Charles Dale. Actor (M).
TV: Colin Fletcher in *A Touch of Frost* (1992); Farmer Hapwell in *Animal Ark* (1997); Maguire in *At Home With The Braithwaites* (1999); Policeman in *Big Deal* (1985); Duncan in *Bramwell* (1996); Billy in *Casualty* (1998); Mike in *Custom and Excise* (1997); Herr Heller in *Genghis Cohen* (1993); Redstone in *Lovejoy* (1991); Gareth in *Morgan's Boy* (1984); Mr Welby in *Out of Hours* (1998); Corporal in *Out of Tune* (1985); George in *Phoebe* (1984); *Pythons On The Mountain* (1984); Security Guard in *Spaced* (1999); Collier in *The Bill* (1995); Michael Cooper in *The Bill* (1997); Police Inspector in *The Famous Five* (1996); Chef in *The Lakes* (1997); Chef in *The Lakes II* (1998); Ambulance Driver in *The Last Romantics* (1991); *The Wars of the Roses* (1990); Whelan in *Touching Evil* (1999); Plesman in *Van Der Valk* (1991).
Films: Paul in *Secret Society* (1999); Gerard Thiery in *The Hour of the Pig* (1992).
Address: c/o The Richard Stone Partnership, 2 Henrietta Street, London WC2E 8PS.

DALE, Jim
Jim Dale. Actor (M). b. Rothwell, 15 August 1935.
Films: *Adolf Hitler: My Part In His Downfall*; *Digby*; *Hot Lead, Cold Feet*; *Joseph Andrews*; *Pete's Dragon*; *Scandalous*; *The American Clock*; *The Hunchback of Notre Dame*; *The Iron Maiden*; *The National Health*; *Carry On* films (various).
Music: *Georgy Girl*; *Joseph Andrews*; *Shalako*; *The Winter's Tale*; *Twinky*.
Address: c/o Eric Glass Ltd, 28 Berkeley Square, London W1X 6HD.

DANAN, Paul
Paul Danan. Actor (M).
TV: Schoolboy in *Chalk*; Clubber in *EastEnders*; Sol Patrick in *Hollyoaks*; *TCC*; Gang member in *The Knock*.
Address: c/o Rossmore Personal Management, Rossmore Road, London NW1 6NJ. Hobbies: football, tennis, badminton, table tennis, basketball.

DANCE, Charles
Charles Dance. Actor (M).
b. Redditch, Worcester, 10 October 1946.
TV: *Bloodlines*; *Edward VII*; *First Born*; *Frost in May*; *Golden Eye*; *Little Eyolf*; *Nancy Astor*; *Out of the Shadows*; *Out on a Limb*; *Phantom of the Opera*; *Rainy Day Woman*; *Rebecca*; *Saigon – The Last Day*; *Skeleton in the Cupboard*; *The Fatal Spring*; *The Jewel in the Crown*; *The Lightning Always Strikes Twice*; *The McGuffin*; *The Secret Servant*; *Thunder Rock*.
Films: *Alien III*; *Blood Oranges*; *Century*; *China Moon*; *Chrono Perambulator*; *Don't Go Breaking My Heart*; *Enemies*; *Exquisite Tenderness*; *For Your Eyes Only*; *Good Morning Babylon*; *Hidden City*; *Hilary and Jackie*; *In The Presence Of Mine*; *Jurji*; *Kabloonak*; *Kalkstein*; *Last Action Hero*; *Limestone*; *Michael Collins*; *Pascali's Island*; *Plenty*; *Shortcut to Paradise*; *Spacetruckers*; *The Golden Child*; *Undertow*; *What Rats Won't Do*; *White Mischief*.
Address: c/o ICM, Oxford House, 76 Oxford Street, London W1N 0AX.

DANDO, Suzanne
Suzanne Dando. Presenter. b. 3 July 1961.
TV: *Noel's House Party*; *Pebble Mill*; *Razzamatazz*; *Record Breakers*; *Run the Gauntlet*; *Sports Extra*; *Sports Saturday*; *Stopwatch*; *Superstars*; *The Generation Game*; *They Think It's All Over*; *Through the Keyhole*; *Trailblazers*; *World's Strongest Man*; *All Well And Good*; *Anything Goes*; *Autocare*; *Bodywatch – This Morning*; *Breakfast Time*; *Children in Need*; *Don't Just Sit There*; *Early Sports Show*; *Fishermania*; *Go-Getters*; *Grandslam Sports*; *Heaven Knows*; *Horse of the Year Show*; *International Open Snooker*; *Miss England*.
Film: *Octopussy*.
Music: *Shape Up and Dance*.

Address: c/o Jane Hughes Management, The Coach House, PO Box 123, Knutsford, Cheshire WA16 9HX.

DANIEL, Brittany

Brittany Daniel. Actor (F).
b. Gainesville, Florida, USA, 17 March 1976.
TV: Eve Whitman in *Dawson's Creek*; Cindy in *Sinkhole*; Brittany in *Sonic Impact*; Mila Rosnovsky in *Swan's Crossing*; Jessica Wakefield in *Sweet Valley High*.
Film: Blinkie in *The Basketball Diaries*.
Address: c/o Michael Amato, 1650 Broadway, Suite 307, New York, New York 10019, USA. Hobbies: in-line skating, working out at the gym.

DANIEL, Cynthia

Cynthia Daniel. Actor (F).
b. Gainesville, Florida, USA, 17 March 1976.
TV: Liz Wakefield in *Sweet Valley High*.
Films: Winkie in *The Basketball Diaries*.
Address: c/o Michael Amato, 1650 Broadway, Suite 307, New York, New York 10019, USA. Hobbies: Rollerblading, bike riding, vegetarianism.

DANIELS, Ben

Ben Daniels. Actor (M).
TV: Ben in *Truth or Dare*; *Inspector Alleyn Mysteries*; Mercutio in *Romeo and Juliet*; *The Crossing*, *Lost Language of Cranes*; *The Aristocrats*; *Silent Witness*; *David*; Ales in *Outside Edge*; *A Touch of Frost*; Captain Wright in *Soldier, Soldier* Colin in *Capital City*; *Murky Waters*; *One by One*; *Great Writers: Thomas Mann*; *Wall of Tyranny*.
Films: Tony in *Beautiful Thing*; Townsend in *Britannic*; Andrew in *Fanny and Elvis*; DJ Bob in *I Want You*; Leopold in *Madeleine*; Augustin in *Passion in the Desert*; Rogers in *The Bridge*; Policeman in *Wish You Were Here?*
Address: c/o Markham & Froggatt Ltd, 4 Windmill Street, London W1P 1HF.

DANIELS, Paul

Paul Daniels. Magician. b. London, 6 April 1938.
TV: *Blackpool Bonanza*; *Blankety Blank*; *Every Second Counts*; *Have I Got News For You*; *The Mrs Merton Show*; *Telly Addicts*; *The Paul Daniels Show*; *Wipeout*; *Wizbit*.
Address: c/o Mervyn O'Horan, 140 Beckett Road, Doncaster, South Yorkshire DN2 4BA. m. Debbie McGee; 1 s. Martin.

DANIELS, Phil

Phil Daniels. Actor (M). b. London, 20 October 1958.
TV: *Big Deal*; *Glitter*; *Hanging Around*; *Harper*; *Holding On*; *Idle Hands*; *Meantime*; *A Midsummer Night's Dream*; *Miss Julie*; *Molly Wopsies*; *Nelson*; *One Foot in the Grave*; *Out of Mecca – The Bride*; *Pickwick Papers*; *Raven*; *Rik Mayall Presents*; *Sex and Chocolate*; *Sex, Chips and Rock 'n' Roll*; *Stand and Deliver*; *Sunnyside Farm*; *Will You Love Me Tomorrow?*
Films: *Bad Behaviour*; *Billy the Kid and the Green Baize Vampire*; *Breaking The Glass*; *Nasty Neighbours*; *Quadrophenia*; *Scum*; *Shore Leave*; *The Bride*; *The Class of Miss McMichael*; *Zulu Dawn*.
Address: c/o ICM, Oxford House, 76 Oxford Street, London W1N 0AX.

DANSON, Jane

Jane Danson. Actor (F). b. Bury, 8 November 1978.
TV: Leanne Battersby in *Coronation Street*; Young Eileen Critchley in *GBH*; Dorothy Pace in *In Suspicious Circumstances*; Chas in *Out of Tune*; Jane in *Science In The Enviroment*; Roz in *Sloggers*; Debbie Fisher in *The Bill*; Monica Jones in *The Grand*; Paula James in *The Ward*; Betty Seagrim in *Tom Jones*.
Address: c/o Pemberton Associates, 193 Wardour Street, London W1V 3FA.

DANSON, Ted

Edward Bridge Danson III. Actor (M).
b. San Diego, California, USA, 29 December 1947.
TV: Tom Spencer in *B.J. and the Bear*; Dr John Becker in *Becker*; Sam Malone in *Cheers*; Dale Weeks in *Cowboy*; himself in *Diagnosis Murder*; *Down Home*; himself in *Ellen*; Sam Malone in *Frasier*; Lemuel Gulliver in *Gulliver's Travels*; Mike Logan in *Ink*; Fireman in *Laverne and Shirley*; Steve in *Magnum PI*; Jack Chenault in *Once Upon A Spy*; Gep in *Our Family Business*; Tom Conway in *Somerset*; Steven Bennett in *Something About Amelia*; Vincenzo Senaca in *Taxi*; Jim Tuite in *Thanks of a Grateful Nation*; *The Chinese Web*; Norman in *The Women's Room*; Danny Kirkwood in *Tucker's Witch*; Nick Vanover in *Veronica's Closet*; *We Are The Children*; Alex in *When The Bow Breaks*.
Films: Spence Holden in *A Fine Mess*; Peter Lowenstein in *Body Heat*; Larry in *Cousins*; Harry Wentworth in *Creepshow*; John Tremont in *Dad*; Ray in *Getting Even With Dad*; Giannin Saletzzo in *Homegrown*; Chip Davis in *Just Between Friends*; Eugene in *Little Treasure*; Dempsey in *Loch Ness*; Hal Jackson in *Made in America*; Jeremy Brockett in *Mumford*; Washington Bellamy in *Pontiac Moon*; Captain Brian Hamill in *Saving Private Ryan*; *She's Having A Baby*; Ian Campbell in *The Onion Field*; Jack Holden in *Three Men and a Baby*; Jack Holden in *Three Men and a Little Lady*.
Address: c/o Wolf/Kasteler, 132 So. Rodeo Drive, Beverly Hills, California 90212 USA. m. 1 Casey Coates

(dis); m. 2 Mary Steenburgen. Hobbies: Shooting hoops, horseback riding.

DANVERS, Ivor

Ivor Danvers. Actor (M). b. Essex, 14 July 1934.
TV: *Angels; Brookside; Crossroads; Graham's Gang;* Gerald Urquhart in *Howard's Way; Juliet Bravo; Keeping up Appearances;* Peter Brown in *Lleifior; Love From Italy; Minder; No Place Like Home; A Sharp Intake Of Breath; Softly, Softly;* Tom Armstrong in *Tenko; Terry and June; The Little Door; The World Walk; We're Going to Be All Right.*
Films: *Electric Eskimo; Give a Dog a Bone; Move; Watch Your Stern.*
Address: c/o April Young, 11 Woodlands Road, Barnes, London SW13 OJZ. m. Henrietta Holmes; 1 d. Lindsey; 1 s. Tommy; mother Violet Danvers. Hobbies: Member of BAFTA, golf, skiing. bridge and chess.

DAVENPORT, Claire

Claire Davenport. Actor (F). b. 24 April 1936.
TV: The Duchess in *Alice in Wonderland;* Mrs Dumphrey in *By the Sword Divided;* Boadicea in *Churchill's People; Dick Emery's Wife; Fawlty Towers; I Didn't Know you Cared;* The Loo Attendant in *In Sickness and in Health;* Hilda, the Char Lady in *Remington Steele;* Nurse Pyne in *Shoulder to Shoulder;* Madame Pace in *Six Characters in Search of an Author;* the Bossy Lizard in *Space Vets;* the Mayoress in *Valentine Park.*
Films: *Birth of the Beatles; Carry On Emanuelle; Crossplot; The Elephant Man; Going Camping; Jubilee; Ladies Who Do; Malakie Cove; On the Buses; Otley; Our Own and Private Place; The Pink Panther; The Return of the Jedi; Some Will, Some Won't; Stick With Me Kid; The Best Pair of Legs; The Lecture; The Tempest; Twinky; Up Jumped A Swagman; War Requiem.*
Address: c/o Alex Jay Personal Management, 137a Kensington High Street, London W8 6SU.

DAVENPORT, Jack

Jack Davenport. Actor (M). b. 1973.
TV: *Couplings; Macbeth; The Moth; The Wyvern Mysteries;* Miles in *This Life; UltraViolet.*
Films: *Career Girls; Fierce Creatures; Talos the Mummy; The Talented Mr Ripley; The Wisdom of Crocodiles.*
Address: c/o Whitehall Artists, 125 Gloucester Road, London SW7 4TE.

DAVENPORT, Nigel

Nigel Davenport. Actor (M). b. 23 May 1928.
TV: *A Choice of Weapons; A Midsummer Night's Dream; A Subject for Scandal and Concern; Bird of Prey; Break-down; David Copperfield* (1999); *Don't Rock the Boat; Double Stakes; Guilty Party; Howard's Way; I Don't Like You; The Island of Dr Moreau; Keeping up Appearances; Longitude* (1999); *Madame Bovary; Masadah; Midsomer Murders; Mosley; Much Ado About Nothing; Oil Strike North; The Picture of Dorian Gray; Point of Return; Return to the Regiment; South Riding; The Apple Cart; The Detectives; The Gioconda Smile; The Good Doctor Bodkin Adams; The Ordeal of Dr Mudd; The Prince Regent; The Travelling Man; The Upper Hand; The Wrong Way Back; To Bury Caesar; Trainer; Until You Are Dead.*
Films: *A High Wind in Jamaica; A Man for all Seasons; An Eye for an Eye; Chariots of Fire; Charlie One Eye; Greystoke; Hotel Shanghai; La Regenta; Life at the Top; Living Free; Mary, Queen of Scots; The Mind of Mr Soames; Nighthawks; Peeping Tom; Phase IV; Play Dirty; Sands of the Kalahari; Sebastian; Sinful Davey; Strata; The Cutter; The London Affair; The Opium Wars; The Return of El Coyote; The Royal Hunt of the Sun; The Third Secret; Villain; Without a Clue; Zulu Dawn.*
Address: c/o Green and Underwood, 2 Conduit Street, London W1R 9TG. 1 d. Laura. 2 s. Hugo, Jack.

DAVID, Alan

Alan David. Actor (M).
b. Merthyr Tydfil, 29 December 1941.
TV: *The Brittas Empire; Casualty; Chris Cross;* Glyn Thomas in *Coronation Street; Cracker; Devil's Advocate; Dirty Work; Foxy Lady; Headhunters; Heartbeat; Inspector Morse; Lovejoy; Maigret;* Bernie in *Making Out; The Merchant of Venice; Peak Practice; Preston Front; Road, Sleepers;* Maurice in *Sam;* Harry in *The Squirrels; The Thin Blue Line; The Vet; A Tour of the Western Isles; Wokenwell.*
Films: *Psychotherapy; Sakharov; The Great Indoors; The Man Who Cried.*
Address: c/o Scott Marshall, 44 Perryn Road, London W3 7NA. m. Jane; 2 s. Harry, Jack.

DAVID, Joanna

Joanna David. Actor (F).
b. Lancaster, 17 January 1947.
TV: *A Touch of Frost; Blind Date; Bramwell; Children of the North; A Dance to the Music of Time;* Mabel Purdy in *Dear Brutus;* Ann in *Fame is the Spur; First Among Equals; Inspector Morse;* Mary Eleanor Pearcey in *Ladykillers; Maigret; Midsomer Murders* (guest lead); *The Mill on the Floss; Miss Marple: The 4.50 From Paddington;* Dora Carrington in *No Need To Lie;* Mrs Gardner in *Pride and Prejudice;* Mrs De Winter in *Rebecca; Rumpole of the Bailey; Secret Friends;* Elinor in *Sense and Sensibility; Sherlock Holmes; Tender is the*

Night; The Dark Room; The Darling Buds of May; The Good Guys; Alice Monroe in *The Last of the Mohicans; Time for Murder;* Queen Victoria in *Treasure Houses; Unexplained Laughter;* Sonia in *War and Peace.*
Films: *Cotton Mary;* Mrs Peter Baring in *Rogue Trader.*
Address: c/o PFD, Drury House, 34–43 Russell Street, London WC2B 5HA. m. Edward Fox; 1 d. Emilia; 1 s. Freddie. Hobbies: Pottery.

DAVIDSON, Jim

Jim Davidson. Comedian/Actor (M)/Presenter.
b. London, 13 December 1954.
TV: *Big Break; Home James; New Faces; Stand Up Jim Davidson; The Generation Game; The Jim Davidson Show; Up the Elephant and Round the Castle; What's on Next?*
Films: *A Zed and Two Noughts.*
Music: *Watching Over You.*
Address: c/o Lake-Smith Griffin Associates, 15 Maiden Lane, London WC2E 7NA.

DAVIDSON, Ross

Ross Davidson. Actor (M). b. Airdrie, 25 August 1949.
TV: *Brookside; Children's TV; Daytime Live;* Andy in *EastEnders; Fell Tiger; Give Us a Clue; POB; Run the Gauntlet; Sky TV; Taggart; The Gentle Touch; The High Road; Widows; Wogan; Young Soldiers; Hollyoaks.*
Films: *Paracelsus; Monty Python's The Meaning of Life; The Pirates of Penzance.*
Address: c/o MCS Promotions, 12 Station Parade, Snaresbrook, London E11 1QF.

DAVIES, Alan

Alan Davies. Actor (M)/Comedian. b. 1966.
TV: *A Many Splintered Thing* (1998); *Auntie's TV Favourites* (1997); *Des O'Connor Tonight* (1995); *Fantasy Football League* (1996); *Film Night* (1997); *Have I Got News For You* (1996); *Jo Brand – Through the Cakehole* (1995); *Jonathan Creek* (1997); *Just For Laughs* (1995); *The Little Picture Show* (1994); *Mondo Rosso* (1995); *One Foot in the Grave;* Simon Treat in *One For The Road* (1995) (lead); *Pebble Mill* (1995); *Room 101* (1997); *Selection Box* (1997); *The South Bank Show* (1993) (comedy special); *Talking Tate* (1997); *The Best Show In The World... Probably* (1998); *The Clive James Show* (1996); *The Comedy Club; The Globe* (1998); *The National Lottery, Live!* (1997); *The Ruby Wax Show* (1997); *The Stand Up Show* (1995); *Top of the Pops* (1996); *Urban Trauma* (1998); *Viva Cabaret* (1993).
Address: c/o International Artistes Ltd, Mezzanine Floor, 235 Regent Street, London W1R 8AX.

DAVIES, Anne

Anne Davies. Actor (F). b. London 1958.
TV: ATS Lady in *A Voyage Around My Father;* Gwen in *After Henry;* Ethel in *All in Good Faith;* Jean in *Doctor Who; EastEnders;* Marjorie in *Equal Terms;* Mrs Ripper in *Ever Decreasing Circles; Grange Hill;* Mrs Copley in *Happy; Keeping up Appearances;* Bridget in *Paradise Postponed;* Matty in *Poldark;* Lucille in *Probation Officer;* Mrs Bates in *Shine on Harvey Moon; The Bill* (two roles); Mrs Halstead in *The Nation's Health;* Dorothy Clarke in *The Sculptress;* Iris Davies in *The Specials;* Mildred in *Windows;* Ettie in *Within These Walls.*
Films: Mrs Branch in *In the Bleak Midwinter;* Geraldine Malik in *Love is Not Enough;* Brenda in *Peter's Friends; The Reaction Time.*
Address: c/o Langford Associates, 17 Westfields Avenue, London SW13 0AT. m. Richard Briers; 2 d. Kate, Lucy. Hobbies: Pets, exercise class, swimming.

DAVIES, Anne-Marie

Anne-Marie Davies. Actor (F). b. 22 October 1975.
TV: Katrina Evans in *Brookside.*
Address: c/o Ray's Northern Casting Agency, 7 Wince Close, Alkington, Middleton, Manchester M24 1UJ. Hobbies: Volleyball (plays for the English national team), Thai boxing, horse riding.

DAVIES, Barry

Barry Davies. Commentator. b. 24 October 1940.
TV: *Commonwealth Games; Olympic Games; Olympic Games* (1968); *The Big Match* (1966); *Wimbledon; The World Cup* (1966); *Match of the Day;* various ice skating championships.
Address: c/o John Byfield, Equity Court, 73–75 Milbrook Road East, Southampton SO15 1RJ.

DAVIES, Diana

Diana Davies. Actor (F). b. 20 July 1936.
TV: Doris Jackson in *A Family At War;* Annie James in *A Touch of Frost;* Mrs Birse in *All Creatures Great and Small;* Sister Swain in *Angels;* Mother in *Brother to the Ox;* Mother in *Celebration;* Norma Ford in *Coronation Street;* Helen in *Dog Food Dan;* Mrs Bates in *Emmerdale; Enemy at the Door* (female lead); Martha Collins in *Heartbeat;* Mother in *How We Used To Live;* Mrs Lipton in *Johnny Jarvis;* Flowershop Woman in *Josie Smith;* Mrs Allen in *Medics;* Val in *Ready When You Are Mr McGill;* Dawn Duckworth in *Sheik of Pickersgill;* Diana Ollerton in *Shoestring;* Sheila Green in *The Cops;* Mrs Grange in *The Grand;* Headteacher in *Where the Heart Is;* Willie's Wife in *Willie's Last Stand;* Tilda in *Wokenwell.*
Address: c/o Pemberton Associates, 193 Wardour Street, London W1V 3FA.

DAVIES, Emma

Emma Davies. Actor (F). b. 7 March 1970.

TV: Amanda in *Bergerac*; Jo in *Boon*; Sarah Francis in *Crown Prosecution*; *Double Trouble*; Juliet Bannerman in *Families*; Melissa in *Family Pride*; Andrea in *Freddie and Max*; *Harry Enfield and Chums*; Rachel in *Heartbeat*; Lady Emily in *Heroes and Villains*; Chloe Brett in *Home James*; Clarinda in *Just William*; *Law and Disorder*; Diana Mitford in *Mosley*; Hermione Bradley in *The Mrs Bradley Mysteries*; Young Woman in *Never the Twain*; Louise in *Shadow of the Noose*; Cindy in *Spatz*; Julie in *The Bill*; Emily in *The Book Tower*; Anne in *The Book Tower*; Iris in *The Tempest*.

Address: c/o Burnett Granger Associates, Prince of Wales Theatre, 31 Coventry Street, London W1V 8AS.

DAVIES, Freddie

Freddie Davies. Actor (M). b. 21 July 1937.

TV: Owen Lovett in *Band of Gold*; Bobby Zee in *Casualty*; Shopkeeper in *Elidor*; George Blade in *Harbour Lights*; Fred in *Heartbeat*; Sturridge in *Hetty Wainthropp Investigates*; Caspar in *Igloo*; Bird Watcher in *Last of the Summer Wine*; Uncle in *Mange Tout*; Harry Miller in *Medics*; Heron Man in *Preston Front*; Denis in *Rik Mayall*; Ray Marshall in *The Tide of Life*.

Films: Bruno Parker in *Funny Bones*; Uncle Val in *La Passione*; Referee in *No.1*; Alfie Duffel in *Treacle*.

Address: c/o Associated International Management, 5 Denmark Street, London WC2H 8LP.

DAVIES, Geoffrey

Geoffrey Davies. Actor (M).

b. Leeds, 15 December 1941.

TV: *Bergerac*; Dick Stuart-Clark in *Doctor at Large*; Dick Stuart-Clark in *Doctor at Sea*; *Doctor on the Go*; Dick Stuart-Clarke in *Doctor Down Under*; Dick Stuart-Clark in *Doctor in Charge*; Dick Stuart-Clark in *Doctor in the House*; *Families*; *Law and Disorder*; *Stick With Me Kid*; *The Bretts*; *The Labours of Erica*.

Films: *Doctor in the Trouble*; Lt. Faversham in *Oh! What a Lovely War*; *Tales From the Crypt*; Lt. Gessel in *The Gap*.

Address: c/o Burnett Granger Associates, Prince of Wales Theatre, 31 Coventry Street, London W1V 8AS.

DAVIES, Martyn

Martyn Davies. Presenter.

b. Bloxwich, West Midlands, 14 January 1956.

TV: *Eye of the Storm*; *National Weather*; *Regional Weather*; *This Morning*.

Address: c/o International Weather Productions, London Television, Studios, Upper Ground, London SE1 9LT. m. Maggie; 1 d. Jordan; 1 s. Nathan. Hobbies: Tennis, motor racing, cooking.

DAVIES, Race

Race Davies. Actor (F).

TV: *Carrott's Lib*; Erica in *Desmond's*; Jackie Owen in *EastEnders*; *In Bed With MeDinner*; Emma Davies in *Insiders*; Teresa Swinton in *Kavanagh QC*; DS Beverly Armitage in *Lazarus and Dingwall*; *Little Armadillos*; Sally Anne in *Men Behaving Badly*; Lydia in *My Wonderful Life*; Gloria in *Papparazzo*; Alien Siren in *Red Dwarf VI*; Margaret Chafer in *Roughnecks*; Rachel in *Sean's Show*; Brenda Cox in *Side by Side*; *The Bill*; *The Ten Percenters*.

Films: Mary in *First Knight*.

Address: c/o Stephen Hatton Management, Suite 24, London Fruit and Wool Exchange, Brushfield Street, London E1 6HB.

DAVIES, Windsor

Windsor Davies. Actor (M).

b. Canning Town, London, 28 August 1930.

TV: *Gormenghast* (1999); *It Ain't Half Hot Mum*; *Mortimer's Law* (1997); *Mosley* (1997); *Never the Twain*; *Oh, Doctor Beeching!* (1997); *Paris* (1994); *Vanity Fair* (1998).

Films: *Adolf Hitler: My Part In His Downfall*; *Carry On Behind*; *Department K*; *Grandslam*; *Hammerhead*; *The Family Way*.

Address: c/o International Artistes Ltd, Mezzanine Floor, 235 Regent Street, London W1R 8AX. m. Lynne; 4 d. Jane, Sarah, Nancy, Beth; 1 s. Daniel. Hobbies: Rugby, reading, walking.

DAVIS, Philip

Philip Davis. Actor (M).

TV: *A Provincial Lady*; *Bergerac*; *Births, Marriages and Deaths*; *Christopher Columbus – The Great Adventure*; *Dead Lucky*; *Gotcha*; *Inspector Morse*; *Moving Story*; *Mystery Stories*; *Nice Town*; *Paradise Club*; *Passmore*; *Robin of Sherwood*; *Rumpole of the Bailey*; *Sexton Blake and the Demon God*; *Tales from the Crypt*; *The Death or Glory Boy*; *The Firm*; *The Flipside of Dominic Hide*; *The Majors Charity*; *Truckers*.

Films: *Alien III*; *Blue Ice*; *Comrades*; *Crimetime*; *Crossing the Border*; *Deep Water*; *Doctor and the Devils*; *Face*; *High Hopes*; *In the Name of the Father*; *Mr Quilp*; *Oliver Twist*; *Photographing Fairies*; *Quadrophenia*; *The Bounty*; *The Canterbury Tales*; *The First Kangaroos*; *The Howling*; *The Wall*; *Underworld*.

Address: William Morris Agency (UK) Ltd, 1 Stratton Street, London W1X 6HB.

DAVISON, Libby

Libby Davison. Actor (F).

TV: *Ain't Misbehavin'*; *Byker Grove*; *Dream On*; *Harry*; *Little Richard Wrecked My Marriage*; *Medics*; *Our Friends in the North*; W.D.C. Rawton in *The Bill*; *The Wedding*.

Films: Miss Warren in *Season Ticket*.

Address: c/o Evans & Reiss, 100 Fawe Park Road, London SW15 2EA.

DAVISON, Peter

Peter Davison. Actor (M). b. London, 13 April 1951.

TV: *A Man You Don't Meet Every Day*; *A Very Peculiar Practice*; *A Very Polish Practice*; *Ain't Misbehavin'*; *All Creatures Great and Small*; *Anna of the Five Towns*; *Blackmail*; *Campion*; *Cuts*; *Dear Nobody*; *Doctor Who*; *Harnessing Peacocks*; *Heavenly Bodies*; *Holding the Fort*; *Jonathan Creek*; *Kinsey*; *Love for Lydia*; *Magnum PI*; *Miss Marple: The Murderer*; *The Mrs Bradley Mysteries: Death of the Opera*; *Sink or Swim*; *Tales of the Unexpected*; *At Home With The Braithwaites*; *The Stalker's Apprentice*; *The Tomorrow People*; *Wuthering Heights*.

Films: *Black Beauty*; *Molly*; *Parting Shots*.

Address: c/o Conway Van Gelder, 18–21 Jermyn Street, London SW1Y 6HP.

DAWN, Elizabeth

Elizabeth Dawn. Actor (F).

b. Leeds, West Yorkshire, 8 November 1939.

TV: Vera Duckworth in *Coronation Street*; *Crown Court* (1975); *How's Yer Father* (1974); *Kisses at Fifty* (1972); *The Larry Grayson Show* (1975); *Leeds United*; *Sam* (1974); *Speech Day* (1972); *Sunset Across the Bay* (1974); *The Green Hill Pals* (1975); *Village Hall* (1974); *Z-Cars* (1974).

Music: *Passing Strangers* (UK Top 20 hit).

Address: c/o Arena Entertainment, Regents Court, 39 Harrogate Road, Leeds, West Yorkshire. m. Don Ibbetson; 3 d. Dawn, Ann, Julie; 1 s. Graham. Hobbies: Charity work, family.

DAWS, Robert

Robert Daws. Actor (M). b. 1959.

TV: *A Bit of Fry and Laurie*; Mark Andrews in *Birds of a Feather*; Simon Eastman in *Casualty*; Tony Jacobs in *Close to Home*; *Embassy*; *Fresh Fields*; Paul Taylor in *Game, Set and Match*; *I Love Keith Allen*; *Jeeves and Wooster*; *John and Yoko*; *The Mystery of Men*; Roger Dervish in *Outside Edge*; *Pie in the Sky*; Hubert De Giscard in *Robin of Sherwood*; *Roger Roger*; Dick Evans in *The Dirty Dozen*; Jack Fellows in *The Great Escape*; Piggy Garstone in *The House of*

Eliott; *The Missing Postman*; *The Paul Merton Show*; *There Comes a Time*; Septimus Warren in *Virginia Woolf*; Seamus Cassidy in *West Two*; Mr Farthington in *Woof*.

Address: c/o ICM, Oxford House, 76 Oxford Street, London W1N 0AX.

DAWSON, Ashley

Ashley Dawson. Actor (M). b. 11 January 1982.

TV: Darren Osborne in *Hollyoaks*.

Address: c/o PHA Casting Management, Tanzaro House, Ardwick Green North, Manchester M12 6FZ.

DAY, Simon

Simon Day. Actor (M).

TV: *A Royal Celebration* (1998); *Shooting Stars* (1998); *The Fast Show*.

Films: *Shakespeare in Love*.

Address: c/o Avalon Promotions, 2nd Floor, Queens House, Leicester Place, Leicester Square, London WC2H 7BP.

DAY, Simon

Simon Day. Actor (M).

TV: *Casualty*; *Pie in the Sky*; *The Great Kandinsky*; *The House of Eliott*; *Red Dwarf*; *London's Burning*; *the Bill*; *the Knock*; *Wycliffe*.

Films: *The Anorak*.

Address: c/o Garricks, 7 Garrick Street, London, WC2E 9AR.

DE CADENET, Amanda

Amanda De Cadenet. Presenter. b. 19 May 1972.

TV: *The Word*.

Films: English prisoner in *Brokendown Palace*; Sarah in *Fall*; Diana in *Four Rooms*; Receptionist in *Grace of My Heart*; Jennifer in *Mascara*.

Address: c/o Storm Artists Management, 47 Brewer Street, London W1R 3FD. m. 1st John Taylor (dis); 1 d. Atlanta.

DE CAUNES, Antoine

Antoine De Caunes. Actor (M)/Presenter.

TV: *Channel Hopping*; *Chorus*; *Eurotrash*; *Eurovision Night* (1998); *Le Show* (1999); *Les Enfants du Rock*; *Nulle Part Ailleurs*; *Rapido*; *Rock Report*; *Surtout l'Après Midi*; *World Cup Special* (1998).

Films: *C'est Pour la Bonne Cause* (1996); *L'Homme est une Femme comme les Autres* (1998); *La Divine Poursuite* (1997); *Les 2 Papas et la Maman* (1995); *Pentimento* (1989).

Address: c/o PBJ Management, 5 Soho Square, London W1V 5DE. 1 d. Emma.

DE LA TOUR, Frances

Frances De La Tour. Actor (F).

b. Bovingdon, Hertfordshire, 30 July 1944.

TV: *A Kind of Living; All Good Men;* Beatrice in *Bejewelled;* Emma Porlock in *Cold Lazarus;* Rosemary in *Downwardly Mobile; Duet For One;* Shirley Silver in *Every Silver Lining; Flickers;* Dr Feuchtwanger in *Genghis Cohen; Housewives' Choice; Murder With Mirrors;* Miss Jones in *Rising Damp; Skirmishes; Stay Lucky; The South Bank Show;* Charlotta in *The Cherry Orchard.*

Address: c/o Kate Feast Management, 10 Primrose Hill Studios, Fitzroy Road, London NW1 8TR.

DE PAUL, Lynsey

Lynsey De Paul. Actor (F)/Singer.

b. London, 11 June 1952.

TV: *A Word in Your Ear; Blankety Blank; Call My Bluff; Dangerous Days; Eve Strikes Back; Holiday; Ladybirds; Living Issues; Living Room Legends; New Faces; Starlite Ballroom; Taking Control; That's Life; The Vinyl Frontier; Through the Keyhole; Woman of Substance.*

Music: *No Honestly; Rock Bottom; Storm in a Teacup; Sugar Me; Won't Somebody Dance With Me?*

Address: c/o Langford Associates, 17 Westfields Avenue, London SW13 0AT. Hobbies: Animal welfare.

DE ROSSI, Portia

Amanda Rogers. Actor (F).

b. Melbourne, Australia, 31 January 1973.

TV: Nelle Porter in *Ally McBeal; Nick Freno; Perfect Assassins;* Maria Hunter in *Too Something.*

Films: *American Intellectuals;* Carla in *Girl;* Sorority Sister Murphy in *Scream 2;* Giddy in *Sirens;* Jennifer Kelliho in *Stigmata;* Joy in *The Invisibles.*

Address: c/o ICM Agency, 8942 Wilshire Blvd., Beverly Hills, California 90211, USA. Hobbies: Playing guitar, reading, poetry.

DEACON, Brian

Brian Deacon. Actor (M). b. Oxford, 13 February 1949.

TV: Alan Woodcourt in *Bleak House;* Brian Brodey in *BUGS; Centre Play – Risking It; Churchill's People; Country Dance;* Neil Kincaid in *Emmerdale;* Oswald in *Ghosts; Good Girl;* Alex in *Inapppropiate Behaviours; Leap In the Dark;* Frank Miles in *Lillie;* Mr Lewisham in *Love and Mr Lewisham;* Jean Pierre in *Me and My Girl;* Clive Gray in *Mr Palfrey of Westminster;* David in *Rewards of Virtue;* Charles in *Separate Tables; Shock of the New; The Emmigrants; The Feathered Serpent; The Guardians; Thirty-Minute Theatre; What's Your Story.*

Films: *A Zed and Two Noughts;* Alan/Martin Yardley in *And The Wall Came Tumbling Down; Il Bacio; Jesus* in *Jesus, His Life and Times;* Gunner Barton in *The Triple Echo; Vampires.*

Address: c/o Kate Feast Management, 10 Primrose Hill Studios, Fitzroy Road, London NW1 8TR.

DEACON, Eric

Eric Deacon. Actor (M). b. Oxford, 25 May 1960.

TV: Les in *A Crowd in the Countryside; A Photograph; A Place Like Home;* Tony Harris in *Brookside; Casualty; Columbus; Contract; Dark Secret; Doctor Who; Hard Cases;* Brian Mansfield in *Heartbeat;* Neil Innes in *Wycliffe; King's Royal; London's Burning* (regular); Dennis Hardwick in *Lovejoy; Maigret; Medics; Only Children; Operation Julie; Penmarric;* Matthew in *Plastic Man; Postcards From SouthSea; Prime Suspect; Spearhead; Stay Lucky; The Bill;* Prison Governor in *The Jump; The Survivors.*

Films: *A Nous Le Petit Anglais; A Zed and Two Noughts; Bitter; Coming of Age; It Could Happen To You; One of the Lads; Wolf; Yesterday's Hero.*

Address: c/o Burdett-Coutts Associates, Riverside Studios, Crisp Road, London W6 9RL.

DEAKIN, Julia

Julia Deakin. Actor (F). b. Lincolnshire.

TV: Jude Jakes in *Hope and Glory;* Gill in *I'm Alan Partridge;* Brucella in *Mother's Ruin;* May in *Oh, Doctor Beeching!;* Stella in *Side by Side;* Carole in *So Haunt Me;* Marsha in *Spaced.*

Films: *Between Two Women;* Berni in *Dancin' Thru The Dark;* Melanie in *Mr Love;* Brenda in *Staggered.*

Address: c/o Scott Marshall, 44 Perryn Road, London W3 7NA.

DEAN, Bill

Bill Dean. Actor (M).

b. Liverpool, Merseyside, 3 September 1921.

TV: *3-7-11; A Turn For The Worst; Brookside; Clarissa; Emmerdale; Heartbeat; Hillsborough; Lovers of the Lake; Oh No, It's Selwyn Froggitt; Priest; Scallagrigg; The Forgotten Army; The Good Companions; The Liver Birds; The Young Indiana Jones Chronicles; Time Out of Mind; When the Boat Comes In.*

Films: Nightclub Proprietor in *Gumshoe; Let Him Have It; Nightwatch.*

Address: c/o Crouch Associates, 9–15 Covent Garden, London WC2H 9PF.

DEAN, Letitia

Letitia Dean. Actor (F). b. 1968.

TV: *Brookside; Casualty;* Weather Girl in *Drop the Dead Donkey;* Sharon in *EastEnders; Grange Hill; Love Story; Lucy Sullivan is Getting Married; Streetwise; The Bill;*

Chris in *The Hello Girls; Timmy and Vicky*.
Films: *England, My England*.
Address: c/o Jonathan Altaras Associates, 13 Shorts Gardens, London WC2H 9AT.

DEAN, Peter

Peter Dean. Actor (M). b. London, 2 May 1939.
TV: *Coronation Street*; Peter Beale in *EastEnders; Minder; Shine on Harvey Moon; Shoestring; The Bill*; Sgt. Wilding in *Woodentop*.
Films: *Sweet William; The Great Rock 'n' Roll Swindle*.
Address: c/o KAL Management, 95 Gloucester Road, Hampton, Middlesex TW12 2UW.

DEAYTON, Angus

Angus Deayton. Presentor/Actor (M).
b. 6 January 1956.
TV: *A History of Alternative Comedy* (1999); *Alexei Sayle's Stuff*; Paul Foot in *Bad Company; Before They Were Famous; Bore of the Year Awards*; Lawyer in *Chelmsford 123*; Quint Hospital Manager in *Doctor at the Top; End of The Year Show* (1995, 1996, 1997); *Friday Night, Saturday Morning Live; Have I Got News For You; In Search of Happiness; KYTV*; Head of MI5 in *Lord of Misrule; Mr Bean* (various); Lord Bernard Nutmeg in *Oliver 2 – Let's Twist Again*; Patrick in *One Foot in the Grave; Temptation Game; The Lying Game*; Performer in *Tiswas; TV Bell*.
Films: Leonard in *Savage Hearts*.
Address: c/o TalkBack Management, 36 Percy Street, London W1P OLN.

DEE, Jack

Jack Dee. Comedian/Presenter.
b. Petts Wood, Winchester, 24 September 1961.
TV: *Aspel and Co.; Big City; Brit Awards; Brucie's Guest Night; Clive Anderson Talks Back; Des O'Connor Tonight; Edinburgh Live; Edinburgh Nights; Glamorama with Jack Dee; It's Only TV... But I Like It; Jack and Jeremy's Police; Jack and Jeremy's Real Lives; Jack Dee's Saturday Night; Just For Laughs; Look Who's Talking; Reportage; Sunday Night Clive; TFI Friday; The Big Breakfast; The Jack Dee Show; This Morning; Top of the Pops; Wogan*.
Address: c/o Off the Kerb Productions, 3rd Floor, Hammer House, 113–117 Wardour Street, London W1V 3TD.

DEELEY, Cat

Cat Deeley. Presenter.
TV: *Amour; CD:UK; Five Night Stand; Girls R Us; Select; SM:tv Live; Stylissimo; The Hit List; Turn on, Tune in, Chill Out Weekend*.

Address: c/o Freud Communications, 19–21 Mortimer Street, London W1N 8DX.

DEGENERES, Ellen

Ellen Degeneres. Actor (F).
b. New Orleans, Louisiana, USA, 26 January 1958.
TV: *Duet*; Ellen Morgan in *Ellen; If These Walls Could Talk 2; Laughing Back: Comedy Takes A Stand*; Nancy MacIntire in *Laurie Hill*; Nancy Bloom in *Mad About You; One Night Stand*; Margo Van Meter in *Open House*; Marriage Counsellor in *Roseanne; Six Comics In Search Of A Generation; The 38th Annual Grammy Awards* (host); herself in *The Larry Sanders Show; Women Of The Night*.
Films: Coach in *Coneheads*; Prologue dog in *Doctor Dolittle*; Cynthia Topping in *Ed TV*; Sgt. Rita Pompano in *Goodbye Lover*; Martha Alston in *Mr Wrong*; Janet Hall in *The Love Letter*; herself in *Wisecracks*.
Address: c/o ICM Agency, 8942 Wilshire Blvd., Beverly Hills, California 90211, USA.

DELANY, Kim

Kim Delany. Actor (F). b. Philadelphia, Pennsylvania, USA, 29 November 1961.
TV: *All Lies End In Murder*; Jenny Gardner Nelson in *All My Children; Hooperman; L.A. Law*; Maggie in *Lady Boss*; Detective Diane Russell in *NYPD Blue; Take My Daughters Please; Tales from the Crypt; Tall, Dark and Deadly; The Broken Cord*; Niki in *The Devil's Child; The Equalizer*; Erica Fontaine in *The Fifth Corner*; Alex Devlin in *Tour of Duty*.
Films: *Body Parts*; Dayna Thomas in *Campus Man; Closer and Closer; Darkman II*; Sister Mary in *Delta Force; Mission To Mars; Rules of Engagement; Serial Killer; That Was Then, This Is Now*; Julia Robbins in *The Drifter*; Sarah in *The Force*.
Address: c/o Gersh Agency, 23rd Floor, 130 West 42nd Street, New York, New York 10036, USA. fiancé Alan Barnette; 1 s. Jack. Hobbies: Biking, swimming, working out.

DENCH, Dame Judi

Judith Dench. Actor (F). b. York, 9 December 1934.
TV: *Hilda Lessways; An Age of Kings; Village Wooing; Major Barbara; Pink String and Sealing Wax; On Giant's Shoulders; Langrishe; Go Down; The Teachers; Z Cars; Love Story; The Funambulists; Jackanory; Parade's End; Marching Song; On Approval; Days to Come; Emilie; Macbeth; Langrishe Go Down; Make and Break; Talking to a Stranger; The Morecambe and Wise Show; Love in a Cold Climate; Going Gently; The Cherry Orchard*; Laura in *A fine Romance; Saigon – Year of the Cat; the Browning Version; Mr & Mrs Edgehill; Ghosts;*

Behaving Badly; Can You Hear Me Thinking; Birthday; Absolute Hell; Jean in *As Time Goes By; The Comedy of Errors; Torch; Middlemarch; The South Bank Show.*
Films: Nora Doel in *84 Charing Cross Road;* Laura in *A Fine Romance;* Mrs Beaver in *A Handful of Dust;* Miss Lavish in *A Room with a View;* Harriet Hawthorne in *After Murder Park;* M in *Goldeneye;* Hecuba in *Hamlet;* Aunt Sadie in *Love In A Cold Climate;* Queen Victoria in *Mrs Brown;* Queen Elizabeth in *Shakespeare in Love;* Arabella in *Tea With Mussolini;* M in *The World is Not Enough;* M in *Tomorrow Never Dies.*
Address: c/o Julian Belfrage Associates, 46 Albemarle Street, London W1X 4PP. m. Michael Williams; 1 d. Finty (Tara Cressida Frances).

DENNIS, Les

Les Dennis. Actor (M)/Comedian/Presenter.
b. Liverpool, 12 October 1954.
TV: *Family Affairs; Family Fortunes; Give Your Mate a Break; Go for It; Les Dennis Laughter Show; London Tonight; Royal Variety Performance; Russ Abbot's Madhouse; The Laughter Show; The Russ Abbot Show; The Smell of Reeves and Mortimer; This is Your Life; Wyrd Sisters.*
Films: Maurice Guppy in *Intimate Relations.*
Address: Lake-Smith Griffin Associates, 15 Maiden Lane, London WC2E 7NA. m. 1 Lynne; m. 2 Amanda Holden; 1 s. Phillip.

DERBYSHIRE, Eileen

Eileen Derbyshire. Actor (F).
b. Manchester, 6 October 1931.
TV: Emily Bishop in *Coronation Street.*
Address: c/o Granada Television, Quay Street, Manchester M60 9EA. m. Thomas Holt; 1 s. Oliver. Hobbies: Literature, music, travel.

DEROSA, Warren

Warren Derosa. Actor (M).
TV: Rob Hawthorn in *Hollyoaks;* Dave in *A Touch of Love.*
Films: Adrian in *Adrian's Debt.*
Address: c/o Ken McReddie Ltd, 91 Regent Street, London W1R 7TB.

DERREN, Litten

Litten Derren. Actor (M).
TV: Mick in *A Touch of Frost;* Mick in *EastEnders;* Steve in *Hands Together; Minder;* Vaughan Rogers in *Perfect World;* DC Guthriel in *Pie in the Sky.*
Address: c/o Evans & Reiss, 100 Fawe Park Road, London SW15 2EA. Hobbies: Magic (member of Magic Circle), juggling, clowning, tumbling.

DESBOROUGH, Bree

Bree Desborough. Actor (F).
b. Sydney, Australia, 22 September 1979.
TV: *GP;* Justine in *Home and Away; Water Rats.*
Address: Seven Network Ltd, Mabbs Lane, Epping, New South Wales 2121, Australia.
Hobbies: Listening to music, going to see bands.

DEU, Amerjit

Amerjit Deu. Actor (M).
b. Punjab, India, 3 September 1960.
TV: *A Touch of Frost;* Udam Singh in *Crimes of the Empire;* Dr Singh in *EastEnders;* Ranjit in *Eldorado; Holby City; Jake's Progress; Lucy Sullivan is Getting Married; Pig Heart Boy; The Bill.*
Films: *Appeal; Caught; Deceivers; Eye of the Storm; Food of Love; Guru in Seven; Mad Cows; Praying for an Elephant; Terminal Eye.*
Address: c/o Scott Marshall, 44 Perryn Road, London W3 7NA. m. Baljinder Deu; 1 d. Gursimran Deu. Hobbies: Sport, theatre, cinema, travel.

DEVANEY, Sue

Sue Devaney. Actor (F)/Presenter.
b. Ashton-under-Lyne, 2 July 1967.
TV: *But First This;* Liz Harker in *Casualty;* Helen in *Common As Muck;* Debbie Webster in *Coronation Street;* 1st Secretary in *dinnerladies;* Amanda in *Exclusive Yarns; Fan TC;* Sandra in *Flying Lady;* Zoe in *Gordon the Gopher;* Betty Bouncer in *Haggard;* Jennifer in *Heartbeat;* Mildred Bailey in *In Loving Memory;* Rita Briggs in *Johnny Briggs; Mating Call;* Treny Wendy in *Model Millie;* Mable in *The Mrs Bradley Mysteries;* Betsy in *Mrs Worthington's Daughter;* Gaynor in *The Mystery of Men;* Jo in *Spatz;* Ruth Harcourt in *The Bill;* Janice in *The Index Has Gone Fishing;* Mad Bastard in *The Real Eddy English;* Ruby in *When We Are Married.*
Address: c/o Marmont Management Ltd, Langham House, 308 Regent Street, London W1R 5AL.

DHIRI, Amita

Amita Dhiri. Actor (F). b. Brighton, Sussex 1968.
TV: Dr Julia Kaash in *Casualty; Dalziel and Pascoe;* Sanita in *Do the Right Thing;* Edna in *Edna Million In A Drop Out Suit;* Rashida in *Indian Tales;* First Witch in *Macbeth;* Delia Vine in *McCallum;* Jandra Nixon in *The Last Train;* Milly in *This Life;* Catherine in *Whatever.*
Films: *24 Hours in London.*
Address: c/o Conway Van Gelder, 18–21 Jermyn Street, London SW1Y 6HP.

DIAMOND, Reed

Reed Diamond. Actor (M). b. New York, 20 July 1964.
TV: *919 5th Avenue*; Jeffrey Baker in *Awake to Murder*; Charlie in *Blind Spot*; Harry Winslow in *Danielle Steel's 'Full Circle'*; Clay Devereaux in *Her Hidden Truth*; Detective Kellerman in *Homicide*; Eddie Jr in *Indefensible: The Truth About Edward Brannigan*; *Ironclads*; Stuart Collins in *Judging Amy*; Christopher Baylor in *Law and Order*; Emil in *O Pioneers!* Thomas Rafferty in *Secrets*; *The Summer of the Swans*.
Films: Bob in *Assassins*; Coast Guard Chief in *Clear and Present Danger*; Skip in *Madison*; Virge in *Memphis Belle*; Ramsay Child in *Two Minute Warning*.
Address: c/o Innovative Artists, 1999 Avenue of the Stars, Los Angeles, California 90067, USA.

DIBLEY, Janet

Janet Dibley. Actor (F).
b. Doncaster, 13 December 1958.
TV: *The Two of Us*; *A Brother's Tale*; Paula in *Band of Gold*; Lorna in *EastEnders*; *Foxy Lady*; Natalia in *Loved By You*; *Lytton's Diary*; Crystal in *The Bill* (1999).
Address: c/o Dalzell and Beresford Ltd, 91 Regent Street, London W1R 7TB.

DICKINSON, Sandra

Sandra Dickinson. Actor (F).
b. Washington DC, USA, 20 October 1940.
TV: *Cover*; *Tales from the Crypt*; *Real Life*; *Stick With Me Kid*; *The Clairvoyant*; *The Des O'Connor Show*; *The Hitch Hiker's Guide to the Galalxy*; *The Tom O'Connor Show*; *The Two Ronnies*; *The Reluctant Vampires*; *Triangle*; *2point4 children*; *What Mad Pursuit*; *What's on Next?*.
Films: *Present Spirits*; *Supergirl*; *Superman III*; *The Final Programme*; *The Hunger*; *The Lonely Lady*.
Address: c/o Kerry Gardner Management, 7 St George's Square, London SW1V 2HX.

DICKSON, Barbara

Barbara Dickson. Actor (F)/Singer.
b. Dunfermline, 27 September 1947.
TV: Anita Braithwaite in *Band of Gold*; Marie Macdonald in *Taggart*; *The Afternoon Show*; Mrs Taylor in *The Missing Postman*.
Music: *All For A Song*; *Answer Me*; *Another Suitcase in Another Hall*; *Coming Alive Again*; *Heartbeats*; *I Know Him Well*; *January, February*; *The Caravan Song*.
Address: c/o Theobald Dickson Productions Ltd, The Coach House, Swinhope Hall, Swinhope, Lincolnshire LN8 6HT. m. Oliver Cookson; 3 s. Colm, Archie, Gabriel.

DICKSON WRIGHT, Clarissa

Clarissa Dickson Wright. Chef/Presenter.
TV: *Clive Anderson All Talk*; *Have I Got News For You*; *Two Fat Ladies*.
Address: c/o BBC, Union House, 65–69 Shepherds Bush Green, London W12 8TX.

DILLANE, Richard

Richard Dillane. Actor (M).
TV: David in *An Evil Streak*; Brian in *Big Women*; Dan in *Emmerdale Christmas Video*; Terry Semple in *Heartbeat*; Ben in *Men Behaving Badly*; Sgt. Brad Connor in *Soldier, Soldier*; Jeroboam in *Solomon*; Villiers in *The Grand*; Robert Horton-Smith in *Verdict*.
Films: Hunter in *Wing Commander*.
Address: c/o Hamilton Asper, 24 Hanway Street, London W1P 9DD.

DILLANE, Stephen

Stephen Dillane. Actor (M).
TV: Gray in *An Affair in Mind*; Karenin in *Anna Karenina*; Peter in *Christabel*; Strickland in *Frankie's House*; Patsy Durack in *Kings In Grass Castles*; Nicholas in *The One Game*; Jonathan in *The Rector's Wife*; Blackmore in *The Widowing of Mrs Holroyd*; John in *The Yellow Wallpaper*; James Woodlay in *You, Me and It*.
Films: Mr Dunlop in *Business as Usual*; Charles in *Firelight*; Horatio in *Hamlet*; *La Chance*; Dr Croly in *Love And Rage*; Noel in *Ordinary Decent Criminal*; Tom in *The Darkest Light*; Evan Morgan in *Two If by Sea*; Michael Henderson in *Welcome to Sarajevo*.
Address: c/o Michelle Braidman Associates, 10–11 Lower John Street, London W1R 3PE.

DIMBLEBY, David

David Dimbleby. Presenter. b. 28 October 1938.
TV: *Twenty-Four Hours*; *An Ocean Apart*; *Panorama*; *People and Power*; *Question Time*; *The Dimbleby Talk-In*; *The White Tribe of Africa*; *This Week, Next Week*.
Address: BBC News, Union House, 65–69 Shepherds Bush Green, London W12 8TX.

DIMMOCK, Charlie

Charlie Dimmock. Gardener. b. 1966.
TV: *The Big Breakfast*; *Charlie's Garden Army*; *Grass Roots*; *Ground Force*; *Night Fever*; *Ready, Steady Cook*.
Address: c/o Arlington Enterprises Ltd, 1–3 Charlotte Street, London W1P 1HD.

DINGWALL, Shaun

Shaun Dingwall. Actor (M).
TV: Van Horne in *A Breed of Heroes*; P.C. Curles in

Between the Lines; Schuster in *Black Easter;* Det. Sgt. Lynch in *Class Act;* Rob Newton in *Hands Together;* James Freeman in *In a Land of Plenty;* Wayne in *Minder; Rocket to the Moon; Screen Two:* Hubsch in *Genghis Cohen;* Steve Evans in *Soldier, Soldier; Stages: Low Level Panic; The Bill;* P.C. Byrne in *The Chief;* Clive in *The Loser;* The Burglar in *The Phoenix and the Carpet;* Rivers in *Touching Evil;* River in *Underground.*
Films: Graham in *Second Best.*
Address: c/o Susan Angel Associates, 1st Floor, 12 D'Arblay Street, London W1V 3FP.

DINSDALE, Reece
Reece Dinsdale. Actor (M).
b. Normanton, West Yorkshire, 6 August 1959.
TV: Rory O'Brien in *Bergerac;* Clive Sussman in *Bliss;* Robert in *Coppers;* Tarquin in *Full Stretch;* Malcolm in *Glamour Night;* Roderick in *Haggard;* Mathew in *Home to Roost;* Tommy Fenn in *Knife Edge;* D.C.I. Sharpe in *Lovejoy;* Tone in *Out on the Floor;* Albert in *Partners in Crime;* Arthur in *Robin of Sherwood;* Sherlock in *Sherlock Holmes and the Case of the Missing Link;* Fearnot in *Story Teller;* Martin in *Take Me Home;* Danny in *The Attractions;* Albert in *The Secret Adversary;* Scott in *Thief Takers;* Jimmy Kemp in *Threads;* Peter in *Young Catherine.*
Films: P.C. Penny in *A Private Function;* Guildenstern in *Hamlet;* John in *ID;* Mike in *Romance and Rejection;* Mal in *Winter Flight.*
Address: c/o William Morris Agency (UK) Ltd, 1 Stratton Street, London W1X 6HB. Hobbies: Huddersfield Town supporter.

DOBIE, Alan
Alan Dobie. Actor (M). b. 2 June 1932.
TV: *A Case of Spirits; A Cold Heart; A Collier's Friday Night; Abracadabra; Age of Innocence; An Inspector Calls; Circus Time; Come and Find Me; Court Case; Dance of Death; Danton; Deadline Midnight; Death of Ivan Lynch; Design for Murder; Diamond Crack Diamond; Dishonoured Bones; Doctor Faustus; Double Dare; Dr Dee; Eleanor Marx; Eustace Diamonds; Everyman; For Services to Myself; Géricault; Hard Times; Hedda Gabler; Heir to Skipton; Horizontal Witness; Kelly and the Spirits; Kessler; Macbeth; Margaret; Master of the Game; Morecambe and Wise; Murder Old Boy; Nanny; Our Young Mr Wignal; Resurrection; Rigleman Harris; Something Old, Something New; Swing Swing Together; The Affair; The Alchemist; The Black Arrow; The Choir That Wouldn't Sing; The Corsican Brothers; The Defector; The Detective Wore Silk Drawers; The Disputation; The Dynamite Party; The Firm of Girdlestone; The Hospice; The House on Kirov Street; The Incident;* *The Last Trumpet; The Lost King; The Madhatter's Holiday; The Man who Fell Apart; The Plane Makers; The Price of Freedom; The Rough and Ready Lot; The Seige of Manchester; The Suicide Club; The Takers; The Verdict is Yours; Thomas Becket; Trouble Shooters; War and Peace; Waxwork; Wobble Together; Zedicular.*
Films: *A Long Day's Dying; Alfred The Great; Battle for the Mind; Charge of the Light Brigade; Dr Syn; Madam Sin; Seven Keys; The Chairman; The Comedy Man; White Bird; White Mischief.*
Address: c/o Jane Lehrer Associates, 100a Chalk Farm Road, London NW1 8EH.

DOBSON, Anita
Anita Dobson. Actor (F). b. London, 29 April 1949.
TV: Miriam Lampter in *Dangerfield;* Angie Watts in *EastEnders;* Eileen Hughes in *Enough Excitement;* Mrs Stitch in *The Famous Five;* Mrs Osbourne in *Get Well Soon;* Mum in *Go Back Out;* Suzi Rudkin in *I'll Be Watching You;* Bertha Birthcanal in *It's a Girl;* Mrs Lawson in *Junk;* Roxanne in *Leave Him to Heaven;* Dorothy in *Nanny;* Esta Quant in *Partners in Crime; Playaway;* Cath in *Rab C. Nesbitt;* Captain Nau in *Red Dwarf VI;* Betty in *Sean's Show;* Gertie in *Smokescreen;* Joyce Potts in *Sunburn;* Improvised characters in *Take the Stage;* Jane Elliot in *The Bill;* Marianne in *The Fireboy; The Lily Savage Show* (various sketches); Roxanne in *The World of Eddie Weary;* Lois in *Up the Elephant and Round the Castle;* Mrs Fuller in *Woof.*
Films: Judith Hamilton in *Beyond Bedlam;* Mrs Hayter in *Dangerous Obsession;* Brenda in *Need;* Blind Concierge in *Seaview Knights;* Mrs Monk in *The Euphoric Scale;* Daphne Teale in *The Revenger's Comedies;* Fanny Lodger in *The Titchborne Claimant.*
Music: *On My Own; Talking of Love.*
Address: c/o CAM London, 19 Denmark Street, London WC2H 8NA. m. Brian May.

DOCHERTY, Jack
Jack Docherty. Actor (M)/Presenter.
b. Edinburgh 1962.
TV: *Absolutely; Acropolis Now; Auld Lang Syne; Edinburgh Nights; Hello Mum; Hogmanay Show; Lenny Henry; Mr Don and Mr George; Queen of the Wild Frontier; Red Dwarf; Saturday Stayback; Spitting Image; The Creatives; The Jack Docherty Show; The Ken Fine Show; The Terry Neason Show; Valhalla.*
Address: c/o PBJ Management, 5 Soho Square, London W1V 5DE.

DODD, Ken
Ken Dodd OBE. Actor (M)/Comedian.
b. Knotty Ash, Liverpool, 8 November 1927.

TV: *An Audience With Ken Dodd; Doddy's Music Box; Doctor Who; Heroes of Comedy; Ken Dodd's Showbiz; Ken Dodd's World of Laughter; The Good Old Days; The Ken Dodd Show; This is Your Life.*

Films: Mr Mouse in *Alice in Wonderland;* Yorick in *Hamlet.*

Music: *Happiness; Love Is Like A Violin; Tears.*

Address: c/o George Bartram Associates, 1 Sherbourne Gate, Birmingham, B16 8DE. Hobbies: Reading, writing, watching horse racing.

DOHERTY, Shannen

Shannen Doherty. Actor (F).

b. Memphis, Tennessee, USA, 12 April 1971.

TV: Jenine in *21 Jump Steet;* Phoebe Danner in *Airwolf;* Brenda Walsh in *Beverly Hills 90210;* Wendy Edwards in *Beverly Hills 90210;* Madeleine Dalton in *Blindfold: Acts of Obsession;* Margaret Mitchell in *Burning Passion;* Prue Halliwell in *Charmed;* Drusilla Shannon in *Father Murphy;* Lindsay Scott in *Freeze Frame;* Heather Romley in *Friends Till The End;* Cindy Dowaliby in *Gone In The Night;* Shelley Fowler in *Highway to Heaven;* Angel in *Jailbreakers; Life Goes On;* Jenny Wilder in *Little House On The Prairie;* Jenny Wilder in *Little House on the Prairie: Look Back To Yesterday;* Jenny Wilder in *Little House: Bless All The Dear Children;* Ima Platt in *Magnum PI* (1983); Lorie Brindel in *Obsessed;* Kris Witherspoon in *Our House; Outlaws;* Kathleen Kennedy in *Robert Kennedy and His Times; Satan's School For Girls;* Rebecca Dubrovich in *Sleeping With The Devil; The Other Lover; The Ticket.*

Films: Katherine Roshak in *Almost Dead;* Maggie Malene in *Girls Just Want to Have Fun;* Heather Duke in *Heathers;* Rene in *Mallrats;* herself in *Naked Gun 33^1/$_3$: The Final Insult;* Bluebird in *Night Shift;* Val Chick 2 in *Nowhere;* Gage Sullivan in *Striking Poses;* Teresa in *The Secret of NIMH.*

Address: c/o United Talent Agency, 9560 Wilshire Blvd, Suite 500, Beverly Hills, California 90212, USA. 1st m. Ashely Hamilton. Hobbies: Passionate about her dogs and horses.

DOLAN, Leo

Leo Dolan. Actor (M).

TV: *Androcles and the Lion; Bottle Boys* (1985); Clulow in *Bramwell* (1994); Ron in *Casualty* (1993); Tony in *Chucklevision* (1995); Dave in *Chucklevision* (1998); Publican in *Crime Monthly* (1996); Removal Man in *Crocodile Shoes* (1996); Sammy in *EastEnders* (1995); Jury Foreman in *Every Woman Knows a Secret* (1998); Tramp in *Family Affairs* (1999); Mr Smith in *Goodnight Sweetheart* (1999); Jack in

Grafters (1998); Officer in *Great Expectations* (1998); Joe in *Hope and Glory* (1999); *In Sickness and in Health* (1986); Debt Collector in *In the Red* (1998); Van Driver in *Jonathan Creek* (1996); Barney in *London's Burning* (1995); *Reservations* (1986) (leading role); *Robin Hood* (1986); Barman in *The Bill* (1995); John in *The Bill* (1989); Mr Brooks in *The Bill* (1992); Mr Taylor in *The Bill* (1994); Mitch in *The Bill* (1998); Peter Yates in *The Bill* (1999); Beckett in *The Detectives* (1994); *The Misanthrope;* Jack in *The Vet* (1995); *Watch This Space; William Tell.*

Films: *Chariots of Fire; Meet Me in Dreamland; My Friend Walter; The Thirty-Nine Steps; The Long Good Friday.*

Address: c/o McIntosh Rae Management, Thornton House, Thornton Road, London SW19 4NG.

DON, Monty

Monty Don. Gardener/Presenter. b. 1957.

TV: *Chelsea Live; Fasten Your Seat Belt; Holiday; Holidays Out; Lost Gardens; Real Gardens; Summer Holiday; This Morning; Tomorrow's World.*

Address: c/o The Roseman Organisation, Suite 9, The Power House, 70 Chiswick Road, London W4 1SY. m. Sarah; 1 d. Freya; 2 s. Tom, Adam.

DONE, Jason

Jason Done. Actor (M).

TV: *Blood and Peaches; It Must Be Love; Merlin; Mother's Ruin; Once upon a Time; Overlanders; The Andersons; The Passion; Where the Heart Is; Wokenwell.*

Films: *The Barber of Siberia; The English Patient.*

Address: c/o ICM, Oxford House, 76 Oxford Street, London W1N 0AX.

DONNELLY, Declan

Declan Donnelly. Actor (M)/Presenter.

b. Newcastle, 25 September 1975.

TV: *Ant and Dec Unzipped* (1997); *Byker Grove; SM:TV Live; The Ant and Dec Show* (1995, 1996); *The Big Breakfast* (1997).

Music: *Falling; Stepping Stone; Tonight I'm Free;* various.

Address: c/o James Grant Management Ltd, Syon Lodge, London Road, Isleworth, Middlesex TW7 5BH.

DONNELLY, Dougie

Dougie Donnelly. Presenter. b. 7 June 1953.

TV: *Commonwealth Games; Friday Night With Dougie Donnelly; Golf; Grandstand; Match of the Day; Rugby Union; Snooker; Olympics; World Cup Football.*

Address: c/o David John Associates, 6 Victoria Crescent Road, Glasgow G12 9DB. m. Linda; 3 d. Kim, Laura, Lisa. Hobbies: Sport, food and wine, travel, reading.

DONOHOE, Amanda

Amanda Donohoe. Actor (F). b. 1962.

TV: *A Connecticut Yankee; A Woman's Guide to Adultery; An Affair in Mind; Briefest Encounter; Deep Secrets; Frasier; Game, Set and Match; Hidden Room; It's Nothing Personal; L.A. Law; Laughter of God; Murder Most Horrid; Shame; Shame 2; The Thorn Birds.*

Films: Lucy Irving in *Castaway;* Gloria in *Circus; Dark Obsession; Foreign Body;* Lady Silvia Marsh in *Lair of the White Worm;* Miranda in *Liar, Liar;* Lady Pembroke in *One Night Stand;* Christine in *Paper Mask;* Ruth in *Thanks for the Memories; The Madness of King George;* Winifred Inger in *The Rainbow;* Laura in *The Substitute; Writer's Block.*

Address: c/o William Morris Agency (UK) Ltd, 1 Stratton Street, London W1X 6HB.

DONOVAN, Daisy

Daisy Donovan. Actor (F).

TV: *Smith and Jones; The 11 O'Clock Show.*

Films: Female reporter in *Still Crazy.*

Address: c/o PFD, Drury House, 34–43 Russell Street, London WC2B 5HA. Father Terence Donovan; mother Diana; brother Terry. Hobbies: Swam the Channel.

DORE, Edna

Edna Doré. Actor (F).

TV: *A Year in Provence;* Mrs Salad in *Anglo-Saxon Attitudes;* Gran in *Brazen Hussies; Brighton Boy; Casualty; Christabel; Class Act; Doctor at Large; Doctor in the House;* Mo Butcher in *EastEnders; Gas and Candles;* Great Grandmother in *How to be a Little Sod; Jo Brand Christmas Special* (1998); *King of the Ghetto; Lizzie's Pictures; Love Hurts;* Stallholder in *Men Behaving Badly; Moving Story;* Grandma in *No Bananas; Open All Hours;* Betty Hidgen in *Our Mutual Friend;* Maisie in *Peak Practice; Reservation; Roger Doesn't Live Here Anymore; Sam's Saturday;* Granny in *Sampson Superslug; Smith and Jones; Streets Apart; Tenko; Terry Scott;* Mrs Essler in *The Bill; The Brothers;* Mrs Umney in *The Canterville Ghost;* Gran in *The Fallen Curtain; The Liver Birds; The Mysteries;* Rose in *Trust Me; Under the Skin;* Iris Cromer in *West Beach.*

Films: *Final Moments; High Hopes;* Edith in *Joint Venture;* The Old Woman in *Les Misérables;* Bag Lady in *My Father, The Liar;* Aunty in *My Little Eye; Nasty Neighbours;* Kath in *Nil By Mouth;* Miss Saville in *Strong Boys;* Mrs Garrett in *The Three Bears;* Iris in *Weak at Denise.*

Address: c/o CDA, 19 Sydney Mews, London SW3 6HL.

DOTRICE, Michele

Michele Dotrice. Actor (F).

b. Cleethorpes, Lincolnshire, 27 September 1947.

TV: *A Month in the Country; Boon;* Lady Cora in *Bramwell;* Mother in *Cause of Death; Celebrity Squares; Chintz; Give Us a Clue;* Lady Percy in *Henry IV: Parts I and II; Midsomer Murders; On the Eve of Publication;* Betty in *Some Mothers Do 'Ave 'Em; That's Showbusiness; The Equalizer; The Morecambe and Wise Show; The Sextet; The Three Sisters;* Catherine Winslow in *The Winslow Boy;* Mrs Sedley in *Vanity Fair.*

Films: *And Soon the Darkness; Captain Jack; Not Now Comrade.*

Address: c/o Eric Glass Ltd, 28 Berkeley Square, London W1X 6HD. m. Edward Woodward; father Roy Dotrice.

DOWIE, Freda

Freda Dowie. Actor (F).

TV: *Alice in Wonderland; Angels; Beck;* Eileen Wolley in *Boon; Cider with Rosie;* Dulcie in *Common As Muck; Cover Her Face; Cranford; Crime Story: What The Butler Did; Crown Court; Death of Socrates; Doctor Finlay's Casebook; Golden Eye;* Muriel Gerard in *Heartbeat; I, Claudius; In Suspicious Circumstances; Insiders; Kinsey; Lillie; Lovejoy;* Jane Waule in *Middlemarch; Moving Story; North and South; Oranges are Not the Only Fruit;* Florrie in *Our Friends in the North; Poirot – The Clapham Cook; Sherlock Holmes; Sophia and Constance; Stay Lucky III;* Maureen Spencer in *Thacker; The Brontës; The Old Curiosity Shop; The Pickwick Papers; The Poisoning of Charles Bravo; The Stone Dance; Upstairs Downstairs; War and Peace; Within these Walls; Zig Zag.*

Films: *A Life In Death; Blackeyes; Butterfly Kiss; Distant Voices, Still Lives; Jude the Obscure; Murder By Degree; Scandalous; The Black Crow; The Monk; The Omen.*

Address: c/o Roxane Vacca Management, 73 Beak Street, London W1R 3LF.

DOWN, Lesley-Anne

Lesley-Anne Down. Actor (F).

b. London, 17 March 1954.

TV: Bridget Conway in *Agatha Christie's Murder Is Easy;* Joan in *Arch of Triumph; Bedtime Stories;* Stephanie Rogers in *Dallas;* Catherine Windson in *Diagnosis Murder;* Anna Novacek in *Family of Cops; Heaven and Hell:* Madeline Main in *North and South;* Anne Kingston in *Indiscreet;* Chloe in *The Last Days of Pompeii;* Geneva in *Nightwalk;* Madeline LaMotte in *North and South;* Diana Carver in *Out of the Unknown; Public Eye; Shivers; Six Dates With Barker;* Olivia in *Sunset Beach; Ten From The Twenties;* Esmerelda in *The*

Hunchback of Notre Dame; Chloe Simpson in *The Nanny*; *The One and Only Phyllis Dixey*; Caroline in *The Sweeney*; *Unity Mitford*; Georgina Worsley in *Upstairs Downstairs*; *When the Boat Comes In*.

Films: Anne Egerman in *A Little Night Music*; *All The Right Noises*; Tessa Hurst in *Assault*; Morgana in *Beastmaster III: The Eye of Braxus*; *Brannigan*; Ilona in *Countess Dracula*; *Creatures From Beyond The Grave/ The Undead*; Olivia Regent in *Death Wish V*; *Hanover Street*; Jean in *In The Heart of Passion II*; Hooker Nurse in *Meet Wally Sparks*; Linda McClelland in *Munchie Strikes Back*; Christine Turner in *Night Trap*; Flax in *Nomads*; *Over The Line*; Cecilia in *Pope Joan*; Gillian Bromley in *Rough Cut*; Lilianne in *Saving Grace*; *Scalawag*; *Scenes From The Goldmine*; *School for Unclaimed Girls*; *Sphinx*; *The Betsy*; Miriam in *The First Great Train Robbery*; *The Pink Panther Strikes Again*; Eve in *The Secret Agent Club*; *Without a Good-bye*; Barbara in *Young Hearts Limited*.

Address: c/o William Morris Agency (UK) Ltd, 1 Stratton Street, London W1X 6HB.

DOWNIE, Anne

Anne Downie. Actor (F). b. Glasgow.

TV: Stella Greg in *High Road*; Judge in *Rough Justice*; *Stand Up Comedy*; *Taggart*; Mary in *The Cow Jumped Over the Moon*; *The Glasgow Kiss*; Guvnor in *You Never Slept in Mine*.

Films: Sheila Lindsay in *Dreams Lost, Dreams Found*; Madame Tarquini in *Handel*.

Address: c/o Pat Lovett PLA, 5 Union Street, Edinburgh EH1 3LT. m. John; 1 d. Susan; 1 s. Mark. Hobbies: Hillwalking, foreign travel, cinema.

DOWNIE, Tim

Tim Downie. Actor (M).

TV: *Cone Zone*; *Conjugal Rights*; *Do the Right Thing*; *Hollyoaks*; *Out of Tune*; *The Bill*.

Address: c/o Lou Coulson, 37 Berwick Street, London W1V 3RF.

DOYLE, Susannah

Susannah Doyle. Actor (F). b. 5 July 1967.

TV: *A Touch of Frost*; *Dirtysomething*; Joy in *Drop the Dead Donkey*; *Handgliding*; *Hospital*; *Maigret*; *Minder*; *Pie in the Sky*; *Soldier, Soldier*; *The Young Indiana Jones Chronicles*; *Work*.

Address: c/o Roxane Vacca Management, 73 Beak Street, London W1R 3LF.

DRAKE, Gabrielle

Gabrielle Drake. Actor (F).

TV: *Family Pride*; *Ffizz*; Diana in *Medics*; Daughter in

Mr H is Late; *Never the Twain*; Harriet Arbuthnot in *No 10 Wellington*; Jill Hammond in *The Brothers*; *The Importance of Being Earnest*; Mrs Kelly Monteith in *The Kelly Monteith Show*; *UFO*; *Crossroads*.

Address: c/o Annette Stone Associates, 2nd Floor, 22 Great Marlborough Street, London W1V 1AF.

DRAYSON, Zac

Zac Drayson. Actor (M).

b. Sydney, Australia, 14 January 1983.

TV: Will Smith in *Home and Away*.

Address: Seven Network Ltd, Mabbs Lane, Epping, New South Wales 2121, Australia. Hobbies: Rugby, surfing, skateboarding, rowing, boxing.

DREYFUS, James

James Dreyfus. Actor (M). b. London 1968.

TV: Chris in *Absolutely Fabulous Special*; Jake in *Being Considered*; *Dame Edna Kisses It Better*; Anthony in *Frontiers*; Tom in *Gimme, Gimme, Gimme*; Professor Fluke in *Gormenghast*; Belunaire in *Paris*; *The All New Alexei Sayle Show*; P.C. Kevin Goody in *The Thin Blue Line*.

Films: *Boyfriends* (lead); Martin in *Notting Hill*; First Subaltern in *Richard III*; Greg in *Thin Ice*.

Address: c/o Cassie Mayer Ltd, 34 Kingly Court, London W1R 5LE.

DRINKEL, Keith

Keith Drinkel. Actor (M). b. 14 November 1944.

TV: Chief Inspector in *Crime Monthly* (1995); Prison Governor in *EastEnders* (1999); Philip Ashton in *Family at War*; The Dauphin in *Henry V*; Julian in *Love and Reason* (1993); Mr Corblimeyone in *Marlene Marlow* (1994); Mark Gaskell in *Miss Marple:*; Dr Bennett in *Picking Up The Pieces* (1998); Sim Hoskin in *Tales of the Unexpected*; John Major in *Thatcher, The Final Days*; The Gas Man in *The Most Beautiful Dress In the World* (1993); John Major in *The Scott Report* (1996); Ernest Beevers in *Time and the Conways*.

Address: c/o McIntosh Rae Management, Thornton House, Thornton Road, London SW19 4NG.

DRINKWATER, Carol

Carol Drinkwater. Actor (F).

b. London, 22 April 1948.

TV: *A Mind to Kill*; Helen Herriot in *All Creatures Great and Small*; *Bill Brand*; *A Bouquet of Barbed Wire*; *Chocky*; *Golden Pennies*; *Master of the Marionettes*; *Public Eye*; *Sam*; *Softly, Softly*; *Tales of the Unexpected*; *The Agatha Christie Hour*; *Ladykillers*; *The Sweeney*; Elizabeth Cook in *The Wind and the Stars*.

Films: *A Clockwork Orange*; *All Creatures Great and*

Small; An Awfully Big Adventure; Father; Joseph Andrews; Magneto; Memoirs of Our Time; Mondo Candido; The Dawnbreakers; The Haunted School; The Shout.
Address: c/o Ken McReddie Ltd, 91 Regent Street, London W1R 7TB. m. Michel Noll.

DRISCOLL, Richard

Richard Driscoll. Actor (M).
TV: Speedy in London's Burning; Steve Ellis in Respect; Frank Skinner in Soldier, Soldier; Greg Lewis in The Bill.
Address: c/o JM Associates, 77 Beak Street, London W1R 3LF.

DRIVER, Betty

Betty Driver. Actor (F). b. Leicester, 20 May 1920.
TV: Betty Williams in Coronation Street; Love on the Dole; Pardon the Expression; This is Your Life.
Films: Facing the Music; Let's Be Famous; Penny Paradise.
Music: MacNamara's Band; Pick the Petals; September in the Rain; The Sailor with the Navy Blue Eyes.
Address: c/o Granada Television, Quay Street, Manchester M60 9EA. Hobbies: art, antiques.

DRIVER, Minnie

Minnie Driver. Actor (F). b. London, 31 January 1970.
TV: Zeena Mitchell in Casualty; Louise Kinsey in Kinsey; Sarah in Lovejoy; Arlette in Maigret; Leah in Mr Wroe's Virgins; Sgt. Val Cole in Murder Most Horrid; Ellie in My Good Friend; Peak Practice; Sally in A Royal Celebration; Flora in The Cruel Train; The Day Today; Mary in The House of Eliott; Jennifer in The Politician's Wife.
Films: Mabel in An Ideal Husband; Beautiful; Phyllis in Big Night; Benny in Circle of Friends; Lydia in God on the Rocks; Irina in Goldeneye; Skylar in Good Will Hunting; Debi Newberry in Grosse Pointe Blank; Karen in Hard Rain; Return To Me; Sachem Farm; Carol in Sleepers; Slowburn; Rachel in That Sunday; Rowina in The Governess; Emily in Zebra Man.
Address: c/o Lou Coulson, 37 Berwick Street, London W1V 3RF.

DRURY, Karen

Karen Drury. Actor (F).
TV: All Creatures Great and Small; The Gay Lord Quex; This Year, Next Year; Book Tower; It's a Whopper; Tiny Revolutions; The Collectors; Comic Strip – The Yob; A Bit of a Do; Lovejoy; Ain't Misbehaving; Men of the World; Susanna Farnham in Brookside.
Films: Cry Freedom.
Address: c/o Lou Coulson, 1st Floor, 37 Berwick Street, London, W1V 3RF.

DU SAUTOY, Carmen

Carmen Du Sautoy. Actor (F).
TV: Absolutely Fabulous; Anglo-Saxon Attitudes; Aristocrats; Astronauts; Marie Chantal in Bergerac; Boon; BUGS; Chess Game; A Dance to the Music of Time; Heartbeat; Hercule Poirot's Casebook; Highlander; La Ronde; Julie Blane in Lost Empires; Mamselle in Orchid House; Paparazzo; Eve in Perfect Scoundrels; Poor Little Rich Girl; Punch Review; Strangers and Brothers; The Barretts of Wimpole Street; The Brothers; The Citadel; Nicole in The Intercom Conspiracy; The Stone Age (lead); The Sweet Scent of Death.
Films: Bert Rigby, You're a Fool; Dracula's Daughter; Jack the Ripper; Praying Mantis; The Man With the Golden Gun.
Address: c/o ICM, Oxford House, 76 Oxford Street, London W1N 0AX.

DUCE, Sharon

Sharon Duce. Actor (F).
b. Sheffield, 17 January 1948.
TV: 99–1; Abel's Will; Big Deal; Braces High; Casualty; Coming Home; Days at the Beach; First Born; Funny Man; Growing Pains; In Loving Memory; Into The Fire; Maisie Raine; Misterioso; Natural Lies; Peak Practice; Renoir; Safe and Sound; Seeing Stars; Send in the Girls; Singles; Tales of the Unexpected; The Bounder; The Hard Word; The House That Jack Built; The Winter Break; Time on Your Hands; The Tomorrow People; Trafford Tanzi; Twelfth Night; Two Men from Derby; Wycliffe.
Films: Buddy's Song; Rogue Trader; Janice in Secret Society; Shooting Stars.
Address: c/o Marmont Management Ltd, Langham House, 308 Regent Street, London W1R 5AL.

DUCHOVNY, David

David Duchovny. Actor (M).
b. New York, USA, 7 August 1960.
TV: David in Baby Snatcher; himself in Dr Katz, Professional Therapist; Richard in Duckman; Agent Mulder in Eek! The Cat; Tom in Frasier; Jake in Red Shoes Diary; Handsome Alvin in Space: Above and Beyond; himself in The Simpsons; Special Agent Fox Mulder in The X-Files; DEA Agent Dennis Bryson in Twin Peaks.
Films: Club goer in Bad Influence; Brad in Beethoven; Rollie Toteroh in Chaplin; John in Denial; Bruce in Don't Tell Mom the Babysitter's Dead; Daniel in Julia Has Two Lovers; Brian Kessler in Kalifornia; Billy in New Year's Day; Eugene Sands in Playing God; Bob Rueland in Return To Me; Officer Tippit in Ruby; Randy in The Rapture; Special Agent Fox Mulder in The X-Files Movie; Dylan in Venice/Venice; Party Guest in Working Girl.

Address: c/o ICM Agency, 8942 Wilshire Blvd, Beverly Hills, California 90211, USA. m. Téa Leoni; 1 d. Madelaine. Hobbies: Sports fan – played scholarship-level basketball and baseball in high school and college, swimming, yoga.

DUDGEON, Neil
Neil Dudgeon. Actor (M).
TV: *Between the Lines; Break Out; Common As Muck; Fatherland; Four Fathers; The Mrs Bradley Mysteries; Night Voice; Our Boy; Out of the Blue; A Piece of Cake; Resnick; Road; Saracen; Sharpe's Eagles; The All New Alexei Sayle Show; The Gift; Tom Jones; A Touch of Frost.*
Address: c/o ICM, Oxford House, 76 Oxford Street, London W1N 0AX.

DUFF, Blythe
Blythe Duff. Actor (F). b. 25 January 1965.
TV: *Antiques Scotland; Get It On; Going, Going, Gone; The Jack Docherty Show; Scottish Passport; Songs of Praise; Spirit of Christmas;* Jackie Reed in *Taggart; Under the Hammer; Win, Lose or Draw.*
Address: c/o Brunskill Management, Suite 8a, 169 Queen's Gate, London SW7 5HE.

DUFFETT, Nicola
Nicola Duffett. Actor (F).
b. Portsmouth, 22 January 1963.
TV: Marjie Harris in *Birds of Feather;* Pam Sharman in *Dangerfield;* Cat in *Family Affair;* Mavis in *Hot Dog Wars;* Ruby Kamara in *Jupiter Moon;* Charlotte in *Maigret – The Hotel Majestic;* Mrs Spence in *Our Boy;* Lil in *Perfect Scoundrels; Shadow of the Noose;* Sandra Vaines in *The Bill; The Fast Show;* Debbie in *East-Enders.*
Films: Angela in *Food of Love;* Jackie Bast in *Howard's End;* Diane in *Mad Dogs and Englishmen;* Mrs Gray in *Shooting Fish.*
Address: c/o Conway Van Gelder, 18–21 Jermyn Street, London SW1Y 6HP. 2 d. Jessica, Poppy.

DUFFY, J.S.
Steven Duffy. Actor (M).
TV: Patrick Francis in *Out of Hours;* Ben in *Psychos;* Andrew Dunbar in *Scotland In The Time of Burns; Slap* (lead); Malcolm Rush in *Taggart; Tinsel Town;* Clerk of the Court in *What About Us;* Liam in *Double Nougat; Hard Nut – A Love Story* (lead); *Looking After Jo Jo.*
Films: Luke Kennedy in *Initiation; No Way Out;* Bobby in *Small Faces;* Frank in *Split Second;* Michael in *Ties.*
Address: c/o Marina Martin Associates, 12–13 Poland Street, London W1V 3DE.

DUNCAN, Lindsay
Lindsay Duncan. Actor (F). b. 7 November 1950.
TV: Lady Bellaston in *Tom Jones;* Helen in *Traffik;* Annie Mayle in *A Year in Provence; Colin's Sandwich;* Barbara Dougal in *GBH;* Louise in *Get Real; Grown Ups;* Monica in *Jake's Progress;* Lady Walton in *Just William;* Pamela in *The Kit Curran Radio Show; Muck and Brass; New Girl in Town;* Elizabeth Leeford in *Oliver Twist;* Dana in *On Approval; One Upmanship;* Karen Miller in *Rainy Day Woman; Redemption; Reilly Ace of Spies;* Marilyn Truman in *Shooting the Past;* Laura Pellin in *Tecx;* Eirwen in *The Childeater;* Anna in *The Rector's Wife; The Wrinkler;* Gutrune in *These Foolish Things.*
Films: Titania in *A Midsummer Night's Dream;* Lady Bertram/Mrs Price in *An Ideal Husband;* Dr Webb in *Body Parts;* Sydney Pappas in *City Hall;* Lily Sacher in *For a Night of Love;* Sally in *Loose Connections;* Lady Markby in *Mansfield Park; Prick Up Your Ears;* Mrs Nankervis in *Samson and Delilah;* Medea in *The Greek Myths;* Dolphin Blue in *The Reflecting Skin.*
Address: c/o Ken McReddie Ltd, 91 Regent Street, London W1R 7TB.

DUNCAN, Peter
Peter Duncan. Actor (M)/Presenter. b. 3 May 1954.
TV: *All Creatures Great and Small; Blue Peter; Duncan Dares;* Bobby in *Fallen Hero;* Robert in *Family Affairs;* Gerry in *Fathers and Families;* Jimmy in *Flockton Flyer;* Deaks in *House of Payne;* John in *John Halifax, Gentleman;* Kerry Hudson in *King Cinder;* Vincent in *Oranges and Lemons;* Mike in *Point of No Return;* Jean Renoir in *Renoir, My Father;* Arthur in *Sons and Lovers;* Driver in *The Big Race;* Peter in *The Childhood Friend;* Milo in *The Devil's Crown;* Ab Dorrit in *Warship.*
Films: Young Treeman in *Flash Gordon;* Kit Nubbles in *Mr Quilp;* Much the Miller in *Robin Hood;* Cantar in *Space 1999 – The Exiles;* Peter in *Stardust;* Richard in *The Lifetaker.*
Music: *Little Tramp; The Card.*
Address: c/o Saraband Associates, 265 Liverpool Road, London N1 1LX.

DUNCAN, Robert
Robert Duncan. Actor (M).
b. St. Austell, Cornwall, 27 July 1952.
TV: *A Different Drummer; Boon;* Peter Hayes in *Casualty;* Gus Hedges in *Drop the Dead Donkey; East-Enders; Enemy at the Door; For Maddie With Love; New World; Squadron; The Bill; The Burston Rebellion; The Good Guys; The Upper Hand.*
Films: *Mr White Goes To Westminster.*
Address: c/o Ken McReddie Ltd, 91 Regent Street, London W1R 7TB. Hobbies: Tennis, golf.

DUNCAN-BREWSTER, Sharon

Sharon Duncan-Brewster. Actor (F).

TV: Janice in *Back Up*; Crystal Gordon in *Bad Girls*; Teenage Girl in *Between the Lines*; Clare Johnson in *Casualty*; Cassie in *Hope I Die Before I Get Old*; *Maisie Raine*; Aisha Bedford in *The Bill*.

Films: Holly Jones in *Body Story*; Bren in *Christmas*.

Address: c/o CAM London, 19 Denmark Street, London WC2H 8NA.

DUNLOP, Joe

Joe Dunlop. Actor (M). b. 16 February 1942.

TV: *Accident*; *Black Silk*; Mr Coulter in *Brookside*; *Chalk and Cheese*; *Chance in a Million*; Jeremy in *Don't Wait Up*; Beattie in *In Suspicious Circumstances*; Jerry in *Keeping up Appearances*; *Sercret Army*; George Hay in *Taggart*; Jack in *Take the High Road*; Walsh in *The Advocates*; *The Incredible Mr Tanner*; *The Week of the Scorpion*; *Danger UXB*; *Upchat Connection*; *What If It's Raining*.

Films: *A Man Called Intrepid*; *Kind of Hero*; *Terrorsome*; *The Whistle Blower*.

Address: c/o Rolf Kruger Management Ltd, 205 Chudleigh Road, London SE4 1EG.

DUNLOP, Lesley

Lesley Dunlop. Actor (F).

b. Newcastle, 10 March 1956.

TV: *A Drive in the Country*; *A Little Princess*; *Angels*; *Black Beauty*; *Boon*; Sara in *Capstick's Law*; Susie Q in *Doctor Who*; Moira Pridwell in *Hetty Wainthropp Investigates*; *Mates*; Zoe in *May to December*; *Our Mutual Friend*; Sally in *Peak Practice*; *Penmarric*; Mo Healy in *Pure Wickedness*; Ellie in *Rich Deceiver*; *Seasons Greetings*; Marrion Wallace in *Silent Witness*; *Smuggler*; *South Riding*; *Stanley*; Joan Durbyfield in *Tess of the D'Urbervilles*; Veronica in *The Bill*; *The Deadly Game*; *The Gathering Storm*; Eliza in *The Phoenix and the Carpet*; *The Red Shift*; *The Rose Garden*; *The White Elephant*; *Waters of the Moon*; Anne in *Where the Heart Is*; Lucky in *Wokenwell*.

Films: *13 At Dinner*; *A Little Night Music*; *Tess*; *The Elephant Man*; *The Monster Club*; *Trick of the Light*.

Address: c/o Annette Stone Associates, 2nd Floor, 22 Great Marlborough Street, London W1V 1AF.

DUNN, Sarah

Sarah Dunn. Actor (F).

TV: Mandy Richardson in *Hollyoaks*.

Address: c/o Channel 4, 124 Horseferry Road, London SW1P 2TX. Hobbies: Singing, guitar, swimming, netball.

DUNNING, Nick

Nick Dunning. Actor (M).

TV: *A Few Short Journeys of the Heart*; *Alive and Kicking*; *Between the Lines*; *Boon*; *Casualty*; *Dangerfield*; *Drop the Dead Donkey*; *El C.I.D.*; *Events at Drimagleen*; *Heaven and Earth*; *Into the Blue*; *Making the Cut*; *Medics*; *Midsomer Murders*; *Minder*; *Remembrance*; *Resnick*; *Saracen*; *Sharman*; *Sister, My Sister*; *Strangers*; *Surgical Two*; *The Ambassador*; *The Bill*; *The Firm*; *The Rita Rudner Show*; *The Rory Bremner Show*; *The Roughest Way*; *The Young Ones*; *Vanity Fair*; Alistair in *Way Upstream*; *Wycliffe*.

Films: *Lamb*; Faulkner in *London Kills Me*; Quentin Agnew in *The Fifth Province*.

Address: c/o Lou Coulson, 37 Berwick Street, London W1V 3RF.

DURHAM, Geoffrey

Geoffrey Durham. Actor (M)/Magician.

TV: *Call My Bluff*; *Countdown*; *Crackerjack!*; *Russell Harty*; *The Best of Magic*; *Through the Keyhole*.

Films: *Wish You Were Here*.

Address: c/o International Artistes Ltd, Mezzanine Floor, 235 Regent Street, London W1R 8AX. m. comedian Victoria Wood.

DURR, Jason

Jason Durr. Actor (M). b. 1967.

TV: Jamie in *A Dark Adapted Eye*; Mark Shuman in *BUGS*; Martin in *Christmas* (lead); Davey Hartey in *Femme Fatale*; Sir Gawain in *Gawain and the Green Knight*; PC Mike Bradley in *Heartbeat*; John Brewster in *Inspector Morse*; Potroculus in *Iphigenia at Aulis*; Lord Kiely in *Sharpe's Battle*; Liam Casey in *The Chief*; Tony Bracciola in *The Paradise Club*.

Films: Graham in *Between Two Worlds*; Johnny in *The Killer Tongue*; Billibud in *Young Soul Rebels*.

Address: c/o Ken McReddie Ltd, 91 Regent Street, London W1R 7TB.

DUTTINE, John

John Duttine. Actor (M).

b. Barnsley, Yorkshire, 15 March 1949.

TV: *A Killing on the Exchange*; *A Pin To See The Peep Show*; *A Woman of Substance*; *Ain't Misbehavin'*; *Casualty*; *Dangerfield*; *Day of the Triffids*; *Family Man*; *Heartbeat*; *Holding On*; *Imaginary Friends*; *Jesus of Nazareth*; *Lame Ducks*; *Long Live The King*; *Lost Property*; *Love Hurts*; *Maisie Raine*; *Master of the Marionettes*; *Noah's Ark*; *Out of the Blue*; *Pilgrim's Rest*; *PSY Warriors*; *Spend, Spend, Spend*; *Taggart*; *Talking to Strange Men*; *The Avenue*; *The Bill*; *The Devil's Crown*; *The Hunt for the Yorkshire Ripper*; *The Inercesser*; *The Mallens*; *Mid-*

somer Murders; The Outsider; Tide Race; To Serve Them All My Days; Touching Evil; Verdict; Wuthering Heights.
Films: *Who Dares Wins.*
Address: c/o Associated International Management, 5 Denmark Street, London WC2H 8LP.

DUTTON, Jonathan

Joathan Dutton. Actor (M).
TV: Wayne 'Tad' Reeves in *Neighbours; Blue Heelers.*
Address: c/o Grundy Television, Grundy House, Barge House Crescent, 34 Upper Ground, London SE1 9PD.

DUTTON, Simon

Simon Dutton. Actor (M).
TV: Will Saltmarsh in *By the Sword Divided;* Sir William Deakin in *Churchill: the Wilderness Years;* Ronny Cox in *Nancherrow; The Man in the Brown Suit* (title role); Lt. Col. Robert Neill in *The Place of the Dead;* Simon Templar in *The Saint.*
Films: The Activist in *A Man From a Far Country;* Ramberti in *Dangerous Beauty;* Eliab in *King David;* Memed in *Memed My Hawk.*
Address: c/o Marmont Management Ltd, Langham House, 308 Regent Street, London W1R 5AL.

DUTTON, Tim

Tim Dutton. Actor (M).   .
TV: *A Man Lay Dead;* Phil in *Against All Odds; Artists in Crime;* Herbert Rhodes in *Cecil Rhodes; Dead Water; Death In a White Tie;* Rockingham in *Frenchman's Creek;* Luke in *Hand in Glove; In the Name Of Love;* Sergeant Bailey in *The Inspector Alleyn Mysteries;* Fothergill in *Lovejoy;* Guy in *Melissa;* Lt. Col. Renfrew in *No Bananas;* Edwin in *Oliver Twist;* DI Arran in *Original Sin;* Tommo Atkins in *Peak Practice;* Toby in *Pie in the Sky;* Mark Owens in *Soldier, Soldier;* James in *Thanks;* Harry in *The Guilty;* Michael Fleet in *The Vet.*
Films: Mark in *Darkness Falls;* Andy Harris in *Death on Everest;* Luke in *In The Name of Love;* Simon Snow in *Murder of Quality;* PC Willis in *Patriot Games;* Francois in *St Ives;* Maurice in *Tom and Viv;* Max in *Too Hard To Forget.*
Address: William Morris Agency (UK) Ltd, 1 Stratton Street, London W1X 6HB.

DWYER, Terri

Terri Dwyer. Actor (F)/Presenter. b. Leicester.
TV: Ruth in *Hollyoaks; TCC.*
Address: c/o John Noel Management, 10a Belmont Street, London NW1 8HH. Hobbies: Swimming, theatre, cinema, drawing.

E

EALEY, Kristian

Kristian Ealey. Actor (M)/Performer. b. 1977.
TV: *Bread; Coronation Street; Hollyoaks; The League of Gentlemen; A Prince Among Men; The Life of John Lennon.*
Address: c/o Ray's Northern Casting Agency, 7 Wince Close, Alkington, Middleton, Manchester M24 1UJ. Hobbies: Swimming, darts, snooker.

EARL, Vince

Vince Earl. Actor (M)/Comedian.
b. Birkenhead, Merseyside, 11 June 1944.
TV: Jimmy Johnson in *Boys from the Blackstuff;* Ron Dixon in *Brookside; Comedians; Entertainment Express; Jimmy Cricket and Friends; Starburst;* Ronnie Barreti in *Turn for the Worse.*
Films: Frank in *No Surrender.*
Address: c/o Irene Earl, 5 Shotwick Park, Saughall, Chester CH1 6BJ. m. Irene; 2 d. Nicole, Kim; 1 s. Stephen. Hobbies: Golf, gym training.

EASTER, David

David Easter. Actor (M). b. 1958.
TV: Darren Appleton in *Bad Boys;* Warren in *Birds of A Feather; Bread;* Pat Hancock in *Brookside;* Pete Callan in *Family Affairs; The Bill; Three Up, Two Down;* Endless in *Wild Blue Dark.*
Films: *Give My Regards to Broad Street;* Christien in *The Harpist;* Howard in *The Music Machine.*
Address: c/o Hilary Gagan Associates, 2nd Floor, Gloucester Mansions, 140a Shaftesbury Avenue, London WC2H 8HD. Hobbies: Sports.

ECCLESTON, Christopher

Christopher Eccleston. Actor (M).
b. Salford, Manchester, 16 February 1964.
TV: *Blood Rights; Boon;* Angel in *Business with Friends; Casualty; Chancer;* Bilborough in *Cracker;* Scharlach/Zunz/Gryphius in *Death and the Compass;* Sean in *Friday on My Mind;* Drew in *Hearts and Minds;* Trevor Hicks in *Hillsborough; Inspector Morse;* Nicky in *Our Friends in the North; Poirot; Rachel's Dream; Roots;* Jim Calvert in *Clocking Off.*
Films: Sender in *A Price Below Rubies;* The Priest in *Anchoress;* Duke of Norfolk in *Elizabeth I;* Levi in *Existenz;* Gary in *Heart;* Wolf in *Invisible Circus;* Jude in *Jude;* Derek Bentley in *Let Him Have It;* David in *Shallow Grave;* Vincent in *With or Without You.*
Address: c/o Hamilton Asper, 24 Hanway Street, London W1P 9DD.

ECCLESTON, Mark

Mark Eccleston. Presenter.
TV: *Coming Up; Exclusive; Screen Grabs.*
Address: John Noel Management, 10a Belmont Street, London NW1 8HH. Hobbies: Snowboarding; surfing; mountain biking; fishing.

ECLAIR, Jenny

Jenny Eclair. Comedienne/Host.
b. Kuala Lumpur, Malaysia, 1960.
TV: *Jenny Eclair Squats* (1997); *Jenny Eclair's Private Function* (1999); *Pick 'n' Mix* (1997); *The Comedy Network* (1997).
Films: *Jenny Eclair: Top Bitch.*
Address: c/o Avalon Promotions, 2nd Floor, Queens House, Leicester Place, Leicester Square, London WC2H 7BP.

EDMONDS, Noel

Noel Edmonds. Presenter/Creator.
b. London, 22 December 1948.
TV: *Juke Box Jury; Late Late Breakfast Show; National Lottery Launch; Noel's Addicts; Noel's House Party; The MultiColoured Swap Shop; Telly Addicts; Telly Years; Top Gear; Top of the Pops.*
Address: c/o Unique Artistes, Avon House, Kensington Village, London W14 8TS. m. Helen; 4 d. Charlotte, Lorna, Olivia, Alice. Hobbies: Aviation, gardening, photography.

EDMONDSON, Adrian

Adrian Edmondson. Actor (M)/Comedian.
b. Bradford, Yorkshire, 24 January 1957.
TV: *Anna Lee; Bad News;* Von Richtofen in *Blackadder Goes Forth; Boom Boom; Bottom; The Comic Strip Presents: Consuela; Filthy Rich and Catflap; Friday Night, Saturday Morning; Happy Families; Hardwicke; If You See God, Tell Him; Jack and the Beanstalk; More Bad News; The Comic Strip Presents: Mr Jolly Lives Next*

Door; Newshounds; Out Go the Lights; Private Enterprise; Snakes and Ladders; The Comic Strip Presents...; The Lenny Henry Show; The Red Nose of Courage; Vyvyan in *The Young Ones*.
Films: *Dirty Movie; Guest House Paradiso; Supergrass; The Magnificent One; The Man; The Pope Must Die.*
Address: c/o Jonathan Altaras Associates, 13 Shorts Gardens, London WC2H 9AT. m. Jennifer Saunders.

EDNEY, Beatie

Beatie Edney. Actor (F). b. London.
TV: Louise in *Dressing for Breakfast;* Louise Grangrind in *Hard Times;* Deborah Burns in *Inspector Morse;* Nancy Ellis in *Lost Empires;* Mary Cavendish in *Poirot;* Susan Covington in *Prime Suspect;* Ester in *The Affair;* Maud Ruthyn in *The Dark Angel;* Annabella Wilmot in *The Tenant of Wildfell Hall;* Cathy Wolsey in *Thief Takers.*
Films: Marjorie in *A Handful of Dust;* Heather in *Highlander;* Carole Richardson in *In the Name of the Father;* Marie Antoinette in *Mesmer;* Celia Rudbeck in *Mister Johnson;* Simone in *The Diary of a Mad Old Man;* Dee in *The Lilac Bus;* Sadie in *Wildflowers.*
Address: c/o Ken McReddie Ltd, 91 Regent Street, London W1R 7TB. Mother Sylvia Syms. Hobbies: Scuba diving.

EDWARDS, Anthony

Anthony Edwards. Actor (M)
b. Santa Barbara, California, USA, 19 July 1962.
TV: Dick Hickock in *In Cold Blood;* Dr Mark Greene in *ER;* Mike Monroe in *Northern Exposure, El Diablo; Hometown Boy Makes Good; Going for Gold: The Bill Johnson Story; High School USA; It Takes Two; The Killing of Randy Webster.*
Films: *Playing By Heart; Us Begins with You; Charlie's Ghost Story; The Client; Sexual Healing; Pet Semetary II; Delta Heat; Landslide; Downtown; Hawks; How I Got Into College; Miracle Mile; Mr. North; Revenge of the Nerds II: Nerds in Paradise; Summer Heat; Top Gun; Gotcha!; The Sure Thing; Revenge of the Nerds; Heart Like a Wheel.*
Address: c/o United Talent Agency, 9560 Wilshire Blvd, Suite 500, Beverly Hills, California 90212, USA. m. Jeanine Lobell, make-up artist; 1 s. Bailey; 1 d. Esme. Hobbies: Surfing

EDWARDS, Gwenan

Gwenan Edwards. Actor (F)/Presenter.
TV: *Aberglasney – A Garden Lost in Time* (1999); *BBC World Television; Cardiff Singer of the World; Decision Time; HTV; News 24* (1999); *Newsroom South East.*
Address: c/o Arlington Enterprises Ltd, 1–3 Charlotte Street, London W1P 1HD.

EDWARDS, Huw

Huw Edwards. News Presenter. b. Bridgend 1961.
TV: *Breakfast News; News 24; One O'Clock News; Six O'Clock News.*
Address: BBC News, Union House, 65–69, Shepherds Bush Green, London W12 8TX. 2 s. Dan, Sam. Hobbies: Piano, French.

EDWARDS, Jez

Jez Edwards. Presenter. b. Knutsford, 3 April 1974.
TV: *Crazy Cottage; Flantastic; K Club; Mashed; Record Breakers; Sticky; The Essential Guide to an Alternative Christmas; The Phonezone.*
Address: c/o Curtis Brown, Haymarket House, 28–29 Haymarket, London SW1Y 4SP. Hobbies: Football.

EELES, Zoe

Zoe Eeles. Actor (F). b. Scotland,.
TV: Elidh in *All Along the Watchtower;* Karen in *Lucy Sullivan is Getting Married.*
Films: Janice Walford in *OBIT.*
Address: c/o Dennis Lyne Agency, 108 Leonard Street, London EC2A 4RH.

EGAN, Peter

Peter Egan. Actor (M).
b. London, 28 September 1946.
TV: *A Day in Summer* (1988); *Ruth Rendell's A New Lease of Death* (1991); *A Touch of Frost* (1998); *Big Breadwinner Hogg* (1968); *The Cater Street Hangman* (1998); Seth in *Cold Comfort Farm* (1967); *Cry Wolf* (1999); Earl of Southampton in *Elizabeth R* (1971); *Ever Decreasing Circles* (1984, 1986, 1987); *Ghost Story* (1994); *Gobble* (1996); *Joint Account* (1988, 1989); Oscar Wilde in *Lillie Langtry* (1978); *MacGyver* (1993); Fothergill in *Reilly Ace of Spies* (1982); *The Ambassador* (1998); *The Chief* (1993); *The Dark Side of the Sun* (1983); Millias in *The Love School* (1974); *The Organisation* (1971); *The Peacock Spring* (1995); *The Perfect Spy* (1986); *The Price of the Bride* (1989); Prince Regent in *The Prince Regent* (1978); *A Woman of Substance.*
Films: *Bean – The Ultimate Disaster Movie; Callan; Chariots of Fire; Hennessy; Paradise Postponed; The Hireling.*
Address: c/o ICM, Oxford House, 76 Oxford Street, London W1N 0AX.

EHLE, Jennifer

Jennifer Ehle. Actor (F).
TV: *Melissa; The Camomile Lawn; the Young Indiana Jones; Mick Love;* Phyllis Maitland in *The Maitlands;* Elizabeth Bennett in *Pride and Prejudice; Self Catering;* Emma in *Pleasure.*

Films: *Sunshine; This Year's Love; Bedrooms and Hallways; Wilde; Paradise Road; Backbeat.*
Address: c/o ICM, Oxford House, 76 Oxford Street, London, W1N OAX.

ELBA, Idris

Idris Elba. Actor (M). b. 6 September 1972.
TV: Hilton in *Absolutely Fabulous*; Charlie in *Bramwell*; Matt Gregory in *Dangerfield*; Tim in *Family Affairs*; Robinson Bennett in *Insiders*; Charlie in *Silent Witness*; Chiswick in *The Governor*; Vaughan Rice in *UltraViolet*.
Films: Gregoire in *Belle Maman*.
Address: c/o Sandra Griffin Management, 6 Ryde Place, Richmond Road, Twickenham, Middlesex TW1 2EH. Hobbies: Music production.

ELIS, Richard

Richard Elis. Actor (M). b. 1975.
TV: Huw in *EastEnders*; Oberon in *Relative Strangers*; *Wales on the Western Front*; Eddie Pensarn in *Y Mapiwr*; *Y Weithred*.
Address: c/o Susan Angel Associates, 1st Floor, 12 D'Arblay Street, London W1V 3FP. Hobbies: Dance, off-road driving.

ELIZONDO, Hector

Hector Elizondo. Actor (M).
b. New York, USA, b. 22 December, 1936.
TV: *Borrowed Hearts; Jonny Quest VS the Cyber Insects; Dr Phillip Watters on Chicago Hope; Aladdin, Jonny's Golden Quest; Mrs Cage; Fish Police; The Burden of Proof; Finding the Way Home; Chains of Gold; Forgotten Prisoners: The Amnesty Files; Dark Avenger; Sparks: The Price of Passion; Your Mother Wears Combat Boots; Kojak; Ariana; Addicted to His Love; Down and Out in Beverly Hills; Natica Jackson; Courage; Foley Square; Murder by Reason of Insanity; a.k.k Pabnle; women of San Quentin; Casablanca; Feel the Heat; Honeyboy; Freebie and the Bean; The Dain Curse; Wanted: The Sundance Woman; Popi.*
Films: *The Other Sister; The Safe House; Entropy; Runaway Bride; Turbulence; Dear God; Perfect Alibi; Beverly Hills Cop III; Backstreet Justice; Exit to Eden; Getting Even with Dad; Being Human; There Goes the Neighbourhood; Frankie and Johnny; Taking Care of Business; Final Approach; Necessary Roughness; Samantha; Pretty Woman; Leviathan; Overboard; Nothing in Common; Private Resort; The Flamingo Kid; Young Doctors in Love; The Fan; American Gigolo; Diary of the Dead; Cuba; Report to the Commissioner; The Taking of Pelham One Two Three; Pocket Money; Deadhead Miles; Stand Up and Be Counted; Valdez is Coming; Born to Win; The Landlord; The Fat Black Pussycat.*
Address: c/o William Morris Agency, 151 El Camino Drive, Beverly Hills, California 90210, USA. m 1. (dis); 1 s.; m. 2. Carolee Campbell. Hobbies: Guitar, singing, dancing.

ELLIOTT, Sue

Sue Elliott. Actor (F). b. 18 December 1950.
TV: The Stick Insect in *Adrian Mole*; Marjorie in *Auf Wiedersehen, Pet*; Mrs Bunn in *Blind Men*; *Casualty*; Zoe in *Chains of Love*; Mum in *Heaven*; *Close to Home*; Julie Dewhurst in *Coronation Street*; *Do It*; Mum in *Goggle Box*; Mrs Bingham in *Henry's Leg*; June Fish in *Home Sweet Home*; *I Love Keith Allen*; *Inspector Morse*; Maureen in *King Leek*; Media Minister in *King of Chaos*; *Poirot*; *Sauna You Than Me*; Ellen Stevens in *The Bill*; Mrs Skillen in *The Glass Virgin*; Diane Springer in *The Missing Postman*; *The Paradise Club*; Mrs Hedges in *The Vanishing Man*; Deliah in *The Worst Witch*; Maggie in *This Life*.
Films: *Girl on a Swing; Robin Hood; Where the Wolves Howl.*
Address: c/o Barry Brown & Partner, 47 West Square London SE11 4SP.

ELLIS, James

James Ellis. Actor (M). b. Belfast.
TV: *Till Death Us Do Part; Accused; All Creatures Great and Small; Ballykissangel; Big Bad World; Billy; Birds of a Feather; Boon; Common As Muck; Crossing the Floor; Doctor Who; Hard Cases; In Sickness and In Health; Little Sir Nicholas; Mike and Angelo; Naming the Names; Nightingales; Noah's Ark; Oliver's Travels;* Paddy Reilly in *One by One*; *Perfect Scoundrels; So, You Think You've Got Troubles; The Blood of the Lamb; The Gathering Seed; The Glory Hole; The Hidden Curriculum; The Holy City; The Long March; The Marksman; The Practice; Tripper's Day; Under the Sun; Woof;* Bert Lynch in *Z Cars*.
Films: *Ill Fares the Land; No Surrender; Resurrection Man; The Near Room; The Shadow of A Gunman; The Teenie Weenies.*
Address: c/o Peter Charlesworth & Associates, 2nd Floor, 68 Old Brompton Road, London SW7 3LQ.

ELLIS, Peter

Peter Ellis. Actor (M). b. 30 May 1936.
TV: *Bill Brand*; Reg Sudworth in *Coronation Street*; Butler in *Edward and Mrs Simpson*; Tom Gould in *First Among Equals*; Colin Gregg in *Remembrance*; Priest in *Squaring the Circle*; MC in *Talent*; Chief Supt. Brownlow in *The Bill*; Starkey in *The Brack Report*.

Films: *An American Werewolf in London; Foreign Body.*
Address: c/o Lou Coulson, 37 Berwick Street,
London W1V 3RF.

ELLISON, Christopher

Christopher Ellison. Actor (M).
b. London, 16 December 1946.
TV: *Birds of A Feather; Bread; Brondo; Brushstrokes;
Crime Traveller; Crossed Wires; Dempsey and Make-
peace;* Ellington in *Ellington; Relative Strangers; Roll
Over Beethoven; Running Scared;* Burnside in *The Bill;
Three Up, Two Down; Up the Elephant and Round the
Castle; Widows; Wolf to the Slaughter.*
Films: *AD; Buster; Give My Regards to Broad Street;
The Last Days of Pompeii; Two Golden Balls; Wolcott.*
Address: c/o Joy Jameson Ltd, 2.19 The Plaza, 535
Kings Road, London SW10 0SZ.

ELLISON, Jennifer

Jennifer Ellison. Actor (F).
TV: *Blue Peter;* Emily Shadwick in *Brookside.*
Address: c/o Mersey Television, Campus Manor,
Chidwall Abbey Road, Chidwall, Liverpool L16 0JP.
Hobbies: Dance, tennis, hockey, netball.

ELLWOOD, Fionnuala

Fionnuala Ellwood. Actor (F).
b. Dublin, Ireland, 3 July 1964.
TV: Melanie in *Brookside; Coronation Street;* Lynn
Whiteley in *Emmerdale; Families;* Sylvia in *Heartbeat;
Prime Suspect; Scruples; Seeking Sarah; The Bill; The
Last Salute; The Legacy of Reggie Perrin; World in
Action.*
Films: *Bluebird; Shaken Not Stirred.*
Address: c/o Emptage Hallett, 24 Poland Street,
London W1V 3DD.

ELMES, John

John Elmes. Actor (M).
TV: Sean in *And the Beat Goes On;* Leo Firman in
Coronation Street; Ian Colvin in *Countdown to War;*
Mr Sanger in *Heartbeat;* James in *The House of Eliott;*
Robert Meadows in *Inspector Morse;* Potter-Pur-
bright in *Jeeves and Wooster;* Jason Jitters in *Julia
Jekyll and Harriet Hyde;* Mr Wattis in *Matt's Millions;*
Horatio in *Norbert Smith;* Edward Tulip in *Smack
and Thistle;* Donaghee in *The Bill;* James in *The
Camomile Lawn;* Sean in *The Grove;* Julian Castle in
The Real Eddy English.
Films: *A Summer Story; Maurice.*
Address: c/o Marmont Management Ltd, Langham
House, 308 Regent Street, London W1R 5AL.

ELPHICK, Michael

Michael Elphick. Actor (M).
b. Chichester 19 September 1946.
TV: *A Pocketful of Dreams; Bird Fancier; Bloom Field;
Boon; CQ; Crown Court; Dangerfield;* Barkiss in *David
Copperfield; Hamlet; Hamp; Harry; Hazel; Holding On;*
Gamekeeper in *Lady Chatterly's Lover; Late Starter;
Metropolis; Much Ado About Nothing; Norma; Oxbridge
Blues;* Private Shultz in *Private Schultz; Privates on
Parade; Roads to Freedom; Smiley's People; The Cherry
Orchard; The Fix* (1996); *The Little Farm;* Schoolmas-
ter in *The Nearly Man; The Professionals; The Sweeney;
The Whole World's a Stage; This Year, Next Year; Three
Up, Two Down.*
Films: *Blind Terror; Blue Remembered Hills; Buddy's
Song; The Element of Crime; Gorky Park; Little Dorritt;
Ordeal by Innocence; Quadrophenia; SS The Supergrass;
The Ballad of Kid Divine; The Cry of the Banshee; The
Curse of the Pink Panther; The Knowledge; The Krays;
Where's Jack?; Withnail and I.*
Address: c/o ICM, Oxford House, 76 Oxford Street,
London W1N 0AX.

ELTON, Ben

Ben Elton. Comedian/Writer/Actor (M).
b. London, 3 May 1959.
TV: *Blackadder Goes Forth; Blackadder II; Blackadder
the Third; Filthy Rich and Catflap; Happy Families;
Stark* (1992); *The Ben Elton Show; The Man from
Auntie; The Thin Blue Line; The Young Ones.*
Films: *Ben Elton Live* (1997) *Maybe Baby* (1999);
Verges in *Much Ado About Nothing.*
Address: c/o McIntyre Management Ltd, 2nd Floor,
35 Soho Square, London W1V 5DG.

EMBERG, Bella

Bella Emberg. Actor (F).
b. Brighton, Sussex, 16 September 1937.
TV: *Birds Fall Down; Pennies from Heaven; Russ Abbot's
Madhouse; Testament of Youth; The Benny Hill Show;
The Royal Variety Show* (1988); *Within these Walls.*
Films: Old Crone in *History of the World – Part 1.*
Address: c/o Mike Hughes Entertainments c/o
Gerald Goss Ltd, Dudley House, 169 Piccadilly,
London W1V 9DD. Hobbies: Driving, opera, read-
ing, cricket, bonsai culture, watching old films.

EMERICK, Louis

Louis Emerick. Actor (M).
b. Liverpool, 10 June 1953.
TV: Mr Ibbotson in *Albion Market;* Mr Fitness in *Balltrap on the Cote Sauvage;* Mick Johnson in *Brookside;*
D.C. Timms in *Floodtide;* Policeman in *Home to*

*Roost; Policeman in *Last of the Summer Wine*; Undertaker in *There was an Old Woman*.
Films: Billy in *The Fruit Machine*.
Address: c/o Pemberton Associates, Suite 35–36, Barton Arcade, Deansgate, Manchester, M3 2BB.

ENFIELD, Harry

Harry Enfield. Actor (M)/Comedian.
b. Sussex, 31 May 1961.
TV: *Albion Parish Council* (1998); *Friday Night Live* (1988); *Gone to the Dogs* (1993); *Harry Enfield and Chums* (1996, 1997); *Harry Enfield and Chums: Christmas Special* (1997, 1998); *Harry Enfield's Guide to the Opera* (1993); *Harry Enfield's Television Programme*; *Men Behaving Badly*; *Norman Ormal* (1998); *Saturday Night Live* (1986); Sir Norbert Smith in *Sir Norbert Smith – A Life* (1993); *Smashie and Nicey – End of an Era* (1994); *Spitting Image* (various); *The New Harry Enfield and Chums* (1998).
Films: *Bob's Birthday*; *Harry Enfield Undressed*; *Roger Mellie, the Man on the Telly*; *The Fantastic Career of Billy the Fish*.
Address: c/o PBJ Management, 5 Soho Square, London W1V 5DE.

ENTWISTLE, Vicky

Vicky Entwistle. Actor (F).
TV: *100 Per Cent*; Beryl White in *Against All Odds*; Janice in *Coronation Street*; *Our Tune*; *The Bill*.
Address: c/o The Narrow Road Company, 21–22 Poland Street, London W1V 3DD. Hobbies: Singing, hockey, dancing, motorbikes.

ESHLEY, Norman

Norman Eshley. Actor (M). b. 30 May 1945.
TV: *Achilles Heel*; Mellors in *William Tell*; *After Henry*; *Between the Wars*; Leigh Dunwell in *Broker's Man*; *Brookside*; Baron Huon in *Cadfael*; Supt. Studley in *Dangerfield*; *Executive Stress*; Jeffrey Fourmile in *George and Mildred*; Martin in *Get Real*; Inspector Priestley in *Goodnight Sweetheart*; The Mayor in *Harbour Lights*; Marcus Vinicius in *I, Claudius*; *Late Expectations*; ATV in *Love Story*; Norman in *Man About the House*; *Maybury*; Rev. Redwood in *Minder*; D.C.I. Reed in *Murder Most Horrid*; Baron Royston in *The New Adventures of Robin Hood*; Insp. Rickles in *One Foot in the Grave*; Debt collector in *Out*; *Taggart*; Terry Riley in *The Bill*; *The Black Tower*; *The Bouncing Boy*; *The Duchess of Duke Street*; *The Fat*; *The Onedin Line*; *The Outsider*; *The Professionals*; The Coward in *The Sweeney*; *The Tell-Tale Heart*; C.I. Sansom in *Thief Takers*; *Vienna 1900*; Bob Last in *Warship*; William in *William Wilson*; Batsman in *Wingate*.

Films: Steve in *Blind Terror*; *House of Mortal Sin*; The Sailor in *The Immortal Story*.
Address: c/o George Heathcote Management, 58 Northdown Street, London N1 9BS.

ESLER, Gavin

Gavin Esler. Presenter/Columnist/Author.
b. Glasgow, 27 February 1953.
TV: Presenter, *BBC News*; Chief North America Correspondent, *BBC News*.
Address: c/o Curtis Brown, Haymarket House, London SW1Y 4SP. Hobbies: Skiing, hiking, backwoods camping.

ESTENSEN, Elizabeth

Elizabeth Estensen. Actor (F). .
TV: Susan in *A Touch of Frost*; Madeline in *Casualty*; Mrs Middleton in *Coronation Street*; Renee Wise in *Cracker*; Miss Gower in *Delta Wave*; Sylvia in *Elizabeth Alone*; Diane Blackstock in *Emmerdale*; Mrs Coggan in *Far From the Madding Crowd*; *Happy Families*; *In The Land of Plenty*; Amanda in *Life Without George*; Wendy in *Marmalade at Work*; Mrs Jones in *Mike and Angelo*; Valerie in *Only You*; Susan in *Our Day Out*; Evelyn in *Pie in the Sky*; T-Bag in *T-Bag*; Mrs Smith in *The Bill*; *The Ladies*; Carol in *The Liver Birds*; Patsy in *The Upper Hand*; *Wing and a Prayer*.
Address: Hillman Threfall, 33 Brookfield, Highgate West Hill, London N6 6AT.

ETIENNE, Treva

Treva Etienne. Actor (M).
TV: Yardie in *Blow Your Mind*; Johnson in *Call Me Mister*; Stuart in *Casualty*; Det. Insp. Judd in *Comics*; Neville in *Desmond's*; Danny in *Funky Black Shorts – The Godsend*; Fireman in *Hale and Pace*; Lloyd Palmer in *Holding On*; Tony Sanderson in *London's Burning*; Father Evans in *Only Fools and Horses*; *Our Friends in the North*; Horace in *Prospects*; Bruno in *Runaway Bay*; Fanshaw in *The Bill*; Sgt. Crawford in *The Fast Show*; Vincent in *The Final Passage*; Mick in *The Last Train*; Phillip in *The Lenny Henry Show*; Sidney in *The Missing Finger*; Mombassa in *The Paradise Club*; *TV Squash*; Graham in *Us Girls*.
Film: *Eyes Wide Shut*.
Address: c/o Kerry Gardner Management, 7 St. George's Square, London SW1V 2HX.

ETTRIDGE, Christopher

Christopher Ettridge. Actor (M).
b. Isleworth, Middlesex, 21 February 1948.
TV: *Hard Times*; *Harry*; *Minder*; *Ragdoll*; *The Bill*; Samson Brass in *The Old Curiosity Shop*; Terry Root in

The Worst Witch; Antony and Cleopatra; Boot Street Band; Bramwell; Casualty; Ollie in *EastEnders; Goodbye Columbus;* Reg Deadman in *Goodnight Sweetheart.*
Films: Sid Thomas in *The Chain;* Hartley in *Warburg;* Hatach in *Esther, Queen of Persia; Kevin and Perry.*
Address: c/o Scott Marshall, 44 Perryn Road, London W3 7NA. Hobbies: Walking, cycling, home decorating, cooking, theatre, cinema.

EVANS, Chris

Chris Evans. Presenter. b. Warrington, 1 April 1966.
TV: *Don't Forget Your Toothbrush; T.F.I. Friday; The Big Breakfast; The Power Station.*
Radio: *Virgin Breakfast Show.*
Address: c/o Ginger Media Group, 1 Golden Square, London W1R 4DJ.

EVANS, Derrick

Derrick Errol Evans. 'Mr Motivator.' Presenter/Fitness instructor. b. Pike, Jamaica, 15 November 1952.
TV: *Alive and Kicking; An Audience With...; Celebrity Squares; Fun in the Sun; Gay Burns Show; Get Up and Give; GMTV; Hearts of Gold; Kilroy; Noel's House Party; Surprise, Surprise; The Gladiators Christmas Special; The Time... The Place; This Morning; Through the Keyhole; TV Travel Shop; Watchdog Health Check; Win, Lose or Draw; Wish You Were Here...?; You Bet.*
Address: c/o Wicked Productions Ltd, PO Box 728, Harrow, Middlesex HA3 0UA. m. Sandra; 2 d. Caroline, Abigail; 1 s. James.

EVANS, Howell

Howell Evans. Actor (M).
b. Glamorgan, Wales, 3 March 1928.
TV: Mr Evans in *Aquila; Coronation Street; Crossroads;* Flint Howells in *District Nurse;* Wales International Rugby Coach in *Old Scores;* Vacuum Cleaner/Salesman in *Open All Hours;* Morgan in *Softly, Softly; The Bill; The Doctors;* Garth in *The Old Devils;* No-Good Boyo in *Under Milk Wood;* William Price in *We are Seven;* Dr Burgess in *You, Me and It; Z-Cars.*
Films: *Behind the Headlines; Chitty Chitty Bang Bang; The Beauty Jungle;* Tom in *The End Window;* Stationmaster in *The Englishman Who Went Up A Hill But Came Down A Mountain; The Ipcress File.*
Address: c/o Alex Jay Personal Management, 137a Kensington High Street, London W8 6SU. m. Patricia Kane; 1 s. Warwick. Hobbies: Photography.

EVANS, Lee

Lee Evans. Comedian. b. Bristol 1962.
TV: *An Evening with Lee Evans* (1993); *Jack Dee*

Variety Show; The World of Lee Evans (1995); *Viva Cabaret* (1993).
Films: Jack in *Funny Bones; Ladies' Man; Mouse Hunt; The Fifth Element;* Tucker in *There's Something About Mary.*
Address: c/o Off The Kerb Productions, 3rd Floor, Hammer House, 113–117 Wardour Street, London W1V 3TD. m. Heather Evans; 1 d. Mollie; father David Evans.

EVANS, Mark

Mark Stuart Evans. Presenter.
b. Leamington Spa, Warwickshire, 9 December 1962.
TV: *Absolutely Animals; All Over the Shop; Barking Mad; Good Morning; Holiday; Landmarks; Live and Kicking; Pet Rescue; Playdays; The Ross King Show; The Wild Bunch; This Morning; Top Gear; TV AM; Why Did the Chicken?; Wildlife Rescue; Wogan; Wood Wizard.*
Address: c/o David Anthony Promotions, PO Box 286, Warrington, Cheshire WA2 6GA. Hobbies: Motor racing, tennis, sailing, gardening.

EVANS, Nicky

Nicky Evans. Actor (M).
TV: Roy Glover in *Emmerdale; Criminal; Harry; Heartbeat; Stay Lucky; Christmas Helpline; Corrigan & Womack; All Creatures Great and Small.*
Address: c/o Sharron Ashcroft Management.

EVANS, Serena

Serena Evans. Actor (F).
TV: *Bad News; Came Out, It Rained, Went Back in Again; The Comic Strip Presents: Consuela;* Lizzie in *Every Woman Knows a Secret; Mr Majeika;* Ms Forelle in *Pie in the Sky; Private Enterprise;* Della in *Ruth Rendell Mysteries; Susie; The Management; The Piglet Files;* Sgt. Patricia Dawkins in *The Thin Blue Line.*
Address: c/o Rebecca Blond Associates, 69a Kings Road, London SW3 4NX.

EVANS, Tenniel

Tenniel Evans. Actor (M).
b. Nairobi, Kenya, 17 May 1926.
TV: *Anna Lee; Bergerac; Big Breadwinner Hogg; Boon; BUGS;* Albert in *Casualty; Crown Court; Dream Stuffing; Driving Ambition; Empty Bottles;* Marquis of Bideford in *Giving Tongue; Harry;* Alec Oxley in *Heartbeat;* Henry VI (Parts I, II and III); Quinlan Royal in *Hetty Wainthropp Investigates; Inside Story; Inspector Morse; Knights of God; Lovejoy; Lytton's Diary; Maria Marten;* Dr Evans in *Mortimer's Law; Moving Story; My Brother's Keeper; One by One;* Mr Lloyd in *Pat and Margaret; Peak Practice; Pie in the*

Sky; Richard III; Matt in *Rides; Rumpole of the Bailey; Run for the Life Boat;* Sir Edward Parkinson-Lewis in *September Song; Shine on Harvey Moon; Strife; Take Three Girls; The Adventures of Sherlock Holmes; The All Electric Amusement Arcade;* Riordan in *The Ambassador; The Avengers; The Bill; The Citadel; The Merry Wives of Windsor;* Mayor of London in *The Prince and the Pauper; The Protest; Ruth Rendell Mysteries;* Paul Merryman in *The Scold's Bridle; The Sullivan Brothers; The Tale of Beatrix Potter; The Two of Us; Thief Takers; To Each His Own; War and Peace;* Charles Stafford in *Wycliffe.*

Films: *10 Rillington Place; Exodus; HMS Valiant; Only Two Can Play; Sakharov; Walk a Crooked Path.*

Address: c/o CDA, 19 Sydney Mews, London SW3 6HL.

EVANS, Victor

Victor Evans. Actor (M).

TV: Faith in *Billy's Christmas Angels; Black First;* Kenny in *Euro Cop; Get Up, Stand Up;* Sam in *Holding On;* Bellamy in *No Problem; Party at the Palace;* Elias in *Storm Damage.*

Films: *Babylon;* Del Bennett in *Burning an Illusion; Carnival; Class of McMichael;* Nester in *Marked for Death;* Ras Seymour in *The Book Liberator.*

Address: c/o Sandra Boyce Management, 1 Kingsway Parade, Albion Road, London N16 0TA.

EWART, Tim

Tim Ewart. Reporter. b. 6 February 1949.

TV: Reporter, *BBC Television North;* Foreign Correspondent *ITN.*

Address: c/o ITN, 200 Gray's Inn Road, London, WC1X 8XZ. m. 1; 2 children; m. 2; 3 children.

EWING, Barbara

Barbara Ewing. Actor (F).

TV: *Alas Smith and Jones; Boon; Brass; Casualty; Chiller; Clouds of Glory; Comrade Dad; Dangerfield; Fallen Curtain; Hard Times; Harry; In Suspicious Circumstances; Lovejoy; Out of the Blue; Peak Practice; Rachel; Sam; September Song; Steven; The Bill; The Little Farm; The Picture Show; The Sweeney; The Vet; Watch with Mother.*

Films: *Dracula Has Risen From the Grave; Eye of the Needle; The Reckoning; Torture Garden; When the Whales Came.*

Address: c/o Scott Marshall, 44 Perryn Road, London W3 7NA.

EYTLE, Tommy

Tommy Eytle. Actor (M).

TV: *Act of Will; Black Silk; Body Contact; Call Me Mister;* Jules in *EastEnders; Johnny Jarvis; The Kelly Monteith Show; The Kenny Everett Show; London's Burning; Never Say Die; Number on End; Playboy of the West Indies (Play For Today); Radical Chambers; Rumpole of the Bailey; Storyboard; The Bill; There's Something Wrong in Paradise; Words and Pictures.*

Address: c/o Crouch Associates, 9–15 Neal Street, London WC2H 9PF.

F

FAIRBRASS, Craig

Craig Fairbrass. Actor (M). b. 1964.

TV: *EastEnders; Big Deal; Duck Patrol; London's Burning; Prime Suspect I* and *II; Shelley; Soldier of Fortune; The Bill; Three Up, Two Down; An Unsuitable Job For a Woman.*

Films: *Beyond Bedlam; Cliffhanger; Darklands; For Queen and Country; Killing Time; Proteus; Real Life; Sour Sweet; Tank Malling; Terminal Force; The Final Frame; Weak at Denise.*

Address: c/o William Morris Agency (UK) Ltd, 1 Stratton Street, London W1X 6HB.

FAITH, Adam

Terence Nelhams. Actor (M).
b. London, 23 June 1940.

TV: *Adam Faith Show; Budgie;* Frank Carver in *Love Hurts; Minder on the Orient Express; The Money Channel.*

Films: *Beat Girl; Foxes; McVicar; Mix Me A Person; Never Let Go; Stardust; What a Carve Up!; What A Whopper; Yesterday's Hero.*

Music: *Poor Me; The First Time; What Do You Want.*

Address: c/o ICM, Oxford House, 76 Oxford Street, London W1N 0AX.

FANCY, Brett

Brett Fancy. Actor (M).
b. Portsmouth, Hampshire, 1 January 1964.

TV: Hex in *BUGS;* Tim Saunders in *Casualty;* Tony in *EastEnders; Jonathan Creek;* Ricky Flood in *Pale Horse; Paparazzo;* The Leveller in *Resort to Murder;* Steve Hood in *Rockliffe's Babies;* Sean Hopper in *Square Deal;* Quincy in *The Bill;* Johnny Lupus in *The Last Salute;* Rob in *The Vet; Unfinished Business.*

Films: *Crimetime;* Tom in *Devil's Treasure;* Colin in *How's Business;* Kevin in *The Frontier.*

Address: c/o Jonathan Altaras Associates, 13 Shorts Gardens, London WC2H 9AT.

FANTHORPE, Reverend

Reverend Fanthorpe. Presenter.
b. Dereham, Norfolk, 9 February 1935.

TV: *Fortean TV* (1997); *Look East* (1958); *News* (1958); *Stations of the Cross* (1999); *Stranger than Fiction* (1998); *The Indie Awards* (1998); *The Real Nostrodamus* (1999); *Through the Keyhole* (1998); various.

Address: c/o Patricia Fanthorpe, 48 Claude Road, Roath, Cardiff CF24 3QA. m. Patricia Alice. 2 d. Stephanie, Fiona. Hobbies: Martial arts, weight training, Harley-Davidson enthusiast.

FARLEIGH, Lynn

Lynn Farleigh. Actor (F). b. Bristol, 3 May 1942.

TV: *Bill Brand; Cakes and Ale; Eyeless in Gaza; Finney;* Mrs Phillips in *Pride and Prejudice; Spooner's Patch;* Marcia in *Steptoe and Son; The Hard Word; Wish Me Luck;* Helen Wycliffe in *Wycliffe.*

Films: *Fairy Tale – A True Story; The Word; Three Into Two Won't Go; Watership Down.*

Address: c/o Conway Van Gelder, 18–21 Jermyn Street, London SW1Y 6HP. m. John Woodvine. Hobbies: Gardening, walking, travelling.

FARRELL, Nicholas

Nicholas Farrell. Actor (M). b. Essex 1955.

TV: Simon in *A Silly Little Habit;* Edward in *Agatha Christie;* R.V. Jones in *April Fool;* Major Hyde in *Bramwell;* Lt. Col. Ian Gowrie in *Breed of Heroes;* Rodrigo in *Bye Bye Columbus;* Phil Byron in *Casualty;* Martin in *Dead Lucky;* Jim in *Donald's Lot;* Martin Jones in *Drop the Dead Donkey;* Harry Pye in *Family Money;* George Hills in *For More Than a Touch of Zen;* Sebastian in *Hold The Dream;* Major Church in *Lipstick on Your Collar;* Dougie in *Lovejoy;* Paul Moran in *MacGyver;* Edmund in *Mansfield Park;* Bob in *Maybury;* John Merrill in *Midsomer Murders;* Bill Thompson in *Portrait of Isa Mulvenny;* Jonathan Sinclair in *Saracen;* Howard Brookes in *Sex, Chips and Rock 'n' Roll;* Lord Fenner in *Sharpe's Regiment;* Leo Beckford in *The Choir;* David Lambert in *The Fools on the Hill;* Father Anthony in *The Ginger Tree;* Teddy Bingham in *The Jewel in the Crown;* Boyd in *The Riff-Raff Element;* Batt Prender in *The Vision Thing;* Larion in *The White Guard;* Mycroft in *To Play the King;* Dr Hayward in *Trials of Oz.*

Films: Dr Mauldy in *Beautiful People;* George Heptner in *Berlin Tunnel 21;* Aubrey Montague in *Chariots of Fire;* Belcher in *Greystroke;* Horatio in *Hamlet;* Bailey in *Harry;* Tom Newman in *In the Bleak Midwinter;*

Mackintosh in *Legionnaires;* Wing Commander Franks in *Matador;* Montana in *Othello;* Derek in *Playing Away;* PM's Secretary in *Plunkett and Macleane;* Lieutenant in *The Eternal Sea;* The Solicitor in *The Rocking Horse Winner;* Antonio in *Twelfth Night.*
Address: c/o Markham & Froggatt Ltd, 4 Windmill Street, London W1P 1HF.

FARRINGTON, Kenneth
Kenneth Farrington. Actor (M).
b. London, 18 April 1936.
TV: *All Creatures Great and Small; An Age of Kings; Armchair Theatre; Boon;* Billy Walker in *Coronation Street; Crown Court;* Jack Gates in *Family Affairs; General Hospital; Grange Hill; Hannay; Heartbeat; Holby City; Juliet Bravo; Love Story; Minder; New Girl in Town; Play for Today; Softly Softly; The Bill; The Borderers; The Saint; The Tomorrow People; Trainer; Tycoon; Valentine Park; Z Cars.*
Films: *Beauty Jungle; Children of the Damned; Danger UXB;* Walter Regan in *Lime Street; One Way Pendulum;* Father in *Party Party; The Contract; The Great Train Robbery.*
Address: c/o Scott Marshall, 44 Perryn Road, London W3 7NA. 1 d. Tessa; 2 s. James, Mark.

FAULKNER, James
James Faulkner. Actor (M). b. London, 18 July 1948.
TV: *A Touch of Frost; Alas Smith and Jones; Apocalypse Watch; Bergerac; Catherine; Chandler and Co.; Chips with Everything; Class Act;* Baron Mullens in *Covington Cross; Crazy Like a Fox; Deceptions;* Rudi Lorimer in *Demob;* Alex Mair in *Devices and Desires;* Simon Kerslake in *First Among Equals; Guinevere; Hamish Macbeth;* Gordon Gregory in *Hazell; Highlander;* Herod in *I, Claudius; Inspector Morse;* Marcus Wolfe in *Just Another Secret; La Femme Nikita; Lace II; Lovejoy; McKenna; Minder; Miss Nightingale; Mr Palfrey of Westminster; Muck and Brass; Napoleon; Pie in the Sky; Poirot; Radical Chambers; Small Country – Big Man; Softly Softly; Space Island One; Stranglers and Brothers; Strike Force; Taggart; Tales of the Unexpected; The Blackheath Poisonings; The Acts of Peter and Paul; The Bill; The Bourne Identity; The Contract; The Hound of the Baskervilles;* Mr K in *The Martian Chronicles; The Professionals; The Shadow Trader; The Sound of the Guns; The Trial of Lord Lucan; The View From Daniel Pike; The Yellow Wallpaper; Wycliffe.*
Films: *One Take Two; Real Life; The Commissioner;* Joseph Strauss in *The Great Waltz; The Maid; The Priest of Love; The Whispering Death; Vigo; Zulu Dawn; A Kid In Aladdin's Court; All The Little Animals; Carry On Columbus;* Millington in *Conduct Unbecoming;*

Crimetime; E= Mc2; Eureka; Genghis Khan; Drummle in *Great Expectations; Lucan; Nulpunkt.*
Address: Jonathan Altaras Associates, 13 Shorts Gardens, London WC2H 9AT. m. Kate; 2 s. Guy and Leo.
Hobbies: sailing; skiing; golf.

FAULKNER, Lisa
Lisa Faulkner. Actor (F). b. 1972.
TV: Christine in *And The Beat Goes On;* Louise Hope in *Brookside;* Cassie in *Casualty;* Alison in *Dangerfield;* Victoria Merrick in *Holby City;* Rachel in *Sisters;* Helen in *The Home.*
Films: Under Matron in *Feast at Midnight;* Helene Lagonelle in *L'Amant;* Barbara in *Les Années Lycées;* Amy Parsons in *Scarlet Tunic;* Fiona in *The Parent Trap.*
Address: c/o Kerry Gardner Management, 7 St. George's Square, London SW1V 2HX.

FAULKNER, Sally
Sally Faulkner. Actor (F).
TV: Mrs Anderson in *Hollyoaks;* Mrs Arthur in *Forgotten;* Sian in *Wycliffe; Grange Hill; Rough Justice; Mirad, A Boy from Bosnia;* Mrs Carpenter in *Frontiers;* Helen Barlow in *Growing Pains;* Mary Coleman in *Oasis;* Barbara *in Emmerdale; The Bill; Kinsey; She Wolf of London;* Mrs Maxwell–Glover in *Coronation Street;* Mrs Straker in *The Return of Sherlock Holmes; Me and My Girl; Murder Not Proven; Jury; Harry Enfield; Hope it Rains; Truman Capote; Bird of Prey; Love Hurts; EastEnders; House of Cards.*
Films: *The Fool; Macbeth; Jaquare Lives; Hot Millions.*
Address: c/o Barry Brown and Partner, 47 West Square, London SE11 4SP.

FAYE, Gaynor
Gaynor Faye. Actor (F). b. 1971.
TV: Judy Mallet in *Coronation Street;* Mandy in *Downwardly Mobile;* Naomi in *Fair Game;* Pauline in *Medics;* WPC Benson in *Men of the World – Long Eye Lashes; Six Sides of Coogan;* Lorraine in *Some Kind of Life;* Mabel in *The Life and Times of Henry Pratt;* Crystal in *The Sharp End;* Fay in *The Wanderer.*
Films: Samantha in *Fanny and Elvis.*
Address: c/o CAM London, 19 Denmark Street, London WC2H 8NA. Mother Kay Mellor.

FEAST, Michael
Michael Feast. Actor (M).
TV: Gerry in *A Touch of Frost;* Edgar Bowker in *Bergerac; Blind Justice;* Snape in *Boon;* Trevor Hine in *BUGS; Casualty;* Mr Dewar in *Clarissa;* Jim Redman in *Eye of the Storm;* Mr Osbourne in *Get Well Soon;* Harry West in *The Inspector Alleyn Mysteries;* Sir Alan

Jackson in *Kavanagh QC*; *Midsomer Murders*; *Night-watch*; Tiarks in *No Final Truth*; Pete Wilson in *Noah's Ark*; Gillis in *Paradise Club*; Harvey Green in *Reach for the Moon*; R.M.P. Major in *Resnick*; Art in *Shadow of the Noose*; Tomlinson in *Soldier, Soldier*; Ronnie Hackett in *South By South East*; Howard in *Studio*; Dieter Krantz in *The Bill*; Det. Ilsley in *The Stephen Lawrence Case*; Harry West in *Touching Evil*; *Under-belly*; Grandin in *Young Blades*.

Films: *Brother Sun, Sister Moon*; *Did You Scream?*; *McVicar*; *Miss Marple: A Caribbean Mystery*; *Prometheus*; *Sleepy Hollow*; *The Draughtman's Contract*; *The Fool*; *The Tribe*.

Address: c/o Conway Van Gelder, 18–21 Jermyn Street, London SW1Y 6HP.

FELLOWES, Julian
Julian Fellowes. Actor (M).

TV: *Acts of Peter and Paul*; *Airey Neave*; Dermot in *All Quiet on the Preston Front*; *Angels*; *Aristocrats*; *Casualty*; *Cold Warrior*; *Covington Cross*; *Dempsey and Make-peace*; *The Duchess of Duke Street*; *For the Greater Good*; *Golden Eye*; *Hotline*; *Just William*; *Kavanagh QC*; *Kean*; *Killing Me Softly*; Morgan in *Knights of God*; *Little Sir Nicholas*; *Lord Elgin and Some Stones of No Importance*; *Love on a Tugboat*; *Love Hurts*; Dr Jobling in *Martin Chuzzlewit*; *Maybury*; *Monarch of the Glen*; *My Son, My Son*; *Old Men at the Zoo*; Claude Seabrook in *Our Friends in the North*; Drummond in *Pie in the Sky*; *Rita Hayworth Story*; *Rumpole*; *Seal Morning*; *Sharpe's Rifles*; Brother Vincent in *Sherwood's Travels*; *Sophia and Constance*; *Swallows and Amazons For Ever*; *The Bunker*; Soames in *The Governor*; *The Great Escape*; *The Nightingale Saga*; *The Scarlet Pimpernel*; Andrew Collins in *The Scott Inquiry*; *The Treaty*; *To Be the Best*; *Tucker's Witch*; *Victorian Scandals*; *Woo*; *The Young Indiana Jones Chronicles*.

Films: *Baby*; *Damage*; *Fellow Traveller*; *Gare au Mâle*; *Jane Eyre*; *Place Vendôme*; Miles in *Priest of Love*; *Shad-owlands*.

Address: c/o ICM, Oxford House, 76 Oxford Street, London W1N 0AX.

FELTZ, Vanessa
Vanessa Feltz. Presenter. b. 1962.

TV: *Shooting Stars*; *The Big Breakfast*; *The Vanessa Show*; *Vanessa*.

Address: BBC, Union House, 65–69 Shepherds Bush Green, London W12 8TX.

FENWICK, Perry
Perry Fenwick. Actor (M).

TV: Billy Mitchell in *EastEnders*; Evans in *London's Burning*; *Out of Hours*; *Our Boy*; *Casualty*; *Thief Takers*; *Daphne and Apollo*; *Turning World*; *Shine on Harvey Moon*; *Ellington*; *Minder*; *Pie in the Sky*; *Love-joy*; *Brittas Empire*; *How to be Cool*; *The Money Men*; *Watching*; *Casualty*; *Evensong*; *Bergerac*; *Reservations*; *The Bill*; *Tucker's Luck*; *To Turn a Blind Eye*; *Tansey Lambert is Dead*; *A Ring of Keys*; *Shall I Be Mother?*; *A Mother Like Him*; *The Squad*.

Films: *Greenwich Meantime*; *Janice Beard 45 wpm*; the *Winslow boy*; the *Tichborne Claimant*; *I.D.*; *Raggedy Rawney*; *Empire State*; *Mona Lisa*; *Success Is the Best revenge*; *Expresso Splasho*; *Party Party*.

Address c/o Burdett-Coutts Associates, Riverside Studios, Crisp Road, London W6 9RL. Hobbies: Music, sports.

FERGUSON, Craig
Craig Ferguson. Actor (M)/Comedian. b. 17 May 1964.

TV: *Almost Perfect*; *High*; *Just For Laughs*; *London Underground*; *Maybe This Time*; *Red Dwarf*; *Saturday Live*; *The Craig Ferguson Show*; *The Craig Ferguson Story*; *The Drew Carey Show*; *The Hitler Diaries*.

Films: *Dreambaby*; *My Friend Hellman*; *Revenant*; *Saving Grace*; *The Big Tease*; *The Bogie Man* (BBC).

Address: William Morris Agency (UK) Ltd, 1 Stratton Street, London W1X 6HB.

FERGUSSON, Jean
Jean Fergusson. Actor (F).

b. Wakefield, Yorkshire, 30 December 1944.

TV: Mrs Minton in *A Woman of Substance*; Mrs Tremayne in *All Creatures Great and Small*; Mrs Mallett in *Coronation Street*; Helen Ashcroft in *Coronation Street*; Caroline Herbert in *Crossroads*; Marina in *Last of the Summer Wine*; Mildred in *Lipstick on Your Collar*; Joyce in *The Practice*.

Address: c/o Scott Marshall, 44 Perryn Road, London W3 7NA. m. Paul Jenkinson. Hobbies: Reading, horse riding, gardening.

FERRIS, Pam
Pam Ferris. Actor (F).

TV: *All Change*; *Casualty*; *Connie*; *Cows*; Ma Larkin in *The Darling Buds of May*; *Death of a Salesman*; *Hard-wick House*; *Ladies in Charge*; *Lizzie's Pictures*; *Middle-march*; *Miss Julie*; *Mr Wakesfield's Insides*; *Mrs Hartley and the Growth Centre*; *Oranges are Not the Only Fruit*; *Our Mutual Friend*; *Roots*; *Sense of Guilt*; *Sisters*; *The Bill*; *The Blues*; *The Rector's Wife*; *The Spheres*; *The Tenant of Wildfell Hall*; *Where the Heart Is*.

Films: *Matilda*; *Meantime*; *The House*; *Winnie*.

Address: c/o Hamilton Asper, 24 Hanway Street, London W1P 9DD.

FIELDING, Douglas

Douglas Fielding. Actor (M). b. London, 6 June 1946.
TV: *Angels*; *Blake's 7*; *Callan*; *Chucklevision*; Roy Quick in *EastEnders* (1985); *Grange Hill*; *Juliet Bravo*; *Softly, Softly*; *The Bill*; *The Knock*; *Whizziwig*; Sgt. Quilley in *Z Cars* (1968).
Films: *Battle of Britain*; *Holding On*; *The Darkening*; *The Day the Fish Came Out*.
Address: c/o The Narrow Road Company, 21–22 Poland Street, London W1V 3DD. m. Sarah-Jane Vant; 1 d. Nicola Sereina; 1 s. Benjamin Frederick.

FIELDING, Yvette

Yvette Fielding. Presenter/Reporter.
TV: *A Weekend's Work*; *Baby, Baby*; *Blue Peter*; *City Hospital*; *Under Offer*.
Address: c/o MPC Entertainment, MPC House, 15–16 Maple Mews, London NW6 5UZ.

FINCH, Felicity

Felicity Finch. Actor (F). b. Teesside, 14 March.
TV: *Agatha Christie*; Jeannie Harris in *Angels*; Rosa in *Bleak House*; Joyce Mickle in *Dangerfield*; *Eve Strikes Back*; Nurse Young in *Little Miss Perkins*; Violet in *Love, Lust and Loneliness*; Lady Lucan in *Lucan*; Lady Lucan in *Murder in Belgravia*; Connie in *No Place Like Home*; Miss Holder in *Out of Sight*; Louise Hammond in *The Bill*; *The Lakes*; *The Lucan Affair*; Julia in *The Piglet Files*; Sally Wyatt in *The Sculptress*; Margaret Pope in *Thomas and Sarah*.
Address: c/o Langford Associates, 17 Westfields Avenue, London SW13 0AT. Hobbies: Dancing, circus skills.

FINCH, Steven

Steven Finch. Actor (M).
b. Maidstone, Kent, 28 December 1961.
TV: Giles Mawhinney in *Agent 2*; *Agent Z and the Penguin From Mars*; Jonathan Gordon-Davies in *Brookside*; Stuart Kydd in *Crown Prosecutor*; James Hewitt in *Fall of the House of Windsor*; John Rae in *Tales of the Unexpected*; *The Bill*; *The Eye of the Yemanger*; Detective Sergeant Rice in *The Jump*; *The Life and Times of John Wycliffe*; Carl Simpson in *The One*; Tony in *What Next?*.
Films: Steve Boyd in *Life at the End of the Line*; David Sterling in *Lin*.
Address: c/o Langford Associates, 17 Westfields Avenue, London SW13 0AT. m. Pam Bennett; 1 d. Emily. Hobbies: Music, running.

FINLAY, Frank

Frank Finlay. Actor (M).
b. Fanworth, Lancashire, 6 August 1926.
TV: *1001 Nights*; Frank Doel in *84 Charing Cross Road*; *Another Bouquet*; *Arc de Triomphe*; Mona in *Aspects of Love*; Napoleon in *Betzi*; *Bouquet of Barbed Wire*; Voltaire in *Candide*; Casanova in *Casanova*; Alcuin in *Charlemagne*; *Count Dracula*; Bridie in *Dear Brutus*; Sancha Panza in *Don Quixote*; Arthur Conan Doyle in *Encounters, The Other Side* (1991); *Exchange of Fire*; *Heartbeat*; *How Do You Want Me?*; *In the Secret State*; Brutus in *Julius Caesar*; Jean Val Jean in *Les Misérables*; *Longitude*; *Mountain of Diamonds* (1990); *Saturday, Sunday, Monday*; *Sherlock Holmes*; *Stalin*; *Tales of the Unexpected*; Adolf Hitler in *The Death of Adolf Hitler*; *The Grand*; *The Last Campaign*; *Leprechauns*; Shylock in *The Merchant of Venice*; *The Verdict of Erebus*; *This Happy Breed*; Andrew Firth in *This Lie*.
Films: Freund in *1919*; Jacob Marley in *A Christmas Carol*; *A Life for Ruth*; *A Study in Terror*; *Assault*; *Cromwell*; *Cthulhu Mansion*; *Dreaming of Joseph Leas*; *Enigma*; *For My Baby*; *Gumshoe*; *Hot Enough for June*; *I'll Never Forget What's 'is Name*; *Inspector Clouseau*; *King of the Wind*; Professor Fallada in *Life Force*; *Limited Edition*; *Neither the Sea nor the Sand*; Iago in *Othello*; *Private Potter*; *Robbery*; *Romance and Rejection*; *Shaft in Africa*; *Murder by Decree*; Father Nunzio in *Sparrow*; *The Comedy Man*; *The Deadly Bees*; *The Four Musketeers*; *The Informers*; *The Jokers*; Nino in *The Key*; *The Loneliness of the Long Distance Runner*; *The Longest Day*; *The Molly Maguires*; *The Ploughman's Lunch*; *The Return of the Soldier*; *The Ring of Darkness*; *The Road to Glory*; *The Sandwich Man*; *The Shoes of the Fisherman*; *The Thief of Baghdad*; *The Three Musketeers*; Priest in *The Wild Geese*; *Twisted Nerve*; *Van Der Valk*; *Victory for Danny Jones*.
Address: c/o Ken McReddie Ltd, 91 Regent Street, London W1R 7TB.

FINNERAN, Siobhan

Siobhan Finneran. Actor (F).
TV: *Cannon and Ball*; Brenda Walsh in *Cops*; Josie Phillips in *Coronation Street*; Heather Hutchins in *Emmerdale*; Janet in *Heartbeat*; *Jackanory*; Milly in *Motormouth*; *Mr Wroe's Virgins*; *New Voices*; Fran in *Out of the Blue*; *Pack of Lies*; Caroline Royal in *Peak Practice*; Lena in *Resort to Murder*; *The Russ Abbot Show*; Tina in *Sharp End*; Julie in *The Factory*; Molly in *The Josie Lawrence Show*; Carol in *Where the Heart Is*.
Films: Rita in *Rita, Sue and Bob Too*.
Address: c/o Shane Collins Associates, 39–41 New Oxford Street, London WC1A 1BH.

FINNEY, Albert

Albert Finney. Actor (M).
b. Salford, Manchester, 9 May 1936.
TV: Reggie in *A Rather English Marriage; Biko Inquest; Cold Lazarus;* Daniel Feeld in *Karaoke; Nostromo; The Endless Game; The Green Man;* Jason Cromwell in *The Image.*
Films: *Breakfast of Champions; Delivering Milo; Erin Brockovich; Forget-Me-Not-Lane; Joan of Arc: The Virgin Warrior; Luther;* Hercule Poirot in *Murder on the Orient Express;* Arthur Seaton in *Saturday Night and Sunday Morning;* George Dunlap in *Shoot the Moon; Simpatico;* Andrew Crocker-Harris in *The Browning Version; The Run of the Country;* Sir in *The Dresser;* Tom Jones in *Tom Jones;* Geoffrey Firmin in *Under the Volcano.*
Address: c/o The Simpkin's Partnership, 45–51 Whitfield Street, London W1P 6AA.

FINNIGAN, Judy

Judy Finnigan. Presenter.
b. Manchester, 16 May 1948.
TV: *Get a Life* (1995); *Judy Finnigan Debate; Regional News* (1974); *Richard and Judy Show* (1992); *This Morning* (1988); *We Can Work It Out* (1998).
Address: c/o Arlington Enterprise Ltd, 1–3 Charlotte Street, London W1P 1HD. m. Richard Madeley.

FIRTH, Colin

Colin Firth. Actor (M).
b. Grayshott, Hampshire, 10 September 1960.
TV: *Camille; Crown Court; Donovan Quick; Dutch Girls; Hostages; Lost Empires; Master of the Moor; Nostromo;* Mr Darcy in *Pride and Prejudice; The Deep Blue Sea; The Widowing of Mrs Holroyd; Tumbledown.*
Films: *1000 Acres; 1919; A Month in the Country; Another Country; Apartment Zero; Circle of Friends; Femme Fatale; Fever Pitch; Londinium; My Life So Far; Relative Values; Secret Laughter of Women; Shakespeare in Love; The English Patient; The Hour of the Pig; The Playmaker; The Turn of the Screw; Valmont; Wings of Fame.*
Address: c/o ICM, Oxford House, 76 Oxford Street, London W1N 0AX.

FIRTH, David

David Firth. Actor (M)/Writer.
TV: *Home James; Keep it in the Family; Shelley; Sorry, I'm a Stranger Here Myself; The Live Rail; These Three; Troilus and Cressida; Up the Elephant and Round the Castle; Yes, Minister.*
Address: c/o Jill Foster Ltd, 9 Barb Mews, Brook Green, London W6 7PA.

FIRTH, Jonathan

Jonathan Firth. Actor (M).
TV: Stephen in *All About Laura;* Paul Gullminton in *Black Velvet Gown;* Chatsworth in *Breed of Heroes;* Joscelin Lucy in *Cadfael;* Roland in *Centrepoint;* Richard in *Covington Cross;* Troy in *Far From the Madding Crowd;* Hal in *Henry IV;* Lord Byron in *Highlander;* Peter Thornton in *Inspector Morse;* Terence in *Kangaroo Palace;* Count Grogan in *Leprechauns;* Stephen Gilmore in *Likeness in Stone;* Fred Vincey in *Middlemarch;* Michael Lacey in *Midsomer Murders;* Nigel Chapman in *Poirot;* Romeo in *Romeo and Juliet; Shoot the Revolution;* Malcolm in *Tales from the Crypt;* Keaton in *Under the Sun;* Michael in *Van Der Valk.*
Films: Cable in *American Friends;* Blade in *Six Pack;* Lord Goring in *The Ideal Husband;* Galois in *Truel;* Linton Heathcliffe in *Wuthering Heights.*
Address: c/o Markham & Froggatt Ltd, 4 Windmill Street, London W1P 1HF.

FIRTH, Peter

Peter Firth. Actor (M).
b. Bradford, Yorkshire, 27 October 1953.
TV: Francis in *And the Beat Goes On* (1996); Dominick Hide in *Another Flip for Dominick* (1982); Joe in *Children Crossing* (1990); Dr James Radcliffe in *Heartbeat* (1994); Scooper in *Here Come the Double Deckers* (1971); Mick in *Holding On* (1997); Henry Tilney in *Northanger Abbey* (1986); Major Henry in *Prisoner of Honour* (1991); Peter in *Resort to Murder* (1996); Roy in *The Aerodrome* (1983); Alex 'Godzilla' Turnball in *The Broker's Man* (1997); Dominick Hide in *The Flipside of Dominick Hide* (1980); Nazi Commandant in *The Garden of Redemption* (1997); Geiger in *The Incident* (1990).
Films: Croft in *Aces High;* Captain Fitzgerald in *Amistad;* Bunny in *An Awfully Big Adventure; Born of Fire;* Jake Stern in *Burndown;* Capt. Andrew Brynner in *Chill Factor; Diamonds on Wheels;* Alan Strong in *Equus;* Major Smith in *Gaston's War;* Joseph Andrews in *Joseph Andrews;* Peter in *Letter to Brezhnev;* Garth in *Mighty Young Joe;* Dr Craig in *Shadowlands;* Angel Clare in *Tess;* Ivan Putin in *The Hunt for Red October;* Steve Clemant in *The Laughter of God;* Dick in *The Pleasure Principle;* Stephen in *When You Comin' Back, Red Ryder?.*
Address: c/o Markham & Froggatt Ltd, 4 Windmill Street, London W1P 1HF.

FISH, Michael

Michael John Fish. Weather Presenter.
b. Eastbourne, East Sussex, 27 April 1944.
TV: *Weather Forecast.*

Address: c/o Arena Entertainment, Regents Court, 39 Harrogate Road, Leeds West, Yorkshire. m. Susan; 2 d. Alison, Nicola. Hobbies: Travel, DIY, genealogy.

FISHEL, Danielle

Danielle Fishel. Actor (F).
b. Mesa, Arizona, USA, 5 May 1981.
TV: Topanga Lawrence in *Boy Meets World*; Jennifer P in *Full House* (1992); *Harry and the Hendersons* (1991).
Films: Cheerleader Gloria in *Jack of All Trades*.
Address: c/o William Morris Agency, 151 El Camino Drive, Beverly Hills, California 90212, USA. Hobbies: Skiing, American football, surfing, snowboarding.

FISHER, Doug

Doug Fisher. Actor (M).
TV: *All in Good Faith; Ellis Island; Feet First; Goodnight Sweetheart; Haggard; Heartbeat; Helen, A Woman of Today; Home to Roost; Jonathan Creek; Keeping In Touch; London's Burning; Maggie; Man About the House; Prime Suspect; Shine on Harvey Moon; Singers Night; Singles; Sorry; Streets Apart; The Bill; The Detectives; The Man Who Almost Knew; The Upper Hand; Yes, Minister.*
Films: *Man About the House; Tess; The Bitch; The Stud.*
Address: c/o The Narrow Road Company, 21–22 Poland Street, London W1V 3DD.

FISHER, Gregor

Gregor Fisher. Actor (M)/Comedian.
TV: *Blood Red Roses; City Lights; End of the Line; Foxy Lady*; The Fly in *Gormenghast; Just a Boy's Game; Naked Video*; Rab C. Nesbitt in *Rab C. Nesbitt; Stan's First Night; The Baldy Man*; Para Handy in *The Tales of Para Handy*.
Films: Parsons in *1984*; Beel in *Another Time, Another Place*; Bill in *The Girl in the Picture*; *To Kill a Priest*; McPherson in *White Mischief; Without a Clue*.
Address: c/o CDA, 19 Sydney Mews, London SW3 6HL.

FISHER, Isla

Isla Fisher. Actor (F). b. 2 February 1977.
TV: Donna in *Australia; Bay City; Clowning Around II*; Melanie in *Haydaze*; Shannon in *Home and Away*; Bett in *Oliver Twist; Paradise Beach; Rip Snorters; Vidiot*; Mandy in *Wavelength*.
Films: Bunny Girl in *Best; Bum Magnet; Furnished Room*; Sheila in *Out of Depth*; Gemma in *Random Acts of Intimacy; The Dive*.
Address: c/o Elaine Murphy Associates, 310 Aberdeen House, 22–24 Highbury Grove, London N52 EA.

FISHER, Jeannie

Jeannie Fisher. Actor (F).
b. Glasgow, Scotland, 18 February 1947.
TV: *Adam Smith; Arthur of the Britons; Canterbury Tales*; Morag Kerr in *High Road; The Silver Sword*.
Address: c/o MGA, Concorde House, 18 Margaret Street, Brighton, Sussex BN2 1TS.

FITZALAN, Marsha

Marsha Fitzalan. Actor (F).
b. Bonn, Germany, 10 March 1953.
TV: *Midsomer Murders; Ruth Rendell Mysteries*; Sarah B'stard in *The New Statesman*.
Films: *An Ideal Husband; Anna Karenina; International Velvet; The Lost Son*.
Address: c/o PFD, Drury House, 34–43, Russell Street, London WC2B 5HA. 2 d. Mariella, Jemima; 1 s. Freddie. Hobbies: Horse riding.

FITZGERALD, Kate

Kate Fitzgerald. Actor (F). b. Liverpool.
TV: Doreen Corkhill in *Brookside*; June Williamson in *Casualty; Daughters of Albion*; Chrissy Atwood in *Peak Practice*; Mrs Delaney in *Queer As Folk*; Mrs Selby in *Secret Society; The Bill*; Ma Cavannagh in *The Lakes*.
Films: *Call Collect*.
Address: c/o Saraband Associates, 265 Liverpool Road, London N1 1LX.

FITZGERALD, Tara

Tara Fitzgerald. Actor (F). b. 18 September 1967.
TV: Dolly in *Anglo-Saxon Attitudes*; Catherine in *Fall From Grace*; Lady Dona St Columb in *Frenchman's Creek*; Beth March in *Little White Lies; Six Characters in Search of an Author*; Victoria Mordant in *The Black Candle*; Polly in *The Camomile Lawn*; Grace in *The Student Prince*; Helen in *The Tenant of Wildfell Hall*; Poppy Carew in *The Vacillations of Poppy Carew*; Marian in The *Woman in White*.
Films: Adele Rice in *A Man of No Importance*; Gloria in *Brassed Off*; Snow Angel in *Childhood*; Daisy in *Conquest*; Nancy Doyle in *Hear My Song*; Kris in *New World Disorder*; Masha in *Rancid Aluminium*; Estella in *Sirens*; Betty from Cardiff in *The Englishman Who Went Up a Hill, But Came Down A Mountain*.
Address: c/o CDA, 19 Sydney Mews, London SW3 6HL.

FLEESHMAN, David

David Fleeshman. Actor (M).
b. Glasgow, Scotland, 11 July 1952.
TV: Sgt. Purkiss in *A Bit of a Do*; Gordon Knight in *After the War; Band of Gold*; Det. Insp. Grucock in

Blind Justice; Boys From the Blackstuff; Dr Burton in
Brookside; Bullman; Capstick's Law; Renshaw in *The
Cater Street Hangman; Children's Ward;* Peter Haines
in *Coronation Street;* Pedro Pedley in *Dalziel and
Pascoe; Dear Enemy;* Soames in *EastEnders;* Det. Sgt.
Jones in *Edge of Darkness;* Charlie Aindow in
Emmerdale; Mr Faber in *Heartbeat; Hetty Wainthropp
Investigates;* Harry in *Highlander – The Raven;* Alexander Houghton in *How We Used To Live;* Thomas Buss
in *In Suspicious Circumstances;* John in *Life Force;
Medics;* Immigration Officer in *Missing Persons; One
By One;* Michael Sterne in *Sam Saturday;* S.O. Stones
in *The Bill; The Outsider; The Practice;* Serge Olsen in
Ruth Rendell Mysteries; The Storyteller; Fletcher in *Trial
and Retribution; Truckers;* Bernard Michaelson in *The
Verdict; Victorian Values.*
Films: *The Nature of the Beast; The Wall.*
Address: c/o Rolf Kruger Management Ltd, 205
Chudleigh Road, London SE4 1EG. m. Sue Jenkins
(Jackie Corkhill in *Brookside*); 2 d. Emily, Rosie; 1 s.
Richard.

FLEET, James
James Fleet. Actor (M). b. Staffordshire.
TV: *A Year in Provence; Advocates II; Boon; Cows;
Cracker; Crossing the Floor; Dance to the Music of Time;
Dempsey and Makepeace;* Mr Brown in *Grange Hill;
Harry Enfield and Chums; Head Hunters; Hess; Lord of
Misrule; Minder; Moll Flanders; Murder Most Horrid;*
Ian Inglis in *Omega Factor; Running Late;* Neil in *Ruth
Rendell Mysteries;* Ashley in *Spark; The Bill; The
Common Pursuit;* Hugo Horton in *The Vicar of Dibley;
They Never Slept; Underworld.*
Films: Simon Liddel in *An Electric Moon;* Jim Thorburn in *Blue Black Permanent; Butterfly Effect;* Mr
Lewis in *Defence of the Realm; Eskimo Day; Exchange
of Fire; Femme Fatale;* Tom in *Four Weddings and a
Funeral; Frenchman's Creek; Milk; Remember Me;* John
Dashwood in *Sense and Sensibility; The Grotesque;
Three Steps to Heaven.*
Address: c/o Scott Marshall, 44 Perryn Road, London
W3 7NA. m. Jane Booker; 1 s. Hamish.

FLEMYNG, Jason
Jason Flemyng. Actor (M). b. London, 1967.
TV: *A Question of Attribution; Beck; Bye Bye Baby;
Doctor Finlay's Casebook; For the Greater Good; Good
Guys; Lovejoy; Tess of the D'Urbervilles; The Double;
Witchcraft; The Young Indiana Jones Chronicles.*
Films: *Alice in Wonderland; Alive and Kicking;
Bruiser; Dancing; Deep Rising; Diamond Swords; Diamonds; Rudyard Kipling's The Jungle Book; Les Carribans; Lock, Stock and Two Smoking Barrels; Rob Roy;*

*Shuttle; Spice World; Stealing Beauty; The Body; The
Commitment; The Hollow Reed; The James Gang; The
Life of Stuff; The Red Violin; The Temptation of Franz
Schubert.*
Address: c/o Conway Van Gelder, 18–21 Jermyn
Street, London SW1Y 6HP.

FLETCHER, Dexter
Dexter Fletcher. Actor (M).
b. London, 31 January 1966.
TV: *Aristophanes; Boon; Dead London; Dread Poets
Society; English File: Text in Time; Murder Most Horrid;
Press Gang; Seven Deadly Sins: Sloth and Lust; Soldier,
Soldier; The Famous Five; The Tempest; Working Week.*
Films: *All Out; Bash; Bugsy Malone; Caravaggio;
Elephant Man; Gothic; Jude the Obscure; Let the Good
Times Roll; Lionheart; Lock, Stock and Two Smoking
Barrels; Revolution; Soloman; The Bounty; The Long
Good Friday; The Mad Monkey; The Rachel Papers; The
Raggedy Rawnety; Topsy Turvy; Watch That Man; When
the Whales Came; Wings of Death.*
Address: c/o ICM, Oxford House, 76 Oxford Street,
London W1N 0AX.

FLETCHER, Diane
Diane Fletcher. Actor (F).
b. Derby, Derbyshire, 17 April 1946.
TV: Nancy Beamish in *A Fairly Secret Army;* The
Duchess of Richmond in *Aristocrats;* Elizabeth
Urquhart in *House of Cards;* Nariona in *Inspector
Morse;* Marcia Tranter in *Midsomer Murders;* Liz in
Murder at the Wedding; Eloise Renaud in *Poirot;*
Emma in *Roger Doesn't Live Here Any More;* Mona
Washburn in *Spoils of Poynton;* Evelyn Tombs in *The
Chamber;* Ada Nieldchew in *The Clarion Van;* Lady
Blakeney in *The Elusive Pimpernel;* Bobby Bennett in
The Irish RM.
Films: *Autobiography of a Princess; Investigation; It's
Good to Talk; Leaving Lily;* Lady Macduff in *Macbeth.*
Address: c/o Scott Marshall, 44 Perryn Road, London
W3 7NA.

FLETCHER, Freddie
Freddie Fletcher. Actor (M). b. Yorkshire.
TV: Mr Derek in *All Creatures Great and Small;* Mr
Smithson in *Children's Ward;* Kenny in *Floodtide;*
Poacher 'Vic' in *GBH;* Sam Carver in *Heartbeat;* Crandon in *How We Used To Live;* George Milton in *Peak
Practice;* Mr Thompson in *Some Kind of Life;* Arnie
Franks in *The Governor;* Gypsy in *The Old Firm.*
Films: Mr Redway in *Brothers in Trouble;* Ronnie Boyd
in *Fox;* Wireless Operator in *Juggernaut;* Jud in *Kes;*
Ned in *Nature of the Beast.*

Address: c/o ATS Casting Ltd, 26 St Michael's Road, Leeds, Yorkshire LS6 3AW.

FLINTOFF, Ian

Ian Flintoff. Actor (M). b. Preston, Lancashire.
TV: Mr Meredith in *A Touch of Frost*; Councillor in *Against All Odds*; Stennings in *Boon*; Chief Supt. Dalyle in *Brookside*; Elliott Needham in *Casualty*; George Urquhart in *Coronation Street*; Kershall in *Evergreen*; The Reporter in *Four Minute Mile*; Edward Palfrey in *The House of Eliott*; Vicar in *Jailbirds*; Daco Humble in *London's Burning*; Richard Rampton QC in *McLibel*; *Play for Tomorrow*; Ch. Insp. Mallory in *Prime Suspect*; Alistair Ellis Brown in *Rides*; Mr Daniels in *The Bill*; *The Greater Good*; Mr Evans in *The Perfect Match*; Maj. Wright in *Trial by Jury*; Neuts in *True Crimes*; Dr Stanley Empson in *A Wing and a Prayer*.
Films: Labour Councillor in *Bad Behaviour*; *Debussy*; Ambassador in *Exchange of Fire*; *I Saw Mummy Kissing Santa*; *Privilege*.
Address: c/o Sheila Bourne Management, Bridge House, Three Mills Island Studios, Three Mills Lane, London E3 3DU.

FLOCKHART, Calista

Calista Flockhart. Actor (F).
b. Freeport, Illinois, USA, 11 November 1964.
TV: Ally McBeal in *Ally McBeal*; Lillian Anderson in *Darrow*; *Lifestories: Family in Crisis* (1992); Elise in *The Guiding Light* (1989); Ally McBeal in *The Practice* (1998).
Films: *Getting In*; *Milk and Money*; *Naked in New York*; Barnard Girl in *Quiz Show*; Diney Majeski in *Telling Lies in America*; Barbara Keeley in *The Birdcage*; Helena in *William Shakespeare's A Midsummer's Night Dream*.
Address: c/o Gersh Agency, 23rd Floor, 130 West 42nd Street, New York, New York 10036, USA. Hobbies: Decorating, pet dog.

FLYNN, Barbara

Barbara Flynn. Actor (F).
b. Hastings, Sussex, 5 August 1948.
TV: *A Flight Fund*; Rose Marie in *A Very Peculiar Practice*; *Afternoon Dancing*; Sue in *Bagthorpes*; Mary Bold in *Barchester Towers*; Jill Swinburne in *The Beiderbecke Connection*; Jane in *Benefactors*; Sheila Green in *Boon*; Dee in *Chandler and Co.*; Judith in *Cracker*; Judy in *Day to Remember*; Joan in *Dear Nobody*; Freda Ashton in *Family at War*; Monica Height in *Inspector Morse*; Marlene in *Keep it in the Family*; Goneril in *King Lear*; Monica in *Love on a Gunboat*; Joanna Lassiter in *Lucky Jim*; Madame Maigret in *Maigret*; Dorothy Kemp in *Maybury*; *Murder Most English*; Margaret Hanson in *No Visible Scar*; Milkwoman in *Open All Hours*; Belinda in *Seasons Greetings*; Sarah Fletcher in *Second Chance*; Heather in *Standing in for Henry*; Jill Swinburne in *The Beiderbecke Affair*; Jill Swinburne in *The Beiderbecke Tapes*; Sandy Whitman in *The Gentle Touch*; Eleanor Goodchild in *The Justice Game*; Shirley in *The Last Song*; Ms Jeffries in *The Vanishing Man*; Jill in *Where Angels Fear*; Miss Browning in *Wives and Daughters*.
Films: Nurse Green in *Britannia Hospital*; Professor Corner in *You're Dead*.
Address: c/o William Morris Agency (UK) Ltd, 1 Stratton Street, London W1X 6HB.

FLYNN, Jerome

Jerome Flynn. Actor (M). b. 16 March 1963.
TV: Nagle in *A Mind To Murder*; Eddie Clapper in *Ain't Misbehavin'*; McCabe in *Badger*; Charlie in *Dirty Dishes*; John Mailer in *Divorce*; Tony Fleming in *Don't Leave me this Way*; *Rat in the Skull*; Paddy Garvey in *Soldier, Soldier*; Freddy in *The Fear*; Franny in *The Monocled Mutineer*; Nigel in *The Russian Soldier*.
Films: *Best*; *Kafka*; *Edward II*; *To Kill a Priest*; *Troubles*; *A Summer Story*.
Address: c/o William Morris Agency (UK) Ltd, 1 Stratton Street, London W1X 6HB.

FLYNN, Judy

Judy Flynn. Actor (F).
TV: Carol in *Albion Market*; Lena in *First of the Summer Wine*; Carol May the Second in *Making Out*; Lynda in *Brookside*; *Casualty*; Carol in *Made in Heaven*; Maureen in *The World of Eddie Weary*; *Soldier, Soldier*; Julie in *The Brittas Empire*; Madge Howell in *The House of Eliott*; Elise in *Closing Numbers*; Marjorie Evans in *Doggin' Around*; *Peak Practice*; *The Bill*; Paula Kenyon in *Hetty Wainthropp Investigates*; *Out of Sight*; *dinnerladies*; *Where the Heart Is*; Jenny Hammond in *Heartbeat*; *Perfect World*; *Heartburn Hotel*.
Films: *Restoration*; Natasha in *Rhythms of the House*.
Address: c/o CDA, 19 Sydney Mews, London SW3 6HL.

FOLEY, Bernadette

Bernadette Foley. Actor (F).
TV: Sara Jackson in *Barriers*; Fran Person in *Brookside*; *Hillsborough*; Maisey Peters in *Rich Deceiver*; Belinda/Trudy in *Watch with Mother*.
Address: c/o Toner Casting, Crane Buildings, Hanover Street, Liverpool L13 DZ.

FORBES, Emma

Emma Forbes. Presenter. b. London, 14 May 1965.
TV: *Esther; Going Live; Good Stuff; Live and Kicking; Speakeasy; Speakeasy Does the Business; Talking Telephone Numbers; The Weekend Show; Tip Top Challenge; What's My Line?*.
Address: c/o James Grant Management Ltd, Syon Lodge, Syon Park, London Road, Middlesex TW7 5BH. 1 d. Lily; 1 s. Sam Theo; mother Nanette Newman, father Brian Forbes.

FORBES, Miranda

Miranda Forbes. Actor (F). b. 11 August 1946.
TV: *A Small Dance; Absolutely Fabulous; As Time Goes By; Ashenden; Back Home; Castle of Adventure; Casualty; Circle of Deceit;* Rosemary in *Faith in the Future; Felix Dexter on TV; French and Saunders; Hancock; Keeping Mum; London's Burning; Lovejoy; May to December; Poirot; Room at the Bottom; Shine on Harvey Moon; The Bill; The Last Romantics; The Prince and the Pauper; The Upper Hand; Waiting for God; Yes, Prime Minister.*
Films: *All Men Are Mortal; Bejewelled; Jane Eyre.*
Address: c/o The Narrow Road Company, 21–22 Poland Street, London W1V 3DD.

FORBES, Natalie

Natalie Forbes. Actor (F).
b. Dorchester, Yorkshire, 1 November.
TV: Maureen in *A Ferry Ride Away;* Brenda in *Blood Money;* Jennifer in *Clapperclaw;* Diana in *Full House;* Cherry Ross in *Happy Feet;* Jean Selby in *Heartbeat;* Amber Python in *Julia Jekyll and Harriet Hyde;* Aquarius in *The Kelly Monteith Show;* Phillipa Thornley in *Lovejoy;* 40D in *Luna;* Tilly Wilcox in *Nanny;* Nadine in *Out on the Floor;* Paula in *Radio;* Annie Dyer in *Shadow of the Noose;* Lorna in *Sharp End;* Kristen in *She-Wolf of London;* WPC Flemming in *The Gentle Touch;* Inga in *The Incredible Mr Tanner;* Astrid in *The Other 'Arf.*
Films: Sally in *Expecting;* Mme Grande in *Napoleon and Josephine; Telephones;* Guinevere in *The Loss Adjuster.*
Address: c/o Susan Angel Associates, 1st Floor, 12 D'Arblay Street, London W1V 3FP.

FORD, Anna

Anna Ford. Newsreader. b. Tewkesbury, Gloucestershire 2 October 1943.
TV: *ITN news programmes; Man Alive; Six O'Clock News; Tomorrow's World* (1978); *TV-am; Heart of the Matter.*
Address: c/o Knight Ayton Management, 10 Argyll Street, London W1V 1AB.

FORD, Julia

Julia Ford. Actor (F).
TV: *A Fatal Intervention; A Skirt Through History; Accused; Anchor Me; Bergerac; Blood and Fire; Casualty; City Central; Eight Hours from Paris; In a Land of Plenty; In Suspicious Circumstances; Insiders; Medics; Peak Practice; Strike Force; The Bill; The Continental; The Healer; The Practice; The Ritz.*
Films: *Butterfly World; Room for Romeo Brass; Soft Sand, Blue Sea.*
Address: c/o Conway Van Gelder Ltd, 18–21 Jermyn Street, London SW1Y 6HP.

FORRESTER, Philippa

Philippa Forrester. Actor (F)/Presenter. b. 1969.
TV: *Barking Mad; Dreamwheels* (1999); *GMTV; Night Fever; Robot Wars; The Broom Cupboard; The Disney Club* (1994); *The Eclipse* (1999); *The O-Zone; The World's Strongest Man* (1997); *This Morning* (1997); *Tomorrow's World; Weekly Echo* (1994); *Zoo Watch.*
Address: c/o Speak-easy Ltd, 90 St Mary's Road, Market Harborough, Leicestershire LEI6 7DX.

FORSYTH, Brigit

Brigit Forsyth. Actor (F). b. Edinburgh, 28 July 1940.
TV: Annie Smith in *Adam Smith;* Bel Bel in *Bazaar and Rummage;* Helen Yeldon in *Boon;* Margaret in *Casualty;* Linda Barton in *Dangerfield;* Mrs Porter in *In Suspicious Circumstances;* Mrs Osman in *Murder Most Horrid;* Rosemary Dobson in *Nice Town;* Francine Pratt in *Playing the Field;* Mrs Todd in *Poirot;* Linda in *Running Wild;* Elsie in *Sharon and Elsie;* Mrs Wells in *Spark;* Miss Maitland in *The Dark Season;* Dr Vincent in *The Practice;* Sylvia Dickinson in *The Ward;* Harriet in *Tom, Dick & Harriet;* Thelma in *Whatever Happened to the Likely Lads?;* Ella Jones in *Wycliffe.*
Films: Hilda Spencer in *Stanley's Vision;* Thelma in *Whatever Happened to the Likely Lads?.*
Address: c/o Pemberton Associates, Suite 35–36, Barton Arcade, Deansgate, Manchester M3 2BB.

FORSYTH, Bruce

Bruce Forsyth. Actor (M)/Presenter/Host.
b. London, 22 February 1928.
TV: *Music Hall; Sunday Night at the London Palladium; The Bruce Forsyth Show; The Canterville Ghost; The Mating Game; The Generation Game; Bring on the Girls; The Muppet Show; Bruce and More Girls; The Entertainers; Bruce Forsyth's Big Night; Play Your Cards Right; Hollywood or bust; Slinger's Day; Sammy and Bruce; You Bet!; Bruce Forsyth's Generation Game; Bruce Forsyth – 50 years in Showbusiness; Bruce Forsyth's Play Your Cards Right; Bruce's Price is Right.*

Films: Swinburne in *Bedknobs and Broomsticks*; Uncle Limelight in *Can Hieronymus Merkin Ever Forget Mercy Humppe and Find True Happiness?*; Clayton in *The Magnificent Seven Deadly Sins*; Arthur Lawrence in *Star!*.

Address: c/o Billy Marsh Associates, 174–178 North Gower Street, London NW1 2NB.

FORTUNE, Jack

Jack Fortune. Actor (M).

TV: *Between The Lines*; *Cardiac Arrest*; *Dangerfield*; *Forever Green*; *Harry Enfield's Television Programme*; *Henry VI*; *Pirates*; *Richard III*; *Soldier, Soldier*; *Taggart*; *Tales of the Unexpected*; *The Advocates*; *The Chelworth Inheritance*; *The Justice Game*; *To Play the King*; *Treasure Island*; *Tumbledown*; *Your Cheatin' Heart*.

Films: *Hawk the Slayer*; *Intimate Strangers*; *The Lovechild*.

Address: c/o Amanda Howard Associates, Ltd, 21 Berwick Street, London W1V 3RG.

FORTUNE, John

John Fortune. Actor (M)/Comedian. b. 1959.

TV: Paul Bentley in *A Very Open Prison*; *BBC3*; *Birds and Well Anyway*; *Bremner, Bird and Fortune*; *Campaign*; *Dramarama*; *First Among Equals*; Chief Executive in *Giving Tongue*; *Haggard*; *Have I Got News For You*; *In the Looking Glass*; *The Lenny Henry Show – Christmas Special*; Long Johns Election Specials; *Not So Much a Programme*; *On the Margin*; Claredon in *Purcell*; *Roger Doesn't Live Here Any More*; *Rory Bremner... Who Else?*; *Round and Round*; *The End of the Pier Show*; *The Good Guys*; *The Late Show*; *The Long Johns*; *The Rory Bremner Show*; *Three Men and a Vote*; *Where Was Spring?*

Films: Acupuncturist in *Maybe Baby*; Melvyn Stott in *Saving Grace*; *The Strange Case of Delfina Potocka*.

Address: c/o The Richard Stone Partnership, 2 Henrietta Street, London WC2E 8PS.

FOSKETT, Wayne

Wayne Foskett. Actor (M).

TV: Elvis in *A Bit of A Do*; *Always and Everyone*; *Between the Lines*; *Birds of a Feather*; Gavin in *Blisters*; *Boon*; *Casualty*; Tommy Lane in *Chancer*; *Cristabel*; Summers in *Framed*; Macca in *GBH*; *Heartbeat*; *Hetty Wainthropp Investigates*; *In Suspicious Circumstances*; Riley in *Love and Reason*; *Lovejoy*; *No Bananas*; *Noah's Ark*; *Peak Practice*; *Soldier, Soldier*; Graham in *Tales of Sherwood Forest*; Malcolm in *Thacker*; *The Blind Men*; *The Widowing of Mrs Holroyd*; *Thief Takers*; *Where the Heart Is*.

Address: c/o Annette Stone Associates, 2nd Floor, 22 Great Marlborough Street, London W1V 1AF.

FOSTER, Barry

Barry Foster. Actor (M). b. Beeston, 21 August 1930.

TV: *A Curious Suicide*; *A Family Affair*; *A Woman Called Golda*; *After Pilkington*; *Born in the Gardens*; *Dan Dan the Charity Man*; *Death of an Expert Witness*; *Divorce His/Hers*; Kaiser Wilhem in *Fall of Eagles*; *Ghosts*; Hamlet in *Hamlet*; *Hotel Du Lac*; *How Many Miles to Babylon?*; *Inspector Morse*; *Jack's Horrible Luck*; *King of the Wind*; *Mogul*; *Old Times*; *Rabbit Pie Day*; *Random Moments in a May Garden*; *Rear Column*; Pieter Eugene in *Roger Roger*; *Smiley's People*; *A Taste of Honey*; *The Soldier's Tale*; *The Three French Men*; *The Three Hostages*; *Under Western Eyes*; Van Der Valk in *Van Der Valk*; *Where the Difference Begins*; *Wingate*; *Woyzeck*.

Films: *The Battle of Britain*; *Frenzy*; *King and Country*; *Rancid Aluminium*; *Sea of Sand*; *The Family Way*; *The Guru*; *Twisted Nerve*.

Address: c/o Ken McReddie Ltd, 91 Regent Street, London W1R 7TB.

FOWLDS, Derek

Derek Fowlds. Actor (M).
b. London, 2 September 1937.

TV: *Affairs of the Heart*; *After That, This...*; *Agony*; *Boon*; *Casualty*; *Chancer*; *Clayhanger*; *Cribb*; Crombie in *Die Kinder*; *Edward VIII*; John Gutteridge in *Firm Friends*; Sgt. Oscar Blaketon (Rtr'd) *in Heartbeat*; *Inspector Morse*; *Intensive Care*; *Miss Jones and Son*; *My Son, My Son*; *Perfect Scoundrels*; *Rings on My Fingers*; Oliver Davidson in *Rules of Engagement*; *Send in the Girls*; *Strangers*; *Darling Buds of May*; *The Doll*; *They Never Slept*; *Walk on the Wild Side*; Bernard Woolley in *Yes, Minister*.

Films: Gilbert Bentley in *After Celia*; *Doctor in Distress*; *East of Sudan*; *Frankenstein Created Woman*; *Hot Enough for June*; *Hotel Paradiso*; *Mistress Pamela*; *Over the Hill*; *The Copler Kids*; *The Loneliness of the Long Distance Runner*; *The Smashing Bird I Used to Know*; *Tower of Evil*; *We Joined the Navy*.

Address: c/o CDA, 19 Sydney Mews, London SW3 6HL.

FOWLER, Harry

Harry Fowler. Actor (M).
b. London, 10 December 1926.

TV: *A Roller Next Year*; *All in Good Faith*; *Big Deal*; *Body Contact*; *Casualty*; *Dead Earnest*; *Doctor Who*; *Educating Marmalade*; *Entertainment Express*; *George and Mildred*; *Gossip*; *Harry's Kingdom*; *High and Dry*; *In Sickness and in Health*; *Little World of Don Camillo*; *Me and the Girls*; *Minder*; *Mitch*; *Room at the Bottom*; *Round and Round*; *Spooner's Patch*; *Supergran*; *The Bill*;

The Bobby Davro Show; The Home Front; The More-cambe and Wise Show; The Professionals; The Suntrap; The Zodiac Game; World's End.

Films: *Chicago Joe and the Showgirl; Fanny Hill; High Rise Donkey; The Lady is a Tramp; Sir Henry at Rawlinson End; The Prince and The Pauper.*

Address: c/o Kenneth Earle Personal Management, 214 Brixton Road, London SW9 6AP.

FOX, 'Doctor' Neil

Neil Fox. Presenter.

TV: *Beat UK; Dr Fox's Chart Update; Dr Fox's Video Jukebox; Major Baseball League; Not the Jack Docherty Show; Pepsi Chart; Sky Sport's Greatest Hits; Speakeasy; WowFabGroovy.*

Address: c/o MPC Entertainment, MPC House, 15–16 Maple Mews, London NW6 5UZ. Hobbies: Harley Davidson enthusiast, flying helicopters, surfing.

FOX, Edward

Edward Fox. Actor (M). b. London, 13 April 1937.

TV: Lord Harry Wrotham in *A Hazard of Hearts; A Midsummer Night's Dream*; Dr Hauser in *Anastasia: The Mystery of Anna*; Sam in *Bermondsey; Black Knight*; Edward in *Edward and Mrs Simpson*; Markham in *Forbidden Territory: Stanley's Search for Livingstone; Girl of My Dreams*; Gen. Limtoc in *Gulliver's Travels*; Harthouse in *Hard Times; Loyalties; Olive*; John Quartermaine in *Quartermaine's Terms*; Prince John in *Robin Hood; School for Scandal*; Archie in *September; Shooting the Chandelier*; Alistair Ross in *The Crucifer of Blood*; Metternich in *The Strauss Dynasty; The Voysey Inheritance*; Monk Scott in *They Never Sleep*.

Films: Lt. Gen. Horrocks in *A Bridge Too Far*; Nils Krogstad in *A Doll's House*; Father in *A Feast at Midnight*; Maj. Wilshaw in *A Month By the Lake; A Passage to India; The Battle of Britain*; Miller in *Force 10 From Navarone*; Cardinal Inquisitor in *Galileo*; Gen. Dyer in *Gandhi*; Walter in *I'll Never Forget What's 'is Name; Lost in Space*; M in *Never Say Never Again; Oh! What a Lovely War*; King Arthur in *Prince Valiant*; Maj. Benford in *Return From the River Kwai; Shaka Zulu*; Bruce Spofford in *Skullduggery*; Col. Rafelli in *Soldaat Van Oranje*; Joe Brody in *The Big Sleep*; Capt. Greenham in *The Bounty; The Breaking of Bumbo*; Hendricks in *The Cat and The Canary*; The Jackal in *The Day of the Jackal*; Oxenby in *The Dresser*; Colonel in *The Duellists*; Norburg's Brother in *The Frozen Dead*; Hugh Trimmingham in *The Go-Between*; Lt. Sprague in *The Jokers*; Hardwicke in *The Long Duel*; Insp. Craddock in *The Mirror Crack'd*; Richie Jackson in *The Naked Runner*; Lord Gilbert Hartlip in *The Shooting Party*; Foreman in

The Squeeze; Alex Faulkner in *Wild Geese II*.

Address: c/o CDA, 19 Sydney Mews, London SW3 6HL. m. 1 Tracy Reid; 1 d. Lucy; m. 2 Joanna David; 1 d. Emilia; 1 s. Freddie.

FOX, Emilia

Emilia Rose Elizabeth Fox. Actor (F).

b. London, 31 July 1974.

TV: Jackie in *Bad Blood*; Ann Devenish in *Bright Hair*; Mrs Copperfield in *David Copperfield*; Georgiana D'Arcy in *Pride and Prejudice*; Jeannie in *Randall & Hopkirk (Deceased)* (2000); Rebecca in *Rebecca*; Spig in *Shooting the Past; Temptation of Franz Schubert; The Round Tower*; Minette in *The Scarlet Pimpernel; Vanessa*.

Films: *Blink; The Ratcatcher.*

Address: c/o PFD, Drury House, 34–43 Russell Street, London WC2B 5HA. Niece of James Fox.

FOX, James

James Fox. Actor (M). b. London 19 May 1939.

TV: *A Perfect Hero; A Question of Attribution; Country; Fall From Grace; Headhunters; Hostage; Love is Old, Love is New; Nancy Astor; Never Come Back; New World; Shadow of the Sun; Shaka Zulu; She's Been Away; Slowly Slowly in the Wind; Sunchild; The Choir; The Dwelling Place; The Old Curiosity Shop; The Road to 1984; These Foolish Things.*

Films: *A Passage to India; Afraid of the Dark; All Forgotten; Anna Karenina; As You Like It; Doomsday Gun; Farewell to the King; Greystoke; Gulliver's Travels; Heart of Darkness; High Season; Jinnah; King Rat; Kings in Grass Castles; Mickey Blue Eyes; Mrs Miniver's Story; Neverever; No Place to Hide; Patriot Games; Performance; The Remains of the Day; Runners; Shadow Run; The Boys in the Island; The Chase; The Loneliness of the Long Distance Runner; The Magnet; The Mighty Quinn; The Russia House; The Servant; The Whistle Blower; Thoroughly Modern Millie; Those Magnificent Men in Their Flying Machines; Up at the Villa.*

Address: c/o ICM, Oxford House, 76 Oxford Street, London W1N 0AX. Father Robin; mother Angela; 2 brothers Edward, Robert; niece Emilia.

FOX, Kerry

Kerry Fox. Actor (F).

b. Wellington, New Zealand, 1966.

TV: *A Village Affair; Déjà Vu* (1999); *Mr Wroe's Virgins; Saigon Baby; The Affair.*

Films: *An Angel at My Table; Country Life; Fanny and Elvis; Friends; Shallow Grave; The Darkest Light; The Hanging Garden; The Last Days of Chez Nous; The Last*

Tattoo; The Sound of One Hand Clapping; To Walk With Lions; Welcome to Sarajevo; The Wisdom of Crocodiles.
Address: c/o ICM, Oxford House, 76 Oxford Street, London W1N 0AX.

FOX, Michael J.
Michael J. Fox. Actor (M).
b. Edmonton, Canada, 9 June 1961.
TV: Dear America: Letters Home from Vietnam (1987); Don't Drink the Water (1994); Alex P. Keaton in Family Ties (1982); Alex P. Keaton in Family Ties Vacation (1985); Jay-Jay Manners in High School USA (1983); I Am Your Child (1997); Ricki in Letters from Frank (1979); Willy-Joe Hall in Palmerstown, USA (1980); Dennis Baxter in Poison Ivy (1985); Sex, Buys and Advertising (1990); Michael Flaherty in Spin City; The Trap (1991); Trapper John (1979).
Films: Back to the Future; Back to the Future Part II; Back to the Future Part III; Pete Maloney in Blue in the Face; Jamie Conway in Bright Lights, Big City; Eriksson in Casualties of War; Arthur in Class of 1984; Tim Alexander in Coldblooded; Dr Benjamin Stone in Doc Hollywood; Doug Ireland in For Love or Money; Daniel McTeague in Greedy; Voice of Chance in Homeward Bound: The Incredible Journey; Voice of Chance in Homeward Bound II: Lost in San Francisco; Michael Chapman in Life with Mikey; Joe Rasnick in Light of Day; Jason Stone in Mars Attacks!; Scott in Midnight Madness; Stuart Little in Stuart Little; Scott Howard in Teen Wolf; Lewis Rothschild in The American President; Frank Bannister in The Frighteners; Nick Lang in The Hard Way; Brantley Foster/Carlton Whitfield in The Secret of My Success; Clayton Farnsworth in Thirty Wishes; Where the Rivers Flow North.
Address: c/o Creative Artists Agency, 9830 Wilshire Boulevard, Beverly Hills, California 90212, USA. m. Tracy Pollan; 1 d. Aquinnah Kathleen; 2 s. Sam Michael, Schuyler Frances. Hobbies: Hockey, guitar.

FOY, Julie
Julie Foy. Actor (F).
b. Bolton, Lancashire, 5 May 1970.
TV: Casualty; Coronation Street; Forever Young; How to be Cool; Jossy's Giants; Missing Persons; Press Gang.
Address: c/o PBR Management, 26 Foubert's Place, Regent Street, London W1V 1HG.

FRANCIS, Clive
Clive Francis. Actor (M). b. London, 26 June 1946.
TV: Amy; As You Like It; Lipstick on Your Collar; May to December; Oedipus at Colonus; Old Flames; Poldark; Quartermaine's Terms; Sharpe's Company; The Ten Percenters; The Bretts; The Far Pavilions; The

Piglet Files; The Plant; The Return of Sherlock Holmes; Longitude.
Films: A Clockwork Orange; Girl Stroke Boy; Inspector Clouseau; The Man Who Had Power Over Women; Villain.
Address: c/o PFD, Drury House, 34–43 Russell Street, London WC2B 5HA. Father Raymond Francis.

FRANCIS, Jan
Jan Francis. Actor (F). b. London, 5 August 1951.
TV: A Chance to Sit Down; Anne of Green Gables; Anne of Avonlea; Country Manners; Death Can Add; The Duchess of Duke Street; Fall of Eagles; Good Companions; Jackanory; Just Good Friends; London Assurance; Love's Labour Lost; Minder; Raffles; Ripping Yarns; Secret Army; Colette in Spark; Stay Lucky; The Party of the First Part; The Plot to Murder Lloyd George; The Ghostbusters of East Finchley; The Lonely Man's Lover; The Long Chase; The Magistrate; QC in The Verdict; Under the Hammer; Sunburn.
Films: Champions; Dracula; The Corvini Inheritance.
Address: c/o Marina Martin Associates, 12–13 Poland Street, London W1V 3DE.

FRANKAU, Nicholas
Nicholas Frankau. Actor (M).
b. Stockport, 16 July 1954.
TV: Carstairs in 'Allo 'Allo; Henry Purvis in C.A.T.S. Eyes; A Bore in Desert of Lies; Lt. Cumby in I Remember Nelson; Stevens in The Last Term; Sennett in The Mixer; Trelawney in Vote for Them.
Films: Sonar Operator in For Your Eyes Only; Ffolkes in Gunbus; Graham in Plenty; Eager Young Man in The Return of the Soldier; Lab Technician in Top Secret.
Address: c/o Waring & McKenna, Lauderdale House, 11 Gower Street, London WC1E 2HB. Hobbies: Cycling, horse riding, swimming, punting.

FRANKLIN, Caryn
Caryn Franklin. Presenter.
b. London, 11 January 1959.
TV: The Clothes Show (1986); GMTV (1999); Network 7 (1987); The Really Useful Show (1996); Style Challenge (1997); Swank (1984); Tracks (1993).
Address: c/o International Artistes Ltd, Mezzanine Floor, 235 Regent Street, London W1R 8AX.

FRANKLIN, Gretchen
Gretchen Franklin. Actor (F). b. London, 7 July 1911.
TV: Blackadder; Danger UXB; Dead Ernest; Ethel Skinner in EastEnders; Fox; George and Mildred; Hallelujah; In Loving Memory; The Kelly Monteith Show; Maybury; Potter; Quatermass; Quincey's Quest; Some Mothers Do

'Ave 'Em; The Casebook of Dr Jekyll; The Dick Emery Show; The Other 'Arf; The Other One; The Victoria Wood Show; You're Only Young Twice.

Address: c/o Burnett Granger Associates, Prince of Wales Theatre, 31 Coventry Street, London W1V 8AS.

FRANKLYN, Sabina

Sabina Franklyn. Actor (F).

b. London, 15 September.

TV: All Creatures Great and Small; Boon; Byron; Covington Cross; Dave Allen; Full House; Keep it in the Family; Miss Marple; Pride and Prejudice (1980); Strangers; The Upper Hand; The Worst Witch; Touch of Love; When the Boat Comes In.

Address: c/o David Daly Associates, 586a Kings Road, London SW6 2DX. m. John Challis; father William Franklyn; mother Margo Johns.

FRANKLYN, William

William Franklyn. Actor (M).

b. London, 22 September 1925.

TV: Charlie Chan; Curtain of Fear; Mountbatten in Diana – Her True Story; Dick and the Duchess; Douglas Fairbanks; GBH; International Detective; Interpol Calling; Burgess in Lovejoy; Maigret; Masterspy; Moon & Son; Neil Simon's London Suite; No Cloak, No Dagger; No Wreath for the General; Paradise Island; Public Eye; Purple Twilight; Red Letter Day; Sir Lancelot; Steam Video Company; The Avengers; The Baron; The Devil's Disciple; The Saracens; The Scarlet Pimpernel; Erick Cooper in The Upper Hand; Top Secret; Trouble Shooters; What's on Next?; General Allenby in The Young Indiana Jones Chronicles.

Films: Above Us The Waves; Cul-De-Sac; Dangers Within; Fury at Smuggler's Bay; Nutcracker; Out of the Clouds; Pit of Darkness; Quatermass II; Robert Rylands in Robert Ryland's Last Journey; Andrews in Splitting Heirs; That Woman Opposite; The Big Day; The Flesh is Weak; The Intelligence Men; The Legend of Young Dick Turpin; The Love Match; The Satanic Rites of Dracula; The Snorkel; Time is the Enemy.

Address: c/o Associated International Management, 5 Denmark Street, London WC2H 8LP.

FRANKS, Philip

Philip Franks. Actor (M).

TV: Patsy's Father in Absolutely Fabulous (1993); Richard Carstone in Bleak House (1984); Sgt. Raymond Craddock in Heartbeat (1997); Tom Pinch in Martin Chuzzlewit (1994); Calvin in Moniker (1994); Giles Dutton in Pie in the Sky (1994); Charlie in Darling Buds of May (1990); God in The Green Man (1990).

Address: c/o The Richard Stone Partnership, 2 Henrietta Street, London WC2E 8PS.

FRANZ, Dennis

Dennis Schlachta. Actor (M).

b. Maywood, Illinois, USA, 28 October 1944.

TV: Angelo Carbone in Bay City Blues (1983); Norman Buntz in Beverly Hills Buntz; Buddy Faro; Joe Gillard in Chicago Story (1982); Civil Wars; ER; Lt. Norman Buntz in Hill Street Blues; Hunter; Bobby Bryant in In the Line of Duty (1992); Kill or Be Killed (1990); Max Fleischer in Kiss Shot (1989); Matlock; Moment of Truth: Caught in the Crossfire (1994); Lieutenant Stan Krieger in Nasty Boys (1990); Andy Sipowicz in NYPD Blue; Riptide; Richard 'Racehorse' Haynes in Texas Justice (1995); The A Team; The Simpsons; TJ Hooker.

Films: Phil in A Fine Mess; Costa in A Perfect Couple; Koons in A Wedding; Don in American Buffalo; Manny Karp in Blow Out; Rubin in Body Double; Nathaniel Messinger in City of Angels; Captain Carmine Lorenzo in Die Hard 2: Die Harder; Detective Marino in Dressed to Kill; Spike in Popeye; Warren Toomey in Psycho II; Remember My Name; Stormy Island; Bob in The Fury; Milan Delich in The Package; himself in The Player.

Address: c/o Paradigm Agency, 25th Floor, 10,100 Santa Monica Boulevard, Los Angeles, California 90067, USA. m. Joanie Zeck; 2 step-daughters Krista, Tricia. Hobbies: skiing, tennis, music, Chicago Cubs supporter.

FRASER, Helen

Helen Fraser. Actor (F).

TV: A Day Out; Sylvia Hollamby in Bad Girls; Box of Delights; Magenta Savannah in Coronation Street; Doctor in Charge; Don't Wait Up; Dramarama; Duty Free; Fairies; In Loving Memory; Intensive Care; Jumbo Spencer; Northanger Abbey; One Foot in the Grave; Rising Damp; Sorry; Tales of the Unexpected; June Howson in The Bill; The Bird Fancier; The Black Madonna; The Dick Emery Show; Trish Pardoe in The Rector's Wife; The Two Ronnies; Charge Nurse in The Uninvited; Under the Moon.

Films: A Kind of Loving; Billy Liar; Gorillas in the Mist; Joseph Andrews; Repulsion; Shadow on the Sun; Something to Hide; Start the Revolution Without Me; Tale From Beyond the Grave; The Birthday Party; The Patricia Neal Story; The Uncle.

Address: c/o International Artistes Ltd, Mezzanine Floor, 235 Regent Street, London W1R 8AX.

FRASER, Hugh

Hugh Fraser. Actor (M). b. London.

TV: Captain Hastings in *ABC Murders*; Kellner in *Bird of Prey*; Gavin Winchell in *Call Me Mister*; the chaplain in *Class of His Own*; Robert Colquhoun in *Cloud Howe*; Peter Jackson in *Codename Kyril*; Bobby Bennett in *Edge of Darkness*; George Hill in *Edge of Darkness*; Sir Anthony Eden in *Edward and Mrs Simpson*; Adrian in *Events at Drimaghleen*; Giles Trent in *Game Set and Match*; Geoff in *Hands*; Dr Stephen Baker in *Heart Attack Hotel*; Saunders in *Heartland*; Captain Hastings in *Hercule Poirot's Casebook*; Rev. Saunders in *Intimate Contact*; Sir Charles Warren in *Jack the Ripper*; Robert in *Lizzie's Pictures*; King James in *Lorna Doone*; Sherlock Holmes in *Murder on the Bluebell Line*; Baxter in *One Fine Day*; Des in *Out*; Wil Langley in *Licking Hitler (Play for Today)*; George Hill in *Reilly: Ace of Spies*; Wellington in *Sharpe's Company*; Wellington in *Sharpe's Enemy*; Wellington in *Sharpe's Honour*; Denzil in *Smuggler*; Chief Insp. Bobby Gault in *Taggart*; Paul Standing in *Tales of the Unexpected*; Preece in *Target*; Naismith in *The Advocates*; Oliver Mortimer in *The Bretts*; Culik in *The Insurance Man*; Zelek Kaydan in *The Lost Tribe*; Terry Wilson in *The Olympian Way*; Richard Lefray in *The Price*; Knightley in *World Cup – A Captain's Tale*; Dearman in *Yesterday's Dreams*.

Films: *101 Dalmatians*; *Deviation*; *Firefox*; *Hanover Street*; *Patriot Games*; *Slade in Flame*; *The Draughtsman's Contract*; *The Man in the Iron Mask*; *The Revenge of the Pink Panther*.

Address: c/o Ken McReddie Ltd, 91 Regent Street, London W1R 7TB.

FRASER, Liz

Liz Fraser. Actor (F). b. London, 14 August 1935.

TV: *Birds of A Feather*; *Capstick's Law*; *Citizen James*; *Demob*; Ma Whistler in *Drover's Gold*; *Eskimos Do It*; *Fairly Secret Army*; *Hero to Zero* (1999); Reggie in *Last of the Summer Wine* (1999); *Minder*; *Miss Marple;*; *Rude Health*; *Shroud for a Nightingale*; *The Bill*; *The Professionals*; *The Saint*; Matron in *Whack-ho*.

Films: Mrs Pike in *Dad's Army*; *Desert Mice*; *Doctor in Love*; *I'm All Right, Jack*; *Live Now, Pay Later*; *The Family Way*; *Two-Way Stretch*; *Up the Junction*.

Address: c/o Peter Charlesworth & Associates, 68 Old Brompton Road, London SW7 3LQ.

FRASER, Shelagh

Shelagh Fraser. Actor (F).
b. Surrey, 25 November 1923.

TV: *A House of Character*; *A Touch of Frost*; Madge in *Absolute Hell*; *Family At War*; *Frankie and Johnny*; *Heartbeat*; *Maigret*; *Midsomer Murders*; *The Old Men at the Zoo*; *The Professionals*; *Z-Cars*.

Films: *Cereal Killer*; Edith in *Edith's Finger*; *Hope and Glory*; *La Bas*; *Merry Hill Millionaires*; *Raising a Riot*; *Staircase*; *The History of Mr Dolly*; *Work Experience*.

Address: c/o Ken McReddie Ltd, 91 Regent Street, London W1R 7TB. Sister Mora Fraser. Hobbies: Writing.

FRAZER, Alison

Alison Frazer. Actor (F). b. 21 May 1947.

TV: *Deadly Confusions*; Nancy in *Oliver Twist*; Princess Mary Tudor in *The Six Wives of Henry VIII*; Princess Lisa Bolkonskya in *War and Peace*.

Films: *Bert Rigby, You're a Fool*; *Murder One, Murder Two*; The Bride in *The Assassin*; Sue in *Three Bites of the Apple* .

Address: c/o Frazer-Skemp Management Ltd, 31 Brompton Street, London SW3 5LA.

FREEMAN, Jane

Jane Freeman. Actor (F).

TV: Helen in *A Taste of Honey*; *All Day at the Sands*; *All Through the Night*; Megaera in *Androcles and the Lion*; Mrs Applebottom in *Blackadder*; *Crossroads*; *Diary of a Young Man*; Mrs Willetts in *Ghost in the Water*; *Hannah*; Ivy in *Last of the Summer Wine*; Florence Jones in *Letty*; *Lynsey*; Social Services Officer in *Maybury*; *Mrs Scully's New Year's Eve*; *On the Move*; *Prince Regent*; Mrs Kimble in *Silas Marner*; *The Fishing Party*; Rosalind Townsley in *The Hard Word*; *The Marriage*; *Within these Walls*; *Zigger Zagger*.

Films: Head Cook in *Who Dares Wins*.

Address: c/o Saraband Associates, 265 Liverpool Road, London N1 1LX.

FREEMAN, Paul

Paul Freeman. Actor (M).
b. Barnet, Hertfordshire, 18 January 1943.

TV: *Cagney and Lacey*; *ER*; *Falcon Crest*; Makepeace in *House of Cards*; *Samson and Delilah*; *The Index Has Gone Fishing*; Martin in *Yesterday's Dreams*; *The Young Indiana Jones Chronicles*.

Films: *An Unsuitable Job for a Woman*; Christopher in *Death of a Princess*; Derek in *Dogs of War*; *Double Team*; *Flight to Berlin*; *Horseman on the Roof*; Aces: *Iron Eagle III*; *Just Like a Woman*; *Mighty Morphin Power Rangers*; Belloc in *Raiders of the Lost Ark*; *Shanghai Surprise*; *Si Elle Dit Oui*; Rebbe in *The Devil's Arithmetic*; Colin in *The Long Good Friday*; Melchior in *The Three Kings*; Moriarty in *Without a Clue*.

Address: c/o Ken McReddie Ltd, 91 Regent Street, London W1R 7TB. Hobbies: Gardening, walking, music, travel.

FRENCH, Dawn

Dawn French. Comedienne/Reader/Actor (F).
b. Holyhead, Wales, 11 October 1957.
TV: *Absolutely Fabulous; The Comic Strip Presents: Bad News Tour/Consuela/Five Go Mad on Mescalin/GLC – The Carnage Continues/Mr Jolly Lives Next Door/ Oxford/ Private Enterprise/Slags/South Atlantic Raiders/ Space Virgins from the Planet Sex/Spaghetti Hoop/ Summer School/Five Go Mad in Dorset/Four Men In A Car;* Mrs Crupp in *David Copperfield; French and Saunders; Girls on Top; Happy Families; Jackanory;* Lisette in *Let Them Eat Cake; Look At the State We're In; Murder Most Horrid; Scoff; Tender Loving Care; The Storyteller;* Rev. Geraldine Granger in *The Vicar of Dibley; Milk;* Bev Bodger in *Sex and Chocolate.*
Films: *The Supergrass.*
Address: c/o PFD, Drury House, 34–43 Russell Street, London WC2B 5HA. m. Lenny Henry; 1 d. Billie.

FRENCH, Michael

Michael French. Actor (M).
TV: Jeff Slade in *Crime Traveller;* David Wicks in *East-Enders;* Nick Jordan in *Holby City.*
Address: c/o Roxane Vacca Management, 73 Beak Street, London W1R 3LF.

FREUD, Emma

Emma Freud. Actor (M)/Presenter.
b. London, 25 January 1962.
TV: *Bliss* (1999); *Edinburgh Nights; Pillow Talk; Plunder; The 6 O'Clock Show; The Big Picture Show; The Incense Train; The Media Show; The Mystery of the Pyramids; The Pulse; The Turner Prize; Theatreland.*
Address: c/o William Morris Agency (UK) Ltd, 1 Stratton Street, London W1X 6HB.

FRICKER, Brenda

Brenda Fricker. Actor (F).
b. Dublin, Ireland, 17 February 1945.
TV: Mother Steed in *A Woman of Independent Means;* Sister Agnes in *Brides of Christ;* Megan Roache in *Casualty;* Maeve in *Durango; Eh Brian, It's a Whopper;* Maureen Lessing in *Growing Pains; Helen: A Woman of Today;* Lottie in *Journey; Just Like Eddie;* Eileen Graham in *Licking Hitler; Mein Kampf;* Virginia Johanson in *Resurrection;* Stella in *Seekers; Stephen D; The Ballroom of Romance; The Picnic; The Practice; The Sinners;* Eliza Graham Bell in *The Sound of Silence; To Have and To Hold; Your Man from the Six Counties.*
Films: Lily Byrne in *A Man of No Importance;* Ethel Twitty in *A Time to Kill;* Maggie Nelson in *Angels in the Outfield;* Iris Greenwood in *Deadly Advice;* Pigeon Lady in *Home Alone II;* Vinnie Moore in *Lethal Innocence;* Claire Maloney in *Masterminds;* Lily Devine in *Meteor;* Mrs Mazzawatti in *Moll Flanders;* Mrs Brown in *My Left Foot;* Annie in *Painted Angels;* Dorcas in *Resurrection Man;* May MacKenzie in *So I Married an Axe Murderer;* Rose Hindmarch in *Swann;* Mrs Bread in *The American;* Maggie McCabe in *The Field;* Mary in *The Woman Who Married Clark Gable;* Marta in *UTZ.*
Address: c/o Cassie Mayer Ltd, 34 Kingly Court, London W1R 5LE.

FRIEL, Anna

Anna Friel. Actor (F). b. 12 July 1976.
TV: *8:15 From Manchester;* Hermia in *A Midsummer Night's Dream;* Beth Jordache in *Brookside;* Sioned in *Cadfael; Coronation Street; GBH; In Suspicious Circumstances;* Bella in *Our Mutual Friend; Tales from the Crypt.*
Films: Hermia in *A Midsummer Night's Dream; All for Love; Everlasting Piece; The Land Girls;* Maddy in *Mad Cows;* Lisa Leeson in *Rogue Trader;* Helen in *The Stringer;* Lizzie in *The Tribe;* Tammy in *Untitled Sunset Strip;* Driver in *You Drive Me.*
Address: c/o Conway Van Gelder Ltd, 18–21 Jermyn Street, London SW1Y 6HP.

FROGGATT, Joanne

Joanne Froggatt. Actor (F).
TV: Rachel in *Bad Girls;* Zoe Tattersall in *Coronation Street;* Sigorney in *dinnerladies; Heartbeat;* Jenny in *Nature Boy;* Becky in *Other People's Children; Rumble; Stick With Me Kid;* Kelly Martin in *The Bill.*
Address: c/o Conway Van Gelder Ltd, 18–21 Jermyn Street, London SW1Y 6HP.

FRONT, Rebecca

Rebecca Front. Actor (F).
TV: Secretary in *Absolutely Fabulous;* Cathy in *Coogan's Run; Fist of Fun;* Claire in *Have Your Cake and Eat It;* Beth in *In the Red;* Heidi in *Jonathan Creek;* Cathy Winslow in *Kavanagh QC; Knowing Me, Knowing You...with Alan Partridge;* Mary in *Knowing Me, Knowing Yule....with Alan Partridge;* Pru in *Norman at the Office;* Juliette Trombaut in *Paris;* Queen Mary in *Purcell; Reeves and Mortimer; Saturday Night Armistice; Saturday Zoo; Smith and Jones; The Day Today;* Melody in *The Lenny Henry Show;* Sarah Seymour in *The Missing Postman;* Debbie in *Tricky Business.*
Address: William Morris Agency (UK) Ltd, 1 Stratton Street, London W1X 6HB.

FROST, David

David Frost. Presenter. b. Kent, 7 April 1939.
TV: *Talking with David Frost; A Gift of Song: The Music*

for UNICEF Concert; Breakfast With Frost; Frost on Sunday; The Spectacular World of Guinness Records; That Was The Week That Was; The David Frost Show; Through the Keyhole.

Address: c/o Noel Gay Artists, 19 Denmark Street, London WC2H 8NA. m. Lady Carina Fitzalan Howard; 3 s. Miles, Wilfred, George; father-in-law Duke of Norfolk.

FROST, Sadie

Sadie Liza Vaugman. Actor (F). b. London.

TV: Nurse in *Boon* (1987); Francesca in *Lake of Darkness*; Jenny Eliot in *Press Gang* (1989); Dominique in *The Cisco Kid.*

Films: Hattie in *A Pyromaniac's Love Story*; Laura Cheveley in *An Ideal Husband*; Max's friend in *Bent*; Lucy Westenra in *Bram Stoker's Dracula*; Tessa in *Captain Jack*; Val in *Crimetime*; Rebecca in *Dark Obsession*; Sadie in *Final Cut*; Natalie in *Flypaper*; *Love, Honour and Obey*; Eva in *Magic Hunter*; *Paper Marriage*; *Presence of Mind*; Sarah in *Rancid Aluminium*; Jo in *Shopping*; Angela in *Splitting Heirs*; Sharon Pellam in *The Krays.*

Address: c/o Julian Belfrage Associates, 46 Albemarle Street, London W1X 4PP.

FROSTRUP, Mariella

Mariella Frostrup. Presenter.

b. Oslo, Norway, 12 November 1962.

TV: *At the Pictures; Big World* (1989); *Censorship; Edinburgh Nights; First Reaction; Four Seasons; Going for a Song; Look Who's Talking; Newman and Baddiel in Pieces; Nigel Plays Brunch; Notes and Queries; Passengers; Relationships* (1991); *Sex in the Movies; Singletons; The Little Picture Show; Video View.*

Address: c/o Noel Gay Artists, 19 Denmark Street, London WC2H 8NA. Hobbies: Tennis, scuba diving.

FRY, Stephen

Stephen Fry. Actor (M)/Comedian.

b. London, 26 August 1957.

TV: *A Bit of Fry and Laurie; Alfresco; Anything More Would be Greedy* (1990); *Blackadder; Blackadder Goes Forth* (1990); *Blackadder the Third; Chance in a*

Million; Mr Mybug in Cold Comfort Farm (1994); *Did You See?; Filthy Rich and Catflap; Gormenghast* (2000); *Happy Families; In the Red* (1998); *Jeeves in Jeeves and Wooster; Mastermind; Not the Nine O'Clock News; Old Flames* (1990); *Saturday Night Live; Stalag Luft* (1993); *The Common Pursuit* (1990); *The Crystal Cube; The Thin Blue Line* (1995); *The Young Ones; This is David Lander* (1988); *Woof.*

Films: *A Civil Action; A Fish Called Wanda; A Handful of Dust; Gossip; I.Q.; Orlando Drake Story; Peter's Friends; Return to Plum Creek; Spice World; The Good Father; The Steal; The Tichbourne Claimant;* The Judge in *The Wind in the Willows; Waterloo; What Ever Happened to Harold Smith?;* Oscar Wilde in *Wilde.*

Address: c/o Hamilton Asper, 24 Hanway Street, London W1P 9DD.

FULFORD, Christopher

Christopher Fulford. Actor (M).

TV: *A Touch of Frost; Bad Boys; Body Contact; Comics; Cracker; Deceit; December Flowers; Hornblower; Inspector Morse; Made in Britain; Moll Flanders; Newshounds; Out of Darkness; Out of Line; Prime Suspect; Proud; Scarlet and Black; The Fix; The Fourth Floor; The Ghostbusters of East Finchley; The Last Train; The Sculptress; The Tempest; Tom Jones; Under the Hammer.*

Films: *A Prayer for the Dying; Bedrooms and Hallways; Detox; Immortal Beloved; Itch; Jack the Ripper; Joyride; Mountains of the Moon; Ploughman's Lunch; Resurrected; Wetherby.*

Address: c/o Conway Van Gelder Ltd, 18–21 Jermyn Street, London SW1Y 6HP.

FULLERTON, Fiona

Fiona Fullerton. Actor (F)/Writer/Presenter.

b. Kaduna, 10 October 1956.

TV: *Angels; Gaugin The Savage; Hold The Dream; Shaka Zulu; The Charmer; To Be The Best.*

Films: *A View To A Kill; Nicholas and Alexandra; Run Wild, Run Free; The Human Factor; Zulu.*

Address: c/o London Management, Noel House, 2–4 Noel Street, London W1V 3RB.

G

G, Ali
Sacha Baron Cohen. Comedian/Actor (M).
TV: *Alternative Queen's Speech '99; Comedy Nation; F2F; Live from the Lighthouse; The 11 O' Clock Show; The Ali G Show; The Best of Ali G.*
Address: c/o PFD, Drury House, 34-43 Russell Street, London WC2B 5HA.

GADDAS, James
James Gaddas. Actor (M).
TV: Vinnie in *Coronation Street*; Pete in *Last Days of Summer*; Eddie Ainsworth in *Heartbeat*; Ian Lake in *Peak Practice*; Ray in *Grafters*; Craig Downey in *Jonathan Creek*; *Playhouse – The Unknown Soldier*; Steve Bentley in *Operation Julie*; Turtleshirt in *Dead Man's Folly*; Prince Amaranth in *The Princess and the Lute Player*; *Wish Me Luck*; Pike in *Troubles*; Robert Prescott in *Coronation Street*; Bendell in *El C.I.D.*; Joe in *Black Candle*; *The Paul Merton Show*; Tony in *The Camomile Lawn*; Guntter in *Secrets*; Markham in *Between the Lines*; *Drop the Dead Donkey*; *The Bill*; Detective Inspector Bob Latham in *Class Act*; Vince in *Stone Cold*; PC Reaper in *Backup*; John Sinclair in *Guillaume*; Dr Robert Nevin in *Medics*; Archer in *Bombay Blue*.
Films: Paul in *Girl's Night*; Franks in *Human Bomb*; *Johnny Loves Suzy*; *Crime in the City*; *Hazard of Hearts*; *The Pied Piper*.
Address: c/o C.C.A. Management, 7 St. George's Square, London SW1V 2HX.

GAFFNEY, Dean
Dean Gaffney. Actor (M)/Presenter.
TV: *All Over the Shop*; Robbie Jackson in *EastEnders*; *EastEnders Magazine Programme*; *Fully Booked*; *Light Lunch*; *Live and Kicking*; *Night Fever*; Mickey Drake in *Oasis*; *Showbiz UK Talk TV*; *Taking the Pitch*; Terry Jakes in *The Bill*.
Films: Youth in *Power of One*; Teenage Boy in *Spice World – The Movie*; Boy in *Young Indie*.
Address: c/o Rossmore Personal Management, Rossmore Road, London NW1 6NJ.

GAINEY, Keeley
Keeley Gainey. Actor (F). b. London.
TV: *Bramwell*; *No Bananas*; *Roger, Roger*.

Films: Martha in *Topsy Turvy*.
Address: c/o Dennis Lyne Agency, 108 Leonard Street, London EC2A 4RH.

GAMBON, Michael
Michael Gambon. Actor (M).
TV: Philip Marlow in *The Singing Detective*; *Expert Witness*; *Faith*; *Mam's Back!*; Archie Rice in *The Entertainer*; Chief Inspector Maigret in *Maigret*; *Minder*; *The Storyteller*; *The Heat of the Day*; *the Breadwinner*; *The Seagull*; *Ghosts*; *Oscar Wilde*.
Films: *The Cook, the Thief, his Wife and her Lover*; *The Gambler*; *Dancing at Lughnasa*; *Plunkett and McLeane*; *The Last September*; *Sleepy Hollow*.
Address: c/o ICM, Oxford House, 76 Oxford Street, London W1N OAX.

GARDEN, Graeme
Graeme Garden. Actor (M). b. Aberdeen, 1943.
TV: *The Goodies* (1972, 1975, 1981); *The Astronauts* (1982); *A Sense of the Past* (1983); *Broaden Your Mind*; *Doctor in the House*; *Mount Olympus*; *Tell the Truth* (1983); *The Goodies and the Beanstalk*; *The Goodies Rule*; *O.K*; *The Whole Hog* (1989); *Surgical Spirit* (1994).
Records: *The Inbetweenies*.
Address: c/o Roger Hancock Ltd, 4 Water Lane, London NW1 8NZ. Hobbies: Painting.

GARRETT, Jeremy
Jeremy Garrett. Actor (M).
b. San Diego, California, USA, 2 April 1976.
TV: *Buffy The Vampire Slayer*; Clay in *Legacy*; *Sabrina, The Teenage Witch*; *Sweet Valley High*.
Address: William Morris Agency, 151 El Camino Drive, Beverly Hills, California 90212, USA. Hobbies: Photography; travel.

GARTSIDE, Kate
Kate Gartside. Actor (F).
TV: Cath in *Back Up*; Karen in *Bathing Elizabeth*; Fiona in *Casualty*; DS Jane McCormack in *City Central*; Emily in *Heartbeat*; Florence in *In Suspicious Circumstances*; Ally in *Preston Front*; Rosy in *Thief Takers*; Helen Mitchell in *Walking on the Moon*.

Films: Paula in *Close My Eyes*; Kathy in *Elephant Juice*; Sister Veronica in *Sister, My Sister*.

Address: c/o Rebecca Blond Associates, 69a Kings Road, London SW3 4NX.

GASCOINE, Jill

Jill Gascoine. Actor (F). b. London, 11 April 1937.

TV: *CATS Eyes*; *Crime and Punishment*; Mrs Williams in *King of the Wind*; Dolly in *Raffles*; Maggie Forbes in *The Gentle Touch*; Lettie Gaunt in *The Onedin Line*; *Trust Me*; *Virtual Murder*.

Films: Mrs Barnwell in *Confessions of a Pop Performer*; *Red Hot*.

Address: c/o CDA, 19 Sydney Mews, London SW3 6HL.

GATISS, Mark

Mark Gatiss. Actor (M). b. 17 October 1966.

TV: *Barking*; *Even further Abroad*; *Harry*; *In the Red*; *Lenny Goes to Town*; *Mash & Peas do US*; *The Devil of Winterborne*; *The Dwelling Place*; *The League of Gentleman*; *The Zero Imperative*; *Unnatural Selection*.

Hobbies: Fencing.

GAUNT, William

William Gaunt. Actor (M).

b. Pudsey, Yorkshire, 3 April 1937.

TV: Edward Capstick in *Capstick's Law*; *Doctor Who*; *Next of Kin*; *No Place Like Home*; *Sergeant Cork*; *The Champions*; *The Far Pavilions*; *The Foundation*; *The Preventers*.

Address: c/o London Management, Noel House, 2–4 Noel Street, London W1V 3RB.

GAYLE, Phil

Phil Gayle. Presenter/Writer.

b. Birmingham, 6 April 1964.

TV: *Big Breakfast News*; *Channel 4 News*; *Find a Fortune*.

Address: c/o Silver Fox Artist Management Ltd, Cameo House, 11 Bear Street, London WC2H 7AS.

GECKS, Nicholas

Nicholas Gecks. Actor (M).

b. Penang, 9 January 1952.

TV: *A Crack in the Ice*; *A Face at the Window*; *A Prisoner of Zenda*; *A Still Small Shout*; *Berlin Break*; *Between the Lines*; *Brookside*; *Chekhov in Yalta*; *Children of the North*; *East Lynne*; *First Tuesday*; *Hunted Down*; *Julius Caesar*; *Making News*; Lawyer Wakeham in *The Mill on the Floss*; *Mrs Capper's Birthday*; *Nicholas Nickleby*; *Not a Penny More, Not a Penny Less*; *Pirates*; *Reilly: Ace of Spies*; *Return of Sherlock Holmes*; *Richard II*; *Rumpole of the Bailey*; *Seeing Red*; *Sherlock Holmes and the Leading Lady*; *Six Centuries of Verse*; *The Bill*; *The Chief*; *The Dark Room*; *The Falklands Factor*; *The Grand Tour*; *The Marlowe Inquest*; *The Secret Agent*; *The South Bank Show*; *Titus Andronicus*; *Two Per Cent*; *Wolf to the Slaughter*; *Wycliffe*.

Films: *Forever Young*; *Parting Shots*; Bushey in *Richard II*; Horatio in *Tai Pan*; Ned in *The Wicked Lady*; Paul Rayley in *To the Lighthouse*.

Address: c/o Conway Van Gelder, 18–21 Jermyn Street, London SW1Y 6HP. m. Heather Wright; 2 d. Maree, Eleanor; 1 s. Joe. **Hobbies:** Music, cricket, golf, travel.

GEE, Robbie

Robbie Gee. Actor (M). b. 24 March 1970.

TV: Jon in *Anna Lee*; *Black Poppies*; Cameron in *Blisters*; *Comin' Atcha*; *Days Like These*; Lee in *Desmonds*; *EastEnders*; *In Exile*; *In Sickness and in Health*; *Midnight Breaks*; *Pie in the Sky*; *Roger, Roger*; *Saracen*; *The Bill*; Snowy in *The Firm*; Tony Morris in *The Manageress*; *The Real McCoy*; *Thief Takers*; *Underbelly*; *Waiting*.

Films: *Greenwich Mean Time*.

Address: c/o Roxanne Vacca Management, 73 Beak Street, London W1R 3LF.

GELLAR, Sarah Michelle

Sarah Michelle Gellar. Actor (F).

b. New York, USA, 14 April 1977.

TV: *Buffy the Vampire Slayer*; *Angel*; *The View*; *Beverly Hills Family Robinson*; *All My Children*; *Swan's Crossing*; *A Woman Named Jackie*; *Girl Talk*; *Spenser for Hire*; *Invasion of Privacy*.

Films: *She's All That*; *Simply Irresistible*; *Cruel Intentions*; Helen Shivers in *I Know What You Did Last Summer*; *Scream 2*; *Small Soldiers*; *High stakes*; *Funny Farm*; *Over Brooklyn Bridge*.

Address: c/o ICM, 8942 Wilshire Blvd., Beverly Hills, California 90211, USA. **Hobbies:** Tae Kwondo.

GEMMEL, Ruth

Ruth Gemmel. Actor (F).

b. Darlington, County Durham.

TV: Gina in *Band of Gold*; Nicola in *Four Fathers* (1998); Elizabeth in *In Suspicious Circumstances* (1994); Jenny Norris in *Kavanagh QC* (1995); Lady Macduff in *Macbeth* (1997); Elizabeth Proctor in *Miller Shorts* (1999); Christine Higson in *Peak Practice* (1996); co-lead in *The Alchemist* (1998); Sue Latham in *The Bill* (1995); Jane in *The Bill* (1999); Jo in *The Perfect Blue* (1997); Staff Nurse Bennett in *You, Me and It*.

Films: Sarah in *Fever Pitch* (1996); Kate in *Safe and Sound* (1996).
Address: c/o Dalzell and Beresford Ltd, 91 Regent Street, London W1R 7TB. Hobbies: Keep fit.

GEORGE, Fenella
Fenella George. Actor (F)/Presenter.
TV: *Adventure Racing* (1999); *Afternoon Live; All the Right Moves; Anybody Out There; Black Run* (1998); *Holiday* (1999); *Late and Live; Magic and Mystery Show* (1996); *The Air Show* (1998); *The Net* (1998); *The Whitbread Round the World Yacht Race* (1998).
Address: c/o Speak-easy Ltd, 90 St Mary's Road, Harborough, Leicestershire LE16 7DX. Hobbies: Travelling, world music.

GEORGESON, Tom
Tom Georgeson. Actor (M).
b. Liverpool, 8 August 1941.
TV: Harry Naylor in *Between the Lines;* Howard in *Liverpool One;* Eddie in *The Manageress.*
Films: George in *A Fish Called Wanda;* Jimmy in *Downtime;* John Lawrence in *Land Girls;* Matty in *Swing.*
Address: c/o Dennis Lyne Agency, 108 Leonard Street, London EC2A 4RH.

GIBSON, Richard
Richard Gibson. Actor (M).
b. Kampala, 1 January 1954.
TV: Herr Flick in *'Allo 'Allo;* Lance in *Armchair Detective;* Edward Beverley in *Children of the New Forest;* Steve Seffon in *Hadleigh;* Charles Butler in *Intimate Exchanges;* Jonathan in *My Father's House;* Colin McFarlane in *Park Ranger;* Hugh Castallack in *Penmarric;* Geoffrey Charles in *Poldark;* Hugh Walton in *Prospects;* Alex in *The Birthday;* Ralph in *The Coral Island;* Peter in *The Gate of Eden;* Stephano in *The Tempest;* Ben Shaw in *The Upper Hand;* Tom Butler in *Three's Company;* Apollo in *Tom Browne's School Days;* William Tredwell in *Tredwell Diaries;* Colin Wainwright in *Wainwright's Law.*
Films: Anthony Farrant in *England Made Me;* British priest in *St. Patrick;* Marcus Maudsley in *The Go-Between;* Major Lawrence in *The Key to Rebecca;* Guy Hamilton in *The Project.*
Address: c/o TN Enterprises, 14 Beech Grove, Booterstown Avenue, Dublin, Ireland. Hobbies: Horse riding, swimming, skating, guitar, violin.

GIEDROYC, Mel
Mel Giedroyc. Actor (F)/Presenter.
TV: *Late Licence* (1994); *Life's A Bitch* (1994); *French and Saunders* (1995); *The Little Picture Show* (1995);

Friday Night Armistice (1996); *Good Stuff* (1996); *Klinik* (1996); *Never Mind the Horrocks* (1996); Mary Timkler in *The Vicar of Dibley* (1996); *Gimme Gimme Gimme* (1998); *Late Lunch; Light Lunch; McCoist and MacAuley* (1998); *Miss World Documentary* (1998); *Never Mind the Buzzcocks* (1998); *With Richard Not Judy* (1998); *Holiday* (1999); Johnny Pumpkin in *Johnny Pumpkin* (1999); *Live and Kicking* (1999).
Address: c/o The Richard Stone Partnership, 2 Henrietta Street, London WC2E 8PS.

GIELGUD, Sir John
Sir John Gielgud. Actor (M).
b. London, 14 April 1904.
TV: *Time After Time* (1985); *Under the Hammer* (1993); *Wagner* (1981); *War and Remembrance* (1986); *Words from Jerusalem* (1995); *A Man For All Seasons* (1988); *Antigone* (1984); *Brideshead Revisited* (1981); *Camille* (1984); *A Dance to the Music of Time* (1996); *Dante and Virgil* (1988); *Gulliver's Travels* (1995); *Inspector Alleyn* (1994); *Inspector Morse* (1992); *Lovejoy – Christmas Special* (1993); *Merlin* (1998); *Oedipus* (1985); *Quartermaine's Terms* (1987); *Romance on the Orient Express* (1984); *Scarlett* (1994); *Summer Day's Dream* (1994); *Summer's Lease* (1989); *The Master of Ballantrae* (1983).
Films: *Appointment With Death; Arthur 2; Bluebeard; First Knight; Getting it Right; Haunted; Inside the Third Reich; Leave all Fair; Loser Takes All; Plenty; Portrait of a Lady; Prospero's Books; Scandalous; Shine; Shining Through; Strauss Dynasty; The Best of Friends; The Canterville Ghost; The Far Pavilions; The Power of One; The Shooting Party; The Titchbourne Claimant; The Whistleblower; The Wicked Lady.*
Address: c/o ICM, Oxford House, 76 Oxford Street, London W1N 0AX.

GILES, Annabel
Annabel Giles. Actor (F).
b. Griffithstown, Wales, 20 May 1959.
TV: *Posh Frocks and New Trousers; Riders; Through the Keyhole; Challenge TV; Hit The Road; Jameson Tonight; Later Than You Think; Monkhouse's Memory Masters; Night Network; Period Rooms.*
Films: *Firelight; The New Look.*
Address: c/o Crawfords, Joseph Jones (After-dinner Speakers). 1 d. Molly; 1 s. Ted. Hobbies: Writing.

GILES, Bill
Bill Giles. Weatherman. b. Dittisham, Devon, 1939.
TV: *This is Your Life* (1988); weather forecasts.
Address: c/o Limelight Management, 33 Newman Street, London W1P 3PD. Hobbies: Golf, cricket.

GILES, Samantha

Samantha Giles. Actor (F).
b. Maidstone, Kent, 2 July 1971.
TV: Rosalind in *Clayton Close*; Kirsty in *Coronation Street*; Amy in *Dangerfield*; Anita in *December*; Karen in *Dominoes*; Bernice in *Emmerdale*; Dr Westwood in *Springhill*; Michelle in *Supplies*; Nurse in *A Winter's Tale*.
Films: Mary in *Midnight Man*.
Address: c/o Emmerdale Press Office, TV Centre, Kirkstall Road, Leeds, Yorkshire LS3 1JS.

GILHOOLY, Brenda

Brenda Gilhooly. Actor (F)/Comedian/Presenter.
b. Epsom, Surrey, 1964.
TV: Lily in *Adam's Family Tree*; *Edinburgh Nights* (1993); *Funny Farm* (1992); *Gayle's World* (1996, 1997); *Good Stuff*; *Harry Hill's Fruit Fancies*; *Jack and Jeremy Real Lives* (1996); *Jack Dee Variety Show* (1995); *Jo Brand Through the Cakehole* (1995); *Jonathan Ross Show* (1992); *Late Licence*; *Moviewatch Christmass Special* (1995); *Nil by Mouth* (1993); *Oddballs* (1996); *Riverside Sitcom Festival* (1999); *Saturday Live* (1996); *Stand Up* (1992); *That's Christmas* (1994); *The Full Monty* (1993); *Tibs and Fibs* (1996); *Top of the Pops* (1995); *Viva Cabaret* (1994); *What's New?* (1992); *WowFabGroovy* (1996).
Films: *King Lear*; *The Crucible*; *As You Like It*; *Greek*.
Address: c/o CDA, 19 Sydney Mews, London SW3 6HL.

GILLESPIE, Robert

Robert Gillespie. Actor (M).
b. Lille, France, 9 November 1933.
TV: *A Soft Touch*; *Agony*; *Bonjour La Classe*; *Born and Bred*; *Butterflies*; *Come Back Mrs Noah*; *Couples*; *Dad's Army*; *Danger Island*; *Doomwatch*; *Escape*; *George and Mildred*; *Hamlet*; *Heroes and Villains*; *Hi Honey I'm Home*; *His and Hers*; *Hotel Paradiso*; *How's Yer Father*; *I Woke Up One Morning*; *Inmates*; *It Ain't Half Hot Mum*; *Keep it in the Family*; *Kipling*; *Limes from Sicily*; *Lucky Jim*; *Marked Personal*; *Mary's Wife*; *Midnight is a Place*; *Mr Digby Darling*; *Naught For Their Comfort*; *No Strings*; *Only When I Laugh*; *Porridge*; *Rasputin*; *Rising Damp*; *Robin's Nest*; *Romeo and Juliet*; *Rosie*; *Sadie, It's Cold Outside*; *Secret Army*; *Selwyn Froggat*; *Singles Weekend*; *So You Think You've Got Troubles*; *Softly, Softly*; *Starting Out*; *The Caucasian Chalk Circle*; *The Drinking Party*; *The Good Life*; *The Haunted House*; *The Life of Riley*; *The Liver Birds*; *The Onedin Line*; *The Queen and The Rebels*; *The Rise and Fall of Reginald Perrin*; *The Sweeney*; *Van Der Valk*; *Vendetta*; *Vile Bodies*; *Warship*; *Whatever Happened to the Likely Lads?*; *Witnesses*; *Z-Cars*.
Films: *A Night to Remember*; *A Severed Head*; *At the Earth's Core*; *Barry McKenzie Holds His Own*; *Carry On up the Front*; *Catch Me a Spy*; *Every Home Should Have One*; *Force 10 From Navarone*; *Midsummer Night's Dream*; *Prince of Denmark Hill*; *Rentadick*; *The Great Escape*; *The Magnificent Seven Deadly Sins*; *The National Health*; *The Prisoner of Zenda*; *The Square Peg*; *The Thirty-Nine Steps*; *Zorn*.
Address: c/o The Jane Nightwork Co, 10 Irving Road, London W14 0JS. Partner Anna Jackson; 1 d. Lucy.
Hobbies: Travel, reading.

GILLETT, Aden

Aden Gillett. Actor (M). b. Yemen, 8 November 1958.
TV: D.S. Lockyer in *The Bill: Bad Chemistry* (1999); Various characters in *Harry Enfield's Television Programme* (1993); Robin of Locksleigh in *Ivanhoe* (1997); Simon Walker in *Out of the Past: The Vet* (1997); D.I. Lightfoot in *Silent Witness* (1999); Tom in *The Guinea Pig* (1998); Jack Maddox in *The House of Elliott* (1994); Reggie Watson in *Touching Evil* (1999); Alan in *Wonderful You* (1999).
Films: Henrich Galeen in *Shadow of a Vampire*; Joe Lender in *The Borrowers*; John Watherston in *The Winslow Boy*; David in *Under the Lighthouse, Dancing*.
Address: c/o Cassie Mayer Ltd, 34 Kingley Court, London W1R 5LE. m. Sara; 1 s. Sam, 1 d. India.

GILLIGAN, Terry

Terry Gilligan. Actor (M). b. Yorkshire.
TV: Richard Barton in *999*; Sales rep in *Ain't Misbehavin'*; Taxi driver in *Always & Everyone*; Punter in *Band of Gold*; Gerry Davott in *Bright Sparks*; Journalist in *Children's Ward*; Shop manager in *Cops*; Sergeant Perriman in *Coronation Street*; Chat Show Host in *Cracker*; Sgt. Sharples in *Emmerdale*; Supt. Adams in *Heartbeat*; Gordon Martindale in *House of Eliot*; Market Researcher in *Last of the Summer Wine*; Police Sergeant in *Lord Lucan*; Cheeky Patient in *My Wonderful Life*; Police Sergeant in *Once Upon A Time in the North*; Paul in *Undercover Customs*.
Address: c/o Sharron Ashcroft Management, Dean Clough, Halifax, Yorkshire HX3 5AX. Hobbies: Singing, dancing, tennis, football, squash.

GILPIN, Peri

Peri Gilpin. Actor (F).
b. Waco, Texas, USA, 27 May 1961.
TV: *21 Jump Street* (1988); *Cheers* (1993); *Fight for Justice* (1995); *Flesh and Blood* (1991); *Frasier* (1993); *Hercules* (1998); *Matlock* (1990); *Superman* (1996); *The Early Edition* (1996); *The Lionhearts* (1998); *The Outer Limits* (1996); *The Secret She Carried* (1996); *Wings* (1993).

Films: *Spring Forward.*
Address: c/o William Morris Agency, 151 El Camino Drive, Beverly Hills, California 90212, USA. m. Christian Vincent Gilpin; Father: Jim O'Brien. Hobbies: Gardening.

GISH, Sheila

Sheila Gish. Actor (F). b. Lincoln.
TV: *Blonde Bombshell; Born in the Gardens; Brighton Belles; Ghostbusters of East Finchley; Jewels; Jonathan Creek; Memories; Pie in the Sky; Playhouse Creatures; Resnick; Small World; Stanley and the Women; Supply and Demand; That Uncertain Feeling; The Perfect Match; The Thin Blue Line.*
Films: *A Day in the Death of Joe Egg; Darling; Highlander; Hitler – The Last Ten Days; Mansfield Park; Quartet; Sea Side; Separate Rooms; The Reckoning.*
Address: c/o ICM, Oxford House, 76 Oxford Street, London W1N 0AX.

GITTINS, Jeremy

Jeremy Gittins. Actor (M). b. 30 January 1956.
TV: *All in Good Faith; Andy Capp; Blackadder Goes Forth; Boon; Casualty; Doctor Who; EastEnders; Fresh Fields; Keeping up Appearances; Lazarus and Dingwall; Masters of the Game; Matlock – The Billionaire; Radio Pictures; Stuck on You; Tales of the Unexpected; Tenko; Terry and June; The Kenny Everett Show; The Kit Curran Show; The Upper Hand; Wink Three Times.*
Films: John in *Anno Domini; Blue Leader Missing; Callan – The Movie; If You Go Down To The Woods; The Bitch.*
Address: c/o Susan Angel Associates, 1st Floor, 12 D'Arblay Street, London W1V 3FP.

GLAISTER, Gabrielle

Gabrielle Glaister. Actor (F).
TV: Carol in *All at Number 20;* Bob in *Blackadder Goes Forth* and *Blackadder II;* Patricia Farnham in *Brookside;* Beverly Jason in *Casualty;* Debs in *Coronation Street;* Joan in *Gaye's World;* Doctor Main in *Get Well Soon;* Mrs Smith in *Grange Hill;* Googie in *Happy Families;* Amy Eshton in *Jane Eyre;* Jane in *Jury;* Janet in *London's Burning;* WPC Tillet in *Rockliffe's Babies;* Frances Chadwick in *The Franchise Affair;* Paula in *The Heart Surgeon;* Various in *The Man from Auntie;* Felicity Hunter in *Wish Me Luck.*
Address: c/o Vivien Wilde Ltd, 193 Wardour Street, London W1V 3FA.

GLEN, Iain

Ian Glen. Actor (M). b. Edinburgh, 24 June 1961.
TV: *Adam Bede; Blood Hunt; Death of a Salesman;*

Painted Lady; Paranoia; Silent Scream; The Fear; The Picnic; Trial and Retribution 2; Will You Love Me Tomorrow?; Wives and Daughters; The Wyvern Mysteries.
Films: *Ferdy Durke; Fools of Fortune; Frankie's House; Gorillas in the Mist; Mountains of the Moon; Painted Lady; Paranoid; Paris By Night;* Hamlet in *Rosencrantz and Guildenstern Are Dead; Young Americans.*
Address: c/o ICM, Oxford House, 76 Oxford Street, London W1N 0AX.

GLENISTER, Philip

Philip Glenister. Actor (M).
TV: *A Fatal Inversion* (1991); *Bergerac* (1990); *Berlin Break* (1993); *Blue Heaven* (1993); *Dressing for Breakfast* (1995); *Drop the Dead Donkey* (1992); *Frontiers* (1994); *Have Your Cake* (1996); *Heartbeat* (1992); *In Suspicious Circumstances* (1992); *Love Hurts* (1991); *Loved Up* (1994); *Minder* (1990); *My Wonderful Life* (1998); *Roger, Roger* (1997, 1998); *Ruth Rendell Mysteries* (1991), *Sharpe's Justice* (1996); *Silent Witness* (1995); *Soldier Soldier VI* (1996); *The Bill* (1994); *The Chief* (1993); *The Factory* (1999); *The Perfect Blue* (1997); *True Love* (1995, 1996); *Vanity Fair* (1998); *Wycliffe Christmas Special* (1997).
Films: *i.d.; London Kills Me.*
Address: c/o Ken McReddie Ltd, 91 Regent Street, London W1R 7TB. Hobbies: Tennis, football, golf, shooting.

GLENISTER, Robert

Robert Glenister. Actor (M).
TV: Aristophanes in *Aristophanes;* Pete in *Blood Rights;* Boon; Sheldon in *Bramwell;* Steve in *Buddy Breathing; Casualty;* Colin in *Chancer; Cover Her Face; Dirty Work;* Keith in *Ending Up;* Boy in *Escape – The Cartland Murder;* Mike Hoskins in *Kinsey;* Jessel in *Landing on the Sun;* Boy in *Little Girls Don't;* Ken in *Lonely Hearts Kid;* Peter in *Long Term Memory* Harry Boy in *Me and the Girls;* Stephen Neilson in *Medics;* Miles in *Only Fools and Horses;* Captain Harville in *Persuasion;* Chris in *Prime Suspect;* Steve in *Sink or Swim;* Ian Henderson in *Soldier, Soldier;* DI Baker in *The Bill;* Miner in *Two Weeks in Winter;* Tom in *Watching;* John Lanman in *Wembley Conference.*
Films: Malevsky in *All Forgotten; Quadrophenia;* Jeremy in *Secret Rapture;* The Earl in *The Visitors.*
Address: c/o Markham & Froggatt Ltd, 4 Windmill Street, London W1P 1HF.

GLOVER, Julian

Julian Glover. Actor (M). b. 27 March 1935.
TV: *Bergerac; Brother Cadfael; By the Sword Divided; Casualty; Cover Her Face; Crown Court; Darling Buds of*

May; Dombey & Son; Henry V; Henry VIII; In Hitler's Shadow; Inspector Alleyn; Invasion; Ladies in Charge; Lovejoy; Magnum; Mandela; Midsomer Murders; Money for Nothing; Mr Palfrey of Westminster; Nancy Astor; Only Yesterday; Oss; QED; Remington Steele; Rumpole of the Bailey; Shakespeare Workshop – King Lear; Six Centuries of Verse; Taggart; Tecx; The Chief; The Fight Master; The Journal of Bridget Hitler; Travelling Man; Wish Me Luck.
Films: Alfred The Great; Anastasia; Cry Freedom; Dead Cert; For Your Eyes Only; Hearts of Fire; Heat and Dust; I was Happy Here; Indiana Jones and the Last Crusade; Ivanhoe; Kim; King Ralph; Never the Sinner; Nicholas and Alexandra; Power and Conflict; QB VII; Quatermass and the Pit; The Adding Machine; The Brute; Star Wars: The Empire Strikes Back; The Fourth Protocol; The Girl with Green Eyes; The Last Grenade; The Magus; The Search for Alexander; The Secret Garden; Tom Jones; Treasure Island; Warburg – Man of Influence; Wuthering Heights; Conde in Vatel.
Address: c/o Jonathan Altaras Associates, 13 Shorts Gardens, London WC2H 9AT.

GODDARD, Liza
Liza Goddard. Actor (F)/Presenter.
b. Smethwick, 20 January 1950.
TV: Phillipa Vale in Bergerac; Brendon Chase; Collector's Lot; Holding On; Just His Luck; Liza's Country; Murder at the Wedding; Pig in the Middle; Queen of a Distant Country; Roll Over Beethoven; Seal Morning; Shostakovitch; Take Three Girls; Take Three Women (1982); Tales of the Unexpected; That's Love; April in The Brothers; The Upchat Line; Wagner; Wodehouse Playhouse; Mrs Jessop in Woof; Yes; Honestly.
Address: c/o Whitehall Artists, 125 Gloucester Road, London SW7 4TE.

GODDARD, Trisha
Trisha Goddard. Presenter.
TV: Kilroy Down Under; Trisha (1999); Various.
Address: c/o ITV Sport, 200 Grays Inn Road, London WC1X 8XZ. 3rd m. Peter Gianfrancesco; 2 d. Madison, Billie.

GODWIN, Christopher
Christopher Godwin. Actor (M). b. 5 August 1943.
TV: A Piece of Cake; Lecturer in After Eskimo Day; Astronauts; Boon II; Cat's Eyes; Charlie Muffin; Don't Be Silly; Don't Write to Mother; Fizz; Holding the Fort; Konrad Dekker in Lovejoy; Anthony Cheever in Mortimer's Law; Moving Story; My Family and Other Animals; Nearly a Happy Ending; Nice Work; Professor Charlesworth in Prince Among Men; Prince Caspian

and the Voyage of the Dawn Treador; Return to Treasure Island; Return to Waterloo; Roll Over Beethoven; Snakes and Ladders; South of the Border; Taking the Floor; The Bill; The Other 'Arf; William Tell.
Films: Bullshot; Handful of Dust; Jinnah; Porridge; The Avengers.
Address: c/o David Daly Associates, 586a Kings Road, London SW6 2DX.

GONET, Stella
Stella Gonet. Actor (F).
TV: Casualty; Down Where the Buffalo Goes; Beatrice Elliot in French and Saunders; Heading Home; Beatrice in House of Eliot; Jane Leyward in Supply & Demand; Alex in The Advocates; The Bill; Marigold in The Common Pursuit; Fiona in The Crow Road; The Shutter Falls; Ellie in To Have and To Hold; Kate in Trip Trap; Alex Horton-Smith in Verdict.
Films: Debbie in For Queen and Country; Zena in Stalin.
Address: c/o Markham & Froggatt Ltd, 4 Windmill Street, London W1P 1HF.

GOODALL, Caroline
Caroline Goodall. Actor (F).
b. London, 13 November 1959.
TV: Ann Bolton in A Royal Love Story; Sally Raglan in After the War; Cassidy in Cassidy; Jean in Function Room; Anne Marie in Gems; Marsha in Madly in Love; Lady Yardley in Poirot – Madly in Love; Quantum Leap; Jenny in Remington Steele; Helen in Ring of Scorpio; Mandy in Royal Celebration; Vanessa Fisk in Spiderman (1995); Mattie Hodges in The Commish (1991); Amy Johnson in The Great Air Race; Estelle in The Moon Stallion; Rebecca in The Outer Limits (1995); Rosalind in The Sculptress; Anne in Trust; Holly in Wink Three Times – Tales of the Unexpected.
Films: Dr Anne Harriman in A Difficult Woman; Annie Summers in Casualties; Kristel in Cliffhanger; Diamond Swords; Susan Hendler in Disclosure; Sally in Everytime We Say Goodbye; Moira Banning in Hook; Meg Moynihan in Hotel Sorrento; Heather Frazer in Opernball; Debra Loomis in Rhapsody in Bloom; Emilie Schindler in Schindler's List; Elyne Mitchell in The Silver Brumby; Katharine Webber in The Webbers; Dr Alice Sheldon in White Squall.
Address: PFD, 34–43 Russell Street, London WC2B 5HA.

GOODMAN, Elinor
Elinor Goodman. Editor/Reporter.
TV: Channel 4 News.
Address: c/o ITN Press Office, 200 Gray's Inn Road, London WC1X 1XB.

GOODWIN, Trudie

Trudie Goodwin. Actor (F).
b. London, 13 November 1951.
TV: *Fox; The Gentle Touch; The Law Machine; Play for Today; Woodentop;* June Ackland in *The Bill.*
Address: c/o Peters, Fraser and Dunlop, Drury House, 34–43 Russell Street, London, WC2B 5HA.
m. Kit Jackson; 2 d. Jessica, Eleanor. Hobbies: Painting, gardening.

GOODYEAR, Julie

Julie Kemp. Actor (F).
b. Heywood, Lancashire, 29 March 1943.
TV: *A Family At War; City '68;* Bet Lynch/Gilroy in *Coronation Street* (1966); *How to be Cool; Nearest and Dearest; Pardon the Expression; The Dustbinmen; The War of Darkie Pilbeam; This is Your Life; Women of the Street.*
Address: c/o 'Spotlight', 7 Leicester Place, London WC2H 7BP. m. 1 Ray Sutcliffe; 1 s. Gary; m. 2 Tony Rudman; m. 3 Richard Skrob (div).

GOOLDEN, Jilly

Jilly Goolden. Presenter.
TV: *Food and Drink; The Great Antiques Hunt; Going, Going, Gone; the Big Breakfast; Noel's House Party; That's Showbusiness; Win, Lose or Draw; Standing Room Only; Mrs Merton Show; Hit the Road; Saturday Disney; You Bet; Horizon; Brain Drain; Jobs for the Girls; Bob Downe Under; Clive Anderson Talks Back; This Morning; Good Morning; A Word in Your Ear.*
Address: c/o Knight Ayton Management, 114 St Martin's Lane, London WC2N 4AZ.

GOOSE, Claire

Claire Goose. Actor (F). b. Norfolk, 1976.
TV: Tina in *Casualty;* Sally in *EastEnders;* Julia Giles in *Landmarks;* Diane in *Loved Up;* Stacey in *The Bill.*
Films: Sally in *Meat;* Jane in *Where's the Loophole.*
Address: c/o CAM, 19 Denmark Street, London WC2H 8NA. Hobbies: Dancing, singing, swimming, roller-skating, horse riding, piano.

GORDON, Hannah

Hannah Gordon. Actor (F).
b. Edinburgh, 9 April 1941.
TV: *A Day in the Life…; Abelard and Heloise; Almost Tomorrow;* Agnes in *David Copperfield; Day After the Fair; Dear Octopus; Exiles; Gardeners Calendar; Good Behaviour; Goodbye Mr Kent;* Estella in *Great Expectations; Great Gardens; Johnson Over Jordan;* Belinda Braithwaite in *Joint Account; Jonathan Creek; Middlemarch;* Bella in *Midsomer Murders;* Mrs Morrison's

Ghost; Mrs Durrell in *My Family and Other Animals; My Wife Next Door; Pobs Programme;* Dr Jean Napier in *Taggart; Telford's Change; The Bond; The Gay Lord Quex; The Lady Killers; The Vase;* The second Mrs Bellamy in *Upstairs Downstairs; What Every Woman Knows.*
Films: *Limited Edition; Spring and Port Wine; Tennis Game; The Elephant Man.*
Address: c/o Conway Van Gelder, 18–21 Jermyn Street, London SW1Y 6HP.

GORDON, Serena

Serena Gordon. Actor (F).
b. London, 3 September 1963.
TV: Lucy Mannette in *A Tale of Two Cities; Act of Will;* Caroline in *Aristocrats; Chillers; Dancing Queen; Hannay; Insiders;* Trisha Mabbot in *Kinsey; Sherlock Holmes: The Master Blackmailer; The Bill; The Shellseekers; Till We Meet Again.*
Films: *House of Mirth; Goldeneye; Maurice; Speak Like a Child; Tom's Midnight Garden.*
Address: c/o Cassie Mayer Ltd, 34 Kingley Court, London W1R 5LE. m. Tim Lawrence; 2 s. Ben, Alfie.

GORDON-LEVITT, Joseph

Joseph Gordon-Levitt. Actor (M).
b. Los Angeles, USA, 17 February.
TV: Tommy in *3rd Rock from the Sun;* George in *Roseanne; Dark Shadows; The Powers That Be; That '70's Show; China Beach; Family Ties; Quantum Leap; LA Law; Stranger on My Land.*
Films: *Picking Up The Pieces; Loving Lulu; 10 Things I Hate About You; Halloween; The Juror; The Great Elephant Escape; Holy Matrimony; Switching Parents; A River Runs Through It; Roadkillers.*
Address: c/o Leslie Siebert, The Gersh Agency, 232 N. Canon Drive, Beverly Hills, California 90210, USA. Hobbies: Roller-blading, gymnastics, playing guitar, programming computers.

GORDON SINCLAIR, John

John Gordon Sinclair. Actor (M). b. Glasgow, 1962.
TV: Robert in *An Actor's Life For Me; Bergerac;* Gordon in *Bouncing; Circles;* Ken in *Frank Stubbs Promotes; Hot Metal;* Walter; Graham in *June;* Colin Cross in *Les Girls;* Michael in *Loved By You; My Summer with Des; Nelson's Column;* Rick in *Raspberry Ripple; Roll Over Beethoven;* Henry in *Self-Catering;* Alex in *Skin Deep;* Gavin in *Snakes and Ladders;* Neil in *Spayer Connection;* Frank in *Your Cheatin' Heart.*
Films: *A Trick of the Light; Britannia Hospital;* Ivar in *Erik the Viking; Gregory's 2 Girls;* Gregory in *Gregory's*

Girl; Richy in *Local Hero*; *That Sinking Feeling*; *The Girl in the Picture*.
Address: c/o ICM, Oxford House, 76 Oxford Street, London W1N 0AX.

GOSH, Shiulie

Shiulie Gosh. Reporter/Presenter. b. Leeds, 1969.
TV: Reporter BBC's *East Midlands Today*; *Countryfile*; Reporter/Presenter *Newsroom South East*; News Correspondent *ITN*.
Address: c/o ITN Press Office, Gray's Inn Road, London WC1X 8XZ.

GOUGH, Sandra

Sandra Gough. Actor (F).
TV: *Bingo*; Irma Barlow Ogden in *Coronation Street*; *Cracker*; Nelli Dingle in *Emmerdale*; Doreen in *Emmerdale*; May in *Foxy Lady*; *Medics*; Feed in *The Kenny Everett Show*; Mother in *The Van Boys*; *Travelling Man*; DHSS Worker in *Yesterday*.
Address: c/o Nyland Management, 20 School Lane, Henton Chapel, Stockport SK4 5DG.

GOWER, David

David Gower. Commentator/Presenter.
b. 1 April 1957.
TV: *Cricket World Cup* (1999); *David Gower's Cricket Monthly*; *Holiday*; *They Think It's All Over*; Test cricket commentairies.
Address: c/o Marquee Group (UK) Ltd, 21 The Green, Richmond, Surrey TW9 1PX. m. Thorunn; 2 d. Alexandra, Samantha. Hobbies: Bobsleighing, photography, safaris, wildlife conservation, collecting (and drinking) fine wines, crosswords.

GRACE, Helen

Helen Grace. Actor (F). b. Hertfordshire, 1972.
TV: Georgia Simpson in *Brookside*; Maggie in *Passion Killers*; Jane Wilkinson in *Poirot*; Chrissie in *Roger Roger*; *The Vanishing Man*.
Films: Woman in *The Leading Man*.
Address: c/o Conway Van Gelder, 18–21 Jermyn Street, London SW1Y 6HP.

GRACE, Nickolas

Nickolas Grace. Actor (M).
b. West Kirby, Merseyside, 21 November 1947.
TV: *Cinderella*; *Merlin*; *The Hunchback of Notre Dame*; Booza Pitt in *The Final Cut*; *Young Indian Jones Chronicles*; *Space Precinct*; *Inside Victor Lewis Smith*; *Sharpe's Honour*; *The Chief*; *Smith and Jones*; Inspector Alleyn Mysteries; *Tonight at 8.30*; *Moon and Son*; *Lovejoy*; *Absolutely Fabulous*; Sonnenschein in *The Green Man*;

Sherlock Holmes; Marcus in *Birds of a Feather*; *Twist of Fate*; *The Man in the Brown Suit*; Hitler in *Unreported Incident*; Nelson in *Napoleon and Josephine*; Grossman in *Max Headroom*; *Candide*; *The Last Place on Earth*; *Lace*; *Huis Clos*; *The Master of Ballantrae*; Sheriff of Nottingham in *Robin of Sherwood*; *Morte d'Arthur*; *Bergerac*; Anthony Blanche in *Brideshead Revisited*; *The Pink Medicine Show*; *The Comedy of Errors*; *The Anarchist*; *The Love School*; *Z-Cars*.
Films: *The Golden Bowl*; *An Ideal Husband*; *Shooting Fish*; *Evita*; Jeroboam in *Solomon and Sheba*; *Just Ask for Diamond*; Oscar Wilde in *Salome's Last Dance*; *Dream Demon*; Lorca in *Death of a Poet*; Harry in *The Heat and the Dust*; *Sleepwalker*; *Europe After the Rain*.
Address: c/o London Management, 2-4 Noel Street, London, W1V 3RB. Hobbies: Cinema, travel, languages, riding, running, swimming.

GRAHAM, Julie

Julia Graham. Actor (F).
TV: Lisa in *99-1*; Megan in *At Home With The Braithwaites*; Sue in *Bookie*; Jane in *Boon*; Sarita in *Bugs*; DS Mary Slater in *Butterfly Collector*; Alison in *Casualty*; Ade Pritchard in *Dalziel and Pascoe*; Sharon in *Downtown Lagos*; Alice in *Harry*; Dorothy in *Heartbeat*; Joan in *Houseman's Tale*; *Let Yourself Go*; Alison in *Life Support*; Rose in *Love Me Tender*; Caroline Bonaparte in *Napoleon and Josephine*; Kylie in *Sharman*; Michelle Stock in *Space Island One*; Jody in *Spender*; Tilly Campbell in *Stan's Wife*; *Strike It Rich*; *Taggart*; Sandra in *The Dark Room*; *The End of the Line: A View of Things*.
Films: Angie in *Bedrooms and Hallways*; Janey in *Blood Red Roses*; Shelly in *Daylight Robbery*; *Nuns on the Run*; Cathy in *Old New Borrowed Blue*; Eugenie in *Preaching to the Perverted*; *Rosebud*; Mandy in *Some Voices*; *The Big Man*; *The Fruit Machine*; Elise in *The Near Room*; *The Silent Scream*.
Address: c/o Sally Hope Associates, 108 Leonard Street, London EC2A 4XS.

GRAHAM, Richard

Richard Graham. Actor (M).
b. Farnborough, Kent, 10 May 1960.
TV: *A Touch of Frost*; *Kavanagh QC*; Mickey Farrel in *Maisie Raine*; Pete in *Real Women*; Michael in *The Passion*; Gordon Bradshaw in *The Thing About Vince*; *Time After Time*.
Films: Gerald Novell in *24 Hours in London*; Mark in *Bravo Two Zero*; Trevor in *ID*; *In the Name of the Father*; Genghis in *My Beautiful Laundrette*; John Mills in *The Bounty*; Quartermaster George Rowe in *Titanic*.

Address: c/o William Morris Agency (UK) Ltd, 1 Stratton Street, London W1X 6HB. m. Yvonne; 1 s. Jack, 1 d. Charlotte. Hobbies: Cricket, supporting Crystal Palace FC.

GRAHAM, Stephen

Syephen Graham. Actor (M).
b. Liverpool, 3 August 1973.
TV: Andrew in *Brothers and Sisters*; Mickey in *Children's Ward*; John in *Forgive and Forget*; Barry Ward in *Heartbeat*; Thewlis in *Liverpool One*; Gary Abdie in *Sex, Guys and Videotapes*; Jason Barrett in *The Bill*; Peter McNulty in *The Jump*; Graham in *The Lakes*; Nick Bowen in *Where the Heart Is*.
Films: Nephew in *Blonde Fist*; Jed in *Dancin' Thru The Dark*; Lead in *Dog Day*; Jacko in *Downtime*.
Address: c/o Pemberton Associates, 193 Wardour Street, London W1V 3FA. Hobbies: Football, singing.

GRAINGER, Gawn

Gawn Grainger. Actor (M).
TV: *A Christmas Carol* (1999); Joseph Newsome in *Boon*; Eden Thackeray in *Dalziel and Pascoe*; George Stephenson in *Doctor Who*; Jack Branagan in *Hetty Wainthropp Investigates*; *Poirot* (1988); Hitler in *Private Schultz* (1981); *The Beggar's Opera*; Bob Loder in *The Black Tower* (1985).
Films: Dr Michael Lloyd in *August*; Henry in *Love and Death on Long Island*.
Address: c/o PFD, Drury House, 34–43 Russell Street, London WC2B 5HA. m. actress Zoe Wanamaker; 1 s. Charlie, 1 d. Eliza. Hobbies: Cricket, darts, snooker, swimming, drives.

GRAMMER, Kelsey

Allen Kelsey Grammer. Actor (M).
b. St Thomas, U.S. Virgin Islands, 21 February 1955.
TV: Snowball in *Animal Farm* (1999); *Another World* (1984); *Beyond Suspicion* (1993); *Cheers* (1984); *Crossings* (1996); *Dance till' Dawn* (1988); *Fired Up* (1997); *Frasier* (1993–); *George Washington* (1984); *Kennedy* (1993); *London Suite* (1997); *The Innocent* (1994); *The Pentagon Wars* (1998); *The Simpsons* (1989); *Top of the Hill* (1989).
Films: Vladimir in *Anastasia*; Zozi in *Bartok the Magnificent*; *Down Periscope*; *Galaxies are Colliding*; *New Jersey Turnpike*; DT Frankenoillie in *Runaway Brain*; Verle in *Standing on Fishes*; Bateson in *Star Trek: First Contact*; *The Real Howard Spitz*; The Prospector in *Toy Story 2*; Detective novelist in *Writer's Block*.
Address: c/o Jeremy Zimmer @ UTA, Suite 500, 9560 Wilshire Blvd, Beverly Hills, California 90210, USA. m. Camille Donatacci; 2 d. Spencer, Greer.

Hobbies: Tennis, darts, billiards, sailing, singing, playing piano, golf.

GRANT, Deborah

Deborah Grant. Actor (F).
b. London, 22 February 1947.
TV: Sarah Francis in *A Bouquet of Barbed Wire*; Debbie in *Bergerac*; Paula in *Bob Martin*; Leonora in *Bread*; Sheila Cody in *Crown Prosecutor*; Antonia Stargerson in *Jonathan Creek*; Stella in *Pat and Margaret*; Carol Johnson in *Peak Practice*; Muriel in *Roger Roger*; Professor Weaver in *Space Island One*; Anthea in *The Thing About Vince*; Various in *Victoria Wood and Friends*; Sarah Preston in *Westbeach*; *Public Eye*; *Minder*; *Bulman*; *Casualty*; *All for Love*; *Clayhanger*; *The Beiderbecke Connection*; *Motherlove*.
Films: *I Want what I want*; *Isadora*; *Otley*; Mrs Profumo in *Scandal*; *The Magic Christian*.
Address: c/o Michelle Braidman Associates, 10-11 Lower John Street, London W1R 3PE. Hobbies: Swimming.

GRANT, Richard E.

Richard E Grant. Actor (M). b. 5 May 1957.
TV: *A Royal Scandal*; *Bed*; *Hard Times*; *Here is the News*; *Honest, Decent, Legal and True*; *Karaoke*; *The Scarlet Pimpernel*; *Suddenly Last Summer*; *Trial and Retribution*.
Films: *Age of Innocence*; *A Christmas Carol*; *Dracula*; *Food of Love*; *Henry and June*; *How To Get Ahead in Advertising*; *Hudson Hawk*; Jack in *Jack And Sarah*; *Keep the Aspidistra Flying*; *Killing Dad*; *La Story*; *Mountains of the Moon*; *Portrait of a Lady*; *Prêt à Porter*; *Serpents Kiss*; *SpiceWorld – The Movie*; *St Ives*; *The Cool Light of Day*; *The Little Vampire*; *The Match*; *The Player*; *Twelfth Night*; *Warlock*; *Withnail and I*.
Address: c/o ICM, Oxford House, 76 Oxford Street, London W1N 0AX.

GRANT, Russell

Russell Grant. Presenter/Astrologer/Journalist.
b. Middlesex, 4 February 1951.
TV: *A Question of Stars*; *Breakfast Time*; *Get Away*; *House Busters*; *Russell Grant's Postcards*; *Russell Grant's All Star Show*; *Russell In New York*; *Star Choice*; *The Zodiac Game*; *This Morning*; *TV-AM*.
Address: c/o Simpson Fox Associates Ltd, 52 Shaftesbury Avenue, London W1V 7DE.

GRANTHAM, Leslie

Leslie Grantham. Actor (M). b. London, 30 April 1947.
TV: *Fort Boyard*; *The Stretch*; *Jake's End*; *The Jewel in the Crown*; *Goodnight and God Bless*; *Hello I Thought You'd*

Gone; Night of the Narrow Boats; Doctor Who; Morons from Outer Space; Knockback; Bulman; EastEnders; Nightwatch; Winners and Losers; Paradise Club; The Good Guys; Woof; Runaway Bay; Gummed Labels; The Detectives; Wild Oats; Cluedo; 99–1; The Uninvited; Shadow Run; Wycliffe; The Bill; The Wedding Tackle; The Bench.
Address: c/o Whitehall Artists, 125 Gloucester Road, London SW7 4TE.

GRAVESON, Jan
Jan Graveson. Actor (F).
TV: WPC Jane Brent in *A Touch of Frost*; Wendy Hallam in *Auf Wiedersehen, Pet*; Lee Brookes in *Casualty*; Cindy Walker in *Casualty*; Rosalyn Greenwood in *Coronation Street*; Lisa O'Brien in *EastEnders*; Angela Brady in *Spender*; Kathleen Tanner in *White Peak Farm*.
Address: c/o David Daly Associates, 586a Kings Road, London SW6 2DX. Hobbies: Tap dancing, piano, singing.

GRAY, Sally
Sally Gray. Actor (F)/Reporter. b. Edinburgh.
TV: *50/50; Around Scotland; Children in Need; Comic Relief; Dear Mr Barker; Dinosaur Detectives; Disney Adventures; Dream Ticket; Feeling Good; Food File; GMTV; Go 4 5; Hype; It'll Never Work; Linford's Record Breakers; Movie Watch; National Lottery* (1998); *National Lottery Big Ticket; NB; Next Generation, Antiques Roadshow; Pulling Power; Scoop; Silverstone TV* (1996); *Summer Holiday; The Mountain Bike Show; The Really Useful Show; Tricks 'n' Tracks; Water Week; Zig Zag.*
Address: c/o Arlington Enterprises Ltd, 1–3 Charlotte Street, London W1P 1HD. Hobbies: Tap dancing, ballet, bungee jumping, keep fit, rugby.

GREAVES, Bob
Bob Greaves. Presenter.
TV: *Holiday; Bob About; World on a Plate; Family Trees, Bob's Bygones; Bob's Century.*
Address: c/o David Anthony Promotions, PO Box 286, Warrington, Cheshire WA2 8GA.

GRECO, Michael
Michael Greco. Actor (M).
TV: Punch in *Academy*; Tino in *Call Red*; Beppe Di Marco in *EastEnders*; Ben in *Faith in the Future*; Waiter in *Love Hurts*.
Films: Matt in *Leo*; Chris in *The Ring*.
Address: c/o CAM London, 19 Denmark Street, London WC2H 8NA.

GREEN, Richard
Richard Green. Actor (M).
TV: *Casualty; Grange Hill; Jupiter Moon; London's Burning; Red Dwarf; Tess of the d'Urbervilles; The Bill; The Upper Hand; To Have and To Hold.*
Address: c/o The Narrow Road Company, 21-22 Poland Street, London W1V 3DD. Hobbies: Swimming, rugby, horse riding, shooting, cricket.

GREEN, Robson
Robson Green. Actor (M).
b. Dudley, Northumberland, 18 December 1964.
TV: Rick in *A Night on the Tyne*; Eric Trapp in *Ain't Misbehavin'*; Jimmy Powell in *Casualty*; Joe Purvis in *Grafters*; John in *Hands*; Owen Springer in *Reckless*; *Rhinoceros*; Dave Tucker in *Soldier, Soldier*; Rory Connor in *The Gambling Man*; Barry Grimes in *The Student Prince*; Creegan in *Touching Evil*; Billy in *Voices of War*; *The Last Musketeer*.
Films: Zak in *Secret of Perfection*.
Address: c/o Coastal Productions Ltd, 250 Broadchare Quayside, Newcastle NE1 3DQ. Hobbies: fishing, supports Newcastle United, runs local theatre.

GREENACRE, Jill
Jill Greenacre. Actor (F). b. 3 June 1965.
TV: *Andy Robson; Meditation; Dramarama; The Bill; Brookside; The Main Event; Library of Romance, A Touch of Love, Sharon and Elsie; Crime Limited; Moonlight and Roses;* Linda in *The Brittas Empire; C15: The New Professionals;* Presenter for *You Can Defend Yourself.*
Address: c/o Langford Associates, 17 Westfields Avenue, London, SW13 0AT. Partner Richard Good. Hobbies: Riding, yoga, meditation.

GREENE, Sarah
Sarah Greene. Actor (F)/Presenter. b. London.
TV: *Airport Watch; BBC Breakfast Time; Blue Peter; Bodycare; Disney Time; Emergency 999; Food for thought* (1999); *Food Network Daily* (1999); *French and Saunders; Friday People; Going Live* (1987); *Good Morning Summer; Holiday* and *Summer Holiday; Hospital Watch; Joy to the world; Life on One; London Plus; Posh Frocks and New Trousers; Royal Weddings; Saturday Superstore; Sky 1 to 3; Take Two; That's Showbusiness; The Exchange; The Longest Running Show on Earth; The Swish of the Curtain; Together; TV-AM's Dream Home;* various award ceremonies; *Wildfilm; Wogan.*
Address: c/o Conway Van Gelder, 18–21 Jermyn Street, London SW1Y 6HP. m. Mike Smith.

GREENHALGH, Andy

Andy Greenhalgh. Actor (M).

TV: *Bad Company; Bostock's Cup; Casualty; Clem; Dressing for Breakfast; Drop the Dead Donkey; EastEnders; Frontiers; Master of the Moor; Minder; Mitch; Murder Most Horrid; Paul Merton; See You Friday; Stick With Me Kid; Sticky Moments; The All New Alexei Sayle Show; The Belfrey Witches; The Blackheath Poisonings; The Charmer; The Hello Girls; The Perfect State; The Vicar of Dibley.*

Films: *A Man Called Sarge; The Canterville Ghost.*

Address: c/o Barry Brown & Partner, 47 West Square, London SE11 4SP.

GREENWOOD, Debbie

Debbie Greenwood. Presenter/Actor (F).

b. Liverpool, 16 September 1959.

TV: *Granada Reports; Weekend; Scramble; Breakfast Time; Lifeline; First Class; Tricks of the Trade; The Tom O'Connor Show; The Garden Party; Streetwise; You Can Do It; TV Weekly; The Paul McKenna Show; Wogan; A Word in Your Ear; Don't Drink the Water; Through the Keyhole; Wheel of Fortune; Pull the Other One; Hello Mum; Polaski; Hold the Back Page.*

Address: c/o Jane Hughes Management, The Coach House, PO Box 123, Knutsford, Cheshire, WA16 9HX. m. Paul Coia (presenter); 1 d. Annalie. Hobbies: Tennis, writing.

GREENWOOD, Kelly

Kelly Greenwood. Actor (F). b. 5 November 1982.

TV: Tracey in *My Wonderful Life; Heartbeat, The Ward.*

Address: c/o Laine Management, Matrix house, 301–303 Chapel Street, Manchester, M3 5JG.

GREENWOOD, Shirley Ann

Shirley Ann Greeenwood. Actor (F).

b. London, 27 July 1935.

TV: Maggie in *London's Burning.*

Films: *Pirates of Penzance; Trial by Jury; Yeomen of the Guard.*

Address: c/o George Heathcote Management, 58 Northdown Street, London N1 9BS. m. Stanley Green; 1 s. Jeremy, 2 d. Deborah, Annabel. Hobbies: Travel, gardening, cooking, reading.

GREGSON, Simon

Simon Alan Gregory. Actor (M)/Presenter.

b. Wythenshawe, Manchester, 2 October 1974.

TV: Steve McDonald in *Coronation Street; Cyber Café; Soccer Skills; The Big Breakfast.*

Address: c/o Langford Associates, 17 Westfields Avenue, London SW13 0AT.

GRIFFIN, Angela

Angela Griffin. Actor (F).

b. Cottingley, Leeds, Yorkshire, 1977.

TV: Jasmine Hopkins in *Holby City;* Presenter on *National Lottery;* Fiona Middleton in *Coronation Street; Live Challenge; Emmerdale Farm; Just Us; Under the Bed Clothes.*

Address: c/o Pemberton Associates, 35–36 Barton Arcade, Deansgate, Manchester M3 2BB.

GRIFFIN, David

David Griffin. Actor (M).

b. Richmond, Surrey, 19 July 1943.

TV: Richard Gardner in *Emmerdale;* Clive Dempster in *Hi De Hi;* Emmet in *Keeping up Appearances;* Sam in *Love's Labour;* Frank Cherryble in *Nicholas Nickleby;* Lt. Attenborough in *Roger of the Raj;* Benvolio in *Romeo and Juliet;* Bobby Van Horath in *Songs of Songs;* Capt. Meredith in *Stalag Luft 211B;* Marcel in *The Copyist;* Miguel in *The Marquise;* Dabiel in *The White Mercedes;* Capt. Douglas in *Till We Meet Again;* Perry in *Waiting in the Wings.*

Films: Chris Ferris in *Battle of Britain;* William in *The Blood Beast Terror;* Tom in *Let's Drink a Toast to a Dear Old Lady;* Jungle Captain in *Privates on Parade;* Patrick Evans in *Screentime;* Peter Johnson in *Singapore Sling;* Freddy in *The Deathshead;* Peter Richards in *Trog.*

Address: c/o Bernard Hunter Associates, 13 Spencer Gardens, London SW14 7AH.

GRIFFITHS, Jaye

Jaye Griffiths. Actor (F).

TV: *A Killing on the Exchange; Anna Lee; Between the Lines; Between the Lines II; Buddha of Suburbia;* Ros in *Bugs; Casualty; Drop the Dead Donkey; EastEnders; Hard Cases; Harry Enfield and Chums; London's Burning; Love Hurts; Maigret; Moon and Son; Open College; Peak Practice; Rockcliffe's Babies; Stephen Sondheim Master Class; Storytime;* DI Sally Johnson in *The Bill; Two Wheels on My Wagon; Underbelly;* Tanya in *Unfinished Business; Watch.*

Address: c/o Susan Angel Associates, 1st Floor, 12 D'Arblay Street, London W1V 3FP.

GRIFFITHS, Richard

Richard Griffiths. Actor (M).

b. Cleveland, 31 July 1947.

TV: *A Kind of Living; A Wanted Man; Amnesty; Anything Legal Considered; Bird of Prey; El CID; Fizz; Gormenghast; In the Red; Inspector Morse; The Merry Wives of Windsor; Mr Wakefield's Crusade; Nobody's Perfect; Perfect Scoundrels; Pie in the Sky; Ted and Ralph; The*

Cleopatra Files; The Good Guys; The Marksman; The World Cup – A Captain's Tale; Whoops, Apocalypse!
Films: *A Private Function; Blame it on the Bellboy; Brittannia Hospital; Chariots of Fire; Funny Bones; Ghandi; Goldeneye; Gorky Park; Greystroke; Guarding Tess; King Ralph; Naked Gun 2; Ragtime; Shanghai Surprise; Sleepy Hollow; Superman II; The French Lieutenant's Woman; Vatel;* Uncle Monty in *Withnail and I.*
Address: c/o Whitehall Artists, 125 Gloucester Road, London SW7 4TE.

GRIFFITHS, Roger
Roger Griffiths. Actor (M)/Producer. b. London.
TV: Cliff in *Captain Butler;* Everton in *Chef!;* Rudi/Writer in *Comin' Atcha.*
Films: Blondie in *Greenwich Mean Time;* Lenny in *Hard Men;* Charlie in *Tube Tales.*
Address: c/o Dennis Lyne Agency, 108 Leonard Street, London EC2A 4RH.

GRIGSON, Sophie
Sophie Grigson. Presenter/Celebrity chef.
b. Broad Town, Swindon, 19 June 1959.
TV: *Arena Food Night; BBC Daytime Live; Feasting For a Fiver* (1999); *Food and Drink; Grow Your Greens, Eat Your Greens* (1993); *Sophie Grigson's Herbs* (1998, 1999); *Taste of the Times* (1997); *This Morning; Who'll Do the Pudding?; Travels a La Carte* (1994*).*
Address: c/o Deborah McKenna Ltd, Claridge House, 29 Barnes High Street, London SW1 3LW. m. William Black; 2 d. Florence, Sidney. Hobbies: Reading, travel.

GROSS, Paul
Paul Gross. Actor (M).
b. Calgary, Canada, 30 April, 1959.
TV: Benton Fraser in *Due South; Murder Most Likely; 20,000 Leagues Under the Sea; Painted Cans; Whale Music; Married to It; Tales of the City; Aspen Extreme; Cold Comfort.*
Films: *Due South; Gross Misconduct; In This Corner.*
Address: c/o Bresler, Kelly and Associates, Suite 510, 11500 West Olympic Blvd, Los Angeles, California 90064, USA. m. Martha Burns; 1 d. Hannah; 1 s. Jack.

GROSSMAN, Loyd
Loyd Grossman. Presenter/Reporter.
b. Boston, Massachusetts, 16 September 1950.
TV: *Conspicuous Consumption* (1996); *Lloyd on Location* (2000); *Lloyd's Louisiana* (1999); *Masterchef; Off Your Trolley* (1994); *Relative Knowledge* (1998); *The Dog's Tale* (1993); *The World on a Plate* (1999); *Through the Keyhole.*

Address: c/o Peter Schbabl, 72 Vincent Square, London SW1P 2PA. m. Deborah; 2 d. Florence, Constance.

GROUT, James
Jame Grout. Actor (M).
b. London, 22 October 1927.
TV: *A Very Peculiar Practice; About Face; All Creatures Great and Small; Born and Bred; Cockles; David Copperfield; Drop the Dead Donkey; Family Money; Goodnight Sweetheart; Henry IV Parts One* and *Two; Inspector Morse; Julie and the Cadillacs; Man and Superman; Mother Love; Mr. Wakefield's Crusade; Northern Lights; Roy's Raiders; Rumpole of the Bailey; September Song; Stay Lucky; The Beiderbecke Affair; The Old Devils; Titmus Regained; Vote for Them; Wonderful You; Yes Minister.*
Address: c/o Crouch Associates, 9–15 Neal Street, London WC2H 9PF.

GRUFFUDD, Ioan
Ioan Gruffudd. Actor (M). b. Cardiff, Wales, 1973.
TV: Defi Lewis in *Austin;* Nigel in *Double Exposure – A Relative Stranger;* Pip in *Great Expectations;* Horatio Hornblower in *Hornblower;* Jack in *Love in the 21st Century;* Gareth Wyn in *Pobol Y Cym;* Jeremy in *Poldark;* Lt. John Feeley in *Warriors;* Arfon in *William Jones.*
Films: Freddy in *Another Life;* Hob in *Pavarotti in Dad's Room;* Solomon in *Solomon and Gaenor;* Fifth Officer Lowe in *Titanic;* John Gray *in Wilde.*
Address: c/o Hamilton Asper, 24 Hanway Street, London W1P 9DD. Hobbies: Horse riding, fencing, oboe.

GRUNDY, Tim
Tim Grundy. Presenter.
TV: *Two's Country; Travelling Light; Pebble Mill, People Today, Showbiz People; See You on Sunday; The Forum.*
Address: c/o David Anthony Promotions, P.O. Box 286, Warrington, Cheshire WA2 8GA. m.; 2 children. Hobbies: Sport, fitness, countryside, music, films.

GUARD, Christopher
Christopher Guard. Actor (M).
b. London, 5 December 1953.
TV: Jim in *A Hymn for Jim; Blackeyes;* Lead in *Bouncing Back;* David Lance in *Bugs III;* Ken in *Casualty;* Cain/Thomas in *Chester Mystery Plays;* David in *David Copperfield;* Pip in *Great Expectations;* Marcellus in *I, Claudius;* John Diamond in *John Diamond;* Lucius in *Julias Caesar;* Clovis Sackbut in *Knight School;* Jonathan Brem in *Life Boat;* Philip Ashley in *My Cousin Rachel;* Alton in *Poirot;* Dr Hatchard in *She Wolf*

in London; Willoughby in *Sherlock Holmes;* Phil Gough in *The Bill;* Ferdinand in *The Tempest;* Wilfred in *Wilfred and Eileen;* Gerald Fairley in *Woman of Substance.*
Films: Erich in *A Little Night Music;* Alec Legg in *Dead Man's Folly;* Marius in *Les Miserables;* Frodo in *Lord of the Rings;* Gerald in *Memoirs of a Survivor;* Peter Quint in *Turn of the Screw.*
Address: c/o The Narrow Road Company, 21-22 Poland Street, London W1V 3DD. Hobbies: Singing, rock guitar, piano, horse riding, football, running.

GUARD, Pippa
Pippa Guard. Actor (F). b. 13 October 1952.
TV: Hermia in *A Midsummer Night's Dream;* Marian in *All or Nothing at All* (1993); Diana in *All's Well that Ends Well* (1980); Ava in *Another Flip for Dominic* (1982); Fiona in *Casualty* (1994); Rebecca Summers in *Circles of Deceit* (1994); *Close to Home* (1990); Miss Glaistow in *Daisies in December* (1995); Claire in *Gobble* (1996); Jan Woolley in *Hope and Glory* (1999); Maggie Tulliver in *The Mill on the Floss* (1978); Maria Marten in *Murder in the Red Barn* (1980); Megan in *Poirot* (1991); Rene in *Roger, Roger* (1998); India Wilkes in *Scarlett* (1994); Carmel in *Space Precinct* (1994); Edwardian Lady in *The Country Diary of an Edwardian Lady* (1983); Lauren in *The Creatives* (1998); Ava in *The Flip Side of Dominic Hyde* (1980); Christina Rossetti in *The Late Show* (1994); Lady Bisset in *The Life and Loves of a She-Devil* (1986); Barbara in *The Mallens* (1979); Rosemary in *The Old Devils* (1991); Phoenix in *The Riff Raff Element* (1992); Miranda in *The Tempest* (1979); Diane Lambton in *The Vet (1995);* Prue in *To The Lighthouse* (1982).
Film: *An Unsuitable Job for a Woman.*
Address: c/o The Richard Stone Partnership, 2 Henrietta Street, London WC2E 8PS.

GUBBA, Tony
Tony Gubba. Commentator/Presenter.
b. Manchester, 23 September 1943.
TV: *Commonwealth Games* (1988); *Match of the Day; News; Sportsnight; The Winter Games; The World Cup;* various sports.
Address: BBC Sport, Union House, 65–69 Shepherds Bush Green, London W12 8TX. 2 d. Claire, Libby. Hobbies: Salmon fishing, DIY, photography.

GUINNESS, Sir Alec
Sir Alec Guinness. Actor (M).
b. London, 2 April 1914.
TV: *A Handful of Dust;* George Smiley in *Smiley's People; Tales from Hollywood; A Foreign Field; Tinker, Tailor, Soldier, Spy.*

Films: *Dr Zhivago;* Herbert Pocket in *Great Expectations;* various in *Kind Hearts and Coronets; The Lavender Hill Mob; Lawrence of Arabia;* Fagin in *Oliver Twist;* Obi-Wan Kenobi in *Star Wars; The Bridge On The River Kwai; The Ladykillers;* Disraeli in *The Mudlark; The Swan; Tunes of Glory.*
Address: c/o Ken McReddie Ltd, 91 Regent Street, London W1R 7TB.

GULATI, Shobna
Shobna Gulati. Actor (F).
TV: Goodness in *Chayatantra the Sixth Story;* Anita in *dinnerladies;* Shobna in *First Sex;* Binni in *In the Mix;* Helen in *London;* Imogen in *Thick and Thin.*
Address: c/o Burnett Granger Associates, Prince of Wales Theatre, 31 Coventry Street, London W1V 8AS. Hobbies: Piano, dancing, guitar.

GUNN, Peter
Peter Gunn. Actor (M). b. 13 February 1963.
TV: Sidney Snell in *A Touch of Frost;* Malcolm in *Casualty;* Simon Thorpe in *Heartburn Hotel;* Bryan Harbour in *Hetty Wainthropp Investigates;* Len Hotton in *Holding On;* Bernard Whelan in *In the Dark Room;* Rawling's Assistant in *Just William;* Mike in *Kiss Me Kate;* Pat Kennedy in *London's Burning;* Devlin in *Love Hurts;* Rev. Walter Stelling in *Mill on the Floss;* Clive in *Minder;* Dean Trussler in *People Like Us;* Pyke in *Pie in the Sky;* Bob Maynard in *Rough Justice;* Private Clayton in *Sharpe's Company;* Paul Shaw in *The Bill;* Geoff Bentham in *The Painted Lady;* Regular in *The Russ Abbot Show.*
Films: Terry in *Blue Juice;* Simmo in *Brassed Off;* Captain Laurent in *Ever After; Felicia's Journey;* Nicky in *Funny Bones;* Bonner in *Resurrection;* The Scientist in *Soup;* Frankie in *Treacle;* Fabian in *Twelfth Night;* Tommy in *When Saturday Comes.*
Address: c/o Barry Brown & Partner, 47 West Square, London SE11 4SP.

GUNNELL, Sally
Sally Gunnell. Presenter.
b. Chigwell, Essex, 29 July 1966.
TV: *Athletics Review of the Year* (1994); *Body Heat;* children's programmes; *This is Your Life* (1997); various sports programmes.
Address: c/o MTC, 10 Kendall Place, London W1H 3AH. m. Jonathan Bigg; 1 s. Finley.

GURNETT, Jane
Jane Gurnett. Actor (F). b. 1959.
TV: Annaliese in *Birds of a Feather;* Rachel in *Casualty;* Dr. Gillian Cramer in *Dangerfield;* Grace in *Day After*

the Fair; Rose in *Days at the Beach*; Annie Ridd in *Lorna Doone*; Bella Frye in *Matilda's England*; Mrs Orton in *Phil and Arthur Go Off*; Chris in *Real Women*; Nesta in *Ruth Rendell – Vanity Dies Hard*; *South of the Border*; Rosalind in *Vote for Them*; Stephanie in *What if it's Raining*; Stephanie in *Widowmaker*.
Films: WPC Sue Ryan in *Closing Ranks*; Nancy/Nelly in *Drowning by Numbers*; Sarah in *Meloncholia*.
Address: c/o Hamilton Asper, 24 Hanway Street, London W1P 9DD.

GURU-MURTHY, Krishnan

Krishnan Guru-Murthy. Reporter/Presenter.
b. Lancashire, 1970.
TV: *Newsround*; *Newsnight*; *BBC World Weekend News*; *BBC News*; *Channel 4 News*.
Address: c/o ITN Press Office, Gray's Inn Road, London WC1X 8XZ.

GUTTERIDGE, Lucy

Lucy Gutteridge. Actor (F).
b. London, 28 November 1956.
TV: Belle in *A Christmas Carol*; *Hitler's SS: Portrait of Evil*; Gloria Morgan in *Little Gloria...Happy at Last*; Linda in *Love in a Cold Climate*; Soroya in *Tales of the Unexpected*; Lorraine Wade in *The Seven Dials Mystery*; *The Woman He Loved*; *Till We Meet Again*.
Films: *Fire In Eden*; *Merlin and the Sword*; *The Greek Tycoon*; *The Hitch Hiker*; *The Trouble With Spies*; *Top Secret*.
Address: Contact via 'Spotlight', 7 Leicester Place, London WC2H 7BP.

GWILYM, Robert

Robert Gwilym. Actor (M).
b. Glamorgan, South Wales.
TV: *Ballroom*; *Casualty*; *Chef II*; *Crocodile Shoes*; *Escape from Sobibor*; *Evil: The Brothers Karamazov*; *Figure of Eight*; *Flying Lady*; *MacGyver*; *Much Ado About Nothing*; *Omnibus: Hildegard*; *Operation Julie*; *Searching*; *Soldier Soldier III*; *South of the Border*; *Taggart*; *The Bill*; *The Devil's Crown*; *The Keep*; *The Paradise Club*; *The Professionals*; *The Zero Option*; *Tiger Bay*; *Unexplained Laughter*.
Films: *Mussolini*; *On The Black Hill*; *Sakharov*.
Address: c/o Joy Jameson Ltd, 2.19 The Plaza, 535 Kings Road, London SW10 0SZ.

H

HACKETT, Claire

Claire Hackett. Actor (F).

TV: Linda in *A Touch of Frost*; WPC Tate in *Between the Lines*; Sandra in *Casualty*; *Cracker*; Dawn in *Dawn and the Candidate*; Tilly in *Gallowglass*; Annie in *Growing Rich*; *Into The Fire*; Madame Homais in *Madame Bovary*; *Medics*; *Terraces*; Lindsay Hewitt in *The Bill*.

Films: *A Nasty Story*; *Dancin' Thru The Dark*; *Man of The Month*; *Women At War*.

Address: c/o Annette Stone Associates, 2nd Floor, 22 Great Marlborough Street, London W1V 1AF.

HALE, Gareth

Gareth Hale. Actor (M)/Comedian.

b. London, 15 January 1953.

TV: *A Pinch of Snuff* (1993); *April Fools Day*; *H&P@BBC*; *Hale and Pace*; *Jobs for the Boys*; *Oddbods* (1998); Ron in *The Management* (1988); *The Scarlet Tunic* (1996).

Address: c/o International Artistes Ltd, Mezzanine Floor, 235 Regent Street, London W1R 8AX.

HALFPENNY, Jill

Jill Halfpenny. Actor (F). b. 15 July 1975.

TV: Rebecca Hopkins in *Coronation Street*; *Birds of a Feather*; *Byker Grove*; *Dangerfield*; *Heartbeat*; *Peak Practice*; *The Bill*; *The Lakes*; *Touching Evil*; *The Round Tower*. Address: c/o Scott Marshall 44 Perryn Road, London, W3 7NA. Hobbies: Shopping, music, singing.

HALL, Cheryl

Cheryl Hall. Actor (F). b. London, 23 July 1950.

TV: *Bramwell*; *Brenda*; *Casualty*; *Citizen Smith*; *Dear Mother*; *Love Albert*; *EastEnders*; *Edna the Inebriate Woman*; *Inspector Morse*; *London's Burning*; *Lucky Feller*; *Man Above Men*; *Oy Vay Maria*; *Silent Witness*; *The Bill*; *The Men's Room*; *Woof*.

Films: *No Sex Please, We're British*; *Safe*; *Seven Deadly Sins*; *The Fourteen*; *Villain*.

Address: c/o Alvarez Management, 86 Muswell Road, London N10 2BE. 2 s. Ben, Josh. Hobbies: Travel.

HALL, Esther

Esther Hall. Actor (F).

TV: Julie Ostrophski in *2020*; Dr Louise Macken in *Always and Everyone*; Lisa Willocks in *Cops*; Maria in *Peak Practice*; Sally in *Playing the Field*; Romey in *Queer as Folk*; Dr Winston in *Where the Heart Is*.

Films: Jan Hall in *Death on Everest*; Mavis in *Land Girls*.

Address: c/o Peters, Fraser and Dunlop, Drury House, 34–43 Russell Street, London WC2B 5HA. Hobbies: Singing, dancing, horse riding, swimming, Tai-Chi.

HALL, Stuart

Stuart Hall. Presenter. b. Hyde, 25 December 1929.

TV: *A Chance to See Again*; *Chefs Sans Frontiers*; *God's Gift*; *Going, Going, Gone*; *It's a Knockout*; *Jeux Sans Frontiers*; *Love Me Do*; *Lucky Numbers*; *North West Tonight*; *Quiz Night*; *Sick as a Parrot*; *Stuart Hall Remembers Flanders*; *Stuart Hall's Christmas in Bosnia*; *Stuart's Hall of Fame*; *The Royal Knockout*; *Travellers Check*; *Virtual World of Sport*.

Address: c/o Jane Hughes Management, The Coach House, PO Box 123, Knutsford, Cheshire WA16 9HX.

HALLAM, John

John Hallam. Actor (M).

b. Lisburn, 28 October 1941.

TV: *Boy Dominic*; *Cadfael*; *Forever Green*; *Haunting Memories*; *Miss Marple*; *Paper Kisses*; *Preston Front*; *The Mallens*; *The Pallisers*; *The Regiment*; *Voyage of the Dawn Treader*; *White Peak Farm*; *Wycliffe*.

Films: *A Walk with Love and Death*; *Anthony and Cleopatra*; *Arabian Nights*; *Flash Gordon*; *Hennessy*; *Kull the Conqueror*; *Last Valley*; *Love and Bullets*; *Marco Polo*; *Murphy's War*; *Nicholas and Alexandra*; *Robin Hood: Prince of Thieves*; *The Offence*; *Under Capricorn*; *Villain*; *When the Whale Comes*; *Zorro*.

Address: c/o Joy Jameson Ltd, 2.19 The Plaza, 535 Kings Road, London SW10 0SZ.

HALLIWELL, Steve

Steve Halliwell. Actor (M).

b. Bury, Lancashire, 19 March 1946.

TV: PC Goole in *All Creatures Great and Small*; Steve in *Brookside*; Clem in *Children of Winter*; Bob in *Coronation Street*; Chief Fire Officer in *Cracker*; PC Mack in *Crown Court*; Zak Dingle in *Emmerdale*; Camping Shop Man in *First and Last*; Buble's Mate in *GBH*; Inspector Newall in *Just Us*; Ringer in *Mannix*; Donovan Dugdale in *Pickersgill People*; Brian Flannery in *The Merrihill Millionaires*; Peter Bishop in *The Practice*; Steve in *Threads*.

Films: Russian Courier in *The Fourth Protocol*.

Address: c/o Pemberton Associates, 53–54 Haymarket, London Sw1Y 4RP. m. Lisa Walsh; 1 d. Charlotte. Hobbies: Jazz, writing, cooking, travel.

HAMILTON, Suzanna

Suzanna Hamilton. Actor (F). b. London, 1960.

TV: *A Masculine Ending; A New Lease of Death;* Sharon in *A Wing and a Prayer; Boon; Casualty; Disraeli; Drovers Gold; Duel of Hearts; Goodbye Days; Hold the Dream; Inspector Morse; Jonathan Creek; McCallum; Murder East, Murder West; Never Come Back; Office Story; Saracen; Small Zones; South Bank Show – Julian Barnes; Strangers; Streetwise; Tecx; The Bill; The Ladies; Victorian Scandals; Wish Me Luck.*

Films: *1984; A Pattern of Roses; A Tale of The Vampire; Birth Of A Nation; Bloody Chamber; Brimstone and Treacle; Devil's Paradise; Goody Two Shoes; Island on Bird Street; Johnny Bull; Maps of Mortal Beauty; Out of Africa; Swallows and Amazons; Tess; The Voice; Wetherby; Wild Cats of St Trinians.*

Address: c/o Emptage Hallett, 24 Poland Street, London W1V 3DD.

HAMPSHIRE, Susan

Susan Hampshire. Actor (F).
b. London, 12 May 1937.

TV: *Andromeda;* Molly in *Monarch of the Glen; Coming Home; Don't Tell Father; Going to Pot; Leaving; My Secret Garden; Nancherrow; The Barchester Chronicles; The First Churchills; The Forsyte Saga; The Grand; The Pallisers; Vanity Fair.*

Films: *David Copperfield; Living Free; Mapertius; Monte Carlo or Bust; Night Must Fall; The Three Lives of Thomasina; Wonderful Life.*

Address: c/o Chatto & Linnit, 123a King's Road, Chelsea, London SW3 4PL. m. 1 Pierre Granier-Deffere (dis); 1 s. Christopher; m. 2 Sir Eddie Kulukundis.

HANCOCK, Martin

Martin Hancock. Actor (M)/Presenter/Host. b. 1973.
TV: *Casualty;* 'Spider' Nugent in *Coronation Street; London's Burning;* Mr Sloppy in *Our Mutual Friend; The Bill; The Milkman; This Life; Wycliffe.*
Address: c/o Crouch Associates, 9-15 Neal Street, London WC2H 9PF.

HANCOCK, Nick

Actor (M)/Presenter/Host.
b. Stoke, 25 October 1962.
TV: *Bostock's Cup; Fantasy Football; Great Railway Journeys – Cuba; Have I Got News For You; Holding the Baby; MAC; The Mary Whitehouse Experience; Mr Bean; Nights; Punt and Dennis; Room 101; Swot or Wot; The Danny Baker Show; The Outsiders; They Think It's All Over; Win, Lose or Draw; You, Me and Him.*
Address: c/o ICM, Oxford House, 76 Oxford Street, London W1N 0AX.

HANCOCK, Sheila

Actor (F). b. Isle of Wight, 22 February 1933.
TV: *An Ape About The House; Bradley; Close Relations; Dangerous Buccaneers; Doctor Who; Entertaining Mr Sloane; Gone to Seed; Gone to the Dogs; Jumping the Queue; Kavanagh QC; My Kingdom for a Horse; Royal Enclosure; Single Voices; The Brighton Belles; The Daughter-in-Law; The Rivals.*
Films: *A Business Affair; Buster; Hawks; Love and Death on Long Island; Making Waves; Night Must Fall; The Clot; The Love Child; The Universe of Dermott Finn; Three Men and a Little Lady.*
Address: c/o ICM, Oxford House, 76 Oxford Street, London W1N 0AX.

HANLY, Peter

Peter Hanly. Actor (M).
TV: Ambrose Egan in *Ballykissangel;* Various in *Commonplaces;* Justin Day in *Radio Waves;* Bosie in *Saint Oscar;* Paul in *The Truth About Claire.*
Films: Prince Edward in *Braveheart;* Ronnie in *Guiltrip;* Barman in *High Spirits.*
Address: c/o Conway Van Gelder, 18-21 Jermyn Street, London SW1Y 6HP.

HANN, Judith

Judith Hann. Presenter.
b. Littleover, Derby, 8 September1942.
TV: *A Taste of Health; Hann at 40; Tomorrow's World; Watchdog Health Check* (1995).
Address: c/o Dave Winslett Associates, 6 Kenwood Ridge, Kenley, Surrey CR8 5JW. m. John Exelby.

HANNAH, John

John Hannah. Actor (M). b. East Kilbride, 1962.
TV: DC Mellis in *Between the Lines;* Johnny in *Bookie;* Willie Connolly in *Boon; Brief Encounter;* Robert in *Brond;* Sturden in *Circle of Deceit;* Don Walker in *Civvies;* Nick in *Faith;* Paul in *Manchester United;* McCallum in *McCallum;* DS Frankie in *Out of the Blue;* Mark in *Paul Calf;* Pretty Boy in *Reasonable Force;*

Danny Bonnar in *Taggart*; Derek Pierce in *The Bill*; Keith in *These Colours Don't Run*; Nick in *Truth or Dare*. **Films:** Leo in *Circus*; *The Final Cut*; Matthew in *Four Weddings and a Funeral*; Neal McBride in *Harbour Beat*; John in *Joan*; Simon in *Kleptophilia*; Terry in *Lazarus and the Hurricane*; Tommy in *Loser's Blues*; *The Love Bug*; Harry in *Madagasgar Skin*; Wordsworth in *Pandemonium*; Darkie Larche in *Resurrection Man*; Tony in *Romance and Rejection*; Jerry in *Sliding Doors*; Spendlove Snr in *The James Gang*; Jonathon in *The Mummy*. Address: William Morris Agency (UK) Ltd, 1 Stratton Street, London W1X 6HB.

HANSEN, Alan

Alan Hansen. Commentator/Analyst.
b. 13 June 1955.
TV: *Match of the Day*; various BBC sports.
Address: c/o Marquee Group (UK) Ltd, 21 The Green, Richmond, Surrey TW9 1PX. Hobbies: Golf, tennis, theatre.

HARDCASTLE, Diana

Diana Hardcastle. Actor (F).
TV: *Boon*; *Bugs*; *East Lynne*; *First Among Equals*; *Frankie and Johnny*; *Love Song*; *Midsomer Murders*; Anna in *Reilly, Ace of Spies*; *Resnick*; *Taggart*; *That's Love* (1988); *The Bill*; *The Fortunes of War*; *The House*; *The Tide Of Life*.
Films: *The House*.
Address: c/o Jonathan Altaras Associates, 13 Short's Gardens, London WC2H 9AT.

HARDIE, Kate

Kate Hardie. Actor (F). b. 1969.
TV: *Travelling Man*; *The Stars of the Roller Skate Disco*; *Casualty*; Rachel in *Thin Air*; Tessa Pascoe in *The Men's Room*; Donna in *A Small Dance*; Ellie in *Under the Sun*; *The Inspector Alleyn Mysteries*; Kaz in *Safe*; *Smokescreen*; *Open Fire*; Susan Christie in *Beyond Reason*.
Films: Rachel in *Runners*; *Number One*; *The Wings of Death*; *Revolution*; Cathy in *Mona Lisa*; Jane Woods in *Cry Freedom*; Carol in *Tree of Hands*; *Conspiracy*; *Melancholia*; Frances in *The Krays*; *Jack and Sarah*; *Sex Crimes – Conform & Deform*; *The Croupier*; *Heart*.
Address: c/o PFD, Drury Houser, 34–43 Russell Street, London WC2B 5HA. m. Rankin Waddell (dis.); 1 s. Lyle; partner David Thewlis; father Bill Oddie.

HARDIMAN, Terrence

Terrence Hardiman. Actor (M).
b. Forest Gate, London, 6 April 1937.
TV: Abbot Radulfus in *Cadfael*; Demon Headmaster in *The Demon Headmaster*; Mr Pooter in *Diary of a*

Nobody; Commander Chiswick in *Prime Suspect III*; Reinhardt in *Secret Army*; *Softly, Softly*; Stuckler in *Wish Me Luck*.
Address: c/o Scott Marshall, 44 Perryn Road, London W3 7NA. m. Rowena Cooper; 1 s. Laurence, 1 d. Eleanor.

HARDY, Jeremy

Jeremy Hardy. Comedian.
TV: *4th Dimension*; Gaoler in *Blackadder*; *Brain Drain*; *Caroline's Comedy World*; *Edinburgh Nights*; Tory Candidate for Toxteth in *Election Confidential*; *Friday Live*; Henry the Alien in *Helping Henry*; *Hysteria*; *If I Ruled the World*; *Jack and Jeremy's Police 4*; *Jack and Jeremy's Real Lives*; *Just a Minute*; *Just For Laughs*; *Last Resort*; *Live from London*; *Loose Talk*; *Monday Night Clive*; Boom Operator in *Now Something Else*; *Paramount City*; *Pillow Talk*; *Rear Windows*; *Right to Reply*; *Saturday Live*; *Scruples*; *The South Bank Show*; *The 39,000 Steps*; *The English Revolution*; *Tonight with Jonathan Ross*; *Up the Junction*; *Wogan*.
Address: c/o Noel Gay Artists, 19 Denmark Street, London WC2H 8NA.

HARDY, Robert

Timothy Sydney Robert Hardy. Actor (M).
b. 29 October 1925.
TV: Siegfried Farnon in *All Creatures Great and Small*; *An Age of Kings*; *Blat*; *Bramwell*; *Bulman – Death by Misadventure*; *Caesar and Clarett*; *Castle Ghosts of England*; *Castle Ghosts of Wales*; *Coriolanus*; *Daniel Deronda*; *David Copperfield*; *Death of the Heart*; *Edward VIII*; *Elizabeth R*; *Fothergill*; *Gulliver's Travels*; *Horses in our Blood*; *Hot Metal*; *Inspector Morse*; *Jenny's War*; *Make or Break*; *Manhunt*; *Middlemarch*; *Midsomer Murders*; *Nancherrow*; *Northanger Abbey*; *Sherlock Holmes – The Master Blackmailer*; *Speed King*; *The Demon Lover*; *The Far Pavilions*; *The Picardy Affair*; *The Tenth Kingdom*; *The Troubleshooters*; *Twelfth Night*; *War and Remembrance*; *Winston Churchill*.
Films: *A Feast at Midnight*; *An Ideal Husband*; *Dark Places*; *How I Won the War*; *La Gifle*; *Le Silencieux*; *Mary Shelley's Frankenstein*; *Mrs Dalloway*; *My Life So Far*; *Paris by Night*; *Robin Hood*; *Sense and Sensibility*; *Sir Gawaine and The Green Knight*; *Ten Rillington Place*, *The Barber of Siberia*; *The Shooting Party*; *The Spy Who Came in from the Cold*; *The Titchborne Claimant*; *The Wilderness Years*; *Yellow Dog*; *The Young Winston*.
Address: c/o Chatto & Linnit, 123a Kings Road, London SW3 4PL. Hobbies: Archery; horses; birds.

HAREWOOD, David

David Harewood. Actor (M).

TV: Daniel in *Agony Too*; Michael Gregory in *Always and Everyone*; Stevie in *Anna Lee*; Bishop in *Ballykissangel*; Trevor Watkins in *Bermuda Grace*; Trevor in *Black Poppies*; Jonathan in *Brothers and Sisters*; Police Sergeant in *Cold Feet*; David West in *For the Greater Good*; Paul Johnson in *Game On*; Stuart in *Great Moments in Aviation*; Terry in *Harnessing Peacocks*; Trevor in *Hearts and Minds*; David Adams in *Kavanagh QC*; MacDuff in *Macbeth on the Estate*; Jonathan in *Murder Most Horrid*; Errol in *South of the Border*; Robbie Coker in *The Bill*; Jammy B in *The Harry Enfield Show*; DS Joe Robinson in *The Vice*; DCI Peterson in *An Unsuitable Job for a Woman*.

Films: Sergeant Street in *Hawk*; Moses in *I Wonder Who's Kissing Her Now*; Jessop in *Mad Dogs and Englishmen*.

Address: c/o Marmont Management Ltd, Langham House, 308 Regent Street, London W1R 5AL.

HARGREAVES, David

David Hargreaves. Actor (M)/Presenter. b. 1940.

TV: Tom Houghton in *1914 All Out*; Derek Owen in *Albion Market*; *All Creatures Great and small* (1989); O'Reilly in *Beck* (1996); Dad in *Bloomin' Marvellous* (1997); Anthony Fairchild in *Bugs* (1997); Donald Saunders and Dennis Martin in *Casualty* (1997); Dennis Martin in *Casualty* (1994); Mr Wix in *Earthfasts* (1993); DS David Doxey in *Expert Witness* (1995); *Forever Young*; Charles Powell in *Hard Cases* (1988); *Harry* (1993); Pendleton in *Heartbeat* (1992); Don Lomax in *Heartbeat* (1999); Picture Editor in *Hetty Wainthropp Investigates* (1995); Supt. Harper in *Inspector Alleyn* (1992); *Juliet Bravo*; Dr Philip Dale in *Justice for Gemma* (1993); Wayne in *Kingdom Come* (1990); *Madly in Love* (1989); *Making Out* (1988); *No Further Cause for Concern*; Rev. Neil Winters in *Peak Practice* (1993); Charlie Fields in *Peak Practice* (1998); Charlie Reeves in *Pie in the Sky* (1996); *Poirot* (1989); Mr Feast in *Ruth Rendell Mysteries* (1993); *Science Workshop*; *Shades of Darkness*; *She's Been Away* (1989); *Shine on Harvey Moon*; John Taylor in *Some Kind of Life* (1995); Alan Robinson in *The Bill* (1996); Jack Brigson in *The Bill* (1994); Alan Slater in *The Bill* (1993); Paul Harvey in *The Bill* (1997); Blue Man in *The Conversion of St Paul* (1990); Lou Clark in *The Mendip Mystery* (1992); Arthur Scargill in *The Miner's Strike* (1989); Dave in *The Passion* (1998); *The Seagreen Man* (1984); Alonso in *The Tempest* (1992); *Truckers* (1987).

Address: c/o The Richard Stone Partnership, 2 Henrietta Street, London WC2E 8PS.

HARGREAVES, Johanna

Johanna Hargreaves. Actor (F). b. 18 June 1963.

TV: *Behind The Screen*; June Marks in *Bergerac*; Linda Jordan in *Between the Lines*; Gale in *Casualty*; Debbie in *Casualty*; Liz Phillips in *Crimewatch – Dreams of Gold*; Sylvie in *Date Rape*; Karen in *Dramarama*; Cindy in *Filthy Rich and Catflap*; Michelle in *Hard Cases*; lead role in *Johnny Jarvis*; *Late Starter*; Sarah in *Let There be Love*; Phyllis Slater in *No Bananas*; Sharon in *Radio Phoenix*; Teacher in *Red Dwarf*; Anna in *S.W.A.L.K.*; *Saturday Action*; *Shine on Harvey Moon*; Angie in *Stay Lucky*; Sandra Blair in *Take the High Road*; Cherry in *Tenko*; Maggie Fisher in *The Bill*; Mrs Higgins in *The Bill*; Julie Watson in *The Bill*; Hattie in *The Glory Boys*; Jane in *The Lenny Henry Show*; Henrietta in *The Little Princess*; *The Quiet Days of Mrs Stafford*; Sandra in *Two People*.

Films: Young Maid in *A Hazard of Hearts*.

Address: c/o George Heathcote Management, 58 Northdown Street, London N1 9BS.

HARKER, Caroline

Caroline Harker. Actor (F). b. 1966.

TV: *A Dance to the Music of Time*; Hazel in *A Touch of Frost*; *Casualty*; *Chancer*; *Covington Cross*; *Growing Rich*; *Harry Enfield and Chums*; Vicky in *Holding On*; Way in *Honey for Tea*; Rowena Featherstonehaugh in *Kavanagh QC*; *Keeping Mum*; Celia in *Middlemarch*; *Moll Flanders*; *Riders*.

Films: *A Woman of the North*; Mrs Fitzherbert in *The Madness Of King George*; Francesca in *War Zone*.

Address: c/o PFD, Drury House, 34–43 Russell Street, London WC2B 5HA. Sister Susannah Harker.

HARKER, Susannah

Susannah Harker. Actor (F).

b. London, 26 April 1965.

TV: Dinah Morris in *Adam Bede*; *Chancer*; *Faith*; Mattie Storin in *House of Cards*; Jane Bennett in *Pride and Prejudice*; *Sherlock Holmes*; Linda in *The Fear*; *The Lady's Not for Burning*; Angela in *Troubles*; *Ultra-Violet*.

Films: Will's Sister in *Burke and Wills*; *A Dry White Season*; *Surviving Picasso*; *White Mischief*.

Address: c/o PFD, Drury House, 34-43 Russell Street, London WC2B 5HA. m. Iain Glen; 1 s. Finlay; sister Caroline.

HARKISHIN, Jimmi

Jimmi Harkishin. Actor (M).

TV: Krishna in *A Killing on the Exchange*; Greg Pratkash in *Casualty*; Ravil in *Close Relations*; Dev in *Coronation Street*; *Crime Story – Gone Too Far*; *Desmond's*; *Eurocops*; *Harry*; Amir Ali in *Heat of the Sun*; Doctor in *Holding* *the Baby*; Gary Lobo in *Jonathan Creek*; Richard Meeran in *Justice for Gemma*; Jay in *Medics*; *Paparazzo*; *Saracen*; Rashid in *Shalom Salaam*; *Solitaire-M*; Krish in *South of the Border*; *Tecx*; *The Bill*; Jose Querro in *Uncle Jack*; *Uncle Jack and the Dark Side of the Moon*.

Films: Ranjit in *Bhaji on the Beach*; Iydaz ali Khan in *East is East*; Sadi in *For Queen and Country*.

Address: Marina Martin Associates, 12–13 Poland Street, London W1V 3DE. Hobbies: Guitar, cricket, parachuting.

HARLEY, Robert

Robert Harley. Actor (M).

TV: *Agony Again* (1995); Estate Agent in *Birds of a Feather* (1996); *Bob Hartley Bostock's Cup* (1999); Sally Smedley lookalike in *Drop the Dead Donkey* (1998); *Fast Forward*; Psychiatrist in *Gayle's World*; *Harry Enfield's Television Programme*; Captain Hook in *I Hate This House* (1995); *Jerry Sadowitz*; *Maxwell's House*; *Murder Most Horrid* (1998); *Noel's House Party*; *Paramount City*; *Paul Merton – The Series*; *Punt and Dennis*; *Rory Bremner, Who Else?* (1996); *Russ Abbott Show* (1995); Max in *The Creatives* (1998); Director in *The Creatives* (1996); *The Morwenna Banks Show* (1997); *The Perverters*; *The Satellite Show*; Cottam in *Underworld* (1997); *Up Yer News*; *What's All This Then?* Address: c/o The Richard Stone Partnership, 2 Henrietta Street, London WC2E 8PS.

HARNETT, Ricci

Ricci Harnett. Actor (M). b. London.

TV: Gary Ashe in *A Certain Justice*; *Roger, Roger*; *Starting Out*.

Address: c/o Dennis Lyne Agency, 108 Leonard Street London EC2A 4RH.

HARPER, Kate

Kate Harper. Actor (F).

TV: Kathy Kane in *Wavelengths*; Iona Datch in *Space Precinct*; Mrs Leroy in *Frank Stubbs Presents*; *Inspector Morse*; *Capital City*; *Poirot*; *She Wolf of London*; *The Upper Hand*; *Spatz*; *Perfect Scoundrels*; Paula Wilson in *Pulaska*; *Hedgehog Weddings*; Felicity Grenville in *The Two Mrs Grenvilles*; *Bergerac*; *Hold the Dream*; *Master of the Game*; *Lace*; *Have a Nice Death*; *Shades of Darkness*; *Tales of the Unexpected – the Mugger*; *Bright Eye*; *Diamonds*; *Dylan*; *Oppenheimer*.

Films: *Stiff Upper Lips*; *Surviving Picasso*; *Passion of Darkly Noon*; *Night Watch*; *Dinosaurs*; *Batman*; *Murder Story*; *Invitation to the Wedding*; *Reds*; *Little Lord Fauntleroy*.

Address: c/o Burdett-Coutts Associates, Riverside Studios, Crisp Road, London W6 9RL.

HARRELSON, Woody

Woodrow Tracy Harrelson. Actor (M).

b. Midland, Texas, USA, 23 August 1961.

TV: Slater in *Bay Coven* (1987); Woodrow Tiberius 'Woody' Boyd in *Cheers* (1993); Henry in *Ellen* (1998); Woody Boyd in *Frasier* (1999); Charlie Long in *Killer Instinct* (1988); Tommy Dugan in *Spin City*; Woody Boyd in *The Simpsons* (1994).

Films: Himself in *Austin Powers: The Spy Who Shagged Me*; Dustin in *Cool Blue*; Hank Gordon in *Doc Hollywood*; Ray Pekurny in *Ed TV*; *Grass*; Big Boy Matson in *Hi-Lo Country*; Ground Zero Hero in *I'll Do Anything*; David Murphy in *Indecent Proposal*; Roy Munson in *Kingpin*; Harris's Boss in *L.A. Story*; Charlie in *Money Train*; Micky Knox in *Natural Born Killers*; Harry Barber in *Palmetto*; *Play it to the Bone*; cameo at end in *She's Having A Baby*; Homeless Vietnam veteran in *Ted and Venus*; Pepper in *The Cowboy Way*; Larry Flynt in *The People vs. Larry Flynt*; Dr Michael Reynolds in *The Sunchaser*; Sgt. Keck in *The Thin Red Line*; Sgt. William Schumann in *Wag the Dog*; Flynn in *Welcome to Sarajevo*; Billy Hoyle in *White Men Can't Jump*; Krushinski in *Wildcats*.

Address: c/o Creative Artists Agency, 9803 Wilshire Boulevard, Beverly Hills, California 90212, USA. m. Laura Louie; 2 d. Deni Montana, Zoe. Hobbies: Yoga, environmental and animal welfare.

HARRIES, Davyd

Davyd Harries. Actor (M).

b. Porthcawl, 31 January 1937.

TV: *Accident*; Derek Gravett in *Accused*; *Angels*; *Anna Karenina*; *Anna Lee*; *Arthur of the Britons*; *Bergerac*; Mr Bowles in *Berkeley Square*; Morris in *Beyond Fear*; *Broke*; *Bugs*; *Cadfael*; Frank Leyland in *Casualty*; Nigel Hughes in *City Central*; *Coming and Going*; *Cousin Bette*; Angus Pelman in *Dalziel and Pascoe*; *Dombey and Son*; DI Spalding in *Emmerdale*; *Ennal's Point*; *Fatal Spring*; *Goodbye Mr Chips*; *Guardians*; *Hair Soup*; *Hannay*; *Hunter's Walk*; *Imaginary Friends*; *In Loving Memory*; *John Brown's Body*; Marric in *Merlin*; *Oliver Twist*; *On Young Shoulders*; Mr Redding in *Out of Sight*; *Owen MD*; *The Racing Game*; *Rough Justice*; *S.W.A.L.K.*; *Secret Army*; *Secret Friends*; *Strife*; *Suez*; *Swish of the Curtain*; *Telford's Change*; *The Bill*; Sam Lester in *The Chief*; *The Citadel*; *The Dark Secret*; *The Dumb Waiter*; *The Knock*; *The Story of Philip Knight*; *The White House Farm Murders*; *Travelling Man*; *You, Me and It*.

Films: *Anno Domini*; *Beautiful Thing*; *Over Lord*; Colonel Hammond in *Sawdust Tales*; PC Atilla Rees in *Under Milk Wood*.

Address: c/o CDA, 19 Sydney Mews, London SW3 6HL.

HARRIOTT, Ainsley

Ainsley Harriott. Presenter/Chef.
b. London, 28 February 1957.
TV: *The Hidden Camera Show; The Big Cook Out; Meals in Minutes; Ainsley's Barbecue Bible; Party of a Lifetime; Celebrity Ready Steady Cook; Can't Cook, Won't Cook; Good Morning with Anne and Nick; The National Lottery Live; The Ainsley Harriott Show.*
Address: c/o Jeremy Hicks Associates, 12 Ogle Street, London W1P 7LG. m. Clare; 1 s. Jimmy; 1 d. Madeleine. Hobbies: Tennis, walking the dog, Arsenal FC supporter.

HARRIS, Jared

Jared Harris. Actor (M).
TV: John Lennon in *Two of Us*.
Films: *B Monkey; Blue in the Face; Bullfighter; Father's Day; Happiness; Hush; I Shot Andy Warhol; Last of the Mohicans; Lost in Space; Nadia; Natural Born Killers; Shadow Magic; Smoke; Sunday; Tall Tale; The Eternal; The Public Eye; The Rachel Papers; The Weekend.*
Address: c/o William Morris Agency (UK) Ltd, 1 Stratton Street, London W1X 6HB.

HARRIS, Richard

Richard Harris. Actor (M).
b. Limerick, Ireland, 1 October 1933.
TV: *The Snow Goose; Camelot; Maigret: The Return; Ricardo; The Great Kandinsky; The Hunchback of Notre Dame; The Iron Harp.*
Films: *A Man Called Horse; A Terrible Beauty; Alive and Kicking; Camelot; Caprice; Cromwell; Cry, the Beloved Country; Echoes of a Summer; Game for Vultures; Golden Rendezvous; Gulliver's Travels; Guns of Navarone; Hawaii; High Point; Juggernaut; Mack the Knife; Major Dundee; Man in the Wilderness; Martin's Day; Mutiny On The Bounty; Orca; Patriot Games; Return of A Man Called Horse; Robin and Marian; Savage Hearts; Shake Hands with the Devil; Silent Tongue; Smilla's Sense of Snow; Tarzan The Ape Man; The Barber of Siberia; The Bible; The Deadly Trackers; The Field; The Hero (aka Bloomfield); The Heroes of Telmark; The Last Word; The Long, the Short and the Tall; The Molly Maguires; The Ravagers; The Red Desert; The Wild Geese; This is the Sea; This Sporting Life; To Walk With Lions; Triumphs of a Man Called Horse; Trojan Eddie; Unforgiven; Wrestling Ernest Hemingway; Your Ticket is No Longer Valid.*
Address: c/o William Morris Agency (UK) Ltd, 1 Stratton Street, London W1X 6HB.

HARRIS, Rolf

Rolf Harris. Presenter/Singer.
b. Perth, Australia, 30 March 1930.
TV: *Animal Hospital; Animal Hospital Down Under; Animal Hospital Goes West; Animal Hospital on the Hoof; Bligh of the Bounty World Navigator; Cartoon Time; Cat Crazy; Coojeebear; Rolf; Rolf on Saturday, OK?; Rolf's Amazing World of Animals; Rolf's Canadian Walkabout; Rolf's Cartoon Club; Rolf's Indian Walkabout; Rolf's Walkabout; The Rolf Harris Show.*
Music: *Bohemian Rhapsody; Bootleg 1; Can You Tell Me What it is Yet?; Digereely Doo All That; Ego Sum Pauper; Jake the Peg; Rolf Rules OK; Stairway to Heaven; Sun Arise; Tie Me Kangaroo Down Sport; Two Little Boys.*
Address: c/o Lake-Smith Griffin Associates, 15 Maiden Lane, London WC2E 7NA.

HARRIS, Russell

Russell Harris. Presenter.
b. Harrogate, 22 November 1957.
TV: *Makalu – The West Face; Room For Improvement; The Arts and Antiques Show; The Beautiful Home Show; The Diceman; The DIY Show; The Great Outdoors; These Four Walls; Time Off; Venture Forth; Wet and Wild.*
Address: David Anthony Promotions, PO Box 286, Warrington, Cheshire WA2 6GA. m. Janette; 1 d. Sophie; 1 s. James. Hobbies: Cookery, motorcycles, guitar, climbing, water-skiing.

HARRISON, Carol

Carol Harrison. Actor (F). b. 1956.
TV: *A Sort of Innocence;* Susie Stansfield in *A Touch of Frost; Bergerac; Black Silk; Broke;* Gloria in *Brushstrokes;* Susan Newman in *Casualty; Danton's Death;* Louise Raymond in *EastEnders;* Loretta in *Get Back; Jessie's Place;* Susan Hutton in *Kavanagh QC; Leaving Home;* Dorothy in *London's Burning;* Michelle in *Metropolis;* Lenny Lemming in *No Sweat; Now and Then; Perfect Scoundrels; Reservations;* Veronica in *Respect;* Lou Pennell in *The Bill; The Chief; The Secret; To Have and To Hold.*
Films: Moff's Mother in *Human Traffic;* Val in *Prince of Denmark Hill; Quadrophenia; Tank Malling; The Elephant Man.*
Address: c/o Associated International Management, 5 Denmark Street, London WC2H 8LP.

HARRY, Jackee

Jackee Harry. Actor (F). b. Winston Salem, North Carolina, USA, 14 August 1956.
TV: *Amen* (1987); Lily Mason in *Another World* (1983); Edna Savage in *Crash Course* (1988); Vanessa Chamberlain in *Designing Women* (1996); Herself in *Dolly* (1987); *Double Your Pleasure* (1989); Lisa Landry in *Sister Sister* (1994); Ruth in *The Royal Family* (1991); Etta Mae in *The Women of Brewster Place* (1989); Ms Blake in *Unhappily Ever After* (1996).

Films: Julie Benson in *Ladybugs;* Charmayne in *Living and Working in Space: The Countdown has Begun; Moscow on the Hudson; The Cotton Club.*
Address: c/o Metropolitan Agency, 4526 Wilshire Boulevard, Los Angeles, California 90010, USA.

HART, Christa

Christa Hart. Presenter/Reporter.
TV: *Afternoon Live* (1997); *All the Right Moves* (1998); *Animal Hospital* (1999); *Animal SOS* (1998); *The Big Breakfast* (1995); *Eddie Mirzeoff* (1995); *Inside Story* (1996); *Remote Control Cooking* (1997); *Schofield's Animal Tales* (1999); *The Word* (1995); *This Morning* (1999).
Address: c/o Arlington Enterprises Ltd, 1–3 Charlotte Street, London W1P 1HD.

HART, Melissa

Melissa Hart. Actor (F).
b. New York, USA, 18 April 1976.
TV: Sabrina Spellman in *Boy Meets World* (1997); Clarissa in *Clarissa Explains It All* (1991); *Kane and Abel* (1985); Sabrina in *Sabrina Down Under* (1999); Sabrina in *Sabrina Goes To Rome* (1999); Sabrina in *Sabrina: The Teenage Witch* (1996); *Silencing Mary* (1998); Sabrina Spellman in *You Wish* (1997).
Films: *Can't Hardly Wait; Drive Me Crazy; Next to You; The Specials.*
Address: c/o William Morris Agency, 1325 Avenue of the Americas, New York, New York 10019, USA. Mother Paula Hart; stepfather Leslie Gilliams. Hobbies: Kickboxing.

HARTMAN, Billy

Billy Hartman. Actor (M).
TV: *99-1; A Touch of Frost; Civvies;* Terry Woods in *Emmerdale; Head over Heels; Heartbeat; In Suspicious Circumstances; Shadow on the Earth; Taggart; Trainer; Vote for Them.*
Films: *April Fool's Day; Doody's Dream; Highlander.*
Address: c/o Barry Brown & Partner, 47 West Square, London SE11 4SP.

HARVEY, Jan

Jan Harvey. Actor (F). b. 1 June 1947
TV: *A Different Drummer; A Family Affair;* Yvonne Newbiggin in *A Touch of Frost;* Queen Witch in *Belfry Witches; Bill Brand;* Jan in *Bugs* (3 and 4); Claire in *Casualty;* Queen Edith in *Churchill's People;* Nicola Gresham in *Dangerfield;* Princess Daisy of Pless in *Edward VIII;* Susan Harvey in *Fell Tiger; Five to Eleven;* Julia in *Holding On;* Jan Howard in *Howard's Way* (Series 1 to 7); Friday Rees in *Inspector Morse; Life and Death of Penelope;* Mary Russell in *Lovejoy;* Barbara Vacant in *Norman Ormal;* Isobel Bailey in *Perfect World; Sam; Second Chance; A Song For Europe; Space 1999; The Forgotten Voyage; The Old Men at the Zoo;* Jane Ratcliffe in *The Round Tower; The Sweeney; Van Der Valk;* Mrs Marsh in *Woof!*
Address: c/o Brunskill Management, Suite 8a, 169 Queen's Gate, London SW7 5HE.

HARVEY, Terence

Terence Harvey. Actor (M).
TV: *A Woman of Style;* Benson in *An Independent Man; And the Beat Goes On; Angels; Bergerac;* Vaughan in *Bodyguards; Boon; Call Me Mister;* Phil Hegarty in *Casualty;* Ch. Insp. George Bernard in *City Central; Class Act; Crown Prosecutor;* Adrian Harding in *EastEnders; El C.I.D.; Families;* Charles Peak in *Grafters;* General Ramsay in *Invasion Earth; Jumping the Queue;* Jock Armstrong in *Kavanagh QC; Making News; Medics;* Presenter in *Melissa; Milner; Miracles Take Longer;* Newsreader in *Mr White Goes To Westminster; Number 10; On The Line; Poirot; Prime Suspect III; Rough Justice; Sam Saturday; Saracens; Spyship;* Bush in *The Ambassador;* Voss in *The Bill;* Gerry in *The Biz;* Supt. Miller in *The Broker's Man; The Chief; The Clarion Van; The Detectives;* Mr Bowyer-Kemp in *The Fragile Heart; The Good Guys; The Life and Loves of a She Devil; The Marksman; The Paper Man; Truckers; Widows.*
Films: *Across the Lake; Big Surprise; The Man Who Knew Too Little.*
Address: c/o CDA, 19 Sydney Mews, London SW3 6HL.

HASSELHOFF, David

David Hasselhoff. Actor (M).
b. Baltimore, Maryland, USA, 17 July 1952.
TV: *AKA Picasso* (2000); Duncan in *Avalanche* (1994); Mitch Buchannon in *Baywatch, Baywatch Nights,* and *Baywatch: Forbidden Paradise;* Don Gregory in *Bridge Across Time* (1995); Jake Gorsky in *Gridlock* (1996); Michael Knight in *Knight Rider* (1982); Michael Knight in *Knight Rider 2000* (1991); Nick Fury in *Nick Fury: Agent of S.H.I.E.L.D.* (1998); *Perry Mason: The Case of 'The Lady in The Lake'* (1988); Scott in *Pleasure Cove* (1979); John Smith D'Artagnan in *Ring of The Musketeers;* Shake Tiller in *Semi-Tough* (1980); Mungo in *Shake Zulu: The Citadel* (2000); Simon in *Starcrash* (1979); Curt Taylor in *The Cartier Affair* (1984); Snapper Foster in *The Young and The Restless* (1982); White Bread in *WB Blue and the Bean* (1989).
Address: c/o Creative Artists Agency, 9830 Wilshire Boulevard, Beverly Hills, California 90212, USA.

m. Pamela Bach; 2 d. Taylor, Hayley. Hobbies: Charity work, musician (vocalist).

HAUGHEY, Michael

Michael Haughey. Actor (M). b. Cumbria.
TV: Dr Alan Moore in *Kavanagh QC*; Frank Barrington in *Peak Practice*; Doctor in *Ruth Rendell Mysteries*; Fisher in *Silent Witness*; Passmore in *The Bill*; Chief Superintendent in *The Chief*; Gentleman Farmer in *The Man Who Cried*.
Films: 1st Servant in *Jacob*; Military Judge in *Prisoner of Honour*.
Address: c/o Roberta Kanal, 82 Constance Road, Twickenham, Middlesex TW2 7JA.

HAVERS, Nigel

Nigel Havers. Actor (M).
b. London, 6 November 1949.
TV: *A Horseman Riding By*; *A Perfect Hero*; *A Question of Guilt*; *A Raging Calm*; *An Englishman's Castle*; *Aspects of Love*; *Bon Voyage*; *Bridge of Time*; *Burning Season*; *Chiller*; *Churchill and the Wilderness Years*; *Coming Out*; Dr Jonathan Paige in *Dangerfield*; *Destiny*; *Don't Wait Up*; *Edward VIII*; *Element of Doubt*; *French Without Tears*; *Goodbye Darling*; *Hold The Dream*; *Leave*; *Lord Elgin and Some Stones of No Importance*; *Murder Most Horrid*; *Nancy Astor*; *Nicholas Nickleby*; *Pennies from Heaven*; *Red Eagle*; *Shabby Tiger*; *Sleepers*; *Soft Target*; *Strangers and Brothers*; *Tales of the Unexpected*; Taylor in *The Charmer*; *The Glass Virgin*; *The Glittering Prizes*; *The Good Guys*; *The Heart Surgeon*; *The Little Princess*; *The White Guard*; *Unity*; *Upstairs Downstairs*; *Woof VII*.
Films: *A Passage to India*; *Burke and Wills*; *Chariots of Fire*; *Empire of the Sun*; *Farewell to the King*; *Naked Under Capricorn*; *Quiet Days In Lucinda Smith*; *The Whistle Blower*.
Address: c/o ICM, Oxford House, 76 Oxford Street, London W1N 0AX. Father: Lord Havers.

HAWKINS, Carol

Carol Hawkins. Actor (F).
b. Barnet, Middlesex, 31 January 1949.
TV: *About Face* (1989); *All at Number 20* (1987); Mrs Sleepwalker in *All Night Long* (1994); Madge in *El C.I.D.* (1989); Sharon in *The Fenn Street Gang*; Make-up girl in *Gayle's World* (1995); *God's Chosen Car Park* (1986); *Hale and Pace* (1996); *Happy Families* (1985); Mrs Matthew in *Hollyoaks*; Doreen in *Leaves on the Line* (1992); *My Husband and I*; Sharon in *Please, Sir!*; Zoe Ripper in *Prince Among Men* (1997); *Relative Strangers* (1986); Charmaine in *Rides* (1992); Ida in *See How they Run*; *The Bill*; Jane

in *The Little Alan Show* (1994); *Together* (1981); Monica Fuller in *Trial and Retribution* (1998).
Films: *Carry On Abroad*; *Carry On Behind*; *Not Now Comrade*; *Please, Sir!*
Address: c/o McIntosh Rae Management, Thornton House, Thornton Road, London SW19 4NG.

HAWTHORNE, Nigel

Nigel Hawthorne. Actor (M).
b. Coventry, West Midlands, 5 April 1929.
TV: *Marie Curie*; *Holocaust*; *Destiny*; *The Knowledge*; *Jessie*; *The Schoolmistress*; *Rod of Iron*; *The Sailor's Return*; *A Tale of Two Cities*; *The Tempest*, Sir Humphrey Appleby in *Yes, Minister* and *Yes, Prime Minister*; *Mapp and Lucia*; *Edward and Mrs Simpson*; *Barchester Chronicles*; *The Fragile Heart*.
Films: *Demolition Man*; *The Clandestine Marriage*; King George III in *The Madness Of King George*; *The Object of My Affection*; *The Winslow Boy*.
Address: c/o Ken McReddie Ltd, 91 Regent Street, London W1R 7TB.

HAYCOCKS, Paddy

Paddy Haycocks. Presenter.
b. Portsmouth, Hampshire, 9 April 1950.
TV: *As it Happens*; *Channel One*; *Give a Pet a Home*; *How Do They Do That?*; *On the Hoof*; *Open House with Gloria Hunniford*; *Six O'Clock Show*; *South Today*; *Southern Eye*; *Streetwise*; *Sunday Best*; *The Travel Show*; *This Way Out*; *Travel Destinations*; *Whoops, Apocalypse!*; *Mum's the Word*; *The South Bank Show Awards*; *The Good Life Guide*; *Weekend World*; *South of Watford*; *Danny Baker On...*
Address: c/o Downes Presenters Agency, 96 Broadway, Bexleyheath, Kent DA6 7DE. Hobbies: Theatre.

HAYDEN, Linda

Linda Hayden. Actor (F).
b. Stanmore, Middlesex, 19 January 1953.
TV: *Cuffy*; *Dick Emery Series*; *Hart to Hart*; *Just Good Friends*; *Minder on the Orient Express*; *Robin's Nest*; *Shillingbury Tales*; *The Bill*; *The Upper Hand*; *Village Hall*.
Films: *Baby Love*; *Blood on Satan's Claw*; *Boys From Brazil*; *Confessions of a Window Cleaner*; *Something to Hide*; *Taste the Blood of Dracula*; *Vampira*.
Address: c/o Silvester Management, 122 Wardour Stree, London W1V 3LA.

HAYES, Melvyn

Melvyn Hayes. Actor (M).
b. London, 11 January 1935.
TV: *Beyond Belief*; *Billy Bunter*; *Black Beauty*; *Bob*

Monkhouse; Cannon and Ball; Cilla Black; Cosmo and Thingy; Dixon of Dock Green; Entertainment Express; Father, Dear Father; Gayle Tuesday; Gunner Beaumont in *It Ain't Half Hot, Mum; Jim Davidson; Jo's Boys; No Friendly Star; No Man's Land; Oliver Twist; Our Mutual Friend; Potter's Picture Palace; Probation Officer; Rex Milligan; Rome Sweet Home; Roy Kinnear; Shadow Squad; Shooting Stars; Sir Yellow; Sky Star Search; Skyport; Song of the March Hare; Spring and Port Wine; Stanley and Livingstone; State of the Union; Taxi; Tearaway; The Bughouse; The Chase; The Cheaters; The Common Man; The Dark is Light Enough; The Double Deckers; The Happening; The Human Jungle; The Krankies; The Lady from Maxims; The Magic Idol; The Ruffians; The Running Tide; The Seven Faces of Jim; The Silver Sword; The Snare of the Fowler; The Sunday Break; The Telescope; The Thin Blue Line; The Unloved; The Wharf Road Mob.*

Films: *A Walk with Love and Death; Adventure in the Hopfields; Bachelor of Arts; Bottoms Up; Carry On England; Crooks in Cloisters; Face the Music; Fun at St Fanny's; Go For a Take; King of the Wind; Love Thy Neighbour; Man About the House; No Trees in the Street; Operation Amsterdam; Santa Claus the Movie; Stars in Your Eyes; Summer Holiday; Tarzan; Blue Peter; The Case of Soho Red; The Curse of Frankenstein; The Flesh and The Fiends; The Good Companions; The Magnificent Seven Deadly Sins; The Magnificent Six and a Half; The Man Who Loved Redheads; The Rainbow Jacket; The Silent Invasion; The Young Ones; The Zany Adventures of Robin Hood; Violent Playground; What's Up Superdoc; Woman in a Dressing Gown.*

Address: c/o Peter Charlesworth & Associates, 68 Old Brompton Road, London SW7 3LQ.

HAYES, Siobhan

Siobhan Hayes. Actor (F).

TV: *Starting Out; Cry Wolf; Birds of a Feather; Bramwell; Dear Dilemma; Park Life; Two Golden Balls; The Bill; Ex; EastEnders; Sharp End; Up the Garden Path; Walrus;* Paula in *Hyper Space Hotel; Middle English: What Adults Say; Middle English: Mr Magus is Waiting; The McGuffin; You and Me; Blue Money; Chinese Detective; Words and Pictures.*

Films: *Omar; MoorCheeba; Cresta Run; Flesh and Blood; A Taste for Healthy Living.*

Address: c/o Anna Scher Theatre Management Ltd, 70–72 Barnsbury Road, London N1 0ES.

HAYGARTH, Tony

Tony Haygarth. Actor (M). 4 February 1945.

TV: *3,7,11; A Touch of Frost; A Tree of Hands; All Change; All Quiet on the Preston Front; Bergerac;*

Between the Lines; Blind Justice; Bramwell; Casualty; Chillers; Devices and Desires; Don Quixote; Duck Patrol; El C.I.D.; Farrington of the F.O.; Finest Family in the Land; Fry and Laurie; Growing Rich; Hardwicke House; Heroes and Villains; Holocaust; I, Claudius; In Hitler's Shadow; Inspector Morse; Kavanagh QC; London Kills Me; Love's Labour Lost; Lovejoy; Making Out; Message For Posterity; Our Friends in the North; Our Geoff; Parnell and the Englishwoman; Perfect Scoundrels; Pie in the Sky; Rosie; Round and Round; Sharpe; Sharpe's Enemy; Shoestring; Space Precinct; The Bill; The Borgias; The Borrowers; The December Rose; The Growing Pains of Adrian Mole; The Insurance Man; The Irons of Wrath; The Things We Do For Love; The Trial; The Wanderer; The Warrior Queen; Travelling Man; Two Gentleman of Verona; Where the Heart Is; Wrinkley.

Films: *A Month In The Country; A Private Function; Chicken Run; Clockwise; Dark River; Dick Turpin; McVicar; Prince of Jutland; Prospects; Scoop; SOS Titanic; Swept From The Sea; The Dressmaker; The Human Factor; The Woodlanders.*

Address: c/o Conway Van Gelder, 18–21 Jermyn Street, London SW1Y 6HP.

HAYWARD, Mike

Mike Hayward. Actor (M).

TV: *A Bouquet of Barbed Wire; Angels; Bergerac; Cockles; Coronation Street; Crown Court; EastEnders; Fallen Hero; Heartland; Juliet Bravo; King Lear; Landmarks; Love Story; Masters and Servants; Shackleton; Strangers; Struggle; The Bill; The Body in Question; The Nearly Men; The Real Eddy English; Tiger Bay; Trail of Guilt; TV Eye; Two People.*

Films: *Captain Stirrick; Secret Places; The Wicked Lady.*

Address: c/o Joy Jameson Ltd, 2.19 The Plaza, 535 Kings Road, London SW10 0SZ.

HAZELDINE, James

James Hazeldine. Actor (M)/Director.

b. Salford, Lancashire, 1948.

TV: *Aren't We All; Beck; Boon; Camille; Chocky; Close Relations; Cruel Earth; Deceit; Emma;* Jimmy Porter in *Forgotten Love Songs; Heartbeat; Inspector Morse;* Gaston in *Isaac Newton; John David; Kids; London's Burning; Look Back In Anger; Macbeth; Miss Marple: Murder at the Vicarage; Murder at the Wedding; My Friend Walter; Omega Factor; On the Palm; One Summer; Pirate Prince; Sam; Sherlock Holmes: The Musgrave Ritual; Small Dance; Streets Apart; The Circle Complex; The Cost of Loving; The Fireboys; The Grand; The Knock; The Trials of Oscar Slater; Truckers; The Vice; Voice From the Callows; Young, Gifted and Broke.*

Films: *Behind the Bleep; Business as Usual; Nicholas*

and Alexandra; Stardust; The Corsican Brothers; The Medusa Touch; The National Health; The Ruling Class.
Address: c/o Conway-Van Gelder, 18–21 Jermyn Street, London SW1Y 6HP.

HAZELGROVE, Jane
Jane Hazelgrove. Actor (F). 17 July 1968.
TV: Maureen Shelby in *A Touch of Frost*; Debbie Taylor in *Albion Market*; Turner in *Band of Gold*; Jane in *Casualty*; Madeline Forrest in *Coronation Street*; Lisa Shepard in *Families*; Marian in *Heartbeat*; Katrina in *Jonathan Creek*; Sandy in *Just a Gigolo*; Yvonne Bradley in *London's Burning*; Yvonne in *Lovejoy*; Rosie in *Making Out*; Rosamund in *Ruth Rendell – You Can't Be Too Careful*; Alison in *Shooting Star*; Lisa Powell in *The Bill*; Sharon Reynolds in *The Cops*; Minnie in *The Grand*; Rosie in *Waterfront Beat*.
Films: *Heidi; The Whipping Boy.*
Address: c/o Barry Brown & Partner, 47 West Square, London SE11 4YD.

HEAD, Anthony
Anthony Head. Actor (M).
TV: *Accident*; Watcher in *Buffy The Vampire Slayer*; Wilfred Kirby in *Eden End*; Clive Martell in *Enemy at the Door*; *Hard Cases*; Alan in *Highlander*; Phil Norton in *Howard's Way*; Adam Faust in *Jonathan Creek*; William in *Lillie*; *Love in a Cold Climate*; Jimmy Price in *Roger, Roger*; *Slags*; *The Detectives*; Terry in *The Ghostbusters of East Finchley*; Chief Hook in *The Grudge Fight*; *The Mallens*; Dominic Elwes in *The Trial of Lord Lucan*; *Zero Option*.
Films: *Devil's Hill; Lady Chatterley's Lover; Prayer For The Dying*; Pittock in *Royce*.
Address: c/o Marina Martin Associates, 12–13 Poland Street, London W1V 3DE. Hobbies: Horse riding, swimming, scuba diving, piano, guitar.

HEALY, Dorian
Forian Healy. Actor (F). b. 1963.
TV: *Capital City; Casualty; Class Act; Hornblower; Johnny Jarvis; Journey's End; No Bananas; Playing the Field; Soldier, Soldier; South of the Border; Statement of Affairs; The Mistress; The Monocled Mutineer; Underbelly; Witchcraft; Wonderful You.*
Films: *For Queen and Country; Her Own Rules; Symbosis; The Human Bomb; Young Soul Rebels.*
Address: c/o ICM, Oxford House, 76 Oxford Street, London W1N 0AX.

HEALY, Tim
Tim Healy. Actor (M).
b. Newcastle-upon-Tyne, 29 January 1952.

TV: *A Perfect Spy; Auf Wiedersehen, Pet; Bostock's Cup; Casualty; Common As Muck; Frank Stubbs Promotes; Heartburn Hotel; Stay Lucky; The Grand; Tom Jones.*
Films: *Bird on a Wire.*
Address: c/o PFD, Drury House, 34–43 Russell Street, London WC2B 5HA.

HEDLEY, Jack
Jack Hedley. Actor (M). b. 1930.
TV: *All Very Well; Dalziel and Pascoe, Space Precinct; Mr Don and Mr George; Trainer; 'Allo 'Allo; Gentlemen and Players; A Quiet Conspiracy; Bobby Davro Show; Hard Cases; Only Fools and Horses Special; Remington Steele; One by One; The Heart of the Matter; Go an Extra Mile; Orient Express; Who Pays the Ferryman?; Hindle Wakes; Cat on a Hot Tin Roof; Colditz; Kate.*
Films: *Karacter; The Plot to Kill Hitler; Three Kinds of Heat; For Your Eyes Only; Goodbye Mr Chips; How I Won the War; Witch and Warlock; The Scarlet Blade; The Very Edge; Room at the Top; The Ring; Kurtulus; Educational History of the World; The Ripper; Brief Encounter; The Anniversary; Secret of Blood Island; Of Human Bondage; In the French Style; Lawrence of Arabia.*
Address: c/o Emptage Hallett, 24 Poland Street, London, W1V 3DD.

HEILBRON, Vivien
Vivien Heilbron. Actor (F). b. 18 May 1944.
TV: Helen Wills in *Brookside* (1992); *Cloud Howe, Gray Granite; EastEnders*; Lile Moor Pickering in *Hetty Wainthropp Investigates* (1997); Lady Celia Romford in *House of Eliott* (1993); Mrs Smith in *In Suspicious Circumstances* (1994); *Kipper and White Wine; Streets Apart; Sunset Song*; Elsa Chambers in *Taggart* (1992); *Take the High Road; Target*; Mrs Ackroyd in *The Murder of Roger Ackroyd* (1999); *The New Statesman; The Unpleasantness at the Bellona Club; This Happy Breed*; Presenter in *Walking Back to Happiness* (1998).
Films: Catriona in *Kidnapped*; Gloria in *Seachange.*
Address: c/o The Richard Stone Partnership, 2 Henrietta Street, London WC2E 8PS.

HENDERSON, Ian
Ian Henderson. Actor (M).
b. Edinburgh, Scotland, 27 August 1968.
TV: Tom Wright in *London Bridge*; *Playdays*; Callum in *Second Thoughts*; Billy in *True Crimes.*
Films: *Mad Dogs and Englishmen*; Byron in *Rhythm and Blues*; Field in *The Dollar Bottom.*
Address: c/o Emptage Hallett, 24 Poland Street, London W1V 3DD.

HENDRICKSE, Sandy

Sandy Hendrickse. Actor (F).

TV: Jean in *Casualty*; Alice Cornwall in *Casualty*; Rita Ryder in *Class Act*; Theresa in *Coasting*; Pamela in *Family Affairs*; Helen in *Heartbeat*; Harmony in *The Lenny Henry Show*; Hannah Craven in *Luv*; Mandy in *Made in Heaven*; Elena in *Men Behaving Badly*; *Motor-mouth*; Connie in *Roughnecks*; Susan in *Tecx*; Christine in *The Bill*; *The Detectives*; Lily Lloyd in *The Man from the Pru*; Phoebe in *The Upper Hand*.

Films: Carol in *Dancin' Thru The Dark*.

Address: c/o Evans & Reiss, 100 Fawe Park Road, London SW15 2EA.

HENDY, Paul

Paul Hendy. Actor (M)/Host/Presenter.

b. 22 July 1966.

TV: *Auf Wiedersehen, Pet*; *Boon*; *Dear Mr. Barker*; *Disney Summer Holidays*; *Don't Try This At Home*; *For Amusements Only*; *Highly Sprung*; *Kicked Into Touch*; *Parallel 9*; *Raise the Roof*; *Stash*; *The Disney Club*; *Travel Bug*.

Address: c/o John Noel Management, 10a Belmont Street, London NW1 8HH. Hobbies: Football.

HENRY, Lenny

Lenny Henry. Actor (M)/Comedian.

b. Dudley, West Midlands, 29 August 1958.

TV: *Alive and Kicking*; *Bernard and the Genie*; *Chef!*; Fred in *Famous Fred* (1996); *Funky Black Shorts*; *Hope and Glory*; *In Dreams*; *Lenny Goes to Town*; *Lenny Henry Gets Wild*; *New Faces*; *New Soul Nation*; *South Bank Show*; *The Lenny Henry Show – Christmas Special*; *The Man*; *The Real McCoy*; *Three of a Kind*; *Tiswas*; *White Goods*.

Films: *True Identity*.

Address: c/o PBJ Management, 5 Soho Square, London W1V 5DE. m. Dawn French.

HENSHALL, Douglas

Douglas Henshall. Actor (M). b. Glasgow, 1967.

TV: Levin in *Anna Karenina*; Eric Shaw in *At The End of Alex Cording*; Johnny in *Boon VI*; Forget in *Common As Muck*; Clive Wandle in *Crossing the Floor*; Louis Jnr in *Down Among The Big Boys*; Stephen in *Firm Friends*; *The Justice Game*; Sammy in *Jute City*; Alex in *Kid In The Corner*; Barry in *Lipstick On Your Collar*; Nash in *Psychos*; Wickham in *Sharpe's Justice*; *South Bank Review* (1989); *Taggart*; Stewart French in *The Bill*; Factory Manager in *The Bill*; Valera in *Theif Takers*; Haig in *Underbelly*; Joop Huizinga in *Van Der Valk*; T. E. Lawrence in *Young Indiana II*.

Films: Edgar in *Angels and Insects*; Benny in *Fast Food*; Victor in *If Only (aka The Man With Rain In His Shoes)*; Ducalon in *Kull the Conqueror*; Michael in

Orphans; Shaw in *Rose Red*; News Reporter in *Silent Scream*; Davie Dawson in *The Big Man*; Danny in *This Year's Love*.

Address: c/o Ken McReddie Ltd, 91 Regent Street, London W1R 7TB.

HENSON, Nicky

Nicky Henson. Actor (M). b. London, 12 May 1945.

TV: Demetrius in *A Midsummer Night's Dream* (1988); Larry Finlay in *A Touch of Frost* (1999); *Absurd Person Singular* (1988); Greg Scarry in *All Quiet on the Preston Front*; Mr O'Rourke in *Anorak of Fire* (1997); Ch. Insp. McGregor in *Between the Lines* (1992); *Boon* (1989); *Call My Bluff* (1997); Sammy Buchanan in *Class Act* (1993); Henri in *Coronation Street* (1995); *Inspector Morse* (1988); *Lovejoy* (1991); CID Man in *Paul Merton In .. ..* (1997); Harrington Smithfield in *Pie in the Sky* (1995); *Seasons Greetings* (1988); Harvey Moon in *Shine on Harvey Moon* (1994); *Startrap* (1988); John Defoe in *The Bill* (1998); *The Bill* (1991); *The Green Man* (1990); Dr Ralph Mathias in *The Healer* (1994); *The Upper Hand* (1990); *Thin Air* (1988).

Films: *Psychomania*.

Address: c/o The Richard Stone Partnership, 2 Henrietta Street, London WC2E 8PS.

HERBERT, Philip

Philip Herbert. Actor (M).

b. London, 28 January 1957.

TV: Factory Boss in *100 Per Cent*; *Amnesty International*; Eamon Trout in *Bodger & Badger*; Steve – Sex Shop Manager in *Brookside*; Peasant Leader in *Cadfael*; Douglas in *Captain Crimson*; Waffling MP in *Carrott Confidential*; Stonker in *Comic Relief* (1991); Compulsive Gambler in *Fortune Numbers*; *Give Up*; *Hysteria III*; *I Love Keith Allen*; *Laughlines*; Steve in *Lonely Hearts Club*; Billy Bloodcup in *Mr Majeka*; Michael in *My Family and Other Animals*; Whitechapel Coachman in *Pickwick Papers*; *Short Change*; Hugh Jelly in *Sticky Moments*; News Photo-grapher in *The Bill*; Cupid in *The Good Sex Guide II*; *The Tub Club*.

Films: Ginger in *Carry On Columbus*; Santa Claus in *Christmas Present*; *Fanny Hill*; Tramp in *Little Shop of Horrors*; Hermie Oodle in *Return of the Jedi*; Servant in *Saboutage*; Drag Host in *Victor/Victoria*.

Address: c/o Elaine Murphy Associates, 310 Aberdeen House, 22–24 Highbury Grove, London N5 2EA. Hobbies: Gym, swimming.

HERRING, Richard

Richard Herring. Host/Comedian.

b. Cheddar, Somerset 1967.

TV: *Fist of Fun*; *The Day Today*; *This Morning with*

Richard Not Judy.
Address: c/o Avalon Promotions, 2nd Floor, Queens House, Leicester Place, Leicester Square, London WC2H 7BP.

HESMONDHALGH, Julie
Julie Hesmondhalgh. Actor (F). b. 1971.
TV: Hayley Cropper in *Coronation Street*; *Dalziel and Pascoe – The Wood Beyond*; *The Bill*; *The A–Z of Dating*; *Pat and Margaret*; Rose in *Catherine Cookson's The Dwelling Place*.
Films: *A Night with a Woman*; *A Day with Charlie*; *A Cry in the Dark*.
Address: c/o Lou Coulson, 1st Floor, 37 Berwick Street, London W1V 3RF.

HEWSON, Sherrie
Sherrie Hewson. Actor (F).
b. Burton Joyce, Nottinghamshire, 1950.
TV: *All at Number 20*; *Alan Bennett Series*; *Barbara*; *Butterflies Don't Count*; *Churchill, the Wilderness Years*; Maureen Naylor-Holdsworth in *Coronation Street*; *Flickers*; *Full House*; *Haggard*; *Home James*; *Home to Roost*; *Honky Tonk Heroes*; *In Loving Memory*; *Kate the Good Neighbour*; *Love for Lydia*; *Lovejoy*; *My Son, My Son*; *Never the Twain*; *Oh! Mr Beeching*; *The Russ Abbott Show*; *Singles*; *The Comedy Crowd*; *The Kindness of Mrs Radcliffe*.
Films: *Carry On Behind*; *Hanover Street*; *The Slipper and the Rose*.
Address: c/o International Artistes Ltd, Mezzanine Floor, 235 Regent Street, London W1R 8AX.

HEYWOOD, Jean
Jean Heywood. Actor (F). b. 15 July 1921.
TV: Olive in *A Touch of Frost*; *Casualty*; Grandma in *Crucial Tales*; Mrs Raisen in *Dangerfield*; Sally Hart in *Family Affairs*; *Harry's Mad*; *Heartbeat*; Enid in *Hetty Wainthropp Investigates*; *Men of the World*; *Our Friends in the North*; Old Lady in *Out of Sight*; Granny in *Paul Merton*; Mrs Love in *The Bill*; Irma Moore in *The Locksmith*; *Trip Trap*; Rita in *Where the Heart Is*.
Films: Ms Comet in *My West*; Sophia in *Red Monarch*; Vera in *Sakharov*.
Address: c/o Burnett Granger Associates, Prince of Wales Theatre, 31 Coventry Street, London W1V 8AS.

HIGGINSON, Huw
Huw Higginson. Actor (M). b. 21 February 1964.
TV: Colin in *Big Deal*; Phil in *Defrosting the Fridge*; *Floodtide*; Roger Brady in *How We Used To Live*; Mike in *Jumbo Spencer*; Southampton's Page in *Shakespeare*; PC George Garfield in *The Bill*.

Address: c/o Evans & Reiss, 100 Fawe Park Road, London SW15 2EA.

HIGHMORE, Edward
Edward Highmore. Actor (M).
b. Kingston-upon-Thames, Surrey, 3 April 1961.
TV: Charles in *Cry of Peacocks*; Malkon in *Doctor Who*; Herr Kandidat in *Heidi*; Leo Howard in *Howard's Way*; Ernie in *Lame Ducks*; Renwick in *Little Orphan Annie*; Dr Woods in *Love Hurts*; Robert in *Master of the Moors*; Derek Johnson in *Mosley*; Ray in *No Child of Mine*; Keith in *See You Friday*; PC Higgins in *Stick With Me Kid*; Dr Stubbs in *The Detectives*; Gary in *The Politician's Wife*; Boll in *Tripods*.
Films: Lord Harewood in *Elizabeth*; Tom in *Trigger Puller*.
Address: c/o William Morris Agency (UK) Ltd, 1 Stratton Street, London W1X 6HB.

HIGSON, Charlie
Charlie Higson. Actor (M)/Writer.
TV: *Bang Bang, It's Reeves and Mortimer*; *Harry Enfield*; *Randall and Hopkirk (Deceased)*; Ralph Mayhew/Aunt Cecilia/Ralph's Father in *Ted and Ralph*; *The Fast Show*; *The Fast Show Live*; *The Smell of Reeves and Mortimer*; *Vic Reeves' Big Night Out*.
Address: c/o London Management, Noel House, 2–4 Noel Street, London W1V 3RB.

HILL, Bernard
Bernard Hill. Actor (M).
b. Manchester, 17 December 1944.
TV: *About Face-Monkey Business*; *Antigone*; *Art of Tripping*; *Boys from the Blackstuff*; *Crime Story: Question of Identity*; *Dirty Something*; *Great Expectations*; *John Lennon – A Journey In Life*; *Lipstick On Your Collar*; *Mill on the Floss*; *Mountain Men*; *New World*; *Once Upon A Time in the North*; *Permanent Red*; *Shepherds On The Rock*; *Shrinks*; *Skallagrigg*; *Squaring the Circle*; *Telltale*; *The Burston Rebellion*; *The Chain*; *The Gospel According to St Luke*; *The Lawlord*; *Triology*.
Films: *A Midsummer Night's Dream*; *Bellman and True*; *Double X*; *Drowning by Numbers*; *Gandhi*; *Ghost and The Darkness*; *Madagascar Skin*; *Mountains of the Moon*; *No Surrender*; *Restless Natives*; *Shirley Valentine*; *The Big Game*; *The Bounty*; *The Gambling Man*; *Titanic*; *True Crime*.
Address: c/o ICM, Oxford House, 76 Oxford Street, London W1N 0AX.

HILL, Dave
Dave Hill. Actor (M).
TV: *Kid in the Corner*; PC Redfern in *City Central*; *The*

Family; Real Women; Highlander; Dalziel and Pasoce; Ice House; Trauma; Cyril in *Chef; The Bill, Cracker, Coronation Street; The All New Alexei Sayle Show;* Andy in *Seaforth; Peak Practice; Harry; Circle of Deceit; Paradise; Game On; Frank Stubbs; Sin Bin; Mike and Angelo; In Suspicious Circumstances; Pie in the Sky; Heartbeat; Casualty; Spender; The Harry Enfield Show; Steps Back; T. Dan Smith;* Frank Webster in *The Monocled Mutineer, Inside Out; Irons of Wrath; Ruth Rendell Mysteries.*

Films: *Still Seven Days to Live; Hope and Glory; Someone Else's Dream; Prometheus; Amy Foster; Black Eyes; The Full Monty; When Saturday Comes; The Draughtsman's Contract; Remembrance; Invitation to a Wedding; The Dress; Car Trouble; Nature of the Beast; The Raggedy Rawney; In Fading Light.*
Address: c/o Marina Martin Associates, 12–13 Poland Street, London W1V 3DE.

HILL, Harry

Harry Hill. Comedian. b. 10 October 1964.
TV: Morrissey in *Celebrity Star in Their Eyes; Harry Hill; Harry Hill's Fruit Fancies; Saturday Live* (1996); *The Royal Variety Performance* (1997).
Address: c/o Avalon Promotions, 2nd Floor, Queens House, Leicester Place, Leicester Square, London WC2H 7BP.

HILL, Katy

Katy Hill. Presenter. b. Poole, Dorset, 1970.
TV: *2000-1; Blue Peter; CBBC in the Park; Children's BAFTA Awards; Millennium Today* (1999); *Nickelodeon; Top of the Pops; UKOK* (1997).
Address: c/o Blue Peter Office, BBC Television, Wood Lane, London W12 7BJ.

HILL, Melanie

Actor (F). b. Newcastle, 1962.
TV: Pauline in *A Night on the Tyne;* Hazel in *Auf Wiedersehen, Pet;* Susan in *Boon;* Avaline in *Bread;* Sister Lockley in *Cardiac Arrest;* Janice in *Casualty;* Angie in *Circle of Deceit;* Emma in *Crocodile Shoes;* Lena in *Finney;* Jean Simpson in *Juliet Bravo;* Rita Dolan in *Playing the Field;* Liz Davies in *Silent Witness;* Sue Hyles in *Spender;* Phyllis in *The Beast in Man;* Polly Beecher in *The Bill;* Lynda Chambers in *The Bill;* Laura in *The Widowing of Mrs Holroyd.*
Films: Sandra in *Brassed Off;* Sarah in *Shopping;* Norma in *The Hawk;* Mary in *When Saturday Comes.*
Address: c/o Markham & Froggatt Ltd, 4 Windmill Street, London W1P 1HF.

HILL, Rose

Rose Hill. Actor (F). b. London, 5 June 1914.
TV: Madame Blanc in *'Allo 'Allo;* Mrs Ryall in *A Touch of Frost; Born and Bred; Caring; Hallelujah; Island Gardens; On the Razzle; Press Gang; Strangers;* Mrs Temple in *The Bill; The Cabbage Patch; The Janet Brown Show; Three Sisters; Waterloo Sunset; Wayne and Albert.*
Films: *Murder East, Murder West; Wild Cats of St Trinians.*
Address: c/o The Richard Stone Partnership, 2 Henrietta Street, London WC2E 8PS.

HILL, Vince

Vince Hill. Singer.
b. Coventry, West Midlands, 16 April 1937.
TV: *Gas Street; The Musical Time Machine; They Sold a Million; This is Your Life.*
Music: *Edelweiss; Look Around; Roses of Picardy.*
Address: c/o George Bartram Associates, 1 Sherbourne Gate, Birmingham B16 8DE. m. Annie; 1 s. Athol.
Hobbies: Cooking, painting, boating, gardening.

HILLMAN, Carly

Carly Hillman. Actor (F).
TV: *Blue Peter; Bright Sparks; CBBC; Diggit;* Nicky Di Marco in *EastEnders; EastEnders Revealed; SMTV: Live.*
Address: c/o Rossmore Personal Management, Rossmore Road, London NW1 6NJ.

HINDLE, Madge

Madge Hindle. Actor (F). b. 19 May 1938.
TV: Mrs Heron in *All Quiet on the Preston Front;* Mrs Sidebottom in *Anorak of Fire;* Doreen in *Barbara;* Judge in *Brothers and Sisters;* Mrs Birtles in *Capstick's Law;* Renee Roberts in *Coronation Street;* Schoolteacher in *Death of a Rebel;* Aunt Annie in *First of the Summer Wine;* Mrs Tiddler in *Gayle's World; Get Some In;* Rose in *Intensive Care;* Maggie in *Jack Point;* Mrs Shurer in *Lost Empires;* Bet Howell in *Mr and Mrs Edgehill;* Betty in *Mr Ellis Versus The People;* Winnie in *My Friend Walter; On the Margin; Open All Hours;* Lady in Hotel in *Pat and Margaret;* Governor's Secretary in *Porridge;* Joyce Webster in *Said The Preacher;* Rose Hackling in *Stan's Last Game;* Miss Prothero in *Sunset Across The Bay;* Marian Grant in *Thank You For Having Her;* Mrs Pain in *The Dwelling Place;* Elaine Dodswell in *The Rector's Wife;* Storyteller in *Tickle on the Tum;* Valerie in *Vinegar Trip.*
Address: c/o Sandra Griffin Management, 6 Ryde Place, Richmond Road, East Twickenham, Middlesex TW1 2EH.

HINDS, Ciaran

Ciaran Hinds. Actor (M). b. Belfast, 1954.

TV: *A Dark Adapted Eye; Between the Lines; Cold Lazarus;* Brian Keenan in *Hostages; Investigation; Ivanhoe;* Mr Rochester in *Jane Eyre;* Captain Wentworth in *Persuasion; Prime Suspect III; Rules of Engagement; Seaforth; Sherlock Holmes; Soldier, Soldier; The Affair; The Long March; The Man Who Cried; We'll Support You Evermore.*

Films: *A Time to Love; The Life of Stuff; The Lost Son; The Lovers; Titanic Town.*

Address: c/o Dalzell and Beresford Ltd, 91 Regent Street, London W1R 7TB.

HINES, Frazer

Frazer Hines. Actor (M).
b. Horsforth, Yorkshire, 22 September 1944.

TV: Jamie McCrimmon in *Doctor Who;* Joe Sugden in *Emmerdale Farm.*

Films: *A King in New York;* Kim in *Peril for the Guy;* Corg in *The Last Valley;* Kim in *The Salvage Gang;* Operator in *Zeppelin.*

Address: c/o Liz Hobbs Management, 6 Cork Street, London W1X 1PB.

HIRD, Dame Thora

Dame Thora Hird. Actor (F).
b. Morecambe, Lancashire, 28 May 1911.

TV: Susan Danby in *The First Lady;* Postmistress in *The Queen's Nose;* Edie Pegden in *Uncle Of The Bride; Wide-Eyed and Legless; Afternoon Off;* Mrs Clarke in *All Creatures Great and Small;* Herself in *Blankety Blank;* Johnson's Daughter in *Bootsie and Snudge; Dinner At Noon;* Enid in *dinnerladies;* Mabel Brassington in *Flesh and Blood;* Captain Emily Ridley in *Hallelujah;* Ivy Unsworth in *In Loving Memory; Intensive Care;* Aunt Edie in *Last of the Summer Wine;* Annie in *Lost for Words; Me! I'm afraid of Virginia Woolf;* Thora Blacklock in *Meet The Wife;* Jean Taylor in *Memento Mori;* Thora Parker in *Ours Is a Nice House;* Jim's Mother in *Pat and Margaret;* Doris in *Talking Heads;* Violet in *Talking Heads 2* (1998).

Films: Mrs Burtshaw in *2,000 Women;* Mrs Bates in *A Boy, a Girl and a Bike;* Mrs Trott in *A Day To Remember;* Mrs Rothwell in *A Kind of Loving;* Mrs Humphries in *Background;* Mrs Jessop in *Bitter Harvest;* Mrs Knowles in *Boys In Brown;* Old Woman in *Corridor of Mirrors;* Agnes O'Connor in *Don't Blame The Stork;* Mrs Cornelius in *Emergency Call;* Mrs Coot in *Fools Rush In;* Mrs Doyle in *For Better, for Worse;* Mrs Galloway in *Further Up The Creek;* Margie Groves in *Home and Away;* Kelly's Landlady in *Lost;* Rosa in *Madness of the Heart;* A.T.S. Girl in

Next Of Kin; Ma Fox in *Once a Jolly Swagman;* Cook in *One Good Turn;* Mrs Carter in *Over The Odds;* Mrs Usher in *Personal Affair;* Mrs Skinner in *Portrait From Life;* Mrs Winthram in *Rattle of a Simple Man;* Mrs Lack in *Sailor Beware!;* Agnes Russell in *Some Will, Some Won't;* Woman at Police Station in *Street Corner;* Mrs Taylor in *Term of Trial;* Joyce, Davis's secretary in *The Black Sheep of Whitehall; The Crowded Day;* Mrs Ada Lapford in *The Entertainer;* Mrs Oakroyd in *The Good Companions;* Miss Rawlings in *The Great Game;* Mrs Pewsley in *The Long Memory;* Sal Brown in *The Love Match;* Mrs Grose in *The Nightcomers;* Maud in *The Courtneys Of Curzon Street;* Rosemary 'Rosie' Elizabeth Rigly in *The Quatermass Experiment;* Mrs Gaye in *The Weaker Sex;* Mrs Larkin in *These Dangerous Years;* Mary in *Tiger By The Tail;* Alice Crouch in *Time Gentlemen Please!;* Mrs Rowan, landlady in *Turn the Key Softly;* Ivy, the Land Girl in *Went the Day Well?;* Gran Ramsey in *Women Without Men.*

Address: c/o Felix De Wolfe, 51 Maida Vale, London W9 1SD. 1 d. Janette Scott.

HISLOP, Ian

Ian Hislop. Presenter. b. 13 July 1960.

TV: *Briefcase Encounter* (1990); *Canterbury Tales* (1996); *Dead on Time* (1995); *Gobble* (1996); *Harry Enfield and Chums* (1997); *Harry Enfield's Television Programme* (1990); *Have I Got News For You* (1999); *He Died a Death* (1991); *Magnez Merveillac* (1994); *School Tales* (1997); *Spitting Image* (1984); *The Case of the Missing* (1991); *The Stone Age* (1989).

Address: c/o PFD, Drury House, 34–43 Russell Street, London WC2B 5HA.

HOBLEY, Tina

Tina Hobley. Actor (F). b. London, 1971.

TV: Waitress in *All in the Game;* Valerie in *Bliss;* Samantha in *Coronation Street;* Carol in *Ghostbusters of East Finchley;* Christine in *Harbour Lights;* Alison in *May and June;* Sarah in *Pie in the Sky;* Jane in *The Bill;* Estate Agent in *The Knock.*

Address: c/o Hillman Threlfall, 33 Brookfield, Highgate West Hill, London N6 6AT.

HODGE, Douglas

Douglas Hodge. Actor (M). b. Plymouth, 1961.

TV: *Anglo-Saxon Attitudes; Capital City; Dance; Fatal Inversion; Middlemarch; Scold's Bridle; The Uninvited.*

Films: *Bliss; Diamond Skulls; Men of The Month; Saigon Baby; Salome's Last Dance; The Trial.*

Address: c/o PFD, Drury House, 34–43 Russell Street, London WC2B 5HA.

HODGE, Patricia

Patricia Hodge. Actor (F). b. 29 September 1946.

TV: *Moonstone; The Legacy of Reginald Perrin; The Cloning of Joanna May; Rich Tea and Sympathy; Rumpole of the Bailey; The Secret Life of Ian Fleming; Inspector Morse; Let's Face the Music of…; Exclusive Yarns; The Life and Loves of a She-Devil; Hotel du Lac; Time for Murder; Sherlock Holmes; O.S.S.; Robin of Sherwood; The Death of the Heart; Hayfever; Jemima Shore Investigates; Holding the Fort; Nanny; The Other 'Arf; The Professional;, Disraeli; Edward and Mrs Simpson; The One and Only Mrs Phyllis Dixey.*

Films: *Betrayal; Heavy Metal; Just Ask for Diamond; Prague Duet; Rosie Dixon; Sunset; The Disappearance; The Elephant Man; The Leading Man; The Waterloo Bridge Handicap; Thieves in the Night.*

Address: c/o ICM, Oxford House, 76 Oxford Street, London W1N 0AX.

HOLDEN, Amanda

Amanda Holden. Actor (F).

b. Bishop's Waltham, Hampshire, 16 February 1971.

TV: *EastEnders; Goodness Gracious Me; Hale and Pace; In Suspicious Circumstances; Jonathan Creek; Kiss Me Kate; Smack the Pony; The Bill; The Grimleys; Thief Takers; We Know Where You Live.*

Films: *Don't Go Breaking My Heart; Intimate Relations; Virtual Sexuality.*

Address: c/o Amanda Howard Associates Ltd, 21 Berwick Street, London W1V 3RG. m. Les Dennis.

HOLDER, Ginny

Ginny Holder. Actor (F).

TV: Cheyney in *A Touch of Frost;* Sue Nbokei in *Crocodile Shoes;* Sarah in *Finney;* Bridget in *No Child of Mine; Panorama;* Lena in *Spiders and Flies;* DS Merle Martin in *Staying Alive;* Charmian in *The Knock;* Harriet Godsell in *An Unsuitable Job for a Woman.*

Films: Agnes in *Her Own Rules;* Georgina in *The Leading Man;* Rita in *The Saint;* Forbes in *Wing Commander.*

Address: c/o William Morris Agency (UK) Ltd, 1 Stratton Street, London W1X 6HB.

HOLDERNESS, Sue

Sue Holderness. Actor (F). b. London, 28 May 1949.

TV: Pamela Huntley-Johnson in *Bless this House;* Prue Saunders in *Both Ends Meet;* Mrs Barton in *Colour Blind;* Maggie in *Dear John; End of Part One;* Sarah in *Fly into Danger;* Mrs Stanley in *Growing Pains;* Jennifer in *Harriet's Back in Town;* Joan Blaketon in *Heartbeat;* Liz in *It Takes a Worried Man;* Sue in *Long Live The King;* Laura in *Minder;* Marlene in *Only*

Fools and Horses; Punchlines; Storyteller in *Rainbow;* Joan Travis in *Revelations;* Lorraine, girlfriend, in *Rowan Atkinson Presents Canned Laughter;* Guest in *Sob Sisters;* Jo Gould in *The Brief;* Cleopatra IV in *The Cleopatra Files;* The Medium in *The New Avengers;* Mildred in *The One and Only Phyllis Dixey;* Marianne in *The Sandbaggers;* Joanna Barrington-Smythe in *Tightrope;* Diane in *Young, Gifted and Broke.*

Films: Ivy in *Lime Street;* Abbey in *Love, Honour and Obey;* Shirley in *That'll be the Day;* Shirley in *The Meat Draw.*

Address: c/o Burnett Granger Associates, Prince of Wales Theatre, 31 Coventry Street, London W1V 8AS.

HOLLAND, Jeffrey

Jefffrey Holland. Actor (M).

b. West Midlands, 17 July 1946.

TV: Spike Dixon in *Hi De Hi;* Cecil Parkin in *Oh, Dr Beeching!;* Richard II; James Twelvetrees in *You Rang M'Lord.*

Address: c/o London Management, Noel House, 2–4 Noel Street, London W1V 3RB.

HOLLAND, Jools

Jools Holland. Musician/Presenter.

b. London, 24 January 1958.

TV: Himself in *Beat Route; Don't Forget Your Toothbrush; French and Saunders; Jool's Holland's Happening; Jool's Hootenanny; Juke Box Jury; Later With Jools Holland;* Himself in *Mr Roadrunner; Name That Tune; Sunday Night; The Beatles Anthology;* Himself in *The Groovy Fellas; The Laughing Prisoner; The Tube;* Himself in *The Young Ones.*

Films: *Hunting Venus; SpiceWorld – The Movie.*

Address: c/o One Fifteen, 28–30 Wood Wharf, Horseferry Place, London SE10 9BT.

HOLLINGBERY, Vilma

Vilma Hollingberry. Actor (F). b 21 July 1932.

TV: Jeanette Conrad in *A Touch of Frost* (1994); Elsie in *Abracadigance* (1988); Ada Hatton in *Casualty* (1993); Gran in *Children's Ward* (1991); Jill Whetstone in *Crime Story* (1993); Evie in *Do Your Own Thing* (1994); Winnie Brown in *London Bridge;* Madame Chartier in *Maigret* (1991); Kitty in *Sitting Pretty;* Alice in *Smitten* (1997); Gloria Mason in *The Bill* (1993); Dorothy Strong in *The Bill* (1990); Hazel Davidson in *The Bill* (1989); Edna Ryland in *The Bill* (1996); Lavinia Crusty in *The Management* (1987); Aunt Betty in *The River* (1988); Mrs Jessop in *Time After Time* (1995); Esme Sutherland in *Waiting for God.*

Films: Mrs Potts in *The Thin Line;* Auntie Panty in *Young Poisoner's Handbook.*

Address: c/o McIntosh Rae Management, Thornton House, Thornton Road, London SW19 4NG.

HOLLOWAY, Julian

Julian Holloway. Actor (M).

b. Watlington, Oxfordshire, 24 June 1944.

TV: *Ellis Island; Grass Roots; Michelangelo; P. G. Wodehouse's Ekridge; Rebecca; Rumpole of the Bailey; The Chief; The Endless Game; The New Avengers; The Punch Review; The Scarlet and The Black; Torch Song.*

Films: *Carry On Camping; Carry On Doctor; Carry On England; Carry On Henry; Carry On Loving; Carry On Up the Khyber; Sammy's Super T-Shirt; Scream and Scream Again.*

Address: c/o Michael Ladkin Personal Management, Suite One, Ground Floor, 1 Duchess Street, London W1N 3DE.

HOLM, Ian

Ian Holm. Actor (M).

b. Goodmayes, Essex, 12 September 1931.

TV: White Knight in *Alice through the Looking Glass* (1999); Himmelstoss in *All Quiet on the Western Front* (1979); Squealer in *Animal Farm* (1999); *Emma's Time* (1970); Bernard Samson in *Game, Set and Match* (1987); Heinrich Himmler in *Holocaust* (1978); Dr Joseph Goebbels in *Inside the Third Reich* (1982); Zerah in *Jesus of Nazareth* (1977); Lear in *King Lear* (1997); Thenardier in *Les Misérables* (1978); Duval in *The Man in the Iron Mask* (1976); *May We Come In?* (1974); *Michelangelo: The Last Giant* (1991); *The Miracle Maker*; David Peters in *Moonlight on the Highway* (1969); Eustace Edgehill in *Mr and Mrs Edgehill* (1985); Hercule Poirot in *Murder by the Book* (1986); Napoleon in *Napoleon and Love* (1974); Alexei in *Play for Today* (1982); *Play of the Month; Play of the Week* (1978); J. Bruce Ismay in *SOS Titanic* (1979); *Strike: The Birth of Solidarity* (1981); *Stuff of Madness* (1990); Narrator in *Television* (1985); *The Bell* (1982); Pod in *The Borrowers* (1993); Andrew Crocker-Harris in *The Browning Version* (1985); Narrator in *The Churchills* (1995); Sir William Collyer in *The Deep Blue Sea* (1994); Control in *The Endless Game* (1990); *The Last Romantics* (1991); J. M. Barrie in *The Lost Boys* (1978); *The Man from Haven* (1972); Pontius Pilate in *The Miracle Maker* (1999); Pod in *The Return of the Borrowers* (1993); The Gatekeeper in *The Thief of Baghdad* (1978); Astrov in *Uncle Vanya* (1991); Richard III in *War of the Roses* (1966); *We, The Accused* (1981).

Films: Naville in *A Life Less Ordinary*; Puck in *A Midsummer Night's Dream*; Ash in *Alien*; Ken in *Another Woman*; Pascal in *Big Night*; Sir Hector in *Blue Ice*; Sam Mussabini in *Chariots of Fire*; Desmond Cussen in *Dance with a Stranger*; Rev. Charles L. Dodgson (aka Lewis Carroll) in *Dreamchild*; *Esther Khan*; Kiri Vinoker in *Existenz*; Capitaine Phillippe D'Arnot in *Greystoke: The Legend of Tarzan, Lord of the Apes*; Polonius in *Hamlet*; Fluellen in *Henry V*; Albertus in *Hour of the Pig*; Joe Gould in *Joe Gould's Secret*; Nicholas Potter in *Juggernaut*; Dr Murnau in *Kafka*; Ben Singleton in *Laughterhouse*; Water Bailiff in *Loch Ness*; Bilbo Baggins in *Lord of the Rings: The Fellowship of the Ring*; El Krim in *March or Die*; The Father in *Mary Shelley's Frankenstein*; David Riccio in *Mary, Queen of Scots*; Tom Frost in *Naked Lunch*; Yakovslev in *Nicholas and Alexandra*; President Poincare in *Oh! What a Lovely War*; Dr Anderson in *Return of the Soldier*; King John in *Robin and Marian*; Martin Lynch-Gibbon in *Severed Head*; *Shergar*; Mohammed in *Shout at the Devil*; *Simon Magus*; Mitchell Stephens in *Sweet Hereafter*; Big Tam in *The Beautiful Game*; Flynn in *The Bofors Gun*; Narrator in *The Fever*; Priest Vito Cornelius in *The Fifth Element*; Grubeshov in *The Fixer*; Lenny in *The Homecoming*; Dr Willis in *The Madness Of King George*; Napoleon in *Time Bandits*; Stanely Pilborough in *Wetherby*; George E. Buckle in *Young Winston*.

Address: c/o Julian Belfrage Associates, 46 Albemarle Street, London W1X 4PP.

HOLMES, Eamonn

Eamonn Holmes. Presenter. b. 4 December 1959.

TV: *A Seat In The Stand; Benson and Hedges Snooker Championship; Check It Out; Cudmore's Call; DIY TV; Friday Live With Eamonn Holmes; Garden Party; GMTV; Good Evening Ulster; Holiday; How Do They Do That?; ITV Telethon; Liverpool Victoria Challenge Snooker Tournament; Miss Northern Ireland; National Television Awards; Oddballs; Open Air; Physical Pursuits; TV Magic and Mystery; World Darts Championships; World Snooker Championship.*

Address: c/o Simpson Fox Associates Ltd, 52 Shaftesbury Avenue, London W1V 7DE.

HOLMES, Katie

Katie Holmes. Actor (F).

b. Toledo, Ohio, USA, 18 December 1978.

TV: Herself in *Access Hollywood* (1998); Josephine Potter in *Dawson's Creek* (1998); Herself in *MTV's Fanatic* (1998); Herself in *TRL* (1999).

Films: Rachel Wagner in *Disturbing Behaviour*; Claire Montgomery in *GO*; Josephine Potter in *Muppets from Space*; Leigh Ann Watson in *Teaching Mrs Tingle*; Libbets Casey in *The Ice Storm*; Hannah Green in *Wonder Boys*.

Address: c/o BWR Agency, 9100 Wilshire Boulevard, 6th Floor, West Tower, Beverly Hills, California 91511, USA. Hobbies: Drinking Starbuck's latte, jelly bellies, reading.

HOLMES, Michelle

Michelle Holmes. Actor (F).
b. Rochdale, Lancashire, 1 January 1967.
TV: *Common As Muck*; Tina (barmaid) in *Coronation Street*; *Firm Friends*; *Goodnight Sweetheart*; *Mr Wroe's Virgins*; *My Dad's a Boring Nerd*.
Films: Sue in *Rita, Sue and Bob Too*.
Address: c/o Roxane Vacca Management, 73 Beak Street, London W1R 3LF.

HOLNESS, Bob

Bob Holness. Actor (M)/Presenter.
b. Vryheid, Natal, South Africa, 12 November 1928.
TV: *All Creatures Great and small* (1989); O'Reillly in *Beck* (1996); *Blockbusters*; Dad in *Bloomin' Marvellous* (1997); Anthony Fairchild in *Bugs* (1997); *Call My Bluff*; *Casualty*; Mr Wix in *Earthfasts* (1993); D.S. Doxey in *Expert Witness* (1995); *Give Us A Clue*; Charles Powell in *Hard Cases* (1988); *Harry* (1993); Don Lomax in *Heartbeat* (1999); Pendleton in *Heartbeat* (1992); Picture Editor in *Hetty Wainthropp Investigates* (1995); Sup. Harper in *Inspector Alleyn* (1992); Dr Philip Dale in *Justice for Gemma* (1993); Wayne in *Kingdom Come* (1990); *Madly in Love* (1989); *Raise the Roof*; *Today*; *A Word in Your Ear*; *Celebrity Catchphrase*; *Home Truths*; *The Generation Game*.
Address: c/o Arlington Enterprises Ltd, 1–3 Charlotte Street, London W1P 1HD.

HOLT, Judy

Judy Holt. Actor (F).
TV: Susan Fairbrother in *And the Beat Goes On* (1996); Mitchell in *Children's Ward* (1995); Mrs Grice in *Coronation Street*; Donna in *Dads*; WPC Lunn in *Emmerdale* (1995); Mrs Lang in *In Suspicious Circumstances* (1994); Mo in *Love is Old, Love is New*; Anna in *My Father's House*; Simmonds in *Old Flames*; *Spring Hill* (1997); Liz in *The Contract*; Mandy in *The Practice*; Susan in *The Road to 1984*; Mitchell in *The Ward* (1995).
Address: c/o Green & Underwood, 2 Conduit Street, London W1R 9TG.

HOOD, Morag

Morag Hood. Actor (F).
b. Glasgow, Scotland, 12 December 1942.
TV: Elizabeth in *A Sense of Guilt*; Carol in *A Taste of Death*; Wolfpack in *After the Party*; *Auf Wiedersehen, Pet*; *Bergerac*; *Crown Court*; *Diversions*; Sue Thompson in *Families*; Dolores in *Hamish Macbeth*; Lady Charlotte Doyle in *Harbour Lights*; *Harry*; Barclay in *Ill Fares the Land*; Mary Musgrove in *Persuasion*; Hilary in *Tell-Tale Heart*; Fensom in *The Big Picnic*; Maggie in *The Camerons*; Irene in *The Cup*; Nora Morgan in *The Governor*; *Travelling Man*; Natasha in *War and Peace*.
Address: c/o Marmont Management Ltd, Langham House, 308 Regent Street, London W1R 5AL.

HOOLEY, Joan

Joan Hooley. Actor (F). b. 13 November 1936.
TV: *Blues for Mr Charlie*; *C.A.B.*; Irma in *Comic Asides*; *Cool for Cats*; *Do Something Addy Man*; Josie in *EastEnders*; Dr Louise Mahler in *Emergency – Ward 10*; Bonetta in *Get Me to the Crematorium on Time*; *Great Moments in Aviation*; Sister Pryce in *Hallelujah Anyhow*; Court Official in *Kavanagh QC*; Teacher in *Little Napoleon*; Older Physio in *Melissa*; *Moon on a Rainbow Shawl*; *Supervisory Management*; Mrs Kirby in *The Bill*; Gloria in *The Bill*; *The Blacks*; Mrs Carter in *To Be the Best*; Ella in *Tygo Road*; Belinda in *Us Girls*.
Address: c/o Chuck Julian Associates, Suite 51, 26 Charing Cross Road, London WC2H 0DH. Partner: Geoffrey Harris; 1 s. Julian Hooley.

HOPE, Richard

Richard Hope. Actor (M).
TV: Simon Watson in *A Perfect State*; Skull in *A Piece of Cake*; Richard in *Band of Gold*; Talbot in *Bramwell*; Lt. Hooper in *Brideshead Revisited*; Dick Trout in *Burning Ambition*; Edmund White in *Casualty*; Donald Spry in *Casualty Of War*; Tom in *Children Crossing*; Heatherstone in *Children of the New Forest*; Doctor in *December Flower*; Owen in *Dogplant*; Colin in *Happy Birthday, Shakespeare*; *Happy Familes*; Steve in *Heartland*; Geoff in *Itch, '4 play'*; *Jackanory*; *Margie and Me*; Colin in *Midsomer Murders*; Roy Shearer in *Peak Practice*; *People Like Us*; Mr Fenton in *Reach for the Moon*; Atillio in *Saturday, Sunday, Monday*; Exton in *Simulated Exercise*; Stuart in *Tears Before Bedtime*; Alan in *The Clinger*; Professor Tom Dexter in *The Demon Headmaster*; Mortimer Tundish in *The Riff Raff Element*; *Victoria Wood Playhouse*; *Wayne and Albert*.
Films: Salto in *Bellman and True*; *Bloody Kids*; Musician in *Breaking Glass*; Squire Wyman in *Feast of July*; *The French Lieutenant's Woman*; Hubert in *Laughterhouse*; Detective in *Scandalous*; *See You At Wembley Frankie Walsh*; *The Last Post*.
Address: c/o PFD, Drury House, 34–43 Russell Street, London WC2B 5HA.

HOPKINS, Sir Anthony

Sir Anthony Hopkins. Actor (M).
b. Port Talbot, Wales, 31 December 1937.
TV: *A Childhood Friend* (1974); *A Company of Five* (1968); Gwyn Thomas in *A Few Selected Exits* (1993); *A Heritage and Its History* (1968); *A Married Man* (1982); Donald Campbell in *Across The Lake* (1988); *All Creatures Great and Small* (1974); *Big Cats* (1993); Guy Burgess in *Blunt* (1986); *Corridors of Power: Strangers and Brothers* (1983); *Cuculus Canorus* (1972); *Danton* (1970); *Dark Victory* (1975); *Decision To Burn* (1970); *Dickens* (1970); *Find Me* (1973); Magwitch in *Great Expectations* (1988); *Guilty Conscience* (1984); *Heartland* (1988); *Hearts and Flowers* (1970); *Hollywood Wives* (1984); *Kean* (1978); *Little Eyolf* (1981); *Lloyd George* (1972); *Mussolini and I* (1984); Othello in *Othello* (1981); Paul in *Peter and Paul* (1980); *Possessions* (1974); *QB VII* (1973); *The Arcata Promise* (1974); *The Arch of Triumph* (1984); Hitler in *The Bunker* (1980); *The Dawning* (1987); *The Good Father* (1985); *The Hunchback of Notre Dame* (1981); *The Lindebergh Kidnapping Case* (1975); *The Peasants Revolt* (1969); *The Poet Game* (1970); *The Tenth Man* (1988); *The Three Sisters* (1969); *The Voyage of The Mayflower* (1979); *Uncle Vanya* (1970); *Victory at Entebbe* (1976); Pierre in *War and Peace* (1971); *War and Peace (Concluded)* (1972).
Films: *84 Charing Cross Road; A Bridge Too Far; A Change of Seasons; A Chorus of Disapproval;* Torvald in *A Doll's House; Audrey Rose; Bookworm; Bram Stoker's Dracula; Chaplin; Desperate Hours;* Claudius in *Hamlet; Howard's End; International Velvet; Juggernaut; Legend of the Fall; Magic; Meet Joe Black; Nixon; One Man's War; Remains of the Day; Shadowlands; Silence of the Lambs; Spotswood; Surviving Picasso;* Captain Bligh in *The Bounty; The Elephant Man; The Girl from Petrovka; The Innocent; The Lion in Winter; The Looking Glass War; The Road to Welville; The Trial; When Eight Bells Toll;* Lloyd George in *Young Winston.*
Address: c/o ICM, Oxford House, 76 Oxford Street, London W1N 0AX. m. 2 Jennifer Lynton; 1 d. Abigail (from 1st m.).

HORNBY, Clive

Clive Hornby. Actor (M).
b. Liverpool, 20 October 1947.
TV: Jack Sugden in *Emmerdale* (1979); *Get Some In; Life at Stake.*
Films: *No Longer Alone; Yanks.*
Address: c/o ALW Associates, 70 Mildmay Road, London N1 4NG. Partner: Helen Weir; 1 s. Tom.

HOROVITCH, David

David Horovitch. Actor (M).
b. London, 11 August 1945.
TV: Bognor in *Bognor;* Inspector Dawson in *Deceit; Drop the Dead Donkey;* Barry in *Finding Sarah; French and Saunders;* Matthew Pocket in *Great Expectations;* Isaac of York in *Ivanhoe;* Mr Brown in *Just William;* Simon Freidman in *Love Hurts;* Inspector Slack in *Miss Marple;* Uncle Kallaway in *Piece of Cake;* Commander Daniels in *Poirot;* Dr Muller in *The Heat of the Sun;* Edward Clark in *The Sculptress;* Hugo in *West Beach.*
Films: *An Unsuitable Job for a Woman; Dirty Dozen III; Paper Marriage;* Isaac in *Solomon and Gaenor.*
Address: c/o Peters, Fraser and Dunlop, Drury House, 34–43 Russell Street, London WC2B 5HA. Hobbies: Walking, cricket, reading.

HORROCKS, Jane

Jane Horrocks. Actor (F)/Performer.
b. Rossendale Valley, Lancashire, 18 January 1964.
TV: Bunny in *Absolutely Fabulous; Bad Girl; Boon; Heartland; Henry IV: Parts I and II; Hunt for Venus; La Nonna;* Natalie in *Leaving Home; Never Mind the Horrocks; Nightlife; Red Dwarf;* Louise in *Road; Roots; Ruth Rendell Mysteries; Some Kind of Life;* The True Bride in *Storyteller; Suffer the Little Children;* Cammy in *Tales from the Crypt; The Garden;* Punk Girl in *Welcome to the Times.*
Films: Marla in *Bring Me the Head of Mavis Davis; Deadly Advice;* Jenny in *Getting it Right;* Nicola in *Life is Sweet;* Faith in *Memphis Belle; Second Best; Self-Catering;* Rita in *The Dressmaker;* Christine Bracken in *The Fifteen Streets;* Laura Hoff (L.V.) in *The Rise and Fall of Little Voice;* Patten the maid in *The Wolves of Willoughby Chase;* Assistant to Chief Witch in *Witches.*
Address: c/o PFD, Drury House, 34–43 Russell Street, London WC2B 5HA.

HORSFALL, Bernard

Bernard Horsfall. Actor (M).
TV: *Between the Lines; Casualty; Chelworth; Death of a Ghost; Doctor Who; Elizabeth; Enemy at the Door; For the Greater Good; Goodbye Days; Grand Duo; Heroes and Villains; Hill of the Red Fox; Minder; Nice Town; Poirot; Strangers and Brothers; Thatcher: The Final Years; The Advocates; The Avengers; The Bill; The Hound of the Baskervilles; Virtual Murder.*
Films: *A Distant Scream; Braveheart; Gandhi; Gold; Guns at Batasi; High Silence; Inside the Third Reich; Nothing to Declare; On Her Majesty's Secret Service; Quest; Shout at the Devil; Steel Bayonet; The Angry Silence; The Brass Target; The One That Got Away.*
Address: c/o Joyce Edwards RJS, 275 Kennington Road, London SE11 6BY.

HOWARD, Anthony

Anthony Howard. Actor (M).
b. Paddington, London, 19 April 1963.
TV: Alan Jackson in *EastEnders*.
Address: c/o London Management, Noel House, 2–4 Noel Street, London W1V 3RB.

HOWARD, Laura

Laura Howard. Actor (F). b. 1977.
TV: Alexandra in *Covington Cross*; Pippa in *Eskimo Day*; Pippa in *Eskimo Day Returns*; Cully Barnaby in *Midsomer Murders*; Tammy Rokeby in *So Haunt Me*; Deborah Osborne in *Soldier, Soldier*; Erica in *The Bill*.
Address: c/o PFD, Drury House, 34–43 Russell Street, London WC2B 5HA.

HOWELLS, Cliff

Cliff Howells. Actor (M). b. London.
TV: Mr McCormack in *A Little Bit of Lippy*; Radio Presenter in *A Very British Coup*; George Jackson in *Brookside*; Crowder in *Coronation Street*; Joseph Cartwright in *GBH*; Donald in *Heartbeat*; Scase in *London's Burning*; Ronnie in *Slap!*; George Leamington in *Snakes and Loofahs*; Man in *Sob Sisters*; Mike Venner in *The Bill*.
Address: c/o Pemberton Associates, 193 Wardour Street, London W1V 3FA.

HOWMAN, Karl

Karl Howman. Actor (M).
b. Woolwich, London, 13 December 1953.
TV: Charlie in *Babes in the Wood* (1998); Wayne Todd in *Bad Boys* (1996); Lenny Bright in *Boon* (1986); Jacko in *Brush Strokes* (1986); Billy Griffiths in *Juliet Bravo* (1980); Danny Varrow in *Minder* (1979); *Mulberry* (1992); Harold Lowe in *SOS Titanic* (1979); Satcey in *The Professionals* (1977); Davey Holmes in *The Sweeney* (1975).
Films: Johnny Reeves in *Party Party*; Stevie in *Stardust*; David in *The Long Good Friday*.
Address: c/o Noel Gay Artists, 19 Denmark Street, London WC2H 8NA. m. Clare; 1 d. Chloe.

HUDD, Roy

Roy Hudd. Actor (M).
b. Croydon, Surrey, 16 May 1937.
TV: *Cold Lazarus*; *Common As Muck*; *Heavy Weather*; *Karaoke*; *Lipstick On Your Collar*; *The Memoirs of Sherlock Holmes*.
Films: *The Alf Garnett Saga*; *The Blood Beast Terror*; *The Magnificent Seven Deadly Sins*; *Up Pompeii*; *Up the Chastity Belt*.

Address: c/o Aza Artistes, 652 Finchley Road, London NW11 7NT.

HUDSON, Robert

Robert Hudson. Actor (M).
b. Sheffield, 24 February 1960.
TV: Harper in *999*; Trevor McBride in *Always and Everyone*; *Asda*; Trevor in *Coronation Street*; Ted Morgan in *Dalziel and Pascoe*; Pete Ryan in *Dempsey and Makepeace*; Reg in *Fresh Fields*; Mal Shanks in *Heartbeat*; Inspector Maxwell in *Peak Practice*; *Poor Circulation*; Don in *Saracen*; *Shredded Wheat*; Roberts in *Slaggers*; Patrick in *Surgical Spirit*; Gordon in *Sylvia's Wedding*; PC 'Yorkie' Smith in *The Bill*; *The Normandy Affair*; Clive Baxter in *The Rock Pool*; *Windsurf*.
Address: c/o Langford Associates, 17 Westfields Avenue, London SW13 0AT. Hobbies: Football, drawing.

HUDSON, Samuel

Samual Hudson. Actor (M).
TV: Luke in *A Touch of Love*; Dorian in *Dangerfield*; Bartholomew in *In Suspicious Circumstances*; Inspector Shaikh; David in *Springhill*; Bob Yob in *The Smiths*; Dave Lee in *Woof*.
Address: c/o Gary Trolan Management, 30 Burrard Road, London NW6 1DB.
Hobbies: Singing, playing guitar, fencing, horse riding, fitness.

HUGHES, Geoffrey

Geoffrey Hughes. Actor (M).
b. Liverpool, 2 February 1944.
TV: Tim in *Boon* (1992); *Coasting* (1990); Eddie Yates in *Coronation Street*; *Doctor Who*; Squire Clodpole in *Good Friday 1663* (1994); various in *I Lovett* (1992); Onslow in *Keeping Up Appearances*; Dilk in *Making Out* (1989,1991); *Needle* (1990); Hopalong Hughes in *Polterguests* (1998); *Spender* (1990); DS Bailey in *The Man from the Pru* (1989); Twiggy in *The Royle Family*; Trinculo in *The Tempest* (1992); *The Upper Hand* (1993); *You Rang M'Lord*; *Z-Cars*.
Films: *'Till Death Us Do Part*; *Hitler, My Part in His Downfall*; *Revenge*; *The Bofors Gun*; *The Man Who Had Power Over Women*; Paul McCartney in *The Yellow Submarine*; *Virgin Soldiers*.
Address: c/o The Richard Stone Partnership, 2 Henrietta Street, London WC2E 8PS.

HUGHES, Nerys

Nerys Hughes. Actor (F)/Presenter.
b. Rhyl, Denbighshire, Wales, 8 November 1941.
TV: *Bathing Elizabeth*; *Bazaar*; *Capital Woman*; *Gallow-*

glass; *Liverpool Mums*; Molly in *Molly*; *Survival of the Fittest*; District Nurse in *The District Nurse*; Sandra in *The Liver Birds*; Glenda in *The Queen's Nose*; *With a Little Help*.
Films: *Second Best*; Maria in *Swing*.
Address: c/o Burnett Granger Associates, Prince of Wales Theatre, 31 Coventry Street, London W1V 8AS. m. Patrick Turley; 1 s. Ben, 1 d. Marie-Claire.

HUGHES, Nicola
Nicola Hughes. Actor (F).
TV: *Heartburn Hotel*; *Night Swimming*; *Trial and Retribution II*.
Address: c/o Marmont Management Ltd, Langham House, 308 Regent Street, London W1R 5AL.

HUGHES, Sean
Sean Hughes. Actor (M)/Comedian.
b. London, 10 November 1965.
TV: *Aaaah Sean*; *Aspel*; *Clive Anderson Talks Back*; *Friday Night Live* (1987); *Life's a Bitch*; *Never Mind the Buzzcocks*; *Sean's Shorts* (1994); *Sean's Show* (1992); *The Signal Box*; *Thirtysomehow* (1995); *Tonight with Jonathan Ross*; *Wogan*.
Films: Einstein in *Rocket Man*; *Snakes and Ladders*; Immigration Officer in *Solo Shuttle*; *The Butcher Boy*; *The Commitments*.
Address: c/o PBJ Management, 5 Soho Square, London W1V 5DE.

HUGILL, Glenn
Glenn Hugill. Actor (M).
TV: Alan Hardy in *Bostock's Cup*; John in *Chandler and Co*; Alan McKenna in *Coronation Street*; Charlie in *Dalziel and Pascoe*; Dave in *Just a Gigolo*; Dave in *Tech Heads*; Waiter in *The Upper Hand*.
Films: Kenny St John in *Up on the Roof*.
Address: c/o Hillman Threlfall, 33 Brookfield, Highgate West Hill, London N6 6AT.

HULL, Ben
Ben Hull. Actor (M).
b. Manchester, 8 November 1972.
TV: Martin Wells in *Children's Ward*; Mark Lacey in *Coronation Street*; Lewis Richardson in *Hollyoaks*; *Revelations*.
Address: c/o Tim Scott Personal Management, 5 Cloisters Business Centre, 8 Battersea Park Road, London SW8 4BG.

HULL, Jenny
Jenny Hull. Presenter/Reporter.
b. London, 30 December 1964.

TV: *Around the South*; *Arts Exchange*; *BBC South Today*; *Children in Need*; *Craftwise*; *Getaways*; *Good Morning With Anne and Nick*; *Holiday* (1997); *How Do They Do That?*; *In Force*; *People and Pets*; *Scene South*; *Shop*; *South of Westminster*; *Summer Getaways*; *Summer Holiday*; *Take a Letter*; *The Science Challenge*.
Address: c/o Unique Artistes, Avon House, Kensington Village, London W14 8TS. m. Nigel Marven.

HULLEY, Annie
Annie Hulley. Actor (F).
b. Wakefield, 23 October 1955.
TV: Eunice in *A Brother's Tale*; Deirdre Burkhill in *A Pinch of Snuff*; Dolores in *Ain't Misbehavin'*; Carol in *Between the Lines*; *Campion*; Lorna Morrow in *Casualty*; Maureen Bradley in *Chandler and Co*; Sarah Sydenham in *City Central*; Gwen Loveday in *Coronation Street*; Joanna in *Eldorado*; *Fame is the Spur*; Janice in *Liverpool 1*; Dee in *London Bridge*; Brelca in *Return of the Antelope*; Di in *September Song*; Sandra in *Sleepers*; Di Higgs in *Sloggers*; *The Bill*; Stella in *The Specials*; Carol Braithwaite in *The Ward*; *Watchdog*.
Address: c/o Barry Brown & Partner, 47 West Square, London SE11 4SP.

HUMBLE, Kate
Kate Humble. Presenter.
TV: *Web Wise*; *Animal Hospital*; *Castaway Science*; *Essential Guide to Rocks* (1998); *Fasten Your Seat Belt* (1998); *GMTV*; *Holiday*; *Holiday on a Shoestring*; *Holidays Out*; *Humble Holidays* (1998); *Summer Holiday*; *Top Gear*; *Waterworld*.
Address: c/o Speak-easy Ltd, 90 St Mary's Road, Market Harborough, Leicestershire LE16 7DX.

HUMPHRIES, Barry
Barry Humphries. Actor (M)/Entertainer. b. Kew, Melbourne, Victoria, Australia, 17 February 1934.
TV: *A Profile of Barry Humphries*; Dame Edna Everage in *An Audience with Dame Edna, Another Audience with Dame Edna, Dame Edna Kisses It Better, Dame Edna's Hollywood, Dame Edna's Neighbourhood Watch*; *The Dame Edna Experience*; *Selling Hitler*; *Single Voices*; *The Barry Humphries Scandals*; *The Bunyip*.
Films: *Barry McKenzie Holds His Own*; *Bliss of Mrs Blossom*; Metternich in *Immortal Beloved*; Sir Les Patterson in *Sir Les Saves the World*; *SpiceWorld*; Barry's Aunt in *The Adventures of Barry McKenzie*; *The Getting of Wisdom*; Humphrey in *The Leading Man*.
Address: c/o Kate Feast Management, 10 Primrose Hill Studios, Fitzroy Road, London NW1 8TR. m. Lizzie Spender; father-in-law Sir Stephen Spender.

HUNNAM, Charlie

Charlie Hunnam. Actor (M).

TV: *All Done With Wires*; Jason in *Byker Grove*; Mark in *Last Night*; Brad in *Microsoap*; Wes in *My Wonderful Life*; Nathan in *Queer as Folk*; Interviewee in *The Fame Game*; Sam in *Three Little Devils*.

Films: Dazz in *Whatever Happened to Harold Smith*.

Address: William Morris Agency (UK) Ltd, 1 Stratton Street, London W1X 6HB.

HUNNICUTT, Gayle

Gayle Hunnicutt. Actor (F).

b. Texas, 6 February 1943.

TV: *A Woman of Substance* (1985); *Affairs of the Heart* (1974); *Dallas* (1989); *Dream West* (1987); *Dylan Thomas* (1983); *Fantomas* (1980); *Humbolt's Gift* (1971); *Lime Street* (1987); *Man and Boy* (1971); *Man Called Intrepid* (1979); *Martian Chronicles* (1978); *Omnibus: The Cat and Culture* (1998); *Philip Marlowe, Private Eye* (1984); *Privilege* (1986); *Sherlock Holmes* (1986); *Strong Medicine* (1986); *Switch* (1975); *Tales from the Crypt* (1995); *Tales of the Unexpected* (1981); *Taxi* (1982); *The Ambassadors* (1975); *The Fall of Eagles*; *The First Modern Olympics* (1985); *The Golden Bowl* (1972); *The Lady Killers* (1981); *The Professionals* (1997); *The Return of the Saint*; *The Ripening Seed* (1973); *The Saint* (1989); *Voices in the Garden* (1991).

Films: *Dream Lover*; *Eye of the Cat*; *Fragment of Fear*; *Legend in Hell House*; *New Face in Hell*; *Once in Paris*; *Return of The Man From U.N.C.L.E.*; *Running Scared*; *Scorpio*; *Silence Like Glass*; *Target*; *The Little Sister*; *The Sell Out*; *The Spiral Staircase*; *Voices*.

Address: c/o William Morris Agency (UK) Ltd, 1 Stratton Street, London W1X 6HB. m. Simon Jenkins; 2 s. Nolan, Edward.

HUNNIFORD, Gloria

Gloria Hunniford. Reporter/Presenter.

b. Portadown, 10 April 1940.

TV: *Big Band Specials*; *Cashwise*; *Children in Need*; *Family Affairs*; *Gloria Live*; *Good Fortune*; *Holiday*; *Open House with Gloria Hunniford* (1998); *Something for the Weekend*; *Songs of Praise*; *Sunday*; *Sunday Live*; *Sunday, Sunday*; *That's Showbusiness*; *This Morning*; *Time Off With…*; *Wogan*.

Address: c/o Unique Artistes, Avon House, Kensington Village, London W14 8TS. d. Caron Keating. Hobbies: Charity work.

HUNT, Gareth

Gareth Hunt. Actor (M). b. London, 7 February 1943.

TV: *An Actor's Life For Me*; *Shaping Up* (1986); *Side by Side*; *The Love School*; *The New Avengers*; *Upstairs Downstairs*.

Films: *A Chorus of Disapproval*; *A Ghost in Monte Carlo*; *A Hazard of Hearts*; *Bloodbath at the House of Death*; *Castle of Adventure*; *Dangerous Love*; *Gabrielle and the Doodlemen*; *It Couldn't Happen Here*; *Licensed To Love and Kill*; *Marco Polo*; *The World is Full of Married Men*; *When the Wall Came Tumbling Down*.

Address: c/o ICM, Oxford House, 76 Oxford Street, London W1N 0AX.

HUNT, Helen

Helen Hunt. Actor (F).

b. Culver City, California, USA, 15 June 1963.

TV: Rebecca Miller in *My Life and Times* (1991); Sarah Sargeant in *Pioneer Woman* (1973); Tami Maida in *Quarterback Princess* (1983); Tracy Calder in *Rollercoaster* (1977); Rene in *Sexual Healing* (1993); Tracey in *Shooter* (1988); Clancy Williams in *St Elsewhere* (1982); Debbie Markham in *Sweet Revenge* (1984); Helga Robinson in *Swiss Family Robinson* (1975); Kerry Gerardi in *The Fitzpatricks* (1977); Bonnie Slaughter in *The Mary Tyler Moore Show* (1970); Kathy Miller in *The Miracle of Kathy Miller* (1981); Kristina Manchett in *The Spell* (1977); Viola in *Twelfth Night* (1998); Jill Prentiss in *Amy Prentiss* (1974); Lizzie Eaton in *Angel Dusted* (1981); Jenny Wells in *Bill: On His Own* (1983); Naomi in *Child Bride of Short Creek* (1981); Cathy in *Choices of the Heart* (1983); Teila Rodriquez in *Death Scream*; Sandy Cameron in *Desperate Lives* (1982); Galter and The Golden Lance* (1985); Gina Pulasky in *In the Company of Darkness* (1993); Jesse in *Incident at Dark River* (1989); Blossom in *Into the Badlands* (1991); Lisa Quinn in *It Takes Two* (1982); Jamie Buchman in *Mad About You* (1992); Pamela Smart in *Murder in New Hampshire* (1991).

Films: Carol Connelly in *As Good As It Gets*; Hospital Reporter – Rose Pondell in *Bob Roberts*; Lynne Stone in *Girls Just Want To Have Fun*; Jennifer in *Miles From Home*; Annie in *Mr Saturday Night*; Jessie Gates in *Next of Kin*; Beth Bodell in *Peggy Sue Got Married*; Teri in *Project X*; Hope Wyatt in *Stealing Home*; Anna in *The Waterdance*; Lena in *Trancers, Trancers III*; Jo Harding in *Twister*; Tracy in *Waiting to Act*.

Address: c/o Creative Artists Agency, 9830 Wilshire Boulevard, Beverly Hills, California 90212, USA. m. Hank Azari (actor). Hobbies: Dancing, yoga, painting.

HUNT, Kathryn

Kathryn Hunt. Actor (F).

TV: Shaz in *Bloomin' Marvellous*; *Brookside*; *Cold Feet*; *Cracker*; *For Amusement Only*; *In Suspicious Circum-*

stances; Irma in *Reckless; Ronson; The Ward;* Cheryl in *Where the Heart Is.*
Films: Val in *Darkest Light;* Nurse Stanley in *Girls' Night.*
Address: c/o Kate Feast Management, 10 Primrose Hill Studios, Fitzroy Road, London NW1 8TR.

HUNTER, Alan
Alan Hunter. Actor (M). b. 24 October 1952.
TV: Don Leaver in *A Touch of Frost;* Robert Young in *Bergerac;* Stephen Butcher in *Crown Court;* Richard Holthouse in *Dangerfield II;* John Woods in *Dangerous Lady;* Baz Taylor in *Dempsey and Makepeace;* Max in *EastEnders;* Guy Slate in *Hannay;* John Vassal; John Reardon in *London's Burning; Minder;* Laurence Moody in *Print Out;* Nick Laughland in *Silent Witness II;* Baz Taylor in *Snakes and Ladders; Spoils of War; Squadron;* Baz Taylor in *Strangers;* Greg Ryder in *Take the High Road;* Terry Green in *The Bill; Truckers.*
Address: c/o Roxane Vacca Management, 73 Beak Street, London W1R 3LF.

HUNTER, Kelly
Kelly Hunter. Actor (F).
TV: *Bergerac; Berlin; Boon; Casualty;* Maddie in *Close Relations;* Dr Amy Webber in *Life Force; Mad and Sandy; Marriage In Cold Blood; Prime Suspect III; Resort to Murder; Say It With Music: Irving; Silent Witness; The Bill; The House of Eliot.*
Films: *Being Human; Les Misérables; Look Me in the Eye; The Hollow Reed; The Luizhin Defence.*
Address: c/o Conway Van Gelder, 18–21 Jermyn Street, London SW1Y 6HP.

HUNTER, Russell
Russel Hunter. Actor (M).
b. Glasgow, 18 February 1925.
TV: *A Touch of Frost; Albert and the Lion; Bud Neill; Casualty; Dad on Arrival; Deacon Brodie; King and Castle; Lovejoy; Rab C Nesbitt; Taggart; The Big Fish; The Detectives;* Ian Sinclair in *The Dunroamin' Rising; The Gaffer; The Justice Game; The Negotiator; Wolf to the Slaughter;* Lonely in *Callan.*
Films: *Shooting Elizabeth.*
Address: c/o Marjorie Abel Ltd, 50 Maddox Street, London W1R 9PA.

HUQ, Konnie
Konnie Huq. Presenter. b. 17 July 1975.
TV: *Eat Your Words* (1997); *HQ* (1993); *Newsround* (1992); *Ratlan II* (1993); *The Rage* (1997); *TVFM* (1993); *VATV* (2000).
Address: c/o Blue Peter Office, BBC Television, Wood Lane, London W12 7RJ.

HURST, Lee
Lee Hurst. Comedian. b. London, 1964.
TV: *Have I Got News For You; Lee Hurst Live; Lee Hurst Live at the Backyard Comedy Club; Saturday Live; They Think It's All Over.*
Address: c/o Backyard Productions, Backyard Comedy Club, 231-337 Cambridge Heath Road, London E2 0EL.

HURST, Samantha
Samantha Hurst. Actor (F). b. Billingham.
TV: *Ain't Misbehavin'* (1996); *Emmerdale; Harry* (1996); Dolores Sharpe in *Heartbeat* (1999); *Lights of Manchester* (1995).
Address: c/o Roxane Vacca Management, 73 Beak Street, London W1R 3LF. **Hobbies:** Painting.

HUTCHINGS, Geoffrey
Geoffrey Hutchings. Actor (M).
b. Dorchester, Dorset, 8 June 1939.
TV: Ralph Tomkins in *A Year in Provence;* PO Swift in *Bye Bye Baby;* Oliver Flint in *Casualty;* Professor Marshall in *Degrees of Error;* Helen's Father in *Drop the Dead Donkey;* Sarge in *Duck Patrol;* Carwyn Phillips in *Filipina Dreamgirls;* Ralph Biggs in *Goodnight Mr Tom;* Bardolph in *Henry IV;* Trevor Gregson in *Kavanagh QC;* Lucas in *Maigret;* Colin Smy in *Midsomer Murders;* Heart Attack in *Minder;* Carvailles in *Monsieur Renard;* Chris Borland in *Mortimer's Law;* John Edwards in *Our Friends in the North;* Jake Gibson in *Peak Practice;* Rochefort in *Pirate Prince;* Douglas Barton in *The Bullion Boys;* The Governor in *Witness Against Hitler.*
Films: Delcommune in *Heart of Darkness;* Nym in *Henry V;* Estate Manager in *Longitude;* Cyril in *The Bench;* Armourer in *Topsy Turvy;* Alec Laing in *White Hunter, Black Heart;* Hubert in *Wish You Were Here.*
Address: c/o Burnett Granger Associates, Prince of Wales Theatre, 31 Coventry Street, London W1V 8AS.

HUTCHISON, Ken
Ken Hutchinson. Actor (M).
TV: *Dixon of Dock Green; Z-Cars; Softly, Softly; The Persuaders; The Protectors; The Sweeney; Shoestring; Hazel; Targets; Space 1999; Bulman; Minder; The Borderers; Sutherland's Law,* Matt Harvey in *The Onedin Line;* Colin in *The Wild West Show,* Heathcliff in *Wuthering Heights; Colin* Wright in *Hideaway;* Inspector Murphy in *Murphy's Mob; Loneliness of the Long Distance Piano Player; Just Another Saturday; Just a Boy's Game; The Red Shift; A Gift from Nessus; The First World Cup; A Touch of Red; One of the Boys; All Quiet on the Western Front; Masada; The Bill; Taggart; 99–1;*

Casualty, The Chief, Hamish Macbeth; Cardiac Arrest; Milner.
Films: *Julius Caesar; Straw Dogs; Wrath of God; Ghandi; Ballon the Slates; Blonde Fist; From the Island.*
Address: c/o Michael Ladkin Personal Management, Suite One, Ground floor, 1 Duchess Street, London W1N 3DE.

HUTTON, Marcus

Marcus Hutton. Actor (M).
TV: Nixon in *Bedlam*; Nathan Cuddington in *Brookside*; Pete in *Bureaucracy of Love*; Henry in *Class Act*; Alan Morton in *Crocodile Shoes*; Phillip in *Diana: Her True Story*; Leigh in *Doctor Who*; Mark in *Inspector Allen*; Wilkins in *Love Hurts*; Lt. Jones in *Lovejoy*; Various in *Smack the Pony*; Co. Pilot James in *The Professionals*.
Address: c/o Elaine Murphy Associates, 310 Aberdeen House, 22–24 Highbury Grove, London N5 2EA.

HYDE, Connie

Connie Hyde. Actor (F).
b. Macclesfield, Cheshire, 2 December 1969.
TV: DS Janet Miller in *City Central*; Synie in *Lifeboat*; DS Susie Blake in *The Dark Room*; Katherine Heywood in *Wing and A Prayer*.
Address: c/o PFD, Drury House, 34–43 Russell Street, London WC2B 5HA. Hobbies: Swimming, running.

HYDE, Jonathan

Jonathan Hyde. Actor (M).
TV: Tigellinus in *A.D.* (1985); Dr Oliver Pleasance in *Bliss* (1995); Godfrid in *Cadfael* (1994); Rosencrantz in *Hamlet, Prince of Denmark* (1980); Caesar in *I Spy Returns* (1994); Duke of Bedford in *Joan Of Arc* (1999); Edward Marshall Hall in *Shadow of the Noose* (1989).
Films: Westridge in *Anaconda*; Van Pelt/Sam Parrish in *Jumanji*; Cadbury in *Richie Rich*; The Egyptologist in *The Mummy*; Ismay in *Titanic*.
Address: c/o PFD, Drury House, 34–43 Russell Street, London WC2B 5HA.

HYDE-PIERCE, David

David Hyde-Pierce. Actor (M).
b. Saratoga Springs, New York, USA, 3 April 1959.
TV: Dr Niles Crane in *Caroline in the City* (1995); Jerry Dorfer in *Dream On* (1992); Dr Niles Crane in *Frasier*; Perry in *Jackie's Back* (1999); Dr Jack Henson in *The Outer Limits* (1996); Theodore Van Home in *The Powers That Be* (1992); Cecil Terwilliger in *The Simpsons* (1997).
Films: Slim in *A Bug's Life*; Delivery Room Doctor in *Addams Family Values*; Bartender in *Bright Lights, Big City*; Mark in *Crossing Delancey*; Daedalus in *Hercules*; Michael Hastings in *Isn't She Great*; Garth in *Little Man Tate*; John Dean in *Nixon*; Monsieur Henri in *Rocket Gibraltar*; Marty Kerner in *Shiny New Enemies*; Dennis Reed in *Sleepless in Seattle*; Lou Rosen in *The Fisher King*; *The Mating Habits of the Earthbound Human*; Theatre Guy in *Vampire's Kiss*; Roy in *Wolf*.
Address: c/o Marilyn Szatmary, Suite 440, 8730 Sunset Boulevard, Los Angeles, California 90069, USA. Hobbies: Piano, skiing.

I

IGBON, Alan

Alan Igbon. Actor (M). b. Manchester, 29 May.

TV: Teddy in *GBH*; *Jake's Progress*; Boswell in *Me! I'm Afraid of Virginia Woolf*; Dennis in *Moving Story*; Danny in *Soul Survivors*; Loggo in *The Boys from the Blackstuff*; Mike in *The Daughter of Albion*; Sheldon in *The Front Line*.

Films: Lenny in *Babylon*; Vic in *Bloody Kids*; Tommy in *One Armed Bandits*; Meakin in *Scum*; Jesus in *Walter*; Lloyd in *Women in Tropical Places*.

Address: c/o Chuck Julian Associates, Suite 51, 26 Charing Cross Road, London WC2H ODH.

ILES, Jon

Jon Iles. Actor (M). b. Ripon, Yorkshire, 17 May 1954.

TV: *C.A.T.'s Eyes*; *Crown Court*; *The Dick Emery Show*; *Fresh Fields*; *Law and Order*; *Never the Twain*; *Supergran*; DC Dashwood in *The Bill*; *The Krypton Factor*; *Three, Seven, Eleven*; *You Bet*.

Address: c/o Hilary Gagan Associates, 2nd Floor, Gloucester Mansions, 140A Shaftesbury Avenue, London WC2H 8HD.

IMRIE, Celia

Celia Imrie. Actor (F). b. 15 July 1952.

TV: *102 Boulevard Haussman*; Mrs Bennett in *A Christmas Carol*; Vera in *A Dark Adapted Eye*; *A Question of Guilt*; Lady Macdonald in *A Tour of the Western Isles*; Victoria Bridgewater in *A Very Open Prison*; *Absolutely Fabulous*; Rachel in *All Good Things*; Marianne in *Bergerac*; The Duchess of Battersea in *Blackhearts in Battersea*; *Blind Justice*; *Bonjour La Classe*; Elsie Queen in *Cloud Howe*; Phillipa in *dinnerladies I & II*; Mrs Calloway in *Duck Patrol*; Gertrude in *Gormenghast*; Sister Muriel Fleming in *Hospital*; *Ice Age*; Nadine in *Into the Blue*; *Jake's Journey*; *Lovejoy*; Victoria Madison in *Mr White Goes To Westminster*; *Old Flames*; Miss Jewsbury in *Oranges Are Not the Only Fruit*; Clare in *Pat and Margaret*; *Say Hello to the Real Dr Snide*; Sheila Armstrong in *Shoestring*; Miss Withers in *Snap*; *Stay Lucky*; *Taggart*; Ann Hadon-Smith in *Thacker*; Lucy Otis in *The Canterville Ghost*; *The Darling Buds of May*; Mum in *The Eggman*; *The Justice Game*; *The New Statesman*; Fiona Paterson in *The Nightmare Man*; Susan Nunsuch in *The Return of the Native*; Joanna Tundish in *The Riff Raff Element*; *The Victoria Wood Christmas Show* (1992); *The World of Eddie Weary*; Kirsty in *The Writing on the Wall*; Polly in *To the Manor Born*; Mrs Miller in *Tom Jones*; Nurse Jenny in *Upstairs Downstairs*; *Van Der Valk*; *Victoria Wood – As Seen On TV*; *Victoria Wood Playhouse*; Jean in *Wokenwell*.

Films: *Assassin*; Barbara in *Blue Black Permanent*; *Death on the Nile*; *Hiccup*; *Highlander*; Iris in *Hilary and Jackie*; Fadge in *In the Bleak Midwinter*; Mrs Moritz in *Mary Shelley's Frankenstein*; *Murder on the Moon*; Fighter Pilot in *Star Wars: The Phantom Menace, Episode 1*; Homilly in *The Borrowers*; *The Harmfulness of Tobacco*; *The House of Whipcord*; *The Wicked Lady*.

Address: c/o CDA, 19 Sydney Mews, London SW3 6HL.

INDRANI, Seeta

Seeta Indrani. Actor (F). b. London, 20 April 1963.

TV: Sita Sharma in *Albion Market*; Haji in *C.A.T.'s Eyes*; Apala in *Damon and Debbie*; Dr Nasir in *Dempsey and Makepeace*; Belinda in *Dido and Aeneas*; Mrs Chastri in *Hunting the Squirrel*; *Inspector Morse: 'The Ghost in the Machine'*; Presenter in *Into Music*; Critina Ramirez in *Maria's Child*; Sam in *Mathspy*; Marjorie in *Spatz*; Presenter in *Storytime*; WPC Norika Datta in *The Bill*; *Timon of Athens*; Katrina in *Tripods*.

Films: Carmen in *Gunbus*; *The Nutcracker*.

Address: c/o Cassie Mayer Ltd, 34 Kingly Court, London W1R 5LE. m. Sergio; 1 d. Milly. Hobbies: Flamenco dancing.

INGLEBY, Lee

Lee Ingleby. Actor (M).

TV: Lloyd in *A Small Addition*; Gary in *A Wing and a Prayer*; *Cadfael*; Kieron in *Dalziel and Pascoe*; Paul in *In the Red*; Spartley in *Jonathan Creek*; Rob in *Junk*; Gordon in *Killer Net*; David in *Nature Boy*; Kevin Fitzpatrick in *Soldier, Soldier*; Bobbie Franklyn in *The Dark Room*.

Films: Leering Lad in *Beer Goggles*; Gustav in *Ever After*.

Address: c/o Conway Van Gelder, 18–21 Jermyn Street, London SW1Y 6HP.

INGLETON, Doreen

Doreen Ingleton. Actor (F).
b. London, 11 January 1966.
TV: Joy Thomas in *EastEnders*; Dusty in *Family Affairs*; Mrs Cooper in *Grange Hill*; Annie Lever in *Inspector Morse*; Opera Singer in *Jonathan Creek*; Mrs Ashley in *Pot Boiler*; Sister Anderson in *Roger, Roger*.
Films: Ray's Mum in *Everybody Loves Sunshine*; Usma in *First It Is Dark*.
Address: c/o Nina Quick Associates, 50 Pembroke Road, London W8 6NX.

INMAN, John

John Inman. Actor (M)/Guest.
b. Preston, 28 June 1935
TV: Mr Humphries in *Are You Being Served?*; *Blankety Blank*; Mr Humphries in *Grace and Favour*; Neville Sutcliffe in *Odd Man Out*; Mr Jones in *Take a Letter Mr Jones*; *The Royal Variety Performance*.
Films: Mr Humphries in *Are You Being Served?*
Address: c/o AMG Ltd, 8 King Street, London WC2E 8HN.

INVERDALE, John

John Inverdale. Presenter. b. Plymouth, 1957.
TV: *On Side; On The Line; Rugby Special; Sunday Grandstand; The World's Strongest Man*.
Address: Contact via 'BBC Sport', Union House, 65–69 Shepherds Bush Green, London W12 8TX.
Hobbies: Pop trivia, rugby.

IRVINE, Hazel

Hazel Irvine. Presenter.
b. St. Andrews, Scotland, 26 May 1965.
TV: *Children in Need; Commonwealth Games; European Championships; Feeling Good; Grandstand; Olympic Games; Outside Now; Ski Sunday; Sportscene; Sunday Grandstand; World Cup Football*.
Address: c/o David John Associates, 6 Victoria Crescent Road, Glasgow G12 9DB. Hobbies: Golf, hill-walking.

IRVINE, John

John Irvine. Reporter/Presenter. b. Belfast, 1964.
TV: Reporter *Ulster Television*; Reporter *ITN*; Ireland Correspondent *ITN*.
Address: c/o ITN, 200 Gray's Inn Road, London,WC1X 8AX. m. Libby; 1 d. Elizabeth.

IRVING, George

George Irving. Actor (M).
TV: Andrew in *A Class of His Own*; *A Night on the Tyne*; Freeman in *A Wing and a Prayer*; Jennings in *Backup*; Jimmy Robinson in *Bad Company*; Ramirez in *Blue Money*; Eddie Lang in *Born Kicking*; DS Ned Cottan in *Bulman*; Tony Underwood in *Bust*; Prior Herluin in *Cadfael*; Will in *Commitments*; Ken Jackson in *Dangerfield*; Tony Royale in *For 4 Tonight*; Meyer in *Holby City*; *In Suspicious Circumstances*; George Henderson in *Inspector Morse*; Alan Jackson in *Juliet Bravo*; Robert in *Made in Heaven*; Dave in *McBride Reading Crime*; Paul in *Night People*; Martin Keel in *Peak Practice*; Justin in *Sitting Pretty*; Humolotin in *South America Journey*; Mdzelevski in *Squaring the Circle*; Joey Buchan in *The Bill*; Preacher in *The Healing*; Det. Insp. Dowler in *The Jazz Detective*; Black Michael in *The Prisoner of Zenda*; David in *The Stars Look Down*; Lawrence Schofield in *This Year, Next Year*; Golaszevski in *Three Days In Szcecin*; Tug in *Tumbledown*; Dave in *Vicious Circle*; Andy in *Village Hall*; Sid in *When The Boat Comes In*; Clive Munson in *Wokenwell*.
Address: c/o Rebecca Blond Associates, 69a Kings Road, London SW3 4NX.

IVORY, William

William Ivory. Actor (M). b. Nottingham, 1964.
TV: Harold Peart in *All Creatures Great and Small*; Thad in *Berlin Breaks*; Andrew Jackson in *Between the Lines II*; Ramsden in *Capstick's Law*; *Chef!*; Vinny in *Common As Muck; Common As Muck II*; Evans in *Confessional*; Eddie Ramsden in *Coronation Street*; Ted in *Deptford Graffiti*; Jed in *Emmerdale Farm*; *Hollyoaks*; *How We Used To Live*; Steve in *Ice Dance*; Ashton in *Merrihill Millionaires*; The Stranger in *Punishment Without Crime*; Mark Divine in *Resnick*; Chris Cheese in *Sardines*; Ephraim Wharmby in *Strike Pay*; *The All New Alexei Sayle Show*; Patrick Dunphy in *Three, Seven, Eleven*; Oggie (lead) in *Vacant Possessions*.
Address: c/o Roxane Vacca Management, 73 Beak Street, London W1R 3LF. Hobbies: Horse riding, guitar, drums, soccer, rugby, cricket.

IZZARD, Eddie

Eddie Izzard. Actor (M)/Comedian.
b. 7 February 1962.
TV: *Aristophanes; Channel Izzard* (1997); *Cows; Lust for Glorious* (1997); *Tales from the Crypt: TX: Je suis a Standup..Definite Article Tour* (1996).
Films: *Hanging Around; The Avengers; The Secret Agent; Velvet Goldmine*.
Address: c/o PBJ Management, 5 Soho Square, London W1V 5DE.

J

JACKSON, Philip

Philip Jackson. Actor (M).

b. Nottingham, 18 June 1948.

TV: Bernard in *Afternoon Off*; Eustace Buckle in *Black Hearts in Battersea*; Jeff in *Blooming Youth*; Ronald in *Bramwell*; Bob in *Camera Club–Glamour Night*; George in *Corn Devils*; Clem in *Downwardly Mobile*; Malcolm in *Exclusive Yarns*; Geoff in *Farmer's Arms*; Clive in *Games Without Frontiers*; Dave in *Girl's Night*; Malachi in *Hamish MacBeth II*; Ken Marsden in *Heartbeat*; Derek in *Honky Tonk Heroes*; Tappy in *Keep An Eye On Albert*; Danny in *Lizzie's Pictures*; Sergeant in *Murder Most Horrid*; Dawlish in *On the Palm*; York in *Our Boy*; Eric Wrathall in *Our Geoff*; Pasmore in *Pasmore*; Dave in *Pennies from Heaven*; Blincoe in *Pickersgill People*; Inspector Japp in *Poirot*; Paul Smith in *Radio*; Detective Harris in *Rat in the Skull*; Abbott Hugo in *Robin of Sherwood*; Jack in *Rogue Male*; Walter in *Skinny Marink*; Arthur in *Sounding Brass*; Milburn in *The Ambassador*; Martin Alloway in *The Consultant*; Greg Oaksey in *The Dark Room*; Rest in *The Fosdyke Saga*; Purgavie in *The Great Paper Chase*; Leonard in *The Last Salute*; The King in *The Luck Child*; Thompson in *The Sea*; Stan in *The Story of Philip Knight*; Wingrove in *The Vice*; Archie in *The Wayward Train*; DS Gilmore in *A Touch of Frost*; The Foreman in *Woe to the Hunter*.

Films: Farmer in *Alien Love Triangle*; Howard Spink in *Bad Behaviour*; Jim in *Brassed Off*; Wasasenburg in *Cousin Bette*; Alan in *Give My Regards to Broad Street*; Martin Burke in *High Hopes*; George in *Little Voice*; White in *Opium War*; Greaves in *Scum*; Simpson in *The Last Dance*; Burkinshaw in *The Fourth Protocol*; Dad in *What Rats Won't Do*.

Address: c/o Markham & Froggatt Ltd, 4 Windmill Street, London W1P 1HF.

JAFFREY, Saeed

Saeed Jaffrey. Actor (M).

TV: *A Killing on the Exchange*; *A Passage to India*; lead in *A View from the Window*; *After Midnight*; *Common As Muck*; Ravi Desai in *Coronation Street*; *Destiny*; *Far Pavilions*; Rafiq in *Gangsters*; *Hard Cases*; *Jewel in the Crown*; *Little Napoleons*; *Love Match*; *Minder*; *Partition*; *Rumpole of the Bailey*; Stay-ing On; *Tales of the Unexpected*; *Tandoori Nights*; *Two Oranges and a Mango*.

Films: Hamidullah in *A Passage to India*; *Courtesans of Bombay*; Patel in *Gandhi*; *Hullabaloo over George and Bonnie's Pictures*; *Masala*; *My Beautiful Laundrette*; *The Deceivers*; *The Guru*; *The Man Who Would Be King*; *The Wilby Conspiracy*.

Address: c/o Magnolia Management, 136 Hicks Avenue, Greenford, Middlesex UB6 8HB. Hobbies: Cricket, snooker, cookery, cartoonist.

JAMES, Clive

Clive James. Presenter/Host.

b. Sydney, New South Wales, Australia, 7 October 1939.

TV: *Cinema*; *Clive James on TV* (1997); *Fame in the Twentieth Century* (1993); *Monday Night Clive* (1999); Postman in *Neighbours* (1996); *Night of 1,000 Years* (1999); *Saturday Night Clive* (1988); *Sunday Night Clive* (1994); *The Clive James Interview* (1991); *The Clive James Show* (1998); *The Late Clive James* (1983); *Various Clive James Postcards From…*

Address: c/o PFD, Drury House, 34–43 Russell Street, London WC2B 5HA.

JAMES, Godfrey

Godfrey James. Actor (M). b. London, 16 April 1931.

TV: *A Very Peculiar Practice*; *About Face*; *Camille*; *Coronation Street*; *Crime Monthly*; *Crime Traveller*; *Criss Cross*; *The Darling Buds of May*; *Dempsey and Makepeace*; *Dickens*; *El C.I.D*; *Emmerdale*; *Fanny by Gaslight*; *Good Guys*; *Hart to Hart*; *Highlander*; *Journey into the Shadows*; *Just a Gigolo*; *Labours of Erica*; *Maigret*; *Minder*; *Mussolini*; *Oliver Twist*; *Poirot*; *Prisoners of Childhood*; *Return of the Antelope*; *Shadow of the Noose*; *Stick With Me Kid*; *The Battle Of Waterloo*; *The Bill*; *Truckers*; *William Tell*; *Wish Me Luck*; *Yes*.

Films: *Highlander*; *Princess*; *Teenie Weenies*; *The Shade of Sandcastle*; *Warburg*; *Women are Weak*.

Address: c/o Scott Marshall, 44 Perryn Road, London W3 7NA.

JAMES, Lennie

Lennie James. Actor (M).

TV: *A Touch of Frost*; *Between the Cracks*; *Civvies*; *Cold Feet*; *Comics*; *Déjà vu*; *Everyman*; *Love Hurts*; *Omnibus*

Artist Unknown; Orchid House; Out of the Blue; People of the Forest; Perfect Blue; Something's Burning; Elias in *Storm Damage; Thief Takers; Undercover Heart.*
Films: *Among Giants;* Sol in *Diamonds;* Graham in *Elephant Juice; Fathers, Sons and Unholy Ghosts; Les Misérables; Lost in Space.*
Address: c/o ICM, Oxford House, 76 Oxford Street, London W1N 0AX.

JAMES, Raji
Raji James. Actor (M). b. London, 24 February 1970.
TV: *A Box Full of Stories; Agony;* Neil in *Blind Men;* Rick in *Call Red;* Frankie in *Chandler and Co; Coronation Street;* Barney in *Crocodile Shoes;* Ben in *Cry Wolf;* Ravi in *Do the Right Thing; Doomwatch;* Junior in *Harry; Heaven on Earth;* Sanjay Kumar in *Holby City; Kid; Mohinda Cheema;* Rafi Sadiki in *Out of the Blue;* Daniels in *Stick With Me;* Andy Hill in *The Bill; The Creatives.*
Films: Hammond in *Action Stations;* Abdul in *East is East.*
Address: c/o Langford Associates, 17 Westfields Avenue, London SW13 0AT. m. Cheryl Innes; 1 s. Shannon.

JAMESON, Louise
Louise Jameson. Actor (F).
b. Wanstead, London, 20 April 1951.
TV: Susan in *Bergerac; Casualty; Cider with Rosie; Degas and Pissaro; Dominic; Doctor Who;* Rosa de Marco in *EastEnders; Emmerdale; Molly; My Friend Walter; Rides; Stick With Me Kid;* Blanche in *Tenko; The Bill; The Game; The Omega Factor; The Pale Horse; The Secret Diary of Adrian Mole; The Tempest; The Terror Game; The Upper Hand; Tom Brown's Schooldays; Wycliffe.*
Address: c/o Conway Van Gelder, 18–21 Jermyn Street, London SW1Y 6HP.

JAMESON, Susan
Susan Jameson. Actor (F).
b. Worcestershire, 13 August 1944.
TV: *All in Good Faith; Archers Goon; Armchair Theatre; Bad Boys; Band of Gold; Boon; Casualty; Circle of Deceit;* Myra in *Coronation Street; Dave Allen; Heartbeat; Hell's Bells; Hi De Hi; Softly, Softly; Space 1999; Strange Report;* Kate in *Take Three Girls;* Christine in *To Serve Them All My Days; U.F.O.;* Jessy Seaton in *When The Boat Comes In; Who Sir, Me Sir?; Woof;* WPC Nelson in *Z-Cars.*
Films: *All Creatures Great and Small;* Catherine in *Brief Lives; Monster; International Velvet; Last of the Long Haired Boys; Little Grey Home in the West; Nine Lives.*

Address: c/o Kate Feast Management, 10 Primrose Hill Studios, Fitzroy Road, London NW1 8TR. m. James Bolam (actor); 1 d. Lucy.

JAMIESON, Kathy
Kathy Jamieson. Actor (F).
TV: *Badger;* Policewoman in *Brookside;* Anne in *Cardiac Arrest;* Sandra Arden in *Coronation Street;* Jo in *Cracker;* Margaret in *Emmerdale;* Sophie in *Heartbeat;* Maggie in *How We Used To Live;* Mum in *Josie Smith; Love and Reason; Medics;* Ellie in *Mr Wroe's Virgins;* Arthur's Mum in *Skallagrig;* Mrs Whitley in *The Ward;* April in *Who's Our Jenny Lind?*
Films: Policewoman in *Business as Usual;* Judith in *Butterfly Kiss;* Kiosk Lady in *The Duke.*
Address: c/o John Markham Associates, 1a Oakwood Avenue, Purley, Surrey CR8 1AR.

JANSON, David
David Janson. Actor (M).
TV: Herr Flick in *'Allo 'Allo;* Chicken Man in *Bad Boys;* Steve in *Brush Strokes;* Billy in *Don't Rock the Boat;* Ellison in *Ever Decreasing Circles;* Ken in *Get Some In;* Mime Artist in *Give Us a Clue;* Murray in *Grundy;* Michael, the Postman in *Keeping up Appearances;* Jimmy in *Newcomers;* Ali Baba in *T-Bag Strikes Again;* various in *The Russ Abbot Show;* Terry in *The Upper Hand.*
Films: Michael in *Diana, Her True Story;* Simon in *The Euphoric Scale.*
Address: c/o Associated International Management, 5 Denmark Street, London WC2H 8LP.

JANUS, Samantha
Samantha Janus. Actor (F). b. 2 November 1972.
TV: Isobel de Pauli in *Liverpool 1;* Ruth in *Babes in the Wood;* Hedda in *Demob;* Mandy in *Game On;* Geraldine in *Grimleys;* Charmaine Wilcox in *Health and Efficiency;* Imogen in *Imogen's Face;* Sharon in *Mama's Back;* Marion in *Minder;* Nicole in *Pie in the Sky;* Louise in *Rampage;* Jane in *Sharman.*
Films: *A Murder of Quality; Dr Jekyll and Mr Hyde;* Hazel in *Up 'n' Under.*
Address: c/o Thelma Wade, 54 Harley Street, London W1.

JARVIS, Chris
Chris Jarvis. Actor (M)/Narrator.
b. Romford, 20 April 1969.
TV: *Broom Cupboard* (1992); *Chucklevision;* Hot Rodney in *Dream Street; Fully Booked; Henry's Cat* (1997); *Look Sharp; Playdays; The Anorak; The Demon Headmaster; The Friday Zone; Wood Lane TV.*

TV AWARD WINNERS 1999

National Television Awards

Most Popular Actress	Amanda Burton
Most Popular Actor	John Thaw
Most Popular Comedy Performer	Nicholas Lyndhurst
Most Popular Newcomer	Tamzin Outhwaite
Most Popular Entertainment Presenter	Lily Savage

She was up against stiff competition from Lisa Riley, Julie Hesmondhalgh, Pam Ferris and Dame Thora Hird, but once again Amanda Burton proved the people's choice for Most Popular Actress.

1999 was a great year for John Thaw. Not only did he scoop the Most Popular Actor award, but his one-off World War Two drama *Goodnight Mister Tom* took the Most Popular Drama prize.

As Rodney Trotter, he'll be forever
Britain's favourite 'plonker', but
Nicholas Lyndhurst's Most
Popular Comedy Performer
award also recognised his work
on *Goodnight Sweetheart*.

In her acceptance speech for
Most Popular Newcomer,
Tamzin Outhwaite thanked her
boyfriend for his 'love and
unconditional support'.
Unfortunately he couldn't be at
the awards ceremony though –
he'd already bought a ticket for
a football match!

Once a social worker called
Paul O'Grady, self-styled 'blonde
bombsite' Lily Savage took the
Most Popular Entertainment
Presenter award for her own
show and *Blankety Blank*.

British Academy Television Awards

Best Light Entertainment Performance	Michael Parkinson
Best Actress	Dame Thora Hird
Best Actor	Tom Courtenay
Best Comedy Performance	Dermot Morgan
Best Newcomer	Tamzin Outhwaite

Parky proved just the ticket for Best Light Entertainment Performance, Yorkshire's best export since flat caps and whippets.

There is nothing like a dame as evergreen Dame Thora Hird showed when she scooped the Best Actress award for Alan Bennett's *Waiting for the Telegram*.

One of Britain's true acting greats Tom Courtenay put in another stunning performance in *A Rather English Marriage* alongside Albert Finney and Joanna Lumley, winning him the Best Actor award.

The award for Best Comedy Performance was given posthumously to Irish actor Dermot Morgan, whose death was made all the more tragic by the fact he'd just made his name in *Father Ted*.

British Soap Awards

Best Actor — Ross Kemp
Best Actress — Barbara Windsor
Sexiest Male — Michael Greco
Sexiest Female — Tamzin Outhwaite
Villain of the Year — Stephen Billington
Best Comedy Performance — John Savident
Lifetime Achievement Award — William Roache

The Krays were eclipsed as the East End's most notorious hard men when the Mitchell brothers walked into Albert Square. This earned Grant, alias Ross Kemp, the Best Actor award.

Wosgoingon? Why it's Grant's mum Peggy, otherwise known as *Carry On* legend Barbara Windsor, collecting her prize for Best Actress.

Michael Greco has hearts fluttering as Walford's very own Italian Stallion, Beppe di Marco. His stud status won him the title of soapland's Sexiest Male.

It could have been rent-an-acceptance-speech year for Tamzin Outhwaite, better known as *EastEnders'* Mel, in 1999. She added Sexiest Female to her long list of awards.

Stephen Billington learned the value of the old treat 'em mean, keep 'em keen adage when *Coronation Street's* nasty Greg earned him the accolade of Villain of the Year.

John Savident's bluff northern humour has made him popular as Weatherfield's Fred Elliott. It also earned him the Best Comedy Performance award.

Where would *Coronation Street* be without the familiar face of Ken Barlow, alias William Roache? He won a Lifetime Achievement award for being on the show since its inception.

Royal Television Society Awards

Best Presenter	David Attenborough
Best Television Performance	Rory Bremner
Best Actor	Ray Winstone
Best Actress	Dame Thora Hird

His whisper may be imitated by impressionists, but no-one has ever come close to mimicking David Attenborough's success as a wildlife film-maker, as evident in his Best Presenter award.

Man of a thousand voices Rory Bremner reverted to his own, albeit one of surprise and gratitude, to accept the award for Best Television Performance.

Ray Winstone's trademark tough guy roles in *Nil By Mouth*, *Births, Marriages and Deaths*, *War Zone* and *Last Christmas* have earned him plaudits. They also won him the Best Actor award.

Television and Radio Industries Club Award

Newscaster of the Year	Trevor McDonald
Sports Personality of the Year	Sue Barker
ITV/Channel 4/	
Channel 5 Personality of the Year	Johnny Vaughan
New TV Talent of the Year	Katie Derham
Satellite/Digital Personality of the Year	Melinda Messenger

She may have given up tennis but Sue Barker certainly added another string to her racquet when she took up presenting. She was named Sports Personality of the Year.

Whether he's informing us about a worldwide disaster or the light-hearted '...and finally' story at the close of the news, Trevor McDonald is the man Britain prefers to deliver our headlines, a status which won him the Newscaster of the Year title.

Something's always cooking when Johnny Vaughan's on *The Big Breakfast*. His wit and wonder won him the commercial television Personality of the Year title.

What Katie Did is an old book title, but when it comes to newswoman Katie Derham the answer's easy – she won the award for New TV Talent of the Year.

Former Page 3 girl Melinda Messenger proved she's got brains as well as beauty by being named Satellite/Digital Personality of the Year.

British Comedy Awards

Best Comedy Actor	Ricky Tomlinson
Best Comedy Actress	Caroline Aherne
Comedy Entertainment Personality	Paul Merton
Best Male Comedy Newcomer	Sacha Baron Cohen (Ali G)
Best Female Comedy Newcomer	Jessica Stevenson
Best New TV Comedy	dinnerladies
Best Comedy Game Show	Have I Got News For You
Best Comedy Talk Show	Graham Norton
Best TV Comedy Drama	Cold Feet
Best Comedy Entertainment Programme	Comic Relief
Best Live Stand-up	Bill Bailey
Lifetime Achievement Award	The Two Ronnies

It was enough to make Mrs Merton's net curtains twitch and the Royles to drop their channel changer – Caroline Aherne clinched the Best Comedy Actress title.

Have we got news for you! Paul Merton, surely the modern-day equivalent of Tony Hancock, scooped the award for Comedy Entertainment Personality.

As a white man playing a black homeboy, Sacha Baron Cohen sparked controversy when he created Ali G. However he deserved the Best Male Comedy Newcomer award for being brave enough to ask Ulster Republicans why they hate the RAC.

Bill Bailey really did come home when he won the Best Live Stand-up award for *The Comedy Store '99* and *Edinburgh '99*.

Victoria Wood's oven quips in
dinnerladies proved the perfect recipe
for the Best New TV Comedy award.

Writing and starring in *Spaced* proved out of
this world for Jessica Stevenson. It earned her
the Best Female Comedy Newcomer award.

There was a case for holding the front page when the *Have I Got News For You* team hit the headlines themselves for winning the Best Comedy Game Show award.

He's camper than a whole field of tents but Graham Norton had exactly the right pitch for the Best Comedy Talk Show award.

Take six thirtysomethings, throw in relationships, careers, children and Manchester and you have *Cold Feet*, the show that was hot enough to win the Best TV Comedy Drama category.

Red Nose Day has now become an institution thanks to Lenny Henry and chums. The charity fund-raiser's annual broadcast, *Comic Relief '99*, won the Best Comedy Entertainment Programme award.

It was hello from me and hello from him when the much-missed double act The Two Ronnies temporarily got back together to collect a Lifetime Achievement award.

Address: c/o Unique Artistes, Avon House, Kensington Village, London W14 8TS. Hobbies: Theatre, gym training, music, disc jockey.

JARVIS, Jamie

Jamie Jarvis. Actor (M).
TV: Troy Harvey in *EastEnders*.
Address: c/o London Management, Noel House, 2–4 Noel Street, London W1V 3RB.

JARVIS, Martin

Martin Jarvis. Actor (M)/Writer.
b. Cheltenham, 4 August 1941.
TV: Linus Frank in *The Absence of War*; *Boon*; Sam Harvey in *Breakaway*; *Casualty*; Uriah Heep in *David Copperfield*; *Doctor Who*; *Extreme Ghostbusters*; Randall Rees in *Inspector Morse*; *Little Women*; *Lovejoy*; *Max Steel*; Maurice Howling in *Murder Most Horrid*; *Murder She Wrote*; Nicholas Nickleby in *Nicholas Nickleby*; *Richie Rich*; Oliver Prude in *Rings on Their Fingers*; *Ross*; M. Renal in *Scarlet and Black*; Neil Biddle in *Sex and Death* (1999); *Space: Above and Beyond*; George Farmlow in *Supply and Demand* (1999); Wilfred Anstey in *The Black Tower*; Jon Forsyte in *The Forsyte Saga*; *The Moonstone*; Frank Greystock in *The Pallisers*; *The Tick*; *The Way of All Flesh*; Harvey Wade in *A Touch of Frost*; *Walker, Texas Ranger*.
Films: Davenport in *Calliope*; Papa in *Emily's Ghost*; Jeremy in *Taste of the Blood of Dracula*; Donald Wilcox in *The Last Escape*; Mr X in *The X-Ray Kid*; Sir Cosmo Duff Gordon in *Titanic*.
Address: c/o London Management, Noel House, 2–4 Noel Street, London W1V 3RB. m. Rosalind Ayres; niece Sophie Langham. Hobbies: Music, growing tangerines.

JASON, David

David Jason. Actor (M).
b. Edmonton, London, 2 Febraury 1940.
TV: Ted Simcock in *A Bit of a Do*; lead role in *A Sharp Intake of Breath*; Inspector Jack Frost in *A Touch of Frost*; Beck in *All the King's Men*; George in *Amongst Barbarians*; Pa Larkin in *The Darling Buds of May*; *David Jason...In His Element*; Shorty Mepstead in *Lucky Feller*; Steven March in *March in the Windy City*; Del Trotter in *Only Fools and Horses*; Granville in *Open All Hours*; Blanco in *Porridge*; Skulliion in *Porterhouse Blue*; The Chemist in *Single Voices: The Chemist*; Billy in *The Bullion Boys*.
Films: *Royal Flash*; Odd Job Man in *The Odd Job*.
Address: c/o The Richard Stone Partnership, 2 Henrietta Street, London WC2E 8PS.

JAYSTON, Michael

Michael Jayston. Actor (M). b. 29 October 1935.
TV: *99-1*; *A Bit of a Do*; *A Guilty Thing Surprised*; *Big Deal*; *Capstick's Law*; *Casualty*; *C.A.T.'s Eyes*; *Churchill's People*; *Cluedo*; *Crazy Like a Fox*; *The Darling Buds of May*; *Doctor Who*; *Element of Doubt*; *Flesh and Blood*; *Haggard*; *Heartburn Hotel*; *Jane Eyre*; *Mad Jack*; *Noah's Ark*; *Only Fools and Horses*; *Outside Edge*; *Press Gang*; *Quiller*; *Room at the Bottom*; *Runaways*; *She Fell Among Thieves*; *Stand By Your Man*; *Stay Lucky*; *Tales of the Unexpected*; *The Disappearance of Lady Francis Fairfax*; *The Good Guys*; *The Ladykillers*; *The Last Romantic*; *The Power Game*; *The Southbank Special*; *There Comes a Time*; *Time For Murder*; *Tinker, Tailor, Soldier, Spy*.
Films: *20,000 Leagues Under The Sea*; *A Midsummer Night's dream*; *Alice in Wonderland*; *Bequest to the Nation*; *Craze*; *Cromwell*; *Dominique*; *Follow Me*; *Highlander III*; *Nicholas and Alexandra*; *The Homecoming*; *The Internecine Project*; *Zulu Dawn*.
Address: c/o Whitehall Artists, 125 Gloucester Road, London SW7 4TE.

JEFFORD, Barbara

Barbara Jefford. Actor (F). b. 26 July 1930.
TV: Lady Mary in *Porterhouse Blue*; Lydia Elliott in *The House of Eliot*.
Films: Magda Goebbels in *Hitler: The Last Ten Days*; Academic woman in *The Saint*; Dr Ruth Faber in *The Shoes of the Fisherman*.
Address: c/o PFD, Drury House, 34–43 Russell Street, London WC2B 5HA.

JENKINS, Sue

Susan Elizabeth Jenkins. Actor (F).
b. Liverpool, 31 July 1959.
TV: Janey in *The Beiderbecke Affair*; Jackie Corkhill in *Brookside*; Julie in *Coasting*; Gloria Todd in *Coronation Street*; Charlotte in *How We Used To Live*; Molly Noselle in *In Suspicious Circumstances*; *Wood and Walters*; *Z Cars*.
Address: c/o Scott Marshall, 44 Perryn Road, London W3 7NA. m. David Fleeshman; 2 d. Emily, Rosie, 1 s. Richard. Hobbies: Water skiing, reading, aromatherapy.

JENNINGS, Alex

Alex Jennings. Actor (M). b. 1958.
TV: Alfonso Bonzo in *Alfonso Bonzo*; *Ashenden, The Spy*; lead role in *Bad Blood*; *Bye Bye Columbus*; *Dread Poets Society*; Bitzer in *Hard Times*; *Inspector Morse*; Siegfried Sassoon in *Poetry of War*; *Shelley*; *Smiley's People*; *The Franchise Affair*; Sebastian Parrish in *The Inspector Alleyn Mysteries*; *The Kit Curran Radio Show*.

Films: *A Midsummer Night's Dream; Solo Shuttle; The Wings of the Dove; War Requiem.*
Address: c/o Marmont Management Ltd, Langham House, 308 Regent Street, London W1R 5AL.

JENSEN, Ashley

Ashley Jensen. Actor (F).
TV: *Bad Boys;* PC Sue Chappel in *City Central;* Rosie in *May to December; Roughnecks.*
Address: c/o Shepherd & Ford, 13 Radnor Walk, London SW3 4BP.

JEPHCOTT, Dominic

Dominic Jephcott. Actor (M).
b. Coventry, West Midlands, 28 July 1957.
TV: Geoffrey Compton in *A Touch of Frost;* Kenneth Fairbrother in *And the Beat Goes On;* Kohler in *Berlin Break;* Peter Gosford in *Casualty;* Alasdair Finch in *Claws;* Sam Fallowfield in *Dalziel and Pascoe;* Inspector Trent in *EastEnders;* Edward Vallance in *Family Album;* Jonathan in *Hold The Dream;* Reggie Brocklehurst in *Jewel in the Crown;* Villeforte in *Napoleon and Josephine;* Harry Maylie in *Oliver Twist;* Magnus Strove in *Paradise Postponed;* Robert St Loup in *Proust – Great Writers;* Moriarty in *Retour De Flamme;* Sandy Ranson in *Rumpole of the Bailey;* Roger Holbrook in *Sam Saturday;* Purvis in *Stalky and Co;* Herbert Howells in *Stars in a Dark Night;* Roger Radcliffe in *Stay Lucky;* Mark in *The Aerodrome;* Hobson in *The Beiderbecke Affair;* Hobson in *The Beiderbecke Connection;* Barrister in *The Bill;* Richard Bayly in *Midsomer Murders;* Dr Chivers in *The Vanishing Man;* Lord Munroe in *Ticket to Ride.*
Films: Peter Leer in *All Quiet on the Western Front;* Reginald in *An African Dream;* Daniel in *Face the Music;* Mount in *Good and Bad at Games;* Dean in *Inseminoid; Interview with a Vampire;* MP in *The Opium War;* Sir Andrew Foulkes in *The Scarlet Pimpernel.*
Address: c/o Markham & Froggatt Ltd, 4 Windmill Street, London W1P 1HF.

JERRICHO, Paul

Paul Jerricho. Actor (M). b. 18 November 1948.
TV: Reg in *American Freak;* Simmons in *Backup;* Doctor in *Chucklevision;* DI Hopwood in *Crime Limited;* Danny Moorcock in *Emmerdale;* Lt. Col. Charles Newman in *For Valour;* Mr Hicks in *Grange Hill;* MP in *Hale and Pace;* Robert Hastings in *Howard's Way;* Jamie Prosser in *Jump;* Officer in *Knights of God;* Dr Wake in *London Bridge;* Bruce Karvis in *Love;* Dave in *Love Hurts; Medicine Through Time;* Cedric in *Melissa;* Harold Merrick in *Mosley;* Police Inspector in *Press Gang;* Wilkin in *The Biko Inquest; The Bill;* The Castel-

lan in *The Five Doctors;* David Maybury in *The Ice House;* Brindith in *The New Adventures of Robin Hood;* Hirschler in *Touch and Go;* Charles Woodhouse in *Triangle.*
Films: *Cry Freedom; Force Ten From Navarone;* Ortutay in *Forced March;* MI5 Officer in *L'Accompagnatrice; The Thirty-None Steps; The Empire Strikes Back.*
Address: c/o McIntosh Rae Management, Thornton House, Thornton Road, London SW19 4NG.

JESSOP, Melanie

Melanie Jessop. Actor (F).
TV: Millicent in *A Touch of Frost;* Bubble's Secretary in *Absolutely Fabulous;* Laurette in *Act of Will;* Jessica in *After the War;* Anne in *Between the Lines;* Belinda in *Chandler and Co;* Helen in *Geh Kinder Geh;* Harry Enfield's TV Show;* Sharon in *Night of the Comic Dead;* Tamara in *Perfect Scoundrels II;* Molly in *Poirot;* Ruby in *Shadow of the Noose;* Lizzie in *Smith and Jones;* Anna in *The Last Word;* Adele in *The Mixer and The Birthday Party.*
Address: c/o Hillman Threlfall, 33 Brookfield, Highgate West Hill, London N6 6AT.

JOHNS, Milton

Milton Johns. Actor (M). b. Bristol, 13 May 1938.
TV: Rev Horsley in *A Horseman Riding By;* Lonny in *Bergerac;* Roland Salmon in *Boon;* Harbutt in *Bread and Blood;* Mr Conran in *Butterflies;* Mr X in *Casualty;* Hugo in *Chalk;* Brendan Scott in *Coronation Street;* Stanley in *Dickens; Doctor Who;* Webb in *El CID;* Dan Danby in *Ever Decreasing Circles;* Customs Officer in *Fresh Fields;* Collinson in *Going Straight;* George Hemlock in *Harry's Mad;* Grim Reaper in *Knight School;* John in *M & M;* Meikel John in *Moll Flanders;* Kistiakcowski in *Oppenheimer;* Perker in *Pickwick Papers;* Cullian in *Play for Today;* William in *Poldark;* Roberts in *Porridge;* John Dashwood in *Sense and Sensibility;* Hopkinson in *Sharpe;* various in *Softly, Softly;* Benham in *Some Mother's Do 'Ave 'Em;* Fred Mitchell in *South Riding;* Mr Adams in *Spearhead;* Mr L. Chop in *Supergran;* Smithson in *The Boy Who Won the Pools;* Fletcher in *The First Churchills;* George Lintz in *The Flaxborough Chronicles;* Ernie in *The Good Life;* Leonard Denbigh in *The Missing Postman;* Sims in *The Professionals;* Vargos in *The Saint; The Scarlet Pimpernel;* Giraud in *The Three Musketeers;* Toms in *The Upper Hand;* Barry Ashwell in *Trainer;* Charles in *Two's Company;* Wilberforce in *Wuffer;* Reg Watson in *Yes, Minister.*
Films: Jarvis in *Black Wood;* German Ambassador in *Mussolini;* Vader's Aide in *Star Wars: The Empire Strikes Back;* Kagan in *The Wall.*

Address: c/o Hilda Physick Agency, 78 Temple Sheen Road, London SW14 7RR. m. Bella; 1 d. Leah, 1 s. Simeon. Hobbies: Cricket (qualified umpire), horse racing, walking.

JOHNSON, Clark

Clark Johnson. Actor (M). b. Philadelphia, Pennsylvania, USA, 10 September 1954.

TV: Mike Delaney in *Coopersmith*; Clarke Roberts in *E.N.G.*; *Forever Knight*; Detective Meldrick Lewis in *Homicide: Life on The Street*; Detective Morton in *Hostage*; Al Pendleton in *Hot Shots*; Guest star in *LA Law*; Sophomore Jinx in *Law and Order*; Master Chang in *Model By Day*; *Nightstick*; Spencer in *Psychic*; *Second City*; Glenn in *Silent Witness: What a Child Saw*; Ray Hamilton in *The Hoop Life*; *The Prosecutors*; *Under African Skies*; Butch in *Women of Brewster Place*.

Films: Black Gang Leader in *Adventures in Babysitting*; Moriarty in *Blindside*; *Blood Brothers*; Lee in *Colors*; Bob Covington in *Drop Zone*; *Fear Of Fiction*; Trevon in *Final Round*; Graves in *Iron Eagle II*; Clive in *Lulu*; Hackney Transportist in *Nick of Time*; Mark Halstead in *Nowhere To Hide*; JJ in *Renegades*; Reece in *Rude*; Dave in *Skullduggery*; Busha in *Soul Survivor*; Winston in *Wild Thing*.

Address: c/o United Talent Agency, Suite 500, 9560 Wilshire Boulevard, Beverly Hills, California 90212, USA.

JOHNSON, Don

Don Johnson. Actor (M).
b. Flat Creek, Missouri, USA, 15 December 1949.

TV: Cowboy in *Amateur Night at the Dixie Bar and Grill* (1979); Bonard Davis in *Beulah Land* (1980); Gandy in *Big Hawaii* (1977); Johnny Wilson in *Cover Girls* (1977); Doug in *Eight is Enough* (1977); Elvis Presley in *Elvis and the Beauty Queen* (1981); Daniel Easton in *First, You Cry* (1979); Jefferson Davis Prewitt in *From Here to Eternity* (1980); Sergeant John Libbey in *In Pursuit of Honor*; *In the Company of Darkness* (1993); Gunther in *Katie: Portrait of a Centrefold* (1978); Nashebo in *Kung Fu* (1973); Quirt in *Law of the Land* (1976); *Life on the Flipside* (1988); Detective James Crockett in *Miami Vice* (1984); Nash Bridges in *Nash Bridges*; *Pressure Point* (1978); Officer Andy Brady in *Revenge of the Stepford Wives* (1980); Deloy Coopersmith in *Sarge* (1971); Mike Sloan in *Ski Lift to Death* (1978); *Tales of the Unexpected* (1979); Sergeant Brian Scott in *The City* (1977); Contestant in *The Dating Game* (1969); Ben Quick in *The Long Hot Summer* (1985); *The Marshal*; Judson Fletcher in *The Rebel* (1979); *The*

Rookies (1972); Officer Larry Wilson in *The Streets of San Francisco* (1976); Bob Howard in *The Two Lives of Carol Letner* (1981); Charlie Morgan in *The Two-Five* (1978).

Films: Vic in *A Boy and His Dog*; Paul Verrall in *Born Yesterday*; Tim Murphy in *Cease Fire*; Jerry Beck in *Dead Bang*; Lt. Falcon in *G.I. Joe: The Movie*; *Good Morning...and Goodbye!*; Ben Dunmore in *Goodbye Lover*; David Greenhill in *Guilty as Sin*; Marlboro in *Harley Davidson and the Marlboro Man*; Documentary Filmmaker in *Heartbeat*; Carl in *Melanie*; Ben Reed in *Paradise*; Harold McKay in *Return to Macon County*; Jacob Gorch in *Soggy Bottom, USA*; Wiley Boon in *Sweet Hearts Dance*; Stanley Cole in *The Harrad Experiment*; Harry Madox in *The Hot Spot*; Stanley Sweetheart in *The Magic Garden of Stanley Sweetheart*; David Simms in *Tin Cup*; Matthew in *Zachariah*.

Music: *Heartbeat*; *Let it Roll*; *Till I Loved You*.

Address: c/o William Morris Agency, 151 El Camino Drive, Beverly Hills, California 90212, USA. m. 1 Melanie Griffith (div); 1 s. Jesse; m. 2 Kelly Phleger; 1 d. Dakota Hobbies: Off-road racing, powerboat racing.

JOHNSON, Meg

Meg Johnson. Actor (F).
b. Upminster, Essex, 30 July 1927.

TV: *A Pattern for Life*; *Children's Ward*; Eunice in *Coronation Street*; *Crown Court*; *Empire Road*; *Hollyoaks*; *Life of Riley*; *Lovejoy*; *Mother Nature's Bloomers*; *Nearest and Dearest*; *Olympian Way*; *Split Ends*; *Strangers*; *Taggart*; *The Good Companions*; *The Harry Worth Show*; *The Practice*; *The Victoria Wood Show*; *Two Up, Two Down*; *Wednesday Love*; *Yanks Go Home*.

Address: c/o John Markham Associates, 1a Oakwood Avenue, Purley, Surrey CR8 1AR.

JOHNSON, Richard

Richard Johnson. Actor (M). b. 30 July 1927.

TV: *A Man For All Seasons*; *Anglo–Saxon Attitudes*; *Breaking The Code*; *The Camomile Lawn*; *Crucifier of Blood*; *Duel of Love*; *Heavy Weather*; *Made in Heaven*; *Midsomer Murders*; Duke of Norfolk in *Murder She Wrote*; *Murder Most Horrid*; *Robert Ryland's Last Journey*; *Supply and Demand*; *The Biko Inquest*; *The Echo*; Squire Trelawney in *Treasure Island*; *Voice Of The Heart*.

Films: *Castaway*; *Hennessy*; *Khartoum*; *Milk*; *Operation Crossbow*; *The Haunting*; *The Lonely Passion of Judith Hearne*; *Turtle Diary*.

Address: c/o Conway Van Gelder, 18–21 Jermyn Street, SW1Y 6HP. Hobbies: Cooking, travel, reading.

163

JOHNSON, Wil

Wil Johnson. Actor (M).

TV: Lysander in *A Midsummer Night's Dream*; DJ in *The Alexi Sayle Show*; Leroy in *Casualty*; DC Skeleton in *Cracker*; Haughton in *Crime Limited 'Haughton'*; Dekko in *Home Front*; Coach in *In the Pink*; Dave in *London's Burning*; Charlie in *Rides*; Leo in *Starting Out*; Lester in *Teaching Matthew*; Carl in *The Bill*; Steve in *The Factory*; Goose in *The Felix Dexter Show*; Drew in *White Goods*.

Address: c/o CAM London, 19 Denmark Street, London WC2H 8NA.

JOHNSTON, Kristen

Kristen Johnston. Actor (F).

b. Washington DC, USA, 20 September 1967.

TV: Sally Solomon in *3rd Rock from the Sun*; *Chicago Hope* (1994); *Christmas in Washington* (1996); Kathie Lee in *Duckman* (1997); Grace Chapman in *London Suite* (1996); Zena in *The Five Mrs Buchanans* (1994); Herself in *The Larry Sanders Show* (1998).

Films: Ivana Humpalot in *Austin Powers: The Spy Who Shagged Me*; Kate in *Backfire*; *McClintock's Peach*; *Running with Scissors*; Alice Kosnick in *The Debt Collector*; Wilma Flintstone in *The Flintstones in Viva Rock Vegas*.

Address: c/o Creative Artists Agency, 9830 Wilshire Boulevard, Beverly Hills, California 90212, USA. Hobbies: Mountain walking, hiking, dogs.

JOHNSTON, Sue

Sue Johnston. Actor (F).

b. Warrington, 7 December 1943.

TV: *A Touch of Frost*; *Bitter Harvest*; Sheila Grant/ Corkhill in *Brookside*; *Coronation Street*; *Crime Traveller*; *Drink the Mercury*; Val in *Duck Patrol*; Grace in *Full Stretch*; Barbara Grade in *Goodbye Cruel World*; Helga Allowby in *Hetty Wainthropp Investigates*; *In Suspicious Circumstances*; Mrs Bailey in *Inspector Morse*; Patricia Candy in *Into The Fire*; Terese Craven in *Luv*; Ruth Parry in *Medics*; *Measure for Measure*; Irma Brookes in *Sex, Chips and Rock 'n' Roll*; Maeve in *The Jump*; Mam in *The Royle Family*; Pat Phoenix in *The Things You Do For Love*; Hazel Devere in *The Verdict*; *Without Walls*.

Films: Vera in *Brassed Off*; *Face*; *Preaching to the Perverted*.

Address: c/o Ken McReddie Ltd, 91 Regent Street, London W1R 7TB. 1 s. Joel.

JONES, Bruce

Bruce Jones. Actor (M). b. Manchester, 1953.

TV: Les Battersby in *Coronation Street*; Tommy Dunn in *A Touch of Frost*; Brian in *Band of Gold*; Garden centre man in *Brookside*; Council Inspector in *Crewe Stories*; Fred Parkin in *Heartbeat*; Camera Man in *Hillsborough*; Terry in *Roughnecks*; Detective in *Waterfront Beat*.

Films: Bob in *Bob's Weekend*; Bob (lead) in *Raining Stones*; Reg in *The Full Monty*.

Address: c/o Nyland Management, 20 School Lane, Henton Chapel, Stockport SK4 5DG.

JONES, Freddie

Freddie Jones. Actor (M).

b. Stoke-on-Trent, 12 September 1927.

TV: *Adam Bede*; *Boon*; *Brensham People*; *Christopher Columbus*; *Cold Comfort Farm*; *Country Girl*; *Dalziel and Pascoe*; *District Nurse*; *Drovers Gold*; *Duck Patrol*; *Fall of the Angels*; *Germinal*; *Ghost*; *Hale and Pace*; *Heartbeat*; *Hotel Room*; *How to be Cool*; *Inspector Morse*; *It Could Be You*; *Lost in London*; *Mr Wroe's Virgins*; *Nan*; *Neverwhere*; *Pennies from Heaven*; *Permanent Red*; *Room at the Bottom*; *Secret Orchards*; *Sherlock Holmes*; *Silas Marner*; *Sob Sisters*; *Sunburn*; *The Bill*; *The Ghost of Motley Hall*; *The Kremlin Farewell*; *The Last Evensong*; *The Life and Crimes of William Palmer*; *The Paper Man*; *The Passion*; *The Secret Diary of Adrian Mole*; *The Temptation of Franz Schubert*; *The Young Indiana Jones Chronicles*; *Through the Looking Glass*; *Tiny Revolutions*; *Vanity Fair*; *Woof*.

Films: *A Pinch of Snuff*; *Accident*; *All Creatures Great and Small*; *And the Ship Sails On*; *Anthony and Cleopatra*; *Appointment with a Killer*; *Assault*; *Captain Stirrick*; *Comrades*; *Consuming Passions*; *Dark River*; *David Copperfield*; *Dead Ringer*; *Doctor in Trouble*; *Dune*; *Ela Nave Va*; *Eleanor, First Lady of the World*; *Erik the Viking*; *Far From The Madding Crowd*; *Firefox*; *Firestarter*; *Following the Ship*; *Frankenstein Must Be Destroyed*; *Gollocks/ There's Plenty of Room in New Zealand*; *Goodbye Gemini*; *Goose Bumps*; *House*; *Juggernaut*; *Kidnapped*; *Krull*; *Lost In London*; *Marat/Sade*; *Married to Malcolm*; *Maschenka*; *Mr Horatio Knibbles*; *Murder is Easy*; *My Life So Far*; *Never Ending Story III*; *Never Too Young to Rock*; *Otley*; *Romance with a Double Bass*; *Seeing Things*; *Silas Marner*; *Sitting Target*; *Son of Dracula*; *Spooks*; *The Black Cauldron*; *The Bliss of Mrs Blossom*; *The Elephant Man*; *The Last Butterfly*; *The Last Vampyre*; *The Man Who Haunted Himself*; *The Mystery of Edwin Drood*; *The Nativity*; *The Paperman*; *The Prince of Jutland*; *The Romantic Englishwoman*; *The Satanic Rites of Dracula*; *The Time to Die*; *The Zany Adventures of Robin Hood*; *Time After Time*; *Vampira*; *What Rats Won't Do*; *White Nights*; *Who's Who*; *Wild at Heart*; *Wisteria Lodge*; *Young Sherlock Holmes*; *Zulu Dawn*.

Address: c/o Ken McReddie Ltd, 91 Regent Street, London W1R 7TB.

JONES, Gemma

Gemma Jones. Actor (F).

b. London, 4 December 1942.

TV: *After the Dance; An Evil Streak; Devices and Desires; Faith; Inspector Morse;* Queen Elizabeth I in *Kenilworth; Longitude; The Borrowers;* Varia in *The Cherry Orchard;* Louisa Trotter in *The Duchess of Duke Street;* Gwendolyn in *The Importance of Being Earnest; The Lie;* Portia in *The Merchant of Venice;* Nina in *The Seagull; An Unsuitable Job for a Woman; Wycliffe.*

Films: *Captain Jack; Cotton Mary; On the Black Hill; Paper House; Sense and Sensibility; The Devils; The Feast of July; The Theory of Flight; The Winslow Boy; Very Like a Whale.*

Address: c/o Conway Van Gelder, 18–21 Jermyn Street, London SW1Y 6HP. 1 s. Luke; Father Griffith Jones; brother Nicholas Jones. Hobbies: Hill walking, all things Tibetan.

JONES, George

George Jones. Actor (M).

b. Chicago, Illinois, USA, 17 October 1948.

TV: Tweedledee in *Alice in Wonderland;* Charlie in *Alien Avengers I,II; Avery Schreiber: Live from the Second City;* Harry Macafee in *Bye Bye Birdie;* Norm Petersen in *Cheers;* Graham McVeigh in *Columbo: Strange Bedfellows;* Warren Kooey in *Hostage for a Day;* Gus Bertoia in *Making the Grade;* George Coleman in *The George Wendt Show;* Les Polonsky in *The Naked Truth;* Sam in *The Price of Heaven;* Mr Sweeney in *The Ratings Game.*

Films: Ticket Agent in *Airplane II;* Charlie Prince in *Dreamscape;* Fat Sam in *Fletch;* Harry in *Forever Young;* Shopkeeper in *Gift of the Magic;* Buster in *Gung Ho;* Harold Gorton in *House; Lakeboat;* Chet Bronski in *Man of The House;* Engineer in *My Bodyguard;* Mr Witten in *Never Say Die;* Jake in *No Small Affair;* Joey in *Outside Providence;* Chet Butler in *Plain Clothes; Prime Gig;* Ivan Bloat in *Rupert's Land;* Keller in *Space Truckers;* Martin Barnfield in *SpiceWorld – The Movie;* Lumberyard Clerk in *The Little Rascals;* Therapist in *The Lovemaster;* Dog catcher in *The Pooch and The Pauper;* Marty Morrison in *Thief of Hearts.*

Address: c/o Ray Reo, Brillstein-Grey, Suite 350, 9150 Wilshire Boulevard, Beverly Hills, California 90210, USA. c/o Paradigm Agency, 25th Floor, 1001 Santa Monica Boulevard, Los Angeles, California 90067, USA. Hobbies: Baseball, reading.

JONES, Peter

Peter Jones. Actor (M). b. Shropshire, 12 June 1920.

TV: *Fist of Fun; It's a Girl; Lifeboat; Minder; One for the Road; Tender Loving Care; The Lift; Midsomer Murders;*
The Upper Hand; Waiting.

Films: *Carry On England; Confessions of a Pop Performer; Milk; Return of the Pink Panther; Seven Nights in Japan.*

Address: c/o Burnett Granger Associates, Prince of Wales Theatre, 31 Coventry Street, London W1V 8AS.

JONES, Simon

Simon Jones. Actor (M).

b. Charlton Park, Wiltshire, 27 July 1950.

TV: *Blackadder II; Brideshead Revisited; Claws; Hart to Hart; The Hitch Hiker's Guide to the Galaxy; King of the Building; Liberty; Murder, She Wrote; Newhart; One Life to Live; Paramour; Remember Wenn; Rock Follies; Shrinks; Tattinger's; The Cosby Mysteries; The News is the News; The Price.*

Films: *American Friends; And Nothing but the Truth; Brazil; Club Paradiso; For Love or Money; Green Card; Miracle on 34th Street; Monty Python's Meaning of Life; Privates on Parade; Reds; Sir Anthony at Rawlinson End; The Devil's Own; Twelve Monkeys.*

Address: c/o ICM, Oxford House, 76 Oxford Street, London W1N 0AX.

JONSSON, Ulrika

Ulrika Jonsson. Presenter.

TV: *Eurovision Song Contest; Gladiators* (1992); *Great Big Election Programme* (1997); *In Bed With Me Dinner; It's Ulrika* (1997); *KYTV; Men Behaving Badly; Men for Sale* (1998); *Royal Variety Performance* (1998); Team Captain in *Shooting Stars* (1995); *The Lenny Henry Series; The National Lottery Dreamworld; TV-AM* (1989); *Ulrika in Euroland* (1998).

Address: c/o Cantor Wise Representation, Osborne House, 111 Bartholomew Road, London NW5 2BJ. 1 s. Cameron.

JORDAN, Desmond

Desmond Jordan. Actor (M). b. Dublin.

TV: *A Goldfish in the Sun; Angel Pavement; Casualty;* James Harris in *Crossroads; Dempsey and Makepeace; Emergency – Ward 10;* Father William in *Father Ted;* Uncle Sid in *London Bridge; Pennies from Heaven; Radio Roo; Shadows and Substance; The Avengers; The File on Harry Jordan; The Heiress of Garth; The Silver Box; The Trial of Captain Calthorpe.*

Address: c/o Langford Associates, 17 Westfields Avenue, London SW13 0AT.

JORDAN, Diane-Louise

Diana-Louise Jordan. Presenter. b. 1960.

TV: *Blue Peter; Bright Sparks; Children in Need; Songs of Praise.*

Address: Contact via BBC, Union House, 65–69 Shepherds Bush Green, London W12 8TX. 1 d. Justine.

JORDAN, Tony

Tony Jordan. Screenwriter.
b. Southport, Merseyside, 21 July 1957.
TV: *April Fool's Day (Hale and Pace); Boon; EastEnders; Eldorado; Minder; Sunburn; Thief Takers; Trainer; Where the Heart Is.*
Address: c/o Bill McLean Personal Management, 23b Deodar Road, London SW15 2NP. m. Tracy; 4 d. Krystal, Leah, Laurel, Lily, 2 s. Anthony, Ben. Hobbies: Boxing, sleeping.

JORDAN, Mark

Mark Jordan. Actor (M).
b. Oldham, 25 January 1965.
TV: PC Hicks in *All Creatures Great and Small;* Tommy in *Away From Home;* Wagger in *Bread;* PC Best in *Coronation Street;* Des in *Dawn and the Candidate; Earthfasts; EastEnders; Emmerdale;* Dave in *How We Used to Live;* Malcolm in *Made in Heaven;* Ian in *Seaview;* George in *Sherlock Holmes; Shoot to Kill;* Grolly in *Strike It Rich;* Reg in *The Last All-British Winner;* Johnno in *Too Nice by Half.*
Address: c/o Evans & Reiss, 100 Fawe Park Road, London SW15 2EA. m. Siobhan Finneran; 1 s. Seamus. Hobbies: Playing with son, watching movies.

JOSEPH, Lesley

Lesley Joseph. Actor (F).
TV: *Macbeth; Absurd Person Singular; My Country 'Tis of Thee; And Mother Makes Five; Sadie; It's Cold Outside; Horizon; The Ballad of Johnny Vanguard; No 10; The Knowledge; Roots; Broke Homes; Les girls; Minder; Exclusive Yarns; A Sleeping Life; P's and Q's;* Dorian in *Birds of Feather; Through the Lace Curtains; Edd the Duck's Megastar Treck; Jack and the Beanstalk; Easy Money;* Ma Pecs in *Rumble; Get Fit With Brittas.*
Address: c/o Silvester Management. m.; 1 s. Andrew; 1 d. Elizabeth.

JOSEPH, Michelle

Michelle Joseph. Actor (F).
TV: *Dr Willoughby; Liverpool 1; Dream Team; Thief Takers;* Della in *EastEnders; Without Walls; As Time Goes By; The Bill.*
Address: c/o CAM, 19 Denmark Street, London WC2N 4AZ.

JOYCE, Paddy

Paddy Joyce. Actor (M).
TV: *All The Fun of the Fair; Anna Lee; Annie's Bar; Attachments; Auf Wiedersehn, Pet; Bowler; Campion; Cathy Come Home; Charlie; Churchill's People; Consternation; Coronation Street; Crown Court; Dick Emery; Dixon of Dock Green; EastEnders; Educating Marmalade; Enigma Files; Father Ted; Frankenstein; Ghost Hour: Rudkin's Fetch; Gone to the Dogs; Grass Arena; Huggy Bear; Into the Labyrinth; Jamaica Inn; Jasper Carrott; King of the Dumpers; Knock Back; The Les Dawson Show; Little and Large; Lloyds of London; Lovejoy; Marya; May to December; Metal Mickey; Minder; Mother Ireland; Peak Practice; Pennies from Heaven; Please Sir; Poor Cow; Profile of a Gentleman; Prospects; The Rolf Harris Show; Rosie; Six Days of Justice; Softly, Softly; S.O.S. Titanic; Stick With Me Kid; Terry and June; The Big Flame; The Bill; The Charmer; The Falklands Factor; The Fenn Street Gang; The Ghost Sonata; The Lump; The Mannions of America; The Melting Pot; The Onedin Line; The Saint; The Walkers; Turtle's Progress; Two's Company; You Rang M'Lord; Z Cars.*
Films: *Brittannia Hospital; Cresta Run; Lamb; Red Monarch; Spirit; The Chain; The Lonely Passion of Judith Hearne.*
Address: c/o Susan Angel Associates, 1st Floor, 12 D'Arblay Street, London W1V 3FP.

JUNKIN, John

John Junkin. Actor (M).
b. Ealing, Middlesex, 29 January 1930.
TV: *Inspector Morse; Mr Bean; Picking Up The Pieces; The Thing About Vince.*
Films: *Chicago Joe and the Showgirl; Confessions From A Holiday Camp; Handful of Dust; A Hard Day's Night.*
Address: c/o Elaine Murphy Associates, 310 Aberdeen House, 22–24 Highbury Grove, London N5 2EA. m. Jennie (sep.); 1 d. Annabel. Hobbies: Crosswords, talking, reading, growing up.

JUPITUS, Phill

Phill Jupitus. Actor (M). b. Isle of Wight.
TV: various in *Comedy Nation;* Gudrun in *Dark Ages* (1999); *Gag Tag; Never Mind the Buzzcocks* (1996); *The Book Quiz* (1998); Dandelion in *Watership Down* (1999).
Address: Off The Kerb, 22 Thornhill Crescent, Lodnon N1 1BJ. Hobbies: West Ham United FC supporter, *Star Wars* fanatic.

K

KANE, Andy
Andy Kane. Handyman. b. London, 25 October 1965.
TV: *A Close Guide To...*; *All Over the Shop*; *Change That*; Handy Andy in *Changing Rooms*; *Election Night Armistice*; *Fully Booked*; *Light Lunch*; *One to Three*; *The National Lottery Big Ticket*; *The Vibe*; *Win, Lose or Draw*.
Address: c/o David Anthony Promotions, PO Box 286, Warrington, Cheshire WA2 6GA. m. Geraldine. Hobbies: Classic and modern cars, music.

KANE, Patricia
Patricia Kane. Actor (F). b. Cardiff.
TV: Mrs Evans in *Aquila*; *District Nurse*; *Magnificent Evans*; *Open All Hours*; Angharad in *Sisters Three*; *Socrates*; *Tender Loving Care*; *That Uncertain Feeling*; *The Bill*; *Unexplained Laughter*; Doris Trott in *The Vicar of Dibley*.
Address: c/o Chuck Julian Associates, Suite 51, 26 Charing Cross Road, London WC2H ODH. m. Howell Evans; 1 s. Warwick. Hobbies: Tennis, tap dancing, crosswords, reading, gardening.

KANE, Sam
Same Kane. Actor (M)/Presenter. b. Liverpool, 1969.
TV: Peter Phelan in *Brookside*; *Night Fever*; *Wish You Were Here?*
Address: c/o Billy Marsh Associates, 174-178 North Gower Street, London NW1 2NB. m. Linda Lusardi (model); 1 d. Lucy, 1 s. Jack.

KANSKA, Joanna
Joanna Kanska. Actor (F).
TV: Magda in *Randall and Hopkirk (Deceased)*; *Peak Practice*; *Grafters*; *Lovejoy*; *Madson*; *Ruth Rendell Mysteries*; *A Very Polish Practice*; *Love Hurts*; *B & B*; *The New Statesman*; *Capital City*; *Sleepers*; *A Slight Hitch*; *Rumpole of the Bailey*.
Films: *The Tall Guy*.
Address: c/o Kate Feast Management, 10 Primrose Hill Studios, Fitzroy Road, London NW1 8TR.

KAPLAN, Juliette
Juliette Kaplan. Actor (F).
b. Bournemouth, Dorset, 2 October 1939.
TV: Mother in *Ad Infinitum*; Mrs Curtis in *Danger-field*; Lucille in *EastEnders*; Rachel in *His Name Was John*; Pearl in *Last of the Summer Wine*; *Life After Birth*; *London's Burning*; Miss Fish in *The Cash Trial Scandal*; Mrs Graham in *The Curse of King Tut*.
Address: c/o Langford Associates, 17 Westfields Avenue, London SW13 0AT. m. Harold Hoser (div.); 1 s. Mark Hoser, 2 d. Perrina Hoser, Tania Hoser. Hobbies: Rifle shooting, bridge, sex.

KAREN, Anna
Anna Karen. Actor (F). b. 1942.
TV: Olive in *On the Buses*; *The Rag Trade*; *Trouble and Strife*; *Roland Rat – The Series*; *Celebrity Squares*; *Play for Today*; *Gayle's World*; *Fantasy Football League*; Aunt Sal in *EastEnders*; *Birds of a Feather*; *Boyz Unlimited*.
Films: *Carry On* series; *Poor Cow*; *Lock Up Your Daughters*; *Stainless Steel*; *Star Spies*; Marlene in *Beautiful Thing*.
Address: c/o George Heathcote Management, 58 Northdown Street, London N1 9BS.

KAY, Barnaby
Barnaby Kay. Actor (M).
TV: Dennis Philby in *Cracker*; DC Spelling in *Jonathan Creek*; *Minder*; Ulf in *The Castle*; *The Ghostbusters of East Finchley*; Tom in *The Vet*.
Films: Alan Lake in *Blonde Bombshell*; *Crucifixion Island*; Wardley Fish in *Oscar and Lucinda*; Noll in *Shakespeare in Love*.
Address: c/o Sally Hope Associates, 108 Leonard Street, London EC2A 4XS.

KAY, Bernard
Bernard Kay. Actor (M).
b. Bolton, Lancashire, 22 February 1938.
TV: *A Very British Coup*; *Bomber Harris*; *Capstick's Law*; *Century Falls*; *Colin's Sandwich*; *Coronation Street*; *Hannay*; *Jonathan Creek*; *Kremlin Farewell*; *London's Burning*; *Minder*; *Robin Hood*; *Rockliffe's Babies*; *Sakharov*; *The Bill*; *The Fourth Floor*; *The Most Dangerous Man in the World*.
Films: *A Ghost in Monte Carlo*; *Dinner Plate*; *Fortunate Pilgrim*; *The Hunting Party*; *The Sewers of Gold*.
Address: c/o Crouch Associates, 9–15 Covent Garden, London WC2H 9PF.

KAY, Charles

Charles Kay. Actor (M). b. Coventry, 31 August 1930.
TV: *The Darling Buds of May; Edge of Darkness; Fall of Eagles; Fiddlers Three; Fortunes of War; Goodnight Mr Tom; Hetty Wainthropp Investigates; My Cousin Rachel; Sherlock Holmes; The Microbe Hunters; To Serve Them All My Days.*
Films: Count Rosenberg in *Amadeus*; George Thornton MP in *Beautiful People*; Canterbury in *Henry V*.
Address: c/o Marmont Management Ltd, Langham House, 308 Regent Street, London W1R 5AL.

KAY, Hilary

Hilary Kay. Antiques expert.
TV: *The Antiques Roadshow*
Address: c/o BBC, Union House, 65–69 Shepherds Bush Green, London W12 8TX.

KAY, Peter

Peter Kay. Actor (M)/Presenter/Comedian.
b. 2 July 1973.
TV: *All Over the Shop; Barking; The Big Breakfast* (1998); *Born to Run; Butterfly Collectors; City Central; Comedy Nation; Coronation Street; Edinburgh Nights; Gas; Let's Get Quizzical; Mad for It; That Peter Kay Thing; The Comedy Store; The Jack Docherty Show;* all the characters in *The Services – Comedy Lab; The Stand Up Show; The Sunday Show; Two Minutes.*
Address: c/o Off the Kerb Productions, 3rd Floor, Hammer House, 113–117 Wardour Street, London W1V 3TD.

KAYE, Gorden

Gorden Kaye. Actor (M).
b. Huddersfield, 7 April 1941.
TV: Mr Bilton in *All Creatures Great and Small*; Rene in *'Allo 'Allo*; Ray Benge in *Born and Bred*; Frank Broadhurst in *Code Name Icarus*; Birley in *Fame is the Spur*; Jem in *God's Wonderful Railway*; Dr Grant in *Mansfield Park*; The Watch in *Much Ado About Nothing*; Clive in *Oh Happy Band*; Vicar in *Rainy Day Women*; Tom Clarke in *Shoestring*; Mr Nickson in *The Bullion Boys*; Mr Thrush in *The Foundation*; PC Knowles in *The Growing Pains of PC Penrose*; Parks in *The Party's Over*; Adam Alexander in *The Strange Affair of Adelaide Harris*.
Films: *Jabberwocky*; Bill in *Pit Ponies*; Harry Dines in *Porridge*; Chubby in *The Waterloo Bridge Handicap*.
Address: c/o Markham & Froggatt Ltd, 4 Windmill Street, London W1P 1HF.

KEARNEY, Gillian

Gillian Kearney. Actor (F).
b. Liverpool, Merseyside, 9 May 1972.
TV: Debbie in *Brookside*; Mandy in *Casualty*; Debbie in *Damon and Debbie*; Susan Watkins in *Heartbeat*; Deborah in *Hetty Wainthropp Investigates*; Julie in *Liverpool 1*; Jenny in *Men of the World*; Ellie Brookes in *Sex, Chips and Rock 'n' Roll*; Cassie in *The Final Frame*; Young Joan in *The Things We Do For Love*; Emily Kennedy in *The Tide Of Life*; Helen in *Waterfront Beat*.
Films: Young Shirley in *Shirley Valentine*; Elizabeth in *The Ruby Ring*.
Address: c/o Jonathan Altaras Associates, 13 Shorts Gardens, London WC2H 9AT.

KEATING, Caron

Caron Keating. Presenter. b. London, 5 October 1962.
TV: *Greenrock; The Visit; Channel One; Blue Peter; 4th Dimension; Wide Angle; Summer Scene; Olympics; Schofield's Quest;* Entertainment Correspondent on *London Tonight; After 5; Routes and Rhythms; Finbar's Class; This Morning.*
Address: c/o James Grant Management Ltd. m.; 2 s. Charlie, Gabriel. Hobbies: Antiques, art, books

KEATING, Tracy

Tracy Keating. Actor (F).
TV: Nurse Peters in *Birds of a Feather*; Sister Dominic in *Body and Soul*; Salvation Army Girl in *Drop the Dead Donkey*; Eva Dobie in *Family Affairs*; Liddy in *Far From The Madding Crowd*; Clare in *Game On*; Mary Shelley in *Highlander*; Nurse Anderson in *Our Friends in the North*; Carolyn in *Prime Suspect IV*; Linda in *The Bill*; Kathy in *The Investigator*; Brenda in *The Peter Principle*; Mrs Stephens in *The Story of Philip Knight*; Geraldine Payne in *Where the Heart Is.*
Address: c/o CAM London, 19 Denmark Street, London WC2H 8NA.

KEEN, Diane

Diane Keen. Actor (F). b. London, 29 July 1946.
TV: *Boon; Brighton Belles; Brookside; Crossroads; The Cuckoo Waltz; Fall of Eagles; Family Affairs; Foxy Lady; Killer Waiting; Oxbridge Blues; Put On By Cunning; Reunion; Rings on their Fingers; Road Rage;* Maid Marion in *Robin Hood; Ruth Rendell Mysteries; September Song; Shillingbury Tales; Sleeps Six; Taggart; The Bill; The Feathered Serpent; The Professionals; The Sandbaggers; White House Murder; You must be the Husband.*
Films: *Here We Go Round the Mulberry Bush; Silver Dream; The Sweeney; The Antechamber; The Visitor.*
Address: c/o Scott Marshall, 44 Perryn Road, London W3 7NA.

KEITH, Penelope

Penelope Keith. Actor (F)/Presenter.
b. Sutton, Surrey, 2 April 1940.
TV: Aunt Louise in *Coming Home* (1998); Caroline Fielding in *Executive Stress* (1986); Wenda Padbury in *Kate* (1970); *Laughter in the House: The Story Of The British Sitcom* (1999); Phillippa Troy in *Law and Disorder* (1994); Sarah Gladwyn in *Moving* (1985); Beatrice in *Much Ado About Nothing* (1978); Maggie in *Next of Kin* (1995); Jean Price in *No Job for a Lady* (1990); Maria Wislack in *On Approval* (1982); Margot Ledbetter in *The Good Life* (1975); Massage Parlour Receptionist in *The Hound of the Baskervilles* (1978); Sarah in *The Norman Conquests: Living Together* (1978); Audrey Forbes-Hamilton in *To the Manor Born* (1979); Helen Lancaster in *Waters of the Moon* (1983).
Films: Lotte Von Gelbstein in *Every Home Should Have One*; Rennie in *Madhouse Mansion*; *Penny Gold*; Dorothy Brett in *Priest of Love*; Reporter in *Rentadick*; Tory Lady in *Take A Girl Like You*.
Address: c/o London Management, Noel House, 2–4 Noel Street, London W1V 3RB. m. Rodney Timson; 2 s. (adopted).

KEITH, Sheila

Sheila Keith. Actor (F). b. Aberdeen, 9 June 1920.
TV: *After Henry; Agony; All in Good Faith; Angels; The Antonia White Quartet; Ballet Shoes; Bless Me Father; Cedar Tree; Crane; Crime Buster; Crossroads; The Darling Buds of May; David Copperfield; Dear Ladies; Dr Finlay's Casebook; Drummonds; Escape; Father Brown; Flaxton Boys; Fresh Fields; George and the Dragon; Hamish Macbeth; Hell's Bells; It's Murder – But It's Art; Kate; The Liver Birds; Love Hurts; Love Story; Lovejoy; Me Mammy; Mog; Moody and Pegg; Mother; Mrs Thursday; Never the Twain; Nicholas Nickleby; Nobody's Conscience; Paradise Club; Play for Today; Present Laughter; Public Eye; Racing Game; The Ronnie Barker Playhouse; Roof Over My Head; Sea Walls; Some Mother's Do 'Ave 'Em; Sophia and Constance; Spring and Autumn; The Brittas Empire; The Dolls; The Kindness of Mrs Radcliffe; The Moonstone; The Other 'Arf; The Pallisers; The Regiment; The Tell Tale Hearts; Ticket to Ride; The Unpleasantness at the Bellona Club; Within these Walls; Z Cars.*
Films: *Clockwise; Frightmare; House of the Long Shadows; House of Whipcord; Ooh You Are Awful!; The Comeback; The Confessional; Venus Peter; Wild Flowers.*
Address: c/o Evans & Reiss, 100 Fawe Park Road, London SW15 2EA.

KELLEGHER, Tina

Tina Kellegher. Actor (F).
TV: *Ballykissangel; Scarlett; Widow's Peak; In The Name*

of the Father; Murder in Eden; The Snapper; Return to Eden.
Address: c/o Conway van Gelder, 18–21 Jermyn Street, London SW1Y 6HP.

KELLY, Chris

Chris Kelly. Presenter/Reporter.
b. Cuddington, Cheshire, 24 April 1940.
TV: *6th Form Challenge; Food and Drink; Kavanagh QC; Saracen; Soldier, Soldier; Wish You Were Here; World in Action; Zoo Time.*
Address: c/o Burnett Granger Associates, Prince of Wales Theatre, 31 Coventry Street, London W1V 8AS. m. Vivien; 1 s. Nicholas, 1 d. Rebecca.

KELLY, Clare

Clare Kelly. Actor (F).
TV: *A Kind of Loving; Casualty; Coronation Street; Dalziel and Pascoe; Heartbeat; Here's A Funny Thing; Keeping up Appearances; Ladykillers; Last of the Summer Wine; No Excuses; Picking up the Pieces; REP; The Bill; The Nesbitts are Coming; The Secret House of Death; The Sharp End; Where the Heart Is; Young at Heart.*
Films: *A Matter of Honor; Best Pair of Legs In The Business; Inadmissible Evidence; Soon The Darkness; Straight on Till Morning.*
Address: c/o The Narrow Road Company, 21–22 Poland Street, London W1V 3DD.

KELLY, Craig

Craig Kelly. Actor (M). b. 1971.
TV: *A Touch of Frost; Casualty; Children of the New Forest; Ellington; Queer as Folk; Running Late;* Stephen Croxley in *The Good Guys; The Young Indiana Jones Chronicles.*
Films: *Killing Joe; Titanic; Undertaker's Paradise; When Saturday Comes; Wing Commander; Young Americans.*
Address: c/o ICM, Oxford House, 76 Oxford Street, London W1N 0AX.

KELLY, David

David Kelly. Actor (M). b. Dublin, 11 July 1929.
TV: *Ballykissangel; Emmerdale;* O'Reilly, the builder, in *Fawlty Towers; Heartbeat; In Sickness and in Health;* One-armed dish-washer in *Robin's Nest; The Ronnie Barker Show; Z-Cars.*
Films: *A Man of No Importance; Greenfingers; The Hunchback of Notre Dame; Into the West; Joyriders; Ordinary Decent Criminal; Philadelphia Here I Come; Pirates; Portrait of an Artist; Red Menace; Run of the Country; The Jigsaw Man; The MacKenzie Break; Trio by Forsythe; Ulysses; Waking Ned* (1999).
Address: c/o Joan Brown Associates, 3 Earl

Road, Barnes, London SW14 7JH. m. Laurie Morton; 1 s.; 1 d.

KELLY, Elizabeth

Elizabeth Kelly. Actor (F).
b. Newcastle-upon-Tyne, 29 May 1921.
TV: Lucy Keen in *Boon*; Auntie Nellie in *EastEnders*; Emily in *How We Used To Live*; Mabel in *Motormouth*; *Out And About*; Olive in *Resnick*; Annie Trotter in *Tilly Trotter*.
Films: Dotty landlady in *Without a Clue*.
Address: c/o Scott Marshall, 44 Perryn Road, London W3 7NA. Widowed; 2 children, 2 grandchildren. Hobbies: Family, reading, gardening, crosswords.

KELLY, Gerard

Gerard Kelly. Actor (M).
TV: Charley Hood in *A Wholly Healthy Glasgow*; MacAllon in *Brat Farrar*; Willie Melvin in *City Lights*; Honsley in *Days at the Beach*; Donal in *Donal and Sally*; Jimmy in *EastEnders*; Jamie in *Gie's a Break*; John Grant in *God's Wonderful Railway 1860*; Arty Jackson in *Goin' Out*; Duggan in *Hamish MacBeth*; Blair in *Holy City*; Jackie in *Jackie McCafferty's Romance*; PC Gallagher in *Juliet Bravo*; David Balfour in *Kidnapped*; Johnny Ross in *Leaving*; Jamie in *Lives of our Own*; Danny in *Loyalties*; Cosimo Latona in *Murder Not Proven*; Tom Abberton in *Nanny*; Student in *Play for Today*; Gary in *Play for Today*; Colin Gilbert in *Rab C Nesbitt*; John in *Shoestring*; Andrew Cameron in *The Camerons*; *The Funny Farm*; George in *The Slab Boys*; Tommy in *The Standard*; Waiter in *The Victoria Wood Show*.
Films: *More Bad News*; *Mr Jolly Lives Next Door*; Andrew in *Thirteenth Reunion*.
Address: c/o Markham & Froggatt Ltd, 4 Windmill Street, London W1P 1HF.

KELLY, Lorraine

Lorraine Kelly. Presenter/Reporter.
b. Glasgow, Scotland, 30 November 1959.
TV: *All Fright on the Night*; *GMTV*; *Kelly's Heroes*; *Live Issue*; *Lorraine Live*; *The Living Room*; *The Ultimate Shopping Guide*; *TV-am*.
Address: c/o SilverFox Artist Management Ltd, Cameo House, 11 Bear Street, London WC2H 7AS. m. Steve; 1 d. Rosie.

KELLY, Matthew

Matthew Kelly. Actor (M)/Presenter.
b. Manchester, 9 May 1950.
TV: *Adventure of a Lifetime*; *Boon*; *Champion of Champions* (1999); *Eureka*; *Funny Man*; *Game for a Laugh*;

Give a Pet a Home (1999); *Holding the Fort* (1980); *Hotel Getaway* (2000); *Madabout*; *Stars in their Eyes*; *The Critic*; *Last of the Summer Wine*; *You Bet*.
Films: *Gabrielle and the Doodleman*.
Address: c/o Stella Richards Management, 42 Hazelbury Road, London SW6. Hobbies: Travelling, swimming, dancing, talking, laughing.

KELLY, Ross

Ross Kelly. Presenter/Reporter.
TV: *Central News*; *Fasten Your Seat Belt*; *GMTV*; *Holiday*; *Lookaround*; *This Morning*; *Whose House?*
Address: c/o The Roseman Organisation, Suite 9, The Power House, 70 Chiswick Road, London W4 1SY. Hobbies: Theatre, walking, packing and ironing for trips!

KELLY, Sam

Sam Kelly. Actor (M).
b. Manchester, 19 December 1943.
TV: Captain Hans Geering in *'Allo 'Allo*; Ron Griffiths in *11 Men Against 11* (1995); Allen Scully in *A Touch of Frost* (1995); Ted in *Barbara* (1998); Mr Snagby in *Bleak House* (1984); Raymond in *Born to Run* (1996); *Boys from the Blackstuff* (1982); Longbehn in *Christabel* (1988); Pete's Dad in *Cold Feet* (1998); Bob Challis in *Coronation Street* (1983); *Dave Allen*; Seedy Man in *Dressing for Breakfast* (1996); *Frankie & Johnny* (1985); Gringe in *Haggard* (1989); *Heart of the Country* (1985); *Hold the Back Page* (1985); Bernard Hotton in *Holding On* (1996); Ted Higgins in *Home to Roost* (1989); *Jenny's War* (1984); Antonio in *Magic With Everything* (1998); Barticle in *Making Out* (1989); Mr Mould in *Martin Chuzzlewit* (1994); Sir Henry Duggitt in *Monster TV* (1999); *Now and Then*; Mr Giles in *Oliver Twist* (1999); Sam in *On the Up*; Sam in *Paul Merton In...*; Frank in *Peak Practice* (1999); *Professional Foul*; Hitler in *Stalag Luft* (1993); Stanley Cox in *Stay Lucky* (1991); Henry in *Thin Air* (1987); *Victoria Wood Special* (1987); *Will You Still Love Me Tomorrow?*(1986).
Films: *Arthur's Hallowed Ground*; Barman in *Blue Ice*; John in *Getaway*; Uncle Sid in *Honest*; Richard Barker in *Topsy Turvy*.
Address: c/o The Richard Stone Partnership, 2 Henrietta Street, London WC2E 8PS.

KELSEY, Ian

Ian Kelsey. Actor (M). b. 1972.
TV: *Adam's Family Tree*; Dr Patrick Spiller in *Casualty*; Dave Glover in *Emmerdale*; *Men Behaving Badly*; *Touching Evil*.
Films: Jo Green in *Black Beauty*; *Wild Justice*.

Address: c/o Joy Jameson Ltd, 2.19 The Plaza, 535 Kings Road, London SW10 0SZ.

KEMP, Jeremy

Jeremy Kemp. Actor (M).
b. Derbyshire, 3 February 1935.
TV: *Cop Out; Duel of Hearts; Duel of Love;* Charles Ampleforth in *Fleet Foremost;* Cromwell in *King Lear;* Patrick Gordon in *Peter The Great; Slip Up; Star Trek;* Buck Kettering in *Summer's Lease; The Adventures of Sherlock Holmes; The Magician;* Baron Von Roon in *The Winds of War; War and Remembrance.*
Films: *Angels and Insects;* Dr Smythe in *Caravans; East of Elephant Rock;* Sir John in *Four Weddings and a Funeral;* Bolt in *Leopard in the Snow; Prisoner of Honour;* Frank in *Return of the Soldier; The 7% Solution;* The Baron in *The Phantom of the Opera;* Black Michael in *The Prisoner of Zenda;* General Strick in *Top Secret; When the Whales.*
Address: c/o Marina Martin Associates, 12–13 Poland Street, London W1V 3DE.

KEMP, Martin

Martin Kemp. Actor (M).
b. London, 10 October 1961.
TV: *Dixon of Dock Green;* Steve Owen in *EastEnders; Glittering Prizes;* Chauffeur in *Growing Rich;* Alfred Cahil in *Highlander; Jackanory; Katherine Mansfield; Mind Where You're Going;* Bill Fontanille in *Murder Between Friends; Oranges and Lemons; Outer Limits; Pygmalion; Rumpole of the Bailey; Scribble;* Eddie McEwan in *Supply & Demand; Tales from the Crypt;* Tom Marsh in *The Bill; The Edwardians; The Tomorrow People.*
Films: Franz in *Aspen;* Reb in *Boca; Desire;* Matthew Greco in *Fleshtone;* David Allenby in *Monk Dawson;* Jack Morris in *Sailor's Tattoo;* Jonesey in *Sugar Town;* Digby Olsen in *The Girl Who Came Late;* Reggie Kray in *The Krays;* Vampire in *Vampire's Embrace;* Frankenstein in *Waxworks II – Lost in Time.*
Address: c/o Associated International Management, 5 Denmark Street, London WC2H 8LP.

KEMP, Ross

Ross Kemp. Actor (M)/Presenter. b. 1 July 1965.
TV: *8.50 to Paddington Green;* Policeman in *Birds of a Feather;* Grant Mitchell in *EastEnders; Emmerdale; London's Burning; Paddington Green; Playing Away; The Chief; The Money Me; Hero of the Hour; Ross Kemp Alive in Alaska.*
Address: c/o PFD, Drury House, 34-43 Russell Street, London WC2B 5HA.

KENDAL, Felicity

Felicity Kendal. Actor (F).
b. Otton, Warwickshire, 25 September 1946.
TV: *Boy Meets Girl; Crimes of Passion; Deadly Earnest; Edward VII; Favourite Things; Home and Beauty; Now is Too Late; Solo; The Camomile Lawn; The Dolly Dialogues;* Barbara Good in *The Good Life; The Marriage Counsellor; The Mayfly and the Frog; The Mistress; The Tenant of Wildfell Hall; The Woodlanders; Twelfth Night.*
Films: *Parting Shots; Shakespeare Wallah; Valentino.*
Address: c/o Chatto & Linnit Ltd, 123a Kings Road, London SW3 4PL. Father Geoffrey Kendal; sister Jennifer Kendal.

KENDALL, Bridget

Bridget Kendall. News Correspondent.
b.Oxford. 27 April 1956.
TV: Moscow Correspondent, *BBC News;* Washington Correspondent, *BBC News;* Diplomatic Correspondent, *BBC News.*
Address: c/o BBC TV Centre, Wood Lane, London W12 7RJ.

KENNEDY, Cheryl

Cheryl Kennedy. Actor (F).
b. Enfield, Middlesex, 29 April 1947.
TV: *Brookside; Loves of Napoleon; Target; The Bill* (1999); *The Mike Yarwood Show; The Professionals; The Strauss Family; The Sweeney; What Every Woman Knows; When the Bough Breaks.*
Films: *Oh You Are Awful!; The Seven Deadly Sins.*
Address: c/o Dalzell and Beresford Ltd, 91 Regent Street, London W1R 7TB.

KENNEDY, James

Jame Kennedy. Actor (M).
TV: *Arise and Go Now; Dalziel and Pascoe; Parole; Prime Suspect II; The Houseman's Tale; Winners and Losers.*
Address: c/o ICM, Oxford House, 76 Oxford Street, London W1N 0AX.

KENNEDY, Kevin

Kevin Kennedy. Actor (M).
b. Manchester, 4 September 1961.
TV: 'Curly' Watts in *Coronation Street;* Pete Bennett in *Keep on Running;* Ken in *The Last Company Car.*
Address: c/o Saraband Associates, 265 Liverpool Road, London N1 1LX.

KENNEDY, Tamara

Tamara Kennedy. Actor (F)/Narrator.
b. Edinburgh, 23 May 1962.
TV: *Heartland FM;* Joanna Ross-Gifford in *Take the*

High Road; Muriel Spark; Orpheus Through the Ages; Rab C Nesbitt; Reel of the 51; Dr Fellowes in Taggart; The Botanics.
Films: *Ra: The Path of the Sun God.*
Address: c/o Young Casting Agency, 7 Beaumont Gate, Glasgow G12 9EE. 1 d. Rosa. Hobbies: Drawing, writing, reading, swimming, art.

KENNEY, Gordon

Gordon Kenney. Actor (M)/Musician/Singer.
b. Cheltenham, 10 February 1950.
TV: PC Jackson in *Arrivederci Millwall*; The Low Downs Blues Band in *The Big Breakfast*; Moss Side Man in *Bullman*; Carlos in *EastEnders*; Vince in *Fire*; Detective in *For Your Hearts Only*; Drunken Soldier in *Tales of Beatrix Potter*; *Telethon*; *The Ellie Lane Show*; General Hugh Reed in *The Middle Man*.
Music: *Incredible Hog.*
Address: c/o Alexander Personal Management Ltd, 16 Roughdown Avenue, Hemel Hempstead, Hertfordshire HP3 9BH. 2 s. Anthony, Ken, 1 d. Nicola. Hobbies: Guitar, harmonica, singing, songwriting.

KEOGH, Barbara

Barbara Keogh. Actor (F). b. Cheshire, 21 April 1929.
TV: *Birds of a Feather; Boon; Bramwell; Brazen Hussies; Casualty*; Various in *Coronation Street*; *Detectives*; Lily in *EastEnders*; *Fenn Street Gang; Heartbeat; Hetty Wainthropp Investigates; Highlander; House of Eliot; Joking Apart; Juliet Bravo; London's Burning*; Gran in *Lost in France; Perfect Spy; Road; Ruth Rendell Mysteries; The Bill*; Nan in *The Grimleys*.
Films: *A Nice Girl like Me; A Pin for a Butterfly; A Touch of Love; Black Joy; Jane Eyre; Paper House; Princess Caraboo; Scrooge; Tai Pan; The Abominable Dr Phibes; The Virgin Soldiers; Whoops Apocalypse.*
Address: c/o London Management, Noel House, 2–4 Noel Street, London W1V 3RB. Hobbies: Collecting little jugs, gardening.

KERMAN, Jill

Jill Kerman. Actor (F). b. 4 July 1956.
TV: Maggie Redman in *Coronation Street; Cosmo and Thingy; Crown Court; Fairly Secret Army*; Nancy in *Oliver; Please, Sir; REP; Softly, Softly; Strangers; The Cuckoo Waltz; The Other One*; Wife in *Then and Now.*
Address: c/o Essany Ltd, 2 Conduit Street, London W1R 9TG.

KERRIGAN, Jonathan

Jonathan Kerrigan. Actor (M). b. 1972.
TV: Mick in *Byker Grove*; Sam Colloby in *Casualty*; Ewan Brodie in *Peak Practice*; Paul in *Reach for the Moon.*

Address: c/o CAM London, 19 Denmark Street, London WC2H 8NA.

KERSHAW, Noreen

Noreen Kershaw. Actor (F)/Director.
b. Jericho, Bury, Lancashire, 16 October 1950.
TV: Lynne Harrison in *Albion Market*; Kathy in *Brookside*; Brenda's mum in *Watching.*
Address: c/o Ken McReddie Ltd, 91 Regent Street, London W1R 7TB.

KILBURN, Melanie

Melanie Kilburn. Actor (F). b. Bradford, Yorkshire.
TV: Hilda in *1914 All Out*; Trudie in *Against All Odds*; Pippa Danes in *All Quiet on the Preston Front*; Carol in *April Fool's Day*; *Brasseye*; Carol in *Casualty*; Angela in *Chancer*; *Hale & Pace*; Rosie in *Heartbeat*; Jo Brand – *Through the Cakehole*; *Juliet Bravo*; Muriel Sands in *Maisie Raine*; Jill Barraclough in *Making Out*; Charlotte in *Moving Story*; Janeen in *Slap*; Carol in *Soldier, Soldier*; Mary in *Stone, Scissors, Paper*; *The Bill*; Maureen in *The Last Company Car*; Edwina Sprott in *The Wimbledon Poisoner*; Jackie in *Vanity Dies Hard*; Sandra in *Where the Heart Is.*
Films: *The Little Drummer Girl*; Kate in *VROOM!*
Address: c/o Markham & Froggatt Ltd, 4 Windmill Street, London W1P 1HF.

KILROY-SILK, Robert

Robert Kilroy-Silk. Presenter/Producer.
b. Birmingham, 19 May 1942.
TV: *Dispatches; Equinox; Kilroy; Panorama.*
Address: c/o Simpson Fox Associates Ltd, 52 Shaftesbury Avenue, London W1V 7DE. m. Jan.

KING, Claire

Claire King. Actor (F)/Presenter.
b. Yorkshire, 10 January 1963.
TV: Mel's Girlfriend in *Alas Smith and Jones*; Angela in *Babes in the Wood*; Kim Tate in *Emmerdale*; *Hale & Pace*; Model in *Hot Metal*; Robert Palmer video girl in *Robbie Coltraine Special*; *Shout!*; Receptionist in *The Bill*; Punk and Hooker in *Watch with Mother*; *Bad Girls.*
Films: *Eat the Rich; Heart of Fire; The Cold Light of Day.*
Address: c/o David Daly Associates, 586a Kings Road, London SW6 2DX. m. Peter Amory.

KINGSTON, Alex

Alex Kingston. Actor (F). b. London, 11 March 1963.
TV: *A Killing on the Exchange; Crocodile Shoes*; Dr Elizabeth Corday in *ER; Foreign Affairs; Hannay; Henry's Leg; I Hate Christmas; Moll Flanders; Soldier, Soldier; The Bill; The Knock; Wanted – Marjorie and Oliver.*

Films: Mrs Soloman in *A Pin for a Butterfly*; Frances Partridge in *Carrington*; *Curran's Wife*; Lisa In *Essex Boys*; Anna in *In Hitler's Shadow*; *The Cook, The Thief, His Wife and Her Lover*; *The Croupier*; Odile in *The St Expurry Story*; *The Wildcats of St Trinians*; The Woman in *The Woman and the Wolf*; Verity Graham in *Weapons of Mass Distraction*.

Address: c/o Lou Coulson, 37 Berwick Street, London W1V 3RF. m. 1 Ralph Fiennes (div). m. 2 Florian Haertel. Hobbies: Shopping at flea markets.

KINGSTON, Mark

Mark Kingston. Actor (M).
b. Greenwich, London, 18 April 1934.
TV: *All Creatures Great and Small*; *Beryl's Lot*; *Boon*; *Broker's Man*; *Chelworth*; *Dr. Finlay's Casebook*; *Driving Ambition*; *Growing Rich*; *Kavanagh QC*; *Lovejoy*; *Moon & Son*; *No Job for a Lady*; *Peak Practice*; *Sarah*; *Shine on Harvey Moon*; *The Avengers*; *Time of My Life*; *Trial of Klaus Barbie*; *United*.
Films: *Ike, The War Years*; *Lady Oscar*; *Melrose*; *St Jack*.
Address: c/o Shepherd & Ford, 13 Radnor Walk, London SW3 4BP. m. Marigold. Hobbies: Reading, travel, music, golf.

KIRKBRIDE, Anne

Anne Kirkbride. Actor (F).
b. Oldham, Lancashire, 21 June 1954.
TV: *Another Sunday and Sweet FA*; Deirdre in *Coronation Street*.
Address: c/o Granada Television, Quay Street, Manchester M60 9EA. m. David Beckett; father Jack Kirkbride. Hobbies: Gardening, photography, reading.

KIRKMAN, Sarah

Sarah Kirkman. Actor (F). b. Manchester.
TV: Clarissa in *Berkeley Square*; Mel in *Bloomin' Marvellous*; Nurse Fido in *Born to Run*; PC Mary Sutcliffe in *City Central*; Sylvie Michaux in *Monsignor Renard*.
Films: Sarah in *Window Shopping*.
Address: c/o CDA, 19 Sydney Mews, London SW3 6HL.

KIRWAN, Dervla

Dervla Kirwan. Actor (F). b. Dublin, 24 October 1971.
TV: Assumpta Fitzgerald in *Ballykissangel*; *Eureka Street* (1999); Assumpta in *Father Ted*; Phoebe in *Goodnight Sweetheart*; *Handful of Stars*; *Happy Birthday Shakespeare* (2000); *Poor Beast in the Rain*; *Ready, Steady, Cook*; *Shades* (2000); *Shooting Stars*; *The Dark Room* (1999); *The Flint Street Nativity* (1999); *The Greatest Store in the World*

(1999); Sister Assumpta in *The Vicar of Dibley*; Bernadette Kennedy in *Time to Dance*; *With or Without You* (1999).
Films: *December Bride*; *Lilac Bus*; *Meteor*; *War of the Buttons*; *With or Without You*.
Address: c/o PFD, Drury House, 34-43 Russell Street, London WC2B 5HA. Hobbies: Running, travel, cinema.

KITCHEN, Gavin

Gavin Kitchen. Actor (M). b. 17 March 1964.
TV: Bryan in *A Visit to a Cousin*; Wheelan in *Badger*; Dexter in *Byker Grove*; Steve Marshall in *Emmerdale*; PC Stokes in *Grafters*; Danny Pearce in *Heartbeat*; Rick Seymour in *Mathspy*; Inspector Davis in *Our Friends in the North*; Sergeant McLelland in *Rough Justice*; Baxter in *Spender*; Billy Patterson in *Strike Force*; Anthony Kerwin in *The Bill*; Kevin Hedworth in *The Manageress*; Baz in *The Paper Lads*.
Address: c/o Burdett-Coutts Associates, Riverside Studios, Crisp Road, London W6 9RL.

KITCHEN, Michael

Michael Kitchen. Actor (M)/Director.
b. Leicester, 31 October 1948.
TV: *A Royal Scandal*; *Caught on the Train*; *Comedy of Errors*; *Dalziel and Pascoe*; *Dirty Old Town*; *Doomsday Gun*; *Freud*; *Home Run*; *Inspector Morse*; *Kidnapped*; *King Lear*; *Love Story*; *Minder*; *Oliver Twist*; *The Railway Children*; *Reckless*; *Staying Put*; *Sunnyside Farm*; *The Benefactors*; *The Browning Version*; *The Buccaneers*; *The Guilty*; *The Hanging Gale*; *The Justice Game*; *The Secret Life of Michael Fry*; *To Play the King*; *Wilderness*; *Young Indiana Jones Chronicles*.
Films: *Balltrap on the Cote Sauvage*; *Breaking Glass*; *Dracula*; *Enchanted April*; *Fatherland*; *Fools of Fortune*; *Mrs Dalloway*; *New Year's Day*; *No Place to Hide*; *Out of Africa*; *Russia House*; *The Dive*; *The Last Contract*; *The Pied Piper*; *The Trial*; *The World is Not Enough*; *Unman, Wittering and Zigo*.
Address: c/o ICM, Oxford House, 76 Oxford Street, London W1N 0AX.

KNIGHTLEY, Will

Will Knightley. Actor (M).
TV: Hockey in *A Touch of Frost* (1995); Nigel in *Casualty* (1994); *Close Relations* (1989); Pathologist in *Cracker* (1995); *Easterman*; *Electric in the City*; *England Summer Sunday*; *Goodbye Cruel World* (1991); Jeremy Marcus in *Harry* (1993); *Hurt Hawkes*; Chaplain in *No Bananas* (1995); *Oscar Wilde*; Dan Jacks in *Peak Practice* (1997); *Preview*; Branston in *The Bill* (1996); John Church in *The Bill* (1997); *The Hound*

of the Baskervilles; The Late Show (1991); *The Life of Shakespeare.*
Films: *Dinosaur; Skinflicker;* Mr Glegg in *The Mill on the Floss.*
Address: c/o The Richard Stone Partnership, 2 Henrietta Street, London WC2E 8PS.

KNOTT, Andrew
Andrew Knott. Actor (M).
b. Salford, Manchester, 22 November 1979.
TV: Garth in *Casualty;* Liam in *Coronation Street;* Darren Featherstone in *Coronation Street; Cracker; Heartbeat;* Steve in *The Ward;* Henry in *Where the Heart Is.*
Films: Joe Green in *Black Beauty;* Dickon in *The Secret Garden.*
Address: c/o Shepherd & Ford, 13 Radnor Walk, London SW3 4BP. Hobbies: Guitar, golf, football, reading.

KNOWLES, Eric
Eric Knowles. Antiques expert.
TV: *Crimewatch UK; Going for a Song; The Antiques Roadshow; The Great Antiques Hunt.*
Address: c/o BBC, Union House, 65–69 Shepherds Bush Green, London W12 8TX.

KNOWLES, Nick
Nick Knowles. Presenter/Director. b. 1962.
TV: *Absolutely Loaded; Central Weekend Live; City Hospital; Coast to Coast; Confidential; DIY SOS; Find a Fortune; GMTV; Holiday Makers; Meridian Tonight; Put it to the Test; Ridgeriders; Road Show; Straight Up; The Great Escape; The Time... The Place; Wish You Were Here?*
Address: c/o Speak-easy Ltd, 90 St Mary's Road, Market Harborough, Leicestershire LEI6 7DX.

KNOX, Barbara
Barbara Knox. Actor (F).
b. Oldham, Lancashire, 1938.
TV: *A Family at War;* Rita Sullivan in *Coronation Street; Emergency – Ward 10; Feel The Width;* Mrs Thursday; *Never Mind the Quality; The Dustbinmen.*
Films: *Goodbye, Mr Chips.*
Address: c/o Arena Entertainment, Regents Court, 39 Harrogate Road, Leeds, West Yorkshire.

KNUTT, Bobby
Bobby Knutt. Actor (M).
b. Yorkshire, 25 November 1945.
TV: *Last of the Summer Wine; Emmerdale; Heartbeat; Common as Muck; Jake's Progress;* Reg Sykes in *Coro-*

nation Street; The Price of Coal; Book Tower; It's A Knutt House.
Films: *Ladder of Swords.*
Address: c/o Tim Scott Personal Management, 5 Cloisters Business Centre, 8 Battersea Park Road, London, SW8 4BG.

KOSSY, Al T
Al T Kossy. Actor (M).
TV: Roy Brabham in *A View of Harry Clarke;* Cockler in *Blood on the Dole;* Nasher Llewlyn in *Boys from the Blackstuff; Bread; Brookside;* Mr Larwood in *The Brothers McGregor;* The Expert in *Cracker;* Cowboy in *Cue Gary;* Manager in *Dancin' thru' the Dark;* Various in *Emo Phillips in London;* The Laughing Man in *GBH;* Parish Priest in *Hillsborough;* Grandad in *Jake's Progress;* Burglar in *The Krankies;* Uncle Tom/Voice overs in *Luv;* Corker in *Making Out;* Old Bobby in *Needle;* Dwarfy Sugden in *Rich Deceiver;* Policeman/Drunk in *Sonny & Hayes;* Grandad in *Springhill;* Yer Man/Singer in *The Gathering Seed;* John (Wino) in *The Lakes;* John Parker/Narrator in *The Man from the Pru;* Wild Rover in *The Marksman;* Roy Bradley in *The Merrihill Millionaires;* Traffic Warden in *The Practice;* Old Man (Jones) in *Under the Skin;* Harold (Barman) in *Watching;* Nobby in *Who's Our Jenny Lind?*
Films: The Porter in *Abilities Not Disabilities;* George in *Bugged;* Bobby in *No Surrender;* Professor Bright in *Rusty and Dusty;* Grandad in *Story World;* Mr Betts in *The Dressmaker;* Frank Riley in *The Life of Riley;* Floor Manager in *This Boy's Story.*
Address: c/o Mersey Television, Campus Manor, Chidwall Abbey Road, Chidwall, Liverpool L16 OJP.

KUDROW, Lisa
Lisa Kudrow. Actor (F)/Host.
b. Encino, California, 30 July 1963.
TV: Kathy Fleisher in *Bob* (1992); Emily in *Cheers* (1989); Nurse Alice in *Coach* (1993); Lauren in *Coach* (1994); Aphrodite in Disney's *Hercules* (1998); Female Beta Maxians in *Duckman* (1994); Amy in *Flying Blind* (1993); Phoebe/Ursula Buffay in *Friends* (1994); Phoebe/Ursula Buffay in *Hope and Gloria* (1995); Herself in *Instant Comedy with the Groundlings* (1998); Stella, a ditzy secretary in *Life Goes On* (1989); Ursula Buffay in *Mad About You;* One of Daryl's Wives in *Newheart* (1990); Herself in *Ruby Wax Meets* (1996); Herself in *Saturday Night Live* (1996); Friend of Perky Girl in *To the Moon, Alice* (1990).
Address: c/o Endeavor Agency, 10th Floor, 9701 Wilshire Boulevard, Beverly Hills, California 90212, USA. m. Michel Stern; 1 s. Julian.

KWANTEN, Ryan

Ryan Kwanten. Actor (M).
b. Sydney, Australia, 28 November 1976.
TV: Vinnie Patterson in *Home and Away*; *Spellbinder II: Land of the Dragon Lords*.
Address: c/o 'Seven Network Ltd, Mabbs Lane, Epping, New South Wales 2121, Australia. Hobbies: Swimming, tennis, snooker, golf, skiing, Ironman events.

KYNMAN, Paul

Paul Kynman. Actor (M). b. 22 October 1967.
TV: Terry in *All or Nothing at All*; Ray in *Casualty*; Steve in *Cut and Run*; Chester in *EastEnders*; Baz in *Firm Friends*; Barry Roache in *Heartbeat*; Slaney in *Hot Dog Wars*; Porky Jup in *Jeeves and Wooster*; Fireman in *Keeping Mum*; Taylor in *Law and Disorder*; Bernie in *Lovejoy*; Phil Bradley in *Sex, Guys and Videotape*; Ben in *Shelley*; Policeman in *The Best Man to Die*; Tony in *The Bill*; Ruud in *The Detectives*; Malahide in *The Governor*; Bouncer in *The Thin Blue Line*; Davies in *Thief Takers*; Frank de Silva in *Touching Evil*; DI Batchley in *Trial and Retribution*; Graham Shuttleworth in *Where the Heart Is*; Eric in *Wonderful You*; Nicholas in *Young Indiana Jones Chronicles*.
Films: Corporal in *Bent*; Mark in *First Knight*; Dragon Legion One in *Kull the Conqueror*; Bruner in *Legionnaire*; Chauffeur in *Shooting Fish*; Ian in *The Darkest Light*.
Address: c/o Michelle Braidman Associates, 10–11 Lower John Street, London W1R 3PE.

L

LaSALLE, Eriq

Eriq LaSalle. Actor (M)/Director/Producer.
b. Hartford, Connecticut, USA, 23 July 1962.
TV: Professor Paul in *A Different World*; *BL Stryker*; Detective Knoll in *Empty Cradle*, Dr Peter Benton in *ER*; *Eyes of a Witness*; *Gideon Oliver*; Dancing Guy in *Magic Moments*; Lucas Davenport in *Mind Prey*; Mike Rivers in *One Life to Live*; Bobby Lee in *Quantum Leap*; *Rebound: The Legend of Earl*; Diego in *The Goat Manigault*; *The Human Factor*; Le Blanc in *Under Suspicion*; Trumayne James in *What Price Victory?*
Films: Anderson in *Colour of Night*; Darryl Jenks in *Coming to America*; Bruford Jamison Jr in *Drop Squad*; Samuel Kemp in *Five Corners*; Inferno in *Diretta*; Frank in *Jacob's Ladder*; *Psalms from the Underground*; *Rappin'*; Deputy Bernie Miles in *Where are the Children?*
Address: c/o Rogers and Cowan, 1888 Century Park East, Los Angeles, California 90067, USA. Hobbies: Martial arts.

LACEY, Ingrid

Ingrid Lacey. Actor (F).
TV: Helen in *A Woman's Guide to Adultery*; Julie in *Dream Kitchen*; Helen Cooper in *Drop the Dead Donkey*; *Getting Hurt*; Mary Widdowson in *Inspector Morse*; Julia in *London's Burning*; Reporter in *Master of the Moor*; Sarah in *Never Come Back*; Eleanor Tilney in *Northanger Abbey*; Cynthia in *Pie in the Sky*; Alice in *Saracen*; Diane in *She-Wolf of London*; Veronica in *Strathblair*; Liora in *Sweating Bullets*; Jane Grant in *The Bill*; Alison Dell in *The Chief*; Inga in *The Endless Game*; Melanie in *Thunder Rock*; Billie Carleton in *White Girls on Dope*.
Films: Mac in *In Love and War*.
Address: c/o Shepherd & Ford, 13 Radnor Walk, London SW3 4BP.

LACEY, Rebecca

Rebecca Lacey. Actor (F). b. Watford, 20 April 1969.
TV: *A Touch of Frost*; Claire in *Badger*; *Bully for Cosmo*; Dr George Woodman in *Casualty*; *Chance in a Million*; *Darling Buds of May*; *Game On*; *Hannay*; *Heavy Weather*; *Home to Roost*; *Lovejoy*; Hilary in *May to December*; *Moving*; *Perfect Scoundrels*; *Shine on Harvey*

Moon; *The Bill*; *The Bretts*; *The New Statesman*; *The Smiths*; *Vanity Dies Hard*; *Vice Versa*; *Who Dares Wins*.
Films: *Second Victory*; *The Romanovs*; *The Shooting Party*.
Address: c/o William Morris Agency (UK) Ltd, 1 Stratton Street, London W1X 6HB. Father Ronald Lacey; mother Mela White; 2 brothers Matthew and Johnathan. Hobbies: Swimming, tennis, table tennis, drawing, painting, reading, writing.

LAHBIB, Simone

Simone Lahbib. Actor (F). b. Stirling, 1965.
TV: Helen Stewart in *Bad Girls*; *Crime Story*; *Dangerfield*; Mary O'Connor in *London Bridge*; *Taggart*; *The Doubles*; Zelda in *The Witch's Daughter*; Lucy McCarthy in *Thief Takers*; Fiona Johnston in *Young Person's Guide to Becoming a Rock Star*.
Films: The Girl in *The Girl in the Picture*; Marie in *The Isle of Voices*.
Address: c/o Ken McReddie Ltd, 91 Regent Street, London W1R 7TB. Hobbies: Books, food, dancing, driving, music, art, photography, films.

LAKE, Ricki

Ricki Lake. Actor (F)/Host. b. Hastings on Hudson, New York, USA, 21 September 1968.
TV: Grace in *Babycakes*; Velour in *Based on an Untrue Story*; Holly Pelegrino in *China Beach*; *Gravedale High*; *Jackie's Back*; *Kate & Allie*; *Murder She Purred: A Mrs Murphy Mystery*; *The Ricki Lake Show*; *The 61st Annual Academy Awards Presentation*; Tammie in *The Chase*; *The Critic*.
Films: Carmen in *A Family Again*; Charlotte in *Buffy the Vampire Slayer*; Figurehead in *Cabin Boy*; Pia in *Cookie*; Pepper in *Cry-Baby*; Tracy Turnblad in *Hairspray*; Bella the Stalker in *Inside Monkey Zetterland*; Donna in *Last Exit to Brooklyn*; Connie/Patricia Winterbourne in *Mrs Winterbourne*; Misty Sutphin in *Serial Mom*; Kerry Tate in *Skinner*; Nicole in *Starlight: A Musical Movie*; *The In Crowd*; Brenda in *Where the Day Takes You*; Bridesmaid in *Working Girl*.
Address: c/o The Gersh Agency, PO Box 5617, Beverly Hills, California 90210, USA. m. Rob Sussman; 1 s. Milo Sebastian. Hobbies: Piano, clarinet, piccolo.

LALLY, Teri

Teri Lally. Actor (F).

b. Coatbridge, Glasgow, 21 April 1961.

TV: Carol McKay in *Take the High Road*.

Films: Shop assistant in *Comfort and Joy*; Margot in *Restless Natives*.

Address: c/o Scottish Television, Cowcaddens, Glasgow, Scotland G2 3PR. m. Scott Ferguson; 2 d. Lucy and Charlotte; 2 s. Gregory and Adam. Hobbies: Family, writing, reading.

LAMARR, Mark

Mark Lamarr. Presenter/Comedian.

b. 7 January 1967.

TV: *4 Goes to Glastonbury*; *Access All Areas*; *The Big Breakfast*; *Big in Japan*; *Big Mouth*; *Craig Miller & Cosgrove at the Festival*; *The Danny Baker Show*; *Edinburgh Nights*; *Funny Farm*; *Jam Down '94*; *Late Night Links*; *London Underground*; *Movie Watch*; *Never Mind the Buzzcocks*, *Packing them In*; *Saturday Zoo*; *Shooting Stars*; *Stand Up*; *The Happening*; *The Jack Docherty Show*; *The Late Show*; *The Mark Lamarr Show*; *The Series From Hell*; *Stand Up Show*; *The World*; *Tonight with Jonathan Ross*; *Top of the Pops*; *Up the Junction*; *Viva Cabaret*; *Wide Angle*.

Address: c/o Off the Kerb Productions, 3rd Floor, Hammer House, 113–117 Wardour Street, London W1V 3TD.

LAMB, Larry

Larry Lamb. Actor (M).

TV: *Annie's Bar* (1996); *Blonde Bombshell*; *Christopher Columbus* (1985); Chase in *Essex Boys*; *Fool's Gold* (1992); *Fox* (1980); *Get Back* (1992); *Harry's Kingdom* (1987); *Little Piece of Sunshine* (1990); *Our Friends in the North* (1995); *Supply and Demand* (1998); *Taggart: Fearful of Lightning*; *The Racing Game* (1979); *Triangle* (1981); *Twist of Fate* (1989); *The Wimbledon Poisoner* (1994).

Films: *Buster*; *Place Vendome*; *Shadey*; *Superman*; *Superman II*; *Superman III*.

Address: c/o Shepherd & Ford, 13 Radnor Walk, London SW34BP.

LAMONT, Glenn

Glenn Lamont. Actor (M).

TV: Richie Carter in *Emmerdale*.

Address: c/o SilverFox Artist Management Ltd, Cameo House, 11 Bear Street, London WC2H 7AS.

LANCASHIRE, Sarah

Sarah Lancashire. Actor (F). b. 1964.

TV: Rebecca in *About Face*; Liz in *Bloomin' Marvellous*;

Wendy in *Bradley*; Raquel Wolstenhulme in *Coronation Street*; Janice Dobbs in *Dramarama*; *Exam Conditions*; *My Secret Desire*; *Seeing Red*; *Showstoppers*; *The Bill*; *The Factory*; *The Verdict*; Alice in *Voices for Change*; Ms Lindon in *Watching*; Ruth in *Where the Heart Is*.

Address: c/o Talent Artists Limited, 4 Mews House, Princes Lane, London N10 3LU. Hobbies: Hockey, horse riding, singing, guitar.

LANDEN, Dinsdale

Dinsdale Landen. Actor (M).

b. Kent, 4 September 1932.

TV: *Devenish*; *Great Expectations*; *Lovejoy*; *Pig in the Middle*; *Play for Today*; Lord Brightlingsea in *The Buccaneers*; *The Fight Against Slavery*; *The Glittering Prizes*; *The Wingless Bird*.

Films: *Digby, The Biggest Dog in the World*; *Every Home Should Have One*; Commander Matteson in *Morons from Outer Space*; *Mosquito Squadron*; *Rasputin: The Mad Monk*; *The Valiant*.

Address: Whitehall Artists, 125 Gloucester Road, London SW7 4TE.

LANG, Belinda

Belinda Lang. Actor (F). b. London, 23 December 1955.

TV: Jill in *2point4children*; Eileen in *A Brother's Tale*; Sheila in *Bust*; Kate in *Dear John*; Agatha Troy in *Inspector Alleyn*; Liza in *Second Thoughts*; Martha in *The Brett*; Beth in *To Serve Them All My Days*.

Address: c/o Ken McReddie Ltd, 91 Regent Street, London W1R 7TB. Father Jeremy Hawk, mother Joan Heal; m. Hugh Fraser; d. Lily Fraser.

LANGFORD, Bonnie

Bonnie Langford. Actor (F)/Dancer/Singer.

b. London, 22 July 1964.

TV: *BBC Big Band on Pebble Mill*; *Children's Royal Variety Shows*; *Doctor Who*; *Saturday Starship*; *Showstoppers*; *This is Your Life*; Emily in *Tonight at 8.30: Family Album*; *Hot Shoe Show*; *Junior Showtime*; Violet Elizabeth in *Just William*; *Lena and Bonnie*; *Little and Large*; *Opportunity Knocks*.

Films: *Bugsy Malone*.

Music: *Bonnie Langford Now*; *Just One Kiss*; *Wuthering Heights, the Musical*.

Address: c/o Lake-Smith Griffin Associates, 15 Maiden Lane, London WC2E 7NA. m. Paul Grunert.

LANGHAM, Chris

Chris Langham. Actor (M). b. London, 14 April 1949.

TV: *Abracadabra*; *Bejewelled*; *Bottom*; *Bouncing Back*; *Clive Anderson Talks Back*; *Cold Harbour*; *Elevator*; *Flip*;

Friday Night with Wogan; Grapevine; Happy Families; History of Pantomime; Douglas in *Kiss Me Kate; Look at the State We're In;* Customs Officer in *Married with Children; Max Headroom; Muppet Show; Murder Most Horrid; Not the Nine O'Clock News; People Like Us; Play for Today; Private Enterprise; Q6; Radio Story; Saturday Live; School for Clowns; Showscan; Silas Marner; Smith and Jones; Spatz; Spike Milligan Special; Spitting Image; Tales from the Poopdeck; The McGuffin.*
Films: *Hollywood Dog; Is it Legal?;* Interviewer in *The Big Tease;* Various in *The Life of Brian.*
Address: c/o David Wilkinson Associates, 115 Hazelbury Road, London SW6 2LX. m. 1 Sue Jones-Davies (div); m. 2 Christine Cartwright; 1 s. Harry; 1 d. Emily. Hobbies: Skiing, diving, computing.

LANGRISHE, Caroline
Caroline Langrishe. Actor (F).
TV: *Cleopatra; Heartbeat; Peak Practice; Mosley; Bombay Blue; Embassy; Sharpe's Return; Cluedo; Lovejoy; Exchange of Fire; Chancer; The Bill; Boon; Shelley; Kenya; Twelfth Night; Pulaski; Fortunes of War; Minder; Let's Run Away to Africa; Sharing Time; Lonely Hearts Kid; No 10; QED; Second's Out; Hammer Horror; Flipside of Dominick Hide; Another Flip for Dominick Hide; Tales of the Unexpected; Degree of Uncertainty; Wuthering Heights; Queen Victoria's Scandals; Anna Karenina; Glittering Prizes.*
Films: *Rogue Trader; Parting Shots; Crimetime; Hawks; Dead Man's Folly; Mistral's Daughter; Michael Bogdanov's Shakespeare; Death Wish; Eagle's Wing; Holocaust 2000.*
Address: c/o Conway van Gelder Ltd, 18–21 Jermyn Street, London SW1 6HP.

LANSBURY, Angela
Angela Lansbury. Actor (F)/Producer.
b. London, 16 October 1925.
TV: *A Talent for Murder; Happy at Last;* Aunt Hortense Boutin in *Lace;* Gertrude Vanderbilt in *Little Gloria;* Agatha McGee in *Love She Sought;* Ada Harris in *Mrs Harris Goes to Paris;* Jessica Fletcher in *Murder, She Wrote;* Marchesa Allabrandi in *Rage of Angels: The Story Continues;* Nan Moore in *Shootdown;* Nellie Lovett in *Sweeney Todd;* Amanda Fenwick in *The Gift of Love: A Christmas Story;* Penelope Keeling in *The Shellseekers.*
Films: Annabell Willart in *All Fall Down;* Eglantine Price in *Bedknobs and Broomsticks;* Sarah Lee Gates in *Blue Hawaii;* Countess Lina in *Breath of Scandal;* Mavis Pruitt in *Dark at the Top of the Stairs;* Phyllis in *Dear Heart;* Salome Otterbourne in *Death on the Nile;* Marguerite in *Four Horsemen of the Apocalypse;*

Nancy Oliver in *Gaslight;* Mama Jean Bello in *Harlow;* Em in *Harvey Girls;* Dusty Willard in *Hoodlum Saint;* Mabel Sabre in *If Winter Comes;* Sybil Logan in *In the Cool of the Day;* Mrs Edwards in *Kind Lady;* Tally Dickson in *Lawless Street;* Doris Hillman in *Life at Stake;* Gloria in *Mister Buddwing* (aka *Woman without a Face*); Leslie in *Mutiny;* Edwina Brown in *National Velvet;* Sibyl Vane in *The Picture of Dorian Gray;* Myra Leeds in *Please Murder Me;* Valeska Chauvel in *Remains to be Seen;* Semadar in *Samson and Delilah;* Countess Herthevon Ornstein in *Something for Everyone* (aka *Black Flowers for the Bride*); Kay Thorndyke in *State of the Union* (aka *The World and His Wife*); Pearl in *Summer of the Seventeenth Doll;* Susan Bratten in *Tenth Avenue Angel;* Lady Blystone in *The Amorous Adventures of Moll Flanders* (aka *Moll Flanders*); Princess Gwendolyn in *The Court Jester;* Claudia in *The Greatest Story Ever Told;* Miss Froy in *The Lady Vanishes;* Mommy Fortuna in *The Last Unicorn;* Minnie Littlejohn in *The Long, Hot Summer;* Mrs Iselin in *The Manchurian Candidate;* Miss Jane Marple in *The Mirror Crack'd;* Clotilde de Marelle in *The Private Affairs of Bel Ami;* Ruth in *The Pirates of Penzance;* Madame Valentine in *The Purple Mask;* Audrey Quail in *The Red Danube;* Mabel Claremon in *The Reluctant Debutante;* Queen Anne in *The Three Musketeers;* Isabel Boyd in *The World of Henry Orient; Till The Clouds Roll By.*
Address: c/o William Morris Agency, 151 El Camino Drive, Beverly Hills, California 90212, USA. m. 1 Richard Cromwell (div); m. 2 Peter Shaw.

LAPOTAIRE, Jane
Jane Lapotaire. Actor (F).
b. Suffolk, 26 December 1944.
TV: *A Curious Suicide; Ain't Misbehavin'; Anthony and Cleopatra; The Big Battalions; Blind Justice; Giving Tongue; Jonny and the Dead; Love Hurts; Macbeth; Marie Curie; McCallum; Seal Morning; Simisola; The Barretts of Wimpole Street; The Captain's Doll; The Dark Angel.*
Films: *Eureka; Lady Jane; Napoleon and Josephine; Performance; Anthony and Cleopatra; Shooting Fish; Surviving Picasso; To Catch a King.*
Address: c/o Storm Artists Management, 47 Brewer Street, London W1R 3FD.

LARKIN, Chris
Chris Larkin. Actor (M).
TV: DS Derek Hill in *Bliss;* Adam Parker in *Casualty;* Toby in *Frank Stubbs Promotes;* Steven Keane in *Highlander; Karaoke;* Cambridge in *Roger, Roger.*

Films: Robin Swinnerton in *Angels and Insects*; Frederick Lynn in *Jane Eyre*; Major Gibson in *Tea With Mussolini*.
Address: c/o CDA, 19 Sydney Mews, London SW3 6HL.

LATHAM, Bernard

Bernard Latham. Actor (M).
b. Manchester, Lancashire, 21 April 1951.
TV: Armitage in *Back Up*; Dr Randall in *Care*; Wayne in *Carrot Del Sol*; Terry in *Casualty*; Rudy Warburton in *Chandler and Co.*; Sid Hope in *Dalziel and Pascoe*; Fire Officer Lazerby in *Dangerfield*; Richard Casey in *Forever Green*; Detective Johnson in *Fox*; Pomeroy in *Ghost Story*; Doctor in *Harvest Moon*; Gordon Cunningham in *Hollyoaks*; Mr Wildman in *Mother Ruin*; Ron Undersworth in *Pobol Y Cym*; Lucien Bex in *Poirot*; Prison Warden in *Rudkins Fetch*; Designer in *Selected Exits*; Bob in *September Song*; Jimmy Salvation in *Supertramp*; Gallagher in *The Bill*; Kev Eccles in *The Practice*; *Who is Rebecca?*; Tregeddick in *Wycliffe*.
Films: RMP Robertson in *Boy Soldier*; Ulf the Unmemorable in *Erik the Viking*; Sir James Penfold in *Rebecca's Daughters*; Handsome in *The Lovers*; Uncle Alfred in *The Rainbow*.
Address: c/o Tim Scott Personal Management, 5 Cloisters Business Centre, 8 Battersea Park Road, London SW8 4BG. Hobbies: Singing, football.

LATHAM, Helen

Helen Latham. Actor (F).
TV: *Big Women*; Miss Farris in *Brookside*; *Crimewatch*; Natalie in *Dream Team*; Various in *Hale & Pace*; *The Jump*.
Films: *The Tenth Kingdom*.
Address: c/o Elaine Murphy Associates, 310 Aberdeen House, 22–24 Highbury Grove, London N5 2EA. Hobbies: Singing, jazz and tap, piano, ballet.

LATHAM, Philip

Philip Latham. Actor (M). b. Leigh-on-Sea, Essex.
TV: Mr Bourne in *Cedar Tree*; *Doctor Who*; *Man from the Pru*; Plantagenet Palliser in *The Pallisers*; *The Fourth Arm*; *The Professionals*; Willie Izzard in *The Troubleshooters*.
Films: *Devil Ship Pirates*; *Dracula Prince of Darkness*; *Force Ten from Navarone*; *The Last Grenade*; *Ring of Spies*; *Spy Story*.
Address: c/o Bryan Drew Ltd, Quadrant House, 80–82 Regent Street, London W1X 3TB. Hobbies: Golf, cricket.

LATHEM, Sam

Sam Lathem. Actor (M). b. London, 30 June 1966.
TV: Gary Parker in *2point4children*; DS Vaines in *Bodyguards*; PC Waterman in *Class Act*; Duggie Porter in *EastEnders*; Oscar in *Exchange of Fire*; *Family Affairs*; *Jack Higgins' Midnight Man*; Matt Vinyl in *London's Burning*; Robbo in *Our Friends in the North*; Eric in *She's Out*, Various in *The Bill*; *The Echo*; *The Tenth Kingdom*; *The Vanishing Man*.
Films: Brian Reilly in *Eye of the Storm*; Fred in *The Mountain Road*.
Address: c/o Langford Associates, 17 Westfields Avenue, London SW13 0AT. Hobbies: Rugby, football.

LAURIE, Hugh

Hugh Laurie. Actor (M)/Comedian/Presenter.
b. Oxford, 11 June 1959.
TV: *Letters from a Bomber Pilot*; *Morris Minor and the Majors*; *Mrs Capper's Birthday*; *Murder Most Horrid*; *Saturday Live*; *South of Watford*; *The Cambridge Footlights*; *The Crystal Cube*; *The Young Ones*; *A Bit of Fry and Laurie*; Uncle in *A Pin for the Butterfly*; *Alfresco Land II*; *All or Nothing at All*; *Blackadder* (1985); *Blackadder Christmas Special*; *Blackadder Goes Forth*; George III in *Blackadder III*; *Friday Live*; Bertie Wooster in *Jeeves and Wooster*.
Films: Jasper in *101 Dalmatians*; *Cousin Bette*; *Maybe Baby*; *Plenty*; *Sense and Sensibility*; *Strapless*; *Stuart Little*; Officer Steady in *The Borrowers*; *The Man in the Iron Mask*; *The Place of Lions*.
Address: c/o Hamilton Asper, 24 Hanway Street, London W1P 9DD.

LAVENDER, Ian

Ian Lavender. Actor (M). b. 16 February 1946.
TV: *A Life on the Box*; *Andrew Neil Show*; *Call My Bluff*; *Casualty*; *Cluedo*; *Come Back Mrs Noah*; *Dad's Army*; *Funny You Ask*; *Goodnight Sweetheart*; *Harry Hill Show*; *Have I Got You Where You Want Me?*; *Keeping up Appearances*; *Mr Big*; *Noel's Telly Years*; *Peak Practice*; *That's Showbusiness*; *The Glums*; *The Hello Goodbye Man*; *West Beach*.
Films: *Dad's Army*.
Address: Hilary Gagan Associates, 2nd Floor, Gloucester Mansions, 140a Shaftebury Avenue, London WC2H 8HD.

LAW, Sally Anne

Sally Anne Law. Actor (F).
TV: *A Time to Dance*; Mrs Baxter in *Aquila*; Mrs Baxter in *Aquila II*; Geraldine in *Birds of a Feather*; *Flying into the Wind*; *S.W.A.L.K.*, *Strangers*, *The Agatha Christie Hour*, Mrs Nixon in *The Bill*; *The Clinger*; *The Glory*

Boys; Linda Danson in *The Knock* (third series); Sarah Ferguson in *Women of Windsor.*
Films: *Party Party; Willow; Women of Windsor.*
Address: c/o David Daly Associates, 586a Kings Road, London SW6 2DX.

LAWLESS, Lucy

Lucille Frances Ryan. Actor (F).
b. Mt Albert, Auckland, New Zealand, 29 March 1968.
TV: *Air New Zealand Holiday; Funny Business;* Lysia in *Hercules and the Amazon Women;* Lyla in *Hercules: The Legendary Adventures;* Xena in *Hercules: The Legendary Journeys;* Sharon List in *High Tide;* Undercover Policewoman in *High Tide; Saturday Night Live;* Herself in *Something So Right;* Sarah McFee in *The Black Stallion;* Liddy Barton in *The Ray Bradbury Theatre;* Herself in *The Simpsons;* Mink Tertius in *Typhon's People;* Xena in *Xena: Warrior Princess.*
Films: Nurse 1 in *A Bitter Song;* Helen in *For The Love of Mike;* Xena in *Hercules and Xena The Animated Movie, the Battle for Mount Olympus; Peach;* Joe's Girl in *The End of the Golden Weather;* Jane Redmond in *The Rainbow Warrior;* Verity in *Within the Law.*
Address: c/o Channel 5, 22 Long Acre, London WC2E 9LY. m. 1 Garth Lawless (dis); 1 d. Daisy; m. 2 Robert Tapert; 1 s. Julius. Hobbies: Yoga, horse riding, music, jazz, singing, martial arts, languages.

LAWLEY, Sue

Sue Lawley. Presenter. b. Dudley, 14 July 1946.
TV: *General Election Nights; Nationwide; 9 O'clock News; Norman Ormal; Question Time; 6 O'clock News; Wogan.*
Address: c/o BBC, Broadcasting House, Portland Place, London W1A 1AA.

LAWRENCE, Josie

Josie Lawrence. Actor (F)/Comedian. b. 6 June 1959.
TV: *Absolutely Fabulous; Alas Smith and Jones;* Linda Prentice in *Campaign; Downwardly Mobile; Duck Patrol; Flint Street Nativity; Friday Night Live; Hercule Poirot; I Love Keith Allen; Jackson Pace; Josie; Norbert Smith;* Janet Wilkins in *Not with a Bang; Outside Edge; Picturebox; Queen of the Wild Frontier;* Rachel in *Rachel and the Roarettes; S.W.A.L.K.;* Lucy in *The Green Man; Whose Line is it Anyway?*
Films: Lottie in *Enchanted April; Married to Malcolm;* Guerrillaette in *The American Way;* Kate in *The Sin Eater.*
Address: c/o ICM, Oxford House, 76 Oxford Street, London W1N 0AX.

LAWSON, Charles

Charles Lawson. Actor (M). b. 1959.
TV: Seamus Duffryn in *Harry's Game;* Billy in *Four*

Days in July; Dossie Wright in *Joyce in June;* Rigg in *The Firm;* Tommy Burns in *Upline;* Yizzel in *Bread;* Jim McDonald in *Coronation Street.*
Films: *Ascendancy; SS; I Cannot Answer That Question; Wilt.*
Address: c/o Barry Brown and Partner, 47 West Square, London SE11 4SP.

LAWSON, Denis

Denis Lawson. Actor (M).
b. Perthshire, 27 September 1947.
TV: *Born Kicking; Love After Lunch; Natural Lies; One Way Out; Royal Scandal; The Ambassador; The Justice Game; The Kit Curran Radio Show; The Uncertain Feeling; The Victoria Wood Show.*
Films: *Local Hero; Providence; Star Wars* (trilogy); *The Chain; The Man in the Iron Mask.*
Address: c/o ICM, Oxford House, 76 Oxford Street, London W1N 0AX

LAWSON, Leigh

Leigh Lawson. Actor (M).
b. Warwickshire, 21 July 1943.
TV: *Kinsey; Lace; O'Pioneers; Queenie; Stick With Me Kid; Tears in the Rain; Travelling Man; An Unsuitable Job for a Woman; Voice of the Heart.*
Films: Bernardo in *Brother Sun, Sister Moon;* Robert in *Ghost Story;* Laurence in *Golden Rendezvous;* Alpie Pratt in *Love Among The Ruins;* Humphrey in *Madame Sousatzka;* Tate in *Out of Depth;* Percy in *Percy's Progress;* Humphrey in *Sword of the Valiant;* Alex D'Urberville in *Tess;* the God King in *The God King;* King Mark in *The Sword and the Fire;* Richard in *The Tiger Lily.*
Address: c/o PFD, Drury House, 34–43 Russell Street, London WC2B 5HA. m. Twiggy.

LAWSON, Quintin

Quintin Lawson. Actor (M).
b. Enniskillen, 17 September 1959.
TV: *Boon; Bread; Crown Court; Harry's Game; Joyce in June; Play for Today ; Playhouse; The Bill; The Hot Potato; The Monocled Mutineer; The Question; The Trap; Up the Elephant and Round the Castle; Upline; Valentine Falls.*
Films: *Four Days in July; The Firm; The SS; Wilt.*
Address: c/o Barry Brown & Partner, 47 West Square, London SE11.

LAWSON, Twiggy

Twiggy Lawson. Actor (F)/Presenter.
b. London, 19 September 1949.
TV: *Bodybags; Charlie the Kid; Heartbeat; Little Match*

Girl; Princesses; Eliza Dolittle in *Pygmalion; Something Borrowed, Something Blue; Sophie's World; Sun Child; Tales from the Crypt; This Morning; Twiggy's People.*
Films: *Club Paradise; Madame Sousatzka; The Boyfriend; The Doctor and the Devils; W; Woundings.*
Music: *If Love Were All; London Pride.*
Address: c/o PFD, Drury House, 34–43 Russell Street, London WC2B 5HA. m. Leigh Lawson.

LAYDEN, Kate
Kate Layden. Actor (F).
TV: Veronica Robinson in *City Central;* Jean Walters in *Coronation Street;* Shadow in *Coronation Street;* Sandra Fowler in *Emmerdale;* Joy Ellis in *Heartbeat;* Maurika Rome in *Hetty Wainthropp Investigates;* Miss Lavengroin in *How We Used To Live;* Brown Owl in *Just Us;* Margaret Sykes in *Manhunt;* Brenda Oldcorn in *Moving Story;* Margaret Bingham in *Poor Edith;* Space Queen in *Search;* Mrs Redmond in *Seeing Red; The Broker's Man,* Veronica in *The Ritz;* Alien Queen in *Vic Reeves' Weekenders;* Mum in *Video Diary of a Nobody;* Mrs Webster in *Where the Heart Is.*
Films: Bee in *The Full Monty.*
Address: c/o North of Watford Actor's Agency, Bridge Hill, Hebden Bridge, West Yorkshire HX7 8EX.

LAYTON, George
George Layton. Actor (M).
b. Bradford, Yorkshire, 2 March 1943.
TV: *Doctor at the Top;* Paul Collier in *Doctor in the House, Doctor at Large, Doctor in Charge;* Bomb Solomon in *It Ain't Half Hot Mum; Len and the River Mob;* Des in *Minder;* PC Brian Booth in *My Brother's Keeper;* Vernon Potter in *Robin's Nest; Sunburn; That's Life; The Likely Lads; The Other Man; The Sweeney.*
Films: *Don't Go Breaking My Heart.*
Address: c/o Amanda Howard Associates Ltd, 21 Berwick Street, London W1V 3RG.

LAZZERI, Martino
Martino Lazzeri. Actor (M)/Presenter.
TV: Simon in *Bad Boyes;* Dan in *Berkeley Square;* Young Urchin in *Blackadder Christmas Carol;* Carlos in *Bluebirds; Boiled Eggs and Soldiers;* Kenny in *Casualty; Fully Booked;* Joe in *Grange Hill;* Alex in *Hollyoaks;* Chairman in *How to be Cool;* Jake in *Pirates;* Luca in *Roger, Roger;* Fizz the Genie in *Tea Bag;* David in *The Bill;* Jimmy in *The Bill;* Kevin in *The Fallen Curtain;* Lawrence in *The Lodge;* Kevin in *The Thief;* Jamie in *The Wild House;* Son in *Who Needs It;* Carlos in *Zorro.*
Address: c/o Rossmore Personal Management, Rossmore Road, London NW1 6NJ. Hobbies: Horse riding, snooker, football.

LE BLANC, Matt
Matt Le Blanc. Actor (M).
b. Newton, Massachusetts, USA, 25 July 1967.
TV: Billy Barton in *Anything to Survive* (1990); Joey Tribbiani in *Friends;* Todd Murphy in *Just the Ten of Us (*1989); Vinnie Verducci in *Married with Children (*1991); *Monsters* (1990); *Red Shoe Diaries* (1993); Vince in *Reform Girls School* (1994); Vinnie Verducci in *Top of the Heap* (1991); Chuck Bender in *TV 101* (1988); Vinnie Verducci in *Vinnie and Bobby* (1992).
Films: Jack 'Deuce' Cooper in *Ed;* Anthony Manetti in *Lookin' Italian;* Major Don West in *Lost in Space;* Terhune in *The Killing Box.*
Address: c/o United Talent Agency, 9560 Wilshire Blvd., Suite 500, Beverly Hills, California 90212, USA. Fiancée Melissa McKnight. Hobbies: Landscape photography, motorcycles.

LE VAILLANT, Nigel
Nigel Le Vaillant. Actor (M).
TV: Etonian in *Brideshead Revisited;* Dr Julian Chapman in *Casualty;* Adam Von Trott ZuSolz in *Christabel;* Dr Paul Dangerfield in *Dangerfield;* Simon in *Honey for Tea; Horizon: Ice Mummies; Jemima Shaw Investigates; Ladies in Charge;* Tom Long in *Tom's Midnight Garden; Wish Me Luck.*
Films: *Personal Services; The Jigsaw Man; White Mischief.*
Address: c/o Shepherd & Ford, 13 Radnor Walk, London SW3 4BP.

LE VELL, Michael
Michael Turner. Actor (M). b. 15 December 1964.
TV: Kevin Webster in *Coronation Street; Fame is the Spur; One by One; The Hard Word.*
Address: c/o Arena Entertainment, Regents Court, 39 Harrogate Road, Leeds, West Yorkshire.

LEACH, Rosemary
Rosemary Leach. Actor (F).
b. Much Wenlock, Shropshire, 18 December 1935.
TV: Connie in *Across the Lake;* Miss Markland in *An Unsuitable Job for a Woman;* Nanny Collons in *Berkeley Square;* Nan in *Blood and Peaches;* Lady Selina Bricklinsea in *Buccaneers; Cider with Rosie; Day to Remember; Don Quixote;* Mrs Bonnet in *French and Saunders;* Joan in *Growing Pains; Hindle Wakes;* Nursie in *If You Meet a Fairy;* lead in *No That's Me Over Here; Once in a Lifetime;* Emilia in *Othello;* Mother in *Paul Merton; Road to Freedom; Shall We Gather at the River;* Grandmother in *Stick With Me Kid;* Nancy Leadbetter in *Summer's Lease;* Mary in *Tender Loving Care;* Joan Plumleigh Bruce in *The*

Charmer; Mrs Dangle in *The Critic*; Aunt Fenny in *The Jewel in the Crown*; Susan Welson in *The Power Game*; *The Three Burrs*; Annie Besant in *The Warrior Returns*; Violet in *The Winslow Boy*; Mrs Forefoot Meadows in *Tilly Trotter*; Dot Curdle in *Titmus Regained*; Mrs Lesley in *Toby*; Aunt Vinny in *Up the Garden Path*; *When We are Married*; *Wild Duck*.

Films: Mrs Hunt in *An Ungentlemanly Act*; Margaret in *Baroness and the Pig*; Mrs Henshaw in *Breathtaking*; *Brief Encounter*; Lady Osborne in *Lucan*; Mrs Honeychurch in *A Room with a View*; *SOS Titanic*; *That'll be the Day*; Golda in *The Bride*; *The Children*; *The Hawk*; Mrs Inchcliff in *Turtle Summer*; Madge in *What Ever Happened to Harold Smith?*.

Address: c/o William Morris Agency (UK) Ltd, 1 Stratton Street, London W1X 6HB. m. Colin Starkey. Hobbies: Gardening, cookery.

LEBOR, Stanley

Stanley Lebor. Actor (M).
b. East Ham, London, 24 September 1934.

TV: *An Independent Man*; *Ever Decreasing Circles*; *Harry's Mad*; *Holocaust*; *Madame Bovary*; *Minder*; *Ready When You Are Mr McGill*; *The Baker Street Boys*; *The Bill*; Uncle Hendreary in *The Borrowers*; *Last of the Summer Wine*; *The Naked Civil Servant*; *The Paul Merton Show*.

Films: *A Bridge Too Far*; *Arabian Nights*; *Flash Gordon*; *Gandhi*; *Oh What A Lovely War*; *Personal Services*; *Superman IV*; *The Medusa Touch*.

Address: c/o Joy Jameson Ltd, 2.19 The Plaza, 535 Kings Road, London SW10 0SZ.

LEDDEN, Emma

Emma Ledden. Presenter. b. Dublin, Ireland, 1977.
TV: *Daily Edition*; *Dance Floor*; *Hit List UK*; *Live & Kicking*; *Select*; *The Den*; *Weekend Edition*.
Address: c/o SilverFox Artist Management Ltd, Cameo House, 11 Bear Street, London WC2H 7AS.

LEDERER, Helen

Helen Lederer. Actor (F)/Comedian.
b. Llanddvery, Wales, 29 September 1958.

TV: *A Word in Your Era*; *Absolutely Fabulous*; *Big Day Out*; *Bottom*; *Bridget Jones Night*; *Casualty*; *Computing for the Terrified*; *Election Special*; *Filthy Rich & Catflap*; *For Amusements Only*; *French and Saunders*; *Friday Night with Wogan*; Felicity in *Girls on Top*; *Going for a Song*; *Hangar 17 – I Hate this House*; Flossie in *Happy Families*; *Harry Enfield and Chums*; *Hello Mum*; *Here's One I Made Earlier*; *Just a Minute*; *Just For Laughs*; *Little Armadillos*; *Modern Times*; *Norland Nannies*; *One Foot in the Grave*; *Pirates*; *Psst – The Really Useful Guide*

to *Alcohol*; *Saturday Night Live*; *The Baldy Man*; *The Funniest Thing*; *The Jack and Jeremy Show*; *The Naked Video*; Anna in *The New Statesman*; *The Pony Club*; *The Refuge*; *The Ruby Wax Show*; *The Survivor's Guide*; *The Young Ones*.

Films: *Dance for Daddy*; *Solitaire for Two*.
Address: c/o Roger Hancock Ltd, 4 Water Lane, London NW1 8NZ. m. Dr Chris Browne; 1 d. Hannah. Hobbies: Films, eating, walking, keep fit.

LEE, Iain

Iain Lee. Reporter/Presenter.
TV: *Political Awards* (1998); *The 11 O'Clock Show*; *The Paul McKenna Show*.
Address: c/o Talkback Management, 36 Percy Street, London W1P 0LN.

LEE, Stewart

Stewart Lee. Comedian/Presenter. b. 1968.
TV: *Festival of Fun*; *Harry Hill*; *Lee & Herring's Fist of Fun*; *This Morning with Richard Not Judy*.
Address: c/o Avalon Promotions, 2nd Floor, Queens House, Leicester Place, Leicester Square, London WC2H 7BP.

LEESLEY, Geoffrey

Geoffrey Leesley. Actor (M).
b. Manchester, 1 June 1949.
TV: Geoff Travis in *Albion Market*; DC Terry Wilson in *Bergerac*; John Harrison in *Brookside*; Keith Cotterill in *Casualty*; Rex in *The Liver Birds*; Frank Matthews in *Waterfront Beat*.
Address: c/o Evans & Reiss, 100 Fawe Park Road, London SW15 2EA.

LEEVES, Jane

Jane Leeves. Actor (F). b. London, 18 April 1962.
TV: Daphne Moon in *Caroline in the City*; Daphne Moon in *Frasier*; Athena in *Hercules*; Annie in *Hooperman*; Gwen Petrie in *Murder She Wrote*; Audrey Cohen in *Murphy Brown*; Rachel Sherwood in *Pandora's Clock*; Holly in *Red Dwarf*; Maria Penny in *Seinfeld*; Maria in *Seinfeld*; Hill's Angel in *The Benny Hill Show*; Blue in *Throb*; Ms Adams in *Who's the Boss?*.

Films: Ladybug in *James and the Giant Peach*; Alberta Leonard in *Miracle on 34th Street*; Wylie in *Mr Write*; Dorothea Van Hauften in *Music of the Heart*; *The Adventures of Tom Thumb and Thumbelina*; Serena in *To Live and Die in LA*; Juliet in *Us Begins with You*.
Address: c/o Talent Artists Limited, 4 Mews House, Princes Lane, London N10 3LU. m. Marshall Coben. Hobbies: Reading, cooking, various sports, dance.

LEEZE, Johnny

Johnny Leeze. Actor (M).
b. Yorkshire, 31 December 1941.
TV: Lionel Brough in *All Creatures Great and Small*; *Book Tower*; Billy Hamilton in *Chimera*; Jack in *Common as Muck*; Harry Clayton in *Coronation Street*; *Cracker*; Prison Officer in *Criminal*; *Cupid's Darts*; Ned Glover in *Emmerdale*; *England's Green and Pleasant Land*; *Hallelujah*; Prison officer in *Harry*; *Heartbeat*; *Intensive Care*; *Juliet Bravo*; *The Last of the Summer Wine*; *Open All Hours*; Custody Sergeant in *Resnick*; Hodges in *Seaforth*; Gamekeeper in *Stay Lucky*; *Strangers*; *Strike*; Inspector Cox in *League of Gentleman*; *Wrathdale*.
Films: Photographer in *Ladder of Swords*; Journalist in *Never Better*.
Address: c/o Sharron Ashcroft Management, Dean Clough, Halifax, Yorkshire HX3 5AX. Hobbies: Dancing, golf, cricket, football, driving.

LEIGH-HUNT, Ronald

Ronald Leigh-Hunt. Actor (M). b. London.
TV: Sir James in *Smart Money*; Alfonce in *Frankenstein*; *Remington Steele*; Monty in *All in Good Faith*; Impy Biggs in *Strong Poison*; *Minder*; *Hilary*; *Doctor Who*; *The Saint*; *The Brothers*; *Freewheelers*.
Films: *The Omen*; *Never Take No for an Answer*; *Le Mans*; *Khartoum*; *Sink the Bismark*; *Mohammed*; *The Nelson Touch*; *Tiger Lily*; *The Story of Private Pooley*; *The Paper Orchid*.
Address: c/o Vincent Shaw, 20 Jay Mews, London SW7 2EP. Hobbies: Motor racing, rugby, tennis, jazz.

LENO, Jay

James Douglas Muir Leno. Actor (M)/Host.
b. New Rochelle, New York, USA, 28 April 1950.
TV: *Alice* (1981); *Almost Heaven* (1979); Don in *Frasier* (1993); Patient in *Good Times* (1974); Jay in *Home Improvement* (1995); Himself in *It's Just a Ride* (1994); Joey Mitchell in *Laverne and Shirley* (1979); Bobby Bitts in *Laverne and Shirley* (1976); Lucky in *Providence* (1999); Kitty in *South Park* (1999); *The Marilyn McCoo and Billy Davis, Jnr Show* (1977); *The Tonight Show with Jay Leno*.
Films: Mookie in *American Hat Wax*; Larry Miller (Poopy Butt) in *Americathon*; Detective Tony Costas in *Collison Course*; Himself in *Contact*; *Doctor Duck's Super Secret All-Purpose Sauce*; Himself in *Ed TV*; Himself in *In & Out*; Himself in *Mad City*; Himself in *Meet Wally Sparks*; Albert Fiore in *Silver Bears*; Himself in *The Birdcage*; Bedrock's Most Wanted Host in *The Flintstones*; *Undercover Angel*; Himself in *Wag the Dog*; Narrator in *What's Up, Hideous Sun Demon*.

Address: c/o Steve Levine, 8942 Wilshire Blvd., Beverly Hills, California 90211, USA. m. Mavis (Nicholson) Leno. Hobbies: Antique Cars, motorcycles.

LENSKA, Rula

Rosa-Marie Leopoldnya Lubienska. Actor (F).
b. St Neots, Cambridgeshire, 30 September 1947.
TV: Renata Cartwright in *Boon*; Mrs Peacock in *Cluedo* (1991); Styles in *Doctor Who* (1984); *Kappatoo* (1990); Kate in *Minder* (1982); Gertrude in *Private Schultz* (1981); Abbess Morgwyn of Ravenscar in *Robin of Sherwood*; Nancy 'Q' Cunard de Longchamps in *Rock Follies of 77*; Isabel Stevens in *Stay Lucky* (1993); Mrs Joan Warner in *Take a Letter Mr Jones* (1981); Herself in *The Full Wax* (1992); Countess Radzsky in *The Seven Dials Mystery* (1982); Mlle. du Toit in *To the Manor Born*.
Films: Louise in *Alfie Darling*; Dee Perry in *Paradise Grove*; Helga in *Royal Flash*.
Address: c/o London Management, Noel House, 2–4 Noel Street, London W1V 3RB. m. Dennis Waterman (actor) (dis).

LEONARD, Jacqueline

Jacqueline Leonard. Actor (F). b. Yorkshire, 1967.
TV: Theresa Kennedy in *A Time to Dance*; Lorraine in *EastEnders*; Lisa Nelkin in *Full Stretch*; Kathleen in *In Suspicious Circumstances*; Miss Spillers in *Inspector Morse*; Mary Peale in *Maisie Raine*; Gwen in *Memento Mori*; Victoria in *Palmer & Co.*; Sarah Preston in *Peak Practice*; Sarah in *Three Miles Up*.
Films: Leora in *Chaplin*; Jack in *ID*.
Address: c/o CAM London, 19 Denmark Street, London WC2H 8NA. Hobbies: Dancing, singing.

LESLIE, John

John Leslie. Presenter. b. Edinburgh, 1965.
TV: *BAFTA Awards*; *Blue Peter*; *Children in Need*; *Entertainment Express*; *Formula One*; *Give Your Mate a Break*; *Good Morning*; *Mainly Men*; *Noel's House Party*; *Royal Tournament*; *Style Challenge*; *Tartan Extra*; *This Morning*; *Was it Good for You?*; *Wheel of Fortune*.
Address: c/o John Noel Management, 10a Belmont Street, London NW1 8HH. Hobbies: Tennis, squash, football (supporter of Hibernian FC), music.

LETTERMAN, David

David Letterman. Actor (M)/Executive producer/Host.
b. Indianapolis, Indiana, USA, 12 April 1947.
TV: Matt Morgan in *Fast Friends* (1979); Himself in *It's Just a Ride* (1994); *The Late Show with David Letterman*; Many guest appearances as himself on programmes like *Spin City*, *Seinfeld*, *The Cosby Show* and *The Larry*

Sanders Show; skit characters in *Mary* (1978); Ellsworth in *Mork and Mindy* (1978); *The Bonnie Hunt* (1995); *The Building* (1993); *The David Letterman Show* (1980); Panellist in *The Gong Show* (1976); *The High Life* (1996); *The Starland Vocal Band Show* (1977).
Films: Motley Crue Roadie in *Beavis and Butt-head Do America;* Old Salt in Fishing Village in *Cabin Boy;* Himself in *Eddie;* Himself in *Private Parts; Steve Martin Live;* Himself in *The Man on the Moon.*
Address: c/o ICM Agency, 8942 Wilshire Blvd., Beverly Hills, California 90211, USA. m. Michele Cook (dis).

LEWIS, Alun

Alun Lewis. Actor (M).
TV: Gifford in *92 Grosvenor Street; A Woman's Place; Angels;* Darryl in *Birds of a Feather;* Bronco Billy in *Boon;* Bobby Boyle in *Bowen; Casualty;* Charley in *Charlie's Aunt; Crown Court;* Vic Windsor in *Emmerdale;* Billy John in *Ennal's Point; Eustace and Hilda; Fearless Frank; Findings on a Late Afternoon; Happy; How We Used To Live;* Gareth in *Jemma Shore Investigates;* Matthew in *Just Another Blues Song; Lifelike; Maybury; Minder;* Bryn in *New Girl in Town;* Terry in *Noah's Castle; Rumpole of the Bailey; The Bill;* Lewis in *The Choir;* Hockey in *The Falkland Factor; The Professionals; The Strange Affair of Adelaide Harris.*
Films: *Bowen;* Hywel in *Experience Preferred But Not Essential; Giro City; Smithfield; Van Der Valk.*
Address: c/o Annette Stone Associates, 2nd Floor, 22 Great Marlborough Street, London W1V 1AF.

LEWIS, Anthony

Anthony Lewis. Actor (M).
b. Leeds, West Yorkshire, 31 March 1983.
TV: Adam in *Adam's Family Tree* (1997); Christopher Nixon in *Cardiac Arrest* (1995); Stephen Nash in *Cracker;* Marc Reynolds in *Emmerdale;* Billy Swinton in *Heartbeat;* Kevin in *My Dad's a Boring Nerd* (1997); Scott Morris in *The Ward* (1998); Stephen Oldfield in *This is Personal* (1999); Barnabas Meyerbridge in *A Touch of Frost* (1995).
Films: Matthew Wilkinson in *Girls' Night.*
Address: c/o Scala Kids Casting, 42 Rufford Avenue, Yeadon, Leeds LS19 7QR. Brother Matthew Lewis. Hobbies: Guitar, watching rugby league, football.

LEWIS, Howard Lew

Howard Lew Lewis. Actor (M). b. 21 August 1939.
TV: *Artrageous; Brushstrokes; Chelmsford 123; Corner House; Flip; Harry's Mad; Jack and the Beanstalk; Look and Read; Maid Marion and Her Merry Men; Monster TV; Mrs Pye; Noel's House Party; Open All Hours; Prospects; Pulaski; The Bill; The Charmer; The Two Ronnies.*

Films: *Brazil; Chaplin; Prince of Thieves; Quills; Shadowlands; Titchborne Claimant.*
Address: c/o The Narrow Road Company, 21–22 Poland Street, London W1V 3DD.

LEWIS, Jonathan

Jonathan Lewis. Actor (M). b. London, 20 May 1963.
TV: Ian Bentley in *Coronation Street;* Stn Officer Chris Hammond in *London's Burning;* Sgt Chris McCleod in *Soldier, Soldier.*
Address: c/o Scott Marshall, 44 Perryn Road, London W3 7NA. m. Miranda Foster; 1 s; father-in-law Barry Foster. Hobbies: Sport, supporter of Tottenham Hotspur FC.

LEWIS, Martyn

Martyn Lewis. Newscaster/Presenter.
b. Swansea, Wales, 7 April 1945.
TV: *Nine O'clock News; One O'clock News; Six O'clock News.*
Address: c/o Simpson Fox Associates Ltd, 52 Shaftesbury Avenue, London, Enland W1V 7DE. m. Liz Carse. Hobbies: Jogging, photography, tennis.

LEWIS, Stephen

Stephen Lewis. Actor (M)/Presenter.
TV: Van Helsing in *2point4 Children; Bodger & Badger; Don't Drink the Water;* Smiler in *The Last of the Summer Wine;* Porter in *London's Burning;* Kid Blumenburg in *Look at it This Way;* Harry Lambert in *Oh Dr Beeching!;* Blakey in *On the Buses;* Bluett in *One Foot in the Grave;* Lead in *REP; The All New Alexei Sayle Show; The Generation Game;* Herbert in *The Great Kandinsky;* Coach Driver in *The Grimleys; The Jugg Brothers; The Maguffin;* Reggie in *The Paradise Club; TV's Greatest Hits.*
Films: *Always Ask for the Best;* Blakey in *Holiday On the Buses;* Blakey in *Mutiny On the Buses;* Blakey in *On the Buses; Sparrows Can't Sing; The Krays; The Staircase.*
Address: c/o Frazer-Skemp Management Ltd, 31 Brompton Street, London SW3 5LA.

LEYSHON, Paul

Paul Leyshon. Actor (M)/Presenter.
TV: *Carlton Kids; Gimme 5; Grange Hill; Hanger 17;* Ollie Benson in *Hollyoaks; Select; The Mag.*
Address: c/o SilverFox Artist Management Ltd, Cameo House, 11 Bear Street, London WC2H 7AS. Hobbies: Singing, disc jockey.

LINDSAY, Robert

Robert Lindsay. Actor (M).
b. Ilkeston, Derbyshire, 12 December 1949.

TV: *All's Well that Ends Well; Brazen Hussies;* Lead in *Citizen Smith; Confessional; Cymbeline; Genghis Cohn; Get Some In; Give Us a Break; Goodbye My Love; Hornblower; Hurt Hawks; Jake's Progress; King Lear; Letter from a Soldier; Midsummer Night's Dream; Nightingales; Oliver Twist; Rose of Eyam; Seconds Out; The Office; The Wimbledon Poisoner; Twelfth Night.*
Films: *Divorcing Jack; Fierce Creatures; Loser Takes All; Remember Me.*
Address: c/o Hamilton Asper, 24 Hanway Street, London W1P 9DD.

LINDSAY, Shona
Shona Lindsay. Actor (F).
b. Edinburgh, 4 December 1969.
TV: Sara Briggs in *Crossroads;* Sandra in *Mother's Ruin;* Barbara Boyer in *The Growing Pains of Adrian Mole;* Lisa in *The Ritz;* Barbara Boyer in *The Secret Diary of Adrian Mole.*
Music: *Aspects of Lloyd Webber; Essential Lloyd Webber II; Goodbye; Grease; Jesus Christ Superstar; Love Songs.*
Address: c/o Eric Glass Ltd, 28 Berkeley Square, London W1X 6HD. Hobbies: Roller skating, horse riding, swimming, badminton, dancing, cycling, piano.

LINEKER, Gary
Gary Lineker. Presenter. b. 30 November 1960.
TV: *Atlanta Olympic Games; Football Focus; Gary Lineker's Golden Boots; Match of the Day; They Think It's All Over.*
Address: c/o Marquee Group (UK) Ltd, 21 The Green, Richmond, Surrey TW9 1PX. m. Michelle Lineker; 4 s. George, Harry, Tobias, Angus. Hobbies: Golf, snooker, cricket.

LINSTEAD, Alec
Alec Linstead. Actor (M).
TV: *Anna Karenina; Crime and Punishment; Doctor Who;* Fincham in *Food of Love;* Vicar in *Frank Stubbs Promotes;* Major Mainwaring in *Goodnight Sweetheart; Juliet Bravo; Love and Mr Lewisham; Nicholas Nickelby;* Chemist in *Poirot; Reilly Ace of Spies;* North country registar in *Sex and Chips and Rock 'n' Roll;* Cross in *Silent Witness;* Dr Werner in *SS Portrait of Evil; The Professionals; The Sweeney.*
Address: c/o Kremer Associates, Cameo House, 11 Bear Street, London WC2H 7AS.

LINTERN, Richard
Richard Lintern. Actor (M).
TV: *After the Dance;* Lord Beaumont in *Cadfael;* Daniel O'Shea in *Covington Cross;* Ralph in *Demob;*

Devlin in *Forever Green;* Trevor in *Holding the Baby;* Daniel Page in *House of Eliott;* Ben in *Imogen's Face;* Tom in *Plotlands;* John Lake in *Poirot;* Big John in *She's Out;* Duncan in *Starlings;* Prince in *The Storyteller;* Fairburn in *Taggart;* Callister in *The Beggar Bride;* Dryden in *The Bill;* Steve in *The Fortunate Pilgrim;* Bruce in *The Good Guys; Victoria Wood's Comedy Playhouse.*
Films: Dominic Corde in *Cater Street Hangman;* Jinnah in *Jinnah;* Graham Schofield in *Lost Souls;* Lord Lucan in *Lucan;* Lead in *Misadventure.*
Address: c/o William Morris Agency (UK) Ltd, 1 Stratton Street, London W1X 6HB.

LIPMAN, Maureen
Maureen Lipman. Actor (F)/Presenter.
b. Hull, 10 May 1946.
TV: *About Face; Absent Friends; Absurd Person Singular; Agony;* Jane Lucas in *Agony Again; Best of British; Bobby Bluesox; Call My Bluff; Casanova; Code Name; Cold Enough for Snow; Couples; Crown Court; Dangerous Davies – The Last Detective; Doctor at Large; Don't Ask Us; Eskimo Day; File it under Fear; Have I Got News For You; Holiday; In a Cottage Hospital; It's Called The Sugar Plum; Last Night Another Dissident; Long Day's Journey Into Night; Love's Labour Lost; On Your Way Riley; Outside Edge; Re: Joyce; Rogue Male; Rolling Home; Room 101; Rooms; See How they Run; Shiftwork; Special Correspondent; Sunny Stories; The Clive Anderson Show; The End of the Year Show; The Evacuees; The Knowledge;* Miss Minchin in *The Little Princess; The Lovers; The Soft Touch; The Witching Hour;* Various *Royal Variety Shows.*
Films: *Captain Jack; Carry On Colombus; Educating Rita; Gumshoe; National Lampoon's European Vacation; Smashing Bird I Used To Know; Solomon and Gaenor;* Miss Higgs in *The Wildcats of St Trinians; Up the Junction; Water.*
Address: c/o Conway Van Gelder, 18–21 Jermyn Street, London SW1Y 6HP. m. Jack Rosenthal (playwright); 1 d. Amy; 1 s. Adam.

LITHGOW, John
John Lithgow. Actor (M).
b. Rochester, New York, USA, 9 October 1945.
TV: Dick Solomon in *3rd Rock from the Sun;* John Walters in *Amazing Stories* (1986); *American Cinema* (1994); Neil Scott in *Baby Girl Scott* (1987); *Big Blond* (1980); Himself in *Christmas in Washington* (1996); Don Quixote in *Don Quixote* (2000); Robert Carter in *Ivory Hunters* (1990); Paul Harrington in *Love, Cheat & Steal* (1993); Wally in *Mom, The Wolfman and Me* (1980); *My Brother's Keeper* (1995); Richard

Carruthers in *Not in Front of the Children* (1982); Laird Riordan in *Redwood Curtain* (1995); Major Kendall Laird in *Resting Place* (1986); Dr Oscar Harles in *Tales from the Crypt* (1995); Artie Margulies in *The Boys* (1991); Joe Huxley in *The Day After*; Marty in *The Glitter Dome* (1984); Senator Conyers in *The Tuskegee Airmen* (1995); Ben Cluett in *Travelling Man* (1989); Roosevelt in *World War II: When Lions Roared* (1994).

Films: Walter Curnow in *2010*; Judge Walter J Skinner in *A Civil Action*; Arthur Fanshawe in *A Good Man in Africa*; Lucas Sergeant in *All That Jazz*; Leslie Huben in *At Play in the Fields of the Lord*; Burke in *Blow Out*; Eric Qualen in *Cliffhanger*; John in *Dealing: Or The Berkeley-To-Boston Forty-Brick Lost-Bag Blues*; Mark Lambert in *Distant Thunder*; Reverend Shaw Moore in *Footloose*; George Henderson in *Harry and the Hendersons*; Thomas Livingston in *Hollow Point*; Malcolm/Robert Sockman in *Homegrown*; Mr Brunner in *I'm Dancing as Fast as I Can*; Sgt Larry Skovik in *Johnny Skidmarks*; Col. Bruce Derringer in *Memphis Belle*; Oliver Thompson in *Mesmerized*; Robert Leslie in *Obsession*; Narrator in *Officer Buckle and Gloria*; Dave Geary in *Out Cold*; *Portofino*; Professor Wilkinson in *Princess Caraboo*; Carter/Cain/Doctor Nix/Josh/Margo in *Raising Cain*; Paul Phillips in *Rich Kids*; Earl Talbott Blake in *Ricochet*; BZ in *Santa Claus the Movie*; Shrek in *Shrek*; Dr Harlinger in *Silent Fall*; Narrator in *Special Effects: Anything Can Happen*; Sam Burns in *Terms of Endearment*; Doctor Emilio Lizardo/Lord in *The Adventures of Buckaroo Banzai Across The Eighth Dimension*; Sam Sebastian/Spitzler in *The Big Fix*; Dr Mathewson in *The Manhattan Project*; Smith Keen in *The Pelican Brief*; John Valentine in *Twilight Zone: The Movie*; Roberta Muldoon in *The World According to Garp*.

Music: *Singin' in the Bathtub* with John Lithgow.

Address: c/o Creative Artists Agency, 9830 Wilshire Boulevard, Beverly Hills, California 90212, USA. m. Mary Yeager; 2 s. Ian, Nathan; 1 d. Phoebe. Hobbies: Painting, writing, reading.

LITTEN, Derren

Derren Litten. Actor (M).

TV: PC Hobbs in *A Touch of Frost*; Mick in *EastEnders*; Steve in *Hands Together*; Vaughan Rogers in *Perfect World*; DC Guthriel in *Pie in the Sky*.

Address: c/o Evans & Reiss, 100 Fawe Park Road, London SW15 2EA. Hobbies: Magic, juggling, singing.

LITTLE, Mark

Mark Little. Actor (M)/Presenter/Comedian.

b. Brisbane, Queensland, Australia, October 1959.

TV: *Countdown Revolution*; Joe Mangel in *Neighbours*; *The Big Breakfast*; *The Feel Good Factor*; *The Flying Doctors*; *Waterfront*.

Films: Lead in *An Indecent Obsession*; Lenny in *Greenkeeping*; Lead in *Nirvana Street Murder*; Curly in *Short Changed*; *Starstruck*; *The Clinic*; *Wills and Burke*.

Address: c/o International Artistes Ltd, Mezzanine Floor, 235 Regent Street, London W1R 8AX.

LITTLE, Natasha

Natasha Little. Actor (F). b. 1971.

TV: Saffron in *Big Women*; Melangel in *Cadfael*; Fanny in *Far From The Madding Crowd*; Jenny in *London's Burning*; Amanda in *Love in the 21st Century*; Receptionist in *Supply & Demand*; Rachel in *This Life*; Becky Sharp in *Vanity Fair*.

Films: Edith Thompson in *Another Life*; Primrose in *Green Fingers*; Fanny in *The Clandestine Marriage*; Sarah in *The Criminal*.

Address: c/o Hamilton Asper, 24 Hanway Street, London W1P 9DD. Hobbies: Dancing, flute, singing.

LITTLE, Ralf

Ralf Little. Actor (M).

TV: Norman Lewis in *Bostock's Cup*; Eddie Tinniswood in *Heartbeat*; Scooby in *Sloggers*; Antony Royle in *The Royle Family*; Robbie in *The Ward*.

Address: c/o JM Associates, 77 Beak Street, London W1R 3LF. Hobbies: Football, cricket, rugby, racquet sports, skiing, snowboarding, horse riding.

LITTLEJOHN, Richard

Richard Littlejohn. Presenter.

TV: *Do I Not Like That*; *Fantasy Football League*; *Have I Got News For You*; *Littlejohn*; *Live & Unleashed*; *Parkinson*; *Question Time*; *Richard Littlejohn*; *Richard Littlejohn – Live & Uncut*; *Six O Six Show*; *Sport in Question*; *The Sundays*; *Thursday Night Live*; *Wanted For*; *Weekendin Live*; *What the Papers Say*.

Address: c/o Noel Gay Artists, 19 Denmark Street, London WC2H 8NA.

LITTLER, Matthew

Matthew Littler. Actor (M). b. 19 March 1982.

TV: Max Cunningham in *Hollyoaks*; Thief in *Moll Flanders*; Patrick in *The Ward*.

Address: c/o Laine Management, Matrix House, 301–303 Chapel Street, Manchester M3 5JG.

LIU, Lucy

Lucy Liu. Actor (F).

b. Jackson Heights, New York USA, 1 December 1968.

TV: Ling Woo in *Ally McBeal*; Nicole in *Coach*;

Mei-Sun Leow in *ER*; Oi-Lan in *Hercules*; Woman Number 3 in *Home Improvement*; Melana in *Jonny Quest*; Alice Woo in *Michael Hayes*; Kim Hsin in *Nash Bridges*; Amy Chu in *NYPD Blue*; Amy Li in *Pearl*; Boomer's girlfriend in *Riot*.

Films: *Austin Powers: The Spy Who Shagged Me*; Alex in *Charlie's Angels: The Movie*; Cathi Rose in *City of Industry*; Former Girlfriend in *Jerry Maguire*; Female's Friend in *Mating Habits of the Earthbound Human*; Brenda in *Molly*; Pearl in *Payback*; *Play it to the Bone*; *Shanghai Noon*; Toy Store Girl in *True Crime*.

Address: c/o PMK Public Relations, 955 South Carillo Drive, Los Angeles, California 90048, USA. Hobbies: Martial arts (including Kali-Eskrima-Silat), fluent in Mandarin Chinese, artist, playing the accordion, rock climbing.

LLEWELLYN, Robert

Robert Llewellyn. Actor (M)/Presenter.
b. Northampton, 10 March 1956.

TV: *Birds of a Feather*; *Bottom*; *I-Camcorder*; Kryten in *Red Dwarf*; *Scrapheap*; *Scrapheap Challenge*; *Smith and Jones*.

Films: *Jim's Gift*.

Address: c/o PFD, Drury House, 34–43 Russell Street, London WC2B 5HA. m. Judy Pascoe; 2 d. Louise, Holly. Hobbies: Gardening, reading, running his own web site.

LLEWELYN-BOWEN, Laurence

Laurence Llewelyn-Bowen. Presenter/Designer.
b. London, 11 March 1965.

TV: *All Over the Shop*; *Bad Boys*; *Change That*; *Changing Rooms*; *Fantasy Rooms*; *Live & Kicking*; *Noel's House Party*; *Party of a Lifetime*; *The Hidden Camera Show*; *Through the Keyhole*; *Tip Top Challenge*.

Address: c/o Michael Ladkin Personal Management, Suite One, Ground Floor, 1 Duchess Street, London W1N 3DE. m. Jacqueline; 2 d. Cecile, Hermione. Hobbies: Visiting museums, visiting art galleries, art and art history.

LLOYD, Jessica

Jessica Lloyd. Actor (F).

TV: Ann in *As Time Goes By*; Catherine in *Casualty*; Alice Willoughby in *Head over Heels*; Clare Sallinger in *Jonathan Creek*; Celia in *Poirot*; Carolyn in *Silent Witness*.

Films: Julia in *Jefferson in Paris*.

Address: c/o Dalzell and Beresford Ltd, 91 Regent Street, London W1R 7TB. Hobbies: Singing, dancing.

LLOYD, Sue

Sue Lloyd. Actor (F). b. 7 August 1940.

TV: *Bergerac*; *Departments*; *Give Us a Clue*; *Hadleigh*; *His and Hers*; *Justice*; *Keeping up Appearances*; *Miss Marple, A Caribbean Mystery*; *Murder on a Midsummer's Eve*; *Randall and Hopkirk (Deceased)*; *Red Nose of Courage*; *Supergran*; *The Baron*; *The Case of Magruder's Millions*; *The Saint*; *The Sweeney*; *The Trouble With Michael Caine*; *The Two Ronnies*; *The Upchat Line*; *Wogan*.

Films: *Bullet to Bejing*; *Corruption*; *Crossbow – The Adventures of William Tell*; *Eat the Rich*; *Innocent Bystander*; *Lady Oscar*; *Percy*; *Spanish Fly*; *The Bitch*; Lead in *The Ipcress File*; *The Revenge of the Pink Panther*; *The Stud*; *UFO*; *Where's Jack*.

Address: c/o Burnett Granger Associates, Prince of Wales Theatre, 31 Coventry Street, London W1V 8AS.

LLOYD PACK, Roger

Roger Lloyd Pack. Actor (M).
b. London, 8 February 1944.

TV: *2point4children*; Jacko in *Alas Smith and Jones*; Hostel Clerk in *Anna Lee*; Quentin in *Archer's Goon*; Ian in *Births, Marriages and Deaths*; Tour Guide in *Blood and Peaches*; Ray Watts in *Boon*; Roy Skarper in *Bouncing Back*; Sydney Bagley in *Brassneck*; Beckett in *Byker Grove*; Captain in *Citizen Locke*; Derek in *Clothes in the Wardrobe*; Phillips in *Dandelion Dead*; Waledemar Chmielewski in *Deliberate Death of a Polish Priest*; Clutch in *Dirty Deeds*; *Dixon of Dock Green*; Dr. Reg Regis in *Health and Efficiency*; Reggie Rawlins in *Heartbeat*; Ronald Selser in *In a Secret State*; Donald Martin in *Inspector Morse*; Alex Watkins in *Kavanagh QC*; Sir Baldwin De'Ath in *Knight School*; Captain Man in *Longitude*; Smallman Smith in *Lovejoy*; Den in *Made in Spain*; Jimmy in *Moving*; Spanish Waiter in *Mr Bean*; Frank Foster in *Murder Most Horrid*; Mr Sowerberry in *Oliver Twist*; Victor in *One For The Road*; Trigger in *Only Fools and Horses*; Fred in *Party Time*; Constable in *Paul Merton in Galton & Simpson's … 'Impasse'*; Bridget's Dad in *Perfect Match*; Melvyn in *Private Schultz*; David Irving in *Selling Hitler*; Earl of Gloucester in *Shakespeare*; Villian in *Softly, Softly*; Eddie Vernon in *Stay Lucky*; Revolutionary in *Survivors*; Manders in *The Brief*; Rudyard in *The Chief*; Glendinning in *The Contractor*; Chambers in *The Crime of Captain Colthurst*; Plitplov in *The Gravy Train*; Victor in *The Macguffin*; Ken Thompson in *The Missing Postman*; Liz in *The Naked Civil Servant*; Frankie in *The Object of Beauty*; Ramos in *The Professionals*; 1st Stairman in *The Trial*; Marvin in *The Vanishing Man*; Anderson in *Tom Jones*; Gordon in *Trust Me*; Owen Nesbitt in *Vicar of Dibley*; Bus Fanatic in

Video Stars; Oliver Cromwell in *What is the Truth – The Putney Debates.*

Films: Waiter in *1984;* Dr Butler in *American Friends;* Doctor in *Bloody Kids;* Nunez in *Cuba;* Rabbi in *Fiddler on the Roof;* Rosencrantz in *Hamlet;* Piano Teacher in *Interview with a Vampire;* Pavlov in *Meetings with Remarkable Men;* Cutts Watson in *Preaching to the Perverted;* Actor 2 in *Prick Up Your Ears;* Judge Haythorn in *Princess Caraboo;* Arnold Crombeck in *The Arnold Crombeck Story;* The Prospero Professor in *The Avengers;* Geoff in *The Cook, The Thief, His Wife and Her Lover;* Charles in *The Go-Between;* Meredith in *The Hollow Reed;* Young Anthony Quinn in *The Magus;* Flat Cleaner in *The Secret Ceremony;* Soldier in *The Virgin Soldiers;* Dr Pitman in *Wilt;* Fred in *The Young Poisoner's Handbook.*

Address: c/o Kate Feast Management, 10 Primrose Hill Studios, Fitzroy Road, London NW1 8TR.

LOCKLEAR, Heather

Heather Locklear. Actor (F).
b. Los Angeles, California, USA, 25 September 1961.
TV: Betsy in *Body Language;* Teenager in *Chips;* Samantha Josephine Reece Carrington Fallmont in *Dynasty;* Samantha Josephine Reece Carrington Fallmont in *Dynasty: The Reunion;* Ingrid in *Eight is Enough;* Victoria in *Fade to Black;* June Edwards in *The Fall Guy;* Alex Burton in *Going Places;* Alex in *Highway Heartbreaker;* Jan Sanderson in *Illusions;* Rita Burwald in *Jury Duty: The Comedy;* Melody Shepherd in *Lethal Charm;* *The Love Boat;* Amanda Woodward Parezi Blake McBride Burns in *Melrose Place;* Tori in *Rich Men, Single Women;* Darcy X in *Rock 'n' Roll Mom;* Suzy in *Shattered Mind;* Caitlin Moore in *Spin City;* Priscilla in *Texas Justice;* Officer Stacy Sheridan in *TJ Hooker;* Cherie Sanders in *Twirl.*
Films: Rita in *The Big Slice;* Katherine in *Double Tap;* Gil Griffin's First Wife in *The First Wives Club;* Grace Cipriani in *Money Talks;* Abby Arcane in *The Return of The Swamp Thing;* Herself in *Wayne's World II.*
Address: c/o Joan Green Management, 1836 Courtney Terrace, Los Angeles, California, USA 90046. Father Bill Locklear, mother Diane Locklear; m. Richie Sambora; 1 d. Ava Elizabeth Sambora.

LOGAN, Phyllis

Phyllis Logan. Actor (F). b. 11 January 1956.
TV: *The White Bird Passes; Scotch & Wry; Off Peak; Time and the Conways;* Lady Jane in *Lovejoy; Out of Time; Extras; Bust; Defrosting the Fridge; And a Nightingale Sang; Sitting Target; Effie's Burning; Goldeneye; Happy Feet; The Cow Jumped Over the Moon; Silent Cries/Guests of the Emperor;* Lou Larson in *Love*

and Reason; Chiller – Here Comes the Mirror Man; Samantha Fisher in *Kavanagh Q.C. – A Family Affair; The Big One;* Julia Stevens in *Inspector Morse – Daughters of Cain;* Anna in *Scene – Skinny Marink;* Miss Leaming in *An Unsuitable Job for a Woman;* Squadron Leader Helen Knox in *Invasion Earth;* Betty in *The Game; Midsomer Murders;* McKendrick in *Holby City; Rab C Nesbitt;* Mary Beck in *All the King's Men;* Harriet Banks Smith in *Randall and Hopkirk (Deceased);* Julia Kendall in *Heartbeat.*
Films: *Another Time, Another Place; Every Picture Tells a Story; The Chain; The Dress; 1984; The Doctor and the Devils; The MacGuffin; The Inquiry; The Kitchen Toto; The White Whale, Il Sole Buio; Soft Top Hard Shoulder;* Frank Kafka's *It's A Wonderful Life;* Monica in *Secrets and Lies;* Mrs Ross in *Shooting Fish.*
Address: c/o CDA, 19 Sydney Mews, London SW3 6HL.

LOGGIN, Sam

Sam Loggin. Actor (F) b. Northamptonshire, 1977.
TV: Jo Jo in *Dangerfield;* Zoe Baker in *Dream Team;* Cat in *Every Woman Knows A Secret;* Lucy Sullivan in *Lucy Sullivan is Getting Married;* Patricia Flint in *The Missing Postman;* Stacey in *Peak Practice;* Jude in *Pie in the Sky;* Madeline Gillingham in *Trial & Retribution.*
Films: *Underground.*
Address: c/o CAM London, 19 Denmark Street, London WC2H 8NA. Hobbies: Horse riding, swimming, athletics.

LOMBARD, Louise

Louise Lombard. Actor (F).
TV: *Bergerac; The Black Velvet Gown; Bodyguards; Capital City; Casualty; Chancer;* Eva Eliot in *French and Saunders;* Eva Eliot in *The House of Eliot.*
Films: *After the Rain; Talos the Mummy.*
Address: c/o PFD, Drury House, 34–43 Russell Street, London WC2B 5HA.

LONERGAN, Kate

Kate Lonergan. Actor (F). b. 1966.
TV: Mrs Took in *Always and Everyone;* Sal Gilks in *The Bill;* Jean in *Casualty;* Dawn in *Four Fathers;* Gwen in *Heartbeat;* Pam in *The Hello Girls;* Dawn in *Hetty Wainthropp Investigates;* Mrs Beath in *Is It Legal?;* Marion in *Maid Marion and Her Merry Men;* Sam in *My Blue Heaven; Parallel 9;* Rene in *Terry and Julian;* Nurse Clark in *Testimony of a Child.*
Films: BP in *Daylight Robbery; The Tall Guy.*
Address: c/o Sally Hope Associates, 108 Leonard Street, London EC2A 4XS.

LONG, Shelley

Shelley Long. Actor (F).
b. Fort Wayne, Indiana, USA, 23 August 1949.
TV: *A Different Kind Of Christmas*; Kate in *A Message from Holly*; Diane Chambers in *Cheers*; Cara in *The Cracker Factory*; Day Ludlow in *Diagnosis Murder*; Eileen Franklin Lipsker in *Fatal Memories*; Diane Chambers in *Frasier*; Ellen Andrews in *Freaky Friday*; Susan De Ruzza in *Good Advice*; Kelly Novak/Kelly in *Kelly Kelly*; Heather in *The Love Boat*; Nurse Mendenhall in *M*A*S*H*; *Memories Of M*A*S*H*; Dottie Wilcox in *Murphy Brown*; Carol in *The Princess and the Cabbie*; Lorraine in *The Promise of Love*; Wicked Witch in *Sabrina: The Teenage Witch*; Penny Sands in *Susie Q*; Anne in *The Women of Spring Break*; Elizabeth in *Vanished Without a Trace*; Truddi Chase in *Voices Within: The Lives of Truddi Chase*.
Films: Sam in *The Advenures of Ragtime*; Carol Brady in *The Brady Bunch Movie*; Tala in *Caveman*; Lizzie Potts in *Don't Tell Her It's Me*; *Dr T and The Women*; Dr Grace Murdock in *Frozen Assets*; Lucy Chadman in *Hello Again*; Lucy Van Pattern Brodsky in *Irreconcilable Differences*; Kathy in *Losin' It*; Anna Crowley in *The Money Pit*; Belinda Keaton in *Night Shift*; Lauren in *Outrageous Fortune*; Alice in *A Small Circle of Friends*; Phyllis Nefler in *Troop Beverly Hills*; Carol Brady in *A Very Brady Sequel*.
Address: c/o Mary Mickelson, 118 South Beverly Drive, Suite 217, Beverly Hills, California 90212, USA. m. Bruce Tyson; 1 d. Juliana.

LONNEN, Ray

Ray Lonnen. Actor (M).
b. Bournemouth, Dorset, 18 May 1940.
TV: John Wood in *20 Steps*; *The Brief*; *Cluedo*; Gareth Oldroyd in *Crime Traveller*; *Crown Court*; *Emergency – Ward 10*; *General Hospital*; *The Gentle Touch*; *Glamour Girls*; *Hammer House of Horror*; Editor in *Harry*; *Harry's Game*; Carsons in *Heartbeat*; *Honey Lane*; James Bowler in *Johnny and the Dead*; *Jubilee*; *Lovejoy*; *Melissa*; *Murder Elite*; Rinstead in *The New Professionals*; *Pathfinders*; *The Power Game*; *Rich Tea and Sympathy*; *Rooms*; *The Sandbaggers*; *Singles*; *Tales of the Unexpected*; *The Troubleshooters*; *Yellowthread Street*; *Z-Cars*.
Films: *Lady Caroline Lamb*; *Maneaters*; *Murder Elite*; *Zeppelin*.
Address: c/o Langford Associates, 17 Westfields Avenue, London SW13 0AT. m. 1 Lynn Dalby; 1 d. Amy; 2 s. Thomas, Rhys; m. 2 Tara Ward. Hobbies: Travel, tennis, cinema, listening to music.

LONSDALE, David

David Lonsdale. Actor (M).
TV: DC Halt in *The Bill*; *Bust*; *The Chief*; Peter Barlow in *Coronation Street*; Evangelist in *CYW Haul*; Fund Manager in *Disaster – Millennium Bug*; *Forever Young*; David in *Heartbeat*; *Inspector Morse*; Police Constable in *Moving Story*; *Rockliffe's Babies*.
Films: *Bert Rigby, You're a Fool*; Hibbert in *Resurrected*; Repossession Man in *The Full Monty*.
Address: c/o Andrew Manson Personal Management, 288 Munster Road, London SW6 6BQ.

LORD, Stephen

Stephen Lord. Actor (M).
b. Salford, Manchester, 1 October 1972.
TV: Steve Jackson in *City Central*; Jonno in *Common As Muck*; Fred Davies in *In Suspicious Circumstances*; Danny in *Into the Fire*; Darwin in *Luv*; Mike in *The Hello Girls*; Luke Baylis in *Wilderness Edge*.
Films: Alf in *Bullion Boys*; Flea in *Fast Food*; Lionel Giddings in *Giving Tongue*; Zed in *Judge Dredd*; Tom Price in *Lie of the Land*; Keith in *The Prince of Denmark Hill*; *Raining Stones*; Simmons in *Shooting Stars*.
Address: c/o Ken McReddie Ltd, 91 Regent Street, London W1R 7TB. Hobbies: Football, running, boxing, yoga, reading.

LOTT, Barbara

Barbara Lott. Actor (F). b. Richmond, 15 May 1920.
TV: Auntie Pearl in *2point4 Children*; *The All Electric Amusement Arcade*; *Angels*; *Ballet Shoes*; *The Croydon Poisonings*; Mrs Carmichael in *Daisies in December*; *The Duchess of Duke Street*; *Enemy at the Door*; *Honeymoon*; *In Suspicious Circumstances*; *Kids*; *The Kit Curran Radio Show*; *Law and Disorder*; *Maybury*; *Nana*; *Nightingales' Boys*; *Noel's House Party*; *Rings on Their Fingers*; *The Sandbaggers*; *Sexton Blake*; *Six Days of Justice*; Mum in *Sorry*; *Spawn*; *The Survivors*; *The Trial of Lady Chatterly*; *Thomas and Sarah*; Mrs Cravat in *Tickle on the Tum*; *War & Peace*; Great-aunt Ruby in *Woof*.
Films: *Electric Moon*; *The Party's Over*; *The Pillow Book*; *Unman, Wittering and Zigo*.
Address: c/o Marmont Management Ltd, Langham House, 308 Regent Street, London W1R 5AL.

LOUIS-DREYFUS, Julia

Julia Louis-Dreyfus. Actor (F)/Comedian.
b. New York, USA, 13 January 1961.
TV: Mollie in *Animal Farm* (1999); *The Art of Being Nick* (1987); Eileen Swift in *Day by Day* (1988); Heather in *Dinosaurs* (1991); Herself in *Dr. Katz, Professional Therapist*; Susan White in *Family Ties*; Debra Dolby in *London Suite* (1996); Herself in *Saturday*

Night Live; Elaine Marie Benes in *Seinfeld*; *Spy Magazine's Hit List: The 100 Most Annoying and Alarming People* (1992).
Films: Princess Atta in *A Bug's Life*; Leslie in *Deconstructing Harry*; Carrie Lawrence in *Father's Day*; Blue Fairy in *Geppetto*; Mary Ann in *Gilligan's Island*; Mary in *Hannah and Her Sisters*; Peggy Etinger in *Jack The Bear*; Margo Chester in *National Lampoon's Christmas Vacation*; North's Mom in *North*; Lisa Simpson in *Soul Man*; Jeanette Cooper in *Troll*.
Address: c/o William Morris Agency, 151 El Camino Drive, Beverly Hills, California 90212, USA. m. Brad Hall; 2 s. Henry, Charles. Hobbies: Cookery, collecting antiques.

LOVE HEWITT, Jennifer
Jennifer Love Hewitt. Actor (F).
b. Waco, Texas, USA, 21 February 1979.
TV: Audrey Hepburn in *Audrey Hepburn*; *Kids Incorporated*; Sarah Reeves in *Party of Five*; *Shaky Ground*; *The Byrds of Paradise*; *Time of your Life*.
Films: *Can't Hardly Wait*; *I Know What You Did Last Summer*; *I Still Know What You Did Last Summer*; *Sister Act 2: Back in the Habit*; *Telling You*; *The Suburbans*.
Music: *Jennifer Love Hewitt*; *Let's Go Bang*; *Love Songs*.
Address: c/o William Morris Agency, 151 El Camino Drive, Beverly Hills, California 90212, USA. Hobbies: Writing, singing, songwriting, dancing, collecting teddy bears, porcelain angels.

LOWRY, Shauna
Shauna Lowry. Presenter. b. Belfast, 6 July 1970.
TV: *Animal Hospital*; *Battersea Dogs Home*; *Bon Voyage*; *Cat's Eyes*; *Children in Need*; *Country Tracks*; *Dreamworld*; *Jo-Maxi*; *Live & Kicking*; *National Lottery Live*; *Style Challenge*; *Summer Holiday*; *VIP*.
Address: c/o Jeremy Hicks Associates, 12 Ogle Street, London W1P 7LG. Hobbies: Wildlife, horse riding, scuba diving, travelling, photography.

LUCAS, Matt
Matt Lucas. Comedian/Actor (M). b. 1975.
TV: *Barking*; *Bernard Chumley's Stately Homes*; *The Comedy Club*; *Crazy Jonathan's*; *It's Ulrika*; *Jilting Joe*; *Le Show*; *London Comedy Festival TV Special*; *Rock Profiles*; George Dawes in *Shooting Stars*; *Spoof O Vision*; *Sunny Side Farm*; *The Smell of Reeves and Mortimer*; *You Are Here*.
Films: *Plunkett and MacLeane*.
Address: c/o ICM, Oxford House, 76 Oxford Street, London W1N 0AX.

LUCAS, William
William Lucas. Actor (M).
b. Manchester, 14 April 1925.
TV: Dr Gordon in *Black Beauty*; *Coronation Street*; Stanley Webb in *Eldorado*; Dr Gordon in *The Further Adventures of Black Beauty*; *Heaven on Earth*; *On the Up*; Lead in *Rigoletto*; *Spoils of War*.
Films: David Medwin in *Bitter Harvest*; Steve in *Calculated Risk*; *Crack in the Mirror*; *Lost*; *Man At The Top*; *Payroll*; Reg Dorking in *Portrait of Alison*; *The Professionals*; *Sons and Lovers*.
Address: c/o Roger Carey Associates, 7 St George's Square, London SW1V 2HX.

LUCKER, Zoe
Zoe Lucker. Actor (F)
TV: *Barbara*; Kirsty Bellamy in *Boyz Unlimited*; Sonia Leech in *Coronation Street*; Carol in *Killer Net*; *Screen Two: Brazen Hussies*; Deirdre in *Wavelength*; Jane in *Where the Heart Is*.
Address: c/o Susan Angel Associates, 1st Floor, 12 D'Arblay Street, London W1V 3FP. Hobbies: Horse riding, cello, singing.

LUMLEY, Joanna
Joanna Lumley. Actor (F)/Presenter. b. 1 May 1946.
TV: *Absolutely Fabulous*; *An Ideal Husband*; *Blithe Spirit*; *Camilla*; *Class Act*; *Cold Comfort Farm*; *Coming Home*; *Coronation Street*; *The Cuckoo Waltz*; *Don't Just Lie There, Say Something*; *The End of My Old Cigar*; *General Hospital*; *Girl Friday*; *The Glory Boys*; *Hedda Gabler*; *In Praise of Rattigan*; *It's Awfully Bad For Your Eyes Darling*; *The Kingdom of The Thunder Dragon*; *The Letter*; *Lovejoy*; *The Mark 2 Wife*; *Mistral's Daughter*; *Move Over Darling*; *Nancherrow*; *The New Avengers*; *The Night After Christmas*; *The Forgotten Toys*; *Noel and Gertie*; *A Perfect Hero*; *The Persuaders*; *Private Lives*; *The Revenger's Comedy*; *Roseanne*; *Sapphire and Steel*; *Starting Out*; *Steptoe and Son*; *That Was Tori*; *The Weather in the Streets*; *The White Rajahs of Sarawak*; *Theatre*; *Up the Workers*; *Who Will I Be Tomorrow*.
Films: *A Rather English Marriage*; *Don't Just Lie There, Say Something*; *Funny Bones*; *Games That Lovers Play*; *Innocent Lies*; *James and the Giant Peach*; *Mad Cows*; *On Her Majesty's Secret Service*; *Parting Shots*; *Prince Valiant*; *Shirley Valentine*; *Some Girls Do*; *Sweeney Todd*; *Tam Lin*; *The Breaking of Bumbo*; *Curse of the Pink Panther*; *The Satanic Rites of Dracula*; *Trail of the Pink Panther*.
Address: c/o ICM, Oxford House, 76 Oxford Street, London W1N 0AX. m. Stephen Barlow.

LUMSDEN, Michael

Michael Lumsden. Actor (M).

TV: Mr Tree in *Bernard's Watch*; Ian in *The Bill*; John Howard in *Brookside*; Derek in *The Buddha of Sub-urbia*; Heslop in *Crocodile Shoes*; Jack Martin in *Firm Friends*; Aubrey in *Floodtide*; Den in *Ghostbusters*; Doctor in *Grown Ups*; Simon in *Health and Efficiency*; Henry in *Letters To Alice*; Con Connors in *London Bridge*; Brian in *My Good Friend*; Tony in *No Pity*; John Bainbridge in *Pig Heart Boy*; Steve in *The Piglet Files*; Young Wood in *Sherlock Holmes*; Jamie in *Victoria Wood's Playhouse*; Nicholas in Watching; *Goodall* in Wish Me Luck.

Address: c/o The Narrow Road Company, 21–22 Poland Street, London W1V 3DD.

LUMSDEN, Norman

Norman Lumsden. Actor (M).

TV: Bob in *Body Story: 'Shut Down'*; *Bruce Forsyth's Generation Game*; *C.A.T.S. Eyes*; *Good Guys*; *Hazell*; *Hercule Poirot's Casebook*; *Jeeves & Wooster*; *Nye*; *One Foot in the Grave*; *Panorama*; *Summer Scene*; *The Brian Conley Series*; *The Two of Us*; *The Word*.

Films: *Act of Will*; *A Handful of Dust*; *Hazard of Hearts*; *Heaven's Gate*; *Minder*; *Paradise Postponed*; *Runners*; *The Big Sleep*; *The Hunchback of Notre Dame*; *The Sweeney*; *White Hunter, Black Heart*.

Address: c/o Chuck Julian Associates, Suite 51, 26 Charing Cross Road, London WC2H ODH.

LUMSDEN, Richard

Richard Lumsden. Actor (M). b. 1956.

TV: *The Brittas Empire*; *Casualty*; Ronald Langland in *Chalk*; Alun in *Coogan's Run*; Darren in *Dangerfield*; Foggy in *First of the Summer Wine*; Hether in *Horn-blower*; Colin in *Is It Legal?*; Tony in *Nelson's Column*; *One Foot in the Grave*; Nutter in *Sharp End*; Pitcher in *Waterfront Beat*; Henry in *Wonderful You*.

Films: Robert Ferrrars in *Sense and Sensibility*; *The Avengers*.

Address: c/o Annette Stone Associates, 2nd Floor, 22 Great Marlborough Street, London W1V 1AF.

LUNGHI, Cherie

Cherie Lunghi. Actor (F). b. London, 4 April 1953.

TV: *Covington Cross*; *David Copperfield*; *Harem*; *Horn-blower*; *Intrigue*; *Litttle White Lies*; *Master of the Game*; *Moloney*; *Much Ado About Nothing*; *Oliver Twist*; *Pray-ing Mantis*; *Strangers and Brothers*; *The Canterville*

Ghost; *The Lady's Not for Burning*; *The Manageress*; *The Mission*; *The Monocled Mutineer*; *The Strauss Dynasty*.

Films: *A Question of Guilt*; *Excalibur*; *Jack And Sarah*; *King David*.

Address: c/o PFD, Drury House, 34–43 Russell Street, London WC2B 5HA.

LYE, Jackie

Jackie Lye. Actor (F). b. Newcastle, 25 July 1969.

TV: Wanda in *Casualty*; Bessie Grant in *Colour Blind*; *Fresh Fields*; Harry's Mum in *Harry's Mad*; Doreen Tidy in *Heartbeat*; *Hell's Bells*; Receptionist in *McCal-lum*; *Mog*; *Sink or Swim*; *The Bill*; Dot in *Tides of Laughter*; *Tripper's Day*; Becky Fleming in *Whizziwig*.

Address: c/o Associated International Management, 5 Denmark Street, London WC2H 8LP.

LYNDHURST, Nicholas

Nicholas Lyndhurst. Actor (M).

b. Emsworth, Hampshire, 20 April 1961.

TV: Davy in *Anne of Avonlea*; *The Burt Bacharach Show*; Adam in *Butterflies*; Uriah Heap in *David Cop-perfield*; *The Dick Emery Show*; Tim in *Fairies*; Phillip in *Father's Day*; Raymond in *Going Straight*; Gary Sparrow in *Goodnight Sweetheart*; *Gulliver's Travels*; Peter in *Heidi*; *The Kenny Everett Christmas Show*; *The Lenny Henry Show*; Phillip in *Losing Her*; Rodney in *Only Fools and Horses*; *Our Show*; Tootles in *Peter Pan*; *The Piglet Files*; Tom Canty/Prince Edward in *The Prince and the Pauper*; Pete Wilson in *Spearhead*; *Sta-lagluft*; *To Serve Them All My Days*; *The Two of Us*; *Wilderness Challenge*.

Films: *Bequest to the Nation*; *Bullshot*; *Endless Nights*; Chalky in *Gunbus*.

Address: c/o Chatto & Linnit Ltd, 123a Kings Road, London SW3 4PL.

LYONS, John

John Lyons. Actor (M).

b. London, 14 September 1943.

TV: *Thirty-minute Theatre*; George Toolan in *A Touch of Frost*; *Catch-Hand*; *Harry Worth Shows*; *On the Buses*; *Play for Today*; *Spooner's Patch*; *The Sweeney*; *The 19th Hole*; *The Doctor series*; *United*.

Films: *Bullseye*; *Dr Jekyll and Sister Hyde*; *Sweeney*; *Yellow Dog*.

Address: c/o June Epstein Associates, Flat 1, 62 Com-pagne Gardens, London NW6 3RY. m. Ann Lyons; 1 d. Laura Ann. Hobbies: Tennis, golf.

M

MACAULAY, Fred

Fred MacAulay. Panellist/Presenter.
b. 29 December 1956.
TV: *Bring Me the Head of Light Entertainment; Gag Tag; Have I Got News For You; Hoots; Loose Talk; McCoist & MacAulay; The Best Show in the World … Probably; The Jools Holland Show; They Think It's All Over.*
Address: c/o BBC Scotland, Broadcasting House, Queen Margaret Drive, Glasgow, Scotland G12 8DG.

MacDONALD, Kenneth

Kenneth MacDonald. Actor (M).
b. Manchester, 20 November 1950.
TV: *And the Beat Goes On; Boon; Capital Lives; Crocodile Shoes; David Copperfield; Heartbeat; Heartburn Hotel; Gunner 'Nobby' Clark in It Ain't Half Hot Mum; Last of the Summer Wine; Moll Flanders; No Bananas; Mike in Only Fools and Horses; Press Gang; Surgical Spirit; The Bill; Touching Evil; Upstairs Downstairs.*
Films: *Breaking Glass; David Copperfield; Hitch in Time; Mixed Doubles; My Night with Reg; Singelton's Pluck; The Class of Miss McMichael.*
Address: c/o Shepherd & Ford, 13 Radnor Walk, London SW3 4BP. m. Sheila; 1 s. William; 1 d. Charlotte.

MacFADYEN, Angus

Angus MacFadyen. Actor (M).
TV: *Care;* Richard Burton in *Destiny – The Elizabeth Taylor Story; God of Happiness; Soldier, Soldier; Takin' Over the Asylum; The Lost Language of Cranes; Two Golden Balls.*
Films: *A Woman's a Helluva Thing;* Robert the Bruce in *Braveheart;* Count Rudolph von Stegenbek in *Brylcreem Boys;* Turner in *Lanai-Loa;* West in *Nevada;* Hitler in *Snide and Prejudice;* Philip in *Still Breathing;* Orson Welles in *The Cradle Will Rock;* Lucius in *Titus Andronicus;* Komodo in *Warrior of Virtue.*
Address: c/o ICM, Oxford House, 76 Oxford Street, London W1N 0AX.

MACKENZIE, Alistair

Alistair MacKenzie. Actor (M).
TV: *Barking; Chef!; Game On; Hamish Macbeth; Lovejoy; Phil Kay Feels; Psychos; Snap; Soldier, Soldier.*

Films: *Boca; California Sunshine; Down in the City; Dragonworld; Horsehair; Misadventures of Margaret; The Moment; Traces.*
Address: c/o Lou Coulson, 37 Berwick Street, London W1V 3RF.

MacKICHAN, Doon

Doon MacKichan. Actor (F)/Guest/Panelist/Voice artist.
TV: Debra in *Agony Again; Brass Eye; Glam Metal Detectives; If I Ruled the World; Knowing Me, Knowing You … With Alan Partridge;* Sophronia Lammle in *Our Mutual Friend; Smack the Pony;* Maria/Allison in *Stressed Eric* (1997); *The Comic Strip Presents …; The Day Today; The Harry Enfield Television Show;* Kirsten in *Beast.*
Films: Various in *Bob and Margaret;* Victoria Lender in *The Borrowers;* Deirdre in *With or Without You.*
Address: c/o Hamilton Asper, 24 Hanway Street, London W1P 9DD. Hobbies: Swimming (swam the Engligh Channel in 1998).

MACKINTOSH, Andrew

Andrew MacKintosh. Actor (M). b. 9 August 1960.
TV: DS Alistair Greig in *The Bill.*
Address: c/o Scott Marshall, 44 Perryn Road, London W3 7NA.

MACKINTOSH, Steven

Steven MacKintosh. Actor (M).
b. Cambridge, 30 April 1967.
TV: *A Dark Adapted Eye; A Touch of Frost; Bad Blood; Between the Lines; Broken Homes; Cadfael; Doctor Who; Ebb Tide; Inspector Morse; Karaoke; Kissing the Gunner's Daughter; Lady Audley's Secret; Maigret; Midnight Movie; Murder in Mind; Murphy's Mob; Nanny; Newshounds; Our Mutual Friend; Poirot; Prime Suspect; Safe; Six Characters in Search of an Author; The Bill; The Browning Version; The Buddah of Suburbia; The Chief; The Luck Child; The Secret Diary of Adrian Mole; Tickets for the Titanic; Undercover Heart; Van Der Valk; Watching; Woman in Black.*
Films: *Blue Juice; Different for Girls; Gare au Male; House of America; It's Good to Talk; Land Girls; Lock, Stock and Two Smoking Barrels; London Kills Me; Memphis Belle; The Muppet Christmas Carol; Prick Up Your Ears; Princess Caraboo; Return of the Native; The Crim-*

inal; *The Grotesque; Treasure Island; Twelfth Night.*
Address: c/o Conway Van Gelder, 18–21 Jermyn Street, London SW1Y 6HP. m. Lisa Jacobs; 2 d. Martha, Blythe.

MacLEOD, Tracy

Tracy MacLeod. Presenter (F).
TV: *A Stab in the Dark; Comic Relief; Do the Right Thing; Edinburgh Nights; Gag Tag; Juke Box Jury; Network 7; Rapido; Sean's Show; The Booker Prize; The Late Show; The Mercury Music Prize; Various* (1985).
Address: c/o PBJ Management, 5 Soho Square, London W1V 5DE.

MacNICHOL, Peter

Peter MacNichol. Actor (M).
b. Dallas, Texas, USA, 10 April 1954.
TV: Roy Dowd in *Abducted: A Father's Love;* John 'The Biscuit' Cage in *Ally McBeal;* Sedgewick in *By Dawn's Early Light;* Mario in *Cheers;* Alan Birch in *Chicago Hope;* Lewis Rickett in *Roswell;* Lawrence Dixon in *Silencing Mary;* Bradley Grist in *The Powers That Be.*
Films: Gary Granger in *Addams Family Values;* Dan Bobbins in *Baby Geniuses;* David Langley in *Bean – The Ultimate Disaster Movie;* Renfield in *Dracula: Dead and Loving it;* Galen in *Dragonslayer;* Janosz Poha in *Ghostbusters II;* Stuart in *Hard Promises;* Cyrus Kinnick in *Heat;* Marty in *Housesitter;* Tyre repairman in *Mojave Moon; Radioland Murders;* Stingo in *Sophie's World.*
Address: c/o Mark Epstein, 940 North Mansfield, Hollywood, California 90038, USA. m. Marsue Cumming. Hobbies: Sir Arthur Conan Doyle/Sherlock Holmes, collecting toy soldiers and movie posters, fishing, model trains, playing the keyboard and the bagpipes.

MacPHERSON, Calum

Calum MacPherson. Actor (M).
TV: PC Roger Tennant (Flub) in *Back Up;* Billy Pumpherston in *Deacon Brodie;* George in *Disaster – Channel Tunnel;* Sgt Patterson in *Inspector Alleyn;* Buster in *Jonathan Creek;* Mr Bignall in *Oliver Twist;* Albert Dobbs in *Return of the Psammead;* Big Dougie in *Roughnecks;* The Village Idiot in *Tenth Kingdom;* Dave in *The Upper Hand;* Brendan Oliver in *Wycliffe.*
Films: James in *Dragonworld.*
Address: c/o CCA Management, 7 St George's Square, London SW1V 2HX.

MacPHERSON, Daniel

Daniel MacPherson. Actor (M).
TV: *Neighbours.*
Address: c/o Grundy Television, Grundy House, Barge House Crescent, 34 Upper Ground, London SE1 9PD.

MacPHERSON, James

James MacPherson. Actor (M). b. 1960.
TV: *Not Fixed;* Michael Jardine in *Taggart.*
Address: c/o Marina Martin Associates, 12–13 Poland Street, London W1V 3DE.

MADELEY, Richard

Richard Madeley. Presenter/Reporter.
b. Romford, Essex, 13 May 1956.
TV: *Calendar; Connections; Eye of the Storm; Get a Life; Granada Reports; Runway; This Morning; Tonight with Richard Madeley and Judy Finnigan.*
Address: c/o Arlington Enterprise Ltd, 1–3 Charlotte Street, London W1P 1HD. m. Judy Finnigan.

MADOC, Phillip

Phillip Madoc. Actor (M). b. 5 July 1934.
TV: *A Mind to Kill;* Sir George Fison in *A Very British Coup;* Dr Lewis in *Another Bouquet;* Jimmy Murphy in *Best; Brookside; Dad's Army;* Lancing in *First Born; Fortunes of War;* Lloyd George in *Lloyd George; Macbeth; Orrible; Porridge;* Magua in *The Last of the Mohicans; Voice of a Nation Concert.*
Films: *Monte Carlo; Operation Crossbow; Operation Daybreak; The Quiller Memorandum; The Spy Who Came in from the Cold;* Trotsky in *Zina.*
Address: c/o Emptage Hallett, 24 Poland Street, Soho, London W1V 3DD.

MADOC, Ruth

Ruth Madoc. Actor (F)/Presenter.
b. Norwich, Norfolk, 16 April 1943.
TV: Lynn in *An Actor's Life for Me;* Dorothy Hope in *Animal Ark;* Katinka in *Arrivederci Rhondda; Blankety Blank;* Miss Terry-Psychic in *Cluedo;* Mrs Jones in *Famous Five; Give Us a Clue;* Gladys Pugh in *Hi De Hi; Hunter's Walk; Lloyd George; Morecambe & Wise;* Mrs Evans in *Oliver's Travels; Over to Our Friends in Wales; Songs of Praise; The Black & White Minstrel Show;* Jean Pryce in *The Gatekeeper; The Good Food Guide;* Sybill Stamfordis in *The Pale Horse.*
Films: *Fiddler on the Roof;* Mrs Ifans in *Pavarotti in Dad's Room; The Prince and The Pauper; Under Milk Wood.*
Address: c/o Saraband Associates, 265 Liverpool Road, London N1 1LX.

MAFHAM, Dominic

Dominic Mafham. Actor (M).
b. Staffordshire, 11 March 1968.
TV: Matthew Castle in *Castles;* Addison in *Chef!;* Ian Chandler in *Degrees of Error;* Mark James in *Long Days, Short Nights; Silent Witness;* Mortimer Lightwood in *Our Mutual Friend;* Julian Wadham in *The*

Ambassador; Daniel Pascoe in *The Fragile Heart*; James Danby in *The Scarlet Pimpernel*; Anthony Sumner in *Trial by Fire*; Justin Winterman in *Uprising*; Owen Mathers in *Wycliffe*.
Films: Roger in *Shooting Fish*; Captain Yardley in *The English Patient*.
Address: c/o Cassie Mayer Ltd, 34 Kingley Court, London W1R 5LE. m. Gwenyth; 2 s. Patrick, Wilfred.
Hobbies: Food, wine, gardening, dogs, motorbikes, fly fishing, horse riding.

MAGNUSSON, Sally
Sally Magnusson. Presenter/Reporter.
b. Glasgow, 11 October 1955.
TV: *A Family of My Own*; *Breakfast News*; *Breakfast Time*; *Current Account*; *Diana, My Sister*; *Dunblane Remembered*; *Living Proof*; *London Plus*; *QED*; *Reporting Scotland*; *Royal Wedding Bells*; *Sixty Minutes*; *Songs of Praise*.
Address: c/o BBC, Union House, 65–69 Shepherds Bush Green, London W12 8TX. 3 s. Jamie, Rossie, Magnus; 2 d. Siggy, Anna Lisa.

MAITLAND, Sandra
Sandra Maitland. Actor (F)/Presenter. b. 1955.
TV: Mandy Jordache in *Brookside*; *Casualty*; *Children's Ward*; *Coronation Street*; *Dangerfield*; *Kinsey*; *The Practice*; *The Really Useful Show*; *The Sharp End*; *The World of Eddie Weary*.
Address: c/o International Artistes Ltd, Mezzanine Floor, 235 Regent Street, London W1R 8AX.

MALAHIDE, Patrick
Patrick Malahide. Actor (M).
b. Pangbourne, Berkshire, 24 March 1945.
TV: *After the War*; *Blackadder*; *Bombing Birmingham*; *Charlie*; *Children of the North*; *Deacon Brodie*; *Dear Enemy*; *Dying Days*; *Inspector Alleyn*; *Inspector Morse*; *Kidnapped*; *Living With Dinosaurs*; *Middlemarch*; *Minder*; *Miss Julie*; *The Pickwick Papers*; *Pity in History*; *Snacker*; *The December Rose*; *The Franchise Affair*; *The One Game*; *The Russian Soldier*; *The Singing Detective*; *The Standard*; *Video Stars*.
Films: *A Man of No Importance*; *A Month In The Country*; *Comfort and Joy*; *Cutthroat Island*; *December Bride*; *Fortress II*; *Heaven*; *Miracle at Midnight*; *Ordinary Decent Criminal*; *The Beautician and the Beast*; *The Killing Fields*; *The Long Kiss Goodnight*; *Till There Was You*; *Two Deaths*; *US Marshals*.
Address: c/o ICM, Oxford House, 76 Oxford Street, London W1N 0AX.

MALLETT, Timmy
Timmy Mallett. Actor (M)/Performer.

TV: *Around the World in 80 Seconds*; *Channel 4 Roadshow*; *CITV Awards* (1997); *Go Getters*; *Night Fever* (1999); *Noel's House Party*; *Oxford Road Show*; *Questions*; *Timmy Towers*; *Top of the Pops*; *Wacaday* (1985); *Way to Go*; *Wide Awake Club* (1984); *Young Person's Guide to Becoming a Rock Star* (1998).
Music: *Gulf Aid*; *Hot, Hot, Hot*; *Huggin an' a Kissin*; *Itsy Bitsy Teeny Weeny Yellow Polka Dot Bikini* (No. 1); *Laughing Policeman*; *Seven Little Girls Sitting in the Back Seat* (No. 13); *The Bump*.
Address: c/o John Miles Organisation, Cadbury Camp Lane, Clapton in Gordano, Bristol BS20 7SB.
Hobbies: Painting.

MALONE, Tina
Tina Malone. Actor (F).
TV: Waitress in *Between the Lines*; Mo McGee in *Brookside*; Moira in *Common As Muck*; Bobbie in *Dinner Ladies*; Mrs P in *The Harry Enfield Show*; Jane in *Nature Boy*; Chrissie in *Sin Bin*; *Something for the Weekend*; Joyce in *Terraces*.
Films: Mrs Crane in *Blonde Fist*; Bernice in *Livertonian*; Tourist in *Married to Malcolm*; Edna Clotworthy in *The Long Day Closes*.
Address: c/o Shane Collins Associates, 39–41 New Oxford Street, London WC1A 1BH.

MANTLE, Clive
Clive Mantle. Actor (M).
b. Barnet, Hertfordshire, 3 June 1957.
TV: *A Bit of Fry and Laurie*; M/Sgt Bud Schultz in *Airbase*; *Alas Smith and Jones*; Jack in *Bloomin' Marvellous*; Dr Mike Barratt in *Casualty* and *Holby City*; *Dempsey and Makepeace*; *Drop the Dead Donkey*; *Hello Mum*; *One Foot in the Grave*; Little John in *Robin of Sherwood*; Cuthbert in *Scoop*; Simon Horton in *The Vicar of Dibley*.
Films: William in *Alien III*; *Foreign Body*; Johnny Ladder in *Mack The Knife*; *Orchard End Murders*; Bobby in *Party Party*; Ellis in *The Secret Life of Ian Fleming*; Harry in *White Hunter, Black Heart*; *Without a Clue*.
Address: c/o Marjorie Abel Ltd, 50 Maddox Street, London W1R 9PA.

MANVILLE, Lesley
Lesley Manville. Actor (F).
TV: *A Statement of Affairs*; *An English Christmas*; *Angels in the Annexe*; *Bad Girls*; *David Copperfield*; *Doctor's Dilemmas*; *Dog Ends*; *Give Us a Break*; *Goggle Eyes*; *Grown Ups*; *Holding On*; *Little Napoleons*; *Moon Over Soho*; *Other People's Children*; *Painted Lady*; *Real Women*; *Sharing Time*; *Silent Witness*; *Soldier, Soldier*; *Spiro*; *The Bite*; *The Firm*; *The Mushroom Picker*; *The Other Couple*; *Top Girls*; *Winnie*.

Films: *Dance with a Stranger; He Came Back to Love; High Hopes; High Season; Milk; Sammy and Rosie Get Laid; Secrets and Lies; Topsy Turvy.*
Address: c/o ICM, Oxford House, 76 Oxford Street, London W1N 0AX.

MANYON, Julian
Julian Manyon. Reporter.
TV: *This Week; Tonight; TV Eye.*
Address: c/o ITN, 200 Grays Inn Road, London WC1X 8XZ.

MARCEL, Rosie
Rosie Marcel. Actor (F).
TV: Michelle Demo in *Bergerac*; Dinah in *Castle of Adventure*; Stella in *Casualty*; Dorothea Mikus in *Casualty*; Donna in *Days Like These*; Lisa Hollingsworth in *Growing Pains*; Sophie in *Press Gang*; Lauara Harris in *Spilt Milk*; Susan in *The Bill*; Carmel Fairly in *The Bill*; Jane in *Weather in the Streets*; Mamie Dickens in *What the Dickens*; Rose Rosenbland in *Young Jung*.
Films: Tavy in *Hyper Sapien*.
Address: c/o Roger Carey Associates, 7 St Georges Square, London SW1V 2HX.

MARCH, Rosalind
Rosalind March. Actor (F).
TV: *Close Relations; Greeks Bearing Gifts; Inspector Morse*; Amanda in *Life Without George*; Liz Kemp in *London Bridge*; Widow in *Oliver Twist*; *Victoria Wood – As Seen On TV.*
Films: Helen Karim in *East is East*.
Address: c/o Evans & Reiss, 100 Fawe Park Road, London SW15 2EA.

MARGOLYES, Miriam
Miriam Margolyes. Actor (F)/Narrator.
b. Oxford, 18 May 1941.
TV: Various in *A Kick Up the Eighties*; Hoffman in *A Rough Stage*; Rosemary in *Alternative Society*; Queen Victoria, Infanta of Spain and Lady Whiteadder in *Blackadder*; Tony Zulu's Mama in *Body Contact*; Dr Kennedy in *City Lights*; Mrs Flagg in *Doss*; *Fall of Eagles*; Wife in *Fat Chance*; Frannie in *Frannie's Turn*; The Baroness in *Freud*; *Girls of Slender Means; Glittering Prizes*; Mrs Wadhurst in *Hands Across The Sea*; Mrs Politter in *Just William; Kizzy*; Nurse Hopkins in *The Life and Loves of a She-Devil*; Wilhemina in *Mr Majeika*; Nelly Quass in *Old Flames*; Mrs Bumble in *Oliver Twist*; Vee Talbot in *Orpheus Descending*; The Cook in *The Phoenix and the Carpet*; Elsa Maxwell in *Poor Little Rich Girl; Scotch and Wry*; Mrs Silverstein in

The Secret Ingredient; Stanley Baxter's Christmas Hamper; Alice in *Strange But True; Supply & Demand; The Finding; The First Schlemeil*; Melissa Todoroff in *The History Man*; Miss Amelia in *The Little Princess; The Lost Tribe; The Widowing of Mrs Holroyd*; Mother in *The Young Ones; Vanity Fair*; Nanny in *Ways and Means*; Queen Victoria in *Without Walls*.
Films: Audrey in *As You Like It*; Fly in *Babe*; Fly in *Babe: Pig in the City; Coming out of the Ice*; Pamela in *Crossing the Border*; Lady in *Dead Again*; Mom in *Ed and his Dead Mother*; Ticket Girl in *Electric Dreams*; *Handel – Honour, Profit and Pleasure*; Mrs Soca in *I Love You to Death; Immortal Beloved*; Aunt Sponge in *James and the Giant Peach*; Flora in *Little Dorrit*; Miss Mack in *Little Shop of Horrors; Mulan*; Rachelle Spira in *Pacific Heights*; Political Activist in *Reds*; Nurse in *Romeo and Juliet*; Officer Jones in *Scrubbers; Stand Up Virgin Soldiers*; Mrs Mingott in *The Age of Innocence*; Landlady in *The Apple*; Dr Kadira in *The Awakening*; Gina in *The Butcher's Wife*; Lady Isabel in *The Fool*; Janey Powell in *The Good Father; The White Horse*; Mrs Rajzman in *Wiesenthal – The Murderer Among Us*; Sarah in *Yentl*.
Address: c/o PFD, Drury House, 34–43 Russell Street, London WC2B 5HA.

MARKS, Gareth
Gareth Marks. Actor (M). b. London.
TV: *Bottom*; Jean Daniel in *BUGS*; Wally Simpkins in *Civvies*; Bill Bowry in *Crocodile Shoes*; Arnie in *Heil Honey, I'm Home*; Dome in *Killer Net*; Wally in *London's Burning*; Mr Soloman in *Lovejoy*; Mr X in *Mike and Angelo*; PC Howard in *Minder*; Cave in *Moon and Son*; Hugo in *New Adventures of Robin Hood*; Harry in *Sam Saturday*; Andy Drake in *The Upper Hand*; Stanley in *The Widow Maker*; Frank in *Time After Time*; Porchester in *Witchcraft*; Jongrann in *Young Indiana Jones Chronicles*.
Films: Gordon Maxwell in *Lazarus*.
Address: c/o Burnett Granger Associates, Prince of Wales Theatre, 31 Coventry Street, London W1V 8AS.

MAROT, Irene
Irene Marot. Actor (F).
TV: *About Face*; Mrs Brandon in *Boon*; DD Dixon in *Brookside*; Paula in *Cracker*; Dolores in *EastEnders*; *Here is the News*; Journalist in *Mother Love*; Mrs Barrett in *The Bill*; *The Chronicles of Narnia*; Ruth in *The Nation's Health*; *Turning Points*; Gloria in *Widows*.
Films: *Dealers*; Dr Faustroll in *Further and Particular*; Sheila in *Getting it Right*; *Intimate Strangers*; Pam in *The Little Drummer Girl*; *Nuns on the Run*.
Address: c/o Lou Coulson, 37 Berwick Street, London W1V3RF.

MARSDEN, Matthew

Matthew Marsden. Actor (M).
TV: *Coronation Street; Emmerdale; Flantastic; Islands.*
Films: *Sister Sun.*
Music: *She's Gone; The Heart's Lone Desire.*
Address: c/o ICM, Oxford House, 76 Oxford Street, London W1N 0AX.

MARSDEN, Roy

Roy Marsden. Actor (M).
b. Stepney, London, 25 June 1941.
TV: *A Certain Justice; A Mind To Murder ; Airline; Cover Her Face; Death of an Expert Witness; Devices and Desires; Frank Stubbs Promotes; Goodbye Mr Chips; Inside Story; Original Sin; Sandbaggers; Shroud for a Nightingale; Taste For Death; The Last Vampyre; Unnatural Causes; Vanity Fair.*
Films: *The Squeeze.*
Address: c/o London Management, Noel House, 2–4 Noel Street, London W1V 3RB.

MARSH, Jean

Jean Marsh. Actor (F)/Writer. b. London, 1 July 1935.
TV: Eliza in *Act of Will* (1989); Lady Lydia in *Adam Adament Lives!* (1967); Barbara in *Bejewelled* (1991); *Cross Examine* (1968); Miss Hunter in *Danny the Champion of the World* (1989); Agatha in *Department S* (1969); Sara Kingdom (1965) and Morgaine (1989) in *Doctor Who*; Mrs Rochester in *Jane Eyre* (1970); Glenda Highsmith in *Murder, She Wrote* (1984); *The Ghost Hunters; The House of Elliott* (1991); Thyrza Gray in *The Pale Horse* (1996); *The Ring* (1996); Culex in *The Tomorrow People* (1992); Rose Buck in *Upstairs Downstairs* (1971).
Films: Joanna Russell in *The Changeling*; Joanna Gray in *The Eagle Has Landed.*
Address: c/o London Management, Noel House, 2–4 Noel Street, London W1V 3RB.

MARSH, Keith

Keith Marsh. Actor (M).
TV: *A Bit of a Do; Agatha Christie; Airline; All Creatures Great and Small; And Mother Makes Three; Andy Capp; The Avengers; The Barchester Chronicles; Bedtime Stories; The Beiderbecke Affair; Beryl; Birds of a Feather; Bottle Boys; Cannon and Ball; Casualty; Coronation Street; Dalziel & Pascoe; The Dick Emery Show; East Lynne; Edna the Inebriated Woman; God Speed Co-operation; Jane Eyre; Langley Bottom; Last of the Summer Wine; London's Burning;* Jacko in *Love Thy Neighbour; Lovejoy; Main Chance; Misterioso; Murphy's Carousel; My Cousin Rachel; Never the Twain; Nice Town; Our Jeff; Owen MD; Passmore; Pennies from Heaven; Rings*

on Their Fingers; Robin's Nest; Softly, Softly; Special Branch; The Bill; The Citadel; The Gaffer; The Practice; The Professionals; Tripods; Tucker's Luck; Vanity Fair; Very Big, Very Soon; Wilfred and Eileen; Young Indiana Jones Chronicles; Z -Cars.
Films: *All Neat in Black Stockings; The Family Way; Staircase.*
Address: c/o Bryan Drew Ltd, Quadrant House, 80–82 Regent Street, London W1X 3TB.

MARSH, Reginald

Reginald Marsh. Actor (M). b. 17 September 1926.
TV: *Coronation Street; Crossroads; Dawson's Connection; George and Mildred; Help; Kelly Monteith; Midnight is a Place; Misleading Cases; Nye; Only When I Laugh; Suez; Terry and June; The Erpingham Camp; The Good Life; The Ratcatchers; The Stone Tape.*
Films: *Jigsaw; QB7; Sky Pirates; The Ragman's Daughter; Young Winston.*
Address: c/o Richard Hatton Ltd, 29 Roehampton Gate, London SW15 5JR.

MARTIN, Derek

Derek Martin. Actor (M).
b. Bow, London, 11 April 1933.
TV: DCI Berwick in *The Chinese Detective; Dempsey and Makepeace; Doctor Who; Fiddlers Three; Hart to Hart; It Ain't Half Hot Mum;* Ron King in *King and Castle;* DI Fred Pyle in *Law and Order; Minder; Only Fools and Horses; Shoestring; Terry and June; The Bill; The Duchess of Duke Street; The Gentle Touch;* Dep. Gov. Gary Marshall in *The Governor; The Professionals; The Sweeney; Upstairs Downstairs.*
Films: *Boston Kickout; Long Days' Dying; Piggy Bank; Priest of Love; Ragtime; The Cutter; The Gift.*
Address: c/o JLM, 242 Acton Lane, London W4 5DL. 2 s. David, Jonathan (twins). Hobbies: Golf (plays in various charity tournaments).

MARTIN, Mel

Mel Martin. Actor (F).
TV: Jane Fanshawe in *A Touch of Frost;* Linda in *An Independent Man;* Jessica Marston in *Boon;* Astola in *Cadfael;* Mrs Jackson in *Casualty;* Beth in *Chandler and Co.;* Deborah Riscoe in *Cover Her Face;* Penny Highsmith in *Dalziel & Pascoe* (1997); Vivien Leigh in *Darlings of the Gods;* Fiona Samson in *Game, Set and Match;* Cicely in *Hancock;* Dawn Longley in *Hetty Wainthropp Investigates;* Rosemary Henderson in *Inspector Morse;* Dorelia MacNeil in *Journey into the Shadows;* Lydia in *Love for Lydia;* Susan Lovejoy in *Lovejoy;* Stella in *Lytton's Diary;* Mrs Otway in *Melba;* Beverley in *Only Fools and Horses;* Persephone in *Orpheus and Eurydice;* Henrietta Mus-

grove in *Persuasion*; Adele in *Playing with Fire*; Charlotte Davenheim in *Poirot*; Demelza in *Poldark*; Rosie in *Summer Lease*; Jennifer in *Talking to a Stranger*; Joanna in *The Big One*; Mrs Bakersby in *The Darling Buds of May*; Jane Carlton in *The Men's Room*; Violet Effingham in *The Pallisers*; Hazel in *Time and the Conways*; Deborah Riscoe in *Unnatural Causes*.

Films: Joan in *Business as Usual*; Lady Ann Howard in *The Adventures of a Lady*; Alice Long in *Tom's Midnight Garden*; Mrs MacGregor in *White Hunter, Black Heart*.
Address: c/o Markham & Froggatt Ltd, 4 Windmill Street, London W1P 1HF.

MASSEY, Jamila
Jamila Massey. Actor (F). b. Simla, 7 January 1934.
TV: Auntie Reena in *A Nice Arrangement*; Shalini in *A Touch of Eastern Promise*; Sushma Sharma in *Albion Market*; Uma Sharma in *Angels*; Safil in *Arabian Nights*; Manju, Nisha's mother in *Brookside*; Priya Kaash in *Casualty*; Jessica in *Chance in a Million*; Mrs Mehrban in *Christmas Present*; Bahu Begum in *Churchill's People: 'Mother India'*; Neelam Kapoor in *EastEnders*; Gita in *Empire Road*; Vashpal Bedi in *Family Pride*; Sister Lucy in *Father Charlie*; Dr Patel in *General Hospital*; Nandini Patel in *Langley Bottom*; Jamila Ranjha in *Mind Your Language*; Mrs Patel in *Minder*; Firoza Begum Shah in *Neighbours*; Mrs Suleiman in *Neighbours*; Sister Kapoor in *Our Flesh and Blood*; Fazia Patel in *Pie in the Sky*; Mrs Krishna in *Pot Boiler*; Auntie in *Pravina's Wedding*; Mrs Beatty in *Six Days of Justice*; Tehmina Nadir in *Sorry, I'm a Stranger Here Myself*; Mrs Patel in *The Bill*; Mrs Ghosh in *The Bill*; Mrs Patel in *The Dick Emery Show*; Mrs Bhular in *The Good Guys*; Maharanee in *The Jewel in the Crown*; Shana in *The Rag Trade*; Dr Cheung in *Together*; The Indian prosecutor in *Tribunal* (1982); Farida in *Within these Walls*; Mrs Kaur in *Worktalk: 'Singh 171'*; Dr Ranjit in *Z-Cars*.
Films: Lal in *Conduct Unbecoming*; Mrs Ahuja in *Madam Sousatzka*; Newsreader in *Sink the Bismark*; Mrs Khan in *Wild West*.
Address: c/o Howard Cooke Associates, 19 Coulson Street, London SW3 3NA. Father Syrah Chohan; m. Reginald Massey; 1 s. Marcus. Hobbies: Reading, tapestry, sewing, gardening, making jam, wine, bread making, rearing peacocks.

MATHESON, Eve
Eve Matheson. Actor (F). b. London.
TV: Catherine Grieve in *Ambassador* (1999); Nina Milyukina in *Grushko* (1993); Zoe in *May to December*; Becky Sharp in *Vanity Fair* (1987).
Address: c/o Scott Marshall, 44 Perryn Road, London W3 7NA.

MATRAVERS, Sarah
Sarah Matravers. Presenter/Reporter.
TV: *Classic Cars; Dance Energy; Fashion Show; Great Escapes; Holiday Maker; Just Kidding; Mad About Pets; Naked in Westminster; Passport to Passion; Rough Guide to Careers; Sunday Disney Club; You Bet.*
Address: c/o John Noel Management, 10a Belmont Street, London NW1 8HH.
Hobbies: water-skiing; mountain biking; street hockey; bungee jumping; cruising in her car.

MATTHEWS, Clare
Clare Matthews. Actor (F).
TV: Clare in *Hollyoaks*; *Rough Justice*; *Ruth Rendell – Fallen Curtain*; *Casualty*; *Crimewatch*; *Choices*; *Dear Dilemma*; *Hitting Home*; *Blood and Fire*; *Ronson's Mission*; *Oasis*; *Woman in Black*.
Films: *Candy; Prince of Thieves.*
Address: c/o Anna Scher Theatre Management Ltd, 70–72 Barnsbury Road, London N1 0ES.

MATTHEWS, Francis
Francis Matthews. Actor (M). b. 2 September 1931.
TV: *The Alexei Sayle Show; Brat Farrar; Crowther Collection; Don't Forget to Write; Follow Me; Ike; Jonathon Creek; Middleman; Moving; Paul Temple; Roof Over My Head; Shall We Gather at the River; Taggart; Tears Before Bedtime; The Detectives; The Gender Gap; Trinity Tales.*
Films: *Crossplot; Dracula Prince of Darkness; Hellfire Club; Just Like a Woman; May We Borrow Your Husband?; Rasputin; The Revenge of Frankenstein; The Battleaxe; The Macguffin; A Woman Possessed.*
Address: c/o Scott Marshall, 44 Perryn Road, London W3 7NA.

MATTHEWS, Sally Ann
Sally Ann Matthews. Actor (F).
b. Oldham, Lancashire, 19 September 1970.
TV: Lady Mullet/Wicked Niece in *Brill*; Jenny Bradley in *Coronation Street*; Librarian in *Dear Nobody*; Paula in *Heartbeat*; Tracey in *Hetty Wainthropp Investigates*; Nurse in *Stay Lucky*; Anjie in *The Bill*; *The Giant Nativity Festivity*; Maria Capstan in *A Wing and A Prayer*.
Films: Waitress in *Brassed Off*.
Address: c/o Sharron Ashcroft Management, Dean Clough, Halifax, Yorkshire HX3 5AX. Hobbies: Photography, piano, harmonica, dancing.

MAUGHAN, Sharon
Sharon Maughan. Actor (F). b. 22 June 1952.
TV: *Cinderella; Dial M for Murder; Dombey and Son;*

The Enigma Files; Hannay; Huggy Bear; Inspector Morse; Justice; Keats; Murder, She Wrote; Ruth Rendell Mysteries; Shabby Tiger; The Bill; The Flame Trees of Thika; The Loner; The Main Chance; The Organisation; Ticket to Ride.
Films: *Another Stakeout.*
Address: c/o ICM, Oxford House, 76 Oxford Street, London W1N 0AX.

MAXWELL, Adam
Adam Maxwell. Actor (M).
b. Glasgow, Scotland; 28 January 1960.
TV: DS Cartwright in *Casualty*; Alex McGarry in *Eve Strikes Back*; Jack Jones in *Green and Pleasant Land*; Sgt Stone in *Inspector Morse*; Brad in *London Bridge*; Ferguson in *Paparazzo*; Dr Seymour in *Peak Practice*; Brodie in *Roughnecks*; Chivers in *Sam Saturday*; *Sometime Never*; DS Eastman/Firefighter Gray/JoeMcKenna in *The Bill*; Wax in *The Detectives*.
Address: c/o Langford Associates, 17 Westfields Avenue, London SW13 0AT.

MAY, Jodhi
Jodhi May. Actor (F). b. 1975.
TV: *For the Greater Good; Signs and Wonders; The Aristocrats; The Gift; Warriors; Turn of the Screw; The House of Mirth.*
Films: *A World Apart; Eminent Domain; House of Mirth; The Last of the Mohicans; Max and Helen; Second Best; Sister, My Sister; The Gambler; The Woodlanders.*
Address: c/o ICM, Oxford House, 76 Oxford Street, London W1N 0AX.

MAYALL, Rik
Rik Mayall. Actor (M)/Comedian/Writer.
b. Droitwich, Worcestershire, 7 March 1958.
TV: Kevin Turvey in *A Kick Up the Eighties*; Flasheart in *Blackadder Goes Forth*; Ritchie in *Bottom*; *Filthy Rich & Catflap*; W De'ath in *In the Red*; *Jackanory*; DI Gideon Pryke in *Jonathan Creek – Special*; *Rik Mayall Presents*; Dangerous Brothers in *Saturday Live*; Alan B'Stard in *The Alan B'Stard Interview, with Brian Walden*; Patrick Massie in *The Bill*; Alan in *The Comic Strip – 4 Men in a Car*; *The Comic Strip Presents …* (1981); *The Frog Prince* (for *Jackanory*); Alan B'Stard in *The New Statesman*; Rick in *The Young Ones*; *Wham Bam Strawberry Jam.*
Films: Sebastian in *A Monkey's Tale*; Marty in *Bring Me the Head of Mavis Davis*; Sultan in *Carry On Columbus*; *Couples and Robbers*; *Drop Dead Fred*; Richie in *Guest House Paradiso*; Wyatt Earp in *Horse Opera*; Hero Baby in *How To Be a Little Sod*; *Jellikins*; *Little Noises*; Merlin in *Merlin – The Return*; Young

William Tell in *Oscar's Orchestra*; Ian in *Remember Me*; Rev. Augustus Dampier in *The Canterville Ghost*; Prince Froglip in *The Princess and the Goblin*; The Robber King in *The Snow Queen*; Toad in *The Willows in Winter*; Toad in *The Wind in the Willows*; Cockney Frogs in *Tom and Vicky*; Keehar in *Watership Down*; Tom Thumb in *The World of Peter Rabbit and Friends: Tale of Two Bad Mice.*
Address: c/o Brunskill Management, Suite 8a, 169 Queen's Gate, London SW7 5HE. m. Barbara; 3 children.

MAYNARD, Bill
Bill Maynard. Actor (M).
b. Farnham, Surrey, 8 October 1928.
TV: *Till Death us do Part; 3-2-1; Andy Robson; Bill Maynard in Person; Celebrity Squares; Coronation Street; Dangerous Davies; Dangerous Days; Death and Glory; Father Brown*; George Trout in *Filipina Dreamgirls*; Claude Jeremiah Greengrass in *Heartbeat*; *Hunter's Walk; Juno & the Paycock; Kisses at Fifty; Looks Familiar; Love Affair; Mike and Angelo; Minder*; Selwyn Froggitt in *Oh No, It's Selwyn Froggitt; Paper Roses; Paradise Island; Play it Again; Spotlight; Tales of the Unexpected*; Fred Moffat in *The Gaffer; The Inheritors*; Frank Riley in *The Life of Riley; The Tale of the Little Pig Robinson; The Way of the World; Trinity Tales; Worzel Gummidge.*
Films: *All Things Bright and Beautiful; Bless This House; Man About the House; Oddball High; Robin and Marion; Carry On Dick; Carry on Henry; Carry on at Your Convenience; Carry on Loving.*
Address: c/o The Richard Stone Partnership, 2 Henrietta Street, London WC2E 8PS.

MAYO, Simon
Simon Mayo. Presenter.
b. London, 21 September 1958.
TV: *Confessions; Doomsday TV.*
Address: c/o James Grant Management Ltd, Syon Lodge, London Road, Syon Park, Middlesex TW7 5BH.

McANDREW, Deborah
Deborah McAndrew. Actor (F).
b. Huddersfield, Yorkshire, 11 October 1967.
TV: Angie Freeman in *Coronation Street*; Liza Everitt in *Heartbeat*; *Songs of Praise; This is the Day.*
Address: c/o Pemberton Associates, 193 Wardour Street, London W1V 3FA.

McARDLE, John
John McArdle. Actor (M).
b. Liverpool, 16 August 1950.
TV: Charlie in *And the Beat Goes On*; Harry in

Bambino Mio; Eddie in *Born to Run*; Billy Corkill in *Brookside*; Paul Garnet in *Gallowglass*; Stuart Laing in *Out of Hours*; DI Ballinger in *Prime Suspect V*; Malc Freeman in *Rich Deceiver*; Dilke in *Skallagrigg*; *The Place of the Dead*.
Address: c/o Dennis Lyne Agency, 108 Leonard Street, London EC2A 4RH.

McCALL, Davina
Davina McCall. Presenter.
b. London, 16 October 1967.
TV: *The Brit Awards*; *Celebrity Confessions*; *Cinematic*; *Comedy Show*; *Comic Relief*; *Dispatches*; *Don't Try this at Home*; *Dream Ticket*; *Girl Power*; *God's Gift*; *Good Stuff*; *Hanging Out*; *MTV Europe Music Awards*; *Prickly Heat*; *Street Mate*; *The Drop Dead Show*; *The Real Holiday Show*; *This Morning*.
Address: c/o John Noel Management, 10a Belmont Street, London NW1 8HH. m. Andrew Leggett (dis); partner Matthew Robertson. Hobbies: Scuba diving; dog walking; supporter of Arsenal FC, horse riding.

McCALLUM, David
David McCallum. Actor (M). b. 19 September 1933.
TV: *Alfred Hitchcock Presents …*; *Behind Enemy Lines*; *Boon*; Professor Plum in *Cluedo*; Flt Lt Simon Carter in *Colditz*; Billy Fawcett in *Coming Home*; *Death Game*; *Frankenstein: The True Story*; *Hauser's Memory*; Ron Cooper in *Heartbeat*; *Kidnapped*; *Lucky Chances*; *March in the Windy City*; *Matlock*; *Mother Love*; *Murder, She Wrote*; *Perry Mason*; Ilya Kuryakin in *Return of the Man from U.N.C.L.E.* (1983); Steel in *Sapphire and Steel*; Frank Cobb in *SeaQuest DSV*; *She Waits*; *Teacher, Teacher*; *The A-Team*; *The Helicopter Spies*; *The Invisible Man*; Ilya Kuryakin in *The Man from U.N.C.L.E.*; *The Man who Lived at The Ritz*; *The Return of Sam McCloud*; *The Screaming Skull*; *Trainer*; *VR5*.
Films: *A Night to Remember*; *Around the World Under the Sea*; *Billy Budd*; Mammy in *Cherry*; *Critical List*; *Diamond Lust*; *Dirty Weekend*; *Fatal Inheritance*; *Freud*; The Jackal in *Healer*; Jim Abbott in *Hear My Son*; *Hell Drivers*; *How to Steal the World*; *Jungle Street*; *King Solomon's Treasure*; *La Cuttura*; *Mosquito Squadron*; *One of Our Spies is Missing*; *One Spy Too Many*; *Robbery Under Arms*; *Sol Madrid*; *The Great Escape*; *The Greatest Story Ever Told*; *The Haunting of Morella*; *The Karate Killers*; *The Long and the Short and the Tall*; *The Secret Place*; *The Spy in the Green Hat*; *The Watcher in the Woods*; *The Wind*; *Violent Playground*.
Address: c/o London Management, Noel House, 2–4 Noel Street, London W1V 3RB. m. 1 Jill Ireland (dis); 3 children; m. 2 Katherine Carpenter; 2 children.

McCARTHY, Jenny
Jenny McCarthy. Actor (F)/Presenter.
b. Chicago, Illinois, USA, 1 November 1972.
TV: Herself in *Baywatch* (1989); Jenny McMillan in *Jenny*; *Silk Stalkings* (1990); *Singled Out* (1995); *The Big Breakfast* (1997); Various in *The Jenny McCarthy Show* (1997); Dani in *Wings* (1990).
Films: Yvette Denslow in *Basketball*; Sugar in *Diamonds*; Sarah Darling in *Scream 3*; Glamorous actress in *The Stupids*; Blond nurse in *Things To Do In Denver When You're Dead*.
Address: c/o ICM Agency, 8942 Wilshire Blvd., Beverly Hills, California 90211, USA. m. John Asher.

McCAUL, Neil
Neil McCaul. Actor (M).
TV: David Bryant in *Wing and a Prayer*; PC Tony Poulson in *Casualty*; Joe Addison in *Class Act*; Ringmaster in *Comedy Nation*; Magician in *Does China Exist?*; Father Terry in *Father Ted*; Raymond in *Get Real*; Adolf Hitler in *Heil Honey, I'm Home*; Martin Short in *Into the Fire*; Harry in *Mary Rose*; DI Salmon in *Minder*; The MD in *People Like Us*; Chief Constable Ryder in *Ruth Rendell Mysteries*; *Sitcom Festival* (6); Mr Salter in *Take Me Home*; Gordon Forbes in *The Peter Principle*; Michael in *The Upper Hand*; *This is David Lander*; Mr Treadwell in *Time after Time*; Demetrius in *Titus Andronicus*; Bill Bailey in *Up the Garden Path*; Keith Harrison in *Where the Heart Is*; Mr Cool in *Woof*.
Films: *Billy the Kid and the Green Baize Vampire*; *The Pirates of Penzance*.
Address: c/o Marmont Management Ltd, Langham House, 308 Regent Street, London W1R 5AL.

McCOIST, Ally
Alistair McCoist MBE. Footballer/Presenter.
b. 24 September 1962.
TV: *A Question of Sport*; *McCoist & MacAulay*.
Address: c/o Carnegie Sports International Ltd, 4 Redheughs Rigg, South Gyle, Edinburgh, Scotland EH12 9DQ. m. Allison; 1 s. Alexander. Hobbies: Reading, listening to music, practical jokes. Awarded MBE in 1996.

McCORMICK, Barry
Barry McCormick. Actor (M).
TV: DS Head in *And the Beat Goes On*; DI Summerfield in *Brookside*; Ray Fields in *BUGS*; PC Davis in *Comics*; Flt. Lt. Taylor in *Disgraceful Conduct*; Nick Trip in *Family Affairs*; Station Officer Grant in *London's Burning*; Det. Rees in *MacGyver*.
Address: c/o Burnett Granger Associates, Prince of Wales Theatre, 31 Coventry Street, London W1V 8AS.

McCUTCHEON, Martine

Martine McCutcheon. Actor (F)
b. Hackney, London, 14 May 1976.
TV: Mandy in *Bluebirds*; Tiffany Mitchell in *EastEnders*; *The Bill*.
Music: *I've Got You*; *Perfect Moment*; *You Me & Us* (album).
Address: c/o PFD, Drury House, 34–43 Russell Street, London WC2B 5HA. Hobbies: Exercising, music, films.

McDANIEL, James

James McDaniel. Actor (M).
b. Washington DC, USA, 25 March 1958.
TV: Jack in *Adventures of Huckleberry Finn*; Officer Franklin Rose in *Cop Rock*; Buzz in *Crime Story*; Jack Casey in *Defenders: Choice of Evils*; Louis in *Fantasy Island*; Mr Mason in *Hill Street Blues*; Fred in *Internal Affairs*; Mikeal Ingrams in *Law and Order*; *Love Kills*; Fred in *Murder in Black and White*; *Murder in Mind*; Fred in *Murder Times Seven*; Lt. Arthur Fancy in *NYPD Blue*; *Queen*; *Road to Galveston*; Daniel Poole in *Scam*; Harry Thiel in *Silencing Mary*; *The Old Man and the Sea*; Spider in *Unforgivable*.
Films: Dorothy's Christmas Party Guest in *Alice*; *Heading Home*; Brother Earl in *Malcolm X*; Policeman in *Rocket Gibraltar*; Roland Halloran in *Strictly Business*; Richard Thompson in *Truth Or Consequences*.
Address: c/o Jennifer Freeland, 20th Century Fox Television, 10201 W. Pico Blvd., Los Angeles, California 90035, USA. m. Hannelore McDaniel.

McDONALD, Jane

Jane McDonald. Host/Singer.
b. Wakefield, Yorkshire, 1963.
TV: *The Royal Variety Show* (1988); *Jane's Cruise to the Stars*; *Mr Gay UK* (1999); *Star for a Night*; *The Cruise*.
Music: *Cruise Into Christmas*.
Address: c/o 'BBC', Union House, 65–69 Shepherds Bush Green, London W12 8TX.

McDONALD, Sir Trevor

Sir Trevor McDonald. Newsreader/Presenter/Reporter.
b. 16 August 1939.
TV: Diplomatic Editor for *Channel 4 News* (1987); Diplomatic Correspondent for *Channel 4 News* (1982); *Channel 4 News* (1989); *ITV Evening News* (1999); *News At 5:40* (1989); *News At Ten*; *The News* (1962); *Tonight* (1999); *Trevor McDonald Meets …* (1998); Diplomatic Correspondent for various news programmes (1980); Northern Ireland Correspondent for various news programmes (1973); Sports Correspondent for various news programmes (1978).

Address: c/o ITN, 200 Grays Inn Road, London WC1X 8XZ. Hobbies: tennis, golf, cricket.

McELWEE, Rob

Rob McElwee. Weather presenter.
b. Burton-on-Trent, 21 January 1961.
TV: *6 O'clock News*; *9 O'clock News*.
Address: c/o Limelight Management, 33 Newman Street, London W1P 3PD. Hobbies: Scottish reeling, rally driving, parachuting, flying gliders.

McENERY, Peter

Peter McEnery. Actor (M).
b. Birmingham, 21 February 1940.
TV: *All Quiet on the Preston Front*; *Berlin Break*; *Boon*; *Midsummer Night's Dream*; *Reach for the Moon*; *Safari*; *The Collection*; *The Florence Nightingale Saga*; *The Mistress*; *Witchcraft*.
Films: *Clayhanger*; *Entertaining Mr Sloane*; *J'ai Tué Rasputin*; *La Curée*; *Le Mur D'Atlantique*; *Moonspinners*; *Negatives, Adventures of Gerard*; *The Aphrodite Inheritance*; *The Cat and The Canary*; *The Fighting Prince of Donegal*; *Tunes of Glory*; *Victim*; *Wonderland*.
Address: c/o ICM, Oxford House, 76 Oxford Street, London W1N 0AX.

McERLANE, Maria

Maria McErlane. Actor (F).
TV: *EuroTrash*; *Good Stuff*; *Hale & Pace*; *House Call*; *In Exile*; *Jack & Jeremy's Real Lives*; *Jo Brand – Through the Cakehole*; *Jo Brand: Like it or Lump it*; *Love in the Afternoon*; *New Year's Eve Triple Whammy*; *Once in a Lifetime*; *Paul Merton In …*; *Press Gang*; *Rory Bremner … Who Else?*; *Sabotage*; *Sean's Show*; *Six Thirty Something*; *Staggering Stories of Ferdinand de Bargos*; *The Fast Show*; *The Paul Merton Show*; *The Rory Bremner Election Special*; *Thirty Somehow*; *This Life*.
Films: *Wisecracks*; *Women in Blue*.
Address: c/o Amanda Howard Associates Ltd, 21 Berwick Street, London W1V 3RG.

McEWAN, Geraldine

Geraldine McEwan. Actor (F).
b. Windsor, Royal Berkshire, 9 May 1932.
TV: *Aspects of Love*; Mrs Proudie in *Barchester Chronicles*; *Candida*; *Come into the Garden Maude*; *Dear Love*; *French & Saunders*; *Hopcraft into Europe*; Lucia in *Mapp and Lucia*; Miss Farnaby in *Mulberry*; Mother in *Oranges are Not the Only Fruit*; *Pandora*; *Play for Today*; *Separate Tables*; *Spring Lenin*; *Tears Before Bedtime*; *The Magistrate*; Miss Jean Brodie in *The Prime of Miss Jean Brodie*; *The Rory Bremner Show*; *Three Months Gone*; *We are Strangers Here*.

Films: *Foreign Body*; Alice in *Henry V*; *Love's Labours Lost*; Miriam in *Moses*; Auntie in *Not Without My Handbag*; *Pit Ponies*; Mortianna in *Prince of Thieves*; *The Love Letter*; *Titus Andronicus*; *Tom Jones*.
Address: c/o Marmont Management Ltd, Langham House, 308 Regent Street, London W1R 5AL.

McFADDEN, Steve
Steve McFadden. Actor (M). b. 1961.
TV: *All Change*; Jones in *Bergerac*; Phil Mitchell in *EastEnders*; *Hard Cases*; *Pygmalion*; *Minder*; *Saracen*; *The Bill*; Billy in *The Firm*; Staff Sgt Ballantine in *Vote for Them*.
Films: *Buster*; *Rossinanti*.
Address: c/o Funky Beetroot Management, PO Box 143, Faversham, Kent ME13 9LP. Hobbies: Boxing, karate, snooker, sailing, horse riding, climbing, playing football.

McGANN, Joe
Joe McGann. Actor (M)/Voice artist/Singer.
b. Liverpool, Merseyside, 24 July 1958.
TV: *Boon*; *Casualty*; Scouser Barry in *Harry Enfield's Television Programme*; *Norbert Smith*; *Rockliffe's Babies*; *The Hanging Gale*; Charlie Burrows in *The Upper Hand*; Masklin in *Truckers*.
Films: *Food of Love*; *No Surrender*; *The Brylcreem Boys*.
Address: c/o Jonathan Altaras Associates, 13 Shorts Gardens, London WC2H 9AT. 3 brothers: Stephen, Mark, Paul; partner actress Julia Graham; 1 d. Lottie.

McGANN, Mark
Mark McGann. Actor (M)/Singer.
b. Liverpool, Merseyside, 1962.
TV: *Casualty*; Gregor Orlaff in *Catherine the Great*; *Deptford Graffiti*; *Les Girls*; *Moving on the Edge*; Tommy in *Murder Most Horrid*; Jiminez in *Pleasure*; *Recording Studio*; Mahal in *Samson & Delilah*; Mad Dog in *Scully*; David Wright in *The Butler Did It*; Jack in *The Golden Collar*; Marcus in *The Grand*; Conor Phelan in *The Hanging Gale*; Michael in *The Last Word*; *The Manageress*; *Yellowthread Street*; Verezz in *Zastrozzi*.
Films: *Abducted*; *Business as Usual*; John Lennon in *John and Yoko – A Love Story*; Niven Craig in *Let Him Have It*; Rock Group Leader in *No Surrender*.
Address: c/o Jonathan Altaras Associates, 13 Shorts Gardens, London WC2H 9AT. 3 brothers: Joe, Stephen, Paul.

McGANN, Paul
Paul McGann. Actor (M)/Singer.
b. Liverpool, Merseyside, 14 November 1960.

TV: *Cariani and the Courtesan*, The Doctor in *Doctor Who*; *Drowning In The Shallow End*; *Fish*; *Forgotten*; Gaskin in *Gaskin*; *Give Us a Break*; *The Monocled Mutineer*; *Nature Boy*; Joe Thompson in *Nice Town*; *Open Space – The War Poets*; Eugene Rayburn in *Our Mutual Friend*; The Soldier in *Russian Night*; Coleridge in *The Ancient Mariner*; *The Gospels*; Liam Phelan in *The Hanging Gale*; *The Importance of Being Earnest*; Colin in *The One That Got Away*; *Two Weeks in Winter*; Norman in *Whistling Wally*.
Films: *Afraid of the Dark*; Potemkin in *Catherine the Great*; *Dealers*; Lead in *Downtime*; Dad in *Fairy Tale – A True Story*; *Paper Mask*; *Streets of Yesterday*; Bassanio in *The Merchant of Venice*; *The Monk*; *The Rainbow*; *The Three Musketeers*; *Tree of Hands*; I in *Withnail & I*.
Address: c/o Marina Martin Associates, 12–13 Poland Street, London W1V 3DE. 3 brothers: Joe, Stephen, Mark.

McGANN, Stephen
Stephen McGann. Actor (M)/Singer.
b. Liverpool, Merseyside, 2 February 1963.
TV: *Brookside*; Alexis Orlov in *Catherine the Great*; Sean Reynolds in *Emmerdale*; Andrei in *Grushko*; Tex in *Help*; *Juliet Bravo*; Mark in *Lifeboat*; *Missing from Home*; Ivor Novello in *Stars in a Dark Night*; *Stay Lucky*; Johann Strauss in *Strauss Dynasty*; Bob in *Streetwise*; Daniel Phelan in *The Hanging Gale*; Jimmy Dunn in *Where the Buffalo Roam*.
Films: *Business as Usual*; Ralph in *Milk*; Henry in *The Harpist*.
Address: c/o Burdett-Coutts Associates, Riverside Studios, Crisp Road, London W6 9RL. 3 brothers: Joe, Mark, Paul.

McGINTY, Lawrence
Lawrence McGinty. Science Journalist. b. 1951.
TV: Science Correspondent *Channel 4 News*; Science and Medical Editor *ITN*.
Address: c/o ITN, 200 Gray's Inn Road, London WC1X 8AX.

McGOUGH, Philip
Philip McGough. Actor (M).
TV: Carey Hinde in *A Sense of Guilt*; Howard Clegg in *And the Beat Goes On*; *Between the Lines*; *Bombshell*; *Boon*; Nick Barber in *Bostock's Cup*; Lennox in *BUGS*; *Casualty*; *EastEnders*; Pryce in *Eye of the Storm*; Jim in *Forever Green*; M Dax in *French Fields*; George Standish in *Hamish MacBeth*; Brian Pierce in *Inspector Morse*; Brickma in *Jonathan Creek*; Edwin Woodall in *The Monocled Mutineer*; Arnie in *Only Fools and Horses*; George Wedley in *Pay and Display*; Harold

Roy in *Resnick*; *Sean's Show*; Provost Marshall in *Sharpe's Gold*; Piers in *So Haunt Me*; *Sunburn*; *The Big One*; *The Bill*; Ken in *The Biz*; Hibbert in *The Magician*; Grekov in *Under the Hammer*; *Wilderness*.
Films: *All Forgotten*; *Bombshell*; *Don't Go Breaking My Heart*; *Forever Young*; *Give us this Day*; *Gulliver's Travels*; *Les Misérables*; *M Butterfly*; *Tale of the City*; *The Final Passage*; *The Fool*.
Address: c/o Barry Brown & Partner, 47 West Square, London SE11.

McGOVERN, Jimmy
Jimmy McGovern. Creator/Writer. b. Liverpool, 1949.
TV: *Brookside*; *Cracker*; *Dockers*; *Heart*; *Hearts & Minds*, *Hillsborough*; *Needle*; *Priest*; *The Lakes*.
Address: c/o The Agency, 370 City Road, London EC1V 2QA.

McGRANGER, Lynne
Lynne McGranger. Actor (F). b. Paddington, Sydney, New South Wales.
TV: Irene Roberts in *Home and Away*; *Seven Deadly Sins*; *Skytrackers*; *Street Angels*; *The Flying Doctors*.
Address: c/o Seven Network Ltd, Mabbs Lane, Epping, New South Wales 2121, Australia.

McGRATH, Rory
Rory McGrath. Actor (M)/Panelist. b. 17 March 1956..
TV: Badvoc in *Chelmsford 123*; *Have I Got News For You*; *Late Lunch*; *Rory McGrath's Commercial Breakdown*; Voice in *The Vicar of Dibley*; *They Think It's All Over*; *Who Dares Wins*; *Whose Line is it Anyway*.
Address: c/o London Management, Noel House, 2–4 Noel Street, London W1V 3RB.

McGUIRE, Victor
Victor McGuire. Actor (M).
TV: Louis in *A Many Splintered Thing*; Andy in *All Good Friends*; Jack Boswell in *Bread*; *Brookside*; Gerry in *Casualty*; Ron in *Goodnight Sweetheart*; Dr Phil Brook in *Health and Efficiency*; Mr Collins in *Liverpool One*; Crawford in *Love Hurts*; *One Summer*; *Robin of Sherwood*; Tony in *Sean's Show*; Louis in *Snap*; Michael in *Sorry About Last Night*; Barry Gage in *Sunburn*; Jake Morgan in *The Bill*; *The Gibraltar Inquest*; Dr Brook in *2point4 Children*; *What Now?*.
Films: Gary in *Lock, Stock and Two Smoking Barrels*.
Address: c/o Lou Coulson, 37 Berwick Street, London W1V3RF.

McINNERNY, Lizzy
Lizzy McInnerny. Actor (F). b. 1960.
TV: *All in the Game*; Birgitta in *An Evening with Gary*

Lineker; *Between the Lines*; Laura Milburn in *Casualty*; *Chains of Love*; Regular in *Gems*; Charlotte in *Intimate Contact*; Clare Galloway in *Looking After Jo Jo*; DJ Kate Miskin in *Original Sin*; *People Like Us*; *The Captain's Doll*; Fleur in *Way Upstream*.
Films: Dona Ursula in *Being Human*; Phoebe in *Daphne and Apollo*; *Ghosts in the Wind*; *Infidelity*; Mary Shelley in *Rowing with the Wind*; Janet in *Summer's Awakening*.
Address: c/o William Morris Agency (UK) Ltd, 1 Stratton Street, London W1X 6HB.

McINNERNY, Tim
Tim McInnerny. Actor (M). b. Cheshire, 1956.
TV: Fiennes in *A Very British Coup*; Yakolev in *Anastasia*; Prendergast in *August Saturday*; Percy in *Blackadder*; Cpt. Kevin Darling in *Blackadder Goes Forth*; Lord Percy in *Blackadder II*; Sir Percy in *Blackadder Millennium Special*; *Casualty*; The Monk in *Catherine the Great*; *The Comic Strip Presents …*; Terry Shields in *Edge of Darkness*; Irwin in *Longitude*; de Pontheim in *Shadow of the Noose*; Vincent Clay in *Sherlock Holmes*; Appleby in *The Great Kandinsky*; Max in *The Vice Story*; *Tracey Takes On …*; Franz Kafka in *Young Indiana Jones Chronicles*.
Films: Alonzo in *101 Dalmatians*; Sven the Berserk in *Erik the Viking*; Ferret in *Fairy Tale – A True Story*; Max in *Notting Hill*; Sir William Gatesby in *Richard III*; Tony Hawes in *Rogue Trader*; John Morgan in *Wetherby*.
Address: c/o CDA, 19 Sydney Mews, London SW3 6HL.

McINTOSH, Neve
Neve McIntosh. Actor (F). b. 1970.
TV: New Ager in *Gobble*; Fuchsia in *Gormenghast*; Lady Audley in *Lady Audley's Secret*; Rachel in *Noah's Ark*; Dr Kate Miller in *Psychos*; Cellini's Maid in *Taggart*.
Films: Wendy in *Look*; Liz in *Plunkett and MacLeane*; Bookshop Assistant in *The Leading Man*; Joy in *Wonderful World*.
Address: c/o Lou Coulson, 37 Berwick Street, London W1V 3RF.

McKAY, Andrew
Andrew McKay. Actor (M).
b. Guildford, Surrey, 18 February 1981.
TV: Barney in *Agent Z and the Penguin From Mars*; Paul in *Crimewatch*; Darren in *London's Burning*; Victor Drake in *The Bill*; Wayne in *The Hill*; James in *Walking on the Moon*.
Address: c/o Italia Conti Agency Ltd, 23 Goswell Road, London EC1M 7AJ.

McKAY, Glenda

Glenda McKay. Actor (F)/Presenter.
b. Leeds, Yorkshire, 2 February 1971.
TV: Rachel Hughes in *Emmerdale; Parish Pump; Tonight.*
Films: Gudrun Brangwen in *The Rainbow.*
Address: c/o Michael Ladkin Personal Management, Suite One, Ground Floor, 1 Duchess Street, London W1N 3DE. Hobbies: Race driving, marathon running.

McKEE, Gina

Gina McKee. Actor (F). b. 14 April 1961.
TV: Sue in *An Actor's Life For Me;* Stephanie Slater in *Beyond Fear; Brass Eye; Chest; Element of Doubt; The Lenny Henry Show; Mothertime;* Mary Cox in *Our Friends in the North; The Passion; Treasure Seekers.*
Films: Kim in *Naked;* Bella in *Notting Hill;* Marion in *The Croupier;* Janis in *The Life of Stuff;* Susan's Mom in *The Loss of Sexual Innocence; Women Talking Dirty;* Nadia in *Wonderland.*
Address: c/o Roxane Vacca Management, 73 Beak Street, London, W1R 3LF.

McKELLEN, Ian

Ian McKellen. Actor (M)/Narrator. b. 25 May 1939.
TV: *Tales of the City; The Last Journey; The Recruiting Officer; The Scarlet Pimpernel; The Trial and Torture of Sir John Rampayne; Walter; Walter and June; Loving Walter; Windmill of the Gods; And the Band Played On; Cold Comfort Farm; Countdown to War; David Copperfield; Dying Day; Edward II; Graceless Go I; Hamlet; Hedda Gabler; Ian McKellen Acting Shakespeare; Ian McKellen's Diary; Keats; Kipling; Macbeth; Mister Shaw's Missing Millions; Othello; Rasputin; Richard II; Ross; So What If It's Green Cheese?; Suleyman the Magnificent; Sunday Out of Season.*
Films: *A Touch of Love/Thank You All Very Much; Alfred The Great; Art Pupil; Bent; Gods and Mothers; I'll Do Anything; Jack and Sarah; The Last Action Hero; Plenty; Priests of Love; Restoration; Richard III; Scandal; Six Degrees of Separation; The Ballad of Little Jo; The Keep; The Promise; The Shadow; X-Men; Zina.*
Address: c/o ICM, Oxford House, 76 Oxford Street, London W1N 0AX.

McKENNA, James

James McKenna. Actor (M).
TV: Brady in *A Touch of Frost; Affairs of the Heart; All in the Game; Between the Lines; Casualty; Collision; Coronation Street; Forever Green; Heartbeat;* Jack Osborne in *Hollyoaks; Mates;* Ray Hebden in *Medics; Perfect Scoundrels; Pie in the Sky; Prima; Roughnecks; Rumpole of the Bailey; September Song; Soldier, Soldier;* Joss Metcalf in *Taggart; Ties of Blood; Waterfront Beat.*

Films: *Bosanova Blues; Highlander;* George McCabe in *When Saturday Comes.*
Address: c/o Annette Stone Associates, 2nd Floor, 22 Great Marlborough Street, London W1V 1AF.

McKENSY, Brendan

Brendan McKensy. Actor (M).
b. Sydney, Australia, 30 October 1985.
TV: *Big Sky;* Titch in *Breakers;* Duncan Stewart in *Home and Away; Police Rescue; Water Rats.*
Address: c/o 'Seven Network Ltd', Mabbs Lane, Epping, New South Wales 2121, Australia. Hobbies: Camping, swimming, trampolining, karting, reading, bike riding, listening to music, drumming, movies.

McKENZIE, Julia

Julia McKenzie. Actor (F)/Singer. b. 17 February 1941.
TV: Mrs Poyser in *Adam Bede; Blankety Blank* (1979); Esther Fields in *French Fields* and *Fresh Fields; Side by Side by Sondheim;* Mrs Jarley in *The Old Curiosity Shop;* Mrs Amberson in *The Shadowy Third.*
Films: *Dick Deadeye;* Gillian in *Shirley Valentine;* Miss Dormancott in *Wild Cats of St Trinians.*
Address: c/o April Young, 11 Woodlands Road, Barnes, London SW13 OJZ.

McKENZIE, Sean

Sean McKenzie. Actor (M)/Narrator. b. Poole, Dorset.
TV: PC Nick Green in *City Central; Coogan's Run; Heartbeat; Heroes and Villains; Jackanory;* Donald in *London's Burning;* Mal Dunlop in *Noah's Ark; Peak Practice; The Bill.*
Films: Nemo in *A Martial Kind of Man;* George in *Go Now;* William in *Jude;* Dickie Deacon in *Old New Borrowed Blue;* Young Beano Baggot in *Still Crazy.*
Address: c/o Scott Marshall, 44 Perryn Road, London W3 7NA. Hobbies: Football (Aston Villa FC fan).

McKERN, Leo

Reginald McKern. Actor (M)/Narrator.
b. Sydney, Australia, 16 March 1920.
TV: *Churchill's People;* Rumpole in *Rumpole of the Bailey; The Adventures of Sherlock Holmes; The Last Romantics; The Lion, the Witch and the Wardrobe;* Number 2 in *The Prisoner.*
Films: *A Man for All Seasons; The French Lieutenant's Woman; Help!; Ryan's Daughter;* Bugenhagen in *The Omen; Travelling North.*
Address: c/o Richard Hatton Ltd, 29 Roehampton Gate, London SW15 5JR. m. Jane; 2 d. Harriet, Abigail.

McKEVITT, Anne

Anne McKevitt. Design consultant/Presenter. b. Thurso.

TV: *Healthcheck; Home Show; Homefront; Homefront in the Garden; This Morning; Value for Money; Watchdog on the House.*
Address: c/o ICM, Oxford House, 76 Oxford Street, London W1N 0AX. Hobbies: Swimming, yoga, walking, environmental and animal welfare.

McLEAN, Andrea

Andrea McLean. Presenter.
b. Glasgow, 5 October 1969.
TV: *Espresso; Food Network Daily; GMTV; The Games Room.*
Address: c/o David Anthony Promotions, PO Box 286, Warrington, Cheshire WA2 6GA. Hobbies: Theatre, cinema, writing, tennis, salsa dancing, bungee jumping, scuba diving.

McLEOD, Shelagh

Shelagh McLeod. Actor (F). b. Vancouver, British Columbia, Canada, 7 May 1960.
TV: *Almost Grown; Boon; Cream in my Coffee;* Camille in *King of the Olympics; Loose Canyon; Lovejoy;* Kate Webster in *Peak Practice; Poirot; Pygmalion; Rockliffe's Babies; Shelley; The A-Team;* Maria Romero in *The Chief; The Cleopatra Files; The Gentle Touch;* Judith Blake in *The Knock; Three of a Kind; Winning Streak; Wish Me Luck;* Jane Trier in *Wycliffe.*
Films: Caroline in *Indian Summer;* Rosalee in *Lady Oscar;* Anna in *Success;* Joanna in *The Last Island.*
Address: c/o Shepherd & Ford, 13 Radnor Walk, London SW3 4BP. Hobbies: Reading, astronomy.

McLYNN, Pauline

Pauline McLynn. Actor (F)/Panellist/Author.
b. 11 July 1962.
TV: Susan Fox-Strangways in *Aristocrats;* Bella Mooney in *Ballykissangel;* Mrs Doyle in *Father Ted; Have I Got News For You; If I Ruled the World; It Happened Next Year; The Dark Ages; Tip Top Challenge; Zig & Zag.*
Films: Aunt Aggie in *Angela's Ashes;* Prostitute in *Far and Away;* Joan in *Guiltrip;* Mother in *My Friend Joe.*
Address: c/o TalkBack Management, 36 Percy Street, London W1P OLN.

McMENAMIN, Ciaran

Ciaran McMenamin. Actor (M)
b. Enniskillen, Northern Ireland, 1974.
TV: Lead in *A Rap at the Door;* Title role in *David Copperfield; The Last Minute;* Jez in *Young Person's Guide to Becoming a Rockstar.*
Films: *County Kilburn; The Trench;* Dino in *Titanic Town.*
Address: c/o Public Eye Communications Ltd, Suite 318 Plaza, 535 King's Road, London SW10 0SZ.

McPARTLIN, Anthony

Anthony McPartlin. Actor (M)/Presenter.
b. Newcastle, 18 November 1975.
TV: *Ant & Dec Unzipped* (1997); PJ in *Byker Grove; SM:tv LIVE; The Ant & Dec Show* (1995); *The Big Breakfast.*
Music: *Falling; Stepping Stone; The Cult of Ant & Dec* (Album); *Tonight I'm Free.*
Address: c/o James Grant Management Ltd, Syon Lodge, London Road, Isleworth, Middlesex TW7 5BH.

McQUARRIE, Stuart

Stuart McQuarrie. Actor (M). b. 19 March 1963.
TV: *Butterfly Collectors;* Sgt Peabody in *Casualty;* Colin in *City Lights;* Dr Sean McKenna in *Doctor Finlay;* Spud in *Four Fathers;* DI McEwan in *Hamish MacBeth;* Struane Byre in *High Life;* Pedro in *Ines de Castro;* Lt Llewellyn in *Invasion Earth;* Magic in *London's Burning;* Spud in *Loose Ends;* Frank in *Love Me Tender;* Roger in *Silent Witness;* Roderick in *Strathblair;* Dougie in *Taggart;* Shug Harvey in *Taggart;* Jock in *The Continental;* Barry in *The Echo;* George in *The Justice Game;* Gordon in *The Peter Principle.*
Films: Leonard in *The Life of Stuff;* Gav in *Trainspotting.*
Address: c/o Hamilton Asper, 24 Hanway Street, London W1P 9DD.

McROBERTS, Briony

Briony McRoberts. Actor (F). b. Welwyn Garden City, Hertfordshire, 10 February 1957.
TV: *Bachelor Father; Brush Strokes; Don't Wait Up; EastEnders;* Samantha Hagen in *High Road; Malice Aforethought; Mr Palfrey of Westminster;* Wendy in *Peter Pan; The Crezz.*
Films: *Captain Nemo and the Underwater City; Fellow Traveller; The Pink Panther Strikes Again.*
Address: c/o Hillman Threlfall, 33 Brookfield, Highgate West Hill, London N6 6AT. m. David Robb. Hobbies: Running, dancing.

McSHANE, Ian

Ian McShane. Actor (M).
b. Blackburn, 29 September 1942.
TV: *Dream Team; Babylon 5; Madson; Soul Survivors; Lovejoy; War and Remembrance; Dallas; Marco Polo; Disraeli.*
Films: *Behind the Iron Mask; Exposed; If It's Tuesday, It Must Be Belgium; Journey into Fear; Ordeal by Innocence; Pussycat, I Love You; Ransom; Sitting Target; Sky West and Crooked; Tamlin; The Battle of Britain; The Last of Sheila; The Wild and the Willing; Torchlight; Yesterday's Hero.*
Address: c/o ICM, Oxford House, 76 Oxford Street, London W1N 0AX. m. Gwen Humble.

McVEY, Esther

Esther McVey. Presenter.
b. Liverpool, Merseyside, 24 October 1968.
TV: *5's Company* (1997); *A Date with Fate* (1998); *CBBC* (1991); *Central Weekend Live* (1998); *Dinner Dates* (1998); *GMTV* (1999); *How Do They Do That?* (1997); *Live At 3* (1996); *Nothing But the Truth* (1998); *Reportage* (1993); *The Heaven and Earth Show* (1999); *The Really Useful Show* (1997); *TV Weekly* (1994).
Address: c/o The Roseman Organisation, Suite 9, The Power House, 70 Chiswick Road, London W4 1SY.
Hobbies: Scuba diving, ballet, hiking, theatre, cinema, stand-up comedy, water-skiing.

MELIA, Michael

Michael Melia. Actor (M). b. 1945.
TV: *A Christmas Present*; *After Henry*; *Bergerac*; *Big Deal*; *Blake's 7*; *Campion*; *Casualty*; *The Chinese Detective*; *Collision Course*; *Coronation Street*; DI Dagley in *Dangerfield*; Donald in *Daylight Robbery* (1999); *Dempsey and Makepeace*; *Diana*; JJ Block in *Dream Team*; Eddie Royle in *EastEnders*; *For 4 Tonight*; *Hazell*; *Here is the News*; *Hollywood Sports*; *How Anthony Made a Friend*; Freddie Mills in *In Suspicious Circumstances*; *Inspector Morse*; *Kiss the Girls and Make them Cry*; *London's Burning*; *Maigret*; *Maybury*; *Minder*; *Reasonable Force*; *Room at the Bottom*; *Rumpole of the Bailey*; *Stay Lucky*; *Strangers*; *The Bill*; *The Detectives*; *The Gentle Touch*; *The Hard Word*; *Travelling Man*; *We, The Accused* ; *When The Boat Comes In*; *Whoops, Apocalypse!*.
Films: *Car Trouble* (1985); Policeman 1 in *Girl on a Swing* (1989).
Address: c/o Burdett-Coutts Associates, Riverside Studios, Crisp Road, London W6 9RL.

MELLINGER, Leonie

Leonie Mellinger. Actor (F). b. Berlin, 24 June 1959.
TV: *All the World's a Stage*; Terry in *Bergerac*; *Children Crossing*; Angela in *Dead Head*; *Fireworks*; Renate in *Frederick Forsyth Presents*; *Ghost Dance*; Veronica Strickland in *Hannay*; Marina in *Lovejoy*; Yvonne in *Maigret*; *Mr Palfrey of Westminster*; Francesca in *Paradise Postponed*; *Partition*; Sylvia in *Play of the Month*; *R*; Angelica/Lily in *Small World*; Miriam in *Sons and Lovers*; *Stay Lucky*; *Strange But True*; Louise St Leger in *Summer Lightning*; Elana in *The Bill*; Clarissa in *The New Statesman*; Caroline in *Whale Music*; Polly Innes in *Wycliffe*; Zina.
Films: *Memed My Hawk*; Emily in *Memoirs of a Survivor*; Mrs Mason in *The Hostage*; *The Young Toscanini*.
Address: c/o Peters, Fraser and Dunlop, Drury House, 34–43 Russell Street, London, WC2B 5HA.
m. Anthony Burton; 1 d. Aurelie. Hobbies: Waterskiing, swimming.

MELLOR, Cherith

Cherith Mellor. Actor (F).
TV: Jill in *A Fine Romance*; Christine in *A Kind of Loving*; Joan in *Casualty*; Mrs Adams in *Casualty*; Norma Trant in *Cracker*; Grace Mitchell in *Devices and Desires*; Susan Pusey in *Drummonds*; Sister Mercer in *Heartbeat*; Amy Bartlett in *Hettie Wainthropp Investigates*; Fiona Hall in *Inspector Morse*; Deirdre De Groot in *Love Hurts*; *Medics*; Helena in *A Midsummer Night's Dream*; Mary Ann Disraeli in *Mrs Brown*; Mrs Leithman in *Orchard Walls*; Carol Wilson in *Some Kind of Life*; Mildred in *Sons and Daughters*; Victoria in *The Bill*; *The Bill*; Hilary Makepeace in *The Final Cut*; *A Touch of Frost*; Carol Cooper in *Upline*; Jean in *West Beach*.
Address: c/o The Narrow Road Company, 21–22 Poland Street, London W1V 3DD.

MELVEY, Justin

Justin Melvey. Actor (M).
b. Sydney, Australia, 7 May 1969.
TV: Harry Keller in *Home and Away*; *Sunset Beach*; *The Young and the Restless*.
Films: *Cloud*; *Mametville Murders*; *The Burning Boys*; *The Debtors*; *The Promised Land*; *Valley of the Dolls*.
Address: c/o Seven Network Ltd, Mabbs Lane, Epping, New South Wales 2121, Australia. Hobbies: Scuba diving, barefoot waterskiing, horseback riding, motorcycle racing, wave skiing, swimming, surfing, piano, guitar, songwriting, karate, boxing.

MEO, Steven

Steven Meo. Actor (M).
TV: Owen in *Bryncoed*; Ensemble in *Comedy Pilot*; Jamie in *Modern Life*; Hairdresser in *The Slate*.
Address: c/o Emptage Hallett, 24 Poland Street, Soho, London W1V 3DD.

MERCIER, Sheila

Sheila Mercier. Actor (F)/Presenter.
b. Hull, Yorkshire, 1 January 1919.
TV: *Dial Rix*; Annie Sugden in *Emmerdale*; *Good Morning*; *Six of Rix*; *Telethon* (1992); *This is Your Life* (1985); *Whose Baby?* (1983).
Films: *The Night We Dropped a Clanger*; *The Night We Got the Bird*.
Address: c/o Mercier Enterprises, Apple Trees, Sponden Lane, Sandhurst, Cranbrook, Kent TN18 5NR.
1 s. Nigel. Hobbies: Reading.

MERRELLS, Jason

Jason Merrells. Actor (M). b. 1968.
TV: Matt in *Casualty*; Banquo in *Macbeth*; Phil Delaney in *Queer as Folk*; McAuliffe in *The Bill*; *The*

Factory; Lunt in *Thief Takers*; *The Verdict*.
Films: *A Small Time Obsession*; *Do Not Disturb*.
Address: c/o Jonathan Altaras Associates, 13 Short Gardens, London WC2H 9AT.

MERTON, Paul

Paul Merton. Actor (M)/Comedian/Writer.
b. London, 17 January 1957.
TV: *An Evening with Gary Lineker*; *Best of the Edinburgh Festival*; *Does China Exist?*; *Have I Got News For You*; *If You See God Tell Him*; *Jack and The Beanstalk*; *Jackanory*; *Just For Laughs*; *Parkinson*; *Paul Merton – The Series*; *Paul Merton in Galton & Simpson's...*; *Paul Merton Live at the Palladium*; *Paul Merton's Life of Comedy*; *Paul Merton's Palladium Story*; *Sticky Moments*; *Terry & Julian*; *Whose Line is it Anyway*.
Address: **c/o** International Artistes Ltd, Mezzanine Floor, 235 Regent Street, London W1R 8AX.

MERTON, Zienia

Zienia Merton. Actor (F).
b. Burma, 11 December 1950.
TV: *Angels*; *Bergerac*; *Beryl's Lot*; *Capital City*; *Casanova*; *Contacts*; *Crime Traveller*; *Dempsey and Makepeace*; Dr Stockley in *EastEnders*; *Ego Hugo*; *Grange Hill*; Barbara Tucker in *Heaven on Earth*; *Hijack to Mogadishu*; *Jackanory Playhouse*; *Kipling*; *Leap in the Dark*; *Lisbon Beat*; *London Bridge*; *Madigan*; *Peak Practice*; Sandra Benes in *Space 1999*; *Tenko*; *Thank You Comrades*; *The Bill*; *The Brief*; *The Floating Man*; *The High Game*; *The History Man*; Mia Stalinska in *The KGB Killings*; *The Lakes*; *Wilde Alliance*.
Films: Sunia in *Masters of Venus*; Lucy Ferner in *Revolution*; Rosa Dax in *The Adventurers*; Ting Ling in *The Most Dangerous Man in the World*; Anna in *The Six Wives of Henry VIII*; Aleya in *Wenn Du Bei Mir Bist*.
Address: c/o Langford Associates, 17 Westfields Avenue, London SW13 0AT. Hobbies: Reading, gardening.

MESSENGER, Melinda

Melinda Messenger. Presenter.
b. Swindon, 23 February 1971.
TV: *Can We Still be Friends?*; *Fort Boyard*; *Melinda Hits Hollywood*; *Melinda's Big Night In*; *Not the Jack Docherty Show*.
Address: c/o Take 3 Management, Osbourne House, 111 Bartholomew Road, London NW5 2BJ. m. Wayne Roberts.

METHVEN, Eleanor

Eleanor Methven. Actor (F).
b. Magherafelt, Co. Londonderry.

TV: *Falling for a Dancer*.
Films: Georgina Flannagan in *A Love Divided*; *Just in Time*; Mrs Parr in *Mad About Mambo*; Patsy McCormick in *The Boxer*; Pat Flynn in *The Disappearance of Finbar*; Obstetrician in *The Snapper*.
Address: c/o Lisa Richards, Haymarket House, 28–29 Haymarket, London, SW1Y 4SP.

MICHIE, John

John Michie. Actor (M).
TV: Alastair Miowich in *Anything More Would be Greedy*; Barry in *Bare Necessities*; Counsellor in *Brookside*; Craig in *BUGS*; Andrew Goodenough in *Dalziel & Pascoe*; *Heartbeat*; Tim in *London Bridge*; *Lovejoy*; Nick in *Master of the Moor*; Trevor Moon in *Moon and Son*; Charlie Green in *Poirot*; Bonnamy in *Rockliffe's Babies*; DI Robbie Ross in *Taggart*; Robbie Meiklejohn in *Taggart*; *The Bill*; Jeff in *The Vet*.
Films: *A Passage to India*; Barry in *Daphne and Apollo*; Monk Dawson in *Monk Dawson*; Roddy in *The Conquest of the South Pole*; Tony Fitzjohn in *To Walk With Lions*; David Baird in *Truth or Dare*.
Address: c/o William Morris Agency (UK) Ltd, 1 Stratton Street, London W1X 6HB.

MIDDLEMASS, Frank

Frank Middlemass. Actor (M).
b. Stockton-on-Tees, Co. Durham, 28 May 1919.
TV: *All in Good Faith*; *As Time Goes By*; *Dance to the Music of Time*; *Dixon of Dock Green*; *Doctor Finlay*; *Great Expectations*; *Heartbeat*; *Miss Marple*; *Oliver Twist*; *Peak Practice*; *Yes, Minister*.
Films: Sir Charles Lyndon in *Barry Lyndon*; Dr Henriques in *Madam Sin*; Bruce in *Otley*; Windsor in *The Island*.
Address: c/o Conway Van Gelder, 18–21 Jermyn Street, London, SW1Y 6HP. Hobbies: Crosswords, reading, talking, theatre.

MIDDLEMISS, Jayne

Jayne Middlemiss. Actor (F)/Presenter.
b. Bedlington, Northumberland, 1971.
TV: *EastEnders Revealed*; *GMTV*; *Rough Cuts*; *Student Choice*; *The O-Zone*; *Top of the Pops*; *Who Wears the Trousers*.
Address: c/o ICM, Oxford House, 76 Oxford Street, London W1N 0AX.

MIDDLEMISS, Philip

Philip Middlemiss. Actor (M)/Presenter.
b. 19 June 1963.
TV: *Body Check*; Bob Phillips in *Bostock's Cup*; *Capital City*; *Christabel*; Des Barnes in *Coronation Street*; *Inspector Morse*; *Ladies in Charge*; Milton in *The Bill*;

Traffik; Barry Smith in *Waterfront Beat*; David Buckley in *Where the Heart Is*.
Address: c/o Barry Brown & Partner, 47 West Square, London SE11.

MILANO, Alyssa

Alyssa Milano. Actor (F).
b. Brooklyn, New York, USA, 19 December 1972.
TV: Sylvia Velliste in *Candles in the Dark* (1993); Amy Fisher in *Casualty of Love: The Long Island Lolita Story* (1993); Phoebe Halliwell in *Charmed* (1998); Rita in *Confessions of a Sorority Girl* (1993); Vanessa Crawford in *Crash Course* (1988); Shelly Sheridan in *Dance 'till Dawn* (1988); Frances Elia Fitz in *Gold Rush* (1998); Jennifer Mancini Campbell in *Melrose Place*; Jennifer in *The Canterville Ghost* (1986); Hannah Valesic in *The Outer Limits* (1995); Amy Winslow in *The Surrogate* (1995); Denise Harris in *To Brave Alaska* (1996); Samantha Micelli in *Who's the Boss* (1984).
Films: Susanne in *Below Utopia*; Jenny in *Commando*; Eve in *Conflict of Interest*; Cristina in *Deadly Sins*; Marion Alagro in *Double Dragon*; Charlotte in *Embrace of the Vampire*; Margo Masse in *Fear*; Chelsea in *Glory Daze*; Hugo Dugay in *Hugo Pool*; Diana in *Little Sister*; Lily in *Poison Ivy II*; Amaryllis in *Public Enemies*; Truck Driver in *Speed Zone!*; Fan in *The Webbers*; Kimmy in *Where the Day Takes You*.
Address: c/o Endeavor Agency, 9701 Wilshire Boulevard, 1oth Floor, Beverly Hills, Calafornia 90212, USA.
Hobbies: Tattoos (she has five), watching ice hockey.

MILES, Annie

Annie Miles. Actor (F). b. 5 May 1958.
TV: Punk in *All in Good Faith*; Linda in *Auf Wiedersehn, Pet*; Tracey in *Back Up*; Sue Sullivan in *Brookside*; Susan Price in *Casualty*; Maria Simons in *Family Affairs*; Sophie in *Harry*; Gail in *Lonely Hearts Kid*; Teacher in *Me and My Girl*; Mrs Jenkins in *Rumble*; Sharon in *Sink or Swim*; Mrs Dawson in *The Bill*; Sally in *The Girl*; Croupier in *The Optomist*; Lisa Watts in *What You Looking At?*.
Address: c/o Jane Lehrer Associates, 100a Chalk Farm Road, London NW1 8EH. m. Bobby. Hobbies: Keep fit, swimming.

MILES, Ben

Ben Miles. Actor (M).
TV: *Couplings*; *Getting it Right*; *Is It Legal?*; *Keep the Aspidistra Flying*; *Measure for Measure*; *Melissa*; *Paris, Brixton*; *Peak Practice*; Richard in *Reach for the Moon*; *The Bill*; Thomas Palmer in *The Life and Crimes of William Palmer*; *The Round Tower*; *Wings of the Dove*; Ray in *Wonderful You*; *Zig Zag*; *Zorro*.

Address: c/o Conway Van Gelder, 18–21 Jermyn Street, London SW1Y 6HP.

MILES, Sarah

Sarah Miles. Actor (F)/Author.
b. Ingatestone, Essex, 31 December 1941.
TV: *Dandelion Dead*; *Dynasty*; *Harem*; *Ring Round the Moon*; *Temple Drake is Missing*; *The Rehearsal*.
Films: *A Ghost in Monte Carlo*; *Blow Up*; *Great Expectations*; *Hope and Glory*; *I was Happy Here*; Lady Caroline Lamb in *Lady Caroline Lamb*; *Ordeal by Innocence*; Rosy Ryan in *Ryan's Daughter*; *Steaming*; *Term of Trial*; *The Big Sleep*; *The Ceremony*; *The Hireling*; *The Man Who Loved Cat Dancing*; *The Priest of Love*; *The Sailor Who Fell From Grace With The Sea*; *The Servant*; *The Silent Touch*; *The Six-Sided Triangle*; *Those Magnificent Men in their Flying Machines*; *Venom*; *Walter & June*; *White Mischief*.
Address: c/o Chatto & Linnit Ltd, 123a Kings Road, London SW3 4PL. Brother Christopher Miles; m. Robert Bolt (deceased). Has written three volumes of memoirs.

MILES, Stuart

Stuart Miles. Presenter. b. 1972.
TV: *Blue Peter* (1994); *News* (1990); *Holiday Maker* (1999); *Saturday Disney* (1993); *SSVC-TV* (1992).
Address: c/o Unique Artistes, Avon House, Kensington Village, London W14 8TS.

MILLEA, Jim

Jim Millea. Actor (M). b. 25 November 1958.
TV: *3-7-11*; *Berkeley Square*; *Big Women*; *Bloomin' Marvellous*; *Children's Ward*; *Circle of Deceit*; *Coronation Street*; *Criminal*; *Dalziel and Pascoe*; *EastEnders*; *Emmerdale*; *Families*; *Heartbeat*; *King Girl*; *Out of Hours*; *Out of the Blue*; *Peak Practice*; *The Braithwaites*; *This is Personal*.
Address: c/o Crouch Associates, 9–15 Covent Garden, London WC2H 9PF. Hobbies: Tennis, football, squash.

MILLER, Ben

Ben Miller. Actor (M)/Comedian/Presenter. b. 1966.
TV: *Armstrong and Miller*; Blake in *Barrier Island*; *The Blind Date*; *Coming Soon*; *Confessions*; *French & Saunders*; *Jerry Sadowitz*; *Murder Most Horrid*; *Passion Killers*; *Paul Merton – The Series* (1993); *Saturday Live*; *Smith and Jones*; *Troma*; *Young Indiana Jones Chronicles*.
Films: *Plunkett and Macleane*; *There's Only One Jimmy Grimble*.
Address: c/o ICM, Oxford House, 76 Oxford Street, London W1N 0AX.

MILLIGAN, Spike

Ahmed Nagar. Actor (M)/Writer/Musician.
b. 16 April 1918.

TV: *A Milligan for all Seasons; Beachcomber; Curry and Chips; Last Laugh Before TV-AM; Muses with Milligan; Oh in Colour; The Marty Feldman Comedy Machine; There's a Lot of it About; Q; Gormenghast.*

Films: *Adolf Hitler: My Part In His Downfall; Alice's Adventures in Wonderland; Digby, The Biggest Dog in the World;* Monsieur Rimbaud in *History of the World – Part I; Life of Brian; Running, Jumping and Standing Still; The Adventures of Barry McKenzie; The Bed Sitting Room; The Cherry Picker;* Policeman in *The Hound of the Baskervilles; The Last Remake of Beau Geste; The Magic Christian; The Magnificent Seven Deadly Sins; The Three Musketeers; Watch Your Stern.*

Address: c/o Norma Farnes, 9 Orme Court, London W2 4RL. m. Shelagh Sinclair; 6 children. Hobbies: Conservation, painting.

MILLIGAN, Stuart

Stuart Milligan. Actor (M).

TV: Alex Newman in *Act of Will;* Art Pepper in *But Beautiful; Disaster; The Harry Enfield Show;* Adam Klaus in *Jonathan Creek;* President in *Newborn;* Harris in *Outpost;* Andy in *Strange But True;* Wallcott in *The Chief; The Intercom Conspiracy; True Crimes;* Paton in *Young Indiana Jones Chronicles.*

Address: c/o Evans & Reiss, 100 Fawe Park Road, London SW15 2EA.

MILLS, Norman

Norman Mills. Actor (M).

TV: Mr Benchmark in *Adam's Family Tree; After the War;* Colin Prendergast in *Brookside; Cardiac Arrest; Child of Darkness;* Frank Jennings in *City Central;* Mr Horner in *Coronation Street; The Darling Buds of May;* Conference Chairman in *Dockers; Emmerdale; Game, Set and Match; GBH;* Mr Kettley in *Heartbeat;* Brown in *Hetty Wainthropp Investigates; In Suspicious Circumstances; Last of the Summer Wine; My Kingdom for a Horse;* PC in *My Wonderful Life;* Frank in *Our Friends in the North;* Mr Rice in *Out of the Blue;* Alan in *Peak Practice;* PC in *Pie in the Sky; Putting on The Ritz;* Train Guard in *Rhinoceros; September Song; Sherlock Holmes;* Mr Wilson in *Some Kind of Life;* Surgeon in *The Ward;* Jailer in *The Wyvern Mystery; A Touch of Frost;* James Nesmith in *Touching Evil;* Court Clerk in *The Verdict.*

Films: *Between Two Women; Wetherby.*

Address: c/o Sharron Ashcroft Management, Dean Clough, Halifax, Yorkshire HX3 5AX. Hobbies: Driving, singing, carpenter, guitar, banjo, ukulele, concertina, harmonica.

MILLSON, Joseph

Joseph Millson. Actor (M). b. 1974.

TV: James in *Dressing for Breakfast;* Raphael in *In Exile; Our Tune;* Sam Morgan in *Peak Practice; The Awful Truth.*

Films: *La Belle Dame Sans Merci; Sophie's World.*

Address: c/o Evans & Reiss, 100 Fawe Park Road, London SW15 2EA. Hobbies: Horse riding, skateboarding, football.

MIRREN, Helen

Helen Mirren. Actor (F)/Narrator/Producer.
b. London, 26 July 1945.

TV: *After the Party; As You Like It;* Ayn Rand in *Ayn Rand; Behind The Scenes; Bellamira;* Alma Rattenbury in *Cause Célèbre; Coffin for the Bridge; Coming Through; Cousin Bette;* Imogen in *Cymbeline; Jackanory; Little Minister;* Chase in *Losing Chase; A Midsummer Night's Dream; Miss Julie; Mrs Reinhart; Mussolini and Claretta Petacci;* Maggie Sullivan in *Painted Lady;* DCI Jane Tennison in *Prime Suspect;* also *Prime Suspect II, III and IV; Quiz Kids; Red King, White Knight; The Apple Cart; The Changeling; The Collection; The Country Wife; The Philanthropist; The Serpent Son – Oresteia.*

Films: *2010; Age of Consent; Bethune, Making of a Hero; Cal; Caligula; Excalibur; Fu Man Chu; Greenfingers; Heavenly Pursuits; Hussy; The Mosquito Coast; O Lucky Man; Pascali's Island; Savage Messiah; Some Mother's Son; The Comfort of Strangers; The Cook, The Thief, His Wife and Her Lover; The Hawk; The Long Good Friday; The Madness of King George; The Prince of Jutland; When the Whales Came; Where Angels Fear to Tread; White Knights.*

Address: c/o Ken McReddie Ltd, 91 Regent Street, London W1R 7TB. m. Taylor Hackford. Father was Russian aristocrat who fled the 1917 revolution.

MIRYLEES, Kika

Kika Mirylees. Actor (F).

TV: Julie J in *Bad Girls;* Andrea in *Canary Wharf;* Lucy Harcourt in *Class Act;* Angela Snow in *The Darling Buds of May;* Zola in *Jonathan Creek;* Corinna in *Lovejoy;* Doc Newton in *Red Dwarf;* Flora Harcourt in *Strathblair;* Miss Watson in *Taggart;* Maria in *The Bill.*

Films: Caroline in *A Man You Don't Meet Every Day;* Patron in *Jackie.*

Address: c/o The Narrow Road Company, 21–22 Poland Street, London W1V 3DD.

MISTRY, Jimi

Jimi Mistry. Actor (M).
b. Scarborough, Yorkshire, 1973.

TV: Kumar in *City Central;* Dr Fred Fonseca in *East-*

Enders; Network East; DC Wright in *Silent Witness;* Mickey Khan in *The Bill;* Bank Clerk in *Thief Takers.*
Films: *East is East;* Sailor in *Hamlet; Illegal Access.*
Address: c/o Glenn Bexfield Personal Management, 55 Kenilworth Road, London E3 5RH.

MITCHELL, Warren

Warren Mitchell. Actor (M).
b. London, 14 January 1926.
TV: Alf Garnett in *A Word with Alf;* Ray Smiles in *Ain't Misbehavin;* Chairman of the Water Board in *Gobble;* Barquentine in *Gormenghast;* Alf Garnett in *In Sickness and in Health;* Ambrose Barberton in *Jackaroo;* Ivan Fox in *So You Think You've Got Troubles; The Dunera Boys;* Franklin D Roosevelt in *The Last Bastion;* Shylock in *The Merchant of Venice;* Alf Garnett in *The Thoughts of Chairman Alf;* Alf Garnett in *Till Death Us Do Part;* Samuel Singer in *Wall of Silence; Waterfront.*
Films: *Carry On Cleo;* Albert in *Crackers;* IQ Patel in *Foreign Body; Help!;* Mr Fishfinger in *Jabberwocky; Knights and Emeralds;* Stan in *Kokoda Crescent;* Gurdjieff's father in *Meetings with Remarkable Men;* Morris in *Norman Loves Rose; The Assassination Bureau;* Bamber in *The Chain; The Jokers; The Roman Spring of Mrs Stone; The Spy Who Came in from the Cold; Two Way Stretch.*
Address: c/o CDA, 19 Sydney Mews, London SW3 6HL.

MOCKFORD, Jeanne

Jeanne Mockford. Actor (F).
b. London, 15 March 1931.
TV: *Bruiser; Dear John; Don't Wait Up;* Marjorie in *Hi De Hi; Julia Jekyll and Harriet Hyde; Keeping up Appearances; Last of the Summer Wine;* Annie Porter in *The Bill; The Bill; The Letter; The Sea;* Senna the Soothsayer in *Up Pompeii.*
Films: Miss Daniels in *Londinium.*
Address: c/o Langford Associates, 17 Westfields Avenue, London SW13 0AT. Hobbies: Crosswords.

MOLINA, Alfred

Alfred Molina. Actor (M). b. London, 24 May 1953.
TV: *A Place of Lions* (1997); Tadeuz in *A Very Polish Practice* (1991); Tony in *A Year in Provence* (1992); George in *Angels* (1991); *Angels in the Annexe* (1984); Eric in *Anyone for Denis?* (1982); General Karmona in *Ashenden* (1991); Ian Spiro in *Atonement* (1993); Gino in *Blat* (1986); *Boon* (1991); Cropper in *C.A.T.S. Eyes* (1985); Spiros in *Drowning in the Shallow End* (1989); Blake in *El CID* (1989); Tony Hancock in *Hancock* (1991); *Joni Jones* (1982); *Meantime* (1982); *Miami Vice* (1987); Hank in *Nativity Blues* (1988); Ira Moss in *Nervous Energy* (1995);

Mulrooney in *Oysters* (1984); Blymokin in *Reilly Ace of Spies* (1982); Jose Morazan in *Saracen* (1989); Lionel in *The Accountant* (1989); *The Losers* (1977); Salvatore Guarnuaccio in *The Marshall* (1992); George Melly in *The Trials of Oz* (1991); Harry in *Trust Me* (1992); Andreus in *Typhon's People* (1993); John Ogden in *Virtuoso* (1988).
Films: *A Further Gesture;* Syme in *American Friends;* Mellersh in *An Enchanted April;* Levin in *Anna Karenina; Before and After; Boogie Nights;* The Professor in *Cabin Boy; Dead Man;* Ceasare in *Ladyhawke;* Sergei in *Letter to Brezhnev;* Avanti in *Manifesto; Maverick; Mojave Moon;* Moody in *Not Without My Daughter;* DC Rodgers in *Number One;* Halliwell in *Prick Up Your Ears;* Satipo in *Raiders of the Lost Ark;* Hamish in *Requiem Apache;* Emil Taquet in *Rescuers: Stories of Courage 55; Scorpion Springs;* Burton in *Ship of Fools; Species;* Dr Jones in *The Hideaway;* Boris in *The Man Who Knew Too Little;* Juan Perez in *The Perez Family;* Cliff in *The Steal;* Titorelli in *The Trial;* Pierre in *Water; When Pigs Fly;* Rev. Dury in *White Fang II – Myth of the White Wolf.*
Address: c/o Lou Coulson, 37 Berwick Street, London W1V 3RF. m. Jill Gascoine.

MOLLOY, Dearbhla

Dearbhla Molloy. Actor (F). b. Dublin, Ireland.
TV: Sister Catherine in *A Secret Slave;* Elizabeth in *Access to the Children;* Asst. Chief Constable Lewis in *Between the Lines;* Eileen Walker in *Casualty;* Elizabeth Clarke in *First Love;* Laura Nelson in *GBH;* Judith in *John David;* Charlotte/Gill in *Killer Exposed;* Marion in *Pentecost;* Dublin Kilkenny in *Pirate Prince;* The Nurse in *Romeo and Juliet;* Mary Ginnelly in *Stay Lucky;* Mother in *Summer Ghost;* Dr Lilith Pascoe in *The Fragile Heart;* Trish McCabe in *Ties of Blood.*
Films: Effa in *Frankie Starlight;* Ava in *Loaded;* Danny's Mother in *Run of the Country;* Ma Stokes in *This is the Sea.*
Address: c/o Cassie Mayer Ltd, 34 Kingley Court, London W1R 5LE.

MOLONEY, Ryan

Ryan Moloney. Actor (M). b. Australia.
TV: Toadfish in *Neighbours; The Purple Pimpernickel; The Bob Morrison Show; Round the Twist; Say a Little Prayer.*
Address: c/o Grundy Television, Grundy House, Barge House Crescent, 34 Upper Ground, London SE1 9PD.

MONCKTON, Patrick

Patrick Arnold. Actor (M).
b. Budapest, Hungary, 9 June 1945.
TV: *Poirot; Alfred Hitchcock Presents …; An Actor's Life*

For Me; Bergerac; Brideshead Revisited; Coronation Street; Dracula: The Series; EastEnders; Handles; Head over Heels; Juliet Bravo; Kung Fu: The Legend Continues; Licking Hitler; Maid of Dunkirk; Michael Winner's True Crimes; Minder; Moon and Son; My Dear Watson; Potter; Professional Foul; Riviera; Screaming; Shadow of the Noose; Sherlock Holmes; So Haunt Me; The Bill; The Brittas Empire; The Gibraltar Trial Inquest; The Growing Pains of Adrian Mole; The Return of Sam McCloud; The Secret Servant; The Upper Hand; Asiz in *Young Indiana Jones Chronicles;* Joe Wilson in *Touching Evil; William The Conqueror; Woof.*

Films: Miklos in *Hannah's War;* Cook in *Robinson Crusoe;* Swag in *The Borrowers;* Mr Perivale in *The First Kangaroos;* Private Kirby in *The Victors;* Peter Pringle in *What Ever Happened to Harold Smith?.*

Address: c/o Langford Associates, 17 Westfields Avenue, London SW13 0AT. m. Gail Monckton. Hobbies: Chess, travel.

MONKHOUSE, Bob

Bob Monkhouse OBE. Actor (M)/Presenter/Writer.
b. Beckenham, Kent, 1 June 1928.
TV: *$64,000 Question; All or Nothing at All; An Audience With Bob Monkhouse; Bob Monkhouse 'On The Spot'; Bob Monkhouse 'Over the Limit'; Bob Monkhouse on Campus; Bob Says: 'Opportunity Knocks'; Bob's Your Uncle; Candid Camera; Celebrity Squares; Family Fortunes; Friends in High Places; Funny For Money; Gag Tag; Jonathan Creek; Monkhouse's Memory Masters; Parkinson; Quick on the Draw; Royal Variety Performance: What a Performance!; Sunday Night at the London Palladium; The Bob Monkhouse Show; The Golden Shot; The ITV Movie Awards; The National Lottery, Live!; Wipeout.*
Films: *Carry On Sergeant; Dentist in the Chair; The Bliss of Mrs Blossom; Weekend with Lulu.*
Address: c/o International Artistes Ltd, Mezzanine Floor, 235 Regent Street, London W1R 8AX. m. Jackie; 1 d. Abigail; 1 s. Simon. Hobbies: Collecting vintage films. Awarded OBE in 1993.

MONTAGUE, Bruce

Bruce Montague. Actor (M).
b. Deal, Kent, 24 March 1939.
TV: Leonard in *Butterflies; Cowboys; Cross Wits; District Nurse;* Phillip in *Ex; For Maddie With Love;* Lord of the Manor in *Keeping up Appearances; Kelly Monteith; Play of the Month; Sharon and Elsie; Special Branch; The Concubine; The Onedin Line; The Secret Army;* Ladak Thoumi in *The Trial of Klaus Barbie;* Director General of the BBC in *The Vision;* Commander Hucklesby in *True Crimes;* Shah in *Whoops, Apocalypse!.*

Films: *A Christmas Carol; A Connecticut Yankie in the Court of King Arthur; George and Mildred; The Thief of Baghdad; Treasure Island.*
Address: c/o Collis Management, 182 Trevelyan Road, London SW17 9LW.

MONTGOMERY, Flora

Flora Montgomery. Actor (F).
b. Belfast, 4 January 1974.
TV: Octavia in *A Certain Justice;* Dorothy in *Heat of the Sun;* Sophie Hamilton in *Metropolis;* Baba Metcalfe in *Moseley; The Governor;* Flora Ackroyd in *The Murder of Roger Ackroyd;* Laura Ferguson in *An Unsuitable Job For a Woman;* Isabella in *Wuthering Heights.*
Films: Sheila in *The Stiff;* Trudy Fortune in *When Brendan Met Trudy.*
Address: c/o Conway Van Gelder, 18–21 Jermyn Street, London SW1Y 6HP.

MOODY, Ron

Ron Moody. Actor (M). b. London, 8 January 1924.
TV: *Dial M for Murder; Discovering Physics – Newton's World; Gunsmoke; Hart to Hart; Hideaway; Last of the Summer Wine; Mike and Angelo; Murder, She Wrote; Nobody's Perfect, Othello, Starsky and Hutch, Tales of the Gold Monkey, Tales of the Unexpected, Telebugs, The Bill, The Caucasian Chalk Circle, The Edwardians, The People's Passion,* Le Brun in *The Word.*
Films: *A Ghost in Monte Carlo;* Merlin in *A Kid In King Arthur's Court; Dogpound Shuffle;* Fagin in *Oliver; Paradise Grove; Summer Holiday; Take Pity; The Flight of the Doves; The Three Kings; The Twelve Chairs; Where is Parsifal?; Wrong is Right.*
Address: c/o Eric Glass Ltd, 28 Berkeley Square, London W1X 6HD.

MOORE, Jonathan

Jonathan Moore. Actor (M).
TV: Frank O'Brian in *Bergerac;* Guppy in *Bleak House;* Riggett in *Campion; Cruel Train; Dalziel & Pascoe;* Woods in *Dragon's Opponent;* Billy the Kid in *Horse Opera;* David Stone in *Inside Story;* Benjamin Bates in *Jack the Ripper;* Baker in *O Fat White Woman; One For The Road; Pie in the Sky;* Prince Alexei in *Rasputin;* Tony in *Selection;* Harry in *Switch On; Tiptoe through the Tulips;* Author and Actor in *Treatment.*
Address: c/o ICM, Oxford House, 76 Oxford Street, London W1N 0AX.

MOORE, Robyn

Robyn Moore. Actor (F).
b. London, 15 September 1963.
TV: *Call Red; Casualty;* Maggie Roswell in *Family*

Affairs; Gloria in *Poirot*; Chloe in *The Bill*.
Address: c/o Ken McReddie Ltd. 91 Regent Street, London W1R 7TB. Father Stephen Moore; Brother Guy Moore; uncle James Hazeldine; 1 d. Harriet; 1 s. Joshua. Hobbies: Gardening, music, dancing.

MOORE, Stephen

Stephen Moore. Actor (M). b. 11 December 1937.
TV: Mr Spofforth in *A Bit of Fry and Laurie*; Third Broker in *A Christmas Carol*; Nicholas Spencer in *And the Beat Goes On*; Trevor in *Bedroom Farce*; Mr Twite in *Black Hearts in Battersea*; Henry Feather in *Blore MP*; Hipkiss in *Boon*; Jasper in *Brideshead Revisited*; Alan in *Casualty*; Kevin in *Casualty*; Charlie in *Clowns*; Col. Beck in *Countdown to War*; Gerald Norland in *Dangerfield*; Graham in *Downwardly Mobile*; The Citizen in *For the People By the People*; Travis in *Happy Autumn Fields*; Kevin's Dad in *Harry Enfield*; Neil in *Just Between Ourselves*; Simon in *Keep Smiling*; Aloysius Jentee in *Leprechauns*; Jeff in *Let's Get Divorced*; William Stephens in *Life and Crimes of William Palmer*; Hugh in *Love Hurts*; Quirk in *Love on a Branch Line*; Lead in *Love on a Gunboat*; Inspector in *Men of the World*; Mr Vincey in *Middlemarch*; Paris in *Paris*; Ron Ellis in *Perfect Scoundrels*; Dr Rymans in *Prince of Hearts*; Jack in *Rock Follies*; Berkley in *Sharpe's Sword*; Professor Swallow in *Small World*; Brig. Chisolm in *Soldier, Soldier*; Farley Smythe in *Soldiers Talking Cleanly*; Danny in *Solo*; Julius Skipton in *Storyboard*; Nicely in *Tales from Hollywood*; Bernard Hadow Smith in *Thacker*; George Mole in *The Growing Pains of Adrian Mole*; Marvin the Paranoid Android (and others) in *The Hitch Hiker's Guide to the Galaxy*; Wilson in *The Last Place on Earth*; Ralph in *The Missing Postman*; Geoffrey in *The Peter Principle*; Mr Parker in *The Queen's Nose*; George Mole in *The Secret Diary of Adrian Mole*; Professor G in *This is Personal*; George in *Three Men in a Boat*; Henson in *Van Der Valk*.
Films: Maj. Steele in *A Bridge Too Far*; *Brassed Off*; Mr Jolly in *Clockwise*; Guy in *Diversion*; Howard in *Pilkington's Pluck*; Young Man in *The White Bus*; Le Blanc in *Truel*; Roscoe in *Under Suspicion*.
Address: c/o Markham & Froggatt Ltd, 4 Windmill Street, London W1P 1HF.

MOORE, William

William Moore. Actor (M). b. Birmingham.
TV: Sgt Turpin in *Coronation Street*; Captain Cottle in *Dombey and Son*; Husband in *My Husband and I*; Cyril (Father) in *Sorry*.
Address: c/o Joan Reddin, Hazel Cottage, Wheeler End Common, Wheeler End, High Wycombe, Bucking-hamshire HP14 3NL. m. Mollie Sugden; 2 s. Simon, Robin (twins). Hobbies: Painting, cricket, golf.

MORAGHAN, Mark

Mark Moraghan. Actor (M).
TV: Greg Shadwick in *Brookside*; Divisional Officer in *Casualty*; DC Payne in *Chandler and Co.*; Coach in *Dream Team*; Barry Scouser in *Harry Enfield and Chums*; Luke in *Heartbeat*; DO Quinn in *London's Burning*; Phil Young in *Peak Practice*; Jonathan in *Real Women*; Trevor Dicks in *Sharman*; DI Reaygo in *The Chief*.
Address: c/o Evans & Reiss, 100 Fawe Park Road, London SW15 2EA.

MORAN, Pauline

Pauline Moran. Actor (F). b. Blackpool, Lancashire.
TV: Teacher in *Afternoon*; Juliet Brody in *BUGS*; Jenny in *Crown Court*; Miss Petowker in *Nicholas Nickleby*; Lesley in *Only a Game*; Sharon in *Our Young Mr Wignal*; Miss Felicity Lemon in *Poirot*; Gypsy in *Romance*; Ruby Ray in *Shadow of the Noose*; Mary Lawrence in *Supernatural*; Cleopatra Berenike in *The Cleopatra Files*; Maisie Maidan in *The Good Soldier*; Antoinette de Mauban in *The Prisoner of Zenda*; Empress of Russia in *The Storyteller*; Gypsy in *The Tent*; Helena in *The Trespasser*; Woman in Black in *The Woman in Black*.
Address: c/o Ken McReddie Ltd, 91 Regent Street, London W1R 7TB. Hobbies: Dressmaking, interior decoration, cookery, cats, textile printing, computers, astrology.

MORAN, Tara

Tara Moran. Actor (F). b. 1 June 1971.
TV: Staff Nurse Mary Skillett in *Casualty*; Christine Carter in *Coronation Street*; *Cracker*; Felicity in *EastEnders*; *Eight Hours from Paris*; Chelsea in *Families*; *Harry*; *Heartbeat*; *Hollyoaks*; *How We Used To Live*; *Sunburn*; Young Conservative in *The New Statesman*; Hannah in *Touching Evil*.
Address: c/o Susan Angel Associates, 1st Floor, 12 D'Arblay Street, London W1V 3FP.

MORGAN, Garfield

Garfield Morgan. Actor (M). b. 19 April 1931.
TV: Chief Inspector in *Alas Smith and Jones*; Curtly in *Born Kicking*; Pilton in *Dangerfield*; A.C.Strain in *Dear Mother, Love Albert*; Roger in *Deceptions*; Wilford in *Jenny's War*; Jolly in *Lovejoy*; Spt. Mason in *Minder*; DI Moss in *Murder Elite*; Superintendent in *Murder on the Orient Express*; Norman in *No Job for a Lady*; Rundle in *One by One*; Desmond in *Shelley*;

Lewis in *Softly, Softly*; Captain in *The 19th Hole*; Haskins in *The Sweeney*; Gerald in *You Must See the Husband*.
Films: *Digby, The Biggest Dog in the World*; *George and Mildred*; *Madigan*; *Our Mother's House*; *Out of Order*; *Perfect Friday*; *Starting Over*; *The Englishman Who Went up a Hill and Came Down a Mountain*; *The Odessa File*; *The Pumpkin Eater*; *The Story of Private Polley*.
Address: c/o Michelle Braidman Associates, 10–11 Lower John Street, London W1R 3PE. Hobbies: Golf, horse riding.

MORIARTY, Paul
Paul Moriarty. Actor (M). b. London, 19 May 1946.
TV: Sgt Wells in *A Touch of Frost*; *Anna Lee*; *Arena*; *Bedtime Stories*; *Between the Lines*; *Casualty*; *Coronation Street*; George Palmer in *EastEnders*; Insp. Bonneau in *Maigret*; *Minder*; *Murder Most Horrid*; *Paradise Club*; *Peak Practice*; Col. Forster in *Pride and Prejudice*; *Russian Roulette*; *Saracen*; *South of the Border*; Frank Hipwood in *The Bill*; *The Chain*; Club Manager in *The Comic Strip Presents …*; Ron in *The Gatekeeper*; *The Gentle Touch*; *The Knock*; Leonard in *The Lodge*; *The Sweeney*; *Troilus and Cressida*; *Trouble Makers*; Abe Geach in *Wycliffe*; *Z Cars*.
Films: *Five Go Mad on Nuclear Fuels*; *Hidden Agenda*.
Address: c/o Emptage Hallett, 24 Poland Street, London W1V 3DD.

MORLEY, Ken
Ken Morley. Actor (M).
b. Chorley, Lancashire, 17 January 1943.
TV: *'Allo 'Allo*; *All Passion Spent*; *Blind Justice*; *Bullman*; *Chelmsford 123*; Reg Holdsworth in *Coronation Street*; *Les Girls*; *Quest*; *Return of the Antelope*; *The Grand*; *The Management*; *Watching*; *Who Dares Wins*; *Woof*; *You Rang M'Lord*.
Films: *Alfie Darling*; *Little Dorrit*.
Address: c/o The Narrow Road Company, 21–22 Poland Street, London W1V 3DD.

MORRIS, Juliet
Juliet Morris. Presenter/Reporter. b. 1956.
TV: *999*; *Breakfast News*; *Good Food Show*; *Good Fortune*; *Here & Now*; *House Detectives*; *Mysteries*; *Newsround Extra*; *Panorama*; *Spotlight*; *The Travel Show*; *Whitbread Literary Awards*.
Address: c/o Speakeasy Ltd, 90 St Mary's Road, Market Harborough, Leicestershire LEI6 7DX.

MORRISSEY, David
David Morrissey. Actor (M).
TV: Marcus in *Available Light*; Inspector Dilke in *Between the Lines*; Leo in *Big Cat*; DC Mills in *Black and Blue*; George Percy Foster in *Cause Célèbre*; Finney in *Finney*; Lawrence in *Framed*; David Snodin in *Holding On*; Michael Ride in *Into the Fire*; Billy in *One Summer*; Bradley Headstone in *Our Mutual Friend*; DS Lewin in *Out of the Blue*; Ray in *Out of Town*; Frank in *Pure Wickedness*; Gerry in *The Knock*; Andy McNab in *The One That Got Away*; Theseus in *Theseus and the Minotaur*.
Films: The Human in *Being Human*; Bellamy in *Drowning by Numbers*; Rob in *Fanny and Elvis*; Kiffer in *Hilary and Jackie*; Little John in *Robin Hood*; Pete in *Some Voices*; Murray Lomax in *The Commissioner*; Joyce in *The Suicide Club*; Rob Wakeman in *The Widow Maker*; Dick in *Waterland*.
Address: c/o ICM, Oxford House, 76 Oxford Street, London W1N 0AX.

MORRISSEY, Neil
Neil Morrissey. Actor (M)/Narrator.
b. Staffordshire, 4 July 1962.
TV: *A Woman's Guide to Adultery*; *Blood Runner*; *Boon*; *C.A.T.S. Eyes*; *Chest*; *Dive to Shark City*; *Ellis Island*; *Follow Through*; *Gentlemen and Players*; *Hunting Venus*; *Jack and the Beanstalk*; Tony in *Men Behaving Badly*; *My Summer with Des*; *Paris*; *Playing Away*; *Pulaski*; *The Smell of Reeves and Mortimer*; *Roger, Roger*; *Roll Over Beethoven*; *Stuck on You*; *The Flint Street Nativity*; *The Journal*; *The Morph Files*; *The Vanishing Man*; *Trafford Tanzi*; *Travellers by Night*.
Films: *The Ballad of Kid Divine*; *The Bounty*; *The Match*; *Up 'n' Under*.
Address: c/o ICM, Oxford House, 76 Oxford Street, London W1N 0AX.

MORTIMER, Bob
Bob Mortimer. Actor (M)/Comedian/Presenter/Writer. b. Middlesbrough, Teeside, 23 May 1959.
TV: *A Night in with Vic and Bob*; *A Nose Through Nature*; *Bang Bang, It's Reeves and Mortimer* (1999); *Christmas Night with the Stars* (1994); *Families at War*; *It's Ulrika*; *Shooting Stars*; *The Smell of Reeves and Mortimer* (1993, 1995); *Vic Reeves' Big Night Out* (1990, 1991); *Vic Reeves' Weekenders*; *Randall and Hopkirk (Deceased)*.
Music: *Abide With Me*; *Born Free*; *Dizzy* (with The Wonderstuff); *I Will Cure You*; *I'm a Believer*; *Let's Dance*.
Address: c/o PBJ Management, 5 Soho Square, London W1V 5DE.

MORTON, Richard
Richard Morton. Actor (M)/Comedian/Presenter.
TV: *Comedy Store Show*; *Dangerous*; *Funny Business*; *Gag Tag*; *Good Stuff*; *Jack and Jeremy's Real Lives*; *Jack*

Dee's Saturday Night; Jack Docherty Show; Night Fever; Our Friends in the North; Richard Morton Live at the Comedy Store; The Richard Morton Christmas Special; The Stand Up Show; Tibs and Fibs; WowFabGroovy.
Address: c/o Off the Kerb Productions, 3rd Floor, Hammer House, 113–117 Wardour Street, London W1V 3TD.

MORTON, Samantha
Samantha Morton. Actor (F). b. 1977.
TV: *Band of Gold; Boon; Cracker;* Harriet in *Emma; Go Wild;* Jane Eyre in *Jane Eyre; Medics; Peak Practice; Soldier, Soldier; Talk, Write and Read; The Vet;* Sophia Weston in *Tom Jones.*
Films: *Dreaming of Joseph Lees;* Michelle in *Jesus's Son;* Sara Coleridge in *Pandemonium;* Hattie in *Sweet and the Lowdown; The Future Lasts a Long Time;* Jackie in *The Last Yellow; The Token King; This is the Sea; Time;* Iris in *Under the Skin.*
Address: c/o Conway Van Gelder, 18–21 Jermyn Street, London SW1Y 6HP.

MOTSON, John
John Motson. Commentator.
b. Hertfordshire, 10 July 1945.
TV: *Match of the Day;* BBC football commentator.
Address: c/o Marquee Group (UK) Ltd, 21 The Green, Richmond, Surrey TW9 1PX. m. Anne; 1 s. Frederick. Hobbies: Reading (particularly thrillers), running half-marathons, cinema.

MOUNT, Peggy
Peggy Mount. Actor (F) b. Leigh-on-Sea, 2 May 1917.
TV: Emma in *George and the Dragon; Lollipop Loves Mr Mole;* Ada Larkin in *The Larkins; What About Stanley?; Winning Widows; You're Only Young Twice.*
Films: *Hotel Paradiso; Oliver; The Ladies Who Do.*
Address: c/o The Richard Stone Partnership, 2 Henrietta Street, London WC2E 8PS. Hobbies: Gardening, cooking, knitting. Awarded OBE in 1976.

MOWRY, Tamara
Tamara Mowry. Actor (F). b. Gelhausen, 6 July 1978.
TV: Evil Chameleon in *Are You Afraid of the Dark?* (1992); Orangejella LaBelle in *Detention* (1999); Denise in *Full House* (1992); Tamara Campbell in *Sister Sister;* Roxanne in *Smart Guy* (1997); Emma C Squared in *The Adventures of Hyperman* (1995).
Films: The Twins in *Holywood Horror.*
Address: c/o Innovative Artists, 1999 Avenue of the Stars, LosAngeles, California 90067, USA. Sister Tia Mowry. Hobbies: Roller blading, ice hockey, street hockey, baseball, horse riding.

MOWRY, Tia
Tia Mowry. Actor (F). b. Gelhausen, 1978.
TV: Judith Ann Webb in *Dangerous Women* (1991); Lemonjella LaBelle in *Detention* (1999); Tia Landry in *Sister Sister.*
Films: The Twins in *Hollywood Horror.*
Address: c/o Innovative Artists, 1999 Avenue of the Stars, LosAngeles, California 90067, USA. Sister Tamara Mowry. Hobbies: Roller blading, ice hockey, street hockey, baseball, horse riding, double-Dutch rope jumping.

MULLANE, Dan
Dan Mullane. Actor (M).
TV: Joey Musgrove in *Brookside;* Young Man in *Chimera;* John in *Ghost Hour.*
Films: The Messenger in *Mighty Aphrodite.*
Address: c/o Kate Feast Management, 10 Primrose Hill Studios, Fitzroy Road, London NW1 8TR.

MULLIN, Lawrence
Lawrence Mullin. Actor (M).
b. Liverpool, Merseyside, 5 August 1953.
TV: *Anna Lee; Between the Lines; Bribes and Corruption; Brookside; Coronation Street; Dear Roy, Love Gillian;* Carl Edwards in *Degrees of Error; Doctor's Dilemmas; Heartbeat; Juliet Bravo; Peak Practice; Rocky O'Rourke; Stoker; The Bill; The Chief; The Endless Game; A Wing and a Prayer.*
Films: *Cuban Breeze;* Travel Agent in *Shirley Valentine.*
Address: c/o Hillman Threlfall, 33 Brookfield, Highgate West Hill, London N6 6AT.

MULLION, Annabel
Annabel Mullion. Actor (F).
TV: Emily Bowley in *A Christmas Carol;* Mona in *Dance to the Music of Time;* Felicity in *Jonathan Creek;* Martha Miller in *Kavanagh QC;* Jemma in *Mr White Goes to Westminster.*
Films: Mary Hutchinson in *Carrington;* Jane Dunbar in *Mission: Impossible.*
Hobbies: Scuba diving, swimming.
Address: c/o London Management, Noel House, 2–4 Noel Street, London W1V 3RB.

MULVILLE, Jimmy
Jimmy Mulville. Actor (M)/Presenter.
b. Liverpool, Merseyside.
TV: *Acropolis Now; Babylon 2;* Aulus Paulinus in *Chelmsford 123;* Philip in *GBH; Going Loco; Holiday '92; Holiday '98;* Derek in *Jake's Progress; Just for Laughs;* Donald Redfarn in *That's Love; The Brain Drain; The Hogmanay Show;* Rayner in *Underworld;*

Who Dares Wins.
Films: *Morons from Outer Space.*
Address: c/o Cassie Mayer Ltd, 34 Kingley Court, London W1R 5LE.

MURNAGHAN, Dermot

Dermot Murnaghan. Newsreader/Presenter/Reporter.
b. 26 December 1957.
TV: *A Whale of a Mess; Britain's Most Wanted; Business Programme; Channel 4 News; ITN Budget Special; ITV Nightly News; News at Ten; Porsche & Tears; Rolling News Service; The Big Breakfast; The Big Story; World News/Channel 4 Daily.*
Address: c/o ITN, 200 Grays Inn Road, London WC1X 8XZ. m. Maria Keegan; 3 d. Kitty, Molly, Alice.

MURPHY, Brian

Brian Murphy. Actor (M).
b. Ventnor, Isle of Wight, 25 September 1933.
TV: Lester Small in *L for Lester*; Greg Sproat in *All in Good Faith*; Buster in *Boon*; Mr Manners in *Brookside*; Walter Burnley in *Casualty*; Ugly Sister in *Cinderella*; Gowing in *Diary of a Nobody* (1964); Mr Woo in *Famous Five*; *Freddie Starr Show*; Bert in *Garnett on Gold*; George Roper in *George and Mildred*; Ken Speed in *Jonathan Creek*; Ansell in *Lame Ducks*; Ricky in *Laugh Until You Die*; George Roper in *Man About The House*; Arthur Capstick in *Mrs Merton and Malcolm*; Arthur Lucan in *On Your Way Riley*; Mr Foskett in *One Foot in the Grave*; Friend in *Paul Merton's Life of Comedy*; Sid in *Sunburn*; Ernest Tanner in *The Incredible Mr Tanner*; Truck Driver in *The Plank*; Stan in *Wizadora*.
Films: George Roper in *George and Mildred*; George Roper in *Man About The House*; Jack in *Sparrers Can't Sing*; Peter in *The Boyfriend*; Adam in *The Devils*.
Address: c/o Saraband Associates, 265 Liverpool Road, London N1 1LX.

MURPHY, Cathy

Cathy Murphy. Actor (F). b. 7 August 1967.
TV: Nurse Mary in *Amy*; Young Housemaid in *Bleak House*; Karen Knight in *Casualty*; Val Milburn in *Casualty*; Miranda McDipper in *December*; *Karaoke*; Lorna in *EastEnders*; Rita Baron in *Expert Witness*; Nurse O'Donnell in *Foreign Bodies*; Tilly in *French & Saunders*; Marion in *Poirot*; Janice in *Hero to Zero*; Tilly in *The House of Elliott*; Lois Loop in *Lucky Sunil*; Val in *Made in Britain*; Patsy in *Maisie Raine*; Sharon Elsworth in *May to December*; *Men Behaving Badly*; Vicky in *Minder*; Jonquil in *My Family and Other Animals*; *Oliver Twist*; Mary Mooney in *Once a Catholic*; *Real Women*; Kathy Dudley in *Rough Justice*; Bryony in *Rumble*; Shelley in *Screaming*; Small Pota-toes; Sharon in *Sorry*; Wendy in *Stanley and the Women*; Paulette in *Stars of the Roller State Disco*; Simone Foxall in *Streetwise*; Margaret in *That's Love*; *The Armando Iannucci Show*; Various in *The Bill*; *The Effects of Gamma Rays on the Man in the Moon*; *Marigolds*; *The Murder of Stephen Lawrence*; Miss Myers in *The Tenant of Wildfell Hall*; Carol in *Time Trouble*; Jane in *Your Place or Mine.*
Films: Linda in *A Love Child*; Cornelia in *AD*; Kerry Nurse in *Angela's Ashes*; Sally in *Captives*; Deborah in *Edge of Sanity*; Waitress in *London Suite*; Polly in *Moll Flanders*; Esta in *Phantom of the Opera*; *Tell Tale Heart*; Tubs in *Those Glory, Glory Days*; Bessie in *UFO.*
Address: c/o Elaine Murphy Associates, 310 Aberdeen House, 22–24 Highbury Grove, London, N52 EA.

MURPHY, Eddie

Eddie Murphy. Actor (M)/Comedian/Voice artist.
b. Brooklyn, New York, USA, 3 April 1961.
TV: *Saturday Night Live*; Superintendent Stubbs in *The PJs* (1999); *What's Alan Watching Now?.*
Films: Reggie Hammond in *48 Hours*; Reggie Hammond in *Another 48 Hours*; Landry in *Best Defense*; Alex Foley in *Beverly Hills Cop*; Axel Foley in *Beverly Hills Cop 2*; Axel Foley in *Beverly Hills Cop 3*; Marcus in *Boomerang*; Kit Ramsey/Jiff Ramsey in *Bowfinger*; Clarence/Prince Akeem/Randy/Watson/Saul in *Coming to America*; Dr John Dolittle in *Doctor Dolittle*; Himself in *Eddie Murphy Raw*; G in *Holy Man*; Rayford Gibson in *Life*; Scott Roper in *Metro*; Musha in *Mulan*; Sherman Klump/Buddy Love in *Nutty II: The Klumps*, Thomas Jefferson Johnson in *The Distinguished Gentleman*; Chandler Jarrel in *The Golden Child*; Sherman Klump/Buddy Love/Lance Perkins/Papa Klump in *The Nutty Professor*; Billy Ray Valentine in *Trading Places*; Maximillian/Preacher Pauly/Guido in *Vampire in Brooklyn.*
Address: c/o William Morris Agency, 151 El Camino Drive, Beverly Hills, California 90212, USA. Brother Charles. m. 2 Tamara Moore; 3 s. Miles Mitchell, Shane Audra (from 1st m.), Christian (from 2nd m.); 1 d. Bria (from 1st m.).

MURPHY, Glen

Glen Murphy. Actor (M).
TV: Mike in *Casualty*; *Doctor Who*; *First Love*; *Harry Carpenter Never Said …*; George in *London's Burning*; *Luna*; *Murphy's Mob*; *Prospects*; *Rockliffe's Babies*; *Scorpion*; *Seconds Out*; *Shine on Harvey Moon*; *The Bill*; *The Other 'Arf*; *Tucker's Luck*; *Up the Elephant and Round the Castle.*
Films: *Clockwork Mice; Cry Freedom; Empire State; Over Exposed; Tank Malling; Victor/Victoria.*

Address: c/o Hillman Threlfall, 33 Brookfield, Highgate West Hill, London N6 6AT.

MURPHY, Katy
Katy Murphy. Actor (F).
TV: Miss Toner in *Tutti Frutti*; Iashbal in *Normal Service*; *John Byrne Show*; *Hercule Poirot's Casebook*; Sarah in *The River*; Doreen in *The Steamie*; *Your Cheatin' Heart*; *Oranges are Not the Only Fruit*; *Up Yer News*; *Itch*; *Bobbing and Weaving*; Freddy in *Spatz*; *B & B*; *The Bill*; Francine in *Takin' Over The Asylum*; *Roughnecks*; Terri Morgan in *Dangerfield*; Denise in *A Mug's Game*; *Mike and Angelo*; *Rab C Nesbitt*; Mary Kee in *Rose – Two Lives*; Third Witch in *Shakespeare's Shorts – MacBeth*; Lucy in *Donovan Quick*; Cancer Nurse in *Nature Boy*; Angela in *Fish*.
Films: *Butterfly Kiss*.
Address: c/o CDA, 19 Sydney Mews, London SW3 6HL.

MURPHY, Sheree
Sheree Murphy. Actor (F). b. London.
TV: Florrie Smith in *Berkeley Square*; Joanne in *Dear Dilemma*; Trish in *Emmerdale*; Dawn in *Only Fools and Horses*; Lizzie in *The Bill*; Laura in *The Bill*; Amy in *The Stolen*.
Films: Hysterical Girl in *Box*; Victorian Child in *Salome's Last Dance*; Virginia in *Tales of a Vampire*.
Address: c/o The Narrow Road Company, 21–22 Poland Street, London W1V 3DD.

MURPHY, Tracey
Tracey Murphy. Actor (F). b. London, 21 April 1979.
TV: Clare Sullivan in *Grange Hill*; Charlotte in *Oliver Twist*; Kelly in *Reach for the Moon*; Sally Spence in *Ruth Rendell Mysteries*; Julie Sefton in *Scold's Bridle*; Isabel in *Sisters*.
Films: Jackie in *The Priest*; Nicola Foster in *Two Bacardis and Coke*; Helen in *Virtual Sexuality*.
Address: c/o PFD, Drury House, 34–43 Russell Street, London WC2B 5HA. Hobbies: Skiing, swimming, tennis, gym training, travel, reading.

MURRAY, Billy
Billy Murray. Actor (M). b. 21 September 1950.

TV: DS Don Beech in *The Bill*; Bill Boxley in *A Touch of Frost*; *Ruth Rendell Mysteries*; *Families*; *EastEnders*; *Bergerac*; *The Bill*; *Casualty*; *Minder*; *Marked Personal*; *Letty*; *Hazell Jemima Shore Investigates*; *Private Shultz*; *Crown Court*; *Target*; *The Rose Medallion*; *Grass*; *Dempsey and Makepeace*; *Family at War*; *Rock Follies*; *Missing From Home*; *Honky Tonk Heroes*; *Softly Softly*; *New Scotland Yard*; *Z Cars*; *Barlow at Large*; *Barney's Last Stand*; *Kids*; *Menace*; *The Silver Collection*; *The Long Sixpence*
Films: *Essex Boys*; *McVicar*; *Buddy's Song*; *My Two Left Feet*; *Lock Up Your Daughters*; *Performance*; *Up the Junction*; *Poor Cow*.
Address: c/o Annette Stone Associates, 2nd floor, 22 Great Marlborough Street, London W1V 1AF.

MURRAY, Bryan
Bryan Murray. Actor (M)/Presenter.
b. Dublin, 13 July 1949.
TV: Shifty in *Bread*; Trevor Jordache in *Brookside*; Mr Roberts in *Casualty*; Mr Roberts in *Holby City*; Own show; Harry Cassidy in *Perfect Scoundrels*; Fitz in *Strumpet City*; Flurry Knox in *The Irish RM*.
Films: Lynch in *Portrait of an Artist*; Ken in *Breakpoint*; Inspector Doyle in *Mrs Santa Claus*; Kieran Clanly in *Sparrows Trap*.
Address: c/o London Management, Noel House, 2–4 Noel Street, London W1V 3RB. m. Juliet; 4 d. Laura, Florence, Gracie, Eva; 1 s. Henry.

MURRAY, Cheryl
Cheryl Frayling-Wright. Actor (F).
b. Liverpool, Merseyside, 13 July 1952.
TV: *3-2-1*; *Billy Liar*; Fiona in *Brookside*; *Celebrity Squares*; Suzie Burchall in *Coronation Street*; *Crown Court*; *Dixon of Dock Green*; *Eleventh Hour*; *Hi De Hi*; *Live at the Lilydrome*; *Microbes and Men*; Dot Dooley in *Midnight at the Starlight*; Arabella in *Our Young Mr Wignall*; *Punch Lines*; Maria in *Rich Deceiver*; *Some You Win*; Jungle Jillian in *Sorry*; *Supernatural*; *That's Entertainment*; *Vienna 1900 – Games with Love and Death*; Julie in *Within these Walls*; Gillian in *Z Cars*; Mother in *Zigger Zagger*.
Address: c/o Nyland Management, 20 School Lane, Henton Chapel, Stockport SK4 5DG.

N

NAIL, Jimmy

Jimmy Nail. Actor (M)/Creator/Writer/Producer.
b. Tyneside, 16 March 1954.
TV: Oz in *Auf Wiedersehen, Pet*; Jed Shepperd in *Crocodile Shoes*; Schmidt in *Master of the Game*; Geordie in *Shoot for the Sun*; *The South Bank Show*; Spender in *Spender*; Wilmos Langfelder in *Wallenburg*.
Films: Tarik in *Crusoe*; Rabbetts in *Danny the Champion of the World*; Paul in *Dream Demon*; Agustin Magaldi in *Evita*; Boyle in *Just Ask For Diamond*; Desmond in *Morons from Outer Space*; Les in *Still Crazy*.
Music: *Ain't No Doubt*; *Crocodile Shoes*; *Crocodile Shoes II*; *Love Don't Live Here Anymore*.
Address: c/o ICM, Oxford House, 76 Oxford Street, London W1N 0AX.

NALLON, Steve

Steve Nallon. Actor (M).
TV: *Call My Bluff*; *C.A.T.S. Eyes*; *Crazy Cottage*; *Jonathan Creek*; *KYTV*; *Noel's Telly Years*; Voice overs (Queen Mother, Margaret Thatcher, Roy Hattersley) in *Spitting Image*; *Spooks*; *The Man from Auntie*; Margaret Thatcher in *The New Statesman*.
Films: *Dreaming*; *Frankie and Johnnie*; *The Girl With Brains In Her Feet*.
Address: c/o Eric Glass Ltd, 28 Berkeley Square London W1X 6HD.

NARASIMHAN, Meera

Meera Narasimhan. Actor (F).
TV: Conceptia in *All At Sea*; Nisha in *Back Up*; Meena in *Casualty*; Kelly Allen in *Dangerfield*; Anna Jones in *Exchange of Fire*; Mina in *In the Picture*; Kalsoom in *Moving Story*; Mira Choudry in *The Bill*; Kumari in *The Lodge*; Sundra in *Thief Takers*.
Films: The Girl in *Love Story*; Kuria in *The Ebb Tide*; Indhira in *The Potting Shed*; Jenny in *The Prom*.
Address: c/o The Narrow Road Company, 21–22 Poland Street, London W1V 3DD. Hobbies: Swimming, yoga, Indian classical dance, roller-skating.

NARDINI, Daniela

Daniela Nardini. Actor (F). b. 1967.
TV: *Art Is Dead Long Live TV*; *Big Women*; *Dr Finlay*; Luchia in *F.O.T.*; *Flying Blind*; *Not Necessarily*; *Reckless*;

Taggart; *Take the High Road*; Anna in *This Life*; *Undercover Heart*; *Your Cheating Heart*.
Films: *A Lonelier Place*; *Dancing*; *Elephant Juice*; *Sick (Tube Tales)*.
Address: c/o ICM, Oxford House, 76 Oxford Street, London W1N 0AX.

NAUGHTIE, James

James Naughtie. Presenter. b. 9 August 1952.
TV: *The Last Night of the Proms*; various opera.
Address: c/o BBC News Union House, 65–69 Shepherds Bush Green, London W12 8TX.

NEALON, Ben

Nealon Ben. Actor (M). b. 1967.
TV: Police Constable in *Between the Lines*; Richard Blencoe in *BUGS*; Luke in *Casualty*; Lieutenant Jeremy Forsythe in *Soldier, Soldier*; John Bell in *The Bill*; Andy Cheevers in *The Bill*.
Address: c/o Kerry Gardner Management, 7 St George's Square, London SW1V 2HX.

NEELY, Bill

Bill Neely. Presenter/ Reporter. b. 21 May 1959.
TV: *Breakfast Time* (1987); ITN news programmes; Sky News.
Address: c/o ITN, 200 Grays Inn Road, London WC1X 8XZ.

NEIL, Andrew

Andrew Neil. Presenter/Commentator. b. 21 May 1949.
TV: *Sixty Minutes*; *Dateline*; *Inside Edition*; *Is This Your Life*; *Look Here*; *Midnight Hour*; *Nationwide*; *Nightline*; *Risk Business*; *Tomorrow's World*.
Address: c/o Arena Entertainment, Regents Court, 39 Harrogate Road, Leeds, West Yorkshire. Hobbies: Dining out in London, New York, South of France and Aspen.

NEILL, Sam

Sam Neill. Actor (M). b. 14 September 1948.
TV: *Amerika*; *Fever*; *Hostage*; *Ivanhoe*; *Kane and Abel*; *Lucinda Brayford*; *Merlin*; *One Against The Wind*; *Reilly, Ace of Spies*; *The Blood of Others*; *The Sinking of the Rainbow Warrior*; *Young Ramsey*.

Films: *A Cry In The Dark; Ashes; Attack Force Z; Bicentennial; Dead Calm; Death in Brunswick; Enigma; Event Horizon; For Love Alone; From a Far Country; In the Mouth of Madness; Jurassic Park; Landfall; Memoirs of an Invisible Man; My Brilliant Career; Plenty; Possession; Revenger's Comedies; Robbery Under Arms; Snow White in the Black Forest; The Final Conflict; The French Revolution; The Good Wife; The Horse Whisperer; The Hunt for Red October; The Journalist; The Jungle Book; The Piano; Until The Ends of the Earth; Victory.*
Address: c/o ICM, Oxford House, 76 Oxford Street, London W1N 0AX.

NEILSON, David
David Neilson. Actor (M).
TV: Wainwright in *Bad Company; Bergerac; Bermuda Grace;* Geoff Woods in *Between the Lines; Blue Heaven; Boys from the Blackstuff;* Blair in *Buccaneers; Casualty; Chimera;* Roy Cropper in *Coronation Street;* Mr Webster in *EastEnders; Goodnight and God Bless; Hard Cases;* Barry in *Heartbeat;* Dacre in *Once Upon a Time in the North;* Millington in *Resnick; Soldiers Talking Cleanly;* Edgar in *Sons and Lovers;* Torchy in *Strangers; Survivors; The Bill;* Norman in *Young at Heart; Z-Cars.*
Films: *Career Girls;* Ashby in *Knights and Emeralds; Life is Sweet;* Jackson in *Mission Critical.*
Address: c/o Lou Coulson, 37 Berwick Street, London W1V 3RF.

NESBITT, James
James Nesbitt. Actor (M). b. 1965.
TV: *Ballykissangel;* Adam in *Cold Feet;* Tony in *Go Now;* John in *Playing the Field;* Bryan Casey in *Soldier, Soldier;* Dave Laney in *Touching Evil; Young Indiana Jones Chronicles.*
Films: *Beachy Head;* Fintan in *Hear My Song;* Uncle Joe in *Jude;* Gerald Clarke in *Jumpers; Loves Lies Bleeding;* Walter in *Thanks for the Memories;* Graham in *The James Gang;* Constable Hubert Porter in *This is the Sea;* Pig Finn in *Waking Ned;* Gregg in *Welcome to Sarajevo;* Stanley in *Women Talking Dirty.*
Address: c/o William Morris Agency (UK) Ltd, 1 Stratton Street, London W1X 6HB.

NESTOR, Eddie
Eddie Nestor. Actor (M).
TV: *Armed and Dangerous* (various); Max in *Black and Blue;* Cyril in *Casualty;* Eddie in *Chilling Out;* Clive in *Dempsey and Makepeace;* Cuthbert in *Desmonds;* Sendwala in *Escape from Kampala;* Harold in *Here and Now;* Ralph in *I'm In Charge Here;* Phil in *Midnight Breaks;* Ian in *Once upon a Time;* Sonny in

Sparks; The Real McCoy; Richard Adams in *The Stephen Lawrence Inquiry.*
Films: Pearce in *Face;* Estate Agent in *Trainspotting.*
Address: c/o Rolf Kruger Management Ltd, 205 Chudleigh Road, London SE4 1EG.

NETTLES, John
John Nettles. Actor (M)/Narrator.
b. St. Austell, Cornwall, 11 October 1943.
TV: *A Family At War; Airport;* Bergerac in *Bergerac; Black Beauty; Boon; Dickens of London; Disaster;* Commander Peter Gilpin in *Hands Across The Sea; Holding On; Reputations;* Lord Capulet in *Romeo and Juliet;* Jim Bergerac in *The Detectives; The Fourth Man; The Hunt; The Liver Birds; The Merchant of Venice;* Inspector Barnaby in *Midsomer Murders; The Phantom Tiger; The Tourist Trap; X-Cars.*
Address: c/o Saraband Associates, 265 Liverpool Road, London N1 1LX.

NETTLETON, John
John Nettleton. Actor (M). b. 5 February 1929.
TV: *A Wing and a Prayer* (1998); Commanding Officer in *Brideshead Revisited* (1982); Rev. Ernest Matthews in *Doctor Who* (1963); The Father in *East of Ipswich* (1986); Sir Francis Bacon in *Elizabeth R* (1971); Smith in *Fairly Secret Army* (1986); Doctor Hugo Swabey in *Rumpole of the Bailey* (1992); Palmer in *The Avengers* (1961); Major in *The Flame Trees of Thika* (1981); Minister in *The Professionals* (1977); Gonzalo in *The Tempest* (1980); Sir Arnold Robinson in *Yes, Prime Minister* (1984).
Films: General Douglas Gracey in *Jinnah* (1997); Minister for the Navy in *Longitude* (2000).
Address: c/o Trevor Ingman, 29 Whitcomb Street, London WC2H 7EP.

NEVILLE, Sarah
Sarah Neville. Actor (F).
TV: Becky Cairns in *Emmerdale;* Gilly Jones in *Annie's Bar; Cuts;* Marlene in *The Buddha of Suburbia;* Stella in *The New Statesman;* Penny Moore in *Stay Lucky;* Virginia in *A Fair and Easy Passage; Bergerac;* Carol Chapman in *Bust II;* Belinda in *A Perfect Spy; Hard Cases;* Carol in *Brookside; The Fourth Floor; Auf Wiedersehen Pet II; The Galactic Garden; Fainthearted Feminist;* Molly Sorrell in *Sorrell and Son;* Wendy in *Kids.*
Address: c/o The Narrow Road Company, 21–22 Poland Street, London W1V 3DD.

NEWMAN, Daniel
Daniel Newman. Actor (M). b. London, 1976.
TV: Steve Marsden in *A Touch of Frost;* Saffi's Child in

Absolutely Fabulous; Toby Skinner in *Back Up*; Hugo Botney in *Bonjour La Classe*; Martin Rydell in *Crown Prosecution*; Eddie in *EastEnders*; Ronnie in *Men of the World*; Tom in *Midsomer Murders*; Boy in *Our Tune*; Dean Turner in *Sometime Never*; Billy in *Speak Like a Child*; David Leigh in *The Bill*; Tommy Newsome in *The Bill*; Spiller in *The Borrowers*; Rick in *The Hello Girls*; Jason Savage in *The Lily Savage Show*; Matthew in *The Waiting Room*; Vince Wilson in *Touching Evil*.
Films: Ian in *Before the Rain*; Cozzer in *Down Amongst the Dead Men*; Paper Boy in *Dracula*; Tar in *Junk*; Elias in *Riddler's Moon*; Wulf in *Robin Hood: Prince of Thieves*; Monkey in *Shopping*; Philip in *The Life and Death of Philip Knight*; Smudger in *The Whipping Boy*.
Address: c/o CAM London, 19 Denmark Street, London WC2H 8NA.

NEWMAN, Nanette

Nanette Newman. Actor (F)/Presenter.
b. Northampton, 29 May 1939.
TV: *Going, Going, Gone*; *Ideal Home Cooks*; Jessie in *Jessie*; *Late Expectations*; *Let There be Love*; *More Calories please*; *Newman Meets …*; *Stay With Me Till Morning*; *The Mixer*; *The Mystery of Edwin Drood*; *TV-am*.
Films: *International Velvet*; *Seance on a Wet Afternoon*; *The Raging Moon*; *The Stepford Wives*; *The Wrong Box*.
Address: c/o Chatto & Linnit Ltd, 123a Kings Road, London SW3 4PL. m. Bryan Forbes; 2 d. Emma Forbes, Sarah.

NICHOLAS, Jeremy

Jeremy Nicholas. Actor (M).
TV: Gerald in *Birds of a Feather*; Tom in *Boon*; Sir John Sibley in *Bright Smiler*; John Maddingham in *Crossroads*; Nick Somers in *The Duchess of Duke Street*; Anthony in *Echoes of Louisa*; Colin Thomas in *Juliet Bravo*; Rodney Finch-Courtney in *King and Castle*; Berrington in *London's Burning*; Pelham Beecher in *Making News*; Hugo Rendell in *Mendip Mystery*; Tom Manners in *Mog*; Bob in *Outside Edge*; Vincent Boyd-Thompson in *People Like Us*; Jocelyn Gummer in *Prospects*; Michael Regan in *Rhinestone Cowboy*; Jeremy Jowling in *Rumpole of the Bailey*; Editor in *Stanley's Dragon*; Drunk in *The Bill*; Inigo Jollifant *The Good Companions*; Nathaniel Winkle in *The Pickwick Papers*; Bertram Potter in *The Tale of Beatrix Potter*; Simon in *The Upper Hand*; J in *Three Men in a Boat*; Frank Truett in *When The Boat Comes In*; Lewis Lake in *Wish Me Luck*; Anthony in *You're Not Watching Me, Mummy*; Geoff Devlin in *Z-Cars*.
Films: *Ishtar*; *Turtle Soup*; *Uncle Bob*.
Address: c/o Louise Hillman Associates, 33 Brookfield, Highgate West Hill, London N6 6AT.

NICHOLLS, Paul

Paul Nicholls. Actor (M).
b. Bolton, Lancashire, 1979.
TV: *City Central*; *Earthfasts*; Joe Wicks in *EastEnders*; *Out of the Blue*; *The Biz*; *The Passion*.
Films: *Love Story*; *Strong Boys*; *The Clandestine Marriage*; *The Trench*.
Address: c/o Roxane Vacca Management, 73 Beak Street, London, W1R 3LF. Hobbies: Skateboarding, basketball, kickboxing, football.

NICHOLLS, Phoebe

Phoebe Nicholls. Actor (F). b. 1958.
TV: Christabel Cavendish in *Blade on the Feather* (1982); Cordelia Flyte in *Brideshead Revisited* (1982); Empress of Lilliput in *Gullivers Travels* (1996); Intended in *Heart of Darkness* (1994); Judith Bendrix in *Second Sight* (1999).
Films: Polly Wright in *Fairy Tale a True Story*; Susannah in *Gentry*; Tina Argyle in *Ordeal by Innocence*; Elizabeth Elliot in *Persuasions*; Merricks Mother in *The Elephant Man*; Deborah Fitzbanks in *The Missionary*.
Address: c/o London Management, 2–4 Noel Street, London W1V 3RB. m. Charles Sturridge.

NICHOLLS, Sue

Sue Nicholls. Actor (F).
b. Walsall, 23 November 1943.
TV: Audrey Roberts in *Coronation Street*; Marlene in *Crossroads*; *Doctor On the Go*; *Heartland*; Lydia in *Jangles*; Brenda in *Not on Your Nellie*; Nadia Popov in *Rentaghost*; *Solo*; *The Duchess of Duke Street*; Joan Greengross in *The Rise and Fall of Reginald Perrin*; *Tycoon*; *Village Hall*; *Wodehouse Playhouse*.
Address: c/o Barry Brown & Partner, 47 West Square, London SE11 4SP.

NICOLSON, John

John Nicolson. Presenter/Reporter. b. Glasgow.
TV: *Assignment*; *Breakfast News*; *DEF II*; *Holiday*; *Newsnight*; *On the Road*; *Open to Question*; *Panorama*; *Public Eye*; *Watchdog*.
Address: c/o Knight Ayton Management, 10 Argyll Street, London W1V 1AB. m. Luis Buitrago Navarro. Hobbies: Travel, food, restoration of derelict houses.

NICOLSON, Steve

Steve Nicolson. Actor (M).
TV: DC Cottam in *A Touch of Frost*; Harry Hadaway in *Babes in the Wood*; Sam Pope in *Bergerac*; PC George Webb in *Between the Lines*; Patrick in *Big Bad World*; Carter in *Bye, Bye, Baby*; Steve in *Casualty*; DI Cloakes in *Comics*; Tim in *Dangerfield*; Dave in *Life*

After Birth; Mark Tapley in *Martin Chuzzlewit*; Peter Storey in *Out of Line*; Packer in *Rules of Engagement*; Adrian in *So, You Think You've Got Troubles*; Marine Green in *Soldier, Soldier*; Stanley in *Still Life – Tonight at 8.30*; DI Roberts in *The Bill*; PC Sachs in *The Chief*; *The Young Indiana Jones Chronicles*.

Films: Prince in *A Foreign Field*; La Foret in *All Men are Mortal*; Dinger in *Bravo Two Zero*; PC Harrison in *Let Him Have It*.

Address: c/o William Morris Agency (UK) Ltd, 1 Stratton Street, London W1X 6HB.

NIGHY, Bill

Bill Nighy. Actor (M). b. 1949.

TV: Hugh Marriner in *Absolute Hell*; Vincent Fish in *Agony*; Howard Nash in *Antonia and Jane*; Barry in *Bergerac*; Deasey in *Deasey's Desperate*; John in *Don't Leave Me This Way*; William in *Dreams of Leaving*; Conor Mullan in *Easter 2016*; Nick in *Fat*; Colin Street in *Fox*; Six Preachers in *God's Messengers*; Mark Gordon in *Insiders*; Claude Culpepper in *Kavanagh QC*; Ian in *Kiss Me Kate*; Alan Sinclair in *Peak Practice*; Goschen in *Reilly, Ace of Spies*; Bill in *Soldiers Talking Cleanly*; Tony in *South of the Border*; Bruno in *Standing In For Henry*; Tom Dickenson in *The Cat Brought It In*; Tom Frewen in *The Eye of the Storm*; Meares in *The Last Place on Earth*; Roger in *The Maitlands*; Mark Carleton in *The Men's Room*; *Thirteen at Dinner*; Dave in *Under the Skin*; Oliver Latham in *Unnatural Causes*; David Cole in *Wycliffe*.

Films: Julian in *Being Human*; AL Gardner in *Fairy Tale a True Story*; Helmut in *Hitler's SS*; Tristan in *Indian Summer*; Ray in *Never Better*; Barton in *Phantom of the Opera*; Ray Simms in *Still Crazy*; Count Bibuloff in *The Bass Player*; Al in *The Little Drummer Girl*; Tiger Brown in *The Threepenny Opera*; Hugh Matheson in *True Blue*.

Address: c/o Markham & Froggatt Ltd, 4 Windmill Street, London W1P 1HF.

NOAKES, John

John Noakes. Actor (M)/Presenter.
b. Halifax, 6 March 1934.

TV: *Blue Peter*; *Chips with Everything*; *Go with Noakes*; *Mad About Pets*; *Next*.

Address: c/o Arlington Enterprise Ltd, 13 Charlotte Street, London W1P 1HD.

NOAR, Amanda

Amanda Noar. Actor (F).

TV: Liz in *Boon*; Rose Finnegan in *Brookside*; Melanie in *Casualty*; Mary in *Coronation Street*; Lindsay in *Danger in Mind*; Natasha Glendenning in *Lovejoy*;

Maisy in *Nanny*; Donna in *Out on the Floor*; Helen in *Starting Out*; Norma in *Stay Lucky*; Susan in *The Benefit*; Susan in *Zero Option*.

Films: Kim in *I Bought a Vampire Motorcycle*; Marian in *The Frontline*; Biba's girlfriend in *The Return of the Jedi*; Vanessa in *The Unkindest Cut*.

Address: c/o The Narrow Road Company, 21–22 Poland Street, LondonW1V 3DD. Hobbies: Horse riding, dancing, swimming, singing.

NOBLE, Emma

Emma Noble. Actor(F)/Presenter.
b. Sidcup, Kent, 26 June 1971.

TV: *Casualty*; *Cold Lazarus*; *Exclusive*; *Jonathan Creek*; *Live 6 Show*; *Sports Talk*; *The Price is Right*; *This Morning*; *Tricky*.

Address: c/o Arcadia Management, 2–3 Golden Square, London, W1R 3AD. m. James Major.

NORDEN, Denis

Denis Norden. Presenter/Writer/Deviser.
b. London, 6 February 1922.

TV: *…On Television*; *21 Years of It'll Be Alright on the Night*; *40 Years of ITV Laughter*; *A Right Royal Song and Dance*; *Denis Norden's Laughter File*; *Denis Norden's Trailer Cinema*; *In On The Act*; *It'll Be Alright on the Night*; *Laughter By Royal Command*; *Looks Familiar*; *Pick of the Pilots*; *The Kids From Alright*; *The Utterly Worst of It'll Be Alright on the Night*; *Thirty Years of Laughter*.

Films: *Buona Sera*; *Every Home should Have One*; *Mrs Campbell*; *The Best House in London*; *The Bliss of Mrs Blossom*; *The Water Babies*; *Twelve Plus One*.

Address: c/o April Young, 11 Woodlands Road, London SW13 OJZ. m. Avril Norden.

NORMAN, Barry

Barry Norman. Presenter/Reporter.
b. London, 21 August 1933.

TV: *Barry Norman's Film Night*; *Film …*; *Hollywood Greats*; *Omnibus* (1982); *Seoul Olympics*; *Talk of the Eighties*; *Talking Pictures*; *The British Greats* (1980).

Address: c/o Curtis Brown, Haymarket House, 28–29 Haymarket, London SW1Y 4SP.

NORMAN, Samantha

Samantha Norman. Film reviewer/Presenter.
b. Hertfordshire, 28 December 1962.

TV: *Dial Midnight*; *Holiday Programme*; *Love Call*; *Party of a Lifetime*; *Stars in Their Eyes*; *The Ticket*; *This Morning*; *Travelogue*; *Weekend*.

Address: c/o Curtis Brown, Haymarket House, 28–29 Haymarket, London SW1Y 4SP. Father Barry

Norman, mother Diana Norman; 2 s. Harry, Charlie. Hobbies: Boxing, films, reading obituaries, children.

NORTON, Graham

Graham Norton. Actor (M)/Comedian/Presenter. b. Bandon, Ireland, 1963.
TV: *Bring Me the Head of Light Entertainment; Carnal Knowledge; Edinburgh Nights;* Father Noel in *Father Ted; Never Mind the Buzzcocks; Not the Jack Docherty Show; Pride Divide; Rock Babylon; So Graham Norton; The Coming Out Party; The Stand Up Show; Unzipped.*
Address: c/o TalkBack Management, 36 Percy Street, London W1P OLN.

NUNN, Judy

Judy Nunn. Actor (F).
b. Melbourne, Australia, 13 April.
TV: *Cop Shop; Holiday Island;* Ailsa Stewart in *Home and Away; Prisoner; Skyways; Sons and Daughters;* Vicky in *The Box; The Onedin Line.*
Address: c/o Seven Network Ltd, Mabbs Lane,

Epping, New South Wales 2121, Australia. m. Bruce Venables.

NUTKINS, Terry

Terry Nutkins. Host/Presenter. b. London.
TV: *Animal Magic; Attractions; Brilliant Creatures; Celebrity Squares; Change Your Life Forever; Diggit; Disney Club; Growing Up Wild; Mashed; Pets Win Prizes; Surprise, Surprise; The Really Useful Show; The Really Wild Roadshow; The Really Wild Show; Vintage Morris; Wake Up in the Wild Room; Zig & Zag.*
Address: c/o John Miles Organisation, Cadbury Camp Lane, Clapton in Gordano, Bristol BS20 7SB

NUTTER, Andrew

Andrew Nutter. Chef/Presenter.
TV: *Afternoon Live; Granada Reports; Mixing It; Quisine; Ready, Steady, Cook; Remote Control Cooking; Simply Baking; Slice of the Action; Super Chefs; Utter Nutter.*
Address: c/o Curtis Brown, Haymarket House, 28–29 Haymarket, London, SW1Y 4SP.

O

OAKLEY, Robin

Robin Oakley. Political editor/Guest panelist.
b. Kidderminster, Worcester, 20 April 1941.
TV: *BBC News; Call My Bluff.*
Address: c/o Knight Ayton Management, 10 Argyll Street, London W1V 1AB. Hobbies: Horse racing, theatre, birdwatching, sport.

OBERMAN, Claire

Claire Oberman. Actor (F). b. 1956.
TV: *Bottle Boys;* Vanguard in *BUGS; Fortunes of War (Mortimer);* Sandy Savage in *Gentlemen and Players;* Caroline Chetwyn in *Griffins;* Daphne Fairbrother in *Hi' De' Hi; Hunter's Gold; Joe and Koro;* Jane Partridge in *Ladies' Night;* Fiona in *Matlock; Mortimer's Patch; Motyhinhan;* Lonny Hope in *Paradise Postponed;* Kate Norris in *Tenko;* Kate Norris in *Tenko Reunion;* Martiana in *The New Adventures of Robin Hood; The Two Ronnies;* Sarah in *To Be the Best;* Alex Ferrel in *Trainer.*
Films: *Das Schone Ende Dieser Welt; Goodbye Pork Pie;* Lady Homes in *Patriot Games.*
Address: c/o Burnett Granger Associates, Prince of Wales Theatre, 31 Coventry Street, London W1V 8AS.

O'BRIEN, Conan

Conan O'Brien. Actor (M)/Writer/Host.
b. Brookline, Massachusetts, USA, 18 April 1963.
TV: *Late Night With Conan O'Brien; Saturday Night Live* (various); Himself in *The Simpsons;* Conan in *Spin City;* Himself in *Veronica's Closet.*
Address: c/o Gavin Polone, Huffin/Polone 9465, Wilshire Blvd, Suite 820 Beverley Hills, California 90212 USA. Hobbies: Guitar enthusiast, tap dancing.

O'BRIEN, Eileen

Eileen O'Brien. Actor (F).
b. Liverpool, 4 December 1945.
TV: Freda Dean in *Boys from the Blackstuff;* Gladys Charlton in *Brookside;* Ivy Pearce in *Casualty;* Celia in *Last of the Summer Wine;* Mrs Dovey in *No Bananas;* Eileen in *Rockliffe's Babies;* Aunty Kate in *The Life and Times of Henry Pratt;* Mrs Bradshaw in *The Life and Crimes of William Palmer;* Sheila Fitzsimmonds in *The Vice.*
Address: c/o Vivien Wilde Ltd, 193 Wardour Street,

London W1V 3FA. Sister Maureen O'Brien.

O'BRIEN, Peter

Peter O'Brien. Actor (M).
b. Murray Bridge, 25 March 1960.
TV: Tom in *Big Sky;* Martin Bridport in *Blue Heelers;* Cycil Smedley in *Cardiac Arrest;* Boris Osman in *Day of the Roses;* Richard Moreland in *Deceit; Gates of Janus;* Steve Elliot in *Halifax FP;* Guy Scott in *In Carol's Arm; Jackanory;* Tim in *Kangaroo Valley; Law of the Land;* Ric Da Silva in *Minty;* Shane in *Neighbours;* Detective Bowen in *Queen Kat Carmel & St Jude;* Cameron in *Queer as Folk;* Don Cassidy in *See How They Run;* Carl in *Spellbinder;* Bill Hamilton in *Taggart;* Sam in *The Flying Doctors;* Jack in *The Gift;* Jim in *The Henderson Kids; The New Alexei Sayle Show;* Detective Sergeant Coffee in *The Stonehouse Affair;* James Anderson in *The Trials of Oz;* Yann in *The Violent Earth;* Martin in *True Crimes; TV Squash;* Trevor in *Water Rats.*
Films: Nick Stevern in *A Kink in the Picasso;* John in *Entertaining Angels Unawares;* Norman in *Hotel de Love;* Dan in *Sally Marshall is Not an Alien;* Captain Robert Dayley in *The Mortal Coil.*
Address: c/o Emptage Hallett, 24 Poland Street, London W1V 3DD.

O'BRIEN, Richard

Richard O'Brien. Actor (M)/Host/Presenter/Writer.
b. Cheltenham, Gloucester, 25 March 1942.
TV: *A Hymn for Jim; Good Stuff; Notes and Queries;* Gulnar in *Robin of Sherwood; Rushton Illustrated; The Brit Awards; The Crystal Maze; The Detectives; The Dick Francis Thriller;* Ink Thief in *The Ink Thief.*
Films: Mr Hand in *Dark City;* Nilus in *Dungeons and Dragons;* Pierre Le Pieu *Ever After – A Cinderella Story;* Fico in *Flash Gordon;* Dr John Dee in *Jubilee;* Lord Hampton in *Revolution; Shock Treatment; Spiceworld;* Batch in *The Odd Job;* Riff-Raff in *The Rocky Horror Picture Show 1975;* James in *The Wolves of Willoughby Chase.*
Music: *Absolute O'Brien.*
Address: c/o Jonathan Altaras Associates, 13 Shorts Gardens, London WC2H 9AT.

O'BRIEN, Simon

Simon O'Brien. Actor (M)/Presenter.
b. Garston, Liverpool, 19 June 1965.
TV: Damon in *Brookside*; Damon in *Damon and Debbie*; *Fraggle Rock*; Phil in *Heartbeat*; *I Can Do That*; Tom Aszewski in *Liverpool 1*; *Move It*; Angus in *Out All the Night*; *Planet Football*; *Power Club*; *Rough Guides*; *Standing Room Only*; Paul Welsh in *The Bill*; Peter in *Young, Gifted and Broke*.
Films: Kav in *Dancin' Thru the Dark*.
Address: c/o Annette Stone Associates, 2nd Floor, 22 Great Marlborough Street, London W1V 1AF.

O'CALLAGHAN, Tony

Tony O'Callaghan. Actor (M).
b. London, 16 June 1956.
TV: *Jockey School*; *Murphy's Mob*; *Me and My Girl*; *Terry and June*; *Dempsey and Makepeace*; *Three Up, Two Down*; *Hannay*; *The Bill*; *Castle of Adventure*; *The Upper Hand*; *A Safe House*; *Children of the North*; *About Face*.
Address: c/o Scott Marshall, 44 Perryn Road, London W3 7NA. m. Siobhan.

O'CONNOR, Des

Des O'Connor. Presenter/Singer.
b. London, 12 January 1932.
TV: *Des O'Connor Tonight*; *Kraft Music Hall*; *Spot the Tune*; *Sunday Night at the London Palladium*.
Music: *1 – 2 – 3 – O'Leary*; *Careless Hands*; *Dick A Dum Dum*; *I Pretend*; *Loneliness*; *Skye Boat Song*; *Tips Of My Fingers*.
Address: c/o Lake-Smith Griffin Associates, 15 Maiden Lane, London WC2E 7NA.

OGILVY, IAN

Ian Ogilvy. Actor (M).
TV: *PS I Luv U*; *Who's the Boss*; *Generations*; *The Return of the Saint*; *Tom, Dick and Harriet*; *Maggie*; *Maigret*; *Over My Dead Body*; *B.L Stryker*; *Three of a Kind*; *Upstairs, Downstairs*; *The Spoils of Poynton*; *Candide*; *Man in the Zoo*; *30 Minute Theatre*; *Menace Unseen*; *I, Claudius*; *Man of Straw*; *Moll Flanders*; *Armchair Theatre*; *The Beaux Strategem*; *Lady Windermere's Fan*; *the Little Minister*; *Anna Karenina*; *Time for Murder*; *Robin Hood*.
Films: *Death Becomes Her*; *Revenge of the Blood Beast*; *The Day the Fish Came Out*.
Address: c/o Whitehall Artists, 125 Gloucester Road, London SW7 4TE.

O'GRADY, Elizabeth

Elizabeth O'Grady. Actor (F). b. 5 November 1982.
TV: Beth Morgan in *Hollyoaks*.

Address: c/o PHA Casting Management, Tanzaro House, Ardwick Green, North Manchester M12 6FZ.

O'HANLON, Ardal

Ardal O'Hanlon. Actor (M)/Presenter/Host/Comédian. b. Monaghan, Ireland.
TV: Eamon in *Big Bad World*; Father Dougal in *Father Ted*; George Sunday/Thermo Man in *My Hero*; *The Stand Up Show*.
Films: Bobby O'Hara in *Another Bobby O'Hara Story*; Johnny Eddy in *Flying Saucer Rock 'n' Roll*; *Moll Flanders*; Mr Purrel in *The Butcher Boy*.
Address: c/o Dawn Sedgwick, 3 Goodwins Court, London WC2N 4LL. m. Melanie; 2 d. Emily, Rebecca.

O'LEARY, Dermot

Dermot O'Leary. Presenter.
TV: *The Bigger Breakfast*; *The Groove*; *Buzz*; *For Better for Worse*; *Fully Booked*; *Inside Rugby*; *Light Lunch*; *No Balls Allowed*; *T4*.
Address: c/o John Noel Management, 10a Belmont Street, London NW1 8HH. Hobbies: Travel; cooking.

OLIVER, Jamie

Jamie Oliver. Chef/Presenter.
b. Southend, 27 May 1975.
TV: *Naked Chef*; *The River Café*.
Address: c/o Deborah McKenna Ltd, Claridge House, 29 Barnes High Street, London SW1 3LW. Fiancée Juliette Norton. Hobbies: Cooking, reading, drumming for his band 'The Scarlet Division', running, cookbooks, pasta and breadmaking, motorcycling.

OLIVER, Tom

Tom Oliver. Actor (M).
TV: *Bellbird*; *Ben Hall*; *Contrabandits*; *Division 4*; *Done Away With*; *Dynasty*; *Going Home*; *Good Morning Mrs Doubleday*; *Here's Dawn*; *Homicide*; *Hunter*; *I've Got a Secret*; *Is Anyone Doing Anything About It*; *Island of Light*; *King's Men*; *Matlock*; Lou Carpenter in *Neighbours*; *Number 96*; *Paul Temple*; *Playschool*; *Point of Departure*; *Riptide*; *Rush*; *Sergeant Musgrave's Dance*; *Silver Backed Brushes*; *Summer Affair*; *The Face of Dick Emery*; *The Group*; *The Right Thing*; *The Ronnie Stevens Show*; *The Shifting Heart*; *30 Minute Theatre*; *Thunderbolt*; *UFO*; *Woobinda*; *You Can't See Around the Corners*.
Films: *Adam's Woman*; *Colour Me Dead*; *Lady from Peking*; *The Nickel Queen*.
Address: c/o Grundy Television, Grundy House, Barge House Crescent, 34 Upper Ground, London SE1 9PD.

OLIVIER, Philip

Philip Olivier. Actor (M).

TV: Tinhead in *Brookside*; *Hearts & Minds*.

Address: c/o Mersey Television, Campus Manor, Chidwall Abbey Road, Liverpool L16 OJP. Hobbies: Horse riding, ice and roller skating, football and rugby, playing the drums.

OLRICH, April

April Olrich. Actor (F). b. Zanzibar, 17 July 1941.

TV: Pru in *Fresh Fields*; Arlette in *Maigret*; Désiree in *Robert's Robots*; *Robin Hood*; June in *Shaping Up*; Isadora in *She-Wolf of London*; Stepdaughter in *Six Characters*; Lucinda in *Teenage Health Freak*; Ivana Trump in *The Gallery*; Senna in *The Howerd Confessions*; *The Lieken Affair*; *The Punch Revue*; The Stripper in *The Seven Deadly Sins*.

Films: *Battle of the River Plate*; *Hussey*; *Macbeth*; *Princess Daisy*; Paula in *Riding High*; *Room at the Top*; *Seven Cities of Atlantis*; Oona in *Supergirl*; Petrovna in *The Intelligence Men*; *The Skull*.

Address: c/o Langford Associates, 17 Westfields Avenue, London SW13 0AT. m. 1 F.D.M. Williams (dis); m. 2 Nigel Pegram. Hobbies: Piano, clothes, swimming.

OLSEN, Gary

Gary Olsen. Actor (M). b. 1958.

TV: Ben Porter in *2point4 Children*; Tweedledum in *Alice Through the Looking Glass*; *Birth of the Beatles*; Geoff Robinson in *Boon*; Dr Michael Jimson in *Health and Efficiency*; PC Litten in *The Bill*; *Wilderness Road*; *Winter Flight*.

Address: c/o PFD, Drury House, 34–43 Russell Street, London WC2B 5HA. m. 1st Candy Davis, 2nd Jane; 1 s. Jake. Hobbies: Tennis, golf, aikido.

O'NEAL, Siri

Siri O'Neal. Actor (F)/Narrator. b. 1972.

TV: Sonia in *Artists in Crime*; *Jackanory*; Sandra in *Lovejoy*; *Masterclass*; Araminta in *Moondial*; Charlotte in *Press Gang*; Juanita in *Sharpe's Battle*; Linda in *Stay Lucky*; Allegra in *Summer's Lease*; Lizzie in *The Bill*; Bethany in *The Cloning of Joanna May*; Christine in *Wycliffe*.

Films: Helen in *An Urban Ghost Story*; Kate in *Jeopardy*; Judith in *The Children*; Suki in *The Rachel Papers*; Helen in *Waterland*.

Address: c/o Marmont Management Ltd, Langham House, 308 Regent Street, London W1R 5AL.

O'NEILL, Maggie

Maggie O'Neill. Actor (F). b. 1964.

TV: *Births, Marriages and Deaths*; *Blore MP*; *Defrosting the Fridge*; *Friday on My Mind*; Dr Amanda Tucker in *Invasion: Earth*; *He's Asking For Me*; *Hero Of The Hour*; *Take Me Home*; *The Life and Times of Henry Pratt*; *Theseus and the Minotaur*.

Films: *Gorillas in the Mist*; *The Artisan*; *Under Suspicion*.

Address: c/o PFD, Drury House, 34–43 Russell Street, London WC2B 5HA.

O'NEILL, Seamus

Seamus O'Neill. Actor (M).

b. Richmond, Yorkshire, 8 December 1952.

TV: *Coronation Street*; *Casualty*; *Band of Gold*; *New Voices*; *The Bill*; *Birds of a Feather*; *Roughnecks*; *Heartbeat*; *Berlin Break*; *Covington Cross*; Harry Travers in *Civvies*; Frank Johnson in *Families*; DC Caplan in *Prime Suspect*; *EastEnders*; *How We Used to Live*; *Brookside*; *Albion Market*; *Cops*; *Emmerdale*.

Address: c/o Myland Management, 20 School Londe, Heaton Chapel, Stockport, SK4 5DG. 1 d. Jennifer; 1 s. Liam. Hobbies: Horses, shooting, blues guitar, stand-up comedy

ONWUKWE, Ben

Ben Onwukwe. Actor (M).

TV: *Bandung File*; Peter Jason in *Bergerac*; Dr Bedi in *Between the Lines*; Greg in *Casualty*; Dr Asante in *Doctor at the Top*; Sean in *Growing Pains*; John in *Hard Cases*; Jefferson in *Inspector Morse*; Recall in *London's Burning*; *Slinger's Day*; *Splitting Up*; Ray Sage in *The Bill*; Steve in *The Biz*; Dr Grivas in *Waiting for God*.

Films: *American Roulette*; *The Chain*.

Address: c/o Barry Brown & Partner, 47 West Square London SE11 4SP.

OPACIC, Paul

Paul Opacic. Actor (M). b. Halifax, 1966.

TV: Weeks in *All in the Game*; Jet in *Birds of a Feather*; *Blind Date with Mr. Bean*; Mark in *British Slaves*; *Deptford Graffiti*; *Ellington*; Steve Marchant in *Emmerdale*; *Love Hurts*; Andrew in *Lovejoy*; Jeff in *Memento Mori*; Steve in *Men of the World*; Jules in *Only Fools and Horses*; PC Stemp in *Running Late*; DC Wickes in *Sam Saturday*; DI Crossley in *The Chief*; Dr Stevens in *The Queen's Nose*; Lt Pascal in *Young Indiana Jones Chronicles*.

Address: c/o Susan Angel Associates 1st Floor, 12 D'Arblay Street, London W1V 3FP. Hobbies: Tennis, cricket, rugby, football.

ORFORD, Richard

Richard Orford. Presenter/Reporter. b. 1971.

TV: *Blankety Blank*; *Find a Fortune*; *Members Only*; *Six O'Clock Show*; *Surprise, Surprise*; *That's Showbusiness*;

The Big Breakfast; The Disney Club; Holiday; The National Hockey League; The Truth About Men; This Morning.
Address: c/o Silver Fox Artist Management Ltd, Cameo House, 11 Bear Street, London WC2H 7AS. Hobbies: Golf, travel, films.

O'SHEA, Kevin
Kevin O'Shea. Actor (M).
b. Enfield, Middlesex, 7 March 1952.
TV: *Crime Monthly; Double Dare;* Max Hargreaves in *Grange Hill;* Calvin Turner in *Kelly Monteith;* Carl in *Second Thoughts; Secret Army;* Johannes Huit in *Shadow of the Noose; Spearhead;* Alienikoff in *Thank You Comrades;* Detective Sergeant Pete Phillips in *The Gentle Touch; The Professional;* Johnny in *We Think the World of You.*
Films: Pilot in *Dirty Dozen III;* Reginald Lee in *SOS Titanic;* Captain in *The Scarlet Pimpernel.*
Address: c/o CAM London, 19 Denmark Street, London WC2H 8NA. Hobbies: Horse riding, swimming, flying gliders.

OSOBA, Tony
Tony Osoba. Actor (M)/Narrator.
TV: Carlos Flores in *A Dance to the Music of Time;* Sultan Badral-din in *Arabian Nights; Between the Lines;* Security Chief in *BUGS;* Peter Ingram in *Coronation Street;* Jarvis in *Dempsey and Makepeace; Doctor Who;* Xicotenga in *Golden Years;* Byrne in *Gruey;* PC Kennedy in *Holby City; Lenny Henry Show;* Freddie in *Making News;* McLaren in *Porridge; Red Eagle; Resnick; Scotch and Wry; Snakes and Ladders;* Dave Cuffrey in *Taggart;* Lynagh in *The Bill; The Bureaucracy (Barrett); The Cage;* Smith in *The Demon Headmaster; Umbrella.*
Films: *Games for the Vultures; Porridge; Red Eagle; Return to Treasure Island; The Flame Trees of Thika; Who Dares Wins.*
Address: c/o Barry Brown & Partner, 47 West Square, London SE11 4SP.

O'SULLIVAN, Aisling
Aisling O'Sullivan. Actor (F). b. 1968.
TV: *Cracker; Life Support; Runaway One.*
Films: *Michael Collins; The American; The Butcher Boy.*
Address: c/o ICM, Oxford House, 76 Oxford Street, London W1N 0AX.

OUTHWAITE, Tamzin
Tamzin Outhwaite. Actor (F)/Presenter. b. 1971.
TV: Mel in *EastEnders;* Karen in *Men Behaving Badly;* Carol in *Tellermate;* Danielle Bannon in *The Bill; The Disney Club.*

Films: Flossie in *Princess in Love;* Young Lover in *The Mystery of Dr Martinu.*
Address: c/o George Heathcote Management, 58 Northdown Street, London N1 9BS. Hobbies: Dancing, roller skating, tennis, ice skating, skiing.

OWEN, Clive
Clive Owen. Actor (M). b. Coventry, 1966.
TV: *An Evening with Gary Lineker; Bad Boys; Chancer; Lorna Doone; Nobody's Children; Precious Bane; Return of the Native; Second Sight; The Magician.*
Films: *Bent; Close My Eyes; Split Second; The Darkening.*
Address: ICM, Oxford House, 76 Oxford Street, London W1N 0AX.

OWEN, Nicholas
Nicholas Owen. Presenter/Reporter.
b. 10 February 1947.
TV: *ITN's Budget Programme; Channel 4 News; Gulf War Midnight Special; Lunchtime News; The Parliament Programme.*
Address: c/o ITN, 200 Grays Inn Road, London WC1X 8XZ. m. 1 d. 1 s. 1 stepd. 1 steps. Hobbies: Trains, writer of history of the trolley bus.

OWEN, Nick
Nick Owen. Commentator/Host/Presenter.
b. Berkhamsted, Hertfordshire, 1 November 1947.
TV: *After the News; Beatles for Sale Auction; Club 22.45; Country Quest; Gardener's World – Live; Good Morning; Hitman Games Show; Midlands Today; North East Tonight; Royal Film Premier; Snooker; Sporting Triangles; Sports Awards; Streetwise; The Football Show; The Time, The Place; This Morning; TV-am; TV-am Sports;* Various News and Sports; *Wish You Were Here; World Cup 1982.*
Address: c/o Knight Ayton Management, 10 Argyll Street, London W1V 1AB.

OWEN, Sid
Sid Owen. Actor (M). b. 12 January 1972.
TV: *Bottle Boys;* Ricky in *EastEnders; Everybody Here; Hale and Pace;* Mick in *Jury; Shackelton; Timmy and Vicky; William Tell; Winter Break.*
Films: Young Ned in *Revolution.*
Address: c/o Sandra Boyce Management, 1 Kingsway, Albion Road, London N16 0TA.

P

PACE, Norman

Norman Pace. Actor (M)/Presenter/Comedian.
b. 17 February 1953.
TV: *A Pinch of Snuff; April Fool's Day; H&P@BBC; Hale & Pace; Jobs for the Boys; Oddbods;* Ron in *The Management.*
Address: c/o International Artistes Ltd, Mezzanine Floor, 235 Regent Street, London W1R 8AX. Hobbies: Horse-racing, fencing.

PACKER, Suzanne

Suzanne Packer. Actor (F). b. 1962.
TV: Barbara in *All Good Friends; Bowen;* Josie Johnson in *Brookside;* Siobhan Etienne in *Brothers and Sisters;* Candice Francis in *Casualty;* Rhiannon in *Dirty Work;* Miss Foster in *Grange Hill;* Helen in *Lifeboat; Megamaths;* Trish in *Porkpie;* Dr Jameson in *Some Kind of Life;* Veronica in *Strangers in the Night;* Catherine Adams in *The Bill;* Maria in *Tiger Bay.*
Address: c/o Kerry Gardner Management, 7 St George's Square, London SW1V 2HX.

PACKHAM, Chris

Chris Packham. Presenter/Naturalist.
TV: *Watch Out; Animal Zone; Disney's Animal Kingdom; Great African Wildlife Rescue; The Really Wild Show; Go Wild; Travel UK; Nature Detectives; Wildshots; Really Wild guide; The Good Sex Guide; The Great Dinosaur Trail; A Week in the Country, Flying Gourmets Guide; The Great British Birdwatch; Smokescreen; Beachwatch; Flamingo Watch; Heading South.*
Address: c/o Arlington Enterprises Ltd, 1–3 Charlotte Street, London, W1P 1HD. Hobbies: motor cars, art, literature, football.

PAGETT, Nicola

Nicola Pagett. Actor (F). b. Cairo, 15 June 1945.
TV: Liz Rodenhurst in *A Bit of a Do* (1988, 1989); Adele Fairley in *A Woman of Substance; Ain't Misbehavin';* Anna Karenina in *Anna Karenina; Blood of Lamb; Cock Hen and Courting Pit; Danger Man; Dangerfield; Dangerous Corner; Flowering Cherry; French Without Tears;* Catherine in *Hand in Glove;* Val in *Redundance – The Wife's Revenge;* Amanda Richardson in *Shadow of the Sun* (1988); *Take the Stage; The Persuaders; Uprising;* Elizabeth Bellamy in *Upstairs Downstairs;* Florence Maybrick in *Wicked Women.*
Films: Princess Mary in *Anne of a Thousand Days; Oliver's Story; Operation Daybreak; Privates on Parade; The Homecoming; There's a Girl in My Soup; Timeless Land.*
Address: c/o Gavin Barker Associates Ltd, 45 South Molton Street, London W1Y 1HD.

PALFREY, Lisa

Lisa Palfrey. Actor (F).
TV: Vilma in *Arrivederci;* Jane in *District Nurse;* Rebecca Longton in *Mind Games;* Kathy in *Out of Line;* Diane Saltmarsh in *Soldier, Soldier;* Lorna Doom in *Swigs;* Mam in *The Deadness of Dad;* Amy in *The Lord of Misrule;* Mother in *Thicker Than Water; Waking Up.*
Films: Mrs Nice in *Guest House Paradiso;* Gwenny in *House of America;* Jan in *Maybe Baby;* Michelle in *Oh Little Town of Bethlehem;* Christine in *Split Second;* Blod in *The Englishman Who Went Up a Hill and Came Down a Mountain.*
Address: c/o Marina Martin Associates, 12–13, Poland Street, London W1V 3DE.

PALIN, Michael

Michael Palin. Actor (M)/Reporter-presenter/Writer.
b. Sheffield, Yorkshire, 5 May 1943.
TV: *Around The World in 80 Days; Do Not Adjust Your Set; East of Ipswich; Full Circle;* Lead in *GBH; Michael Palin's Hemingway Adventure; Monty Python's Flying Circus; Number 27; Pole to Pole; Ripping Yarns; The Frost Report; The Two Ronnies; Tomkinson's Schooldays.*
Films: *A Fish Called Wanda; A Private Function; American Friend; Brazil; Fierce Creatures; Jabberwocky; Monty Python and the Holy Grail; Monty Python's Life of Brian; Monty Python's Meaning of Life; Time Bandits.*
Address: c/o BBC, Union House, 65-69 Shepherds Bush Green, London W12 8TX. Hobbies: Self-confessed 'dromomaniac' (travel addict).

PALLISTER, Kevin

Kevin Pallister. Actor (M). b. London.
TV: Graham Clark in *Emmerdale;* Duane Waverley in *Head over Heels.*

Films: Charlie Runnel in *Robin Hood*.
Address: c/o Emptage Hallett, 24 Poland Street, London W1V 3DD.

PALMER, Geoffrey

Geoffrey Palmer. Actor (M)/Narrator.
b. London, 4 June 1927.
TV: *A Little Rococo; A Midsummer Night's Dream; A Question of Attribution; A Story to Frighten the Children; Absurd Person Singular; After the War; As Time Goes By; Bergerac; Blackadder Goes Forth; Butterflies; Cheap Day; Churchill's People; Colditz; Death of an Expert Witness; Executive Stress;* Harry Truscott in *Fairly Secret Army; Fawlty Towers;* Sir Stanley Birkin in *Full Throttle; Games; Hot Metal; Inspector Morse; Maiden's Trip; Natural World; Radio Pictures; Reckless;* Bernard in *Season's Greetings; Smack and Thistle; Stalag Luft; Tales from the Riverbank; The Avengers; The Fall and Rise of Reginald Perrin; The Houseboy; The Inspector Alleyn Mysteries; The Insurance Man; The Legacy of Reginald Perrin; The Liberation of Eileen; The Professionals; The Scorpion Factor; The Shopper; The Sweeney; Waters of the Moon; Who is Sylvia?*.
Films: *A Fish Called Wanda; A Zed and Two Noughts;* The White King in *Alice Through the Looking Glass; Anna & the King; Clockwise; Hawks; Mrs Brown; O Lucky Man; The Honorary Consul;* Warren in *The Madness of King George; The Outsider; Tomorrow Never Dies*.
Address: c/o Marmont Management Ltd, Langham House, 308 Regent Street, London W1R 5AL.

PALMER, Toni

Toni Palmer. Actor (F).
b. London, 17 September 1932.
TV: *Bergerac; Cuckoo Sister; London's Burning; Mog; Only Fools and Horses; Paul Merton In...; Real Women; Return of the Antelope; Rumpole of the Bailey; The Bill; The Ghostbusters of East Finchley; The Rag Trade; Up the Elephant and Round the Castle*.
Films: *Ellis Island; Personal Services; Sir Henry at Rawlinson's End; Splitting Heirs; The Doctor and the Devils; The French Lieutenant's Woman; The Young Americans*.
Address: c/o Barry Brown & Partner, 47 West Square, London SE11 4SP.

PAPE, Daniel

Daniel Pape. Actor (M).
TV: Thug in *Battered Britain;* Boyfriend in *Mad for It; The Sunday Show*.
Address: Inter-city Casting, Portland Tower, Portland Street, Manchester M1 3LF. Hobbies: sports.

PAPILLON, Louise

Louise Papillon. Actor (F). b. Bristol, 4 May 1945.
TV: Wendy Stagg in *Bad Company;* Waitress in *Cruel Train;* Mrs Saltaire in *Dalziel and Pascoe;* Pathologist in *Dangerfield;* Mrs Hollies in *Good Health;* Mrs Spencer in *Just Us*.
Films: Agatha in *Pirates of Penzance*.
Address: c/o Magnet Personal Management, Unit 743, Big Peg, 120 Vyse Street, Birmingham B18 69F.

PARFITT, Judy

Judy Parfitt. Actor (F). b. Sheffield, Yorkshire.
TV: *Alice Through the Looking Glass; Daughters of the Colonel; Goodbye My Love; Guest of the Emperor; Jewel in the Crown; Post Mortem; Shoulder to Shoulder; Stormy Weather; The Charmer;* Edith Nesbitt in *The Edwardians; The Family Dance; The Ruby Ring; The Secret Orchard; Well, Thank You Thursday*.
Films: *Diamond Skulls; Dolores Claibourne; Even After Falling Through; Galileo; Hamlet; Maurice; The Chain; The Mind of Mr Soames; Wilde*.
Address: c/o Conway Van Gelder, 18–21 Jermyn Street, London SW1Y 6HP. m. Tony Steedman. Hobbies: Cooking, walking, talking, painting, interior decor, browsing antique shops.

PARIS, Dan

Dan Paris. Actor (M).
TV: Drew Kirk in *Neighbours*.
Address: c/o Grundy Television, Grundy House, Barge House Crescent, 34 Upper Ground, London SE1 9PD. Hobbies: Swimming, surfing, triathlon.

PARISI, Cliff

Cliff Parisi. Actor (M)/Creator.
TV: *A Bit of Fry and Laurie;* Dave Perry in *A Prince Among Men;* Gary Foster in *Bermuda Grace;* Preston in *Boon;* Daniel Bentley in *Bramwell; Can You Hear Me Thinking;* Lunchbox in *Chance; Darling Buds of May;* Edgar in *Dirty Dishes; Gone to Seed;* Stanley in *Gone to the Dogs;* Ken in *Growing Pains;* Vic Morrish in *Hero to Zero;* Tom Buckley in *Kavanagh QC;* Tony in *Kiss Me Kate; KYTV;* Mickey in *London's Burning;* Draper in *Longitude;* Jeff in *Our Boy;* Sproutt in *Paul Merton In... The Wrong Man; Pie in the Sky;* Plato Potatoes in *Pirates;* Marshall in *Reach for the Moon;* Tino in *Revolver; Sean's Show; Sharman;* Reggi Roach in *Sunburn II;* PC Todd in *Tales of Sherwood; The Bill;* Cliffy in *The Guilty; The Harry Enfield Show; The Paul Merton Series*.
Films: *Northern Crescent; Queen of Hearts; The Man Who Knew Too Little;* Policeman in *The Pleasure Principle;* Pub Waiter in *The Saint; The Wisdom of Crocodiles*.

Address: c/o CDA, 19 Sydney Mews, London SW3 6HL.

PARKER, Nathaniel

Nathaniel Parker. Actor (M). b. London, 1962.

TV: *A Village Affair*; *Absolute Hell*; *Away Day*; Tom Cranmer in *Dangerous Games*; David in *David*; Rob Hall in *Death on Everest*; Gabriel Oak in *Far From The Madding Crowd*. Ivan Lyon in *Heroes II*; *Inspector Morse*; *Look At It This Way*; *McCallum*; *Never Come Back*; *Piece of Cake*; *Poirot*; Lionel in *The Black Candle*; *The Vision Thing*; *Trust*; Rawdon Crawley in *Vanity Fair*; *Without Walls*; *Wizards*.

Films: *Beverly Hills Ninja*; Laertes in *Hamlet*; Thomas Dermer in *Indian Warrior*; Cassio in *Othello*; Clive in *The Bodyguard*; *Unsigned*; Wilfred Owen in *War Requiem*; Rochester in *Wide Sargasso Sea*.

Address: c/o ICM, Oxford House, 76 Oxford Street, London W1N 0AX.

PARKIN, Simon

Simon Parkin. Presenter. b. Manchester, 11 April 1967.

TV: *Alarm Alert*; *Broom Cupboard*; *But First This*; *CBBC 2*; *Chromazone*; *East Midlands Children in Need*; *Eat Your Words*; *Getaways*; *Go Getters*; *It's Not!*; *Junior Choice*; *Livetime*; *Midweek National Lottery Live*; *Now On Two*; *Parkin's In …*; *Parkin's Posse*; *Postcards*; *Rewind*; *The Early Years*; *The Listings*; *The O-Zone*; *Top of the Pops*; *Unwind*; *UP2U*.

Address: c/o David Anthony Promotions, PO Box 286, Warrington, Cheshire WA2 8GA. m. Celina; 1 d. Emily, 1 s. Charlie. Hobbies: Sleeping, eating, clearing up after children.

PARKINSON, Michael

Michael Parkinson. Host/Interviewer/Presenter/Producer/Reporter. b. Barnsley, 28 March 1935.

TV: *All Star Secrets*; *Auntie's All Time Greats*; *Ghostwatch*; *Give Us a Clue*; *Going for a Song*; *Parkinson*, (1971, 1998); *Parkinson – One to One*; *Parkinson: The Interviews*; *Parky*; *Teabreak*; *The Help Squad*; *The Michael Parkinson Show*; *The Movie Game*; *Twenty-Four Hours*; *Where in the World*; *World in Action*.

Address: c/o J W International, 74 Wimpole Street, London WIM 7DD. m. Mary Parkinson. Hobbies: Golf and cricket.

PARRY, Ken

Ken Parry. Actor (M).
b. Ince, Wigan, Lancashire, 20 June 1930.

TV: Snout in *A Midsummer Night's Dream*; Chef at Handyman Hall in *Blott on the Landscape*; Jack Crossley in *Children's Ward*; Benny Stone in *Coronation Street*; Fat Man in *Crime Story*; Leo Dolman in *Crossroads*; Spurty in *Filthy Rich and Catflap*; Vicar in *Good Sex Guide*; Mr B Bumble in *Honey for the Prince*; God in *Medieval Mystery Plays*; Madhouse Keeper in *Nicholas Nickleby*; Mr Vainridden in *Oliver Twist*; Madame Noel in *Saracen*; Norman in *Seeing a Beauty Queen Home*; Mr Arbuthnot in *The Avengers*; Marty Cranwell in *The Baron*; Royston Bloat in *The House of Windsor*; Old Gobbo in *The Merchant of Venice*; Mr Pickwick in *The Pickwick Papers*; Judge in *The Rose Garden*; Fat Eric in *The Sweeney*; Minion in *The Young Ones*; *Z-Cars*.

Films: Charlie in *A Hole Lot of Trouble*; Barclay in *Benjamin Franklin*; Potsnap in *Come Play with Me*; Thomas in *Hawk the Slayer*; Sykes in *Lifeforce*; Rossini in *Lisztomania*; Mr Orchestra in *Sherlock Holmes' Smarter Brother*; Pawnbroker in *Spring and Port Wine*; Dr Beulea in *Start the Revolution Without Me*; The Porter in *That's Your Funeral*; John the Carpenter in *The Miller's Tale*; Snow in *The Rainbow Thief*; Tailor in *The Taming of the Shrew*.

Address: c/o PBR Management, 26 Foubert's Place, Regent Street, London W1V 1HG. Hobbies: Listening to good music, reading, clairvoyance.

PARRY, Vivien

Vivien Parry. Actor (F).

TV: Reception Nurse in *A Separate Peace*; Gracey in *About Face*; Sally Reynolds in *Aquila*; Valerie in *Bodyguards*; *Chimera*; Sergeant McPhearson in *EastEnders*; Hotel Receptionist in *Lovejoy*; Josie in *Medics*; Angela in *Take Me Home*; Pauline Parker in *The Bill*.

Address: c/o CCA Management, 7 St George's Square, London SW1V 2HX.

PARSONS, Nicholas

Nicholas Parsons. Actor (M)/Presenter.
b. Grantham, Lincolnshire, 10 October 1928.

TV: *Alphabet Quiz*; *Laughlines*; *Sale of the Century*; *The Benny Hill Show*.

Films: *Don't Raise the Bridge Lower the River*; *Spy Story*.

Address: c/o Arena Entertainment, Regents Court, 39 Harrogate Road, Leeds, West Yorkshire. Hobbies: Cricket, golf.

PARTRIDGE, David

David Partridge. Actor (M). b. Salisbury, Wiltshire.

TV: Dr David Scobie in *Always and Everyone*; Biff in *Death of a Salesman*; DS Ben Dalton in *The Bill*; Simon in *The Vice*.

Films: Simpson in *The Browning Version*.

Address: c/o Ken McReddie Ltd, 91 Regent Street, London W1R 7TB.

PASCO, Richard

Richard Pasco. Actor (M). b. London, 18 July 1926.
TV: *Bramwell; Dance to the Music of Time; Drummonds; Hannay; Hetty Wainthropp Investigates; Inspector Morse; Kavanagh QC; Sorrel & Son; The Absence of War; The Man from the Pru.*
Films: *A Watcher in the Woods; Arch of Triumph; Hot Enough for June; Lady Jane; Mrs Brown; Rasputin; Room at the Top; The Gorgon; Wagner; Yesterday's Enemy.*
Address: c/o Whitehall Artists, 125 Gloucester Road, London SW7 4TE.

PATERSON, Bill

Bill Paterson. Actor (M). b. 1945.
TV: *Auf Wiedersehen, Pet; Boon;* Mole in *Dutch Girls;* Victor in *God's Chosen Car Park;* Stephen Blackpool in *Hard Times; It's My City; Licking Hitler;* Colin in *Lily My Love;* Cameron in *Melissa;* Mr White in *Mr White Goes to Westminster;* Baxter in *Oliver's Travels; One of Ourselves;* Mr Mildew in *Out of Sight;* Matt Hennessey in *Shrinks; Smiley's People; Stan's Last Game;* Anthony Steadman in *Tell Tale Hearts; The Cherry Orchard; The Cheviot, The Stag and the Black Black Oil;* Kenneth in *The Crow Road; The Ghostbusters of East Finchley;* Chase in *The Interrogation of John; The Lost Tribe;* Sir Nicol McLean in *The Secret Adventures of Jules Verne; The Singing Detective;* The Producer in *The Story of a Recluse;* James Webb in *The Turnaround; The Vanishing Army;* Bull in *The Writing on the Wall; Traffick; United Kingdom; Wall of Silence;* Mr Gibson in *Wives and Daughters; Yellowbacks.*
Films: Wormold in *A Private Function;* Baron Munchausen; *Charlie; Comfort and Joy;* MacLeod in *Defence of the Realm;* Sullivan in *Friendship's Death;* Kreitman in *Heart;* Anthony in *Hidden City;* Bill Pleeth in *Hilary and Jackie;* Ratcliffe in *Richard III;* Café Owner in *Spice Girls – The Movie;* Minister of Justice in *Sunshine;* Jordan in *The Bearskin;* McIntyre in *The Killing Fields;* Tommy in *The Match; The Object of Beauty; The Ploughman's Lunch; The Rachel Papers;* Charles I in *The Return of the Musketeers;* Father in *The Witches;* Sandy in *Truly, Madly, Deeply;* Captain in *Victory.*
Address: c/o Marina Martin Associates, 12–13 Poland Street, London W1V 3DE.

PATRICK, Anna

Anna Patrick. Actor (F).
TV: *Broken English; Inspector Morse; Maisie;* Vicki in *Rachel's Dream; Reckless;* Julia Lawson in *She's Out; Sixth Sense; South of the Border; Top Girls;* Linda in *You, Me and It.*
Films: Aphrodite in *A Little Loving; A Short Cut; An Ideal Husband;* Emilia in *Othello.*

Address: c/o Roxane Vacca Management, 73 Beak Street, London W1R 3LF.

PAUL, Andrew

Andrew Paul. Actor (M). b. 17 March 1961.
TV: *After Image; Barnet; Don't Wait Up; Gentlemen and Players; Goin' Out; Help: The Setbacks; Inspector Morse; Missing Persons; Mrs Capper's Birthday; Out; Out of Tune; Sizzler; Slinger's Day; The Bill; Time of My Life; Timmy and Vicky; Tripper's Day; Vote For Hitler; Vote for Them.*
Films: *Bellman and True; Scum; The Pirates of Penzance.*
Address: c/o Scott Marshall, 44 Perryn Road, London W3 7NA.

PAXMAN, Jeremy

Jeremy Paxman. Presenter/Reporter.
b. Leeds, Yorkshire, 11 May 1950.
TV: *Breakfast News; Called To Account; Newsnight; Panorama; Six O'Clock News; Tonight; University Challenge; You Decide With Paxman.*
Address: c/o BBC, Union House, 65–69 Shepherds Bush Green, London W12 8TX. Hobbies: Fly-fishing.

PAYNE, Tris

Tristan Payne. Host/Presenter. b. 1968.
TV: *Family Pet; Homemaker; House Doctors; Night Time; On Foot with Tristan Payne; Overdrive; Pet Rescue; Pet Roadshow; The Car Show; Weekly Echo; Wish You Were Here.*
Address: c/o John Noel Management, 10a Belmont Street, London NW1 8HH. Hobbies: Horse riding, cycling, swimming, hiking, everything Italian.

PEACE, Heather

Heather Peace. Actor (F).
b. Bradford, West Yorkshire, 16 June 1975.
TV: *The Bill; Dangerfield;* Miss Cullen in *Emmerdale;* Sally Fields in *London's Burning.*
Address: c/o Cassie Mayer Ltd, 34 Kingley Court, London W1R 5LE. Hobbies: music, football, most sports, eating out, cooking, guitar, piano.

PEACOCK, Daniel

Daniel Peacock. Actor (M)/Writer/Director.
TV: *Anything's Possible; Bang Liberty; Chest;* Dad in *Diary of a Teenage Health Freak; Girlfriends; Hanger 17; Jackson Pace: The Great Years; Life, Love and Everything;* Gilby in *Men of the World; Mud; Sister Said; The Comic Strip Presents ...The Yob; The Museum Thing; Very Big, Very Soon.*
Films: Tonto the Torch in *Carry On Columbus;* Terence in *Eat the Rich;* Youth in *Gandhi;* Buzzer in *I Bought a Vampire Motorcycle;* Rock Promoter in *Jewel*

of the Nile; Toby in *Party Party;* Rudge in *Porridge;* Danny in *Quadrophenia;* Bull in *Robin Hood;* Jim Jarvis in *Supergrass;* Dominic in *Whoops Apocalypse.* Address: c/o JM Associates, 77 Beak Street, London W1R 3LF. Father: Trevor Peacock.

PEACOCK, Trevor

Trevor Peacock. Actor (M). b. 19 May 1931.
TV: Old Joe in *A Christmas Carol;* Crook in *Bejewelled;* Dr Sinclair Lewis in *Boon; Born and Bred;* Jack Cade in *Henry VI (Part I);* Talbot in *Henry VI (Part II);* Jacom in *Highlander;* Old Bailey in *Neverwhere;* Chorus in *Oedipus at Colonus;* Boult in *Pericles;* Trevor in *The Gift;* Fatha Wanka in *The Gravy Train Goes East;* Matthew Skipps in *The Lady's Not for Burning;* Trotti in *The Vicar of Dibley;* Titus in *Titus Andronicus;* Feste in *Twelfth Night;* Dad Middlemass in *Underworld.*
Films: Taxi Thief/AD Humphries in *Antonia and Jane;* Iaccoponi in *Roseanna's Grave;* Examining Magistrate in *The Trial.*
Address: c/o BBC, Union House, 65–69 Shepherds Bush Green, London W12 8TX. s. Daniel Peacock.

PEAKE, Maxine

Maxine Peake. Actor (F). b. Lancashire.
TV: Belinda Peach in *Coronation Street;* Twinkle in *dinnerladies;* Sharon Wilkinson in *Girls' Night;* Caroline in *Hetty Wainthropp Investigates;* Marion Cretiss in *Jonathan Creek;* Lucy in *Picking Up the Pieces;* Sue in *Sunburn;* Marie in *The Factory;* Geraldine Evans in *The Ward.*
Address: c/o Burnett Granger Associates, Prince of Wales Theatre, 31 Coventry Street, London W1V 8AS.
Hobbies: Horse-riding, football, rugby, swimming.

PEARCE, Joanne

Joanne Pearce. Actor (F).
TV: *For the Greater Good; Jumping the Queue; Lovejoy; Reilly, Ace of Spies; Shakespeare Workshop; Silent Witness; The Comedy of Errors; The Two Gentleman of Verona; Way Upstream.*
Films: *Morons from Outer Space; Murder East, Murder West; Whoops Apocalypse.*
Address: c/o ICM, Oxford House, 76 Oxford Street, London W1N 0AX.

PEARSON, Neil

Neil Pearson. Actor (M). b. 1959.
TV: *Bell Run; Between the Lines; Bostock's Cup; Chelmsford 123; Dirty Work; Drop the Dead Donkey; Eskimos Do It; Feverpitch; Heaven on Earth; Intimate Contact;*

Les Girls; Mystery of Men; Oi for England; Rhodes; Secret Rapture; See You Friday; Submariners; Gary in *That's Love; The Magician's House; This is David Lander; Upline.*
Films: *Privates on Parade.*
Address: c/o ICM, Oxford House, 76 Oxford Street, London W1N 0AX.

PEART, David

David Peart. Actor (M).
TV: Dr Weatherhead in *A Wing and a Prayer;* Doorman in *BUGS;* Ted Cooper in *Coronation Street;* Consultant in *Dalziel and Pascoe;* Mr Unpleasant in *Extremely Dangerous;* Police Sergeant in *Hot Metal;* Footman in *Jeeves and Wooster;* Steve Longford in *Johnny and the Dead;* Undertaker in *London's Burning;* Governor in *Nelson's Column;* Jehovah's Witness in *One Foot in the Grave;* Assistant Commissioner in *Open Fire;* University Don in *Silent Witness;* Fire Officer in *The Bill;* Tango Two in *The Knock;* Coroner in *Uninvited.*
Address: c/o Waring & McKenna, Lauderdale House, 11 Gower Street, London WC1E 2HB.

PEASGOOD, Julie

Julie Peasgood. Actor (F).
TV: *Alas Smith and Jones; Beaux Strategem; The Bill; Boon; Brookside; Brush Strokes; BUGS; Chains of Love; Chandler & Co; Cherryripe and the Lugworm; Clayhanger; Dancers – Feel Free; Digger;* Jo in *Emmerdale; First Born; Five Red Herrings; Good Sex Guide; Imaginary Friends; The Law Centre; Luv; Men of the World; Mountain Men; Murder Most Horrid; The Optimist; Perfect Scoundrels; September Song; Seven Faces of Woman; Simisola; Small World; Spender; Survivors; Taggart; 10 Percenters; This Year, Next Year; 2point4children; Van der Valk; Whistling Wally; A Woman's Guide to Adultery.*
Films: *The House of the Long Shadows; The Lake.*
Address: c/o Scott Marshall, 44 Perryn Road, London W3 7NA.

PECK, Brian

Brian Peck. Actor (M)/Storyteller. b. Hull, Yorkshire.
TV: *An Englishman's Castle; Codename; Coronation Street; Crossroads; Dixon of Dock Green; Gracie; Hell's Bells;* Will Mossop in *Hobson's Choice; Jackanory; Killers; Last of the Summer Wine; London's Burning; Minder;* Smike in *Nicholas Nickleby; Ride on the Donkeys;* Rigsby's Brother in *Rising Damp; SAB; Six Days of Justice; Softly, Softly; Sorry; The Bill; The Dragon's Opponent; The Exiles; The Long Street; This Happy Breed; Trial; Walk on the Grass; Z Cars.*
Films: *Christopher Columbus; Echo of Barbara; Quatermass and the Pit; Seven Keys; Star; Tarnished Heroes;*

Peter Joe in *The Adventures of Peter Joe*; *The Pit and the Pendulum*; *The Set Up*; *Twisted Nerve*.
Address: c/o PBR Management, 26 Foubert's Place, London W1V 1HG. m. Jennifer Wilson; 1 d. Melanie. Hobbies: Gardening, collecting paintings and antiques.

PECK, Ian
Ian Peck. Actor (M).
TV: *A Touch of Frost*; Phillips in *Bombe*; *Brighton Boy*; *Captives*; *Class Act*; *Dangerfield*; *Food For Love*; Fred in *Stanley's Dragon*; *The Bill*; *The Day Today*; *The Legacy of Reginald Perrin*; *The Merrihill Millionaires*; *Wokenwell*.
Address: c/o Susan Angel Associates, 1st Floor, 12 D'Arblay Street, London W1V 3FP.

PEEBLES, Alison
Alison Peebles. Actor (F).
TV: Moira McNulty in *Albert and the Lion*; Sarah Petersen in *Casualty*; Inez in *Inez De Castro*; Linda in *Miles is Better*; Anne Cowan in *Psychos*; Miss Danvers in *Rab C Nesbitt*; Pheemie in *Strathblair*; Arm Fairley in *Taggart*; Isla McLenn in *Taggart*; Vivien Liddell in *The Advocate*; Betsy Bourke in *The Final Cut*; DCI Robertson in *The Priest and the Pirate*.
Films: Mrs McDougall in *Braveheart*; Nancy in *Bumping the Odds*; Fran in *Mirror/Mirror*; Mother in *The Acid House Trilogy*; Auntie Betty in *The Star*; Reporter in *Witches*.
Address: c/o Vivien Wilde Ltd, 193 Wardour Street, London W1V 3FA.

PEEL, Edward
Edward Peel. Actor (M).
TV: *London's Burning*; *Casualty*; *Emmerdale*; *Cracker*; *The Bill*; *Underbelly*; *Watt on Earth*; *F.L.I.P.*; *Castle of Adventure*; *Eurocops*; *A Wanted Man*; *Doctor Who*; *Truckers*; *Coast to Coast*; *By the Sword Divided*; *Juliet Bravo*; *The Fourth Arm*; *The Grudge Fight*; *Pillion*; *The Comedians*; *Boys from the Black Stuff*.
Films: *The First Kangaroos*; *Shogun*; *Caleb Williams*; *Britannia Hospital*; *A Nightingale Sang in Berkeley Square*; *Star Wars: The Empire Strikes Back*.
Address: c/o The Narrow Road Company, 21–22 Poland Street, London, W1V 3DD. Hobbies: Marathon running.

PEERS, Kerry
Kerry Peers. Actor (F).
TV: Christine in *Chimera*; *September Song*; WDC Suzi Croft and Jenny in *The Bill*; Linda in *The Marshall and the Madwoman*; Tracy in *The Touch*; Angharad in *We are Seven*; *Where the Heart Is*; *With Two Lumps of Ice*.

Address: c/o Roxane Vacca Management, 73 Beak Street, London W1R 3LF.

PEGG, Simon
Simon Pegg. Actor (M)/Writer.
b. Bristol, 14 February 1970.
TV: *Big Train*; Ray in *Hippies*; Jools in *Faith in the Future*; Justin Pope in *Randall and Hopkirk (Deceased)*; Tim in *Spaced*.
Films: Mr Nice in *Guest House Paradiso*; *Laugh Until You Die*; Bank Teller in *Tube Tales*.
Address: c/o Dawn Sedgwick, 3 Goodwins Court, London WC2N 4LL. Hobbies: Music, films, science fiction, snowboarding.

PEGRAM, Nigel
Nigel Pegram. Actor (M).
TV: *Can We Get On Now Please?*; *Capital City*; Mr Elton in *Crown Prosecution*; *Diana – Her True Story*; *Drop the Dead Donkey*; *Fresh Fields*; *Get Some In*; *Hinckley House*; *Leave it to Charlie*; Mervyn Griffith-Jones QC in *Look of Love*; *Lovejoy*; Doctor in *Melissa*; *Metal Mickey*; *Never Come Back*; *Newshounds*; Nigel in *Outside Edge*; *Pulaski*; Headmaster in *Renford Rejects*; *Robert's Robots*; Owen Struther in *Ruth Rendell Mysteries – Inspector Wexford*; *South by South East*; *Squaring the Circle*; *The Front Line*; *The Gibraltar Inquest*; *The Inquest of Neil Aggett*; *The Other One*; *The Professionals*; *The Singing Detective*; *The Tomorrow People*; *Tom, Dick & Harriet*; *Under the Hammer*; *Van Der Valk*.
Films: *Charles & Diana – A Royal Love Story*; Father Bridgley in *Driven*; *Funny Money*; *Power of One*; *Princess Daisy*; Dr Shelley in *Proteus*; *Split Second*; Willa Westinghouse in *The American Way*.
Address: c/o Associated International Management, 5 Denmark Street, London WC2H 8LP.

PELKA, Kazia
Kazia Pelka. Actor (F). b. Dewsbury, Yorkshire, 1961.
TV: Anna Wolska in *Brookside*; *Coronation Street*; *Full House*; Maggie Bolton in *Heartbeat*; *How We Used To Live*; *Rides*; *Space Precinct*; *The Chief*; *Think About Science*; *Urban Jungle*.
Films: *Dirty Dozen*.
Address: c/o Conway Van Gelder, 18–21 Jermyn Street, London SW1Y 6HP.

PELLEGRINO, Vince
Vince Pellegrino. Actor (M). b. 1967.
TV: Derek 'Sunny' Sunderland in *Casualty* and *Holby City*; Snotter in *Crocodile Shoes*; *Dalziel and Pascoe*; Sam in *Famous Five*; Specko in *Lenny Henry Show*;

Grange in *Out of the Blue*; DC Kerly in *Pie in the Sky*; Ian Phillips in *The Bill*; Chris in *Where the Heart Is.*
Films: Terry in *Peggy Sue*; *The Fifth Element.*
Address: c/o The Narrow Road Company, 21–22 Poland Street, London W1V 3DD.

PEMBERTON, Steve

Steve Pemberton. Actor (M)/Writer.
b. 1 September 1967.
TV: Mosolov in *Alice in Russialand*; *Barking*; *Friday Night Armistice*; *In the Red*; *Lenny Goes to Town*; *Smith and Jones*; *The League of Gentlemen*; *Gormenghast*; *Randall and Hopkirk (Deceased)*..
Films: *This Year's Love.*
Address: c/o PBJ Management, 5 Soho Square, London W1V 5DE.

PENHALIGON, Susan

Susan Penhaligon. Actor (F). b. Manila, 3 July 1949.
TV: *A Fine Romance*; *A Kind of Loving*; *Bergerac*; Pru in *A Bouquet of Barbed Wire*; *Brassnecks*; *Casualty*; *Doctor Who*; *Dracula*; *Fearless Frank*; Natalie in *Heart of the Country*; *Ruth Rendell Mysteries*; *Seven Faces of Women*; *Tales of the Unexpected*; *Upstairs Downstairs*; *Wycliffe.*
Films: *No Sex Please, We're British*; *Private Road*; *Survival Run*; *The Land That Time Forgot*; *The Last Chapter*; Mae Rose Cottage in *Under Milk Wood.*
Address: c/o Conway Van Gelder, 18–21 Jermyn Street, London SW1Y 6HP. 1 s. Truan Munro. Hobbies: Writing scripts.

PENK, Steve

Steve Penk. Presenter. b. 1963.
TV: *The Way They Were*; *TV Nightmares*; *When Athletes Attack*; *Would I Lie to You?.*
Address: c/o MPC Entertainment, MPC House, 15–16 Maple Mews, London NW6 5UZ.

PENROSE, Tricia

Tricia Penrose. Actor (F)/Performer/Presenter.
b. Liverpool, 9 April 1970.
TV: *Brookside*; *Celebrity Stars in Their Eyes*; *Emmerdale*; Gina Ward in *Heartbeat*; *Medics*; *Soap Fever.*
Address: c/o AMG Ltd, 8 King Street, London WC2E 8HN. Hobbies: Aerobics, shopping, music, singing, theatre.

PERCIVAL, Lance

Lance Percival. Actor (M)/Creator/Writer.
b. Sevenoaks, Kent, 26 July 1933.
TV: *Comic Relief*; *Countdown*; *Noel's Telly Years*; *Pro-Celebrity Golf*; *That Was The Week That Was*; *Through the Keyhole*; *Tricks of the Trade*; *Whodunnit?.*

Films: *Carry On* (various); *Too Late The Hero*; *The Big Job*; *Darling Lili*; *Yellow Submarine.*
Address: c/o Michelle Braidman Associates, 10–11 Lower John Street, London W1R 3PE. 1 s. Jamie Percival. Hobbies: Golf, crosswords.

PERKINS, Sue

Sue Perkins. Performer/Presenter/Reporter. b. 1969.
TV: *100 Per Cent Unofficial Friends*; *Clive Anderson All Talk*; *Fist of Fun*; *French & Saunders*; *Friday Night Armistice*; *Gimme, Gimme, Gimme*; *Good Stuff*; *Have I Got News For You*; *Holiday*; *If I Ruled the World*; *Late Licence*; *Late Lunch*; *Life's a Bitch*; *Light Lunch*; *Live & Kicking*; *McCoist & MacAuley*; *Monday Night Clive*; *Promo Trailers*; *Saturday Night Armistice*; *The Little Picture Show*; *The Mel & Sue Project*; *The Week is Dead*; *With Richard Not Judy.*
Address: c/o The Richard Stone Partnership, 2 Henrietta Street, London WC2E 8PS.

PERRY, Matthew

Matthew Perry. Actor (M). b. Williamstown, Massachusetts, USA, 19 August 1969.
TV: Roger Azarian in *Beverly Hills 90210*; Desi Arnaz Jr in *Call Me Anna*; Chandler Bing in *Caroline in the City*; Ed Stanley in *Charles in Charge*; George Westerfield in *Deadly Relations* (1993); Alex in *Dream On*; Bill at 18 in *Empty Nest* (1989); Chandler in *Friends*; Sandy in *Growing Pains*; *Highway to Heaven*; Matt Bailey in *Home Free*; Steven in *John Larroquette Show*; Ed in *Just the Ten of Us*; Willie Morrison in *Parallel Lives*; Chazz Russell in *Second Chance*; Davey in *Silver Spoons*; Billy Kells in *Sydney*; Benjamin in *Who's the Boss.*
Films: Fred Roberts in *A Night In The Life Of Jimmy Reardon* (1988); Leslie Edwards in *Almost Heroes*; Alex Whitman in *Fools Rush In*; Randall Burns in *Getting In*; Timothy in *She's Out of Control*; *The Whole Nine Yards* (2000); Oscar Novak in *Three To Tango* (1999).
Address: c/o William Morris Agency, 151 El Camino Drive, Beverly Hills, California 90212, USA. Father John Bennett Perry, mother Suzanne Perry Morrison, stepfather Keith Morrison. Hobbies: Ice hockey, tennis.

PERTWEE, Bill

Bill Pertwee. Actor (M)/Storyteller.
b. Amersham, Buckinghamshire, 21 July 1926.
TV: *Blankety Blank*; *Chance in a Million*; Mr Hodges in *Dad's Army*; *Jackanory*; *Noel's House Party*; *Spy Trap*; *Super Troupers*; *The Generation Game*; *Today's the Day*; *Wogan*; *Woof*; *You Rang M'Lord.*
Address: c/o The Richard Stone Partnership, 2 Henrietta Street, London WC2E 8PS.

PERTWEE, Sean

Sean Pertwee. Actor (M). b. 1965.
TV: *A Touch of Frost; Bodyguards; Boon; Cadfael; Chancer; Clarissa; Cleopatra; For One Night Only: Errol Flynn; Hard Cases; Kissing the Gunner's Daughter; Lockerbie; Macbeth; Peak Practice; Poirot; Speed; The Changeling; The Chief; The Harry Enfield Show; The Last Laugh; Virtual Murder; Young Indiana Jones Chronicles.*
Films: *Blue Juice; Coping With Cupid; Deadly Voyage; Dirty Weekend; Event Horizon; Five Seconds To Spare; ID; Leon the Pig Farmer; London Kills Me; Love, Honour and Obey; Prick Up Your Ears; Sex Crimes – Conform and Deform; Shopping; Soldier; Stiff Upper Lips; Still Seven Days To Live; Swing Kids; Talos the Mummy; Tube Tales.*
Address: c/o William Morris Agency (UK) Ltd, 1 Stratton Street, London W1X 6HB.

PETERS, Andi

Andi Peters. Presenter/Producer/Director.
b. London, 29 July 1970.
TV: *An Audience with the Spice Girls; Andi Meets ... Britney Spears; Andi Meets ... Gary Barlow; BoyZone Special; Broom Cupboard; But First This; CBBC2; Children in Need; EEK; Free Time; Good Fortune; Live & Kicking; Live & Kicking Red Nose Awards; Short Change; Take Two; The Noise; The O-Zone (1989, 1993); The Travel Quiz; The Weekend Show (1997); Train 2 Win (1997).*
Address: c/o James Grant Management Ltd, Syon Lodge, London Road, Middlesex TW7 5BH.

PETRIE, Alistair

Alistair Petrie. Actor (M).
TV: *999; All Quiet on the Preston Front; Dalziel and Pascoe; Demob; Emma; Game On; Jonathan Creek; Murder in the Family; Poirot; Scarlet and Black; The History File; This Way Out.*
Films: Herbert in *Mrs Dalloway.*
Address: c/o Roxane Vacca Management, 73 Beak Street, London W1R 3LF.

PETTIFER, Julian

Julian Pettifer. Reporter/Writer presenter.
b. Malmesbury, Wiltshire, 21 July 1935.
TV: *Automania; Correspondent; Diamonds in the Sky; Global Sunrise; Missionaries; Naturewatch; Panorama; The Living Isles; The Vietnam War; Tonight; Twenty-Four Hours.*
Address: c/o Curtis Brown, Haymarket House, 28–29 Haymarket, London SW1Y 4SP.

PHILBIN, Maggie

Maggie Philbin. Presenter/Reporter.
b. Manchester, 23 June 1955.

TV: *At Home With Maggie Philbin; Countdown to Christmas; Family Matters; Good For You; Help Your Child with Reading; Hospital Watch; Lifeline; Out of the Doll's House; Primetime; QED; Staying Alive; Swap Shop; The Bodymatters Roadshow; The Learning Zone; The Right Thing; The Show Me Show; This Morning; Time Off; Tomorrow's World; TW – Time Machine; Wideworld; Wildscreen – The Inside Story.*
Address: c/o Dave Winslett Associates, 6 Kenwood Ridge, Kenley, Surrey CR8 5JW. Hobbies: Marathon running.

PHILLIPS, Fiona

Fiona Phillips. Presenter/Reporter.
b. Canterbury, Kent, 1 January 1961.
TV: *GMTV; Good Stuff; Start the Weekend.*
Address: c/o Knight Ayton Management, 10 Argyll Street, London W1V 1AB.

PHILLIPS, Leslie

Leslie Phillips. Actor (M). b. London, 20 April 1924.
TV: *Bermuda Grace; Blanding's Castle; Boon; Casanova; Chancer; Comic Strip; Dalziel and Pascoe; Foreign Affairs; Honey for Tea; Impasse; Life After Life; Love on a Branch Line; Lovejoy; Monte Carlo; Morning Departure; Mr Palfrey of Westminster; My Wife Jacqueline; Our Man at St Marks; Redundance – or The Wife's Revenge; Royal Celebration; Rumpole; Summer's Lease; Tales from the Crypt; Thacker; The Canterville Ghost; The Changeling; The Gong Game; The House of Windsor; The Kensington Cats; The Pale Horse; The Reluctant Debutante; The Suit; The Trials of Oz; The Very Fine Line; Who Bombed Birmingham?; Woof.*
Films: *August; Carry On Nurse; Crooks Anonymous; Doctor in Clover; Empire of the Sun; Fast Lady; Ferdinando; Gamma People; High Flight; In the Doghouse; King Ralph; Les Girls; Mad Cows; Seven Deadly Sins; Maroc 7; Mountains of the Moon; Out of Africa; Pool of London; Scandal; Some Will, Some Won't; Spanish Fly; The Glass Slipper; The Longest Day; The Other Eden; The Smallest Show on Earth; Train of Events; Very Important Person; You Must Be Joking; Doctor in Love; Doctor in Trouble.*
Address: c/o Storm Artists Management, 47 Brewer Street, London W1R 3FD.

PHILLIPS, Sally

Sally Phillips. Actor (F)/Writer/Performer.
b. 10 May 1970.
TV: *A Night In with Comic Relief;* Sarah Sampson-Superchrist in *Brass Eye; Comedy Nation; Comic Relief Debt Wish Live;* Pinky in *Cows;* Whore in a Helicopter in *Election Night Armistice; Fist of Fun;*

Friday Night Armistice (Various); *Funny Girls Weekend*; Jill in *Hippies*; Laura in *Holding the Baby*; Sophie in *I'm Alan Partridge*; Gemma in *In the Red*; Natalie in *Kiss Me Kate*; Miss Lowe in *My Dad's a Boring Nerd*; *Saturday Night Armistice*; *Six Pairs of Pants*; *Smack the Pony*; *Smith and Jones*; Waitress in *With Friends Like You*.

Address: c/o TalkBack Management, 36 Percy Street, London W1P 0LN.

PHILLIPS, Sian

Sian Phillips. Actor (F).
b. Bettws, Carmarthenshire, 14 May 1934.
TV: *A Killing on the Exchange*; Rachel Hardcastle in *A Mind to Kill*; *A Painful Case*; Red Queen in *Alice Through the Looking Glass*; *Barriers*; The Baroness in *Cinderella*; *Crime and Punishment*; *Don Juan in Hell*; *Emlyn's Moon*; *Ewok 11*; *Freddie and Max*; *George Borrow*; *Hands Across the Sea*; *Heartbreak House*; *Home for Xmas*; Mam in *House of America*; *How Green Was My Valley*; *How Many Miles to Babylon*; *I, Claudius*; Eleanor of Aquitaine in *Ivanhoe*; Founder of SECTION in *La Femme Nikita*; *Lady Windermere's Fan*; Rhiannon in *Nearest and Dearest*; *Off to Philadelphia in the Morning*; *Perfect Scoundrels*; *Platonov*; *Sean*; *Shoulder to Shoulder*; *Siwan*; *Smiley's People*; *Summer Silence*; *The Achurch Letters*; Emily in *The Aristocrats*; *The Astonished Heart*; *The Black Candle*; *The Carpathian Eagle*; *The Chestnut Soldier*; *The Garden of Loneliness*; Meg in *The Magician's House*; *The Oresteia*; *The Quiet Man*; Matilda Gillespie in *The Scold's Bridle*; *The Sex Game*; *The Shadow of the Noose*; *The Snow Spider*; *The Tortoise and the Hare*; *The Two Mrs Grenvilles*; *The Wilderness Years*; *Tinker, Tailor, Soldier, Spy*; *Treason*; *Vanity Fair*; *Ways and Means*.
Films: *Beckett*; *Clash of the Titans*; *Dune*; *Goodbye Mr Chips*; *Heidi*; *Murphy's War*; *Out of Time*; *The Age of Innocence*; *The Borrowers*; *The Doctor and the Devils*; *Under Milk Wood*; *Valmont*.
Address: c/o Saraband Associates, 265 Liverpool Road, London N1 1LX.

PHILLIPS, Trevor

Trevor Phillips. Presenter/Producer/Reporter.
b. London, 31 December 1953.
TV: *Black on Black*; *Club Mix*; *Crosstalk*; *Diana – Portrait of a Princess*; *Eyewitness*; *Richard Littlejohn – Live and Uncut*; *Sunday*; *The Inside Track*; *The London Programme*; *The Making of Britain*; *The Midnight Hour*; *This Week*; *Trial of Enoch*; *Untold – Britain's Slave Trade*; *Windrush – England My England*.
Address: c/o Jacques Evans Management Ltd, 4 Gorlestone Street, London W14 8XS.

PICCIRILLI, Michael

Michael Piccirilli. Actor (M). b. 10 June 1971.
TV: James Fraser in *Home and Away*.
Address: c/o Seven Network Ltd, Mabbs Lane, Epping, NSW 2121, Australia. Hobbies: Photography.

PICKARD, John

John Pickard. Actor (M)/Presenter. b. 1978.
TV: David Porter in *2point4 Children*; *Alexei Sayle's Stuff*; *Cyberstar*; *Dangerous Boys*; Danny in *DJ Kat Show*; Kevin in *EastEnders*; Neil in *Grange Hill*; *Road Hog*; Young Terry in *Run for the Life Boat*; Ryan Eastwood in *Sunburn*; McLaren in *The Ghosts of Oxford Street*; John Otterson in *Timewatch*; Jason in *What Shall We Tell the Children*.
Films: Boy in *Just Like a Woman*; Young Man in *Monster Maker*; Peter in *More Than Dreams*; Thomas in *Rage*; *The Train*.
Music: *The Ghosts of Oxford Street*.
Address: c/o Rossmore Personal Management, Rossmore Road, London NW1 6NJ. Brother Nick Pickard. Hobbies: Football.

PICKARD, Nick

Nick Pickard. Actor (M).
TV: Rosco in *Brookside Video*; Ben in *Erasmus Microman*; Tony in *Hollyoaks*; Lee in *If You Were Me*; Prince Charming in *Jim'll Fix It*; Ian in *Now That It's Morning*; *Return to 2001*; Anthony in *Sex Now*; Harold in *The Saving of Aunt Esther*; Sean in *Us Girls*; Jim in *You Rang M'Lord*.
Films: Mio in *Mio My Mio*.
Address: c/o Rossmore Personal Management, Rossmore Road, London NW1 6NJ. Brother John Pickard.

PICKARD, Raymond

Raymond Pickard. Actor (M).
b. Liverpool, 31 July 1982.
TV: Danny in *Rhinoceros*; Brian Longman in *Seaforth*; Norman Starkey in *Spywatch*; Washington in *The Canterville Ghost*; Brendan in *The Vice*; Wim in *The Writing on the Wall*.
Films: Spiller in *The Borrowers*.
Address: c/o Evans & Reiss, 100 Fawe Park Road, London SW15 2EA. Hobbies: Go-karting, ju-jitsu, poetry.

PICKLES, Carolyn

Carolyn Pickles. Actor (F). b. Halifax, 8 February 1952.
TV: Jeanetta in *The Preston Front*; Bluebell in *Bluebell*; Simone in *May to December*; Sally Bilton in *We'll Meet Again*.

Films: Charlotte Fisher in *Agatha; Brothers & Sisters; Champions;* Miss Giles in *Mirror Crack'd;* Marian in *Tess.* Address: c/o Conway Van Gelder, 18–21 Jermyn Street, London SW1Y 6HP. Great-uncle: Wilfred Pickles; Aunt Christina Pickles, father James Pickles.

PICKUP, Ronald

Ronald Pickup. Actor (M). b. 7 June 1940.
TV: Felix D'Arcy in *Case of Coincidence: A Murder of Quality;* The Banker in *A Time To Dance; All Good Men; Bergerac; Boon; Casualty;* Captain Lancaster in *Danny, the Champion of the World; Dalziel and Pascoe;* Prince Yakimov in *Fortunes of War;* Henry VIII in *Henry VIII; Hetty Wainthropp Investigates; Hornblower: The Duchess and the Devil; Inspector Morse;* Prince John in *Ivanhoe;* Lord Randolph Churchill in *Jennie: Lady Randolph Churchill;* Edgar in *King Lear;* Edmund Tyrone in *Long Day's Journey Into Night; Lovejoy;* Jocelyn Fry in *Milner; Pope John Paul II; Romeo and Juliet;* William Pitt in *The Fight Against Slavery;* Howard Joyce in *The Letter;* Aslan in *The Lion, the Witch and the Wardrobe;* Putzi Hanfstaengl in *The Nightmare Years;* Daniel Byrne in *The Rector's Wife;* Giuseppe Verdi in *Verdi;* Julian Winterhalter in *Waters of the Moon.*
Films: Spiro in *Eleni;* Elliot in *Never Say Never Again;* Igor Stravinsky in *Nijinsky;* The Forger in *The Day of the Jackal;* Hunter in *The Mission;* Bayliss in *The Thirty-Nine Steps;* Baron Tusenbach in *The Three Sisters;* Lieutenant Harford in *Zulu Dawn.*
Address: c/o London Management, Noel House, 2–4 Noel Street, London W1V 3RB.

PIERCEY, Jennifer

Jennifer Piercey. Actor (F).
TV: Sister Grant in *A Big Romping Boy;* Antonia in *Absolutely Fabulous;* Olivia Mosgrove in *Desmonds;* Peggy Irvine in *Dialogue in the Dark;* Lady Ailsa McKenzie in *Dr Finlay;* Gloria in *Duck Patrol;* Mrs Hanson in *Escape to Somerset;* Mrs Scott in *Grange Hill;* Mrs Thompson in *Inspector Morse;* Kitty in *Jonathan Creek;* Mrs Pye in *Love on a Branch Line;* WI Chairman in *Lovejoy;* Mrs Dear in *Mud;* Isa Mulvenny in *Portrait of Isa Mulvenny;* Chairwoman in *Rumpole of the Bailey;* Heather Lomax in *The Advocates;* Mrs Maureen Salmon in *The Chief;* Mrs Campbell in *The Dunroamin' Rising;* Shop Assistant in *The Last Salute;* Lilian in *The Two of Us;* Giselle in *The Workshop.*
Films: Kirsty in *Another Time, Another Place;* Mrs Evers in *Friend or Foe.*
Address: c/o Rolf Kruger Management Ltd, 205 Chudleigh Road, London SE4 1EG.

PIERSON, Emma

Emma Pierson. Actor (F). b. Plymouth, 30 April 1981.
TV: Jackie in *Days Like These;* Becky in *Grange Hill.*
Films: Nymph in *Guest House Paradiso;* Nadya in *The Whisper;* Fiona in *Virtual Sexuality.*
Address: c/o Associated International Management, 5 Denmark Street, London WC2H 8LP.

PIGOTT-SMITH, Tim

Pigott-Smith. Actor (M). b. Rugby, 13 May 1946.
TV: Hubert in *Bullion Boys; Calcutta Chronicles;* Dick Staveley in *Eustace and Hilda;* Shawcross in *Fame is the Spur;* Hotspur in *Henry IV (Part I);* Ronald Merrick in *Jewel in the Crown;* Francis Crick in *Life Story;* Angelo in *Measure for Measure;* Timothy Perkins in *School Play;* Chief Constable John Stafford in *The Chief; The Shadowy Third;* Brendan Bracken in *Wilderness Years.*
Films: *Aces High; Clash of the Titans; Escape to Victory; Hunchback of Notre Dame; Lucky Village; Richard's Things; Sweet William;* Ben in *The Remains of the Day.* Address: c/o PFD, Drury House, 34–43 Russell Street, London WC2B 5HA. m. Pamela Miles; 1 s. Tom. Hobbies: Reading, music, writing.

PILEGGI, Mitch

Mitch Pileggi. Actor (M).
b. Portland, Oregon, 5 April 1952.
TV: *China Beach; Dallas; Doctor, Doctor; Players; That 70s Show;* FBI Assistant Director Skinner in *The X-Files; Walker, Texas Ranger.*
Films: Internal Affairs Investigator in *Basic Instinct; Death Wish IV: The Crackdown;* Sarge in *Return of the Living Dead, Part II;* Horace Pinker in *Shocker;* Dexter in *Takedown;* Walter Skinner in *X-Files The Movie.*
Address: c/o Pacula King Associates, Suite 315, 9229 Sunset Blvd, Los Angeles, California 90069, USA. m. 1st (dis.) Debbie Andrews, 2nd Arlene Rempel. Hobbies: Wrestling, football.

PILGER, John

John Pilger. Film-maker/Journalist. b. 9 October 1939.
TV: *Apartheid Did Not Die; Breaking The Mirror – The Murdoch Effect; Burp! Pepsi vs Coke in the Ice Cold War; Cambodia Year One; Cambodia: The Betrayal; Death of A Nation; Do You Remember Vietnam?; Guilty Until Proven Innocent; Mr Nixon's Secret Legacy; Nicaragua; Nobody's Children; One British Family; Other People's Wars; Palestine Is Still The Issue; Paying the Price: The Killing of the Children of Iraq; Pilger in Australia; Pyramid Lake Is Dying; Street of Joy; Thalidomide: The 98 We Forgot; The Battle of Chile; The Most Powerful Politician in America; The Secret Country; The Timor Con-*

spiracy; The Truth Game; Vietnam: Still America's War; Welcome to Australia; Year Zero.
Address: c/o David Higham Management, 528 Lower John Street, London W1R 4HA.

PILKINGTON, Lorraine

Lorraine Pilkington. Actor (F). b. Dublin, Ireland.
TV: *Extra Extra;* Christy Bannham in *Four Fathers; Her Own Rules;* Katrina in *Monarch of the Glen;* Maggie Clarke in *Runway One; West End Girls.*
Films: Eileen in *All Things Bright and Beautiful; Breathtaking; Durango;* Rose in *Gold in the Streets; Human Traffic;* Irene in *L'Irelandaise;* Josephine in *The Boxer;* Jo in *The Cake;* Katie in *The Disappearance of Finbar;* Jayne in *The Last of The High Kings; The Miracle;* Patricia in *The Nephew.*
Address: c/o ICM, Oxford House, 76 Oxford Street, London W1N 0AX.

PINCHER, Mark

Mark Pincher. Actor (M).
b. Birmingham, 29 May 1970.
TV: *Andi Peters Show;* Vince in *Sex Starved Years of Harry and Cosh; The Generation Game; Theatre Award.*
Address: c/o SCA Management, 23 Goswell Road, London EC1.

PINDER, Steven J

Steven J Pinder. Actor (M). b. Lancashire.
TV: Max Farnham in *Brookside; Cat's Eyes;* Roy Lambert in *Crossroads; Crown Court;* Owen in *Foxy Lady; Hollywood Sports; Now and Then; Scotch and Wry.*
Address: c/o Conway Van Gelder, 18–21 Jermyn Street, London SW1Y 6HP.

PIPER, Ailsa

Ailsa Piper. Actor (F).
TV: *A Country Practice; Embassy; GP; Have a Go; House Rules; Kelly; Lift Off; Man of Letters;* Ruth Wilkinson in *Neighbours; Prime Time; The Flying Doctors.*
Films: *Vincent and the Shadow.*
Address: c/o Grundy Television, Grundy House, Barge House Crescent, 34 Upper Ground, London SE1 9PD.

PIPER, Jacki

Jacki Piper. Actor (F). b. Birmingham, 3 August 1948.
TV: Jane Fordham in *Back Up;* Margaret Talbot in *Dangerfield;* Avril in *Don't Dilly Dally;* Pearl in *Hogg's Back;* Moneyfeather in *Kelly Montieth;* Harriet in *Men of Affairs; Strange But True;* Lynne Cox in *The Bill;* Esther Pidgeon in *The Rise and Fall of Reginald Perrin;* Jane in *The Rough With the Smooth;* Doreen in *The Things You Do for Love;* Natasha in *Thriller.*

Films: Myrtle Plummer in *Carry On At Your Convenience;* Sally Martin in *Carry On Loving;* Sister Williams in *Carry on Matron;* June in *Carry On Up the Jungle;* Sue in *Doctor in Trouble;* Ida in *Mr Love;* Carrie in *The Love Ban;* Lyn Greer in *The Man Who Haunted Himself.*
Address: c/o Langford Associates, 17 Westfields Avenue, London SW13 0AT. m. Douglas Barrell; 2 s. Nick, Tim. Hobbies: Watercolour art, tennis, music-hall, reading.

PIRIE, Jacqueline

Jacqueline Pirie. Actor (F)/Presenter.
b. Stirling, 10 October 1985.
TV: Eileen Whinge in *Arthur Square;* Mary Lou/Billy Sue/Cindy in *Campus Capers;* Carrie in *Casualty;* Annabel Chivers in *Chalkface;* Linda in *Coronation Street; DJ Kat Show;* Tina Dingle in *Emmerdale; Gas Street; General Accident; Lifeline;* Shirley Anne Turtledove in *Palace Hill II;* Jess in *Stars; Which Way Now.*
Films: Mary in *Chasing the Deer;*
Address: c/o Lou Coulson, 37 Berwick Street, London W1V 3RF.

PITT, Ingrid

Ingrid Pitt. Actor (F). b. 21 November 1938.
TV: *Bulman; Comedy of Errors;* Dr Salow/Queen of Atlantis in *Doctor Who; Ironside; Jason King; Nadine;* Elvira in *Smiley's People; The House; The Zoo Gang;* Dachsie in *Unity; Where the Action Is.*
Films: *Asylum;* Countess Bathory in *Countess Dracula; El Lobo; Green Fingers; Hannah's War; Parker; Prehistoric Sound; Splendour of Andalucia; The House that Dripped Blood; The Omegans; The Vampire Lovers; The Wicker Man;* Heidi in *Where Eagles Dare; Who Dares Wins; Wild Geese 2.*
Address: c/o Langford Associates, 17 Westfields Avenue, London SW13 0AT. m. Tony Rudlin; 1 d. Steffanie Pitt.

PITT, Steffanie

Steffanie Pitt. Actor (F). b. Colorado, USA.
TV: *Annie's Bar; C.A.T.S. Eyes; DJ Kat Show; Gaucho Girl; Gentlemen and Players; Kane and Abel; Make and Break; Matt's Million; Mr Knowall; Smith and Jones; The Bill; The Lady and the Highwayman; The New Statesman; The Russian Soldier; The Upper Hand.*
Films: *Asylum; Biggles; Bullseye; Death Wish III.*
Address: c/o Great Management Ltd, Pinewood Studios, Pinewood Road, Iver Heath, Buckinghamshire SL0 0NH. m. Arthur Blake; mother Ingrid Pitt. Hobbies: Swimming, skiing, horse riding, golf.

PIVARO, Nigel

Nigel Pivaro. Actor (M). b. 11 December 1960.
TV: Terry Duckworth in *Coronation Street*; Colin Wardle in *Expert Witness*; Sergeant Pearce in *Hetty Wainthropp Investigates*.
Films: *Meet Me Tonight in Dreamland*; *Sunny Side of the Street*.
Address: c/o Hilary Gagan Associates, 2nd Floor, Gloucester Mansions, 140a Shaftesbury Avenue, London WC2H 8HD.

PLANER, Nigel

Nigel Planer. Actor (M). b. London, 22 February 1953.
TV: David in *Blackeyes*; Lawrence in *Bonjour la Classe*; Jocelyn in *Cuts*; Lester in *Jonathan Creek*; David Castle in *King and Castle*; Veitch in *Number 27*; Nigel Cochrane in *Roll Over Beethoven*; Lou Lewis in *Shine on Harvey Moon*; Colville in *The Bill*; *The Comic Strip Presents …*; Nicholas Craig in *The Naked Actor – Masterclass*; John Peel in *The Trials of Oz*; Neil in *The Young Ones*; Sam in *Two Lumps of Ice*.
Films: Den Dennis in *Bad News Tour*; Charlie (Department of Works) in *Brazil*; Gerald in *Land Girls*; Gunter in *Supergrass*; Mansell in *Yellowbeard*.
Address: c/o PFD, Drury House, 34–43 Russell Street, London WC2B 5HA. m. Frankie; 3 s. Stanley, Marlon, Harvey.

PLEASENCE, Angela

Angela Pleasence. Actor (F).
TV: *Barchester Chronicles*; Liz in *Birthday*; Charlotte in *Charlotte Brontë*; *Churchill's People – The Conquerors*; *Cider with Rosie*; Laura in *Coronation Street*; *Crime Traveller*; Alice in *Dixon of Dock Green*; Jackson in *Joan – The Ladies*; *Mansfield Park*; *Midsomer Murders*; Pam in *Murder at the Wedding*; Betty in *Paul Temple*; Lottie in *September*; *Silas Marner*; St Joan in *St Joan*; *The Bill*; Tina Seymore in *The Expert*; Miss Cutts in *The Hothouse*; Marie Shatov in *The Possessed*; *The Walls of Jericho*; The Wife in *The Whole Truth*.
Films: *Abelard and Héloïse*; *Here We Go Round the Mulberry Bush*; Trude in *Hitler, The Last Ten Days*; *The Love Ban*; Fantine in *Les Misérables*; Helen in *Symptoms*; Emily in *Tales From Beyond the Grave*; *A Christmas Carol*; *The Favour, the Watch and the Very Big Fish*; Victoria in *The Gaunt Woman*; The Stranger in *The Godsend*.
Address: c/o Scott Marshall, 44 Perryn Road, London W3 7NA. Father Donald Pleasence; sister Miranda Pleasence.

PLEASENCE, Miranda

Miranda Pleasence. Actor (F).
TV: WPC Holland in *A Touch of Frost*; Alison Pyke in *BUGS*; *Casualty*; *Karaoke*; *Pie in the Sky*; *The Bill*; *The Phoenix and the Carpet*; *The Plant*; Eliza in *The Tenant of Wildfell Hall*; Louise in *The Visitor*; Heather in *Wonderful You*.
Films: Rachel in *Safe Haven*; Pippa in *Tip of My Tongue*.
Address: c/o Annette Stone Associates, 2nd Floor, 22 Great Marlborough Street, London W1V 1AF. Father Donald Pleasence; sister Angela Pleasence.

POLLARD, Su

Su Pollard. Actor (F)/Host.
b. Nottingham, 7 November 1949.
TV: Peggy in *Hi De Hi*; *Oh, Doctor Beeching*; *Penny Crayon*; *Take the Plunge*; *Two Up, Two Down*; Ivy in *You Rang M'Lord*.
Music: *Starting Together*.
Address: c/o Noel Gay Artists, 19 Denmark Street, London WC2H 8NA.

POLLITT, Michael

Michael Pollitt. Actor (M). b. Bolton, Lancashire, 13 March 1990.
TV: *Where the Heart Is*.
Address: c/o Laine Management, Matrix House, 301–303 Chapel Street, Salford, M3 5JG. Hobbies: Dancing, drama.

POLLOCK, Eileen

Eileen Pollock. Actor (F). b. Belfast, 18 May 1947.
TV: Lilo Lil in *Bread*.
Films: Molly Kay (Brothel Keeper) in *Far and Away*; Carmel in *Four Days in July*; Magistrate in *Thanks for the Memories*; Mrs Pottinger in *A Love Divided*; Mrs Finnucane in *Angela's Ashes*.
Address: c/o George Heathcote Management, 58 Northdown Street, London N1 9BS. Hobbies: Writing, travelling, dining, theatre, swimming, browsing in markets.

POLYCARPOU, Peter

Peter Polycarpou. Actor (M). b. Brighton.
TV: Chris in *Birds of a Feather*; Paul in *Rich Tea and Sympathy*; Yiannis in *Sunburn*.
Films: Mecante in *Evita*; Phil Green in *Julie and the Cadillacs*.
Address: c/o Burnett Granger Associates, Prince of Wales Theatre, 31 Coventry Street, London W1V 8AS.

PORRETT, Susan

Susan Porrett. Actor (F).
TV: Doris Watson in *Absolute Hell*; Mrs Webb in *Alphonzo Bonzo*; Carol Trapnell in *Bam! Pow! Zapp!*;

Rachel in *Big Women*; Mrs Webb in *Billy Webb*; Freda in *Blott on the Landscape*; Beth's Mum in *Cold Lazarus*; Beverley Trendall in *Crimewatch; Days Like These*; Doreen in *Gallowglass*; Mrs Thomas in *Grange Hill*; Joyce Parmby in *Hetty Wainthropp Investigates*; Model in *How Do You Want Me?*; Lady Holland in *Landsee*; Mrs Wederben in *Life and Times of Henry Pratt*; Florence in *Malice Aforethought*; Tantripp in *Middlemarch*; Trotter in *Poirot*; Hotel Receptionist in *Poppyland*; Mrs Oxdriver in *Precious Bane*; Magda in *The Adventures of Don Quick*; Mrs Cataclysm in *The Adventures of Frank*; Mrs Tarrant/Eve in *The Bill*; Mrs Cramm in *The Citadel*; Morgan in *The Duchess of Duke Street*; Alice in *Upstairs Downstairs*; Sister in *Wednesday's Child*.

Films: Mrs Medcalf in *A Private Function*; Mrs Ward in *Full Circle*; Vanessa Tweed in *Harmfulness of Tobacco*; Receptionist in *Madame Sousatzka*; Daphne in *One of Our Dinosaurs is Missing*; Lady Newbold in *Plunkett and MacLeane*; Porcelain Young-Thing in *Sir Henry at Rawlinson End*; Amorous Boy's Mother in *The Company of Wolves*; Nun in *The Saint*; Security Officer in *The Whistle Blower*; Maureen in *The Wrong Blonde*.

Address: c/o Kate Feast Management, 10 Primrose Hill Studios, Fitzroy Road, London NW1 8TR.

PORTER, Dr Mark

Dr Mark Porter. Presenter.

TV: *Evening Surgery; Fit to Win; Get Fit with Brittas; Good Health; Good Morning with Anne & Nick; Morning Surgery; Watchdog Health Check*.

Address: c/o The Roseman Organisation Suite 9, The Power House, 70 Chiswick Road, London W4 1SY.

PORTER, Gail

Gail Porter. Presenter/Reporter. b. Edinburgh, 1972.

TV: *The Big Breakfast; Electric Circus; Fully Booked; Gail Porter's Big 90s; Net-Aid; Not Melinda's Big Night In; One Night Stand; That Internet Show; The Movie Chart Show; Scratchy & Co; Top of the Pops; Wish You Were Here*.

Films: *Just The Ticket*.

Address: c/o Unique Artistes, Avon House, Kensington Village, London W14 8TS.

POSTLETHWAITE, Pete

Pete Postlethwaite. Actor (M).

b. Warrington, Cheshire, 7 February 1945.

TV: *A Day Out*; McCabe in *Blind Justice*; McLoughlin in *Boon*; Kecks in *Coast to Coast; Debut on Two*; Vince the Mince in *El CID*; Deric in *Lost for Words*; Montague Tigg in *Martin Chuzzlewit*; Eric 'Luggo' Lawson in *Minder*; Kerrigan in *Needle*; Becket in *Number 27*;

Hakeswill in *Sharpe's Rifles*; Mitch in *Sin Bin*; Rick in *Tales of Sherwood Forest*; Ray Galler in *The Bill*; McKeown in *The Butterfly Collectors*; Danny Dagan in *The Muscle Market*; Panter in *They Never Slept*; Thwum in *Thwum*; Major Knox in *Tumbledown*; Stuart Shooter in *Watching*; Calleja in *Zorro – The Masked Man*.

Films: The Butcher in *A Private Function*; Carpenter in *Alice in Wonderland; Aliens III*; Saunders in *Amistad*; Ray in *Among Giants*; Jones in *Animal Farm*; Danny in *Brassed Off*; Sincai in *Brute*; Sidney in *Crimetime*; Dad in *Distant Voices, Still Lives*; Gilbert in *Dragonheart*; Player King in *Hamlet*; Reid in *Hearts and Bones*; Giuseppe Conlon in *In the Name of the Father*; The Old Man in *James and the Giant Peach*; Captain Beams in *Last of the Mohicans; Letters from a Wayward Son*; Friar Lawrence in *Romeo and Juliet*; Glover in *Suite 16*; Uncle Reg in *The Divine Ryans*; Jack in *The Dressmaker*; Roland Tembo in *The Lost World*; Smithers in *The Serpent's Kiss*; Kobayashi in *The Usual Suspects; Though the Sky Falls*; Piot in *To Kill a Priest*; George Merry in *Treasure Island; Waterland*; Ken in *When Saturday Comes*.

Address: c/o Markham & Froggatt Ltd, 4 Windmill Street, London W1P 1HF.

POWELL, Gwyneth

Gwyneth Powell. Actor (F). b. 1946.

TV: Kitty in *A Touch of Frost*; Mrs McCloskey in *Grange Hill*; Matilda in *Magic With Everything*.

Films: *Return to the Secret Garden*.

Address: c/o Dennis Lyne Agency, 108 Leonard Street, London EC2A 4RH.

POWELL, Jenny

Jenny Powell. Reporter/Presenter.

b. Ilford, Essex, 8 April 1968.

TV: *7-A-Side Football Tournament; Cat's Eyes; Disney Adventures; Disney Club; Eureka! Roman Britain; Gimme 5; GMTV; Go Getters; Live 6 Show; Live Challenge; National Lottery Live; No Limits; Soapfever; This Morning; Top of the Pops; Trinidad and Tobago; Two by Two; UK's Strongest Man; What's Up Doc?; Wheel of Fortune; World's Weirdest Animals; World's Weirdest Television*.

Address: c/o Arlington Enterprise Ltd, 1–3 Charlotte Street, London W1P 1HD.

POWELL, Robert

Robert Powell. Actor (M). b. Salford, 1 June 1944.

TV: Toby Wren in *Doomwatch; Frankenstein*; Richard Hannay in *Hannay*; Jesus in *Jesus of Nazareth; Jude the Obscure; Looking for Clancy*; Ambrosius in *Merlin and the Crystal Cave; Mr Rolls and Mr Royce; Mrs Warren's Profession; Shaka Zulu; Shelley; The Detectives*.

Films: *Asylum; Beyond Good and Evil; Harlequin; Imperative; Jane Austen in Manhattan; Mahler in Mahler; Once on Chunuk Bair; Running Scared; Secrets;* Richard Hannay in *The 39 Steps; The Asphyx; The Jigsaw Man; The Long Conversation with a Bird; The Mystery of Edwin Drood; The Survivor;* Captain Walker in *Tommy; What Waits Below.*
Address: c/o Jonathan Altaras Associates, 13 Short's Gardens, London WC2H 9AT.

POWLEY, Mark

Mark Powley. Actor (M).
b. Chelmsford, Essex, 4 October 1963.
TV: *Bergerac;* Admiral Tudor in *Bluefields;* John in *Casualty;* Liam Hammond in *Emmerdale;* Jason in *Game On; Lovejoy;* Roger Ellis in *May to December;* Ray Burnside in *Moon & Son; Next of Kin; Noah's Ark; Peak Practice; Rockliffe's Babies;* Herr Kopfler in *Sherlock Holmes;* PC Ken Melvin in *The Bill; The Politician's Wife; Victoria Wood.*
Films: Brad in *Time Warp Terror; Wing Commander.*
Address: c/o Scott Marshall, 44 Perryn Road, London W3 7NA. m. Janis; 2 d. Bel, Honor. Hobbies: Snooker, rugby, scuba diving, horse-riding.

PRAED, Michael

Michael Praed. Actor (M).
b. Gloucestershire, 1 April 1960.
TV: Marty in *Crown Prosecutor; Dynasty; For One Night Only;* Jake in *Riders; Robin of Sherwood; Rothko; The Adventures of Jules Verne; The Entertainers.*
Films: *Dangerous Obsession; Nightflyers;* Gary in *Staggered.*
Address: c/o ICM, Oxford House, 76 Oxford Street, London W1N 0AX.

PRESTON, Duncan

Duncan Preston. Actor (M).
TV: *Buddy;* Mr Kennedy in *Chalk; Coogan's Run;* Stan in *dinnerladies; Gentry; Happy Since I Met You;* Kevin's Dad in *Harry Enfield and Chums;* David Cousins in *Holby City;* Slim Jim in *Holed;* William Shakespeare in *In Search of Hamlet;* Colin Cooper in *Midsomer Murders;* Rev. Thomas in *Noah's Ark; Noble House;* Jim in *Pat and Margaret; Press Gang; Shades of Darkness;* Ivor Braun in *Snap; Sun Child;* Haslam in *Surgical Spirit; The New Statesman; Victoria Wood – As Seen On TV.*
Films: *A Passage to India; If Tomorrow Comes; Macbeth;* Sergeant Wilson in *Milk; Porridge; Robin Hood; Scandalous.*
Address: c/o CDA, 19 Sydney Mews, London SW3 6HL.

PRINGLE, Bryan

Bryan Pringle. Actor (M). b. 19 January 1935.
TV: Superintendent of Police in *A Crack in the Ice;* Maurice in *A Night on the Tyne;* Vince Herbert in *A Prince Among Men;* Dennis in *After Henry;* Mr Hardwood in *Alfonso Bonzo;* Grimsdale in *All Creatures Great and Small;* David Charnley in *Blind Justice;* Bull in *Boon;* Turnball in *Capstick's Law;* George in *Casualty;* Paddy in *Coracle;* Superintendent in *Crimestrike;* John Huby in *Dalziel and Pascoe;* Smith, the Butler in *Dance to the Music of Time;* Father in *Debut on Two;* Mr Porter in *Diary of a Nobody;* Jimmy Fisher in *Flying Lady;* Hodgkins in *Hardwick House;* Ned in *Heartbeat;* Pirbright in *Heavy Weather;* Barker in *Inspector Morse;* Ted in *Jo Brand: Like It or Lump It;* George Fosse in *King and Castle;* Bunduck in *Ladies' Night;* Malcolm in *Leaving Home;* Leslie in *Les Girls;* Tandy in *Lovejoy;* Bramwell Ritchie in *Moving Story;* Franklyn in *Murder Most Horrid;* Len in *My Kingdom for a Horse;* Chorus in *Oedipus at Colonus;* Barry in *Ollie's Prison;* Len in *On Giant's Shoulders;* Percy Bigwell in *Paradise Postponed;* Jim Barraclough in *Peak Practice;* Wally Butters in *Perfect Scoundrels;* Inspector Flaubert in *Pleasure;* Pathologist in *Prime Suspect;* Stan in *Roots;* Ben Baker in *Rumpole;* So *Haunt Me;* Kail in *Tess of the D'Urbervilles;* Morris Muscle in *The Beast in Man;* Grandfather in *The Day Grandad Went Blind;* Father in *The Detectives;* Henry in *The Dog It Was;* Merton Mitchum in *The Good Companions;* Peregrine Crusty in *The Management;* Commissionaire in *The Office Life;* Alan in *The Oldest Goose in the Business;* Nimrod in *The Ragged Trousered Philanthropist;* The Cook in *The Storyteller;* Raggles in *Vanity Fair;* Sergeant Match in *What the Butler Saw;* Father Martin in *Wish Me Luck;* Stanley in *Wokenwell;* Float in *Young Indiana Jones Chronicles.*
Films: Stefan in *All Forgotten;* Maskell in *American Friends;* Goodchild in *B Monkey;* Spiro in *Brazil;* Waiter in *Bullshot;* Gatekeeper in *Consuming Passions;* Morrilles in *Dark River;* Mr Hayter in *Darkness Falls;* Jake in *Drowning by Numbers;* Mr Lamb in *Getting it Right;* Pfister in *Haunted Honeymoon;* Gate Guard in *Jabberwocky;* Jim in *Lawrence of Arabia;* Employee in *Legend of the Pianist;* Mr Taylor in *Passion;* Man at End of Pier in *Remains of the Day;* Father Gilbert in *Snow White in the Black Forest;* Mr Brown in *The Boyfriend;* Doorman in *The Steal;* Minnit in *The Young Visitors.*
Address: c/o Markham & Froggatt Ltd, 4 Windmill Street, London W1P 1HF.

PROTHEROE, Brian

Brian Protheroe. Actor (M).
b. Salisbury, Wiltshire, 16 June 1944.

TV: Band Leader in *Bavarian Nights*; Ralph Whatman in *Dr Willoughby*; Beaufort in *Gentlemen and Players*; Edward IV in *Henry VI*; Bannock in *Highlander*; Conway in *Leave Him to Heaven*; Matt in *Natural Lies*; James Bigsley in *Not a Penny More Not a Penny Less*; Rosten in *Pie in the Sky*; Frank in *Real Women*; Grammaticoff in *Reilly Ace of Spies*; Edward IV in *Richard III*; Leo Brompton in *Shrinks*; Peter Paterson in *The Hello Girls*; Saterninus in *Titus Andronicus*; Ollie in *To Have and to Hold*; Dunbar in *Wolverine*.

Films: Professor Walker in *Commedia*; Co-pilot in *Superman*; Gang Member in *The Biggest Bank Robbery*.

Address: c/o Marmont Management Ltd, Langham House, 308 Regent Street, London W1R 5AL.

PRYCE, Jonathan

Jonathan Pryce. Actor (M). b. Holywell, 1 June 1947.

TV: Henry Kravis in *Barbarians at the Gate*; *Daft as a Brush*; Saul in *David*; Constable in *Doomwatch*; Duncan Stewart in *Great Moments in Aviation*; Mr Wroe in *Mr Wroe's Virgins*; Mr Ellsworthy in *Murder is Easy*; Gethin Price in *The Comedians*; *For Tea on Sunday*; *Play Things*; Christian Magny in *Praying Mantis*; Gerd Heidemann in *Selling Hitler*; Herod in *The Day Christ Died*; William Wallace in *The Man from the Pru*; *The Storyteller*; *The Union Game – A History of Rugby*; Sam in *Thicker Than Water*; Timon in *Timon of Athens*; *Whose Line is it Anyway?*; The Master in *Doctor Who – The Curse of Fatal Death (Comic Relief)*.

Films: Alec Bolton in *A Business Affair*; Alan in *A Troll in Central Park*; Sam Lowry in *Brazil*; Ken in *Breaking Glass*; Lytton Strachey in *Carrington*; *Commedia*; Mr Farris in *Consuming Passions*; Dr Ted Philips in *Deadly Advice*; Juan Perón in *Evita*; Trilby in *Freddie the Frog*; James Ling in *Glengarry Glen Ross*; Charles in *Haunted Honeymoon*; Henry Higgins/The Engineer in *Hey Mr Producer! – The Musical World of Cameron Mackintosh*; Jack in *Jumpin' Jack Flash*; Taylor in *Loophole*; *Man on Fire*; *Pavarotti in Dad's Room*; Dr William Rivers in *Regeneration*; Seamus in *Ronin*; Conway in *Shopping*; Mr Dark in *Something Wicked This Way Comes*; Cardinal Daniel Houseman in *Stigmata*; Horation Jackson in *The Adventures of Baron Munchausen*; Monsieur Rivière in *The Age of Innocence*; Robert Fallon in *The Doctor and the Devils*; Himself/The Engineer in *The Heat is On*; James Penfield in *The Ploughman's Lunch*; Norman in *The Rachel Papers*; *Titanic – Answers from the Abyss*; Elliot Carver in *Tomorrow Never Dies*; Joseph Menasse in *Voyage of the Damned*.

Address: c/o Julian Belfrage Associates, 46 Albemarle Street, London W1X 4PP.

PUCKRIK, Katie

Katie Puckrik. Actor (F)/Film Critic/Presenter/Writer/Reporter.

TV: *01 For London*; *4 Goes to Glastonbury*; *Access All Areas*; *All Over the Shop*; Nurse in *Ant & Dec Unzipped*; *Cyber Café*; *Don't Drink the Water*; *Dream Ticket*; *Fab FM: End of an Era*; *Five's Company*; *Good Stuff*; *Heaven and Hell Live*; *Icons*; *Ikea: A New Religion*; *It's Not Just Saturday*; *Late Edition*; *Night Fever*; *Not Fade Away*; *Pyjama Party*; *Rowland Rivron Bites the Bullet*; *The Basement*; *The Goods*; *The Jack Docherty Show*; *The Sunday Show*; *The Take*; *The Time, The Place*; *The Word*; *Truth About Sex Appeal*; *Virgin Channel Entertainment Guide*; *You Don't Know Me But*; *Zig & Zag's Dirty Deeds*.

Address: c/o The Richard Stone Partnership, 2 Henrietta Street, London WC2E 8PS.

PULESTON-DAVIES, Ian

Ian Puleston-Davies. Actor (M).

TV: DC Barrett in *Between the Lines*; Ben in *Boon*; Stephen in *Brookside*; Daniel Meredith in *Dirty Work*; Steve Lipton in *Dr Willoughby*; Jimmy in *EastEnders*; John in *Grange Hill*; Rick the Intelligent in *Harpur*; Terry in *Hollyoaks*; Derek Reid in *Jack of Hearts*; Connor Tierney in *Liverpool One*; Paparazzi in *Metropolis*; PC Carter in *The Ruth Rendell Mysteries*; Don in *Satellite City*; *The Bill*; Young Charlie in *The Old Devils*; Youth Host in *The Politician's Wife*.

Films: Kevin in *Business as Usual*; *Plunkett & MacLeane*; *Room to Rent*; Typewriter Man in *Rosebud*.

Address: c/o Sally Hope Associates, 108 Leonard Street, London EC2A 4XS.

PUNCH, Lucy

Lucy Punch. Actor (F).

TV: Regan in *Cinderella*; Helen Foreman in *Days Like These*; Eveline in *Let Them Eat Cake*.

Address: c/o London Management, Noel House, 2–4 Noel Street, London W1V 3RB.

PUREFOY, James

James Purefoy. Actor (M). b. Somerset, 3 June 1964.

TV: Nicholas Jenkins in *A Dance to the Music of Time*; *Angel Train*; *Bright Hair*; *Calling the Shots*; *Don Quixote*; *Have Your Cake and Eat It*; *Metropolis*; *Sharpe's Sword*; *Tears Before Bedtime*; *Tenant of Wildfell Hall*; *The Cloning of Joanna May*; Darius Guppy in *The Prince*; *The Prince and the Pauper*; *The Tide of Life*.

Films: Brendan in *Bedrooms and Hallways*; *Blink*; Jedd in *Feast of July*; Joe in *Jilting Joe*; *Mansfield Park*; *Maybe Baby*; *The Lighthouse*; *The Wedding Tackle*; *Women Talking Dirty*.

Address: c/o ICM, Oxford House, 76 Oxford Street, London W1N 0AX.

PURVES, Peter

Peter Purves. Actor (M)/Presenter.
b. Preston, Lancashire, 10 February 1939.
TV: *Babble; Blue Peter; Breed All About It; Bullseye; Crimewatch Midlands; Cruft's Dog Show; Darts;* Steven in *Doctor Who; Pets Go Public; Super Dogs.*
Address: c/o Downes Presenter's Agency, 96 Broadway, Bexleyheath, Kent DA6 7DE. m. Kathryn Evans; 1 d. Cleo, 1 s. Matthew. Hobbies: Golf, classic cars, dogs (especially Newfoundlands), animals, cinema, computers, antiques, cooking.

Q

QUAYLE, Anna

Anna Quayle. Actor (F).
b. Birmingham, 6 October 1937.
TV: *A Degree of Frost;* Celia Spookfinder in *Adam's Family Tree III;* Nancy Tallboys in *Brideshead Revisited; Father Charlie; Flying High; Girls About Town;* Mrs Munroe in *Grange Hill; Grubb Street; Henry V; In the Looking Glass; James and the Giant Peach; Lytton's Diary;* Olga Braceley in *Mapp and Lucia;* Mrs Moorhouse in *Marjorie and Men; Never the Twain; Not Only … But Also; Rolling Home; Sakharov; The People of the Forest; Sloggers; Spate of Speight; The Avengers; The Beauty Operators; The Clan McCallaghan; The Georgian House; The Light Princess.*
Films: *A Hard Day's Night; Adventures of a Private Eye; Casino Royale; Chitty Chitty Bang Bang; Drop Dead Darling; Eskimo Nell; Mistress Pamela; Never Take Yes for an Answer; SOS Titanic; Smashing Time; The Sandwich Man; The Seven Per Cent Solution; The Tower of Babel; Three for All; Up the Chastity Belt.*
Address: c/o CDA, 19 Sydney Mews, London SW3 6HL.

QUENTIN, Caroline

Caroline Quentin. Actor (F)/Presenter.
b. 11 June 1960.
TV: *All or Nothing at All;* Monica in *An Evening with Gary Lineker; Bouncing Back; Casualty; Fry and Laurie; Galton & Simpson – The Missing Pages; Have I Got News for You; Home Front;* Maddy in *Jonathan Creek;* Kate in *Kiss Me Kate;* Dorothy in *Men Behaving Badly; Mr Bean; Once in a Lifetime; Paul Merton – The Series; This is David Lander; Travelogue; Upline; Videostars.*
Address: c/o Amanda Howard Associates Ltd, 21 Berwick Street, London W1V 3RG.

QUILLEY, Denis

Denis Quilley. Actor (M).
b. London, 26 December 1927.
TV: *After the War; Gladstone; Murder of a Moderate Man; Rich Tea and Sympathy; Sherlock Holmes; The Interrogation of John.*
Films: *Evil Under the Sun; Foreign Bodies; Masada; Mr Johnson; Murder on the Orient Express; Privates on Parade.*
Address: c/o Bernard Hunter Associates, 13 Spencer Gardens, London SW14 7AH.

QUIRKE, Pauline

Pauline Quirke. Actor (F)/Narrator/Presenter.
b. London, 8 July 1959.
TV: *A Name for a Day; Adventures of Oliver Twist; Ain't Many Angels; Angels; Baby Talk;* Sharon in *Birds of a Feather; Canterville Ghost; Casualty; Crown Court; David Copperfield; Deadly Summer; Dixon of Dock Green; Double Nougat; First Sign of Madness; Girls on Top; Hardwicke House; Jackanory; Jenny Can't Work any Faster; Jobs for the Girls; Life After Death; Lovely Couple; Maisie Raine; Maisie Raine II; Our Boy; Pauline's Quirkes; Pauline's PC Perils; Pauline's People; Real Women; Rockliffe's Babies; Shine on Harvey Moon; The Duchess of Duke Street; The Sculptress; The Travel Show; The Treasure Seekers; TV Club; Very Big, Very Soon; You Must be Joking.*
Films: *Check-Out Girl; Getting it Right; Little Dorrit; Still Lives – Distant Voices; The Elephant Man; The Return of the Soldier.*
Address: c/o DB Management, Pinewood Studios, Iver, Buckinghamshire SLO ONH. m. Steve; 1 d. Emily, 1 s. Charlie.

R

RADCLIFFE, Naomi
Naomi Radcliffe. Actor (F).
TV: Sarah in *Band of Gold*; Tina in *Cold Feet*; Alison Wakefield in *Coronation Street*; Beulah Turner in *In Suspicious Circumstances*; Claire Alcock in *Sunburn*; Lynne Milligan in *The Grand*.
Address: c/o Marina Martin Associates, 12–13 Poland Street, London W1V 3DE.

RAFFERTY, Barbara
Barbara Rafferty. Actor (F).
TV: Betty Hood in *Blagadoon*; Flora in *Dr Finlay; Go Now*; Agnes Meldrum in *Hamish Macbeth*; *Medical Ethics*; Madame Isis in *Para Handy*; Mrs Dougi in *Playing for Real*; Ella Cotter in *Rab C Nesbitt*; *Taggart*; Alice in *Take the High Road*; *Tinsel Town*; *Tutti Frutti*; *Young Person's Guide to Becoming a Rock Star*; Shirley in *Your Cheatin' Heart*.
Films: *Blood Red Roses*; *Slab Boys*; *The Wicker Man*; *Women Talking Dirty*.
Address: c/o ICM, Oxford House, 76 Oxford Street, London W1N 0AX.

RAFFIELD, Paul
Paul Raffield. Actor (M). b. London, 19 June 1957.
TV: Adam in *2point4 Children*; Dr Stirling in *Coronation Street*; Angus in *Grange Hill*; Robert in *Joking Apart*; Tom in *Karaoke*; King of Spades/Jack of Hearts in *MegaMaths*; Vicar in *Real Women*; Morgan in *The Gay Lord Quex*.
Films: Music shop owner in *Buddy's Song*.
Address: c/o Ken McReddie Ltd, 91 Regent Street, London W1R 7TB.

RAGGETT, Nick
Nick Raggett. Actor (M).
TV: Gavin in *Arcadia*; Dennis in *Darling Buds of May*; Freddie in *Get Back*; Danny Holmes in *IT For the Terrified*; Charlie in *Inspector Morse*; Derek in *Lovejoy*; Johnny in *Minder*; Henderson in *Pie in the Sky*; Simon Matthews in *Seconds Out*; Jake in *Streetwise*; Burgess/Yates in *The Bill*; Barry in *The Fear*.
Films: Bill in *Remote Control*.
Address: c/o Hillman Threlfall, 33 Brookfield, West Hill, London N6 6AT. Hobbies: Guitar, most sports.

RAMSAY, Gordon
Gordon Ramsay. Presenter/Chef. b. 1967.
TV: *Food and Drink*; *Masterchef*; *Passion for Flavour*.

RAMSAY, Louie
Louie Ramsay. Actor (F).
TV: Dora Wexford in *The Ruth Rendell Mysteries: A Sleeping Life, From Doon with Death, Kissing the Gunner's Daughter, No Crying He Makes, Shake Hands Forever, Simisola, Some Lie and Some Die, Wolf to the Slaughter*; *Road Rage*; *Softly, Softly*; Lady Bentley in *Strike It Rich*; *When the Boat Comes In*.
Address: c/o Brunskill Management, Suite 8a, 169 Queen's Gate, London SW7 5HE. m. 1 Ronan O'Casey (dis.); m. 2 George Baker.

RANTZEN, Esther
Esther Rantzen. Presenter. b. 22 June 1940.
TV: *Braden's Week*; *Esther*; *Hearts of Gold*; *Man Alive*; *Room 101*; *That's Esther*; *That's Life*.
Address: c/o Noel Gay Artists, 19 Denmark Street, London WC2H 8NA. m. Desmond Wilcox; 2 d. Emily, Rebecca, 1 s. Joshua.

RAPHAEL, Sally Jesse
Sally Jesse Raphael. Actor (F)/Executive producer/Host. b. Euston, Pennsylvania, USA, 25 February 1943.
TV: Judge in *No One Would Tell*; Herself in *Sabrina The Teenage Witch*; *Sally Jesse Raphael*; Herself in *The Nanny*; *The Third Twin*.
Films: Herself in *Meet Wally Sparks, Resident Alien, She Devil, The Addams Family, The Associate*.
Address: c/o Lee Fryd, c/o The Sally Show, 1510 Plaza, OF2, New York 10001, USA. m. Karl Soderlund; 2 children; 1 adopted child; 2 stepchildren. Hobbies: Designed her homes in Nice, Pawling, New York and Manhattan.

RASHLEIGH, Andrew
Andrew Rashleigh. Actor (M).
b. London, 23 January 1949.
TV: Pathologist in *Bad Company*; Brannigan in *Bomber*; Uniformed Constable in *Brideshead Revisited*; Ritchie Mason in *Casualty*; Customs Officer in

Harry Enfield Show; Cliff in *Heartbeat;* Mr Gardner in *Hollyoaks;* Jamie in *Lovejoy;* Trev in *Making Out;* Police Sergeant in *Minder;* DI Hilbury in *The Bill;* Hastings in *The Broker's Man;* Ron Cook in *The White House Farm Murders.*

Films: Simon (lead) in *Acceptable Levels;* Reporter in *Funny Bones;* Jailer in *Richard III;* Policeman in *Whatever Happened to Harold Smith.*

Address: c/o Michelle Braidman Associates, 10–11 Lower John Street, London W1R 3PE. Hobbies: Badminton, canoeing, sailing.

RATZENBERGER, John

John Ratzenberger. Actor (M)/Director/Voice artist/ Writer. b. Bridgeport, Connecticut, 6 April 1947.

TV: Marvin Schector in *Camp Cucmonga;* Rigger in *Captain Planet;* Clifford 'Cliff' C Clavin Jr in *Cheers; Dog's Best Friend;* Tom Phillips in *Friends in Space;* Bill Sweeny in *Goliath Awaits;* Jimmy in *The Good Soldier;* General Joe Brodsky in *Timestalkers.*

Films: PT Flea in *A Bug's Life;* American Lieutenant in *Gandhi;* Phil in *One Night Stand;* Controller in *Superman I* and *II;* Dusty in *That Darn Cat;* Major Bren Derlin *The Empire Strikes Back;* Clay Fairfield in *Tick Tock;* Hamm in *Toy Story 1* and *2.*

Address: c/o Stone Manner's Agency, Suite 740, 8436 W. 3rd Street, Los Angeles California 90048, USA. 2 children. Hobbies: Sailing, world history, fishing, carpentry, motorcycling, rowing, farming.

RAVENS, Jan

Jan Ravens. Actor (F).

b. Bebington, Merseyside, 14 May 1958.

TV: *Alexei Sayle's Stuff; An Actor's Life for Me; Carrott's Lib; C.A.T.S. Eyes; Duck Patrol; Harry Enfield and Chums; Have I Got News for You; Luv; No Frills; One Foot in the Grave; Spitting Image; The Final Frame; The Grimleys; Whose Line is it Anyway?.*

Films: *Fireworks;* Mama in *La Passione.*

Address: c/o Hillman Threlfall, 33 Brookfield, West Hill London, N6 6AT.

RAVENSCROFT, Christopher

Christopher Ravenscroft. Actor (M). b. 1946.

TV: *Coronation Street; John Halifax, Gentleman; Mind to Murder, PD James; Pericles; Secret Army; The Hound of the Baskervilles; The Levels;* Inspector Burden in *Ruth Rendell Mysteries; Twelfth Night.*

Films: *Henry V.*

Address: c/o The Narrow Road Company, 21–22 Poland Street, London W1V 3DD.

RAWLE, Jeff

Jeff Rawle. Actor (M). b. Birmingham, 20 July 1951.

TV: *A Perfect Hero; Bergerac;* Billy in *Billy Liar;* Barry in *Blood and Peaches; Boon; Call Me Mister; Casualty; Claire; Country and Irish; Doctor Who;* George in *Drop the Dead Donkey; EastEnders;* Paul in *Faith in the Future;* Anthony in *Fish; Fortunes of War; Juliet Bravo; Look at the State We're In;* Barry in *Lords of Misrule; Love on the Dole; Medics;* Colin Parker in *Microsoap; Minder; Moon and Son;* Neville in *Neville's Island; Play for Today; Remington Steele; Rides; Run for the Lifeboat;* Lang in *Sharman; Singles; Singles Weekend; South of the Border; The Chief; The Gift; The Life and Times of Henry Pratt; The Water Maiden; Vote for Them; Wilde Alliance.*

Films: *A Hitch in Time; Awayday; Baal; Correction Please; Crystal Gazing; Doctors and Devils; Duchamp; Inspector Calls II; Laughterhouse; Rating Norman.*

Address: c/o Annette Stone Associates, 2nd Floor, 22 Great Marlborough Street, London W1V 1AF.

RAWLINGS, Adrian

Adrian Rawlings. Actor (M).

b. Stoke-on-Trent, 27 March 1958.

TV: Chris in *An Evil Streak;* Oliver in *Forgotten; Insiders; Liverpool 1; Soldier, Soldier; Tears Before Bedtime; The Ginger Tree; Woman in Black.*

Films: *Blood;* Dr Richardson in *Breaking the Waves; Ghost Writers; Mountains of the Moon; Revolution.*

Address: c/o Ken McReddie Ltd, 91 Regent Street, London W1R 7TB. Hobbies: Travel.

RAWLINGS, Ian

Ian Rawlings. Actor (M).

TV: *Mission Impossible;* Philip Martin in *Neighbours; Some Kind of Friend; Sons and Daughters; The Power and the Passion.*

Address: c/o Grundy Television, Grundy House, Barge House Crescent, 34 Upper Ground, London SE1 9PD.

RAY, Andrew

Andrew Ray. Actor (M). b. London, 31 May 1939.

TV: King George VI in *Edward and Mrs Simpson; Inspector Morse; Our Mutual Friend;* Dr John Reginald in *Peak Practice; Tales of the Unexpected; Upstairs Downstairs.*

Films: *Gideon's Day; Paris by Night; Prize of Gold; Roughcut; Serious Charge;* Title Role in *The Mudlark; Twice Around the Daffodils; Woman in a Dressing Gown; Yellow Balloon.*

Address: c/o Chuck Julian Associates, Suite 51, 26 Charing Cross Road, London WC2 ODH. m. Susan

Ray; 1 d. Madeleine, 1 s. Mark; father Ted; brother Robin. Hobbies: Supporter of Arsenal FC.

REDDINGTON, Ian

Ian Reddington. Actor (M). b. Sheffield.

TV: *Boon; Cadfael; Casualty; Doctor Who; EastEnders; Holby City; Inspector Morse; Peak Practice; Play for Today; Snap; The Bill; The Queen's Nose; The Sculptress; The Sharp End; Three Up, Two Down.*

Films: *Crime Strike; Highlander; Speak Like a Child; Who Needs a Heart.*

Address: c/o Ken McReddie Ltd, 91 Regent Street, London W1R 7TB.

REDFERN, Michael

Michael Redfern. Actor (M).

TV: *Alas Smith and Jones;* Police Sup't Johnson in *An Independent Man;* George in *Between the Lines;* Police Inspector in *Boon;* Mr Cooper in *Bottom;* Drill Sergeant in *Bye Bye Baby; Carrott Confidential; Checkpoint Chiswick;* Sean Thompson in *Crime Expert; Filthy Rich and Catflap;* Boyce in *Fool's Gold; Girls on Top;* Mr Warner in *Health and Efficiency;* Ted in *Hope and Glory;* Mr Roberts in *Hope it Rains;* Fitness Instructor in *I Charles De Gaulle;* PC in *In Sickness and in Health; In the Secret State;* Lewis in *Library of Romance;* Air Traffic Controller in *London's Burning; Money and Magee; Relative Strangers;* Lord Glister in *Robin Hood; Sorry;* Mechanic in *Stick With Me Kid;* Jack in *The 19th Hole;* Harry Ford in *The Bill;* Mr Warner in *The Detectives; Three Up, Two Down;* Chief Sup't Fleming in *True Crimes 1991.*

Films: Commissionaire in *Hubcap;* George in *Square Eyed Junkie.*

Address: c/o McIntosh Rae Management, Thornton House, Thornton Road, London SW19 4NG. Hobbies: Golf.

REDGRAVE, Jemma

Jemma Redgrave. Actor (F). b. 1965.

TV: *A Time to Die;* Elaine in *All Good Things;* Gale in *Blue Murder;* Eleanor Bramwell in *Bramwell;* Dr Wolf in *Cry Wolf;* Joanna in *Fish;* Pip Campbell in *Mixing It;* Cynthia Mosley in *Mosley; The Buddha of Suburbia;* Pamela in *The Real Charlotte;* Caroline Croon in *The Trials of Oz.*

Films: *Dream Demon; Howard's End; Power and Conflict; The Acid House.*

Address: c/o Conway Van Gelder, 18–21 Jermyn Street, London SW1Y 6HP.

REDING, Nick

Nick Reding. Actor (M). b. London, 31 August 1962.

TV: Parker in *A Touch of Frost;* Marusko in *BUGS;* Dave in *Frank Stubbs;* Edward, Prince of Wales in *Henry VI (Part III);* Basil Pilgrim in *Inspector Alleyn Mysteries;* Tim in *Lake of Darkness;* Older Campbell in *Longitude;* George in *My Family and Other Animals;* Harry Stokes in *Paradise Postponed;* Edward, Prince of Wales in *Richard III;* DI Connor in *Silent Witness;* Albert in *Sponoza; Sunburn;* PC Ramsey in *The Bill;* Cazeaux in *The Count of Solar;* Haki in *The Final Frame;* Tommy Dixon in *The House of Elliott;* Cruickshank in *The Monocled Mutineer;* Alex Turner/Tim Ellis in *Where There's Smoke.*

Films: Skag in *Attenborough;* Giles Cremorne in *Croupier;* Tring in *Mr Johnson;* Mellor in *Murder of Quality;* Pete in *Real Life.*

Address: c/o Markham & Froggatt Ltd, 4 Windmill Street, London W1P 1HF.

REDMAN, Amanda

Amanda Redman. Actor (F).

TV: *To Have and to Hold; On the Line; La Ronde; Pericles; The Rivals; The Importance of Being Earnest; Oxbridge Blues; Streets Apart; The Lorelei;* Sally in *The Men's Room;* Rosie Bromley in *El C.I.D.;* Wexford – *From Doom with Death; Body and Soul;* Janet in *Demob;* Joanna Stevens in *Dangerfield;* Julie Carson in *Taggart – Black Orchid;* Susan Townsend in *The Secret House of Deth; Beck;* Prudence in *Close Relations;* Regan in *King Lear;* Diana Dors in *Blonde Bombshell;* Debbie Bryan in *Hope and glory;* Alison Braithwaite in *At Home With the Braithwaites.*

Films: *Richard's Things; Give My Regards to Broad Street; For Queen and Country;* Petula in *The Wedding Tackle;* Deedee in *Sexy Beast.*

Address: c/o CDA, 19 Sydney Mews, London SW3 6HL.

REDMOND, Siobhan

Siobhan Redmond. Actor (F).
b. Glasgow, Scotland, 27 August 1959.

TV: *Alfresco; At the End of Alex Cording; Between the Lines; Bulman; Casualty; Dad on Arrival; Deacon Brodie; End of the Line; Every Woman Knows A Secret; Gravy Train; Hard Cases; In the Red; Look Back In Anger; Nervous Energy; Nothing To Worry About; Rab C Nesbitt; Relative Stranger; Rides; Sorry About Last Night; Sweet Nothings; Taggart; Tea Bags; The Bill; The Dunroman Rising; The High Life; Throwaways; Wokenwell.*

Films: *Beautiful People; Captives; Duet for One; Karmic Mothers.*

Address: c/o Conway Van Gelder, 18–21 Jermyn Street SW1Y 6HP.

REES, Maureen

Maureen Rees. Actor (F)/Presenter.
b. Cardiff, 25 February 1942.
TV: *All Over the Shop; Ant and Dec Show;* Herself in *Barbara; Holiday; Children in Need; Confessions; Dreamworld; Driving School; Esther; Here and Now; Maureen's Motors; National Television Awards; Night Fever; Record Breakers; Speculate to Accumulate; Style Challenge; The Eleventh Hour; The Generation Game; The Jack Dee Show; The Making of Maureen; The National Lottery Live; The Really Useful Show; The Time the Place; This is Your Life.*
Films: *Dad's Room.*
Music: *I Like Driving in My Car* (No. 50).
Address: c/o David Anthony Promotions, PO Box 286, Warrington, Cheshire WA2 6GA. m. David Rees; 1 s. Leyton. 2 d. Mandy, Hayley. Hobbies: Reading, classical music, history, charity work.

REES, Roger

Roger Rees. Actor (M). b. Aberystwyth, 5 May 1944.
TV: *A Christmas Carol; Bouquet of Barbed Wire; Comedy of Errors; Double Platinum; Imaginary Friends; Liberty! The American Revolution; Macbeth; Saigon: The Year of the Cat; The Crossing; The Ebony Tower; Nicholas Nickleby; Singles; Cheers.*
Films: *Black Male; If Looks could Kill; Jump; Midsummer Night's Dream; Next Stop Wonderland; Star 80; Stop! Or my Mom Will Shoot; Sudden Manhattan; The Bumblebee Flies Anyway; The Voysey Inheritance; Trouble on the Corner; Under Western Eyes.*
Address: c/o ICM, Oxford House, 76 Oxford Street, London W1N 0AX.

REEVES, Saskia

Saskia Reeves. Actor (F). b. London, 1962.
TV: Antonia in *Antonia and Jane;* Lady Mordaunt in *Citizen Locke;* Pietrovska in *Bandung;* Helen in *Border Country;* Rosie in *Children Crossing;* Mrs Cratchitt in *A Christmas Carol;* Serena in *Cruel Train;* Greta in *Metamorphosis;* Phillippa Monaghan in *My Defence;* Bridget in *Perfect Match;* Carol in *Plotlands;* Irene in *Summer's Day Dream.*
Films: Miriam in *Butterfly Kiss;* Natalie in *Close My Eyes;* Sarah in *December Bride;* Jean in *Different for Girls;* Sarah in *Faith;* Maria in *Heart;* Linda in *ID;* Joy in *LA Without a Map;* Isobel in *The Bridge;* Louis in *Traps.*
Address: c/o Markham & Froggatt Ltd, 4 Windmill Street, London W1P 1HF.

REEVES, Vic

Jim Moir. Comedian/Writer/Presenter.
b. Darlington, 24 January 1959.

TV: *A Night in with Vic and Bob; A Nose Through Nature; Bang Bang, It's Reeves and Mortimer; Christmas Night with the Stars; Families at War; It's Ulrika; Shooting Stars; The Smell of Reeves and Mortimer; Vic Reeves' Big Night Out; Weekenders.*
Music: *Abide With Me; Born Free; Dizzy* (No. 1); *I Will Cure You; I'm A Believer.*
Address: c/o PBJ Management, 5 Soho Square, London W1V 5DE.

REGAN, Linda

Linda Regan. Actor (F). b. London, 5 November 1959.
TV: *Harry and Cosh;* April in *Hi De Hi; Minder; The Bill; The Knock.*
Films: *Carry On England; Holding On; The Hiding Place.*
Address: c/o George Heathcote Management, 58 Northdown Street, London N1 9BS. m. Brian Murphy; Sister: Carol Drinkwater. Hobbies: Magic, writing.

REGAN, Vincent

Vincent Regan. Actor (M). b. 1966.
TV: *99–1; A Touch of Frost; Between the Lines; Boon; Call Red; Chandler and Co.; Eureka Street; Heaven; Invasion Earth; Jeremiah; London's Burning; Moving Story; Over the Rainbow; Paul Calf Video Diary; Peak Practice; Ruth Rendell Mysteries; The Bill.*
Films: *B Monkey; Black Beauty; Fork in the Road; Hard Men; Joan of Arc; When Animals Attack.*
Address: c/o Conway Van Gelder, 18–21 Jermyn Street, London SW1Y 6HP.

REID, Anne

Anne Reid. Actor (F).
TV: *A Bit of Fry and Laurie;* Gwendoline in *A Close Shave – Wallace and Gromit; Bleak House; Boon; Buggin's Ermine; Casualty; Coronation Street; dinnerladies; Doctor Who; Fathers and Families; Firm Friends; Heartbeat; Hetty Wainthropp Investigates; Heydays Hotel; In Hitler's Shadow; Inappropiate Behaviours; Josie Smith; Lost for Words; Matchfit; Medics; Mickey Love; Mrs Worthington's Daughter; My Father's House; Next of Kin; Pat and Margaret; Paul Merton in... 'Don't Dilly Dally', 'The Lift' and 'Visiting Day'; Peak Practice; Playing the Field; Rich Tea and Sympathy; Roughnecks; Ruth Rendell Mysteries; Seaforth; Shine on Harvey Moon; Sometime Never; Spark; The Bill; The Mallens; The Upper Hand; Very Big, Very Soon; Victoria Wood's Comedy Playhouse.*
Films: *Love and Death on Long Isand; The Wingless Bird.*
Address: c/o Crouch Associates, 9-15 Neal Street, London WC2H 9PF.

REID, Mike

Mike Reid. Actor (M)/Presenter.
b. London, 19 January 1940.
TV: *The Saint; The Baron; The Comedians; Runaround; Yes My Dear; Big Deal; Minder; The Detectives;* Frank Butcher in *EastEnders.*
Address: c/o Curtis Brown, Haymarket House, 28–29 Haymarket, London SW1Y 4SP.

REID, Tim

Tim Reid. Actor (M).
b. Norfolk, Virginia, USA, 19 December 1944.
TV: *Blue Moon;* Frank Parrish in *Frank's Place;* Mike Hanlon in *IT; Linc;* Tillson in *Little Lulu;* Chip Chatsworth in *Mastergate; Samurai Pizza Cats;* Downtown Brown in *Simon and Simon;* Ray Campbell in *Sister, Sister;* Michael Horne in *Teachers Only;* Donald in *You Can't Take It With You;* Joe in *You Must Remember This.*
Films: *Asunder;* Chief Dixon in *Dead Bang; Once Upon a Time, When We Were Coloured;* Detective Wilson in *Out of Sync; Say a Little Prayer; Spirit Lost;* Lt Col. Clark in *The Fourth War.*
Address: c/o New Millennium Studios, 1 New Millennium Drive, Petersburg, Virginia 23805, USA.
m. Daphne Maxwell-Reid. Hobbies: Lives on a farm and boards horses.

REILLY, Kelly

Kelly Reilly. Actor (F).
TV: Kathleen Le Saux in *Bramwell;* Patience in *Children of the New Forest;* Tina in *Pie in the Sky;* Clowance Poldark in *Poldark;* Polly Henry in *Prime Suspect VI;* Clarice in *Rebecca;* Julie in *Sex and Death;* Sophie Bright in *Sharman; The Ruth Rendell Mysteries: Simisola;* Laura in *The Biz;* Nancy Miller in *Tom Jones;* Nancy in *Wonderful You.*
Films: Nimnh in *Maybe Baby;* Cherry in *Peaches.*
Address: c/o Lou Coulson, 37 Berwick Street, London W1V 3RF.

REISER, Paul

Paul Reiser. Actor (M).
b. New York, USA, 30 March 1957.
TV: Modell in *Diner; Loved By You;* Paul Buchman in *Mad About You;* Michael Taylor in *My Two Dads; The 20th Annual People's Choice Awards* (1994); *The 37th Annual Grammy Awards* (1995); *The 48th Annual Prime Time Emmy Awards* (1996); Tony Minot in *The Tower;* Dexter Bunche in *You Ruined My Life;* Ivan Turbell in *Remington Steele.*
Films: Carter J Burke in *Aliens;* Jeffrey in *Beverly Hills Cop;* Jeffrey in *Beverly Hills Cop II;* Donny in *Bye, Bye,*

Love; Stephen in *Crazy People;* Himself in *Get Bruce;* Charlie in *Mr Write; One Night at McCool's;* Marty in *The Story of Us.*
Address: c/o William Morris Agency, 151 El Camino Drive, Beverly Hills, California 90212, USA.

RHIND-TUTT, Julian

Julian Rhind-Tutt. Actor (M).
b. Middlesex, 20 July 1968.
TV: Philip in *An Unsuitable Job for a Woman; Hippies; Let Them Eat Cake; Reckless;* Forester in *The Tribe* (1998); *Under the Sun;* Stan in *The Vacillations of Poppy Carew.*
Films: Journalist in *Notting Hill;* Duke of York in *The Madness of King George; The Trench.*
Address: c/o PFD, Drury House, 34–43 Russell Street, London WC2B 5HA.

RHODES, Gary

Gary Rhodes. Chef/Presenter.
b. London, 22 April 1960.
TV: *Gary Rhodes* (1996); *Gary's Perfect Christmas; Rhodes Around Britain; Open Rhodes Around Britain; Roald Dahl's Revolting Recipes; This is Your Life.*
Address: c/o Deborah McKenna Ltd, Claridge House, 29 Barnes High Street, London SW13 9LW. m. Jenny; 2 s. Samuel, George. Hobbies: Fast cars, fashion, music.

RHYS-JONES, Griff

Griff Rhys-Jones. Actor (M)/Presenter/Writer.
b. Cardiff, Wales, 16 November 1953.
TV: Harry Clarke in *A View of Harry Clarke; Boat People; Bookworm;* Ian in *Demob;* Patrick in *Ex;* Jones in *Not the Nine O'clock News;* Carrington in *Porterhouse Blue;* Maurice/Colin/Boz/Rev. Andrew Pennycuick in *Small Doses; Smith and Jones; The Nation's Favourite Comic Poem; Alas Smith and Jones; The World According to Smith and Jones.*
Films: Touchstone in *As You Like It;* Graham Sweetley in *Morons from Outer Space;* Guiseppe in *Pinocchio; Staggered;* Ray Mason in *Up 'n' Under;* Henry Wilt in *Wilt.*
Address: c/o TalkBack Management, 36 Percy Street, London W1P OLN.

RICE, Anneka

Anneka Rice. Presenter.
b. Cowbridge, Wales, 4 October 1958.
TV: *Capital Woman; CBTV; Challenge Anneka; Family Trees; News; Passport; Sporting Chance; Treasure Hunt; TV–am; Wish You Were Here.*
Address: c/o Simpson Fox Associates Ltd, 52 Shaftes-

bury Avenue, London W1V 7DE. m. 1 Nick Allott (dis.); Partner: Tom Gutteridge (dis); 3 s. Thomas Allott, Joshua Allott, Sam Gutteridge. Hobbies: scuba diving.

RICHARD, Wendy

Wendy Richard. Actor (F)/Presenter.
b. Middlesbrough, 20 July 1946.
TV: *A Big Night Out*; Shirley Brahms in *Are You Being Served?*; *Big Breakfast*; *Blankety Blank*; *Both Ends Meet*; *Call My Bluff*; *Circus*; *Dad's Army*; *Danger Man*; *Dixon of Dock Green*; *Don't Turn Out the Lights*; Pauline Fowler in *EastEnders*; *Esther*; *Give Us a Clue*; Shirley Brahms in *Grace & Favour*; *Harpers West One*; *HMS Paradise*; *Holly Road Rig*; *It's Only TV But I Like It*; *Jim'll Fix It*; *Jobs for the Boys*; *Joe Nobody*; *Little and Large*; *London Wall*; *No Hiding Place*; *Noel's House Party*; *Not on Your Nellie*; *On the Buses*; *Play for Today*; *Please, Sir*; *Spooner's Patch*; *Telly Addicts*; *That's Life*; *The Dick Emery Show*; *The Fenn Street Gang*; *The Generation Game*; *The History of the Jack Russell*; *The Likely Lads*; *The Making of Jericho*; *The Newcomers*; *Up Pompeii*; *Wogan*; *You Bet*; *Z-Cars*.
Films: *Are You Being Served?*; *Bless this House*; *Carry On Girls*; *Carry on Matron*; *Doctor in Clover*; *Gumshoe*; *Help!*; *No Blade of Grass*; *On the Buses*.
Address: c/o Associated International Management, 5 Denmark Street, London WC2H 8LP.

RICHARDS, Michael

Michael Richards. Actor (M)/Comedian.
b. Van Nuys, Los Angeles, USA, 24 July 1949.
TV: Eddie Gordon in *Cheers*; Mr Micawber in *David Copperfield*; *Fridays*; Dr Herndon P. Stool in *Herndon*; Rick the gardener in *Marblehead Manor*; Cosmo Kramer in *Seinfeld*; Himself in *The Larry Sanders Show*; Kessier in *The Seinfeld Chronicles*.
Films: Doug Beech in *Airheads*; Motel Clerk in *Coneheads*; Martin Beck in *Problem Child*; The Wolf in *Redux Riding Hood*; Obituary writer in *So I Married an Axe Murderer*; Fejos in *Transylvania 6–5000*; Richard 'Rick' Rietti in *Trial and Error*; Acrobat in *Whoops Apocalypse*.
Address: c/o Jay Cooper, Manatt Phelps Philips, 11555 West Olympic Blvd, Los Angeles, California 90064, USA. m. Cathleen Richards (dis.); 1 d. Sophia; partner Michele Correy. Hobbies: Travelling, book collecting.

RICHARDSON, Ian

Ian Richardson. Actor (M). b. Edinburgh, 7 April 1934.
TV: *A Royal Scandal*; *Alice Through the Looking Glass*; *All's Well That Ends Well*; Rex Hunt in *An Ungentle-*

mantly Act; *Canterbury Tales*; *Charlie Muffin*; *Churchill and the Generals*; *Dirty Weekend*; *Gormenghast* (2000); *Highlander*; Francis in *House of Cards*; *Monsignor Quixote*; *Much Ado About Nothing*; *Porterhouse Blue*; *Private Schultz*; *Six Centuries of Verse*; *Star Quality*; *The Canterville Ghost*; *The Devil's Disciple*; *The Final Cut*; *The Gravy Train*; *The Gravy Train Goes East*; Sherlock Holmes in *The Hound of the Baskervilles*; The Magician in *The Magician's House*; *The Master of Ballantrae*; *The Phantom of the Opera*; *The Sign of Four*; *The Treasure Seekers*; *The Winslow Boy*; *The Woman in White*; *To Play the King*; *Tinker, Tailor, Soldier, Spy*.
Films: *Dark City*; *Man of La Mancha*; *Marat/Sade*; Captain Fitzroy in *The Darwin Adventure*; *The Fourth Protocol*; *Whoops Apocalypse*.
Address: c/o London Management, Noel House, 2–4 Noel Street, London W1V 3RB.

RICHARDSON, Joely

Joely Richardson. Actor (F)/Voice artist.
b. London, 9 January 1965.
TV: Serafina in *Behaving Badly*; Janetta Wheatland in *Heading Home*; Lady Chatterley in *Lady Chatterley*; Amanda Powell in *The Echo*; *The Storyteller*; Emily in *The Tribe*; *Poirot: The Dream*.
Films: Anita in *101 Dalmatians*; Dominique in *Body Contact*; Cissie Colpitts in *Drowning by Numbers*; Rhiannon in *Rebecca's Daughters*; Young Jean Travers in *Wetherby*.
Address: c/o PFD, Drury House, 34–43 Russell Street, London WC2B 5HA.

RICHARDSON, Miranda

Miranda Richardson. Actor (F).
b. Southport, Lancashire, 3 March 1959.
TV: *Alice*; *Blackadder II* and *III*; *Die Kinder*; *Fatherland*; *Jackanory*; *Merlin*; *Redemption*; *Sweet As You Are*; *Ted and Ralph*; *The Scold's Bridle*; *The Storyteller*.
Films: *All for Love*; *Blackadder – Millennium Dome*; *Damage*; *Empire of the Sun*; *Kansas City*; *La Nuit et le Moment*; *Sleepy Hollow*; *Space Virgins*; *Swann*; *The Chicken Run*; *The Crying Game*; *Tom and Viv*.
Address: c/o ICM, Oxford House, 76 Oxford Street, London W1N 0AX.

RICHARDSON, Natasha

Natasha Richardson. Actor (F).
b. London, 11 May 1963.
TV: *Ghosts*; *In a Secret State*; *Suddenly Last Summer*; *The Barringtons*; *The Copper Beeches*; *Zelder*.
Films: *A Month In The Country*; *Dangerous Woman*; *Fat Man and Little Boy*; *Gothic*; *Nell*; *Past Midnight*; *Patty Hearst*; *The Comfort of Strangers*; *The Favor, the*

Watch and the Very Big Fish; The Handmaid's Tale; The Parent Trap; Widow's Peak.
Address: c/o ICM, Oxford House, 76 Oxford Street, London W1N 0AX.

RICHARDSON, Patricia

Patricia Richardson. Actor (F).
b. Bethesda, Maryland, 23 February 1951.
TV: Beth McConnell in *Double Trouble*; Jill Taylor in *Home Improvement*; Cassie Maguire in *Parent Trap III*; Laurel Vega in *Undue Influence*.
Films: Cindy in *In Country*; Connie Hope in *Ulee's Gold*.
Address: c/o Jonathan Howard, 151 El Camino Drive, Beverly Hills, California 90212, USA.

RICHIE, Shane

Shane Richie. Presenter/Actor (M).
b. London, 11 March 1964.
TV: *Caught in the Act; Love Me Do; Lucky Numbers; Run the Risk; The Shane Richie Experience; Win, Lose or Draw.*
Films: Nicos Malmatakis in *Dead Clean*; Paul in *Distant Shadow*; Porter in *Macbeth*.
Address: AMG Ltd, 8 King Street, London WC2E 8HN. m. Coleen Nolan; 2 s. Shane, Jake. Hobbies: Collecting *Planet of the Apes* memorabilia.

RICKITT, Adam

Adam Rickitt. Actor (M). b. Cheshire, 29 May 1978.
TV: Nick Tilsley in *Coronation Street*.
Music: *Everything My Heart Desires; Good Times; I Breathe Again* (No. 5).
Address: c/o Polydor Ltd, 1 Sussex Place, London W6 9XS. Father Peter Rickitt; mother Gill Rickitt; 3 brothers Tim, Mark, Sam. Hobbies: Rugby, boxing, surfing, horse riding, driving, Manchester City supporter.

RICKWOOD, Christopher

Christopher Rickwood. Actor (M).
TV: PC Keith Stringer in *A Touch of Frost*; Father Nathan in *Big Bad World*; PC Roberts in *Sam Saturday*; Robert in *The Bill*.
Address: c/o Storm Artists Management, 47 Brewer Street, London W1R 3FD.

RIDDINGTON, Ken

Ken Riddington. Producer. b. Leicester.
TV: *A Horseman Riding By; A Very Peculiar Practice; An Unofficial Rose; Anna Karenina; Breakaway; Campion; Diana; House of Cards; Late Call; Mother Love; Tenko; Tenko Reunion; The Brothers; The Citadel; The Legend of King Arthur; To Serve Them All My Days.*
Address: c/o Bernard Hunter Associates, 13 Spencer

Gardens, London SW14 7AH.

RIDER, Steve

Steve Rider. Sports presenter/Reporter.
TV: *Blankety Blank; Commonwealth Games; French & Saunders; Goodnight Sweetheart; Grandstand; Motormouth; Olympic Games; Sportsnight; Cricket World Cup,* (1999); *The Full Wax; Wimbledon; Winter Olympics; World of Sport; The Boat Show.*
Address: c/o Blackburn Sachs Associates, Eastgate House, 16–19 Eastcastle Street, London W1N 7PA.
Hobbies: Golf, watching motor racing (particularly British Touring Car Championships).

RIGG, Diana

Diana Rigg. Actor (F).
b. Doncaster, Yorkshire, 20 July 1938.
TV: *Bleak House; Hedda Gabler; King Lear; Little Eyolf; Mother Love;* Mrs Danvers in *Rebecca; Samson and Delilah;* Emma Peel in *The Avengers; The Worst Witch; Witness for the Prosecution; The Mrs Bradley Mysteries.*
Films: *A Good Man in Africa; A Little Night Music; A Midsummer Night's Dream; Evil Under the Sun; On Her Majesty's Secret Service; The Hospital.*
Address: c/o PFD, Drury House, 34–43 Russell Street, London WC2B 5HA.

RILEY, Lisa

Lisa Riley. Actor (F)/Presenter.
b. Bury, Lancashire, 13 July 1976.
TV: Mandy Dingle in *Emmerdale; You've Been Framed.*
Films: *Butterfly Kiss; Secret Society.*
Address: c/o AMG Ltd, 8 King Street, London WC2E 8HN.

RIMMER, Simon

Simon Rimmer. Chef/Presenter.
TV: *Battle of the Chefs; Granada Tonight; Livetime; Shop!; This Morning.*
Address: c/o Curtis Brown, Haymarket House, 28–29 Haymarket, London SW1Y 4SP.

RINGHAM, John

John Ringham. Actor (M).
TV: *Birds of a Feather;* Smythe in *Bramwell; Casanova; Casualty;* Captain Bailey in *Dad's Army; Darling Buds of May; Doctor Who; Flambards;* Norman in *Just Good Friends; London's Burning;* Norman in *Melissa; New Scotland Yard;* Captain in *New World;* Mr Hassocks in *Out of Sight; Pennies from Heaven; Poldark; The* Doctor in *Shadowlands; Sherlock Holmes; Taggart; The Avengers;* Lawyer Finney in *The Barchester Chronicles; The Bill; The Cantor of St Thomas;* Judge Simms in *The*

Governor (1994); Major Maxwell in *The Piglet Files; The Saint;* Mr Blocker in *Woof.*

Address: c/o Michael Ladkin Personal Management, Suite One, Ground Floor, 1 Duchess Street, London W1N 3DE.

RINTOUL, David

David Rintoul. Actor (M). b. 29 November 1948.

TV: Linus in *AD; Crown Court;* Boswell in *Dialogue in the Dark;* Dr Finlay in *Dr Finlay; Henry VIII;* Sir John Phillips in *Inspector Alleyn Mysteries;* Wheatley in *Kinsey; Ladies in Charge; Lillie; Lord Peter Whimsey; Much Ado About Nothing;* John Cavendish in *Mysterious Affair at Styles; One Chance in Four; Poirot;* Darcy in *Pride and Prejudice;* Dr Carter in *Private Practice; Rabbit Pie Day; Taggart; The Big Deal;* Yasha in *The Cherry Orchard;* Rev. Douglas in *The Dunroamin' Rising;* Ewan Cameron in *The Flight of the Heron; The Hunchback of Notre Dame; The Mallens; The Member for Chelsea; The Prince Regent; The Shadow of the Noose; Warship;* Archie Weir in *Weir of Hermiston.*

Films: Werewolf in *The Legend of the Werewolf.*

Address: c/o Ken McReddie Ltd, 91 Regent Street, London W1R 7TB.

RIPLEY, Fay

Fay Ripley. Actor (F). b. London, 1966.

TV: *Cold Feet; Karaoke; One for the Road; Rumble; The Bill; The Broker's Man; The Prince; Without Walls.*

Films: *A Mute Witness; Eclipsed; Roseanna's Grave; The Announcement.*

Address: c/o ICM, Oxford House, 76 Oxford Street, London W1N 0AX.

RIPPON, Angela

Angela Rippon. Presenter.

b. Plymouth, Devon, 12 October 1944.

TV: *A Game of War; Angela Rippon Meets; Antiques Roadshow; Come Dancing; Eurovision Song Contest; Face Value; Healthcheck; In the Country; Masterteam; Matchpoint; Open House; The Key to the White House; The Morecambe and Wise Christmas Show; The Nobel Prize; The Wedding of HRH Prince Charles and Lady Diana Spencer; The Windsor's Sale of a Lifetime; Those Were the Days; Top Gear; What's My Line.*

Address: c/o Knight Ayton Management, 10 Argyll Street, London W1V 1AB.

RITCHIE, Kate

Kate Ritchie. Actor (F). b. Goulburn, New South Wales, Australia, 14 August 1978.

TV: *Cyclone Tracy;* Sally Fletcher in *Home & Away.*

Address: c/o Seven Network Ltd, Mabbs Lane,

Epping, NSW 2121, Australia. Hobbies: Singing, videos, cinema, scuba diving, the beach.

RITTER, John

John Ritter. Actor (M).

b. Burbank, California, USA, 17 September 1948.

TV: Judge Harold Benton in *A Smoky Mountain Christmas;* Dr Carter Elston in *Dead Husbands;* John Heartman in *Hearts Afire;* Joe Cass in *Holy Joe;* Detective Harry Hooperman in *Hooperman; In Love with an Older Woman;* Ben Hanscom in *IT;* Donald Bridges in *It Came From The Sky;* Dr David Farris in *Lethal Vows;* Rick Knowlton in *The Colony* (1995); Walter Wingate in *The Night That Panicked America;* Jeremy Carlisle in *The Only Way Out;* Paul in *The Summer My Father Grew Up;* Rev. Matthew Fordwick in *The Waltons;* Jack Tripper in *Three's Company* and *Three's a Crowd;* Donald Todsen in *Tricks of the Trade;* Paul Hegstrom in *Unforgivable.*

Films: President Roosevelt in *Americathon;* Warren Kincaid in *Bride of Chucky;* Robert Forrest in *I Woke Up Early the Day I Die; Believe in You;* Christian Therapist in *Lost in The Perishing Point Hotel;* Ward Nelson in *North;* Little Ben Healy in *Problem Child;* Ben Healy in *Problem Child 2;* Steven Mayer in *Shadow of Doubt;* Peter Dickenson in *The Flight of Dragons;* The Rider in *The Other;* Tom Williams in *Tripfall;* Satan in *Wholly Moses.*

Address: c/o ICM, Oxford House, 8942 Wilshire Blvd., Beverly Hills, California 90211, USA. m. 1 Nancy Morgan (dis.); 1 d; m. 2 Amy Yasbeck; 2 s.; 1 d.; father Tex Ritter; mother Dorothy Fay; brother Tom.

RITTERS, Rebecca

Rebecca Ritters. Actor (F). b. 26 January 1984.

TV: Hannah Martin in *Neighbours.*

Address: c/o Grundy Television, Grundy House, Barge House Crescent, 34 Upper Ground, London SE1 9PD. Hobbies: Travel, animal welfare.

ROACH, Pat

Pat Roach. Actor (M). b. Birmingham.

TV: *A Roller Next Year; Auf Wiedersehen, Pet; Bullseye; Casualty; Coasting; Ellington; Gangsters; Give Us a Kiss, Christabel; Harry's Kingdom; Hazell; Heartbeat; Jack and Jeremy Police; Jim Davidson Show; Juliet Bravo;* PC Evans in *Last Place on Earth; Marlene Marlow Investigates; Minder; Pirates; Saturday Starship; Sea Dragon; Space Precinct; Telly Addicts; The Bill; The Detectives; The Lenny and Jerry Show; The New Adventures of Robin Hood; Three Wishes for Jamie; True Tilda.*

Films: *A Clockwork Orange; Barry Lydon; Clash of the Titans; Conan the Barbarian II; Flash Gordon; I Love You Love Me Love; Indiana Jones and the Last Crusade;*

Indiana Jones and the Raiders of the Lost Ark; Indiana Jones and the Temple of Doom; Kill the Conquerer; Never Say Never Again; Red Sonja; Robin Hood Prince of Thieves; The Big Man; The Monster Club; The Portrait of a Lady; The Return of the Musketeers; The Spaceman and King Arthur; Kael in *Willow.*

Address: c/o Peter Charlesworth & Associates, 68 Old Brompton Road, London SW7 3LQ.

ROACHE, Linus

Linus Roache. Actor (M).
b. Burnley, Lancashire, 1 February 1964.
TV: Richard Davidson in *A Sort of Innocence;* Christ in *Animated World Faiths – The Life of Christ;* Detective Sergeant Brian Tait in *Black and Blue;* Peter Barlow in *Coronation Street;* Tom in *Keeping Tom Nice;* Vincent Van Gogh in *Omnibus: Vincent Van Gogh;* Daniel McAvaddy in *Saracen;* Bob Langman in *Seaforth;* Vlado in *Shot Through the Heart; The Onedin Line.*
Films: Denis Law in *Best; Link;* Ulster Boy in *No Surrender;* Sam Coleridge in *Pandemonium;* Father Greg Pilkington in *Priest;* Perry in *Siam Sunset;* Count Jacko/Count Giaccomo in *The Venice Project;* Merton Densher in *The Wings of the Dove.*
Address: c/o Kate Feast Management, 10 Primrose Hill Studios, Fitzroy Road, London NW1 8TR. Father William Roache.

ROACHE, William

William Roache. Actor (M).
b. Ilkeston, Derbyshire, 25 April 1932.
TV: Ken Barlow in *Coronation Street; Knight Errant Limited; Marking Time; Royal Variety Performance; Skyport; The Bulldog Breed.*
Films: *Behind the Mask; His and Hers; The Queen's Guards.*
Address: c/o Granada Television, Quay Street, Manchester M60 9EA. m. 1 (dis.) Anna Cropper; 1 s. Linus Roache; 1 d. Vanya; m. 2 Sara McEwen; 1 s. William James; 2 d. Verity Elizabeth, Edwina.

ROBB, David

David Robb. Actor (M). b. London, 23 August 1947.
TV: *Casualty;* Andrew Foster in *First Among Equals;* Michael Heseltine in *Half the Picture;* Laertes in *Hamlet; Highlander;* Germanicus in *I Claudius;* Lancelot du Lac in *Le Morte D'Arthur; Midsomer Murders;* Captain O'Shea in *Parnell and the Englishwoman;* Tybalt in *Romeo and Juliet;* Andrew Menzies in *Strathblair; Taggart;* Urville in *The Crow Road;* Robin Grant in *The Flame Trees of Thika;* Donald Davidson in *The Glittering Prizes.*

Films: *Cold to the Touch; Conduct Unbecoming; Regeneration; Swing Kids; The Deceivers; The Four Feathers.*
Address: c/o London Management, Noel House, 2–4 Noel Street, London W1V 3RB. m. Briony McRoberts. Hobbies: Rugby, military history.

ROBERTS, Ben

Ben Roberts. Actor (M). b. Bangor, Clwyd, 1 July 1950.
TV: *Angels; Parents & Teenagers; Tales of Sherwood;* Chief Inspector Conway in *The Bill; The Bretts; The Mortician's Tea Party; The Professionals.*
Address: c/o The Narrow Road Company, 21–22 Poland Street, London W1V 3DD. Hobbies: Flying.

ROBERTSON, Clive

Clive Robertson. Actor (M).
b. London, 17 December 1965.
TV: Ben Evans in *Sunset Beach;* Greg in *London Bridge; Paparazzo; The Bill; Before the Killing Starts; Topper; Secret Weapon.*
Address: c/o Langford Associates, 17 Westfields Avenue, London SW13 0AT. Partner Libby Purvis.

ROBINSON, Anne

Anne Robinson. Presenter/Writer.
b. Crosby, Liverpool, 26 September 1944.
TV: *Afternoon Plus; Breakfast Time; Points of View; Questions; The Write Stuff; Watchdog.*
Address: c/o Penrose Media, 19 Victoria Grove, London W8 5RW. m. John Penrose; 1 d. Emma. Hobbies: Dogs, gossip, food, houses.

ROBINSON, Jancis

Jancis Robinson. Presenter/Writer.
b. Cumbria, 22 April 1950.
TV: *Jancis Robinson Meets …; The Design Awards; The Dump; The Wine Programme.*
Address: c/o Arena Entertainment, Regents Court, 39 Harrogate Road, Leeds, West Yorkshire.

ROBINSON, Lucy

Lucy Robinson. Actor (F).
TV: Susan in *A Rather English Marriage;* Di in *A Small Dance;* Sophie in *Big Bad World;* Margaret in *Casualty;* Debs in *Clarissa;* Sarah in *Dressing for Breakfast;* Mrs Elton in *Emma;* Janet in *Flip;* Susie in *Get Real;* Mother in *If You Meet a Fairy;* Laura Cox in *Nancherrow;* Kim in *Preston Front;* Mrs Hurst in *Pride and Prejudice;* Rachel in *Revelations;* Carol Bryant in *The Bill;* Mayoress in *Thin Blue Line.*
Address: c/o Kate Feast Management, 10 Primrose Hill Studios, Fitzroy Road, London NW1 8TR.

ROBINSON, Tony

Tony Robinson. Actor (M)/Presenter/Voice artist.
b. 15 August 1946.
TV: *Alas Smith and Jones*; Shlomo Denkovitz in *Bergerac*; Titch in *Big Jim and the Figaro*; Baldrick in *Blackadder*; *Blood and Honey*; Kenneth Mills in *Blue Heaven*; *Boudicca*; *Bulman*; *City Farm*; Francis Skeffington in *Crime of Capt. Colthurst*; Dr Grace in *Doctor at Large*; *Great Journey*; Hugh in *Holed*; Ernie in *Joey*; Godwin the Idiot in *Knight School*; Pringle in *Law and Disorder*; Sheriff of Nottingham in *Maid Marion and Her Merry Men*; Willy the Weed in *Minder*; Humphrey in *Miracle Brother Humphrey*; *Musical Tales*; Alan in *My Wonderful Life*; *Nellie the Elephant*; *Oydsseus – The Greatest Hero of them All*; Rev. Timothy White in *Pastoral Care*; *Play for Today (Beyond the Pale/Black and Blue/Doran's Box)*; *Stay Tooned*; *Storyworld*; *Stretch and Slim*; *Sunday Brunch*; *Tale from Fat Tulip's Garden*; Head Teacher in *Teenage Health Freak*; *The English Programme*; *The Fairy Oak*; *The Good Book Guide*; *The Good Sex Guide*; *The Last Evensong*; *The Lenny Henry Show*; Dr Hamilton in *The Silent Twins*; *The Toucan Tecs*; *The Young Ones*; *This is David Lander*; *Time Team*; Roger Smith in *Virtual Murder*; *Who Dares Wins*; *Wild about Essex*; Marcus in *Women's Guide to Adultery*; *Wrestling with the Big One*; Pierre Duclos in *Young Indiana Jones Chronicles*.
Films: Baldrick in *Blackadder – Millennium Dome*; *Branigan*; Engywook in *The Never Ending Story III*.
Address: c/o Kate Feast Management, 10 Primrose Hill Studios, Fitzroy Road, London NW1 8TR.

ROBSON, Linda

Linda Robson. Actor (F). b. 13 March 1958.
TV: Mary in *Agony*; Tracy in *Birds of a Feather*; *Going Out*; *Harry's Game*; *Jobs for the Girls*; *Pauline's Quirkes*; Maggie Moon in *Shine on Harvey Moon*; *The Gentle Touch*.
Address: c/o Holland Associates.

ROCK, Crissy

Crissy Rock. Actor (F). b. Liverpool, 1958.
TV: *Born to Run*; *Brazen Hussies*; *Butterfly Collectors*; Jean in *Dockers*; *Peak Practice*; *Shellfish*; *Springhill*; *Des O'Connor Tonight*; *Vanessa*.
Films: *Ladybird Ladybird*.
Address: c/o Kenneth Earle Personal Management, 214 Brixton Road, London SW9 6AP.

RODGER, Struan

Struan Rodger. Actor (M)/Producer. b. 1956.
TV: Jack Greenwood in *A Captain's Tale*; Major White

in *A Woman at War*; Fergusson in *An Unsuitable Job for a Woman*; Smith in *Bergerac*; Grenville Barker in *Blood Rights*; Father Daniel Thomas in *Boys from the Blackstuff*; David in *Chandler and Co.*; Christopher Columbus in *Christopher Columbus*; Squadron Leader Alec Dywer in *Circle of Deceit*; Commissioner Brownlow in *Come Home Charlie and Face Them*; Mac in *Edge of Darkness*; Matthew Sheridan in *Faith*; Morgan in *Game Set and Match*; Bonnie Prince Charlie in *Highlander*; Michael O'Rourke in *Life After Death*; Hugh McBrail in *Lost Belongings*; Sidelski in *Lovejoy*; Gaston in *Maigret*; The Interrogator in *Mirad: A Boy From Bosnia*; Mr Richardson in *Moll Flanders*; Parris in *Moon & Son*; Van Braks in *Poirot*; Superintendent Halliday in *Prime Suspect III*; Northumberland in *Richard II*; Inspector Brush in *Rumpole of the Bailey*; Peter the Hair in *Spender*; Hickson in *Sweet Nothings*; Father Popieiuszko in *The Deliberate Death of a Polish Priest*; Major Naughton in *The Detective*; David in *The Lonely Man's Lover*; GB Shaw in *The Love School*; The Mayor of Casterbridge in *The Mayor of Casterbridge*; David Hinkley in *The Vice*; Perkins in *The Waiting Time*.
Films: *A Child From the South*; *Afraid of the Dark*; *Chariots of Fire*; *Diamond Sculls*; *Four Weddings and a Funeral*; *Hitler – A Portrait of Evil*; *Les Misérables*; *Reunion*; *The Innocent Sleep*; *The Madness of King George*; *The Manions of America*; *Too Many Chefs*.
Address: c/o Marina Martin Associates, 12–13 Poland Street, London W1V 3DE. Hobbies: Sports.

RODGERS, Anton

Anton Rodgers. Actor (M).
b. Wisbech 10 January 1933.
TV: *A Gift of Tongues*; *Affairs of the Heart*; *After the Dance*; *After the War*; *Border Music*; *Comeback*; *Coming Out*; *Disraeli*; *Fathers and Families*; *French Fields*; *Fresh Fields*; *Goodbye and I Hope We Meet Again*; *Jamie on a Flying Visit*; *Justice*; *Lilly*; *May to December*; *Nightingales' Boys*; *Noah's Ark*; *Red Letter Day*; *Secret Agent*; *Sharing Time*; *Something in Disguise*; *Star Struck*; *Talking Takes Two*; *The Dinner Party*; *The Flaxborough Chronicles*; *The Gay Lord Quex*; *The Guest*; *The Leftovers*; *The Old Curiosity Shop*; *The Organisation*; *Thomas and Sarah*; *Underdog*; *Uprising*; *You are My Heart's Desire*; *Young Guy Seeks Part-time Work*; *Zodiac*.
Films: *Dirty Rotten Scoundrels*; *East of Elephant Rock*; *Impromptu*; *Intimate Reflections*; *Rotten to the Core*; *Scrooge*; *Son of the Pink Panther*; *The Day of the Jackal*; *The Fourth Protocol*; *The Man Who Haunted Himself*; *Tick Tock*.
Address: c/o Whitehall Artists, 125 Gloucester Road, London SW7 4TE.

RODGERS, Bill

Bill Rodgers. Actor (M).

TV: Wilf in *Adam's Family Tree*; *All Creatures Great and Small*; Security Guard in *Always and Everyone*; Fête MC in *Berkeley Square*; Bob Broadhurst in *Cardiac Arrest*; Harry Holmes in *City Central*; Dawson in *Common As Muck*; Punter in *Cops*; *Coronation Street*; *Cracker*; *Emmerdale*; Removal Man in *Girl's Night Out*; Lisa's Punter in *Gold*; Barry Watson in *Heartbeat*; *Into The Fire*; *Oranges are Not the Only Fruit*; Bill Collins in *Peak Practice*; *Rough Justice*; *Scab*; *Sleepers*; *Smokescreen*; George Abbey in *The Life and Crimes of William Palmer*; *Where the Heart Is*.

Films: Friend in *Bert Rigby You're a Fool*; Bouncer in *Crime Strike*; Tourist in *Married to Malcolm*; *The Innocent*; Bluto in *VROOM!*.

Address: c/o Sharron Ashcroft Management, Dean Clough, Halifax, Yorkshire HX3 5AX. Hobbies: Driving, singing, dancing (ballroom), bass tuba, guitar, drums, fire-blowing.

RODSKA, Christian

Christian Rodska. Actor (M).

TV: Bernard in *Bergerac*; Dr O'Rourke in *Brookside*; *Campion*; Leonard Davidson in *Chandler and Co.*; Shaston Driver in *Doomwatch*; Ron Strycker in *Follyfoot*; Client in *Kiss Me Kate*; Hawthorne in *Licensed To Live*; Sergeant Moers in *Maigret*; Bill Hayes in *Maisie Raine*; Sergeant Moers in *Medics*; *Night People*; Gordon in *People Like Us*; Hedley in *The Bill*; *The Diary of Anne Frank*; Serial Lead in *The Eagle of the Ninth*; *The Exercise*; Dr Carr in *The Round Tower*; Arthur Barras in *The Stars Look Down*; Tant in *This Year, Next Year*; Felix in *Wish Me Luck*.

Address: c/o Evans & Reiss, 100 Fawe Park Road, London SW15 2EA.

RODWAY, Norman

Norman Rodway. Actor (M)/Narrator.

TV: *The Gospels*; Coroner in *The Lakes*; Dr Gilchrist in *The Mirror Crack'd*; Henry Kensal in *The Professionals*; Lead in *The Speaker of Mandarin*; *The War that Never Ends*; Hesse in *The World Walk*; *The Young Indiana Jones Chronicles*; Apemantus in *Timon of Athens*; Lead in *A Month in the Country*; *A Tour of the Western Isles*; Michael in *Best of Friends*; Alec in *Cheap Day*; Jacques de Bois in *Cockles*; William Hopkins in *Coming Through*; Danton in *Danton's Death*; Dr McCulloch in *Don't Write to Mother*; Roly in *Inspector Morse*; Mayor in *Jeeves and Wooster*; Bunyan in *John Bunyan*; Gloucester in *King Lear*; *Murder Not Proven*; Husband in *Not as Bad as They Seem*; Corinthian Messenger in *Oedipus*; Queensbury in

Oscar Wilde; Bryce in *Out*; *Oxbridge Blues*; Cleon in *Pericles*; Gaukroger in *Pity in History*; Cummings in *Reilly, Ace of Spies*; *Rumpole of the Bailey*; De Stogumer in *St Joan*; Dr McBride in *Staying Alive*; Lead in *The Bretts*; Mr Dangle in *The Critic*.

Films: Hotspur in *Chimes at Midnight*; Mr Bollox in *Country Kilburn*; Lead in *Four in the Morning*; Werner Noth in *Mother Night*; Adolf Hitler in *The Empty Mirror*.

Address: c/o William Morris Agency (UK) Ltd, 1 Stratton Street, London W1X 6HB.

ROE, Owen

Owen Roe. Actor (M). b. 30 May 1959.

TV: Dooley in *Ballykissangel*; Mick in *Fair City*; Mathewson in *Loving*; Paul Hyland in *Making the Cut*; Tim O'Hara in *Scarlett*; Robbie in *Shannongate*; Joe Smeeton in *The Broker's Man*; Ron in *The Governor*; Charles G Duffy in *The Treaty*.

Films: Senior Officer in *Frankie Starlight*; Arthur Griffith in *Michael Collins*; Joe in *Soft Sand Blue Sea*; Billy in *Three and Two*; Lead in *Undercurrent*.

Address: c/o Lisa Richards, Haymarket House, 28–29 Haymarket, London SW1Y 4SP.

ROËVES, Maurice

Maurice Roëves. Actor (M).

b. Sunderland, 19 March 1937.

TV: *919 5th Avenue*; God in *Acid House Trilogy, 'Ciranton Star Cause'*; *Forgive and Forget*; Lennie in *Grafters*; *Hillsborough*; *Negotiator*.

Films: God in *The Acid House*; Ronnie McMinn in *Creatures*; Donald McNeep in *Donald McNeep Has Lost His Sheep*; Colonel Monro in *Last of the Mohicans*.

Address: c/o Michelle Braidman Associates, 10-11 Lower John Street, London W1R 3PE. Partner Vanessa; 1 d. Hobbies: Holidays.

ROGERS, Chris

Chris Rogers. Presenter/Writer.

b. Middlesbrough, 13 November 1974.

TV: *A Life of Knowledge*; *BBC Schools*; *Brilliant Creatures*; *Newsround*; *Newsround 24*; *Newsround Extra*; *Sky News*; *Top Gear*.

Address: c/o Unique Artistes, Avon House, Kensington Village, London W14 8TS. m. Sheree Rogers.

ROGERS, Katherine

Katherine Rogers. Actor (F). b. London.

TV: Josie in *London's Burning*; Eva in *Springhill*; Princess Cardine in *The Aristocrats*.

Address: c/o Dennis Lyne Agency, 108 Leonard Street, London EC2A 4RH.

RONAY, Shebah

Shebah Ronay. Actor (F)/Presenter. b. London, 1972.
TV: *Game On; GMTV; Hollyoaks; The Club; The House of Elliott; The Man Who Cried; Vanessa.*
Films: *Reunion; The Things We Do for Love.*
Address: c/o Panic 2, Mortimer House, Furmage Street, London SW18 4DF. Mother Edina Ronay; grandfather Egon Ronay.

ROOKE, Lynda

Lynda Rooke. Actor (F).
TV: Sister Chalfont in *Angels;* Gloria Skinner in *Back Up; Berkeley Square;* Jill Lester in *Casualty;* Laura Collins in *Coronation Street;* Stacy in *Criminal; Good Companions;* Mrs Matthews in *Grange Hill;* Jill Patrick in *Hollyoaks; No More Dying Then;* Celia Darling in *Once Upon a Time in the North;* Gloria in *Operation Julie;* Bella in *Pat and Margaret;* Rita in *Perfect Scoundrels; Play for Today;* Phyliss in *The Biz III;* Iris in *The Sculptress;* Mrs Hill in *This is Personal; The Hunt for the Yorkshire Ripper.*
Films: *Naked.*
Address: c/o Kate Feast Management, 10 Primrose Hill Studios, Fitzroy Road, London NW1 8TR.

ROOPER, Jemima

Jemima Rooper. Actor (F).
b. Hammersmith, London, 24 October 1981.
TV: George in *The Famous Five;* Anne in *Heatwave;* Vicky in *Higher Mortals;* Gemma in *Junk;* Siren in *Lifeforce;* Julie in *Summer in the Suburbs;* Alice in *The Passion;* Roberta in *The Railway Children;* Lizzie in *Wives and Daughters.*
Films: Maggie in *OWD Bob;* Vicky in *The Higher Mortals;* Annabel in *Willy's War.*
Address: c/o Conway Van Gelder, 18–21 Jermyn Street, London SW1Y 6HP. Hobbies: Singing, dancing, painting, theatre, films.

ROOT, Amanda

Amanda Root. Actor (F). b. 1963.
TV: *Anna Karenina; Big Cat; Breaking the Code;* Producer in *Buddha of Suburbia; Dangerfield;* Clair Claremont in *Gothic – South Bank Show; Harry Enfield and Chums;* Polly in *Ladies in Charge;* Miss Mounsey in *Love on a Branch Line;* Julia in *Worlds Beyond;* Mary Rose in *Mary Rose;* Rachel in *Mortimer's Law;* Ricardis in *Omnibus; Original Sin; Sunny Side Farm;* Adela in *The House of Bernarda Alba;* Hilda Maxwell in *The Man Who Cried;* Sarah Penwarden in *Time For Murder; Turning World.*
Films: Kate in *In The West;* Miss Temple in *Jane Eyre;* Anne in *Persuasion; Whatever Happened to Harold Smith?*

Address: c/o ICM, Oxford House, 76 Oxford Street, London W1N 0AX.

ROPER, Tony

Tony Roper. Actor (M). b. Glasgow, 19 August 1941.
TV: Ian Guthrie in *All Along the Watchtower; Naked Video; Only an Excuse;* James Coiter in *Rab C Nesbitt; Scotch and Wry;* Stanley Powell in *The Bill.*
Address: c/o Tim Scott Personal Management, 5 Cloisters Business Centre, 8 Battersea Park Road, London SW8 4BG.

ROSEN, Doraly

Doraly Rosen. Actor (F).
TV: Angie Lynch in *Casualty;* Miriam Jacobs in *Kavanagh QC;* Jennifer in *The Alchemist.*
Films: *Angel;* Split in *Graves End;* Rachel in *Hidden Lives.*
Address: c/o Storm Artists Management, 47 Brewer Street, London W1R 3FD.

ROSENTHAL, Jim

Jim Rosenthal. Sports presenter.
b. Oxford, 6 November 1947.
TV: *Big Fight Live; European Football Championship; Formula One; ITV Sports; Olympic Games; On the Ball; World Cup Football; Rugby World Cup; World of Sport.*
Films: Himself in *Renford Rejects; The Manageress.*
Address: c/o ITV Sport, 200 Grays Inn Road, London WC1X 8XZ. m. Chrissy; 1 s. Tom. Hobbies: All sports.

ROSLIN, Gaby

Gaby Roslin. Presenter/Host/interviewer.
b. London, 12 July 1964.
TV: *Children in Need; City Hospital; Cruft's; EastEnders Tribute; Friends with Gaby; Hippo; Holby – A Morning in Casualty; Holiday; Motormouth Live; Predators; Telethon '90; The Big Breakfast; The Gaby Roslin Show; The Real Christmas Show; The Real Holiday Show; The Real Wedding Show; TV's Greatest Hits; Whatever You Want.*
Address: c/o PBJ Management, 5 Soho Square, London W1V 5DE.

ROSS, David

David Ross. Actor (M).
TV: *A Wing and a Prayer; Ain't Misbehavin'; Band of Gold; Bergerac; Boys from the Blackstuff; Brookside; Casualty; Cold Enough for Snow;* Lester Fontayne in *Coronation Street; Days at the Beach; Eskimo Day; Fair Game; Further Adventures of Sherlock Holmes; GBH; Get Away; Goodbye and I Hope We Meet Again; Good-*

night Sweetheart; Harbour Lights; Hard Cases; Home Video; In Suspicious Circumstances; Jake's Progress; Josie Lawrence Special; Juliet Bravo; Last Company Car; Leave it to Charlie; London's Burning; May to September; Melissa; Oliver Twist; Parole; Red Dwarf; Roger, Roger; Scully; Seaforth; Shooting Stars; Storyboard II; The Bill; The Brittas Empire; The Outsider; The Riff-Raff Element; This is David Lander; Time After Time; Vanity Fair; Watching; Wycliffe; Xyyman; Yanks Go Home; Zero Option.

Films: Basil; Heirs and Graces; Mary Reilly.

Address: c/o Susan Angel Associates, 1st Floor, 12 D'Arblay Street, London W1V 3FP.

ROSS, Jonathan

Jonathan Ross. Host/Presenter. b. 17 November 1960.
TV: British Comedy Awards; Film '99; Gagtag; It's Only TV But I Like It; One Hour with Jonathan Ross; Saturday Zoo; The Incredibly Strange Film Show; The Last Resort; The Late Jonathan Ross; They Think it's all Over; Tonight with Jonathan Ross; French and Saunders; Shooting Stars; The Mrs Merton Show; Have I Got News For You; The Lenny Henry Show; Wogan; Sunday Night Clive; 30 Years of Monty Python; Never Rewind the Buzzcocks.

Films: Himself in Spiceworld.

Address: c/o Off the Kerb Productions, 3rd Floor, Hammer House, 113–117 Wardour Street, London W1V 3TD. m. Jane Goldman; brother Paul Ross.

ROSS, Lee

Lee Ross. Actor (M). b. 1971.
TV: Phil Mitchell in 99–1; Ray in Casualty; Ryan Pratt in Playing the Field; Lead in SAB; Roy in Shine On Harvey Moon; Neil Simpson in The Bill; Paul Swan in The Negotiator; Gary in The Upper Hand; Bill Smurthwaite in Thief Takers; Peter James in Trial & Retribution; Chris Comer in West Beach.

Films: Jason in Buddy's Song; Oscar Levy in Burning Up; Andy Walton in Dockers; Harry in Dreaming of Joseph Lees; Speed in Hard Man; Gumbo in ID; Freddy in Island on Bird Street; Danny in Life's a Gas; Tom in Metroland; Danny Argyropoulos in Rogue Trader; Paul in Secrets and Lies; Phil in Sweet Nothings; Gordon in The Crane; Spalding in The English Patient.

Address: c/o CAM London, 19 Denmark Street, London WC2H 8NA.

ROSS, Paul

Paul Ross. Actor (M)/Presenter/Reporter.
TV: All Over the Shop; Big Breakfast; Daily Live; Gladiators Celebrity Special; Junior Masterchef; Make Yourself Useful Week; The Other Half Celebrity Special; Work!;

Lenny Goes to Town.
Address: c/o Partners in Crime. Brother Jonathan Ross.

ROUSE, Simon

Simon Rouse. Actor (M).
TV: A Ticket To Ride; Billy Liar; Bread; C.A.T.S. Eyes; Casualty; Cricket; Crime and Punishment; Crown Court; Dead Romantic; Dead Shepherd; Doctor Who; Even Solomon; Free as a Bird; Hard Cases; Here is the News; Juliet Bravo; Kipper; Marked Personal; Minder; One Bumper News Day; Operation Julie; Portrait In Black; Robin of Sherwood; Sam; Sheppey; Softly, Softly; St Joan; Tecx; DCI Meadows in The Bill; The Brief; The Master Builder; The Practice; Wednesday Love; Wilderness Edge; You Never Get What You Want.

Films: Blood Royal; Bones; Butley; Dick Turpin; Operation Julie; Retribution; Smuggler; The Cure; The Manions of America; The Professionals; The Ragman's Daughter; The Saint; White Bird.

Address: c/o Representation Joyce Edwards RJS, 275 Kennington Road, London SE11 6BY.

ROUTLEDGE, Patricia

Patricia Routledge. Actor (F)/Voice artist.
b. Birkenhead, 17 February 1929.
TV: A Visit from Mrs Protheroe; A Woman of No Importance; Cost of Loving; Crown Court; David Copperfield; Face the Music; First and Last; Five to Eleven; Green Forms; Hetty Wainthropp in Hetty Wainthropp Investigates; Aunt Dodo in Home Video; Jackanory; Hyacinth Bucket in Keeping Up Appearances; Let's; Marjorie in Marjorie and Men; Barbara Pym in Miss Pym's Day Out; Nicholas Nickleby; Omnibus: Hildegarde of Bingen; Plain Jane; Cousin Ribby in Samuel Whiskers; Mars Baines in Sophia and Constance; Steptoe and Son; Miss Ruddock in Talking Heads – Lady of Letters; The Beggar's Opera; The Imitation Game; The Old Wives' Tale; The Two Ronnies; Cousin Ribby in Tom Kitten; Kitty in Victoria Wood – As Seen On TV; Maria Halliwell in When We Are Married.

Address: c/o Marmont Management Ltd, Langham House, 308 Regent Street, London W1R 5AL.

ROWE, Christopher

Christopher Rowe. Actor (M)/Presenter.
TV: Ian Wage in Bostock's Cup; Dangerfield; PC Warren in Eurocops; Eye Spy; Mr Potter in Goggle Eyes; Hold the Pickle; Auctioneer in Moon and Son; No Limit; Harry in Perfect Crime; The Prince in Playdays; PC Paper in Radio Roo; Jeffrey Lucus in Teenage Health Freak.

Address: c/o Kerry Gardner Management, 7 St George's Square, London SW1V 2HX.

ROWLANDS, Patsy

Patsy Rowlands. Actor (F).

b. London, 19 January 1934.

TV: Betty in *Bless this House*; Lil Potato in *Bottom*; Mrs Dunphy in *Cater Street Hangman*; *Charlie the Kid*; Mrs Harty in *Femme Fatale*; Mrs Clayton in *Get Well Soon*; Madame Jocasta in *Gone to Seed*; Sister Alice Meredith in *Hallelujah*; Doris Johnson in *Harry's Mad*; *Hewitt E.*; *Imaginary Friends*; *In Loving Memory*; Mrs Webley in *Inside George Webley*; *Jackanory*; *Mooncat and Company*; *My Son, My Son*; *Never the Twain*; *Play for Today*; *Rainbow*; *Robin's Nest*; *Supergran*; Shirley in *That's Love*; Dol Common in *The Alchemist*; Rachel Armfield in *The Bill*; *The Dick Emery Show*; *The History of Mr Polly*; *The Les Dawson Show*; *The Little Princess*; *The Nesbitts are Coming*; Susan in *The Squirrels*; *This Company*; *Two's Company*; Mrs Tinkler in *Vanity Fair*; *Wilfred and Eileen*.

Films: *A Kind of Loving*; Annie Southurst in *Alice in Wonderland*; *Carry On* (various); Madame Kempinsi in *Crimestrike*; *Joseph Andrews*; Miss Dibble in *Little Lord Fauntleroy*; Mrs Brooks in *Tess*; Mrs Simpkin in *The Canterbury Tales*; Honor in *Tom Jones*.

Address: c/o Dalzell & Beresford Ltd, 91 Regent Street, London W1R 7TB.

ROYLE, Carol

Carol Royle. Actor (F). b. Blackpool, 10 February 1954.

TV: *Bergerac*; *Blackeyes*; *Blake's 7*; *Casualty*; *Crime Traveller*; *Girl Talk*; *Heartbeat*; *Ladies in Charge*; *Life Without George*; *London Embassy*; *Oxbridge Blues*; *Racing Game*; *Cedar Tree*; *The Outsider*; *Thief Takers*.

Films: *Deadline*; *Tuxedo Warrior*.

Address: c/o Shepherd & Ford, 13 Radnor Walk, London SW3 4BP. m. Julian Spear; 1 s. Taran, 1 d. Talitha.

ROYLE, David

David Royle. Actor (M).

b. Salford, Manchester, 16 June 1961.

TV: Searcher in *Cold Lazarus*; Gay Man in *Coogan's Run*; Detective Sergeant Weild in *Dalziel & Pascoe*; Guensche in *Hitler, The Final Report*; Policeman in *London's Burning*; Range Officer in *Soldier, Soldier*; Customs Officer in *The Knock*.

Address: c/o JM Associates, 77 Beak Street, London W1R 3LF. Hobbies: Parachuting, swimming, singing, driving.

RUSSELL, Catherine

Catherine Russell. Actor (F). b. London, 1966.

TV: Madeline Kohler in *Airbase*; Issy in *Always and Everyone*; Caroline Chilos in *An Unsuitable Job for a Woman*; Elly Chandler in *Chandler and Co.*; Tish Anstey in *Chelworth*; Bridget in *Holding On*; Martha Jusserend in *Maigret*; Katrina Reiger in *Poirot*; Grace Dunbar in *Sherlock Holmes*; Wendy Timms/Julie Gardener in *The Bill*; Deborah in *Wilderness*.

Films: Polly in *Clockwork Mice*; Margaret in *Soft Top, Hard Shoulder*; Julie Parris in *Solitaire for Two*; Suzanne in *The Lake*.

Address: c/o PFD, Drury House, 34-43 Russell Street, London WC2B 5HA. m. Richard Holmes; 2 children. Hobbies: Cooking, singing.

RUSSELL, Clive

Clive Russell. Actor (M).

TV: *Hope and Glory*; *Great Expectations*; *Heartburn Hotel*; *Bodywork*; *Rab C Nesbitt*; *Sunny Side Farm*; *A Perfect State*; *Lord of Misrule*; *Crossing the Floor*; *Atletico Partick*; *Deacon Brodie*; *Murder Most Horrid*; *Bad Boys*; *Cracker*; *The Peter Principle*; *Finney*; *Ruffian Hearts*; *I.M. Jolly*; *Roughnecks*; *Parahandy*; *Middlemarch*; *The Vision*; *Seconds Out*; *Tell-Tale Hearts*; *Jute City*; *The Grass Arena*; *For the Greater Good*; *Do Not Disturb*; *The Gift*; *Tumbledown*.

Films: *Oliver Twist*; *All Forgotten*; *the Thirteenth Warrior*; *My Life So Far*; *For My Baby*; *Oscar and Lucinda*; *Margaret's Museum*; *Fatherland*; *The Hawk*; *The Power of One*; *The 13th Warrior*.

Address: c/o The Narrow Road Company, 21-22 Poland Street, London W1V 3DD.

RUTTER, Barrie

Barrie Rutter. Actor (M).

b. Hull, Yorkshire, 12 December 1946.

TV: *Boon*; Ted in *Casualty*; Danny in *Coasting*; Bandit Leader in *Covington Cross*; Barry Ryan in *Crown Prosecutor*; Mr Maskell in *Heartbeat*; Inspector Judd in *Kavanagh QC*; Tom in *The Bill*; Andrew Macintyre in *Verdict*; Keith in *Way Upstream*.

Address: c/o Michelle Braidman Associates, 10-11 Lower John Street, London W1R 3PE. Hobbies: Driving, riding motorcycles.

RYAN, Francesca

Francesca Ryan. Actor (F).

TV: Linda Spencer in *Brookside*; Jennifer in *Casualty*; *Celebration*; Miranda in *Coronation Street*; *Happy Families*; Elaine in *Heartburn Hotel*; DS Green in *Hollyoaks*; *Last of the Summer Wine*; Dr Claire Armstrong in *Medics*; *My Father's House*; Marianne in *Prime Suspect*; *Split Ends*; Kate (DSE) in *The Bill*; *Trust Me*; *Wait on Earth*; *The World of Eddie Weary*.

Address: c/o Jane Lehrer Associates, 100a Chalk Farm Road, London NW1 8EH.

RYAN, Helen

Helen Ryan. Actor (F). b. Liverpool, 16 June 1938.

TV: Princess Alexandra in *Edward VII*; Anna in *Fathers and Families*; Hannah in *Hannah – Miss Mole*; Babushka in *Hannay*; Lady Jevney in *Harry*; Betty Preston in *Heartbeat*; Aunt Phoebe in *Just William*; Lavinia in *My Brother Jonathan*; Celia in *My Father's House*; Princess Alexandra/Mrs McFarlane in *Sherlock Holmes*; Mrs Keating in *The Christmas Tree*; Wiz in *Captain Crimson*; Mary in *C.A.T.S. Eyes*; Olive in *The Duchess of Duke Street*.

Films: Gertrude Bell in *Clash of Loyalties*; Princess Alexandra in *The Elephant Man*; Mrs Crowther in *The Hawk*; Aunt in *The Legend of Crystalstone*; Lucy in *The Misunderstood*.

Address: c/o The Lisa Richards Agency, Haymarket House, 28–29 Haymarket, London SW1Y 4SP.

RYDER RICHARDSON, Anna

Anna Ryder Richardson. Interior designer/Presenter/Co-presenter/Team captain. b. 1968.

TV: *All the Right Moves; Change That; Changing Rooms; House Invaders; Night Fever; Party of a Lifetime; The Terrace; Whose House.*

Address: c/o Lake-Smith Griffin Associates, 15 Maiden Lane, London WC2E 7NA.

RYDER RICHARDSON, Katie

Katie Ryder Richardson. Actor (F).
b. Aylesbury, Buckinghamshire, 4 June 1969.

TV: Loveday in *Coming Home*; Loveday in *Nancherrow*; Emily in *The Cater Street Hangman*.

Address: c/o Evans & Reiss, 100 Fawe Park Road, London SW15 2EA. m. Ben Smith. Hobbies: Driving, horse riding, interior design, Photoshop owener, cats.

RYECART, Patrick

Patrick Ryecart. Actor (M). b. 9 May 1952.

TV: *After All; Arms and the Man; Beautiful Lies; Coming Home; Crime Squad; Dalziel and Pascoe; Dick Turpin; Heart of Darkness; Hotel Shanghai; Lillie; The Mystery of Doctor Martinu; Mendelssohn in Scotland; My Son, My Son; Nancherrow; Pas De Deux; Perfect Hero; Pericles; Poirot; Romeo and Juliet; Rumpole of the Bailey; Silas Marner; South of the Border; The Bretts; The Dame of Sark; The High Life; The Professionals; The Rag Nymph; The Rivals; The Talisman; Trainer; Young Indy.*

Films: *21; A Bridge too Far; Arthur The King; Camille; Casanova; Dick Turpin; Goldeneye; Jenny's War; Lace II; Nancy Wake; Prisoner of Honor; Silver Dream Racer; Tai Pan.*

Address: c/o ICM, Oxford House, 76 Oxford Street, London W1N 0AX.

S

SACHS, Andrew

Andrew Sachs. Actor (M)/Presenter and Co-writer/
Voice artist. b. 7 April 1930.

TV: Moise Davidson in *Bergerac*; Einstein in *Einstein*;
Nat Silver in *Every Silver Lining*; Manuel in *Fawlty
Towers*; Peter Pryce in *Jack of Hearts*; Sidney in
Minder; Mr Jones in *Pirates*; *QED: Whatever Happened
to the Leisure Age*; Mr Polly in *The History of Mr Polly*;
Teddeus in *The Mushroom Picker*; Trinculo in *The
Tempest*; *When In Spain*; *Wiggly Park*; *William's Wish
Wellington*.

Films: Registrar in *Hitler – The Last Ten Days*; Dust-
man in *It's Your Move*; Minister in *Taxandra*; Durdles
in *The Mystery of Edwin Drood*.

Address: c/o The Richard Stone Partnership, 2 Henrietta Street, London WC2E 8PS.

SADOWITZ, Jerry

Jerry Sadowitz. Presenter. b. 4 June 1961.

TV: Magician in *The Pallbearer's Review*; Magician in
The People vs Jerry Sadowitz.

Address: c/o London Management, Noel House, 2–4
Noel Street, London W1V 3RB. Hobbies: Magic.

SALEM, Pamela

Pamela Salem. Actor (F)/Guest lead.

TV: Monica in *Buccaneer*; Sandra in *Don't Leave Me
This Way*; Joanne in *EastEnders*; The Hooker in *EL
C.I.D*; *ER*; Chantal in *French Fields*; *Lytton's Diary*;
Zenith in *Paradise Club*; Lindsey Singleton in *Trainer*.

Films: *After Darkness*; *Gods and Monsters*; *Magnum*;
Miss Moneypenny in *Never Say Never Again*; *Night
Train To Remember*; Herodias in *Salome*; *Succubus*; *The
Bitch*; *Thirteen at Dinner*.

Address: c/o Burdett-Coutts Associates, Riverside
Studios, Crisp Road, London W6 9RL. Hobbies:
Swimming, scuba diving, fencing, horse riding and
water-skiing.

SALLIS, Peter

Peter Sallis. Actor (M)/Voice artist. b. 1 February 1921.

TV: *Come Home Charlie and Face Them*; His Own
Father in *First of the Summer Wine*; Clegg in *Last of the
Summer Wine*; *Leave it to Charlie*; *Mountain Men*;
Rumpole; *She Loves Me*; *The Armchair Theatres*; The
Bretts; Peyps in *The Diary Of Samuel Pepys*; *The Moon-
stone*; *The New Statesman*; Wallace in *Wallace And
Gromit, A Close Shave*, *Wallace And Gromit, A Grand
Day Out*, *Wallace And Gromit, The Wrong Trousers*.

Films: *Anastasia*; *Charlie Bubbles*; *Doctor in Love*; *Taste
the Blood of Dracula*; *The Curse of the Warewolf*; *Witness for the Prosecution*.

Address: c/o Jonathan Altaras Associates, 13 Shorts
Gardens, London WC2H 9AT.

SALTHOUSE, John

John Salthouse. Actor (M)/Narrator/Writer.
b. 16 June 1951.

TV: *Abigail's Party*; *Buy Your Way to Heaven*; *Daylight
Robbery*; *Dream Team*; *Heartbeat*; *Home On The Range*;
Kick; *Making Out*; *Ruth Rendell Mysteries*; *Taggart*; DI
Galloway in *The Bill*.

Address: c/o Marquee Group (UK) Ltd, 21 The
Green, Richmond, Surrey TW9 1PX. Hobbies:
Coaching children in both football and cricket.

SANDERSON, Kate

Kate Sanderson. Presenter/Reporter. b. 1971.

TV: *Attractions*; *Electric Circus*; *Festival of the Sea*; *Holiday*; *Live and Kicking*; *Newsround*; *Record Breakers*;
Spotlight; *The List*.

Address: c/o Speakeasy Ltd, 90 St Mary's Road,
Market Harborough, Leicestershire LEI6 7DX.

SANDIFORD, Benedict

Benedict Sandiford. Actor (M).

TV: Tony Richards in *A Touch of Frost*; Mr Brunskill in
At Home With The Braithwaites; Neil in *Barbara*;
Tutilo in *Cadfael*; Neil in *Cold Enough for Snow*; Brad
in *Cuts*; Tom in *Harry Enfield and Chums*; Tom in
Harry Enfield and Chums: Christmas Special; Tom
Phillips in *Heartbeat*; James in *In The Name of Love*;
Maurice in *Love Amongst The Haystacks*; Jamie in *May
to December*; Vernon in *Men of the World*; Edward in
Mr White Goes To Westminster; Peter in *Only You*;
Jason Fairburn in *Peak Practice*; Kevin in *Pie in the
Sky*; Pierre in *Pierre and Jean*; Malcolm in *Smith and
Jones*; James/Paul Morrell in *Sons and Lovers*; Joe Sul-
livan in *The Ward*; Brian Moss in *This Life*; Eddie
Walker in *Touching Evil*; Davey in *Where the Heart Is*.

Films: Neil in *Eskimo Day*; Alfred Wood in *Wilde*.
Address: c/o Representation Joyce Edwards RJS, 275 Kennington Road, London SE11 6BY.

SANDON, Henry

Henry Sandon. Antiques expert.
TV: *The Antiques Roadshow*.
Address: c/o BBC, Union House, 65–69 Shepherds Bush Green, London W12 8TX. Hobbies: Archaeology.

SARPONG, June

June Sarpong. Presenter. b. London.
TV: *Dancefloor Chart Show*; *Planet Pop*; *Select*.
Brother Sam Sarpong.

SATCHWELL, Brooke

Brooke Satchwell. Actor (F). b. 14 November 1980.
TV: Anne Wilkinson in *Neighbours*.
Address: c/o Pearson Television, 1 Stephen Street, London W1P 1PJ.

SAUNDERS, Jennifer

Jennifer Saunders. Actor (F)/Writer/Presenter/Voiceover. b. Sleaford, Lincolnshire, 12 July 1958.
TV: Edina Monsoon in *Absolutely Fabulous*; Jennifer Saunders in *French and Saunders*; Andrea Waltham in *Friends*; Jennifer Marsh in *Girls on Top*; Granny Fuddle/Cassie/Madeline/Joyce/Roxane in *Happy Families*; Herself in *How To Be Absolutely Fabulous*; Colombine in *Let Them Eat Cake*; Edina Monsoon in *Roseanne*; Various characters in *The Comic Strip Presents*; The Rat in *The Magician's House*; Princess Badsister in *The Storyteller*; Sue/Helen Mucus in *The Young Ones*.
Films: Roanna in *Fanny and Elvis*; Fashionable Woman in *SpiceWorld*.
Address: c/o PFD, Drury House, 34–43 Russell Street, London WC2B 5HA. m. Adrian Edmondson; 3 d. Freya, Beattie, Ella.

SAVAGE, Ben

Ben Savage. Actor (M).
b. Chicago, Illinois, USA, 13 September 1980.
TV: Chris Bankston in *A Family For Joe*; Cory Matthews in *Boy Meets World*; Matthew Lacey in *Dear John*; Stuart in *Party of Five*; Andy in *She Woke Up*; Cory Matthews in *Teen Angel*; Cupit Boy in *The Wonder Years*; Coty Wycoff in *Wild Palms*.
Films: Sam in *Big Girls Don't Cry … They Get Even*; Roger in *Clifford*; Eric in *Little Monsters*.
Address: c/o William Morris Agency, 151 El Camino Drive, Beverly Hills, California 90212, USA. Brother Fred; sister Kala. Hobbies: Music, reading novels, tennis, watching the Chicago Bulls.

SAVAGE, Lily

Paul O'Grady. Comedian/Presenter.
b. Liverpool, 14 June 1955.
TV: *An Evening with Lily Savage*; *Blankety Blank*; *Life Swaps*; *Smash Hits Poll Winner's Party*; *The Big Breakfast*; *The Lily Savage Show*; *Top of the Pops*.
Address: c/o Well Bred Productions Ltd, 189 Bermondsey Street, London SE1 3UW.

SAVAGE, Mike

Mike Savage. Actor (M).
b. Co. Clare, Ireland, 20 May 1943.
TV: *Frankie Howerd Specials*; *George and Mildred*; *Man About the House*; *Radio Phoenix*; *Mummy and Daddy*; *Kean*; *Danger UXB*; *The Sweeney*; *The Professionals*; *Couples*; *Jingle Bells*; *Crossroads*; *Coronation Street*; *Softly Softly*; *Ghost Squad*; *Barlow at Large*; *Z-Cars*; *Dixon of Dock Green*; *The Album*; *From the Top*; *Dempsey and Makepeace*; *Turtle's Progress Close to Home*; *Charles & Diana – A Royal Romance*; *On the Line*; *Dangerous Davis – The Last Detective*; *Fox*; *Rude Health*; *Confessions from a Holiday Camp*; *Stagg's Night*; *Running Wild*; *Eureka*; *The Deceivers*; *Out of Tune*; *Mike Read's Mates and Music*; *The Wednesday Illustrated Review*; *Grange Hill*; *Mitch*; *Minder*; *Doppleganger*; *Pennies from Heaven*; *Porterhouse Blue*; *Outside Edge*; *The Charmer*; *The Bill*; *Shoot to Kill – The Stalker Affair*; *Defrosting the Fridge*; *Echoes*; *Growing Pains*; *Casualty*; *On the Up*; *Lovejoy*; *House of Elliott*; *Covington Cross*; *Eskimo Day*; Del in *Prospects*; Frank Makepeace in *Noah's Ark*; *Gulliver's Travels*; M.C. in *Goodnight Sweetheart*; Alex Davis in *The Vice*; Roy in *Harbour Lights*; DCS Clark in *This Is Personal – the Hunt for the Yorkshire Ripper*.
Address: c/o Hilda Physick, 78 Temple Sheen Road, London SW14 7RR. m. Christine; 1 d. Melanie; 1 s. Paul.

SAVIDENT, John

John Savident. Actor (M).
TV: *Blake's 7*; *Boon*; *Chance in a Million*; *Clapperclaw*; *Coronation Street*; *Doctor Who*; *Dream Gardens*; *Father Charlie*; *Fresh Fields*; *Fry and Laurie*; *.Good Friday 1666*; *Jane*; *Jeeves and Wooster*; *Juliet Bravo*; *Let There be Love*; *Lovejoy*; Raffles in *Middlemarch*; *Mike and Angelo*; *Moll Flanders*; *Mr Bean*; *Mrs Arris Goes to Paris*; *Parnell and the Englishwoman*; *PG Wodehouse*; *Starting Out*; *Strange True Tale*; *Tea Bag*; *The Bill*; *The Black Adder*; *The Chinese Detective*; *The Cleopatras*; *The Professionals*; *The Rory Bremner Show*; *The Silent Twins*; *The Unknown Enchantment*; *The Various Ends of Mrs F's Friends*; *This Office Life*; *Tolpuddle Martyrs*; *Treasure Seekers*; *Two's Company*; *Woman*; *Young Indy*.

Films: *A Clockwork Orange; A Summer Story; Battle of Britain; Before Winter Comes; Duel for Love; Ghandi; Heart of Darkness; Hudson Hawk; Impromptu; Lame Ducks; Little Dorrit; Mountains of the Moon; Oliver Twist; Othello; Remains of the Day; The Wicked Lady; Tom and Viv; Trial By Combat; Waterloo.*
Address: c/o Conway Van Gelder, 18–21 Jermyn Street, London SW1Y 6HP.

SAVILE, Sir Jimmy

Sir Jimmy Savile. Disc-jockey/Presenter.
b. Leeds, 31 October 1926.
TV: *20 Years of Jim'll Fix It; Jim'll Fix It; The Obituary Show; Top of the Pops.*
Hobbies: Cycling, running, walking. Knighted 1990.

SAWALHA, Julia

Julia Sawalha. Actor (F).
b. London, 9 September 1968.
TV: Saffron in *Absolutely Fabulous; Bottom; Casualty; El CID; Faith in the Future; French and Saunders; Inspector Morse; Lovejoy; Martin Chuzzlewit; Press Gang; Pride and Prejudice; Second Thoughts; Tales from the Crypt; The Flint Street Nativity.*
Films: *Buddy's Song; Chicken Run; In the Bleak Midwinter; The Wind in the Willlows.*
Address: c/o PFD, Drury House, 34–43 Russell Street, London WC2B 5HA. Sister Nadia; father Nadim.

SAWALHA, Nadia

Nadia Sawalha, Actor (F).
TV: *Bottom;* Noor in *Call Red;* Dr Rosalind Anderson in *Casualty;* Annie Palmer in *EastEnders; Loose Women; Michael Winner's True Crimes;* Julie in *Page 3;* Gina in *Second Thoughts;* Temesa in *The Darkening;* Katherine in *The Vanishing Man;* Co-lead Pilot in *Which Way To The War.*
Films: Amanda in *Caught in the Act; Slave of Dreams;* Lea in *Sleeping With The Fishes; Soloman and Sheba;* Stewardess in *Top Tips.*
Address: c/o Associated International Management, 5 Denmark Street, London WC2H 8LP. Father Nadim; sister Julia.

SAWALHA, Nadim

Nadim Sawalha. Actor (M). b. 1935.
TV: Seko in *Abraham;* Prem in *Blue Heaven;* Syrian Ambassador in *Chess Game;* Dr Shaaban Hamada in *Dangerfield;* Dr Samson Perera in *Expert Witness;* Salim in *Frederick Forsyth Presents;* Mr Buhtu in *Hawk;* Turkish Bank Manager in *House of Cards;* Dr Hassan in *Inspector Morse;* Ishmaelite in *Joseph;* Uncle Said in

Lovejoy; Minder; Miracles Take Longer; Mr Gupta in *Open All Hours;* Doctor in *Pirates;* Mr Amjad in *Remember;* Sheika Mansour in *Saracens; Sorry I'm a Stranger Here Myself;* Makram Alias in *Streets of Yesterday;* Zayid in *Tales of the Unexpected;* Joseph Charadi in *Tangier Cop;* Ahmed in *The Big Battalions; The Bill;* Sheikh in *The Care of Time; The Professionals; The Sweeney;* Sheikh Suleiman in *Trainer;* Charan Singh in *West of Paradise.*
Films: *A Touch of Class;* Rico in *Abraham;* Judge Zadic in *Arabian Nights;* Mardian in *Cleopatra;* Karim in *Half Moon Street; Knights and Emeralds;* The Turkish Pasha in *Pascali's Island;* Faisal in *Russian Roulette; Sinbad and the Eye of the Tiger;* Lugash Agent in *Son of the Pink Panther; Sphinx;* World Council Minister in *The Avengers; The Awakening; The Children's Crusade; The Hawk; The Living Daylights; The Spy Who Loved Me; The Wind and the Lion.*
Address: c/o Associated International Management, 5 Denmark Street, London WC2H 8LP. 2 d. Julia, Nadia.

SAYLE, Alexei

Alexei Sayle. Actor (M)/Comedian/Presenter/Voice over/Writer. b. Liverpool, 7 August 1952.
TV: Rittblatt in *'4 play' Itch;* The Puppeteer in *Tom Jones; Alexei Sayle's Comedy Hour; Alexei Sayle's Merry-go-round; Alexei Sayle's Stuff;* Bacbac in *Arabian Nights; BBC Design Awards;* Lavrenti in *Caucasian Chalk Circle;* Reg in *Common As Muck;* Carl/Stirling Moss in *Didn't You Kill My Brother?;* DJ in *Doctor Who; Drive;* Sergei in *Golden Palace; Great Bus Journeys of the World; Great Railway Journeys;* The X-ray Operator in *Hospital; Jackanory, 'Diary of a Killer Cat';* The Father in *Le Kiss; Lenin of the Rovers;* Freddie the Phone in *Lovejoy;* James Bond in *My Uncle Monty, One For the Road;* Clarence in *Night Voice; Northern Songs; OTT;* Alain Degout in *Paris; Pigeon Pie;* Inspector in *Queen of the Wild Frontier; Sex, Drugs and Dinner;* Sir Roland Crust/Winston Crust in *Small World;* Andy in *Sorry About Last Night; The All New Alexei Sayle Show; The Big Three-O;* Milcic in *The Gravy Train; The History of the Ford Cortina;* The Balowski Family in *The Young Ones;* Bernie in *Two Minutes;* Melvyn Coombes in *Upline; You Make Me Feel Like Dancing.*
Films: Seemuller in *A Circle of Sharks;* Ahmed in *Carry On Columbus;* Uncle Henry in *Don't Walk;* Golodkin in *Gorky Park;* The Sultan in *Indiana Jones and the Last Crusade;* The Voice of the Toilet in *Love Child;* Turnpike Keeper in *Mr Corbett's Ghost;* Wib in *Reckless Kelly;* Beluga in *Rhinoceros Hunting In Budapest;* Cabbie in *Siesta;* Traffic Cop in *Supergrass;*

Mighty Mac in *Swing*; Margar in *The Bride*; Slav in *Whoops Apocalypse*.

Address: c/o Cassie Mayer Ltd, 34 Kingley Court, London W1R 5LE.

SCALES, Prunella

Prunella Scales. Actor (F).

b. Sutton Abinger, 22 June 1933.

TV: *A Nice Girl Like You*; *A Question of Attribution*; *A Wife Like The Moon*; *After Henry*; *Bergerac*; *Beyond The Pale*; *Breaking The Code*; *Dalziel and Pascoe*; *Doris and Doree*; *Emma*; *Fair Game*; *Fawlty Towers*; *Home Cooking*; *Jackanory*; *Keeping Mum*; *Little Pig Robinson*; *Mapp and Lucia*; *Midsomer Murders*; *Mr Big*; *Natural Causes*; *Never the Twain*; *Outside Edge*; *Searching*; *Sherwood Travels*; *Signs and Wonders*; *Singles*; *Slimming Down*; *Target*; *The Ghost of Grenville Hall*; *The Index Has Gone Fishing*; *The Lord of Misrule*; *The Merry Wives of Windsor*; *The Rector's Wife*; *What the Butler Saw*; *When We Are Married*; *Woodcock*.

Films: *An Awfully Big Adventure*; *Chorus of Disapproval*; *Consuming Passions*; *Howard's End*; *Mad Cows*; *Second Best*; *Stiff Upper Lips*; *The Boys from Brazil*; *The Hound of the Baskervilles*; *The Lonely Passion of Judith Hearne*; *The Wicked Lady*; *Wagner*; *Wolf*.

Address: c/o Conway Van Gelder, 18–21 Jermyn Street, London SW1Y 6HP.

SCANLAN, Joanna

Joanna Scanlan. Actor (F).

TV: *A Rather English Marriage*; *Casualty*; *Coming Soon*; *Cry Wolf*; *History File*; *How Do You Want Me?*; *Inspector Wexford*; *Jane Eyre*; *Kid in the Corner*; *Morwenna Banks Show*; *Morwenna Banks Show Special*; *Murder Most Horrid*; *Peak Practice*; *Picking Up the Pieces*; *The Bill*; *Vanity Fair*.

Address: c/o Casarotto Ramsay & Associates Ltd, National House, 60–66 Wardour Street, London WV1 4ND.

SCHNEIDER, David

David Schneider. Actor (M)/Presenter.

b. London, 22 May 1963.

TV: *Go Now*; *Hangar 17*; *Heading Home*; Tony Hayers in *I'm Alan Partridge*; *Kavanagh QC*; *Knowing Me, Knowing You*; The Judo Instructor in *Mr Bean*; *The Day Today*; *The Friday Night Armistice*; Bradley in *The Peter Principle*; *Up to Something*.

Films: Train Driver in *Mission: Impossible*; Ian in *You're Dead*.

Address: c/o London Management Noel House, 2–4 Noel Street, London W1V 3RB. m. Sandy McDade; 2 d. Clara, Miriam

SCHOFIELD, Leslie

Leslie Schofield. Actor (M).

TV: *Casualty*; *Chucklevision*; *Coronation Street* ; Jeff in *EastEnders*; *Fall and Rise of Reginald Perrin*; *Famous Five*; *Gentlemen and Players*; *Get Back*; *Good Guys*; *Heartbeat*; *Holding On*; Mr Briggs in *Jonny Briggs*; Reggie Tripper in *Juliet Bravo*; *King Leek*; *Minder*; *Moving Story*; Patterer in *Oliver Twist*; *Sherlock Holmes*; *The Bill*; *The Brittas Empire*; Dr Teegal in *The Exercise: Master of the Game*; *The Tide of Life*; *This is David Lander*; *Tricky Business*; *Wokenwell*; *Wycliffe*.

Films: *Anneke*; *Clockwise*; *Dead Man's Folly*; *Force 10 From Navarone*; *Lost In London*; *Master of the Game*; *Night of the Fox*; *Star Wars*; *The Moth*; *Villain*; *Wild Geese*.

Address: c/o Evans & Reiss, 100 Fawe Park Road, London SW15 2EA.

SCHOFIELD, Phillip

Phillip Schofield. Presenter/Actor (M).

b. Oldham, Manchester, 1 April 1962.

TV: *Broom Cupboard*; *Going Live*; *Now We're Talking*; *One In A Million*; *Schofield's Adventures in Hawaii*; *Schofield's Europe*; *Schofield's Quest*; *Schofield's TV Gold*; *Take Two*; *Talking Telephone Numbers*; *Television's Greatest Hits*; *Tenball*; *The Movie Game*.

Address: c/o James Grant Management Ltd, Syon Lodge, London Road, Middlesex TW7 5BH. 2 d. Molly, Ruby.

SCHONFIELD, Stephanie

Stephanie Schonfield. Actor (F).

TV: Andrea in *Crocodile Shoes*. Dr Carey in *Darling Buds of May*; Stella in *Emmerdale*; Gambler in *Expert Witness*; Clara Barley in *Great Expectations*; *Harry Enfield's TV Programme* (various); Janice Bolton in *Hollyoaks*; Handmaiden in *Nice Work*; Marietta Liptrott in *Rumpole of the Bailey*.

Films: Debbie in *Ford's on Water*; Magda Pike in *The Apocalypse Watch*.

Address: c/o Sheila Bourne Management, Bridge House, Three Mills Island Studios, Three Mills Lane, London E3 3DU.

SCHRODER, Rick

Rick Schroder. Actor (M).

b. Staten Island, New York, USA, 13 April 1970.

TV: Terry O'Neil in *A Son's Promise*; Jimmy Pearls in *Blood River*; John Thornton in *Call Of The Wild*; Jason Copeland in *Detention: Siege at Johnson High School*; Sam Benson in *Ebenezer*; Isaiah in *Heart Full Of Rain*; Newt Dobbs in *Lonesome Dove*; Frank Reily in *Miles From Nowhere*; Johnny in *My Son Johnny*;

Detective Danny Sorenson in *NYPD Blue*; Danny Evetts in *Out on the Edge*; Newt Dobbs in *Return to Lonesome Dove*; Otto MacNab in *Texas*; Mark in *The Stranger Within*; Joey Cutter in *To My Daughter with Love*; Nick Donahue in *Too Close to Home*.

Films: Billy Maloney in *Across the Tracks*; Lt Paul Hellerman in *Crimson Tide*; TJ Flynn in *The Champ*; Shawn Daley in *The Earthling*; Bobby in *The Last Flight of Noah's Ark*; Stick in *There Goes My Baby*.

Address: c/o ICM, Oxford House, 76 Oxford Street, London W1N 0AX. **Hobbies:** Built his own 2,500 square foot log cabin on his ranch in the summer of 1998. Owns 800 head of cattle, quarter horses, 2,000 deer and three trout lakes.

SCHWIMMER, David

David Schwimmer. Actor (M).
b. Queens, New York, USA, 12 November 1966.
TV: *A Deadly Silence*; Sonny Padalero in *Blossom*; Dr Christopher Saunders in *Breast Men*; Dr Karubian in *ER*; Ross in *Friends*; Himself in *Happy Birthday Elizabeth: A Celebration of Life*; Dana Romney in *LA Law*; Greg Richardson in *Monty*; Josh in *NYPD Blue*; Ross Geller in *The Single Guy*; Michael in *The Wonder Years* (1991, 1992).
Films: Chris in *All the Rage*; Edward French in *Apt Pupil*; John Anderson in *Crossing the Bridge*; Duty Officer in *Flight of the Intruder*; Max Abbitt in *Kissing a Fool*; Father Leo Jerome in *Picking up the Pieces*; Robert S Levitt in *Since You've Been Gone*; Frank Martin in *Six Days, Seven Nights*; *The Waiter*; Neil Campbell in *Twenty Bucks*; Cop 2 in *Wolf*.
Address: c/o The Gersh Agency, PO Box 5617, Beverly Hills, California 90210, USA. **Hobbies:** Theatre.

SCOGGINS, Tracy

Tracy Scoggins. Actor (F).
b. Dickinson, Texas, USA, 13 November 1959.
TV: Captain Elizabeth Lochley in *Babylon 5: A Call to Arms, Babylon 5: The River of Souls, Babylon 5, Crusade*; Anita Smithfield in *Dallas: War of the Ewings, Dallas: JR Returns*; Vala Duvalle in *Dan Turner, Hollywood Detective*; Monica Colby in *Dynasty*; Irene Gorley in *Hawaiian Heat*; Melanie Corrigan in *Jake Lassiter: Justice on the Bayou*; Hope Hathaway in *Jury Duty: The Comedy*; Cat Grant in *Lois and Clark: The New Adventures of Superman*; Amanda Carpenter in *Lonesome Dove: The Outlaw Years*; Tracy in *Renegades*; Monica Colby in *The Colbys*; Cindy Ryan in *Twirl*.
Films: Ariel in *Alien Intruder*; Marla Beaumont in *Dead On, Dead On: Relentless II*; Judith Grey in *Demonic Toys, Dollman vs Demonic Toys*; Tricia Merritt in *Play Murder For Me*; Rita Benson in *The Gumshoe*

Kid; Blue in *Timebomb*; Monique in *Toy Soldiers*; Samantha Stewart in *Ultimate Desires*; Barbara White in *Watchers II*.
Address: c/o Media Artists Group, 6404 Wilshire Blvd, Suite 950, Los Angeles, California 90048, USA. **Hobbies:** Cycling, swimming, jogging.

SCOTT, Brough

Brough Scott. Chief racing presenter/Racing presenter. b. 12 December 1942.
TV: *Channel 4 Racing*; *Horse Racing*.
Address: c/o Marquee Group (UK) Ltd, 21 The Green, Richmond, Surrey TW9 1PX. m. Susan; 2 s. Charlie, Jamie; 2 d. Sophie, Tessa.

SCOTT, Selina

Selina Scott. Presenter/Producer/Reporter.
b. Yorkshire, 13 May.
TV: *A Prince Among Islands*; *A Year of Spain*; *Breakfast Time*; *Entertainment Express*; *News*; *Election 'Specials'*; *Selina Scott Show*; *The Clothes Show*; *The King Of Greece*; *The Royal Wedding of HRH The Prince and Princess of Wales*; *West 57th*.
Address: c/o Knight Ayton Management, 10 Argyll Street, London W1V 1AB.

SCOTT THOMAS, Kristen

Kristen Scott Thomas. Actor (F)/Narrator.
b. Redruth, Cornwall, 24 May 1960.
TV: Alice in *Belle Époque*; Sister Gabriel/Anna Gibson in *Body and Soul*; Kate in *Framed*; Immortal Gatekeeper in *Gulliver's Travels*; Victoria in *Look at it This Way*; *Microcosmos*; Nancy in *Mistral's Daughter*; *Precious*; *Sentimental Journey*; Caroline in *The Endless Game*; Leda St Gabriel in *The Secret Life of Ian Fleming*; Thérèse in *The Tenth Man*; Jenny Sidonia in *Titmus Regained*; Elizabeth in *Weep No More, My Lady*.
Films: Brenda Last in *A Handful of Dust*; Sarah in *Amour et Confusions*; Matty Crompton in *Angels & Insects*; L'Institutrice in *Aux Yeux du Monde*; Clara in *Bille em Tete*; Fiona in *Bitter Moon*; *Djamel et Juliette*; Katia in *Force Majeur*; Fiona in *Four Weddings and a Funeral*; Julie in *L'Argent Troubel*; Marie in *La Meridienne*; *La Salade*; *La Tricheuse*; Marie Forestier in *Le Bal du Gouverneur*; Assistant to Hitchcock in *Le Confessional*; Mary-Jane Cooper in *Les Milles*; Sabine in *Mio Caro Dottor Grassler*; Sarah Davies in *Mission: Impossible*; Kay Chandler in *Random Hearts*; Imogen Staxton-Billing in *Revenger's Comedies*; Lady Anne in *Richard III*; *Somebody to Love*; *Souvenir*; Katherine Clifton in *The English Patient*; Annie MacLean in *The Horse Whisperer*; Caroline in *The Pompatus of Love*; Marie-Thérèse Von Debretsky in *Un Été Inoubliable*;

Mary Sharon in *Under the Cherry Moon*; Mary Panton in *Up at the Villa* (2000).
Address: c/o ICM, Oxford House, 76 Oxford Street, London W1N 0AX. m. François Oliviennes; 1 d. Hannah; 1 s. Joseph; sister Serena Scott Thomas

SCOTT THOMAS, Serena
Serena Scott Thomas. Actor (F). b. 1962.
TV: *After All; Bermuda Grace; Diana – Her Story; Harnessing Peacocks; Headhunters; Inspector Alleyn; Nash Bridges; Nostromo; Poirot; She-Wolf of London; Sherwood Travels; The Green Man; The Guilty; The Way to Dusty Death.*
Films: *Let Him Have It; Relax … It's Just Sex; The World is not Enough.*
Address: c/o ICM, Oxford House, 76 Oxford Street, London W1N 0AX. Sister: Kristen Scott Thomas.

SCULLY, Hugh
Hugh Scully. Presenter.
b. Bradford-on-Avon, Wiltshire, 5 May 1943.
TV: *Antiques Roadshow; Nationwide; Spotlight South West.*
Address: c/o QXL.com plc, Landmark House, Hammersmith Bridge Road, London W6 9DP. Hobbies: Antiques.

SCURFIELD, Matthew
Matthew Scurfield. Actor (M).
TV: Major Finn in *A Dance to the Music of Time; A Guilty Thing Surprised; A Murder of Quality;* Dave Chaplin in *A Touch of Frost; Blue Heaven; Brookside;* Dennis Hardy in *Casualty;* Jack McHine in *Cosmic Sucker;* Martin Ryder in *Dangerfield III; Heart of the Country;* Trevor in *Here Comes the Mirror Man;* Oliver Hardiman in *Hetty Wainthropp Investigates;* Impatient patient in *Karaoke;* Dr Ralph Dutton Jones in *Kavanagh QC; Look Me in the Eye;* Frankie in *Minder; Mornin' Sarge;* Alan Dace in *Out of Hours;* Roger Hoskins in *Pie in the Sky; Piglet Files; Scoop;* The Slaughterman in *Sharpe's Honour; Shelley;* Big Smithy's Crony in *Smokescreen;* The Kidnapper in *Tales from the Crypt; The Bill;* Inspector Jack Harris in *The Chief; The Hitch Hiker's Guide to the Galaxy;* Detective Sergeant Dawes in *Time After Time;* DS Rinnick in *Wycliffe; Young Indiana Jones Chronicles; Zorro.*
Films: *1984; Amy Foster; Black Beauty; Dakota Road; McVicar; Monster Make; Raiders of the Lost Ark; The Jigsaw Man; The Loss Adjuster; The Sweeney II; Wedekind.*
Address: c/o Rebecca Blond Associates, 69a Kings Road, London SW3 4NX.

SEAGROVE, Jenny
Jenny Seagrove. Actor (F).
b. Kuala Lumpur, 4 July 1958.
TV: *A Woman of Substance; Deadly Games; Diana; Hold The Dream; In Like Flynn; Incident At Victoria Falls; Killer; Lucy Walker; Magic Moments; Some Other Spring; The Betrothed; The Brack Report; The Eye of the Beholder; The Woman in White.*
Films: *A Chorus of Disapproval; A Shocking Accident; Appointment With Death; Bullseye!; Don't Go Breaking My Heart; Local Hero; Miss Beatty's Children; Nate and Hayes* (US)/*Savage Islands* (UK); *Sherlock Holmes: The Sign of Four; Tattoo; To Hell and Back In Time For Breakfast.*
Address: c/o Marmont Management Ltd, Langham House, 308 Regent Street, London W1R 5AL.

SECOMBE, Sir Harry
Sir Harry Secombe. Actor (M)/Presenter/Singer/Comedian. b. Swansea, South Wales, 8 September 1921.
TV: *Highway; Pepys; Secombe and Friends; Secombe Here; Songs of Praise.*
Films: *Davy;* Mr Bumble in *Oliver; Song of Norway; Sun Struck.*
Address: c/o Ruth Levene, 179 North Ways, College Crescent, London NW3 5DL. m. Myra; 2 d. Jennifer, Katy; 2 s. Andrew, David. Knighted 1981.

SEED, Graham
Graham Seed. Actor (M).
TV: *After the Dance; Ashenden; Brideshead Revisited; Brookside; Death or Glory Boys; Dinner Ladies; Edward VII; Freddie and Max; Good and Bad at Games; I, Claudius; Jeeves and Wooster; Madson; Nature Boy; Old Flames; Prime Suspect; Resnick; The Bill; The Upper Hand; Victoria Wood Sketches.*
Films: *Gandhi; Honest; Little Dorrit .*
Address: c/o Dalzell & Beresford Ltd, 91 Regent Street, London W1R 7TB.

SEINFELD, Jerry
Jerry Seinfeld. Actor (M)/Comedian/Producer/Host/Writer. b. Brooklyn, New York, USA, 29 April 1954.
TV: Host in *Abbott & Costello meet Jerry Seinfeld;* Frankie in *Benson;* 'Comp-u-Comp' in *Dilbert;* Himself in *Jerry Seinfeld Stand Up Confidential, Larry David: Curb Your Enthusiasm, Mad About You, New WKRP in Cincinnati, Newsradio, Playboy's Comedy Roast: Tommy Chong; Seinfeld;* Host in *Spy Magazine Presents How To Be Famous; The 43rd Annual Primetime Emmy Awards;* Himself in *The Larry Sanders Show;* Network Rep in *The Ratings Game; The Seinfeld Chronicles.*
Films: *Doctor Duck's Super Secret All Purpose Sauce.*

Address: c/o Elizabeth Clark, 11 Beach Street, 4th Floor, New York City 10013, USA. Fiancée: Jessica Sklar. Hobbies: Has practised Zen meditation since the early 1970s, watching ball games, collects Porsches and Nike tennis shoes.

SELBY, Tony

Tony Selby. Actor (M). b. 26 February 1938.

TV: *Ace of Wands; Casualty; Doctor Who; Hero to Zero; Holby City; Law and Disorder; Love Hurts; Mike and Angelo; My Summer with Des; Real Women; The Bill; The Changeling; The Detectives; The Gentleman Caller; The Good Life; The Informer; The Lady is a Tramp; The Vanishing Man; The World of Lee Evans; Up the Junction.*

Films: *Adolf Hitler, My Part in His Downfall; Alfie; Press for Time.*

Address: c/o Associated International Management, 5 Denmark Street, London, WC2H 8LP.

SERKIS, Andy

Andy Serkis. Actor (M).

TV: Cassian in *Arabian Nights;* Tom in *Finney;* Pytor in *Grushko;* MEM O'Brian in *Kavanagh QC; Made in Spain;* Morris Minor and the Motors; Bill Sykes in *Oliver Twist;* Sergeant Corrigan in *Pale Horse;* Max in *Pie in the Sky; Saracen;* Owen in *Streetwise; The Bill;* Jacko in *The Chief;* Greville in *The Darling Buds of May;* Stephen in *The Jump; The New Statesman; The Poliakoff Trilogy;* Lawler in *Touching Evil.*

Films: *Among Giants; Career Girls; Clueless;* Chester in *Five Seconds to Spare; Insomnia; Loop;* Potts in *Mojo;* Thelwall in *Pandemonium;* Fitz in *Stella Does Tricks;* Leo in *Sweeney Barrett; The Near Room;* Torsten in *The Prince of Jutland.*

Address: c/o Lou Coulson, 37 Berwick Street, London W1V 3RF.

SESSIONS, John

John Sessions. Actor (M)/Comedy actor/Voice artist. b. 11 January 1953.

TV: Charles Dickens in *Ackroyd's Dickens;* Larry in *Boon;* Crosera in *Day In Summer; Educating Marmalade;* Nigel in *Girls on Top;* Prunesquallor in *Gormenghast;* Gramsci in *Gramsci;* Blake in *Happy Families;* Hercules in *In the Red; Laugh, I Nearly Paid My Licence Fee;* Daniel in *My Night With Reg; Spitting Image; Stella Street; The Lenny Henry Show;* Lord Pennistone in *The New Statesman;* John Michaels in *The Pope Must Die;* Fielding in *Tom Jones;* Boswell in *Tour of the Western Isles;* Silly Man in *Whoops Apocalypse; Whose Line is it Anyway?.*

Address: c/o Markham & Froggatt Ltd, 4 Windmill Street, London W1P 1HF.

SEYMOUR, Carolyn

Carolyn Seymour. Actor (F).

b. Aylesbury, Buckinghamshire, 6 November 1947.

TV: *Alfred Hitchcock Presents …; Ally McBeal; Babylon 5; Cagney and Lacey; Civil Wars; Class of '96; Condor; Family Ties; Girls of the White Orchid; Hart to Hart; Jack's Place; Justice; LA Law; Magnum PI; Masquerade; Matlock; Murder, She Wrote; Over My Dead Body; Poor Little Rich Girl; Quantum Leap; Reform School Girls (TVM); Remington Steele; Return of the Man from U.N.C.L.E.; Return of the Saint; Star Trek: The Next Generation;* Jenny in *Take Three Girls II; The Chicago Trial Conspiracy;* Abby Grant in *The Survivors; The Trials of Rosie O'Neill; Twilight Zone.*

Films: *Congo; Destination Unknown; Gumshoe; Midnight Cabaret; Mr Mom; Steptoe and Son; The Bitch; The Gay Blade; The Odd Job; The Ruling Class; Unman, Wittering and Zigo; Zorro.*

Address: c/o Langford Associates, 17 Westfields Avenue, London SW13 0AT. 1st m. (dis.) Peter Medak (film director); 1 s. Joshua, 1 d. Daisy. Hobbies: Pets, cooking, travel.

SEYMOUR, Jane

Joyce Frankenberg. Actor (F)/Producer.

b. Hillingdon, Middlesex, 15 February 1951.

TV: Anna Robinson in *A New Swiss Family Robinson;* Alison Reid in *Absolute Truth;* Laura in *Angel Of Death;* Adrienne Wells in *Are You Lonesome Tonight;* Serina in *Battlestar Galactica;* Margie Parks in *Benny & Barney: Las Vegas Undercover;* Marjorie Chisholm Armagh in *Captains and Kings;* Hillary Burnham in *Crossings;* Laura Cole in *Dallas Cowboys Cheerleaders;* Leigh Cullen/Tracey Cullen in *Dark Mirror;* Dr Michaela Quinn in *Dr Quinn Medicine Woman, Dr Quinn Medicine Woman – The Movie;* Agatha/Prima in *Frankenstein: The True Story;* Fraulein Rottenmeier in *Heidi;* Emma in *Jack the Ripper;* Mary Yellan in *Jamaica Inn;* Jan in *Killer On Board;* Hadley Norman in *Matters of The Heart;* Diane Putnam in *Obsessed With A Married Woman;* Maria Callas in *Onassis: The Richest Man In The World;* Bella Wilfer in *Our Mutual Friend;* Hazel Brannon Smith in *Passion For Justice;* Linda Crandell in *Praying Mantis;* Eva Meyers in *Seventh Avenue;* Catherine Alexander in *Sidney Sheldon's Memories of Midnight;* Teresa in *Sunstroke;* Genny Luckett in *The Awakening Land;* Ethne Eustace in *The Four Feathers;* Herself in *The Grand Knockout Tournament* (1987); Julia Evans in *The Haunting Passion;* Emma Fogarty in *The Onedin Line;* Maria Gianelli in *The Phantom of the Opera;* Marguerite in *The Scarlet Pimpernel;* Bathsheba in *The Story of David; The Strauss Family;* Brett Ashley in *The Sun Also Rises;*

Wallis Simpson in *The Woman He Loved*; Natalie Henry in *War and Rememberance*.

Films: Maria in *El Tunel*; Jane Caldwell in *Head Office*; Marie Antoinette in *La Révolution Française*; Sara in *Lassite*; Solitaire in *Live And Let Die*; Jackie in *Oh Heavenly Dog*; Lady Juliana in *Quest for Camelot*; Farah in *Sinbad And The Eye Of The Tiger*; Elise McKenna in *Somewhere in Time*; Lillian Stein in *The Only Way*; Pamela Plowden in *Young Winston*.

Address: c/o Chris Barrett, Metropolitan Agency, 4526 Wilshire Blvd, Los Angeles, California 90010, USA. Dick Guttman & Associates, 11850 Beverly Drive, Suite 201, Beverly Hills, California, USA. m. 1 (dis.) Michael Attenborough; m. 2 James Keach; 1 d. Kate Flynn, 3 s. John Stacey Keach, Kristopher Steven Keach, Sean Flynn. Hobbies: Ballet dancing, interior decorating, painting, spokesman for UNICEF, received OBE in 1999.

SHAKESBY, Patricia

Patricia Shakesby. Actor. b. Yorkshire.

TV: *Brighton Rock*; *Coronation Street*; *Detective*; Polly in *Howard's Way*; *Tall, Fat and Ugly*; *The Pity of it All*; *Twelfth Night*; *War and Peace*; *Yes, Minister*.

Films: *The Welcome*.

Address: c/o Bryan Drew Ltd, Quadrant House, 80–82 Regent Street, London W1X 3TB.

SHANDLING, Garry

Garry Shandling. Actor (M)/Comedian/Host/Presenter. b. Tuscon, Arizona, USA, 29 November 1949.

TV: *Caroline In The City*; Himself in *Dr Katz, Professional Therapist*; *It's Garry Shandling's Show*; Jack in *Mother Goose Rock 'n' Rhyme*; Himself in *The Ben Stiller Show*; Larry Sanders in *The Larry Sanders Show*; Himself in *Young Comedians Show*.

Films: Male Pigeon (voice) in *Dr Dolittle*; *Doctor Duck's Super Secret All Purpose Sauce*; Artie in *Hurlyburly*; Kip De May in *Love Affair*; Stanley Tannenbaum in *Mixed Nuts*; *Town And Country*; *What Planet Are You From?*.

Address: c/o United Talent Agency, Nick Stevens, Suite 500, 9560 Wilshire Blvd, Beverly Hills California 90212, USA. Pat Kingsley, PMK Public Relations, Suite 200, 955 South Carrillo Drive, Los Angeles, California 90048, USA. Hobbies: Meditation, health-food nut, reading.

SHANE, Paul

Paul Shane. Actor (M). b. 19 June 1940.

TV: *A Day Out*; Grayson in *Common As Muck*; Ted Bovis in *Hi De Hi*; Jack Skinner in *Oh! Doctor Beeching*; Stokes in *You Rang M'Lord*.

Films: Ted in *Hilltop Hospital*; Papa in *La Passione*.

Address: c/o ATS Casting Ltd, 26 St Michael's Road, Leeds, Yorkshire LS6 3AW.

SHANNON, Johnny

Johnny Shannon. Actor (M). b. London, 29 July 1932.

TV: *Angels*; Wacky in *Beryl's Lot*; Billy Bunyan in *Big Deal*; *Blackhearts in Battersea*; *Budgie*; *Bust*; *Chinese Detective*; *Coast to Coast*; *Dixon of Dock Green*; Alfie the boxing promoter in *EastEnders*; *Fawlty Towers*; *Give Us a Break*; Lenny in *Give Us a Break Special*; *Go for Gold*; *Hazell and the Greasy Gunners*; *High Street Blues*; Mr Ryder in *Keep it in the Family*; *Keeping Score*; *Minder*; *Morecambe & Wise*; *Old Dog with New Tricks*; *Pursuit*; *Queenie*; *Secret Army*; *Six Faces of a Man*; *Supergran*; *Tales of the Unexpected*; *The Bill*; Winston in *The Boy Who Won The Pools*; *The Bright Side*; *The Dick Emery Show*; *The Donati Conspiracy*; Cyril in *The Enigma Files*; *The Gold Robbers*; *The Kenny Everett Show*; Ron in *The Operation*; *The Other One*; *The Professionals*; *The Sweeney*; Charlie Warren in *The XYZ Man*; Lord Slipper Meat in *Union Castle*; *Z Cars*.

Address: c/o Chatto & Linnit Ltd, 123a Kings Road, London SW3 4PL.

SHARMA, Paul

Paul Sharma. Actor (M).

TV: Mukesh Gupta in *Accused*; Rashid in *Casualty*; Ashok in *Choices*; *Maisie Raine*; Rajiv in *Roger, Roger*; *Success*; Steve in *Watford Gap*; Elvis in *What You Looking At?*.

Films: Jamie in *A–Z*; Mumtaz in *The Drive*; Assistant in *Wild Justice*.

Address: c/o Garricks, 7 Garrick Street, London WC2E 9AR.

SHARROCK, Ian

Ian Sharrock. Actor (M).

TV: *A Play For Love: Games*; *Agent Z and the Penguin From Mars*; *Ain't Misbehavin'*; *Behind the Palace Walls*; *Casualty*; *Crime Traveller*; *Dads*; Jackie Merrick in *Emmerdale*; *Heartbeat*; *Hospital*; *I'm Alan Partridge*; *In The Name Of Love*; *Lynda La Plante's Killer Net*; *Peter Pan*; *Picking Up The Pieces*; *She-Wolf of London*; *Smike*; *The Bill*; *Where the Heart Is*.

Films: *Candleshoe*.

Address: c/o Susan Angel Associates, 1st Floor, 12 D'Arblay Street, London W1V 3FP. Hobbies: Singing, golf, driving.

SHAW, Joe

Joe Shaw. Actor (M). b. London, 15 November 1972.

TV: Dominic McAlister in *Bad Girls*; Octavius in

House of Angels; Jerry in *Junk*; Cecil Rhodes in *Rhodes*.
Films: Dalgar in *Kull the Conqueror*; Eric Burns in *Le Policier De Tangier*.
Address: c/o Ken McReddie Ltd, 91 Regent Street, London W1R 7TB. Father Martin Shaw.

SHAW, Martin

Martin Shaw. Actor (M).
b. Birmingham, 21 January 1945.
TV: *A Woman of Today*; *Achilles Heel*; Robert Kingsford in *Always and Everyone*; *Beasts: Buddyboy*; *Black and Blue*; *Cassidy*; *Classic Two: Exiles*; *Cream in My Coffee*; *Doctor in the House*; Lead in *East Lynne*; *Electra*; *For the Greater Good*; Lead in *Hamlet*; *Intrigue*; *Jubilee: Our Kids*; *Love's Labour Lost*; Cecil Rhodes in *Rhodes*; *Spice Island Farewell*; Lead in *The Chief III*, *The Chief IV*, *The Chief V*; *The Explorers*; Scott in *The Last Place on Earth*; Lead in *The Most Dangerous Man in the World*; *The Pigeon Fancier*; Lead in *The Professionals*; *The Scarlet Pimpernel*; *The System*; *The Villains*; *Two Feet off the Ground*; *Who Bombed Birmingham?*.
Films: *Ladder of Swords*; *Macbeth*; *Seven Men at Daybreak*; *Sinbad's Golden Voyage*.
Address: c/o Jonathan Altaras Associates, 13 Shorts Gardens, London WC2H 9AT.

SHAW, Tracy

Tracy Shaw. Actor (F). b. 27 January 1973.
TV: Maxine in *Coronation Street*.
Address: c/o Arena Entertainment, Regents Court, 39 Harrogate Road, Leeds, West Yorkshire.

SHEARSMITH, Reece

Reece Shearsmith. Actor (M).
TV: *Alexei Sayle's Merry-go-round*; *In the Red*; *Lenny Goes to Town*; *The Devil of Winterbourne*; *The Ghost of Winterbourne*; *The League of Gentlemen*.
Films: *This Year's Love*.
Address: c/o PBJ Management, 5 Soho Square, London W1V 5DE. Hobbies: Conjuring.

SHEPARD, Vonda

Vonda Shepard. Performer/Lyricist.
b. New York, USA, 7 July 1963.
TV: Herself in *Ally McBeal*.
Music: *Ally* (TV series – half-hour version); *Ally McBeal Soundtrack*; *Ally McBeal Soundtrack II*; *By 7.30*; *It's Good Eve* (album); *Songs From Ally McBeal*; *The Radical Light* (album); *Vonda Shepard* (album).
Address: c/o Gail Gellerman, 23853 Pacific Coast Highway, Suite 920, Malibu, California 90265, USA. Father Richmond Shepard.

SHEPHARD, Ben

Ben Shephard. Actor (M)/Presenter.
b. 11 December 1974.
TV: *T4*; *The Bigger Breakfast*; *Bedrock*; *Control Freaks*.
Address: c/o James Grant Management Ltd, Syon Lodge, London Road, Isleworth, Middlesex TW7 5BH.

SHEPHERD, Cybill

Cybill Shepherd. Actor (F)/Producer/Writer.
b. Memphis, Tennessee, USA, 18 February 1950.
TV: Debbie in *Baby Brokers*; Cybill Sheridan in *Cybill*; Janice in *Journey Of The Heart*; Carla in *Masquerade*; Reeny Perdew in *Memphis*; Maddie Hayes in *Moonlighting*; Elaine in *Secrets of a Married Man*; Samantha Weathers in *Stormy Weathers*; Faith Kelsey in *Telling Secrets*; Eula Verner in *The Long Hot Summer*; Colleen Champion in *The Yellow Rose*; Julie in *There Was A Little Boy*; Karen Parsons in *Which Way Home*; Judy Stokes in *While Justice Sleeps*.
Films: Nancy Brill in *Alice*; Golden Girl in *Americathon*; Brooke Carter in *At Long Last Love*; Connie Jeffries in *Chances Are*; Annie P/'Daisy' Miller in *Daisy Miller*; Kelly in *The Heartbreak Kid*; June Nordstrom in *Marine Life*; Claire in *Married To It*; Marilyn Schwary in *Once Upon A Crime*; Debbie Lickman in *Silver Bears*; Mary Jane in *Special Delivery*; Betsy in *Taxi Driver*; Jacy Furrow in *Texasville* (1990); Amanda Kelly in *The Lady Vanishes*; Jacy Furrow in *The Last Picture Show*; Kiki Taylor in *The Last Word*; Herself in *The Muse*; Jennifer in *The Return*.
Music: *Mad About The Boy*; *Somewhere Down The Road*; *Talk Memphis To Me* (album); *Vanilla*.
Address: c/o ICM, 8942 Wilshire Blvd, Beverly Hills, CA 90211, USA. Hobbies: A nutrition and physical fitness enthusiast, walking, swimming, cycling and reading with her children, singing.

SHEPHERD, Jack

Jack Shepherd. Actor. b. 20 October 1940.
TV: Peplow in *A Day in Summer*; Brodi in *A Murderer Among Us*; Van Santen in *A Room for the Winter*; Mr Brown in *A Separate Piece*; Son in *All Good Men*; Joe Marriot in *Balltrap on the Côte Sauvage*; Commander Neame in *Between the Lines*; Nick Shepherd in *Calling the Shots*; Goya in *Cracking Up*; DPP in *Crimestrike*; Allsop in *Cripples*; Reinfield in *Dracula*; Itzhak Lightmann in *Escape from Sobibor*; Rudi in *Girls of Slender Means*; Harry in *Hard Travelling*; Marcus Maybury in *Hospice*; Jamie in *Lovejoy*; , Mr Bi in *Mr and Mrs Bureaucrat*; Paul in *Mysterioso*; Yuri in *Nina*; Gramsci in *Occupations*; Gauguin in *Omnibus – Vincent Van Gogh*; Butler in *Over Here*; Rev. Williams

in *Pastoral Care*; Pidgeon in *Pidgeon Hawk or Dove?*; Director in *Ready When You Are Mr MacGill*; Corker in *Scoop*; Stalker in *Shoot To Kill*; Baxter Dawes in *Sons and Lovers*; Bertold Brecht in *Tales from Hollywood*; Johann Frank in *The Act*; Thomas à Becket in *The Devil's Crown*; Chinaman in *The Holy City*; Lead in *The Killing*; Sloman in *The Party*; Lomas in *The Tunnel*; Trainee in *Through the Night*; Blake in *Trust Me*; Tobias in *Woman at War*; Wycliffe in *Wycliffe, Wycliffe Special*.

Films: Dwyer in *All Neat and Back*; Dr Price in *Angry Earth*; Philip in *Blue Black Permanent*; Stevens in *Blue Ice*; Teo in *Luces y Sombras*; Dyscart in *No Escape*; Mr Slaughter in *Object of Beauty*; Edward Groves in *Scarlet Tunic*; Bill in *Snarl Up*; Underwater Vicar in *The Bedsitting Room*; Referee in *The Big Man*; Eskerson in *The Last Valley*; Sergeant Wellbeloved in *The Virgin Soldiers*; Kenneth in *Twenty-One*.

Address: c/o Markham & Froggatt Ltd, 4 Windmill Street, London W1P 1HF.

SHEPHERD, Simon

Simon Shepherd. Actor. b. Bristol, 20 August 1956.

TV: Duncan Racallister in *Beyond Reason*; Sam Bliss in *Bliss*; Piers Garfield-Ward in *Chancer*; Peter Taylor in *Life for a Life*; Dr Will Preston in *Peak Practice*; Mark Sopwith in *Tilly Trotter*; Major Stone in *Warriors*.

Films: Gloucester in *Henry V*; Rupert in *Nine Lives*; Peter Norris in *Rogue Trader*; Edgar Linton in *Wuthering Heights*.

Address: c/o PFD, Drury House, 34–43 Russell Street, London WC2B 5HA. Hobbies: Children, horses.

SHEPHERD, Steve

Steve Shepherd. Actor (M).

TV: Lee Shotton in *An Unsuitable Job for a Woman*; Chef in *Christmas*; David O'Neil in *Forgive and Forget*; George Kyprianou in *Maisie Raine*; *The One That Got Away*; Joe in *This Life*.

Films: Sam in *Greenwich Mean Time*; Sam in *I Want You*; Rudy in *RPM*; Jason in *Virtual Sexuality*.

Address: c/o ICM, Oxford House, 76 Oxford Street, London W1N 0AX.

SHERIDAN, Dinah

Dinah Sheridan. Actor (F).

TV: *All Night Long*; *An Ideal Husband*; *Don't Wait Up*; *Lovejoy*.

Films: *29 Acacia Avenue*; Eve Canyon in *Appointment in London*; *Behind Your Back*; *Calling Paul Temple*; *Father Steps Out*; Stella White in *For You Alone*; *Full Speed Ahead*; Wendy in *Genevieve*; Mary Pemberton in *Get Cracking*; *Irish and Proud of It*; Dinah Shaw in *Landslide*; *Merely Mr Hawkins*; *Murder in Reverse*; *No Trace*; *Paul Temple's Triumph*; Evie in *Salute John Citizen*; Eileen Hannay in *The Hills of Donegal*; Jane Hugget in *The Huggets Abroad*; *The Mirror Crack'd*; Mother in *The Railway Children*; Jess Peel in *The Sound Barrier*; Grace Marston in *The Story of Gilbert and Sullivan*; Shirley Yorke in *The Story of Shirley Yorke*; Mary Payton in *Where No Vultures Fly*.

Address: c/o ICM, Oxford House, 76 Oxford Street, London W1N 0AX.

SHIELDS, Brooke

Christa Shields. Actor (F)/Guest/Voice artist.

b. New York, USA, 31 May 1965.

TV: Erika Ford in *Friends*; Laura Black in *I Can Make You Love Me*; Dr Beth Taft in *Nothing Lasts Forever*; Vanessa Foster in *Quantum Leap*; Susan Keane in *Suddenly Susan*; Norma in *Tales from the Crypt*; Cyndee Lafrance in *The Almost Perfect Bank Robbery*; Herself in *The Muppet Show*; Kristin in *The Prince Of Central Park*; Herself in *The Simpsons*; Laura in *Wet Gold*.

Films: Stevie in *Backstreet Dreams*; Sam in *Black And White*; Brenda Starr in *Brenda Starr*; Jade in *Endless Love*; Skye Daley in *Freaked*; Mimi Wolverton in *Freeway*; Karen Spages in *Holy Terror*; Kate in *Just You And Me, Kid*; Tita in *King of the Gypsies*; Violet in *Pretty Baby*; Christine Shaye in *Running Wild*; Dale in *Sahara*; Stewardess/Herself in *Speed Zone!*; *The Bachelor*; Emmeline in *The Blue Lagoon*; Lily in *The Misadventures of Margaret*; Kate Fletcher in *The Seventh Floor*; Nina in *The Weekend*; Tilt (Louise Davenport) in *Tilt*; Wanda Nevada in *Wanda Nevada*.

Address: c/o William Morris Agency, 151 El Camino Drive, Beverly Hills, California 90212, USA. m. 1 (dis.) André Agassi; Father Frank Shields; mother Teri Shields; sister Marina. Hobbies: Lends her voice to issues supporting children's welfare and education.

SHIMMIN, Sadie

Sadie Shimmin. Actor (F).

TV: *Blackadder*; *Bramwell*; *Casualty*; *Dirty Dishes*; *EastEnders*; *Hard Cases*; *History File*; *Mornin' Sarge*; *Off Limits*; *Prime Suspect*; *Ruth Rendell Mysteries*; *Silent Witness*; *The Bill*; *The Real McCoy*.

Address: c/o Crouch Associates, 9–15 Long Acre, London WC2H 9PF.

SHIPTON, Cathy

Cathy Shipton. Actor (F). b. 27 March 1957.

TV: Mother in *The Bill*; Sister Duffy in *Casualty*;

Dulcie in *Little Sir Nicholas*; Mrs Burridge in *One Foot in the Grave*; Sarah Price in *Taggart*.
Films: Midwife in *Spice World*.
Address: c/o Marina Martin Associates, 12–13 Poland Street, London W1V 3DE. Hobbies: Long-distance running.

SILVA, Adele
Adele Silva. Actor (F). Guest.
TV: *Blankety Blank*; Squeak in *Doctor Who*; Beth in *EastEnders*; Kelly in *Emmerdale*; Fenella Fudd in *Mr Majeika*; Abagail Benson in *The Chain*; *The T-Spot*.
Address: c/o Rossmore Personal Management, Rossmore Road, London NW1 6NJ.

SILVERA, Carmen
Carmen Silvera. Actor (F). b. Toronto, 1980.
TV: Edith in *'Allo 'Allo*; *Before Water Lilies*; *Cluedo*; Camilla Hope in *Compact*; *Dad's Army*; *Doctor Who*; *La Passione*; *Tales of the Unexpected*; *Two Women*; *Whoops Apocalypse*; *Within these Walls*; *Z Cars*.
Address: c/o Burnett Granger Associates, Prince of Wales Theatre, 31 Coventry Street, London W1V 8AS.

SIMM, John
John Simm. Actor (M). b. Leeds, Yorkshire, 1971.
TV: *Between the Lines*; *Chillers – The Man In the Mirror*; *Cracker*; *Forgive and Forget*; *Heartbeat*; *Meat*; *Men of the World*; *Oasis*; *Pinch of Snuff*; *Rumpole of the Bailey*; *The Bill*; *The Lakes*; *The Locksmith*.
Films: *Boston Kickout*; *Diana and Me*; *Human Traffic*; *Understanding Jane*; *Wonderland*.
Address: c/o ICM, Oxford House, 76 Oxford Street, London W1N 0AX.

SIMON, Charles
Charles Simon. Actor (M).
b. Tettenhall Wood, 4 February 1909.
TV: *The Singing Detective*; *Kavanagh QC*; *Poirot*; *Wives and Daughters*; *Midsomer Murders*; *Summer in the Suburbs*.
Films: *Echio Pinoccio*; *Topsy Turvey*; *Paradise Grove*; *Whatever Happened to Harold Smith*.
Address: c/o Vincent Shaw, 20 Jay Mews, London, SW7 2EP.

SIMONS, William
William Simons. Actor (M).
TV: *Auf Wiedersehen, Pet*; *Boon*; Jim Cawley in *Coronation Street*; Mr Watson in *Darling Buds of May*; *Dempsey and Makepeace*; *Doctor Who*; *Emmerdale*; *Enemy at the Door*; Alf Ventress in *Heartbeat*; Inspector Fox in *Inspector Allen*; *Juliet Bravo*; *Julius Caesar*;

Boyd in *Love Hurts*; Goodis in *Lovejoy*; *Minder*; *Rumpole of the Bailey*; *Tales of Mystery and Imagination*; *The Last Party*; *The Sweeney*; Keckwick in *The Woman in Black*.
Address: c/o Saraband Associates, 265 Liverpool Road, London N1 1LX.

SIMPSON, Joe
Joe Simpson. Actor (M). b. Manchester.
TV: PC in *Always and Everyone*; Brent in *Cracker*; Sgt Roper in *Coronation Street*; Robber in *Crimewatch UK*; Ray Thorpe in *Emmerdale*; Reed in *Heartbeat*; Hospital porter in *Peak Practice*; Army Spotter in *Rhinoceros*; journalist in *The Things You do for Love*; Surveillance Officer in *Undercover Customers*; Skin in *Walk with a Purpose*.
Address: c/o Sharron Ashcroft Management, Dean Clough, Halifax, Yorkshire HX3 5AX. Hobbies: Singing, dancing, football. Takes an active part in theatre workshops and production and direction.

SIMPSON, Junior
Junior Simpson. Comedian/Panelist/Presenter/Team captain.
TV: *Bring Me the Head of Light Entertainment*; *Cutting Edge at the Comedy Store*; *In the Dark with Junior Simpson*; *Live at Jongleurs*; *Never Mind the Buzzcocks*; *Night Fever*; *The Hit Man*; *The Real McCoy*.
Address: c/o Off the Kerb Productions, 3rd Floor, Hammer House, 113–117 Wardour Street, London W1V 3TD.

SIMS, Joan
Joan Sims. Actor (F). b. Laindon, Essex, 9 May 1930.
TV: *As Time Goes By*; *Martin Chuzzlewit*; *My Good Friend*; *On the Up*; *Only Fools and Horses*; *Spark*; *The Canterville Ghost*; *The Dick Emery Show*; *The Stanley Baxter Show*; *The Two Ronnies*; *Till Death us do Part*; *Victoria Wood Show*.
Films: *Carry On (various)*; *Doctor in Trouble*; *Love Among the Ruins*; *The Fool*.
Address: c/o Richard Hatton Ltd, 29 Roehampton Gate, London SW15 5JR.

SINCLAIR, Belinda
Belinda Sinclair. Actor (F).
TV: *A Touch of Frost*; *Casualty*; *Heartbeat*; *Ladykillers*; *Maggie's Baby*; *Minder*; *Mouse in the Corner*; *Moving Story*; *No Frills*; *Ruth Rendell*; *Saracen*; *Shelley*; *Silent Witness*; *Small Zones*; *South of the Border*; *Spatz*; *The Bill*; *The Dancing Years*; *The Honeysiege*; *The Ice House*; *The Indiscretion of an American Wife*; *Two for One*; *Upline*; *You, Me and It*.

Films: *Loose Connections; The Beggar's Opera.*
Address: c/o Conway Van Gelder, 18–21 Jermyn Street, London SW1Y 6HP.

SINCLAIR, Suzanne

Suzanne Sinclair. Actor (F). b. London 12 Jan 1960.
TV: Jackie Kinnaird in *Back Up; Fool of Me; Grange Hill; L'Escale; Le Bal d'Irene; Le Loufiat; Ne M'Appelez Plus Gloria; Newsfile; Saturday Stayback;* WPC Mulvaney/Angela Thorpe in *The Bill; The Dressing Room; The Lenny Henry Show; There's a Lot of it About; Under the Moon; Victoria Wood – As Seen on TV.*
Films: Andie in *Bellona; Hard Facts;* Mona in *Quadrophenia;* Thorn in *White Angel.*
Address: c/o Langford Associates, 17 Westfields Avenue, London SW13 0AT. Hobbies: Running marathons, karate.

SINDEN, Marc

Marc Sinden. Actor (M). b. 9 May 1954.
TV: *Against All Odds; Bergerac; Century Falls; Country Boy; Crossroads; Emmerdale; Home Front;* Chas Floyd in *Magnum PI; Never the Twain;* Martin Pryce in *Politician's Wife; Rumpole of the Bailey; The Island.*
Films: *Carry On Columbus; Clash of Loyalties; Manges D'Homme;* Group Captain White in *The Brylcreem Boys;* Mr Honeythunder in *The Mystery of Edwin Drood; The Wicked Lady; White Nights.*
Address: c/o Hilary Gagan Associates, 2nd Floor, Gloucester Mansions, 140a Shaftesbury Avenue, London WC2H 8HD.

SINGLETON, Valerie

Valerie Singleton. Presenter/Continuity Announcer. b. 9 April 1937.
TV: *Blue Peter* (1962); *Blue Peter Royal Safari* (1971); *Blue Peter Special Assignment* (1980); *Blue Peter Special Assignment* (1974); *Echoes of Germany* (1980); *Migrant Workers in Europe* (1980); *Nationwide* (1972); *Open University; The Money Programme* (1980); *The Royal Wedding of Princess Anne and Captain Mark Phillips; Tonight* (1978); *Tonight in Town* (1978); *Val Meets the VIPs* (1976).
Address: c/o Arlington Enterprises Ltd, 1–3 Charlotte Street , London W1P 1HD.

SINSTADT, Gerald

Gerald Sinstadt. Presenter. b. 19 Feb 1930.
TV: *Eastern Sport; Grandstand; Kick Off; Match of the Day; Sportsnight.*
Address: c/o Peter Schnabl, 72 Vincent Square, London SW1P 2PA.

SKEPPER, Catrina

Catrina Skepper. Entertainment Correspondent/ Fashion Correspondent/Presenter/Showbiz Correspondent.
TV: *Good Morning with Anne & Nick* (1995); *Heaven and Earth; Live at Three; This Morning; VIP.*
Address: c/o Knight Ayton Management, 10 Argyll Street, London W1V 1AB. Hobbies: Art history, music, yoga, horse riding and diving.

SKIDMORE, Graham

Graham Skidmore. Voice over.
TV: 'Our Graham' in *Blind Date; Families at War; GMTV; Shooting Stars; The Reeves and Mortimer; This Morning.*
Address: c/o Roberta Kanal, 82 Constance Road, Twickenham, Middlesex TW2 7JA.

SKINNER, Claire

Claire Skinner. Actor (F).
TV: *A Dance to the Music of Time; Capital Lives; Chef!; Inspector Morse; Second Sight; Six Sides of Steve Coogan; South of the Border; The Peter Principle; The Wingless Bird; Two Golden Balls.*
Films: *Clockwork Mice; i.d.; Life is Sweet; Naked; Sleepy Hollow; Wrong Blonde; You're Dead.*
Address: c/o ICM Oxford House, 76 Oxford Street, London W1N 0AX.

SKINNER, Frank

Frank Skinner. Comedian/Host.
b. Oldbury, West Midlands, 28 January 1957.
TV: *Balls to Africa for Comic Relief* (1996); *Fantasy Football League* (1998); *Fantasy Football League* (1994); *The Frank Skinner Show* (1995); *Wogan* (1993); *World Cup Grandstand* (1994).
Music: *Three Lions (It's Coming Home)* (No. 1).
Address: c/o Avalon Promotions, 2nd Floor, Queens House, Leicester Place, London WC2H 7BP.

SLATTERY, Tony

Tony Slattery. Actor (M)/Comedian/Writer.
b. London 9 November 1959.
TV: *Alas Smith and Jones; Behind the Bikesheds; Clive Anderson Talks Back; Footlights Revue; Gems; Going for a Song; Have I Got News For You; Just a Gigolo; Just a Minute; Metropolis; Murder Most Horrid; Ps and Qs; Red Dwarf VIII; Renford Rejects; Ruby Wax – Stripped; S & M; Saturday Night at the Movies; Saturday Stayback; Sixty Minutes; That's Love; The Easter Stories; The Lenny Henry Show; The Music Game; This Is David Harper; Tibs and Fibs; Up Yer News; Ways and Means; Whose Line is it Anyway?; Wodehouse on Broadway.*

Films: *Carry On Columbus; Drowning in the Shallow End; How to Get Ahead in Advertising; Peter's Friends; The Crying Game; To Die For; Up 'n' Under.*
Address: c/o Paul Becker Ltd, 193 Wardour Street, London W1V 3FA.

SLAVIN, Jane

Jane Slavin. Actor (F).
TV: *D C Muir* in *202; Cathy Jordan* in *Always and Everyone;* WDS Doyle in *Band of Gold;* Starr Faithful in *In Suspicious Circumstances;* Jane in *Maigret;* Georgy Kepler in *Peak Practice;* Debbie in *The Bill;* Sarah Franks in *The Bill;* Danni in *Ultra Violet;* Arabella in *Unfinished Business;* Clare in *Wrestling with the Big One;* Hazel Formby in *Wycliffe.*
Films: Melody in *Night Swimming.*
Address: c/o David Daly Associates, 586a Kings Road, London SW6 2DX.

SMALL, Sharon

Sharon Small. Actor (F).
TV: Nicola in *An Independent Man;* Annie in *Hamish MacBeth;* Linda in *No Child of Mine;* Bernadette in *Roughnecks;* Carol in *Sunburn;* Michelle Gibson in *Taggart;* Jayne Smith in *The Bill.*
Films: Alison in *Bite;* Lead in *Bumping The Odds;* Caroline in *Driven.*
Address: c/o Marina Martin Associates, 12–13 Poland Street, London W1V 3DE.

SMILLIE, Carol

Carol Smillie. Presenter.
b. Glasgow, Scotland, 23 December 1961.
TV: *BBC Hogmanay; Changing Rooms; Hearts of Gold; Holiday; Holiday Memories; Holiday Swaps; National Lottery; Smillie's People; Summer Holiday; Wheel of Fortune.*
Address: c/o David Anthony Promotions, PO Box 286, Warrington, Cheshire WA2 6GA. m. Alex Knight; 2 d. Christie, Jodie; 1 s. Robbie. Hobbies: Sculpting, DIY, driving.

SMITH, Claire

Claire Smith. Presenter.
TV: *A Close Guide To...; Kilroy; Knight Riders; Sky Travel Show; Steve Wright's People Show; The Time, the Place; This Morning.*
Address: c/o David Anthony Promotions, PO Box 286 Warrington, Cheshire WA2 6GA. Father Bill Smith.

SMITH, Elaine

Elaine Smith. Actor (F)/Panelist.
TV: *City Lights; Elaine TA Hogmanay; Hubbub; Jo Brand Show; Laugh, I Nearly Paid My Licence Fee; Naked*

Video; Only the Lady; Rab C Nesbitt; Scottish Question Time; Split Second; The Last Witch.
Films: *Every Picture Tells a Story; Women Talking Dirty.*
Address: c/o ICM, Oxford House, 76 Oxford Street, London W1N 0AX.

SMITH, Ian

Ian Smith. Actor (M)
TV: *Prisoner Cell Clock H;* Harold Bishop in *Neighbours.*
Address: c/o Pearson Television, 1 Stephen Street, London W1P 1JP.

SMITH, Kirk

Kirk Smith. Actor (M). b. Liverpool.
TV: Keith Roowey in *Brookside;* Tony Jackson in *Children's Ward;* Pete Collins in *Emmerdale.*
Address: c/o Yorkshire Television, The Television Centre, Kirkstall Road, Leeds, Yorkshire W12 8TX.
Hobbies: Weight training, cinema, running.

SMITH, Liz

Liz Smith. Actor (F).
TV: *All in Good Faith; Bad Voodoo; Bootsie & Snudge; Bottom; Bust; Casualty; Christmas is Coming; City Central; Cluedo; Crown Court; Doggin' Around; Donovan Quick; Dunrulin'; El CID; Emmerdale Farm; For One Night Only – Margaret Rutherford; Good Parenting Guide; Haunted; I Didn't Know You Cared; Imaginary Friends; In Loving Memory; Jake's Progress; Karaoke; King and Castle; La Nona; Little Dorrit; Making Out; Making Waves; Mr Right; Murder Rap; Nicholas Nickleby; No, Honestly; Now and Then; Oliver Twist; Partners in Crime; Pirates; Road; Rory Bremner... Who Else?; Russ Abbott's Madhouse; Russian Night 1941; Ruth Rendell Mysteries; Separate Tables; Singles; Spend, Spend, Spend; The All Electric Amusement Arcade; The Bill; The Dick Emery Show; The Fortune Hunters; The Hunchback of Notre Dame; The Life and Loves of a She-Devil; The Mask; The Prodigal Mother; The Queen's Nose;* Nanna in *The Royle Family; The Sweeney; The Vicar of Dibley; Tinniswoods North Country; 2point4 Children; Underbelly; Valentine's Park; Welcome to the Times; Wise Children; Words of Love; Young Charlie; Young Indiana Jones Chronicles.*
Films: *A Private Function; Agatha; Alice in Wonderland; All Things Bright and Beautiful; Apartment Zero; Bert Rigby, You're a Fool; Dakota Road; Dardanelles; Dracula; Revenger's Comedies; Sir Henry at Rawlinson End; The Cook, The Thief, His Wife and Her Lover; The Duellists; The French Lieutenant's Woman; The Monster Club; The Pink Panther; We Think the World of You;*

Whoops Apocalypse; High Spirits; Keep the Aspidistra Flying; Princess.
Address: c/o Conway Van Gelder, 18–21 Jermyn Street, London SW1Y 6HP.

SMITH, Mel

Mel Smith. Actor (M)/Writer/Director/Producer.
b. London 3 December 1952.
TV: *Alas Smith and Jones;* Colin in *Colin's Sandwich;* Father Xmas in *Father Xmas;* Jumbo Whiffy in *Filthy Rich and Catflap;* Milner in *Milner;* Cyril Ash in *Minder;* Tom Craig in *Muck and Brass; Not the Nine O'clock News;* Giles, Derek, Sam and Rev. Bottomley in *Small Doses; Smith and Jones; The World According to Smith and Jones.*
Films: Alan in *Babylon; Bean – The Ultimate Disaster Movie; Bloody Kids;* Crouch in *Bullshot;* Rocco in *Lame Ducks;* Bernard in *Morons from Outer Space;* Gus Halsey in *National Lampoon's Vacation II;* Billy Evans in *Number One;* Albino Torturer in *Princess Bride; Radioland Murders;* Pyle in *Restless Natives;* Jack Abbatt in *Slayground; The Tall Guy;* Sir Toby Belch in *Twelfth Night;* Inspector Flint in *Wilt;* Grimshaw in *Wolves of Willoughby Chase.*
Records: *Bitter and Twisted; Rockin' Around the Christmas Tree; Scratch 'n' Sniff.*
Address: c/o TalkBack Management, 36 Percy Street, London W1P OLN.

SMITH, Mike

Mike Smith. Presenter.
b. Hornchurch, Essex, 23 April 1955.
TV: *Body Heat; Channel Tunnel Opening; Dream Wheels; First: AIDS; Hearts of Gold; Hospital Watch; Late Late Breakfast Show; Live Aid; Royal Tournament; That's Showbusiness.*
Address: c/o Arlington Enterprises Ltd, 1–3 Charlotte Street, London W1P 1HD. m. Sarah Greene.

SMITH, Penny

Penny Smith. Anchor/Presenter. b. 1961.
TV: *6 o'clock News; Crime File; Crime Monthly; Crime Net; Crime Weekly; GMTV News; Going for a Song; Most Wanted; Sky News; Sky News Sunrise; Super Chefs; The Reuter's News Hour.*
Address: c/o The Roseman Organisation, Suite 9, The Power House, 70 Chiswick Road, London W4 1SY. Hobbies: Opera, tennis, yoga, eating, drinking red wine, shoes.

SMURFIT, Victoria

Victoria Smurfit. Actor (F). b. Dublin, Ireland, 1973.
TV: Orla O'Connell in *Ballykissangel;* Hannah in

Berkley Square; Rowena in *Ivanhoe.*
Films: Weather girl in *The Beach;* Annabel in *The Leading Man;* Annagh Lee in *The Run of the Country;* Clodagh in *The Wedding Tackle.*
Address: c/o ICM, Oxford House, 76 Oxford Street , London W1N 0AX. Hobbies: Horse riding, skiing, ice skating.

SNAPE; Ruby

Ruby Snape. Actor (F). b. Llangollen, North Wales.
TV: Denise in *Daylight Robbery,* Miss Thing in *The Grimleys, Dirty Work,* Tracey in *Grafters, Kiss Me Kate, Married for Life, Grange Hill, It Might Be You, Agony Again, Wild Justice, Going Their Way.*
Films: Melissa in *Parting Shots.*
Address: c/o PBR Management, 1st Floor, 26 Foubert's Place, London W1V 1HG.

SNOW, Jon

Jon Snow. News Presenter/Reporter/Foreign Correspondent. b. 28 September 1958.
TV: *Channel 4 News; Election Night; ITN* News Programmes; Live coverage of historic news events including the release of Nelson Mandela; Monica Lewinsky interview for *Channel 4 News;* Three-hour news marathon for *Channel 4 News* on President Clinton; *Weekly Planet.*
Address: c/o ITN, 200 Grays Inn Road, London WC1X 8XZ. Cousin Peter Snow.

SNOW, Peter

Peter Snow. Newscaster/Reporter/Presenter.
b. 20 April 1938.
TV: *Election Night; ITN* news programmes; *Newsnight; Nine O'clock News; Tomorrow's World; Tomorrow's World Plus.*
Address: c/o BBC. m. Ann MacMillan; 3 d. Rebecca, Kate, Shauna; 3 s. Daniel, Shane, Matthieus; cousin Jon Snow.

SNOWDEN, Jane

Jane Snowden. Actor (F).
TV: Sister Beth in *A Touch of Frost;* Sarah in *A Very Peculiar Practice;* Deborah in *All Passion Spent;* Mary in *Gaudy Night;* Maureen Dysin in *Inspector Morse;* Vanity in *Pirates;* Jennie in *The Frog Prince;* Emily in *Wish Me Luck.*
Address: c/o Amanda Howard Associates Ltd, 21 Berwick Street, London W1V 3RG.

SOMERVILLE, Geraldine

Geraldine Somerville. Actor (F). .
TV: Miss Julie in *After Miss Julie;* Ruth in *Casualty;*

Penhaligon in *Cracker*; Val in *Daylight Robbery*; Deborah in *Heaven on Earth*; Pauline Weatherby in *Poirot*; Juliet in *Romeo and Juliet*; Emily in *The Aristocrats*; Biddy in *The Black Velvet Gown*; Ann Welch in *The Deep Blue Sea*.

Films: Augustine in *Augustine*; Elizabeth in *Bathing Elizabeth*; Kate in *Haunted*; Olivia in *Jilting Joe*; Ruth in *True Blue*.

Address: c/o William Morris Agency (UK) Ltd, 1 Stratton Street, London W1X 6HB.

SOMERVILLE, Julia
Julia Somerville. Presenter/Newsreader.
b. 14 July 1947.
TV: *1987 Royal Review of the Year*; *3D*; *ITV Lunchtime News*; *News at One*; *Nine O'clock News*; *Royal Review* (1987).
Address: c/o ITN, 200 Grays Inn Road, London WC1X 8XZ.

SORBO, Kevin
Kevin Sorbo. Actor (M)/Co-writer/Director/Guest
b. Mound, Minnesota, USA, 24 September 1958.
TV: *Aspen*; *Critical Condition*; *Cybill*; Hercules in *Hercules and the Amazon Women* (1994); *Hercules and the Circle of Fire* (1994); *Hercules in the Maze of the Minotaur* (1994); *Hercules in the Underworld* (1994); *Hercules: The Legendary Adevtures*; *Hercules and the Lost Kingdom* (1994); *Murder, She Wrote*; *The Commish*; Hercules in *Xena: Warrior Princess*.
Films: *Hercules and Xena – The Animated Movie*; Hercules in *The Battle for Mount Olympus* (1998); Kull in *Kull the Conqueror* (1997); John Willison in *Slaughter of the Innocents* (1994).
Address: c/o ICM, Oxford House, 76 Oxford Street, London W1N 0AX. m. Sam Jenkins. Hobbies: Basketball, golf, baseball, American football, jogging, swimming.

SPALL, Timothy
Timothy Spall. Actor (M).
b. London 27 February 1957.
TV: Pilot in *A Class Act*; Sgt. Baxter in *A Cotswold Death*; Phil in *A Nice Day at the Office*; himself in *African Footsteps*; Clevor Trevor in *Arena- Movie Nights*; Barry in *Auf Wiedersehen, Pet*; Paul in *Body Contact*; Webster in *Boon*; Francis Meakes in *Broke*; *Dead Poets' Society*; Lyndon in *Dutch Girls*; Frank Stubbs in *Frank Stubbs Promotes*; Paul in *Great Writers – Dostoyevsky*; Hawkins in *Guest of a Nation*; Hawkins in *Home Sweet Home*; Chico in *La Nona*; pathologist in *Murder Most Horrid*; Gordon in *Neville's Island*; Mr Venus in *Our Mutual Friend*; Kevin in *Outside Edge*;

Jimmy Beales in *Roots*; Oswald Bates in *Shooting the Past*; Donald Caudell in *Stolen*; Shorty in *The Brylcream Boys*; Pig Robinson in *The Tale of Little Pig Robinson*; Yepikhodov in *The Three Sisters*; Wainwright in *Vanishing Army*.
Films: Rambrode in *1871*; Peck in *Dream Demon*; Polidari in *Gothic*; Rosencrantz in *Hamlet*; Aubrey in *Life is Sweet*; Don Armado in *Love's Labour Lost*; Harry in *Quadrophenia*; Douglas in *Remembrance*; Rev. Miln in *Robinson Crusoe*; Morris in *Secrets & Lies*; Jim in *SOS Titanic*; Beano in *Still Crazy*; Paulus in *The Bride*; Sterling in *The Clandestine Marriage*; Nick Watt in *The Nihilist's Double Vision*; Eric Lyle in *The Sheltering Sky*; *The White Hunter*; Hodkins in *Black Heart*; Healey in *The Wisdom of Crocodiles*; Igor in *To Kill a Priest*; Cunningham in *Young Indy*.
Address: c/o Markham & Froggatt Ltd, 4 Windmill Street, London W1P 1HF.

SPEED, Lucy
Lucy Speed. Actor (F).
TV: Sandy in *An Unsuitable Job for a Woman*; Martha in *Children of the New Forest*; Rose Penfold in *Dodgem*; Natalie in *EastEnders*; Nell Gwynn in *My*; Susan in *King and Castle*; Beki in *Rides 1 and 2*; Vicky Thurleigh in *Saracen*; Nan in *The Prince and the Pauper*; Lorraine in *Unsolved Mysteries*.
Films: *Impromptu*; *Keep the Aspidistra Flying*; *Metroland*; *Shakespeare in Love*.
Address: c/o Annette Stone Associates, 2nd Floor, 22 Great Marlborough Street, London W1V 1AF.

SPEER, Hugo
Hugo Speer. Actor (M).
TV: Davey in *An Englishman in New York*; *Men Behaving Badly*; Dr Aidan Petit in *McCallum*; *Sharman*; *The Bill*; Nick Sexton in *Thieftakers*; Chris Rawlings in *Heartbeat*; *Woof*; and Terry in *So Haunt Me*.
Film: Martin in *Swing*; Guy in *The Full Monty*; Andy in *The Bhaji on the Beach*; *Mainline Run*.
Address: c/o Rebecca Blond Associates, 69a King's Road, London SW3 4NX.

SPENCER, Jansen
Jansen Spencer. Actor (M). b. 5 May 1981.
Films: *Lucky Break*; Paul McClain in *Neighbours*; *Skippy*; *The Flying Doctors*.
Address: c/o Pearson Television, 1 Stephen Street, London W1P 1PJ.

SPENCER, Jesse
Jesse Spencer. Actor (M). b. 12 February 1979.
TV: Billy Kennedy in *Neighbours*; *Time Trax*.

Films: *Doodles.*
Address: c/o Pearson Television, 1 Stephen Street, London W1P 1PJ. Hobbies: Violin, guitar.

SPENDLOVE, Rob

Rob Spendlove. Actor (M).
TV: *A Taste for Death; All Change; Back Up; Broker's Man; Casualty; Children of the New Forest; Class Act; Closing Ranks; Dangerfield; EastEnders; EL C.I.D.; Fools Gold; Golden Years; Hard Cases; Lovejoy; Natural Lies; Noah's Ark; Rachel's Dream; Soldier, Soldier; Taggart; Tecx; That's Love; The Choir; Where There's Smoke.*
Films: *Backbeat; In the Name of the Father; Queenie; Tai Pan; Winds of War.*
Address: c/o Scott Marshall, 44 Perryn Road, London W3 7NA.

SPIRO, Alyson

Alyson Spiro. Actor (F).
TV: Alison Gregory in *Brookside;* WPC Bryant in *Casualty;* Sarah Sugden in *Emmerdale;* Kath Borrow in *Fell Tiger;* Naomi in *Flat Bust; If You See God,* Mary Ramis in *Tell Him;* Mary Divine in *Kings Royal;* Jane in *Northern Crescent;* Margaret Speel in *Prime Suspect III;* Cheryl Stacey in *Sam Saturday;* Anita in *She'll Be Wearing Pink Pyjamas;* Joann in *The Amnesty Files;* Mrs Hill in *The Bill;* Julie Hart in *The Bill;* Astrid *The Birth of the Beatles;* Liz in *The Enigma Files.*
Address: c/o Cassie Mayer Ltd, 34 Kingley Court, London W1R 5LE.

SPRIGGS, Elizabeth

Elizabeth Spriggs. Actor (F). b. Birmingham.
TV: Connie Fox in *Fox;* Mother Radcliffe in *Frost In May;* Madame Laginsky in *Impromptu;* Calpurnia in *Julius Caesar;* Sairey Gamp in *Martin Chuzzlewit;* Mae in *Oranges are Not the Only Fruit;* Dilecta in *Prometheus;* Nan in *Shine on Harvey Moon;* Witch in *Simon and the Witch;* Lady Muriel Royce in *Strangers and Brothers;* Grandmother in *Taking Over the Asylum;* Mrs Radcliffe in *The Kindness of Mrs Radcliffe;* Mistress Quickley in *The Merry Wives of Windsor;* Hannah in *Victorian Scandals;* Wife in *We the Accused;* Maud Lowther in *Wings of a Dove.*
Films: *Sahkahrov;* Mrs Jennings in *Sense & Sensibility; The Cold Room; The Hour of the Pig; Unsuitable Job for a Woman; Yellow Pages.*
Address: c/o ICM, Oxford House, 76 Oxford Street, London W1N 0AX.

SPRINGER, Jerry

Jerry Springer. Actor/Producer/Host.
b. London, 13 January 1944.

TV: Himself in: *Jerry Springer on Sunday* (1999*); Jerry Springer UK* (1999); *Love Boat: The Next Wave* (1998); *Mad TV* (1999); Himself in *Sabrina the Teenage Witch* (1999); Photographer in *Since You've Been Gone* (1998); Jerry Feller in *Sunset Beach* (1999); Himself in *Talk Soup* (1997); *The Jerry Springer Show* (1991).
Films: Himself in: *Austin Powers: The Spy Who Shagged Me* (1999*); Kissing A Fool* (1998); *Meet Wally Sparks* (1997); Jerry Farrelly in *Ringmaster* (1998*).
Address: c/o William Morris Agency, 151 El Camino Drive, Beverly Hills, California 90212, USA.

SQUIRES, Graeme

Graeme Squires. Actor (M).
b. Sydney, Australia, 13 May 1980.
TV: Tom Nash in *Home & Away.*
Address: c/o Seven Network Ltd, Mabbs Lane, Epping, New South Wales 2121, Australia. Hobbies: Snorkelling, surfing, fishing, gourmet food, action movies.

ST CLEMENT, Pam

Pam St Clement. Actor (F).
TV: Mrs Bainbridge in *Angels;* Joan Foster in *Bottle Boys;* Mrs Badlock in *Can We Get On Now Please?;* Pat in *EastEnders;* Mrs Beckersley in *Emmerdale;* Fat Molly in *Enemy at the Door;* Ann Scott in *Indelible Evidence;* Linda Silvers in *Labour of Love;* Mrs Baker in *Minder;* Connie in *Not for the Likes of Us;* Mary Chater in *Root of All Evil/Lady Killers;* Carmel in *Shall I See You Now;* Gladys Robinson in *Shoestring;* Lady Constance Lytton in *Shoulder to Shoulder;* Aunt Daisy in *Tap Dancer/The Chinese Detective;* Crockett in *The Clergyman's Daughter;* Noreen Mullin in *Together;* Frau Heinz in *Tripods;* Elsie Foster in *We'll Meet Again;* Marlene Ward in *Within these Walls.*
Films: Mother Superior in *Biggles;* Berthe in *Hedda; Scrubbers;* Barmaid in *SS; The Nation's Health.*
Address: c/o Saraband Associates, 265 Liverpool Road, London N1 1LX.

ST JOHN, Ian

Ian St John. Commentator/Presenter. b. 7 June 1938.
TV: *European Championships; On the Ball* (1979); *Saint & Greavsie* (1984); *World Cup.*
Address: c/o Marquee Group (UK) Ltd, 21 The Green, Richmond, Surrey TW9 1PX.

STABB, Dinah

Dinah Stabb. Actor (F).
TV: Mrs Waring in *A Respectable Trade;* Gwen Meredith in *Artemis* (1981); Carole in *As Man and Wife;*

Wakenham QC in *EastEnders*; Julie in *Emergency Channel*; Ella Parsons in *Hetty Wainthropp*; Barbara in *In the Name of Love*; DI Dunne in *Lovejoy*; Angela in *Marked Personal*; Helen Lomax in *Medics*; Jane Marsh in *Moon and Son*; Mrs Fangunwa in *Prime Suspect II*; Princess Caroline in *Prince Regent*; Muriel Reith in *Reith*; Millie in *South of the Border*; Julia in *The Ambassador*; Helen Collins in *The Broker's Man*; Virginia Chapel in *The Chief*; Cousin Hilda in *The Life and Times of Henry Pratt*; Miss Agafya in *The Marriage*; Margaret Bainbridge in *The Piglet Files*; Nancy Powell in *Village Hall*; Celia Jordan in *Wycliffe*.

Films: *Almost Time for Tea*; Mrs Frobisher in *The Browning Version*; Louise in *The Riddle of the Sphinx*; Louisa in *The Trespasser*; Rose in *The Whistle Blower*.

Address: c/o Sally Hope Associates, 108 Leonard Street, London EC2A 4XS.

STABLEFORD, Howard

Howard Stableford. Actor (M)/Presenter.
b. Preston, Lancashire.

TV: *Animal Zone*; *Beat the Teacher*; *Jigsaw*; *Newsround*; *Open Saturday for the Open University*; *Puzzle Trail*; *The Leisure Hour*; *Tomorrow's World*.

Address: c/o Dave Winslett Associates, 6 Kenwood Ridge, Kenley, Surrey CR8 5JW. Hobbies: Scuba diving, long-distance running.

STACY, Neil

Neil Stacy. Actor (M).
b. Stowupland, Suffolk, 15 May 1941.

TV: Fenton in *Barlow at Large*; Robert in *Duty Free*; Mr Walpole in *Get Well Soon*; Sir Robert in *House of Windsor*; Captain Scott in *Shackleton*; Herbert in *Strangers and Brothers*; Colonel Squires in *The Fourth Arm*; Lawrence Fitzgibbon in *The Pallisers*; Dawson in *The Standard*; Giles in *Three Up, Two Down*; Carter in *To Serve Them All My Days*; Boris Drubetzkoy in *War & Peace*.

Address: c/o Shepherd & Ford, 13 Radnor Walk, London SW3 4BP.

STAFF, Kathy

Minnie Higginbottom. Actor (F).
b. Dukinfield, Cheshire, 12 July 1928.

TV: Flower Lady in *Camille*; *Castle Haven*; Doris Luke in *Crossroads*; Winnie Purvis in *Emmerdale*; *Hadleigh*; Nora Batty in *Last of the Summer Wine*; Mrs Blewett in *Open All Hours*; Mabel in *Separate Tables*; *The Benny Hill Show*; *Within these Walls*.

Films: Mrs Oliphant in *A Kind of Loving*; Bombazine woman in *The Dresser*.

Address: c/o London Management, Noel House, 2–4 Noel Street, London W1V 3RB. m. John; 2 d. Susan, Katherine. Hobbies: Church work.

STANDING, John

John Standing. Actor (M). b. 16 August 1934.

TV: *A Dance to the Music of Time*; *Gulliver's Travels*; *Harvest Moon*; *Joan of Arc*; *LA Law*; *Murder, She Wrote*; *Pygmalion*; *Riders*; *The Battle of Waterloo*; *The Choir*; *The Woman in White*; *Visitors*; *Ways and Means*.

Films: *Eight and a Half Women*; *King Rat*; *Mad Cows*; *Mrs Dalloway*; *The Eagle Has Landed*; *The Elephant Man*; *The Psychopath*; *Walk Don't Run*; *Zee and Co*.

Address: c/o ICM, Oxford House, 76 Oxford Street, London W1N 0AX. Grandfather is theatre actor Sir Guy Standing; mother is film actress Kay Hammond.

STANDING, Richard

Richard Standing. Actor (M).

TV: Danny in *Coronation Street*; *Dalziel and Pascoe*; Chris in *Families*; DC Wear in *Harry*; various in *Jo Brand Show*; Michael Lowther in *Picking Up the Pieces*; Dean Barry in *The Bill*; Steve Greer in *The Bill*; Jerry in *The Change*; Fred Willet in *The Grand*.

Films: Les in *A Martial Kind of Man*; Charlie in *Neighbours*.

Address: c/o Evans & Reiss, 100 Fawe Park Road, London SW15 2EA.

STAPLETON, Jacinta

Jacinta Stapleton. Actor (F). b. 6 June 1979.

TV: *Becca*; *Blue Heelers*; *Colin Carpenter*; *Flying Doctors*; *Full Frontal*; *Genie from Down Under*; *Merle*; Amy Greenwood in *Neighbours*; *Ocean Girl*; *Rose Against the Odds*.

Films: *Boulevard of Broken Dreams*; *What the Moon Saw*.

Address: c/o Pearson Television, 1 Stephen Street, London W1P 1PJ.

STAPLETON, John

John Stapleton. Presenter. b. 24 February 1946.

TV: *30 Minutes*; *Central Weekend Live*; *My Favourite Hymns*; *Nationwide*; *News Hour*; *Newsnight*; *Panorama*; *The Time, The Place*; *Watchdog*.

Address: c/o Arlington Enterprise Ltd, 1–3 Charlotte Street, London W1P 1HD. Hobbies: Supporter of Manchester City.

STARKE, Michael

Michael Starke. Actor (M).
b. Liverpool, 13 November 1957.

TV: Sinbad in *Brookside*; *Making Out*.

Films: Dave in *Distant Voices, Still Lives*; *No Surrender*.

Address: c/o Dennis Lyne Agency, 108 Leonard Street, London EC2A 4RH. m. Lyn; 2 d.

STARR, Freddie

Freddie Starr. Comedian/Host/Actor (M).
b. Liverpool, 10 January 1944.
TV: *40 Years of Freddie Starr* (1999); *An Audience with Freddie Starr; Beat the Crusher; Freddie Starr the Game Show Host; The Freddie Starr Show* (1998); Lance Izzard in *Lynda La Plante's Supply and Demand*.
Films: Teddy in *Squeeze*; Short Unser-Eaker in *Mr Itislake*.
Address: c/o Hazemead Ltd, 3rd floor, 18 Hanover Street, London W1R 9HG. Hobbies: Breeding thoroughbred racehorses.

STAUNTON, Imelda

Imelda Staunton. Actor (F)/Panellist/Presenter.
TV: Various in *A Bit of Fry and Laurie*; Bridget Bennet in *A Masculine Ending*; Stephanie Saunders in *An Englishman's Wife*; Mrs Micawber in *David Copperfield*; *Don't Leave Me This Way; Easy Money*; Muriel n *If You See God Tell Him; Is It Legal?; Jackanory – Delilah and the Dishwasher*; Edith in *Ladies in Charge; Midsomer Murders*; Deirdre in *Revenge; Tales from the Crypt*; Nurse White in *The Singing Detective*; Dwarfish in *They Never Slept*; Issy in *Up the Garden Path*; Cheryl in *Yellowbacks*.
Films: Ethel Graydon in *Another Life*; Mrs Burakova in *Citizen X*; Beth in *Deadly Advice*; Margaret in *Much Ado About Nothing*; Mary in *Peter's Friends*; Conchita in *Rat*; Charlotte Palmer in *Sense & Sensibility*; the nurse in *Shakespeare in Love; Twelfth Night*.
Address: c/o PFD, Drury House, 34–43 Russell Street, London WC2B 5HA. m. Jim Carter.

STEADMAN, Alison

Alison Steadman. Actor (F)/Voice Artist.
b. Liverpool, 26 August 1946.
TV: *A Small Morning; Abigail's Party*; Marge in *Crapston Villas; Esther Waters; Girl; Gone to Seed; Gone to the Dogs; Hard Labour; He's Gone; Let Them Eat Cake; News Hounds; No Bananas; Nuts in May; Our Flesh and Blood; Passmore; Pride and Prejudice; Selling Hitler*; Mrs Perfect in *Stressed Eric; The Missing Postman; The Singing Detective; The Wimbledon Poisoner; Through the Night; Virtuoso*.
Films: *A Private Function; Adventures of Baron Munchausen; Blame it on the Bellboy; Champions; Clockwise; Life is Sweet; Number One; P'Tang Yang Kipperbang; Shirley Valentine; Stormy Monday*.
Address: c/o Peters, Fraser and Dunlop, Drury House, 34–43 Russell Street , London WC2B 5HA. m. Director Mike Leigh (dis.); 2 s. Toby, Leo.

STEED, Maggie

Maggie Steed. Actor (F).
TV: Flavia in *All Change*; Tess Baker in *Blood Rights; Brideshead Revisited; Clapperclaw*; Mrs Raffald in *Clothes in the Wardrobe*; Margaret Thatcher in *Dispatches – The Scott Enquiry*; Mother in *French and Saunders Christmas Special; Gravy Train; Growing Rich*; Maggie McTeer in *Hard Cases*; Angela Storrs in *Inspector Morse; Let Them Eat Cake; Lipstick on Your Collar; Little Richard Wrecked My Marriage; Lovejoy*; Mrs Todgers in *Martin Chuzzlewit*; Ellen in *Olly's Prison*; Margaret Crabbe in *Pie in the Sky; Red Dwarf; Ruth Rendel Mysteries – Speaker of Mandarin*; Rita Moon in *Shine on Harvey Moon*; Myra Beamish in *The History Man*.
Films: Mrs Costello in *Kings in Grass*; Muttchen in *Simon Magus*.
Address: c/o Jonathan Altaras Associates, 13 Short sGardens, London WC2H 9AT.

STEED, Tim

Tim Steed. Actor (M).
TV: *Blonde Bombshell; Happy Birthday Shakespeare; Poirot*.
Address: c/o Jonathan Altaras Associates, 13 Shorts Gardens, London WC2H 9AT. Hobbies: Judo, contemporary movement and clowning.

STEEN, Steve

Steve Steen. Actor (M)/Panellist/Voice Artist.
TV: *Blackadder III; Clive Anderson; Crapston Villas*; Bob in *Days Like These; Family Affairs; Have I Got News For You; Jackanory*; various in *Jo Brand Through the Cakehole; Kenny Everett Show*; various in *Lenny Henry Show*; various in *Paul Merton Show; Press Gang; Red Dwarf*; various in *Rory Bremner... Who Else?*; Tommy Price in *The Bill; Truly, Madly, Weekly; Whose Line is it Anyway?*
Address: c/o Richard Stone Partnership, 2 Henrietta Street, London WC2E 8PS.

STELFOX, Shirley

Shirley Stelfox. Actor (F). b. 11 April 1941.
TV: *'Get Calf' Six Sides of Coogan; A Pin to See the Peepshow; Bergerac; Bloomin' Marvellous; Brookside; Casualty; Common As Muck; Coronation Street; Crown Court; Family Affairs; General Hospital; Harry's Mad III; Heartbeat; Hope and Glory; Keeping up Appearances; Making Out; Pat and Margaret; The Bill; The Broker's Man; Z-Cars*.
Films: Shirley in *Personal Services* (1984).
Address: c/o Associated International Management, 5 Denmark Street, London WC2H 8LP.

STEPHENSON, Debra

Debra Stephenson. Actor (F)/Presenter/Voice artist.
TV: Michelle Dockley in *Bad Girls* (1999); Corrie in *Cone Zone* (1996); various in *Hale and Pace* (1996); Kitty Carmichael in *Midsomer Murders* (1997); *No Sweat* (1998); Zoe in *People Like Us* (1999); Diane Powell in *Playing the Field* (1997); Michelle in *Reckless* (1996); *Opportunity Knocks*; team member in *The Friday Zone* (1997).
Address: c/o The Richard Stone Partnership, 2 Henrietta Street, London WC2E 8PS.

STEPHENSON, Denise

Denise Stephenson. Actor (F).
TV: *Bad Blood; Berlin Brea; Gaugin' the Savage; Nobody's Perfect; Out of the Blue; Peak Practice; Pie in the Sky; Piglet Files; Saracens; Second Thoughts; The Bill; Thief Takers; This Life; Ticket to Ride; Touch and Go;* Mrs Henderson in *Waterfront Beat; Winners and Losers.*
Films: *An American Werewolf in London; An Ideal Husband; Made in Heaven; SpiceWorld; What Rats Won't Do.*
Address: c/o Emptage Hallett, 24 Poland Street, London W1V 3DD.

STEPHENSON, Nicola

Nicola Stephenson. Actor (F). b. 5 July 1971.
TV: Jennifer in *Big Bad World;* Margaret Clemence in *Brookside;* Karen in *Can't Buy Me Love;* Sister Julie Fitzjohn in *Casualty/Holby City;* Amanda in *Children's Ward;* Priscilla Millbanks in *Coronation Street;* Sam in *Go Back Out;* Reynolds in *Kiss and Tell;* Susie in *Medics;* Carol in *Mirage Land;* Gail in *My Wonderful Life;* Lizzie in *Day at the Office;* Jessica in *Ocean View;* Lucy Shore in *Out of the Blue.*
Films: *The Final Frame;* Karen in *The Last Yellow;* Ethel in *The Rainbow.*
Address: c/o Lou Coulson, 37 Berwick Street, London W1V 3RF.

STEVENS, Ronnie

Ronnie Stevens. Actor (M). b. 2 September 1930.
TV: *About Face; As Time Goes By; Casualty; Chance in a Million; Cover Her Face; Ever Decreasing Circles; For the Greater Good; Goodnight Sweetheart; Harvey Moon; Hetty Wainthropp Investigates; Hi De Hi; May to December; Minder; Only When I Laugh; Roll Over Beethoven; Rumpole of the Bailey; Tales of the Unexpected; Terry and June; That's Love; The Bill; Twelfth Night; Yes Minister.*
Films: *Blame it on the Bellboy; Brassed Off; Carry On Cruising; Killing Dad; Morons from Outer Space; SOS Titanic; The Parent Trap.*

Address: c/o CDA, 19 Sydney Mews, London SW3 6HL.

STEVENSON, Jessica

Jessica Stevenson. Actor (F)//Writer/. b. Brighton.
TV: Maggie in *Tears Before Bedtime;* Judith Lessiter in *Midsomer Murders; After the Hotty; Armstrong and Miller; Asylum;* Various in *Barking;* Jackie South in *Crown Prosecutor;* various in *Harry Enfield Xmas Special;* Charlotte Parker in *House of Elliott;* Cheryl in *The Royle Family; Spaced;* Alice Timpson in *Staying Alive.*
Films: Helga in *Swing Kids;* First Midwife in *The Baby of Macon.*
Address: c/o Jonathan Altaras Associates, 13 Shorts Gardens, London WC2H 9AT.

STEVENSON, Juliet

Juliet Stevenson. Actor (F)/Presenter/Writer.
b. Essex, 30 October 1956.
TV: Lucy Sadler in *Amy;* Antigone in *Antigone;* Fliss in *Bazaar and Rummage;* Annie Lee in *Cider with Rosie;* Elizabeth von Reitburg in *Freud; Great Journeys;* Isabella Eberhart; Margaret in *In The Border Country;* Rosalin in *Life Story;* Vicky in *Living With Dinosaurs;* Joanne Langton in *Maybury;* Antigone in *Oedipus at Colonus;* Rape Victim in *Omnibus – Rape;* Ruth in *Out of Love;* Hilda Spencer in *Stanley;* Jean in *Stone, Scissors, Paper;* Nora in *The Doll's House;* Barbara Mallens in *The Mallens;* Claire in *The March;* Flora in *The Politician's Wife;* Helen West in *Trial by Fire;* Nina in *Truly, Madly, Deeply.*
Films: Isobel in *A Secret Rapture;* Cissie in *Drowning by Numbers;* Mrs Elton in *Emma;* Alice in *Ladder of Swords;* Frau Burstner in *The Trial;* Nina in *Truly, Madly, Deeply; Who Dealt?*
Address: c/o Markham & Froggatt Ltd, 4 Windmill Street, London W1P 1HF.

STEVENSON, Ray

Ray Stevenson. Actor (M)/Agony Uncle.
TV: Steve in *Band of Gold;* DI Tony Baynham in *City Central;* Armstrong in *Drover's Gold; Making Love in the 21st Century;* Jow Higson in *Peak Practice; Real Women;* Clim in *Return of the Native;* Steve Taylor in *Some Kind of Life;* Matthew in *The Dwelling Place; The Theory of Flight;* Larry Birch in *The Tide of Life.*
Address: c/o Dalzell and Beresford Ltd, 91 Regent Street, London W1R 7TB. Hobbies: Driving, singing, rugby.

STEWART, Alastair

Alastair Stewart. News anchor/Presenter.
b. 22 June 1952.

TV: *Channel Four News; ITN; ITN specials; London Tonight; Missing; News at One; News at Ten;* Presenter for Pan Am crash over Locherbie and Memorial Service; *Police Camera Action; Sunday Programme; The Parliament Programme.*
Address: c/o Simpson Fox Associates Ltd, 52 Shaftesbury Avenue, London W1V 7DE.

STEWART, French
Stewart French. Actor (M)/Host.
b. Albuquerque, New Mexico, USA, 20 February 1964.
TV: Harry Solomon in *3rd Rock from the Sun* (1996); himself in *Christmas in Washington;* Icarus in *Hercules* (1998); Steven/Mr Mayer/Puppetmaster in *Just Shoot Me* (1998); Guest Host in *Mad TV* (1996); Razor Dee in *New WKRP in Cincinnati* (1992); Office Temp Worker in *Newsradio* (1997); Manager in *Seinfeld* (1994); Tellus Colony Survivor in *Space Above and Beyond* (1995).
Films: IR Crewman in *Broken Arrow* (1996); Interviewer in *Dick* (1999); Dennis in *Glory Daze* (1996); Businessman 2 in *Leaving Las Vegas* (1996); Seth Winnick in *Love Stinks* (1999); Supperstein in *Magic Island* (1995); Happy in *Mchale's Navy* (1997); Lieutenant Fereth in *Stargate* (1994).
Address: c/o JC Robbins, 2114 Glendon Avenue, Los Angeles, California, USA. James Anderson, c/o Carsey Werner, 4024 Radford Avenue, Studio City, California 91604, USA. m. Katharine La Nasa.

STEWART, Jeff
Jeff Stewart. Actor (M).
TV: Zak in *Angels;* Harry Fellows in *Crossroads;* Dukka in *Doctor Who;* Steve in *Give Us a Break;* Tinsnip Eddie in *Help;* Police Constable in *Hi De Hi;* Young Boxer in *Lytton's Diary;* Mick in *Minder;* Jenkins in *Reilly, Ace of Spies;* John in *Roots;* PC Hollis in *The Bill;* Davy Drummond in *The Nightmare Man.*
Address: c/o McIntosh Rae Management, Thornton House, Thornton Road, London SW19 4NG. Hobbies: Long-distance running.

STEWART, William G
William G Stewart. Actor (M)/Presenter.
TV: *15–1; Bless this House; Doctors Down Under; Father Dear Father in Australia; The Many Wives of Patrick.*
Address: c/o Regent Productions, The Mews, 6 Putney Common, London SW15 1HL.

STOCKBRIDGE, Peter
Peter Stockbridge. Actor (M).
b. Brighton, Sussex, 11 January 1920.
TV: Walter in *Animal Ark;* Wilfred White in *Casualty;*

Stan in *EastEnders;* Grandpa Kemp in *London Bridge;* Jack Stalleybrass in *Lovejoy;* Billy in *Pure Wickedness;* Mr Warburton/Brian Macey in *The Bill;* Mr Penrose in *Wycliffe.*
Films: Lord Chamberlain in *Elizabeth;* Mr Wilson in *Foreign Moon;* Lord Jenkins in *Mad Dogs and Englishmen;* Mr Bennett in *Secrets and Lies;* Old Porter in *Tom and Viv.*
Address: c/o Chuck Julian Associates, Suite 51, 26 Charing Cross Road, London WC2H ODH. m. Sheila; 2s. John, Tony. Hobbies: Walking, reading.

STOCKBRIDGE, Sara
Sara Stockbridge. Actor (F)/Writer.
TV: Leslie in *Babes in the Wood;* Rosie Wilcox in *Casualty;* Midge in *Days Like These;* Louise Gray in *EastEnders;* Megan in *Lucy Sullivan is Getting Married;* Babs in *Mickey Love;* Harriet Handmaiden in *Red Dwarf V;* Sharon in *Space Virgins from the Planet Sex;* Carol Tate in *The Bill;* Alana Miller in *The Bill;* various in *The Comic Strip Series;* Janet in *The Crying Game; The Glam Metal Detectives;* Vendercise in *Then; Young Person's Guide to Becoming a Rock Star.*
Films: Simone in *24 Hours in London;* Night Huntress in *Best;* Nurse Andrews in *Bloodrunners;* Nina in *Carry On Columbus;* Witch in *David;* Lisa in *Fierce Creatures;* Estelle in *Interview with a Vampire;* Tara in *Random Acts of Intimacy;* Tiffany in *Split Second;* Felicity in *The Wedding Tackle.*
Address: c/o Elaine Murphy Associates, 310 Aberdeen House, 22–24 Highbury Grove, London N52 EA.

STOCKHAM, Jo-Anne
Jo-Anne Stockham. Actor (F).
TV: Clare in *Alas Smith and Jones;* Voluptua in *Bottom;* doctor in *Cold Feet;* DC Novello in *Dalziel and Pascoe;* Martha in *Frontiers;* Clare in *London Bridge;* Cathy Taylor in *The Bill;* Anne Carter in *Wycliffe.*
Address: c/o Tim Scott Personal Management, 5 Cloisters Business Centre, 8 Battersea Park Road, London SW8 4BG.

STOOKE, Liz
Liz Stooke. Actor (F). b. Kent.
TV: *Day in Summer; Brookside; Coronation Street; Emmerdale; First Among Equals; Heartbeat;* Angela Cunningham in *Hollyoaks; Parallel 9;* Kathy Swift in *The Ward.*
Films: *The Final Frame.*
Address: c/o The Actors Group, 4 Newton Street, Piccadilly, Manchester M1 2AW. Hobbies: Horse riding, swimming.

STOTT, Ken

Ken Stott. Actor (M). b. Edinburgh, 1955.

TV: McCaffrey in *A Mug's Game*; Lawrence in *All Good Things*; Bernie in *Anna Lee*; Joe Hickey in *Bad Company*; Tom Walton in *Dockers*; Curran in *King Lear*; Barney Barnarto in *Rhodes*; Sgt. Bob Clare in *Silent Witness*; Redfern in *Stone, Scissors, Paper*; Taggart in *Dr McNaughten*; Eddie in *Takin' Over the Asylum*; Jeremy Twitcher in *The Beggar's Opera*; *The Singing Detective*; Pat Chappell in *The Vice*; Martin Cahill in *Vicious Circle*; Fraser Boyle in *Your Cheatin' Heart*.

Films: Gaspar Dias in *Being Human*; Ted Thickbroom in *Fever Pitch*; Franz Kafka's *It's A Wonderful Life*; Chance in *Plunkett & MacLeane*; Prevot in *Saint Ex*; Detective McCall in *Shallow Grave*; Ike in *The Boxer*; *The Debt Collector*.

Address: c/o Jonathan Altaras Associates, 13 Shorts Gardens, London WC2H 9AT.

STOURTON, Edward

Edward Stourton. Presenter/Reporter.
b. Lagos, Nigeria, 24 November 1957.

TV: *BBC News* (1988); *Channel Four News* (1982); *Channel Four News* (1986); *Channel Four News* (1984); ITN News Programmes (1990); *One O'clock News*.

Address: c/o BBC News, Union House, 65–69 Shepherds Bush Green, London W12 8TX.

STRACHAN, Michaela

Michaela Strachan. Presenter.

TV: *The Really Wild Show*; *The Hitman and Her*; *The Wide Awake Club*; *Wacaday*; *Shark Rerscue*.

Address: c/o Michael Ladkin Personal Management, Suite One, Ground Floor, 1 Duchess Street, London W1N 3DE.

STRAKER, Mark

Mark Straker. Actor (M). b. London 9 March 1956.

TV: *A Wing and a Prayer*; *Absent Friends*; Nigel Parnaby in *Birds of a Feather*; Dinsdale in *Boot Street Band*; *Casualty*; Hanham/NCO in *Chips with Everything*; *Dangerfield*; Carter in *Doctor Who*; Perez in *Down to Earth*; James Jefferson in *EastEnders*; *For Valour*; *Henry's Leg*; *Kindred Spirits*; Manners in *Lovejoy*; *Melissa*; *Number 73*; *Punt and Dennis*; *Radio Phoenix*; *Randall and Hopkirk (Deceased)*; Michael Moss in *Rocket to the Moon*; *The Bill*; *The Lakes*; *The Wild House*; *They Came from Somewhere Else*; David Fletcher in *Trial by Jury*.

Films: Matthew in *End of the Real*; Petrie in *Exchange of Fire*; Peter in *Sick Call*; *The Idiot*.

Address: c/o Langford Associates, 17 Westfields Avenue, London SW13 0AT.

STREET-PORTER, Janet

Janet Bull. Presenter/Producer.
b. 27 December 1946.

TV: *A to Z of Belief*; *Cathedral Calls* (1999); *As the Crow Flies*; *Design Awards*; *Full Wax*; *Midnight Hour*; *Paintbox* (1998); *Reportage*; *Rough Guide to Careers*; *The London Weekend Show* (1975); *Twentieth Century Box* (1981).

Address: c/o Well Bred Productions Ltd, 189 Bermondsey Street, London SE1 3UW. Hobbies: Walking.

STRINGER, Nick

Nick Stringer. Actor (M).

TV: *About Face*; *Auf Wiedersehen, Pet*; *Bergerac*; *Black and Blue Lamp*; Bill Turner in *Blind Justice*; *Boon*; *Cat's Eyes*; Jumpin' Jack in *Coronation Street*; *Dempsey and Makepeace*; *Devil's Crown*; Max Derwin in *Family Affairs*; Mr Curtain in *Famous Five*; Tommy Kingdom in *Goodnight Sweetheart*; *Home Front*; *Johnny Jarvis*; *Lucky Jim*; *Minder*; *New Statesman*; Jumbo in *Only Fools and Horses*; *Open All Hours*; Pete in *Peak Practice*; *Pickersgill People*; *Press Gang*; *Shadow of the Sun*; *Showstring*; PC Smollett in *The Bill*; *The Affront*; *The Collectors*; Farmer Flint in *The Missing Postman*; *The Professionals*; *The Sweeney*; Doug Mellis in *The Ward*; *This is David Lander*.

Films: Det. Sgt Rice in *Clockwise*; Baker in *Personal Services*; Edward in *Stella Does Tricks*; *Terence Davies Trilogy*; *The Long Good Friday*; *The Shout*.

Address: c/o Kerry Gardner Management, 7 St George's Square, London SW1V 2HX.

STRONG, Gwyneth

Gwyneth Strong. Actor (F).
b. London 2 December 1959.

TV: Charlie in *99–1*; *Bloody Kids*; Denise Longden in *Forgotten*; Teacher in *Living With Dinosaurs*; Lucy Sullivan is Getting Married; Linda in *Nice Town*; Cassandra in *Only Fools and Horse*; Janet in *Real Women*; Jan in *The Flockton Flyer*; WPC Rachel McMahon in *The Missing Postman*.

Films: Blind Mother with Baby in *Afraid of the Dark*; Gwenda in *Crimetime*; Girl at Funeral in *Cry Freedom*; Mary Valley in *Nothing But the Night*; Sharon in *The Story of Ruth*.

Address: c/o PFD, Drury House, 34–43 Russell Street, London WC2B 5HA.

STRONG, Mark

Mark Strong. Actor (M).

TV: Timson in *Not Even God is Wise Enough*; Tosker Cox in *Our Friends in the North*; Inspector Hall in

Prime Suspect III; Producer in *The Buddah of Suburbia*; Michael Mitcham in *Trust*; Oblonski in *Anna Karenina*; Terry in *Births, Marriages and Deaths*; Colonel Forsyth in *Bomber*; Mr Knightley in *Emma*; Chris in *In the Name of Love*.

Films: Kenny English in *Captives*; Detective in *Century*; Frank in *Elephant Juice*; Steve in *Fever Pitch*; Dave in *If Only*; Scheider in *One Against the Wind*; Istvan in *The Tate of Sunshine*.

Address: c/o ICM, Oxford House, 76 Oxford Street, London W1N 0AX.

STRONG, Rider

Rider Strong. Actor (M).

b. San Francisco, California, USA, 11 December 1979.

TV: Shawn Hunter in *Boy Meets World* (1993); *Davis Rules*; *Empty Nest*; *Evening Shade*; *Home Improvement* (1992); *Invasion America* (1998); *Julie* (1992); *Long Road Home*; *Maybe This Time*; *Millie*; *Nurses* (1991); *Party of Five* (1996); *Summertime Switch* (1994); *The Last Hit* (1993); *The Practice* (1999); *Time Trax* (1993).

Films: *Benefit of the Doubt* (1993); Justin Allen in *My Giant* (1998); Lenny Dalton in *The Pact* (1999).

Address: c/o Judt Savage, 6212 Banner Avenue, Los Angeles, California 90038, USA. Traci Harper, 800 S. Robertson Blvd, Suite 2, Los Angeles, California, USA. Hobbies: Soccer, swimming, white-water rafting, snowboarding, roller blading, cycling, land sports, IBM computers, music, writing, reading poetry.

STUBBS, Imogen

Imogen Stubbs. Actor (F).

b. Newcastle, 20 February 1961.

TV: Megan in *After the Dance*; Anna Lee in *Anna Lee*; Suzie in *Mothertime*; Desdemona in *Othello*; Ginny in *Relatively Speaking*; Marie in *Sandra: A Love Story*; Ursula in *The Rainbow*.

Films: Magan in *A Summer Story*; Roniy in *Deadline*; Princess Aud in *Erik the Viking*; Sarah in *Traveller*; Sarah in *Jack and Sarah*; Nanou in *Nanou*; Zena in *Pin for the Butterfly*; Lucy Steele in *Sense and Sensibility*; Diana Stiles in *True Colours*; Viola in *Twelfth Night*.

Address: c/o William Morris Agency, 151 El Camino Drive, Beverly Hills, California 90212, USA. m. Director Trevor Nunn; 1 d. Ellie; 1 s. Jesse.

STUBBS, Ray

Ray Stubbs. Producer/Presenter/Reporter.

TV: *A Question of Sport*; *Football Focus*; *Grandstand*; *Match of the Day*; *On the Line*; *Sportsnight*.

Address: c/o BBC, Union House, 65–69 Shepherds Bush Green, London W12 8TX

STUBBS, Una

Una Stubbs. Actor (F)/Panelist/Presenter.

b. 1 May 1937.

TV: Rita in *Till Death Us Do Part*; Mother in *Christmas Lantern*; Social Worker in *Deltawaves*; Fifi La Touche in *Educating Marmalade*; Alice in *Fawlty Towers*; *Give Us a Clue*; *Happy Families*; *Heartbeat*; *In Sickness and in Health*; *Keeping up Appearances*; Selina Jennings in *Midsomer Murders*; *Morris Minor's Marvellous Motor*; *The Morecambe and Wise Show*; Miss Bat in *The Worst Witch*; Jo Ransley in *Them and Us*; Mrs Breeze in *Tricky Business*; *Woolcraft/Threads/Off the Cuff*; Aunt Sally in *Worzel Gummidge*.

Films: *Summer Holiday*; *Wonderful Life*; *The Bargee*.

Address: c/o Rebecca Blond Associates, 69a Kings Road, London SW3 4NX.

STYLER, Trudie

Trudie Styler. Actor (F)/Producer.

b. Birmingham, 6 January 1957.

TV: *Apocalyptic Butterflies*; *Boys from Brazil*; *Carnival*; *Cockles*; *Funny Man*; *Head Girl*; *Miss Marple*; *Moving the Mountain*; *Nativity Blues*; *Poldark*; *The Bell*; *The Body in the Library*; *The Gentle Touch*; *The Kelly Monteith Show*; *The Mayor of Casterbridge*; *Midsomer Murders*; *The Scold's Bridle*.

Films: *Fair Game*; *Grave Indiscretion*; *In the QT*; *Lock, Stock and Two Smoking Barrels*; *Modigliani*; *The American Bride*; *The Dress*; *The Grotesque*.

Address: c/o William Morris Agency (UK) Ltd, 1 Stratton Street, London W1X 6HB. m. Sting; 4 children.

SUCHET, David

David Suchet. Actor (M). b. London, 2 May 1946.

TV: Reilly in *Reilly, Ace of Spies*; Poirot in *Agatha Christie's Poirot*; *Being Normal*; Shakespeare in *Bingo*; Blott in *Blott on the Landscape*; Judge O'Connor in *Cause Célèbre*; *Jackanory*; *King and Castle*; *Murrow*; *Nobody Here but Us Chickens*; Glougauer in *Once in a Lifetime*; Edward Teller in *Oppenheimer*; Colin in *Oxbridge Blues*; *Playing Shakespeare*; Tom Kempinski in *Separation*; *The Last Day*; *The Last Innocent Man*; Freud in *The Life of Freud*; Adolf Verloc in *The Secret Agent*; *Time to Die*; Timon in *Timon of Athens*; Leopold Bloom in *Ulysses*.

Films: *A Tale of Two Cities*; *A World Apart*; *Gulag*; *Harry and the Hendersons*; *Iron Eagle*; *Little Drummer Girl*; *Master of the Game*; *Mussolini*; *Red Monarch*; Louis B Meyer in *RKO*; Napoleon in *Sabotage*; *Song for Europe*; *The Falcon and the Snowman*; *The Hunchback of Notre Dame*; *The Lucona Affair*; *The Trenchcoat*; *Thirteen at Dinner*; *To Kill a Priest*; *Why the Whales Came*.

Address: c/o ICM Oxford House, 76 Oxford Street, London W1N 0AX. m. Sheila Ferris; 1 s. Robert; 1 d. Katherine; brother John Suchet. Hobbies: Music, photography, ornithology.

SUCHET, John

John Suchet. Presenter/Washington correspondent.
b. 29 March 1944.
TV: *Early Evening News* (1992); ITN news programmes (1981); *ITV Lunchtime News; News at Ten* (1992); *Who? What? Why?* (1998).
Address: c/o ITN, 200 Grays Inn Road, London WC1X 8XZ. Brother David Suchet. Hobbies: Classical music.

SUE PATT, Terry

Terry Sue Patt. Actor (M).
TV: Yusef in *The Firm;* Nurse Luke in *Cardiac Arrest;* Silent Partner in *Black and Blue;* Garfield in *Making News;* Lloyd in *Desmonds; The Ball Trap and Côte Sauvage;* Michael Squire in *The Bill: 'Chasing the Dragon'; Going to Work;* Snapper in *Brick is Beautiful.*
Films: Albert Dyer in *Little Napoleon;* Slitt in *The Dark Horse; The Best Ever Fallout Shelter; Wings of Death; Blind Man's Bluff; Life School.*
Address: c/o Sandra Boyce, 1 Kingsway Parade, Albion Road, London N16 0TA.

SUGDEN, Mollie

Mollie Sugden. Actor (F).
b. Keighley, Yorkshire, 21 July 1922.
TV: Mrs Betty Slocombe in *Are You Being Served?* (1972); Mrs White in *Cluedo* (1991); Mrs Noah in *Come Back Mrs Noah* (1977); Nellie Harvey in *Coronation Street;* Mrs Goddard in *Emma* (1972); Mrs Betty Slocombe in *Grace & Favour* (1992); *Hugh and I* (1962); Mum in *Just Jimmy* (1964); Mrs Hutchinson in *Liver Birds* (1969); Nora Powers in *My Husband and I* (1987); Mrs Robinson in *Oliver's Travels* (1995); Mum in *Son of the Bride* (1973); *Steptoe and Son* (1972); Ida Willis in *That's My Boy* (1981); Minister for Trade and Domestic Affairs in *The Goodies* (1970).
Films: Mrs Betty Slocombe in *Are You Being Served?* (1977); Mary in *BFG* (1989).
Address: c/o Joan Reddin, Hazel Cottage, Wheeler End Common, Wheeler End, High Wycombe, Buckinghamshire HP14 3NL. m. William Moore; 2 s. (twins) Robin, Simon. Hobbies: Gardening, cooking, knitting.

SUGGS, Graeme

Graeme Suggs. Presenter.
b. Hastings, Sussex, 13 January 1961.
TV: *Night Fever* (1996); *Suggs on Saturday* (1986).
Films: Nasty Book Publisher in *Don't Go Breaking My Heart* (1997); Himself in *Take It or Leave It* (1983); Rock Star in *The Final Frame* (1986).
Music: (Madness lead singer) 24 Top Twenty Hits; *Divine Madness* (comeback album); (Solo) *The Lone Ranger; The Pyramids Club*
Address: c/o Noel Gay Artists, 19 Denmark Street, London WC2H 8NA.

SULLIVAN, Dean

Dean Sullivan. Actor (M)/Presenter.
b. Liverpool, 7 June 1955.
TV: *All I Want for Christmas;* Jimmy Corkhill in *Brookside.*
Address: c/o Mersey Television, Campus Manor, Chidwall Abbey Road, Chidwall, Liverpool L16 0JP. Hobbies: Theatre, reading, art.

SUTTON, Dudley

Dudley Sutton. Actor (M). b. 6 April 1933.
TV: *Armchair Theatre; Bergerac; Blackheart the Pirate; Deltawave;* Mr Magic in *Emmerdale; In Suspicious Circumstances; Juno & the Paycock;* Tinker Dill in *Lovejoy; Notable Host; Radio;* Ken in *Randall and Hopkirk (Deceased); Shine on Harvey Moon; Smiley's People; The Beiderbecke Affair;* Dr Terry Kane in *The Famous Five; Widows.*
Films: *A Town Called Bastard; Casanova; Chain Reaction; Una Rosa Al Naso;* Mr Dick in *David Copperfield; Diamonds on Wheels; Edward II;* Offul in *Incognito; Lamb; Madam Sin;* Mr White in *Marbles; Moses; One More Time; Orlando; Rotten to the Core; The Big Sleep; The Boys; The Devils; The Island; The Leather Boys; The London Connection; The Prince and the Pauper; The Rainbow;* Onslow in *The Tichbourne Claimant;* Harold Atkinson in *Up at the Villa; Valentino.*
Address: c/o Kerry Gardner Management, 7 St George's Square, London SW1V 2HX.

SUZMAN, Janet

Janet Suzman. Actor (F).
b. South Africa, 9 January 1939.
TV: Cleopatra in *Anthony & Cleopatra;* Charlotte in *Charlotte Brontë;* Hilda in *Clayhanger;* Hedda in *Hedda Gabler; Inspector Morse;* Lady Macbeth in *Macbeth;* Florence Nightingale in *Miss Nightingale;* Lady Mountbatten in *Mountbatten – The Last Viceroy;* Joan in *St Joan;* Clytemnestra in *The Greeks;* Nicola in *The Singing Detective;* Masha in *Three Sisters;* Viola in *Twelfth Night.*

Films: *A Day in the Death of Joe Egg; A Dry White Season;* Fellini in *And the Boat Sails On; Leon the Pig Farmer;* Alexandra in *Nicholas and Alexandra; Nuns on the Run; The Black Windmill; The Draughtsman's Contract; The House on Garibaldi Street;* Frieda Lawrence in *The Priest of Love; The Voyage of the Damned; The Zany Adventures of Robin Hood.*
Address: c/o William Morris Agency, 151 El Camino Drive, Beverly Hills, California 90212, USA.

SWEENEY, Claire

Claire Sweeney. Actor (F)/Singer.
TV: *Bread;* Lindsey Corkhill in *Brookside; Top Town; World in Action.*
Address: c/o Mersey Television, Campus Manor, Chidwall Abbey Road, Chidwall, Liverpool L16 OJP.
Hobbies: Scuba diving, roller skating, reading.

SWIFT, Clive

Clive Swift. Actor (M). b. 9 February 1936.
TV: LP Brantley in *Bare Heaven;* Sir Horace Wilson in *Churchill: The Wilderness Years;* Albert Benbow in *Clayhanger;* Major Bagstock in *Dombey and Son;* Pimpkin in *First Among Equals;* Lord North in *Goodbye America;* Richard Bucket in *Keeping up Appearances;* Tupman in *Pickwick Papers;* Huggins in *South Riding;* Bishop Proudie in *The Barchester Chronicles.*
Address: c/o Roxane Vacca Management, 73 Beak Street, London W1R 3LF.

SWIFT, Jeremy

Jeremy Swift. Actor (M).
TV: Bob in *A Christmas Carol;* Waldemar Krystoff in *An Actor's Life For Me;* Lead in *Blind Men;* Bob in *Bostock's Cup;* David Fermie in *Dalziel and Pascoe;* Ant in *Next of Kin;* JB Chancer in *Pirates;* Ric the Vic in *Roger, Roger;* David Jeffries in *The Grand;* Shoplifter in *The Paul Merton Show;* Office Manager in *The S Club;* Shaggy in *The Student Prince; The Tenth Kingdom;* Dr Ven in *The Thing About Vince;* Jos Sedley in *Vanity Fair.*
Films: Projectionist in *Mr Love.*
Address: c/o Marina Martin Associates, 12–13 Poland Street, London W1V 3DE.

SWINTON, Tilda

Tilda Swinton. Actor (F).
TV: *Your Cheatin' Heart.*
Films: *Zastrozzi; Caravaggio; The Open Universe; Aria; Friendship's Death; The Last of England; War Requiem; Mozart and Salieri; The Garden; Edward II; Man to Man; Orlando; Wittgenstein; Female Perversions; The War Zone; Protagonist; The Beach.*

Address: c/o Hamilton Asper management, Ground Floor, 24 Hanway Street, London W1P 9DD.

SYKES, Eric

Eric Sykes. Actor/Comedian/Writer.
b. Oldham, Lancashire, 4 May 1923.
TV: *Curry and Chips; Dress Spectaculars; Eric Sykes Show;* Mollocks in *Gormenghast; It's Your Move; Mr H is Late; Pantomania, Opening Night; Sykes and A;* Golf Club Secretary in *The Nineteenth Hole; The Plank.*
Films: *If You Go Down to the Woods Today; Invasion Quartet; Kill or Cure; Monte Carlo or Bust; One Way Pendulum; Rhubarb; The Spy With the Cold Nose; The Plank; Watch Your Stern.*
Address: c/o Norma Farnes, 9 Orme Court, London W2 4RL. m. Edith; 3 d. Catherine, Susan, Julie; 1 s. David.

SYKES, Melanie

Melanie Sykes. Actor (F)/Presenter/Reporter.
b. Mossley, Manchester, 7 August 1970.
TV: *Dream Ticket; Hit List UK; Holiday Programme; ITV Disney Special; Melanie Sykes' Southall Stories; Real TV UK; Smash Hits Poll Winners Party; The Big Breakfast.*
Address: c/o James Grant Management Ltd, Syon Lodge, London Road, Isleworth, Middlesex TW7 5BH.

SYLVESTRE, Cleo

Cleo Sylvestre. Actor (F)/Presenter.
b. Hitchin, Hertfordshire.
TV: *Callan;* Nurse in *Catherine; Crime Ltd;* Melanie Harper in *Crossroads; Grange Hill;* Melanie Harper in *Happy Families;* Mrs Williams in *If You See God Tell Him; Merry-Go-Round; Play for Today; Playschool;* Mother Superior in *Rockliffe's Babies; The Best of Who Do You Do?; The Bill; The Gemini Factor; Thirty Minute Theatre; Who Do You Do?; You and Me.*
Films: *The Attendant; The Love Child; Three; Tube Tales.*
Address: c/o Elaine Murphy Associates, 310 Aberdeen House, 22–24 Highbury Grove, London N5 2EA. m. Ian Palmer (dis.); 2 d, Zoe, Lucy, 1 s. Rupert. Hobbies: Gardening, walking, music, birdwatching.

SYMMS, Natasha

Natasha Symms. Actor (F)/Dancer. b. 20 April 1978.
TV: *Comic Relief; Crystal Rose Show;* Contestant in *Live TV.*
Films: *Billy Badmouth.*
Address: c/o A & B Presonal Management, 5th Floor, Plaza Suite, 114 Jermyn Street, London SW1Y 6LJ.
Hobbies: Dancing, swimming.

SYMS, Sylvia

Sylvia Syms. Actor (F).

b. Woolwich, London, 6 January 1936.

TV: Marion in *At Home With the Braithwaites* (2000); Lilian Crown in *A Sleeping Life* (1989); Mrs Eversley in *Blood and Fire*; Margaret Thatcher in *Half the Picture*; Peggy Tatton in *Heartbeat*; Annie Stanhope in *Intimate Contacts* (1987); wife in *It's Your Move* (1982); Claudia in *Kavanagh QC*; Stephen's mother in *Master of the Moor* (1994); Mrs Easterbrook in *Miss Marple* (1985); Lady with Poodle in *Mr H is Late* (1987); Sylvia Gibbons in *My Good Woman* (1972); Nanaire in *Nancy Astor* (1984); Harriet in *Natural Lies* (1992); Mrs Campness in *Neville's Island* (1998); Esma Carling in *Original Sin* (1996); Isabel de Gines in *Peak Practice*; Margaret Thatcher in *Thatcher, The Final Days*; Alice in *The Fight Master*; Lady Constance in *The Glass Virgin* (1995); Mrs Thorn in *The Orchard Walls.*

Films: Rebecca Huntley-Pike in *A Chorus of Disapproval* (1988); Cynthia Eve in *Absolute Beginners* (1986); Ruth in *Asylum* (1972); Sister Mitya in *Conspiracy of Hearts* (1960); *Dancing*; Mrs Crosby in *Dirty Weekend* (1993); Margaret Woodville in *East of Sudan* (1964); Maisie King in *Espresso Bongo* (1960); *Food of Love* (1997); Sheila Larkin in *Hostile Witness* (1968); *House of Angelo* (1997); Sister Diana Murdoch in *Ice Cold in Alex* (1958); *It Happens Every Thursday* (1953); *Mad Wedding* (1995); Janet Carr in *My Teenage Daughter* (1956); Constance Babington Smith in *Operation Crossbow* (1965); Mrs Ransome in *Run Wild, Run Free* (1969); Linda's mother in *Shining Through* (1992); Headmistress in *Shirley Valentine* (1989); Margaret in *Staggered* (1994); Jean Scott in *The Birthday Present* (1957); Laura Galt in *The Desperados* (1969); Diana in *The Laughter of God* (1990); Ann Wyndham in *The Moonraker* (1957); Delia Pinner in *The Punch and Judy Man* (1963); Kathleen in *The Quare Fellow* (1962); Margaret Stephenson in *The Tamarind Seed* (1974); Kay O'Neill in *The World of Suzie Wong* (1960); Ursula Westerby in *There Goes the Bride* (1979); Laura Farr in *Victim* (1961); Georgie Harlow in *Woman in a Dressing Gown* (1957).

Address: c/o Barry Brown & Partner, 47 West Square, London SE11. 1 d. Beatie Edney.

T

TACEY, Will

Will Tacey. Actor (M). b. London, 23 February 1948.
TV: Dr McAllie in *Brookside* (1995); DS Nicholls in *Brookside* (1985); Keith in *Casualty*; Alan Aldridge in *City Central*; Dr Keane in *Coronation Street* (1997); DI Snow in *Coronation Street* (1995); Insurance Salesman in *Coronation Street* (1983); Sergeant in *Coronation Street* (1989); Owen in *Goodbye Cruel World*; Mr Wimbourne in *Miss Marple*; Mr Peters in *The Bill*; Greg in *Titmus Regained*.
Address: c/o Jane Hollowood & Associates Ltd, 7 Manley Road, Manchester M16 8PN. 1 s. Sam. Hobbies: Cricket, fly-fishing.

TALBOT, Fred

Fred Talbot. Presenter/Weather Presenter.
TV: *Fully Booked; Granada Tonight; Kelly; Mad Science; Shooting Stars; This Morning.*
Address: c/o David Anthony Promotions, PO Box 286, Warrington, Cheshire WA2 6GA. Hobbies: Astronomy.

TAMM, Mary

Mary Tamm. Actor (F).
b. Dewsbury, West Yorkshire, 22 March 1950.
TV: *Agatha Christie's Poirot*; Antonia Kent in *Animal Ark; Bergerac*; Penny Crosbie in *Brookside; Casualty*; Pauline Ogden in *Coronation Street*; Mary Chandler in *Crime Traveller*; Romana in *Doctor Who*; Selina in *Girls of Slender Means*; Marilyn in *Heartbeat; Hunter's Walk; Jane Eyre*; Jan Bishop in *London Bridge*; Diane Caldwell in *Loved By You; Not the Nine O'clock News; Only When I Laugh; Perfect Scoundrels; Quest for Love*; Julie in *Raging Calm; Return of the Saint*; Jill Frazer in *The Assassination Run; The Bill; The Darkenin; The Donati Conspiracy; The Hello-Goodbye Man; The Inheritors*; Alice in *The New Adventures of Robin Hood*; Maggie Llewellyn in *The New Professionals; The Scarlet Woman; The Treachery Game; Three Kinds of Heat*; Maddie in *Uprising; Warship; Whodunnit?; Worlds Beyond.*
Films: *Melody is Her Second Name; Pressing Engagement; Rampage; The Doubt; The Likely Lads*; Sigi in *The Odessa File; The Sweet Life; Wallflowers; Witness Madness.*
Address: c/o Langford Associates, 17 Westfields Avenue, London SW13 0AT. m. Marcus Ringrose; 1 d. Lauren Zoe. Hobbies: Pets, horse riding, computer Scrabble, painting, reading.

TANDY, Mark

Mark Tandy. Actor (M). b. Athlone, 8 February 1957.
TV: Gerry in *A Small World*; Professor Adams in *A Time to Dance*; Ragdale in *A Touch of Frost*; Frank Packenham in *A Vote for Hitler*; Mark in *Absolutely Fabulous*; Charles in *As Time Goes By*; WB Yeats in *Aubrey Beardsley*; Sheridan Thurleigh in *Call Me Mister*; Dr Wishart in *Catherine*; Montague Barnes in *Eye of the Storm*; Lysander Pilot in *Fall From Grace*; Jamie in *Hedgehog Wedding*; Collins in *Inspector Morse*; Gerry in *Jewel in the Crown*; Robin Butler-Cook in *Killer Net*; Cheesman in *Kiss & Tell*; Guy Andrews in *Liverpool 1*; Whiston in *Longitude*; Graham Rose in *Murder Not Proven; Nicholas Nickleby*; Sugden in *Poirot*; Reggie Cooper in *Portrait of a Marriage*; Vet in *Prince; Pulaski*; Miles Gordon in *Saracen; Scarfe on Art*; Tom in *So Haunt Me*; Lord Seadown in *The Buccaneers*; William Winter in *The Chess Sultan; The Gibraltar Inquest*; Peter Vansittart in *The Waiting Time.*
Films: Hammond in *Captive*; Philip Henderson in *Defence of the Realm*; Jackson in *Duel of Hearts*; Robin in *Food of Love*; Mr Villiers in *Howard's End*; Loser Takes All*; Father in *Luzhin Defense*; Lord Risley in *Maurice*; Jim Hutton in *Mrs Dalloway*; Manus Dempsey in *Railway Station Man*; William Shakespeare in *Sophie's World*; Minister of Information in *Soup*; the composer in *Wings of Fame.*
Address: c/o CDA, 19 Sydney Mews, London SW3 6HL.

TARBUCK, Jimmy

Jimmy Tarbuck. Comedian/Actor (M)/Compère.
b. Liverpool, 6 February 1940.
TV: *An Audience with Jimmy Tarbuck; Brazen Hussies*; made TV debut in *Comedy Bandbox; Fantasy Football; Full Swing; It's Tarbuck; Live from Her Majesty's; Live from the Piccadilly; Room 101*; Resident compère in *Sunday Night at the London Palladium* (1965); *Tarbuck's Late; Tarbuck's Luck; Tarby After Ten; Tarby and Friends; Tarby's Frame Game; The Jimmy Tarbuck Show; The Mrs Merton Show; The National Lottery Live!; Winner Takes All.*

Address: c/o International Artistes Ltd, Mezzanine Floor, 235 Regent Street, London W1R 8AX. m. Pauline; 2 d. Liza, Cheryl; 1 s. James. Hobbies: Supporter of Liverpool FC, golf.

TARBUCK, Liza
Liza Tarbuck. Actor (F)/Presenter/Host/Voice artist.
b. Liverpool, 21 November 1964.
TV: *Burnt Bits*; *Chimera*; *Homemaker II*; *I Suppose You Think That's Funny*; Dana in *Mens Sana in Thingummy Doodah, Victoria Wood*; Facility in *Mr Majeika*; *Music for the Millennium*; *Passport to the Sun* (2000); *Round the Houses*; *She's Gotta Have It*; *Soap Fever*; *The Big Breakfast*; *The Weekend Show*; *This Morning*; Angie in *Tumbledown*; Pamela in *Watching*.
Address: c/o Roger Hancock Ltd, 4 Water Lane, London NW1 8NZ. Father Jimmy Tarbuck. Hobbies: art, DIY, embroidery, gardening, reading, mosaic.

TARMEY, William
William Tarmey. Actor (M).
b. Manchester, 4 April 1941.
TV: Jack Duckworth in *Coronation Street*; *Crown Court*; *King Lear*; *Play for Today*; *Rising Star*; *Strangers*; *The Ghosts of Motley Hall*; *The Glamour Girls*; *Thicker Than Water*; *This is Your Life*.
Music: *A Gift of Love*; *I'll Be with You Soon*; *One Voice*.
Address: c/o Arena Entertainment, Regents Court, 39 Harrogate Road, Leeds, West Yorkshire. m. Alma; 1 s; 1 d.

TARRANT, Chris
Chris Tarrant. Presenter.
b. Reading, Berkshire, 10 October 1946.
TV: *Man O Man*; *OTT*; *Pop Quiz*; *Stayback*; *Tarrant on TV*; *The Main Event*; *The Opposite Sex*; *TisWas*; *Who Wants To Be a Millionaire?*
Address: c/o PHA Casting Management, Tanzaro House, Ardwick Green North, Manchester M12 6FZ.

TARRANT, Colin
Collin Tarrant. Actor (M).
TV: Insp. Andrew Monroe in *The Bill*; Will Brangwen in *The Rainbow*.
Address: c/o CAM London, 19 Denmark Street, London WC2H 8NA.

TAVARE, Jim
Jim Tavare. Performer/Writer.
TV: *Beethoven's Not Dead*; *Clive Anderson*; *Jim Tavare Pictures Presents . . .*(1994); *Royal Variety Performance*; *The Comedy Network*; *The Des O'Connor Show*; *The Jim Tavare Show*.

Address: c/o Avalon Promotions, 2nd Floor, Queens House, Leicester Place, London WC2H 7BP.

TAYLFORTH, Gillian
Gillian Taylforth. Actor (F).
b. London 14 August 1955.
TV: *Big Cat*; *Big Jim and the Figaro Club*; Kathy in *EastEnders*; *Eleanor*; *Fast Hands*; *It's a Lovely Day Tomorrow*; *Law and Disorder*; *The Rag Trade*; *Little Girls Don't*; *Lost in France*; *Phyllis Dixey*; *Saving it for Albie*; *Shelley*; *Stars of the Roller Disco*; *The Copyist*; *Thunder Cloud*; *White Light*; *Zigger Zagger*.
Films: *Possessions*; *The Long Good Friday*.
Address: c/o Roxane Vacca Management, 73 Beak Street, London W1R 3LF.

TAYLFORTH, Kim
Kim Taylforth. Actor (F). b. 1958.
TV: *Bloody Kids*; Nancy in *London's Burning*.
Films: Blondie in *Face*; *Radio On*; *The Knowledge*.
Address: c/o Roxane Vacca Management, 73 Beak Street, London W1R 3LF.

TAYLOR, Benedict
Benedict Taylor. Actor (M)/Storyteller.
b. London 14 August 1955.
TV: *92 Grosvenor Street*; *A Flame to the Phoenix*; *A Perfect Spy*; *An Actor's Life for Me*; *Barriers*; *Beau Geste*; *Bergerac*; *Deadman's Tales*; *Drums Along Balmoral Drive*; *Family*; *In Exile*; *Jackanory*; *Jewels*; *Mitch*; *My Brother Jonathan*; *Play for Today*; *Play of the Week*; Gavin Davis in *Psychos*; *Sharpe's Company*; *Tales of the Unexpected*; *The Corsican Brothers*; *The Darling Buds of May*; *The Dirty Dozen*; *The First Modern Olympics*; *The Gentle Touch*; *The Last Days of Pompeii*; *The Ten Percenters*; *The Three Musketeers*; *The Young Indiana Jones Chronicles*; *Thirteen at Dinner*; *Vanity Fair*; *Zorro*.
Films: *Duel of Hearts*; *Every Time We Say Goodbye*; Winterman in *Monk Dawson*; *Say Hello to Yesterday*; Bravo Two in *Star Wars: The Phantom Menace*; *The Black Arrow*; *The Far Pavilions*; *The Innocents*; *The Water in the Woods*.
Address: c/o Jonathan Altaras Associates, 13 Shorts Gardens, London WC2H 9AT. Hobbies: Music (composition and production), dancing, painting, illustration, photography, skiing.

TAYLOR, Georgia
Georgia Taylor. Actor (F). b. 26 February 1980.
TV: Toyah Battersby in *Coronation Street*.
Address: c/o Inter-city Casting, Portland Tower, Portland Street, Manchester M1 3LF.

TAYLOR, Gwen

Gwen Taylor. Actor (F).
b. Derbyshire, 19 February 1939.
TV: Rita Simcock in *A Bit of a Do; A Perfect State; Antigone;* Barbara in *Barbara; Class Act; Colin's Sandwich; Conjugal Rights; Duty Free; Forever Young; Happy Christmas, I Love You; Holby City; Inspector Morse; Keeping Tom Nice; Moving Story; Murder Most Horrid; Pilgrim's Rest; Ripping Yarns; Sauce for the Goose; Screaming; Sharp End; Sob Sisters; Some Kind of Life; The Billy Plays; Ties of Blood; Wycliffe; Yes, Prime Minister.*
Films: *Monty Python's Life of Brian; Richard's Things.*
Address: c/o Gavin Barker Associates Ltd, 45 South Molton Street, London W1Y 1HD. m. Graham Reid.

TAYLOR, Kerrie

Kerrie Taylor. Actor (F).
TV: Viv in *Brookside;* Jean Abbott in *Heartbeat;* Lucy Benson in *Hollyoaks.*
Films: Jane in *Synchronicity;* Marie in *The Regular.*
Address: c/o Sally Hope Associates, 108 Leonard Street, London EC2A 4XS.

TAYLOR, Roberta

Roberta Taylor. Actor (F).
TV: *After the Dance; Dangerfield; Demob; EastEnders; In Suspicious Circumstances; Inspector Morse; One Way Out; Sharman; Silent Witness; The Bill; The Knock; The Passion; The Turnaround.*
Films: *The Witches; Tom & Viv.*
Address: c/o Roxane Vacca Management, 73 Beak Street, London W1R 3LF.

TEALE, Owen

Owen Teale. Actor (M).
b. Swansea, Wales, 20 May 1961.
TV: Conor in *Ballykissangel;* Philip Braithwaite in *Boon;* Tom in *Bryncoe;* Dave Chapman in *Dangerfield;* Terry in *Dangerous Lady;* Ham Peggoty in *David Copperfield;* Happy in *Death of a Salesman;* Maldak in *Doctor Who;* Bentley Drummond in *Great Expectations;* Dai in *Knights of God;* priest in *Love in the House of Our Lord; One by One; Strife;* lawyer in *The Bureaucracy of Love;* John O'Brien in *The Fifteen Streets;* Bob North in *The Secret House of Death;* Edmund in *The Vacillations of Poppy Carew;* Gary in *The Thin Blue Line;* Mike McCarthy in *Waterfront Beat;* Nic in *Way Out of Order;* Dan in *Wilderness.*
Films: Grattius in *Cleopatra;* Alan in *La Guerre des Moutons; Marco Polo;* Will Scarlet in *Robin Hood;* Lopahin in *The Cherry Orchard;* Ken Marsh in *The Hawk;* Unknown Soldier in *War Requiem.*

Address: c/o Markham & Froggatt Ltd, 4 Windmill Street, London W1P 1HF.

TELFORD, Zoe

Zoe Telford. Actor (F).
TV: Louise Reynolds in *Invasion Earth;* Sarah in *Peak Practice;* Chloe in *Soldier Soldier;* Helen in *The Bill;* Roe in *The Last Train.*
Address: c/o Lisa Richards, Haymarket House, 28–29 Haymarket, London SW1Y 4SP.

TERRIS, Malcolm

Malcolm Terris. Actor (M). b. Sunderland, 1941.
TV: Eric Firman in *Coronation Street;* Sir Christopher Bell in *The Secret;* Roger Ackroyd in *Poirot; Underworld; A Touch of Frost; Spender.*
Films: *The First Great Train Robbery; Mutiny on the Bounty; Revolution; Comrades; Mata Hari; McVicar; Red Monarch.*
Address: c/o Tim Scott Personal Management, 5 Cloisters Business Centre, 8 Battersea Park Road, London SW8 4BG.

TEWSON, Josephine

Josephine Tewson. Actor (F).
b. London, 26 February 1939.
TV: *Coronation Street;* Mildred Bates in *Hark at Barker* (1969); Mildred Bates in *His Lordship Entertains* (1972); Elizabeth in *Keeping up Appearances;* Penelope Marshall in *No Appointment Necessary* (1977); Dorothy in *Odd Man Out* (1977); *Shelley;* Miss McDowdie in *Son of the Bride;* Louise in *Sunburn II; Terry and June; The Dick Emery Show; The Les Dawson Show.*
Address: c/o London Management, Noel House, 2–4 Noel Street, London W1V 3RB. m. 1 Leonard Rossiter (dis.); m. 2 Harry Newman; cousin John Inman. Hobbies: Opera, watching cricket.

THAW, John

John Thaw. Actor (M). b. Manchester, 3 January 1942.
TV: *A Year in Provence; Goodnight Mr Tom; Home to Roost;* Chief Inspector Morse in *Inspector Morse; Into the Blue;* Hubert de Burgh in *King John;* Mitch in *Mitch;* Joe MacConnell in *Plastic Man; Redcap; Thick as Thieves; Regan; Bomber Harris; Stairheads; Stanley and the Women; The Sweeney; The Waiting Time; We'll Support You Evermore; Kavanagh QC; Monsignor Renard.*
Films: *Business as Usual;* Fred Karno in *Chaplin;* Kruger in *Cry Freedom; The Grass is Singing.*
Address: c/o John Redway Associates, 5 Denmark Street, London WC2H 8LP. m. Sheila Hancock; 2 d. Abigail, Joanna; 1 step-d Melanie.

THAW, Melanie

Melanie Thaw. Actor (F).

TV: *A Touch of Frost; Bergerac; Fever; Great Expectations; Peak Practice; Pie in the Sky; Trainer; Van Der Valk; Wedded.*

Address: c/o ICM, Oxford House, 76 Oxford Street, London W1N 0AX. Step-father John Thaw; mother Sheila Hancock.

THEAKSTON, Jamie

Jamie Theakston. Presenter. b. 31 January 1970.

TV: *Landmarks; Live & Kicking; The Priory; Name Droppers; The O-Zone;* Eclipse coverage for BBC; *Top of the Pops.*

Address: c/o ICM, Oxford House, 76 Oxford Street, London W1N 0AX.

THEROUX, Louis

Louis Theroux. Reporter/Presenter. b. 20 May 1970.

TV: *Louis Theroux's Weird Weekends; Michael Moore's TV Nation.*

Address: c/o Julia Kreitman, 24 Pottery Lane, London W11 4LZ.

THOMAS, Gareth

Gareth Thomas. Actor (M).

TV: *Bergerac* (1983); Roj Blake in *Blake's 7* (1978); Bill Stone in *Boon* (1989); Adam Brake in *Children of the Stones* (1977); Harold Thomson in *Crown Prosecution* (1995); Rev. Gruffyd in *How Green Was My Valley* (1975); Owen in *Knights of God* (1987); Area Commander Bulstrode in *London's Burning* (1988); *Medics* (1994); Morgan Thomas in *Morgan's Boy* (1984); Briggs in *Public Eye* (1971); Tom Lewis in *Public Eye* (1971); Joseph Harrison in *Sherlock Holmes* (1984); *Space Cadets* (1997); Shem in *Star Maidens* (1976); Philip Denny in *The Citadel* (1983); Policeman in *The Creatives* (1998); Dan Mackay in *The Witch's Daughter* (1996).

Films: Liverpool joiner in *Juggernaut* (1974); Blaze in *Merlin* (1998); Corrado in *Storia di una Capinera* (1993); Publican in *Waterland* (1992).

Address: c/o Julian Belfrage Associates, 46 Albemarle Street, London W1X 4PP.

THOMAS, Jonathan

Jonathan Thomas. Actor (M).

b. Bethlehem, Pennsylvania, USA.

TV: *Behind Closed Doors;* Randy Taylor in *Home Improvement;* Kevin McAllister in *In Living Colour;* Kevin Brady in *The Bradys; The Making of The Lion King.*

Films: Jake in *I'll Be Home for Christmas;* Ben Archer in *Man of the House;* Steven in *Speedway Junky;* Voice of Pinocchio in *The Adventures of Pinocchio;* Young Simba in *The Lion King;* Tom Sawyer in *Tom and Huck; Walking Across Egypt;* Marshall Stouffer in *Wild America.*

Address: c/o ICM Agency, 8942 Wilshire Blvd, Beverly Hills, California 90211, USA. Hobbies: Fishing, watching movies, collecting sports cards, listening to music.

THOMAS, Mark

Mark Thomas. Comedian/Presenter/Reporter.

TV: *Christmas Moviewatch; Comics; Crapston Villas; Cyber Café; Dento; Dispatches; Frost Programme; Johnny Vaughan Film Show; Kosovo Special; Late Licence; Lie of the Land: Dispatches Follow Up; Mark Thomas Comedy Product; Mark Thomas Comedy Product Repackages; Never Mind the Buzzcocks; Not Fade Away; Saturday Zoo; Searching for a Star; The Beat; The Comedy Story; The Obituary Show; The Rory Bremner Show; You Don't Know Me But.*

Address: c/o The Richard Stone Partnership, 2 Henrietta Street, London WC2E 8PS.

THOMAS, Sarah

Sarah Thomas. Actor (F). b. London, 5 June 1952.

TV: *Auntie's Niece; Blackadder; Death in Devon; Happy Families; Heartbeat;* Glenda in *Last of the Summer Wine; Moses; Rumpole of the Bailey; Shroud for a Nightingale; Special Branch; The Bill; Together;* Enid in *Worzel Gummidge.*

Address: c/o Langford Associates, 17 Westfields Avenue, London SW13 0AT. Hobbies: Travel, birdwatching.

THOMASON, Marsha

Marsha Thomason. Actor (F). b. 1975.

TV: Sheena in *Brazen Hussies;* Lous in *Love in the 21st Century;* Sally in *Pie in the Sky;* Shazza in *Playing the Field;* Janice Lafferty in *Prime Suspect;* Sinita in *Skinny Marink;* Jacqui Richards in *Where the Heart Is.*

Films: Wendy in *Safe;* Nurse in *The Priest.*

Address: c/o William Morris Agency, 1 Stratton Street, London W1X 6HB.

THOMPSON, Derek

Derek Thompson. Actor (M).

TV: Will Thurley in *Brookside;* Charlie Fairhead in *Casualty;* Bruce Curran in *Fighting Back;* Jonathan in *Hard to Get;* Billy Downes in *Harry's Game;* Spooner in *Me! I'm Afraid of Virginia Woolf;* Harry Moon in *Rock Follies of '77;* Tom Richards in *The Danedyke Mystery;* DS Jimmy Fenton in *The Gentle Touch;* Chad in *The Photograph;* Frank in *The Price.*

Films: Andy in *Breaking Glass;* Herbie in *Resurrection*

Man; Jeff in *The Long Good Friday;* Hourigan in *Wild Geese II;* Ken in *Yanks.*
Address: c/o Jonathan Altaras Associates, 13 Shorts Gardens, London WC2H 9AT.

THOMPSON, Emma
Emma Thompson. Actor (F)/Writer.
b. London, 15 April 1959.
TV: *Alfresco; Celebration; Cheers; Ellen* (1998); Harriet Pringle in *Fortunes of War; Friday Night, Saturday Morning; Jasper Carrott's Election Night Special; Knuckle; Saturday Live; The Blue Boy; The Crystal Cube; The Winslow Boy; Thompson* (1988); Suzi Kettles in *Tutti Frutti; Up for Grabs.*
Films: *Carrington; Dead Again; Henry V* (1988); Margaret Schlegel in *Howard's End* (1991); Duchess in *Impromptu* (1989); Gareth Pierce in *In the Name of the Father; Judas Kiss* (1998); *Junior;* Beatrice in *Much Ado About Nothing* (1992); Maggie in *Peter's Friends* (1992); *Primary Colors* (1998); Miss Kenton in *The Remains of the Day* (1992); *Sense and Sensibility* (1995); *The Tall Guy; The Winter Guest* (1996).
Address: c/o Hamilton Asper, 24 Hanway Street, London W1P 9DD. m. Kenneth Branagh (dis.); partner Greg Wise; father Eric Thompson; mother Phyllida Law.

THOMPSON, Sophie
Sophie Thompson. Actor (F).
TV: *A Traveller in Time;* Gillian Player in *Message to Posterity;* Clare in *Nelson's Column;* Mary in *Speakers of Mandarin;* Val in *The Complete Guide to Relationships;* Aggie in *The Master Blackmailer.*
Films Francesca in *21;* Rose in *Dancing at Lughnasa;* Miss Bates in *Emma;* Lydia in *Four Weddings and a Funeral;* Mary Musgrove in *Persuasion.*
Address: c/o Jonathan Altaras Associates, 13 Shorts Gardens, London WC2H 9AT.

THORN, Barbara
Barbara Thorn. Actor (F).
TV: Valerie in *Careering Ahead; EastEnders;* Sommersby in *Elizabeth Alone;* Doris in *Game, Set and Match;* Diane Cole in *Grange Hill;* Carol in *Holby City;* Muriel in *Hope it Rains;* Mrs Pope in *Law and Disorder;* Sandy in *Love and Marriage;* Mrs Chambers in *Off Limits;* Jo in *Partners;* Judith Ingleby in *Pie in the Sky;* Sarah in *Tecx;* Inspector Frazer in *The Bill;* various in *The Business;* Dorrie in *The Tripods;* child protection officer in *Trial and Retribution.*
Films: Sheila in *84 Charing Cross Road.*
Address: c/o Jane Lehrer Associates, 100a Chalk Farm Road, London NW1 8EH.

THORNE, Angela
Angela Thorne. Actor (F). b. Karachi, 25 January 1939.
TV: *Anyone for Denis?; Cold Comfort Farm; Drummonds; Dunrulin'; Elizabeth R; Farrington of the FO; Mistral's Daughter; Noah's Ark; Paying Guests; The Good Guys; The Lady's Not for Burning; The Rocking Horse Winner; The Woodlanders; Three Up, Two Down; To the Manor Born; That Was The Week That Was.*
Films: *Bullshot; Oh! What a Lovely War; Yellow Dog.*
Address: c/o Whitehall Artists, 125 Gloucester Road, London SW7 4TE.

THORNTON, Frank
Frank Thornton. Actor (M).
b. London, 15 January 1921.
TV: *All Rise for Julian Clary;* Captain Peacock in *Are You Being Served?; Five to Eleven;* Captain Peacock in *Grace & Favour;* Mr Trabb in *Great Expectations; Green Fingers; Last of the Summer Wine; Noel's House Party;* Gremio in *Taming of the Shrew;* Rev. Hale in *Upper Hand.*
Films: *A Flea in Her Ear; A Funny Thing Happened on the Way to the Forum; The Bed-Sitting Room; The Old Curiosity Shop; The Return of the Three Musketeers.*
Address: c/o David Daly Associates, 586a Kings Road, London SW6 2DX.

THORNTON, Kate
Kate Thornton. Presenter/Reporter.
b. 7 February 1973.
TV: *A406; Dishes; Don't Try This at Home* (1999); *Hit for Six; SFX; Straight Up* (1997); *This Morning; Top of the Pops.*
Address: c/o John Noel Management, 10a Belmont Street, London NW1 8HH. Hobbies: Writing articles, books, scripts.

THORP, Richard
Richard Thorp. Actor (M). b. 2 January 1932.
TV: Dr Rennie in *Emergency Ward 10;* Alan Turner in *Emmerdale;* Market in *Honey Lane; Oxbridge* (2000); *Strangers; The Benny Hill Show; The Harry Worth Show.*
Films: *Dambusters; Good Companions; Lancelot & Guinevere; Mystery Submarine; The £20,000 Kiss; The Green Mask; There's Always Thursday.*
Address: c/o David Daly Associates, 586a Kings Road, London SW6 2DX.

THRELFALL, David
David Threlfall. Actor (M).
b. Manchester, 12 October 1953.
TV: *A Statement of Affairs* (1992); Prince Charles in *Diana – Her True Story* (1992); *Dog Ends* (1984);

Gemma (1993); *I Want to be Like You*; Hugh Warner in *Jumping the Queue* (1987); Edgar in *King Lear* (1982); *Kiss of Death*; Lenny in *Men of the World*; *Murder of Quality* (1990); *Murderers Among Us* (1994); Smike in *Nicholas Nickleby*; *Nightingales* (1989, 1992); *On the Good Ship Yaki Hicki*; *Doola*; Leslie Titmus in *Paradise Postponed* (1985); Andy in *Person to Person* (1988); *Scum*; *Seeing in the Dark* (1989); *Sex, Chips and Rock 'n' Roll* (1999); *The Brylcreem Boys*; *The Clothes in the Wardrobe* (1992); *The Gathering Seed* (1982); Weaver in *The Marksman* (1987); *Thief Takers* (1996); Leslie Titmus in *Titmus Regained* (1991); *When the Whales Came* (1988).
Films: *Casualty of War* (1989); *Patriot Games* (1991); Vasily in *The Red Monarch* (1982); *The Russia House* (1989).
Address: c/o Chatto & Linnit Ltd, 123a Kings Road, London SW3 4PL.

TIERNAN, Andrew

Andrew Tiernan. Actor (M). b. Birmingham.
TV: Billy Pink in *99–1*; David Panter in *Between the Lines*; Operator in *Capital Sins*; Sean Kerrigan in *Cracker*; Bunting in *Hornblower*; Gary in *In a Land of Plenty*; Lenny in *Jonathan Creek*; Banquo in *Macbeth on the Estate*; Mr Dagley in *Middlemarch*; DC Rosper in *Prime Suspect*; DC Rosper in *Prime Suspect II*; Duggie in *Safe*; Billy Dodds in *Soldier, Soldier*; Mark in *Some Kind of Life*; Davey Royce in *Thacker*; Leo in *The Guilty*; Gary O'Brien in *The Sculptress*; John Isles in *Thief Takers*.
Films: Orlando/Oliver in *As You Like It*; Visitor in *Being Human*; Gaveston in *Edward II*; Chris in *Face*; Cyril in *Playing God*; Scar in *Snow White in the Black Forest*; Mohamed in *The Protagonists*; Muller in *The Scarlet Tunic*; Berthold in *The Trial*; Captain Jorgu in *Two Deaths*; the hitchhiker in *You Drive Me*.
Address: c/o Hamilton Asper, 24 Hanway Street, London W1P 9DD. Hobbies: Kickboxing, bass guitar.

TIERNEY, Malcolm

Malcolm Tierney. Actor (M).
TV: *A Bit of a Do*; *All the World's a Stage*; *Bergerac*; *Cat's Eyes*; *Collision Course*; *Crime & Punishment*; *Crown Court*; *Dalziel and Pascoe*; *Doctor Who*; *Expert Witness*; *Family Life*; *Hannay*; *House of Cards*; *Kiszko*; *Love on the Dole*; Charlie Gimbert in *Lovejoy*; *LS Lowry – A Private View*; *Poldark*; *Pope John Paul II*; *Put on by Cunning*; *Room at the Bottom*; *Spoils of War*; *Spyship*; *The Barretts of Wimpole Street*; *The Bill*; *The Broker's Man*; *The Gentle Touch*; *The Homefront*; *The Love School*; *The Main Chance*; *The Wilsons*; *True Crimes*; *Van Der Valk*; *Where Adam Stood*.

Films: *All Neat*; *Apocalypse Watch*; *Braveheart*; *Escape to Athena*; *Family Life*; *In the Name of the Father*; *LA Without a Map*; *Little Dorrit*; *McVicar*; *Star Wars*; *The Eagle Has Landed*; *The Medusa Touch*; *The Saint*; *The Sweet Life*.
Address: c/o International Artistes Ltd, Mezzanine Floor, 235 Regent Street, London W1R 8AX.

TILBROOK, Paula

Paula Tilbrook. Actor (F).
TV: Flo in *Andy Capp*; *Brookside*; *Butterfly Kiss*; *Coronation Street*; Betty in *Emmerdale*; *Last of the Summer Wine*; *Play for Today*; *To Play the King*.
Films: *A Private Function*; *Wetherby*; *Yanks*.
Address: c/o Spotlight, 7 Leicester Place, London WC2H 7BP.

TIMOTHY, Christopher

Christopher Timothy. Actor (M).
b. Gwynedd, Wales, 14 October 1940.
TV: James Herriot in *All Creatures Great and Small*; *Doctors*; Chris Collins in *Holby City II*; Storyteller in *Jackanory Playhouse*; Det. Sgt Love in *Murder Most English*; Clive in *See How They Run*; Himself in *Spirit of Christmas* ; Paul Duffield in *The Bill*; Kevin in *The Kitchen*; *Take Three Girls*; *Take Three Women*; Himself in *The Les Dennis Show*; Corporal in *The Moon Shines Bright on Charlie Chaplin*; Fedotic in *Three Sisters*.
Films: *Alfred The Great*; Spike in *Here We Go Round the Mulberry Bush*; Corporal Brook in *The Virgin Soldiers*.
Address: c/o Kate Feast Management, 10 Primrose Hill Studios, Fitzroy Road, London NW1 8TR.

TITCHMARSH, Alan

Alan Titchmarsh. Presenter/Reporter.
b. Yorkshire, 2 May 1949.
TV: *Gardener's World*; *Ground Force*; *Points of View*; *Songs of Praise*; *Sweet Inspiration*; *The Chelsea Flower Show*; *The Word*; *Titchmarsh's Travels*.
Address: c/o Arlington Enterprise Ltd, 1–3 Charlotte Street, London W1P 1HD. Hobbies: Gardening, writing.

TITUS-ADAMS, Troy

Troy Titus-Adams. Actor (F).
TV: Sharon in *Birth of a Nation*; Nina Harris in *EastEnders*; Lizzie Simpson in *Rhino*.
Films: Torch singer in *Black Banana*; Sadie in *Knights and Emerald*; Carol in *L'Air Du Temps*; ex-patriot in *The Brit Pack*; Kath in *The Rachel Papers*.
Address: c/o Sandra Boyce Management, 1 Kingsway Parade, Albion Road, London N16 0TA.

TODD, Saira

Saira Todd. Actor (F).

TV: *Rocket to the Moon*; Lisa in *Queer as Folk*; *The Bill*; Gabrielle in *Playing the Field*; *Police 2020*; *Drop the Dead Donkey*; *Holding On*; *Punt and Dennis*; *A Touch of Frost*; *Bliss, A Few Short Journeys of the Heart*. *Casualty*; *Life and Times of Howard McGovern*, *Without Walls*; *Perfect Scoundrels*; *Ruth Rendell – A Fatal Inversion*; Hilary in *Capital City*.

Films: *Bring Me Your Love*; *Secret Rapture*; *Bad Behaviour*.

Address: c/o Kate Feast Management, 10 Primrose Hill Studios, Fitzroy Road, London NW1 8TR.

TOLSON, Dickon

Dickon Tolson. Actor (M). b. 24 March 1973.

TV: *Sunburn*; Lee Simms in *Peak Practice*; *An Unsuitable Job for a Woman*; *999*; *Grange Hill*; *Mud*; *Casualty*; *Crime Monthly*; *The Upper Hand*; *Anna Lee*; *Growing Pains*; *Full Stretch*; *Between the Lines*; *Rescue 999*; *London's Burning*; *The Bill*; *Hidden Fears*; *Troublemakers*; *Runaways*; *Skulduggery*; *Only Fools and Horses*.

Films: *Deep in You*; *Beer Goggles*; *Pulp Misshapes*; *Indian Summer*; *Staggered*; *Buddy's Song*; *1984*; *Sacred Hearts*; *Hats Off for Christmas*.

Address: c/o Anna Scher Theatre Management Ltd, 70–72 Barnsbury Road, London N1 0ES.

TOMELTY, Frances

Frances Tomelty. Actor (F).

TV: Commander Stone in *99–1*; *A Celebration of Irish Culture*; *A Perfect Spy*; Fionnula in *Ballykissangel*; Gwenda in *Bazaar and Rummage*; Theresa in *Blue Money*; *Bookworm*; Nina in *Boon*; Kate McGann in *Casualty*; Mrs Lang in *Cracker*; *English File*; Eva Mount Stephens in *In Suspicious Circumstances*; Grace Craven in *Inspector Morse*; Ruby in *Iris in the Traffic, Ruby in the Rain*; Calpurnia in *Julius Caesar*; Juno in *Juno & the Paycock*; Gina Lomax in *Kavanagh QC*; *Lee Harvey Oswald – The Minsk Years*; Connie Sullivan in *Lucy Sullivan is Getting Married*; Laura Grey in *Lytton's Diary*; Danielle Farge in *Nobody's Children*; *Panorama*; Patricia in *Perfect Scoundrels*; Monagh in *Play for Today*; Susannah Prine in *Radio Pictures*; Lorraine Hope in *Rear Window*; Stella in *Stella*; Sister Milroy in *Testament of Youth*; Sheila Hatch in *The File on Jill Hatch*; *The Late Show*; Linda Doran in *The Strangers*; Norma O'Sullivan in *Trial & Retribution*; Polly in *Under the Skin*; Mrs O'Dowd in *Vanity Fair*; *Vapours and Capers*; Julia in *Work*.

Films: Anna in *Bellman and True*; Countess von Bruno in *Bullshot*; Moira in *Half a Shave*; Matron in *High Boot Benny*; Mrs Kane in *Lamb*; Mrs Carter in *Monk Dawson*; the widow in *The Field*.

Address: c/o Mayer Management, 34 Kingly Court, Beak Street, London W1R 5LE.

TOMLINSON, Ricky

Ricky Tomlinson. Actor (M). b. Liverpool, 1940.

TV: Doctor in *Boys from the Blackstuff*; Bobby Grant in *Brookside*; DCI Wise in *Cracker*; Tommy in *Dockers*; John Glover in *Hillsborough*; Jim Pratt in *Playing the Field*; Cinders in *Roughnecks*; Bodyguard in *Strike*; *That's Entertainment*; *The Alexei Sayle Show*; Gordon in *The Fix*; Dad in *The Royle Family*; Glyn in *Where the Buffalo Roam*.

Films: Robert in *Butterfly Kiss*; *Das Leben ist eine Baustelle*; Ezra in *Mojo*; Mr Peach in *Nasty Neighbours*; Fibbin Gibbon in *Preaching to the Perverted*; Tommy in *Stones*; Larry in *Riff Raff*; *United Kingdom*.

Address: c/o Nyland Management, 20 School Lane, Heaton Chapel, Stockport SK4 5DG.

TOMPKINSON, Stephen

Stephen Tompkinson. Actor (M). b. 1967.

TV: Jeremy Craig in *A Very Open Prison*; Julian in *After Henry*; Spock in *All Quiet on the Preston Front*; Eric in *And a Nightingale Sang*; Father Peter in *Ballykissangel*; Tony Mitten in *Casualty*; Marcus Worton in *Chancer*; Mark in *Downwardly Mobile*; Damien in *Drop the Dead Donkey*; Copper Clive in *First Signs of Madness*; Trevor in *Grafters*; Woody in *Made in Heaven*; PC Clark in *Minder*; Jim Harper in *Oktober*; Kevin in *Tales of Sherwood Forest*; Philip Welch in *The Deep Blue Sea*; Jim Wilson in *The Manageress*.

Films: Phil in *Brassed Off*; Dezmond in *Hotel Splendide*; Stephen in *Treacle*.

Address: c/o Barry Brown & Partner, 47 West Square, Southwark, London SE11 4SP.

TOWNSEND, Stanley

Stanley Townsend. Actor (M).

TV: Sean Cassidy in *A Touch of Frost*; Mickey Keeler in *Ballykissangel*; Dr Barry Sullivan in *Bliss*; *Career Opportunities*; Gregory in *DDU (Making the Cut)*; the Ranny Gazoo in *Fortycoats*; Dr Clancy in *Glenroe*; Insp. Sam Barrison in *Jonathan Creek*; Geraghty in *Lapsed Catholics*; Journalist in *Lost Belongings*; Boris in *Nighthawks*; Thomas Sedton in *Parnell*; Keith Johnson in *Peak Practice*; Jim Kerr in *The Bill*; Pete in *The Governor*.

Films: John Horan in *Beyond Reason*; Interrogator in *Blue Ice*; Dr Boyle in *Good Girls*; *In the Name of the Father*; *Into the West*; Consultant in *Jake's Progress*; Co-star in *Joe My Friend*; *Les Misérables*; Goldsmith in *Moll Flanders*; *Taffin*; *The Miracle*; *The Van*.

Address: c/o Marina Martin Associates, 12–13 Poland Street, London W1V 3DE.

TRAVIS, William

William Travis. Actor (M).
TV: Del in *Emmerdale*; Michaux in *Monsignor Renard*; Higgis in *The Bill*; Dick Lampard in *Where the Heart Is*.
Address: c/o Annette Stone Associates, 2nd Floor, 22 Great Marlborough Street, London W1V 1AF.

TREACHER, Bill

Bill Treacher. Actor (M). b. London, 4 June 1936.
TV: *Angels; Bergerac; Bless This House; Dad's Army; Dixon of Dock Green; Down the Gate;* Arthur Fowler in *EastEnders; Fanny by Gaslight; Grange Hill; Maggie and Her; Minder; New Scotland Yard; Softly, Softly; Spooner's Patch; Spy Trap; Sweet Sixteen; The Agatha Christie Hour; The Black Tulip; The Bright Side; The Lady is a Tramp; The Other 'Arf; The Professionals; The Sporting Club Dinner; Warship; Who Sir, Me Sir?*
Films: Mr Carpenter in *Pop Pirates*; Stuart in *Talos the Mummy*.
Address: c/o Glyn Management, The Old School House, Brettenham, Ipswich IP7 7QP. m. Kate Kessey; 1 d. Sophie, 1 s. Jamie. Hobbies: Gardening, painting.

TREMAIN, Eleanor

Eleanor Tremain. Actor (F). b. London, 16 July 1972.
TV: *BUGS; Common as Muck;* Saskia in *Heartburn Hotel; Just William; Kiss Me Kate;* Dorothy Manners in *The Mrs Bradley Mysteries; The Vet*.
Address: c/o Ken McReddie Ltd, 91 Regent Street, London W1R 7TB. Mother Rose Tremain.

TREMARCO, Christine

Christine Tremarco. Actor (F).
TV: Nicky in *City Central*; Debbie in *Dance*; Paula in *Dockers*; Cathy Thompson in *Heartbeat*; Michelle in *Liverpool 1*; Maria in *Pretending to be Judith*; Trish Freeman in *Springhill*; Catherine in *The Factory*; Cheryl in *Trial and Retribution*.
Films: Louise Pearson in *Bordertown*; Sarah in *Face*; Jo in *Family Ties; Hold Back the Night*; Lisa Ushworth in *Priest*; Lili O'Mara in *The Leaving of Liverpool*; Vron in *Under the Skin*.
Address: c/o Marina Martin Associates, 12–13 Poland Street, London W1V 3DE.

TREVES, Frederick

Frederick Treves. Actor (M).
b. Margate, 29 March 1925.
TV: *A Certain Justice; A Taste of Sunshine; After the War; Antigone; Between the Lines; Casualty; Downtown Lagos; Drop the Dead Donkey; Easy Listening; For the Greater Good; Game, Set and Match; God on the Rocks; Hetty Wainthropp Investigates; Inspector Alleyn; Inspector Morse; Just William; Lipstick on My Collar; Mr Bean; Noah's Ark; Paper Mask; Poirot; Ruth Rendell Mysteries; Silas Marner; Silent Witness; Summer's Lease; The Ambassador; The Bill; The Cherry Orchard; The Glass Virgin; The Jewel in the Crown; The Politician's Wife; The Rector's Wife; The Vet; To Play the King; Underbelly; Unknown Soldier; Wynne & Penkovsky*.
Films: *Afraid of the Dark; Defence of the Realm; The Elephant Man; The Fool*.
Address: c/o Whitehall Artists, 125 Gloucester Road, London SW7 4TE.

TROUGHTON, David

David Troughton. Actor (M). b. London, 9 June 1950.
TV: *A Very Peculiar Practice;* King George V in *All the King's Men; Angels; Bergerac; Braces High; Chips with Everything;* Uncle Sid in *Cider with Rosie; Crime & Punishment; David Copperfield; Doctor Who;* Roy Merchant Jnr in *Drop the Dead Donkey; Executive Stress; Frank Muir on Children; Full House;* Blenkiron in *Heartbeat;* DCI Bob Kelso in *Kavanagh QC; Last Night Another Dissident; Lloyd George Knew My Father;* Homais in *Madame Bovary; Midsomer Murders; Moliere;* Emmett in *One Inch over the Horizon; Our Mutual Friend; P G Wodehouse Playhouse; Potter; School Play; Smuggler; Tales of Sherwood Forest; Tealeaf on the Roof; The Love School; The Norman Conquest; The Rainbow; The Winslow Boy;* Ryan in *Undercover Heart;* Martin in *Underworld; Wessex Tales; Wings*.
Address: c/o Markham & Froggatt Ltd, 4 Windmill Street, London W1P 1HF. Father Patrick Troughton; brother Michael Troughton.

TROUGHTON, Michael

Michael Troughton. Actor (M).
b. London, 2 March 1955.
TV: *2point4 Children; A Crack in the Ice; A Picture of a Place; Angels; Blake's 7; Bookmark; Boon; Cat's Heart; Crown Prosecutor; Death of the Heart; God's Chosen Car Park; Goodnight Sweetheart;* Harry in *Hetty Wainthropp Investigates; Is It Legal?; Love Story;* Ivor in *Lucy Sullivan is Getting Married; Minder; Morgan's Boy;* Inspector Stanley in *The Mrs Bradley Mysteries; Nancy Astor; Night Life; Occupation Democrat;* Lord of Leeds in *Poldark;* Dirk in *Retrace; Sean's Show; Shall We Gather at the River;* Allen Symonds in *Silent Witness; Singles; Sorrel & Son; Space Vets; Squadron; Strangers and Brothers;* Derek Halliday in *Taggart; Take Three Women; Testament of Youth; The Barretts of Wimpole Street; The Chain; The Fatal Spring; The Gingerbread*

Girl; The Grassless Grave; The Grudge Fight; Bill Lester in *The Heart Surgeon; The Member for Chelsea; The Mill on the Floss; The New Statesman; Timebusters; We, the Accused;* Mr Walters in *Woof.*
Address: c/o JM Associates, 77 Beak Street, London W1R 3LF. Father Patrick Troughton; brother David Troughton

TULLY, Susan
Susan Tully. Actor (F)/Narrator/Presenter.
b. London, 20 October 1967.
TV: *Big Deal;* Michelle Fowler in *EastEnders; Gender Quake; Grange Hill; Holiday Reps; Jackanory; Our Show; Shop Till You Drop; The Saturday Banana; Why Can't I Go Home?*
Films: *Second to the Right and on Till Morning;* June in *Up 'n' Under.*
Address: c/o Saraband Associates, 265 Liverpool Road, London N1 1LX.

TURNER, Anthea
Anthea Turner. Presenter. b. 1960.
TV: *Best of Magic; Blue Peter; But First This; Change Your Life Forever; GMTV; National Lottery Big Ticket Show; National Lottery Live; Pet Power; Top of the Pops; Turner Round the World; UP2U; Wish You Were Here...?*
Address: c/o James Grant Management Ltd, Syon Lodge, London Road, Isleworth, Middlesex TW7 5BH. Partner Grant Bovey; sister Wendy Turner-Webster.

TURNER, Gideon
Gideon Turner. Actor (M).
TV: Robin Dunstan in *Bad Girls;* Michael in *Casualty;* young Partridge in *Dalziel and Pascoe;* DC Joe Christian in *Dangerfield;* Young David in *David;* Ronnie Harvey in *Heartbeat;* Marcus in *The Stalker's Apprentice.*
Films: Jason in *Loop;* Adam in *Poppy's Present.*
Address: c/o Jonathan Altaras Associates, 13 Shorts Gardens, London WC2H 9AT.

TURNER, Stephanie
Stephanie Turner. Actor (F).
b. Bradford, Yorkshire, 25 May 1944.
TV: *A Touch of Frost; An Ideal Husband; Boon; Casualty;* Miss Armitage in *Hello Girls;* Insp. Darblay in *Juliet Bravo; Peak Practice; The Bill; The Blood That's in You; Van Der Valk.*
Address: c/o Kerry Gardner Management, 7 St George's Square, London SW1V 2HX.

TURNER, Zara
Zara Turner. Actor (F).
TV: Lucy Kennedy in *The Blind Date;* Yvonne in *Dah Dit Dah;* Laura Sweeney in *Father Ted;* Natalie in *Forgotten;* Chris in *Hearts and Minds;* Angela in *McCallum;* Fiona Lang in *Out of Line;* WPC Tamsin in *The Bill;* Tracey in *The Waiting Time;* Penny in *The Writing Game;* Alison in *Touch and Go;* Kate in *Where There's Smoke;* Annabel in *Wycliffe.*
Films: Elizabeth in *Resurrection Man;* Anna in *Sliding Doors.*
Address: c/o William Morris Agency (UK) Ltd, 1 Stratton Street, London W1X 6HB.

TURNER-WEBSTER, Wendy
Wendy Turner-Webster. Presenter.
TV: *Animals; Cruft's; Pet Rescue; Revelations; Video Box.*
Address: c/o Billy Marsh Associates, 174–178 North Gower Street, London NW1 2NB. m. Gary Webster; sister Anthea Turner. Hobbies: International animal welfare, writing cookery books.

TYSON, Cathy
Cathy Tyson. Actor (F).
b. Kingston, Surrey, 12 June 1965.
TV: *Angels;* Carol in *Band of Gold* (1995); Lucy in *Medics; Always and Everyone.*
Films: *Mona Lisa.*
Address: c/o PFD, Drury House, 34–43 Russell Street, London WC2B 5HA. m. Craig Charles (dis.); 1 s. Jack.

U

ULLMAN, Tracey

Tracey Ullman. Actor (F)/Comedian.

b. Buckinghamshire, 30 December 1959.

TV: *A Kick up the Eighties;* Dr Tracey Clark in *Ally McBeal; Best of Tracey Takes on ...; Girls on Top; The Full Wax; The Tracey Ullman Show; Three of a Kind; Tracey Takes on New York; Tracey Takes on ...*

Films: *Give My Regards to Broad Street; I Love You to Death; I'll Do Anything; Jumpin' Jack Flash; Plenty; Robin Hood: Men in Tights; Small Time Crooks.*

Address: c/o ICM, Oxford House, 76 Oxford Street, London W1N 0AX.

UNWIN, Ben

Ben Unwin. Actor (M).

b. Sydney, Australia, 15 August 1977.

TV: Adam in *GP;* Jesse in *Home and Away.*

Address: c/o Seven Network Ltd, Mabbs Lane, Epping, New South Wales 2121, Australia. Hobbies: Singing, guitar, songwriting, reading, art, films, music.

URE, Gudrun

Gudrun Ure. Actor (F). b. 12 March 1926.

TV: *The Crow Road; Life After Life; Moon and Son; Second Thoughts; Stick with Me Kid; Streets Apart;* Supergran in *Supergran; The Tenth Kingdom.*

Films: *Doctor in the House; Million Pound Note; Thirty-six Hours.*

Address: c/o Joy Jameson Ltd, 2.19 The Plaza, 535 Kings Road, London SW10 0SZ.

USTINOV, Sir Peter

Sir Peter Ustinov. Actor (M)/Narrator/Presenter.

b. London, 16 April 1921.

TV: Hercule Poirot in *13 at Dinner; Alice in Wonderland; Around The World in 80 Days; Barefoot in Athens; Einstein's Universe; Gideon; Inside the Vatican;* Hercule Poirot in *Murder in Three Acts; Occasional Political Commentaries; Omnibus – Life of Samuel Johnson; Peter Ustinov in China; Peter Ustinov's Russia; Planet Ustinov; Russia Now; Secret Identity of Jack the Ripper; Storm in Summer; The Ballerinas; The Hermitage; The Mighty Continent; The Mozart Mystique; The Old Curiosity Shop; The Well Tempered Bach; Ustinov Meets Pavarotti; Ustinov on the Orient Express.*

Films: *Appointment with Death; Ashanti; Big Truck and Poor Clare; Billy Bud; Blackbeard's Ghost; Charlie Chan and the Curse of the Dragon Queen; Death on the Nile; Evil Under the Sun; Hammersmith is Out; Hot Millions; John Goldfarb, Please Come Home; Lorenzo's Oil; Memed My Hawk; One of Our Dinosaurs is Missing; Purple Taxi; Romanoff and Juliet; Spartacus; Stiff Upper Lip; The Bachelor; The Comedians; The French Revolution; The Last Remake of Beau Geste; The Phoenix and the Magic Carpet; The Thief of Baghdad; Topkapi; Viva Max.*

Address: c/o William Morris Agency, 151 El Camino Drive, Beverly Hills, California 90212, USA.

V

VALENTINE, Anthony
Anthony Valentine. Actor (M).
b. Blackburn, 17 August 1939.
TV: *A Father's Revenge; After the War; Age of Treason; Airline; An Age of Kings; Bergerac; Billy Bunter; Body and Soul; Boon IV; Callan; Children of the New Forest; Codename; Colditz; Dangerous Corner; Hannay; I Have Been Here Before; John Gabriel Borkman; Justice; Killer Exposed; Lime Street; Love Me to Death; Lovejoy; Masada; Mencius Was a Bad Boy; Minder; Moon and Son; Murder is Easy; Murder, Mystery and Suspense; Pulaski; Raffles; Riders; Robin of Sherwood; Sherlock Holmes; Stay Lucky; Sunset Song; The Carpathian Eagle; The Dancing Years; The Detectives; The Donati Conspiracy; The Fear; The Fifth Corner; The House of Eliott; The Knock; The Second Holmes; Trainer; Van Der Valk; Vice Versa; Whirligig.*
Films: *American Cuisine; Escape to Athena; Fatal Mission; Girl on the Pier; House of Angelo; No Way Back; People's Princess; Performance; The Damned; The Monster Club; To the Devil a Daughter; West II.*
Address: c/o ICM, Oxford House, 76 Oxford Street, London W1N 0AX.

VALENTINE, Kym
Kim Valentine. Actor (F). b. 24 May 1977.
TV: *Adult Illiteracy at Bathurst; Brides of Christ; Candid Camera; Cheez TV; Home and Away; Hoops TV; My Two Wives;* Libby Kennedy in *Neighbours; Swap Shop.*
Address: c/o Pearson Television, 1 Stephen Street, London W1P 1PJ.

VAN CAUWELAERT, Jean-Paul
Jean-Paul Van Cauwelaert. Actor (M).
b. Dublin, Ireland, 31 March 1975.
TV: *Fair City; Glenroe;* Skinny in *Mystic Knights of Tir Na Nog.*
Films: Messenger in *Braveheart;* George in *Love and Death on Rapid Transit;* David in *Midnight Kitchen;* Jay in *Playing Alice.*
Address: c/o Eric Glass Ltd, 28 Berkeley Square, London W1X 6HD. Hobbies: Birdwatching, carpentry.

VAN DER BEEK, James
James Van Der Beek. Actor (M). b. 8 March 1977.
TV: Stephen Anderson in *As the World Turns;* Paulie in *Clarissa Explains It All;* Dawson Leery in *Dawson's Creek; Howie Mandel Show.*
Films: Rick Sandford in *Angus; Castle in the Sky; Harvest; I Love You, I Love You Not; Texas Rangers; Varsity Blues.*
Address: c/o Endeavor Agency, 10th Floor, 9701 Wilshire Boulevard, Beverly Hills, California, CA 90212, USA. Mother Melinda Van Der Beek; father Jim Van Der Beek. Hobbies: Football.

VAN GYSEGHEM, Joanna
Joanna Van Gyseghem. Actor (F).
TV: Sgt Vicky Hicks in *Fraud Squad; The Linden Tree; Intimate Strangers; Within These Walls; Secret Army;* Mary in *The Challengers; Funny Man;* Susan in *Pig in the Middle; Kelly Monteith; Feet Foremost;* Linda in *Duty Free; The Giftie;* Marigold in *Rumpole of the Bailey; The Darling Buds of May;* Helen in *Down to Earth;* Dorothy Horncastle in *Dalziel and Pascoe;* Mrs Bennett *Dangerfield;* Psychologist in *Peak Practice;* Katrina in *Grafters.*
Address: c/o CDA, 19 Sydney Mews, London SW3 6HL.

VAN OUTEN, Denise
Denise Van Outen. Actor (F)/Presenter.
b. 27 May 1974.
TV: Leigh in *Babes in the Wood; Jack and the Beanstalk; Men for Sale; Prickly Heat; Record of the Year; Scratchy & Co.; Something for the Weekend; The Big Breakfast; The Bill.*
Films: Maureen in *Love, Honour and Obey;* Alex in *Tube Tales.*
Music: *Especially for You.*
Address: c/o SilverFox Artist Management Ltd, Cameo House, 11 Bear Street, London WC2H 7AS.

VANDENBERGH, Sarah
Sarah Vandenbergh. Actor (F)/Presenter.
TV: *Celebrity Squares; Fully Booked; Gamesmaster; Gimme 5; Good Morning; Hey Hey It's Saturday;* Sarah in *Hollyoaks; Live and Kicking;* Lauren Carpenter in *Neighbours; Parallel 9; Puzzle Maths; That's*

Showbusiness; The Big Breakfast; What's Up Doc?
Films: *Out of Depth; The Inbetweeners; The People's Princess.*
Address: c/o. Eric Glass Ltd, 28 Berkeley Square, London W1X 6HD.

VARMA, Indira
Indira Varma. Actor (F). b. 1972.
TV: Kerosin in *Courage;* Sonya in *In the Land of Plenty;* Martine in *Psychos;* Emma in *The Grove.*
Films: Kitty in *Clancy's Kitchen;* Bonnie in *Dope Opera;* Jinnah's young wife in *Jinnah;* Co-lead in *Kama Sutra;* Maneet in *Phoenix;* Amy in *Trying to Grow.*
Address: c/o Marina Martin Associates, 12-13 Poland Street, London, W1V 3DE. Hobbies: singing, piano, oboe, fencing, skiing, ballet.

VAUGHAN, Johnny
Johnny Vaughan. Host/Presenter. b. London, 1966.
TV: *Best Night; Bog Standard TV Show; Coca Cola Hit Mix; Here's Johnny; Icons* (1995); *Johnny Meets Madonna* (1998); *Late Licence* (1994); *Light Lunch; Moviewatch* (1993); *Naked City* (1994); *Student Choice; Talking About Sex* (1994); *The Big Breakfast; The Brit Awards* (1999); *The Fall Guy; The Good Sex Guide; The One Where Johnny Makes Friends* (1998); *This Morning* (1995); *Win, Lose or Draw* (1995).
Music: *Especially For You.*
Address: c/o The Richard Stone Partnership, 2 Henrietta Street, London WC2E 8PS.

VAUGHAN, Peter
Peter Vaughan. Actor (M).
b. Shropshire, 4 April 1923.
TV: *Birds of a Feather; Bleak House; C.A.T.S. Eyes; Celebration; Chancer; Circle of Deceit; Citizen Smith; Coast to Coast; Codename Kyril; Countdown to War; Crown Court; Czech Mate; Dandelion Dead; Dayndyke; Fox; Freedom of the Dig; Game Set and Match; Harry's Kingdom; Hornblower; Jamaica Inn; Monte Carlo; Morecambe and Wise; Murder Most Horrid; Nightingales; Oliver's Travels; Our Friends in the North; Our Geoff; Our Mutual Friend; Philby, Burgess and Maclean; Rab C Nesbitt; Season's Greetings; Shelley; Sins; Spot Effects Man; Strife; The Bourne Identity; The Doombolt Chase; The Moonstone; The Wilderness Years; Under a Dark Angel's Eyes; War and Remembrance; When We are Married; Winston Churchill.*
Films: *An Ideal Husband; Brazil; Coming Out of the Ice; Face; Fatherland; Forbidden; Haunted Honeymoon; Heart of Darkness; Hotel Splendide; King of the Wind; Les Misérables; Longitude; Mountain of the Moon; Porridge; Prisoner of Honour; The Remains of the Day; Straw Dogs; The Crucible; The French Lieutenant's*

Woman; The Missionary; The Razor's Edge; The Secret Agent; Time Bandits; Zulu Dawn.
Address: c/o ICM, Oxford House, 76 Oxford Street, London W1N 0AX.

VENISON, Barry
Barry Venison. Football expert b. 1965.
TV: *ITV Soccer; Sky Soccer.*
Address: c/o Park Associates, 68 South Lambeth Road, London SW8 1RL. Hobbies: Tennis, walking, cars, wine.

VENTHAM, Wanda
Wanda Ventham. Actor (F).
TV: *Thriller; You're Not Watching Me Mummy; Home is the Sailor; UFO; Fallen Hero; Union Castle; The Lotus Eaters; No Place Like Home; Minder; The Gentle Touch; Only When I Laugh; The Bracke Report; The Sweeney; A Family At War; The Trouble Shooters; Love Story; Doctor Who;* Sylvia in *Executive Stress; Lost Empires;* Alexandra in *Out of the Shadows;* Mrs Ridge in *All Creatures Great and Small; Only Fools and Horses; Capstick's Law;* Marion Kershaw in *Boon; Just a Gigolo;* Rosie in *Next of Kin;* Fiona in *Heartbeat; Alas Smith and Jones;* Deborah's mother in *Men Behaving Badly;* Margaret Balshaw in *Hetty Wainthropp Investigates;* Mrs Braithwaite in *The Vanishing Man; Casualty;* Ilena Courtney in *Dangerfield; Verdict;* Mrs Fullcup in *Randall & Hopkirk (Deceased).*
Films: *The Knack; Death's Head; Mister Ten Per Cent; Doctor Kronos.*
Address: c/o CDA, 19 Sydney Mews, London SW3 6HL.

VICKERAGE, Lesley
Lesley Vickerage. Actor (F). b. London, 1961.
TV: Jenny Dean in *Between the Lines;* Susan Vorholt in *Bugs;* Francine in *Get Real;* Viv in *Grafters;* WPC in *Inspector Morse;* Ellie in *My Good Friend II;* Chrissie in *Roger, Roger; Silent Witness;* Kate Butler in *Soldier, Soldier;* Trisha in *The Bill;* Ceebie Singleton in *The Chamber.*
Films: Hermione in *Keep the Aspidistra Flying.*
Address: c/o Hamilton Asper, 24 Hanway Street, London W1P 9DD. Hobbies: Singing.

VINCENT, Tim
Tim Vincent. Actor (M)/Presenter.
b. Wrexham, 4 November 1972.
TV: *The Big Breakfast; Blue Peter* (1993); Billy Ryan in *Children's Ward;* Marty in *Dangerfield;* Vet in *Emmerdale* (2000); *Fully Booked; Short Change; The Clothes Show.*

Address: c/o James Grant Management Ltd, Syon Lodge, London Road, Syon Park, Middlesex TW7 5BH.

VIRGO, John

John Virgo. Presenter/Commentator.
b. Manchester, 3 April 1946.
TV: *Big Break; Snooker.*
Address: Mike Hughes Entertainments, c/o Gerald Goss Ltd, Dudley House, 169 Piccadilly, London W1V 9DD.

VORDERMAN, Carol

Carol Vorderman. Presenter.
b. Prestatyn, Wales, 24 December 1960.
TV: *Ask No Questions* (1987); *Better Homes* (1999); *Breaking Glass* (1995); *Car Wise (1990); Celebrity 15 to 1; Celebrity Stars in Their Eyes* (1998); *Cher in Celebrity Wheel of Fortune; Cluedo; Computers Don't Bite* (1997); *Countdown* (1982); *Crosswits; Dream House* (1999); *Entertainment Today; Find a Fortune* (1999); *Gibberish; Give a Pet a Home* (1999); *Go-Getters; Going Live* (1991); *Hot Gadgets* (1997); *How 2; Jim'll Fix It* (1991); *Just One Chance* (1997); *Kid's Kafé* (1986); *Micro Mindstretchers* (1988); *Millennium Science; Mrs Merton; Music On TV; Mysteries with Carol Vorderman; Noel's House Party; Notes and Queries; On Your Marks; Open College: Powerbase Series; Out of this World; Parkinson* (1999); *Pick of the Week* (1992); *Points of View; Postcards from Down Under* (1991); *Put it to the Test* (1995); *So We Bought a Computer* (1988); *Sounds Good* (1986); *Sum Chance* (1990); *Take Nobody's Word for It; Tested to Destruction* (1999); *Testing, Testing* (1997); *The Antiques Inspectors; The Game* (1985); *The Hypnotic Experience* (1992); *The National Lottery* (1997); *The Software Show* (1989); *The Vorderman Report* (1990); *This is Your Life* (1997); *This Morning; Chips; Through the Keyhole* (1988); *Tomorrow's World* (1994); *What Will They Think of Next?* (1998); *Wide Awake Club; World Chess Championship; You Bet.*
Address: c/o John Miles Organisation, Cadbury Camp Lane, Clapton in Gordano, Bristol BS20 7SB.

VOSBURGH, Tilly

Tilly Vosburgh. Actor (F).
b. London, 17 December 1960.
TV: Ella Twite in *Black Hearts in Battersea; Blind Justice; Casualty; Darling Buds of May;* Susan Rose in *EastEnders;* Layla in *Frank Stubbs II;* Jules in *Full Stretch; Good Guys; Hold the Back Page;* Gabby Reedy in *Holding On; Maria Martin; Meantime; Minder; Morning Sarge;* Paul Merton's Mum in *Paul Merton's Life of Comedy; Peak Practice; Perfect Scoundrels; Poirot; Raspberry; The New Alexei Sayle Show; The Rory Bremner Show; Starting Out; Strong Poison;* Mum in *Teenage Health Freak; The Bill;* Daphne in *The Life and Crimes of Henry Pratt;* Della in *The Men's Room; The Victoria Wood Show; This is David Lander; Two People; Will You Love Me Tomorrow?; Wycliffe; You'll Never See Me Again;* Mrs Newton in *Young Indiana.*
Films: *Erik the Viking;* Toby in *Paranoia;* Mrs Taylor in *Shopping; The Missionary; The Pirates of Penzance; Tight Trousers.*
Address: c/o Marina Martin Associates, 12–13 Poland Street, London W1V 3DE.

VOSS, Phillip

Phillip Voss. Actor (M).
TV: Sir Robert Grifford in *A Royal Scandal;* Richard Jordan in *A Village Affair;* Chief Inspector Stewart in *Bad Company;* Jeremy Walters in *Boon;* Mr Jenkins in *C.A.T.S. Eyes;* Walter Fallon in *Crossroads;* Cunningham in *Dwelling Place;* Shumann in *Escape – Mogadishu;* Ivan in *Fish;* Vicar in *Floodtide;* Thomas in *Goodnight and Godbless George;* Coroner in *Inspector Morse;* Auguste De Meane in *Ladykillers;* The Physician in *Let Them Eat Cake;* Edward Carson in *Lillie;* Professor Lemarch in *Me and the Girls;* Chief Inspector in *Melissa; Northern Crescent;* Polish Man in *Rescuers Talking;* Bogus Vicar in *Shine on Harvey Moon;* Solms in *Spy Trap;* Drayford in *The Paradise Club;* Gerald in *Where the Heart Is.*
Films: Headmaster in *Clockwise;* Laura's Father in *Four Weddings and a Funeral; Frankenstein and the Monster from Hell; Hopscotch;* Duncan in *Indian Summer;* Herald in *Lady Jane;* Colonel Rigby in *Mountains of the Moon;* Censor in *Murrow;* Auctioneer in *Octopussy;* Senior Civil Servant in *Secret Rapture.*
Address: c/o Kate Feast Management, 10 Primrose Hill Studios, Fitzroy Road, London NW1 8TR.

W

WADDINGTON, Steven

Steven Waddington. Actor (M). b. Leeds, 1968.

TV: Title Role in *Ivanhoe* (1997); Neville in *Resort to Murder* (1995); Dinger in *The One That Got Away* (1996).

Films: Bartolome in *1492 – Conquest of Paradise* (1992); Ralph Partridge in *Carrington* (1995); Jerry Hoff in *Don't Get Me Started* (1994); Title Role *Edward II* (1991); Stevie in *Face* (1997); Heyward in *Last of the Mohicans* (1992); Ribold in *Prince of Jutland* (1994); Murray Ritchie in *Seconds Out* (1993); Killian in *Sleepy Hollow (1999)*; Nigel Ravens in *Tarzan and the Lost City* (1998).

Address: c/o Julian Belfrage Associates, 46 Albemarle Street, London W1X 4PP.

WADDLE, Justine

Justine Waddle. Actor (F).

TV: Estella in *Great Expectations*; Tess in *Tess of the D'Urbervilles*; Laura Fairlie in *The Woman in White*; Molly in *Wives and Daughters*.

Films: Countess Nordstrom in *Anna Karenina*; Sorrel in *Free Falling*; Julia in *Mansfield Park*; Young girl in *Misadventures of Margaret*.

Address: c/o ICM, Oxford House, 76 Oxford Street, London W1N 0AX.

WADE, Stuart

Stuart Wade. Actor (M). b. Halifax, Yorkshire, 1971.

TV: Bif in *Emmerdale*; *T.A.P.S.*

Film: *Drug Abuse*.

Address: c/o Sharron Ashcroft, Dean Clough, Halifax HX3 5AX.

WADIA, Nina

Nina Wadia. Actor (F).

TV: Viv Thomas in *EastEnders*; *English Express*; Comedian in *First Sex*; *Goodness Gracious Me*; *Jesus Green*; *Kiss Me Kate*; Maggie in *Perfect World*; *The Bill*; Sharma in *2point4 Children*; Asha/Nisha in *Women of the Dust*.

Films: Sumita in *Flight*; Geeta in *Momo Aur Nippal*; Priya Mohan in *Moti Roti*; Dolly in *Sixth Happiness*.

Address: c/o Garricks, 7 Garrick Street, London WC2E 9AR.

WAKEFIELD, Lou

Lou Wakefield. Actor (F). b. Leicester.

TV: Silent Maid in *An Imaginative Woman*; Barbara Haydon in *Casualty*; Pippa in *Girls of Slender Means*; Jane Barratt in *Growing Pains*; Dianah in *Happy Families*; Carla in *Inside Out*; Dr Key in *Inspector Morse*; Pat in *Joggers*; Suffragette in *Shoulder to Shoulder*; Inger in *Tecx*; DS Kellner in *The Bill*; Edith Westmore in *The Linden Tree*; Dee Dee in *The Refuge*; Jackie Pearce in *This is David Lander*; DCC Roth in *Wycliffe*.

Address: c/o Cassie Mayer Ltd, 34 Kingly Court, London W1R 5LE.

WALDEN, Ben

Ben Walden. Actor (M). .

TV: Marcus in *99 – 1*; Fitch in *Between the Lines*; Walter in *Camomile Lawn*; Young Martin in *Martin Chuzzlewit*; Miles in *Message For Posterity*; 'Widows' Billy in *Moving Story*; Black and Tan Aux in *Shadow of a Gunman*; Holland in *The Bill*; Dick Mason in *The Man Who Cried*.

Address: c/o William Morris Agency (UK) Ltd, 1 Stratton Street, London W1X 6HB.

WALDHORN, Gary

Gary Waldhorn. Actor (M). b. London, 3 July 1943.

TV: *After Pilkington*; Lionel in *Brush Strokes*; Campaign*; Gallowglass*; Heartbeat*; Lovejoy*; Missing Persons*; David Horton in *The Vicar of Dibley*.

Films: *Sir Henry at Rawlinson End*; Tornado in *The Chain*; *Zeppelin*.

Address: c/o Jonathan Altaras Associates, 13 Shorts Gardens, London WC2H 9AT. Partner Jo James; 1 s. Joshua David. Hobbies: Walking, reading, travel.

WALKER, Amanda

Amanda Walker. Actor (F).

TV: Mrs Conyers in *A Dance to the Music of Time*; Mary in *A Statement of Affairs*; Amanda Lederman in *All or Nothing at All*; Mrs Johnson in *Bramwell*; Joan Harrison in *City Central*; Mavis Marsh in *Dalziel and Pascoe*; Bessie in *Dandelion Dead*; Mrs F in *Deptford Graffiti*; Dorothy Headlam in *Faith*; Barbara in *Fish*; Debbie Davidson in *From Doon with Death*; Barbara Scott in *Hamish MacBeth*; Miss Apthwaite in *Hetty Wainthropp*

Investigates; Pamcia in *Intimate Contact*; Alison's Mother in *Joking Apart*; Sheila in *Kinsey II*; Hepzibah McKinly in *Life Force*; Molly Clifford in *Medics*; Edwina in *Midsomer Murders III*; Mrs Wilson in *Norbert Smith*; *Paul Merton*; Mrs Tengelly in *Poirot*; sketches in *Punt and Dennis Show*; elderly lady in *Roger, Roger*; Dr Tulcan in *The Bill*; Mortitana in *The New Adventures of Robin Hood*; Marjorie in *The Passion*; Mrs Ransome in *The Railway Children*; The Queen in *The Royal Family*; Mary Queen of Scots in *The Tudors*; Betty Lawson Johnson in *The Woman He Loved*.

Films: Old noblewoman in *Cinderella*; Secretary in *Fierce Creatures*; Lady Mackleworth in *Heat and Dust*; Mme Scalinger in *Nostradamus*; Neighbour in *Rhythms of the House*; *Room with a View*; Elizabeth Farrel in *Seven Days to Live*; Nurse Graham in *Shadow of the Sun*; Mother in *The Big Man*; Lady Hampton in *The English Patient*; *Wild Flowers*.

Address: c/o Michelle Braidman Associates, 10–11 Lower John Street, London W1R 3PE.

WALKER, Anna

Anna Walker. Actor (F)/Host/Presenter/Reporter. b. 4 December 1964.

TV: *Alphabet Game*; *Big Strong Boys*; *Calendar*; *Fantasy Football*; *Frank Stubbs Promotes*; *Full Swing*; *Goals on Sunday*; *Grandstand*; *Hale and Pace*; *Heart of the Country*; *Holiday Maker*; *King of the Road*; *Live at Five*; *National Lottery*; *Noel's House Party*; *On the Line*; *Pick of the Week*; *Pull the Other One*; *Ski Sunday*; *Sky TV's Telethon*; *Sportsnight*; *Summer Olympics*; *Sunrise*; *Tecx*; *That's Showbusiness*; *The London International Boat Show*; *Through the Keyhole*; *Tomorrow's World*; *TV-AM*; *Underbelly*; *Walker's Wildside*; *Walker's World*; *Wildlife Police*; *Win, Lose or Draw*; *Winter Olympics*; *Wish You Were Here...?*; *Women's Soccer*; *You Bet*.

Address: c/o Jane Hughes Management, The Coach House, PO Box 123, Knutsford, Cheshire WA16 9HX. Hobbies: Skiing, off-piste heli-skiing, golf, fitness training, scuba diving, tennis, bungee jumping, water-skiing, running.

WALKER, Chris

Chris Walker. Actor (M). b. Yorkshire.

TV: Jim Fairfield in *An Ungentlemanly Act*; Company Sergeant Major in *Breed of Heroes*; Mike Smith in *Brookside*; *Casualty*; George in *Class Act*; Ray Thorpe in *Coronation Street*; Keith in *Danger in Mind*; Dave in *Defrosting the Fridge*; Mr Ellis in *Getting Hurt*; Pullen in *Harry*; Eddie King in *Heartbeat*; Lord Athelstane in *Ivanhoe*; Roy in *Loved By You*; Fire Chief in *One Foot in the Grave*; DCI Paul Boyd in *Our Friends in the North*; Danny Jackson in *Peak Practice*; Matthew

Mullen in *Playing the Field*; DS King in *Stay Lucky*; Fred Stephens in *Sunny's Ear*; PC Nick Shaw in *The Bill*; Tez in *The Continental*; David 'Bronco' Lane in *The Fix*; Brian Rimmer in *The Manageress*.

Films: Grisha in *Final Warning*; Screw in *Swing*; Skinhead in *The Fourth Protocol*; Morgan in *The Funny Man*; Paul in *The King is Alive*; Mac in *When Saturday Comes*.

Address: c/o CAM London, 19 Denmark Street, London WC2H 8NA.

WALKER, Murray

Murray Walker. Commentator. b. 10 October 1923.

TV: *Driving Force*; *Grand Prix*.

Address: c/o Arena Entertainment, Regents Court, 39 Harrogate Road, Leeds, West Yorkshire. Hobbies: Motorbikes.

WALKER, Nicola

Nicola Walker. Actor (F).

TV: Gypsy Jones in *A Dance to the Music of Time*; Slave/Dionysius/Polixenes in *Aristophanes*; Susy Travis in *Chalk*; Shirley in *Cows*; Harriet Ambrose in *Cruel Earth*; Sally in *Faith*; WPC Fay Radnor in *Jonathan Creek*; Colette in *Milner*; Lucy Diver in *Moll Flanders*; Carol in *Pie in the Sky*; Susan Taylor in *Touching Evil*.

Address: c/o Rebecca Blond Associates, 69a Kings Road, London SW3 4NX.

WALKER, Roger

Roger Walker. Actor (M)/Presenter. b. Bristol, 22 December 1944.

TV: *A Time to Dance*; Kipper in *Big Deal*; *Blackeyes*; *Bodger & Badger*; *Bread*; *Brookside*; *Casualty*; *County Hall*; Bunny in *Eldorado*; *Emmerdale*; *Gentlemen and Players*; *Harry Enfield*; *Heartbeat*; *Oranges are Not the Only Fruit*; *Out of Sight*; Barry in *Picking Up the Pieces*; *Rainbow*; *Squadron*; *Terry and June*; *The Bill*; *The Darling Buds of May*; *The Detectives*; *The Moonstone*; *The Paul Merton Show*; *The Sooty Show*; Jim in *The Upper Hand*; *Waterfront Beat*; *Whizziwig*; *Woof*.

Address: c/o Evans & Reiss, 100 Fawe Park Road, London SW15 2EA. 2 d. Anna, Sarah. Hobbies: Computers, crosswords, cycling, sailing (transatlantic yachtsman).

WALKER, Romla

Romla Walker. Actor (F). b. London, 31 March 1970.

TV: Claudia Fielding in *EastEnders*; *The Bill*; Sophie in *The Vice*.

Films: Fiona in *Soldier's Leap*.

Address: c/o Conway Van Gelder, 18–21 Jermyn Street, London SW1Y 6HP. m. Andrew Pleavin. Hobbies: Motorcycles, skiing, snowboarding, fencing, cooking.

WALKER, Roy

Roy Walker. Comedian/Presenter/Host.
b. Belfast, 31 July 1940.
TV: *A Night of a Hundred Stars; Catchphrase; Licensed for Singing and Dancing; New Faces; Summertime Special; The Comedians; The Laughter Show; The Russ Abbot Show; This is Your Life; Wogan.*
Address: c/o Lake-Smith Griffin Associates, 15 Maiden Lane, London WC2E 7NA. 2 s. Mark and Phil; 1 d. Josie. Hobbies: Golf, horses, skiing, sailing.

WALKER, Rudolph

Actor (M). b. 28 September 1939.
TV: Winston Wainwright in *A Perfect State*; Johnny Johnson in *Bitter Harvest*; Larry Scott in *Black Silk*; Gage in *Bugs*; Major Kimmumwe in *Escape from Kampala*; Bill Reynolds in *Love Thy Neighbour*; The Invigilator in *Mr Bean*; Cartwright in *Rules of Engagement*; Berry Bryan in *The Book Liberator*; PC Gladstone in *Thin Blue Line*.
Films: Leonard Baptiste in *Bhaji on the Beach*; Tony in *Big George Is Dead*; Somers in *Fight Master*; King Mulambon in *King Ralph*; Bill Reynolds in *Love Thy Neighbour*; Kamau in *The Last Giraffe*; Newton in *The Pirate Prince*; Martin in *The Spaghetti House Siege*; Mbote in *Universal Soldier*.
Address: c/o Mayer Management, 34 Kingly Court, Beak Street, London W1R 5LE. m. Dounne Alexander-Walker; 1 s. 1 d. Hobbies: Cricket, tennis, walking, reading.

WALLACE, Julie T.

Julie T. Wallace. Actor (F). b. 28 May 1961.
TV: Valerie the Violent in *Adam's Family Tree*; *Anchoress*; *Heartbeat*; *Les Dogs*; *Lovejoy*; *Morning Sarge*; Matron in *Mr Wymi*; *Queen of the Wild Frontier*; *Rory Bremner Who Else?*; *Selling Hitler*; *Sharpe*; *Sharpe's Rifles*; *Stay Lucky*; Lynda in *Stolen*; *The Full Wax*; Mrs Avery in *Last of the Summer Wine*; Ruth in *The Life and Loves of a She-Devil*; *The Life and Times of Henry Pratt*; *The Lunatic*.
Films: *B Monkey*; *Hawks*; *Neverwhere*; *The Beautician and the Beast*; *The Fifth Element*; Rosika in *The Living Daylights*; Coaxer in *The Threepenny Opera*; *True Tilda*.
Address: c/o Annette Stone Associates, 2nd Floor, 22 Great Marlborough Street, London W1V 1AF.

WALSH, Richard

Richard Walsh. Actor (M).
TV: Sicknote in *London's Burning*.
Address: c/o The Narrow Road Company, 21–22 Poland Street, London W1V 3DD. Hobbies: Singing.

WALSH, Sally

Sally Walsh. Actor (F). b. Bradford, 31 July 1979.
TV: Catherine Tebbit in *Children of Winter*; Lynn Hutchinson in *Emmerdale*; Jane Cunningham and Jean in *Heartbeat*; Chrissie Gallant in *Smokescreen*; Denise in *The Ward*; *Tumbledown Farm*.
Films: Little Nell in *The Old Curiosity Shop*.
Address: c/o Pemberton Associates, 193 Wardour Street, London W1V 3FA. Hobbies: Dancing.

WALSH, Tommy

Tommy Walsh. Landscape gardener.
TV: *Ground Force*; *Whose House*.
Address: c/o Arlington Enterprises Ltd, 1–3 Charlotte Street, London W1P 1HD.

WALTER, Harriet

Harriet Walter. Actor (F).
b. London, 24 September 1950.
TV: *A Dance to the Music of Time*; *Amy*; *Dalziel and Pascoe*; Esther Martin in *Inspector Morse*; Queen Morag in *Leprechauns*; Felicity in *Norman Ormal*; Varya in *The Cherry Orchard*; Harriet Vane in *The Dorothy Sayers Mysteries*; Cathy Raine in *The Imitation Game*; Charity in *The Men's Room*; Frances Carr in *The Price*; *Unfinished Business*.
Films: Sybil in *Bedrooms and Hallways*; Jeanine the Witch in *Hour of the Pig*; Julia in *Keep the Aspidistra Flying*; Lily in *Milou en Mai*; Madame Larina in *Onegin*; Ottilie in *Reflections*; Fanny in *Sense and Sensibility*; Emmy in *The Good Father*; Mrs Cavendish in *The Governess*; Harriet in *Turtle Diary*.
Address: c/o Conway Van Gelder, 18–21 Jermyn Street, London SW1Y 6HP. m. Peter Blythe; uncle Christopher Lee. Hobbies: Languages, travelling, classical music.

WALTER, Natalie

Natalie Walter. Actor (F). b. 1975.
TV: Carolyn in *Babes in the Wood*; Beryl in *Get Well Soon*; Molly in *Harry Enfield and Chums*; Sally in *Perfect State*; Tanya in *Road Rage*; Karen in *Stalker's Apprentice*; Chloe in *The Peter Principle*; Elf in *The Thin Blue Line*.
Films: *If Only*; Georgina in *Remember Me*.
Address: c/o SilverFox Artist Management Ltd, Cameo House, 11 Bear Street, London WC2H 7AS.

WALTERS, Julie

Julie Walters. Actor (F)/Host.
b. Birmingham, 22 February 1950.
TV: *Bambino Mio; Boys from the Blackstuff; Brazen Hussies; Clothes in the Wardrobe*; Petula in *dinnerladies*; *GBH; Get-*

aways; Girls Night; Green Card; Intensive Care; Fairy Godmother in *Jack and the Beanstalk; Jake's Progress; Julie Walters and Friends; Melissa; Oliver Twist; Pat and Margaret; Roald Dahl's Little Red Riding Hood; Say Something Happened; Talking Heads; The All Day Breakfast Show; The Birthday Party; The Secret Diary of Adrian Mole; Victoria Wood – As Seen on TV; Wide Eyed and Legless.*
Films: June Edwards in *Buster; Car Trouble;* Rita in *Educating Rita; Intimate Relations; Just Like a Woman; Killing Dad; One Fell Swoop;* Christine Painter in *Personal Services;* Elsie Orton (Joe Orton's Mother) in *Prick Up Your Ears;* Fran in *She'll be Wearing Pink Pyjamas; Sister, My Sister; Stepping Out; Titanic Town.*
Address: c/o ICM, Oxford House, 76 Oxford Street, London W1N 0AX. m. Grant Roffey, 1 d. Maisie.

WANAMAKER, Zoë
Zoë Wanamaker. Actor (F).
b. New York, USA, 13 May 1949.
TV: *A Christmas Carol;* Lady Anne in *A Dance to the Music of Time; All the World's a Stage; Baal; Balltrap on the Côte Sauvage; Blackheath Poisonings; Confederacy of Wives; Countess Alice; Crown Court; Danton's Death;* Jane Murdstone in *David Copperfield; Edge of Darkness; Enemies of the State; Glad Day;* Cora in *Gormenghast; Inspector Morse; Jennie;* Mary Muldoon in *Leprechauns;* Tessa Piggit in *Love Hurts; Memento Mori; Once in a Lifetime; Othello; Paradise Postponed; Poor Little Rich Girl;* Moira in *Prime Suspect;* Lady Anne in *Richard III; Spy Trap; Strike; Tales of the Unexpected; Beaux Stratagem; The Devil's Crown; Dog It Was It Died; The English Programme; The English Wife; The History of Panto; The Widowing of Mrs Holroyd; Village Hall.*
Address: c/o Conway Van Gelder, 18–21 Jermyn Street, London SW1Y 6HP. Father Sam Wanamaker.

WARBURTON, Lee
Lee Warburton. Actor (M).
b. Cheshire, 27 June 1972.
TV: Tony Horrocks in *Coronation Street;* Tony Elliott in *Hope and Glory;* Stryker in *Queer as Folk;* Shaun Douglas in *A Wing and A Prayer.*
Films: Macca in *Dogtribe.*
Address: c/o Langford Associates, 17 Westfields Avenue, London SW13 0AT. Hobbies: Sports, running marathons.

WARD, Ali
Ali Ward. Actor (F)/Host. b. Nottingham, 1966.
TV: *Gardener of the Year Award; Gardening Neighbours.*
Address: c/o BBC, Union House, 65–69 Shepherd's Bush Green, London W12 8TX.

WARD, Simon
Simon Ward. Actor (M). b. London, 19 October 1941.
TV: *'Allo Beatrice; Around the World in 80 Days; Breakthrough; Diamonds; Dracula; The Corsican Brothers; The Four Feathers; The Misfit.*
Films: *Aces High; All Creatures Great and Small; Calf Love; Children of Rage; Deadly Strangers; Die Standarte (Battle Flag); Dominique; Double X; Frankenstein Must Be Destroyed; Hitler: The Last Ten Days; Holocaust (2000); I Start Counting; L'Etincelle; La Sabina; Leave All Fair; Quest for Love; Supergirl; The Four Musketeers; The Monster Club; The Three Musketeers; Young Winston; Zulu Dawn.*
Address: c/o Shepherd & Ford, 13 Radnor Walk, London SW3 4BP. 1 d. Sophie Ward.

WARD, Sophie
Sophie Ward. Actor (F).
b. London, 30 December 1964.
TV: *A Caribbean Mystery;* Eden Hilliyard in *A Dark Adapted Eye; Casanova; Class of '61; MacGyver; The Shell Seekers.*
Films: *A Summer Story; Aria; Little Dorrit; Return to Oz; Wuthering Heights; Young Sherlock Holmes; Young Toscanini.*
Address: c/o Shepherd & Ford, 13 Radnor Walk, London SW3 4BP. Father Simon Ward; 2 s. Nathaniel, Josh.

WARD, Zander
Zander Ward. b. 9 October 1979.
TV: Paul Millington in *Hollyoaks;* Crispin in *The Wild House;* Joe in *The Boot Street Band;* Andy Walker in *Grange Hill.*
Films: Vince in *Look Like the Innocent.*
Address: c/o SCA Management, 23 Goswell Road, London EC1M.

WARING, Derek
Derek Waring. Actor (M). b. London, 26 April 1930.
TV: *After Henry; Emmerdale Farm; George and Mildred; Law and Disorder; Love After Lunch; Moody and Pegg; Never the Twain; Partners; Pastoral Care; Rings on Their Fingers; Suntrap; Take the High Road; The Avengers; The Flaxborough Chronicles; The Funnyside; The Happy Apple; The Heart of the Country; The Killers; Thundercloud; Unofficial Rose; Wings;* Inspector Goss in *Z Cars.*
Films: *Barnacle Bill; Charlie Chan; Dunkirk; Hitler; I Accuse; Indian Summer; Ivanhoe; No Time to Die; Robin Hood; The Last Ten Days; The Truth About Women; VC.*
Address: c/o Burnett Granger Associates, Prince of Wales Theatre, 31 Coventry Street, London W1V 8AS. m. Dorothy Tutin; 1 d. Amanda; 1 s. Nick.

WARING, George

George Waring. Actor (M).
b. Eccles, Lancashire, 20 February 1927.
TV: *Agatha Christie Hour*; Reardon in *Airline*; Clifford in *Andy Capp*; *As Time Goes By*; Tom Meek in *Castlehaven*; *Churchill's People*; Arnold Swain in *Coronation Street*; *Cribb*; Donald Miller in *Crown Court*; *Doctor Who*; Reg Padgett in *Emmerdale*; Hambley in *Forever Green*; Norman in *Hazell*; Edward Simpson in *Mixed Blessings*; Joe Lever in *Mrs Thursday*; Prefect in *Prisoner of Zenda*; Fawcett in *Sam*; Clerk in *Six Days of Justice*; *Softly, Softly*; Scantlebury in *Strife*; *The Cleopatra Files*; Trainer in *The Racing Game*; *The War of Darkie Pilbeam*; *The Winter Ladies*; Father in *Tightrope*; *Z-Cars*.
Films: Bishop Tunstall in *God's Outlaw*; Polish Ambassador in *Squaring the Circle*.
Address: c/o Janet Welch Personal Management, 46 The Vineyard, Richmond, Surrey TW10 6AN. m. Geraldine Gwyther; 1 s. Geoffrey; 1 d. Georgina. Hobbies: Reading, tennis, classical music.

WARING, Stephanie

Stephanie Waring. Actor (F).
TV: Cindy Cunningham in *Hollyoaks*.
Address: c/o Piccadilly Management, Unit 123, 23 New Mount Street, Manchester M4 4DS. Hobbies: Dancing, swimming, gymnastics.

WARK, Kirsty

Kirsty Wark. Presenter/Producer. b. Dumfries, 3 February 1955.
TV: *Agenda*; *Breakfast Time*; *Current Account*; *Edinburgh Nights*; *Nelson Mandela Concert*; *One Foot in the Past*; *Reporting Scotland*; *Ruth Ellis: A Life for a Life* (1999); *Seven Days*; *The Kirsty Wark Show* (1999); *The Late Show*; *Words Apart*; *Words with Wark*; *Newsnight*.
Address: c/o Clements & Co., The Production Centre, The Tollgate, Marine Crescent, Glasgow. m. Alan Clements; 1 d. Caitlin, 1 s. James.

WARREN, Marcia

Marcia Warren. Actor (F). b. Watford, Hertfordshire.
TV: *Behaving Badly*; *Casualty*; Angela in *Dangerfield*; *I Woke Up One Morning*; Miss Poll in *Just William*; *Keeping Up Appearances*; Miss Pym's Day Out; *No Place Like Home*; *Now and Then*; *Searching*; *September Song*; *The Bill*; *Virtual Murder*; *We'll Think of Something*.
Films: *Don't Start Me Up*; *Mr Love*; *South by South East*; *Spotters*.
Address: c/o Scott Marshall, 44 Perryn Road, London W3 7NA. Hobbies: Food, gardening.

WATERMAN, Denise

Denise Waterman. Host/Presenter.
TV: *Bringing Up Baby*; *Room For Improvement*; *The Close Guide*.
Address: c/o David Anthony Promotions, PO Box 286, Warrington, Cheshire WA2 6GA.

WATERMAN, Dennis

Dennis Waterman. Actor (M)/Producer/Presenter/ Singer. b. Clapham, London, 24 February 1948.
TV: *The Sweeney*; *Circles of Deceit*; *Fair Exchange*; *Just William*; *Match of the Seventies*; *Member of the Wedding*; Terry in *Minder*; *On the Up*; *Stay Lucky*; *The First World Cup – A Captain's Tale*; *The Harry Secombe Show*; *The Lives and Loves of a She Devil*; *The Sweeney*; *The Val Doonican Show*; *Who's Our Little Jenny Lind*; *With a Little Help from My Friends*.
Films: *Cold Justice*; *Man in the Wilderness*; *Murder on the Orient Express*; *Scars of Dracula*; *Smashing Bird I Used To Know*; *The Belstone Fox*; *The Eyes Have It*; *The Sweeney*; *The Sweeney II*; *Up the Junction*.
Address: c/o Music Media Management, 1st Floor, 754 Fulham Road, London SW6 5SH.

WATKINS, Howie

Howie Watkins. Presenter. b. London, 17 July 1969.
TV: *Country File*; *Country Files*; *Crazy Creatures*; *GMTV*; *Live At 3*; *Science in Action*; *The Complete Guide to the Twentieth Century*; *The Countryside Hour*; *The Essential Guide to Weather*; *The Really Wild Guide to Britain*; *The Really Wild Show*; *The Weather Show*.
Address: c/o Curtis Brown, Haymarket House, 28–29 Haymarket, London SW1Y 4SP. m. Louisa Watkins. Hobbies: Violin, animal conservation.

WATKINS, Jason

Jason Watkins. Actor (M).
TV: *Annie's Bar*; *Between the Lines*; Tommy Bennett in *Bostock's Cup*; *Casualty*; Paul in *Couples*; Taz in *Duck Patrol*; Gerry Fairweather in *EastEnders*; *Good Guys*; Bob in *Grown Ups*; *Pie in the Sky*; Mick Luger in *Sex 'n' Death*; *Soldier, Soldier*; *The Bill*; *The Buddha of Suburbia*.
Films: *Circus*; *Eugene Onegin*; *High Hopes*; *Sabotage*; *Split Second*.
Address: c/o The Jules Bennett Agency, PO Box 25, Moreton-in-Marsh, Gloucestershire GL56 9YJ.

WATSON, Emily

Emily Watson. Actor (F). b. 1965.
TV: *A Summer Day's Dream*; *The Mill on the Floss*.
Films: *Angela's Ashes*; *Breaking the Waves*; *Hilary and Jackie*; *Metroland*; *The Boxer*; *The Cradle Will Rock*.

Address: c/o ICM, Oxford House, 76 Oxford Street, London W1N 0AX.

WATSON, Kylie

Kylie Watson. Actor (F).
b. Sydney, Australia, 7 May 1978.
TV: Shauna Bradley in *Home and Away.*
Address: c/o Seven Network Ltd, Mabbs Lane, Epping, New South Wales, NSW 2121, Australia. Hobbies: Dance, painting, art, interior decorating, swimming, roller blading, snowboarding, wake boarding, boating, drums and piano, music.

WATSON, Moray

Moray Watson. Actor (M).
b. Sunningdale, Berkshire, 25 June 1928.
TV: *Campion; Churchill: The Wilderness Years; Compact; Medics; Miss Marple; Nobody's Perfect;* Sir Donald Stiffy in *Norbet Smith;* Mr Bennett in *Pride and Prejudice; Rumpole of the Bailey; Seal Morning; Tales of Mystery and Imagination;* The Brigadier in *The Darling Buds of May; The Pallisers; The Vicar of Dibley.*
Films: *Operation Crossbow; Sea Wolves;* Novelist/Butler in *The Grass is Greener; The Valiant.*
Address: c/o Whitehall Artists, 125 Gloucester Road, London SW7 4TE.

WATT, Tom

Tom Watt. Actor (M)/Presenter.
b. London, 14 February 1956.
TV: *And a Nightingale Sang; Boon; Dads;* Lofty in *EastEnders; In the Club; A Kind of Loving; Rookies; South of the Border; Stuck on You.*
Films: *Patriot Games.*
Address: c/o ICM, Oxford House, 76 Oxford Street, London W1N 0AX.

WAUGH, Gillian

Gillian Waugh. Actor (F).
b. Bradford, West Yorkshire, 9 December 1962.
TV: Gail Bevan in *Children's Ward;* Student and young mum in *Coronation Street;* Mrs Easton in *Coronation Street;* Ellen Charlton in *Heartbeat.*
Films: Speech therapist in *Lost for Words.*
Address: c/o Amber Personal Management, 28 St Margaret's Chambers, 5 Newton Street, Manchester M1 1HL. 1 s. Oliver; 1 d. Evie. Hobbies: Being with friends and her children.

WAX, Ruby

Ruby Wax. Actor (F)/Presenter/Producer/Writer.
b. Evanston, Chicago, USA, 19 April 1953.
TV: Candy in *Absolutely Fabulous;* Shelley Du Pont in *Girls on Top;* Sue in *The Comic Strip Presents;* Herself in *Don't Miss Wax; East Meets Wax; Late Lunch; Ruby; Ruby Takes a Trip; Ruby Wax Meets ... ; Ruby's American Pie* (1999); *Ruby's Health Quest; Sunday Night Clive; The Full Wax ; The Ruby Wax Show; The Ruby Wax Show; Wax Cracks Cannes; Wax Cracks Hollywood* and *Wax on Wheels.*
Address: c/o PFD, Drury House, 34-43 Russell Street, London WC2B 5HA. 2 d. Marina, Madeline; 1 s. Max.

WEBB, Danny

Danny Webb. Actor (M).
TV: Marcus in *2point4 Children;* Johnny in *A Perfect State; A Touch of Frost; A Woman's Guide to Adultery; Cardiac Arrest; Comics;* Doc Hiller in *Dalziel and Pascoe;* Warden in *Disaster at the Mall;* William in *Frenchman's Creek;* Vic Morley in *Harbour Lights; Head Hunters; Intimate Contact;* Liam Keller in *King of Chaos;* Vicar in *Mrs Hartley and the Growth Centre; Murder Most Horrid; Our Friends in the North;* Mr Boyd in *Out of Hours; Poirot; Sharman; Tales of Sherwood Forest;* Sammy in *The Bill;* Nathan Weiss in *The Cleopatra Files;* Davey in *The Jump;* Huck in *True Tilda;* John in *Venus Hunters.*
Films: *Alien 3;* Sid in *Billy the Kid and the Green Baize Vampire;* Paul in *Defence of the Realm;* Captain Will in *Henry V;* Dad in *In the Name of Love United;* John in *Love and Death on Long Island;* Stranger in *No Exit;* Clive Ewing in *Still Crazy; The Unapproachable;* David in *The Year of the Quiet Sun;* Steve in *True Blue.*
Address: c/o Markham & Froggatt Ltd, 4 Windmill Street, London W1P 1HF.

WEBB, Shelley

Shelley Webb. Presenter/Reporter.
b. 26 August 1963.
TV: *110%; History of Football; Live and Dangerous; Mirror Group TV; Standing Room Only; The Football Show; Women's FA Cup.*
Address: c/o Marquee Group (UK) Ltd, 21 The Green, Richmond, Surrey TW9 1PX. m. Neil Webb, 2 s. Luke, Joshua. Hobbies: Lifelong Chelsea fan, member of the Women in Film and Television five-a-side team, Gold Friends member of NSPCC, amateur dramatics and film, sponsor of Children in Uganda and India through Action Aid.

WEBSTER, Gary

Gary Webster. Actor (M).
b. London, 3 February 1964.
TV: Dickie Dawson in *Blonde Bombshell;* Paul in *Boon; Inspector Morse; London's Burning;* Ray Daley in

Minder; Lawrie Johnson in *My Wonderful Life*; Steve in *Real Women*; *Taggart*; *The Bill*.
Address: c/o London Management, Noel House, 2–4 Noel Street, London W1V 3RB.

WEDDERBURN, Clive
Clive Wedderburn. Actor (M)/Presenter.
TV: Torrington in *Black and Blue*; Clyde in *Buddy's Story*; Miller in *Hampton Celeste*; *Jackanory*; Devon in *Look at it This Way*; *Saturday Disney*; PC Gary McCann in *The Bill*.
Films: Aubrey in *Knights and Emeralds*.
Address: c/o Waring & McKenna, Lauderdale House, 11 Gower Street, London WC1E 2HB. Hobbies: Singing, riding, sailing, tennis, football.

WEIR, Arabella
Arabella Weir. Actor (F). b. 1957.
TV: *99–1*; *Alexei Sayle's Stuff*; *Blood Hunt*; *Bonjour La Classe*; *Harry Enfield and Chums*; *Harry Enfield's Television Programme*; *Honest, Decent and True*; *KYTV*; *Les Girls*; *Metro*; *My Summer with Des*; *No Country for Old Men*; *One Foot in the Grave*; *Othello*; *Paradise Club*; *Randall and Hopkirk (Deceased)*; *Takin' Over the Asylum*; *The All New Alexei Sayle Show*; *The Creatives*; *The Demon Lover*; *The Fast Show*; *The Fast Show Christmas Special*; *The Lenny Henry Show – Christmas Special*; *This is David Lander*; *Traffik*.
Films: *Shooting Fish*; *The French Lieutenant's Woman*; *The Frog Prince*.
Address: c/o Roxane Vacca Management, 73 Beak Street, London W1R 3LF. Father former British ambassador Sir Michael Weir. Hobbies: She has written two books.

WEIR, Simon
Simon Weir. Actor (M). b. Glasgow, 5 May 1973.
TV: James Stewart in *Hidden History*; Paul Lafferty in *High Road*; Burglar in *Snug & Cozi*; Andrew Carnegie in *Victorian Scots*.
Films: Ronnie Verton in *33 – 1*; Michael Palmer in *Frank's*; David in *OBIT*; Tambo in *The Acid House*.
Address: c/o Young Casting Agency, 7 Beaumont Gate, Glasgow, Scotland G12 9EE. Hobbies: Football, boxing, weight training, motorcycling.

WEISZ, Rachel
Rachel Weisz. Actor (F). b. 1972.
TV: *Dirty Something*; *Inspector Morse*; *My Summer with Des*; *Scarlet and Black*; *White Goods*.
Films: Amy Foster in *Swept from the Sea*; *Chain Reaction*; *I Want You*; *Night of the Creatures*; *Stealing Beauty*; *Sunshine*; *The Land Girls*; *The Mummy*.

Address: c/o ICM, Oxford House, 76 Oxford Street, London W1N 0AX.

WELCH, Denise
Denise Welch. Actor (F). b. 1958.
TV: *A Kind of Living*; Jean in *Auf Wiedersehen, Pet*; Jane Tompkins in *Barriers*; Polly Bell in *Byker Grove*; Natalie Horrocks in *Coronation Street*; *Harry*; Vanessa in *See You Friday*; Marcia in *Soldier, Soldier*; Frances Spender in *Spender*; Sheila Hayman in *The Bill*.
Films: Jessie in *The Glass Virgin*.
Address: c/o Burnett Granger Associates, Prince of Wales Theatre, 31 Coventry Street, London W1V 8AS. m. Tim Healy.

WELLAND, Colin
Colin Welland. Actor (M).
b. Liverpool, 4 July 1934.
TV: *Blue Remembered Hills*; *Bramwell*; *Femme Fatale*; *The Fix*; *The Verdict is Yours*; *Trial & Retribution*; *United Kingdom*; PC Graham in *Z Cars*.
Films: *A Dry White Season*; *Chariots of Fire*; *Dancin' in the Dark*; *Twice in a Lifetime*; *Yanks*.
Address: c/o Peter Charlesworth & Associates, 68 Old Brompton Road, London SW7 3LQ.

WELLING, Albert
Albert Welling. Actor (M).
b. London, 29 February 1952.
TV: *A Touch of Frost*; *A Voyage Around my Father*; *Brass Eye*; *Bugs*; *Drop the Dead Donkey*; *Friday Night Armistice*; *Heartbeat*; *In the Red*; *Kavanagh QC*; *Lovejoy*; *On the Edge of the Sand*; *Our Young Mr Wignal*; *Pie in the Sky*; *Poirot*; *Prime Suspect V*; *Rabbit Pie Day*; *Raspberry Ripple*; *Rumpole's Return*; *Ruth Rendell Mysteries*; *Sergeant Cribb*; *Shine on Harvey Moon*; *Stronger Than the Sun*; *Telford's Change*; *The Blonde Bombshell*; *The First Olympics*; *The Murder of Stephen Lawrence*; *Underworld*; *Wing and A Prayer*; *Wycliffe*.
Address: c/o Sally Hope Associates, 108 Leonard Street, London EC2A 4XS.

WELLS, Colin
Colin Wells. Actor (M).
TV: *A Scottish Soldier*; *An Independent Man*; Luke in *Birds of a Feather*; Greg in *Casualty*; *Haig*; Dick Manderville in *Hello Girls*; *Iphigenia at Aulis*; *Man From Aunty*; *Mr Bean*; John Adams in *Peak Practice II*; *The Bill*; Greg in *The Grove*; Sam Curtis in *The Professionals*.
Films: *Land of Gentlemen*; *Things of No Importance*; Martius Andronicus in *Titus Andronicus*.
Address: c/o Eric Glass Ltd, 28 Berkeley Square, London W1X 6HD.

WELLS, Maggie
Maggie Wells. Actor (F).
TV: *A Divorce*; *A Winter's Tale*; *Alexander the Greatest*; *Black Silk*; *Harlequinade*; *London Bridge*; Dimple Potts in *Love on a Branch Line*; *Marked Personal*; *Mates*; Liz Adams in *Peak Practice*; *Queen of Hearts*; *Saturday, Sunday, Monday*; *She'll Have to Do*; *Shelley*; *T Bag Strikes Again*; *The Bill*; Mrs Penruthlan in *The Famous Five*; *The Kitchen*; *The Three Graces*; *The Wind Blew Her Away*; *Upstairs Downstairs*; Patricia Illingsworth in *Where the Heart Is*.
Films: *Foreign Affairs*; *Photographing Fairies*.
Address: c/o Evans & Reiss, 100 Fawe Park Road, London SW15 2EA.

WELSH, Cameron
Cameron Welsh. Actor (M). b. 9 March 1977.
TV: Mitch McColl in *Home and Away*; *Wildside*.
Films: *Sadness*; *Talking*.
Address: c/o Seven Network Ltd, Mabbs Lane, Epping, New South Wales, NSW 2121, Australia. Hobbies: Guitar, theatre.

WENDT, George
George Wendt. Actor (M).
b. Chicago, Illinois, USA, 17 October 1948.
TV: Tweedledee in *Alice in Wonderland* (1999); Charlie in *Alien Avengers* (1996) and *Alien Avengers II* (1997); *Avery Schreiber: Live From the Second City* (1980); Harry MacAfee in *Bye Bye Birdie* (1995); Norm Peterson in *Cheers*; Graham McVeigh in *Columbo: Strange Bedfellows* (1995); Warren Kooey in *Hostage For a Day* (1994); Gus Bertoia in *Making the Grade* (1982); *The George Wendt Show* (1995); Les Polonsky in *The Naked Truth* (1997); Sam in *The Price of Heaven* (1997); Mr Sweeney in *The Ratings Game* (1984).
Films: Ticket agent in *Airplane II* (1982); Charlie Prince in *Dreamscape* (1984); Fat Sam in *Fletch* (1985); Harry in *Forever Young* (1992); Shopkeeper in *Gift of the Magi* (1980); Buster in *Gung Ho* (1986); Harold Gorton in *House* (1986); Chet Bronski in *Man of the House* (1995); Engineer in *My Bodyguard* (1980); Mr Witten in *Never Say Die* (1988); Jake in *No Small Affair* (1984); Joey in *Outside Providence* (1999); Chet Butler in *Plain Clothes* (1988); Ivan Bloat in *Rupert's Land* (1998); *Somewhere in Time* (1980); Keller in *Space Truckers* (1997); Martin Barnfield in *SpiceWorld* (1997); Lumberyard clerk in *The Little Rascals* (1994); Therapist in *The Lovemaster* (1997); Dog catcher in *The Pooch and the Pauper* (1999); Marty Morrison in *Thief of Hearts* (1984).
Address: c/o Paradigm Agency, 25th Floor, 1001 Santa Monica Blvd, Los Angeles, CA 90067, USA. m. Bernadette Birkett. Hobbies: Basketball, reading.

WEST, Sam
Sam West. Actor (M)/Narrator. b. 19 June 1966.
TV: *A Breed of Heroes*; *All in the Genes*; *As Time Goes By*; *Battle of the Sexes*; Prince Edward in *Edward VII*; *Equinox – Against Nature*; Johnny in *Frankie & Johnny*; *Heavy Weather*; Major Edrington in *Hornblower*; *I Hate Christmas Too*; *In Excess*; *Inspector Alleyn*; *Making a Killing – Nazi Art*; James Lamerton in *Nanny*; *Neighbours at War*; Archie in *Over Here*; *Persuasion*; Caspian in *Prince Caspian and the Voyage of the Dawn Treader*; Stephen in *Stanley and the Women*; *The Guccis*; *The Maitlands*; *The Nazis – A Warning from History*; *The Planets*; *The Vacillations of Poppy Carew*; Mark in *Voices in the Garden*; *Young Man in a Hurry*.
Films: *Archipel*; *Carrington*; *Costumes*; *A Feast at Midnight*; Leonard in *Howard's End*; *Notting Hill*; *Reunion*; *Rupert's Land*; *Stiff Upper Lips*; *The Dance of Shiva*; *The Ripper*; James in *The Skip*.
Address: c/o PFD, Drury House, 34–43 Russell Street, London WC2B 5HA. Father Timothy West; mother Prunella Scales. Hobbies: Cricket.

WEST, Timothy
Timothy West. Actor (M). b. Bradford, Yorkshire, 1934.
TV: *A Shadow on the Sun*; *A Very Peculiar Practice*; *Beecham*; *Blore MP*; *Bramwell*; *Brass*; *Breakthrough at Reykjavik*; *Churchill and the Generals*; *Crime and Punishment*; *Cuts*; *Edward VII*; *Eleven Men Against Eleven*; *Framed*; *Goodnight Sweetheart*; *Hard Times*; *Harry's Kingdom*; *Horatio Bottomley*; *King Lear*; *Murder Most Horrid*; *Reith to the Nation*; *Smokescreen*; *Survival of the Fittest*; *The Contractor*; *The Monocled Mutineer*; *The Place of the Dead*; *What the Butler Saw*; *When We are Married*; *Why Lockerbie?*.
Films: *The Thirty-Nine Steps*; *Agatha*; *Cry Freedom*; *Ever After*; *Hedda*; *Joan of Arc*; *Joseph Andrews*; *Masada*; *Nicholas and Alexandra*; *Oliver Twist*; *Rough Cut*; *The Day of the Jackal*.
Address: c/o Gavin Barker Associates Ltd, 45 South Molton Street, London W1Y 1HD. m. Prunella Scales; 1 s. Sam West. Hobbies: Narrow boating.

WESTBROOK, Daniella
Daniella Westbrook. Actor (F)/Presenter.
b. 5 November 1973.
TV: *Baby, Baby*; *Cape to Cod*; Sam Mitchell in *EastEnders*; *EastEnders Revealed*; Dawn in *Frank Stubbs Promotes*; *Gayle's World*; *Ghost Train*; *Go-getters*; *Granada Talk TV*; *Motormouth*; *Night Fever*; *Noel's Garden Party*; *The Broom Cupboard*; *The Good Sex*

Guide; The London Programme; The Ross King Morning Show; This Morning; UK Raw.

Films: Girl in *Taking Liberties.*

Address: c/o Rossmore Personal Management, Rossmore Road, London NW1 6NJ. Hobbies: Horse riding.

WEYBRIDGE, Simon

Simon Weybridge. Actor (M).

b. Surrey, 17 June 1973.

TV: *Being with You;* Damien Harris in *Boyz Unlimited; Friday Night Armistice; Malagaska; Safe Sex in Ireland; TGI Friday;* PC Hayes in *The Bill; The Christmas Armistice; Without Walls.*

Films: Colin in *Look Like the Innocent; Someday We'll Love.*

Address: c/o Langford Associates, 17 Westfields Avenue, London SW13 0AT. Hobbies: Football, gym training, travel.

WHATELY, Kevin

Kevin Whately. Actor (M). b. 6 February 1951.

TV: *A Murder is Announced;* Neville in *Auf Wiedersehen, Pet;* Steve Shepherd in *B & B; Fair Stood the Wind for France; Geordie Racer;* Colin Worsfield in *Gobble;* DS Lewis in *Inspector Morse; Night Voice;* Jack Kerruish in *Peak Practice;* Geoff Meadows in *Pure Wickedness; Shackleton;* Hopkins in *Skallagrig;* Jimmy Griffin in *The Broker's Man; The Dig;* Ian Armstrong in *Trip Trap;* Dr Carr in *What Katy Did.*

Films: *Hawk the Slayer ;* Clive in *Paranoid; Return of the Soldier;* Hardy in *The English Patient.*

Address: c/o CDA, 19 Sydney Mews, London SW3 6HL.

WHEATLEY, John

John Wheatley. Actor (M).

TV: *A Very Peculiar Practice; Attachments;* Hector Jerome in *Bugs;* Jack Edwards in *Casualty;* Joe Broughton in *Coronation Street;* Peter Temple in *Crown Prosecutor;* Bob in *Do the Right Thing;* Martin Hopkins in *Fallen Hero;* Julian McKenzie in *Game, Set and Match;* Dale in *Kavanagh QC;* Ronnie Hopwood in *Kiss of Death; Maybury; Nanny;* Spike in *Operation Green Ice;* Percy Blackburrow in *Shackleton;* Vaisey in *Silent Witness;;* Dave Nugent and Mick Evans in *The Bill;* David Shilton in *The Bill;* Michael in *The Light That Shines; The Thirteenth Day of Christmas;* Robert Smythe in *Theory of Chaos;* Keith McPhail in *This is Personal;* Atterley in *Vote for Them;* Moyle in *Wycliffe.*

Address: c/o Barry Brown & Partner, 47 West Square, London SE11.

WHEATLEY, Rebecca

Rebecca Wheatley. Actor (F)/Singer.

TV: Amy in *Holby City;* Amy in *Casualty.*

Music: *Everlasting Love, Stay With Me Baby;* two albums.

Address: c/o Roxanne Vacca Management, 73 Beak Street, London, W1R 3LF.

WHILEY, Jo

Jo Whiley. Presenter/Disc-jockey.

b. Northampton, 1965.

TV: *Glastonbury Festival; Jo Whiley; Top of the Pops.*

Address: c/o BBC Press and Publicity, 152–156 Great Portland Street, London W1N 6AJ.

WHITBY, Martyn

Martyn Whitby. Actor (M).

b. Nottingham, 10 December 1949.

TV: Alfred in *Cadfael;* Norman Pascoe in *Casualty;* Malley in *Dempsey and Makepeace;* Neil Bradley in *EastEnders;* David Hughes in *Emmerdale;* DI Franks in *Harry; Harry Enfield's Television Programme;* PC Steven in *In the Cold Light of the Day;* Roger in *Jobs for the Boys;* John in *Killing Me Softly;* Custody Sgt in *Love Hurts;* Policeman in *Magnum PI;* Aldridge in *Minder;* Meeting Heckler in *Moseley;* Harbourmaster in *No Bananas; Patagonia;* DI Hall in *Rough Justice;* Lennie in *Sam Saturday;* Davey in *Soldier, Soldier;* Graham Horder, Frank O'Connell and Councillor Williams in *The Bill;* Gilroy in *The Detectives;* Jack in *The District Nurse;* Bar manager in *The Hello Girls;* Mr Hebdon in *The World of Eddie Weary;* Smart in *Van Der Valk;* Sydney in *White Goods;* Insp. Phillips in *Wycliffe.*

Films: Mikhail in *Sakharov; Success is the Best Revenge.*

Address: c/o Walmsley Associates, 37a Crimsworth Road, London SW8 4RJ. m. Penny; 2 d. Claudia, Harriet.

WHITCHURCH, Philip

Philip Whitchurch. Actor (M). b. 30 January 1951.

TV: *Coronation Street;* Cyril McGregor in *Brothers McGregor;* Scully in *Castanets;* Frankie Murphy in *GBH; The Bill,* Captain Fredrickson in *Sharpe;* Blind Billy in *Plotlands;* Dennis Hill in *Hope and Glory;* Tyler in *My Herd.*

Films: *To Kill a Priest; Blue Isle; Treasure Island; Shot Through the Heart;* Corporal Dade in *The English Patient.*

Address: c/o Evans & Reiss, 100 Fawe Park Road, London, SW15 2EA . Partner Sally Ann Edwards; 1 s. Matthew; 1 d. Isabelle.

WHITE, Eve

Eve White. Actor (F).

TV: Sarah in *Chandler and Co.*; WPC Booth in *Crime Monthly*; Natalie in *Galleria*; Kathy in *Hale & Pace*; Lisa in *Hanging Fire*; Mrs Morgan in *Hollyoaks*; Lin in *Microtherapy*; Peasant in *Miss Julie*; Sue Jenkins in *Peak Practice*; Staff Nurse in *Perfect Scoundrels*; Jennifer Carmichael in *Positive Driving*; Mrs Heller in *The Bill*; Jane Mooney in *The Bill*; Sarah in *The Grass Arena*; Miss Smythe and Carla in *Them and Us*; Chemist in *True Crimes*; Jane in *Well Man*.

Address: c/o Tim Scott Personal Management, 5 Cloisters Business Centre, 8 Battersea Park Road, London SW8 4BG. Hobbies: Singing, dance, ukulele, swimming, badminton, trampoline, wrestling, weight training, driving, puppetry.

WHITE, Frances

Frances White. Actor (F)/Presenter.

b. Leeds, 1 November 1938.

TV: Linda Clark in *A Little Bit of Wisdom*; *A Perfect Spy*; Dorothy in *A Very Peculiar Practice*; *Blue and White*; *Casualty*; *Chelworth*; *Cluedo*; Kate Hamilton in *Crossroads*; Molly Cramer in *Dangerfield*; *Dusky Ruth*; *Frances and Richard*; *Game On*; *Hale and Pace*; *Harry's Mad*; *Hero With a Past*; Christine Jarvis in *Hunter's Walk*; Julia in *I, Claudius*; *I Woke Up One Morning*; *Justice*; *Looking for Vicky*; *Lord Raingo*; Miss Vera Flood/Mrs Vera Tipple in *May to December*; *Nobody's Perfect*; *Omnibus*; *Out of Sight*; *Paradise Postponed*; Margaret Shaw in *Peak Practice*; Mrs Avery in *Plotlands*; Queen Charlotte in *Prince Regent*; Andrea Warner in *Raging Calm*; *Rumpole of the Bailey*; *Summer and Winter*; Ann in *The Last Salute*; *The New Men*; *The Secret Agent*; *The Stick Insect*; Mrs Truman in *The Unknown Soldier*; *The Victorian Chaise Longue*; *They Don't Make Summers*; *Thief Takers*; *Wednesday's Child*; Marian Pierce in *Wycliffe*.

Films: Mary Fleming in *Mary Queen of Scots*; Liz Bartlett in *Press for Time*; Dinah in *The Pumpkin Eater*.

Address: c/o Langford Associates, 17 Westfields Avenue, London SW13 0AT. Father Frank White; m. Anthony Hone (deceased); 1 d. Kate. Hobbies: Cats, gardening, reading, listening to music.

WHITE, Sheila

Sheila White. Actor (F). b. London, 18 October 1947.

TV: Alice in *Alice in Wonderland*; *Billy Dainty Series*; *Casualty*; *Dear Mother, Love Albert*; *Don't Rock the Boat*; Carol Hanley in *EastEnders*; Moyra Sheffield in *Framed*; Messalina in *I, Claudius*; *Minder*; Karen in *Poldark*; *Royal Variety Performance*; *Starburst*; Annie Miller in *The Love School*; Avril in *Very Big, Very Soon*.

Films: *Alfie*; *Darling*; *Confessions of a Window Cleaner*; *Here We Go Round the Mulberry Bush*; *Mrs Brown You've Got a Lovely Daughter*; *Oliver!*; *Silver Dream Racer*; *The Spaceman and King Arthur*; *Villain*.

Address: c/o Burnett Granger Associates, Prince of Wales Theatre, 31 Coventry Street, London W1V 8AS.

WHITEFORD, Lindy

Lindy Whiteford. Actor (F).

TV: *By Common Consent*; *Minder*; *Skin Deep*; *Matlock*; *A Very Peculiar Practice*; *Casualty*; *Boon*; *Bust*; *The Bill*; *Bergerac*; *Sam Saturday*; *A Touch of Frost*; *Taggart*; *Headhunters*; *The Brown Man*; *Dr Finlay*; *Lifeboat*; *Between the Lines*; *Beyond Fear*; Jean Allen in *Boyz Unlimited*.

Films: *Soft Top Hard Shoulder*; *Company*; *Secrets*.

Address: c/o CDA, 19 Sydney Mews, London SW3 6HL.

WHITEHEAD, Geoffrey

Geoffrey Whitehead. Actor (M). b. 1 October 1939.

TV: *A Very Open Prison*; *Alas Smith and Jones*; *Between the Lines*; *Catherine the Great*; *Chelmsford 123*; *Crossing the Floor*; *Executive Stress*; *Faith*; *Hitler and The Third Reich*; *House of Eliott*; *Jewels*; *Johnny and the Dead*; *Look At the State We're In*; *Lords of Misrule*; *Paul Merton – The Series*; *Peter the Great*; *Pinkerton's Progress*; *Red Fox*; *Reilly, Ace of Spies*; *Second Thoughts*; *Shelley*; *Sherlock Holmes and Doctor Watson*; *Soldier, Soldier*; *The Brief*; *The Cleopatra Files*; *The Foundation*; *The Fourth Floor*; *The Lift*; *The Strauss Dynasty*; *The Sweeney*; *Upstairs Downstairs*; *War and Remembrance*; *Women at War*; *Young Indiana Jones Chronicles*; *Z Cars*.

Address: c/o Bryan Drew Ltd, Quadrant House, 80–82 Regent Street, London W1X 3TB.

WHITEHOUSE, Paul

Paul Whitehouse. Actor (M)/Writer. b. 1958.

TV: *Clive Anderson All Talk*; Pawnbroker in *David Copperfield*; *Harry Enfield and Chums*; *Harry Enfield's Television Programme*; *Late Lunch*; Mike Smash in *Smashie and Nicey – End of an Era*; *Ted and Ralph*; various in *The Fast Show* and *The Fast Show Live*; Jimmy Lea from Slade in *The Smell of Reeves and Mortimer*.

Address: c/o London Management, Noel House, 2–4 Noel Street, London W1V 3RB.

WHITELAW, Billie

Billie Whitelaw. Actor (F).

b. Coventry, Warwickshire, 6 June 1932.

TV: *A Tale of Two Cities*; *Beckett* triple bill – *Footfalls, Rockaby* and *Eh Joe*; *Born to Run*; *Camille*; *Dr Jekyll and Mr Hyde*; *Firm Friends*; *Jamaica Inn*; *Murder of Quality*;

The Chain; The Fifteen Streets; The Picnic; The Poet Game; The Secret Garden.

Films: *Charlie Bubbles; Dark Crystal; Duel of Love; Eagle in a Cage; Frenzy; Gumshoe; Hell is a City; Jane Eyre; Leo the Last; Lorna Doone; Nightwatch; No Job For Woman; No Love For Jonnie; Payroll; Shadey; Start the Revolution Without Me; The Adding Machine; The Dressmaker; The Krays; The Omen; The Water Babies; Twisted Nerve.*

Address: c/o ICM, Oxford House, 76 Oxford Street, London W1N 0AX.

WHITELEY, Richard

John Richard Whiteley. Presenter.

b. 28 December 1943.

TV: *Calendar; Calendar Countdown; Countdown; First Face; Richard Whiteley Unbriefed* (1999).

Address: c/o The Richard Stone Partnership, 2 Henrietta Street, London WC2E 8PS. 1 s. James. Hobbies: Walking, horse racing, socialising.

WHITELY, Arkie

Arkie Whitely. Actor (F).

TV: *A Family Man; A Town Like Alice; Bullets; But Beautiful; Casualty; Drowning In the Shallow End; Gallowglass; Kavanagh QC; Love Hurts; McCallum; Natural Lies; People Like Us; Perfect Scoundrels; Slippery Slide;* Madame Euphrasine in *The Grand;* Elizabeth Fraser in *The Last Musketeer; Van Der Valk.*

Films: *Mad Max III;* Betty in *Princess Caraboo; Razorback; Scandal; The Killing of Angel Street; The Secret Life of Ian Fleming.*

Address: c/o PFD, Drury House, 34–43 Russell Street, London WC2B 5HA.

WHITFIELD, June

June Whitfield. Actor (F).

b. London, 11 November 1925.

TV: Mother in *Absolutely Fabulous; All Rise for Julian Clary;* Mrs Birkshead in *Catherine Cookson's The Secret; Friends; Happy Ever After;* June in *Terry and June;* Nurse in *The Blood Donor; This is Your Life;* Queen Victoria in *Timekeepers of the Millennium.*

Films: Various in *Carry On . . .*

Address: c/o April Young, 11 Woodlands Road, Barnes, London SW13 0JZ. Awarded OBE in 1985 and CBE in 1998.

WHITROW, Benjamin

Benjamin Whitrow. Actor (M).

b. Oxford, 17 February 1937.

TV: *A Crack in the Ice; A Few Selected Exits; A Moment in Time; All For Love; Bergerac; Blonde Bombshell;* *Brookside; Chancer; Coming Through; Embassy; Fizz; Harry's Game; Hayfever; Inspector Morse; Jonathan Creek; Kiss Me Kate; Men of the World; The Merchant of Venice; Minor Complications; Moving Story; Natural Causes; On Approval; One Fine Day; Partners in Crime; Pastoral Care; Paying Guests; Peak Practice; Pride and Prejudice; Shackleton; The Spoils of War; Starlite Ballroom; Tales of the Unexpected; The Bill; The Factory; The New Statesman; Tom Jones; Troilus and Cressida; Victoria Wood As Seen On TV; We Think the World of You; What Have You Been Up to Lately.*

Films: *A Man for All Seasons; A Shocking Accident; Brimstone & Treacle; Charlie; Clockwise; Damage; Golden Afternoon; Jilting Joe; On the Black Hill; Personal Services; Project Samurai; Restoration; Sauce for the Goose; Sharma and Beyond; The Opium Wars; The Saint.*

Address: c/o Lou Coulson, 37 Berwick Street, London W1V 3RF.

WHITTAKER, Sally

Sally Whittaker. Actor (F).

b. Middleton, Lancashire, 30 May 1963.

TV: *Coronation Street; Hold Tight; Juliet Bravo; The Practice.*

Address: c/o Barry Brown & Partner, 47 West Square, Southwark, London SE11. m. Tim; 1 d. Phoebe; 1 s. Samuel.

WILBY, James

James Wilby. Actor (M).

b. Rangoon, Burma, 20 February 1958.

TV: *A Tale of Two Cities; Adam Bede; Crocodile Shoes; Dutch Girls; Lady Chatterley; Mother Love; Original Sin; Storyteller; Tell Me That You Love Me; The Dark Room; Treasure Seekers; Witness Against Hitler; You Me and It.*

Films: *A Handful of Dust; An Ideal Husband; Cotton Mary; Howard's End; Immaculate Conception; Maurice; Regeneration; Tom's Midnight Garden; Un Partie d'Echec.*

Address: c/o William Morris Agency, 151 El Camino Drive, Beverly Hills, California 90212, USA.

WILCOX, Paula

Paula Wilcox. Actor (F).

b. Manchester, 13 December 1949.

TV: Ivy Sandford in *Blue Heaven;* Dorothy West in *Boon;* Barrister in *Brookside;* Cathy in *Caseload;* Rosalind Paynter in *Casualty;* Ros in *Fiddlers Three;* Sylvia in *Life After Birth;* Chrissie in *Man About the House;* Elizabeth Jones in *Miss Jones and Son;* Maureen in *Mrs Capper's Birthday; Only You;* Amanda Blake in *Peak Practice; Peter Cook and Friends;* Ros in *Present*

Spirits; *Remember the Lambeth Walk?*; Sara Bean in *Smokescreen*; Cynthia Bright in *The Bright Side*; Beryl in *The Lovers*; Audrey Parker in *The Queen's Nose*; Mrs Walwyn in *The Stalker's Apprentice*.
Address: c/o Kate Feast Management, 10 Primrose Hill Studios, Fitzroy Road, London NW1 8TR.

WILLCOX, Toyah
Toyah Willcox. Actor (F). b. 18 May 1958.
TV: The cat in *A Tale of Pig Robinson*; Stop Press Sadie in *Adam's Family Tree*; Aunt Boomerang in *Barmy Aunt Boomerang*; *Dr Jekyll and Mr Hyde*; Debbie in *Function Room*; *Glitter*; Deborah Drake in *Kavanagh QC*; *Little Girls Don't*; *Look Here*; Gigi in *Maigret and the Hotel Majestic*; *Shoestring*; Marigold in *Tales of the Unexpected*; *The Ebony Tower*; The dog in *The Ink Thief*; Dialta Downes in *Tomorrow Calling*; *Toyah – A Documentary*.
Films: Pauline in *Anchoress*; Mad in *Jubilee*; Barbara Gifford in *Julie and the Cadillacs*; Billy in *Midnight Breaks*; Monkey in *Quadrophenia*; *The Corn is Green*; Dr Johnson in *The Most Fertile Man In Ireland*; *The Tempest*; *Tied Up in Tallinn*.
Address: c/o Emptage Hallett, 24 Poland Street, London W1V 3DD.

WILLIAMS, Lia
Lia Williams. Actor (F). b. Birkenhead, 1965.
TV: Maida in *A Shot Through the Heart*; *Bad Blood*; *Bread*; Carrie in *Casualty*; Fern in *Filthy Lucre*; Janet in *Flowers of the Forest*; Josephine in *Happy Families*; Amanda in *Imogen's Face*; *Les Girls*; Joanna in *Mr Wroe's Virgins*; Mary in *Nightingales*; *No Place Like Home*; Paula in *Seaforth*; Linda Goswell in *Shrinks*; Melissa in *The Uninvited*; Lucy in *The Yob*.
Films: Gabrielle in *Different for Girls*; Bella in *Dirty Weekend*; Constance in *Firelight*; Diana in *The Fifth Province*; Amanda in *The King is Alive*.
Address: c/o Hamilton Asper, 24 Hanway Street, London W1P 9DD. 1 s. Josh. Hobbies: Dance, advanced jazz, ballet, contemporary and tap, singing.

WILLIAMS, Mark
Mark Williams. Actor (M)/Writer.
TV: Samms in *99–1*; *Bad Company*; *Bottom*; *Casualty*; *Chef!*; *Coppers*; *Dead at Thirty*; Perch in *Gormenghast*; *Great Expectations*; Various in *Harry Enfield's Television Programme*; *Health and Efficiency*; Peter in *Hunting Venus*; Danny in *Kinsey*; *Making Out*; *Merlin*; *Peak Practice*; *Red Dwarf*; Gerald in *Searching*; *Storyteller*; *Stuff*; *Ted & Ralph*; Tommy in *The Big Game*; various in *The Fast Show* and *The Fast Show Christmas Special*; *The Honeymoon's Over*; Flynn in *The Strangerers*; Whipping Warden in *The Trial*; *Tumbledown*.

Films: Horace in *101 Dalmatians*; Juke box man in *Fever*; *High Season*; *Out of Order*; Aslak in *Prince of Jutland*; Wilf in *Privileged*; Wabash in *Shakespeare in Love*; Exterminator Jeff in *The Borrowers*; Roland Thornton in *Whatever Happened to Harold Smith*.
Address: c/o CDA, 19 Sydney Mews, London SW3 6HL.

WILLIAMS, Michael
Michael Williams. Actor (M).
b. Manchester, 9 July 1935.
TV: Ted Jeavons in *A Dance to the Music of Time* (1997); Mike in *A Fine Romance* (1981); Goronwy Rees in *Blunt* (1985); Kevin in *Can You Hear Me Thinking* (1990); Barry in *Conjugal Rights* (1993); Duc d'Alençon in *Elizabeth R* (1971); *Ice Age* (1978); Davey Warbeck in *Love in a Cold Climate* (1980); *My Son, My Son* (1979); *Playing Shakespeare* (1984); *Quest of Eagles* (1979); Dromio of Syracuse in *The Comedy of Errors* (1978); Alan Crowe in *The Hanged Man* (1975).
Films: Professor Eric Hawthorne in *After Murder Park* (1979); *Dead Cert* (1974); Barry O'Meara in *Eagle in a Cage* (1971); Brian in *Educating Rita* (1983); Hirsch in *Enigma* (1982); William in *Henry V* (1989); Herlad in *Marat/Sade* (1966); *The Benefit of the Doubt* (1967).
Address: c/o Julian Belfrage Associates, 46 Albemarle Street, London W1X 4PP. m. Judi Dench; 1 d. Finty.

WILLIAMS, Paulette
Paulette Williams. Actor (F).
TV: *Bobby Davro Special*; Angela in *Casualty*; Amanda Kennett in *Cops*; Charlotte in *Highlander*; *Les Dawson Special*; *Les Dennis Laughter Show*; *Top of the Pops*; Jacqui in *Where the Heart Is*.
Films: Daisy in *Alice Through the Looking Glass*.
Address: c/o Evans & Reiss, 100 Fawe Park Road, London SW15 2EA. Hobbies: Dancing, martial arts, athletics, walking, t'ai chi, sign language, climbing, yoga, cycling, cookery, music, meditation, singing.

WILLIAMS, Rhodri
Rhodri Williams. Analyst/Presenter/Host.
b. Cardiff, Wales, 10 May 1968.
TV: *2000 Today*; *5's Company*; *Animal Hospital*; *Animal Hospital Roadshow*; *Children in Need*; *Don't Look Back*; *Driver of the Year*; *Give Me 5*; *Heno*; *Holiday*; *Pacio*; *Rugby Union World Cup*; *Sky Sports News*; *The Big Weekend*; *The Front Row*; *Trio*; *Up for It*.
Address: c/o The Jules Bennett Agency, PO Box 25, Moreton-in-Marsh, Gloucestershire GL56 9YJ. m. Carla. Hobbies: Golf, skiing, weight training, roller blading, bungee jumping, running.

WILLIAMS, Simon

Simon Williams. Actor (M).
b. Windsor, Berkshire, 16 June 1946.
TV: *Agony Again; Alfred Hitchcock Presents; Don't Wait Up; First Among Equals; Law and Disorder; Sam McCloud in London; The Mixer; The Return of the Man from U.N.C.L.E.; Upstairs Downstairs.*
Films: *Joanna; No Longer Alone; The Breaking of Bumbo; The Fiendish Plot of Fu Manchu; The Incredible Sarah; The Odd Job; The Prisoner of Zenda.*
Address: c/o Rebecca Blond Associates, 69a Kings Road, London, UK SW3 4NX. m. Lucy Fleming; 1 s. Tom; 1 d. Amy. Hobbies: Tennis, walking.

WILLIAMS, Sylvester

Sylvester Williams. Actor (M).
TV: Victor in *A Mother Like You;* Cary in *August Wilson;* Delroy in *Black Silk;* Celebrity in *Comin' Atcha;* Cleveland Davis in *Desmond's;* Mick in *EastEnders; South Bank Show;* John Henry in *The Rear Column;* Hudson in *Thief Takers.*
Films: Juka in *Sheena;* Wesley in *Simple.*
Address: c/o Sandra Boyce Management, 1 Kingsway Parade, Albion Road, London N16 0TA.

WILLIAMS, Tam

Tam Williams. Actor (M).
TV: *A Dance to the Music of Time; Anorak; Casualty; Cold Enough for Snow;* Scott Miller in *Killer Net; Martin Chuzzlewit; Silent Witness.*
Films: Thomas in *A Time to Love; The Trench; Unforgettable; War Poem.*
Address: c/o Jonathan Altaras Associates, 13 Shorts Gardens, Covent Garden, London WC2H 9AT. Hobbies: Trombone, keyboards.

WILLIAMSON, Shaun

Shaun Williamson. Actor (M). b. London.
TV: *Call My Bluff;* Taxi Driver in *Crime Monthly;* Supergrass in *Crime Monthly;* Barry Evans in *EastEnders;* Cashier in *Inspector Morse;* Chris in *London's Burning; Night Fever;* Ken in *Stick With Me Kid;* Dale in *That's English;* SO19 Officer in *The Bill;* Removal Man in *The Geeks;* Brown in *Waiting for God; Win, Lose or Draw.*
Films: Peter's driver in *Stella Does Tricks.*
Address: c/o McIntosh Rae Management, Thornton House, Thornton Road, London SW19 4NG.

WILLSON, Quentin

Quentin Willson. Narrator/Presenter.
b. Leicester, 23 July 1957.
TV: *All the Right Moves; Bangers & Cash; Driving School; Menzone* (1996); *The Car's the Star; Top Gear;*
War & Piste.
Films: *Janice Beard* (1999).
Address: c/o Mezzo Consultancy Ltd, Sycamore House, Main Street, Hungarton, Leicester, LE7 9JR.

WILMOT, Gary

Gary Wilmot. Actor (M)/Host/Presenter.
b. London, 8 May 1954.
TV: *Cue Gary; Mike Reid's Mates and Music; New Faces; Saturday Gang; Showstoppers; This is Your Life; You and Me.*
Address: c/o Dee O'Reilly Management, 112 Gunnersbury Avenue, London W5 4HB. m. Johanne Murdock, 2 d. Kate, Georgia. Hobbies: Football, DIY.

WILSON, Jennifer

Jennifer Wilson. Actor (F). b. London, 25 April 1937.
TV: *A Doll's House; A Man of Our Times; Antigone; Collect Your Hand Baggage; Dixon of Dock Green; Dr Finlay's Casebook; Hobson's Choice;* Maggie in *Hobson's Choice;* Kate Nickleby in *Nicholas Nickleby; Softly, Softly;* Jennifer Kinsley/Hammond in *The Brothers; This Happy Breed;* Kay in *Time and the Conways;* Title Role in *The Widowing of Mrs Holroyd;* Gloria in *You Never Can Tell; Z Cars.*
Films: Mrs Pooley in *Private Pooley; Sammy Going South; The Yellow Rolls Royce.*
Address: c/o PBR Management, 26 Foubert's Place, Regent Street, London W1V 1HG. m. Brian Peck; 1 d. Melanie. Hobbies: Reading, cooking, collecting, painting.

WILSON, Richard

Richard Wilson. Actor (M)/Director. b. 9 July 1936.
TV: *A Wholly Healthy Glasgow; Changing Step; Cluedo; The Commitments; Crown Court; Duck Patrol; Emmerdale; Father Ted; Fatherland; High and Dry; Hot Metal; In the Red; Inspector Morse; Life Support; Mr Bean; Murder by the Book; My Good Woman; Normal Service;* Victor Meldrew in *One Foot in the Grave* and *One Foot in the Algarve; Only When I Laugh; Other Animals; Poppyland; Remainder Man; Room at the Bottom; Selling Hitler; Sharp Intake of Breath; Sherlock Holmes; The Holy City; The Lord of Misrule; The Sweeney; The Vision Thing; The Woman I Love; Tutti Frutti; Under the Hammer; Unnatural Pursuits; Virginia Fly is Drowning; Walking the Plank.*
Films: *A Dry White Season; A Passage to India; Carry On Columbus; Fellow Travellers; Gulliver's Travels; How to Get Ahead in Advertising; Prick Up Your Ears; Soft Top, Hard Shoulder; Watch That Man; Women Talking Dirty.*
Address: c/o Conway Van Gelder, 18–21 Jermyn Street, London SW1Y 6HP.

WILSON, Sean

Sean Wilson. Actor (M).
b. Crumpsall, Manchester, 4 April 1965.
TV: *Crown Court*; *Mozart's Unfinished*; *Travelling Man*; Martin Platt in *Coronation Street*.
Address: c/o Granada Television, Quay Street, Manchester M60 9EA.

WILSON-JONES, Anna

Anna Wilson-Jones. Actor (F).
TV: *Berkeley Square*; Katie May in *Boyz Unlimited*; Justine in *Monarch of the Glen*; Sarah in *Spaced*; Maria in *Streetlife*; *The Bill*; *The Skip*; Gina in *Wonderful You*.
Films: Genya Lozinska in *Vigo*.
Address: c/o Rebecca Blond Associates, 69a Kings Road, London SW3 4NX.

WILTON, Penelope

Penelope Wilton. Actor (F).
b. Scarborough, 3 June 1946.
TV: White Queen in *Alice Through the Looking Glass*; Anne Bryce in *Ever Decreasing Circles*; Regan in *King Lear*; Desdemona in *Othello*; *Screaming*; Rosemary in *Talking Heads 2*; Homily in *The Borrowers*; Hester Collyer in *The Deep Blue Sea*; Lady Angela Forbes in *The Monocled Mutineer*; Annie in *The Norman Conquests*; Marjorie in *This Could Be the Last Time*; *The Widowing of Mrs Holroyd*.
Films: Patricia Fulford in *Blame it on the Bellboy*; Lady Ottoline Morrell in *Carrington*; Pat Garden in *Clockwise*; Wendy Woods in *Cry Freedom*; Alice Singleton in *Laughterhouse*; Sonia in *The French Lieutenant's Woman*; Marion French in *The Secret Rapture*; Aunt Melbourne in *Tom's Midnight Garden*.
Address: c/o Julian Belfrage Associates, 46 Albemarle Street, London W1X 4PP.

WINDING, Victor

Victor Winding. Actor (M).
b. London, 30 November 1929.
TV: *A Winter Harvest*; *Angels*; *Armchair Thriller*; *Benjamin Sweet*; *Bognor*; Victor Lee in *Crossroads*; *Dixon of Dock Green*; Dr Fairfax in *Emergency – Ward 10*; *It Takes a Worried Man*; *Jemima Shaw Investigates*; *Little and Large*; *Menace Unseen*; *No Hiding Place*; *Probation Officer*; Baxter in *Strike It Rich*; *The Bill*; Insp. Fleming in *The Expert*; *The Farm*; *The Flaxton Boys*; Kenneth Piggot in *The Mendip Mystery*; *Yes, Prime Minister*; *Z-Cars*.
Films: *The Sailor's Return*; *The Medusa Touch*; *The System*; *The Village*.
Address: c/o The Richard Stone Partnership, 2 Henrietta Street, London WC2E 8PS.

WINDSOR, Barbara

Barbara Windsor. Actor (F). b. London, 6 August 1937.
TV: *Dreamers Highway*; Peggy Mitchell in *EastEnders*; *Six Five Special*; *The Jack Jackson Show*; *The Rag Trade*; *This is Your Life*.
Films: *A Study in Terror*; various in *Carry On...*; *Chitty Chitty Bang Bang*; *Comrades*; *Double Vision*; *Flame in the Street*; *Hair of the Dog*; *Lost*; *On the Fiddle*; *Sparrers Can't Sing*; *The Boyfriend*; *Too Hot to Handle*.
Music: *Sparrers Can't Sing*.
Address: c/o Burnett Granger Associates, Prince of Wales Theatre, 31 Coventry Street, London W1V 8AS.

WINDSOR, Frank

Frank Windsor. Actor (M).
b. Walsall, Staffordshire, 12 July 1927.
TV: *All Creatures Great and Small*; *Boon*; *Casualty*; *Chancer*; *Doctor Who*; *Finding Sarah*; *First Among Equals*; Harry Bradley in *Flying Lady*; *Headmaster*; *Kidnapped*; *Lovejoy*; *Middlemen*; *Midsomer Murders*; Sophocles in *Oedipus at Colonus*; *Peak Practice*; *September Song*; *Softly Softly*; *Task Force*; *The Detectives*; *The Fifteen Streets*; *The Real Eddy English* ; *Touch and Go*; *Trip Trap*; *Z-Cars*.
Films: *Dropout*; *Revolution*; *Spring and Port Wine*; *Sunday Bloody Sunday*; *The London Connection*; *The Shooting Party*; *This Sporting Life*; *Too Many Chefs*; *Twentyfour Seven*.
Address: c/o Scott Marshall, 44 Perryn Road, London W3 7NA.

WINFREY, Oprah

Oprah Winfrey. Actor (F)/Host/Producer/Voice artist.
b. Kosciusko, Mississippi, USA, 29 January 1954.
TV: *About Us: The Dignity of Children*; *All American Girl*; Miss Zora in *Before Women Had Wings*; Mattie Michael in *Brewster Place*; *David and Lisa*; Therapist in *Ellen*; Elizabeth Keckley in *Lincoln*; *Overexposed*; *The Oprah Winfrey Show*.
Films: Sethe in *Beloved*; *Listen Up: The Lives of Quincy Jones*, Mrs Thomas in *Native Son*; Sofia in *The Color Purple*; Herself in *Throw Momma From the Train*.
Address: c/o Creative Artists Agency, 9830 Wilshire Boulevard, Beverly Hills, California 90212, USA. Fiancé Stedman Graham; father Vernon Winfrey; mother Vernita Lee. Hobbies: Her dog.

WING, Anna

Anna Wing. Actor (F). b. London, 30 October 1914.
TV: Mrs Tutt in *Bonjour La Classe*; Binnie in *Casualty*; Grandma in *Collision Course*; Lou Beale in *EastEnders*; *French and Saunders Christmas Special*; Chairwoman in *Jake's Progress*; Mrs Green in *Men of the World*;

Auntie Jeannie in *Mike and Angelo*; Elsie in *Real Women*; Lou in *Spatz*; *The Detectives*; Gran in *The Groves*; *The Invisible Man*; *The Late Show*; *The Old Men at the Zoo*; Jo's mum in *Through the Cakehole*; Isobel Harrison in *Watt on Earth*.
Films: Pensioner with dog in *101 Dalmatians*; Grandmother in *Chez Moi*; Mrs Stubbs in *Darkest England*; Mrs Lacey in *In the Flesh*; Jean in *Last Rites*; Mag in *Meet Me In Dreamland*; *Runners*; *The Ploughman's Lunch*.
Address: c/o McIntosh Rae Management, Thornton House, Thornton Road, London SW19 4NG.

WINGETT, Mark
Mark Wingett. Actor (M).
b. Melton Mowbray, Leicestershire, 1 January 1961.
Television: *Private Schultz*; *Quadrophenia*; PC/DC Jim Carver in *The Bill*; *The Professionals*; *Woodentop*.
Address: c/o London Management, Noel House, 2–4 Noel Street, London W1V 3RB.

WINSLET, Beth
Beth Winslet. Actor (F).
TV: *Bodywork*.
Films: Ruth Lascelles in *The Scold's Bridle*.
Address: c/o Jonathan Altaras Associates, 13 Shorts Gardens, Covent Garden, London WC2H 9AT. Sister Kate Winslet.

WINSTONE, Ray
Ray Winstone. Actor (M).
b. London, 19 February 1957.
TV: Gangster in *A Fairly Secret Army*; PC Molson in *Absolute Hell*; Bill Haden in *Bergerac*; Sgt Godley in *Between the Lines*; Malcolm – Prison Officer/Elvis in *Birds of a Feather*; Alan in *Births, Marriages and Deaths*; Charlie Brett Smith in *Black and Blue*; Stanley Castilano in *Blore*; Terry Brennan in *Casualty*; Father Charlie in *Father Matthews' Daughter*; Kenny in *Fox*; *Get Back*; Martin Sweet in *Get Back*; CPO Jack Evans in *Kavanagh QC*; King Duncan in *Macbeth on the Estate*; Arnie in *Minder*; Man Upstairs in *Mr Right*; Weaver in *Mr Thomas*; Terry in *Murder Most Horrid*; Ed in *Nice Town*; Woody in *Our Boy*; Mike in *Paint*; *Palmer*; *Playing for Time*; Chief Detective Ford in *Pulaski*; Will Scarlet in *Robin of Sherwood*; Carlin in *Scum*; George Bright in *Sharman*; Con #1 in *Space Precinct*; School Bully in *Sunshine Over Brixton*; Thane in *The Ghostbusters of East Finchley*; TA in *The Lonely Hearts Kid*; Jack Swan in *The Negotiator*; William Parker in *Thief Takers*; Collins in *Underbelly*.
Films: Billy in *All Washed Up*; John in *Dangerous*

Obsession; Dave in *Face*; Dave in *Fanny & Elvis*; Ray in *Final Cut*; Vincent in *Five Seconds to Spare*; Peters in *Ladybird Ladybird*; Pederson in *Martha Meet Frank, Daniel and Thomas*; Ray in *Nil By Mouth*; Kevin in *Quadrophenia*; Carlin in *Scum*; Gal in *Sexy Beast*; Title role in *Tank Malling*; Billy in *That Summer*; Mr Billy in *The Mammy*; Chas in *The Sea Change*; Dad in *The Warzone*; Colonel in *Woundings*; *Yellow*.
Address: c/o CAM London, 19 Denmark Street, London WC2H 8NA.

WINTON, Dale
Dale Winton. Host/Presenter. b. 22 May 1955.
TV: *Gimme Gimme Gimme*; *Pets Win Prizes*; *Supermarket Sweep*; *The Frank Skinner Show*; *The National Lottery Live*; *The Other Half*; *Trainspotting*; *Winton's Wonderland*.
Address: c/o Noel Gay Artists, 19 Denmark Street, London WC2H 8NA.

WISDOM, Tom
Tom Wisdom. Actor (M).
TV: *Black Hearts in Battersea*; Edward in *Children of the New Forest*; Tom Ferguson in *Coronation Street*; Matthew in *Escape to Somerset*; Will in *The Castle*; Jan Turek in *The Good King*; Russell in *Wavelength*; *Wycliffe*.
Address: c/o Emptage Hallett, 24 Poland Street, London W1V 3DD.

WISE, Greg
Greg Wise. Actor (M).
b. Northumberland, 15 May 1966.
TV: The Red Knight in *Alice Through the Looking Glass*; Henry in *Covington Cross*; Dr Jim Nightingale in *Hospital*; Grimes in *House of Frankenstein*; Rodolphe in *Madame Bovary*; Jamie in *Masculine Ending*; Greg Martin in *Taggart*; Justin in *Tales from the Crypt*; Guy Thwaite in *The Buccaneers*; Franklyn in *The Moonstone*; Hugh Brittain in *The Place of the Dead*; Alistair in *The Riff Raff Element*; Cato McGill/Adam Prime in *Typhon's People*; Marshall in *Wonderful You*.
Films: Dyson in *Judas Kiss*; Alex in *Mad Cows*; Willoughby in *Sense and Sensibility*; Arch Wilson in *The Feast of July*.
Address: c/o Markham & Froggatt Ltd, 4 Windmill Street, London W1P 1HF. Partner Emma Thompson.

WITCHELL, Nicholas
Nicholas Witchell. Newsreader/Presenter.
b. Cosford, Shropshire, 23 September 1953.
TV: Reporter, *BBC Northern Ireland*; Reporter *BBC News London*; *BBC Ireland* Correspondent; Presenter

6 o'clock News; Presenter *BBC Breakfast News*; Correspondent for *Panorama*; Diplomatic Correspondent, *BBC News*; Associate Producer *News '39*, *News 44*, *News '45*.
Address: c/o BBC TV Centre, Wood Lane, London, W12 7RJ. m. Carolyn Stephenson; 2 d. Arabella, Giselle.

WOGAN, Katherine

Katherine Wogan. Actor (F). b. 1974.
TV: Mary Richmond in *Aristocrats*; Dr Pat Robinson in *Dalziel and Pascoe*; Clare Costello in *Grafters*; Georgia in *Sixteen Minutes*.
Address: c/o Burnett Granger Associates, Prince of Wales Theatre, 31 Coventry Street, London W1V 8AS. Father Terry Wogan. Hobbies: Riding, swimming, tennis, snow- and water-skiing, jazz, salsa dancing, flamenco dancing, singing.

WOGAN, Terry

Terry Wogan. Presenter/Disc-jockey.
b. Limerick, Ireland, 3 August 1938.
TV: *Auntie's Bloomers*; *Auntie's Sporting Bloomers*; *Blankety Blank*; *Children in Need*; *Do the Right Thing*; *Friday Night with Terry Wogan Live*; *The Eurovision Song Contest*; *The National Lottery Live*; *Wogan* (1982); *Wogan's Island*; *Wogan's Web*
Address: c/o J. Gurnett Personal Management Ltd, 2 New Kings Road, London SW6 4SA. m. Helen; 2 s. Alan, Mark; 1 d. Katherine.

WOLF, Rita

Rita Wolf. Actor (F).
b. Calcutta, India, 25 February 1960.
TV: Yasmin in *A Wing and a Prayer*; Meena in *Albion Market*; Atima Mehta in *Calling the Shots*; Felicity Khan in *Coronation Street*; Young girl in *Debut on Two*; Emily in *Debut on Two*; Zu in *Eye Contact*; Nayana Singh in *Kavanagh QC*; *Kuhush*; Kamala in *Mohammed's Daughter*; Jackie in *One by One*; Sonia Souhami in *Rockliffe's Babies*; Satinder in *Romance, Romance*; Princess Rania in *Saracen*; Karen in *Shelley*; Dr Kantons in *Spender*; Asha in *Tandoori Nights*; Vritra in *Wild Justice*.
Films: Shopkeeper's wife in *Girl 6*; Fauzia in *Majhar*; Tania in *My Beautiful Launderette*; Maya in *Slipstream*; Carrie in *The Chain*.
Address: c/o Burdett-Coutts Associates, Riverside Studios, Crisp Road, London W6 9RL. Hobbies: Singing, riding, swimming.

WOOD, Aleetza

Aleetza Wood. Actor (F).
TV: Peta Janossi in *Home and Away*

Films: *Fetch*; *The Boys*.
Address: c/o Seven Network Ltd, Mabbs Lane, Epping, New South Wales 2121, Australia.

WOOD, Jake

Jake Wood. Actor (M). b. Prestwich, 15 May 1953.
TV: *A Breed of Heroes*; *A Touch of Frost*; *Bramwell*; *Casualty*; *Eleven Men Against Eleven*; *Gobble*; *Holding On*; *It Could Be You*; *Red Dwarf*; *The Governor*; *The Wilsons*; *Thin Blue Line*; *Trial and Retribution*.
Films: *Crime Time*; *Dad Savage*; *Flesh and Blood*; *Never Come Morning*; *Revolution*; *Skullduggery*.
Address: c/o ICM, Oxford House, 76 Oxford Street, London W1N 0AX.

WOOD, Victoria

Victoria Wood. Actor (F)/Presenter/Singer/Writer.
b. Prestwich, Lancashire, 19 May 1953.
TV: *An Audience With Victoria Wood*; Bren in *dinnerladies*; *Great Railway Journeys*; *Happy Since I Met*; investigative films for *Comic Relief*; *Nearly a Happy Ending*; *New Faces*; *Pat and Margaret*; *South Bank Show*; *Talent*; *That's Life*; *Victoria Wood – As Seen On TV*; *Victoria Wood's All Day Breakfast*; *Wood and Walters*.
Films: Tea Lady in *The Wind in the Willows*.
Address: c/o McIntyre Management Ltd, 2nd Floor, 35 Soho Square, London W1V 5DG. m. Geoffrey Durham.

WOODBURNE, Jackie

Jackie Woodburne. Actor (F).
TV: *1915*; *A Country Practice*; *Blinky Bill*; *Carson's Law*; *Cop Shop*; *Fast Lane*; *GP*; *Kings*; *Law of the Land*; *Learned Friends*; Susan Kennedy in *Neighbours*; *Outbreak of Love*; *Patchwork Hero*; *Prisoner*; *Sarah Dane*; *Saturday, Saturday*; *Skyways*; *Special Squad*; *The Flying Doctors*; *Words Fail Me*; *Young Doctors*.
Address: c/o Pearson Television, 1 Stephen Street, London W1P 1PJ.

WOODFORD, Kevin

Kevin Woodford. Chef/Presenter.
b. Isle of Man, 4 June 1950.
TV: *A Day at the Pictures with Kevin Woodford*; *All Over the Shop*; *Big Kevin, Little Kevin*; *Bob Monkhouse's Birthday Special*; *Can't Cook, Won't Cook*; *Fasten Your Seat Belt*; *Holiday*; *Noel's House Party*; *Ready, Steady, Cook*; *Songs of Praise*; *Summer Holiday*; *The Heaven and Earth Show*; *The National Lottery Show*; *Win, Lose or Draw*.
Address: c/o David Anthony Promotions, PO Box 286, Warrington, Cheshire WA2 6GA. m. Jean. Hobbies: Golf, aerobics, work.

WOODLEY, David

David Woodley. Actor (M)/Stuntman.
b. Brisbane, Australia, 7 December 1960.
TV: *Big Sky*; Joel Nash in *Home and Away*; *Mission Impossible*; *Paradise Beach*; *Time Trax*.
Address: c/o Seven Network Ltd, Mabbs Lane, Epping, New South Wales 2121, Australia.

WOODVINE, John

John Woodvine. Actor (M).
b. South Shields, 21 July 1929.
TV: *A Month in the Country*; *A Pinch of Snuff*; *A Tale of Two Cities*; *All Creatures Great and Small*; *All in Good Faith*; *An Actor's Life for Me*; *Blue Smoke, Red Moon*; *Dr Finlay*; *Edge of Darkness*; *Faith*; *Finney*; *Heartbeat*; *Knights of God*; *Les Girls*; *Medics*; *New Statesman*; *Peak Practice*; *Perfect State*; *Pontius Pilate*; *Romeo and Juliet*; *Room at the Bottom*; *Runaway Bay*; *Spender*; *Tell Tale Heart*; *The Black and Blue Lamp*; *The Browning Version*; *The Dog It Was That Died*; *The Marlowe Inquest*; *The Merchant of Venice*; *The Pirate Prince*; *Verdict*; *Who Bombed Birmingham?*
Films: *A Nightingale Sang*; *An American Werewolf in London*; *Countdown to War*; *Danny Champion of the World*; *Deceptions*; *Dragonworld*; *Fatherland*; *Murder With Mirrors*; *Squaring the Circle*; *The Trial*; *Vote For Hitler*; *Wuthering Heights*.
Address: c/o Scott Marshall, 44 Perryn Road, London W3 7NA.

WOODWARD, Edward

Edward Woodward. Actor (M)/Presenter.
b. Croydon, Surrey, 1 June 1930.
TV: Kyle in *1990*; *A Bit of a Holiday*; *A Christmas Carol*; Scott Fitzgerald in *A Dream Divided*; *Blunt Instrument*; Lead role in *Callan*; *In Suspicious Circumstances*; Nev in *Common As Muck*; *Emergency Ward 10*; *Evelyn*; *Hands of a Murderer*; Teddy Harrison in *Harrison: The Shamrock Conspiracy and the Cry of the City*; Cassius in *Julius Caesar*; *Killer Contract*; *Love is Forever*; *Merlin and the Sword*; *Nice Work*; Title role in *Othello*; Maxwell Beckett in *Over My Dead Body*; Lead role in *Rod of Iron*; Luigi in *Saturday, Sunday, Monday*; *Skyport*; *The Baron*; *The Base Player and the Blonde*; Lopakin in *The Cherry Orchard*; *The Defenders*; *The Edward Woodward Show*; Robert McCall in *The Equalizer*; Guy Crouchback in *The Evelyn Waugh Trilogy*; *The Man in the Brown Suit*; *The Prisoner*; *The Professionals*; *The Saint*; Melvyn Griffiths-Jones QC in *The Trial of Lady Chatterley*; *Uncle Tom's Cabin*.
Films: *A Christmas Reunion*; *Beckett*; *Callan*; *Champions*; *Comeback*; *Deadly Advice*; *Hunted*; *King David*; *Mister Johnson*; *Sitting Target*; *Stand Up Virgin Soldiers*; *The File of the Golden Goose*; *The Wicker Man*; *Where*

There's a Will; *Who Dares Wins*; *Young Winston*.
Address: c/o Eric Glass Ltd, 28 Berkeley Square, London W1X 6HD. m. Michele Dotrice. 2 s. Peter, Tim; 2 d. Sarah, Emily.

WOODWARD, Tim

Tim Woodward. Actor (M). b. London, 24 April 1953.
TV: *A Killing on the Exchange*; *A Piece of Cake*; *All the World's a Stage*; *Blue Murder*; *Bramwell*; Pip in *Chips with Everything*; *Closing Number*; *Cousin Phyllis*; *Crown Court*; *East Lynne*; *Go Back Out the Way You Came In*; *Guests of the Nation*; *Heartbeat*; *Iphigenia at Aulis*; *Lady Windermere's Fan*; *MacGyver*; *Prime Suspect*; *Space Island One*; *Spooky – The Keeper*; *The Affair of the Pin Pearl*; *The Antonia White Quartet*; *The Bill*; *The Case of the Frightened Lady*; *The Dark Angel*; *The Equaliser*; *The File of Bridget Hitler*; *The File on Jill Hatch*; *The Governor*; *The House of Angelo*; *The Irish RM*; *The Vice*; *Under the Sun*; Mr Osborne in *Vanity Fair*; *Wings*.
Films: *B Monkey*; *Galileo*; *King David*; *Personal Services*; *Pope John Paul*; Jack Warner in *RKO 281*; *Salome*; *Some Mother's Son*; *The Europeans*; *The Scarlet Letter*.
Address: c/o Dalzell & Beresford Ltd, 91 Regent Street, London W1R 7TB. Father Edward Woodward.

WOODYATT, Adam

Adam Woodyatt. Actor (M).
b. Woodford, Essex, 28 June 1968.
TV: Shiner in *Baker Street Boys*; *Big Free for All*; *Celebrity 15 to 1*; *Computers Don't Bite*; *Dreamhouse*; Ian Beale in *EastEnders*; *Family Fortunes*; *Guiding Stars*; *National Lottery Live*; *Noel's House Party*; *On the House*; *That's Showbusiness*; *The Big Breakfast*; *Value for Money*; *Wish You Were Here...?*; Dave Firkettle in *Witches and the Grinnygog*; *Wogan*.
Address: c/o Associated International Management, 5 Denmark Street, London WC2H 8LP.

WOOF, Emily

Emily Woof. Actor (F). b. 1969.
TV: Nancy in *Oliver Twist* (1999); Paula in *Daylight Robbery* (1999); Susie in *Killer Net* (1998); Lydgate's maid in *Middlemarch* (1994).
Films: *Fast Food*; *Passion*; *Photographing Fairies*; *The Full Monty*; *This Year's Love*; *Velvet Goldmine*; *The Woodlanders*.
Address: c/o ICM, Oxford House, 76 Oxford Street, London W1N 0AX.

WORRALL THOMPSON, Antony

Henry Antony Cardew Worrall Thompson. Chef.
b. Stratford-upon-Avon, 1 May 1951.

TV: *Have I Got News For You; Hot Chefs; It's Only TV But I Like It; Ready, Steady, Cook; Shooting Stars.*
Address: c/o Limelight Management, 33 Newman Street, London W1P 3PD. m. Jacinta; 4 children Blake, Sam, Toby-Jack, Billie-Lara; godfather Richard Burton; godfather to child, Rory Bremner.

WORTH, Helen
Cathryn Helen Wigglesworth. Actor (F).
b. Leeds, Yorkshire, 7 January 1951.
TV: Gail Platt in *Coronation Street*; Mary Ashe in *Doctor Who* (1963); Schoolgirl in *The Prime of Miss Jean Brodie* (1969).
Address: c/o Arena Entertainment, Regents Court, 39 Harrogate Road, Leeds, West Yorkshire.

WRAGG, Kaye
Kaye Wragg. Actor (F).
TV: Nimmy in *Born to Run*; Melanie in *Coronation Street*; Joanna in *Prime Suspect*; Sheryl Fogarty in *Slap*; Jaqui in *The Anorak*; Hannah in *The Home (True stories)*; Lucy in *The Lakes*; Vicki in *Where the Heart Is*.
Films: Anne Ridley in *Lyddie* .
Address: c/o Shepherd & Ford, 13 Radnor Walk, London SW3 4BP. Hobbies: Singing, swimming, running.

WRAY, Emma
Emma Wray. Actor (F).
b. Birkenhead, 22 March 1965.
TV: Pandora in *Boon*; Minty Goodenough in *Defrosting the Fridge*; Tracy in *Minder*; Donna in *My Wonderful Life*; Pippa in *Stay Lucky*; Julie in *The Big Game*; Donna in *True Love*; Brenda in *Watching*.
Address: c/o Burdett-Coutts Associates, Riverside Studios, Crisp Road, London W6 9RL. Hobbies: Gymnastics, ballet dancing.

WRIGHT, Ian
Ian Wright. Commentator/Presenter/Host.
b. London, 3 November 1963.
TV: *An Audience with Lennox Lewis; Friday Night's All Wright; Guinness Book of Records; Match of the Day; Question of Sport; They Think It's All Over.*
Address: c/o Jerome Anderson Management, 248 Station Road, Edgware, Middlesex HA8 7AU. m. Debbie.

WYLTON, Tim
Tim Wylton. Actor (M).
TV: Rodney Sillitoe in *A Bit of a Do*; *A Question of Commitment* (1989); Garwood in *A Touch of Frost*; *A Very Peculiar Practice* (1989); George in *All Creatures Great and Small*; *Anna Lee* (1992); Reg in *Annie's Bar* (1996); Lol in *As Time Goes By*; *Big Women*; *Boon* (1991); *Bugs* (1998); *Cadfael*; *Capital City* (1990); *Casualty* (1991); George Griff in *Cockles*; Ron in *Darling Buds of May*; George in *Desert of Lies*; *Dodgem* (1990); *Emmerdale* (1993); *Fatal Inversion* (1991); *French and Saunders* (1992); *Haggard* (1990); *Hamlet*; Father in *Haunted Harmony*; *Heartbeat* (1996); Fluellen in *Henry V*; Franks in *Wycliffe*; Malcolm in *Instant Enlightenment*; *Just William*; Edward Thorpe in *Lifeboat* (1993); *Lobiz* (1992); Smiler in *Minder*; FK Henderson in *Mog*; Stanley in *My Hero*; Menzies Wilson in *Peak Practice*; *Playing the Field*; de la Fontaine in *Poirot*; Mr Gardiner in *Pride and Prejudice* (1994); *Rumpole of the Bailey* (1992); *Stay Lucky* (1990); The vicar in *The Bell*; *The Bill* (1989); *The Bill* (1993); Sutton in *The Bretts*; Eric in *The Dustbinmen*; Tom Jones in *The Treaty*; *Trainer* (1992); *Underbelly* (1991); Pilot in *Wings* (1995).
Films: *Carrycot; Melody; Pink Panther; Under Milk Wood.*
Address: c/o Hillman Threfall, 33 Brookfield, Highgate West Hill, London N6 6AT.

Y

YARDLEY, Stephen

Stephen Yardley. Actor (M).
b. Yorkshire, 24 March 1942.
TV: Ken Lewis in *Bergerac*; Reeve in *Blake's 7*; James Drew in *Blood Money*; Grieves in *Breakpoint*; Gilbert in *Brighton Belles*; Beckett in *Bugs*; Bob Connelly in *Casualty*; Brabley in *Chariots of Fire*; Webber in *Conduct of Prejudice*; *Coronation Street*; Dr John Thanet in *Crown Court*; Richard in *Dangerfield*; The Stranger in *Danger Man*; Joseph in *Doctor and the Devils*; Henry Fisher in *Doctors*; Arak in *Doctor Who*; Martin in *Executive Stress*; Vince in *Family Affairs*; Duke Hopwood in *Fanny by Gaslight*; Brian Bulman in *Flying Swan*; Jules Plogov in *Germinal*; Jacko Lyall in *Goodbye Darling*; Patrick Baker in *Harriet's Back in Town*; George in *Heartbeat*; Ken Masters in *Howard's Way*; Adler in *Juliet Bravo*; Toby in *Just William*; Mason in *Law and Disorder*; Mike Baxter in *Marriage Lines*; Alan in *Morgan's Boy*; Charles in *Nana*; Marshall Lannes in *Napoleon in Love*; DI Carroll in *New Scotland Yard*; The Lover in *Norma*; Ralph Carter in *Public Eye*; Clayton in *Rivals of Sherlock Holmes*; Chasserian in *Roads to Freedom*; Will in *Sister Dora*; John Wilmot in *Strange But True*; Defarge in *Tale of Two Cities*; Tony in *The Bender*; Ian in *The Brothers*; John in *The Day of the Triffids*; Blanden in *The Gentle Touch*; Hughes in *The Mask of Janus*; Mervans in *The Poisoners*; Swetman in *The Professionals*; Max in *Secret Army*; Laker in *The Sweeney*; Erskine in *The Villains*; Spyder Scott in *The XYY Man*; Maurice in *Three Months Gone*; Lieutenant Sims in *Tom Gratton's War*; Kenny Craig in *United*; Inspector Cadogan in *Virtual Murder*; Ramballe in *War and Peace*; Wolfgang in *War of Darkie Pilbeam*; Vic Morgan in *Widows*; John Wright in *Within These Walls*; PC May in *Z-Cars*.
Films: Lieutenant Martin in *Adolf Hitler, My Part in His Downfall*; Marty in *Atlantic Wall*; Ridley in *Funny Money*; Tony Hogg in *Jane Brown's Body*; Toms in *Private Eye*; Kemodov in *Remington Steele*; Chiarkos in *RPM*; Turner in *Slayground*; Pieter in *The Champions*; Knowles in *The Corvini Inheritance*; Pearson in *The First Day*; Drago in *The Innocent Sleep*; Maidment in *The Shooting Party*.
Address: c/o Brunskill Management, Suite 8a, 169 Queen's Gate, London SW7 5HE. Hobbies: Squash, golf, cycling.

YATES, Marjorie

Marjorie Yates. Actor (F).
b. Birmingham, 13 April 1941.
TV: *Heartbeat*; Mrs Ashton in *Danny's Story*; *Where the Heart Is*; *Wycliffe*; Joan Fairlie in *Annie's Bar*; Dr Miles in *Guardians*; *The Bill*; Mrs Redwood in *The Governor*; *Fighting for Gemma*; *Ruth Rendell – The Speaker of Mandarin*; *Leaving of Liverpool*; *Underbelly*; *Boon*; *June*; *A Very British Coup*; *Suffer Little Children*; *Morgan's Boy*; *Forever*; *Marks*; *Mitch*; *Great Expectations*; *A Change in Time*; *Life for Christine*; *Passmore*; *Connie*; *All Day on the Sand*; *The Cost of Loving*; *The Sweeney*; *Couples*; *Against the Crowd*; *It's A Lovely Day Tomorrow*; *Suspicion*; *Justice*; *Better than the Movies*; *Villains*; *Bouncing Boy*.
Films: *Bin Liners*; *The Long Day Closes*; *Stardust*; *Dean Men's Folly*; *Optimists*; *Albert's Memorial*; *Legend of the Werewolf*; *Wetherby*.
Address: c/o Kate Feast Management, 10 Primrose Hill Studios, Fitzroy Road, London NW1 8TR. 1 d. Polly; 1 s. Carl. Hobbies: Wildlife conservation.

YIP, David

David Nicholas Yip. Actor (M). b. 4 June 1951.
TV: *It Ain't Half Hot Mum*; *Savages*; *Whodunnit?*; *Spies*; *The Cuckoo Waltz*; *Doctor Who*; *The Professionals*; *The Chinese Detective*; Dr Michael Choi in *Brookside*; *Wail of the Banshee*; *White Girls on Dope*, *Every Silver Lining*, Rick Ramon in *Rich Deceivers*; Jimmy Mac in *Thieftakers*; Chuku in *Bugs*; Dr Lawrence in *Bliss*; *The Rory Bremner Show*.
Films: *Indiana Jones and the Temple of Doom*; *A View to a Kill*; *Ping Pong*; *Empire of the Sun*; *Highlander*; *Out of Order*; *Hawks*; *Destiny San Francisco*; *Chinese Method*; *Goodbye Hong Kong*.
Address: c/o Evans and Reiss, 100 Fawe Park Road, London SW15 2EA. m. 1 Liz Bagley (dis); m. 2 Lynn Farleigh. Hobbies: Tennis, swimming.

YORATH, Gabby

Gabrielle Yorath. Anchor/Presenter/Reporter.
b. 24 April 1973.
TV: *Britain's Strongest Man* (1996); *Central Sports Special* (1998); *Champions League Highlights* (1999); *Goals on Sunday* (1996); *Ice Hockey* (1997); *Late Tackle*

(1998); *Late Tackle* (1999); *On the Ball* (1998); *The Locker* (1998); *The Sports Centre* (1996); Celebrity interviewer for *Tonight* (1996); *Wish You Were Here..?* Address: c/o Marquee Group (UK) Ltd, 21 The Green, Richmond, Surrey TW9 1PX. Hobbies: Tennis, half marathons, travelling.

YORK, Michael
Michael York-Johnson. Actor (M)/Narrator.
b. Fulmer, Buckinghamshire, 27 March 1942.
TV: *A Christmas Carol* (1997); *A Knight in Camelot* (1998); *A Man Called Intrepid* (1978); Merlin in *A Young Connecticut Yankee in King Arthur's Court* (1995); *Actors on Acting* (1984); *Are You My Mother* (1986); *Babylon 5: A Late Delivery from Avalon* (1995); *CBS Reports: Hitler and Stalin* (1994); *Dark Mansions* (1985); *David Copperfield's Christmas* (1993); *Dead Man's Gun* (1998); *Duel of Hearts* (1990); *Fall From Grace* (1994); *For Those I Loved* (1982); *Gardens of the World* (1993); John the Baptist in *Jesus of Nazareth* (1976); *Magic and Beyond* (1999); Benedick in *Much Ado About Nothing* (1978); *Nicolas Slonimski: A Touch of Genius* (1994); *Not of this Earth* (1995); *Perfect Little Angels* (1998); *Politically Incorrect* (1997); *Ponce de Leon* (1986); *River of Gold* (1992); *Seaquest* (1995); *September* (1995); *Sliders: This Side of Paradise* (1997); *Sophocles' Theban Plays* (1988); *Space* (1984); *Sword of Gideon* (1986); *Teklab* (1994); *The Far Country* (1985); Young Jolyon in *The Forsyte Saga* (1966); *The Four Minute Mile* (1988); *The Great War* (1996); *The Heat of the Day* (1988); *The Hunt for Stolen War Treasure* (1989); *The Lady and the Highwayman* (1988); *The Long Way Home* (1997); *The Magic Flute* (1994); *The Magic School Bus* (1995); *The Magnificat* (1997); *The Master of Ballantrae* (1983); *The Naked Truth* (1995); Rommel in *The Night of the Fox* (1989); *The Out of Towner* (1994); *The Phantom of the Opera* (1982); *The Ring* (1996); *The Ripper* (1997); *The Road to Avonlea* (1990); *The Search for Nazi Gold* (1998); *Magic and Beyond*; *The Secret of the Sahara* (1987); *The Story of Anglicanism* (1989); *The Weather in the Streets* (1983); *The White Lions* (1979); *Till We Meet Again* (1989); Dietrich Bonhoeffer in *True Patriot* (1977); *True Women* (1997); *Twilight Theatre* (1982); *Un Coup de Baguette Magique* (1997); Robinson Crusoe in *Vendredi* (1981).
Films: *A Monkey's Tale* (1999); *Accident* (1966); *Alfred the Great* (1968); *Austin Powers: International Man of Mystery* and *Austin Powers: The Spy Who Shagged Me* (1999); *British Rock: The First Wave* (1985); Brian Roberts in *Cabaret* (1971); *Conduct Unbecoming* (1974); *Dark Planet* (1997); *Dawn* (1985); *Discretion Assured* (1993); *Eline Vere* (1992); *England Made Me* (1971); *Fedora* (1977); *Final Assignment* (1979); *Good-*

bye America (1997); *Gospa* (1996); *Great Expectations* (1974); *Justine the Great* (1968); *La Poudre D'Escampette* (1970); *Lethal Obsession* (1987); Logan in *Logan's Run* (1975); *Lost Horizon* (1972); *Lovers and Liars* (1999); *Merchants of Venus* (1999); *Midnight Cop* (1988); *Murder on the Orient Express* (1974); *One Hell of a Guy* (1999); *Phantom of Death* (1987); *Rochade* (1992); *Romeo and Juliet* (1967); *Seven Nights in Japan* (1975); *Smashing Time* (1967); *Something for Everyone* (1969); *Studio 54* (1998); *Success is the Best Revenge* (1984); D'Artagnan in *The Four Musketeers* (1974); *The Ghostly Rental* (1999); *The Golden Globe Awards* (1985); *The Guru* (1968); *The Island of Dr Moreau* (1976); Beau Geste in *The Last Remake of Beau Geste* (1976); *The Long Shadow* (1991); *The Magic Paintbrush* (1992); *The Code* (1999); D'Artagnan in *The Return of the Musketeers* (1988); *The Riddle of the Sands* (1978); *The Shadow of a Kiss* (1993); *The Strange Affair* (1967); *The Taming of the Shrew* (1966); D'Artagnan in *The Three Musketeers*; *The Revenge of Milady*; *The Queen's Diamonds*; *The Treat* (1998); *The Wanderer* (1991); *Timeless India* (1994); *Wide Sargasso Sea* (1992); *Wrongfully Accused* (1998); *Zeppelin* (1970).
Address: c/o Andrew Manson Personal Management, 288 Munster Road, London SW6 6BQ. m. Pat. Hobbies: Chairman of the California Youth Theatre, writing books.

YOUDALE, Diane
Diana Youdale. Gladiator/Presenter.
b. Billingham, Cleveland, 1970.
TV: *Children in Need* (1997); *Games Mistress*; Jet in *Gladiators*; *Mountain Bike Show*; *Ouch*; *Out and About*; *Pulling Power*; *Two Wheels Better*; *You Bet*.
Address: c/o Arlington Enterprise Ltd, 1–3 Charlotte Street, London W1P 1HD. Hobbies: Works for eating disorder organisations, psychology.

YOUNG, Barbara
Barbara Young. Actor (F).
b. Brighouse, Yorkshire, 19 February 1936.
TV: *Casualty*; Barbara Platt in *Coronation Street*; Dot Stockwell in *Coronation Street*; Sadie Hargreaves in *Family Affairs*; Dot in *Hazell*; Agrippinilla in *I, Claudius*; *The Bill*; *The Perfect Spy*; *War and Peace*, Sadie Hargreaves in *Family Affairs*.
Films: *Hidden City*; *Jane Eyre*; *White City*.
Address: c/o Grantham Hazeldine, 51 Blenheim Street, London W1Y 9LB. 2 d. Cory Jane, Liza Kate.

YOUNG, Helen
Helen Young. Presenter. b. Sussex, 1969.
TV: *BBC Weather Forecast*

Address: c/o Limelight Management, 33 Newman Street, London W1P 3PD. Hobbies: Running, swimming, volleyball, squash, canoeing, skiing, playing the clarinet, painting.

YOUNG, Kirsty

Kirsty Young. Presenter/Newsreader/Reporter.
b. Stirling, Scotland, 1969.
TV: *5 News* (1997); *Film '96* (1996); *Holiday '96* (1996); *Holidays Out* (1996); *Kirsty* (1994); *Late Edition* (1994); *Scotland Today* (1992); *Scotland Today at Lunchtime* (1992); *The Street* (1996); *The Time, The Place* (1996); *ITV News* (2000).
Address: c/o ITN, 200 Grays Inn Road, London WC1X 8XZ.

YOUNG, Paul

Paul Young. Actor (M).
b. Edinburgh, Scotland, 3 June 1944.
TV: *Albert and the Lion*; *Dr Finlay*; *Hooked*; *No Job for a Lady*; *Poirot*; *Soldier, Soldier*; *Sunset Song*; *Taggart*; *The Bill*; *The Crow Road*; *The House on the Hill*; *The Last Salute*; *The Tales of Para Handy*.
Films: Dougal in *Another Time, Another Place*; Brady Logan in *Chato's Land*; Frank in *Complicity*; Wee Geordie in *Geordie*; Dr Gebbie in *My Life So Far*; Dr Brock in *Regeneration*; First Officer Murdoch in *SOS Titanic*; Lt Quentin in *Submarine X-1*.
Address: Shepherd & Ford Associates, 13 Radnor Walk, Chelsea, London SW3 4BP. m. Sheila Duffy; 2 d. Hannah, Katie. Hobbies: Reading, gardening, crosswords, good food and wine, fishing.

YOUNG, Stacey

Stacey Young. Presenter/Reporter. b. Rochford, 1965.
TV: *GMTV*; *Mr & Mrs*; *This Morning*; *Wish You Were Here...?*.
Address: c/o Panic, 2 Mortimer House, Furmage Street, London SW18 4DF.

Z

ZETA JONES, Catherine

Catherine Zeta Jones. Actor (F).
b. Swansea, 25 September 1969.
TV: Catherine in *Catherine the Great*; Mariette in *Darling Buds of May*; *Out of the Blue*; Eustacia in *The Return of the Native*; *The Cinder Path*; *Young Indiana Jones Chronicles*; *Titanic*.
Films: Chloë in *Blue Juice*; Beatriz in *Columbus*; Marie in *Coup de Foudre*; *Entrapment*; Theodora in *The Haunting*; *Scheherazade*; *Splitting Heirs*; Elena in *The Mask of Zorro*; Sala in *The Phantom*.
Address: c/o ICM, Oxford House, 76 Oxford Street, London W1N 0AX. Fiancé Michael Douglas.

ZIEGLER, Matilda

Matilda Ziegler. Actor (F). b. 1964.
TV: *Casualty*; Donna Ludlow in *EastEnders*; Jane Ford in *Harbour Lights*; *In Suspicious Circumstances*; Irma Gobb in *Mr Bean*; *Mr White Goes to Westminster*; *The Bill*; Hilary Hampson in *An Unsuitable Job for a Woman*.
Films: *Jilting Joe*.
Address: c/o London Management, Noel House, 2–4 Noel Street, London W1V 3RB.

ZOVKIC, Lidija

Lidija Zovkic. Actor (F).
TV: The Angel in *I Saw You*; Elena in *Dangerfield*.
Films: *The Beach*; *Maybe Baby*.
Address: c/o Storm Artists Management, 1st Floor, 47 Brewer Street, London W1R 3FD.

USEFUL ADDRESSES

TELEVISION COMPANIES

Anglia Television

Anglia House
Norwich
Norfolk NR1 3JG
tel: 01603 615151
fax: 01603 631032

Associated New Media
60 Charlotte Street
London W1P 2AX
tel: 020 7209 1234
fax: 020 7209 1235

BBC Television
BBC Television Centre
Wood Lane
London W12 7RJ
tel: 020 8743 8000
fax: 020 8749 7520

BBC Birmingham
Broadcasting Centre
Pebble Mill Road
Birmingham B5 7QQ
tel: 0121 432 8888
fax: 0121 432 8634

BBC Bristol
Broadcasting House
Whiteladies Road
Bristol BS8 2LR
tel: 0117 9732211

BBC Northern Ireland
Broadcasting House
Ormeau Avenue
Belfast BT2 8HQ
tel: 02890 338000

BBC Scotland
Broadcasting House
Queen Margaret Drive
Glasgow G12 8DG
tel: 0141 339 8844

BBC Wales
Broadcasting House
Llandaff
Cardiff CF5 2YQ
tel: 02920 322000

BBC World Service
PO Box 76
Bush House
Strand
London WC2B 4PH
tel: 020 7240 3456

Border Television
Television Centre
Durranhill
Carlisle
Cumbria CA1 3NT
tel: 01228 525101
fax: 01228 541384

BSkyB
Grant Way
Isleworth
Middlesex TW7 5QD
tel: 020 7705 3000
fax: 020 7705 3030

Cable News Network International
CNN House
19–22 Rathbone Place
London W1P 1DF
tel: 020 7637 6800
fax: 020 7637 6868

Carlton Westcountry
Langage Science Park
Western Wood Way
Plymouth
Devon PL7 5BQ
tel: 01752 333333
fax: 01752 333444

Carlton Television
101 St Martin's Lane
London WC2N 4AZ
tel: 020 7240 4000
fax: 020 7240 4171

Carlton Television
Central Court
Gas Street
Birmingham B1 2JT
tel: 0121 643 9898

Channel 4
124 Horseferry Road
London SW1P 2TX
tel: 020 7396 4444
fax: 020 7306 8356

Channel 5
22 Long Acre
London WC2E 9LY
tel: 020 7550 5555
fax: 020 7497 5222

Channel Television
The Television Centre
La Pouquelaye
St Helier
Jersey
Channel Islands JE1 3ZD
tel: 01534 816816
fax: 01534 816817

Discovery Channel
160 Great Portland Place
London W1N 5TB
tel: 020 7462 3600
fax: 020 7462 3700

Flextech Television
160 Great Portland Street
London W1N 5TB
tel: 020 7299 5000
fax: 020 7299 6000

GMTV
The London Television Centre
Upper Ground
London SE1 9TT
tel: 020 7827 7000
fax: 020 7827 7100

Grampian Television
Queen's Cross
Aberdeen
AB15 4XJ
tel: 01224 846846
fax: 01224 846800

Granada Television
Quay Street
Manchester
M60 9EA
tel: 0161 832 7211
fax: 0161 953 0283

HTV
Television Centre
Bath Road
Bristol BS4 3HG
tel: 0117 9722722
fax: 0117 9722400

HTV Wales
The Media Centre
Culverhouse Cross
Cardiff CF5 6XJ
tel: 01222 590590
fax: 01222 597183

ITN
200 Gray's Inn Road
London WC1X 8XZ
tel: 020 7833 3000

ITV Network Centre
200 Gray's Inn Road
London WC1X 8XZ
tel: 020 7843 8000

LWT
The London Television Centre
Upper Ground
London SE1 9LT
tel: 020 7620 1620

Meridian Broadcasting
Television Centre
Southampton
Hampshire SO14 OPZ
tel: 01703 222555
fax: 01703 335050

MTV Networks Europe Inc
Hawley Crescent
London NW1 8TT
tel: 020 7284 7777
fax: 020 7284 7788

NBC Europe
4th Floor
3 Shortlands
Hammersmith
London W6 8HX
tel: 020 8600 6600
fax: 020 8600 6601

Sci-Fi
77 Charlotte Street
London W1P 2DD
tel: 020 7805 6100
fax: 020 7805 6150

Scottish Television
Cowcaddens
Glasgow G2 3PR
tel: 0141 300 3000
fax: 0141 300 3030

S4C
Parc Ty Glas
Llanishen
Cardiff CF14 5DU
tel: 01222 747444
fax: 01222 754444

Teletext Ltd
101 Farm Lane
Fulham
London SW6 1QJ
tel: 020 7386 5000
fax: 020 7386 5002

Tyne Tees Television
Television Centre
City Road
Newcastle upon Tyne
NE1 2AL
tel: 0191 261 0181
fax: 0191 261 2302

Ulster Television
Havelock House
Ormeau Road
Belfast BT7 1EB
tel: 01232 328122
fax: 01232 246695

Warner Bros
98 Theobald's Road
London WC1X 8WB
tel: 020 7984 5400
fax: 020 7984 5001

Yorkshire Television
The Television Centre
Leeds
West Yorkshire LS3 1JS
tel: 0113 2438283
fax: 0113 2445107

TELEVISION PRODUCTION COMPANIES

Absolutely Productions
8th Floor
Alhambra House
27–31 Charing Cross Road
London WC2H OAU
tel: 020 7930 3113
fax: 020 7930 4114

Action Time
Wrendal House
2 Whitworth Street West
Manchester M1 5WX
tel: 0161 236 8999
fax: 0161 236 8845

Alomo Productions
1 Stephen Street
London W1P 1PJ
tel: 020 7691 6000
fax: 020 7691 6081

Antelope (UK)
29b Montague Street
London WC1B 5BH
tel: 020 7209 0099
fax: 020 7209 0098

Bazal Productions
Broadcast Communications
46–47 Bedford Square
London WC1B 3DP
tel: 020 7462 9000
fax: 020 7462 9998

Blue Heaven Productions
45 Leather Lane
London EC1N 7JT
tel: 020 7404 4222
fax: 020 7404 4266

Carlton Productions
35–38 Portman Square
London W1H ONU
tel: 020 7486 6688
fax: 020 7486 1132

Carnival (Films and Theatre) Ltd
12 Raddington Road
Ladbroke Grove
London W10 5TG
tel: 020 8968 0968/1818/1717
fax: 020 8968 0155/0177

Channel X Communications
22 Stephenson Way
London NW1 2HD
tel: 020 7387 3874
fax: 020 7387 0738

Chatsworth Television
97–99 Dean Street
London W1V 5RA
tel: 020 7734 4302
fax: 020 7437 3301

Childsplay Productions
8 Lonsdale Road
London NW6 6RD
tel: 020 7328 1429
fax: 020 7328 1416

Diverse Productions
Gorleston Street
London W14 8XS
tel: 020 7603 4567
fax: 020 7603 2148

Elstree (Production) Co Ltd
Shepperton Studios
Studios Road
Shepperton
Middlesex TW17 0QD
tel: 01932 572680/1
fax: 01932 572682

Feelgood Fiction
49 Goldhawk Road
London W12 8QP
tel: 020 8746 2535
fax: 020 8740 6177

Friday Productions
23a St Leonard's Terrace
London SW3 4QG
tel: 020 7730 0608
fax 020 7730 0608

Handmade Films Ltd
19 Beak Street
London W1R 3LB
tel: 020 7434 1434
fax: 020 7434 3143

Hartswood Films Ltd
Twickenham Studios
The Barons
St Margaret's
Twickenham
Middlesex TW1 2AW
tel: 020 8607 8736
fax: 020 8607 8744

Hat Trick Productions
10 Livonia Street
London W1V 3PH
tel: 020 7434 2451
fax: 020 7287 9791

Holmes Associates
38–42 Whitfield Street
London W1P 5RF
tel: 020 7813 4333
fax: 020 7637 9024

Initial Film and Television
Broadcast Communications
46–47 Bedford Square
London WC1B 3DP
tel: 020 7462 9000
fax: 020 7462 9001

Jim Henson Productions
30 Oval Road
London NW1 7DE
tel: 020 7428 4000
fax: 020 7428 4001

Kingfisher Television Productions
Carlton Studios
Lenton Lane
Nottingham NG7 2NA
tel: 0115 964 5262
fax: 0115 964 5263

Landseer Film and Television Productions
140 Royal College Street
London NW1 0TA
tel: 020 7485 7333
fax: 020 7485 7573

Mike Mansfield Television
5th Floor
41–42 Berners Street
London W1P 3AA
tel: 020 7580 2581
fax: 020 7580 2582

Mentorn Films
43 Whitfield Street
London W1 6TG
tel: 020 7258 6800
fax: 020 7258 6888

Mersey Television Company
Campus Manor
Childwall Abbey Road
Liverpool L16 OJP
tel: 0151 722 9122
fax: 0151 722 6839

Noel Gay Television
1 Albion Court
Albion Place
Hammersmith
London W6 0QT
tel: 020 8600 5200
fax: 020 8600 5222

Pearson Television
1 Stephen Street
London W1P 1PJ
tel: 020 7691 6000
fax: 020 7691 6100

Picture Palace Films
13 Egbert Street
London NW1 8LJ
tel: 020 7586 8763
fax: 020 7586 9048

Planet 24
195 Marsh Wall
London E14 9SG
tel: 020 7345 2424
fax: 020 7345 9400

Portman Productions
167 Wardour Street
London W1V 3TA
tel: 020 7468 3400
fax: 020 7468 3499

Primetime
Southern Star
45–49 Mortimer Street
London W1N 7TD
tel: 020 7636 9421
fax: 020 7436 7426

Red Rooster Television Entertainment
14–15 D'Arblay Street
London W1V 3FP
tel: 020 7439 6969
fax: 020 7439 6767

Talisman Films Ltd
5 Addison Place
London W11 4RJ
tel: 020 7603 7474
fax: 020 7602 7422

TalkBack Productions
36 Percy Street
London W1P 0LN
tel: 020 7323 9777
fax; 020 7637 5105

Tiger Aspect Productions
5 Soho Square
London W1V 5DE
tel: 020 7434 0672
fax: 020 7287 1448

United Film and Television Productions
48 Leicester Square
London WC2H 7FB
tel: 020 7389 8555
fax: 020 7930 8499

United Media Ltd
68 Berwick Street
London W1V 3PE
tel: 020 7287 2396
fax: 020 7287 2398

Wall to Wall Television
8–9 Spring Place
London NW5 3ER
tel: 020 7485 7424
fax: 020 7267 5292

Warner Sisters Film and TV Ltd
The Cottage
Pall Mall Deposit
124 Barlby Road
London W10 6BL
tel: 020 8960 3550
fax: 020 7960 3880

Working Title Films Ltd
Oxford House
76 Oxford Street
London W1N 9FD
tel: 020 7307 3000
fax: 020 7307 3001/2/3

Zenith Productions Ltd
43–45 Dorset Street
London W1H 4AB
tel: 020 7224 2440
fax: 020 7224 3194

RADIO

BBC Radio
Broadcasting House
Langham Place
London W1A 1AA
tel: 020 7580 4468

Classic FM
PO Box 2834
London W1A 5NT
tel: 020 7343 9000
fax: 020 7344 2700

talkSPORT
18 Hatfields
London SE1 8DJ
tel: 020 7959 7800

Virgin Radio
1 Golden Square
London W1R 4DJ
tel: 020 7434 1215
fax: 020 7434 1197